W9-BVI-775

Personalized Learning

In MyEconLab you are treated as an individual with specific learning needs.

Auto-Graded Tests and Assignments

- MyEconLab comes with two pre-loaded sample tests for each chapter so you can self-assess your understanding of the material.

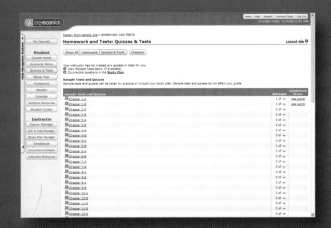

Personalized Study Plan

- A study plan is generated based on your results on sample tests and instructor assignments. You can clearly see which topics you have mastered and, more importantly, which topics you need to work on!

Practice Problems

- Use the study plan exercises to get practice where you need it. To check how you're doing, click "results" to get an overview of all your scores.

Save Time. Improve Results. www.myeconlab.com

Pearson eText

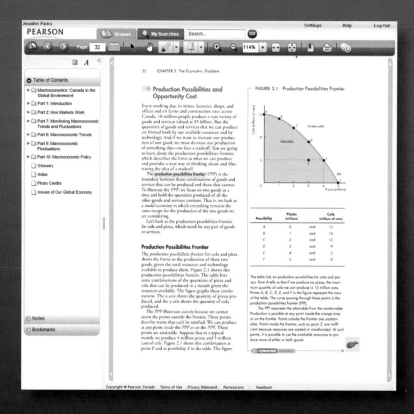

Pearson eText gives you access to the text wherever you can access the internet. eText pages look exactly like the printed text, offering powerful new functionality for students and instructors.

Users can create notes, highlight text in different colours, create bookmarks, zoom, click hyperlinked words and phrases to view definitions, and choose single-page or two-page view.

Pearson eText allows for quick navigation using a table of contents and provides full-text search. The eText may also offer links to associated media files, enabling users to access videos and animations.

Save Time. Improve Results. www.myeconlab.com

myeconlab ®

Get Ahead of the Curve

Improve Your Grade

It's easy to prepare wisely with practice quizzes and tutorials. MyEconLab offers a wide variety of problems that let you practise the theories and models being learned.

Graphing Tools and Questions

MyEconLab offers questions that allow you to draw graphs and plot data, as well as manipulate interactive model-based graphs.

Practice Problems

Many study plan and instructor-assigned problems contain algorithmically generated values to ensure you get the practice you need to prepare for tests and exams.

Go to www.myeconlab.com and follow the simple registration instructions on the Student Access Code Card provided with the text. Your unique access code is hidden there.

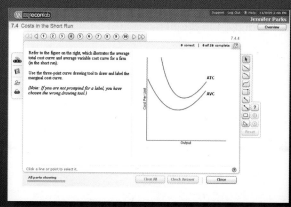

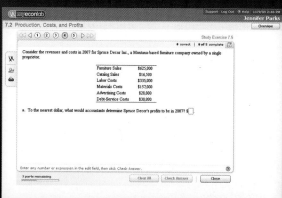

Save Time. Improve Results. www.myeconlab.com

Get Ahead of the Curve

Save Time.

Improve Results.

More than 3 million students have used a Pearson MyLab product to get a better grade.

MyEconLab is an all-in-one learning and testing environment for introductory economics. This easy-to-navigate site provides students with a variety of resources, including

- An interactive Pearson eText

- Personalized learning opportunities—YOU choose what, where, and when you want to study

- Self-assessment tests that create a personalized study plan to guide you on making the most efficient use of study time

- Dynamic resources including videos and animated graphs to enhance your learning experience

To take advantage of all that MyEconLab has to offer, you will need an access code. If you do not already have an access code, you can buy one online at **www.myeconlab.com.**

THE ECONOMICS

OF MONEY, BANKING,

AND FINANCIAL

MARKETS

FREDERIC S. MISHKIN
COLUMBIA UNIVERSITY

APOSTOLOS SERLETIS
UNIVERSITY OF CALGARY

THE ECONOMICS OF MONEY, BANKING, AND FINANCIAL MARKETS

FOURTH CANADIAN EDITION

Pearson Canada
Toronto

To Aglaia

Library and Archives Canada Cataloguing in Publication

Mishkin, Frederic S.
The economics of money, banking and financial markets / Frederic S.
Mishkin, Apostolos Serletis. — 4th Canadian ed.

Includes bibliographical references and index.
ISBN 978-0-321-58471-7

1. Finance—Textbooks. 2. Money—Textbooks. 3. Banks and banking— Textbooks.
I. Serletis, Apostolos, 1954– II. Title.

HG173.M58 2011   332   C2009-906674-2

Copyright © 2011, 2008, 2005, 2002 Pearson Canada Inc., Toronto, Ontario.

Pearson Addison Wesley. All rights reserved. This publication is protected by copyright and permission should be obtained from the publisher prior to any prohibited reproduction, storage in a retrieval system, or transmission in any form or by any means, electronic, mechanical, photocopying, recording, or likewise. For information regarding permission, write to the Permissions Department.

Original edition published by Pearson Education, Inc., Upper Saddle River, New Jersey, USA. Copyright © 2010, 2007, 2004 Pearson Education, Inc. *Parts of Financial Markets and Institutions,* First Canadian Edition, copyright © 2004 by Pearson Education Canada Inc., and *The Economics of Money, Banking, and Financial Markets: Business School Edition,* Second Edition, copyright © 2010, 2007 by Pearson Education, Inc., were also used in the Canadian edition. This edition is authorized for sale only in Canada.

ISBN 978-0-321-58471-7

Vice President, Editorial Director: Gary Bennett
Acquisitions Editors: Don Thompson, Claudine O'Donnell
Sponsoring Editor: Alexandra Dyer
Marketing Manager: Leigh-Anne Graham
Developmental Editor: Christina Lee
Production Editors: Leanne Rancourt, Cheryl Jackson
Copy Editor: Laura Neves
Proofreader: Kelli Howey
Production Coordinator: Deborah Starks
Compositor: Nelson Gonzalez
Permissions Researcher: Sandy Cooke
Art Director: Julia Hall
Cover and Interior Designer: Quinn Banting

For permission to reproduce copyrighted material, the publisher gratefully acknowledges the copyright holders listed below tables and figures throughout the text, which are considered extensions of this copyright page.

Statistics Canada information is used with the permission of Statistics Canada. Users are forbidden to copy the data and redisseminate them, in an original or modified form, for commercial purposes, without permission from Statistics Canada. Information on the availability of the wide range of data from Statistics Canada can be obtained from Statistics Canada's Regional Offices, its World Wide Web site at http://www.statcan.gc.ca, and its toll-free access number 1-800-263-1136.

3 4 5   14 13 12 11

Printed and bound in the United States of America.

Brief Contents

Contents

Preface

HALLMARKS

Although this text has undergone a major revision, it retains the basic hallmarks that have made it the best-selling textbook on money and banking over the past three editions:

- A unifying, analytic framework that uses a few basic economic principles to organize students' thinking about the structure of financial markets, the foreign exchange markets, financial institution management, and the role of monetary policy in the economy
- A careful, step-by-step development of models (an approach found in the best principles of economics textbooks), which makes it easier for students to learn
- The complete integration of an international perspective throughout the text
- A thoroughly up-to-date treatment of the latest developments in monetary theory
- Special features called "Financial News" to encourage reading of financial newspapers
- An applications-oriented perspective with numerous applications and special-topic boxes that increase students' interest by showing them how to apply theory to real-world examples

WHAT'S NEW IN THE FOURTH CANADIAN EDITION

In addition to the expected updating of all data through the end of 2008 whenever possible, there is major new material in every part of the text.

The Subprime Financial Crisis

The subprime financial crisis in the United States led to a series of events that have completely changed the structure of the financial system and the way central banks operate. This has required a rewriting of almost the entire textbook, including two new chapters, a rewrite of two whole chapters, and the addition of many timely new sections, applications, and boxes throughout the rest of the book.

New Chapter 9: Financial Crises and the Subprime Meltdown

With the onset of the subprime financial crisis, a money and banking course would not be complete without an extensive analysis of why financial crises like the subprime crisis occur and why they have such devastating effects on the economy. Using an economic analysis of the effects of asymmetric information on financial markets and the economy, this new chapter examines why financial crises occur and why they have such devastating effects. This analysis is used to explain the course of events in a number of past financial crises throughout the world, with a particular focus on explaining the most recent subprime crisis. Because the events in the subprime crisis have been so dramatic, the material in this chapter is very exciting for students.

New Chapter 12: Nonbank Financial Institutions

Banking is not the only type of financial intermediation in the economy. Nonbank finance also plays an important role, and in recent years the process of financial innovation has increased the importance of nonbank finance and blurred the distinction between different types of financial institutions. A money and banking book would not be complete without a detailed examination of the institutions engaged in nonbank finance. Chapter 12 examines how institutions engaged in nonbank finance (insurance companies, pension funds, finance companies, mutual funds, hedge funds, and private equity and venture capital funds) operate and how they are regulated. It also examines recent trends in nonbank finance and how nonbank financial institutions were affected by the subprime meltdown.

Reordering of Part III, Financial Institutions, and Rewrite of Chapter 10, Economic Analysis of Financial Regulation

In past editions, the chapter on the structure of the banking industry was followed by the chapter on banking regulation. This ordering no longer makes sense in the aftermath of the subprime financial crisis, because nonbank financial institutions like investment banks have for the most part disappeared as free-standing institutions and are now part of banking organizations. To reflect the new financial world that we have entered, we first discuss the financial industry as a whole and then look at the specifics of how the now more broadly based banking industry is structured. To do this, we have placed the chapter on regulation before the chapter on the structure of the banking industry and have rewritten it to focus less on bank regulation and more on regulation of the overall financial system.

Compelling New Material Throughout the Text

The subprime financial crisis in the United States has had such far-reaching effects on the field of money and banking that almost every chapter in this book has required changes to reflect what has happened. Throughout the book, we have also added a large amount of substantive new material on the impact of the subprime financial crisis including:

- A new application on the subprime collapse and the BAA-Treasury spread (Chapter 5)
- A new application on the subprime financial crisis and the stock market (Chapter 7)
- A new box on credit rating agencies and the subprime financial crisis (Chapter 8)
- A new box on Canada's asset-backed commercial paper saga (Chapter 9)
- A new box on mark-to-market accounting and financial stability (Chapter 10)
- A new box on the subprime mortgage crisis and consumer protection regulation (Chapter 10)
- A new section on where financial regulation is heading after the subprime financial crisis (Chapter 10)
- A new box on the money market mutual fund panic of 2008 (Chapter 11)
- A new box on the subprime financial crisis and the demise of large, free-standing investment banks (Chapter 11)
- A new box on the AIG blowup (Chapter 12)
- A new box on the subprime financial crisis and the monoline insurers (Chapter 12)
- A new application on how a capital crunch caused a credit crunch in 2008 (Chapter 13)

- A new application on lessons from the subprime financial crisis: when are financial derivatives likely to be a worldwide time bomb? (Chapter 14)

- A new section on monetary policy at the effective lower bound for the overnight interest rate (Chapter 17)

- A new Inside the Central Bank box on monetary policy at times of crisis (Chapter 17)

- A new section on preemptive strikes against economic downturns and financial disruption during the subprime meltdown (Chapter 18)

- A new section on lessons from the subprime crisis as to how central banks should respond to asset-price bubbles (Chapter 18)

- A new application on the subprime crisis and the dollar (Chapter 19)

- A new box on the subprime financial crisis and the IMF (Chapter 20)

- A new application on the perfect storm of shocks: negative supply shocks and the subprime financial crisis (Chapter 24)

- A new application on the subprime recession (Chapter 25)

Additional New Material on Financial Markets and Institutions

There have also been changes in financial markets and institutions in recent years that have not been directly related to the subprime financial crisis, and we have added the following new material to keep the text current:

- A new section on the positive role that lawyers play in our financial system, entitled "Let the Lawyers Live!" (Chapter 8)

- A new box on subprime mortgages in Canada (Chapter 9)

- A new box on how well Basel 2 will work (Chapter 10)

- A rewritten section on financial innovation and the growth of the "shadow banking system" (Chapter 11)

- A new section on credit insurance (Chapter 12)

- A new section on private equity and venture capital funds (Chapter 12)

- A new box on sovereign wealth funds and whether they pose a danger (Chapter 12)

- A new box on the Montreal Exchange and the Canadian Derivatitives Clearing Corporation (Chapter 14)

New Material on Monetary Theory and Policy

We have added new material on monetary theory and policy over and above that which was related to the subprime financial crisis:

- A rewrite of Chapter 17 to reflect recent developments in Bank of Canada operating procedures

- Expanded discussion of the Taylor Rule (Chapter 18)

- A new section on preemptive strikes against inflation (Chapter 18)

- A new section on preemptive strikes against economic downturns and financial disruptions (Chapter 18)

Further Simplification of the Supply and Demand Analysis of the Foreign Exchange Market

The chapter on the determination of exchange rates has always been challenging for some students. In the Third Edition, we moved the analysis closer to a more traditional supply and demand analysis to make it more intuitive. Although this change has been very well received by instructors, we decided that the model of exchange rate determination could be made even easier for students if we relegated the calculation comparing expected returns and the interest parity conditions to an appendix. Doing so in the fourth Canadian edition simplifies discussion appreciably and should make the analysis of exchange rate determination much more accessible to students.

Improved Exposition and Organization

Helpful comments from reviewers prompted us to improve the exposition throughout the book. The reviewers convinced us that we could simplify and condense the discussion of how the money supply is determined by combining Chapters 15 and 16 from the third Canadian edition into a new chapter. The resulting new Chapter 16, entitled "The Money Supply Process," does not lose any content and works even better in the classroom than the two chapters in the Third Edition. Also, at the suggestion of several reviewers, we simplified the exposition at the beginning of Chapter 24 of how the aggregate demand curve is derived.

Appendices and Mini-Cases on the Web

The MyEconLab website that accompanies this book (**www.myeconlab.com**) is an essential resource for additional content.

The web appendices for the fourth Canadian edition of *The Economics of Money, Banking, and Financial Markets* include:

Chapter 1:   Defining Aggregate Output, Income, the Price Level, and the Inflation Rate

Chapter 4:   Measuring Interest Rate Risk: Duration

Chapter 5:   Models of Asset Pricing

Chapter 5:   Applying the Asset Market Approach to a Commodity Market: The Case of Gold

Chapter 7:   Evidence on the Efficient Market Hypothesis

Chapter 10:   Banking Crises Throughout the World

Chapter 13:   Measuring Bank Performance

Chapter 13:   Nonbanking Financial Institutions and Duration Analysis

Chapter 15:   The Price Stability Goal and the Nominal Anchor

Chapter 16:   The Bank of Canada's Balance Sheet and the Monetary Base

Chapter 16:   The M2+ Money Multiplier

Chapter 19:   The Interest Parity Condition

Chapter 20:   The Canadian Balance of Payments

Chapter 21:   A Mathematical Treatment of the Baumol-Tobin and Tobin Mean-Variance Models

Chapter 21:   Empirical Evidence on the Demand for Money

Chapter 23:   Algebra of the *ISLM* Model

Mini-cases available on MyEconLab include:

Chapter 4:   Interest Rates, Bond Yields, and Duration

Chapter 5:   The Behaviour of Interest Rates

Chapter 6:	Yield Curve Hypotheses and the Effects of Economic Events
Chapter 7:	Adaptive Expectations, Rational Expectations, and Optimal Forecasts
Chapter 11:	The Changing Landscape for Domestic and Global Financial Markets
Chapter 13:	Bank Performance Analysis
Chapter 13:	Calculating and Comparing Gap, Duration, and Risk-Management Alternatives
Chapter 14:	Micro Hedge, Macro Hedge, Managing Interest-Rate Risk, and Duration
Chapter 19:	The Foreign Exchange Market and Financial Derivatives

Instructors can either use these web appendices and mini-cases in class to supplement the material in the textbook, or recommend them to students who want to expand their knowledge of the money and banking field. The answers to the web mini-cases are available in the Instructor's Manual.

FLEXIBILITY

In using previous editions, adopters, reviewers, and survey respondents have continually praised this text's flexibility. There are as many ways to teach money, banking, and financial markets as there are instructors. To satisfy the diverse needs of instructors, the text achieves flexibility as follows:

- Core chapters provide the basic analysis used throughout the book, and other chapters or sections of chapters can be used or omitted according to instructor preferences. For example, Chapter 2 introduces the financial system and basic concepts such as transaction costs, adverse selection, and moral hazard. After covering Chapter 2, the instructor may decide to give more detailed coverage of financial structure by assigning Chapter 8, or may choose to skip Chapter 8 and take any of a number of different paths through the book.

- The text also allows instructors to cover the most important issues in monetary theory and policy without having to use the *ISLM* model in Chapters 22 and 23, while more complete treatments of monetary theory make use of the *ISLM* chapters.

- The internationalization of the text through marked international sections within chapters, as well as through complete separate chapters on the foreign exchange market and the international monetary system, is comprehensive yet flexible. Although many instructors will teach all the international material, others will not. Instructors who want less emphasis on international topics can easily skip Chapter 19 on the foreign exchange market and Chapter 20 on the international financial system and monetary policy. The international sections within chapters are self-contained and can be omitted with little loss of continuity.

To illustrate how this book can be used for courses with varying emphases, several course outlines are suggested for a semester teaching schedule. More detailed information about how the text can be used flexibly in your course is available in the Instructor's Manual.

- *General Money and Banking Course:* Chapters 1–5, 10–13, 17, 18, 24, and 26, with a choice of six of the remaining fourteen chapters.
- *General Money and Banking Course with an International Emphasis:* Chapters 1–5, 10–13, 16–20, 24, and 26, with a choice of four of the remaining eleven chapters.
- *Financial Markets and Institutions Course:* Chapters 1–13, with a choice of seven of the remaining fourteen chapters.
- *Monetary Theory and Policy Course:* Chapters 1–5, 15–18, 21, 24, and 27, with a choice of five of the remaining thirteen chapters.

PEDAGOGICAL AIDS

In teaching theory or its applications, a textbook must be a solid motivational tool. To this end, we have incorporated a wide variety of pedagogical features to make the material easy to learn:

1. **Previews** at the beginning of each chapter tell students where the chapter is heading, why specific topics are important, and how they relate to other topics in the book.

2. **Applications**, numbering around 50, demonstrate how the analysis in the book can be used to explain many important real-world situations.

3. **Financial News boxes** introduce students to relevant news articles and data that are reported daily in the press and explain how to read them.

4. **Inside the Central Bank boxes** give students a feel for what is important in the operation and structure of central banks.

5. **Global boxes** include interesting material with an international focus.

6. **FYI boxes** highlight dramatic historical episodes, interesting ideas, and intriguing facts related to the subject matter.

7. **Key statements** are important points set in boldface italic type so that students can easily find them for later reference.

8. **Graphs** with captions, numbering more than 150, help students clearly understand the interrelationship of the variables plotted and the principles of analysis.

9. **Summaries** at the end of each chapter list the main points covered.

10. **Key terms** are important words or phrases, boldface when they are defined for the first time and listed by page number at the end of the chapter.

11. **End-of-chapter questions and problems**, numbering more than 400, help students learn the subject matter by applying economic concepts, including a special class of problems that students find particularly relevant, under the heading "Predicting the Future."

12. **Web Exercises** encourage students to collect information from online sources or use online resources to enhance their learning experience.

13. **Glossary** at the back of the book provides definitions of all the key terms.

AN EASIER WAY TO TEACH: SUPPLEMENTS TO ACCOMPANY THE FOURTH CANADIAN EDITION

The Economics of Money, Banking, and Financial Markets, Fourth Canadian Edition, includes the most comprehensive program of supplements of any money, banking, and financial markets textbook. These items are available to qualified domestic adopters but in some cases may not be available to international adopters.

MyEconLab is the premier online assessment and tutorial system, pairing rich online content with innovative learning tools. The MyEconLab course for the fourth Canadian edition of *The Economics of Money, Banking, and Financial Markets* includes all end-of-chapter problems from the text as well as additional questions for further study, which can be easily assigned and automatically graded.

STUDENTS AND MYECONLAB   This online homework and tutorial system puts students in control of their own learning through a suite of study and practice tools correlated with the online, interactive version of the textbook and other media tools. Within MyEconLab's structured environment, students practise what they learn, test their understanding, and then pursue a study plan that MyEconLab generates for them based on their performance on practice tests.

INSTRUCTORS AND MYECONLAB   MyEconLab provides flexible tools that allow instructors to easily and effectively customize online course materials to suit their needs. Instructors can create and assign tests, quizzes, or homework assignments. MyEconLab saves time by automatically grading all questions and tracking results in an online grade book. MyEconLab can even grade assignments that require students to draw a graph.

After registering for MyEconLab, instructors have access to downloadable supplements such as an instructor's manual, PowerPoint lecture notes, and the test bank. The test bank can also be used within MyEconLab, giving instructors ample material from which they can create assignments.

Additional MyEconLab features include:

- *Animated Figures*. Key figures from the textbook are presented in step-by-step animations with audio explanations of the action.

- *Applications*. A selection of the applications from the text are available with assignable questions.

- *Mishkin Interviewed on the Financial Crisis*. Watch video footage from a recent interview with one of the authors.

For more information and to register, please visit **www.myeconlab.com**.

Additional Instructor Resources

1. **Instructor's Resource CD-ROM**   This edition of the book comes with a powerful teaching tool: an Instructor's Resource CD-ROM. Fully compatible with Windows and Macintosh computers, the CD-ROM contains Word and PDF files for the entire contents of the Instructor's Manual, PowerPoint slides, and TestGen. Using this supplement, instructors can prepare such student handouts as solutions to problem sets made from end-of-chapter problems or the outline of the lecture of the day. TestGen is a valuable test preparation tool that allows

professors to view, edit, and add questions. The Instructor's Manual, PowerPoint slides, and TestGen are also available online at **http://vig. pearsoned.ca**.

2. **Instructor's Manual** Prepared by the authors, the Instructor's Manual provides conventional elements such as sample course outlines, chapter outlines, and answers to questions and problems in the text.

3. **PowerPoint® Slides** A complete set of slides that are specifically designed for or culled from the textbook is available electronically.

4. **TestGen** The computerized test bank allows the instructor to produce exams efficiently. This product consists of multiple-choice and short answer questions and offers editing capabilities. It is available in Windows and Macintosh versions.

Additional Student Resources

1. **Technology Specialists** Pearson's Technology Specialists work with faculty and campus course designers to ensure that Pearson technology products, assessment tools, and online course materials are tailored to meet your specific needs. This highly qualified team is dedicated to helping schools take full advantage of a wide range of educational resources by assisting in the integration of a variety of instructional materials and media formats. Your local Pearson Education sales representative can provide you with more details on this service program.

2. **CourseSmart** is a new way for instructors and students to access textbooks online anytime from anywhere. With thousands of titles across hundreds of courses, CourseSmart helps instructors choose the best textbook for their class and give their students a new option for buying the assigned textbook as a lower cost eTextbook. For more information, visit **www.coursesmart.com**.

3. **Study Guide** Fully revised and updated, the Study Guide includes chapter synopses and completions, exercises, self-tests, and answers to the exercises and self-tests.

ACKNOWLEDGMENTS

This book is the result of efforts by many people. We are extremely grateful to Alexandra Dyer, Sponsoring Editor; Don Thompson and Claudine O'Donnell, Acquisitions Editors; Christina Lee, Developmental Editor; Leanne Rancourt and Cheryl Jackson, Production Editors, and Laura Neves, Copy Editor; and the many others at Pearson Education Canada who have contributed to the completion of this edition.

We are also grateful to all of the many people who commented on various chapters of the book, made valuable suggestions, and kindly provided us with data. We would particularly like to thank the following reviewers whose comments on the manuscript contributed to the development of this edition:

Kam Hon Chu, Memorial University

Yolina Denchev, Camosun College

Michael Ho, University of Toronto

Frank Ingold, George Brown College

Suzanne Iskander, Humber College

Jean-Paul Lam, University of Waterloo

Marc Prudhomme, University of Ottawa

Duane Rockerbie, University of Lethbridge

Shanker Seetharam, Centennial College

Lance Shandler, Kwantlen University College

Amy Sopinka, University of Victoria

Thomas Velk, McGill University

Although we have done our best to make this edition as complete and error-free as possible, as most of you know, perfection is impossible. We would greatly appreciate any suggestions for improvement. Please send your comments to serletis@ucalgary.ca.

Frederic S. Mishkin
Apostolos Serletis
2009

About the Authors

Frederic S. Mishkin is the Alfred Lerner Professor of Banking and Financial Institutions at the Graduate School of Business, Columbia University. He is also a Research Associate at the National Bureau of Economic Research and past president of the Eastern Economics Association. Since receiving his Ph.D. from the Massachusetts Institute of Technology in 1976, he has taught at the University of Chicago, Northwestern University, Princeton University, and Columbia. He has also received an honorary professorship from the People's (Renmin) University of China. From 1994 to 1997, he was Executive Vice President and Director of Research at the Federal Reserve Bank of New York and an associate economist of the Federal Open Market Committee of the Federal Reserve System. From September 2006 to August 2008, he was a member (governor) of the Board of Governors of the Federal Reserve System.

Professor Mishkin's research focuses on monetary policy and its impact on financial markets and the aggregate economy. He is the author of more than fifteen books, including *Financial Markets and Institutions*, Sixth Edition (Addison-Wesley, 2009); *Monetary Policy Strategy* (MIT Press, 2007); *The Next Great Globalization: How Disadvantaged Nations Can Harness Their Financial Systems to Get Rich* (Princeton University Press, 2006); *Inflation Targeting: Lessons from the International Experience* (Princeton University Press, 1999); *Money, Interest Rates, and Inflation* (Edward Elgar, 1993); and *A Rational Expectations Approach to Macroeconometrics: Testing Policy Ineffectiveness and Efficient Markets Models* (University of Chicago Press, 1983). In addition, he has published more than 150 articles in such journals as *American Economic Review, Journal of Political Economy, Econometrica, Quarterly Journal of Economics, Journal of Finance*, and *Journal of Monetary Economics*.

Professor Mishkin has served on the editorial board of *American Economic Review* and has been an associate editor at *Journal of Business and Economic Statistics,* the *Journal of Applied Econometrics,* and *Journal of Money, Credit and Banking;* he also served as the editor of the Federal Reserve Bank of New York's *Economic Policy Review.* He is currently an associate editor (member of the editorial board) at six academic journals, including *Macroeconomics and Monetary Economics Abstracts; Journal of International Money and Finance; International Finance; Finance India; Economic Policy Review;* and *Emerging Markets, Finance and Trade.* He has been a consultant to the Board of Governors of the Federal Reserve System, the World Bank, and the International Monetary Fund, as well as to many central banks throughout the world. He was also a member of the International Advisory Board to the Financial Supervisory Service of South Korea and an adviser to the Institute for Monetary and Economic Research at the Bank of Korea. Professor Mishkin was a Senior Fellow at the Federal Deposit Insurance Corporation's Center for Banking Research and was an academic consultant to and served on the Economic Advisory Panel of the Federal Reserve Bank of New York.

Apostolos Serletis is Professor of Economics and Finance at the University of Calgary. Since receiving his Ph.D. from McMaster University in 1984, he has held visiting appointments at the University of Texas at Austin, the Athens University of Economics and Business, and the Research Department of the Federal Reserve Bank of St. Louis.

Professor Serletis' teaching and research interests focus on monetary and financial economics, macroeconometrics, and nonlinear and complex dynamics. He is the author of eight books, including *Macroeconomics: A Modern Approach* (First Canadian Edition) with Robert J. Barro (Nelson, 2010), *The Demand for Money: Theoretical and Empirical Approaches* (Springer, 2007), *Financial Markets and Institutions: Canadian Edition*, with Frederic S. Mishkin and Stanley G. Eakins (Addison-Wesley, 2004), and *The Theory of Monetary Aggregation*, co-edited with William A. Barnett (Elsevier, 2000). In addition, he has published over 150 articles in such journals as *Journal of Economic Literature; Journal of Monetary Economics; Journal of Money, Credit, and Banking; Journal of Econometrics; Journal of Applied Econometrics; Journal of Business and Economic Statistics; Macroeconomic Dynamics; Journal of Banking and Finance; Journal of Economic Dynamics and Control; Economic Inquiry; Canadian Journal of Economics;* and *Studies in Nonlinear Dynamics and Econometrics.*

Professor Serletis is Associate Editor of *Macroeconomic Dynamics* and a member of the editorial board at two academic journals, *Journal of Economic Asymmetries* and *Journal of Economic Studies.* He is listed in a variety of directories, including *Who's Who in Economics* and *Who's Who in the World.*

PART I

Introduction

THE SUBPRIME CRISIS: AN INTRODUCTION

The subprime financial crisis that started in the United States in August 2007 was the result of a credit-driven, asset-price bubble in the U.S. housing market. When that bubble burst, the value of mortgage-backed securities held by financial institutions plummeted. The crisis ended up bringing down the financial system, which not only led to an economic downturn and a rise in unemployment in the United States, but also to a global recession. Governments around the world worked on full-scale banking bailouts and rescue packages adding up to trillions of dollars.

The view held by the popular press and most politicians is that Wall Street professionals, bankers, and homeowners are to blame for having taken excessive, self-destructive risks out of "greed." Another view is that bankers and homeowners are the victims of the financial crisis and that the causes of the crisis were inadequate supervision and regulation of financial firms, inadequate consumer protection regulation, and low-quality data produced and supplied by the Federal Reserve and other central banks around the world. Regarding the latter, poor or inadequate data originating at central banks produced the misperceptions of superior monetary policy and an incorrect assessment of systemic risk, and thereby supported greater risk-taking by lenders and borrowers.

Chapter 1 begins with a road map of the money, banking, and financial markets field. In Chapter 2, we examine the basic functions performed by financial markets, describe the principal financial-market instruments, and discuss why the financial system is the most heavily regulated sector of the economy. Chapter 3 looks at some of the monetary statistics produced and supplied by the central bank.

CHAPTER 1

Why Study Money, Banking, and Financial Markets?

LEARNING OBJECTIVES

After studying this chapter you should be able to

1. outline what is involved in the study of financial markets (such as bonds, stocks, and foreign exchange markets)
2. identify what it means to study financial institutions (i.e., banks, insurance companies, mutual funds)
3. describe why money is a major influence on inflation, business cycles, and interest rates

PREVIEW

On the evening news you hear that the Bank of Canada is raising the bank rate by one-half of a percentage point. What effect might this have on the interest rate of an automobile loan when you finance your purchase of a sleek new sports car? Does it mean that a house will be more or less affordable in the future? Will it make it easier or harder for you to get a job next year?

This book provides answers to these and other questions by examining how financial markets (such as those for bonds, stocks, and foreign exchange) and financial institutions (chartered banks, trust and mortgage loan companies, credit unions and *caisses populaires,* insurance companies, mutual fund companies, and other institutions) work and by exploring the role of money in the economy. Financial markets and institutions not only affect your everyday life but also involve flows of billions of dollars of funds through our economy, which in turn affect business profits, the production of goods and services, and even the economic well-being of countries other than Canada. What happens to financial markets, financial institutions, and money is of great concern to politicians and can even have a major impact on elections. The study of money, banking, and financial markets will reward you with an understanding of many exciting issues. In this chapter we provide a road map of the book by outlining these issues and exploring why they are worth studying.

WHY STUDY FINANCIAL MARKETS?

Part II of this book focuses on **financial markets**, markets in which funds are transferred from people who have an excess of available funds to people who have a shortage. Financial markets such as bond and stock markets are crucial to promoting greater economic efficiency by channelling funds from people who do not have a productive use for them to those who do. Well-functioning financial markets are a key factor in producing high economic growth and poorly performing financial markets are one reason that many countries in the world remain desperately poor. Activities in financial markets also have direct effects on personal wealth, the behaviour of businesses and consumers, and the cyclical performance of the economy.

The Bond Market and Interest Rates

A **security** (also called a *financial instrument*) is a claim on the issuer's future income or **assets** (any financial claim or piece of property that is subject to ownership). A **bond** is a debt security that promises to make payments periodically for a specified period of time.[1] The bond market is especially important to economic activity because it enables corporations and governments to borrow to finance their activities and because it is where interest rates are determined. An **interest rate** is the cost of borrowing or the price paid for the rental of funds (usually expressed as a percentage of the rental of $100 per year). There are many interest rates in the economy—mortgage interest rates, car loan rates, and interest rates on many different types of bonds.

Interest rates are important on a number of levels. On a personal level, high interest rates could deter you from buying a house or a car because the cost of financing it would be high. Conversely, high interest rates could encourage you to save because you can earn more interest income by putting aside some of your earnings as savings. On a more general level, interest rates have an impact on the overall health of the economy because they affect not only consumers' willingness to spend or save but also businesses' investment decisions. High interest rates, for example, may cause a corporation to postpone building a new plant that would ensure more jobs.

Because changes in interest rates have important effects on individuals, financial institutions, businesses, and the overall economy, it is important to explain fluctuations in interest rates that have been substantial over the past twenty years. For example, the interest rate on three-month treasury bills peaked at over 20% in August 1981. This interest rate then fell to a low of less than 3% in 1997, rose to near 5% in the late 1990s, fell to a low of 2% in the early 2000s, and rose to above 4% by 2007, only to fall to less than 1% in 2009.

Because different interest rates have a tendency to move in unison, economists frequently lump interest rates together and refer to "the" interest rate. As Figure 1-1 shows, however, interest rates on several types of bonds can differ substantially. The interest rate on three-month treasury bills, for example, fluctuates more than the other interest rates and is lower on average. The interest rate on long-term corporate bonds is higher on average than the other interest rates, and the spread between it and the other rates fluctuates over time.

In Chapter 2 we study the role of bond markets in the economy, and in Chapters 4 through 6 we examine what an interest rate is, how the common movements in interest rates come about, and why the interest rates on different bonds vary.

The Stock Market

A **common stock** (typically just called a *stock*) represents a share of ownership in a corporation. It is a security that is a claim on the earnings and assets of the corporation. Issuing stock and selling it to the public is a way for corporations to

---

[1] The definition of *bond* used throughout this book is the broad one in common use by academics, which covers short- as well as long-term debt instruments. However, some practitioners in financial markets use the word *bond* only to describe specific long-term debt instruments such as corporate bonds or Canada bonds.

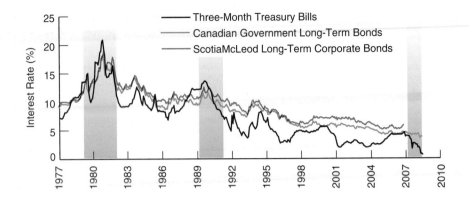

FIGURE 1-1   Interest Rates on Selected Bonds, 1977–2009

Note: Shaded areas represent recessions.

Source: Statistics Canada CANSIM II Series V122531, V122544, and V122518.

raise funds to finance their activities. The stock market, in which claims on the earnings of corporations (shares of stock) are traded, is the most widely followed financial market in almost every country that has one (that's why it is often called simply "the market"). A big swing in the prices of shares in the stock market is always a big story on the evening news. People often speculate on where the market is heading and get very excited when they can brag about their latest "big killing," but they become depressed when they suffer a big loss. The attention the market receives can probably be best explained by one simple fact: it is a place where people get rich—and poor—quickly.

As Figure 1-2 indicates, stock prices are extremely volatile. After the market rose in the 1980s, on "Black Monday," October 19, 1987, it experienced the worst one-day drop in its entire history, with the S&P/TSX Composite falling by 11%. From then until 2000, the stock market experienced one of the great bull markets in its history, with the S&P/TSX climbing to a peak of over 11 000. With the collapse of the high-tech bubble in 2000, the stock market fell sharply, dropping by over 40% by late 2002. It then recovered again to over the 14 000 level in early

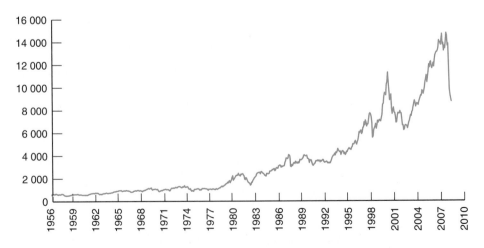

FIGURE 1-2   Stock Prices as Measured by the S&P/TSX Composite Index, 1956–2009

Source: Statistics Canada CANSIM II Series V122620.

2008, and then fell again by almost 50% by early 2009. These considerable fluctuations in stock prices affect the size of people's wealth and, as a result, may affect their willingness to spend.

The stock market is also an important factor in business investment decisions because the price of shares affects the amount of funds that can be raised by selling newly issued stock to finance investment spending. A higher price for a firm's shares allows the firm to raise a larger amount of funds that can be used to buy production facilities and equipment.

In Chapter 2 we examine the role that the stock market plays in the financial system, and we return to the issue of how stock prices behave and respond to information in the marketplace in Chapter 7.

WHY STUDY FINANCIAL INSTITUTIONS AND BANKING?

Part III of this book focuses on financial institutions and the business of banking. Banks and other financial institutions are what make financial markets work. Without them, financial markets would not be able to move funds from people who save to people who have productive investment opportunities. Thus they play a crucial role in the economy.

Structure of the Financial System

The financial system is complex, comprising many different types of private sector financial institutions, including banks, insurance companies, mutual funds, finance companies, and investment banks, all of which are heavily regulated by the government. If an individual wanted to make a loan to Bombardier or Nortel, for example, they would not go directly to the president of the company and offer a loan. Instead, they would lend to such companies indirectly through **financial intermediaries**, institutions that borrow funds from people who have saved and in turn make loans to others.

Why are financial intermediaries so crucial to well-functioning financial markets? Why do they extend credit to one party but not to another? Why do they usually write complicated legal documents when they extend loans? Why are they the most heavily regulated businesses in the economy?

We answer these questions in Chapter 8 by developing a coherent framework for analyzing financial structure in Canada and in the rest of the world.

Financial Crises

At times, the financial system seizes up and produces **financial crises**, major disruptions in financial markets that are characterized by sharp declines in asset prices and failures of many financial and nonfinancial firms. Financial crises have been a feature of capitalist economies for hundreds of years and are typically followed by the worst business-cycle downturns. Starting in August of 2007, the United States economy was hit by the worst financial disruption since the Great Depression when defaults in subprime residential mortgages led to major losses in financial institutions, producing not only numerous bank failures, but also the demise of Bear Stearns, the largest investment bank in the United States.

Chapter 9 discusses why these crises occur and how they can do so much damage to the economy.

Banks and Other Financial Institutions

Banks are financial institutions that accept deposits and make loans. Included under the term *banks* are firms such as chartered banks, trust and mortgage loan companies, and credit unions and *caisses populaires*. Banks are the financial intermediaries that the average person interacts with most frequently. A person who needs a loan to buy a house or a car usually obtains it from a local bank. Most Canadians keep a large proportion of their financial wealth in banks in the form of chequing accounts, savings accounts, or other types of bank deposits. Because banks are the largest financial intermediaries in our economy, they deserve the most careful study. However, banks are not the only important financial institutions. Indeed, in recent years, other financial institutions such as insurance companies, finance companies, pension funds, mutual funds, and investment banks have been growing at the expense of banks, and so we need to study them as well.

In Chapter 11 we look at the banking industry, examine how the competitive environment has changed in the industry and learn why some financial institutions have been growing at the expense of others. In Chapter 11 we extend the economic analysis from Chapter 8 to understand why bank regulation takes the form it does and what can go wrong in the regulatory process. In Chapter 12 we identify the differences between banks and nonbank financial institutions and explain the regulation of nonbank financial institutions in the context of adverse selection and moral hazard problems.

In Chapter 13 we examine how banks and other financial institutions manage their assets and liabilities to make profits. Because the economic environment for banks and other financial institutions has become increasingly risky, these institutions must find ways to manage risk. How they manage risk with financial derivatives is the topic of Chapter 14.

Financial Innovation

In the good old days, when you took cash out of the bank or wanted to check your account balance, you got to say hello to a friendly human teller. Nowadays you are more likely to interact with an automated teller machine (ATM) when withdrawing cash and you can get your account balance from your home computer. To see why these options have developed, we study why and how financial innovation takes place in Chapter 11, with particular emphasis on how the dramatic improvements in information technology have led to new means of delivering financial services electronically, known as **e-finance**. We also study financial innovation because it shows us how creative thinking on the part of financial institutions can lead to higher profits. By seeing how and why financial institutions have been creative in the past, we obtain a better grasp of how they may be creative in the future. This knowledge provides us with useful clues about how the financial system may change over time and will help keep our knowledge about banks and other financial institutions from becoming obsolete.

WHY STUDY MONEY AND MONETARY POLICY?

Money is defined as anything that is generally accepted in payment for goods or services or in the repayment of debts. Money is linked to changes in economic variables that affect all of us and are important to the health of the economy. The final two parts of the book examine the role of money in the economy.

Money and Business Cycles

In 1981–1982, total production of goods and services (called **aggregate output**) in the economy fell and the number of people out of work rose to close to 12% of the labour force. After 1982, the economy began to expand rapidly, and by 1989, the **unemployment rate** (the percentage of the available labour force unemployed) had declined to 7.5%. In 1990, the eight-year expansion came to an end, and the economy began to decline again, with unemployment rising above 11%. The economy bottomed out in 1991, and the subsequent recovery has been the longest in Canadian history, with unemployment rates falling to around 6% in 2008, before rising above 7% in early 2009 in the aftermath of the subprime financial crisis.

Why did the economy boom from 1982 to 1990, contract in 1990–1991, boom again from 1991 to 2007, and slow down in late 2008? Evidence suggests that money plays an important role in generating **business cycles**, the upward and downward movement of aggregate output produced in the economy. Business cycles affect all of us in immediate and important ways. When output is rising, for example, it is easier to find a good job; when output is falling, finding a good job might be difficult. Figure 1-3 shows the movements of the rate of money growth from 1968 to 2008, with the shaded areas representing **recessions**, periods of declining aggregate output. What we see is that every recession has been preceded by a decline in the rate of money growth, indicating that changes in money might be a driving force behind business cycle fluctuations. However, not every decline in the rate of money growth is followed by a recession.

We explore how money might affect aggregate output in Chapters 21 through 27, where we study **monetary theory**, the theory that relates changes in the quantity of money to changes in aggregate economic activity and the price level.

Money and Inflation

Twenty years ago, the movie you may have paid $13 to see last week would have set you back only a couple of dollars. In fact, for $13 you could probably have had dinner, seen the movie, and bought yourself a big bucket of hot buttered popcorn. As shown in Figure 1-4, which illustrates the movement of average prices in the Canadian economy from 1968 to 2008, the prices of most items are quite a bit higher now. The average price of goods and services in an economy is called the **aggregate price level** or, more simply, the *price level* (a more precise definition is found in the web appendix to this chapter). **Inflation**, a continual increase in the price level, affects individuals, businesses, and the government. It is generally regarded as an important problem to be solved and is often at the top of political and policymaking agendas. To solve the inflation problem, we need to know something about its causes.

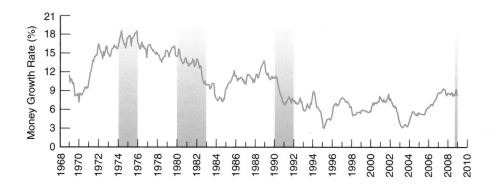

FIGURE 1-3 Money Growth (M2++ (Gross) Annual Rate) and the Business Cycle in Canada, 1968–2008

Note: Shaded areas represent recessions.

Source: Statistics Canada CANSIM II Series V41552801.

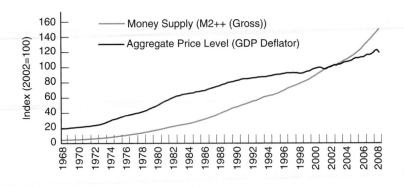

FIGURE 1-4   Aggregate Price Level and the Money Supply in Canada, 1968–2008

Source: Statistics Canada CANSIM II Series V1997756 and V41552801.

What explains inflation? One clue to answering this question is found in Figure 1-4. As we can see, the price level and the money supply generally move closely together. These data seem to indicate that a continuing increase in the money supply might be an important factor in causing the continuing increase in the price level that we call inflation.

Further evidence that inflation may be tied to continuing increases in the money supply is found in Figure 1-5. For a number of countries, it plots the average **inflation rate** (the rate of change of the price level, usually measured as a percentage change per year) from 1995 to 2007 against the average rate of money growth over the same period. As you can see, there is a positive association between infla-

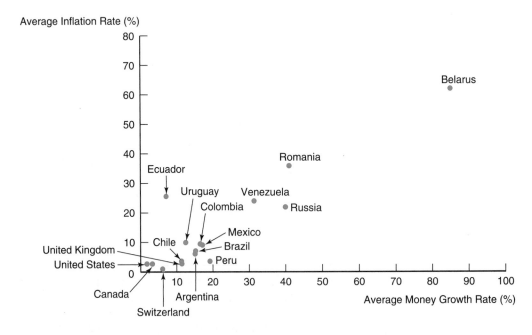

FIGURE 1-5   Average Inflation Rate Versus Average Rate of Money Growth for Selected Countries, 1995–2007

Source: IMF International Financial Statistics.

tion and the growth rate of the money supply: the countries with the highest inflation rates are also the ones with the highest money growth rates. Belarus, Romania, Russia, and Venezuela, for example, experienced high inflation during this period, and their rates of money growth were high. By contrast, Canada and the United States had low inflation rates over the same period, and their rates of money growth have been low. Such evidence led Milton Friedman, a Nobel laureate in economics, to make the famous statement "Inflation is always and everywhere a monetary phenomenon."[2] We look at money's role in creating inflation in Chapter 26.

Money and Interest Rates

In addition to other factors, money plays an important role in the interest-rate fluctuations that are of such great concern to businesses and consumers. Figure 1-6 shows the changes in the interest rate on long-term Canada bonds and the rate of money growth. As the money growth rate rose in the late 1970s, the long-term bond rate rose with it. However, the relationship between money growth and interest rates has been less clear-cut since 1980. We analyze the relationship between money and interest rates when we examine the behaviour of interest rates in Chapter 5.

Conduct of Monetary Policy

Because money can affect many economic variables that are important to the well-being of our economy, politicians and policymakers throughout the world care about the conduct of **monetary policy**, the management of money and interest rates. The organization responsible for the conduct of a nation's monetary policy is the **central bank**. Canada's central bank is the **Bank of Canada** (also called simply **the Bank**). In Chapters 15–18, we study how central banks like the Bank of Canada can affect interest rates and the quantity of money in the economy and then look at how monetary policy is actually conducted in Canada and elsewhere.

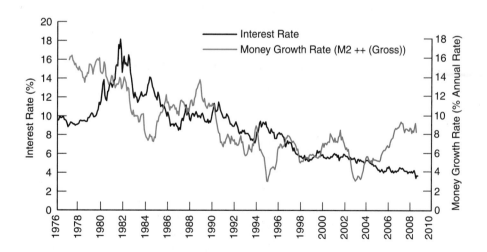

FIGURE 1-6   M2 ++ (Gross) Money Growth (Over 12 Months) and Interest Rates (Long-Term Government of Canada Bonds), 1977–2008

Source: Statistics Canada CANSIM II Series V41552801 and V122544.

---

[2] Milton Friedman, *Dollars and Deficits* (Upper Saddle River, N.J.: Prentice Hall, 1968), p. 39.

Fiscal Policy and Monetary Policy

Fiscal policy involves decisions about government spending and taxation. A **budget deficit** is the excess of government expenditures over tax revenues for a particular time period (typically a year), while a **budget surplus** arises when tax revenues exceed government expenditures. The government must finance any deficit by borrowing, while a budget surplus leads to a lower government debt burden. As Figure 1-7 shows, the budget deficit, relative to the size of our economy, peaked in 1992 at 8.7% of national output (as calculated by the gross domestic product, or GDP, a measure of aggregate output described in the web appendix to this chapter). Since then, the budget deficit declined and the budget actually went into surplus in recent years. Budget deficits have been the subject of bitter battles between Canadian politicians. Some argue that deficits increase the national debt and make us vulnerable to increases in world interest rates. They propose to cut government spending to pay down the debt and to reduce taxes. Others argue that the ability to issue public debt allows the government to smooth taxes and inflation over time.

You may have seen or heard statements in newspapers or on TV that budget surpluses are a good thing while deficits are undesirable. We explore the accuracy of such claims in Chapters 8 and 18 by seeing how budget deficits might lead to a financial crisis, as they did in Argentina in 2001. In Chapter 26, we examine why deficits might result in a higher rate of money growth, a higher rate of inflation, and higher interest rates.

WHY STUDY INTERNATIONAL FINANCE?

The globalization of financial markets has accelerated at a rapid pace in recent years. Financial markets have become increasingly integrated throughout the world, with Canadian companies often borrowing in foreign financial markets and foreign companies borrowing in Canadian financial markets. Banks and other financial institutions have become increasingly international and often have operations in many countries throughout the world. Part VI of this book explores the foreign exchange market and the international financial system.

FIGURE 1-7 Government Budget Surplus or Deficit as a Percentage of Gross Domestic Product, 1961–2008

Source: Statistics Canada CANSIM II Series V498316, V498326, and V498086.

The Foreign Exchange Market

For funds to be transferred from one country to another, they have to be converted from the currency in the country of origin (say, dollars) into the currency of the country to which they are going (say, euros). The **foreign exchange market** is where this conversion takes place and it is instrumental in moving funds between countries. It is also important because it is where the **foreign exchange rate**, the price of one country's currency in terms of another's, is determined.

Because the foreign exchange rate is the relative price of two national currencies, there are two ways of quoting an exchange rate: either as the amount of domestic currency that can be purchased with a unit of foreign currency or as the amount of foreign currency that can be purchased with a unit of domestic currency. Throughout this book, we always use the latter quoting convention—that is, we express the exchange rate as units of foreign currency per Canadian dollar. In these terms, when the exchange rate increases so that a Canadian dollar buys more units of foreign currency, we say that the Canadian dollar has had an **appreciation**. A decline in the exchange rate is associated with a **depreciation** of the Canadian dollar.

Figure 1-8 shows the exchange rate for the Canadian dollar from 1971 to 2008 in terms of the U.S. dollar. The exchange rate is defined as the U.S. dollar price of one Canadian dollar. Clearly, the exchange rate has experienced five long swings over this period. The first is a 30.8% depreciation from January 1973 to February 1986; the second is a 26.0% appreciation from February 1986 to January 1992; the third is a 26.7% depreciation from January 1992 to October 2002; the fourth is a 62% appreciation from October 2002 to November 2007; and the fifth is a 21% depreciation from November 2007 to January 2009.

What have these fluctuations in the exchange rate meant to the Canadian public and businesses? A change in the exchange rate has a direct effect on Canadian consumers because it affects the cost of foreign goods. In particular, a weaker dollar leads to more expensive foreign goods, makes vacationing abroad more expensive, and raises the cost of indulging your desire for imported delicacies. When the value of the dollar drops, Canadians decrease their purchases of foreign goods and increase their consumption of domestic goods (such as travel within Canada).

Conversely, a strong dollar means that Canadian goods exported abroad will cost more in foreign countries and foreigners will buy fewer of them. Exports of steel, for example, declined sharply when the dollar strengthened in the late 1980s.

FIGURE 1-8 Exchange Rate for the Canadian Dollar, 1971–2008

Source: Statistics Canada CANSIM II Series V37426.

A strong dollar benefited Canadian consumers by making foreign goods cheaper but hurt Canadian businesses and eliminated some jobs by cutting both domestic and foreign sales of their products. The increase in the value of the dollar since 2002 has had a similar effect: it has made foreign goods less expensive but has made Canadian businesses less competitive. Fluctuations in the foreign exchange markets have major consequences in the Canadian economy.

In Chapter 19 we study how exchange rates are determined in the foreign exchange market in which dollars are bought and sold for foreign currencies.

The International Financial System

The tremendous increase in capital flows between countries means that the international financial system has a growing impact on domestic economies. Whether a country fixes its exchange rate to that of another is an important determinant of how monetary policy is conducted. Whether there are capital controls that restrict mobility of capital across national borders has a large effect on domestic financial systems and the performance of the economy. What role international financial institutions such as the International Monetary Fund should play in the international financial system is very controversial. All of these issues are explored in Chapter 20.

HOW WE WILL STUDY MONEY, BANKING, AND FINANCIAL MARKETS

This textbook stresses the economic way of thinking by developing a unifying framework to study money, banking, and financial markets. This analytic framework uses a few basic economic concepts to organize your thinking about the determination of asset prices, the structure of financial markets, bank management, and the role of money in the economy. It encompasses the following basic concepts:

- A simplified approach to the demand for assets
- The concept of equilibrium
- Basic supply and demand to explain behaviour in financial markets
- The search for profits
- An approach to financial structure based on transaction costs and asymmetric information
- Aggregate supply and demand analysis

The unifying framework used in this book will keep your knowledge from becoming obsolete and make the material more interesting. It will enable you to learn what *really* matters without having to memorize a mass of dull facts that you will forget soon after the final exam. This framework will also provide you with the tools to understand trends in the financial marketplace and in variables such as interest rates, exchange rates, inflation, and aggregate output.

To help you understand and apply the unifying analytic framework, simple models are constructed in which the variables held constant are carefully delineated, each step in the derivation of the model is clearly and carefully laid out, and the models are then used to explain various phenomena by focusing on changes in one variable at a time, holding all other variables constant.

To reinforce the models' usefulness, this text uses case studies, applications, and special-interest boxes to present evidence that supports or casts doubts on the theories being discussed. This exposure to real-life events and empirical data should dissuade you from thinking that all economists make abstract assumptions and develop theories that have little to do with actual behaviour.

To function better in the real world outside the classroom, you must get into the lifelong habit of regularly following the financial news that appears in leading financial publications such as *The Globe and Mail: Report on Business* and the *National Post: Financial Post*. To help and encourage you to read the financial section of the newspaper, this book contains two special features. The first is a set of special boxed inserts titled "Financial News" that contain actual columns and data from the media that appear daily or periodically. These boxes give you the detailed information and definitions you need to evaluate the data being presented.

In addition to these applications, this book also contains nearly 400 end-of-chapter problems that ask you to apply the analytic concepts you have learned to other real-world issues. Particularly relevant is a special class of problems headed "Predicting the Future." So that you can work on these problems on your own, answers to half of them are found at the end of the book. These give you an opportunity to review and apply many of the important financial concepts and tools presented throughout the book.

EXPLORING THE WEB

The Internet has become an extremely valuable and convenient resource for financial research. We emphasize the importance of this tool in several ways. First, wherever we utilize the web to find information to build the charts and tables that appear throughout the text, we include the source site's URL. These sites often contain additional information and are updated frequently. Second, we have added Web Exercises to the end of each chapter. These exercises prompt you to visit sites related to the chapter and work with real-time data and information. We have also provided Web References on the MyEconLab that accompanies this book (**www.pearsoned.ca/myeconlab**) that list the URLs of sites related to the material being discussed. Visit these sites to further explore a topic you find of particular interest.

Collecting and Graphing Data

The following sample Web Exercise is especially important because it demonstrates how to export data from a website into Microsoft Excel for further analysis. We suggest you work through this problem on your own so that you will be able to perform this activity when prompted in subsequent Web Exercises.

SAMPLE WEB EXERCISE

You have been hired by Risky Ventures Ltd. as a consultant to help the company analyze interest rate trends. Your employers are initially interested in determining the historical relationship between short-term interest rates. The biggest task you must immediately undertake is collecting market interest-rate data. You know the best source of this information is the web.

1. You decide that your best indicators of short-term interest rates are the bank rate, the one-month bankers' acceptances rate, and the three-month prime corporate rate. Your first task is to gather historical data. Go to **www.bankofcanada.ca** and select "Rates and Statistics" and then "Canadian Interest Rates." The site should look like the screen shown on page 14.

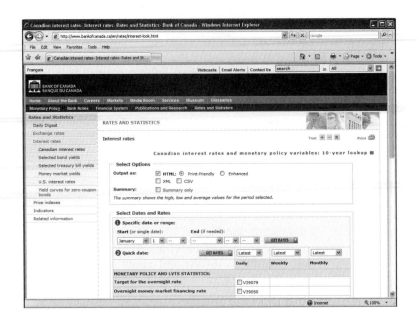

Source: Bank of Canada, www.bankofcanada.ca/en/rates/interest-look.html.

2. Although you have located an accurate source of historical interest rate data, getting it onto a spreadsheet will be very tedious. You recall that Excel (Microsoft® Excel) will let you convert text data into columns. Begin by indicating that you want to display the data in CSV format, sorted by date. Under the monthly series frequency, click on "V122530," "V122504," and "V122491," specify dates by choosing the start and end dates, and click on "Get Rates." A new screen should appear with a link to download the CSV data to your computer.

3. You now want to analyze the interest rates by graphing them. Use Excel to open the CSV file you downloaded. Click on the Chart Wizard icon on the tool bar (or INSERT/CHART). Select scatter diagram and choose any type of scatter diagram that connects the dots. Let the Excel wizard take you through the steps of completing the graph.

CONCLUDING REMARKS

The topic of money, banking, and financial markets is an exciting field that directly affects your life—interest rates influence earnings on your savings and the payments on loans you may seek on a car or a house, and monetary policy may affect your job prospects and the prices of goods in the future. Your study of money, banking, and financial markets will introduce you to many of the controversies about the conduct of economic policy that are hotly debated in the political arena and will help you gain a clearer understanding of economic phenomena you hear about in the news media. The knowledge you gain will stay with you and benefit you long after your course is done.

SUMMARY

1. Activities in financial markets have direct effects on individuals' wealth, the behaviour of businesses, and the efficiency of our economy. Three financial markets deserve particular attention: the bond market (where interest rates are determined), the stock market (which has a major effect on people's wealth and on firms' investment decisions), and the foreign exchange market (because fluctuations in the foreign exchange rate have major consequences for the Canadian economy).

2. Banks and other financial institutions channel funds from people who might not put them to productive use to people who can do so and thus play a crucial role in improving the efficiency of the economy.

3. Money appears to have a major influence on inflation, business cycles, and interest rates. Because these economic variables are so important to the health of the economy, we need to understand how monetary policy is and should be conducted. We also need to study government fiscal policy because it can be an influential factor in the conduct of monetary policy.

4. This textbook stresses the economic way of thinking by developing a unifying analytic framework for the study of money, banking, and financial markets using a few basic economic principles. This textbook also emphasizes the interaction of theoretical analysis and empirical data.

KEY TERMS

aggregate output, p. 6
aggregate price level, p. 7
appreciation, p. 11
asset, p. 3
Bank of Canada (the Bank), p. 9
banks, p. 5
bond, p. 3
budget deficit, p. 10
budget surplus, p. 10
business cycles, p. 7

central bank, p. 9
common stock, p. 3
depreciation, p. 11
e-finance, p. 6
financial crises, p. 5
financial intermediaries, p. 5
financial markets, p. 2
fiscal policy, p. 10
foreign exchange market, p. 11
foreign exchange rate, p. 11

inflation, p. 7
inflation rate, p. 8
interest rate, p. 3
monetary policy, p. 9
monetary theory, p. 7
money, p. 6
recession, p. 7
security, p. 3
unemployment rate, p. 6

QUESTIONS

You will find the answers to the questions marked with an asterisk in the Textbook Resources section of your MyEconLab.

1. Has the inflation rate in Canada increased or decreased in the past few years? What about interest rates?

*2. If history repeats itself and we see a decline in the rate of money growth, what might you expect to happen to
   a. real output
   b. the inflation rate, and
   c. interest rates?

3. When was the most recent recession?

*4. When interest rates fall, how might you change your economic behaviour?

5. Can you think of any financial innovation in the past ten years that has affected you personally? Has it made you better off or worse off? Why?

*6. Is everybody worse off when interest rates rise?

7. What is the basic activity of banks?

*8. Why are financial markets important to the health of the economy?

9. What is the typical relationship among interest rates on three-month treasury bills, long-term Canada bonds, and long-term corporate bonds?

*10. What effect might a fall in stock prices have on business investment?

11. What effect might a rise in stock prices have on consumers' decisions to spend?

*12. How does a fall in the value of the pound sterling affect British consumers?

13. How does an increase in the value of the pound sterling affect Canadian businesses?

*14. Looking at Figure 1-8 (page 11), in what years would you have chosen to visit the Canadian Rockies rather than Washington, D.C.?

15. When the dollar is worth more in relation to currencies of other countries, are you more likely to buy Canadian-made or foreign-made jeans? Are Canadian companies that make jeans happier when the dollar is strong or when it is weak? What about a Canadian company that is in the business of importing jeans into Canada?

QUANTITATIVE PROBLEMS

CANSIM Questions

1. The following table lists monthly foreign exchange rates between the U.S. dollar and the Canadian dollar (in $/US$) for 2008 (this is CANSIM II series V41589522).

January	1.011132
February	0.999086
March	1.002025
April	1.013886
May	0.999371
June	1.016733
July	1.012695
August	1.054395
September	1.058295
October	1.184750
November	1.218174
December	1.234500

   a. Which month would have been the best month to convert Canadian dollars into U.S. dollars? Which month would have been the worst?
   b. Did the Canadian dollar appreciate or depreciate in 2008?
   c. What was the percentage appreciation or depreciation of the Canadian dollar?
   d. If you convert the monthly observations into an annual observation (by taking the arithmetic average), how representative will the annual observation be of the exchange rate during 2008?

*2. The following table lists monthly stock prices in Canada as measured by the S&P/TSX Composite Index (this is CANSIM II series V122620) for 2008.

January	13 155.10
February	13 582.69
March	13 350.13
April	13 937.04
May	14 714.73
June	14 467.03
July	13 592.91
August	13 771.25
September	11 752.90
October	9 762.76
November	9 270.62
December	9 987.70

   a. Which month would have been the worst month to buy the index?
   b. What was the percentage decline in the index from January to December?

3. Get the monthly data for 1970 to 2009 on the M3 (gross) monetary aggregate (CANSIM series V41552794) from the Textbook Resources area of the MyEconLab.
   a. Calculate the money growth rate over the entire period and present a time series plot of the series (that is, graph the money growth rate series against time).
   b. Calculate the average monetary growth rate and its standard deviation over each of the last four decades.
   c. Which decade had the lowest money growth? The highest?
   d. Which decade had the lowest money growth volatility? The highest?

WEB EXERCISES

1. In this exercise we will practise collecting data from the web and graphing it using Excel. Use the example on page 14 as a guide. Go to **www.forecasts.org/data/index.htm**, click on "Stock Index Data" at the top of the page, and then choose the U.S. Stock Indices—Monthly option. Finally, choose the Dow Jones Industrial Average option.
   a. Move the data into an Excel spreadsheet.
   b. Using the data from part (a), prepare a graph. Use the graphing wizard to properly label your axes.

2. In Web Exercise 1 you collected and graphed the Dow Jones Industrial Average. This same site reports forecast values of the DJIA. Go to **www.forecasts. org**. Click on the Dow Jones Industrials link under 6 Month Forecasts in the far left column.
   a. What is the Dow forecast to be in three months?
   b. What percentage increase is forecast for the next three months?

Be sure to visit the MyEconLab website at **www.myeconlab.com**. This online homework and tutorial system puts you in control of your own learning with study and practice tools directly correlated to this chapter content.

On the MyEconLab website you will find the following appendix for this chapter:
Appendix 1.1: Defining Aggregate Output, Income, the Price Level, and the Inflation Rate

CHAPTER 2

An Overview of the Financial System

LEARNING OBJECTIVES

After studying this chapter you should be able to

1. summarize the basic function performed by financial markets
2. explain why financial markets are classified as debt and equity markets, primary and secondary markets, exchanges and over-the-counter markets, and money and capital markets
3. describe the principal money market and capital market instruments
4. express why the government regulates financial markets and financial intermediaries (i.e., chartered banks, trust and mortgage loan companies, credit unions and *caisses populaires*, insurance companies, mutual fund companies, and other institutions)

PREVIEW

Inez the Inventor has designed a low-cost robot that cleans house (even does windows), washes the car, and mows the lawn, but she has no funds to put her wonderful invention into production. Walter the Widower has plenty of savings, which he and his wife accumulated over the years. If Inez and Walter could get together so that Walter could provide funds to Inez, Inez's robot would see the light of day, and the economy would be better off: we would have cleaner houses, shinier cars, and more beautiful lawns.

Financial markets (bond and stock markets) and financial intermediaries (banks, insurance companies, pension funds) have the basic function of getting people like Inez and Walter together by moving funds from those who have a surplus of funds (Walter) to those who have a shortage of funds (Inez). More realistically, when Apple invents a better iPod, it may need funds to bring it to market. Similarly, when a local government needs to build a road or a school, it may need more funds than local property taxes provide. Well-functioning financial markets and financial intermediaries are crucial to economic health.

To study the effects of financial markets and financial intermediaries on the economy, we need to acquire an understanding of their general structure and operation.

In this chapter we learn about the major financial intermediaries and the instruments that are traded in financial markets as well as how these markets are regulated.

This chapter presents an overview of the fascinating study of financial markets and institutions. We return to a more detailed treatment of the regulation, structure, and evolution of financial markets in Chapters 8 through 12.

FUNCTION OF FINANCIAL MARKETS

Financial markets perform the essential economic function of channelling funds from households, firms, and governments who have saved surplus funds by spending less than their income to those who have a shortage of funds because they wish to spend more than they earn. This function is shown schematically in Figure 2-1. Those who have saved and are lending funds, the lender-savers, are at the left, and those who must borrow funds to finance their spending, the borrower-spenders, are at the right. The principal lender-savers are households, but business enterprises and the government (particularly provincial and local government), as well as foreigners and their governments, sometimes also find themselves with excess funds and so lend them out. The most important borrower-spenders are businesses and the government (particularly the federal government), but households and foreigners also borrow to finance their purchases of cars, furniture, and houses. The arrows show that funds flow from lender-savers to borrower-spenders via two routes.

In *direct finance* (the route at the bottom of Figure 2-1), borrowers borrow funds directly from lenders in financial markets by selling them *securities* (also called *financial instruments*), which are claims on the borrower's future income or assets. Securities are assets for the person who buys them but **liabilities** (IOUs or debts) for the individual or firm that sells (issues) them. For example, if Research In Motion (RIM) needs to borrow funds to pay for a new factory to manufacture new products, it might borrow the funds from savers by selling them *bonds*, debt securities that promise to make payments periodically for a specified period of time, or *stocks*, securities that entitle the owners to a share of the company's profits and assets.

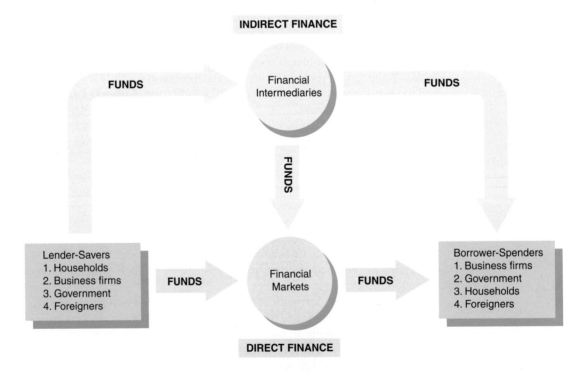

FIGURE 2-1   Flows of Funds Through the Financial System

Why is this channelling of funds from savers to spenders so important to the economy? The answer is that the people who save are frequently not the same people who have profitable investment opportunities available to them, the entrepreneurs. Let's first think about this on a personal level. Suppose that you have saved $1000 this year, but no borrowing or lending is possible because there are no financial markets. If you do not have an investment opportunity that will permit you to earn income with your savings, you will just hold on to the $1000 and will earn no interest. However, Carl the Carpenter has a productive use for your $1000: he can use it to purchase a new tool that will shorten the time it takes him to build a house, thereby earning him an extra $200 per year. If you could get in touch with Carl, you could lend him the $1000 at a rental fee (interest) of $100 per year, and both of you would be better off. You would earn $100 per year on your $1000, instead of the zero amount that you would earn otherwise, while Carl would earn $100 more income per year (the $200 extra earnings per year minus the $100 rental fee for the use of the funds).

In the absence of financial markets, you and Carl the Carpenter might never get together. You would both be stuck with the status quo, and both of you would be worse off. Without financial markets, it is hard to transfer funds from a person who has no investment opportunities to one who has them; financial markets are thus essential to promoting economic efficiency.

The existence of financial markets is beneficial even if someone borrows for a purpose other than increasing production in a business. Say that you are recently married, have a good job, and want to buy a house. You earn a good salary, but because you have just started to work, you have not saved much. Over time you would have no problem saving enough to buy the house of your dreams, but by then you would be too old to get full enjoyment from it. Without financial markets, you are stuck; you cannot buy the house and must continue to live in your tiny apartment.

If a financial market were set up so that people who had built up savings could lend you the funds to buy the house, you would be more than happy to pay them some interest in order to own a home while you are still young enough to enjoy it. Then, over time, you would pay back your loan. If this loan could occur, you would be better off, as would the persons who made you the loan. They would now earn some interest, whereas they would not if the financial market did not exist.

Now we can see why financial markets have such an important function in the economy. They allow funds to move from people who lack productive investment opportunities to people who have such opportunities. Financial markets are critical for producing an efficient allocation of capital, which contributes to higher production and efficiency for the overall economy. Indeed, as we will explore in Chapter 9, when financial markets break down during financial crises (as they have in Mexico, East Asia, and Argentina in recent years), severe economic hardship results, which can even lead to dangerous political instability.

Well-functioning financial markets also directly improve the well-being of consumers by allowing them to time their purchases better. They provide funds to young people to buy what they need and can eventually afford without forcing them to wait until they have saved up the entire purchase price. Financial markets that are operating efficiently improve the economic welfare of everyone in the society.

STRUCTURE OF FINANCIAL MARKETS

Now that we understand the basic function of financial markets, let's look at their structure. The following descriptions of several categorizations of financial markets illustrate essential features of these markets.

Debt and Equity Markets

A firm or an individual can obtain funds in a financial market in two ways. The most common method is to issue a debt instrument, such as a bond or a mortgage, which is a contractual agreement by the borrower to pay the holder of the instrument fixed dollar amounts at regular intervals (interest and principal payments) until a specified date (the maturity date), when a final payment is made. The **maturity** of a debt instrument is the number of years (term) until that instrument's expiration date. A debt instrument is **short-term** if its maturity is less than a year and **long-term** if its maturity is ten years or longer. Debt instruments with a maturity between one and ten years are said to be **intermediate-term**.

The second method of raising funds is by issuing **equities**, such as common stock, which are claims to share in the net income (income after expenses and taxes) and the assets of a business. If you own one share of common stock in a company that has issued one million shares, you are entitled to one-millionth of the firm's net income and one-millionth of the firm's assets. Equities often make periodic payments (**dividends**) to their holders and are considered long-term securities because they have no maturity date. In addition, owning stock means that you own a portion of the firm and thus have the right to vote on issues important to the firm and to elect its directors.

The main disadvantage of owning a corporation's equities rather than its debt is that an equity holder is a *residual claimant*; that is, the corporation must pay all its debt holders before it pays its equity holders. The advantage of holding equities is that equity holders benefit directly from any increases in the corporation's profitability or asset value because equities confer ownership rights on the equity holders. Debt holders do not share in this benefit because their dollar payments are fixed. We examine the pros and cons of debt versus equity instruments in more detail in Chapter 8, which provides an economic analysis of financial structure.

Primary and Secondary Markets

A **primary market** is a financial market in which new issues of a security, such as a bond or a stock, are sold to initial buyers by the corporation or government agency borrowing the funds. A **secondary market** is a financial market in which securities that have been previously issued can be resold.

The primary markets for securities are not well known to the public because the selling of securities to initial buyers often takes place behind closed doors. An important financial institution that assists in the initial sale of securities in the primary market is the **investment bank**. It does this by **underwriting** securities: it guarantees a price for a corporation's securities and then sells them to the public.

The Toronto Stock Exchange (TSX) and the TSX Venture Exchange, in which previously issued stocks are traded, are the best-known examples of Canadian secondary markets, although the bond markets, in which previously issued bonds of major corporations and the Canadian government are bought and sold, actually have a larger trading volume. Other examples of secondary markets are foreign exchange markets, futures markets, and options markets. Securities brokers and dealers are crucial to a well-functioning secondary market. **Brokers** are agents of investors who match buyers with sellers of securities; **dealers** link buyers and sellers by buying and selling securities at stated prices.

When an individual buys a security in the secondary market, the person who has sold the security receives money in exchange for the security, but the corporation that issued the security acquires no new funds. A corporation acquires new funds only when its securities are first sold in the primary market. Nonetheless, secondary markets serve two important functions. First, they make it easier to sell these financial instruments to raise cash; that is, they make the financial instruments more **liquid**. The increased liquidity of these instruments then makes them more desirable and thus easier for the issuing firm to sell in the primary market. Second, they determine the price of the security that the issuing firm sells in the primary market. The investors that buy securities in the primary market will pay the issuing corporation no more than the price they think the secondary market will set for this security. The higher the security's price in the secondary market, the higher will be the price that the issuing firm will receive for a new security in the primary market and hence the greater the amount of financial capital it can raise. Conditions in the secondary market are therefore the most relevant to corporations issuing securities. It is for this reason that books like this one, which deal with financial markets, focus on the behaviour of secondary markets rather than that of primary markets.

Exchanges and Over-the-Counter Markets

Secondary markets can be organized in two ways. One is to organize **exchanges**, where buyers and sellers of securities (or their agents or brokers) meet in one central location to conduct trades. The Toronto Stock Exchange for stocks and the Winnipeg Commodity Exchange for commodities (wheat, oats, barley, and other agricultural commodities) are examples of organized exchanges. The Montreal Exchange (ME) is another example of an organized exchange, offering a range of equity, interest rate, and index derivative products.

The other method of organizing a secondary market is to have an **over-the-counter (OTC) market**, in which dealers at different locations who have an inventory of securities stand ready to buy and sell securities "over the counter" to anyone who comes to them and is willing to accept their prices. Because over-the-counter dealers are in computer contact and know the prices set by one another, the OTC market is very competitive and not very different from a market with an organized exchange.

Many common stocks are traded over the counter, although a majority of the largest corporations have their shares traded at organized stock exchanges. The Canadian government bond market, by contrast, is set up as an over-the-counter market. Dealers establish a "market" in these securities by standing ready to buy and sell Canadian government bonds. Other over-the-counter markets include those that trade other types of financial instruments such as negotiable certificates of deposit, overnight funds, and foreign exchange.

Money and Capital Markets

Another way of distinguishing between markets is on the basis of the maturity of the securities traded in each market. The **money market** is a financial market in which only short-term debt instruments (generally those with original maturity of less than one year) are traded; the **capital market** is the market in which longer-term debt (generally those with original maturity of one year or greater) and equity instruments are traded. Money market securities are usually more widely traded than longer-term securities and so tend to be more liquid. In addition, as we will see in Chapter 4, short-term securities have smaller fluctuations in prices than long-term securities, making them safer investments. As a result, corporations and banks actively use the money market to earn interest on surplus funds that they expect to have only temporarily. Capital market securities, such as stocks and long-term bonds, are often held by financial intermediaries such as insurance companies and pension funds, which have more certainty about the amount of funds they will have available in the future.

FINANCIAL MARKET INSTRUMENTS

To complete our understanding of how financial markets perform the important role of channelling funds from lender-savers to borrower-spenders, we need to examine the securities (instruments) traded in financial markets. We first focus on the instruments traded in the money market and then turn to those traded in the capital market.

Money Market Instruments

Because of their short terms to maturity, the debt instruments traded in the money market undergo the least price fluctuations and so are the least risky investments. The money market has undergone great changes in the past three decades, with the amount of some financial instruments growing at a far more rapid rate than others.

The principal money market instruments are listed in Table 2-1, along with the amount outstanding at the end of 1980, 1990, 2000, and 2008. The *National Post: Financial Post* reports money market rates in its "Bond Yields and Rates" column (see the Financial News: Money Rates box on page 24).

GOVERNMENT OF CANADA TREASURY BILLS These short-term debt instruments of the Canadian government are issued in 1-, 3-, 6-, and 12-month maturities to finance the federal government. They pay a set amount at maturity and have no interest payments, but they effectively pay interest by initially selling at a discount, that is, at a price lower than the set amount paid at maturity. For instance, you might pay $9600 in May 2010 for a one-year treasury bill that can be redeemed in May 2011 for $10 000.

Treasury bills are the most liquid of all the money market instruments because they are the most actively traded. They are also the safest of all money market instruments because there is almost no possibility of *default*, a situation in which the party issuing the debt instrument (the federal government, in this case) is unable to make interest payments or pay off the amount owed when the instrument matures. The federal government is always able to meet its debt obligations, because it can raise taxes to pay off its debts. Treasury bills are held mainly by banks, although households, corporations, and other financial intermediaries hold small amounts.

TABLE 2-1 Principal Money Market Instruments

Type of Instrument	Amount Outstanding ($ millions)			
	1980	1990	2000	2008
Treasury bills				
Government of Canada	13 709	113 654	76 633	116 706
Provincial governments	905	12 602	17 541	24 646
Municipal governments	113	514	188	155
Short-term paper				
Commercial paper	2 555	12 971	24 330	13 063

Source: Statistics Canada CANSIM II series V37377, V122256, V122257, and V122652.

CERTIFICATES OF DEPOSIT A *certificate of deposit* (CD) is a debt instrument sold by a bank to depositors that pays annual interest of a given amount and at maturity pays back the original purchase price. CDs are often negotiable, meaning that they can be traded, and in bearer form (called **bearer deposit notes**), meaning that the buyer's name is neither recorded in the issuer's books nor on the security itself. These negotiable CDs are issued in multiples of $100 000 and with maturities of 30 to 365 days, and can be resold in a secondary market, thus offering the purchaser both yield and liquidity.

Chartered banks also issue non-negotiable CDs. That is, they cannot be sold to someone else and cannot be redeemed from the bank before maturity without paying a substantial penalty. Non-negotiable CDs are issued in denominations ranging from $5000 to $100 000 and with maturities of one day to five years. They are also known as **term deposit receipts** or **term notes**.

CDs are also an extremely important source of funds for trust and mortgage loan companies. These institutions issue CDs under a variety of names; for example, DRs (Deposit Receipts), GTCs (Guaranteed Trust Certificates), GICs (Guaranteed Investment Certificates), and GIRs (Guaranteed Investment Receipts).

COMMERCIAL PAPER *Commercial paper* is an unsecured short-term debt instrument issued in either Canadian dollars or other currencies by large banks and well-known corporations, such as Microsoft and Bombardier. Because commercial paper is unsecured, only the largest and most creditworthy corporations issue commercial paper. The interest rate the corporation is charged reflects the firm's level of risk. The interest rate on commercial paper is low relative to those on other corporate fixed-income securities and slightly higher than rates on government of Canada treasury bills.

Sales finance companies also issue short-term promissory notes known as **finance paper**. Finance and commercial paper are issued in minimum denominations of $50 000 and in maturities of 30 to 365 days for finance paper and 1 to 365 days for commercial paper. Most finance and commercial paper is issued on a discounted basis. Chapter 11 discusses why the commercial paper market has had such tremendous growth.

REPURCHASE AGREEMENTS *Repurchase agreements*, or *repos*, are effectively short-term loans (usually with a maturity of less than two weeks) for which treasury bills serve as *collateral*, an asset that the lender receives if the borrower does not pay back the loan. Repos are made as follows: a large corporation, such as Bombardier, may have some idle funds in its bank account, say $1 million, which it would like to lend for a week. Bombardier uses this excess $1 million to buy treasury bills from a bank, which agrees to repurchase them the next week at a price slightly above Bombardier's purchase price. The effect of this agreement is that Bombardier makes a loan of $1 million to the bank and holds $1 million of the bank's treasury bills until the bank repurchases the bills to pay off the loan. Repurchase agreements are a fairly recent innovation in financial markets, having been introduced in 1969. They are now an important source of bank funds, with the most important lenders in this market being large corporations.

OVERNIGHT FUNDS These are typically overnight loans by banks to other banks. The *overnight funds* designation is somewhat confusing, because these loans are not made by the federal government or by the Bank of Canada, but rather by banks to other banks. One reason why a bank might borrow in the overnight funds market is that it might find it does not have enough settlement

FINANCIAL NEWS

Money Rates

The *Globe and Mail* and the *National Post* publish daily a listing of interest rates on many different financial instruments. In the *National Post: Financial Post*, this listing can be found in the "Bond Yields and Rates" column.

The interest rates in the "Bond Yields and Rates" column that are discussed most frequently in the media are as follows:

Bank rate: The interest rate charged by the Bank of Canada on loans made to members of the Canadian Payments Association.

Overnight money market (financing) rate: A measure of the collateralized overnight rate compiled by the Bank of Canada.

Prime rate: The base interest rate on corporate bank loans, an indicator of the cost of business borrowing from banks.

Treasury bill rates: The interest rates on Government of Canada treasury bills, an indicator of general interest rate movements.

Selected U.S. interest rates: Selected U.S. interest rates such as treasury bill rates, commercial paper rates, the discount rate, the prime rate, and the federal funds rate. These are indicators of general interest rate movements in the United States.

London interbank offer rate (or *Libor*): The British Bankers' Association average of interbank rates for dollar deposits in the London market.

BOND YIELDS AND RATES

CANADIAN YIELDS

	Latest	Prev day	Wk ago	4 Wks ago
T-Bills				
1-month	0.30	0.27	0.49	0.53
3-month	0.40	0.43	0.60	0.72
6-month	0.49	0.49	0.65	0.72
1-year	0.55	0.57	0.75	0.80
Bonds				
2-year	0.95	0.93	1.14	1.14
5-year	1.85	1.81	2.05	1.93
7-year	2.07	2.03	2.25	2.36
10-year	2.93	2.91	3.12	3.04
30-year	3.61	3.55	3.70	3.76
Banker's acceptances (ask prices)				
1-month	0.62	0.65	0.75	0.95
3-month	0.61	0.62	0.75	0.90
6-month	0.80	0.85	1.10	1.30
3-mth forward rate agreement				
3-month	0.51	0.49	0.65	0.63
6-month	0.45	0.46	0.70	0.59
9-month	0.56	0.54	0.86	0.71

U.S. YIELDS

	Latest	Prev day	Wk ago	4 Wks ago
T-Bills				
1-month	0.05	0.08	0.13	0.21
3-month	0.19	0.19	0.24	0.28
6-month	0.38	0.37	0.43	0.42
Bonds				
2-year	0.94	0.88	0.97	0.99
5-year	1.88	1.79	1.99	1.96
10-year	2.53	2.47	2.68	2.98
30-year	2.87	2.81	3.02	3.69
Commercial paper				
1-month	0.24	0.21	0.27	0.34
3-month	0.35	0.34	0.51	0.43
6-month	1.48	1.58	1.58	1.28
3-mth forward rate agreement				
3-month	1.43	1.32	1.28	1.07
6-month	1.44	1.36	1.34	1.15
9-month	1.57	1.49	1.50	1.35

INTERNATIONAL

		Latest	Prev day	Wk ago	4 Wks ago
Euro-deposit rates (bid)					
US$	1-month	0.47	0.45	0.43	1.20
	3-month	1.45	1.24	1.21	1.13
	6-month	1.85	1.69	1.64	1.56
C$	3-month	1.21	1.21	1.35	1.52
euro	3-month	1.70	1.66	1.49	1.99
Yen	3-month	0.90	0.32	0.78	0.65
£	3-month	1.71	1.61	1.78	1.69
London interbank offer rate US$					
US$	1-month	n.a	0.53	0.50	0.45
	3-month	n.a	1.28	1.26	1.24
	6-month	n.a	1.83	1.80	1.75

BANK RATES

Canada		United States	
Bank of Canada	0.75	Discount	0.50
Overnight Money		Prime	3.25
Market Financing	0.30	Federal Funds	0.22
Prime	2.50		
Call Loan Average	0.45		

Source: National Post: Financial Post, March 7, 2009, p. FP13. All rights reserved. Republication or redistribution of Thomson Reuters content, including by framing or similar means, is expressly prohibited without the prior written consent of Thomson Reuters. Thomson Reuters and its logo are registered trademarks or trademarks of the Thomson Reuters group of companies around the world. © Thomson Reuters 2009. Thomson Reuters journalists are subject to an *Editorial Handbook,* which requires fair presentation and disclosure of relevant interests.

deposits at the Bank of Canada. It can then borrow these balances from another bank with excess settlement balances.

The overnight market is very sensitive to the credit needs of the deposit-taking institutions, so the interest rate on overnight loans, called the **overnight interest rate**, is a closely watched barometer of the tightness of credit market conditions in the banking system and the stance of monetary policy. When it is high, it indicates that the banks are strapped for funds, whereas when it is low, banks' credit needs are low.

Capital Market Instruments

Capital market instruments are debt and equity instruments with maturities of greater than one year. They have far wider price fluctuations than money market instruments and are considered to be fairly risky investments. The principal capital market instruments are listed in Table 2-2, which shows the amount outstanding at the end of 1980, 1990, 2000, and 2008.

STOCKS   *Stocks* are equity claims on the net income and assets of a corporation. Their value was $324.1 billion at the end of 2008. The amount of new stock issues in any given year is typically quite small—less than 1% of the total value of shares outstanding. Individuals hold around half of the value of stocks; pension funds, mutual funds, and insurance companies hold the rest.

MORTGAGES   *Mortgages* are loans to households or firms to purchase housing, land, or other real structures, where the structure or land serves as collateral for the loans. The mortgage market is the largest debt market in Canada, with the amount of residential mortgages (used to purchase residential housing) outstanding more than tenfold the amount of commercial and farm mortgages. Trust and mortgage loan companies and credit unions and *caisses populaires* were the primary lenders in the residential mortgage market until 1967. The revision of the Bank Act in 1967, however, extended the authority of chartered banks to make conventional residential mortgage loans and chartered banks entered this market very aggressively.

Banks and life insurance companies make the majority of commercial and farm mortgages. The federal government also plays an active role in the mortgage market via the Canada Mortgage and Housing Corporation (CMHC), which provides funds to the mortgage market by selling bonds and using the proceeds to buy mortgages.

CORPORATE BONDS   These are long-term bonds issued by corporations with very strong credit ratings. The typical *coporate bond* sends the holder an interest payment twice a year and pays off the face value when the bond matures. Some

TABLE 2-2   Principal Capital Market Instruments

Type of Instrument	Amount Outstanding ($ billions)			
	1980	**1990**	**2000**	**2008**
Corporate stocks (market value)	42.9	109.8	242.1	324.1
Residential mortgages	91.9	245.3	431.2	863.8
Corporate bonds	30.0	72.8	187.6	274.6
Government of Canada securities (marketable)	27.8	124.5	301.9	223.1
Bank commercial loans	58.7	102.7	132.0	185.0
Consumer loans	39.2	90.9	189.8	398.6
Nonresidential and farm mortgages	15.1	56.1	49.7	77.1

Source: Statistics Canada CANSIM II series V122642, V122746, V122640, V37378, V122631, V122707, V122656, V122657, V122658, V122659, V800015, and the authors' calculations.

corporate bonds, called *convertible bonds*, have the additional feature of allowing the holder to convert them into a specified number of shares of stock at any time up to the maturity date. This feature makes convertible bonds more desirable to prospective purchasers than regular bonds, and allows the corporation to reduce its interest payments, because these bonds can increase in value if the price of the stock appreciates sufficiently. Because the outstanding amount of both convertible and nonconvertible bonds for any given corporation is small, they are not nearly as liquid as other securities such as Government of Canada bonds.

Although the size of the corporate bond market is substantially smaller than that of the stock market, the volume of new corporate bonds issued each year is substantially greater than the volume of new stock issues. Thus the behaviour of the corporate bond market is probably far more important to a firm's financing decisions than the behaviour of the stock market. The principal buyers of corporate bonds are life insurance companies; pension funds and households are other large holders.

GOVERNMENT OF CANADA BONDS   Intermediate-term bonds (those with initial maturities from one to ten years) and long-term bonds (those with initial maturities greater than ten years) are issued by the federal government to finance its deficit. Because they are the most widely traded bonds in Canada, they are the most liquid security traded in the capital market. They are held by the Bank of Canada, banks, households, and foreign investors.

These debt instruments are issued in either bearer or registered form and in denominations of $1000, $5000, $25 000, $100 000, and $1 million. In the case of **registered bonds**, the name of the owner appears on the bond certificate and is also recorded at the Bank of Canada. Some issues have the additional **call** (or **redemption**) feature of allowing them to be "called" on specified notice (usually 30 to 60 days).

CANADA SAVINGS BONDS   These are nonmarketable bonds issued by the government of Canada and sold each year from early October through to April 1. *Canada Savings Bonds* (CSBs) are floating-rate bonds, available in denominations from $100 to $10 000, and offered exclusively to individuals, estates, and specified trusts. They are issued as registered bonds and can be purchased from financial institutions or through payroll savings plans.

CSBs are different from all other bonds issued by the government of Canada in that they do not rise or fall in value, like other bonds do. They have the valuable option of being redeemable at face value plus accrued interest, at any time prior to maturity, by being presented at any financial institution. In October 1998 the government of Canada introduced another type of bond that is similar to CSBs—Canada Premium Bonds (CPBs). CPBs offer a slightly higher coupon rate than the CSBs, but can be redeemed only once a year, on the anniversary of the issue date and during the month after that date.

PROVINCIAL AND MUNICIPAL GOVERNMENT BONDS   Provincial and municipal governments also issue bonds to finance expenditures on schools, roads, and other large programs. The securities issued by provincial governments are referred to as **provincial bonds** or **provincials** and those issued by municipal governments as **municipal bonds** or **municipals**—the securities issued by the federal government are referred to as **Canadas**. Provincials and municipals are denominated in either domestic currency or foreign currencies, mostly U.S. dollars, Swiss francs, and Japanese yen. They are mainly held by trusteed pension plans, social security funds (predominantly the Canada Pension Plan), and foreigners.

GOVERNMENT AGENCY SECURITIES   These are long-term bonds issued by various government agencies such as the Ontario Municipal Improvement Corporation and the Alberta Municipal Financing Corporation to assist municipalities to finance such items as mortgages, farm loans, or power-generating equipment. The provincial governments guarantee many of these securities. They function much like Canadas, provincials, and municipals and are held by similar parties.

CONSUMER AND BANK COMMERCIAL LOANS   These are loans to consumers and businesses made principally by banks, but—in the case of consumer loans—also by finance companies.

INTERNATIONALIZATION OF FINANCIAL MARKETS

The growing internationalization of financial markets has become an important trend. Before the 1980s, U.S. financial markets were much larger than financial markets outside the United States, but in recent years the dominance of U.S. markets has been disappearing (see the Global box, Are U.S. Capital Markets Losing Their Edge?).

The extraordinary growth of foreign financial markets has been the result of both large increases in the pool of savings in foreign countries such as Japan and the deregulation of foreign financial markets, which has enabled foreign markets to expand their activities. Canadian corporations and banks are now more likely to tap international capital markets to raise needed funds, and Canadian investors often seek investment opportunities abroad. Similarly, foreign corporations and banks raise funds from Canadians, and foreigners have become important investors in Canada. A look at international bond markets and world stock markets will give us a picture of how this globalization of financial markets is taking place.

International Bond Market, Eurobonds, and Eurocurrencies

The traditional instruments in the international bond market are known as **foreign bonds**. Foreign bonds are sold in a foreign country and are denominated in that country's currency. For example, if the German automaker Porsche sells a bond in Canada denominated in Canadian dollars, it is classified as a foreign bond. Foreign bonds have been an important instrument in the international capital market for centuries. In fact, a large percentage of U.S. railroads built in the nineteenth century were financed by sales of foreign bonds in Britain.

A more recent innovation in the international bond market is the **Eurobond**, a bond denominated in a currency other than that of the country in which it is sold—for example, a bond issued by a Canadian corporation that is denominated in Japanese yen and sold in Germany. Currently, over 80% of the new issues in the international bond market are Eurobonds, and the market for these securities has grown very rapidly.

A variant of the Eurobond is **Eurocurrencies**, which are foreign currencies deposited in banks outside the home country. The most important of the Eurocurrencies are **Eurodollars**, which are U.S. dollars deposited in foreign banks outside the United States or in foreign branches of U.S. banks. Because these short-term deposits earn interest, they are similar to short-term Eurobonds. Canadian banks borrow Eurodollar deposits from other banks or from their own foreign branches, and Eurodollars are now an important source of funds for Canadian banks.

GLOBAL   Are U.S. Capital Markets Losing Their Edge?

Over the past few decades the United States lost its international dominance in a number of manufacturing industries, including automobiles and consumer electronics, as other countries became more competitive in global markets. Recent evidence suggests that financial markets are now undergoing a similar trend: Just as Ford and General Motors have lost global market share to Toyota and Honda, U.S. stock and bond markets recently have seen their share of sales of newly issued corporate securities slip. In 2008 the London and Hong Kong stock exchanges each handled a larger share of initial public offerings (IPO) of stock than did the New York Stock Exchange, which had been by far the dominant exchange in terms of IPO value just five years before. Likewise, the portion of new corporate bonds issued worldwide that are initially sold in U.S. capital markets has fallen below the share sold in European debt markets in each of the past two years.*

Why do corporations that issue new securities to raise capital now conduct more of this business in financial markets in Europe and Asia? Among the factors contributing to this trend are quicker adoption of technological innovation by foreign financial markets, tighter immigration controls in the United States following the terrorist attacks in 2001, and perceptions that listing on American exchanges will expose foreign securities issuers to greater risks of lawsuits. Many people see burdensome financial regulation as the main cause, however, and point specifically to the Sarbanes-Oxley Act of 2002. The U.S. Congress passed this act after a number of accounting scandals involving U.S. corporations and the accounting firms that audited them came to light. Sarbanes-Oxley aims to strengthen the integrity of the auditing process and the quality of information provided in corporate financial statements. The costs to corporations of complying with the rules and procedures are high, especially for smaller firms, but largely avoidable if firms choose to issue their securities in financial markets outside the United States. For this reason, there is much support for revising Sarbanes-Oxley to lessen its alleged harmful effects and induce more securities issuers back to United States financial markets. However, there is not conclusive evidence to support the view that Sarbanes-Oxley is the main cause of the relative decline of U.S. financial markets and therefore in need of reform.

Discussion of the relative decline of U.S. financial markets and debate about the factors that are contributing to it likely will continue.

*"Down on the Street," *The Economist*, November 25, 2006, pp. 69–71.

Note that the name of the European currency, the euro, can create some confusion about the terms Eurobond, Eurocurrencies, and Eurodollars. A Eurobond is typically not a bond that is denominated in euros. A bond denominated in euros is called a Eurobond only if *it is sold outside the countries that have adopted the euro*. Similarly, Eurodollars have nothing to do with euros, but are instead U.S. dollars deposited in banks outside the United States.

World Stock Markets

Until recently, the U.S. stock market was by far the largest in the world, but stock markets in other countries have been growing in importance (see Table 2-3). Now the United States is not always number one: in the mid-1980s, the value of stocks

TABLE 2-3 Top 10 Stock Exchanges in the World (by Domestic Market Capitalization at Year-End 2008)

Exchange	Value (in billions of US$)	Rank in 2008
NYSE	9 209	1
Tokyo	3 116	2
Nasdaq	2 396	3
Euronext	2 102	4
London	1 868	5
Shanghai	1 425	6
Hong Kong	1 329	7
Deutsche Börse	1 111	8
Toronto	1 033	9
BME Spanish Exchanges	948	10

Source: World Federation of Exchanges, *2008 Market Highlights*, www.world-exchanges.org/statistics.

traded in Japan had at times exceeded the value of stocks traded in the United States. The increased interest in foreign stocks has prompted the development in Canada of mutual funds that specialize in trading in foreign stock markets. Canadian investors now pay attention not only to the Canadian stock markets (the Toronto Stock Exchange and the TSX Venture Exchange) but also to stock price indexes for foreign stock markets such as the Dow Jones Industrial Average (New York), the Nikkei 225 Average (Tokyo), and the Financial Times–Stock Exchange 100-Share Index (London) (see Financial News: Foreign Stock Market Indexes).

The internationalization of financial markets is having profound effects on Canada. Foreigners not only are providing funds to corporations in Canada but also are helping finance the federal government. Without these foreign funds, the Canadian economy would have grown far less rapidly in the last twenty years. The internationalization of financial markets is also leading the way to a more integrated world economy in which flows of goods and technology between countries are more commonplace. In later chapters we will encounter many examples of the important roles that international factors play in our economy.

FUNCTION OF FINANCIAL INTERMEDIARIES: INDIRECT FINANCE

As shown in Figure 2-1 (page 18), funds can move from lenders to borrowers by a second route, called *indirect finance* because it involves a financial intermediary that stands between the lender-savers and the borrower-spenders and helps transfer funds from one to the other. A financial intermediary does this by borrowing funds from the lender-savers and then using these funds to make loans to borrower-spenders. For example, a bank might acquire funds by issuing a liability to the public (an asset for the public) in the form of savings deposits. It might then use the funds to acquire an asset by making a loan to Canadian Pacific or by buying a Canadian Pacific bond in the financial market. The ultimate result is that funds have been transferred from the public (the lender-savers) to Canadian Pacific (the borrower-spender) with the help of the financial intermediary (the bank).

FINANCIAL NEWS

Foreign Stock Market Indexes

Foreign stock market indexes are published daily in the financial pages of newspapers and on the web. The entries from Bloomberg, shown here, are explained in the text.

The first column identifies the market index: for example, the shaded entry for the S&P/TSX Composite Index. The second column, "Value," gives the closing value of the index, which was 11 508.53 for the S&P/TSX Composite on December 7, 2009. The "Change" column indicates the change in the index, −2.27. The "% Change" column indicates the percentage change in the index, −0.02%.

WORLD INDEXES

NORTH/LATIN AMERICA

Index	Value	Change	% Change
Dow Jones Industrial Average	10 409.38	20.48	0.20
S&P 500 Index	1 106.86	0.88	0.08
NASDAQ Composite Index	2 194.04	−0.31	−0.01
S&P/TSX Composite Index	11 508.53	−2.27	−0.02
Mexico Bolsa Index	32 111.59	6.20	0.02
Brazil Bovespa Stock Index	68 102.76	499.23	0.74

EUROPE/AFRICA/MIDDLE EAST

Index	Value	Change	% Change
DJ Euro Stoxx 50 € Pr	2 900.71	−9.62	−0.33
FTSE 100 Index	5 321.87	−0.49	−0.01
CAC 40 Index	3 844.65	−1.97	−0.05
DAX Index	5 793.66	−23.99	−0.41
IBEX 35 Index	12 027.90	−4.30	−0.04
FTSE MIB Index	22 839.62	−86.41	−0.38
AEX-Index	321.14	0.01	0.00
OMX Stockholm 30 Index	966.98	0.01	0.00
Swiss Market Index	6 476.82	−24.34	−0.37

ASIA PACIFIC

Index	Value	Change	% Change
Nikkei 225	10 167.60	145.01	1.45
Hang Seng Index	22 324.96	173.19	−0.77
S&P/ASX 200 Index	4 676.50	−25.70	−0.55

Source: Reprinted from Bloomberg.com with permission on December 7, 2009.

The process of indirect finance using financial intermediaries, called **financial intermediation**, is the primary route for moving funds from lenders to borrowers. Indeed, although the media focus much of their attention on securities markets, particularly the stock market, financial intermediaries are a far more important source of financing for corporations than securities markets are. This is true not only for Canada but for other industrialized countries as well (see the Global box, The Importance of Financial Intermediaries to Securities Markets: An International Comparison). Why are financial intermediaries and indirect finance so important in financial markets? To answer this question, we need to understand the role of transaction costs, risk sharing, and information costs in financial markets.

GLOBAL	The Importance of Financial Intermediaries to Securities Markets: An International Comparison

Patterns of financing corporations differ across countries, but one key fact emerges. Studies of the major developed countries, including Canada, the United States, Great Britain, Japan, Italy, Germany, and France, show that when businesses go looking for funds to finance their activities, they usually obtain them indirectly through financial intermediaries and not directly from securities markets.* Even in Canada and the United States, which have the most developed securities markets in the world, loans from financial intermediaries are far more important for corporate finance than securities markets are. The countries that have made the least use of securities markets are Germany and Japan; in these two countries, financing from financial intermediaries has been almost ten times

greater than that from securities markets. However, after the deregulation of Japanese securities markets in recent years, the share of corporate financing by financial intermediaries has been declining relative to the use of securities markets.

Although the dominance of financial intermediaries over securities markets is clear in all countries, the relative importance of bond versus stock markets differs widely across countries. In the United States, the bond market is far more important as a source of corporate finance. On average, the amount of new financing raised using bonds is ten times the amount using stocks. By contrast, countries such as France and Italy make more use of equities markets than of bond markets to raise capital.

*See, for example, Colin Mayer, "Financial Systems, Corporate Finance, and Economic Development," in *Asymmetric Information, Corporate Finance, and Investment*, ed. R. Glenn Hubbard (Chicago: University of Chicago Press, 1990), pp. 307–332.

Transaction Costs

Transaction costs, the time and money spent in carrying out financial transactions, are a major problem for people who have excess funds to lend. As we have seen, Carl the Carpenter needs $1000 for his new tool, and you know that it is an excellent investment opportunity. You would like to lend him the funds, but to protect your investment, you have to hire a lawyer to write up the loan contract that specifies how much interest Carl will pay you, when he will make these interest payments, and when he will repay you the $1000. Obtaining the contract will cost you $500. When you include this transaction cost for making the loan, you realize that you can't earn enough from the deal (you spend $500 to make perhaps $100) and reluctantly tell Carl that he will have to look elsewhere.

This example illustrates that small savers like you or potential borrowers like Carl might be frozen out of financial markets and thus be unable to benefit from them. Can anyone come to the rescue? Financial intermediaries can.

Financial intermediaries can substantially reduce transaction costs because they have developed expertise in lowering costs and because their large size allows them to take advantage of **economies of scale**, the reduction in transaction costs per dollar of transactions as the size (scale) of transactions increases. For example, a bank knows how to find a good lawyer to produce an airtight loan contract, and this contract can be used over and over again in its loan transactions, thus lowering the legal cost per transaction. Instead of a loan contract (which may not be all that well written) costing $500, a bank can hire a topflight lawyer for $5000 to draw up an airtight loan contract that can be used for 2000 loans at a cost of $2.50 per loan. At a cost of $2.50 per loan, it now becomes profitable for the financial intermediary to lend Carl the $1000.

Because financial intermediaries are able to reduce transaction costs substantially, they make it possible for you to provide funds indirectly to people like Carl with productive investment opportunities. In addition, a financial intermediary's low transaction costs mean that it can provide its customers with **liquidity services**, services that make it easier for customers to conduct transactions. For example, banks provide depositors with chequing accounts that enable them to pay their bills easily. In addition, depositors can earn interest on chequing and savings accounts and yet still convert them into goods and services whenever necessary.

Risk Sharing

Another benefit made possible by the low transaction costs of financial institutions is that they can help reduce the exposure of investors to **risk**, that is, uncertainty about the returns investors will earn on assets. Financial intermediaries do this through **risk sharing**: they create and sell assets with risk characteristics that people are comfortable with, and the intermediaries then use the funds they acquire by selling these assets to purchase other assets that may have far more risk. Low transaction costs allow financial intermediaries to share risk at low cost, enabling them to earn a profit on the spread between the returns they earn on risky assets and the payments they make on the assets they have sold. This process of risk sharing is also sometimes referred to as **asset transformation**, because, in a sense, risky assets are turned into safer assets for investors.

Financial intermediaries also promote risk sharing by helping individuals to diversify and thereby lower the amount of risk to which they are exposed. **Diversification** entails investing in a collection (**portfolio**) of assets whose returns do not always move together, with the result that overall risk is lower than for individual assets. (Diversification is another name for the old adage that "you shouldn't put all your eggs in one basket.") Low transaction costs allow financial intermediaries to do this by pooling a collection of assets into a new asset and then selling it to individuals.

Asymmetric Information: Adverse Selection and Moral Hazard

The presence of transaction costs in financial markets explains, in part, why financial intermediaries and indirect finance play such an important role in financial markets. An additional reason is that in financial markets, one party often does not know enough about the other party to make accurate decisions. This inequality is called **asymmetric information**. For example, a borrower who takes out a loan usually has better information about the potential returns and risk associated with the investment projects for which the funds are earmarked than the lender does. Lack of information creates problems in the financial system on two fronts: before the transaction is entered into and after.

Adverse selection is the problem created by asymmetric information *before* the transaction occurs. Adverse selection in financial markets occurs when the potential borrowers who are the most likely to produce an undesirable *(adverse)* outcome—the bad credit risks—are the ones who most actively seek out a loan and are thus most likely to be selected. Because adverse selection makes it more likely that loans might be made to bad credit risks, lenders may decide not to make any loans even though there are good credit risks in the marketplace.

To understand why adverse selection occurs, suppose that you have two aunts to whom you might make a loan—Aunt Sheila and Aunt Louise. Aunt Louise is a conservative type who borrows only when she has an investment she is quite sure will pay off. Aunt Sheila, by contrast, is an inveterate gambler who has just come across a get-rich-quick scheme that will make her a millionaire if she can just borrow $1000 to invest in it. Unfortunately, as with most get-rich-quick schemes, there is a high probability that the investment won't pay off and that Aunt Sheila will lose the $1000.

Which of your aunts is more likely to call you to ask for a loan? Aunt Sheila, of course, because she has so much to gain if the investment pays off. You, however, would not want to make a loan to her because there is a high probability that her investment will turn sour and she will be unable to pay you back.

If you knew both your aunts very well—that is, if your information were not asymmetric—you wouldn't have a problem because you would know that Aunt Sheila is a bad risk and so you would not lend to her. Suppose, though, that you don't know your aunts well. You are more likely to lend to Aunt Sheila than to Aunt Louise because Aunt Sheila would be hounding you for the loan. Because of the possibility of adverse selection, you might decide not to lend to either of your aunts, even though there are times when Aunt Louise, who is an excellent credit risk, might need a loan for a worthwhile investment.

Moral hazard is the problem created by asymmetric information *after* the transaction occurs. Moral hazard in financial markets is the risk (*hazard*) that the borrower might engage in activities that are undesirable (*immoral*) from the lender's point of view because they make it less likely that the loan will be paid back. Because moral hazard lowers the probability that the loan will be repaid, lenders may decide that they would rather not make a loan.

As an example of moral hazard, suppose that you made a $1000 loan to another relative, Uncle Melvin, who needs the money to purchase a computer so he can set up a business inputting students' term papers. Once you have made the loan, however, Uncle Melvin is more likely to slip off to the track and play the horses. If he bets on a 20-to-1 long shot and wins with your money, he is able to pay you back your $1000 and live high off the hog with the remaining $19 000. But if he loses, as is likely, you don't get paid back, and all he has lost is his reputation as a reliable, upstanding uncle. Uncle Melvin therefore has an incentive to go to the track because his gains ($19 000) if he bets correctly may be much greater than the cost to him (his reputation) if he bets incorrectly. If you knew what Uncle Melvin was up to, you would prevent him from going to the track, and he would not be able to increase the moral hazard. However, because it is hard for you to keep informed about his whereabouts—that is, because information is asymmetric—there is a good chance that Uncle Melvin will go to the track and you will not get paid back. The risk of moral hazard might therefore discourage you from making the $1000 loan to Uncle Melvin, even if you were sure that you would be paid back if he used it to set up his business.

The problems created by adverse selection and moral hazard are an important impediment to well-functioning financial markets. Again, financial intermediaries can alleviate these problems.

With financial intermediaries in the economy, small savers can provide their funds to the financial markets by lending these funds to a trustworthy intermediary, say, the Honest John Bank, which in turn lends the funds out either by making loans or by buying securities such as stocks or bonds. Successful financial intermediaries have higher earnings on their investments than small savers because they are better equipped than individuals to screen out good from bad credit risks, thereby reducing losses due to adverse selection. In addition, financial intermediaries have high earnings because they develop expertise in monitoring the parties they lend to, thus reducing losses due to moral hazard. The result is that financial intermediaries can afford to pay lender-savers interest or provide substantial services and still earn a profit.

As we have seen, financial intermediaries play an important role in the economy because they provide liquidity services, promote risk sharing, and solve information problems, thereby allowing small savers and borrowers to benefit from the existence of financial markets. The success of financial intermediaries performing this role is evidenced by the fact that most Canadians invest their savings with them and obtain loans from them. Financial intermediaries play a key role in improving economic efficiency because they help financial markets channel funds from lender-savers to people with productive investment opportunities. Without a well-functioning set of financial intermediaries, it is very hard for an economy to reach its full potential. We will explore further the role of financial intermediaries in the economy in Part III.

TYPES OF FINANCIAL INTERMEDIARIES

We have seen why financial intermediaries play such an important role in the economy. Now we look at the principal financial intermediaries and how they perform the intermediation function. They fall into three categories: depository institutions (banks and near banks), contractual savings institutions, and investment intermediaries. Table 2-4 provides a guide to the discussion of the financial intermediaries that fit into these three categories by describing their primary liabilities (sources of funds) and assets (uses of funds). The relative size of these intermediaries in Canada is indicated in Table 2-5.

Depository Institutions (Banks)

Depository institutions (which for simplicity we refer to as *banks* throughout this text) are financial intermediaries that accept deposits from individuals and institutions and make loans. The study of money and banking focuses special attention on this group of financial institutions because they are involved in the creation of deposits, an important component of the money supply. These institutions include chartered banks and the so-called near banks: trust and mortgage loan companies, and credit unions and *caisses populaires*.

CHARTERED BANKS   These financial intermediaries raise funds primarily by issuing chequable deposits (deposits on which cheques can be written), savings deposits (deposits that are payable on demand but do not allow their owner to write cheques), and term deposits (deposits with fixed terms to maturity). They then use these funds to make commercial, consumer, and mortgage loans and to buy Canadian government securities and provincial and municipal bonds. There are 73 chartered banks in Canada, and as a group they are the largest financial intermediary and have the most diversified portfolios (collections) of assets.

TRUST AND MORTGAGE LOAN COMPANIES (TMLs)   These depository institutions, numbering 70, obtain funds primarily through chequable and nonchequable savings deposits, term deposits, guaranteed investment certificates, and debentures. In the past, these institutions were constrained in their activities and mostly made mortgage loans for residential housing. Over time, these restrictions have been

TABLE 2-4 Primary Assets and Liabilities of Financial Intermediaries		
Type of Intermediary	**Primary Liabilities (Sources of Funds)**	**Primary Assets (Uses of Funds)**
Depository Institutions (Banks)		
Chartered banks	Deposits	Loans, mortgages, government bonds
Trust and mortgage loan companies	Deposits	Mortgages
Credit unions and *caisses populaires*	Deposits	Mortgages
Contractual Savings Institutions		
Life insurance companies	Premiums from policies	Corporate bonds and mortgages
Property and casualty insurance companies	Premiums from policies	Corporate bonds and stocks
Pension funds	Retirement contributions	Corporate bonds and stocks
Investment Intermediaries		
Finance companies	Finance paper, stock, bonds	Consumer and business loans
Mutual funds	Shares	Stocks and bonds
Money market mutual funds	Shares	Money market instruments

loosened so that the distinction between these depository institutions and chartered banks has blurred. These intermediaries have become more alike and are now more competitive with each other.

CREDIT UNIONS AND *CAISSES POPULAIRES* (CUCPs)   Credit unions and *caisses populaires* are very small cooperative lending institutions organized around a particular group: union members, employees of a particular firm, and so forth. They acquire funds from deposits and primarily make mortgage and consumer loans.

Contractual Savings Institutions

Contractual savings institutions, such as insurance companies and pension funds, are financial intermediaries that acquire funds at periodic intervals on a contractual basis. Because they can predict with reasonable accuracy how much they will have to pay out in benefits in the coming years, they do not have to worry as much as depository institutions about losing funds. As a result, the liquidity of assets is not as important a consideration for them as it is for depository institutions, and they tend to invest their funds primarily in long-term securities such as corporate bonds, stocks, and mortgages.

LIFE INSURANCE COMPANIES   Life insurance companies, numbering 94, insure people against financial hazards following a death and sell annuities (annual income payments upon retirement). They acquire funds from the premiums that people pay to keep their policies in force and use them mainly to buy corporate bonds and mortgages. They also purchase stocks but are restricted in the amount

TABLE 2-5 Relative Shares of Financial Institutions and Pension Plans Regulated by OSFI (as of March 31, 2008)

Type of Intermediary	Number	Total assets ($ millions)	Percent (%)
Chartered Banks			
Domestic	20	2 596 712	67.92
Foreign bank subsidiaries	24	139 523	3.65
Foreign bank branches	29	79 191	2.07
Trust and Loan Companies			
Bank-owned	31	243 163	6.36
Other	39	23 292	0.61
Cooperative Credit Associations	8	21 152	0.55
Life Insurance Companies			
Canadian-incorporated	46	456 440	11.94
Foreign branches	48	15 275	0.40
Fraternal Benefit Societies			
Canadian-incorporated	10	5 809	0.15
Foreign branches	8	1 775	0.05
Property and Casualty Insurance Companies			
Canadian-incorporated	96	78 256	2.05
Foreign branches	100	30 873	0.81
Pension Plans	1 350	131 765	3.44
Total		3 823 226	100.00

Source: Office of the Superintendent of Financial Institutions Canada (OSFI), *2007–2008 Annual Report*.

that they can hold. Currently, with about $472 billion of assets, they are among the largest of the contractual savings institutions.

PROPERTY AND CASUALTY (P&C) INSURANCE COMPANIES   These companies, numbering 196, insure their policyholders against loss from theft, fire, and accidents. They are very much like life insurance companies, receiving funds through premiums for their policies, but they have a greater possibility of loss of funds if major disasters occur. For this reason, they use their funds to buy more liquid assets than life insurance companies do. Their largest holding of assets is government bonds and debentures; they also hold corporate bonds and stocks.

PENSION FUNDS AND GOVERNMENT RETIREMENT FUNDS   Private pension funds and provincial and municipal retirement funds provide retirement income in the form of annuities to employees who are covered by a pension plan. Funds are acquired by contributions from employers and/or from employees, who either have a contribution automatically deducted from their paycheques or contribute voluntarily. The largest asset holdings of pension funds are corporate bonds and stocks. The establishment of pension funds has been actively encouraged by the federal government both through legislation requiring pension plans and through tax incentives to encourage contributions.

Investment Intermediaries

This category of financial intermediaries includes finance companies, mutual funds, and money market mutual funds.

FINANCE COMPANIES Finance companies raise funds by selling commercial paper (a short-term debt instrument) and by issuing stocks and bonds. They lend these funds to consumers, who make purchases of such items as furniture, automobiles, and home improvements, and to small businesses. Some finance companies are organized by a parent corporation to help sell its product. For example, Ford Credit makes loans to consumers who purchase Ford automobiles.

MUTUAL FUNDS These financial intermediaries acquire funds by selling shares to many individuals and use the proceeds to purchase diversified portfolios of stocks and bonds. Mutual funds allow shareholders to pool their resources so that they can take advantage of lower transaction costs when buying large blocks of stocks or bonds. In addition, mutual funds allow shareholders to hold more diversified portfolios than they otherwise would. Shareholders can sell (redeem) shares at any time, but the value of these shares will be determined by the value of the mutual fund's holdings of securities. Because these fluctuate greatly, the value of mutual fund shares will too; therefore, investments in mutual funds can be risky.

MONEY MARKET MUTUAL FUNDS These financial institutions have the characteristics of mutual funds but also function to some extent as depository institutions because they offer deposit-type accounts. Like most mutual funds, they sell shares to acquire funds that are then used to buy money market instruments that are both safe and very liquid. The interest on these assets is paid out to shareholders.

REGULATION OF THE FINANCIAL SYSTEM

The financial system is among the most heavily regulated sectors of the Canadian economy. The government regulates financial markets for three main reasons: to increase the information available to investors, to ensure the soundness of the financial system, and to improve control of monetary policy. We will examine how these three reasons have led to the present regulatory environment. As a study aid, the principal regulatory agencies of the Canadian financial system are listed in Table 2-6.

Increasing Information Available to Investors

Asymmetric information in financial markets means that investors may be subject to adverse selection and moral hazard problems that may hinder the efficient operation of financial markets. Risky firms or outright crooks may be the most eager to sell securities to unwary investors, and the resulting adverse selection problem may keep investors out of financial markets. Furthermore, once an investor has bought a security, thereby lending money to a firm, the borrower may have incentives to engage in risky activities or to commit outright fraud. The presence of this moral hazard problem may also keep investors away from financial markets. Government regulation can reduce adverse selection and moral hazard problems in financial markets and increase their efficiency by increasing the amount of information available to investors.

Provincial securities commissions, the most significant being the Ontario Securities Commission (OSC), administer provincial acts requiring corporations issuing securities to disclose certain information about their sales, assets, and earn-

TABLE 2-6 Principal Regulatory Agencies of the Canadian Financial System

Regulatory Agency	Subject of Regulation	Nature of Regulations
Provincial securities and exchange commissions	Organized exchanges and financial markets	Requires disclosure of information and restrict insider trading
Bank of Canada	Chartered banks, TMLs, and CUCPs	Examines the books of the deposit-taking institutions and coordinates with the federal agencies that are responsible for financial institution regulation: OSFI and CDIC
Office of the Superintendent of Financial Institutions Canada (OSFI)	All federally regulated chartered banks, TMLs, CUCPs, life insurance companies, P&C insurance companies, and pension plans	Sets capital adequacy, accounting, and board-of-directors responsibility standards; conducts bank audits and coordinates with provincial securities commissions
Canada Deposit Insurance Corporation (CDIC)	Chartered banks, TMLs, CUCPs	Provides insurance of up to $100 000 for each depositor at a bank, examines the books of insured banks, and imposes restrictions on assets they can hold
Québec Deposit Insurance Board	TMLs and credit cooperatives in Québec	Similar role as the CDIC
Canadian Life and Health Insurance Compensation Corporation (CompCorp)	Life insurance companies	Compensates policyholders if the issuing life insurance company goes bankrupt
P&C Insurance Compensation Corporation (PACIC)	Property and casualty insurance companies	Compensates policyholders if the issuing P&C insurance company goes bankrupt

ings to the public and restrict trading by the largest stockholders in the corporation. By requiring disclosure of this information and by discouraging insider trading, which could be used to manipulate security prices, regulators hope that investors will be better informed and be protected from abuses in financial markets. Indeed, in recent years, the OSC has been particularly active in prosecuting people involved in insider trading in Canada's largest stock exchange, the Toronto Stock Exchange (TSX).

Ensuring the Soundness of Financial Intermediaries

Asymmetric information can lead to the widespread collapse of financial intermediaries, referred to as a **financial panic**. Because providers of funds to financial intermediaries may not be able to assess whether the institutions holding their funds are sound or not, if they have doubts about the overall health of financial intermediaries they may want to pull their funds out of both sound and unsound institutions. The possible outcome is a financial panic that produces large losses for the public and causes serious damage to the economy. To protect the public and the economy from financial panics, the government has implemented various types of regulations.

RESTRICTIONS ON ENTRY Provincial banking and insurance commissions, the Bank of Canada, and the Office of the Superintendent of Financial Institutions (OSFI), an agency of the federal government, have created tight regulations governing who is allowed to set up a financial intermediary. Individuals or groups that want to establish a financial intermediary, such as a bank or an insurance company, must obtain a charter from the provincial or federal government. Only if they are upstanding citizens with impeccable credentials and a large amount of initial funds will they be given a charter.

DISCLOSURE There are stringent reporting requirements for financial intermediaries. Their bookkeeping must follow certain strict principles, their books are subject to periodic inspection, and they must make certain information available to the public.

RESTRICTIONS ON ASSETS AND ACTIVITIES There are restrictions on what financial intermediaries are allowed to do and what assets they can hold. Before you put your funds into a chartered bank or some other such institution, you would want to know that your funds are safe and that the financial intermediary will be able to meet its obligations to you. One way of doing this is to restrict the financial intermediary from engaging in certain risky activities. Another way to limit a financial intermediary's risk behaviour is to restrict it from holding certain risky assets, or at least from holding a greater quantity of these risky assets than is prudent. For example, chartered banks and other depository institutions are not allowed to hold common stock because stock prices experience substantial fluctuations. Insurance companies are allowed to hold common stock, but their holdings cannot exceed a certain fraction of their total assets.

DEPOSIT INSURANCE The government can insure people's deposits so that they do not suffer any financial loss if the financial intermediary that holds these deposits fails. The most important government agency that provides this type of insurance is the Canada Deposit Insurance Corporation (CDIC), created by an act of Parliament in 1967. It insures each depositor at a member deposit-taking financial institution up to a loss of $100 000 per account. Except for certain wholesale branches of foreign banks, credit unions, and some provincial institutions, all deposit-taking financial institutions in Canada are members of the CDIC. All CDIC members make contributions into the CDIC fund, which are used to pay off depositors in the case of a bank's failure. The Québec Deposit Insurance Board, an organization similar to CDIC and set up at the same time as CDIC, provides insurance for TMLs and credit cooperatives in Québec.

LIMITS ON COMPETITION Politicians have often declared that unbridled competition among financial intermediaries promotes failures that will harm the public. Although the evidence that competition has this effect is extremely weak, provincial and federal governments at times have imposed restrictive regulations. For example, from 1967 to 1980 the entry of foreign banks into Canadian banking was prohibited. Since 1980, however, the incorporation of foreign bank subsidiaries has been regulated, but Canada still ranks low with respect to the degree of competition from foreign banks.

In later chapters we will look more closely at government regulation of financial markets and will see whether it has improved their functioning.

Financial Regulation Abroad

Not surprisingly, given the similarity of the economic systems here and in the United States, Japan, and the nations of Western Europe, financial regulation in these countries is similar to financial regulation in Canada. The provision of information is improved by requiring corporations issuing securities to report details about assets and liabilities, earnings, and sales of stock, and by prohibiting insider trading. The soundness of intermediaries is ensured by licensing, periodic inspection of financial intermediaries' books, and the provision of deposit insurance.

The major differences between financial regulation in Canada and abroad relate to bank regulation. In the past, for example, the United States was the only industrialized country to subject banks to restrictions on branching, which limited banks' size and restricted them to certain geographic regions. These restrictions were abolished by legislation in 1994. U.S. and Canadian banks are also the most restricted in the range of assets they may hold. Banks in other countries frequently hold shares in commercial firms; in Japan and Germany, those stakes can be sizable.

SUMMARY

1. The basic function of financial markets is to channel funds from savers who have an excess of funds to spenders who have a shortage of funds. Financial markets can do this either through direct finance, in which borrowers borrow funds directly from lenders by selling them securities, or through indirect finance, which involves a financial intermediary that stands between the lender-savers and the borrower-spenders and helps transfer funds from one to the other. This channelling of funds improves the economic welfare of everyone in the society. Because they allow funds to move from people who have no productive investment opportunities to those who have such opportunities, financial markets contribute to economic efficiency. In addition, channelling of funds directly benefits consumers by allowing them to make purchases when they need them most.

2. Financial markets can be classified as debt and equity markets, primary and secondary markets, exchanges and over-the-counter markets, and money and capital markets.

3. The principal money market instruments (debt instruments with maturities of less than one year) are treasury bills, certificates of deposit, commercial paper, repurchase agreements, overnight funds, and Eurodollars. The principal capital market instruments (debt and equity instruments with maturities greater than one year) are stocks, mortgages, corporate

bonds, Canadian government securities, Canada Savings Bonds, government agency securities, provincial and municipal government bonds, and consumer and bank commercial loans.

4. An important trend in recent years is the growing internationalization of financial markets. Eurobonds, which are denominated in a currency other than that of the country in which they are sold, are now the dominant security in the international bond market. Eurodollars, which are dollars deposited in foreign banks, are an important source of funds for Canadian banks.

5. Financial intermediaries are financial institutions that acquire funds by issuing liabilities and in turn use those funds to acquire assets by purchasing securities or making loans. Financial intermediaries play an important role in the financial system because they reduce transaction costs, allow risk sharing, and solve problems created by adverse selection and moral hazard. As a result, financial intermediaries allow small savers and borrowers to benefit from the existence of financial markets, thereby increasing the efficiency of the economy.

6. The principal financial intermediaries fall into three categories: (a) banks—chartered banks, trust and mortgage loan companies, and credit unions and *caisses populaires*; (b) contractual savings institutions—life insurance companies, property and casu-

alty insurance companies, and pension funds; and (c) investment intermediaries—finance companies, mutual funds, and money market mutual funds.

7. The government regulates financial markets and financial intermediaries for three main reasons: to increase the information available to investors, to ensure the soundness of the financial system, and to improve control of monetary policy. Regulations include requiring disclosure of information to the public, restrictions on who can set up a financial intermediary, restrictions on what assets financial intermediaries can hold, and the provision of deposit insurance.

KEY TERMS

adverse selection,   p. 32

asset transformation,   p. 32

asymmetric information,   p. 32

bearer deposit notes,   p. 23

brokers,   p. 20

call (redemption)   p. 26

Canadas,   p. 26

capital market,   p. 21

dealers,   p. 20

diversification,   p. 32

dividends,   p. 20

economies of scale,   p. 31

equities,   p. 20

Eurobond,   p. 27

Eurocurrencies,   p. 27

Eurodollars,   p. 27

exchanges,   p. 21

finance paper,   p. 23

financial intermediation,   p. 30

financial panic,   p. 38

foreign bonds,   p. 27

intermediate-term,   p. 20

investment bank,   p. 20

liabilities,   p. 18

liquid,   p. 21

liquidity services,   p. 32

long-term,   p. 20

maturity,   p. 20

money market,   p. 21

moral hazard,   p. 33

municipal bonds (municipals),   p. 26

over-the-counter (OTC) market,   p. 21

overnight interest rate,   p. 24

portfolio,   p. 32

primary market,   p. 20

provincial bonds (provincials),   p. 26

registered bonds,   p. 26

risk,   p. 32

risk sharing,   p. 32

secondary market,   p. 20

short-term,   p. 20

term deposit receipts (term notes),   p. 23

transaction costs,   p. 31

underwriting,   p. 20

QUESTIONS

You will find the answers to the questions marked with an asterisk in the Textbook Resources section of your MyEconLab.

*1. Why is a share of Microsoft common stock an asset for its owner and a liability for Microsoft?

2. If I can buy a car today for $5000 and it is worth $10 000 in extra income next year to me because it enables me to get a job as a travelling anvil seller, should I take out a loan from Larry the Loan Shark at a 90% interest rate if no one else will give me a loan? Will I be better or worse off as a result of taking out this loan? Can you make a case for legalizing loan-sharking?

*3. Some economists suspect that one of the reasons that economies in developing countries grow so slowly is that they do not have well-developed financial markets. Does this argument make sense?

4. Describe how authority over deposit-based financial intermediaries is split among the Bank of Canada, the OSFI, and the CDIC.

*5. "Because corporations do not actually raise any funds in secondary markets, these markets are less important to the economy than primary markets." Comment.

6. If you suspect that a company will go bankrupt next year, which would you rather hold, bonds issued by the company or equities issued by the company? Why?

*7. How can the adverse selection problem explain why you are more likely to make a loan to a family member than to a stranger?

8. Think of one example in which you have had to deal with the adverse selection problem.

*9. Why do loan sharks worry less about moral hazard in connection with their borrowers than some other lenders do?

10. If you are an employer, what kinds of moral hazard problems might you worry about with your employees?

*11. If there were no asymmetry in the information that a borrower and a lender had, could there still be a moral hazard problem?

12. "In a world without information and transaction costs, financial intermediaries would not exist." Is this statement true, false, or uncertain? Explain your answer.

*13. Why might you be willing to make a loan to your neighbour by putting funds in a savings account

earning a 5% interest rate at the bank and having the bank lend her the funds at a 10% interest rate rather than lend her the funds yourself?

14. How does risk sharing benefit both financial intermediaries and private investors?

*15. Discuss some of the manifestations of the globalization of world capital markets.

WEB EXERCISES

1. One of the single best sources of information about financial institutions is the financial data produced by the OSFI. Go to **www.osfi-bsif.gc.ca**, click on "Banks" and then "Financial Data–Banks" and answer the following.
   a. What percent of assets do domestic chartered banks hold in loans? What percentage of assets are held in mortgage loans?
   b. What percent of assets do trust companies hold in mortgage loans?
   c. What percent of assets do cooperatives hold in mortgage loans and in consumer loans?

2. The most famous financial market in the world is the New York Stock Exchange. Go to **www.nyse.com**.
   a. Click on "Information for Media" and summarize the activity in the market in terms of movements in the Dow Jones Industrial Average and the NYSE Composite Index.
   b. Firms must pay a fee to list their shares for sale on the NYSE. What would be the fee for a firm with 5 million common shares outstanding?

Be sure to visit the MyEconLab website at **www.myeconlab.com**. This online homework and tutorial system puts you in control of your own learning with study and practice tools directly correlated to this chapter content.

CHAPTER 3

What Is Money?

LEARNING OBJECTIVES

After studying this chapter you should be able to

1. describe the meaning of the word *money*
2. distinguish among the three primary functions of money: a medium of exchange, a unit of account, and a store of value
3. illustrate how information technology has paved the way for e-money, e-banking, and e-commerce
4. explain money measurement matters

PREVIEW

If you lived in Canada before the creation of the central bank (the Bank of Canada) in 1935, your money might have consisted primarily of gold and silver coins and paper notes, called *banknotes*, issued by private banks. Today you use not only coins and dollar bills as means of payment, but also cheques written on accounts held at banks, credit cards, debit cards, stored-value cards, and electronic cash and cheques. Money has been different things at different times, but it has always been important to people and to the economy.

To understand the effects of money on the economy, we must understand exactly what money is. In this chapter we develop precise definitions by exploring the functions of money, looking at why and how it promotes economic efficiency, tracing how its forms have evolved over time, and examining how money is currently measured.

MEANING OF MONEY

As the word *money* is used in everyday conversation, it can mean many things, but to economists it has a very specific meaning. To avoid confusion, we must clarify how economists' use of the word *money* differs from conventional usage.

Economists define *money* as anything that is generally accepted in payment for goods or services or in the repayment of debts. Currency, consisting of dollar bills and coins, clearly fits this definition and is one type of money. When most people talk about money, they're talking about **currency** (paper money and coins). If, for example, someone comes up to you and says, "Your money or your life," you should quickly hand over all your currency rather than ask, "What exactly do you mean by 'money'?"

To define money merely as currency is much too narrow for economists. Because cheques are also accepted as payment for purchases, chequing account deposits are considered money as well. An even broader definition of money is often needed because other items such as savings deposits can in effect function as money if they can be quickly and easily converted into currency or chequing account deposits. As you can see, there is no single, precise definition of money or the money supply, even for economists.

To complicate matters further, the word *money* is frequently used synonymously with *wealth*. When people say, "Joe is rich—he has an awful lot of money," they probably mean that Joe not only has a lot of currency and a high balance in his chequing account but also has stocks, bonds, four cars, three houses, and a yacht. Thus while "currency" is too narrow a definition of money, this other popular usage is much too broad. Economists make a distinction between money in the form of currency, demand deposits, and other items that are used to make purchases, and **wealth**, the total collection of pieces of property that serve to store value. Wealth includes not only money but also other assets such as bonds, common stock, art, land, furniture, cars, and houses.

People also use the word *money* to describe what economists call *income*, as in the sentence "Sheila would be a wonderful catch; she has a good job and earns a lot of money." **Income** is a *flow* of earnings per unit of time. Money, by contrast, is a stock: it is a certain amount at a given point in time. If someone tells you that he has an income of $1000, you cannot tell whether he earned a lot or a little without knowing whether this $1000 is earned per year, per month, or even per day. But if someone tells you that she has $1000 in her pocket, you know exactly how much this is.

Keep in mind that the money discussed in this book refers to anything that is generally accepted in payment for goods and services or in the repayment of debts and is distinct from income and wealth.

FUNCTIONS OF MONEY

Whether money is shells or rocks or gold or paper, it has three primary functions in any economy: as a medium of exchange, as a unit of account, and as a store of value. Of the three functions, its function as a medium of exchange is what distinguishes money from other assets such as stocks, bonds, and houses.

Medium of Exchange

In almost all market transactions in our economy, money in the form of currency or cheques is a **medium of exchange**; it is used to pay for goods and services. The use of money as a medium of exchange promotes economic efficiency by eliminating much of the time spent in exchanging goods and services. To see why, let's look at a barter economy, one without money, in which goods and services are exchanged directly for other goods and services.

Take the case of Ellen the Economics Professor, who can do just one thing well: give brilliant economics lectures. In a barter economy, if Ellen wants to eat, she must find a farmer who not only produces the food she likes but also wants to learn economics. As you might expect, this search will be difficult and time-consuming, and Ellen may spend more time looking for such an economics-hungry farmer than she will teaching. It is even possible that she will have to quit lecturing and go into farming herself. Even so, she may still starve to death.

The time spent trying to exchange goods or services is called a *transaction cost*. In a barter economy, transaction costs are high because people have to satisfy a "double coincidence of wants"—they have to find someone who has a good or service they want and who also wants the good or service they have to offer.

Let's see what happens if we introduce money into Ellen the Economics Professor's world. Ellen can teach anyone who is willing to pay money to hear her lecture. She can then go to any farmer (or his representative at the supermarket) and buy the food she needs with the money she has been paid. The problem of the double coincidence of wants is avoided and Ellen saves a lot of time, which she may spend doing what she does best: teaching.

As this example shows, money promotes economic efficiency by eliminating much of the time spent exchanging goods and services. It also promotes efficiency by allowing people to specialize in what they do best. Money is therefore essential in an economy: it is a lubricant that allows the economy to run more smoothly by lowering transaction costs, thereby encouraging specialization and the division of labour.

The need for money is so strong that almost every society beyond the most primitive invents it. For a commodity to function effectively as money, it has to meet several criteria: (1) It must be easily standardized, making it simple to ascertain its value; (2) it must be widely accepted; (3) it must be divisible so that it is easy to "make change"; (4) it must be easy to carry; and (5) it must not deteriorate quickly. Forms of money that have satisfied these criteria have taken many unusual forms throughout human history, ranging from wampum (strings of beads), used by Native Americans, to tobacco and whiskey, used by the early American colonists, to cigarettes, used in prisoner-of-war camps during World War II. The diversity of forms of money that have been developed over the years is as much a testament to the inventiveness of the human race as the development of tools and language. See, for example, the FYI box, Money in a Prisioner-of-War Camp and Modern Prisons.

Unit of Account

The second role of money is to provide a **unit of account**; that is, it is used to measure value in the economy. We measure the value of goods and services in terms of money, just as we measure weight in terms of kilograms or distance in terms of kilometres. To see why this function is important, let's look again at a barter economy where money does not perform this function. If the economy has only three goods, say, peaches, economics lectures, and movies, then we need to know only three prices to tell us how to exchange one for another: the price of peaches in terms of economics lectures (that is, how many economics lectures you have to pay for a peach), the price of peaches in terms of movies, and the price of economics lectures in terms of movies. If there were ten goods, we would need to know 45 prices in order to exchange one good for another; with 100 goods, we would need 4950 prices; and with 1000 goods, 499 500 prices.[1]

---

[1] The formula for telling us the number of prices we need when we have N goods is the same formula that tells us the number of pairs when there are N items. It is

$$\frac{N(N-1)}{2}$$

In the case of ten goods, for example, we would need

$$\frac{10(10-1)}{2} = \frac{90}{2} = 45$$

FYI   Money in a Prisoner-of-War Camp and Modern Prisons

An extremely entertaining article on the development of money in a prisoner-of-war camp during World War II is R. A. Radford's "The Economic Organization of a P.O.W. Camp."* He describes his experience with the economy of a German prisoner-of-war camp where cigarettes had become the primary medium of exchange, with most prices expressed in units of cigarettes.

Cigarettes have also been used as currency in prisons in the United States and other countries in much the same way. Recently, however, with the enactment of a ban on smoking (and therefore the prohibition of the cigarette pack) in federal prisons in the United States, a substitute currency has evolved: pouches of mackerel—in prison lingo, "macks."

In particular, inmates in modern federal prisons in the United States get credits in their commissary accounts from prison jobs, which pay about 40 cents per hour, and use these credits to buy goods such as food and toiletries from the commissary. Prisoners are not allowed to possess cash, but they have developed a substitute medium of exchange by using their commissary account credits to buy macks, which they then use as currency. That is, they use macks to pay for gambling debts and to buy goods and services from other prisoners, such as haircuts and shoeshines. Macks are a good substitute for the U.S. dollar because they each cost about US$1.

Economica 12 (November 1945): 189–201.

Imagine how hard it would be in a barter economy to shop at a supermarket with 1000 different items on its shelves, having to decide whether chicken or fish is a better buy if the price of a kilogram of chicken were quoted as 4 kilograms of butter and the price of a kilogram of fish as 8 kilograms of tomatoes. To make it possible to compare prices, the tag on each item would have to list up to 999 different prices, and the time spent reading them would result in very high transaction costs.

The solution to the problem is to introduce money into the economy and have all prices quoted in terms of units of that money, enabling us to quote the price of economics lectures, peaches, and movies in terms of, say, dollars. If there were only three goods in the economy, this would not be a great advantage over the barter system because we would still need three prices to conduct transactions. But for ten goods we now need only ten prices; for 100 goods, 100 prices; and so on. At the 1000-good supermarket, there are now only 1000 prices to look at, not 499 500!

We can see that using money as a unit of account reduces transaction costs in an economy by reducing the number of prices that need to be considered. The benefits of this function of money grow as the economy becomes more complex.

Store of Value   Money also functions as a **store of value**; it is a repository of purchasing power over time. A store of value is used to save purchasing power from the time income is received until the time it is spent. This function of money is useful because most of us do not want to spend our income immediately upon receiving it but rather prefer to wait until we have the time or the desire to shop.

Money is not unique as a store of value; any asset, whether money, stocks, bonds, land, houses, art, or jewellery, can be used to store wealth. Many such assets have advantages over money as a store of value: they often pay the owner a higher interest rate than money, experience price appreciation, and deliver services such as providing a roof over one's head. If these assets are a more desirable store of value than money, why do people hold money at all?

The answer to this question relates to the important economic concept of **liquidity**, the relative ease and speed with which an asset can be converted into a medium of exchange. Liquidity is highly desirable. Money is the most liquid asset of all because it is the medium of exchange; it does not have to be converted into anything else in order to make purchases. Other assets involve transaction costs when they are converted into money. When you sell your house, for example, you have to pay a brokerage commission (usually 5% to 7% of the sales price), and if you need cash immediately to pay some pressing bills, you might have to settle for a lower price in order to sell the house quickly. The fact that money is the most liquid asset, then, explains why people are willing to hold it even if it is not the most attractive store of value.

How good a store of value money is depends on the price level, because its value is fixed in terms of the price level. A doubling of all prices, for example, means that the value of money has dropped by half; conversely, a halving of all prices means that the value of money has doubled. During a period of high inflation, when the price level is increasing rapidly, money loses value rapidly, and people will be more reluctant to hold their wealth in this form. This is especially true during periods of extreme inflation, known as **hyperinflation**, in which the inflation rate exceeds 50% per month.

Hyperinflation occurred in Germany after World War I, with inflation rates sometimes exceeding 1000% per month. By the end of the hyperinflation in 1923, the price level had risen to more than 30 billion times what it had been just two years before. The quantity of money needed to purchase even the most basic items became excessive. There are stories, for example, that near the end of the hyperinflation, a wheelbarrow of cash would be required to pay for a loaf of bread. Money was losing its value so rapidly that workers were paid and given time off several times during the day to spend their wages before the money became worthless. No one wanted to hold on to money, and so the use of money to carry out transactions declined and barter became more and more dominant. Transaction costs skyrocketed, and as we would expect, output in the economy fell sharply.

EVOLUTION OF THE PAYMENTS SYSTEM

We can obtain a better picture of the functions of money and the forms it has taken over time by looking at the evolution of the **payments system**, the method of conducting transactions in the economy. The payments system has been evolving over centuries, and with it the form of money. At one point, precious metals such as gold were used as the principal means of payment and were the main form of money. Later, paper assets such as cheques and currency began to be used in the payments system and viewed as money. Where the payments system is heading has an important bearing on how money will be defined in the future.

Commodity Money

To obtain perspective on where the payments system is heading, it is worth exploring how it has evolved. For any object to function as money, it must be universally acceptable; everyone must be willing to take it in payment for goods and services. An object that clearly has value to everyone is a likely candidate to serve as money, and a natural choice is a precious metal such as gold or silver. Money made up of precious metals or another valuable commodity is called **commodity money**, and from ancient times until several hundred years ago commodity money functioned as the medium of exchange in all but the most primitive societies. The problem with a payments system based exclusively on precious metals is that such a form of money is very heavy and is hard to transport from one place to another. Imagine the holes you'd wear in your pockets if you had to buy things only with coins! Indeed, for large purchases such as a house, you'd have to rent a truck to transport the money payment.

Fiat Money

The next development in the payments system was paper currency (pieces of paper that function as a medium of exchange). Initially, paper currency embodied a promise that it was convertible into coins or into a quantity of precious metal. However, currency has evolved into **fiat money**, paper currency decreed by governments as legal tender (meaning that legally it must be accepted as payment for debts) but not convertible into coins or precious metal. Paper currency has the advantage of being much lighter than coins or precious metal, but it can be accepted as a medium of exchange only if there is some trust in the authorities who issue it and printing has reached a sufficiently advanced stage that counterfeiting is extremely difficult. Because paper currency has evolved into a legal arrangement, countries can change the currency that they use at will. Indeed, this is what many European countries did when they abandoned their currencies for the euro in 2002.

Major drawbacks of paper currency and coins are that they are easily stolen and can be expensive to transport because of their bulk if there are large amounts. To combat this problem, another step in the evolution of the payments system occurred with the development of modern banking: the invention of *cheques*.

Cheques

A cheque is an instrument from you to your bank used to transfer money from your account to someone else's account when she deposits the cheque. Cheques allow transactions to take place without the need to carry around large amounts of currency. The introduction of cheques was a major innovation that improved the efficiency of the payments system. Frequently, payments made back and forth cancel each other; without cheques, this would involve the movement of a lot of currency. With cheques, payments that cancel each other can be settled by cancelling the cheques, and no currency need be moved. The use of cheques thus reduces the transportation costs associated with the payments system and improves economic efficiency. Another advantage of cheques is that they can be written for any amount up to the balance in the account, making transactions for large amounts much easier. Cheques are advantageous in that loss from theft is greatly reduced, and they provide convenient receipts for purchases.

There are, however, two problems with a payments system based on cheques. First, it takes time to get cheques from one place to another, a particularly serious problem if you are paying someone in a different location who needs to be paid quickly. In addition, if you have a chequing account, you know that it usually takes several business days before a bank will allow you to make use of the funds from a cheque you have deposited. If your need for cash is urgent, this feature of paying by cheque can be frustrating. Second, all the paper shuffling required to process cheques is costly.

Electronic Payment

The development of inexpensive computers and the spread of the Internet now make it cheap to pay bills electronically. In the past, you had to pay your bills by mailing a cheque, but now banks provide websites that allow you to log on, make a few clicks, and thereby transmit your payment electronically. Not only do you save the cost of the stamp, but paying bills becomes (almost) a pleasure, requiring little effort. Electronic payment systems provided by banks now even spare you the step of logging on to pay bills. Instead, recurring bills can be automatically deducted from your bank account. Estimated cost savings when a bill is paid electronically rather than by cheque exceed one dollar. Electronic payment is thus becoming far more common in Canada and the United States.

E-Money

Electronic payment technology can not only substitute for cheques, but can substitute for cash, as well, in the form of **electronic money** (or **e-money**), money that exists only in electronic form. The first form of e-money was the *debit card*. Debit cards, which look like credit cards, enable customers to purchase goods and services by electronically transferring funds directly from their bank accounts to a merchant's account. Debit cards are used in many of the same places that accept credit cards and are now often becoming faster to use than cash. At most supermarkets, for example, you can swipe your debit card through the card reader at the checkout station, press some buttons, and the amount of your purchases is deducted from your bank account. Most banks and credit card companies such as Visa and MasterCard issue debit cards, and your ATM card typically can function as a debit card.

A more advanced form of e-money is the *stored-value card*. The simplest form of stored-value card is purchased for a preset dollar amount that the consumer pays up front, like a prepaid phone card. The more sophisticated stored-value card is known as a **smart card**. It contains a computer chip that allows it to be loaded with digital cash from the owner's bank account whenever needed. In Asian countries such as Japan and Korea, cell phones now have a smart card feature that raises the expression "pay by phone" to a new level. Smart cards can be loaded from ATMs, personal computers with a smart card reader, or specially equipped telephones.

A third form of electronic money is often referred to as **e-cash**, which is used on the Internet to purchase goods or services. A consumer gets e-cash by setting up an account with a bank that has links to the Internet and then has the e-cash transferred to her PC. When she wants to buy something with e-cash, she surfs to a store on the web and clicks the "buy" option for a particular item, whereupon the e-cash is automatically transferred from her computer to the merchant's computer. The merchant can then have the funds transferred from the consumer's bank account to his before the goods are shipped.

Given the convenience of e-money, you might think that we would move quickly to a cashless society in which all payments are made electronically. However, this hasn't happened, as discussed in the FYI box, Are We Headed for a Cashless Society?

MEASURING MONEY

The definition of money as anything that is generally accepted in payment for goods and services tells us that money is defined by people's behaviour. What makes an asset money is that people believe it will be accepted by others when making payment. As we have seen, many different assets have performed this role over the centuries, ranging from gold to paper currency to chequing accounts. For that reason, this behavioural definition does not tell us exactly what assets in our

FYI   **Are We Headed for a Cashless Society?**

Predictions of a cashless society have been around for decades, but they have not come to fruition. For example, *Business Week* predicted in 1975 that electronic means of payment "would soon revolutionize the very concept of money itself," only to reverse itself several years later. Pilot projects in recent years with smart cards to convert consumers to the use of e-money have not been a success. Mondex, one of the widely touted, early stored-value cards that was launched in Britain in 1995, is only used on a few British university campuses. In Germany and Belgium, millions of people carry bank cards with computer chips embedded in them that enable them to make use of e-money, but very few use them. Why has the movement to a cashless society been so slow in coming?

Although e-money might be more convenient and may be more efficient than a payment system based on paper, several factors work against the disappearance of the paper system. First, it is very expensive to set up the computer, card reader, and telecommunications networks necessary to make electronic

money the dominant form of payment. Second, electronic means of payment raise security and privacy concerns. We often hear media reports that an unauthorized hacker has been able to access a computer database and to alter information stored there. Because this is not an uncommon occurrence, unscrupulous persons might be able to access bank accounts in electronic payment systems and steal funds by moving them from someone else's accounts into their own. The prevention of this type of fraud is no easy task, and a whole new field of computer science has developed to cope with security issues. A further concern is that the use of electronic means of payment leaves an electronic trail that contains a large amount of personal data on buying habits. There are worries that government, employers, and marketers might be able to access these data, thereby encroaching on our privacy.

The conclusion from this discussion is that, although the use of e-money will surely increase in the future, to rephrase Mark Twain, "the reports of cash's death are greatly exaggerated."

economy should be considered money. To measure money, we need a precise definition that tells us exactly what assets should be included.

The Bank of Canada's Monetary Aggregates

The Bank of Canada (the Bank), the central banking authority responsible for monetary policy in Canada, has conducted many studies on how to measure money. The problem of measuring money has become especially crucial because extensive financial innovation has produced new types of assets that might properly belong in a measure of money.

Since 1980, the Bank of Canada has modified its measures of money several times. More recently, financial innovation and the removal of reserve requirements have made it difficult to distinguish between demand and notice deposits and prompted the Bank of Canada to terminate a number of money aggregate time series and replace them with alternative series that do not rely on the distinction between demand and notice deposits. Moreover, the new measures include private sector **float** (funds in transit between the time a cheque is deposited and the time the payment is settled) because of the declining importance of float. Recently, the Bank of Canada settled on the following measures of the money supply, which are also referred to as **monetary aggregates** (also shown in Table 3-1).[2]

The **M2** (gross) monetary aggregate includes currency outside banks, personal deposits at chartered banks, and non-personal demand and notice deposits at chartered banks. The currency component of M2 (gross) includes only paper money and coins in the hands of the nonbank public and does not include cash that is held in ATMs or bank vaults. Surprisingly, there is close to $1500 cash in the hands of each person in Canada and more than US$2000 in the hands of each person in the United States (see the FYI box, Where Are All the Dollars?).

The **M3** (gross) aggregate includes M2 (gross) plus chartered bank nonpersonal term deposits and foreign currency deposits of Canadian residents. The nonpersonal term deposits are held by provincial and municipal governments, corporations, and

---

TABLE 3-1 Measures of Monetary Aggregates

M2 (gross)

Currency outside banks

Personal deposits at chartered banks

Non-personal demand and notice deposits at chartered banks

M3 (gross) = M2 (gross) plus the following:

Non-personal term deposits at chartered banks

Foreign currency deposits of residents at chartered banks

M2+ (gross) = M2 (gross) plus the following:

Deposits at trust and mortgage loan companies (TMLs)

Deposits at credit unions and *caisses populaires* (CUCPs)

Life insurance company individual annuities

Personal deposits at government-owned savings institutions

Money market mutual funds

M2++ (gross) = M2+ (gross) plus the following:

Canada Savings Bonds and other retail instruments

Non–money market mutual funds

M1+ (gross)

Currency outside banks

All chequable deposits at chartered banks, TMLs, and CUCPs

M1++ (gross) = M1+ (gross) plus the following:

All non-chequable deposits at chartered banks, TMLs, and CUCPs.

Notes: Monetary aggregates exclude inter-bank deposits and include continuity adjustments. In January 2007, the monetary aggregates were redefined to reflect: (i) the elimination of demand deposits and (ii) the inclusion of private-sector float.

---

[2] For more details regarding the Bank of Canada's recent changes to the monetary aggregates, see Tracy Chan, Ramdane Djoudad, and Jackson Loi, "Changes in the Indicator Properties of Narrow Monetary Aggregates," *Bank of Canada Review* (Summer 2005): 3–10.

FYI   Where Are All the Dollars?

The close to $1500 currency per person in Canada, and over US$2000 of U.S. currency per person in the United States, are surprisingly large numbers. Currency is bulky, can be easily stolen, and pays no interest, so it doesn't make sense for most of us to hold a lot of it. Do you know anyone who carries $1500 in their pockets? We have a puzzle: where are all these dollars and who is holding them?

One group that holds a lot of dollars are criminals. If you were engaged in illegal activity, you would not conduct your transactions with cheques because they are traceable and therefore a potentially powerful piece of evidence against you. This is why Tony Soprano had so much cash in his backyard.

Some businesses also like to hold a lot of cash because if they operate as a cash business, which makes their transactions less traceable, they can avoid declaring income on which they would have to pay taxes.

The other group that holds Canadian and (to a larger extent) U.S. dollars are foreigners. In many countries, people do not trust their own currency because they often experience high inflation, which erodes the value of their currency; these people hold dollars as a hedge against this inflation risk. Lack of trust in the ruble, for example, has led Russians to hold enormous amounts of U.S. dollars. In fact, over half the quantity of U.S. dollars are held abroad.

institutions, and also include deposits held by one bank with another, known as *interbank deposits.* The foreign currency deposits are mostly denominated in U.S. dollars. Notice that the M2 and M3 monetary aggregates do not include deposits with near banks, such as trust and mortgage loan companies (TMLs) and credit unions and *caisses populaires* (CUCPs).

The **M2+** (gross) monetary aggregate includes M2 (gross) plus deposits at near banks, life insurance company annuities, and money market mutual funds. Finally, **M2++** (gross) adds to M2+ (gross) Canada Savings Bonds and non–money market mutual funds (i.e., bond and equity mutual funds). This broader monetary aggregate is good at capturing information about the long-run spending plans and expectations of the household sector of the economy.[3]

With the financial innovation that has occurred, TMLs and CUCPs can also offer deposits that function as media of exchange. The Bank of Canada has responded to this by introducing new measures of money. The **M1+** monetary aggregate includes currency outside banks and chequable deposits at chartered banks plus other assets that have cheque-writing features—all chequable (personal or non-personal) notice deposits at TMLs and CUCPs. These assets are also extremely liquid because they can be turned into cash quickly at very little cost. The **M1++** (gross) aggregate includes M1+ (gross) plus all nonchequable (personal or non-personal) deposits at chartered banks, TMLs, and CUCPs. Both the M1+ (gross) and M1++ (gross) monetary aggregates internalize the substitution between demand and notice deposits and are good at capturing information about changes in savings behaviour, as well as transaction intentions.

[3] Joseph Atta-Mensah and Loretta Nott, "Recent Developments in the Monetary Aggregates and Their Implications," *Bank of Canada Review* (Spring 1999): 5–19, provide an excellent discussion of the recent behaviour of Canada's monetary aggregates.

Because we cannot be sure which of the monetary aggregates is the true measure of money, it is logical to wonder if their movements closely parallel one another. If they do, then using one monetary aggregate to predict future economic performance and to conduct policy will be the same as using another, and the fact that we are not sure of the appropriate definition of money for a given policy decision is not too costly. However, if the monetary aggregates do not move together, then what one monetary aggregate tells us is happening to the money supply might be quite different from what another monetary aggregate would tell us. The conflicting stories might present a confusing picture that would make it hard for policymakers to decide on the right course of action.

Figure 3-1 plots the growth rates of M2 (gross), M1++ (gross), and M2++ (gross) from 1969 to 2008. The growth rates of these three aggregates do tend to move together. Yet some glaring discrepancies exist in the movements of these aggregates. The average growth rate of money in the 1970s was 14.2% according to M2 (gross), 11.9% according to M1++ (gross), and 15% according to M2++ (gross). The average monetary growth rate in the 1990s was 3.6% according to M2 (gross), 2.7% according to M1++ (gross), and 6.6% according to M2++ (gross). Thus, the different measures of money tell a very different story about the course of monetary policy.

From the data in Figure 3-1, you can see that obtaining a single precise, correct measure of money does seem to matter and that it does make a difference which monetary aggregate policymakers and economists choose as the true measure of money.

Money as a Weighted Aggregate

The measures of the money supply listed in Table 3-1 make black-and-white decisions about whether a given asset is money by including it or excluding it. In addition, these measures are simple-sum indices in which all monetary components are assigned a constant and equal (unitary) weight. This index is M in

$$M = x_1 + x_2 + \ldots + x_n$$

where x_j is one of the n monetary components of the monetary aggregate M. This summation index implies that all monetary components contribute equally to the money total and it views all components as dollar-for-dollar perfect substitutes. Such an index, there is no question, represents an index of the stock of nominal monetary wealth, but cannot, in general, represent a valid structural economic variable for the services of the quantity of money.

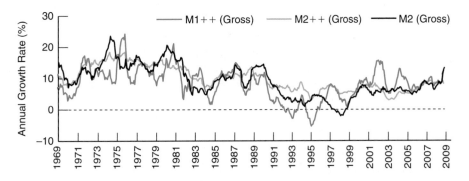

FIGURE 3-1   Growth Rates of M2 (Gross), M1++ (Gross), and M2++ (Gross), 1969–2008

Source: Statistics Canada CANSIM II Series V41552796, V37152, V41552801.

Over the years, there has been a steady stream of attempts at properly weighting monetary components within a simple-sum aggregate. With no theory, however, any weighting scheme is questionable. Recently, attention has been focused on the gains that can be achieved by a rigorous use of microeconomic theory, aggregation theory, and index number theory. This new approach to monetary aggregation led to the construction of *weighted monetary aggregates*.[4] These aggregates represent a viable and theoretically appropriate alternative to the simple-sum aggregates. Moreover, recent research indicates that these new measures of money seem to predict inflation and the business cycle somewhat better than more conventional measures.[5]

HOW RELIABLE ARE THE MONEY DATA?

The difficulties of measuring money arise not only because it is hard to decide what is the best definition of money but also because the Bank of Canada frequently revises earlier estimates of the monetary aggregates by large amounts later on. There are two reasons why the Bank revises its figures. First, because small depository institutions need to report the amounts of their deposits only infrequently, the Bank has to estimate these amounts until these institutions provide the actual figures at some future date. Second, the adjustment of the data for seasonal variation is revised substantially as more data become available. To see why this happens, let's look at an example of the seasonal variation of the money data around Christmastime. The monetary aggregates always rise around Christmas because of increased spending during the holiday season; the rise is greater in some years than in others. This means that the factor that adjusts the data for the seasonal variation due to Christmas must be estimated from several years of data, and the estimates of this seasonal factor become more precise only as more data become available. When the data on the monetary aggregates are revised, the seasonal adjustments often change dramatically from the initial calculation.

The conclusion we can draw is that the initial data on the monetary aggregates reported by the Bank of Canada are not a reliable guide to what is happening to short-run movements in the money supply, such as the one-month growth rates. However, the initial money data are reasonably reliable for longer periods, such as a year. The moral is that **we probably should not pay much attention to short-run movements in the money supply numbers but should be concerned only with longer-run movements.**

---

[4] William Barnett, Douglas Fisher, and Apostolos Serletis, "Consumer Theory and the Demand for Money," *Journal of Economic Literature* 30 (1992): 2086–2119, provide a state-of-the-art survey of this literature. See also William Barnett and Apostolos Serletis, *The Theory of Monetary Aggregation* (Amsterdam: North-Holland, 2000), and Apostolos Serletis, *The Demand for Money: Theoretical and Empirical Approaches,* 2nd edition (Springer, 2007).

[5] See, for example, Apostolos Serletis and Terence E. Molik, "Monetary Aggregates and Monetary Policy." In *Money, Monetary Policy, and Transmission Mechanisms*, Bank of Canada (2000): 103–135.

SUMMARY

1. To economists, the word *money* has a different meaning from income or wealth. Money is anything that is generally accepted as payment for goods or services or in the repayment of debts.

2. Money serves three primary functions: as a medium of exchange, as a unit of account, and as a store of value. Money as a medium of exchange avoids the problem of double coincidence of wants

that arises in a barter economy, lowers transaction costs, and encourages specialization and the division of labour. Money as a unit of account reduces the number of prices needed in the economy, which also reduces transaction costs. Money also functions as a store of value but performs this role poorly if it is rapidly losing value due to inflation.

3. The payments system has evolved over time. Until several hundred years ago, the payments system in all but the most primitive societies was based primarily on precious metals. The introduction of paper currency lowered the cost of transporting money. The next major advance was the introduction of cheques, which lowered transaction costs still further. We are currently moving toward an electronic payments system in which paper is eliminated and all transactions are handled by computers. Despite the potential efficiency of such a system, obstacles are slowing the movement to the chequeless society and the development of new forms of electronic money.

4. The Bank of Canada has defined six different measures of the money supply—M1+, M1++, M2, M2+, M2++, and M3. These measures are not equivalent and do not always move together, so they cannot be used interchangeably by policymakers. Obtaining the precise, correct measure of money does seem to matter and has implications for the conduct of monetary policy.

5. Another problem in the measurement of money is that the data are not always as accurate as we would like. Substantial revisions in the data do occur; they indicate that initially released money data are not a reliable guide to short-run (say, month-to-month) movements in the money supply, although they are more reliable over longer periods of time, such as a year.

KEY TERMS

commodity money, p. 48	liquidity, p. 47	medium of exchange, p. 44
currency, p. 43	M1+, p. 52	monetary aggregates, p. 51
e-cash, p. 49	M1++, p. 52	payments system, p. 47
electronic money (e-money), p. 49	M2, p. 51	smart card, p. 49
fiat money, p. 48	M2+, p. 52	store of value, p. 46
float, p. 50	M2++, p. 52	unit of account, p. 45
hyperinflation, p. 47	M3, p. 51	wealth, p. 44
income, p. 44		

QUESTIONS

You will find the answers to the questions marked with an asterisk in the Textbook Resources section of your MyEconLab.

1. Which of the following three expressions uses the economists' definition of money?
   a. "How much money did you earn last week?"
   b. "When I go to the store, I always make sure that I have enough money."
   c. "The love of money is the root of all evil."

*2. There are three goods produced in an economy by three individuals:

Good	Producer
Apples	Orchard owner
Bananas	Banana grower
Chocolate	Chocolatier

If the orchard owner likes only bananas, the banana grower likes only chocolate, and the chocolatier likes only apples, will any trade among these three persons take place in a barter economy? How will introducing money into the economy benefit these three producers?

3. Why did cavemen not need money?

*4. Why were people in Canada in the nineteenth century sometimes willing to be paid by cheque rather than with gold, even though they knew that there was a possibility that the cheque might bounce?

5. In ancient Greece, why was gold a more likely candidate for use as money than wine was?

*6. Was money a better store of value in Canada in the 1950s than it was in the 1970s? Why or why not? In which period would you have been more willing to hold money?

7. Would you be willing to completely give up your chequebook and use an electronic means of payment for everything exclusively? Why or why not?

8. Rank the following assets from most liquid to least liquid:
   a. Chequing account deposits
   b. Houses
   c. Currency
   d. Washing machines
   e. Savings deposits
   f. Common stock

*9. Why have some economists described money during hyperinflation as a "hot potato" that is quickly passed from one person to another?

10. In Brazil, a country that was undergoing a rapid inflation before 1994, many transactions were conducted in dollars rather than in reals, the domestic currency. Why?

*11. Suppose that a researcher discovers that a measure of the total amount of debt in the Canadian economy over the past 20 years was a better predictor of inflation and the business cycle than M1+, M1++, M2, M2+, M2++, or M3. Does this discovery mean that we should define money as equal to the total amount of debt in the economy?

12. In a weighted monetary aggregate, which of the following assets would probably receive the highest weights? Which would receive the lowest weights?
   a. Currency
   b. Savings account deposits
   c. Foreign currency deposits
   d. Canada Savings Bonds
   e. Houses
   f. Furniture

*13. Why are revisions of monetary aggregates less of a problem for measuring long-run movements of the money supply than they are for measuring short-run movements?

QUANTITATIVE PROBLEMS

1. Look up the M1+, M1++, M2, M2+, M2++, and M3 numbers in the *Bank of Canada Banking and Financial Statistics* for the most recent one-year period. Have their growth rates been similar? What implications do their growth rates have for the conduct of monetary policy?

*2. Which of the Bank of Canada's measures of the monetary aggregates, M1+, M1++, M2, M2+, M2++, or M3, is composed of the most liquid assets? Which is the largest measure?

CANSIM Question

3. Get the monthly data from 1970 to 2009 on the M2 (gross) monetary aggregate (CANSIM series V41552796) from the Textbook Resources area of the MyEconLab.
   a. Calculate the money growth rate over the entire period and present a time series plot of the series (that is, graph the money growth rate series against time).
   b. Calculate the average monetary growth rate and its standard deviation over each of the last four decades.
   c. Which decade had the lowest money growth? The highest?
   d. Which decade had the lowest money growth volatility? The highest?

WEB EXERCISES

1. Go to **www.bankofcanada.ca** and click on "Rates and Statistics" and then "Summary of key monetary policy variables."
   a. What has been the growth rate in M1+, M1++, and M2++ over the last 12 months?
   b. From what you know about the state of the economy, does this seem expansionary or restrictive?

2. Go to **www.bankofcanada.ca** and click on "Monetary Policy." Select one policy on which the Bank of Canada has a written policy. Write a one-paragraph summary of this policy.

Be sure to visit the MyEconLab website at **www.myeconlab.com**. This online homework and tutorial system puts you in control of your own learning with study and practice tools directly correlated to this chapter content.

PART II

Financial Markets

CRISIS AND RESPONSE: CREDIT MARKET TURMOIL AND THE STOCK MARKET CRASH IN OCTOBER 2008

The subprime financial crisis began snowballing in the U.S. as the value of mortgage-backed securities on financial institutions' balance sheets plummeted. A "flight to quality" drove three-month Treasury bill rates down to almost zero, which had last happened during the Great Depression of the 1930s. Credit spreads—an indicator of risk—shot through the roof, with the U.S. Treasury bill to Eurodollar rate (TED) spread going from around 40 basis points (0.40 percentage points) before the subprime crisis started to over 450 basis points in mid-October, the highest value in its history. After earlier sharp declines, the stock market crashed further, with the week beginning on October 6, 2008, showing the worst weekly decline in history.

The subprime crisis in the United States illustrates how volatile financial markets can be. This volatility hit financial consumers directly with difficulty getting loans, falling home values, declining retirement account values, and jobs in jeopardy. How can policy respond to disruptions in financial markets? We begin addressing this question by examining the inner workings of financial markets, particularly interest rate dynamics. Chapter 4 explains what an interest rate is, and the relationship between interest rates, bond prices, and returns. Chapter 5 examines how the overall level of interest rates is determined. In Chapter 6, we extend the analysis of the bond market to explain changes in credit spreads and the relationship of long-term to short-term interest rates. Chapter 7 looks at the role of expectations in the stock market and what drives stock prices.

CHAPTER 4

Understanding Interest Rates

LEARNING OBJECTIVES

After studying this chapter you should be able to

1. detail the present value concept and the meaning of the term *interest rate*
2. discern among the ways of measuring the interest rate: the yield to maturity, the current yield, and the yield on a discount basis
3. illustrate how bond prices and interest rates are negatively related: when interest rates rise, bond prices fall, and vice versa
4. explain the difference between nominal and real interest rates
5. assess the difference between interest rates and rates of return

PREVIEW   Interest rates are among the most closely watched variables in the economy. Their movements are reported almost daily by the news media because they directly affect our everyday lives and have important consequences for the health of the economy. They affect personal decisions such as whether to consume or save, whether to buy a house, and whether to purchase bonds or put funds into a savings account. Interest rates also affect the economic decisions of businesses and households, such as whether to use their funds to invest in new equipment for factories or to save their money in a bank.

Before we can go on with the study of money, banking, and financial markets, we must understand exactly what the phrase *interest rates* means. In this chapter we see that a concept known as the *yield to maturity* is the most accurate measure of interest rates; the yield to maturity is what economists mean when they use the term *interest rate*. We discuss how the yield to maturity is measured. We'll also see that a bond's interest rate does not necessarily indicate how good an investment the bond is because what it earns (its rate of return) does not necessarily equal its interest rate. Finally, we explore the distinction between real interest rates, which are adjusted for inflation, and nominal interest rates, which are not.

Although learning definitions is not always the most exciting of pursuits, it is important to read carefully and understand the concepts presented in this chapter. Not only are they continually used throughout the remainder of this text, but a firm grasp of these terms will give you a clearer understanding of the role that interest rates play in your life as well as in the general economy.

MEASURING INTEREST RATES

Different debt instruments have very different streams of cash payments to the holder (known as **cash flows**) with very different timing. Thus we first need to understand how we can compare the value of one kind of debt instrument with another before we see how interest rates are measured. To do this, we make use of the concept of *present value*.

Present Value

The concept of **present value** (or **present discounted value**) is based on the commonsense notion that a dollar paid to you one year from now is less valuable to you than a dollar paid to you today: this notion is true because you can deposit a dollar in a savings account that earns interest and have more than a dollar in one year. Economists use a more formal definition, as explained in this section.

Let's look at the simplest kind of debt instrument, which we will call a **simple loan**. In this loan, the lender provides the borrower with an amount of funds (called the *principal*) that must be repaid to the lender at the *maturity date*, along with an additional payment for the interest. For example, if you made your friend, Jane, a simple loan of $100 for one year, you would require her to repay the principal of $100 in one year's time along with an additional payment for interest—say, $10. In the case of a simple loan like this one, the interest payment divided by the amount of the loan is a natural and sensible way to measure the interest rate. This measure of the so-called *simple interest rate, i*, is:

$$i = \frac{\$10}{\$100} = 0.10 = 10\%$$

If you made this $100 loan, at the end of the year you would have $110, which can be rewritten as:

$$\$100 \times (1 + 0.10) = \$110$$

If you then lent out the $110, at the end of the second year you would have:

$$\$110 \times (1 + 0.10) = \$121$$

or, equivalently,

$$\$100 \times (1 + 0.10) \times (1 + 0.10) = \$100 \times (1 + 0.10)^2 = \$121$$

Continuing with the loan again, you would have at the end of the third year:

$$\$121 \times (1 + 0.10) = \$100 \times (1 + 0.10)^3 = \$133$$

Generalizing, we can see that at the end of n years, your $100 would turn into:

$$\$100 \times (1 + i)^n$$

The amounts you would have at the end of each year by making the $100 loan today can be seen in the following timeline:

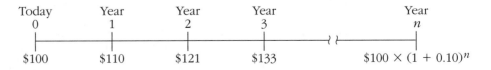

Today 0	Year 1	Year 2	Year 3	Year n
$100	$110	$121	$133	$100 \times (1 + 0.10)^n$

This timeline immediately tells you that you are just as happy having $100 today as having $110 a year from now (of course, as long as you are sure that Jane will pay you back). Or that you are just as happy having $100 today as having $121 two years from now, or $133 three years from now, or $100 × (1 + 0.10)^n n years from now. The timeline tells us that we can also work backward from future amounts to the present: for example, $133 = $100 × (1 + 0.10)^3 three years from now is worth $100 today, so that:

$$\$100 = \frac{\$133}{(1 + 0.10)^3}$$

APPLICATION   How to Use Your Financial Calculator

The same answer can be obtained by using a financial calculator. Assuming that you have the Texas Instruments BA-35 Solar calculator, set it in the "FIN" mode by pressing the "MODE" key until the word "FIN" appears on the screen, and clear it by pushing the "2nd" key and then the "CE/C" key.

1. Enter 133 and push the "FV" key
2. Enter 10 and push the "%i" key
3. Enter 3 and push the "N" key
4. Enter 0 and push the "PMT" key
5. You want to solve for the present value, so push the "CPT" key and then the "PV" key

The answer is 99.9249.

The process of calculating today's value of dollars received in the future, as we have done above, is called *discounting the future.* We can generalize this process by writing today's (present) value of $100 as *PV*, the future cash flow (payment) of $133 as *CF*, and replacing 0.10 (the 10% interest rate) with *i*. This leads to the following formula:

$$PV = \frac{CF}{(1 + i)^n} \tag{1}$$

Intuitively, what Equation 1 tells us is that if you are promised $1 of cash flow for certain ten years from now, this dollar would not be as valuable to you as $1 is today because if you had the $1 today, you could invest it and end up with more than $1 in ten years.

The concept of present value is extremely useful, because it allows us to figure out today's value (price) of a credit market instrument at a given simple interest rate, *i*, by just adding up the individual present values of all the future payments received. This information allows us to compare the value of two instruments with very different timing of their payments.

| APPLICATION | Simple Present Value |

What is the present value of $250 to be paid in two years if the interest rate is 15%?

Solution

The present value would be $189.04. Using Equation 1:

$$PV = \frac{CF}{(1 + i)^n}$$

where

CF = cash flow in two years = $250
i = annual interest rate = 0.15
n = number of years = 2

Thus

$$PV = \frac{\$250}{(1 + 0.15)^2} = \frac{\$250}{1.3225} = \$189.04$$

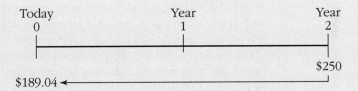

To solve using a financial calculator (such as the Texas Instruments BA-35 Solar calculator):

1. Enter 250 and push the "FV" key
2. Enter 15 and push the "%*i*" key
3. Enter 2 and push the "N" key
4. Enter 0 and push the "PMT" key
5. Push the "CPT" key and then the "PV" key

The answer is 189.0359.

| APPLICATION | How Much Is That Jackpot Worth? |

As an example of how the present value concept can be used, let's assume that you just hit the $20 million jackpot in a lottery, which promises you a payment of $1 million for the next twenty years. You are clearly excited, but have you really won $20 million?

Solution

No, not in the present value sense. In today's dollars, that $20 million is worth a lot less. If we assume an interest rate of 10% as in the earlier examples, the first payment of $1 million is clearly worth $1 million today, but the next payment next year is only worth \$1 million/(1 + 0.10) = \$909,091, a lot less than \$1 million. The following year the payment is worth \$1 million/(1 + 0.10)^2 = \$826,446 in today's dollars, and so on. When you add all these up, they come to \$9.4 million. You are still pretty excited (who wouldn't be?), but because you understand the concept of present value, you recognize that you are the victim of false advertising. You didn't really win \$20 million, but instead won less than half as much.

Four Types of Credit Market Instruments

In terms of the timing of their cash flow payments, there are four basic types of credit market instruments:

1. A simple loan, which we have already discussed, in which the lender provides the borrower with an amount of funds that must be repaid to the lender at the maturity date along with an additional payment for the interest. Many money market instruments are of this type: for example, commercial loans to businesses.

2. A **fixed-payment loan** (which is also called a **fully amortized loan**) in which the lender provides the borrower with an amount of funds, which must be repaid by making the same payment every period (such as a month) consisting of part of the principal and interest for a set number of years. For example, if you borrowed \$1000, a fixed-payment loan might require you to pay \$126 every year for 25 years. Instalment loans (such as auto loans) and mortgages are frequently of the fixed-payment type.

3. A **coupon bond** pays the owner of the bond a fixed interest payment (coupon payment) every year until the maturity date, when a specified final amount (**face value** or **par value**) is repaid. The coupon payment is so named because the bondholder used to obtain payment by clipping a coupon off the bond and sending it to the bond issuer, who then sent the payment to the holder. Nowadays, it is no longer necessary to send in coupons to receive these payments. A coupon bond with \$1000 face value, for example, might pay you a coupon payment of \$100 per year for ten years and at the maturity date repay you the face value amount of \$1000. (The face value of a bond is usually in \$1000 increments.)

   A coupon bond is identified by three pieces of information. First is the corporation or government agency that issues the bond. Second is the maturity date of the bond. Third is the bond's **coupon rate**, the dollar amount of the yearly coupon payment expressed as a percentage of the face value of the bond. In our example, the coupon bond has a yearly coupon payment of \$100 and a face value of \$1000. The coupon rate is then \$100/\$1000 = 0.10, or 10%. Canada bonds and corporate bonds are examples of coupon bonds.

4. A **discount bond** (also called a **zero-coupon bond**) is bought at a price below its face value (at a discount), and the face value is repaid at the maturity date. Unlike a coupon bond, a discount bond does not make any interest payments; it just pays off the face value. For example, a discount bond with a face value of \$1000 might be bought for \$900 and in a year's time the owner would be repaid the face value of \$1000. Canadian government treasury bills and long-term zero-coupon bonds are examples of discount bonds.

These four types of instruments require payments at different times: simple loans and discount bonds make payment only at their maturity dates, whereas fixed-payment loans and coupon bonds have payments periodically until maturity.

How would you decide which of these instruments provides you with more income? They all seem so different because they make payments at different times. To solve this problem, we use the concept of present value to provide us with a procedure for measuring interest rates on these different types of instruments.

Yield to Maturity

Of the several common ways of calculating interest rates, the most important is the **yield to maturity**, the interest rate that equates the present value of cash flow payments received from a debt instrument with its value today.[1] Because the concept behind the calculation of yield to maturity makes good economic sense, economists consider it the most accurate measure of interest rates.

To understand yield to maturity better, we now look at how it is calculated for the four types of credit market instruments. In all these examples, the key to understanding the calculation of the yield to maturity is equating today's value of the debt instrument with the present value of all of its future cash flows.

SIMPLE LOAN   Using the concept of present value, the yield to maturity on a simple loan is easy to calculate. For the one-year loan we discussed, today's value is $100, and the payments in one year's time would be $110 (the repayment of $100 plus the interest payment of $10). We can use this information to solve for the yield to maturity i by recognizing that the present value of the future payments must equal today's value of a loan.

APPLICATION   Yield to Maturity on a Simple Loan

If Pete borrows $100 from his sister and next year she wants $110 back from him, what is the yield to maturity on this loan?

Solution

The yield to maturity on the loan is 10%.

$$PV = \frac{CF}{(1 + i)^n}$$

where

PV = amount borrowed   = $100
CF = cash flow in one year = $110
n = number of years   = 1

Thus

$$\$100 = \frac{\$110}{(1 + i)}$$

$$(1 + i)\,\$100 = \$110$$

$$(1 + i) = \frac{\$110}{\$100}$$

$$i = 1.10 - 1 = 0.10 = 10\%$$

---

[1] In other contexts, it is also called the *internal rate of return.*

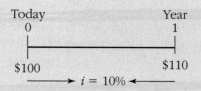

To find the yield to maturity using a financial calculator:

1. Enter 100 and push the "PV" key
2. Enter 110 and push the "FV" key
3. Enter 1 and push the "N" key
4. Enter 0 and push the "PMT" key
5. Push the "CPT" key and then the "%*i*" key

The answer is 10.

This calculation of the yield to maturity should look familiar because it equals the interest payment of $10 divided by the loan amount of $100; that is, it equals the simple interest rate on the loan. An important point to recognize is that *for simple loans, the simple interest rate equals the yield to maturity.* Hence the same term *i* is used to denote both the yield to maturity and the simple interest rate.

FIXED-PAYMENT LOAN   Recall that this type of loan has the same cash flow payment every period throughout the life of the loan. On a fixed-rate mortgage, for example, the borrower makes the same payment to the bank every month until the maturity date, when the loan will be completely paid off. To calculate the yield to maturity for a fixed-payment loan, we follow the same strategy we used for the simple loan—we equate today's value of the loan with its present value. Because the fixed-payment loan involves more than one cash flow payment, the present value of the fixed-payment loan is calculated as the sum of the present values of all payments (using Equation 1).

In the case of our earlier example, the loan is $1000 and the yearly cash flow payment is $126 for the next 25 years. The present value is calculated as follows: at the end of one year there is a $126 payment with a *PV* of $126/(1 + *i*); at the end of two years there is another $126 payment with a *PV* of $126/(1 + *i*)²; and so on until at the end of the twenty-fifth year, the last payment of $126 with a *PV* of $126/(1 + *i*)²⁵ is made. Making today's value of the loan ($1000) equal to the sum of the present values of all the yearly payments gives us

$$\$1000 = \frac{\$126}{1 + i} + \frac{\$126}{(1 + i)^2} + \frac{\$126}{(1 + i)^3} + \cdots + \frac{\$126}{(1 + i)^{25}}$$

More generally, for any fixed-payment loan,

$$LV = \frac{FP}{1 + i} + \frac{FP}{(1 + i)^2} + \frac{FP}{(1 + i)^3} + \cdots + \frac{FP}{(1 + i)^n} \qquad (2)$$

where

$$LV = \text{loan value}$$
$$FP = \text{fixed yearly payment}$$
$$n = \text{number of years until maturity}$$

For a fixed-payment loan amount, the fixed yearly payment and the number of years until maturity are known quantities, and only the yield to maturity is not. So we can solve this equation for the yield to maturity i. Because this calculation is not easy, many pocket calculators have programs that allow you to find i given the loan's numbers for LV, FP, and n. For example, in the case of the 25-year loan with yearly payments of $126, the yield to maturity that solves Equation 2 is 12%. Real estate brokers always have a pocket calculator that can solve such equations so that they can immediately tell the prospective house buyer exactly what the yearly (or monthly) payments will be if the house purchase is financed by taking out a mortgage.

APPLICATION   **Yield to Maturity on a Fixed-Payment Loan**

You decide to purchase a new home and need a $100 000 mortgage. You take out a loan from the bank that has an interest rate of 7%. What is the yearly payment to the bank to pay off the loan in 20 years?

Solution   The yearly payment to the bank is $9439.29.

$$LV = \frac{FP}{1+i} + \frac{FP}{(1+i)^2} + \frac{FP}{(1+i)^3} + \cdots + \frac{FP}{(1+i)^n}$$

where

$LV = \text{loan value amount} = \$100\ 000$
$i\ = \text{annual interest rate} = 0.07$
$n\ = \text{number of years} = 20$

Thus

$$\$100\ 000 = \frac{FP}{1+0.07} + \frac{FP}{(1+0.07)^2} + \frac{FP}{(1+0.07)^3} + \cdots + \frac{FP}{(1+0.07)^{20}}$$

To find the yearly payment for the loan using a financial calculator:

1. Enter $-100\ 000$ and push the "PV" key
2. Enter 0 and push the "FV" key
3. Enter 20 and push the "N" key
4. Enter 7 and push the "%i" key
5. Push the "CPT" and "PMT" keys

The answer is 9439.29.

COUPON BOND   To calculate the yield to maturity for a coupon bond, follow the same strategy used for the fixed-payment loan: equate today's value of the bond with its present value. Because coupon bonds also have more than one cash flow payment, the present value of the bond is calculated as the sum of the present values of all the coupon payments plus the present value of the final payment of the face value of the bond.

The present value of a $1000-face-value bond with ten years to maturity and yearly coupon payments of $100 (a 10% coupon rate) can be calculated as follows: at the end of one year, there is a $100 coupon payment with a *PV* of $100/(1 + *i*); at the end of the second year, there is another $100 coupon payment with a *PV* of $100/(1 + *i*)^2; and so on until, at maturity, there is a $100 coupon payment with a *PV* of $100/(1 + *i*)^{10} plus the repayment of the $1000 face value with a *PV* of $1000/(1 + *i*)^{10}. Setting today's value of the bond (its current price, denoted by *P*) equal to the sum of the present values of all the cash flow payments for this bond gives

$$P = \frac{\$100}{1+i} + \frac{\$100}{(1+i)^2} + \frac{\$100}{(1+i)^3} + \cdots + \frac{\$100}{(1+i)^{10}} + \frac{\$1000}{(1+i)^{10}}$$

More generally, for any coupon bond,[2]

$$P = \frac{C}{1+i} + \frac{C}{(1+i)^2} + \frac{C}{(1+i)^3} + \cdots + \frac{C}{(1+i)^n} + \frac{F}{(1+i)^n} \qquad (3)$$

where

P = price of coupon bond
C = yearly coupon payment
F = face value of the bond
n = years to maturity date

In Equation 3, the coupon payment, the face value, the years to maturity, and the price of the bond are known quantities, and only the yield to maturity is not. Hence we can solve this equation for the yield to maturity *i*. Just as in the case of the fixed-payment loan, this calculation is not easy, so business-oriented pocket calculators have built-in programs that solve this equation for you.

APPLICATION   Yield to Maturity on a Coupon Bond

Find the price of a 10% coupon bond with a face value of $1000, a 12.25% yield to maturity, and eight years to maturity.

Solution

To solve using the Texas Instruments BA-35 Solar calculator:

1. Enter 1000 and push the "FV" key
2. Enter 8 and push the "N" key
3. Enter 12.25 and push the "%*i*" key
4. Enter 100 and push the "PMT" key
5. Push the "CPT" and "PV" keys

The answer is 889.1977.

---

[2] Most coupon bonds actually make coupon payments on a semi-annual basis rather than once a year as assumed here. The effect on the calculations is only very slight and will be ignored here.

Table 4-1 shows the yields to maturity calculated for several bond prices. Three interesting facts emerge:

1. When the coupon bond is priced at its face value, the yield to maturity equals the coupon rate.

2. The price of a coupon bond and the yield to maturity are negatively related; that is, as the yield to maturity rises, the price of the bond falls. As the yield to maturity falls, the price of the bond rises.

3. The yield to maturity is greater than the coupon rate when the bond price is below its face value.

These three facts are true for any coupon bond and are really not surprising if you think about the reasoning behind the calculation of the yield to maturity. When you put $1000 in a bank account with an interest rate of 10%, you can take out $100 every year and you will be left with the $1000 at the end of ten years. This is similar to buying the $1000 bond with a 10% coupon rate analyzed in Table 4-1, which pays a $100 coupon payment every year and then repays $1000 at the end of ten years. If the bond is purchased at the par value of $1000, its yield to maturity must equal 10%, which is also equal to the coupon rate of 10%. The same reasoning applied to any coupon bond demonstrates that if the coupon bond is purchased at its par value, the yield to maturity and the coupon rate must be equal.

It is straightforward to show that the bond price and the yield to maturity are negatively related. As *i,* the yield to maturity, rises, all denominators in the bond price formula must necessarily rise. Hence a rise in the interest rate as measured by the yield to maturity means that the price of the bond must fall. Another way to explain why the bond price falls when the interest rate rises is that a higher interest rate implies that the future coupon payments and final payment are worth less when discounted back to the present; hence the price of the bond must be lower.

The third fact, that the yield to maturity is greater than the coupon rate when the bond price is below its par value, follows directly from facts 1 and 2. When the yield to maturity equals the coupon rate, then the bond price is at the face value, and when the yield to maturity rises above the coupon rate, the bond price necessarily falls and so must be below the face value of the bond.

There is one special case of a coupon bond that is worth discussing because its yield to maturity is particularly easy to calculate. This bond is called a **consol** or a **perpetuity**; it is a perpetual bond with no maturity date and no repayment of principal that makes fixed coupon payments of $*C* forever. Consols were first sold by the British Treasury during the Napoleonic Wars and are still traded today;

TABLE 4-1   Yields to Maturity on a 10% Coupon-Rate Bond Maturing in Ten Years (Face Value = $1000)

Price of Bond ($)	Yield to Maturity (%)
1200	7.13
1100	8.48
1000	10.00
900	11.75
800	13.81

they are quite rare, however, in Canadian capital markets. The formula in Equation 3 for the price of the consol P simplifies to the following:[3]

$$P_c = \frac{C}{i_c} \tag{4}$$

where
P_c = price of the perpetuity (consol)
C = yearly payment
i_c = yield to maturity of the perpetuity (consol)

One nice feature of perpetuities is that you can immediately see that as i_c goes up, the price of the bond falls. For example, if a perpetuity pays $100 per year forever and the interest rate is 10%, its price will be $1000 = $100/0.10. If the interest rate rises to 20%, its price will fall to $500 = $100/0.20. We can also rewrite this formula as

$$i_c = \frac{C}{P_c} \tag{5}$$

The formula in Equation 5, which describes the calculation of the yield to maturity for a perpetuity, also provides a useful approximation for the yield to maturity on coupon bonds. When a coupon bond has a long term to maturity (say, 20 years or more), it is very much like a perpetuity, which pays coupon payments forever. This is because the cash flows more than 20 years in the future have such small present discounted values that the value of a long-term coupon bond is very close to the value of a perpetuity with the same coupon rate. Thus i_c in Equation 5 will be very close to the yield to maturity for any long-term bond. For this reason, i_c, the yearly coupon payment divided by the price of the security, has been given the name **current yield** and is frequently used as an approximation to describe interest rates on long-term bonds.

DISCOUNT BOND   The yield-to-maturity calculation for a discount bond is similar to that for the simple loan. Let us consider a discount bond such as a one-year Canadian treasury bill, which pays off a face value of $1000 in one year's time. If the current purchase price of this bill is $900, then equating this price to the pre-

---

[3] The bond price formula for a consol is

$$P = \frac{C}{1 + i} + \frac{C}{(1 + i)^2} + \frac{C}{(1 + i)^3} + \cdots$$

which can be written as

$$P = C(x + x^2 + x^3 + \cdots)$$

in which $x = 1/(1 + i)$. The formula for an infinite sum is:

$$1 + x + x^2 + x^3 + \cdots = \frac{1}{1 - x} \quad \text{for } x < 1$$

and so

$$P = C\left(\frac{1}{1 - x} - 1\right) = C\left(\frac{1}{1 - 1/(1 + i)} - 1\right)$$

which by suitable algebraic manipulation becomes

$$P = C\left(\frac{1 + i}{i} - \frac{i}{i}\right) = \frac{C}{i}$$

APPLICATION   Yield to Maturity on a Perpetuity

What is the yield to maturity on a bond that has a price of $2000 and pays $100 annually forever?

Solution   The yield to maturity would be 5%.

$$i_c = \frac{C}{P_c}$$

where

C = yearly payment = $100
P_c = price of perpetuity (consol) = $2000

Thus

$$i_c = \frac{\$100}{\$2000}$$

$$i_c = 0.05 = 5\%$$

To solve using the Texas Instruments BA-35 Solar calculator:

1. Enter 2000 and push the "PV" key
2. Enter 0 and push the "FV" key
3. Enter 999 (to approximate an infinite number of payments) and push the "N" key
4. Enter 100 and push the "PMT" key
5. Push the "CPT" and "%i" keys

The answer is 5.

sent value of the $1000 received in one year, using Equation 1 (page 60), gives

$$\$900 = \frac{\$1000}{1 + i}$$

and solving for i,

$$(1 + i) \times \$900 = \$1000$$

$$\$900 + \$900i = \$1000$$

$$\$900i = \$1000 - \$900$$

$$i = \frac{\$1000 - \$900}{\$900} = 0.111 = 11.1\%$$

More generally, for any one-year discount bond, the yield to maturity can be written as

$$i = \frac{F - P}{P} \tag{6}$$

where F = face value of the discount bond
         P = current price of the discount bond

In other words, the yield to maturity equals the increase in price over the year, $F - P$, divided by the initial price P. In normal circumstances, investors earn positive returns from holding these securities and so they sell at a discount, meaning that the current price of the bond is below the face value. Therefore, $F - P$ should be positive, and the yield to maturity should be positive as well. However, this is not always the case, as recent extraordinary events in Japan indicate (see the Global box, Negative T-Bill Rates? Japan Shows the Way).

An important feature of this equation is that it indicates that for a discount bond, the yield to maturity is negatively related to the current bond price. This is the same conclusion that we reached for a coupon bond. For example, Equation 6 shows that a rise in the bond price from \$900 to \$950 means that the bond will have a smaller increase in its price at maturity, and the yield to maturity falls from 11.1% to 5.3%. Similarly, a fall in the yield to maturity means that the price of the discount bond has risen.

SUMMARY   The concept of present value tells you that a dollar in the future is not as valuable to you as a dollar today because you can earn interest on this dollar. Specifically, a dollar received n years from now is worth only $\$1/(1 + i)^n$

GLOBAL   Negative T-Bill Rates? Japan Shows the Way

We normally assume that interest rates must always be positive. Negative interest rates would imply that you are willing to pay more for a bond today than you will receive for it in the future (as our formula for yield to maturity on a discount bond demonstrates). Negative interest rates therefore seem like an impossibility because you would do better by holding cash that has the same value in the future as it does today.

The Japanese have demonstrated that this reasoning is not quite correct. In November 1998, interest rates on Japanese six-month treasury bills became negative, yielding an interest rate of −0.004%, with investors paying more for the bills than their face value. This is an extremely unusual event because no other country in the world has seen negative interest rates during the last fifty years. How could this happen?

As we will see in Chapter 5, the weakness of the Japanese economy and a negative inflation rate drove Japanese interest rates to low levels, but these two factors can't explain the negative rates. The answer is that large investors found it more convenient to hold these six-month bills as a store of value rather than holding cash because the bills are denominated in larger amounts and can be stored electronically. For that reason, some investors were willing to hold them, despite their negative rates, even though in monetary terms the investors would be better off holding cash. Clearly, the convenience of T-bills only goes so far, and thus their interest rates can go only a little bit below zero.

today. The present value of a set of future cash flow payments on a debt instrument equals the sum of the present values of each of the future payments. The yield to maturity for an instrument is the interest rate that equates the present value of the future payments on that instrument to its value today. Because the procedure for calculating yield to maturity is based on sound economic principles, this is the measure that economists think most accurately describes the interest rate.

Our calculations of the yield to maturity for a variety of bonds reveal the important fact that ***current bond prices and interest rates are negatively related: when the interest rate rises, the price of the bond falls, and vice versa.***

THE DISTINCTION BETWEEN INTEREST RATES AND RETURNS

Many people think that the interest rate on a bond tells them all they need to know about how well off they are as a result of owning it. If Irving the Investor thinks he is better off when he owns a long-term bond yielding a 10% interest rate and the interest rate rises to 20%, he will have a rude awakening: as we will see shortly, if he has to sell the bond, Irving has lost his shirt! How well a person does by holding a bond or any other security over a particular time period is accurately measured by the **return** or, in more precise terminology, the **rate of return**. The concept of *return* discussed here is extremely important because it is used continually throughout this book and understanding it will make the material presented later in the book easier to follow. For any security, the rate of return is defined as the payments to the owner plus the change in its value, expressed as a fraction of its purchase price. To make this definition clearer, let us see what the return would look like for a $1000-face-value coupon bond with a coupon rate of 10% that is bought for $1000, held for one year, and then sold for $1200. The payments to the owner are the yearly coupon payments of $100, and the change in its value is $1200 − $1000 = $200. Adding these together and expressing them as a fraction of the purchase price of $1000 gives us the one-year holding-period return for this bond:

$$\frac{\$100 + \$200}{\$1000} = \frac{\$300}{\$1000} = 0.30 = 30\%$$

You may have noticed something quite surprising about the return that we have just calculated: it equals 30%, yet as Table 4-1 (page 67) indicates, initially the yield to maturity was only 10%. This demonstrates that ***the return on a bond will not necessarily equal the yield to maturity on that bond.*** We now see that the distinction between interest rate and return can be important, although for many securities the two may be closely related.

More generally, the return on a bond held from time t to time $t + 1$ can be written as

$$RET = \frac{C + P_{t+1} - P_t}{P_t} \tag{8}$$

where

RET = return from holding the bond from time t to time $t + 1$

P_t = price of the bond at time t

P_{t+1} = price of the bond at time $t + 1$

C = coupon payment

APPLICATION   **Calculating the Rate of Return**

What would the rate of return be on a bond bought for $1000 and sold one year later for $800? The bond has a face value of $1000 and a coupon rate of 8%.

Solution

The rate of return on the bond for holding it one year is −12%.

$$RET = \frac{C + P_{t+1} - P_t}{P_t}$$

where

$$
\begin{aligned}
C &= \text{coupon payment} = \$1000 \times 0.08 = \$80 \\
P_{t+1} &= \text{price of the bond one year later} = \$800 \\
P_t &= \text{price of the bond today} = \$1000
\end{aligned}
$$

Thus

$$RET = \frac{\$80 + (\$800 - \$1000)}{\$1000} = \frac{-\$120}{\$1000} = -0.12 = -12\%$$

A convenient way to rewrite the return formula in Equation 8 is to recognize that it can be split into two separate terms:

$$RET = \frac{C}{P_t} + \frac{P_{t+1} - P_t}{P_t}$$

The first term is the current yield i_c (the coupon payment over the purchase price):

$$\frac{C}{P_t} = i_c$$

The second term is the **rate of capital gain**, or the change in the bond's price relative to the initial purchase price:

$$\frac{P_{t+1} - P_t}{P_t} = g$$

where g = rate of capital gain. Equation 8 can then be rewritten as

$$RET = i_c + g \tag{9}$$

which shows that the return on a bond is the current yield i_c plus the rate of capital gain g. This rewritten formula illustrates the point we just discovered. Even for a bond for which the current yield i_c is an accurate measure of the yield to maturity, the return can differ substantially from the interest rate. Returns will differ from the interest rate especially if there are sizable fluctuations in the price of the bond that produce substantial capital gains or losses.

APPLICATION | **Calculating the Rate of Capital Gain**

Calculate the rate of capital gain or loss on a ten-year zero-coupon bond for which the interest rate has increased from 10% to 20%. The bond has a face value of $1000.

Solution

The rate of capital gain or loss is -49.7%.

$$g = \frac{P_{t+1} - P_t}{P_t}$$

where

P_{t+1} = price of the bond one year from now $= \dfrac{\$1000}{(1 + 0.20)^9} = \$193.81$

P_t = price of the bond today $= \dfrac{\$1000}{(1 + 0.10)^{10}} = \$385.54$

Thus

$$g = \frac{\$193.81 - \$385.54}{\$385.54}$$

$$g = -0.497 = -49.7\%$$

To explore this point even further, let's look at what happens to the returns on bonds of different maturities when interest rates rise. Table 4-2 calculates the one-year return using Equation 9 on several 10%-coupon-rate bonds all purchased at par when interest rates on all these bonds rise from 10% to 20%. Several key findings in this table are generally true of all bonds:

- The only bond whose return equals the initial yield to maturity is one whose time to maturity is the same as the holding period (see the last bond in Table 4-2).
- A rise in interest rates is associated with a fall in bond prices, resulting in capital losses on bonds whose terms to maturity are longer than the holding period.
- The more distant a bond's maturity, the greater the size of the percentage price change associated with an interest-rate change.
- The more distant a bond's maturity, the lower the rate of return that occurs as a result of the increase in the interest rate.
- Even though a bond has a substantial initial interest rate, its return can turn out to be negative if interest rates rise.

At first it frequently puzzles students (as it puzzles poor Irving the Investor) that a rise in interest rates can mean that a bond has been a poor investment. The trick to understanding this is to recognize that a rise in the interest rate means that the price of a bond has fallen. A rise in interest rates therefore means that a capital loss has occurred, and if this loss is large enough, the bond can be a poor

TABLE 4-2   One-Year Returns on Different-Maturity 10%-Coupon-Rate Bonds
When Interest Rates Rise from 10% to 20%

(1) Years to Maturity When Bond Is Purchased	(2) Initial Current Yield (%)	(3) Initial Price ($)	(4) Price Next Year* ($)	(5) Rate of Capital Gain (%)	(6) Rate of Return (2 + 5) (%)
30	10	1000	503	−49.7	−39.7
20	10	1000	516	−48.4	−38.4
10	10	1000	597	−40.3	−30.3
5	10	1000	741	−25.9	−15.9
2	10	1000	917	−8.3	+1.7
1	10	1000	1000	0.0	+10.0

*Calculated with a financial calculator using Equation 3.

investment indeed. For example, we see in Table 4-2 that the bond that has 30 years to maturity when purchased has a capital loss of 49.7% when the interest rate rises from 10% to 20%. This loss is so large that it exceeds the current yield of 10%, resulting in a negative return (loss) of −39.7%. If Irving does not sell the bond, his capital loss is often referred to as a "paper loss." This is a loss nonetheless because if he had not bought this bond and had instead put his money in the bank, he would now be able to buy more bonds at their lower price than he presently owns.

Maturity and the Volatility of Bond Returns: Interest-Rate Risk

The finding that the prices of longer-maturity bonds respond more dramatically to changes in interest rates helps explain an important fact about the behaviour of bond markets: ***prices and returns for long-term bonds are more volatile than those for shorter-term bonds.*** Price changes of +20% and −20% within a year, with corresponding variations in returns, are common for bonds more than 20 years away from maturity.

We now see that changes in interest rates make investments in long-term bonds quite risky. Indeed, the riskiness of an asset's return that results from interest-rate changes is so important that it has been given a special name, **interest-rate risk**.[4] Dealing with interest-rate risk is a major concern of managers of financial institutions and investors, as we will see in later chapters (see also the FYI box Helping Investors to Select Desired Interest-Rate Risk).

Although long-term debt instruments have substantial interest-rate risk, short-term debt instruments do not. Indeed, bonds with a maturity that is as short as the

---

[4] Interest-rate risk can be quantitatively measured using the concept of duration. This concept and how it is calculated are discussed in an appendix to this chapter, which can be found on this book's MyEconLab **www.pearsoned.ca/myeconlab.**

FYI	Helping Investors to Select Desired Interest-Rate Risk

Because many investors want to know how much interest-rate risk they are exposed to, some mutual fund companies try to educate investors about the perils of interest-rate risk, as well as to offer investment alternatives that match their investors' preferences.

For example, one U.S. company, Vanguard Group, offers eight separate high-grade bond mutual funds. In its prospectus, Vanguard separates the funds by the average maturity of the bonds they hold and demonstrates the effect of interest-rate changes by computing the percentage change in bond value resulting from a 1% increase and decrease in interest rates.

Three of the bond funds invest in bonds with average maturities of one to three years, which Vanguard rates as having the lowest interest-rate risk. Three other funds hold bonds with average maturities of five to ten years, which Vanguard rates as having medium interest-rate risk. Two funds hold long-term bonds with maturities of 15 to 30 years, which Vanguard rates as having high interest-rate risk.

By providing this information, Vanguard hopes to increase its market share in the sale of bond funds. Not surprisingly, Vanguard is one of the most successful mutual fund companies in the business.

---

holding period have no interest-rate risk.[5] We see this for the coupon bond at the bottom of Table 4-2, which has no uncertainty about the rate of return because it equals the yield to maturity, which is known at the time the bond is purchased. The key to understanding why there is no interest-rate risk for any bond whose time to maturity matches the holding period is to recognize that (in this case) the price at the end of the holding period is already fixed at the face value. The change in interest rates can then have no effect on the price at the end of the holding period for these bonds, and the return will therefore be equal to the yield to maturity known at the time the bond is purchased.[6]

---

[5] The statement that there is no interest-rate risk for any bond whose time to maturity matches the holding period is literally true only for discount bonds and zero-coupon bonds that make no intermediate cash payments before the holding period is over. A coupon bond that makes an intermediate cash payment before the holding period is over requires that this payment be reinvested. Because the interest rate at which this payment can be reinvested is uncertain, there is some uncertainty about the return on this coupon bond even when the time to maturity equals the holding period. However, the riskiness of the return on a coupon bond from reinvesting the coupon payments is typically quite small, and so the basic point that a coupon bond with a time to maturity equalling the holding period has very little risk still holds true.

[6] In the text, we are assuming that all holding periods are short and equal to the maturity on short-term bonds and are thus not subject to interest-rate risk. However, if an investor's holding period is longer than the term to maturity of the bond, the investor is exposed to a type of interest-rate risk called *reinvestment risk*. Reinvestment risk occurs because the proceeds from the short-term bond need to be reinvested at a future interest rate that is uncertain.

To understand reinvestment risk, suppose that Irving the Investor has a holding period of two years and decides to purchase a $1000 one-year bond at face value and will then purchase another one at the end of the first year. If the initial interest rate is 10%, Irving will have $1100 at the end of the year. If the interest rate rises to 20%, as in Table 4-2, Irving will find that buying $1100 worth of another one-year bond will leave him at the end of the second year with $1100 × (1 + 0.20) = $1320. Thus Irving's two-year return will be ($1320 − $1000)/$1000 = 0.32 = 32%, which equals 14.9% at an annual rate. In this case, Irving has earned more by buying the one-year bonds than if he had initially purchased the two-year bond with an interest rate of 10%. Thus when Irving has a holding period that is longer than the

(Continued on next page)

Summary

The return on a bond, which tells you how good an investment it has been over the holding period, is equal to the yield to maturity in only one special case: when the holding period and the maturity of the bond are identical. Bonds whose term to maturity is longer than the holding period are subject to interest-rate risk: changes in interest rates lead to capital gains and losses that produce substantial differences between the return and the yield to maturity known at the time the bond is purchased. Interest-rate risk is especially important for long-term bonds, where the capital gains and losses can be substantial. This is why long-term bonds are not considered to be safe assets with a sure return over short holding periods.

THE DISTINCTION BETWEEN REAL AND NOMINAL INTEREST RATES

So far in our discussion of interest rates, we have ignored the effects of inflation on the cost of borrowing. What we have up to now been calling the interest rate makes no allowance for inflation, and it is more precisely referred to as the **nominal interest rate**. We distinguish it from the **real interest rate**, the interest rate that is adjusted by subtracting expected changes in the price level (inflation) so that it more accurately reflects the true cost of borrowing. This interest rate is more precisely referred to as the *ex ante real interest rate* because it is adjusted for *expected* changes in the price level. The *ex ante* real interest rate is most important to economic decisions, and typically it is what economists mean when they make reference to the "real" interest rate. The interest rate that is adjusted for *actual* changes in the price level is called the *ex post real interest rate*. It describes how well a lender has done in real terms after the fact.

The real interest rate is more accurately defined by the *Fisher equation*, named for Irving Fisher, one of the great monetary economists of the twentieth century. The Fisher equation states that the nominal interest rate i equals the real interest rate i_r plus the expected rate of inflation π^e.[7]

$$i = i_r + \pi^e \tag{10}$$

---

[6] *(continued)* term to maturity of the bonds he purchases, he benefits from a rise in interest rates. Conversely, if interest rates fall to 5%, Irving will have only $1155 at the end of two years: $1100 × (1 + 0.05). Thus his two-year return will be ($1155 − $1000)/$1000 = 0.155 = 15.5%, which is 7.5% at an annual rate. With a holding period greater than the term to maturity of the bond, Irving now loses from a fall in interest rates.

We have thus seen that when the holding period is longer than the term to maturity of a bond, the return is uncertain because the future interest rate when reinvestment occurs is also uncertain—in short, there is reinvestment risk. We also see that if the holding period is longer than the term to maturity of the bond, the investor benefits from a rise in interest rates and is hurt by a fall in interest rates.

[7] A more precise formulation of the Fisher equation is

$$i = i_r + \pi^e + (i_r \times \pi^e)$$

because

$$1 + i = (1 + i_r)(1 + \pi^e) = 1 + i_r + \pi^e + (i_r \times \pi^e)$$

and subtracting 1 from both sides gives us the first equation. For small values of i_r and π^e, the term $i_r \times \pi^e$ is so small that we ignore it, as in the text.

Rearranging terms, we find that the real interest rate equals the nominal interest rate minus the expected inflation rate:

$$i_r = i - \pi^e \qquad (11)$$

To see why this definition makes sense, let us first consider a situation in which you have made a one-year simple loan with a 5% interest rate ($i = 5\%$) and you expect the price level to rise by 3% over the course of the year ($\pi^e = 3\%$). As a result of making the loan, at the end of the year you expect to have 2% more in **real terms**, that is, in terms of real goods and services you can buy. In this case, the interest rate you expect to earn in terms of real goods and services is 2%; that is,

$$i_r = 5\% - 3\% = 2\%$$

as indicated by the Fisher definition.

A similar distinction can be made between nominal returns and real returns. Nominal returns, which do not allow for inflation, are what we have been referring to as simply "returns." When inflation is subtracted from a nominal return, we have the real return, which indicates the amount of extra goods and services that can be purchased as a result of holding the security.

The distinction between real and nominal interest rates is important because the real interest rate, which reflects the real cost of borrowing, is likely to be a better indicator of the incentives to borrow and lend. It appears to be a better guide to how people will be affected by what is happening in credit markets. Figure 4-1,

APPLICATION   Calculating Real Interest Rates

Solution

What is the real interest rate if the nominal interest rate is 8% and the expected inflation rate is 10% over the course of a year?

The real interest rate is −2%. Although you will be receiving 8% more dollars at the end of the year, you will be paying 10% more for goods. The result is that you will be able to buy 2% fewer goods at the end of the year, and you will be 2% worse off in real terms.

$$i_r = i - \pi^e$$

where

$$i = \text{nominal interest rate} = 0.08$$
$$\pi^e = \text{expected inflation rate} = 0.10$$

Thus

$$i_r = 0.08 - 0.10 = -0.02 = -2\%$$

As a lender, you are clearly less eager to make a loan in this case because in terms of real goods and services you have actually earned a negative interest rate of 2%. By contrast, as the borrower, you fare quite well because at the end of the year, the amounts you will have to pay back will be worth 2% less in terms of goods and services—you as the borrower will be ahead by 2% in real terms. ***When the real interest rate is low, there are greater incentives to borrow and fewer incentives to lend.***

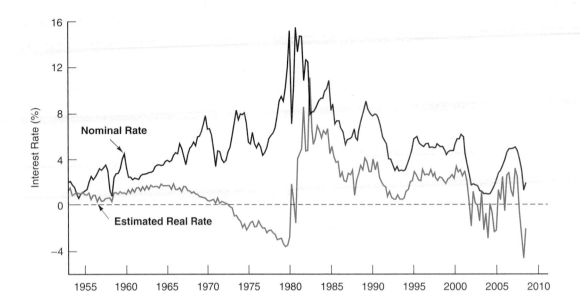

FIGURE 4-1   Real and Nominal Interest Rates (Three-Month Treasury Bill), 1953–2008

Sources: Nominal rates from www.federalreserve.gov/releases/H15. The real rate is constructed using the procedure outlined in Frederic S. Mishkin, "The Real Interest Rate: An Empirical Investigation," *Carnegie-Rochester Conference Series on Public Policy* 15 (1981): 151–200. These procedures involve estimating expected inflation as a function of past interest rates, inflation, and time trends and then subtracting the expected inflation measure from the nominal interest rate.

which presents estimates from 1953 to 2008 of the real and nominal interest rates on three-month U.S. Treasury bills, shows us that nominal and real rates often do not move together. (This is also true for nominal and real interest rates in Canada and the rest of the world.) By the standard of nominal interest rates, you would have thought that credit market conditions were tight in this period because it was expensive to borrow. However, the estimates of the real rates indicate that you would have been mistaken. In real terms, the cost of borrowing was actually quite low.[8]

---

[8] Because most interest income in Canada is subject to income taxes, the true earnings in real terms from holding a debt instrument are not reflected by the real interest rate defined by the Fisher equation but rather by the *after-tax real interest rate*, which equals the nominal interest rate *after income tax payments have been subtracted*, minus the expected inflation rate. For a person facing a 30% tax rate, the after-tax interest rate earned on a bond yielding 10% is only 7% because 30% of the interest income must be paid to the CRA. Thus the after-tax real interest rate on this bond when expected inflation is 5% equals 2% (= 7% − 5%). More generally, the after-tax real interest rate can be expressed as

$$i(1 - \tau) - \pi^e$$

where τ = the income tax rate.

This formula for the after-tax real interest rate also provides a better measure of the effective cost of borrowing for many corporations in Canada because in calculating income taxes, they can deduct interest payments on loans from their income. Thus if you face a 30% tax rate and take out a business loan with a 10% interest rate, you are able to deduct the 10% interest payment and thus lower your business taxes by 30% of this amount. Your after-tax nominal cost of borrowing is then 7% (10% minus 30% of the 10% interest payment), and when the expected inflation rate is 5%, the effective cost of borrowing in real terms is again 2% (= 7% − 5%).

As the example (and the formula) indicates, after-tax real interest rates are always below the real interest rate defined by the Fisher equation. For a further discussion of measures of after-tax real interest rates, see Frederic S. Mishkin, "The Real Interest Rate: An Empirical Investigation," *Carnegie-Rochester Conference Series on Public Policy* 15 (1981): 151–200.

Formerly, real interest rates in Canada were not observable; only nominal rates were reported. This all changed on December 10, 1991, when the government of Canada began to issue **indexed bonds**, whose interest and principal payments are adjusted for changes in the price level (see the FYI box With Real Return Bonds, Real Interest Rates Have Become Observable in Canada).

FYI — With Real Return Bonds, Real Interest Rates Have Become Observable in Canada

On December 10, 1991, the Canadian government issued coupon bonds whose coupon payment and face value are indexed to the Consumer Price Index (CPI). These securities are known as *Real Return Bonds* and are designed to provide investors with a known real return if held to maturity. Other countries such as the United Kingdom, Australia, and Sweden also issue similar indexed securities, and the U.S. Treasury joined the group (in September 1998) by issuing TIPS (Treasury Inflation Protection Securities).

These indexed securities have successfully acquired a niche in the bond market, enabling governments to raise more funds. In addition, because their interest and principal payments are adjusted for changes in the price level, the interest rate on these bonds provides a direct measure of a real interest rate. These indexed bonds are very useful to policymakers, especially monetary policymakers, because by subtracting their interest rate from a nominal interest rate on a nonindexed bond, they generate more insight into expected inflation, a valuable piece of information.

For example, on January 28, 2009, the interest rate on long-term Canada bonds was 3.72%, while that on the long-term Real Return Bond was 2.26%. Thus, the implied expected inflation rate, derived from the difference between these two rates, was 1.46%. The private sector finds the information provided by Real Return Bonds very useful: Many financial institutions routinely publish the expected Canadian inflation rate derived from these bonds.

APPLICATION — Calculating the Principal and Coupon Payment of Real Return Bonds

Consider a real return bond with a face value of $1000 and a coupon yield of 2%. Calculate the principal and coupon payment after one year if the inflation rate is 3%.

Solution

After a year, to account for inflation, the principal will be increased by 3%, from $1000 to $1030. The coupon yield is still 2%, but applies to the new principal of $1030, instead of $1000. Hence, the coupon payment will be 0.02 × $1030 = $20.60.

SUMMARY

1. The yield to maturity, which is the measure that most accurately reflects the interest rate, is the interest rate that equates the present value of future payments of a debt instrument with its value today. Application of this principle reveals that bond prices and interest rates are negatively related: when the interest rate rises, the price of the bond must fall, and vice versa.

2. The return on a security, which tells you how well you have done by holding this security over a stated period of time, can differ substantially from the interest rate as measured by the yield to maturity. Long-term bond prices have substantial fluctuations when interest rates change and thus bear interest-rate risk. The resulting capital gains and losses can be large, which is why long-term bonds are not considered to be safe assets with a sure return.

3. The real interest rate is defined as the nominal interest rate minus the expected rate of inflation. It is a better measure of the incentives to borrow and lend than the nominal interest rate, and it is a more accurate indicator of the tightness of credit market conditions than the nominal interest rate.

KEY TERMS

cash flows,   p. 59

consol (perpetuity),   p. 67

coupon bond,   p. 62

coupon rate,   p. 62

current yield,   p. 68

discount bond
   (zero-coupon bond),   p. 62

face value (par value),   p. 62

fixed-payment loan
   (fully amortized loan),   p. 62

indexed bond,   p. 79

interest-rate risk,   p. 74

nominal interest rate,   p. 76

present discounted value,   p. 59

present value,   p. 59

rate of capital gain,   p. 72

real interest rate,   p. 76

real terms,   p. 77

return (rate of return),   p. 71

simple loan,   p. 59

yield to maturity,   p. 63

QUESTIONS

You will find the answers to the questions marked with an asterisk in the Textbook Resources section of your MyEconLab.

*1. Write down the formula that is used to calculate the yield to maturity on a 20-year 10% coupon bond with $1000 face value that sells for $2000.

2. If there is a decline in interest rates, which would you rather be holding, long-term bonds or short-term bonds? Why? Which type of bond has the greater interest-rate risk?

*3. Francine the Financial Adviser has just given you the following advice: "Long-term bonds are a great investment because their interest rate is over 20%." Is Francine necessarily right?

QUANTITATIVE PROBLEMS

*1. Would a dollar tomorrow be worth more to you today when the interest rate is 20% or when it is 10%?

2. You have just won $20 million in a provincial lottery, which promises to pay you $1 million (tax-free) every year for the next 20 years. Have you really won $20 million?

*3. If the interest rate is 10%, what is the present value of a security that pays you $1100 next year, $1210 the year after, and $1331 the year after that?

4. If the security in Problem 3 sold for $4000, is the yield to maturity greater or less than 10%? Why?

5. What is the yield to maturity on a $1000 face-value discount bond maturing in one year that sells for $800?

*6. What is the yield to maturity on a simple loan for $1 million that requires a repayment of $2 million in five years' time?

7. To pay for university, you have just taken out a $1000 government loan that makes you pay $126 per year for 25 years. However, you don't have to start making these payments until you graduate from university two years from now. Why is the yield to maturity necessarily less than 12%, the yield to maturity on a normal $1000 fixed-payment loan in which you pay $126 per year for 25 years?

*8. Which $1000 bond has the higher yield to maturity, a 20-year bond selling for $800 with a current yield of 15% or a one-year bond selling for $800 with a current yield of 5%?

9. Pick five Canada bonds from the bond page of the newspaper, and calculate the current yield. Note when the current yield is a good approximation of the yield to maturity.

*10. You are offered two bonds, a one-year Canada bond with a yield to maturity of 9% and a one-year treasury bill with a yield on a discount basis of 8.9%. Which would you rather own?

11. If mortgage rates rise from 5% to 10% but the expected rate of increase in housing prices rises from 2% to 9%, are people more or less likely to buy houses?

*12. Interest rates were lower in the mid-1980s than they were in the late 1970s, yet many economists have commented that real interest rates were actually much higher in the mid-1980s than in the late 1970s. Does this make sense? Do you think that these economists are right?

13. You borrowed $1000 on January 1 and must repay a total amount of $1060 exactly a year later.
    a. What is the interest paid?
    b. What is the interest rate?

*14. Consider a perpetuity that has a coupon of $100 per year.
    a. What is the price of the perpetuity if the yield to maturity is 5%?
    b. If the yield to maturity doubles, what will happen to the price?

*15. Suppose that the interest rate is 5%. Which of the following statements are true and which are false?
    a. $57 today is equivalent to $61 one year from now.
    b. $5000 today is equivalent to $5250 one year from now.
    c. $37.80 one year from now is equivalent to $36 today.

CANSIM Questions

16. Get the quarterly data from 1953 to 2009 on the three-month T-bill rate (CANSIM series V122541) and the total consumer price index (series V41690973) from the Textbook Resources area of the MyEconLab.
    a. Calculate the (actual) annual inflation rate, using the formula
    $$\pi_t = 4 \times 100 \times (P_{t+1} - P_t)/P_t$$
    b. Plot the nominal interest rate, i, and the inflation rate, π_t.
    c. Assume that the expected inflation rate is the same as the actual inflation rate (a restrictive assumption!) and calculate the real interest rate, i_r.
    d. Plot the nominal and real interest rates on a graph.
    e. What is the relationship between the nominal interest rate, i, and the real interest rate, i_r, over this period?

17. Get the monthly data from 1991 to 2009 for the interest rate on long-term Canada Real Return Bonds (CANSIM series V122553) from the Textbook Resources area of the MyEconLab.
    a. Plot this real interest rate, i_r.
    b. Has the real interest rate been rising or falling over the sample period?
    c. What is the mean real interest rate over the sample period? What is its standard deviation (the standard deviation is the square root of the variance)?

WEB EXERCISES

1. Investigate the data on interest rates available from the Bank of Canada at **www.bankofcanada.ca**. Answer the following questions.
    a. What is the difference in the interest rates on 10-year and 2-year bonds?
    b. What is the difference in the interest rate on long-term government of Canada bonds and Real Return Bonds?
    c. What is the difference in the interest rate on long-term Government of Canada bonds and corporate bonds?

2. Figure 4-1 (page 78) shows the estimated real and nominal rates for three-month U.S. treasury bills. Go to **www.martincapital.com/main/charts.html** and click on the relevant link under "Charts of Interest Rates and Yields."
    a. Compare the three-month real rate to the long-term real rate. Which is greater?
    b. Compare the short-term nominal rate to the long-term nominal rate. Which appears most volatile?

 Be sure to visit the MyEconLab website at **www.myeconlab.com**. This online homework and tutorial system puts you in control of your own learning with study and practice tools directly correlated to this chapter content.

On the MyEconLab website you will find the following appendix and mini-case for this chapter:
Appendix 4.1: Measuring Interest Rate Risk: Duration
Mini-Case 4.1: Interest Rates, Bond Yields, and Duration

CHAPTER 5

The Behaviour of Interest Rates

LEARNING OBJECTIVES

After studying this chapter you should be able to

1. describe how the demand and supply analysis for bonds provides one theory of how nominal interest rates are determined
2. explain how the demand and supply analysis for money, known as the liquidity preference framework, provides an alternative theory of interest-rate determination
3. outline the factors that cause interest rates to change
4. characterize the effects of monetary policy on interest rates: the liquidity effect, the income effect, the price-level effect, and the expected-inflation effect

PREVIEW

In the early 1950s, nominal interest rates on three-month treasury bills were about 1% at an annual rate; by 1981, they had reached over 20%; in the early 2000s and in 2008 they fell below 2%. What explains these substantial fluctuations in interest rates? One reason why we study money, banking, and financial markets is to provide some answers to this question.

In this chapter we examine how the overall level of *nominal* interest rates (which we refer to as simply "interest rates") is determined and what factors influence their behaviour. We learned in Chapter 4 that interest rates are negatively related to the price of bonds, so if we can explain why bond prices change, we can also explain why interest rates fluctuate. We make use of supply and demand analysis for markets for bonds and money to examine how interest rates change.

In order to derive a demand curve for assets like money or bonds, the first step in our analysis, we must first understand what determines the demand for these assets. We do this by developing an economic theory known as the *theory of asset demand,* which outlines criteria that are important when deciding how much of an asset to buy. Armed with this theory, we can then go on to derive the demand curve for bonds or money. After deriving supply curves for these assets, we develop the concept of market equilibrium, the point at which the quantity supplied equals the quantity demanded. Then we use this model to explain changes in equilibrium interest rates.

Because interest rates on different securities tend to move together, in this chapter we will act as if there is only one type of security and one interest rate in the entire economy. In the following chapter, we expand our analysis to look at why interest rates on different types of securities differ.

DETERMINANTS OF ASSET DEMAND

Before going on to our supply and demand analysis of the bond market and the market for money, we must first understand what determines the quantity demanded of an asset. Recall that an asset is a piece of property that is a store of value. Items such as money, bonds, stocks, art, land, houses, farm equipment, and manufacturing machinery are all assets. Facing the question of whether to buy and hold an asset or whether to buy one asset rather than another, an individual must consider the following factors:

1. **Wealth**, the total resources owned by the individual, including all assets
2. **Expected return** (the return expected over the next period) on one asset relative to alternative assets
3. **Risk** (the degree of uncertainty associated with the return) on one asset relative to alternative assets
4. **Liquidity** (the ease and speed with which an asset can be turned into cash) relative to alternative assets.

Wealth

When we find that our wealth has increased, we have more resources available with which to purchase assets, and so, not surprisingly, the quantity of assets we demand increases. Therefore, the effect of changes in wealth on the quantity demanded of an asset can be summarized as follows: ***holding everything else constant, an increase in wealth raises the quantity demanded of an asset.***

Expected Return

In Chapter 4 we saw that the return on an asset (such as a bond) measures how much we gain from holding that asset. When we make a decision to buy an asset, we are influenced by what we expect the return on that asset to be. If a Bell Canada bond, for example, has a return of 15% half the time and 5% the other half of the time, its expected return (which you can think of as the average return) is 10% ($= 0.5 \times 15\% + 0.5 \times 5\%$).[1] If the expected return on the Bell bond rises relative to expected returns on alternative assets, holding everything else constant, then it becomes more desirable to purchase it, and the quantity demanded increases. This can occur in either of two ways: (1) when the expected return on the Bell bond rises while the return on an alternative asset—say, stock in TD Canada Trust—remains unchanged or (2) when the return on the alternative asset, the TD Canada Trust stock, falls while the return on the Bell bond remains unchanged. To summarize, ***an increase in an asset's expected return relative to that of an alternative asset, holding everything else unchanged, raises the quantity demanded of the asset.***

Risk

The degree of risk or uncertainty of an asset's returns also affects the demand for the asset. Consider two assets, stock in Fly-by-Night Airlines and stock in Feet-on-the-Ground Bus Company. Suppose that Fly-by-Night stock has a return of 15% half the time and 5% the other half of the time, making its expected return

---

[1] If you are interested in finding out more information on how to calculate expected returns, as well as standard deviations of returns that measure risk, you can look at an appendix to this chapter that describes models of asset pricing on this book's MyEconLab at **www.pearsoned.ca/myeconlab.** This appendix also describes how diversification lowers the overall risk of a portfolio and has a discussion of systematic risk and basic asset pricing models such as the capital asset pricing model and arbitrage pricing theory.

10%, while stock in Feet-on-the-Ground has a fixed return of 10%. Fly-by-Night stock has uncertainty associated with its returns and so has greater risk than stock in Feet-on-the-Ground, whose return is a sure thing.

A *risk-averse* person prefers stock in Feet-on-the-Ground (the sure thing) to Fly-by-Night stock (the riskier asset), even though the stocks have the same expected return, 10%. By contrast, a person who prefers risk is a *risk preferrer* or *risk lover*. Most people are risk-averse, especially in their financial decisions: everything else being equal, they prefer to hold the less-risky asset. Hence, **holding everything else constant, if an asset's risk rises relative to that of alternative assets, its quantity demanded will fall.**

Liquidity

Another factor that affects the demand for an asset is how quickly it can be converted into cash at low cost—its liquidity. An asset is liquid if the market in which it is traded has depth and breadth, that is, if the market has many buyers and sellers. A house is not a very liquid asset because it may be hard to find a buyer quickly; if a house must be sold to pay off bills, it might have to be sold for a much lower price. And the transaction costs in selling a house (broker's commissions, lawyer's fees, and so on) are substantial. A Canadian government treasury bill, by contrast, is a highly liquid asset. It can be sold in a well-organized market where there are many buyers, so it can be sold quickly at low cost. **The more liquid an asset is relative to alternative assets, holding everything else unchanged, the more desirable it is, and the greater will be the quantity demanded.**

Theory of Asset Demand

All the determining factors we have just discussed can be assembled into the **theory of asset demand**, which states that, holding all of the other factors constant:

1. The quantity demanded of an asset is positively related to wealth.
2. The quantity demanded of an asset is positively related to its expected return relative to alternative assets.
3. The quantity demanded of an asset is negatively related to the risk of its returns relative to alternative assets.
4. The quantity demanded of an asset is positively related to its liquidity relative to alternative assets.

These results are summarized in Table 5-1.

TABLE 5-1   Response of the Quantity of an Asset Demanded to Changes in Income or Wealth, Expected Returns, Risk, and Liquidity

Variable	Change in Variable	Change in Quantity Demanded
Wealth	↑	↑
Expected return relative to other assets	↑	↑
Risk relative to other assets	↑	↓
Liquidity relative to other assets	↑	↑

Note: Only increases (↑) in the variables are shown. The effect of decreases in the variables on the change in demand would be the opposite of those indicated in the rightmost column.

SUPPLY AND DEMAND IN THE BOND MARKET

Our first approach to the analysis of interest-rate determination looks at supply and demand in the bond market to see how the price of bonds is determined. With our understanding of how interest rates are measured from the previous chapter, we then recognize that each bond price is associated with a particular level of interest rates. Specifically, the negative relationship between bond prices and interest rates means that when we see that the bond price rises, the interest rate falls (or vice versa).

The first step in the analysis is to obtain a bond **demand curve**, which shows the relationship between the quantity demanded and the price when all other economic variables are held constant (that is, values of other variables are taken as given). You may recall from previous economics courses that the assumption that all other economic variables are held constant is called *ceteris paribus*, which means "other things being equal" in Latin.

Demand Curve

To clarify our analysis, let us consider the demand for one-year discount bonds, which make no coupon payments but pay the owner the $1000 face value in a year. If the holding period is one year, then, as we saw in Chapter 4, the return on the bonds is known absolutely and is equal to the interest rate as measured by the yield to maturity. This means that the expected return on this bond is equal to the interest rate i, which, using Equation 6 from Chapter 4 (page 70), is

$$i = RET^e = \frac{F - P}{P}$$

where
$$i = \text{interest rate} = \text{yield to maturity}$$
$$RET^e = \text{expected return}$$
$$F = \text{face value of the discount bond}$$
$$P = \text{initial purchase price of the discount bond}$$

This formula shows that a particular value of the interest rate corresponds to each bond price. If the bond sells for $950, the interest rate and expected return is

$$\frac{\$1000 - \$950}{\$950} = 0.053 = 5.3\%$$

At this 5.3% interest rate and expected return corresponding to a bond price of $950, let us assume that the quantity of bonds demanded is $100 billion, which is plotted as point A in Figure 5-1.

At a price of $900, the interest rate and expected return are

$$\frac{\$1000 - \$900}{\$900} = 0.111 = 11.1\%$$

Because the expected return on these bonds is higher, with all other economic variables (such as income, expected returns on other assets, risk, and liquidity) held constant, the quantity demanded of bonds will be higher as predicted by the theory of asset demand. Point B in Figure 5-1 shows that the quantity of bonds demanded at the price of $900 has risen to $200 billion. Continuing with this reasoning, if the bond price is $850 (interest rate and expected return = 17.6%), the quantity of bonds demanded (point C) will be greater than at point B. Similarly, at

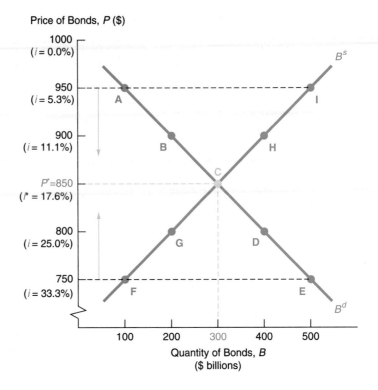

Price of Bonds, P ($)

FIGURE 5-1   Supply and Demand for Bonds

Equilibrium in the bond market occurs at point C, the intersection of the demand curve B^d and the bond supply curve B^s. The equilibrium price is $P^* = \$850$, and the equilibrium interest rate is $i^* = 17.6\%$. (*Note:* P and i increase in opposite directions.)

the lower prices of $800 (interest rate = 25%) and $750 (interest rate = 33.3%), the quantity of bonds demanded will be even higher (points D and E). The curve B^d, which connects these points, is the demand curve for bonds. It has the usual downward slope, indicating that at lower prices of the bond (everything else being equal), the quantity demanded is higher.[2]

Supply Curve

An important assumption behind the demand curve for bonds in Figure 5-1 is that all other economic variables besides the bond's price and interest rate are held constant. We use the same assumption in deriving a **supply curve**, which shows the relationship between the quantity supplied and the price when all other economic variables are held constant.

When the price of the bonds is $750 (interest rate = 33.3%), point F shows that the quantity of bonds supplied is $100 billion for the example we are considering. If the price is $800, the interest rate is the lower rate of 25%. Because at this interest rate it is now less costly to borrow by issuing bonds, firms will be willing to borrow more through bond issues, and the quantity of bonds supplied is at the higher level of $200 billion (point G). An even higher price of $850, corresponding to a lower interest rate of 17.6%, results in a larger quantity of bonds supplied

---

[2] Note that although our analysis indicates that the demand curve is downward-sloping, it does not imply that the curve is a straight line. For ease of exposition, however, we will draw demand curves and supply curves as straight lines.

of $300 billion (point C). Higher prices of $900 and $950 result in even greater quantities of bonds supplied (points H and I). The B^s curve, which connects these points, is the supply curve for bonds. It has the usual upward slope found in supply curves, indicating that as the price increases (everything else being equal), the quantity supplied increases.

Market Equilibrium

In economics, **market equilibrium** occurs when the amount that people are willing to buy (*demand*) equals the amount that people are willing to sell (*supply*) at a given price. In the bond market, this is achieved when the quantity of bonds demanded equals the quantity of bonds supplied:

$$B^d = B^s \qquad (1)$$

In Figure 5-1, equilibrium occurs at point C, where the demand and supply curves intersect at a bond price of $850 (interest rate of 17.6%) and a quantity of bonds of $300 billion. The price of $P^* = \$850$, where the quantity demanded equals the quantity supplied, is called the *equilibrium* or *market-clearing* price. Similarly, the interest rate of $i^* = 17.6\%$ that corresponds to this price is called the equilibrium or market-clearing interest rate.

The concepts of market equilibrium and equilibrium price or interest rate are useful because there is a tendency for the market to head toward them. We can see that it does in Figure 5-1 by first looking at what happens when we have a bond price that is above the equilibrium price. When the price of bonds is set too high, at, say, $950, the quantity of bonds supplied at point I is greater than the quantity of bonds demanded at point A. A situation like this, in which the quantity of bonds supplied exceeds the quantity of bonds demanded, is called a condition of **excess supply**. Because people want to sell more bonds than others want to buy, the price of the bonds will fall, and this is why the downward arrow is drawn in the figure at the bond price of $950. As long as the bond price remains above the equilibrium price, there will continue to be an excess supply of bonds, and the price will continue to fall. This will stop only when the price has reached the equilibrium price of $850, where the excess supply of bonds will be eliminated.

Now let's look at what happens when the price of bonds is below the equilibrium price. If the price of the bonds is set too low, say at $750, the quantity demanded at point E is greater than the quantity supplied at point F. This is called a condition of **excess demand**. People now want to buy more bonds than others are willing to sell, and so the price of bonds will be driven up. This is illustrated by the upward arrow drawn in the figure at the bond price of $750. Only when the excess demand for bonds is eliminated by the price rising to the equilibrium level of $850 is there no further tendency for the price to rise.

We can see that the concept of equilibrium price is a useful one because it indicates where the market will settle. Because each price on the vertical axis of Figure 5-1 shows a corresponding interest rate value, the same diagram also shows that the interest rate will head toward the equilibrium interest rate of 17.6%. When the interest rate is below the equilibrium interest rate, as it is when it is at 5.3%, the price of the bond is above the equilibrium price, and there will be an excess supply of bonds. The price of the bond then falls, leading to a rise in the interest rate toward the equilibrium level. Similarly, when the interest rate is above the equilibrium level, as it is when it is at 33.3%, there is excess demand for bonds, and the bond price will rise, driving the interest rate back down to the equilibrium level of 17.6%.

Supply and Demand Analysis

Our Figure 5-1 is a conventional supply and demand diagram with price on the left vertical axis and quantity on the horizontal axis. Because the interest rate that corresponds to each bond price is also marked on the vertical axis, this diagram allows us to read the equilibrium interest rate, giving us a model that describes the determination of interest rates. It is important to recognize that a supply and demand diagram like Figure 5-1 can be drawn for *any* type of bond because the interest rate and price of a bond are *always* negatively related for any type of bond, whether a discount bond or a coupon bond.

An important feature of the analysis here is that supply and demand are always in terms of *stocks* (amounts at a given point in time) of assets, not in terms of *flows*. The **asset market approach** for understanding behaviour in financial markets—which emphasizes stocks of assets rather than flows in determining asset prices—is now the dominant methodology used by economists because correctly conducting analyses in terms of flows is very tricky, especially when we encounter inflation.[3]

CHANGES IN EQUILIBRIUM INTEREST RATES

We will now use the supply and demand framework for bonds to analyze why interest rates change. To avoid confusion, it is important to make the distinction between *movements along* a demand (or supply) curve and *shifts in* a demand (or supply) curve. When quantity demanded (or supplied) changes as a result of a change in the price of the bond (or, equivalently, a change in the interest rate), we have a *movement along* the demand (or supply) curve. The change in the quantity demanded when we move from point A to B to C in Figure 5-1, for example, is a movement along a demand curve. A *shift in* the demand (or supply) curve, by contrast, occurs when the quantity demanded (or supplied) changes *at each given price (or interest rate)* of the bond in response to a change in some other factor besides the bond's price or interest rate. When one of these factors changes, causing a shift in the demand or supply curve, there will be a new equilibrium value for the interest rate.

In the following pages we will look at how the supply and demand curves shift in response to changes in variables, such as expected inflation and wealth, and what effects these changes have on the equilibrium value of interest rates.

Shifts in the Demand for Bonds

The theory of asset demand developed at the beginning of the chapter provides a framework for deciding what factors cause the demand curve for bonds to shift. These factors include changes in four parameters:

1. Wealth

2. Expected returns on bonds relative to alternative assets

3. Risk of bonds relative to alternative assets

4. Liquidity of bonds relative to alternative assets

---

[3] The asset market approach developed in the text is useful in understanding not only how interest rates behave but also how any asset price is determined. A second appendix to this chapter, which is on this book's MyEconLab at **www.pearsoned.ca/myeconlab**, shows how the asset market approach can be applied to understanding the behaviour of commodity markets, in particular, the gold market. The analysis of the bond market that we have developed here has another interpretation using a different terminology and framework involving the supply and demand for loanable funds. This loanable funds framework is discussed in a third appendix to this chapter, which is also on MyEconLab.

To see how a change in each of these factors (holding all other factors constant) can shift the demand curve, let us look at some examples. (As a study aid, Table 5-2 summarizes the effects of changes in these factors on the bond demand curve.)

TABLE 5-2	Factors That Shift the Demand Curve for Bonds		
Variable	Change in Variable	Change in Quantity Demanded at Each Bond Price	Shift in Demand Curve
Wealth	↑	↑	P → B_1^d B_2^d B
Expected interest rate	↑	↓	P ← B_2^d B_1^d B
Expected inflation	↑	↓	P ← B_2^d B_1^d B
Riskiness of bonds relative to other assets	↑	↓	P ← B_2^d B_1^d B
Liquidity of bonds relative to other assets	↑	↑	P → B_1^d B_2^d B

Note: Only increases (↑) in the variables are shown. The effect of decreases in the variables on the change in demand would be the opposite of those indicated in the remaining columns.

WEALTH   When the economy is growing rapidly in a business cycle expansion and wealth is increasing, the quantity of bonds demanded at each bond price (or interest rate) increases, as shown in Figure 5-2. To see how this works, consider point B on the initial demand curve for bonds B_1^d. With higher wealth, the quantity of bonds demanded at the same price must rise, to point B'. Similarly, the higher wealth causes the quantity demanded at the same bond price to rise to point D'. Continuing with this reasoning for every point on the initial demand curve B_1^d, we can see that the demand curve shifts to the right from B_1^d to B_2^d as is indicated by the arrows.

The conclusion we have reached is that *in a business cycle expansion with growing wealth, the demand for bonds rises and the demand curve for bonds shifts to the right.* Using the same reasoning, *in a recession, when income and wealth are falling, the demand for bonds falls, and the demand curve shifts to the left.*

Another factor that affects wealth is the public's propensity to save. If households save more, wealth increases and, as we have seen, the demand for bonds rises and the demand curve for bonds shifts to the right. Conversely, if people save less, wealth and the demand for bonds will fall and the demand curve shifts to the left.

EXPECTED RETURNS   For a one-year discount bond and a one-year holding period, the expected return and the interest rate are identical, so nothing besides today's interest rate affects the expected return.

For bonds with maturities of greater than one year, the expected return may differ from the interest rate. For example, we saw in Chapter 4, Table 4-2 (page 74), that a rise in the interest rate on a long-term bond from 10 to 20% would lead to a sharp decline in price and a very negative return. Hence, if people begin to think that interest rates will be higher next year than they had originally anticipated, the

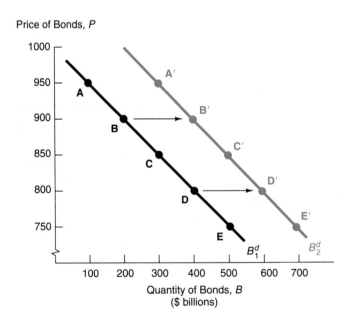

FIGURE 5-2   Shift in the Demand Curve for Bonds

When the demand for bonds increases, the demand curve shifts to the right as shown.

expected return today on long-term bonds will fall, and the quantity demanded will fall at each interest rate. ***Higher expected interest rates in the future lower the expected return for long-term bonds, decrease the demand, and shift the demand curve to the left.***

By contrast, a revision downward of expectations of future interest rates would mean that long-term bond prices would be expected to rise more than originally anticipated, and the resulting higher expected return today would raise the quantity demanded at each bond price and interest rate. ***Lower expected interest rates in the future increase the demand for long-term bonds and shift the demand curve to the right*** (as in Figure 5-2).

Changes in expected returns on other assets can also shift the demand curve for bonds. If people suddenly became more optimistic about the stock market and began to expect higher stock prices in the future, both expected capital gains and expected returns on stocks would rise. With the expected return on bonds held constant, the expected return on bonds today relative to stocks would fall, lowering the demand for bonds and shifting the demand curve to the left.

A change in expected inflation is likely to alter expected returns on physical assets (also called *real assets*) such as automobiles and houses, which affects the demand for bonds. An increase in expected inflation, say, from 5% to 10%, will lead to higher prices on cars and houses in the future and hence higher nominal capital gains. The resulting rise in the expected returns today on these real assets will lead to a fall in the expected return on bonds relative to the expected return on real assets today and thus cause the demand for bonds to fall. Alternatively, we can think of the rise in expected inflation as lowering the real interest rate on bonds, and the resulting decline in the relative expected return on bonds causes the demand for bonds to fall. ***An increase in the expected rate of inflation lowers the expected return for bonds, causing their demand to decline and the demand curve to shift to the left.***

RISK If prices in the bond market become more volatile, the risk associated with bonds increases, and bonds become a less attractive asset. ***An increase in the riskiness of bonds causes the demand for bonds to fall and the demand curve to shift to the left.***

Conversely, an increase in the volatility of prices in another asset market, such as the stock market, would make bonds more attractive. ***An increase in the riskiness of alternative assets causes the demand for bonds to rise and the demand curve to shift to the right*** (as in Figure 5-2).

LIQUIDITY If more people started trading in the bond market and as a result it became easier to sell bonds quickly, the increase in their liquidity would cause the quantity of bonds demanded at each interest rate to rise. ***Increased liquidity of bonds results in an increased demand for bonds, and the demand curve shifts to the right*** (see Figure 5-2). ***Similarly, increased liquidity of alternative assets lowers the demand for bonds and shifts the demand curve to the left.*** The reduction of brokerage commissions for trading common stocks that occurred when the fixed-rate commission structure was abolished in 1975, for example, increased the liquidity of stocks relative to bonds, and the resulting lower demand for bonds shifted the demand curve to the left.

Shifts in the Supply of Bonds

Certain factors can cause the supply curve for bonds to shift, among them:

1. Expected profitability of investment opportunities
2. Expected inflation
3. Government activities

We will look at how the supply curve shifts when each of these factors changes (all others remaining constant). (As a study aid, Table 5-3 summarizes the effects of changes in these factors on the bond supply curve.)

EXPECTED PROFITABILITY OF INVESTMENT OPPORTUNITIES   The more profitable plant and equipment investments that a firm expects it can make, the more willing it will be to borrow in order to finance these investments. When the economy is growing rapidly, as in a business cycle expansion, investment opportunities that are expected to be profitable abound, and the quantity of bonds supplied at any given bond price will increase (see Figure 5-3). *Therefore, in a business cycle expansion, the supply of bonds increases, and the supply curve shifts to the right. Likewise, in a recession, when there are far fewer expected profitable invest-*

TABLE 5-3   Factors That Shift the Supply Curve of Bonds

Variable	Change in Variable	Change in Quantity Supplied at Each Bond Price	Shift in Supply Curve
Profitability of investments	↑	↑	
Expected inflation	↑	↑	
Government deficit	↑	↑	

Note: Only increases (↑) in the variables are shown. The effect of decreases in the variables on the change in supply would be the opposite of those indicated in the remaining columns.

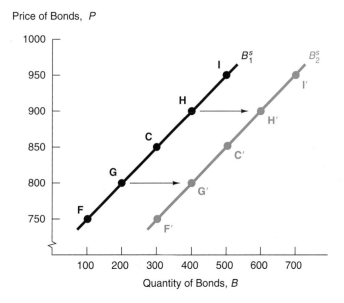

FIGURE 5-3 Shift in the Supply Curve for Bonds

When the supply of bonds increases, the supply curve shifts to the right.

ment opportunities, the supply of bonds falls and the supply curve shifts to the left.

EXPECTED INFLATION As we saw in Chapter 4, the real cost of borrowing is more accurately measured by the real interest rate, which equals the (nominal) interest rate minus the expected inflation rate. For a given interest rate (and bond price), when expected inflation increases, the real cost of borrowing falls; hence the quantity of bonds supplied increases at any given bond price. *An increase in expected inflation causes the supply of bonds to increase and the supply curve to shift to the right* (see Figure 5-3).

GOVERNMENT BUDGET The activities of the government can influence the supply of bonds in several ways. The Canadian government issues bonds to finance government deficits, the gap between the government's expenditures and its revenues. When these deficits are large, the government sells more bonds, and the quantity of bonds supplied at each bond price increases. *Higher government deficits increase the supply of bonds and shift the supply curve to the right* (see Figure 5-3). *On the other hand, government surpluses, as have occurred in recent years, decrease the supply of bonds and shift the supply curve to the left.*

Provincial and municipal governments and other government agencies also issue bonds to finance their expenditures, and this can also affect the supply of bonds. We will see in later chapters that the conduct of monetary policy involves the purchase and sale of bonds, which in turn influences the supply of bonds.

We now can use our knowledge of how supply and demand curves shift to analyze how the equilibrium interest rate can change. The best way to do this is to pursue several applications that are particularly relevant to our understanding of how monetary policy affects interest rates. In going through these applications, keep two things in mind:

1. When you examine the effect of a variable change, remember that we are assuming that all other variables are unchanged; that is, we are making use of the *ceteris paribus* assumption.

2. Remember that the interest rate is negatively related to the bond price, so when the equilibrium bond price rises, the equilibrium interest rate falls. Conversely, if the equilibrium bond price moves downward, the equilibrium interest rate rises.

APPLICATION   **Changes in the Interest Rate Due to Expected Inflation: The Fisher Effect**

We have already done most of the work to evaluate how a change in expected inflation affects the nominal interest rate in that we have already analyzed how a change in expected inflation shifts the supply and demand curves. Figure 5-4 shows the effect on the equilibrium interest rate of an increase in expected inflation.

Suppose that expected inflation is initially 5% and the initial supply and demand curves B_1^s and B_1^d intersect at point 1, where the equilibrium bond price is P_1. If expected inflation rises to 10%, the expected return on bonds relative to real assets falls for any given bond price and interest rate. As a result, the demand for bonds falls, and the demand curve shifts to the left from B_1^d to B_2^d. The rise in expected inflation also shifts the supply curve. At any given bond price and interest rate, the real cost of borrowing has declined, causing the quantity of bonds supplied to increase, and the supply curve shifts to the right, from B_1^s to B_2^s.

When the demand and supply curves shift in response to the change in expected inflation, the equilibrium moves from point 1 to point 2, the intersection of B_2^d and B_2^s. The equilibrium bond price has fallen from P_1 to P_2, and because the bond price is negatively related to the interest rate, this means that the interest rate has risen. Note that Figure 5-4 has been drawn so that the equilibrium

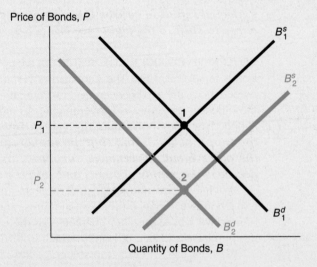

Price of Bonds, *P*

Quantity of Bonds, *B*

FIGURE 5-4   Response to a Change in Expected Inflation

When expected inflation rises, the supply curve shifts from B_1^s to B_2^s, and the demand curve shifts from B_1^d to B_2^d. The equilibrium moves from point 1 to point 2, with the result that the equilibrium bond price falls from P_1 to P_2 and the equilibrium interest rate rises.

quantity of bonds remains the same for both point 1 and point 2. However, depending on the size of the shifts in the supply and demand curves, the equilibrium quantity of bonds could either rise or fall when expected inflation rises.

Our supply and demand analysis has led us to an important observation: ***when expected inflation rises, interest rates will rise.*** This result has been named the **Fisher effect**, after Irving Fisher, the economist who first pointed out the relationship of expected inflation to interest rates. The accuracy of this prediction is shown in Figure 5-5 for the United States; a similar figure exists for Canada. The interest rate on three-month U.S. Treasury bills has usually moved along with the expected inflation rate. Consequently, it is understandable that many economists recommend that inflation must be kept low if we want to keep interest rates low.

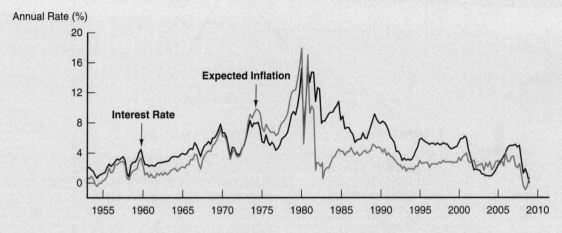

FIGURE 5-5   Expected Inflation and Interest Rates (Three-Month Treasury Bills), 1953–2008

Source: Expected inflation calculated using procedures outlined in Frederic S. Mishkin, "The Real Interest Rate: An Empirical Investigation," *Carnegie-Rochester Conference Series on Public Policy 15* (1981): 151–200. These procedures involve estimating expected inflation as a function of past interest rates, inflation, and time trends.

APPLICATION

Changes in the Interest Rate Due to a Business Cycle Expansion

Figure 5-6 analyzes the effects of a business cycle expansion on interest rates. In a business cycle expansion, the amount of goods and services being produced in the economy rises, so national income increases. When this occurs, businesses will be more willing to borrow because they are likely to have many profitable investment opportunities for which they need financing. Hence at a given bond price, the quantity of bonds that firms want to sell (that is, the supply of bonds) will increase. This means that in a business cycle expansion, the supply curve for bonds shifts to the right (see Figure 5-6) from B_1^s to B_2^s.

Expansion in the economy will also affect the demand for bonds. As the business cycle expands, wealth is likely to increase, and the theory of asset demand tells

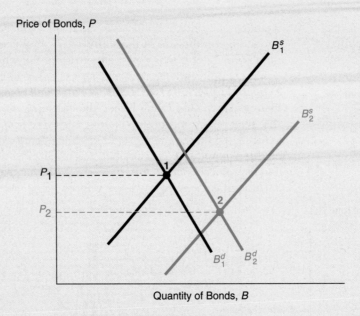

Price of Bonds, P

Quantity of Bonds, B

FIGURE 5-6 Response to a Business Cycle Expansion

In a business cycle expansion, when income and wealth are rising, the demand curve shifts rightward from B_1^d to B_2^d, and the supply curve shifts rightward from B_1^s to B_2^s. If the supply curve shifts to the right more than the demand curve, as in this figure, the equilibrium bond price moves down from P_1 to P_2, and the equilibrium interest rate rises.

us that the demand for bonds will rise as well. We see this in Figure 5-6, where the demand curve has shifted to the right, from B_1^d to B_2^d.

Given that both the supply and demand curves have shifted to the right, we know that the new equilibrium reached at the intersection of B_2^d and B_2^s must also move to the right. However, depending on whether the supply curve shifts more than the demand curve or vice versa, the new equilibrium interest rate can either rise or fall.

The supply and demand analysis used here gives us an ambiguous answer to the question of what will happen to interest rates in a business cycle expansion. The figure has been drawn so that the shift in the supply curve is greater than the shift in the demand curve, causing the equilibrium bond price to fall to P_2, leading to a rise in the equilibrium interest rate. The reason the figure has been drawn so that a business cycle expansion and a rise in income lead to a higher interest rate is that this is the outcome we actually see in the data. Figure 5-7 plots the movement of the interest rate on three-month treasury bills from 1962 to 2008 and indicates when the business cycle is undergoing recessions (shaded areas). As you can see, the interest rate tends to rise during business cycle expansions and fall during recessions, which is what the supply and demand diagram indicates.

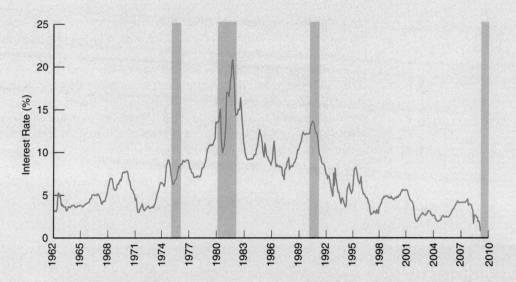

FIGURE 5-7 Business Cycles and Interest Rates (Three-Month Treasury Bills), 1962–2008

Shaded areas indicate periods of recession. The figure shows that interest rates rise during business cycle expansions and fall during contractions, which is what Figure 5-6 suggests would happen.

Source: Statistics Canada CANSIM II Series V122531.

APPLICATION | Explaining Low Japanese Interest Rates

In the 1990s and early 2000s, Japanese interest rates became the lowest in the world. Indeed, in November 1998, an extraordinary event occurred: interest rates on Japanese six-month treasury bills turned slightly negative (see Chapter 4). Why did Japanese rates drop to such low levels?

In the late 1990s, Japan experienced a prolonged recession, which was accompanied by deflation, a negative inflation rate. Using these facts, analysis similar to that used in the preceding application explains the low Japanese interest rates.

Negative inflation caused the demand for bonds to rise because the expected return on real assets fell, thereby raising the relative expected return on bonds and in turn causing the demand curve to shift to the right. The negative inflation also raised the real interest rate and therefore the real cost of borrowing for any given nominal rate, thereby causing the supply of bonds to contract and the supply curve to shift to the left. The outcome was then exactly the opposite of that graphed in Figure 5-4 (page 94): the rightward shift of the demand curve and leftward shift of the supply curve led to a rise in the bond price and a fall in interest rates.

The business cycle contraction and the resulting lack of investment opportunities in Japan also led to lower interest rates by decreasing the supply of bonds and shifting the supply curve to the left. Although the demand curve also would shift to the left because wealth decreased during the business cycle contraction, we have seen in the preceding application that the demand curve would shift less than the supply curve. Thus, the bond price rose and interest rates fell (the opposite outcome to that in Figure 5-6, page 96).

Usually, we think that low interest rates are a good thing because they make it cheap to borrow. But the Japanese example shows that just as there is a fallacy in the adage "You can never be too rich or too thin" (maybe you can't be too rich, but you can certainly be too thin and do damage to your health), there is a fallacy in always thinking that lower interest rates are better. In Japan, the low and even negative interest rates were a sign that the Japanese economy was in real trouble, with falling prices and a contracting economy. Only when the Japanese economy returns to health will interest rates rise back to more normal levels.

APPLICATION   Have Low Savings Rates in Canada Led to Higher Interest Rates?

Since 1980, Canada has experienced a sharp drop in personal savings rates, with record lows in recent years. Many commentators, including high officials of the Bank of Canada, have blamed the profligate spending habits of the Canadian public for high interest rates. Are they right?

Our supply and demand analysis of the bond market indicates that they could be right. The decline in savings means that the wealth of Canadian households is lower than would otherwise be the case. This smaller amount of wealth decreases the demand for bonds and shifts the demand curve to the left from B_1^d to B_2^d, as shown in Figure 5-8. The result is that the equilibrium bond price drops from P_1

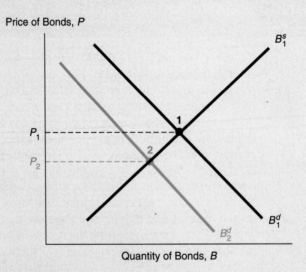

FIGURE 5-8   Response to a Lower Savings Rate

With a lower savings rate, all other things equal, wealth decreases, and the demand curve shifts from B_1^d to B_2^d. The equilibrium moves from point 1 to point 2, with the result that the equilibrium bond price drops from P_1 to P_2 and the equilibrium interest rate rises.

to P_2 and the interest rate rises. Low savings can thus raise interest rates, and the higher rates may retard investment in capital goods. The low savings rate of Canadians may therefore lead to a less-productive economy and is of serious concern to both economists and policymakers. Suggested remedies for the problem range from changing the tax laws to encourage saving to forcing Canadians to save more by mandating increased contributions into retirement plans.

SUPPLY AND DEMAND IN THE MARKET FOR MONEY: THE LIQUIDITY PREFERENCE FRAMEWORK

Instead of determining the equilibrium interest rate using the supply of and demand for bonds, an alternative model developed by John Maynard Keynes, known as the **liquidity preference framework**, determines the equilibrium interest rate in terms of the supply of and demand for money. Although the two frameworks look different, the liquidity preference analysis of the market for money is closely related to the loanable funds framework of the bond market.[4]

The starting point of Keynes's analysis is his assumption that there are two main categories of assets that people use to store their wealth: money and bonds. Therefore, total wealth in the economy must equal the total quantity of bonds plus money in the economy, which equals the quantity of bonds supplied B^s plus the quantity of money supplied M^s. The quantity of bonds B^d and money M^d that people want to hold and thus demand must also equal the total amount of wealth, because people cannot purchase more assets than their available resources allow. The conclusion is that the quantity of bonds and money supplied must equal the quantity of bonds and money demanded:

$$B^s + M^s = B^d + M^d \qquad (2)$$

Collecting the bond terms on one side of the equation and the money terms on the other, this equation can be rewritten as

$$B^s - B^d = M^d - M^s \qquad (3)$$

The rewritten equation tells us that if the market for money is in equilibrium ($M^s = M^d$), the right-hand side of Equation 3 equals zero, implying that $B^s = B^d$, meaning that the bond market is also in equilibrium.

Thus it is the same to think about determining the equilibrium interest rate by equating the supply and demand for bonds or by equating the supply and demand for money. In this sense, the liquidity preference framework, which analyzes the market for money, is equivalent to a framework analyzing supply and demand in the bond market. In practice, the approaches differ because by assuming that there are only two kinds of assets, money and bonds, the liquidity preference approach implicitly ignores any effects on interest rates that arise from changes in the expected

---

[4] Note that the term *market for money* refers to the market for the medium of exchange, money. This market differs from the *money market* referred to by finance practitioners, which is the financial market in which short-term debt instruments are traded.

returns on real assets such as automobiles and houses. In most instances, however, both frameworks yield the same predictions.

The reason that we approach the determination of interest rates with both frameworks is that the bond supply and demand framework is easier to use when analyzing the effects from changes in expected inflation, whereas the liquidity preference framework provides a simpler analysis of the effects from changes in income, the price level, and the supply of money.

Because the definition of money that Keynes used includes currency (which earns no interest) and chequing account deposits (which in his time typically earned little or no interest), he assumed that money has a zero rate of return. Bonds, the only alternative asset to money in Keynes's framework, have an expected return equal to the interest rate i.[5] As this interest rate rises (holding everything else unchanged), the expected return on money falls relative to the expected return on bonds, and as the theory of asset demand tells us, this causes the demand for money to fall.

We can also see that the demand for money and the interest rate should be negatively related by using the concept of **opportunity cost**, the amount of interest (expected return) sacrificed by not holding the alternative asset—in this case, a bond. As the interest rate on bonds, i, rises, the opportunity cost of holding money rises, and so money is less desirable and the quantity of money demanded must fall.

Figure 5-9 shows the quantity of money demanded at a number of interest rates, with all other economic variables, such as income and the price level, held constant. At an interest rate of 25%, point A shows that the quantity of money

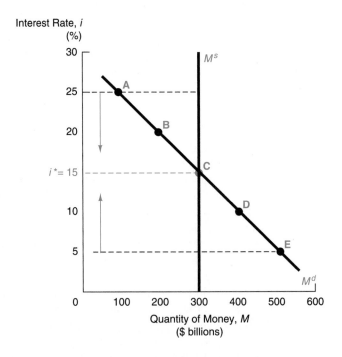

FIGURE 5-9   Equilibrium in the Market for Money

---

[5] Keynes did not actually assume that the expected returns on bonds equalled the interest rate but rather argued that they were closely related. This distinction makes no appreciable difference in our analysis.

demanded is $100 billion. If the interest rate is at the lower rate of 20%, the opportunity cost of money is lower, and the quantity of money demanded rises to $200 billion, as indicated by the move from point A to point B. If the interest rate is even lower, the quantity of money demanded is even higher, as is indicated by points C, D, and E. The curve M^d connecting these points is the demand curve for money, and it slopes downward.

At this point in our analysis, we will assume that a central bank controls the amount of money supplied at a fixed quantity of $300 billion, so the supply curve for money M^s in the figure is a vertical line at $300 billion. The equilibrium where the quantity of money demanded equals the quantity of money supplied occurs at the intersection of the supply and demand curves at point C, where

$$M^d = M^s \tag{4}$$

The resulting equilibrium interest rate is at $i^* = 15\%$.

We can again see that there is a tendency to approach this equilibrium by first looking at the relationship of money demand and supply when the interest rate is above the equilibrium interest rate. When the interest rate is 25%, the quantity of money demanded at point A is $100 billion, yet the quantity of money supplied is $300 billion. The excess supply of money means that people are holding more money than they desire, so they will try to get rid of their excess money balances by trying to buy bonds. Accordingly, they will bid up the price of bonds, and as the bond price rises, the interest rate will fall toward the equilibrium interest rate of 15%. This tendency is shown by the downward arrow drawn at the interest rate of 25%.

Likewise, if the interest rate is 5%, the quantity of money demanded at point E is $500 billion, but the quantity of money supplied is only $300 billion. There is now an excess demand for money because people want to hold more money than they currently have. To try to obtain more money, they will sell their only other asset—bonds—and the price will fall. As the price of bonds falls, the interest rate will rise toward the equilibrium rate of 15%. Only when the interest rate is at its equilibrium value will there be no tendency for it to move further, and the interest rate will settle to its equilibrium value.

CHANGES IN EQUILIBRIUM INTEREST RATES

Analyzing how the equilibrium interest rate changes using the liquidity preference framework requires that we understand what causes the demand and supply curves for money to shift.

Shifts in the Demand for Money

In Keynes's liquidity preference analysis, two factors cause the demand curve for money to shift: income and the price level.

INCOME EFFECT   In Keynes's view, there were two reasons why income would affect the demand for money. First, as an economy expands and income rises, wealth increases and people will want to hold more money as a store of value. Second, as the economy expands and income rises, people will want to carry out more transactions using money, with the result that they will also want to hold more money. The conclusion is that ***a higher level of income causes the demand for money at each interest rate to increase and the demand curve to shift to the right.***

PRICE-LEVEL EFFECT   Keynes took the view that people care about the amount of money they hold in real terms, that is, in terms of the goods and services that it can buy. When the price level rises, the same nominal quantity of money is no longer as valuable; it cannot be used to purchase as many real goods or services. To restore their holdings of money in real terms to their former level, people will want to hold a greater nominal quantity of money, so *a rise in the price level causes the demand for money at each interest rate to increase and the demand curve to shift to the right.*

Shifts in the Supply of Money

We will assume that the supply of money is completely controlled by the central bank, which in Canada is the Bank of Canada. (Actually, the process that determines the money supply is substantially more complicated, involving banks, depositors, and borrowers from banks. We will study it in more detail later in the book.) For now, all we need to know is that *an increase in the money supply engineered by the Bank of Canada will shift the supply curve for money to the right.*

APPLICATION   Changes in the Equilibrium Interest Rate Due to Changes in Income, the Price Level, or the Money Supply

To see how the liquidity preference framework can be used to analyze the movement of interest rates, we will again look at several applications that will be useful in evaluating the effect of monetary policy on interest rates. In going through these applications, remember to use the *ceteris paribus* assumption: when examining the effect of a change in one variable, hold all other variables constant. (As a study aid, Table 5-4 summarizes the shifts in the demand and supply curves for money.)

Changes in Income

When income is rising during a business cycle expansion, we have seen that the demand for money will rise, as shown in Figure 5-10 by the shift rightward in the demand curve from M_1^d to M_2^d. The new equilibrium is reached at point 2 at the intersection of the M_2^d curve with the money supply curve M^s. As you can see, the equilibrium interest rate rises from i_1 to i_2. The liquidity preference framework thus generates the conclusion that *when income is rising during a business cycle expansion (holding other economic variables constant), interest rates will rise.* This conclusion is unambiguous when contrasted to the conclusion reached about the effects of a change in income on interest rates using the bond supply and demand framework.

Changes in the Price Level

When the price level rises, the value of money in terms of what it can purchase is lower. To restore their purchasing power in real terms to its former level, people will want to hold a greater nominal quantity of money. A higher price level shifts the demand curve for money to the right from M_1^d to M_2^d (see Figure 5-10). The equilibrium moves from point 1 to point 2, where the equilibrium interest rate has risen from i_1 to i_2, illustrating that *when the price level increases, with the supply of money and other economic variables held constant, interest rates will rise.*

TABLE 5-4 Factors That Shift the Demand for and Supply of Money

Variable	Change in Variable	Change in Money Demand (M^d) or Supply (M^s) at Each Interest Rate	Change in Interest Rate	
Income	↑	M^d↑	↑	
Price level	↑	M^d↑	↑	
Money supply	↑	M^s↑	↓	

Note: Only increases (↑) in the variables are shown. The effect of decreases in the variables on the change in demand would be the opposite of those indicated in the remaining columns.

Changes in the Money Supply

An increase in the money supply due to an expansionary monetary policy by the Bank of Canada implies that the supply curve for money shifts to the right. As is shown in Figure 5-11 by the movement of the supply curve from M_1^s to M_2^s, the equilibrium moves from point 1 down to point 2, where the M_2^s supply curve intersects with the demand curve M^d and the equilibrium interest rate has fallen from i_1 to i_2. **When the money supply increases (everything else remaining equal), interest rates will decline.**[6]

---

[6] This same result can be generated using the supply and demand for bonds framework.

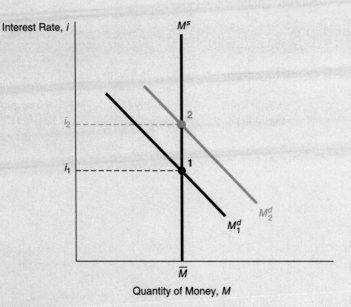

FIGURE 5-10   Response to a Change in Income or the Price Level

In a business cycle expansion, when income is rising, or when the price level rises, the demand curve shifts from M_1^d to M_2^d. The supply curve is fixed at $M^s = \overline{M}$. The equilibrium interest rate rises from i_1 to i_2.

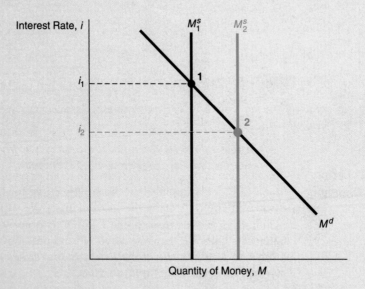

FIGURE 5-11   Response to a Change in the Money Supply

When the money supply increases, the supply curve shifts from M_1^s to M_2^s, and the equilibrium interest rate falls from i_1 to i_2.

| APPLICATION | Money and Interest Rates |

The liquidity preference analysis in Figure 5-11 seems to lead to the conclusion that an increase in the money supply will lower interest rates. This conclusion has important policy implications because it has frequently caused politicians to call for a more rapid growth of the money supply in order to drive down interest rates.

But is this conclusion that money and interest rates should be negatively related correct? Might there be other important factors left out of the liquidity preference analysis in Figure 5-11 that would reverse this conclusion? We will provide answers to these questions by applying the supply and demand analysis we have used in this chapter to obtain a deeper understanding of the relationship between money and interest rates.

Milton Friedman, a Nobel laureate in economics, has raised an important criticism of the conclusion that a rise in the money supply lowers interest rates. He acknowledges that the liquidity preference analysis is correct and calls the result—that an increase in the money supply (*everything else remaining equal*) lowers interest rates—the *liquidity effect*. However, he views the liquidity effect as merely part of the story: an increase in the money supply might not leave "everything else equal" and will have other effects on the economy that may make interest rates rise. If these effects are substantial, it is entirely possible that when the money supply rises, interest rates too may rise.

We have already laid the groundwork to discuss these other effects because we have shown how changes in income, the price level, and expected inflation affect the equilibrium interest rate.

1. *Income Effect.* Because an increasing money supply is an expansionary influence on the economy, it should raise national income and wealth. Both the liquidity preference and bond supply and demand frameworks indicate that interest rates will then rise (see Figure 5-6 on page 96 and 5-10 on page 104). Thus **the income effect of an increase in the money supply is a rise in interest rates in response to the higher level of income.**

2. *Price-Level Effect.* An increase in the money supply can also cause the overall price level in the economy to rise. The liquidity preference framework predicts that this will lead to a rise in interest rates. So **the price-level effect from an increase in the money supply is a rise in interest rates in response to the rise in the price level.**

3. *Expected-Inflation Effect.* The higher inflation rate that results from an increase in the money supply also affects interest rates by affecting the expected inflation rate. Specifically, an increase in the money supply may lead people to expect a higher price level in the future—hence the expected inflation rate will be higher. The supply and demand for bonds framework has shown us that this increase in expected inflation will lead to a higher level of interest rates. Therefore, **the expected-inflation effect of an increase in the money supply is a rise in interest rates in response to the rise in the expected inflation rate.**

At first glance it might appear that the price-level effect and the expected-inflation effect are the same thing. They both indicate that increases in the price level induced by an increase in the money supply will raise interest rates. However, there is a subtle difference between the two, and this is why they are discussed as two separate effects.

Suppose that there is a onetime increase in the money supply today that leads to a rise in prices to a permanently higher level by next year. As the price level rises over the course of this year, the interest rate will rise via the price-level effect. Only at the end of the year, when the price level has risen to its peak, will the price-level effect be at a maximum.

The rising price level will also raise interest rates via the expected-inflation effect because people will expect that inflation will be higher over the course of the year. However, when the price level stops rising next year, inflation and the expected inflation rate will return to zero. Any rise in interest rates as a result of the earlier rise in expected inflation will then be reversed. We thus see that in contrast to the price-level effect, which reaches its greatest impact next year, the expected-inflation effect will have its smallest impact (zero impact) next year. The basic difference between the two effects, then, is that the price-level effect remains even after prices have stopped rising, whereas the expected-inflation effect disappears.

An important point is that the expected-inflation effect will persist only as long as the price level continues to rise. As we will see in our discussion of monetary theory in subsequent chapters, a onetime increase in the money supply will not produce a continually rising price level; only a higher rate of money supply growth will. Thus a higher rate of money supply growth is needed if the expected-inflation effect is to persist.

Does a Higher Rate of Growth of the Money Supply Lower Interest Rates?

We can now put together all the effects we have discussed to help us decide whether our analysis supports the politicians who advocate a greater rate of growth of the money supply when they feel that interest rates are too high. Of all the effects, only the liquidity effect indicates that a higher rate of money growth will cause a decline in interest rates. In contrast, the income, price-level, and expected-inflation effects indicate that interest rates will rise when money growth is higher. Which of these effects are largest, and how quickly do they take effect? The answers are critical in determining whether interest rates will rise or fall when money supply growth is increased.

Generally, the liquidity effect from the greater money growth takes effect immediately because the rising money supply leads to an immediate decline in the equilibrium interest rate. The income and price-level effects take time to work because it takes time for the increasing money supply to raise the price level and income, which in turn raise interest rates. The expected-inflation effect, which also raises interest rates, can be slow or fast, depending on whether people adjust their expectations of inflation slowly or quickly when the money growth rate is increased.

Three possibilities are outlined in Figure 5-12; each shows how interest rates respond over time to an increased rate of money supply growth starting at time T. Panel (a) shows a case in which the liquidity effect dominates the other effects so that the interest rate falls from i_1 at time T to a final level of i_2. The liquidity effect operates quickly to lower the interest rate, but as time goes by the other effects start to reverse some of the decline. Because the liquidity effect is larger than the others, however, the interest rate never rises back to its initial level.

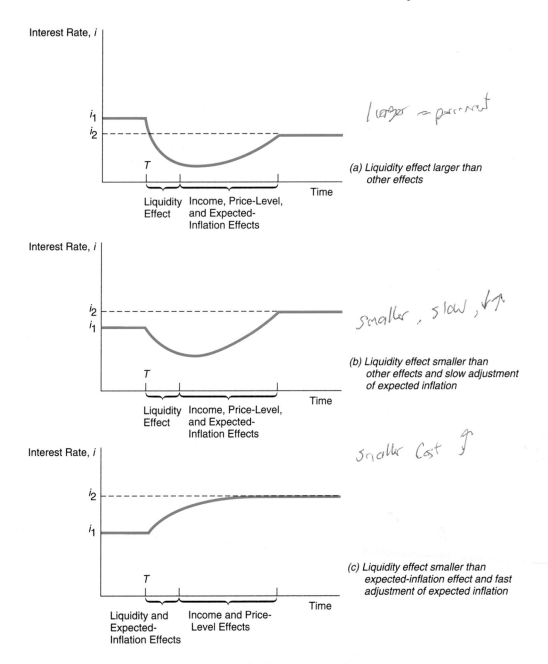

larger → permanent

(a) Liquidity effect larger than other effects

smaller, slow, ↓↑

(b) Liquidity effect smaller than other effects and slow adjustment of expected inflation

smaller Cost ↑

(c) Liquidity effect smaller than expected-inflation effect and fast adjustment of expected inflation

FIGURE 5-12   Response over Time to an Increase in Money Supply Growth

Panel (b) has a smaller liquidity effect than the other effects, with the expected-inflation effect operating slowly because expectations of inflation are slow to adjust upward. Initially, the liquidity effect drives down the interest rate. Then the income, price-level, and expected-inflation effects begin to raise it. Because these effects are dominant, the interest rate eventually rises above its initial level to i_2. In the short run, lower interest rates result from increased money growth, but eventually they end up climbing above the initial level.

Panel (c) has the expected-inflation effect dominating as well as operating rapidly because people quickly raise their expectations of inflation when the rate of money growth increases. The expected-inflation effect begins immediately to over-power the liquidity effect, and the interest rate immediately starts to climb. Over time, as the income and price-level effects start to take hold, the interest rate rises even higher, and the eventual outcome is an interest rate that is substantially above the initial interest rate. The result shows clearly that increasing money supply growth is not the answer to reducing interest rates; rather, money growth should be reduced in order to lower interest rates!

An important issue for economic policymakers is which of these three scenarios is closest to reality. If a decline in interest rates is desired, then an increase in money supply growth is called for when the liquidity effect dominates the other effects, as in panel (a). A decrease in money growth is appropriate if the other effects dominate the liquidity effect and expectations of inflation adjust rapidly, as in panel (c). If the other effects dominate the liquidity effect but expectations of inflation adjust only slowly, as in panel (b), then whether you want to increase or decrease money growth depends on whether you care more about what happens in the short run or the long run.

Which scenario does the evidence support? The relationship of interest rates and money growth from 1968 to 2008 is plotted in Figure 5-13. When the rate of money supply growth began to climb in the late-1970s, interest rates rose, indicating that the price-level, income, and expected-inflation effects dominated the liquidity effect. By the early 1980s, interest rates reached levels unprecedented in the post–World War II period, as did the rate of money supply growth.

The scenario depicted in panel (a) of Figure 5-12 seems doubtful, and the case for lowering interest rates by raising the rate of money growth is much weakened. Looking back at Figure 5-5 (page 95), which shows the relationship between inter-est rates and expected inflation, you should not find this too surprising. The rise in the rate of money supply growth in the 1960s and 1970s is matched by a large rise in expected inflation, which would lead us to predict that the expected-inflation effect would be dominant. It is the most plausible explanation for why interest rates rose in the face of higher money growth. However, Figure 5-13 does not really tell

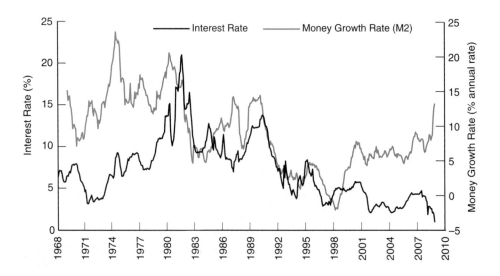

FIGURE 5-13   Money Growth (M2, Annual Rate) and Interest Rates (Three-Month Treasury Bills), 1968–2008

Source: Statistics Canada CANSIM II Series V122531 and V41552796.

us which one of the two scenarios, panel (b) or panel (c) of Figure 5-12, is more accurate. It depends critically on how fast people's expectations about inflation adjust. However, recent research using more sophisticated methods than just looking at a graph like Figure 5-13 do indicate that increased money growth temporarily lowers short-term interest rates (this is also indicated in Figure 5-13 in the 2000s).[7] However, as you can see in the FYI box Forecasting Interest Rates, interest rate forecasting is a perilous business.

FYI   Forecasting Interest Rates

Forecasting interest rates is a time-honoured profession. Economists are hired (sometimes at very high salaries) to forecast interest rates because businesses need to know what the rates will be in order to plan their future spending, and banks and investors require interest-rate forecasts in order to decide which assets to buy.

The media frequently report interest rate forecasts by leading prognosticators. These forecasts are produced using a wide range of statistical models and a number of different sources of information. One of the most popular methods is based on the bond supply and demand framework described earlier in the chapter. Using this framework, analysts predict what will happen to the factors that affect the supply of and demand for bonds and then use the supply and demand analysis outlined in the chapter to come up with their interest-rate forecasts.

An alternative method of forecasting interest rates makes use of econometric models, models whose equations are estimated with statistical procedures using past data. Many of these econometric models are quite large, involving hundreds and sometimes over a thousand interlocking equations. They produce simultaneous forecasts for many variables, including interest rates, under the assumption that the estimated relationships between variables do not change over time.

Good forecasts of future interest rates are extremely valuable to households and businesses, which, not surprisingly, would be willing to pay a lot for accurate forecasts. Unfortunately, forecasting interest rates is a perilous business. To their embarrassment, even the top experts are frequently far off in their forecasts.

[7] See Lawrence J. Christiano and Martin Eichenbaum, "Identification and the Liquidity Effect of a Monetary Policy Shock," in *Business Cycles, Growth, and Political Economy,* ed. Alex Cukierman, Zvi Hercowitz, and Leonardo Leiderman (Cambridge, Mass.: MIT Press, 1992), pp. 335–370; Eric M. Leeper and David B. Gordon, "In Search of the Liquidity Effect," *Journal of Monetary Economics* 29 (1992): 341–370; Steven Strongin, "The Identification of Monetary Policy Disturbances: Explaining the Liquidity Puzzle," *Journal of Monetary Economics* 35 (1995): 463–497; Adrian Pagan and John C. Robertson, "Resolving the Liquidity Effect," *Federal Reserve Bank of St. Louis Review* 77 (May–June 1995): 33–54; and Ben S. Bernanke and Illian Mihov, "Measuring Monetary Policy," *Quarterly Journal of Economics* 63 (August 1998): 869–902.

SUMMARY

1. The theory of asset demand tells us that the quantity demanded of an asset is (a) positively related to wealth, (b) positively related to the expected return on the asset relative to alternative assets, (c) negatively related to the riskiness of the asset relative to alternative assets, and (d) positively related to the liquidity of the asset relative to alternative assets.

2. The supply and demand analysis for bonds provides one theory of how interest rates are determined. It predicts that interest rates will change when there is a change in demand because of changes in income (or wealth), expected returns, risk, or liquidity or when there is a change in supply because of changes in the attractiveness of investment opportunities, the real cost of borrowing, or government activities.

3. An alternative theory of how interest rates are determined is provided by the liquidity preference framework, which analyzes the supply of and demand for money. It shows that interest rates will change when there is a change in the demand for money because of changes in income or the price level or when there is a change in the supply of money.

4. There are four possible effects of an increase in the money supply on interest rates: the liquidity effect, the income effect, the price-level effect, and the expected-inflation effect. The liquidity effect indicates that a rise in money supply growth will lead to a decline in interest rates; the other effects work in the opposite direction. The evidence seems to indicate that the income, price-level, and expected-inflation effects dominate the liquidity effect such that an increase in money supply growth leads to higher rather than lower interest rates.

KEY TERMS

asset market approach,   p. 88

demand curve,   p. 85

excess demand,   p. 87

excess supply,   p. 87

expected return,   p. 83

Fisher effect,   p. 95

liquidity,   p. 83

liquidity preference framework,
    p. 99

market equilibrium,   p. 87

opportunity cost,   p. 100

risk,   p. 83

supply curve,   p. 86

theory of asset demand,
    p. 84

wealth,   p. 83

QUESTIONS

You will find the answers to the questions marked with an asterisk in the Textbook Resources section of your MyEconLab.

1. Explain why you would be more or less willing to buy a share of Air Canada stock in the following situations:
   a. Your wealth falls.
   b. You expect the stock to appreciate in value.
   c. The bond market becomes more liquid.
   d. You expect gold to appreciate in value.
   e. Prices in the bond market become more volatile.

*2. Explain why you would be more or less willing to buy a house under the following circumstances:
   a. You just inherited $100 000.
   b. Real estate commissions fall from 6% of the sales price to 5% of the sales price.
   c. You expect Air Canada stock to double in value next year.
   d. Prices in the stock market become more volatile.
   e. You expect housing prices to fall.

3. Explain why you would be more or less willing to buy gold under the following circumstances:
   a. Gold again becomes acceptable as a medium of exchange.
   b. Prices in the gold market become more volatile.
   c. You expect inflation to rise, and gold prices tend to move with the aggregate price level.
   d. You expect interest rates to rise.

*4. Explain why you would be more or less willing to buy long-term Air Canada bonds under the following circumstances:
   a. Trading in these bonds increases, making them easier to sell.
   b. You expect a bear market in stocks (stock prices are expected to decline).
   c. Brokerage commissions on stocks fall.
   d. You expect interest rates to rise.
   e. Brokerage commissions on bonds fall.

5. What would happen to the demand for Rembrandts if the stock market undergoes a boom? Why?

Answer each question by drawing the appropriate supply and demand diagrams.

*6. An important way in which the Bank of Canada decreases the money supply is by selling bonds to the public. Using a supply and demand analysis for bonds, show what effect this action has on interest rates. Is your answer consistent with what you would expect to find with the liquidity preference framework?

7. Using both the liquidity preference and supply and demand for bonds frameworks, show why interest rates are procyclical (rising when the economy is expanding and falling during recessions).

*8. Why should a rise in the price level (but not in expected inflation) cause interest rates to rise when the nominal money supply is fixed?

9. What effect will a sharp increase in personal savings rates have on Canadian interest rates?

10. What effect will a sudden increase in the volatility of gold prices have on interest rates?

*11. How might a sudden increase in people's expectations of future real estate prices affect interest rates?

12. Explain what effect a large federal deficit might have on interest rates.

*13. Using both the supply and demand for bonds and liquidity preference frameworks, show what the effect is on interest rates when the riskiness of bonds rises. Are the results the same in the two frameworks?

14. If the price level falls next year, remaining fixed thereafter, and the money supply is fixed, what is likely to happen to interest rates over the next two years? (Hint: Take account of both the price-level effect and the expected-inflation effect.)

*15. Will there be an effect on interest rates if brokerage commissions on stocks fall? Explain your answer.

Predicting the Future

16. The governor of the Bank of Canada announces in a press conference that he will fight the higher inflation rate with a new anti-inflation program. Predict what will happen to interest rates if the public believes him.

*17. The governor of the Bank of Canada announces that interest rates will rise sharply next year, and the market believes him. What will happen to today's interest rate on long-term corporate bonds?

18. Predict what will happen to interest rates if the public suddenly expects a large increase in stock prices.

*19. Predict what will happen to interest rates if prices in the bond market become more volatile.

20. If the next governor of the Bank of Canada has a reputation for advocating an even slower rate of money growth than the current governor, what will happen to interest rates? Discuss the possible resulting situations.

QUANTITATIVE PROBLEMS

1. The demand curve and supply curve for one-year T-bills (with a face value of $1000) were estimated using the following equations:

$$B^d: Price = -\frac{2}{5}Quantity + 940$$

$$B^s: Price = Quantity + 100$$

a. What is the expected equilibrium price and quantity of T-bills in this market?
b. Given your answer in (a), which is the expected interest rate in this market?

*2. The demand curve and supply curve for one-year T-bills (with a face value of $1000) were estimated using the following equations:

$$B^d: Price = -\frac{2}{5}Quantity + 940$$

$$B^s: Price = Quantity + 100$$

Following a dramatic decline in the value of the stock market, the demand for bonds increased and this resulted in a parallel shift in the demand curve for bonds, such as the price of bonds at all quantities increased $100. Assuming no change in the supply function for bonds, what is the new equilibrium price and quantity? What is the new market interest rate?

CANSIM Questions

3. Get the monthly data from 1976 to 2009 on the M2 (gross) monetary aggregate (CANSIM series V41552796) and the three-month T-bill rate (series V122531) from the Textbook Resources area of the MyEconLab.

a. Calculate the annual money growth rate, using the formula

$$\mu_t = 100 \times (M_{t+12} - M_t)/M_t$$

b. Plot the monetary growth rate, μ_t, and the nominal interest rate, i_t.
c. What is the correlation coefficient between the money growth, μ_t, and the nominal interest rate, i_t? Do you find anything interesting?

4. Get the monthly data from 1976 to 2009 on the three-month T-bill rate (CANSIM series V122531) from the Textbook Resources area of the MyEconLab.

   a. Plot the nominal interest rate, i_t.

   b. Calculate the change in i_t.

   $$\Delta i_t = i_{t+1} - i_t$$

   c. Plot Δi_t. Has the nominal interest rate become more or less volatile over the sample period?

WEB EXERCISES

1. One of the largest single influences on the level of interest rates is inflation. There are a number of sites that report inflation over time. Go to **www.bankofcanada.ca/en/cpi.htm** and review the data. What has the average rate of inflation been since 1995? What year had the lowest level of inflation? What year had the highest level of inflation?

2. Increasing prices erode the purchasing power of the dollar. It is interesting to calculate how much goods would have cost at some point in the past after adjusting for inflation. Click on **www. bankofcanada.ca/en/inflation_calc.htm.** What is the cost today of a car that cost $10 000 the year that you were born?

3. One of the points made in this chapter is that inflation erodes investment returns. Go to **www.moneychimp.com/articles/econ/inflation_calculator.htm** and review how changes in inflation alter your real return. What happens to the difference between the adjusted value of an investment compared to its inflation-adjusted value as:

   a. Inflation increases?

   b. The investment horizon lengthens?

   c. Expected returns increase?

Be sure to visit the MyEconLab website at **www.myeconlab.com**. This online homework and tutorial system puts you in control of your own learning with study and practice tools directly correlated to this chapter content.

On the MyEconLab website you will find the following appendices and mini-case for this chapter:

Appendix 5.1: Models of Asset Pricing

Appendix 5.2: Applying the Asset Market Approach to a Commodity Market: The Case of Gold

Mini-Case 5.1: The Behaviour of Interest Rates

CHAPTER 6

The Risk and Term Structure of Interest Rates

LEARNING OBJECTIVES

After studying this chapter you should be able to

1. describe how default risk, liquidity, and tax considerations affect interest rates
2. explain how interest rates on bonds with different maturities are related by applying the expectations theory, the segmented markets theory, and the liquidity premium theory
3. predict the movement of short-term interest rates in the future using the yield curve

PREVIEW

In our supply and demand analysis of interest-rate behaviour in Chapter 5, we examined the determination of just one interest rate. Yet we saw earlier that there are enormous numbers of bonds on which the interest rates can and do differ. In this chapter we complete the interest-rate picture by examining the relationship of the various interest rates to one another. Understanding why they differ from bond to bond can help businesses, banks, insurance companies, and private investors decide which bonds to purchase as investments and which ones to sell.

We first look at why bonds with the same term to maturity have different interest rates. The relationship among these interest rates is called the **risk structure of interest rates**, although risk and liquidity both play a role in determining the risk structure. A bond's term to maturity also affects its interest rate, and the relationship among interest rates on bonds with different terms to maturity is called the **term structure of interest rates**. In this chapter we examine the sources and causes of fluctuations in interest rates relative to one another and look at a number of theories that explain these fluctuations.

RISK STRUCTURE OF INTEREST RATES

Figure 6-1 shows the yields to maturity for several categories of long-term bonds from 1978 to 2008. It shows us two important features of interest-rate behaviour for bonds of the same maturity: interest rates on different categories of bonds differ from one another in any given year, and the spread (or difference) between the interest rates varies over time. The interest rates on corporate bonds, for example, are above those on Canada bonds and provincial bonds. In addition, the spread between the interest rates on corporate bonds and Canada bonds is very large during the 1980–1982 and

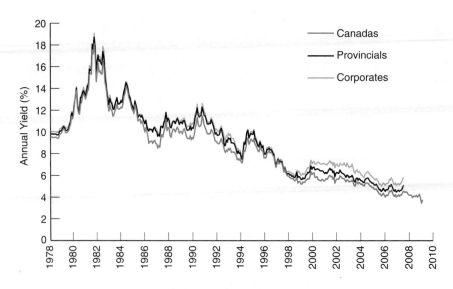

FIGURE 6-1   Long-Term Bond Yields, 1978–2008

Source: Statistics Canada CANSIM II Series V122544, V122517, and V122518.

1990–1991 recessions, is smaller during the mid-1990s, and then widens again afterwards. What factors are responsible for these phenomena?

Default Risk

One attribute of a bond that influences its interest rate is its **risk of default**, which occurs when the issuer of the bond is unable or unwilling to make interest payments when promised or pay off the face value when the bond matures. A corporation suffering big losses might be more likely to suspend interest payments on its bonds. The default risk on its bonds would therefore be quite high. By contrast, Canadian government bonds have usually been considered to have no default risk because the federal government can always increase taxes to pay off its obligations. Bonds like these with no default risk are called **default-free bonds**. The spread between the interest rates on bonds with default risk and default-free bonds, called the **risk premium**, indicates how much additional interest people must earn in order to be willing to hold that risky bond. Our supply and demand analysis of the bond market in Chapter 5 can be used to explain why a bond with default risk always has a positive risk premium and why the higher the default risk is, the larger the risk premium will be.

To examine the effect of default risk on interest rates, let us look at the supply and demand diagrams for the default-free (Canadian government) and corporate long-term bond markets in Figure 6-2. To make the diagrams somewhat easier to read, let's assume that initially corporate bonds have the same default risk as Canada bonds. In this case, these two bonds have the same attributes (identical risk and maturity); their equilibrium prices and interest rates will initially be equal ($P_1^c = P_1^T$ and $i_1^c = i_1^T$), and the risk premium on corporate bonds ($i_1^c - i_1^T$) will be zero.

If the possibility of a default increases because a corporation begins to suffer large losses, the default risk on corporate bonds will increase, and the expected return on these bonds will decrease. In addition, the corporate bond's return will be more uncertain as well. The theory of asset demand predicts that because the expected return on the corporate bond falls relative to the expected return on the default-free

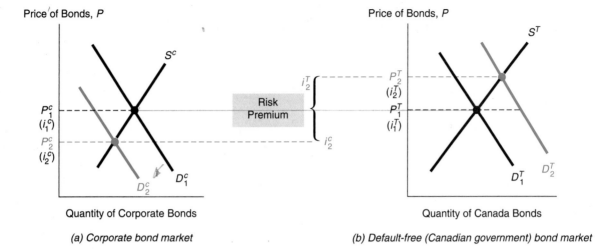

FIGURE 6-2   Response to an Increase in Default Risk on Corporate Bonds

An increase in default risk on corporate bonds shifts the demand curve from D_1^C to D_2^C. Simultaneously, it shifts the demand curve for Canada bonds from D_1^T to D_2^T. The equilibrium price for corporate bonds falls from P_1^C to P_2^C, and the equilibrium interest rate on corporate bonds rises to i_2^C. In the Canada bond market, the equilibrium bond price rises from P_1^T to P_2^T, and the equilibrium interest rate falls to i_2^T. The brace indicates the difference between i_2^C and i_2^T, the risk premium on corporate bonds.

Canada bond while its relative riskiness rises, the corporate bond is less desirable (holding everything else equal), and demand for it will fall. Another way of thinking about this is that if you were an investor, you would want to hold (demand) a smaller amount of corporate bonds. The demand curve for corporate bonds in panel (a) of Figure 6-2 then shifts to the left, from D_1^C to D_2^C.

At the same time, the expected return on default-free Canada bonds increases relative to the expected return on corporate bonds while their relative riskiness declines. The Canada bonds thus become more desirable, and demand rises, as shown in panel (b) by the rightward shift in the demand curve for these bonds from D_1^T to D_2^T.

As we can see in Figure 6-2, the equilibrium price for corporate bonds falls from P_1^C to P_2^C, and since the bond price is negatively related to the interest rate, the equilibrium interest rate on corporate bonds rises to i_2^C. At the same time, however, the equilibrium price for the Canada bonds rises from P_1^T to P_2^T, and the equilibrium interest rate falls to i_2^T. The spread between the interest rates on corporate and default-free bonds—that is, the risk premium on corporate bonds—has risen from zero to $i_2^C - i_2^T$. We can now conclude that ***a bond with default risk will always have a positive risk premium, and an increase in its default risk will raise the risk premium.***

Because default risk is so important to the size of the risk premium, purchasers of bonds need to know whether a corporation is likely to default on its bonds. This information is provided by **credit-rating agencies**, investment advisory firms that rate the quality of corporate and municipal bonds in terms of the probability of default. Table 6-1 provides the ratings and their description for the two largest credit-rating agencies, Dominion Bond Rating Service (DBRS) and Standard & Poor's Corporation (S&P)—in the United States, Moody's Investor Service and Standard & Poor's Corporation provide similar information. Bonds with relatively low risk of default are called *investment-grade* securities and have a rating of BBB

TABLE 6-1	Bond Ratings by Standard & Poor's and DBRS
Rating	**Definitions**
AAA	Highest quality
AA	Superior quality
A	Satisfactory quality
BBB	Adequate quality
BB	Speculative
B	Highly speculative
CCC, CC, C	Very highly speculative
D	In default

and above. Bonds with ratings below BBB have higher default risk and have been aptly dubbed speculative-grade or **junk bonds**. Because these bonds always have higher interest rates than investment-grade securities, they are also referred to as high-yield bonds. Investment-grade securities whose rating has fallen to junk levels are referred to as **fallen angels**.

Next let's look back at Figure 6-1 and see if we can explain the relationship between interest rates on corporate and Canada bonds. Corporate bonds always have higher interest rates than Canada bonds because they always have some risk of default, whereas Canada bonds do not. Because corporate bonds have a greater default risk than Canada bonds, their risk premium is greater, and the corporate bond rate therefore always exceeds the Canada bond rate. We can use the same analysis to explain the huge jump in the risk premium on corporate bond rates during the 1980–1982, 1990–1991, and 2000 recessions (Figure 6-3). The recession periods saw a very high rate of business failures and defaults. As we would expect, these factors led to a substantial increase in default risk for bonds issued by vulnerable corporations, and the risk premium for corporate bonds reached unprecedented high levels.

FIGURE 6-3   Corporates–Canadas Spread, 1978–2008

Source: Statistics Canada CANSIM II Series V122518 and V122544.

APPLICATION	**The Subprime Collapse and the BAA-Treasury Spread in the United States**

Starting in August 2007, the collapse of the subprime mortgage market in the U.S. led to large losses in American financial institutions (which will be discussed more extensively in Chapter 9). As a consequence of the subprime collapse, many investors began to doubt the financial health of corporations with low credit ratings, such as BAA, and even the reliability of the ratings themselves. The perceived increase in default risk for BAA bonds made them less desirable at any given interest rate, decreased the quantity demanded, and shifted the demand curve for BAA bonds to the left. As shown in panel (a) of Figure 6-2, the interest rate on BAA bonds should have risen, which is indeed what happened. Interest rates on BAA bonds rose by 280 **basis points** (2.80 percentage points) from 6.63% at the end of July 2007 to 9.43% at the most virulent stage of the crisis in mid October 2008. But the increase in perceived default risk for BAA bonds after the subprime collapse made default-free U.S. Treasury bonds relatively more attractive and shifted the demand curve for these securities to the right—an outcome described by some analysts as a "flight to quality." Just as our analysis predicts in Figure 6-2, interest rates on U.S. Treasury bonds fell by 80 basis points, from 4.78% at the end of July 2007 to 3.98% in mid-October 2008. The spread between interest rates on BAA and Treasury bonds rose by 360 basis points from 1.85% before the crisis to 5.45% afterward.

Liquidity

Another attribute of a bond that influences its interest rate is its liquidity. As we learned in Chapter 5, a liquid asset is one that can be quickly and cheaply converted into cash if the need arises. The more liquid an asset is, the more desirable it is (holding everything else constant). Canada bonds are the most liquid of all long-term bonds because they are so widely traded that they are the easiest to sell quickly and the cost of selling them is low. Corporate bonds are not as liquid because fewer bonds for any one corporation are traded; thus it can be costly to sell these bonds in an emergency because it may be hard to find buyers quickly.

How does the reduced liquidity of corporate bonds affect their interest rates relative to the interest rate on Canada bonds? We can use supply and demand analysis with the same figure that was used to analyze the effect of default risk, Figure 6-2, to show that the lower liquidity of corporate bonds relative to Canada bonds increases the spread between the interest rates on these two bonds. Let us start the analysis by assuming that initially corporate and Canada bonds are equally liquid and all their other attributes are the same. As shown in Figure 6-2, their equilibrium prices and interest rates will initially be equal: $P_1^c = P_1^T$ and $i_1^c = i_1^T$. If the corporate bond becomes less liquid than the Canada bond because it is less widely traded, then as the theory of asset demand indicates, its demand will fall, shifting its demand curve from D_1^c to D_2^c, as in panel (a). The Canada bond now becomes relatively more liquid in comparison with the corporate bond, so its demand curve shifts rightward from D_1^T to D_2^T, as in panel (b). The shifts in the curves in Figure 6-2 show that the price of the less-liquid corporate bond falls and its interest rate rises, while the price of the more-liquid Canada bond rises and its interest rate falls.

The result is that the spread between the interest rates on the two bond types has risen. Therefore, the differences between interest rates on corporate bonds and Canada bonds (that is, the risk premiums) reflect not only the corporate bond's default risk but its liquidity too. This is why a risk premium is more accurately a "risk and liquidity premium," but convention dictates that it be called a *risk premium*.

⇲ Income Tax Considerations

In Canada, coupon payments on fixed-income securities are taxed as ordinary income in the year they are received. In some other countries, however, certain government bonds are not taxable. In the United States, for example, interest payments on municipal bonds are exempt from federal income taxes, and these bonds have had lower interest rates than U.S. Treasury bonds for at least 40 years. How does taxation affect the interest rate on bonds?

Let us imagine that you have a high enough income to put you in the 40% income tax bracket, where for every extra dollar of income you have to pay 40 cents to the government. If you own a $1000-face-value taxable bond that sells for $1000 and has a coupon payment of $100, you get to keep only $60 of the payment after taxes. Although the bond has a 10% interest rate, you actually earn only 6% after taxes.

Suppose, however, that you put your savings into a $1000-face-value tax-exempt bond that sells for $1000 and pays only $80 in coupon payments. Its interest rate is only 8%, but because it is a tax-exempt security, you pay no taxes on the $80 coupon payment, so you earn 8% after taxes. Clearly, you earn more on the tax-exempt bond, so you are willing to hold the bond even though it has a lower interest rate than the taxable bond. Notice that the tax-exempt status of a bond becomes a significant advantage when income tax rates are very high.

APPLICATION   Tax-Exempt versus Taxable Bonds

Suppose you had the opportunity to buy either a tax-exempt bond or a taxable bond, both of which have a face value and purchase price of $1000. Assume both bonds have identical risk. The tax-exempt bond has coupon payments of $60 and a coupon rate of 6%. The taxable bond has coupon payments of $80 and an interest rate of 8%. Which bond would you choose to purchase, assuming a 40% tax rate?

Solution

You would choose to purchase the tax-exempt bond because it will earn you $60 in coupon payments and an interest rate after taxes of 6%. In this case, you pay no taxes on the $60 coupon payments and earn 6% after taxes. However, you have to pay taxes on taxable bonds. You will keep only 60% of the $80 coupon payment because the other 40% goes to taxes. Therefore, you receive $48 of the coupon payment and have an interest rate of 4.8% after taxes. Buying the tax-exempt bond would yield you higher earnings.

APPLICATION	Effects of the Bush Tax Cut on Bond Interest Rates in the United States

The Bush tax cut passed in 2001 scheduled a reduction of the top income tax bracket from 39% to 35% over a ten-year period. What is the effect of this income tax decrease on interest rates in the municipal bond market relative to those in the U.S. Treasury bond market?

A supply and demand analysis similar to that in Figure 6-2 provides the answer. A decreased income tax rate for wealthy people means that the after-tax expected return on tax-free municipal bonds relative to that on U.S. Treasury bonds is lower because the interest on Treasury bonds is now taxed at a lower rate. Because municipal bonds now become less desirable, their demand decreases, shifting the demand curve to the left, which lowers their price and raises their interest rate. Conversely, the lower income tax rate makes U.S. Treasury bonds more desirable; this change shifts their demand curve to the right, raises their price, and lowers their interest rates.

Our analysis thus shows that the Bush tax cut has caused interest rates on municipal bonds to rise relative to interest rates on Treasury bonds. With the possible repeal of the Bush tax cuts that may occur with the Obama administration, this analysis would be reversed. Higher tax rates would raise the after-tax expected return on tax-free municipal bonds relative to Treasuries. Demand for municipal bonds would increase, shifting the demand curve to the right, which would raise their price and lower their interest rate. Conversely, the higher tax rate would make Treasury bonds less desirable, shifting their demand curve to the left, lowering their price, and raising their interest rate. Higher tax rates would thus result in lower interest rates on municipal bonds relative to the interest rate on Treasury bonds.

Summary

In general, the risk structure of interest rates (the relationship among interest rates on bonds with the same maturity) is explained by three factors: default risk, liquidity, and the income tax treatment of the bond's interest payments. As a bond's default risk increases, the risk premium on that bond (the spread between its interest rate and the interest rate on a default-free Canadian government bond) rises. The greater liquidity of Canada bonds also explains why their interest rates are lower than interest rates on less liquid bonds. If a bond has a favourable tax treatment, as do municipal bonds in the United States whose interest payments are exempt from federal income taxes, its interest rate will be lower.

TERM STRUCTURE OF INTEREST RATES

We have seen how risk, liquidity, and tax considerations (collectively embedded in the risk structure) can influence interest rates. Another factor that influences the interest rate on a bond is its term to maturity: bonds with identical risk, liquidity, and tax characteristics may have different interest rates because the time remaining to maturity is different. A plot of the yields on bonds with differing terms to maturity but the same risk, liquidity, and tax considerations is called a **yield curve**, and it describes the term structure of interest rates for particular types of bonds, such as government bonds. The Financial News box Yield Curves shows several

FINANCIAL NEWS

Yield Curves

The *Wall Street Journal* publishes a daily plot of the yield curves for U.S. Treasury securities, an example of which is presented here. It is found in the Money and Investing section. The *Globe and Mail: Report on Business* publishes similar yield curves for Government of Canada securities.

The numbers on the vertical axis indicate the interest rate for the U.S. Treasury security, with the maturity given by the numbers on the horizontal axis.

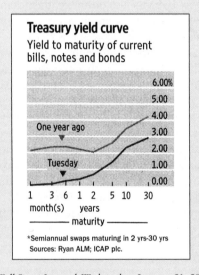

Source: *Wall Street Journal*, Wednesday, January 21, 2009, p. C4.

yield curves for U.S. Treasury securities that were published in the *Wall Street Journal*. Similar yield curves are reported for Canada in the *Globe and Mail: Report on Business*. Yield curves can be classified as upward-sloping, flat, and downward-sloping (the last sort is often referred to as an **inverted yield curve**). When yield curves slope upward, as in the Financial News box, the long-term interest rates are above the short-term interest rates; when yield curves are flat, short- and long-term interest rates are the same; and when yield curves are inverted, long-term interest rates are below short-term interest rates. Yield curves can also have more complicated shapes in which they first slope up and then down, or vice versa. Why do we usually see upward slopes of the yield curve?

Besides explaining why yield curves take on different shapes at different times, a good theory of the term structure of interest rates must explain the following three important empirical facts:

1. As we see in Figure 6-4, interest rates on bonds of different maturities move together over time.

2. When short-term interest rates are low, yield curves are more likely to have an

FIGURE 6-4   Movements over Time of Interest Rates on Government of Canada Bonds with Different Maturities, 1962–2008

Source: Statistics Canada CANSIM II Series V122531, V122485, and V122487.

upward slope; when short-term interest rates are high, yield curves are more likely to slope downward and be inverted.

3. Yield curves almost always slope upward, like the yield curves in the Financial News box.

Four theories have been put forward to explain the term structure of interest rates, that is, the relationship among interest rates on bonds of different maturities reflected in yield-curve patterns: (1) the expectations theory, (2) the segmented markets theory, (3) the liquidity premium theory, and (4) the preferred habitat theory. The expectations theory does a good job of explaining the first two facts on our list but not the third. The segmented markets theory can explain fact 3 but not the other two facts, which are well explained by the expectations theory. Because each theory explains facts that the others cannot, a natural way to seek a better understanding of the term structure is to combine features of all four theories, which leads us to the liquidity premium and preferred habitat theories, which can explain all three facts.

If the liquidity premium and preferred habitat theories do a better job of explaining the facts and are hence the most widely accepted theories, why do we spend time discussing the other two theories? There are two reasons. First, the ideas in these two theories provide the groundwork for the liquidity premium and preferred habitat theories. Second, it is important to see how economists modify theories to improve them when they find that the predicted results are inconsistent with the empirical evidence.

Expectations Theory

The **expectations theory** of the term structure states the following common-sense proposition: the interest rate on a long-term bond will equal an average of short-term interest rates that people expect to occur over the life of the long-term bond. For example, if people expect that short-term interest rates will be 10% on average over the coming five years, the expectations theory predicts that the interest rate on bonds with five years to maturity will be 10% too. If short-term interest rates were expected to rise even higher after this five-year period so that the average short-term interest rate over the coming 20 years is 11%, then the interest rate on 20-year bonds would equal 11% and would be higher than the interest rate on five-year bonds. We can see that the explanation provided by the expectations theory for why interest rates on bonds of different maturities differ is that short-term interest rates are expected to have different values at future dates.

The key assumption behind this theory is that buyers of bonds do not prefer bonds of one maturity over another, so they will not hold any quantity of a bond if its expected return is less than that of another bond with a different maturity. Bonds that have this characteristic are said to be *perfect substitutes*. What this means in practice is that if bonds with different maturities are perfect substitutes, the expected return on these bonds must be equal.

To see how the assumption that bonds with different maturities are perfect substitutes leads to the expectations theory, let us consider the following two investment strategies:

1. Purchase a one-year bond, and when it matures in one year, purchase another one-year bond.
2. Purchase a two-year bond and hold it until maturity.

Because both strategies must have the same expected return if people are holding both one- and two-year bonds, the interest rate on the two-year bond must equal the average of the two one-year interest rates.

APPLICATION   Expectations Theory

The current interest rate on a one-year bond is 9%, and you expect the interest rate on the one-year bond next year to be 11%. What is the expected return over the two years? What interest rate must a two-year bond have to equal the two one-year bonds?

Solution

The expected return over the two years will average 10% per year ([9% + 11%]/2 = 10%). The bondholder will be willing to hold both the one- and two-year bonds only if the expected return per year of the two-year bond equals 10%. Therefore, the interest rate on the two-year bond must equal 10%, the average interest rate on the two one-year bonds. Graphically, we have:

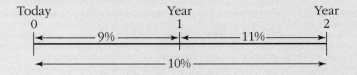

We can make this argument more general. For an investment of $1, consider the choice of holding, for two periods, a two-period bond or two one-period bonds. Using the definitions

i_t = today's (time t) interest rate on a one-period bond

i^e_{t+1} = interest rate on a one-period bond expected for next period (time $t + 1$)

i_{2t} = today's (time t) interest rate on the two-period bond

the expected return over the two periods from investing $1 in the two-period bond and holding it for the two periods can be calculated as

$$(1 + i_{2t})(1 + i_{2t}) - 1 = 1 + 2i_{2t} + (i_{2t})^2 - 1 = 2i_{2t} + (i_{2t})^2$$

After the second period, the $1 investment is worth $(1 + i_{2t})(1 + i_{2t})$. Subtracting the $1 initial investment from this amount and dividing by the initial $1 investment gives the rate of return calculated in the above equation. Because $(i_{2t})^2$ is extremely small—if $i_{2t} = 10\% = 0.10$, then $(i_{2t})^2 = 0.01$—we can simplify the expected return for holding the two-period bond for the two periods to

$$2i_{2t}$$

With the other strategy, in which one-period bonds are bought, the expected return on the $1 investment over the two periods is

$$(1 + i_t)(1 + i^e_{t+1}) - 1 = 1 + i_t + i^e_{t+1} + i_t(i^e_{t+1}) - 1 = i_t + i^e_{t+1} + i_t(i^e_{t+1})$$

This calculation is derived by recognizing that after the first period, the $1 investment becomes $1 + i_t$, and this is reinvested in the one-period bond for the next period, yielding an amount $(1 + i_t)(1 + i^e_{t+1})$. Then, subtracting the $1 initial investment from this amount and dividing by the initial investment of $1 gives the expected return for the strategy of holding one-period bonds for the two periods. Because $i_t(i^e_{t+1})$ is also extremely small—if $i_t = i^e_{t+1} = 0.10$, then $i_t(i^e_{t+1}) = 0.01$—we can simplify this to

$$i_t + i^e_{t+1}$$

Both bonds will be held only if these expected returns are equal, that is, when

$$2i_{2t} = i_t + i^e_{t+1}$$

Solving for i_{2t} in terms of the one-period rates, we have

$$i_{2t} = \frac{i_t + i^e_{t+1}}{2} \qquad (1)$$

which tells us that the two-period rate must equal the average of the two one-period rates. Graphically, this can be shown as:

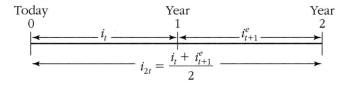

We can conduct the same steps for bonds with a longer maturity so that we can examine the whole term structure of interest rates. Doing so, we will find that the interest rate of i_{nt} on an n-period bond must equal

$$i_{nt} = \frac{i_t + i_{t+1}^e + i_{t+2}^e + \cdots + i_{t+(n-1)}^e}{n} \tag{2}$$

Equation 2 states that the n-period interest rate equals the average of the one-period interest rates expected to occur over the n-period life of the bond. This is a restatement of the expectations theory in more precise terms.[1]

APPLICATION   Expectations Theory and the Yield Curve

The one-year interest rate over the next five years is expected to be 5%, 6%, 7%, 8%, and 9%. Given this information, what are the interest rates on a two-year bond and a five-year bond? Explain what is happening to the yield curve.

Solution

The interest rate on the two-year bond would be 5.5%.

$$i_{nt} = \frac{i_t + i_{t+1}^e + i_{t+2}^e + \cdots + i_{t+(n-1)}^e}{n}$$

where

$$i_t = \text{year 1 interest rate} = 5\%$$

$$i_{t+1}^e = \text{year 2 interest rate} = 6\%$$

$$n = \text{number of years} = 2$$

Thus

$$i_{2t} = \frac{5\% + 6\%}{2} = 5.5\%$$

The interest rate on the five-year bond would be 7%.

$$i_{nt} = \frac{i_t + i_{t+1}^e + i_{t+2}^e + \cdots + i_{t+(n-1)}^e}{n}$$

where

$$i_t = \text{year 1 interest rate} = 5\%$$

$$i_{t+1}^e = \text{year 2 interest rate} = 6\%$$

$$i_{t+2}^e = \text{year 3 interest rate} = 7\%$$

$$i_{t+3}^e = \text{year 4 interest rate} = 8\%$$

$$i_{t+4}^e = \text{year 5 interest rate} = 9\%$$

$$n = \text{number of years} = 5$$

---

[1] The analysis here has been conducted for discount bonds. Formulas for interest rates on coupon bonds would differ slightly from those used here but would convey the same principle.

Thus

$$i_{5t} = \frac{5\% + 6\% + 7\% + 8\% + 9\%}{5} = 7.0\%$$

Using the same equation for the one-, three-, and four-year interest rates, you will be able to verify the one-year to five-year rates as 5.0%, 5.5%, 6.0%, 6.5%, and 7.0%, respectively. The rising trend in short-term interest rates produces an upward-sloping yield curve along which interest rates rise as maturity lengthens.

The expectations theory is an elegant theory that explains why the term structure of interest rates (as represented by yield curves) changes at different times. When the yield curve is upward-sloping, the expectations theory suggests that short-term interest rates are expected to rise in the future, as we have seen in our numerical example. In this situation, in which the long-term rate is currently above the short-term rate, the average of future short-term rates is expected to be higher than the current short-term rate, which can occur only if short-term interest rates are expected to rise. This is what we see in our numerical example. When the yield curve is inverted (slopes downward), the average of future short-term interest rates is expected to be below the current short-term rate, implying that short-term interest rates are expected to fall, on average, in the future. Only when the yield curve is flat does the expectations theory suggest that short-term interest rates are not expected to change, on average, in the future.

The expectations theory also explains fact 1, that interest rates on bonds with different maturities move together over time. Historically, short-term interest rates have had the characteristic that if they increase today, they will tend to be higher in the future. Hence, a rise in short-term rates will raise people's expectations of future short-term rates. Because long-term rates are the average of expected future short-term rates, a rise in short-term rates will also raise long-term rates, causing short- and long-term rates to move together.

The expectations theory also explains fact 2, that yield curves tend to have an upward slope when short-term interest rates are low and are inverted when short-term rates are high. When short-term rates are low, people generally expect them to rise to some normal level in the future, and the average of future expected short-term rates is high relative to the current short-term rate. Therefore, long-term interest rates will be substantially above current short-term rates, and the yield curve would then have an upward slope. Conversely, if short-term rates are high, people usually expect them to come back down. Long-term rates would then drop below short-term rates because the average of expected future short-term rates would be below current short-term rates and the yield curve would slope downward and become inverted.[2]

---

[2] The expectations theory explains another important fact about the relationship between short-term and long-term interest rates. As you can see looking back at Figure 6-4, short-term interest rates are more volatile than long-term rates. If interest rates are *mean-reverting*—that is, if they tend to head back down after they are at unusually high levels or go back up when they are at unusually low levels—then an average of these short-term rates must necessarily have lower volatility than the short-term rates themselves. Because the expectations theory suggests that the long-term rate will be an average of future short-term rates, it implies that the long-term rate will have lower volatility than short-term rates.

The expectations theory is an attractive theory because it provides a simple explanation of the behaviour of the term structure, but unfortunately it has a major shortcoming: it cannot explain fact 3, that yield curves usually slope upward. The typical upward slope of yield curves implies that short-term interest rates are usually expected to rise in the future. In practice, short-term interest rates are just as likely to fall as they are to rise, and so the expectations theory suggests that the typical yield curve should be flat rather than upward-sloping.

Segmented Markets Theory

As the name suggests, the **segmented markets theory** of the term structure sees markets for different-maturity bonds as completely separate and segmented. The interest rate for each bond with a different maturity is then determined by the supply of and demand for that bond with no effects from expected returns on other bonds with other maturities.

The key assumption in the segmented markets theory is that bonds of different maturities are not substitutes at all, so the expected return from holding a bond of one maturity has no effect on the demand for a bond of another maturity. This theory of the term structure is at the opposite extreme to the expectations theory, which assumes that bonds of different maturities are perfect substitutes.

The argument for why bonds of different maturities are not substitutes is that investors have very strong preferences for bonds of one maturity but not for another, so they will be concerned with the expected returns only for bonds of the maturity they prefer. This might occur because they have a particular holding period in mind, and if they match the maturity of the bond to the desired holding period, they can obtain a certain return with no risk at all.[3] (We have seen in Chapter 4 that if the term to maturity equals the holding period, the return is known for certain because it equals the yield exactly, and there is no interest-rate risk.) For example, people who have a short holding period would prefer to hold short-term bonds. Conversely, if you were putting funds away for your young child to go to college, your desired holding period might be much longer, and you would want to hold longer-term bonds.

In the segmented markets theory, differing yield curve patterns are accounted for by supply and demand differences associated with bonds of different maturities. If, as seems sensible, investors have short desired holding periods and generally prefer bonds with shorter maturities that have less interest-rate risk, the segmented markets theory can explain fact 3, that yield curves typically slope upward. Because in the typical situation the demand for long-term bonds is relatively lower than that for short-term bonds, long-term bonds will have lower prices and higher interest rates, and hence the yield curve will typically slope upward.

Although the segmented markets theory can explain why yield curves usually tend to slope upward, it has a major flaw in that it cannot explain facts 1 and 2. Because it views the market for bonds of different maturities as completely segmented, there is no reason for a rise in interest rates on a bond of one maturity to

[3] The statement that there is no uncertainty about the return if the term to maturity equals the holding period is literally true only for a discount bond. For a coupon bond with a long holding period, there is some risk because coupon payments must be reinvested before the bond matures. Our analysis here is thus being conducted for discount bonds. However, the gist of the analysis remains the same for coupon bonds because the amount of this risk from reinvestment is small when coupon bonds have the same term to maturity as the holding period.

affect the interest rate on a bond of another maturity. Therefore, it cannot explain why interest rates on bonds of different maturities tend to move together (fact 1). Second, because it is not clear how demand and supply for short- versus long-term bonds change with the level of short-term interest rates, the theory cannot explain why yield curves tend to slope upward when short-term interest rates are low and to be inverted when short-term interest rates are high (fact 2).

Because each of our two theories explains empirical facts that the other cannot, a logical step is to combine the theories, which leads us to the liquidity premium and preferred habitat theories.

Liquidity Premium and Preferred Habitat Theories

The **liquidity premium theory** of the term structure states that the interest rate on a long-term bond will equal an average of short-term interest rates expected to occur over the life of the long-term bond plus a liquidity premium (also referred to as a term premium) that responds to supply and demand conditions for that bond.

The liquidity premium theory's key assumption is that bonds of different maturities are substitutes, which means that the expected return on one bond *does* influence the expected return on a bond of a different maturity, but it allows investors to prefer one bond maturity over another. In other words, bonds of different maturities are assumed to be substitutes but not perfect substitutes. Investors tend to prefer shorter-term bonds because these bonds bear less interest-rate risk. For these reasons, investors must be offered a positive liquidity premium to induce them to hold longer-term bonds. Such an outcome would modify the expectations theory by adding a positive liquidity premium to the equation that describes the relationship between long- and short-term interest rates. The liquidity premium theory is thus written as:

$$i_{nt} = \frac{i_t + i^e_{t+1} + i^e_{t+2} + \cdots + i^e_{t+(n-1)}}{n} + l_{nt} \tag{3}$$

where l_{nt} = the liquidity (term) premium for the n-period bond at time t, which is always positive and rises with the term to maturity of the bond, n.

Closely related to the liquidity premium theory is the **preferred habitat theory**, which takes a somewhat less-direct approach to modifying the expectations hypothesis but comes up with a similar conclusion. It assumes that investors have a preference for bonds of one maturity over another, a particular bond maturity (preferred habitat) in which they prefer to invest. Because they prefer bonds of one maturity over another, they will be willing to buy bonds that do not have the preferred maturity (habitat) only if they earn a somewhat higher expected return. Because investors are likely to prefer the habitat of short-term bonds to that of longer-term bonds, they are willing to hold long-term bonds only if they have higher expected returns. This reasoning leads to the same Equation 3 implied by the liquidity premium theory with a term premium that typically rises with maturity.

The relationship between the expectations theory and the liquidity premium and preferred habitat theories is shown in Figure 6-5. There we see that because the liquidity premium is always positive and typically grows as the term to maturity increases, the yield curve implied by the liquidity premium and preferred habitat theories is always above the yield curve implied by the expectations theory and has a steeper slope. (Note that for simplicity we are assuming that the expectations theory yield curve is flat.)

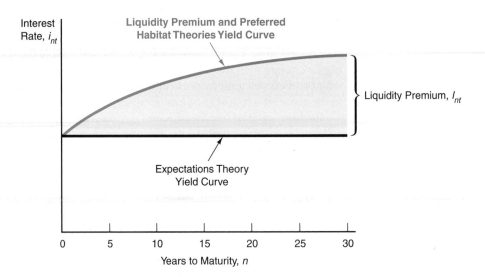

FIGURE 6-5   The Relationship Between the Liquidity Premium and Preferred Habitat Theories and Expectations Theory

Because the liquidity premium is always positive and grows as the term to maturity increases, the yield curve implied by the liquidity premium and preferred habitat theories is always above the yield curve implied by the expectations theory and has a steeper slope. Note that the yield curve implied by the expectations theory is drawn under the scenario of unchanging future one-year interest rates.

APPLICATION   Liquidity Premium Theory

Let's suppose that the one-year interest rate over the next five years is expected to be 5%, 6%, 7%, 8%, and 9%. Investors' preferences for holding short-term bonds have the liquidity premiums for one-year to five-year bonds as 0%, 0.25%, 0.5%, 0.75%, and 1.0%, respectively. What is the interest rate on a two-year bond and a five-year bond? Compare these findings with the answer in the previous Application dealing with the pure expectations theory.

Solution   The interest rate on the two-year bond would be 5.75%.

$$i_{nt} = \frac{i_t + i_{t+1}^e + i_{t+2}^e + \cdots + i_{t+(n-1)}^e}{n} + l_{nt}$$

where

$$i_t = \text{year 1 interest rate} = 5\%$$
$$i_{t+1}^e = \text{year 2 interest rate} = 6\%$$
$$l_{2t} = \text{liquidity premium} = 0.25\%$$
$$n = \text{number of years} = 2$$

Thus

$$i_{2t} = \frac{5\% + 6\%}{2} + 0.25\% = 5.75\%$$

The interest rate on the five-year bond would be 8%.

$$i_{nt} = \frac{i_t + i_{t+1}^e + i_{t+2}^e + \cdots + i_{t+(n-1)}^e}{n} + l_{nt}$$

where

$$i_t = \text{year 1 interest rate} = 5\%$$
$$i_{t+1}^e = \text{year 2 interest rate} = 6\%$$
$$i_{t+2}^e = \text{year 3 interest rate} = 7\%$$
$$i_{t+3}^e = \text{year 4 interest rate} = 8\%$$
$$i_{t+4}^e = \text{year 5 interest rate} = 9\%$$
$$l_{5t} = \text{liquidity premium} = 1\%$$
$$n = \text{number of years} = 5$$

Thus

$$i_{5t} = \frac{5\% + 6\% + 7\% + 8\% + 9\%}{5} + 1\% = 8.0\%$$

If you did similar calculations for the one-, three-, and four-year interest rates, the one-year to five-year interest rates would be as follows: 5.0%, 5.75%, 6.5%, 7.25%, and 8.0%, respectively. Comparing these findings with those for the pure expectations theory, we can see that the liquidity preference theory produces yield curves that slope more steeply upward because of investors' preferences for short-term bonds.

Let's see if the liquidity premium and preferred habitat theories are consistent with all three empirical facts we have discussed. They explain fact 1, that interest rates on different-maturity bonds move together over time: a rise in short-term interest rates indicates that short-term interest rates will, on average, be higher in the future, and the first term in Equation 3 then implies that long-term interest rates will rise along with them.

They also explain why yield curves tend to have an especially steep upward slope when short-term interest rates are low and to be inverted when short-term rates are high (fact 2). Because investors generally expect short-term interest rates to rise to some normal level when they are low, the average of future expected short-term rates will be high relative to the current short-term rate. With the additional boost of a positive liquidity premium, long-term interest rates will be substantially above current short-term rates, and the yield curve would then have a steep upward slope. Conversely, if short-term rates are high, people usually expect them to come back down. Long-term rates would then drop below short-term rates because the average of expected future short-term rates would be so far below current short-term rates that despite positive liquidity premiums, the yield curve would slope downward.

The liquidity premium and preferred habitat theories explain fact 3, that yield curves typically slope upward, by recognizing that the liquidity premium rises with a bond's maturity because of investors' preferences for short-term bonds. Even if short-term interest rates are expected to stay the same on average in the future, long-term interest rates will be above short-term interest rates, and yield curves will typically slope upward.

How can the liquidity premium and preferred habitat theories explain the occasional appearance of inverted yield curves if the liquidity premium is positive? It must be that at times short-term interest rates are expected to fall so much in the future that the average of the expected short-term rates is well below the current short-term rate. Even when the positive liquidity premium is added to this average, the resulting long-term rate will still be below the current short-term interest rate.

As our discussion indicates, a particularly attractive feature of the liquidity premium and preferred habitat theories is that they tell you what the market is predicting about future short-term interest rates just from the slope of the yield curve. A steeply rising yield curve, as in panel (a) of Figure 6-6, indicates that short-term interest rates are expected to rise in the future. A moderately steep yield curve, as in panel (b), indicates that short-term interest rates are not expected to rise or fall much in the future. A flat yield curve, as in panel (c), indicates that short-term rates are expected to fall moderately in the future. Finally,

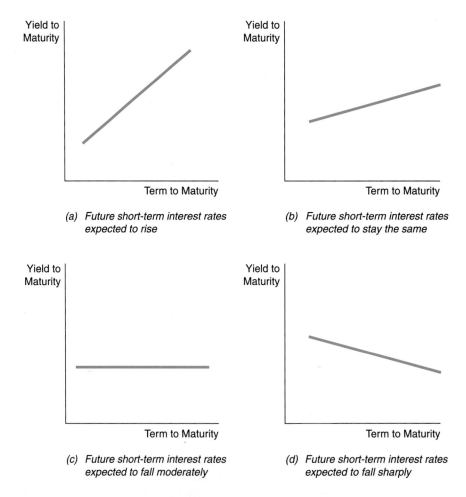

(a) *Future short-term interest rates expected to rise*

(b) *Future short-term interest rates expected to stay the same*

(c) *Future short-term interest rates expected to fall moderately*

(d) *Future short-term interest rates expected to fall sharply*

FIGURE 6-6   Yield Curves and the Market's Expectations of Future Short-Term Interest Rates According to the Liquidity Premium and Preferred Habitat Theories

an inverted yield curve, as in panel (d), indicates that short-term interest rates are expected to fall sharply in the future.

The Predictive Power of the Yield Curve

People often think that the slope of the yield curve can be used to forecast future short-term interest rates. The yield curve has this practical use only if it is determined by the expectations theory of the term structure that views long-term interest rates as equalling the average of future short-term interest rates. If, however, there are liquidity (term) premiums in the term structure, then it will be difficult to extract a reliable forecast of future short-term interest rates without good measures of these premiums.

In the 1980s, researchers examining the term structure of interest rates questioned whether the slope of the yield curve provides information about movements of future short-term interest rates.[4] They found that the spread between long- and short-term interest rates does not always help predict future short-term interest rates, a finding that may stem from substantial fluctuations in the liquidity (term) premium for long-term bonds. More recent research using more discriminating tests now favours a different view. It shows that the term structure contains quite a bit of information for the very short run (over the next several months) and the long run (over several years) but is unreliable at predicting movements in interest rates over the intermediate term (the time in between).[5] Research also finds that the yield curve helps forecast future inflation and business cycles (see the FYI box).

Summary

The liquidity premium and preferred habitat theories are the most widely accepted theories of the term structure of interest rates because they explain the major empirical facts about the term structure so well. They combine the features of both the expectations theory and the segmented markets theory by asserting that a long-term interest rate will be the sum of a liquidity (term) premium and the average of the short-term interest rates that are expected to occur over the life of the bond.

The liquidity premium and preferred habitat theories explain the following facts: (1) Interest rates on bonds of different maturities tend to move together over time, (2) yield curves usually slope upward, and (3) when short-term interest rates are low, yield curves are more likely to have a steep upward slope, whereas when short-term interest rates are high, yield curves are more likely to be inverted.

The theories also help us predict the movement of short-term interest rates in the future. A steep upward slope of the yield curve means that short-term rates are expected to rise, a mild upward slope means that short-term rates are expected to

---

[4] Robert J. Shiller, John Y. Campbell, and Kermit L. Schoenholtz, "Forward Rates and Future Policy: Interpreting the Term Structure of Interest Rates," *Brookings Papers on Economic Activity* 1 (1983): 173–217; N. Gregory Mankiw and Lawrence H. Summers, "Do Long-Term Interest Rates Overreact to Short-Term Interest Rates?" *Brookings Papers on Economic Activity* 1 (1984): 223–242.

[5] Eugene Fama, "The Information in the Term Structure," *Journal of Financial Economics* 13 (1984): 509–528; Eugene Fama and Robert Bliss, "The Information in Long-Maturity Forward Rates," *American Economic Review* 77 (1987): 680–692; John Y. Campbell and Robert J. Shiller, "Cointegration and Tests of the Present Value Models," *Journal of Political Economy* 95 (1987): 1062–1088; John Y. Campbell and Robert J. Shiller, "Yield Spreads and Interest Rate Movements: A Bird's Eye View," *Review of Economic Studies* 58 (1991): 495–514.

FYI

The Yield Curve as a Forecasting Tool for Inflation and the Business Cycle

Because the yield curve contains information about future expected interest rates, it should also have the capacity to help forecast inflation and real output fluctuations. To see this, recall from Chapter 5 that rising interest rates are associated with economic booms and falling interest rates with recessions. When the yield curve is either flat or negatively sloped, it suggests that future short-term interest rates will be falling and therefore that the economy is more likely to enter a recession. Indeed, the yield curve is found to be an accurate predictor of the business cycle.[1]

In Chapter 4, we also learned that a nominal interest rate is composed of a real interest rate and expected inflation, implying that the yield curve contains information not only about the future path of nominal interest rates, but about future inflation as well. A steep yield curve does predict a future rise in inflation, while a flat or negatively sloped yield curve forecasts a future fall in inflation.[2]

The ability of the yield curve to forecast business cycles and inflation is one reason why the slope of the yield curve is in the toolkit of many economic forecasters and is often viewed as a useful indicator of the stance of monetary policy, with a steep yield curve indicating loose policy and a flat or negatively sloped yield curve indicating tight policy.

[1] E.g., see Arturo Estrella and Frederic S. Mishkin, "Predicting U.S. Recessions: Financial Variables As Leading Indicators," *Review of Economics and Statistics* 80 (February 1998): 45–61.

[2] Frederic S. Mishkin, "What Does the Term Structure Tell Us About Future Inflation?" *Journal of Monetary Economics* 25 (January 1990): 77–95; and "The Information in the Longer-Maturity Term Structure About Future Inflation," *Quarterly Journal of Economics* 55 (August 1990): 815–28.

remain the same, a flat slope means that short-term rates are expected to fall moderately, and an inverted yield curve means that short-term rates are expected to fall sharply.

APPLICATION   Interpreting Yield Curves, 1990–2009

Figure 6-7 illustrates several yield curves that have appeared for Canadian government bonds in recent years. What do these yield curves tell us about the public's expectations of future movements of short-term interest rates?

The inverted yield curve that occurred in January 1990 indicated that short-term interest rates were expected to decline sharply in the future. In order for longer-term interest rates with their positive liquidity premium to be well below the short-term interest rate, short-term interest rates must be expected to decline so sharply that their average is far below the current short-term rate. Indeed, the public's expectations of sharply lower short-term interest rates evident in the yield curve were realized soon after January 1990; by March 1991, three-month treasury bill rates had declined from over 12% to less than 9%.

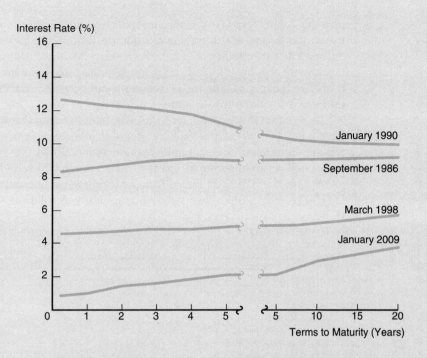

FIGURE 6-7   Yield Curves for Government of Canada Bonds, 1986–2009

Source: Statistics Canada CANSIM II Series V122531, V122532, V122533, V122538, V122539, V122540, V122543, and V122544, and the authors' calculations.

The upward-sloping yield curve in January 2009 indicates that short-term interest rates would climb in the future. The long-term interest rate is above the short-term interest rate when short-term interest rates are expected to rise because their average plus the liquidity premium will be above the current short-term rate. The moderately upward-sloping yield curve in September 1986 indicates that short-term interest rates were expected neither to rise nor to fall in the near future. In this case, their average remains the same as the current short-term rate, and the positive liquidity premium for longer-term bonds explains the moderate upward slope of the yield curve.

APPLICATION   Using the Term Structure to Forecast Interest Rates

Interest-rate forecasts are extremely important to managers of financial institutions because future changes in interest rates have a significant impact on the profitability of their institutions. Furthermore, interest-rate forecasts are needed when managers of financial institutions have to set interest rates on loans that are promised to customers in the future. Our discussion of the term structure of interest rates has indicated that the slope of the yield curve provides general information about the market's prediction of the future path of interest rates. For example, a steeply upward-sloping yield curve indicates that short-term interest rates are predicted to rise in the future, and a downward-sloping yield curve indicates that short-term interest rates are predicted to fall. However, a financial institution manager needs much more specific information on interest-rate forecasts than this. Here we show how the manager of a financial institution can generate specific forecasts of interest rates using the term structure.

To see how this is done, let's start the analysis using the approach we took in developing the expectations theory. Recall that because bonds of different maturities are considered perfect substitutes, we assumed that the expected return over two periods from investing \$1 in a two-period bond, which is $(1 + i_{2t})(1 + i_{2t}) - 1$, must equal the expected return from investing \$1 in one-period bonds, which is $(1 + i_t)(1 + i_{t+1}^e) - 1$. This is shown graphically as follows:

Today   Year   Year
0   1   2

$\longleftarrow 1 + i_t \longrightarrow \quad \longleftarrow 1 + i_{t+1}^e \longrightarrow$

$\longleftarrow (1 + i_{2t})(1 + i_{2t}) \longrightarrow$

In other words,

$$(1 + i_t)(1 + i_{t+1}^e) - 1 = (1 + i_{2t})(1 + i_{2t}) - 1$$

Through some tedious algebra we can solve for i_{t+1}^e:

$$i_{t+1}^e = \frac{(1 + i_{2t})^2}{1 + i_t} - 1 \tag{4}$$

This measure of i_{t+1}^e is called the **forward rate** because it is the one-period interest rate that the pure expectations theory of the term structure indicates is expected to prevail one period in the future. To differentiate forward rates derived from the term structure from actual interest rates that are observed at time t, we call these observed interest rates **spot rates**.

Going back to the Application Expectations Theory and the Yield Curve (p. 124), which we used to discuss the expectations theory earlier in this chapter, at time t the one-year interest rate is 5% and the two-year rate is 5.5%. Plugging these numbers into Equation 4 yields the following estimate of the forward rate one period in the future:

$$i_{t+1}^e = \frac{(1 + 0.055)^2}{1 + 0.05} - 1 = 0.06 = 6\%$$

Not surprisingly, this 6% forward rate is identical to the expected one-year interest rate one year in the future. This is exactly what we should find, as our calculation here is just another way of looking at the pure expectations theory.

We can also compare holding the three-year bond against holding a sequence of one-year bonds, which reveals the following relationship:

$$(1 + i_t)(1 + i_{t+1}^e)(1 + i_{t+2}^e) - 1 = (1 + i_{3t})(1 + i_{3t})(1 + i_{3t}) - 1$$

and plugging in the estimate for i_{t+1}^e derived in Equation 4, we can solve for i_{t+2}^e:

$$i_{t+2}^e = \frac{(1 + i_{3t})^3}{(1 + i_{2t})^2} - 1$$

Continuing with these calculations, we obtain the general solution for the forward rate n periods into the future:

$$i^e_{t+n} = \frac{(1 + i_{n+1t})^{n+1}}{(1 + i_{nt})^n} - 1 \tag{5}$$

Our discussion indicated that the expectations theory is not entirely satisfactory because investors must be compensated with liquidity premiums to induce them to hold longer-term bonds. Hence, we need to modify our analysis, as we did when discussing the liquidity premium theory, by allowing for these liquidity premiums in estimating predictions of future interest rates.

Recall from the discussion of those theories that because investors prefer to hold short-term rather than long-term bonds, the n-period interest rate differs from that indicated by the pure expectations theory by a liquidity premium of ℓ_{nt}. So to allow for liquidity premiums, we need merely subtract ℓ_{nt} from i_{nt} in our formula to derive i^e_{t+n}:

$$i^e_{t+n} = \frac{(1 + i_{n+1t} - \ell_{n+1t})^{n+1}}{(1 + i_{nt} - \ell_{nt})^n} - 1 \tag{6}$$

This measure of i^e_{t+n} is referred to, naturally enough, as the *adjusted forward-rate forecast.*

In the case of i^e_{t+1}, Equation 6 produces the following estimate:

$$i^e_{t+1} = \frac{(1 + i_{2t} - \ell_{2t})^2}{1 + i_t} - 1$$

Using the example from the Liquidity Premium Theory Application on page 128, at time t the ℓ_{2t} liquidity premium is 0.25%, $\ell_{1t} = 0$, the one-year interest rate is 5%, and the two-year interest rate is 5.75%. Plugging these numbers into our equation yields the following adjusted forward-rate forecast for one period in the future:

$$i^e_{t+1} = \frac{(1 + 0.0575 - 0.0025)^2}{1 + 0.05} - 1 = 0.06 = 6\%$$

which is the same as the expected interest rate used in the Application on expectations theory, as it should be.

Our analysis of the term structure thus provides managers of financial institutions with a fairly straightforward procedure for producing interest-rate forecasts. First they need to estimate ℓ_{nt}, the values of the liquidity premiums for various n. Then they need merely apply the formula in Equation 6 to derive the market's forecasts of future interest rates.

A customer asks a bank if it would be willing to commit to making the customer a one-year loan at an interest rate of 8% one year from now. To compensate for the costs of making the loan, the bank needs to charge one percentage point more than the expected interest rate on a Canada bond with the same maturity if it is to make a profit. If the bank manager estimates the liquidity premium to be 0.4%, and the one-year Canada bond rate is 6% and the two-year bond rate is 7%, should the manager be willing to make the commitment?

Solution

The bank manager is unable to make the loan because at an interest rate of 8%, the loan is likely to be unprofitable to the bank.

$$i^e_{t+n} = \frac{(1 + i_{n+1t} - \ell_{n+1t})^{n+1}}{(1 + i_{nt} - \ell_{nt})^n} - 1$$

where

$$
\begin{aligned}
i_{n+1t} &= \text{two-year bond rate} &&= 0.07 \\
\ell_{n+1t} &= \text{liquidity premium} &&= 0.004 \\
i_{nt} &= \text{one-year bond rate} &&= 0.06 \\
\ell_{1t} &= \text{liquidity premium} &&= 0 \\
n &= \text{number of years} &&= 1
\end{aligned}
$$

Thus

$$i^e_{t+1} = \frac{(1 + 0.07 - 0.004)^2}{1 + 0.06} - 1 = 0.072 = 7.2\%$$

The market's forecast of the one-year Canada bond rate one year in the future is therefore 7.2%. Adding the 1% necessary to make a profit on the one-year loan means that the loan is expected to be profitable only if it has an interest rate of 8.2% or higher.

SUMMARY

1. Bonds with the same maturity will have different interest rates because of three factors: default risk, liquidity, and tax considerations. The greater a bond's default risk, the higher its interest rate relative to other bonds; the greater a bond's liquidity, the lower its interest rate; and bonds with tax-exempt status will have lower interest rates than they otherwise would. The relationship among interest rates on bonds with the same maturity that arises because of these three factors is known as the risk structure of interest rates.

2. Four theories of the term structure provide explanations of how interest rates on bonds with different terms to maturity are related. The expectations theory views long-term interest rates as equalling the average

of future short-term interest rates expected to occur over the life of the bond; by contrast, the segmented markets theory treats the determination of interest rates for each bond's maturity as the outcome of supply and demand in each market in isolation. Neither of these theories by itself can explain the fact that interest rates on bonds of different maturities move together over time and that yield curves usually slope upward.

3. The liquidity premium and preferred habitat theories combine the features of the other two theories and by so doing are able to explain the facts just mentioned. They view long-term interest rates as equalling the average of future short-term interest rates expected to

occur over the life of the bond plus a liquidity premium. These theories allow us to infer the market's expectations about the movement of future short-term interest rates from the yield curve. A steeply upward-sloping curve indicates that future short-term rates are expected to rise, a mildly upward-sloping curve indicates that short-term rates are expected to stay the same, a flat curve indicates that short-term rates are expected to decline slightly, and an inverted yield curve indicates that a substantial decline in short-term rates is expected in the future.

KEY TERMS

basis point,   p. 117

credit-rating agencies,   p. 115

default-free bonds,   p. 114

expectations theory,   p. 121

fallen angels,   p. 116

forward rate   p. 134

inverted yield curve,   p. 120

junk bonds,   p. 116

liquidity premium theory,   p. 127

preferred habitat theory,   p. 127

risk of default, p. 114

risk premium,   p. 114

risk structure of interest rates,   p. 113

segmented markets theory,   p. 126

spot rate   p. 134

term structure of interest rates,   p. 113

yield curve,   p. 119

QUESTIONS

You will find the answers to the questions marked with an asterisk in the Textbook Resources section of your MyEconLab.

1. Which should have the higher risk premium on its interest rates, a corporate bond with an S&P BBB rating or a corporate bond with a C rating? Why?

*2. Why do Canadian treasury bills have lower interest rates than large-denomination negotiable bank CDs?

3. Risk premiums on corporate bonds are usually anti-cyclical; that is, they decrease during business cycle expansions and increase during recessions. Why is this so?

*4. "If bonds of different maturities are close substitutes, their interest rates are more likely to move together." Is this statement true, false, or uncertain? Explain your answer.

5. If yield curves, on average, were flat, what would this say about the liquidity (term) premiums in the term structure? Would you be more or less willing to accept the expectations theory?

*6. If a yield curve looks like the one shown in (a), what is the market predicting about the movement of future short-term interest rates? What might the yield curve indicate about the market's predictions about the inflation rate in the future?

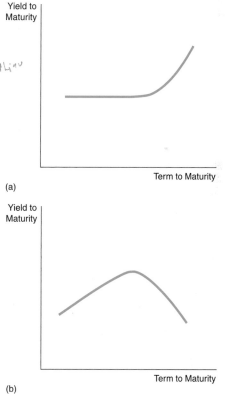

(a)

(b)

7. If a yield curve looks like the one shown in (b), what is the market predicting about the movement of future short-term interest rates? What might the yield curve indicate about the market's predictions about the inflation rate in the future?

*8. What are the financial implications of a firm with a high default risk?

Predicting the Future

9. Predict what will happen to interest rates on a corporation's bonds if the federal government guarantees today that it will pay creditors if the corporation goes bankrupt in the future. What will happen to the interest rates on Canada bonds?

*10. Predict what would happen to the risk premiums on corporate bonds if brokerage commissions were lowered in the corporate bond market.

11. Predict what would happen to yield spreads in response to the following macroeconomic events: recession, high inflation, and stock market increase.

*12. If the yield curve suddenly becomes steeper, how would you revise your predictions of interest rates in the future?

13. If expectations of future short-term interest rates suddenly fall, what would happen to the slope of the yield curve?

QUANTITATIVE PROBLEMS

*1. Assuming that the expectations theory is the correct theory of the term structure, calculate the interest rates in the term structure for maturities of one to five years, and plot the resulting yield curves for the following series of one-year interest rates over the next five years:
(a) 5%, 7%, 7%, 7%, 7%
(b) 5%, 4%, 4%, 4%, 4%
How would your yield curves change if people preferred shorter-term bonds to longer-term bonds?

2. Assuming that the expectations theory is the correct theory of the term structure, calculate the interest rates in the term structure for maturities of one to five years, and plot the resulting yield curves for the following path of one-year interest rates over the next five years:
(a) 5%, 6%, 7%, 6%, 5%
(b) 5%, 4%, 3%, 4%, 5%
How would your yield curves change if people preferred shorter-term bonds to longer-term bonds?

*3. Rates on one-year T-bills over the next four years are expected to be 3%, 4%, 5%, and 5.5%. If four-year Canada bonds are yielding 4.5%, what is the liquidity premium on this bond?

4. Suppose that you are forecasting one-year T-bill rates as follows:

Year	1-year rate (%)
1	4.25
2	5.15
3	5.50
4	6.25
5	7.10

You have a liquidity premium of 0.25% for the next year and 0.50% thereafter. Would you be willing to purchase a four-year Canada bond at a 5.75% interest rate?

CANSIM Questions

5. Get the monthly data from 1978 to 2006 on the three-month T-bill rate (CANSIM series V122531), the interest rate on long-term corporate bonds (series V122518), and the interest rate on long-term Canada bonds (series V122544) from the Textbook Resources area of the MyEconLab.

   a. Present a time series plot of these interest rate series and comment on their long-run movements.

   b. Calculate the mean and standard deviation as well as the maximum and minimum values for each series over the sample period.

   c. Which were the worst and best years in terms of interest rates?

6. Get the monthly data from 1978 to 2006 on long-term Canada bonds (CANSIM series V122544), the interest rate on long-term provincial bonds (series V122517), and the interest rate on long-term corporate bonds (series V122518) from the Textbook Resources area of the MyEconLab.

   a. Present a time series plot of these interest rates and comment on their long-term movements.

   b. Which series exhibit the strongest correlations? The weakest? Do the correlation patterns you identified here manifest in the graphical representation of the series?

   c. Compare the contemporaneous correlations over the whole period with those in the 1960s, 1970s, 1980s, 1990s, and 2000s.

   d. Calculate the corporate-Canada spread and the corporate-provincials spread and plot these series.

   e. Continuing from (d), comment on the time paths of the risk premiums.

WEB EXERCISES

1. Go to **www.bloomberg.com** and click on "Market Data" and then "Rates & Bonds" to find information about the yield curve in Australia, Brazil, Germany, Hong Kong, Japan, the United Kingdom, and the United States. What does each of these yield curves tell us about the public's expectations of future movements of short-term interest rates?

2. Investment companies attempt to explain to investors the nature of the risk the investor incurs when buying shares in their mutual funds. For example, Vanguard (a U.S. company) carefully explains interest rate risk and offers alternative funds with different interest rate risks. Go to **http://flagship.vanguard.com/VGApp/ hnw/FundsStocksOverview**.

   a. Select the bond fund you would recommend to an investor who has very low tolerance for risk and a short investment horizon. Justify your answer.

   b. Select the bond fund you would recommend to an investor who has very high tolerance for risk and a long investment horizon. Justify your answer.

Be sure to visit the MyEconLab website at **www.myeconlab.com**. This online homework and tutorial system puts you in control of your own learning with study and practice tools directly correlated to this chapter content.

On the MyEconLab website you will find the following mini-case for this chapter:
Mini-Case 6.1: Yield Curve Hypotheses and the Effects of Economic Events

CHAPTER 7

The Stock Market, the Theory of Rational Expectations, and the Efficient Market Hypothesis

LEARNING OBJECTIVES

After studying this chapter you should be able to

1. illustrate how stocks are valued as the present value of dividends
2. determine how information in the market affects asset prices: the theory of efficient capital markets, according to which current asset prices fully reflect all available information

PREVIEW

Rarely does a day go by that the stock market isn't a major news item. We have witnessed huge swings in the stock market in recent years. The 1990s were an extraordinary decade for stocks: the S&P/TSX Composite in Canada and the Dow Jones and S&P 500 indexes in the United States increased more than 400%, while the tech-laden NASDAQ index rose more than 1000%. By May 2002, these indexes had reached record highs. Unfortunately, the good times did not last, and many investors lost their shirts in the recent spectacular decline of the stock market.

Because so many people invest in the stock market and the price of stocks affects the ability of people to retire comfortably, the market for stocks is undoubtedly the financial market that receives the most attention and scrutiny. In this chapter, we look first at how this important market works.

We begin by discussing the fundamental theories that underlie the valuation of stocks. These theories are critical to understanding the forces that cause the value of stocks to rise and fall minute by minute and day by day. Once we have learned the methods for stock valuation, we need to explore how expectations about the market affect its behaviour. We do so by examining the *theory of rational expectations*, which has more general implications for how markets in other securities besides stocks operate. When this theory is applied to financial markets, the outcome is the *efficient market hypothesis*. The theory of rational expectations is also central to debates about the conduct of monetary policy, to be discussed in Chapter 27.

COMPUTING THE PRICE OF COMMON STOCK

Common stock is the principal way that corporations raise equity capital. Holders of common stock own an interest in the corporation consistent with the percentage of outstanding shares owned. This ownership interest gives **shareholders**—those who hold stock in a corporation—a bundle of rights. The most important are the right to vote and to be the **residual claimant** of all funds flowing into the firm (known as **cash flows**), meaning that the stockholder receives whatever remains after all other claims against the firm's assets have been satisfied. Stockholders are paid dividends from the net earnings of the corporation. **Dividends** are payments made periodically, usually every quarter, to stockholders. The board of directors of the firm sets the level of the dividend, usually upon the recommendation of management. In addition, the stockholder has the right to sell the stock.

One basic principle of finance is that the value of any investment is found by computing the value today of all cash flows the investment will generate over its life. For example, a commercial building will sell for a price that reflects the net cash flows (rents – expenses) it is projected to have over its useful life. Similarly, we value common stock as the value in today's dollars of all future cash flows. The cash flows a stockholder might earn from stock are dividends, the sales price, or both. To develop the theory of stock valuation, we begin with the simplest possible scenario: you buy the stock, hold it for one period to get a dividend, and then sell the stock. We call this the *one-period valuation model.*

The One-Period Valuation Model

Suppose that you have some extra money to invest for one year. After a year, you will need to sell your investment to pay tuition. After watching the financial news on TV, you decide that you want to buy Royal Bank stock. You call your broker and find that Royal Bank is currently selling for $50 per share and pays $1.25 per year in dividends. The analyst on the financial news predicts that the stock will be selling for $60 in one year. Should you buy this stock?

To answer this question, you need to determine whether the current price accurately reflects the analyst's forecast. To value the stock today, you need to find the present discounted value of the expected cash flows (future payments) using the formula in Equation 1 of Chapter 4 (page 60). Note that in this equation, the discount factor used to discount the cash flows is the required return on investments in equity rather than the interest rate. The cash flows consist of one dividend payment plus a final sales price. When these cash flows are discounted back to the present, the following equation computes the current price of the stock:

$$P_0 = \frac{Div_1}{(1 + k_e)} + \frac{P_1}{(1 + k_e)} \tag{1}$$

where P_0 = the current price of the stock. The zero subscript refers to time period zero, or the present

Div_1 = the dividend paid at the end of year

k_e = the required return on investments in equity

P_1 = the price at the end of the first period; the assumed sales price of the stock

To see how Equation 1 works, let's compare the price of the Royal Bank stock given the figures reported above. You will need to know the required return on equity to find the present value of the cash flows. Since a stock is more risky than a bond, you will require a higher return than that offered in the bond market. Assume that after careful consideration you decide that you would be satisfied to earn 12% on the investment.

Solution

Putting the numbers into Equation 1 yields the following:

$$P_0 = \frac{\$1.25}{1 + 0.12} + \frac{\$60}{1 + 0.12} = \$1.12 + \$53.57 = \$54.69$$

Based on your analysis, you find that the stock is worth $54.69. Since the stock is currently available for $50 per share, you would choose to buy it. Why is the stock selling for less than $54.69? It may be because other investors place a different risk on the cash flows or estimate the cash flows to be less than you do.

The Generalized Dividend Valuation Model

Using the same concept, the one-period dividend valuation model can be extended to any number of periods: The value of stock is the present value of all future cash flows. The only cash flows that an investor will receive are dividends and a final sales price when the stock is ultimately sold in period n. The generalized multi-period formula for stock valuation can be written as:

$$P_0 = \frac{D_1}{(1 + k_e)^1} + \frac{D_2}{(1 + k_e)^2} + \cdots + \frac{D_n}{(1 + k_e)^n} + \frac{P_n}{(1 + k_e)^n} \quad (2)$$

If you tried to use Equation 2 to find the value of a share of stock, you would soon realize that you must first estimate the value the stock will have at some point in the future before you can estimate its value today. In other words, you must find P_n in order to find P_0. However, if P_n is far in the future, it will not affect P_0. For example, the present value of a share of stock that sells for $50 seventy-five years from now using a 12% discount rate is just one cent [$50/(1.12^{75}) = \$0.01]$. This reasoning implies that the current value of a share of stock can be calculated as simply the present value of the future dividend stream. The **generalized dividend model** is rewritten in Equation 3 without the final sales price:

$$P_0 = \sum_{t=1}^{\infty} \frac{D_n}{(1 + k_e)^t} \quad (3)$$

Consider the implications of Equation 3 for a moment. The generalized dividend model says that the price of stock is determined only by the present value of the dividends and that nothing else matters. Many stocks do not pay dividends, so how is it that these stocks have value? *Buyers of the stock expect that the firm will pay dividends someday.* Most of the time a firm institutes dividends as soon as it has completed the rapid growth phase of its life cycle.

The generalized dividend valuation model requires that we compute the present value of an infinite stream of dividends, a process that could be difficult, to say the least. Therefore, simplified models have been developed to make the calculations easier. One such model is the **Gordon growth model**, which assumes constant dividend growth.

The Gordon Growth Model

Many firms strive to increase their dividends at a constant rate each year. Equation 4 rewrites Equation 3 to reflect this constant growth in dividends:

$$P_0 = \frac{D_0 \times (1 + g)^1}{(1 + k_e)^1} + \frac{D_0 \times (1 + g)^2}{(1 + k_e)^2} + \cdots + \frac{D_0 \times (1 + g)^\infty}{(1 + k_e)^\infty} \tag{4}$$

where
D_0 = the most recent dividend paid
g = the expected constant growth rate in dividends
k_e = the required return on an investment in equity

Equation 4 has been simplified using algebra to obtain Equation 5.[1]

$$P_0 = \frac{D_0 \times (1 + g)}{(k_e - g)} = \frac{D_1}{(k_e - g)} \tag{5}$$

This model is useful for finding the value of stock, given a few assumptions:

1. *Dividends are assumed to continue growing at a constant rate forever.* Actually, as long as they are expected to grow at a constant rate for an extended period of time, the model should yield reasonable results. This is because errors about distant cash flows become small when discounted to the present.

2. *The growth rate is assumed to be less than the required return on equity, k_e.* Myron Gordon, in his development of the model, demonstrated that this is a reasonable assumption. In theory, if the growth rate were faster than the rate demanded by holders of the firm's equity, in the long run the firm would grow impossibly large.

---

[1] To generate Equation 5 from Equation 4, first multiply both sides of Equation 4 by $(1 + k_e)/(1 + g)$ and subtract Equation 4 from the result. This yields:

$$\frac{P_0 \times (1 + k_e)}{(1 + g)} - P_0 = D_0 - \frac{D_0 \times (1 + g)^\infty}{(1 + k_e)^\infty}$$

Assuming that k_e is greater than g, the term on the far right will approach zero and can be dropped. Thus, after factoring P_0 out of the left-hand side:

$$P_0 \times \left[\frac{1 + k_e}{1 + g} - 1 \right] = D_0$$

Next, simplify by combining terms to:

$$P_0 \times \frac{(1 + k_e) - (1 + g)}{1 + g} = D_0$$

$$P_0 = \frac{D_0 \times (1 + g)}{(k_e - g)} = \frac{D_1}{(k_e - g)}$$

Stock Valuation, Constant Growth

To see how Equation 5 works, let's compute the current market price of Coca-Cola stock, assuming dividends grow at a constant rate of 10.95%, $D_0 = \$1.00$, and the required return is 13%.

Solution

$$P_0 = \frac{D_0 \times (1 + g)}{k_e - g}$$

$$P_0 = \frac{\$1.00 \times (1.1095)}{0.13 - 0.1095}$$

$$P_0 = \frac{\$1.1095}{0.0205} = \$54.12$$

Coca-Cola stock should sell for $54.12 if the assumptions regarding the constant growth rate and required return are correct.

Price Earnings Valuation Method

Theoretically, the best method of stock valuation is the dividend valuation approach. Sometimes, however, it is difficult to apply. If a firm is not paying dividends or has a very erratic growth rate, the results may not be satisfactory. Other approaches to stock valuation are sometimes applied. Among the more popular is the price earnings ratio.

The **price earnings ratio (PE)** is a widely watched measure of how much the market is willing to pay for $1 of earnings from a firm. A high PE has two interpretations:

1. A higher than average PE may mean that the market expects earnings to rise in the future. This would return the PE to a more normal level.

2. A high PE may alternatively indicate that the market feels the firm's earnings are very low risk and is therefore willing to pay a premium for them.

The PE ratio can be used to estimate the value of a firm's stock. Note that algebraically the product of the PE ratio times expected earnings is the firm's stock price.

$$\frac{P}{E} \times E = P \qquad (6)$$

Firms in the same industry are expected to have similar PE ratios in the long run. The value of a firm's stock can be found by multiplying the average industry PE times the expected earnings per share.

APPLICATION	Stock Valuation, PE Ratio Approach

The average industry PE ratio for restaurants similar to Applebee's, a pub restaurant chain, is 23. What is the current price of Applebee's if earnings per share are projected to be $1.13?

Solution

Using Equation 6 and the data given we find:

$$P_0 = P/E \times E$$
$$P_0 = 23 \times \$1.13 = \$25.99$$

The PE ratio approach is especially useful for valuing privately held firms and firms that do not pay dividends. The weakness of the PE approach to valuation is that by using an industry average PE ratio, firm-specific factors that might contribute to a long-term PE ratio above or below the average are ignored in the analysis. A skilled analyst will adjust the PE ratio up or down to reflect unique characteristics of a firm when estimating its stock price.

HOW THE MARKET SETS STOCK PRICES

Suppose you went to an auto auction. The cars are available for inspection before the auction begins, and you find a little Mazda Miata that you like. You test-drive it in the parking lot and notice that it makes a few strange noises, but you decide that you would still like the car. You decide $5000 would be a fair price that would allow you to pay some repair bills should the noises turn out to be serious. You see that the auction is ready to begin, so you go in and wait for the Miata to enter.

Suppose there is another buyer who also spots the Miata. He test-drives the car and recognizes that the noises are simply the result of worn brake pads that he can fix himself at a nominal cost. He decides that the car is worth $7000. He also goes in and waits for the Miata to enter.

Who will buy the car and for how much? Suppose only the two of you are interested in the Miata. You begin the bidding at $4000. He ups your bid to $4500. You bid your top price of $5000. He counters with $5100. The price is now higher than you are willing to pay, so you stop bidding. The car is sold to the more-informed buyer for $5100.

This simple example raises a number of points. First, the price is set by the buyer willing to pay the highest price. The price is not necessarily the highest price the asset could fetch, but it is incrementally greater than what any other buyer is willing to pay. Second, the market price will be set by the buyer who can take best advantage of the asset. The buyer who purchased the car knew that he could fix the noise easily and cheaply. Because of this he was willing to pay more for the car than you were. The same concept holds for other assets. For example, a piece of property or a building will sell to the buyer who can put the asset to the most productive use.

Finally, the example shows the role played by information in asset pricing. Superior information about an asset can increase its value by reducing its risk. When you consider buying a stock, there are many unknowns about the future cash flows. The buyer who has the best information about these cash flows will discount them at a lower interest rate than will a buyer who is very uncertain.

Now let us apply these ideas to stock valuation. Suppose that you are considering the purchase of stock expected to pay a $2 dividend next year. Market analysts expect the firm to grow at 3% indefinitely. You are uncertain about both the constancy of the dividend stream and the accuracy of the estimated growth rate. To compensate yourself for this uncertainty (risk), you require a return of 15%.

Now suppose Jennifer, another investor, has spoken with industry insiders and feels more confident about the projected cash flows. Jennifer requires only a 12% return because her perceived risk is lower than yours. Bud, on the other hand, is dating the CEO of the company. He knows with more certainty what the future of the firm actually is, and thus requires only a 10% return.

What are the values each investor will give to the stock? Applying the Gordon growth model yields the following stock prices:

Investor	Discount Rate	Stock Price
You	15%	$16.67
Jennifer	12%	$22.22
Bud	10%	$28.57

You are willing to pay $16.67 for the stock. Jennifer would pay up to $22.22, and Bud would pay $28.57. The investor with the lowest perceived risk is willing to pay the most for the stock. If there were no other traders but these three, the market price would be between $22.22 and $28.57. If you already held the stock, you would sell it to Bud.

We thus see that the players in the market, bidding against each other, establish the market price. When new information is released about a firm, expectations change and with them, prices change. New information can cause changes in expectations about the level of future dividends or the risk of those dividends. Since market participants are constantly receiving new information and revising their expectations, it is reasonable that stock prices are constantly changing as well.

APPLICATION   Monetary Policy and Stock Prices

Stock market analysts tend to hang on every word that the governor of the Bank of Canada utters because they know that an important determinant of stock prices is monetary policy. But how does monetary policy affect stock prices?

The Gordon growth model in Equation 5 tells us how. Monetary policy can affect stock prices in two ways. First, when the Bank of Canada lowers interest rates, the return on bonds (an alternative asset to stocks) declines, and investors are likely to accept a lower required rate of return on an investment in equity (k_e). The resulting decline in k_e would lower the denominator in the Gordon growth model (Equation 5), lead to a higher value of P_0, and raise stock prices. Furthermore, a lowering of interest rates is likely to stimulate the economy, so that the growth rate in dividends, g, is likely to be somewhat higher. This rise in g also causes the denominator in Equation 5 to fall, which also leads to a higher P_0 and a rise in stock prices.

As we will see in Chapter 26, the impact of monetary policy on stock prices is one of the key ways in which monetary policy affects the economy.

APPLICATION	The Subprime Financial Crisis and the Stock Market

The subprime financial crisis in the United States that started in August 2007 led to one of the worst bear markets in the last 50 years. Analysis of stock price valuation, again using the Gordon growth model, can help us understand how this event affected stock prices.

The subprime financial crisis had a major negative impact on the economy, leading to a downward revision of the growth prospects for companies, thus lowering the dividend growth rate (g) in the Gordon model. The resulting increase in the denominator in Equation 5 would lead to a decline in P_0 and hence a decline in stock prices.

Increased uncertainty for the economy and the widening credit spreads resulting from the subprime crisis also raised the required return on investment in equity. A higher k_e also led to an increase in the denominator in Equation 5, a decline in P_0, and a general fall in stock prices.

In the early stages of the financial crisis, the decline in growth prospects and credit spreads were moderate and so, as the Gordon model predicts, the stock market decline was also moderate. However, when the crisis entered a particularly virulent stage in October of 2008, credit spreads shot through the roof, the economy tanked, and as the Gordon model predicts, the stock market crashed, falling by over 40% from its peak value a year earlier.

THE THEORY OF RATIONAL EXPECTATIONS

The analysis of stock price evaluation we have outlined in the previous section depends on people's expectations—especially of cash flows. Indeed, it is difficult to think of any sector in the economy in which expectations are not crucial; this is why it is important to examine how expectations are formed. We do so by outlining the *theory of rational expectations*, currently the most widely used theory to describe the formation of business and consumer expectations.

In the 1950s and 1960s, economists regularly viewed expectations as formed from past experience only. Expectations of inflation, for example, were typically viewed as being an average of past inflation rates. This view of expectation formation, called **adaptive expectations**, suggests that changes in expectations will occur slowly over time as past data change (see the FYI box, Adaptive Expectations). So if inflation had formerly been steady at a 5% rate, expectations of future inflation would be 5% too. If inflation rose to a steady rate of 10%, expectations of future inflation would rise toward 10%, but slowly: In the first year, expected inflation might rise only to 6%; in the second year, to 7%; and so on.

Adaptive expectations have been faulted on the grounds that people use more information than just past data on a single variable to form their expectations of that variable. Their expectations of inflation will almost surely be affected by their predictions of future monetary policy as well as by current and past monetary policy. In addition, people often change their expectations quickly in the light of new information. To meet these objections to adaptive expectations, John Muth developed an alternative theory of expectations, called **rational expectations**, which

FYI   Adaptive Expectations

The adaptive expectations hypothesis can be stated as follows

$$x_t^e - x_{t-1}^e = \theta(x_t - x_{t-1}^e),\ 0 < \theta < 1 \quad (7)$$

where x_t is the value of x at time t and x_t^e is the expected value of x for period $t+1$, with the expectation held at time t. Equation 7 says that the change in the expected value of x, $x_t^e - x_{t-1}^e$, is proportional to the forecast error, which is the discrepancy between the current actual and last period's expected value of x.

- if expectations realize (i.e., $x_t = x_{t-1}^e$), then $x_t^e = x_{t-1}^e$
- if x turns out to be surprisingly high (i.e., $x_t > x_{t-1}^e$), then $x_t^e > x_{t-1}^e$
- if x turns out to be surprisingly low (i.e., $x_t < x_{t-1}^e$), then $x_t^e < x_{t-1}^e$

Clearly, the formulation in Equation 7 expresses the ability of economic agents to learn from their past mistakes. This is why it is also known as the **error-learning hypothesis**. Equation 7 can be written as

$$x_t^e = \theta x_t + (1-\theta)x_{t-1}^e$$

and by continuous back substitution yields

$$x_t^e = \theta x_t + \theta(1-\theta)x_{t-1} + \theta(1-\theta)^2 x_{t-2} + \cdots$$

In short, the adaptive expectation hypothesis implies that the expected value of x at time t, x_t^e, is a weighted average of current and past values of x. The weighting scheme can be thought of as a "memory." In fact,

- as $\theta \to 0$, the weights decline slowly and the economic agent is said to have "long memory," in the sense that information from the distant past influences significantly the formation of expectations for the future.
- as $\theta \to 1$, the weights decline quickly and the economic agent is said to have "short memory," in the sense that only information from the recent past influences the formation of expectations for the future.

can be stated as follows: ***Expectations will be identical to optimal forecasts (the best guess of the future) using all available information.***[2]

What exactly does this mean? To explain it more clearly, let's use the theory of rational expectations to examine how expectations are formed in a situation that most of us encounter at some point in our lifetimes: our drive to work. Suppose that when Joe Commuter travels when it is not rush hour, it takes an average of 30 minutes for his trip. Sometimes it takes him 35 minutes, other times 25 minutes, but the average non–rush-hour driving time is 30 minutes. If, however, Joe leaves for work during the rush hour, it takes him, on average, an additional 10 minutes to get to work. Given that he leaves for work during the rush hour, the best guess of the driving time—the **optimal forecast**—is 40 minutes.

If the only information available to Joe before he leaves for work that would have a potential effect on his driving time is that he is leaving during the rush hour, what does rational expectations theory allow you to predict about Joe's expecta-

[2] John Muth, "Rational Expectations and the Theory of Price Movements," *Econometrica* 29 (1961): 315–335.

tions of his driving time? Since the best guess of his driving time using all available information is 40 minutes, Joe's expectation should also be the same. Clearly, an expectation of 35 minutes would not be rational, because it is not equal to the optimal forecast, the best guess of the driving time.

Suppose that the next day, given the same conditions and the same expectations, it takes Joe 45 minutes to drive because he hits an abnormally large number of red lights, and the day after that he hits all the lights right and it takes him only 35 minutes. Do these variations mean that Joe's 40-minute expectation is irrational? No, an expectation of 40 minutes' driving time is still a rational expectation. In both cases, the forecast is off by 5 minutes, so the expectation has not been perfectly accurate. However, the forecast does not have to be perfectly accurate to be rational—it need only be the *best possible* given the available information; that is, it has to be correct *on average*, and the 40-minute expectation meets this requirement. Since there is bound to be some randomness in Joe's driving time regardless of driving conditions, an optimal forecast will never be completely accurate.

The example makes the following important point about rational expectations: ***Even though a rational expectation equals the optimal forecast using all available information, a prediction based on it may not always be perfectly accurate.***

What if an item of information relevant to predicting driving time is unavailable or ignored? Suppose that on Joe's usual route to work there is an accident that causes a two-hour traffic jam. If Joe has no way of ascertaining this information, his rush-hour expectation of 40 minutes' driving time is still rational, because the accident information is not available to him for incorporation into his optimal forecast. However, if there was a radio or TV traffic report about the accident that Joe did not bother to listen to or heard but ignored, his 40-minute expectation is no longer rational. In light of the availability of this information, Joe's optimal forecast should have been two hours and 40 minutes.

Accordingly, there are two reasons why an expectation may fail to be rational:

1. People might be aware of all available information but find it takes too much effort to make their expectation the best guess possible.

2. People might be unaware of some available relevant information, so their best guess of the future will not be accurate.

Nonetheless, it is important to recognize that if an additional factor is important but information about it is not available, an expectation that does not take account of it can still be rational.

Formal Statement of the Theory

We can state the theory of rational expectations somewhat more formally. If X stands for the variable that is being forecast (in our example, Joe Commuter's driving time), X^e for the expectation of this variable (Joe's expectation of his driving time), and X^{of} for the optimal forecast of X using all available information (the best guess possible of his driving time), the theory of rational expectations then simply says:

$$X^e = X^{of} \qquad (8)$$

That is, the expectation of X equals the optimal forecast using all available information.

Rationale Behind the Theory

Why do people try to make their expectations match their best possible guess of the future using all available information? The simplest explanation is that it is costly for people not to do so. Joe Commuter has a strong incentive to make his expectation of the time it takes him to drive to work as accurate as possible. If he underpredicts his driving time, he will often be late to work and risk being fired. If he overpredicts, he will, on average, get to work too early and will have given up sleep or leisure time unnecessarily. Accurate expectations are desirable, and there are strong incentives for people to try to make them equal to optimal forecasts by using all available information.

The same principle applies to businesses. Suppose that an appliance manufacturer—say, General Electric—knows that interest-rate movements are important to the sales of appliances. If GE makes poor forecasts of interest rates, it will earn less profit, because it might produce either too many appliances or too few. There are strong incentives for GE to acquire all available information to help it forecast interest rates and use the information to make the best possible guess of future interest-rate movements.

The incentives for equating expectations with optimal forecasts are especially strong in financial markets. In these markets, people with better forecasts of the future get rich. The application of the theory of rational expectations to financial markets (where it is called the **efficient market hypothesis** or the **theory of efficient capital markets**) is thus particularly useful.

Implications of the Theory

Rational expectations theory leads to two commonsense implications for the forming of expectations that are important in the analysis of both the stock market and the aggregate economy:

1. ***If there is a change in the way a variable moves, the way in which expectations of this variable are formed will change as well.*** This tenet of rational expectations theory can be most easily understood through a concrete example. Suppose that interest rates move in such a way that they tend to return to a "normal" level in the future. If today's interest rate is high relative to the normal level, an optimal forecast of the interest rate in the future is that it will decline to the normal level. Rational expectations theory would imply that when today's interest rate is high, the expectation is that it will fall in the future.

    Suppose now that the way in which the interest rate moves changes so that when the interest rate is high, it stays high. In this case, when today's interest rate is high, the optimal forecast of the future interest rate, and hence the rational expectation, is that it will stay high. Expectations of the future interest rate will no longer indicate that the interest rate will fall. The change in the way the interest-rate variable moves has therefore led to a change in the way that expectations of future interest rates are formed. The rational expectations analysis here is generalizable to expectations of any variable. Hence when there is a change in the way any variable moves, the way in which expectations of this variable are formed will change too.

2. ***The forecast errors of expectations will on average be zero and cannot be predicted ahead of time.*** The forecast error of an expectation is $X - X^e$, the difference between the realization of a variable X and the expectation of the variable; that is, if Joe Commuter's driving time on a particular day is 45 minutes and his expectation of the driving time is 40 minutes, the forecast error is 5 minutes.

    Suppose that in violation of the rational expectations tenet, Joe's forecast error is not, on average, equal to zero; instead, it equals 5 minutes. The forecast error is now predictable ahead of time because Joe will soon notice that he is, on average, 5 minutes late for work and can improve his forecast by increasing it by 5 minutes. Rational expectations theory implies that this is exactly what Joe will do because he will want his forecast to be the best guess possible. When Joe has revised his forecast upward by 5 minutes, on average, the forecast error will equal zero so that it cannot be predicted ahead of time. Rational expectations theory implies that forecast errors of expectations cannot be predicted.

THE EFFICIENT MARKET HYPOTHESIS: RATIONAL EXPECTATIONS IN FINANCIAL MARKETS

While the theory of rational expectations was being developed by monetary economists, financial economists were developing a parallel theory of expectation formation in financial markets. It led them to the same conclusion as that of the rational expectations theorists: expectations in financial markets are equal to optimal forecasts using all available information.[3] Although financial economists gave their theory another name, calling it the *efficient market hypothesis*, in fact their theory is just an application of rational expectations to the pricing of not only stocks but other securities.

The efficient market hypothesis is based on the assumption that prices of securities in financial markets fully reflect all available information. You may recall from Chapter 4 that the rate of return from holding a security equals the sum of the capital gain on the security (the change in the price), plus any cash payments, divided by the initial purchase price of the security:

$$R = \frac{P_{t+1} - P_t + C}{P_t} \tag{9}$$

where R = rate of return on the security held from time t to $t + 1$ (say, the end of 2010 to the end of 2011)

P_{t+1} = price of the security at time $t + 1$, the end of the holding period

P_t = price of the security at time t, the beginning of the holding period

C = cash payment (coupon or dividend payments) made in the period t to $t + 1$

Let's look at the expectation of this return at time t, the beginning of the holding period. Because the current price P_t and the cash payment C are known at the beginning, the only variable in the definition of the return that is uncertain is the price next period, P_{t+1}.[4] Denoting the expectation of the security's price at the end of the holding period as P^e_{t+1}, the expected return R^e is:

$$R^e = \frac{P^e_{t+1} - P_t + C}{P_t}$$

---

[3] The development of the efficient market hypothesis was not wholly independent of the development of rational expectations theory, in that financial economists were aware of Muth's work.

[4] There are cases where C might not be known at the beginning of the period, but that does not make a substantial difference to the analysis. We would in that case assume that not only price expectations but also the expectations of C are optimal forecasts using all available information.

The efficient market hypothesis also views expectations of future prices as equal to optimal forecasts using all currently available information. In other words, the market's expectations of future securities prices are rational, so that:

$$P_{t+1}^e = P_{t+1}^{of}$$

which in turn implies that the expected return on the security will equal the optimal forecast of the return:

$$R^e = R^{of} \tag{10}$$

Unfortunately, we cannot observe either R^e or P_{t+1}^e, so the rational expectations equations by themselves do not tell us much about how the financial market behaves. However, if we can devise some way to measure the value of R^e, these equations will have important implications for how prices of securities change in financial markets.

The supply and demand analysis of the bond market developed in Chapter 5 shows us that the expected return on a security (the interest rate, in the case of the bond examined) will have a tendency to head toward the equilibrium return that equates the quantity demanded to the quantity supplied. Supply and demand analysis enables us to determine the expected return on a security with the following equilibrium condition: The expected return on a security R^e equals the equilibrium return R^*, which equates the quantity of the security demanded to the quantity supplied; that is,

$$R^e = R^* \tag{11}$$

The academic field of finance explores the factors (risk and liquidity, for example) that influence the equilibrium returns on securities. For our purposes, it is sufficient to know that we can determine the equilibrium return and thus determine the expected return with the equilibrium condition.

We can derive an equation to describe pricing behaviour in an efficient market by using the equilibrium condition to replace R^e with R^* in the rational expectations equation (Equation 10). In this way, we obtain:

$$R^{of} = R^* \tag{12}$$

This equation tells us that ***current prices in a financial market will be set so that the optimal forecast of a security's return using all available information equals the security's equilibrium return.*** Financial economists state it more simply: In an efficient market, a security's price fully reflects all available information.

APPLICATION	The Efficient Market Hypothesis

Suppose that a share of Microsoft had a closing price yesterday of $90, but new information was announced after the market closed that caused a revision in the forecast of the price next year to go to $120. If the annual equilibrium return on Microsoft is 15%, what does the efficient market hypothesis indicate the price will go to today when the market opens? (Assume that Microsoft pays no dividends.)

Solution

The price would rise to $104.35 after the opening.

$$R^{of} = \frac{P^{of}_{t+1} - P_t + C}{P_t} = R^*$$

where

$$\begin{aligned}
R^{of} &= \text{optimal forecast of the return} = 15\% = 0.15 \\
R^* &= \text{equilibrium return} = 15\% = 0.15 \\
P^{of}_{t+1} &= \text{optimal forecast of price next year} = \$120 \\
P_t &= \text{price today after opening} \\
C &= \text{cash (dividend) payment} = 0
\end{aligned}$$

Thus

$$0.15 = \frac{\$120 - P_t}{P_t}$$

$$P_t \times 0.15 = \$120 - P_t$$

$$P_t(1.15) = \$120$$

$$P_t = \$104.35$$

Rationale Behind the Theory

To see why the efficient market hypothesis makes sense, we make use of the concept of **arbitrage**, in which market participants (*arbitrageurs*) eliminate **unexploited profit opportunities** (i.e., returns on a security that are larger than what is justified by the characteristics of that security). There are two types of arbitrage, *pure arbitrage*, in which the elimination of unexploited profit opportunities involves no risk, and the type of arbitrage we discuss here in which the arbitrageur takes on some risk when eliminating the unexploited profit opportunities.

To see how arbitrage leads to the efficient market hypothesis, suppose that, given its risk characteristics, the normal return on a security—say, Nexen common stock—is 10% at an annual rate, and its current price P_t is lower than the optimal forecast of tomorrow's price P^{of}_{t+1} so that the optimal forecast of the return at an annual rate is 50%, which is greater than the equilibrium return of 10%. We are now able to predict that, on average, ExxonMobil's return would be abnormally high, so that there is no unexploited profit opportunity. Knowing that, on average, you can earn such an abnormally high rate of return on ExxonMobil because $R^{of} > R^*$, you would buy more, which would in turn drive up its current price P_t relative to the expected future price P^{of}_{t+1}, thereby lowering R^{of}. When the current price had risen sufficiently so that R^{of} equals R^* and the efficient market condition (Equation 12) is satisfied, the buying of ExxonMobil will stop, and the unexploited profit opportunity will have disappeared.

Similarly, a security for which the optimal forecast of the return is −5% and the equilibrium return is 10% ($R^{of} < R^*$) would be a poor investment, because, on average, it earns less than the equilibrium return. In such a case, you would sell the security and drive down its current price relative to the expected future price until R^{of} rose to the level of R^* and the efficient market condition is again satisfied. What we have shown can be summarized as follows:

$$R^{of} > R^* \ \rightarrow \ P_t\uparrow \rightarrow R^{of}\downarrow$$

$$R^{of} < R^* \ \rightarrow \ P_t\downarrow \ \rightarrow \ R^{of}\uparrow$$

until

$$R^{of} = R^*$$

Another way to state the efficient market condition is this: ***In an efficient market, all unexploited profit opportunities will be eliminated.***

An extremely important factor in this reasoning is that ***not everyone in a financial market must be well informed about a security or have rational expectations for its price to be driven to the point at which the efficient market condition holds.*** Financial markets are structured so that many participants can play. As long as a few (often referred to as "smart money") keep their eyes open for unexploited profit opportunities, they will eliminate the profit opportunities that appear, because in so doing, they make a profit. The efficient market hypothesis makes sense, because it does not require everyone in a market to be cognizant of what is happening to every security.

Stronger Version of the Efficient Market Hypothesis

Many financial economists take the efficient market hypothesis one step further in their analysis of financial markets. Not only do they define an efficient market as one in which expectations are rational—that is, equal to optimal forecasts using all available information—but they also add the condition that an efficient market is one in which prices reflect the true fundamental (intrinsic) value of the securities. Thus in an efficient market, all prices are always correct and reflect **market fundamentals** (items that have a direct impact on future income streams of the securities). This stronger view of market efficiency has several important implications in the academic field of finance. First, it implies that in an efficient capital market, one investment is as good as any other because the securities' prices are correct. Second, it implies that a security's price reflects all available information about the intrinsic value of the security. Third, it implies that security prices can be used by managers of both financial and nonfinancial firms to assess their cost of capital (cost of financing their investments) accurately and hence that security prices can be used to help them make the correct decisions about whether a specific investment is worth making or not. The stronger version of market efficiency is a basic tenet of much analysis in the finance field.

APPLICATION **Practical Guide to Investing in the Stock Market**

The efficient market hypothesis has numerous applications to the real world.[5] It is especially valuable because it can be applied directly to an issue that concerns many of us: how to get rich (or at least not get poor) in the stock market. The Financial News box, Stock Prices, shows how stock prices are quoted. A practical guide to investing in the stock market, which we develop here, provides a better understanding of the use and implications of the efficient market hypothesis.

How Valuable Are Published Reports by Investment Advisers?

Suppose you have just read in the *Globe and Mail: Report on Business* that investment advisers are predicting a boom in oil stocks because an oil shortage is developing. Should you proceed to withdraw all your hard-earned savings from the bank and invest them in oil stocks?

The efficient market hypothesis tells us that when purchasing a security, we cannot expect to earn an abnormally high return, a return greater than the equilibrium return. Information in newspapers and in the published reports of investment advisers is readily available to many market participants and is already reflected in market prices. So acting on this information will not yield abnormally high returns, on average. As we have seen, the empirical evidence for the most part confirms that recommendations from investment advisers cannot help us outperform the general market. Indeed, as the FYI box, Should You Hire an Ape as Your Investment Adviser? suggests, human investment advisers in San Francisco do not on average even outperform an orangutan!

Probably no other conclusion is met with more skepticism by students than this one when they first hear it. We all know or have heard of somebody who has been successful in the stock market for a period of many years. We wonder, "How could someone be so consistently successful if he or she did not really know how to predict when returns would be abnormally high?" The following story, reported in the press, illustrates why such anecdotal evidence is not reliable.

A get-rich-quick artist invented a clever scam. Every week, he wrote two letters. In letter A, he would pick team A to win a particular football game, and in letter B, he would pick the opponent, team B. A mailing list would then be separated into two groups, and he would send letter A to the people in one group and letter B to the people in the other. The following week he would do the same thing but would send these letters only to the group who had received the first letter with the correct prediction. After doing this for ten games, he had a small cluster of people who had received letters predicting the correct winning team for every game. He then mailed a final letter to them, declaring that since he was obviously an expert predictor of the outcome of football games (he had picked winners ten weeks in a row) and since his predictions were profitable for the recipients who bet on the games, he would continue to send his predictions only if he were paid a substantial amount of money. When one of his clients figured out what he was up to, the con man was prosecuted and thrown in jail!

---

[5] The empirical evidence on the efficient market hypothesis is discussed in an appendix to this chapter on this book's MyEconLab at **www.pearsoned.ca/myeconlab**.

FINANCIAL NEWS

Stock Prices

Stock prices are available online from the *Globe and Mail.* The site provides quotations for companies listed on the Toronto Stock Exchange and the TSX Venture Exchange in Canada as well as for companies listed on the New York, NASDAQ, and other American stock exchanges. To access the information go to the *Globe and Mail* website at **www.theglobeandmail.com** and click on "Report on Business," then "Globe Investor," and then "Stock Quotes." Enter a company name or its stock symbol to view the latest quote and related information.

Stock prices are quoted in the following format (a company listed on the Toronto Stock Exchange is used as an example):

| Company | Symbol | Latest Price | Change | | | | 52 Weeks | |
			Net	%	Time	High	Low	Volume	High	Low
Nexen Inc.	NXY-T	18.370	0.040	0.22	13:39	18.570	17.900	1 112 122	43.450	13.330

Source: Globeinvestor.com, "Quotes," www.globeinvestor.com/v5/content/quotes.html, accessed January 29, 2009.

The following information is included in each column. Nexen common stock is used as an example.

Company: Company name: Nexen Inc.

Symbol: Symbol that identifies company: NXY-T

Latest Price: Last price that time: 18.370

Net Change: Change in the price from the previous day: 0.040

% Change: Percentage change in the price from the previous day: 0.22%

Time: Time of quote: 13:39 (on January 29, 2009)

High: Highest price of a share that day: 18.570

Low: Lowest price of a share that day: 17.900

Volume: Number of shares traded that day: 1 112 122

52-week high: Highest price of a share in the past 52 weeks: 43.450 for Nexen stock

52-week low: Lowest price of a share in the past 52 weeks: 13.330 for Nexen stock

---

What is the lesson of the story? Even if no forecaster is an accurate predictor of the market, there will always be a group of consistent winners. A person who has done well regularly in the past cannot guarantee that he or she will do well in the future. Note that there will also be a group of persistent losers, but you rarely hear about them because no one brags about a poor forecasting record.

Should You Be Skeptical of Hot Tips?

Suppose your broker phones you with a hot tip to buy stock in the Happy Feet Corporation (HFC) because it has just developed a product that is completely effective in curing athlete's foot. The stock price is sure to go up. Should you follow this advice and buy HFC stock?

The efficient market hypothesis indicates that you should be skeptical of such news. If the stock market is efficient, it has already priced HFC stock so that its

---

FYI   **Should You Hire an Ape as Your Investment Adviser?**

The *San Francisco Chronicle* came up with an amusing way of evaluating how successful investment advisers are at picking stocks. They asked eight analysts to pick five stocks at the beginning of the year and then compared the performance of their stock picks to those chosen by Jolyn, an orangutan living at Marine World/Africa USA in Vallejo, California. Consistent with the results found in the "Investment Dartboard" feature of the *Wall Street Journal*, Jolyn beat the investment advisers as often as they beat her. Given this result, you might be just as well off hiring an orangutan as your investment adviser as you would be hiring a human being!

---

expected return will equal the equilibrium return. The hot tip is not particularly valuable and will not enable you to earn an abnormally high return.

You might wonder, though, if the hot tip is based on new information and would give you an edge on the rest of the market. If other market participants have gotten this information before you, the answer is no. As soon as the information hits the street, the unexploited profit opportunity it creates will be quickly eliminated. The stock's price will already reflect the information, and you should expect to realize only the equilibrium return. But if you are one of the first to gain the new information, it can do you some good. Only then can you be one of the lucky ones who, on average, will earn an abnormally high return by helping eliminate the profit opportunity by buying HFC stock.

Do Stock Prices Always Rise When There Is Good News?

If you follow the stock market, you might have noticed a puzzling phenomenon: When good news about a stock, such as a particularly favourable earnings report, is announced, the price of the stock frequently does not rise. The efficient market hypothesis and the random-walk behaviour of stock prices explain this phenomenon.

Because changes in stock prices are unpredictable, when information is announced that has already been expected by the market, the stock price will remain unchanged. The announcement does not contain any new information that should lead to a change in stock prices. If this were not the case and the announcement led to a change in stock prices, it would mean that the change was predictable. Because that is ruled out in an efficient market, **stock prices will respond to announcements only when the information being announced is new and unexpected.** If the news is expected, there will be no stock price response. This is exactly what the evidence we described earlier, which shows that stock prices reflect publicly available information, suggests will occur.

Sometimes an individual stock price declines when good news is announced. Although this seems somewhat peculiar, it is completely consistent with the workings of an efficient market. Suppose that although the announced news is good, it is not as good as expected. HFC's earnings may have risen 15%, but if the market expected earnings to rise by 20%, the new information is actually unfavourable, and the stock price declines.

Efficient Market Prescription for the Investor

What does the efficient market hypothesis recommend for investing in the stock market? It tells us that hot tips, investment advisers' published recommendations, and technical analysis—all of which make use of publicly available information—cannot help an investor outperform the market. Indeed, it indicates that anyone without better information than other market participants cannot expect to beat the market. So what is an investor to do?

The efficient market hypothesis leads to the conclusion that such an investor (and almost all of us fit into this category) should not try to outguess the market by constantly buying and selling securities. This process does nothing but boost the income of brokers, who earn commissions on each trade.[6] Instead, the investor should pursue a "buy-and-hold" strategy—purchase stocks and hold them for long periods of time. This will lead to the same returns, on average, but the investor's net profits will be higher, because fewer brokerage commissions will have to be paid.

It is frequently a sensible strategy for a small investor, whose costs of managing a portfolio may be high relative to its size, to buy into a mutual fund rather than individual stocks. Because the efficient market hypothesis indicates that no mutual fund can consistently outperform the market, an investor should not buy into one that has high management fees or that pays sales commissions to brokers, but rather should purchase a no-load (commission-free) mutual fund that has low management fees.

As we have seen, the evidence indicates that it will not be easy to beat the prescription suggested here, although some of the anomalies to the efficient market hypothesis suggest that an extremely clever investor (which rules out most of us) may be able to outperform a buy-and-hold strategy.

APPLICATION

What Do the Black Monday Crash of 1987 and the Tech Crash of 2000 Tell Us About Rational Expectations and Efficient Markets?

On October 19, 1987, dubbed "Black Monday," the Dow Jones Industrial Average declined more than 20%, the largest one-day decline in U.S. history. The collapse of the high-tech companies' share prices from their peaks in March 2000 caused the heavily tech-laden NASDAQ index to fall from around 5000 in March 2000 to around 1500 in 2001 and 2002, for a decline of well over 60%. These two crashes have caused many economists to question the validity of efficient market theory and rational expectations. They do not believe that a rational marketplace could have produced such a massive swing in share prices. To what degree should these stock market crashes make us doubt the validity of rational expectations and the efficient market hypothesis?

Nothing in rational expectations theory rules out large changes in stock prices. A large change in stock prices can result from new information that produces a

---

[6] The investor may also have to pay Canada Revenue Agency (CRA) capital gains taxes on any profits that are realized when a security is sold—an additional reason why continual buying and selling does not make sense.

dramatic decline in optimal forecasts of the future valuation of firms. However, economists are hard-pressed to come up with fundamental changes in the economy that can explain the Black Monday and tech crashes. One lesson from these crashes is that factors other than market fundamentals probably have an effect on stock prices. Hence, these crashes have convinced many economists that a stronger version of the efficient market hypothesis, which states that asset prices reflect the true fundamental (intrinsic) value of securities, is incorrect. They attribute a large role in determination of stock prices to market psychology and to the institutional structure of the marketplace. However, nothing in this view contradicts the basic reasoning behind rational expectations or the efficient market hypothesis—that market participants eliminate unexploited profit opportunities. Even though stock market prices may not always solely reflect market fundamentals, this does not mean that rational expectations do not hold. As long as stock market crashes are unpredictable, the basic lessons of the theory of rational expectations hold.

Some economists have come up with theories of what they call *rational bubbles* to explain stock market crashes. A **bubble** is a situation in which the price of an asset differs from its fundamental market value. In a rational bubble, investors can have rational expectations that a bubble is occurring because the asset price is above its fundamental value but continue to hold the asset anyway. They might do this because they believe that someone else will buy the asset for a higher price in the future. In a rational bubble, asset prices can therefore deviate from their fundamental value for a long time because the bursting of the bubble cannot be predicted and so there are no unexploited profit opportunities.

However, other economists believe that the Black Monday crash of 1987 and the tech crash of 2000 suggest that there may be unexploited profit opportunities and that the theory of rational expectations and the efficient market hypothesis might be fundamentally flawed. The controversy over whether capital markets are efficient or expectations are rational continues.

BEHAVIOURAL FINANCE

Doubts about the efficient market hypothesis, particularly after the stock market crash of 1987, have led to a new field of study, **behavioural finance**, which applies concepts from other social sciences like anthropology, sociology, and, particularly, psychology to understand the behaviour of securities prices.[7]

As we have seen, the efficient market hypothesis assumes that unexploited profit opportunities are eliminated by "smart money" market participants. But can smart money dominate ordinary investors so that financial markets are efficient? Specifically, the efficient market hypothesis suggests that smart money participants sell when a stock price goes up irrationally, with the result that the stock falls back down to a price that is justified by fundamentals.

---

[7] Surveys of this field can be found in Hersh Shefrin, *Beyond Greed and Fear: Understanding of Behavioral Finance and the Psychology of Investing* (Harvard Business School Press: Boston, 2000); Andrei Shleifer, *Inefficient Markets* (Oxford University Press: Oxford, 2000); and Robert J. Shiller, "From Efficient Market Theory to Behavioral Finance," Cowles Foundation Discussion Paper No. 1385 (October 2002).

For this to occur, however, smart money must be able to engage in **short sales:** that is, they borrow stock from brokers and then sell it in the market, with the hope that they earn a profit by buying the stock back again ("covering the short") after it has fallen in price. However, work by psychologists suggests that people are subject to loss aversion: that is, they are more unhappy when they suffer losses than they are happy from making gains. Short sales can result in losses far in excess of an investor's initial investment if the stock price climbs sharply above the price at which the short sale is made (and losses have the possibility of being unlimited if the stock price climbs to astronomical heights).

Loss aversion can thus explain an important phenomenon: very little short selling actually takes place. Short selling may also be constrained by rules restricting it because it seems unsavoury for someone to make money from another person's misfortune. That there is so little short selling can explain why stock prices sometimes get overvalued. Not enough short selling can take place by smart money to drive stock prices back down to their fundamental value.

Psychologists have also found that people tend to be overconfident in their own judgements. As a result, investors tend to believe that they are smarter than other investors. Because investors are willing to assume that the market typically doesn't get it right, they trade on their beliefs and not pure facts. This theory can explain why securities markets have such a large trading volume, something that the efficient market hypothesis does not predict.

Overconfidence and social contagion (fads) provide an explanation for stock market bubbles. When stock prices go up, investors attribute their profits to their intelligence and talk up the stock market. This word-of-mouth enthusiasm and the media then can produce an environment in which even more investors think stock prices will rise in the future. The result is a positive feedback loop in which prices continue to rise, producing a speculative bubble, which finally crashes when prices get too far out of line with fundamentals.[8]

The field of behavioural finance is a young one, but it holds out hope that we might be able to explain some features of securities markets' behaviour that are not well explained by the efficient market hypothesis.

SUMMARY

1. Stocks are valued as the present value of future dividends. Unfortunately, we do not know very precisely what these dividends will be. This uncertainty introduces a great deal of error to the valuation process. The Gordon growth model is a simplified method of computing stock value that depends on the assumption that the dividends are growing at a constant rate forever. Given our uncertainty regarding future dividends, this assumption is often the best we can do.

2. The interaction among traders in the market is what actually sets prices on a day-to-day basis. The trader that values the security the most (either because of less uncertainty about the cash flows or because of greater estimated cash flows) will be willing to pay the most.

As new information is released, investors will revise their estimates of the true value of the security and will either buy or sell it depending upon how the market price compares to their estimated valuation. Because small changes in estimated growth rates or required return result in large changes in price, it is not surprising that the markets are often volatile.

3. The efficient market hypothesis states that current security prices will fully reflect all available information, because in an efficient market, all unexploited profit opportunities are eliminated. The elimination of unexploited profit opportunities, necessary for a financial market to be efficient, does not require that all market participants be well informed.

---

[8] See Robert J. Shiller, *Irrational Exuberance* (Broadway Books: New York, 2001).

4. The efficient market hypothesis indicates that hot tips, investment advisers' published recommendations, and technical analysis cannot help an investor outperform the market. The prescription for investors is to pursue a buy-and-hold strategy—purchase stocks and hold them for long periods of time. Empirical evidence generally supports these implications of the efficient market hypothesis in the stock market.

5. The stock market crash of 1987 and the tech crash of 2000 have convinced many financial economists that the stronger version of the efficient market hypothesis, which states that asset prices reflect the true fundamental (intrinsic) value of securities, is not correct. It is less clear that the stock market crash shows that the weaker version of the efficient market hypothesis is wrong. Even if the stock market was driven by factors other than fundamentals, these crashes do not clearly demonstrate that many of the basic lessons of the efficient market hypothesis are no longer valid, as long as these crashes could not have been predicted.

6. The new field of behavioural finance applies concepts from other social sciences like anthropology, sociology, and particularly psychology to understand the behaviour of securities prices. Loss aversion, overconfidence, and social contagion can explain why trading volume is so high, stock prices get overvalued, and speculative bubbles occur.

KEY TERMS

adaptive expectations, p. 147

arbitrage, p. 153

behavioural finance, p. 159

bubble, p. 159

cash flows, p. 141

dividends, p. 141

efficient market hypothesis, p. 150

error-learning hypothesis, p. 148

generalized dividend model, p. 142

Gordon growth model, p. 143

market fundamentals, p. 154

optimal forecast, p. 148

price earnings ratio (PE), p. 144

rational expectations, p. 147

residual claimant, p. 141

shareholders, p. 141

short sales, p. 160

theory of efficient capital markets, p. 150

unexploited profit opportunity, p. 153

QUESTIONS

You will find the answers to the questions marked with an asterisk in the Textbook Resources section of your MyEconLab.

1. What basic principle of finance can be applied to the valuation of any investment asset?

*2. Identify the cash flows available to an investor in stock. How reliably can these cash flows be estimated? Compare the problem of estimating stock cash flows to estimating bond cash flows. Which security would you predict to be more volatile?

3. Some economists think that the central banks should try to prick bubbles in the stock market before they get out of hand and cause later damage when they burst. How can monetary policy be used to prick a bubble? Explain how it can do this using the Gordon growth model.

*4. "Forecasters' predictions of inflation are notoriously inaccurate, so their expectations of inflation cannot be rational." Is this statement true, false, or uncertain? Explain your answer.

5. "Whenever it is snowing when Joe Commuter gets up in the morning, he misjudges how long it will take him to drive to work. Otherwise, his expectations of the driving time are perfectly accurate. Considering that it snows only once every ten years where Joe lives, Joe's expectations are almost always perfectly accurate." Are Joe's expectations rational? Why or why not?

*6. If a forecaster spends hours every day studying data to forecast interest rates but his expectations are not as accurate as predicting that tomorrow's interest rate will be identical to today's interest rate, are his expectations rational?

7. "If stock prices did not follow a random walk, there would be unexploited profit opportunities in the market." Is this statement true, false, or uncertain? Explain your answer.

*8. Suppose that increases in the money supply lead to a rise in stock prices. Does this mean that when you see that the money supply has had a sharp rise in the past week, you should go out and buy stocks? Why or why not?

*9. If I read in the *Globe and Mail: Report on Business* that the "smart money" on Bay Street expects stock prices to fall, should I follow that lead and sell all my stocks?

10. If my broker has been right in her five previous buy and sell recommendations, should I continue listening to her advice?

*11. Can a person with rational expectations expect the price of a share of Google to rise by 10% in the next month?

12. "If most participants in the stock market do not follow what is happening to the monetary aggregates, prices of common stocks will not fully reflect information about them." Is this statement true, false, or uncertain? Explain your answer.

*13. "An efficient market is one in which no one ever profits from having better information than the rest." Is this statement true, false, or uncertain? Explain your answer.

14. If higher money growth is associated with higher future inflation and if announced money growth turns out to be extremely high but is still less than the market expected, what do you think would happen to long-term bond prices?

*15. "Foreign exchange rates, like stock prices, should follow a random walk." Is this statement true, false, or uncertain? Explain your answer.

16. Can we expect the value of the dollar to rise by 2% next week if our expectations are rational?

*17. "Human fear is the source of stock market crashes, so these crashes indicate that expectations in the stock market cannot be rational." Is this statement true, false, or uncertain? Explain your answer.

QUANTITATIVE PROBLEMS

1. Compute the price of a share of stock that pays a $1-per-year dividend and that you expect to be able to sell in one year for $20, assuming you require a 15% return.

*2. After careful analysis, you have determined that a firm's dividends should grow at 7% on average in the foreseeable future. Its last dividend was $3. Compute the current price of this stock, assuming the required return is 18%.

3. If the public expects a corporation to lose $5 a share this quarter and it actually loses $4, which is still the largest loss in the history of the company, what does the efficient market hypothesis say will happen to the price of the stock when the $4 loss is announced?

*4. An index has an average (geometric) mean return over 20 years of 3.8861%. If the beginning index value was 100, what was the final index after 20 years?

CANSIM Question

5. Get the monthly data from 1956 to 2009 on the S&P TSX Composite Index (CANSIM series V122620) from the Textbook Resources area of the MyEconLab.
   a. Present a time series plot of this series and comment on its long-run movements.
   b. Calculate the mean and standard deviation as well as the maximum and minimum values for this series.
   c. Which were the worst and best years in terms of the stock market?
   d. Calculate monthly changes and plot the new series. Does the magnitude of the changes in the index increase towards the end of the sample?

WEB EXERCISES

1. Go to **www.finance.yahoo.com** and download daily data on the Dow Jones Industrial Average (DJIA) since 1928.
   a. Sort the series from oldest to newest, present a time series plot of the Dow Jones Industrial Average over the last 80 years, and comment on its long-run movements.
   b. Which were the worst and best years in the U.S. stock market?
   c. Calculate daily changes and plot the new series. Does the magnitude of the changes in the Dow Jones Industrial Average increase towards the end of the sample?
   d. Continuing from (c), can you conclude that the U.S. stock market has been more volatile towards the end of the sample? Why or why not?

2. There are a number of indexes that track the performance of the U.S. stock market. It is interesting to review how they track along each other. Go to **www.bloomberg.com**. Click on the "Charts" tab at the top of the screen. Alternatively, choose to display the DJIA, S&P 500, NASDAQ, and the Russell 2000. Set the time frame to five years. Click on "Get Chart."
   a. Which index has been most volatile over the last five years?
   b. Which index has posted the greatest gains over the last five years?
   c. Now adjust the time frame to intraday. Which index has performed the best today? Which has been most volatile?

3. Visit **www.forecasts.org/data/index.htm**. Click on "Stock Index Data" at the very top of the page. Now choose "International Stock Indices-Monthly." Review the indices for the Nikkei 225, DAX, Hang Seng, FTSE 100, and S&P/TSX (identified as TSE 300). Which index appears most volatile? In which index would you rather have invested in 1990 if the investment had been allowed to compound until now?

Be sure to visit the MyEconLab website at **www.myeconlab.com**. This online homework and tutorial system puts you in control of your own learning with study and practice tools directly correlated to this chapter content.

On the MyEconLab website you will find the following appendix and mini-case for this chapter:
Appendix 7.1: Evidence on the Efficient Markets Hypothesis
Mini-Case 7.1: Adaptive Expectations, Rational Expectations, and Optimal Forecast

PART III

Financial Institutions

CRISIS AND RESPONSE: BAILOUT PACKAGES IN THE TRILLIONS OF DOLLARS

In response to the subprime crisis in the United States, governments and central banks around the world departed significantly from their traditional policy tools and introduced new facilities, pouring trillions of dollars into financial institutions. In the United States, for example, the House of Representatives passed the Emergency Economic Stabilization Act on October 3, 2008. This stunning $700 billion bailout package sought to promote recovery from the subprime financial crisis by authorizing the U.S. Treasury to purchase troubled mortgage assets from struggling financial institutions or to inject capital into banking institutions. To calm fears further, the Act raised the federal deposit insurance limit temporarily from $100 000 to $250 000.

The initial bill was voted down on September 29 when constituents flooded their representatives with complaints about bailing out the greedy Wall Street executives behind the crisis. The debate in the United States pitted Wall Street against Main Street: Bailing out financial institutions was seen as being in opposition to helping struggling homeowners. How could injecting capital into the financial system help those fearful of losing their job or, worse yet, suddenly without work?

The central role of financial institutions in the working of the economy—the focus of Part III—was overlooked. Banks and other financial institutions make financial markets work by moving funds from people who save to people who have productive investment opportunities. That bank branch on Main Street was not going to be able to lend freely to a small business owner or recent university graduate looking to fund a new car purchase until capital once again flowed.

The financial crisis highlights how the financial system changes over time, be it from financial innovations or hard lessons from crises such as the one at hand. Chapter 8 analyzes financial structure in Canada and in the rest of the world. In Chapter 9, we develop a framework to understand the dynamics of financial crises—and focus in particular on the red-hot subprime crisis of 2007–2008. In Chapter 10, we extend the economic analysis developed in Chapter 8 to understand the motivations for bank regulation and we examine the pitfalls in the regulatory process. Chapter 11 examines the development of the Canadian banking system over time and the growing internationalization of banking. In Chapter 12, we look at the business of nonbank financial institutions.

CHAPTER 8

An Economic Analysis of Financial Structure

LEARNING OBJECTIVES

After studying this chapter you should be able to

1. depict how asymmetric information results in adverse selection and moral hazard problems that interfere with the efficient functioning of financial markets
2. express how government regulation, the private production and sale of information, and financial intermediaries can lessen, but cannot eliminate, asymmetric information problems
3. discuss why securities regulators are introducing new rules and regulations, such as the Sarbanes-Oxley Act in the United States

PREVIEW

A healthy and vibrant economy requires a financial system that moves funds from people who save to people who have productive investment opportunities. But how does the financial system make sure that your hard-earned savings get channelled to Paula the Productive Investor rather than to Benny the Bum?

This chapter answers that question by providing an economic analysis of how our financial structure is designed to promote economic efficiency. The analysis focuses on a few simple but powerful economic concepts that enable us to explain features of our financial system such as why financial contracts are written as they are and why financial intermediaries are more important than securities markets for getting funds to borrowers. The analysis also demonstrates the important link between the financial system and the performance of the aggregate economy, which is the subject of the last part of the book.

BASIC FACTS ABOUT FINANCIAL STRUCTURE THROUGHOUT THE WORLD

The financial system is complex in structure and function throughout the world. It includes many different types of institutions: banks, insurance companies, mutual funds, stock and bond markets, and so on—all of which are regulated by government. The financial system channels billions of dollars per year from savers to people with productive investment opportunities. If we take a close look at financial structure all over the world, we find eight basic facts, some of which are quite surprising, that we need to explain in order to understand how the financial system works.

The bar chart in Figure 8-1 shows how Canadian businesses financed their activities using external funds (those obtained from outside the business itself) in the period 1970–2002 and compares the Canadian data to those of Germany, Japan, and the United States. The *Bank Loans* category is made up primarily of loans from depository institutions; *Nonbank Loans* is composed primarily of loans by other financial intermediaries; the *Bonds* category includes marketable debt securities such as corporate bonds and commercial paper; and *Stock* consists of new issues of new equity (stock market shares).

Now let us explore the eight facts.

1. ***Stocks are not the most important source of external financing for businesses.*** Because so much attention in the media is focused on the stock market, many people have the impression that stocks are the most important sources of financing for Canadian corporations. However, as we can see from the bar chart in Figure 8-1, the stock market accounted for only a small fraction of the external financing of businesses in the 1970–2002 period: 12%.[1]

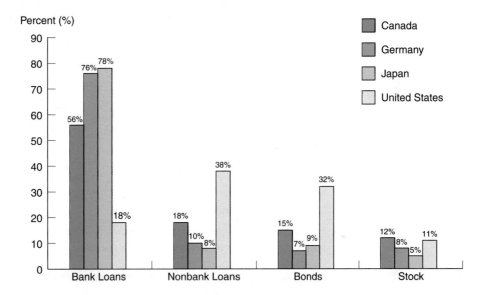

FIGURE 8-1   Sources of External Funds for Nonfinancial Businesses: A Comparison of Canada with Germany, Japan, and the United States

The data are for the 1970–2002 period for Canada and for the 1970–2000 period for Germany, Japan, and the United States.

Sources: Andreas Hackethal and Reinhard H. Schmidt, "Financing Patterns: Measuring Concepts and Empirical Results," Johann Wolfgang Goethe-Universitat Working Paper No. 125, January 2004; and Apostolos Serletis and Karl Pinno, "Corporate Financing in Canada," *Journal of Economic Asymmetries* 3 (2006); 1–20.

---

[1] The 12% figure for the percentage of external financing provided by stocks is based on the flows of external funds to corporations. However, this flow figure is somewhat misleading, because when a share of stock is issued, it raises funds permanently, whereas when a bond is issued, it raises funds only temporarily until they are paid back at maturity. To see this, suppose that a firm raises $1000 by selling a share of stock and another $1000 by selling a $1000 one-year bond. In the case of the stock issue, the firm can hold on to the $1000 it raised this way, but to hold on to the $1000 it raised through debt, it has to issue a new $1000 bond every year. If we look at the flow of funds to corporations over a 33-year period, as in Figure 8-1, the firm will have raised $1000 with a stock issue only once in the 33-year period, while it will have raised $1000 with debt 33 times, once in each of the 33 years. Thus it will look as though debt is 33 times more important than stocks in raising funds, even though our example indicates that they are actually equally important for the firm.

Similarly small figures apply in the other countries presented in Figure 8-1 as well. Why is the stock market less important than other sources of financing in Canada and other countries?

2. ***Issuing marketable debt and equity securities is not the primary way in which businesses finance their operations.*** Figure 8-1 shows that bonds are a more important source of financing than stocks in Canada (15% versus 12%). However, stocks and bonds combined (27%), which make up the total share of marketable securities, still supply less than one-third of the external funds corporations need to finance their activities. The fact that issuing marketable securities is not the most important source of financing is true elsewhere in the world as well. Indeed, as we see in Figure 8-1, other countries (except the United States) have a much smaller share of external financing supplied by marketable securities than Canada. Why don't businesses use marketable securities more extensively to finance their activities?

3. ***Indirect finance, which involves the activities of financial intermediaries, is many times more important than direct finance, in which businesses raise funds directly from lenders in financial markets.*** Direct finance involves the sale to households of marketable securities such as stocks and bonds. The 27% share of stocks and bonds as a source of external financing for Canadian businesses actually greatly overstates the importance of direct finance in our financial system. In general, only a small fraction of newly issued corporate bonds, commercial paper, and stocks are sold directly to Canadian households. The rest of these securities are bought primarily by financial intermediaries such as insurance companies, pension funds, and mutual funds. Because in most countries marketable securities are an even less important source of finance than in Canada, direct finance is also far less important than indirect finance in the rest of the world. Why are financial intermediaries and indirect finance so important in financial markets? In recent years, indirect finance has been declining in importance. Why is this happening?

4. ***Financial intermediaries, particularly banks, are the most important source of external funds used to finance businesses.*** As we can see in Figure 8-1, the primary source of external funds for businesses throughout the world are loans made by banks and other nonbank financial intermediaries such as insurance companies, pension funds, and finance companies (56% in the United States, but over 70% in Japan, Germany, and Canada). In other industrialized countries, bank loans are the largest category of sources of external finance and so the data suggest that banks in these countries have the most important role in financing business activities. In developing countries, banks play an even more important role in the financial system than they do in the industrialized countries. What makes banks so important to the workings of the financial system? Although banks remain important, their share of external funds for businesses has been declining in recent years. What is driving their decline?

5. ***The financial system is among the most heavily regulated sectors of the economy.*** The financial system is heavily regulated in Canada and all other developed countries. Governments regulate financial markets primarily to promote the provision of information, and to ensure the soundness (stability) of the financial system. Why are financial markets so extensively regulated throughout the world?

6. ***Only large, well-established corporations have easy access to securities markets to finance their activities.*** Individuals and smaller businesses that are not well established are less likely to raise funds by issuing marketable securities. Instead, they most often obtain their financing from banks. Why do only large, well-known corporations find it easier to raise funds in securities markets?

7. ***Collateral is a prevalent feature of debt contracts for both households and businesses.*** **Collateral** is property that is pledged to a lender to guarantee payment in the event that the borrower is unable to make debt payments. Collateralized debt (also known as **secured debt** to contrast it with **unsecured debt**, such as credit card debt, which is not collateralized) is the predominant form of household debt and is widely used in business borrowing as well. The majority of household debt in Canada consists of collateralized loans: Your automobile is collateral for your auto loan, and your house is collateral for your mortgage. Commercial and farm mortgages, for which property is pledged as collateral, make up one-quarter of borrowing by nonfinancial businesses; corporate bonds and other bank loans also often involve pledges of collateral. Why is collateral such an important feature of debt contracts?

8. ***Debt contracts typically are extremely complicated legal documents that place substantial restrictions on the behaviour of the borrower.*** Many students think of a debt contract as a simple IOU that can be written on a single piece of paper. The reality of debt contracts is far different, however. In all countries, bond or loan contracts typically are long legal documents with provisions (called **restrictive covenants**) that restrict and specify certain activities that the borrower can engage in. Restrictive covenants are not just a feature of debt contracts for businesses; for example, personal automobile loan and home mortgage contracts have covenants that require the borrower to maintain sufficient insurance on the automobile or house purchased with the loan. Why are debt contracts so complex and restrictive?

As you may recall from Chapter 2, an important feature of financial markets is that they have substantial transaction and information costs. An economic analysis of how these costs affect financial markets provides us with explanations of the eight facts, which in turn provide us with a much deeper understanding of how our financial system works. In the next section, we examine the impact of transaction costs on the structure of our financial system. Then we turn to the effect of information costs on financial structure.

TRANSACTION COSTS

Transaction costs are a major problem in financial markets. An example will make this clear.

How Transaction Costs Influence Financial Structure

Say you have $500 you would like to invest, and you think about investing in the stock market. Because you have only $500, you can buy only a small number of shares. Even if you use online trading, your purchase is so small that the brokerage commission for buying the stock you picked will be a large percentage of the purchase price of the shares. If instead you decide to buy a bond, the problem is even worse because the smallest denomination for some bonds you might want to buy is as much as $10 000 and you do not have that much to invest. You are disappointed and realize that you will not be able to use financial markets to earn a return on your hard-earned savings. You can take some consolation, however, in the fact that you are not alone in being stymied by high transaction costs. This is a fact of life for many of us.

You also face another problem because of transaction costs. Because you have only a small amount of funds available, you can make only a restricted number of investments, because a large number of small transactions would result in very high transaction costs. That is, you have to put all your eggs in one basket, and your inability to diversify will subject you to a lot of risk.

How Financial Intermediaries Reduce Transaction Costs

This example of the problems posed by transaction costs and the example outlined in Chapter 2 when legal costs kept you from making a loan to Carl the Carpenter illustrate that small savers like you are frozen out of financial markets and are unable to benefit from them. Fortunately, financial intermediaries, an important part of the financial structure, have evolved to reduce transaction costs and allow small savers and borrowers to benefit from the existence of financial markets.

ECONOMIES OF SCALE   One solution to the problem of high transaction costs is to bundle the funds of many investors together so that they can take advantage of *economies of scale,* the reduction in transaction costs per dollar of investment as the size (scale) of transactions increases. Bundling investors' funds together reduces transaction costs for each individual investor. Economies of scale exist because the total cost of carrying out a transaction in financial markets increases only a little as the size of the transaction grows. For example, the cost of arranging a purchase of 10 000 shares of stock is not much greater than the cost of arranging a purchase of 50 shares of stock.

The presence of economies of scale in financial markets helps explain why financial intermediaries developed and have become such an important part of our financial structure. The clearest example of a financial intermediary that arose because of economies of scale is a mutual fund. A *mutual fund* is a financial intermediary that sells shares to individuals and then invests the proceeds in bonds or stocks. Because it buys large blocks of stocks or bonds, a mutual fund can take advantage of lower transaction costs. These cost savings are then passed on to individual investors after the mutual fund has taken its cut in the form of management fees for administering their accounts. An additional benefit for individual investors is that a mutual fund is large enough to purchase a widely diversified portfolio of securities. The increased diversification for individual investors reduces their risk, thus making them better off.

Economies of scale are also important in lowering the costs of things such as computer technology that financial institutions need to accomplish their tasks. Once a large mutual fund has invested a lot of money in setting up a telecommunications system, for example, the system can be used for a huge number of transactions at a low cost per transaction.

EXPERTISE   Financial intermediaries also arise because they are better able to develop expertise to lower transaction costs. Their expertise in computer technology enables them to offer customers convenient services like being able to call a toll-free number for information on how well their investments are doing and to write cheques on their accounts.

An important outcome of a financial intermediary's low transaction costs is the ability to provide its customers with *liquidity services,* services that make it easier for customers to conduct transactions. Some money market mutual funds, for example, not only pay shareholders high interest rates, but also allow them to write cheques for convenient bill-paying.

ASYMMETRIC INFORMATION: ADVERSE SELECTION AND MORAL HAZARD

The presence of transaction costs in financial markets explains in part why financial intermediaries and indirect finance play such an important role in financial markets (fact 3). To understand financial structure more fully, however, we turn to the role of information in financial markets.[2]

Asymmetric information—one party's having insufficient knowledge about the other party involved in a transaction to make accurate decisions—is an important aspect of financial markets. For example, managers of a corporation know whether they are honest or have better information about how well their business is doing than the stockholders do. The presence of asymmetric information leads to adverse selection and moral hazard problems, which were introduced in Chapter 2.

Adverse selection is an asymmetric information problem that occurs *before* the transaction occurs: potential bad credit risks are the ones who most actively seek out loans. Thus the parties who are the most likely to produce an undesirable outcome are the ones most likely to want to engage in the transaction. For example, big risk takers or outright crooks might be the most eager to take out a loan because they know that they are unlikely to pay it back. Because adverse selection increases the chances that a loan might be made to a bad credit risk, lenders may decide not to make any loans even though there are good credit risks in the marketplace.

Moral hazard arises *after* the transaction occurs: the lender runs the risk that the borrower will engage in activities that are undesirable from the lender's point of view because they make it less likely that the loan will be paid back. For example, once borrowers have obtained a loan, they may take on big risks (which have possible high returns but also run a greater risk of default) because they are playing with someone else's money. Because moral hazard lowers the probability that the loan will be repaid, lenders may decide that they would rather not make a loan.

The analysis of how asymmetric information problems affect economic behaviour is called **agency theory**. We will apply this theory here to explain why financial structure takes the form it does, thereby explaining the facts described at the beginning of the chapter.

THE LEMONS PROBLEM: HOW ADVERSE SELECTION INFLUENCES FINANCIAL STRUCTURE

A particular characterization of how the adverse selection problem interferes with the efficient functioning of a market was outlined in a famous article by Nobel Prize winner George Akerlof. It is called the "lemons problem" because it resem-

---

[2] An excellent survey of the literature on information and financial structure that expands on the topics discussed in the rest of this chapter is contained in Mark Gertler, "Financial Structure and Aggregate Economic Activity: An Overview," *Journal of Money, Credit and Banking* 20 (1988): 559–588.

bles the problem created by lemons in the used-car market.[3] Potential buyers of used cars are frequently unable to assess the quality of the car; that is, they can't tell whether a particular used car is a car that will run well or a lemon that will continually give them grief. The price that a buyer pays must therefore reflect the *average* quality of the cars in the market, somewhere between the low value of a lemon and the high value of a good car.

The owner of a used car, by contrast, is more likely to know whether the car is a peach or a lemon. If the car is a lemon, the owner is more than happy to sell it at the price the buyer is willing to pay, which, being somewhere between the value of a lemon and a good car, is greater than the lemon's value. However, if the car is a peach, the owner knows that the car is undervalued at the price the buyer is willing to pay, and so the owner may not want to sell it. As a result of this adverse selection, few good used cars will come to the market. Because the average quality of a used car available in the market will be low and because few people want to buy a lemon, there will be few sales. The used-car market will function poorly, if at all.

Lemons in the Stock and Bond Markets

A similar lemons problem arises in securities markets, that is, the debt (bond) and equity (stock) markets. Suppose that our friend Irving the Investor, a potential buyer of securities such as common stock, can't distinguish between good firms with high expected profits and low risk and bad firms with low expected profits and high risk. In this situation, Irving will be willing to pay only a price that reflects the *average* quality of firms issuing securities—a price that lies between the value of securities from bad firms and the value of those from good firms. If the owners or managers of a good firm have better information than Irving and *know* that they are a good firm, they know that their securities are undervalued and will not want to sell them to Irving at the price he is willing to pay. The only firms willing to sell Irving securities will be bad firms (because his price is higher than the securities are worth). Our friend Irving is not stupid; he does not want to hold securities in bad firms, and hence he will decide not to purchase securities in the market. In an outcome similar to that in the used-car market, this securities market will not work very well because few firms will sell securities in it to raise capital.

The analysis is similar if Irving considers purchasing a corporate debt instrument in the bond market rather than an equity share. Irving will buy a bond only if its interest rate is high enough to compensate him for the average default risk of the good and bad firms trying to sell the debt. The knowledgeable owners of a good firm realize that they will be paying a higher interest rate than they should, and so they are unlikely to want to borrow in this market. Only the bad firms will be willing to borrow, and because investors like Irving are not eager to buy bonds issued by bad firms, they will probably not buy any bonds at all. Few bonds are likely to sell in this market, and so it will not be a good source of financing.

---

[3] George Akerlof, "The Market for 'Lemons': Quality, Uncertainty and the Market Mechanism," *Quarterly Journal of Economics* 84 (1970): 488–500. Two important papers that have applied the lemons problem analysis to financial markets are Stewart Myers and N. S. Majluf, "Corporate Financing and Investment Decisions When Firms Have Information That Investors Do Not Have," *Journal of Financial Economics* 13 (1984): 187–221, and Bruce Greenwald, Joseph E. Stiglitz, and Andrew Weiss, "Information Imperfections in the Capital Market and Macroeconomic Fluctuations," *American Economic Review* 74 (1984): 194–199.

The analysis we have just conducted explains fact 2—why marketable securities are not the primary source of financing for businesses in any country in the world. It also partly explains fact 1—why stocks are not the most important source of financing for Canadian businesses. The presence of the lemons problem keeps securities markets such as the stock and bond markets from being effective in channelling funds from savers to borrowers.

Tools to Help Solve Adverse Selection Problems

In the absence of asymmetric information, the lemons problem goes away. If buyers know as much about the quality of used cars as sellers so that all involved can tell a good car from a bad one, buyers will be willing to pay full value for good used cars. Because the owners of good used cars can now get a fair price, they will be willing to sell them in the market. The market will have many transactions and will do its intended job of channelling good cars to people who want them.

Similarly, if purchasers of securities can distinguish good firms from bad, they will pay the full value of securities issued by good firms, and good firms will sell their securities in the market. The securities market will then be able to move funds to the good firms that have the most productive investment opportunities.

PRIVATE PRODUCTION AND SALE OF INFORMATION The solution to the adverse selection problem in financial markets is to eliminate asymmetric information by furnishing people supplying funds with full details about the individuals or firms seeking to finance their investment activities. One way to get this material to saver-lenders is to have private companies collect and produce information that distinguishes good from bad firms and then sell it. In Canada, companies such as Standard & Poor's and the Dominion Bond Rating Service gather information on firms' balance sheet positions and investment activities, publish these data, and sell them to subscribers (individuals, libraries, and financial intermediaries involved in purchasing securities).

The system of private production and sale of information does not completely solve the adverse selection problem in securities markets, however, because of the so-called **free-rider problem**. The free-rider problem occurs when people who do not pay for information take advantage of the information that other people have paid for. The free-rider problem suggests that the private sale of information will be only a partial solution to the lemons problem. To see why, suppose that you have just purchased information that tells you which firms are good and which are bad. You believe that this purchase is worthwhile because you can make up the cost of acquiring this information, and then some, by purchasing the securities of good firms that are undervalued. However, when our savvy (free-riding) investor Irving sees you buying certain securities, he buys right along with you, even though he has not paid for any information. If many other investors act as Irving does, the increased demand for the undervalued good securities will cause their low price to be bid up immediately to reflect the securities' true value. Because of all these free riders, you can no longer buy the securities for less than their true value. Now because you will not gain any profits from purchasing the information, you realize that you never should have paid for this information in the first place. If other investors come to the same realization, private firms and individuals may not be able to sell enough of this information to make it worth their while to gather and produce it. The weakened ability of private firms to profit from selling information will mean that less information is produced in the marketplace, and so adverse selection (the lemons problem) will still interfere with the efficient functioning of securities markets.

GOVERNMENT REGULATION TO INCREASE INFORMATION   The free-rider problem prevents the private market from producing enough information to eliminate all the asymmetric information that leads to adverse selection. Could financial markets benefit from government intervention? The government could, for instance, produce information to help investors distinguish good from bad firms and provide it to the public free of charge. This solution, however, would involve the government in releasing negative information about firms, a practice that might be politically difficult. A second possibility (and one followed by Canada and most governments throughout the world) is for the government to regulate securities markets in a way that encourages firms to reveal honest information about themselves so that investors can determine how good or bad the firms are. In Canada, government regulation exists that requires firms selling securities to have independent **audits**, in which accounting firms certify that the firm adheres to standard accounting principles and discloses information about sales, assets, and earnings. Similar regulations are found in other countries. However, disclosure requirements do not always work well, as the recent collapse of Enron and accounting scandals at other corporations, such as WorldCom and Parmalat (an Italian company) suggest (see the FYI box, The Enron Implosion).

The asymmetric information problem of adverse selection in financial markets helps explain why financial markets are among the most heavily regulated sectors in the economy (fact 5). Government regulation to increase information for investors is needed to reduce the adverse selection problem, which interferes with the efficient functioning of securities (stock and bond) markets.

FYI   **The Enron Implosion**

Until 2001, Enron Corporation, a firm that specialized in trading in the energy market, appeared to be spectacularly successful. It had a quarter of the energy-trading market and was valued as high as US$77 billion in August 2000 (just a little over a year before its collapse), making it the seventh largest corporation in the United States at that time. Toward the end of 2001, however, Enron came crashing down. In October 2001, Enron announced a third-quarter loss of US$618 million and disclosed accounting "mistakes." The U.S. SEC then engaged in a formal investigation of Enron's financial dealings with partnerships led by its former finance chief. It became clear that Enron was engaged in a complex set of transactions by which it was keeping substantial amounts of debt and financial contracts off its balance sheet. These transactions enabled Enron to hide its financial difficulties.

Despite securing as much as US$1.5 billion of new financing from JPMorgan Chase and Citigroup, the company was forced to declare bankruptcy in December 2001, making it the largest bankruptcy in U.S. history.

The Enron collapse illustrates that government regulation can lessen asymmetric information problems but cannot eliminate them. Managers have tremendous incentives to hide their companies' problems, making it hard for investors to know the true value of the firm.

The Enron bankruptcy not only increased concerns in financial markets about the quality of accounting information supplied by corporations, but it also led to hardship for many of the former employees who found that their pensions had become worthless. Outrage against executives at Enron was high, and several were indicted, convicted, and sent to jail.

Although government regulation lessens the adverse selection problem, it does not eliminate it. Even when firms provide information to the public about their sales, assets, or earnings, they still have more information than investors: there is a lot more to knowing the quality of a firm than statistics can provide. Furthermore, bad firms have an incentive to make themselves look like good firms because this would enable them to fetch a higher price for their securities. Bad firms will slant the information they are required to transmit to the public, thus making it harder for investors to sort out the good firms from the bad.

FINANCIAL INTERMEDIATION So far we have seen that private production of information and government regulation to encourage provision of information lessen but do not eliminate the adverse selection problem in financial markets. How, then, can the financial structure help promote the flow of funds to people with productive investment opportunities when there is asymmetric information? A clue is provided by the structure of the used-car market.

An important feature of the used-car market is that most used cars are not sold directly by one individual to another. An individual considering buying a used car might pay for privately produced information by subscribing to a magazine like *Consumer Reports* to find out if a particular make of car has a good repair record. Nevertheless, reading *Consumer Reports* does not solve the adverse selection problem because even if a particular make of car has a good reputation, the specific car someone is trying to sell could be a lemon. The prospective buyer might also bring the used car to a mechanic for a once-over. But what if the prospective buyer doesn't know a mechanic who can be trusted or if the mechanic charges a high fee to evaluate the car?

Because these roadblocks make it hard for individuals to acquire enough information about used cars, most used cars are not sold directly by one individual to another. Instead, they are sold by an intermediary, a used-car dealer who purchases used cars from individuals and resells them to other individuals. Used-car dealers produce information in the market by becoming experts in determining whether a car is a peach or a lemon. Once they know that a car is good, they can sell it with some form of a guarantee: either a guarantee that is explicit, such as a warranty, or an implicit guarantee in which they stand by their reputation for honesty. People are more likely to purchase a used car because of a dealer's guarantee, and the dealer is able to make a profit on the production of information about automobile quality by being able to sell the used car at a higher price than the dealer paid for it. If dealers purchase and then resell cars on which they have produced information, they avoid the problem of other people free-riding on the information they produced.

Just as used-car dealers help solve adverse selection problems in the automobile market, financial intermediaries play a similar role in financial markets. A financial intermediary such as a bank becomes an expert in producing information about firms so that it can sort out good credit risks from bad ones. Then it can acquire funds from depositors and lend them to the good firms. Because the bank is able to lend mostly to good firms, it is able to earn a higher return on its loans than the interest it has to pay to its depositors. The resulting profit that the bank earns allows it to engage in this information production activity.

An important element in the bank's ability to profit from the information it produces is that it avoids the free-rider problem by primarily making private loans rather than by purchasing securities that are traded in the open market. Because a private loan is not traded, other investors cannot watch what the bank is doing and bid up the loan's price to the point that the bank receives no compensation for the information it has produced. The bank's role as an intermediary that holds mostly nontraded loans is the key to its success in reducing asymmetric information in financial markets.

Our analysis of adverse selection indicates that financial intermediaries in general, and banks in particular because they hold a large fraction of nontraded loans, should play a greater role in moving funds to corporations than securities markets do. Our analysis thus explains facts 3 and 4: why indirect finance is so much more important than direct finance and why banks are the most important source of external funds for financing businesses.

Another important fact that is explained by the analysis here is the greater importance of banks in the financial systems of developing countries. As we have seen, when the quality of information about firms is better, asymmetric information problems will be less severe, and it will be easier for firms to issue securities. Information about private firms is harder to collect in developing countries than in industrialized countries; therefore, the smaller role played by securities markets leaves a greater role for financial intermediaries such as banks. A corollary of this analysis is that as information about firms becomes easier to acquire, the role of banks should decline. A major development in the past 20 years has been huge improvements in information technology. Thus the analysis here suggests that the lending role of financial institutions such as banks should have declined, and this is exactly what has occurred.

Our analysis of adverse selection also explains fact 6, which questions why large firms are more likely to obtain funds from securities markets, a direct route, rather than from banks and financial intermediaries, an indirect route. The better known a corporation is, the more information about its activities is available in the marketplace. Thus it is easier for investors to evaluate the quality of the corporation and determine whether it is a good firm or a bad one. Because investors have fewer worries about adverse selection with well-known corporations, they will be willing to invest directly in their securities. Our adverse selection analysis thus suggests that there should be a pecking order for firms that can issue securities. Hence we have an explanation for fact 6: The larger and more established a corporation is, the more likely it will be to issue securities to raise funds.

COLLATERAL AND NET WORTH   Adverse selection interferes with the functioning of financial markets only if a lender suffers a loss when a borrower is unable to make loan payments and thereby defaults. Collateral, property promised to the lender if the borrower defaults, reduces the consequences of adverse selection because it reduces the lender's losses in the event of a default. If a borrower defaults on a loan, the lender can sell the collateral and use the proceeds to make up for the losses on the loan. For example, if you fail to make your mortgage payments, the lender can take title to your house, auction it off, and use the receipts to pay off the loan. Lenders are thus more willing to make loans secured by collateral, and borrowers are willing to supply collateral because the reduced risk for the lender makes it more likely they will get the loan in the first place and perhaps at a better loan rate. The presence of adverse selection in credit markets thus provides an explanation for why collateral is an important feature of debt contracts (fact 7).

Net worth (also called **equity capital**), the difference between a firm's assets (what it owns or is owed) and its liabilities (what it owes), can perform a similar role to collateral. If a firm has a high net worth, then even if it engages in investments that cause it to have negative profits and so defaults on its debt payments, the lender can take title to the firm's net worth, sell it off, and use the proceeds to recoup some of the losses from the loan. In addition, the more net worth a firm has in the first place, the less likely it is to default because the firm has a cushion of assets that it can use to pay off its loans. Hence when firms seeking credit have high net worth, the consequences of adverse selection are less important and lenders are more willing to make loans. This analysis lies behind the often-heard lament, "Only the people who don't need money can borrow it!"

Summary

So far we have used the concept of adverse selection to explain seven of the eight facts about financial structure introduced earlier: the first four emphasize the importance of financial intermediaries and the relative unimportance of securities markets for the financing of corporations; the fifth, that financial markets are among the most heavily regulated sectors of the economy; the sixth, that only large, well-established corporations have access to securities markets; and the seventh, that collateral is an important feature of debt contracts. In the next section we will see that the other asymmetric information concept of moral hazard provides additional reasons for the importance of financial intermediaries and the relative unimportance of securities markets for the financing of corporations, the prevalence of government regulation, and the importance of collateral in debt contracts. In addition, the concept of moral hazard can be used to explain our final fact (fact 8) of why debt contracts are complicated legal documents that place substantial restrictions on the behaviour of borrowers.

HOW MORAL HAZARD AFFECTS THE CHOICE BETWEEN DEBT AND EQUITY CONTRACTS

Moral hazard is the asymmetric information problem that occurs after the financial transaction takes place, when the seller of a security may have incentives to hide information and engage in activities that are undesirable for the purchaser of the security. Moral hazard has important consequences for whether a firm finds it easier to raise funds with debt than with equity contracts.

Moral Hazard in Equity Contracts: The Principal–Agent Problem

Equity contracts, such as common stock, are claims to a share in the profits and assets of a business. Equity contracts are subject to a particular type of moral hazard called the **principal–agent problem**. When managers own only a small fraction of the firm they work for, the stockholders who own most of the firm's equity (called the *principals*) are not the same people as the managers of the firm, who are the *agents* of the owners. This separation of ownership and control involves moral hazard in that the managers in control (the agents) may act in their own interest rather than in the interest of the stockholder-owners (the principals) because the managers have less incentive to maximize profits than the stockholder-owners do.

To understand the principal–agent problem more fully, suppose that your friend Steve asks you to become a silent partner in his ice-cream store. The store requires an investment of $10 000 to set up and Steve has only $1000. So you purchase an equity stake (shares) for $9000, which entitles you to 90% of the ownership of the firm, while Steve owns only 10%. If Steve works hard to make tasty ice cream, keeps the store clean, smiles at all the customers, and hustles to wait on tables quickly, after all expenses (including Steve's salary), the store will have

$50 000 in profits per year, of which Steve receives 10% ($5000) and you receive 90% ($45 000).

But if Steve doesn't provide quick and friendly service to his customers, uses the $50 000 in income to buy artwork for his office, and even sneaks off to the beach while he should be at the store, the store will not earn any profit. Steve can earn the additional $5000 (his 10% share of the profits) over his salary only if he works hard and forgoes unproductive investments (such as art for his office). Steve might decide that the extra $5000 just isn't enough to make him want to expend the effort to be a good manager; he might decide that it would be worth his while only if he earned an extra $10 000. If Steve feels this way, he does not have enough incentive to be a good manager and will end up with a beautiful office, a good tan, and a store that doesn't show any profits. Because the store won't show any profits, Steve's decision not to act in your interest will cost you $45 000 (your 90% of the profits if he had chosen to be a good manager instead).

The moral hazard arising from the principal–agent problem might be even worse if Steve were not totally honest. Because his ice-cream store is a cash business, Steve has the incentive to pocket $50 000 in cash and tell you that the profits were zero. He now gets a return of $50 000, and you get nothing.

Further indications that the principal–agent problem created by equity contracts can be severe are provided by recent corporate scandals in corporations such as Enron and Tyco International, in which managers have been accused of diverting funds for personal use. Besides pursuing personal benefits, managers might also pursue corporate strategies (such as the acquisition of other firms) that enhance their personal power but do not increase the corporation's profitability.

The principal–agent problem would not arise if the owners of a firm had complete information about what the managers were up to and could prevent wasteful expenditures or fraud. The principal–agent problem, which is an example of moral hazard, arises only because a manager, like Steve, has more information about his activities than the stockholder does—that is, there is asymmetric information. The principal–agent problem would also not arise if Steve alone owned the store and there were no separation of ownership and control. If this were the case, Steve's hard work and avoidance of unproductive investments would yield him a profit (and extra income) of $50 000, an amount that would make it worth his while to be a good manager.

Tools to Help Solve the Principal–Agent Problem

PRODUCTION OF INFORMATION: MONITORING   You have seen that the principal–agent problem arises because managers have more information about their activities and actual profits than stockholders do. One way for stockholders to reduce this moral hazard problem is for them to engage in a particular type of information production, the monitoring of the firm's activities: auditing the firm frequently and checking on what the management is doing. The problem is that the monitoring process can be expensive in terms of time and money, as reflected in the name economists give it, **costly state verification**. Costly state verification makes the equity contract less desirable, and it explains, in part, why equity is not a more important element in our financial structure.

As with adverse selection, the free-rider problem decreases the amount of information production that would reduce the moral hazard (principal–agent) problem. In this example, the free-rider problem decreases monitoring. If you know that other stockholders are paying to monitor the activities of the company you hold shares in, you can take a free ride on their activities. Then you can use the money you save by not engaging in monitoring to vacation on a Caribbean island. If you can do this, though, so can other stockholders. Perhaps all the stockholders will go to the islands, and no one will spend any resources on monitoring the firm. The moral hazard problem for shares of common stock will then be severe, making it hard for firms to issue them to raise capital (providing an explanation for fact 1).

GOVERNMENT REGULATION TO INCREASE INFORMATION   As with adverse selection, the government has an incentive to try to reduce the moral hazard problem created by asymmetric information, which provides another reason why the financial system is so heavily regulated (fact 5). Governments everywhere have laws to force firms to adhere to standard accounting principles that make profit verification easier. They also pass laws to impose stiff criminal penalties on people who commit the fraud of hiding and stealing profits. However, these measures can only be partly effective. Catching this kind of fraud is not easy; fraudulent managers have the incentive to make it very hard for government agencies to find or prove fraud.

FINANCIAL INTERMEDIATION   Financial intermediaries have the ability to avoid the free-rider problem in the face of moral hazard, and this is another reason why indirect finance is so important (fact 3). One financial intermediary that helps reduce the moral hazard arising from the principal–agent problem is the **venture capital firm**. Venture capital firms pool the resources of their partners and use the funds to help budding entrepreneurs start new businesses. In exchange for the use of the venture capital, the firm receives an equity share in the new business. Because verification of earnings and profits is so important in eliminating moral hazard, venture capital firms usually insist on having several of their own people participate as members of the managing body of the firm, the board of directors, so that they can keep a close watch on the firm's activities. When a venture capital firm supplies start-up funds, the equity in the firm is not marketable to anyone *but* the venture capital firm. Thus other investors are unable to take a free ride on the venture capital firm's verification activities. As a result of this arrangement, the venture capital firm is able to garner the full benefits of its verification activities and is given the appropriate incentives to reduce the moral hazard problem.

Venture capital firms have been important in the development of the high-tech sector in Canada and the United States, which has resulted in job creation, economic growth, and increased international competitiveness.

DEBT CONTRACTS   Moral hazard arises with an equity contract, which is a claim on profits in all situations, whether the firm is making or losing money. If a contract could be structured so that moral hazard would exist only in certain situations, there would be a reduced need to monitor managers, and the contract would be more attractive than the equity contract. The debt contract has exactly these attributes because it is a contractual agreement by the borrower to pay the lender *fixed* dollar amounts at periodic intervals. When the firm has high profits, the lender receives the contractual payments and does not need to know the exact profits of the firm. If the managers are hiding profits or are pursuing activities that are personally beneficial but don't increase profitability, the lender doesn't care as long as these activities do not interfere with the ability of the firm to make its debt payments on time. Only when the firm cannot meet its debt payments, thereby being in a state of default, is there a need for the lender to verify the state of the firm's profits. Only in this situation do lenders involved in debt contracts need to act more like equity holders; now they need to know how much income the firm has in order to get their fair share.

The less frequent need to monitor the firm, and thus a lower cost of state verification, helps explain why debt contracts are used more frequently than equity contracts to raise capital. The concept of moral hazard thus helps explain fact 1, why stocks are not the most important source of financing for businesses.[4]

HOW MORAL HAZARD INFLUENCES FINANCIAL STRUCTURE IN DEBT MARKETS

Even with the advantages just described, debt contracts are still subject to moral hazard. Because a debt contract requires the borrowers to pay out a fixed amount and lets them keep any profits above this amount, the borrowers have an incentive to take on investment projects that are riskier than the lenders would like.

For example, suppose that because you are concerned about the problem of verifying the profits of Steve's ice-cream store, you decide not to become an equity partner. Instead, you lend Steve the $9000 he needs to set up his business and have a debt contract that pays you an interest rate of 10%. As far as you are concerned, this is a surefire investment because there is a strong and steady demand for ice cream in your neighbourhood. However, once you give Steve the funds, he might use them for purposes other than you intended. Instead of opening up the ice-cream store, Steve might use your $9000 loan to invest in chemical research equipment because he thinks he has a 1-in-10 chance of inventing a diet ice cream that tastes every bit as good as the premium brands but has no fat or calories.

Obviously, this is a very risky investment, but if Steve is successful, he will become a multimillionaire. He has a strong incentive to undertake the riskier investment with your money because the gains to him would be so large if he succeeded. You would clearly be very unhappy if Steve used your loan for the riskier investment because if he were unsuccessful, which is highly likely, you would lose most, if not all, of the money you loaned him. And if he were successful, you wouldn't share in his success—you would still get only a 10% return on the loan because the principal and interest payments are fixed. Because of the potential moral hazard (that Steve might use your money to finance a very risky venture), you would probably not make the loan to Steve, even though an ice-cream store in the neighbourhood is a good investment that would provide benefits for everyone.

Tools to Help Solve Moral Hazard in Debt Contracts

NET WORTH AND COLLATERAL   When borrowers have more at stake because their net worth (the difference between their assets and liabilities) or the collateral they have pledged to the lender is high, the risk of moral hazard—the temptation to act in a manner that lenders find objectionable—will be greatly reduced because the borrowers themselves have a lot to lose. Let's return to Steve and his ice-cream business. Suppose that the cost of setting up either the ice-cream store or the

---

[4] Another factor that encourages the use of debt contracts rather than equity contracts is our tax laws. Debt interest payments are a deductible expense for Canadian firms, whereas dividend payments to equity shareholders are not.

research equipment is $100 000 instead of $10 000. So Steve needs to put $91 000 of his own money into the business (instead of $1000) in addition to the $9000 supplied by your loan. Now if Steve is unsuccessful in inventing the no-calorie nonfat ice cream, he has a lot to lose, the $91 000 of net worth ($100 000 in assets minus the $9000 loan from you). He will think twice about undertaking the riskier investment and is more likely to invest in the ice-cream store, which is more of a sure thing. Hence when Steve has more of his own money (net worth) in the business, you are more likely to make him the loan.

Similarly, if you have pledged your house as collateral, you are less likely to go to Las Vegas and gamble away your earnings that month because you might not be able to make your mortgage payments and might lose your house.

One way of describing the solution that high net worth and collateral provides to the moral hazard problem is to say that it makes the debt contract **incentive-compatible**; that is, it aligns the incentives of the borrower with those of the lender. The greater the borrower's net worth and collateral pledged, the greater the borrower's incentive to behave in the way that the lender expects and desires, the smaller the moral hazard problem in the debt contract and the easier it is for the firm or household to borrow. Conversely, when the borrower's net worth and collateral is lower, the moral hazard problem is greater, and it is harder to borrow.

MONITORING AND ENFORCEMENT OF RESTRICTIVE COVENANTS   As the example of Steve and his ice-cream store shows, if you could make sure that Steve doesn't invest in anything riskier than the ice-cream store, it would be worth your while to make him the loan. You can ensure that Steve uses your money for the purpose *you* want it to be used for by writing provisions (restrictive covenants) into the debt contract that restrict his firm's activities. By monitoring Steve's activities to see whether he is complying with the restrictive covenants and enforcing the covenants if he is not, you can make sure that he will not take on risks at your expense. Restrictive covenants are directed at reducing moral hazard either by ruling out undesirable behaviour or by encouraging desirable behaviour. There are four types of restrictive covenants that achieve this objective:

1. ***Covenants to discourage undesirable behaviour.*** Covenants can be designed to lower moral hazard by keeping the borrower from engaging in the undesirable behaviour of undertaking risky investment projects. Some covenants mandate that a loan can be used only to finance specific activities, such as the purchase of particular equipment or inventories. Others restrict the borrowing firm from engaging in certain risky business activities, such as purchasing other businesses.

2. ***Covenants to encourage desirable behaviour.*** Restrictive covenants can encourage the borrower to engage in desirable activities that make it more likely that the loan will be paid off. One restrictive covenant of this type requires the breadwinner in a household to carry life insurance that pays off the mortgage upon that person's death. Restrictive covenants of this type for businesses focus on encouraging the borrowing firm to keep its net worth high because higher borrower net worth reduces moral hazard and makes it less likely that the lender will suffer losses. These restrictive covenants typically specify that the firm must maintain minimum holdings of certain assets relative to the firm's size.

3. ***Covenants to keep collateral valuable.*** Because collateral is an important protection for the lender, restrictive covenants can encourage the borrower to keep the collateral in good condition and make sure that it stays in the possession of the borrower. This is the type of covenant ordinary people encounter most often. Automobile loan contracts, for example, require the car owner to maintain a minimum amount of collision and theft insurance and prevent the sale of the car unless the loan is paid off. Similarly, the recipient of a home mortgage must have adequate insurance on the home and must pay off the mortgage when the property is sold.

4. ***Covenants to provide information.*** Restrictive covenants also require a borrowing firm to provide information about its activities periodically in the form of quarterly financial statements, thereby making it easier for the lender to monitor the firm and reduce moral hazard. This type of covenant may also stipulate that the lender has the right to audit and inspect the firm's books at any time.

We now see why debt contracts are often complicated legal documents with numerous restrictions on the borrower's behaviour (fact 8): debt contracts require complicated restrictive covenants to lower moral hazard.

FINANCIAL INTERMEDIATION   Although restrictive covenants help reduce the moral hazard problem, they do not eliminate it completely. It is almost impossible to write covenants that rule out *every* risky activity. Furthermore, borrowers may be clever enough to find loopholes in restrictive covenants that make them ineffective.

Another problem with restrictive covenants is that they must be monitored and enforced. A restrictive covenant is meaningless if the borrower can violate it knowing that the lender won't check up or is unwilling to pay for legal recourse. Because monitoring and enforcement of restrictive covenants are costly, the free-rider problem arises in the debt securities (bond) market just as it does in the stock market. If you know that other bondholders are monitoring and enforcing the restrictive covenants, you can free-ride on their monitoring and enforcement. But other bondholders can do the same thing, so the likely outcome is that not enough resources are devoted to monitoring and enforcing the restrictive covenants. Moral hazard therefore continues to be a severe problem for marketable debt.

As we have seen before, financial intermediaries, particularly banks, have the ability to avoid the free-rider problem as long as they primarily make private loans. Private loans are not traded, so no one else can free-ride on the intermediary's monitoring and enforcement of the restrictive covenants. The intermediary making private loans thus receives the benefits of monitoring and enforcement and will work to shrink the moral hazard problem inherent in debt contracts. The concept of moral hazard has provided us with additional reasons why financial intermediaries play a more important role in channelling funds from savers to borrowers than marketable securities do, as described in facts 3 and 4.

Summary

The presence of asymmetric information in financial markets leads to adverse selection and moral hazard problems that interfere with the efficient functioning of those markets. Tools to help solve these problems involve the private production and sale of information, government regulation to increase information in financial markets, the importance of collateral and net worth to debt contracts, and the use of monitoring and restrictive covenants. A key finding from our analysis is that the existence of the free-rider problem for traded securities such as stocks and bonds indicates that financial intermediaries, particularly banks, should play a greater role than securities markets in financing the activities of businesses. Economic analysis of the consequences of adverse selection and moral hazard has helped explain the basic features of our financial system and has provided solutions to the eight facts about our financial structure outlined at the beginning of this chapter.

To help you keep track of the tools that help solve asymmetric information problems, Table 8-1 provides a listing of the asymmetric information problems and tools that can help solve them. In addition, it lists how these tools and asymmetric information problems explain the eight facts of financial structure described at the beginning of the chapter.

TABLE 8-1 Asymmetric Information Problems and Tools to Solve Them

Asymmetric Information Problem	Tools to Solve It	Explains Fact No.
Adverse selection	Private production and sale of information	1, 2
	Government regulation to increase information	5
	Financial intermediation	3, 4, 6
	Collateral and net worth	7
Moral hazard in equity contracts (principal–agent problem)	Production of information: monitoring	1
	Government regulation to increase information	5
	Financial intermediation	3
	Debt contracts	1
Moral hazard in debt contracts	Net worth and collateral	7
	Monitoring and enforcement of restrictive covenants	8
	Financial intermediation	3, 4

Note: List of facts:

1. Stocks are not the most important source of external financing.
2. Marketable securities are not the primary source of finance.
3. Indirect finance is more important than direct finance.
4. Banks are the most important source of external funds.
5. The financial system is heavily regulated.
6. Only large, well-established firms have easy access to securities markets.
7. Collateral is prevalent in debt contracts.
8. Debt contracts have numerous restrictive covenants.

APPLICATION   Financial Development and Economic Growth

Recent research has found that an important reason why many developing countries or ex-communist countries like Russia (which are referred to as transition countries) experience very low rates of growth is that their financial systems are underdeveloped (a situation referred to as *financial repression*).[5] The economic analysis of financial structure helps explain how an underdeveloped financial system leads to a low state of economic development and economic growth.

The financial systems in developing and transition countries face several difficulties that keep them from operating efficiently. As we have seen, two important tools used to help solve adverse selection and moral hazard problems in credit markets are collateral and restrictive covenants. In many developing countries, the system of property rights (the rule of law, constraints on government expropriation, absence of corruption) functions poorly, making it hard to make effective use of these two tools. In these countries, bankruptcy procedures are often extremely slow and cumbersome. For example, in many countries, creditors (holders of debt) must first sue the defaulting debtor for payment, which can take several years, and then once a favourable judgement has been obtained, the creditor has to sue again to obtain title to the collateral. The process can take in excess of five years, and by the time the lender acquires the collateral, it may have been neglected and thus have little value. In addition, governments often block lenders from foreclosing on borrowers in politically powerful sectors such as agriculture. Where the market is unable to use collateral effectively, the adverse selection problem will be worse because the lender will need even more information about the quality of the borrower in order to screen out a good loan from a bad one. The result is that it will be harder for lenders to channel funds to borrowers with the most productive investment opportunities. There will be less productive investment and hence a slower-growing economy. Similarly, a poorly developed or corrupt legal system may make it extremely difficult for lenders to enforce restrictive covenants. Thus they may have a much more limited ability to reduce moral hazard on the part of borrowers and so will be less willing to lend. Again the outcome will be less-productive investment and a lower growth rate for the economy. The importance of an effective legal system in promoting economic growth suggests that lawyers play a more positive role in the economy than we give them credit for (see the FYI box, Let the Lawyers Live!).

Governments in developing and transition countries often use their financial systems to direct credit to themselves or to favoured sectors of the economy by setting interest rates at artificially low levels for certain types of loans, by creating so-called development finance institutions to make specific types of loans, or by directing existing institutions to lend to certain entities. As we have seen, private institutions have an incentive to solve adverse selection and moral hazard problems and lend to borrowers with the most productive investment opportunities. Governments have less incentive to do so because they are not driven by the profit motive and so their directed credit programs may not channel funds to sectors that will produce high growth for the economy. The outcome is again likely to result in less-efficient investment and slower growth.

---

[5] See World Bank, *Finance for Growth: Policy Choices in a Volatile World* (World Bank and Oxford University Press, 2001) for a survey of the literature linking economic growth to financial development and a list of additional references.

In addition, banks in many developing and transition countries are owned by their governments. Again because of the absence of the profit motive, these **state-owned banks** have little incentive to allocate their capital to the most productive uses. Not surprisingly, the primary loan customer of these state-owned banks is often the government, which does not always use the funds wisely.

FYI   Let the Lawyers Live!

Lawyers are often an easy target for would-be comedians. Countless jokes centre on ambulance-chasing and shifty filers of frivolous lawsuits. Hostility to lawyers is not just a recent phenomenon: in Shakespeare's *Henry VI*, written in the late sixteenth century, Dick the Butcher recommends, "The first thing we do, let's kill all the lawyers." Is Shakespeare's Dick the Butcher right?

Most legal work is actually not about ambulance chasing, criminal law, and frivolous lawsuits. Instead, it involves the writing and enforcement of contracts, which is how property rights are established. Property rights are essential to protect investments. A good system of laws, by itself, does not provide incentives to invest, because property rights without enforcement are meaningless. This is where lawyers come in. When some-

one encroaches on your land or makes use of your property without your permission, a lawyer can stop him or her. Without lawyers, you would be unwilling to invest. With zero or limited investment, there would be little economic growth.

Canada and the United States have more lawyers per capita than many other countries in the world. They are also among the richest countries in the world with a financial system that is superb at getting capital to new productive uses such as the technology sector. Is this just a coincidence? Or could the legal system actually be beneficial to its economy? Recent research suggests the American legal system, which is based on the Anglo-Saxon legal system, is actually a big advantage for the U.S. economy.*

*See Rafael La Porta, Florencio Lopez-de-Silanes, Andrei Shleifer, and Robert W. Vishny, "Legal Determinants of External Finance," *Journal of Finance* 52 (3), pp. 1131–1150; and Rafael La Porta, Florencio Lopez-de-Silanes, Andrei Shleifer, and Robert W. Vishny, "Law and Finance," *Journal of Political Economy* 106 (6), pp. 1113–1155.

We have seen that government regulation can increase the amount of information in financial markets to make them work more efficiently. Many developing and transition countries have an underdeveloped regulatory apparatus that retards the provision of adequate information to the marketplace. For example, these countries often have weak accounting standards, making it very hard to ascertain the quality of a borrower's balance sheet. As a result, asymmetric information problems are more severe, and the financial system is severely hampered in channelling funds to the most productive uses.

The institutional environment of a poor legal system, weak accounting standards, inadequate government regulation, and government intervention through directed credit programs and state ownership of banks all help explain why many countries stay poor while others grow richer.

Is China a Counter Example to the Importance of Financial Development?

Although China appears to be on its way to becoming an economic powerhouse, its financial development is still in its early stages. The country's legal system is weak so that financial contracts are difficult to enforce, while accounting standards are lax so that high-quality information about creditors is hard to find. Regulation of the banking system is still in its formative stages, and the banking sector is dominated by large state-owned banks. Yet China has had one of the highest growth rates in the world over the last twenty years. How has China been able to grow so rapidly given its low level of financial development?

As noted above, China is in an early state of development with a per capita income that is still less than US$5000, one-eighth that in the United States. With an extremely high savings rate averaging around 40% over the last two decades, it has been able to rapidly build up its capital stock and shift a massive pool of underutilized labour from the subsistence agriculture sector into higher-productivity activities that use capital. Even though available savings have not been allocated to their most productive uses, the huge increase in capital, when combined with the gains in productivity from moving labour out of low-productivity subsistence agriculture, has been enough to produce high growth.

As China gets richer, however, this strategy is unlikely to work. The Soviet Union provides a graphic example. In the 1950s and 60s, the Soviet Union had many similarities to China. It had high growth fuelled by a high savings rate, a massive buildup of capital, and shifts of a large pool of underutilized labour from subsistence agriculture to manufacturing. During this high-growth phase, the Soviet Union was unable to develop the institutions to allocate capital efficiently. As a result, once the pool of subsistence labourers was used up, the Soviet Union's growth slowed dramatically and it was unable to keep up with the West. Today no one considers the Soviet Union to have been an economic success story, and its inability to develop the institutions necessary to sustain financial development and growth was an important reason for the demise of this once superpower.

To get to the next stage of development, China will need to allocate its capital more efficiently, and to do this it has to improve its financial system. The Chinese leadership is well aware of this challenge: The government has announced that state-owned banks are being put on the path to privatization. In addition, the government is engaged in legal reform to make financial contracts more enforceable. New bankruptcy law is being developed so that lenders have the ability to take over the assets of firms that default on their loan contracts. Whether the Chinese government will be successful in developing a first-rate financial system, thereby enabling China to join the ranks of developed countries, is a big question mark.

CONFLICTS OF INTEREST

Earlier in the chapter, we saw how financial institutions play an important role in the financial system. Specifically, their expertise in interpreting signals and collecting information from their customers gives them a cost advantage in the production of information. Furthermore, because they are collecting, producing, and distributing this information, the financial institutions can use the information over and over again in as many ways as they would like, thereby obtaining economies of scale. By providing multiple financial services to their customers, such as providing them with bank loans or selling their bonds for them, they can also obtain **economies of scope**—that is, they can lower the cost of information production for each service by applying one information resource to many different services. A bank, for example, can evaluate how good a credit risk a corporation is when making them a loan, which then helps the bank decide whether it would be easy for it to sell the bonds of this corporation to the public. Additionally, by providing multiple financial services to their customers, financial institutions develop broader and longer-term relationships with firms. These relationships further reduce the cost of producing information, and further increase economies of scope.

Although the presence of economies of scope may substantially benefit financial institutions, it also creates potential costs in terms of **conflicts of interest**. Conflicts of interest are a type of moral hazard problem that arise when a person or institution has multiple objectives (interests) and, as a result, has conflicts between those objectives. Conflicts of interest are especially likely to occur when a financial institution provides multiple services. The potentially competing interests of those services may lead an individual or firm to conceal information or disseminate misleading information. Here we use the analysis of asymmetric information problems to understand why conflicts of interest are important, why they arise, and what can be done about them.

Why Do We Care About Conflicts of Interest?

We care about conflicts of interest because a substantial reduction in the quality of information in financial markets increases asymmetric information problems and prevents financial markets from channelling funds into productive investment opportunities. Consequently, the financial markets and the economy become less efficient.

Why Do Conflicts of Interest Arise?

Three types of financial service activities have led to prominent conflict-of-interest problems in financial markets in recent years:[6] underwriting and research in investment banks, auditing and consulting in accounting firms, and credit assessment and consulting in credit-rating agencies. Why do combinations of these activities so often produce conflicts of interest?

UNDERWRITING AND RESEARCH IN INVESTMENT BANKING Investment banks perform two tasks: They *research* companies issuing securities, and they *underwrite* these securities by selling them to the public on behalf of the issuing corporations. Investment banks often combine these distinct financial services because information synergies are possible: That is, information produced for one task may also be useful in the other task. A conflict of interest arises between the brokerage and underwriting services because the banks are attempting to simulta-

---

[6] Another important type of conflict of interest arises in universal banking, in which banks engage in multiple financial service activities, including commercial banking, investment banking, and insurance. For further analysis of these conflicts of interest, see Andrew Crockett, Trevor Harris, Frederic S. Mishkin, and Eugene N. White, *Conflicts of Interest in the Financial Services Industry: What Should We Do About Them?*, Geneva Reports on the World Economy 4 (International Center for Monetary and Banking Studies and Centre for Economic Policy Research: Geneva and London, 2003).

neously serve two client groups—the security-issuing firms and the security-buying investors. These client groups have different information needs. Issuers benefit from optimistic research, whereas investors desire unbiased research. However, the same information will be produced for both groups to take advantage of economies of scope. When the potential revenues from underwriting greatly exceed the brokerage commissions from selling, the bank will have a strong incentive to alter the information provided to investors to favour the issuing firm's needs or else risk losing the firm's business to competing investment banks. For example, an internal Morgan Stanley memo excerpted in the *Wall Street Journal* on July 14, 1992, stated, "Our objective . . . is to adopt a policy, fully understood by the entire firm, including the Research Department, that we do not make negative or controversial comments about our clients as a matter of sound business practice."

Because of directives like this one, analysts in investment banks might distort their research to please issuers, and indeed this seems to have happened during the stock market tech boom of the 1990s. Such actions undermine the reliability of the information that investors use to make their financial decisions and, as a result, diminish the efficiency of securities markets.

Another common practice that exploits conflicts of interest is **spinning**. Spinning occurs when an investment bank allocates hot, but underpriced, **initial public offerings (IPOs)**—that is, shares of newly issued stock—to executives of other companies in return for their companies' future business with the investment bank. Because hot IPOs typically immediately rise in price after they are first purchased, spinning is a form of kickback meant to persuade executives to use that investment bank. When the executive's company plans to issue its own shares, he or she will be more likely to go to the investment bank that distributed the hot IPO shares, which is not necessarily the investment bank that would get the highest price for the company's securities. This practice may raise the cost of capital for the firm, thereby diminishing the efficiency of the capital market.

AUDITING AND CONSULTING IN ACCOUNTING FIRMS   Traditionally, an auditor checks the books of companies and monitors the quality of the information produced by firms to reduce the inevitable information asymmetry between the firm's managers and its shareholders. In auditing, threats to truthful reporting arise from several potential conflicts of interest. The conflict of interest that has received the most attention in the media occurs when an accounting firm provides its client with both auditing services and nonaudit consulting services such as advice on taxes, accounting, management information systems, and business strategy. Supplying clients with multiple services allows for economies of scale and scope, but creates two potential sources of conflicts of interest. First, auditors may be willing to skew their judgements and opinions to win consulting business from these same clients. Second, auditors may be auditing information systems or tax and financial plans put in place by their nonaudit counterparts within the firm, and therefore may be reluctant to criticize the systems or advice. Both types of conflicts may lead to biased audits, with the result that less reliable information is available in financial markets and investors find it difficult to allocate capital efficiently.

Another conflict of interest arises when an auditor provides an overly favourable audit to solicit or retain audit business. The unfortunate collapse of Arthur Andersen—once one of the five largest accounting firms in the United States—suggests that this may be the most dangerous conflict of interest.

Credit Assessment and Consulting in Credit-Rating Agencies

Investors use credit ratings (e.g., AAA or BAA) that reflect the probability of default to determine the creditworthiness of particular debt securities. As a consequence, debt ratings play a major role in the pricing of debt securities and in the regulatory process. Conflicts of interest can arise when multiple users with divergent interests (at least in the short term) depend on the credit ratings. Investors and regulators are seeking a well-researched, impartial assessment of credit quality; the issuer needs a favourable rating. In the credit-rating industry, the issuers of securities pay a rating firm such as Standard & Poor's or Moody's to have their securities rated. Because the issuers are the parties paying the credit-rating agency, investors and regulators worry that the agency may bias its ratings upward to attract more business from the issuer.

Another kind of conflict of interest may arise when credit-rating agencies also provide ancillary consulting services. Debt issuers often ask rating agencies to advise them on how to structure their debt issues, usually with the goal of securing a favourable rating. In this situation, the credit-rating agencies would be auditing their own work and would experience a conflict of interest similar to the one found in accounting firms that provide both auditing and consulting services. Furthermore, credit-rating agencies may deliver favourable ratings to garner new clients for the ancillary consulting business. The possible decline in the quality of credit assessments issued by rating agencies could increase asymmetric information in financial markets, thereby diminishing their ability to allocate credit. Such conflicts of interest came to the forefront because of the damaged reputations of the credit-rating agencies during the subprime financial crisis starting in 2007 (see the FYI box, Credit-Rating Agencies and the Subprime Financial Crisis.)

What Has Been Done to Remedy Conflicts of Interest?

Two major policy measures were implemented in the United States to deal with conflicts of interest: the Sarbanes-Oxley Act and the Global Legal Settlement.

SARBANES-OXLEY ACT OF 2002   The public outcry over the corporate and accounting scandals in the United States led in 2002 to the passage of the Public Accounting Reform and Investor Protection Act, more commonly referred to as the Sarbanes-Oxley Act, after its two principal authors in Congress. This act increased supervisory oversight to monitor and prevent conflicts of interest:

- It established a Public Company Accounting Oversight Board (PCAOB), overseen by the SEC, to supervise accounting firms and ensure that audits are independent and controlled for quality.
- It increased the SEC's budget to supervise securities markets.

Sarbanes-Oxley also directly reduced conflicts of interest:

- It made it illegal for a registered public accounting firm to provide any non-audit service to a client contemporaneously with an impermissible audit (as determined by the PCAOB).

Sarbanes-Oxley provided incentives for investment banks not to exploit conflicts of interest:

- It beefed up criminal charges for white-collar crime and obstruction of official investigations.

FYI   Credit-Rating Agencies and the Subprime Financial Crisis

Credit-rating agencies have come under severe criticism for the role they played during the subprime financial crisis in the U.S. Credit-rating agencies advised clients on how to structure complex financial instruments that paid out cash flows from subprime mortgages. At the same time, they were rating these identical products, leading to the potential for severe conflicts of interest. Specifically, the large fees they earned from advising clients on how to structure products that they were rating meant they did not have sufficient incentives to make sure their ratings were accurate.

When housing prices began to fall and subprime mortgages began to default, it became crystal clear that the rating agencies had done a terrible job of assessing the risk in the subprime products they had helped to structure. Many AAA-rated products had to be downgraded over and over again until they reached junk status. The resulting massive losses on these assets were one reason why so many financial institutions that were holding them got into trouble, with absolutely disastrous consequences for the economy.

Criticisms of the credit-rating agencies led the U.S. Securities and Exchange Commision (SEC) to propose comprehensive reforms in 2008. The SEC concluded that the credit-rating agencies' models for rating subprime products were not fully developed and that conflicts of interest may have played a role in producing inaccurate ratings. To address conflicts of interest, the SEC prohibited credit-rating agencies from structuring the same products they rate, prohibited anyone who participates in determining a credit rating from negotiating the fee that the issuer pays for it, and prohibited gifts from bond-issuers to those who rate them in any amount over $25. In order to make credit-rating agencies more accountable, the SEC's new rules also required more disclosure of how the credit-rating agencies determine ratings. For example, credit-rating agencies were required to disclose historical ratings performance, including the dates of downgrades and upgrades, information on the underlying assets of a product that were used by the credit-rating agencies to rate a product, and the kind of research they used to determine the rating. In addition, the SEC required the rating agencies to differentiate the ratings on structured products from those issued on bonds. The expectation is that these reforms will bring increased transparency to the ratings process and reduce the conflicts of interest that played such a large role in the subprime debacle.

Sarbanes-Oxley also had measures to improve the quality of information in the financial markets:

- It required a corporation's chief executive officer (CEO) and chief financial officer (CFO), as well as its auditors, to certify the accuracy of periodic financial statements and disclosures of the firm (especially regarding off-balance-sheet transactions) (Section 404).

- It required members of the audit committee (the subcommittee of the board of directors that oversees the company's audit) to be "independent"; that is, they cannot be managers in the company or receive any consulting or advisory fee from the company.

FYI   The Demise of Arthur Andersen

In 1913, Arthur Andersen, a young accountant who had denounced the slipshod and deceptive practices that enabled companies to fool the investing public, founded his own firm. Up until the early 1980s, auditing was the most important source of profits within this firm. However, by the late 1980s, the consulting part of the business experienced high revenue growth with high profit margins, while audit profits slumped in a more competitive market. Consulting partners began to assert more power within the firm, and the resulting internal conflicts split the firm in two. Arthur Andersen (the auditing service) and Andersen Consulting were established as separate companies in 2000.

During the period of increasing conflict before the split, Andersen's audit partners had been under increasing pressure to focus on boosting revenue and profits from audit services. Many of Arthur Andersen's clients that later went bust—Enron, WorldCom, Qwest, and Global Crossing—were also the largest clients in Arthur Andersen's regional offices. The combination of intense pressure to generate revenue and profits from auditing and the fact that some clients dominated regional offices translated into tremendous incentives for regional office managers to provide favourable audit stances for these large clients. The loss of a client like Enron or WorldCom would have been devastating for a regional office and its partners, even if that client contributed only a small fraction of the overall revenue and profits of Arthur Andersen.

The Houston office of Arthur Andersen, for example, ignored problems in Enron's reporting. Arthur Andersen was indicted in March 2002 and then convicted in June 2002 for obstruction of justice for impeding the SEC's investigation of the Enron collapse. Its conviction—the first ever against a major accounting firm—barred Arthur Andersen from conducting audits of publicly traded firms. This development contributed to the firm's demise.

GLOBAL LEGAL SETTLEMENT OF 2002   The second major policy measure arose out of a lawsuit brought by New York Attorney General Eliot Spitzer against the ten largest investment banks (Bear Stearns, Credit Suisse First Boston, Deutsche Bank, Goldman Sachs, J.P. Morgan, Lehman Brothers, Merrill Lynch, Morgan Stanley, Salomon Smith Barney, and UBS Warburg). A global settlement was reached on December 20, 2002, with these investment banks by the SEC, the New York Attorney General, NASD, NASAA, NYSE, and state regulators. Like Sarbanes-Oxley, this settlement directly reduced conflicts of interest:

- It required investment banks to sever the links between research and securities underwriting.
- It banned spinning.

The Global Legal Settlement also provided incentives for investment banks not to exploit conflicts of interest:

- It imposed US$1.4 billion in fines on the accused investment banks.

The global settlement had measures to improve the quality of information in financial markets:

- It required investment banks to make their analysts' recommendations public.
- Over a five-year period, investment banks were required to contract with at least three independent research firms that would provide research to their brokerage customers.

CONTROL ATTESTATION IN CANADA   A great deal of regulatory initiatives with respect to corporate governance have also occupied public attention in Canada in recent years, in reaction to the issues raised by the corporate and accounting scandals in the United States. For example, in October 2002, the Ontario government introduced Bill 198, in response to the strong reforms taking place in the United States. Similar to the Sarbanes-Oxley Act, Bill 198 made several reforms to the securities laws in Ontario, including auditor independence, CEO and CFO accountability for financial reporting, enhanced penalties for illegal activities, and faster disclosure to the public. Moreover, in February 2005 the Canadian Securities Administrators released for comment the Internal Control Instrument and the Certification Instrument, two proposed instruments that substantially mirror the requirements of the Sarbanes-Oxley Act in the United States.

Summary

It is too early to evaluate the impact of the Sarbanes-Oxley Act and the Global Legal Settlement, but the most controversial elements were the separation of functions (research from underwriting, and auditing from nonaudit consulting). Although such a separation of functions may reduce conflicts of interest, it might also diminish economies of scope and thus potentially lead to a reduction of information in financial markets. In addition, there is a serious concern that implementation of these measures, particularly Sarbanes-Oxley, is too costly and is leading to a decline in U.S. capital markets (see the FYI box, Has Sarbanes-Oxley Led to a Decline in U.S. Capital Markets?).

SUMMARY

1. There are eight basic facts about financial structure throughout the world. The first four emphasize the importance of financial intermediaries and the relative unimportance of securities markets for the financing of corporations; the fifth recognizes that financial markets are among the most heavily regulated sectors of the economy; the sixth states that only large, well-established corporations have access to securities markets; the seventh indicates that collateral is an important feature of debt contracts; and the eighth presents debt contracts as complicated legal documents that place substantial restrictions on the behaviour of borrowers.

2. Transaction costs freeze many small savers and borrowers out of direct involvement with financial markets. Financial intermediaries can take advantage of economies of scale and are better able to develop expertise to lower transaction costs, thus enabling savers and borrowers to benefit from the existence of financial markets.

3. Asymmetric information results in two problems: adverse selection, which occurs before the transaction, and moral hazard, which occurs after the transaction. Adverse selection refers to the fact that bad credit risks are the ones most likely to seek loans, and moral hazard refers to the risk of the borrower's engaging in activities that are undesirable from the lender's point of view.

4. Adverse selection interferes with the efficient functioning of financial markets. Tools to help reduce the adverse selection problem include private production and sale of information, government regulation to increase information, financial intermediation, and collateral and net worth. The free-rider problem

FYI	Has Sarbanes-Oxley Led to a Decline in U.S. Capital Markets?

There has been much debate in the United States in recent years regarding the impact of Sarbanes-Oxley, especially Section 404, on U.S. capital markets. Section 404 requires both management and company auditors to certify the accuracy of their financial statements. There is no question that Sarbanes-Oxley has led to increased costs for corporations, and this is especially true for smaller firms with revenues of less than US$100 million, where the compliance costs have been estimated to exceed 1% of sales. These higher costs could result in smaller firms listing abroad and discourage IPOs in the United States, thereby shrinking U.S. capital markets relative to those abroad. However, improved accounting standards could work to encourage stock market listings and IPOs because better information could raise the valuation of common stocks.

Critics of Sarbanes-Oxley have cited it, as well as higher litigation and weaker shareholder rights, as the cause of declining U.S. stock listings and IPOs, but other factors are likely at work. The European financial system experienced a major liberalization in the 1990s, along with the introduction of the euro, that helped make its financial markets more integrated and efficient. As a result, it became easier for European firms to list in their home countries. The fraction of European firms that list in their home countries has risen to over 90% currently from around 60% in 1995. As the importance of the United States in the world economy has diminished because of the growing importance of other economies, the U.S. capital markets have become less dominant over time. This process is even more evident in the corporate bond market. In 1995, corporate bond issues in the U.S. were double Europe's, while issues of corporate bonds in Europe now exceed those in the United States.

occurs when people who do not pay for information take advantage of information that other people have paid for. This problem explains why financial intermediaries, particularly banks, play a more important role in financing the activities of businesses than securities markets do.

5. Moral hazard in equity contracts is known as the principal–agent problem because managers (the agents) have less incentive to maximize profits than stockholders (the principals). The principal–agent problem explains why debt contracts are so much more prevalent in financial markets than equity contracts. Tools to help reduce the principal–agent problem include monitoring, government regulation to increase information, and financial intermediation.

6. Tools to reduce the moral hazard problem in debt contracts include net worth, monitoring and enforcement of restrictive covenants, and financial intermediaries.

7. Conflicts of interest arise when financial service providers or their employees are serving multiple interests and develop incentives to misuse or conceal information needed for the effective functioning of financial markets. We care about conflicts of interest because they can substantially reduce the amount of reliable information in financial markets, thereby preventing them from channelling funds to those with productive investment opportunities. Two types of financial service activities that have had the greatest potential for conflicts of interest are underwriting and research in investment banking, and auditing and consulting in accounting firms. In the United States, two major policy measures have been implemented to deal with conflicts of interest: the Sarbanes-Oxley Act and the Global Legal Settlement of 2002 arising from the lawsuit by the New York Attorney General against the ten largest investment banks.

KEY TERMS

agency theory,   p. 171

audits,   p. 174

collateral,   p. 169

conflict of interest,   p. 187

costly state verification,   p. 178

economies of scope,   p. 187

free-rider problem,   p. 173

incentive-compatible,   p. 181

initial public offerings (IPO),
    p. 188

net worth (equity capital),   p. 176

principal–agent problem,   p. 177

restrictive covenants,   p. 169

secured debt,   p. 169

spinning,   p. 188

state-owned banks,   p. 185

unsecured debt,   p. 169

venture capital firm,   p. 179

QUESTIONS

You will find the answers to the questions marked with an asterisk in the Textbook Resources section of your MyEconLab.

1. How can economies of scale help explain the existence of financial intermediaries?

*2. Describe two ways in which financial intermediaries help lower transaction costs in the economy.

3. Would moral hazard and adverse selection still arise in financial markets if information were not asymmetric? Explain.

*4. How do standard accounting principles help financial markets work more efficiently?

5. Do you think the lemons problem would be more severe for stocks traded on the Toronto Stock Exchange or those traded over the counter? Explain.

*6. Which firms are most likely to use bank financing rather than to issue bonds or stocks to finance their activities? Why?

7. How can the existence of asymmetric information provide a rationale for government regulation of financial markets?

*8. Would you be more willing to lend to a friend if she put all of her life savings into her business than you would if she had not done so? Why?

9. Rich people often worry that others will seek to marry them only for their money. Is this a problem of adverse selection?

*10. The more collateral there is backing a loan, the less the lender has to worry about adverse selection. Is

this statement true, false, or uncertain? Explain your answer.

11. How does the free-rider problem aggravate adverse selection and moral hazard problems in financial markets?

*12. Explain how the separation of ownership and control in Canadian corporations might lead to poor management.

13. Why can the provision of several types of financial services by one firm lead to a lower cost of information production?

*14. How does the provision of several types of financial services by one firm lead to conflicts of interest?

15. How can conflicts of interest make financial service firms less efficient?

*16. Describe two conflicts of interest that occur when underwriting and research are provided by a single investment firm.

17. How does spinning lead to a less efficient financial system?

*18. Describe two conflicts of interest that can occur in accounting firms.

19. Which provisions of Sarbanes-Oxley do you think are beneficial, and which do you think are not?

*20. Which provisions of the Global Legal Settlement do you think are beneficial, and which do you think are not?

WEB EXERCISES

1. In this chapter we discuss the lemons problem and its effect on the efficient functioning of a market. This theory was initially developed by George Akerlof. Go to **www.nobel.se/economics/laureates/2001/public.html**. This site reports that Akerlof, Spence, and Stiglitz were awarded the Nobel Prize in economics in 2001 for their work. Read this report down through the section on George Akerlof. Summarize his research ideas in one page.

Be sure to visit the MyEconLab website at **www.myeconlab.com**. This online homework and tutorial system puts you in control of your own learning with study and practice tools directly correlated to this chapter content.

CHAPTER 9

Financial Crises and the Subprime Meltdown

LEARNING OBJECTIVES

After studying this chapter you should be able to

1. discuss the factors that lead to financial crises
2. explain how increases in adverse selection and moral hazard cause financial crises
3. discuss the most recent financial crisis, the subprime financial crisis of 2007–2008, which led to a number of banking crises around the world and a decline in global economic activity

PREVIEW

Financial crises are major disruptions in financial markets characterized by sharp declines in asset prices and firm failures. Beginning in August of 2007, defaults in the subprime mortgage market in the United States (for borrowers with weak credit records) sent a shudder through the financial markets, leading to the worst financial crisis since the Great Depression and to a number of banking crises throughout the world. In Congressional testimony, Alan Greenspan, former Chairman of the U.S. Federal Reserve, described the subprime financial crisis as a "once-in-a-century credit tsunami." Wall Street firms and commercial banks suffered hundreds of billions of dollars of losses. Households and businesses found they had to pay higher rates on their borrowings—and it was much harder to get credit. Stock markets crashed all over the world, falling by over 40% from their peak. Many financial firms, including commercial banks, investment banks, and insurance companies, went belly up.

Why did this financial crisis occur? Why have financial crises been so prevalent throughout history, and what insights do they provide on the current crisis? Why are financial crises almost always followed by severe contractions in economic activity? We will examine these questions in this chapter by developing a framework to understand the dynamics of financial crises. Building on Chapter 8, we make use of agency theory, the economic analysis of the effects of asymmetric information (adverse selection and moral hazard) on financial markets and the economy, to see why financial crises occur and why they have such devastating economic effects. We will then apply the analysis to explain the course of events in a number of past financial crises throughout the world, including the most recent subprime crisis in the United States.

FACTORS CAUSING FINANCIAL CRISES

In the previous chapter we saw that a well-working financial system solves asymmetric information problems so that capital is allocated to its most productive uses. A financial crisis occurs when an increase in asymmetric information from a disruption in the financial system causes severe adverse selection and moral hazard problems that render financial markets incapable of channelling funds efficiently from savers to households and firms with productive investment opportunities. When financial markets fail to function efficiently, economic activity contracts sharply.

To understand why financial crises occur and, more specifically, how they lead to contractions in economic activity, we need to examine the factors that cause them. Six categories of factors play an important role in financial crises: asset market effects on balance sheets, deterioration in financial institutions' balance sheets, banking crises, increases in uncertainty, increases in interest rates, and government fiscal imbalances. We will examine each of these factors and their impact on lending, investment, and economic activity.

Asset Market Effects on Balance Sheets

The state of borrowers' balance sheets has important implications for the severity of asymmetric information problems in the financial system.

STOCK MARKET DECLINE   A sharp decline in the stock market is one factor that can cause a serious deterioration in borrowing firms' balance sheets. In turn, this deterioration can increase adverse selection and moral hazard problems in financial markets and provoke a financial crisis. A decline in the stock market means that the net worth of corporations has fallen, because share prices are the valuation of a corporation's net worth. The decline in net worth makes lenders less willing to lend because, as we have seen, the net worth of a firm plays a role similar to that of collateral. When the value of collateral declines, it provides less protection to lenders, meaning that losses on loans are likely to be more severe. Because lenders are now less protected against the consequences of adverse selection, they decrease their lending, which in turn causes investment and aggregate output to decline. In addition, the decline in corporate net worth as a result of a stock market decline increases moral hazard by providing incentives for borrowing firms to make risky investments, as they now have less to lose if their investments go sour. The resulting increase in moral hazard makes lending less attractive—another reason why a stock market decline and the resultant decline in net worth leads to decreased lending and economic activity.

UNANTICIPATED DECLINE IN THE PRICE LEVEL   In economies with moderate inflation, which characterizes most industrialized countries, many debt contracts with fixed interest rates are typically of fairly long maturity (ten years or more). In this institutional environment, unanticipated declines in the aggregate price level also decrease the net worth of firms. Because debt payments are contractually fixed in nominal terms, an unanticipated decline in the price level raises the value of borrowing firms' liabilities in real terms (increases the burden of their debt) but does not raise the real value of firms' assets. The result is that net worth in real terms (the difference between assets and liabilities in real terms) declines. A sharp drop in the price level therefore causes a substantial decline in real net worth for borrowing firms and an increase in adverse selection and moral hazard problems facing lenders. An unanticipated decline in the aggregate price level thus leads to a drop in lending and economic activity.

UNANTICIPATED DECLINE IN THE VALUE OF THE DOMESTIC CURRENCY
Because of uncertainty about the future value of the domestic currency in developing countries (and in some industrialized countries), many nonfinancial firms, banks, and governments in developing countries find it easier to issue debt denominated in foreign currencies rather than in their own currency. This can lead to a financial crisis in a similar fashion to an unanticipated decline in the price level. With debt contracts denominated in foreign currency when there is an unanticipated decline in the value of the domestic currency the debt burden of domestic firms increases. Since assets are typically denominated in domestic currency, there is a resulting deterioration in firms' balance sheets and a decline in net worth, which then increases adverse selection and moral hazard problems along the lines just described. The increase in asymmetric information problems leads to a decline in investment and economic activity.

ASSET WRITE-DOWNS Asset price declines also lead to write-downs of the value of the assets side of the balance sheets of financial institutions. This deterioration in their balance sheets can also lead to a contraction of lending, as the next factor indicates.

Deterioration in Financial Institutions' Balance Sheets

Financial institutions, particularly banks, play a major role in financial markets because they are well positioned to engage in information-producing activities that facilitate productive investment for the economy. The state of banks' and other financial intermediaries' balance sheets has an important effect on lending. Suppose financial institutions suffer deterioration in their balance sheets and so have a substantial contraction in their capital. They will have fewer resources to lend, and lending will decline. The contraction in lending then leads to a decline in investment spending, which slows economic activity.

Banking Crises

If the deterioration in financial institutions' balance sheets is severe enough, the institutions will start to fail. Fear can spread from one institution to another, causing even healthy ones to go under. Because banks have deposits that can be pulled out very quickly, they are particularly prone to contagion of this type. A **bank panic** occurs when multiple banks fail simultaneously. The source of the contagion is asymmetric information. In a panic, depositors, fearing for the safety of their deposits (in the absence of or with limited amounts of deposit insurance) and not knowing the quality of banks' loan portfolios, withdraw their deposits to the point that the banks fail. When a large number of banks fail in a short period of time, there is a loss of information production in financial markets and a direct loss of banks' financial intermediation.

The decrease in bank lending during a banking crisis decreases the supply of funds available to borrowers, which leads to higher interest rates. Bank panics result in an increase in adverse selection and moral hazard problems in credit markets. These problems produce an even sharper decline in lending to facilitate productive investments and lead to an even more severe contraction in economic activity.

Increases in Uncertainty

A dramatic increase in uncertainty in financial markets, due perhaps to the failure of a prominent financial or nonfinancial institution, a recession, or a stock market crash, makes it hard for lenders to screen good from bad credit risks. The resulting inability of lenders to solve the adverse selection problem makes them less willing to lend, which leads to a decline in lending, investment, and aggregate economic activity.

Increases in Interest Rates

As we saw in Chapter 8, individuals and firms with the riskiest investment projects are those who are willing to pay the highest interest rates. If increased demand for credit or a decline in the money supply drives up interest rates sufficiently, good credit risks are less likely to want to borrow while bad credit risks are still willing to borrow. Because of the resulting increase in adverse selection, lenders will no longer want to make loans. The substantial decline in lending will lead to a substantial decline in investment and aggregate economic activity.

Increases in interest rates also play a role in promoting a financial crisis through their effect on cash flow, the difference between cash receipts and expenditures. A firm with sufficient cash flow can finance its projects internally, and there is no asymmetric information because it knows how good its own projects are. (Indeed, businesses in Canada and the United States fund around two-thirds of their investments with internal funds.) An increase in interest rates and therefore in household and firm interest payments decreases their cash flow. With less cash flow, the firm has fewer internal funds and must raise funds from an external source, say, a bank, which does not know the firm as well as its owners or managers. How can the bank be sure if the firm will invest in safe projects or instead take on big risks and then be unlikely to pay back the loan? Because of increased adverse selection and moral hazard, the bank may choose not to lend even to firms that are good risks and want to undertake potentially profitable investments. Thus, when cash flow drops as a result of an increase in interest rates, adverse selection and moral hazard problems become more severe, again curtailing lending, investment, and economic activity.

Government Fiscal Imbalances

In emerging-market countries (Argentina, Brazil, Ecuador, Russia, and Turkey are recent examples), government fiscal imbalances may create fears of default on government debt. As a result, demand from individual investors for government bonds may fall, causing the government to force financial institutions to purchase them. If the debt then declines in price—which, as we have seen in Chapter 6, will occur if a government default is likely—financial institutions' balance sheets will weaken and their lending will contract for the reasons described earlier. Fears of default on the government debt can also spark a foreign exchange crisis in which the value of the domestic currency falls sharply because investors pull their money out of the country. The decline in the domestic currency's value will then lead to the destruction of the balance sheets of firms with large amounts of debt denominated in foreign currency. These balance sheet problems lead to an increase in adverse selection and moral hazard problems, a decline in lending, and a contraction of economic activity.

DYNAMICS OF PAST CANADIAN FINANCIAL CRISES

Canada had a number of financial and banking crises in the nineteenth and twentieth centuries—in 1866, 1879, 1923, and 1930–1933. Our analysis of the factors that lead to a financial crisis can explain why these crises took place and why they were so damaging to the Canadian economy. We will now examine trends in past Canadian crises and uncover insights into present-day challenges along the way.

Financial crises in Canada have progressed in two and sometimes three stages. To help you understand how these crises have unfolded, refer to Figure 9-1, a diagram that identifies the stages and sequence of events in Canadian financial crises.

Stage One: Initiation of Financial Crisis

There are several possible ways that financial crises start: mismanagement of financial liberalization or innovation, asset price booms and busts, spikes in interest rates, or a general increase in uncertainty when there are failures of major financial institutions (see the top row of Figure 9-1).

MISMANAGEMENT OF FINANCIAL LIBERALIZATION/INNOVATION   The seeds of a financial crisis are often sown when countries engage in **financial liberalization**, the elimination of restrictions on financial markets and institutions, or when major financial innovations are introduced to the marketplace, as occurred recently with subprime residential mortgages. Financial innovation or liberalization is highly beneficial in the long run because it facilitates the process of financial development discussed in the previous chapter, which leads to a more efficient financial system that can allocate capital better. However, financial liberalization or innovation has a dark side: if managed improperly, it can lead financial institutions to take on excessive risk. With restrictions lifted or new financial products introduced, financial institutions frequently go on a lending spree, often called a **credit boom**, and expand their lending at a rapid pace. Unfortunately, the managers of these financial institutions may not have the expertise to manage risk appropriately in these new lines of business. Even if the required managerial expertise is initially present, the rapid growth of credit will likely outstrip the information resources available to these institutions, leading to overly risky lending.

As we will discuss in Chapter 10, most governments try to prevent bank panics and encourage banks to keep on lending during bad times by providing a government safety net. If depositors and other providers of funds to banks are protected from losses, they will keep on supplying banks with funds so banks can continue to lend and will not fail. However, there is a catch: The government safety net weakens market discipline for the bank. With a safety net, depositors know that they will not lose anything if a bank fails. Thus, the bank can still acquire funds even if it takes on excessive risk. The government safety net therefore increases the moral hazard incentive for banks to take on greater risk than they otherwise would, because if their risky, high-interest loans pay off, the banks make a lot of money; if they don't and the bank fails, taxpayers pay most of the bill for the safety net that protects the banks' depositors. In other words, banks can play the game of "heads, I win: tails, the taxpayer loses."

The presence of a government safety net requires regulation and government supervision of the financial system to prevent excessive risk taking. However, new lines of business and rapid credit growth stretch the resources of the government's supervisory agencies. Financial supervisors find themselves without the expertise or the additional resources needed to appropriately monitor the new lending activities. Without this monitoring, risk-taking can explode.

Eventually, this risk-taking comes home to roost. Losses on loans begin to mount and the drop in the value of the loans (on the asset side of the balance sheet) falls relative to liabilities, thereby driving down the net worth (capital) of banks and other financial institutions. With less capital, these financial institutions cut back on their lending, a process that is called **deleveraging**. Furthermore, with less capital, banks and other financial institutions become riskier, causing depositors and other potential lenders to these institutions to pull out their funds. Fewer

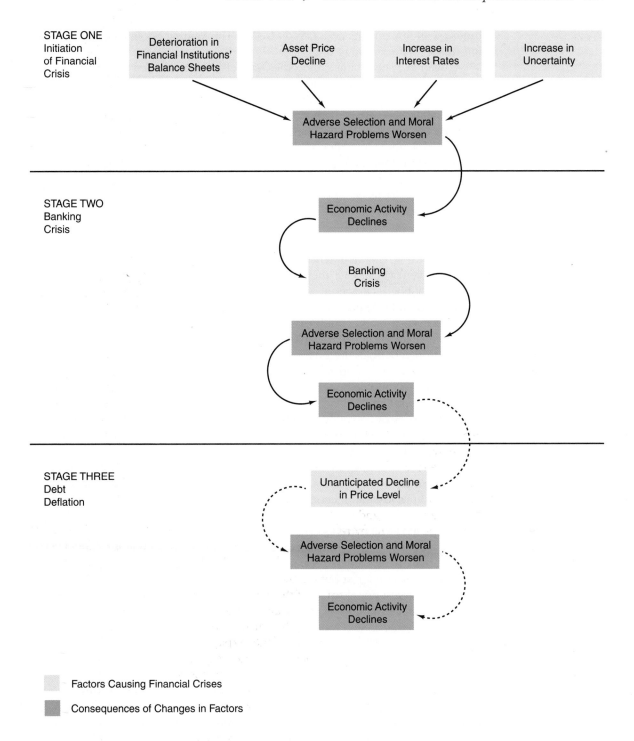

FIGURE 9-1 Sequence of Events in Canadian Financial Crises

The solid arrows in Stages One and Two trace the sequence of events in a typical financial crisis; the dotted arrows show the additional set of events that occur if the crisis develops into a debt deflation, Stage Three in our discussion.

funds mean fewer loans and a credit freeze. The lending boom turns into a lending crash.

As we have seen, banks and other financial intermediaries play a crucial role in financial markets because they are well suited to collect information about businesses and industries. This ability in turn enables these institutions to distinguish good loan prospects from bad ones. When financial intermediaries deleverage and cut back on their lending, no one else can step in to collect this information and make these loans. The ability of the financial system to cope with the asymmetric information problems of adverse selection and moral hazard is therefore severely hampered (as shown in the arrow pointing from the first factor in the top row of Figure 9-1). As loans become scarcer, firms are no longer able to fund their attractive investment opportunities; they decrease their spending and economic activity contracts.

ASSET PRICE BOOM AND BUST   Asset prices, in the stock market and real estate, can be driven well above their fundamental economic values by investor psychology (dubbed "irrational exuberance" by Alan Greenspan when he was Chairman of the U.S. Federal Reserve). The result is an **asset-price bubble**, such as the tech stock-market bubble of the late 1990s or the recent housing-price bubble in the United States that we will discuss later in this chapter.

Asset-price bubbles are often also driven by credit booms, in which the large increase in credit is used to fund purchases of assets, thereby driving up their price. When the bubble bursts and asset prices realign with fundamental economic values, the resulting decline in net worth increases asymmetric information (as shown by the arrow pointing from the second factor in the top row of Figure 9-1), making borrowers less credit-worthy and causing a contraction in lending and spending along the lines we discussed in the previous section.

The asset-price bust can also, as we have seen, lead to a deterioration in financial institutions' balance sheets, which causes them to deleverage, further contributing to the decline in economic activity.

SPIKES IN INTEREST RATES   Many Canadian financial crises were precipitated by increases in interest rates, either when interest rates shot up in the United States or when bank panics led to a scramble for liquidity in Canada that produced sharp upward spikes in interest rates.

Higher interest rates lead to declines in cash flow for households and firms and a reduction in the number of good credit risks who are willing to borrow, both of which increase adverse selection and moral hazard (as shown by the arrow pointing from the third factor in the top row of Figure 9-1), causing a decline in economic activity.

INCREASE IN UNCERTAINTY   Canadian financial crises have almost always started when uncertainty is high, either after a recession has begun or the stock market has crashed. The failure of a major financial institution is a particularly important source of heightened uncertainty that features prominently in financial crises. Examples in Canadian history are the Bank of Upper Canada in 1866, the Home Bank in 1923, and the bank panic of 1879. Since good financial information is harder to come by in a period of high uncertainty, adverse selection and moral hazard problems increase, leading to a decline in lending and economic activity (as shown by the arrow pointing from the last factor in the top row of Figure 9-1).

Stage Two: Banking Crisis

Because of the worsening business conditions and uncertainty about their banks' health, depositors begin to withdraw their funds from banks and a banking crisis or bank panic often ensues. The resulting decline in the number of banks results in a loss of their information capital and worsening adverse selection and moral hazard problems in the credit markets, leading to a further spiralling down of the economy. Figure 9-1 illustrates this progression in the Stage Two portion. Bank panics were a feature of all Canadian financial crises during the nineteenth and twentieth centuries, occurring in 1866, 1879, 1923, and 1930–1933. Bank panics were also a feature of all U.S. financial crises until World War II, occurring every twenty years or so in 1819, 1837, 1857, 1873, 1884, 1893, 1907, and 1930–33.

For the typical Canadian financial crisis, there is then a sorting out of firms that were insolvent (had a negative net worth) from healthy firms by bankruptcy proceedings. The same process occurs for banks, often with the help of public and private authorities. Once this sorting out is complete, uncertainty in financial markets declines, the stock market recovers, and interest rates fall. The overall result is that adverse selection and moral hazard problems diminish and the financial crisis subsides. With the financial markets able to operate well again, the stage is set for the recovery of the economy, bringing us to the next possible stage.

Stage Three: Debt Deflation

If, however, the economic downturn leads to a sharp decline in prices, the recovery process can be short-circuited. In this situation, shown as Stage Three in Figure 9-1, a process called **debt deflation** occurs, in which a substantial unanticipated decline in the price level sets in, leading to further deterioration in firms' net worth because of the increased burden of indebtedness. With debt deflation, the adverse selection and moral hazard problems continue to increase so that lending, investment spending, and aggregate economic activity remain depressed for a long time. The most significant financial crisis that included debt deflation was the Great Depression, the worst economic contraction in history.

APPLICATION   **The Mother of All Financial Crises: The Great Depression in the United States**

In 1928 and 1929, prices doubled in the U.S. stock market. Federal Reserve officials viewed the stock market boom as excessive speculation. To curb it, they pursued a tight monetary policy to raise interest rates; the Fed got more than it bargained for when the stock market crashed in October 1929, falling by more than 60%.

Although the 1929 crash had a great impact on the minds of a whole generation, most people forget that by the middle of 1930, more than half of the stock market decline had been reversed. Indeed, credit market conditions remained quite stable and there was little evidence that a major financial crisis was underway.

What might have been a normal recession turned into something far different, however, when adverse shocks to the agricultural sector led to bank failures in agricultural regions that then spread to the major banking centres. A sequence of bank panics followed from October 1930 until March 1933. More than one-third of U.S. banks went out of business.

The continuing decline in stock prices after mid-1930 (by mid-1932 stocks had declined to 10% of their value at the 1929 peak) and the increase in uncertainty from the unsettled business conditions created by the economic contraction worsened adverse selection and moral hazard problems in the credit markets. The loss of one-third of the banks reduced the amount of financial intermediation. Intensified adverse selection and moral hazard problems decreased the ability of financial markets to channel funds to firms with productive investment opportunities. As our analysis predicts, the amount of outstanding commercial loans fell by half from 1929 to 1933, and investment spending collapsed, declining by 90% from its 1929 level.

The short-circuiting of the process that kept the economy from recovering quickly, which it does in most recessions, occurred because of a fall in the price level by 25% in the 1930–1933 period. This huge decline in prices triggered debt deflation in which net worth fell because of the increased burden of indebtedness borne by firms. The decline in net worth and the resulting increase in adverse selection and moral hazard problems in the credit markets led to a prolonged economic contraction in which unemployment rose to 25% of the labour force. The financial crisis in the Great Depression was the worst ever experienced, and it explains why this economic contraction was also the most severe ever experienced by the United States.[1]

THE SUBPRIME FINANCIAL CRISIS OF 2007–2008

Now that our framework for analyzing financial crises is in place, we are prepared to tackle the most recent financial crisis, the subprime financial crisis of 2007–2008 in the United States. Mismanagement of financial innovation in the subprime residential mortgage market and the bursting of a bubble in housing prices were the underlying driving forces behind the U.S. financial crisis of 2007–2008.

Financial Innovations Emerge in the Mortgage Markets

Before 2000, only the most credit-worthy (prime) borrowers were able to obtain residential mortgages. Advances in computer technology and new statistical techniques, known as data mining, however, led to enhanced, quantitative evaluation of the credit risk for a new class of riskier residential mortgages. **Subprime mortgages** are mortgages for borrowers with less-than-stellar credit records. **Alt-A mortgages** are mortgages for borrowers with higher expected default rates than prime (A-paper), but with better credit records than subprime borrowers. Households with credit records could now be assigned a numerical credit score, known in the United States as a FICO score (named after the Fair Isaac Corporation that developed it), that would predict how likely they would be to default on their loan payments. In addition, by lowering transaction costs, computer technology enabled the bundling together of smaller loans (like mortgages) into standard debt securities, a process known as **securitization**.

---

[1] For a discussion of the role of asymmetric information problems in the Great Depression period, see Ben Bernanke, "Nonmonetary Effects of the Financial Crisis in the Propagation of the Great Depression," *American Economic Review* 73 (1983): 257–276; and Charles Calomiris, "Financial Factors and the Great Depression," *Journal of Economic Perspectives* (Spring 1993): 61–85.

The ability to cheaply bundle and quantify the default risk of the underlying high-risk mortgages in a standardized debt security called **mortgage-backed securities** provided a new source of financing for these mortgages. The financial innovation of subprime and alt-A mortgages was born. Financial innovation didn't stop there. **Financial engineering**, the development of new, sophisticated financial instruments, led to **structured credit products** that are derived from cash flows of underlying assets and can be tailored to have particular risk characteristics that appeal to investors with differing preferences. Particularly notorious were **collateralized debt obligations (CDOs)**, which paid out the cash flows from subprime mortgage-backed securities in different tranches, with the highest-rated tranche paying out first, while lower ones paid out less if there were losses on the mortgage-backed securities. There were even CDO2s and CDO3s that sliced and diced risk even further, paying out the cash flows from CDOs and CDO2s.

Housing Price Bubble Forms

Aided by liquidity from cash flows surging into the United States from countries like China and India, the subprime mortgage market took off after the recession was over in 2001, becoming over a trillion dollar market by 2007. The development of the subprime mortgage market was lauded by economists and politicians alike because it led to a "democratization of credit" and helped raise U.S. homeownership rates to the highest levels in history. The asset price boom in housing, which took off after the 2000–2001 recession was over, also helped stimulate the growth of the subprime market. Higher housing prices meant that subprime borrowers could refinance their houses with even larger loans when their homes appreciated in value. Subprime borrowers were also unlikely to default because they could always sell their house to pay off the loan, making investors happy because the securities backed by cash flows from subprime mortgages had high returns. The growth of the subprime mortgage market, in turn, increased the demand for houses and so fuelled the boom in housing prices.

Agency Problems Arise

But all was not well in the subprime mortgage market. All the agency problems described in the previous chapter were coming to the fore. The subprime mortgage market was based on a so-called **originate-to-distribute** business model, in which the mortgage was originated by a separate party, typically a mortgage broker, and then distributed to an investor as an underlying asset in a security. Unfortunately, the originate-to-distribute model is subject to the principal–agent problem because the agent for the investor, the mortgage originator, has little incentive to make sure that the mortgage is a good credit risk. Once the mortgage broker earns her fee, why should she care if the borrower makes good on his payment? The more volume the broker originates, the more she makes.

Not surprisingly, given these incentives, mortgage brokers often did not make a strong effort to evaluate whether the borrower could pay off the loan. Adverse selection then became especially severe: risk-loving investors were able to obtain loans to acquire houses that would be very profitable if housing prices went up, but they could just "walk away" from the house if housing prices went down. The principal–agent problem also created incentives for mortgage brokers to encourage households to take on mortgages they could not afford, or to commit fraud by falsifying information on a borrower's mortgage applications in order to qualify them for their mortgages. Compounding this problem was lax regulation of originators, who were not required to disclose information to borrowers that would have helped them assess whether they could afford the loans.

The agency problems went even deeper. Commercial and investment banks, which were earning large fees by underwriting mortgage-backed securities and structured credit products like CDOs, also had weak incentives to make sure that the ultimate holders of the securities would be paid off. The credit rating agencies that were evaluating these securities also were subject to conflicts of interest: they were earning fees from rating them *and* from advising clients on how to structure the securities to get the highest ratings. The integrity of these ratings was thus more likely to be compromised.

Information Problems Surface

Although financial engineering has the potential to create products and services that better match investors' risk appetites, it also has a dark side. Structured products like CDOs, CDO2s, and CDO3s can get so complicated that it can be hard to value the cash flows of the underlying assets for a security or to determine who actually owns these assets. Indeed, in a speech in October 2007, Ben Bernanke, the Chairman of the Federal Reserve, joked that he "would like to know what those damn things are worth." In other words, the increased complexity of structured products can actually destroy information, thereby making asymmetric information worse in the financial system and increasing the severity of adverse selection and moral hazard problems.

Housing-Price Bubble Bursts

As housing prices rose and profitability for mortgage originators and lenders was high, the underwriting standards for subprime mortgages fell to lower and lower standards. Riskier borrowers were able to obtain mortgages, and the amount of the mortgage relative to the value of the house, the loan-to-value ratio (LTV), rose. Borrowers were often able to get piggyback, second, and third mortgages on top of their original 80% LTV mortgage, so that they had to put almost no money down on their houses. When asset prices rise too far out of line with fundamentals, however, they must come down, and eventually the housing-price bubble burst. With housing prices falling after their peak in 2006, the rot in the U.S. financial system began to be revealed. The decline in housing prices led to many subprime borrowers finding that their mortgages were "underwater," that is, the value of the house fell below the amount of the mortgage. When this happened, struggling homeowners had tremendous incentives to walk away from their homes and just send the keys back to the lender. Defaults on mortgages shot up sharply, eventually leading to over 1 million mortgages in foreclosure.

Crisis Spreads Globally

Although the problem originated in the United States, the wake-up call came from Canada and Europe, a sign of how extensive the globalization of financial markets had become. After Fitch and Standard & Poor's announced ratings downgrades on mortgage-backed securities and CDOs totalling more than $10 billion, the asset-based commercial paper market seized up and a French investment house, BNP Paribas, suspended redemption of shares held in some of its money market funds on August 7, 2008. Despite huge injections of liquidity into the financial system by the European Central Bank and the Federal Reserve, banks began to hoard cash and were unwilling to lend to each other. As can be seen in Figure 9-2, the U.S. Treasury bill-to-Eurodollar rate (TED) spread, a good measure of liquidity in the interbank market, shot up from an average of 40 basis points (0.40 percentage points) during the first half of 2007 to a peak of 240 by August 20, 2007. The drying up of credit led to the first major bank failure in the United Kingdom in over

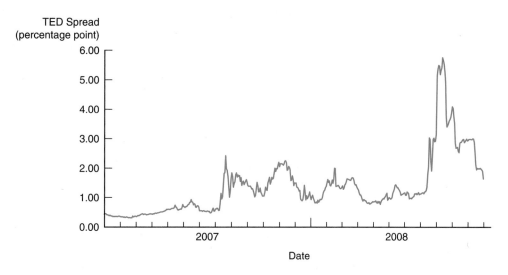

FIGURE 9-2 Treasury Bill-to-Eurodollar Rate (TED) Spread

The TED spread is a good indicator of liquidity in the interbank market

Source: www.federalreserve.gov/releases/h1S/data.htm

100 years when Northern Rock, which had relied on wholesale short-term borrowing rather than deposits for its funding, collapsed in September 2008.

In Canada, the early symptom of the U.S. subprime crisis was the freezing of the asset-backed commercial paper (ABCP) market in August 2007. It caused a sharp decrease in liquidity in short-term Canadian credit markets, including the overnight interbank market and the overnight repurchase market. In order to restore confidence and liquidity in the ABCP market, and prevent significant write-offs for banks that would have reduced their capital and raised concerns about their solvency, market participants reached an agreement, known as the Montreal Accord, to restructure the frozen ABCP market and minimize the costs to the Canadian taxpayer (see the FYI box, Canada's Asset-Backed Commercial Paper Saga, for more details).

**Banks'
Balance
Sheets
Deteriorate**

The decline in U.S. housing prices, which now accelerated, led to rising defaults on mortgages. As a result, the value of mortgage-backed securities and CDOs collapsed, leading to ever-larger write-downs at banks and other financial institutions. The balance sheets of these institutions deteriorated because of the losses from their holdings of these securities and because many of these institutions had to take back onto their balance sheets some of the structured investment vehicles (SIVs) they had sponsored. **Structured investment vehicles** are similar to CDOs in that they pay out cash flows from pools of assets such as mortgages; instead of issuing long-term debt as in CDOs, they issued asset-backed commercial paper. With weaker balance sheets, these banks and other financial institutions began to deleverage, selling off assets and restricting the availability of credit to both households and businesses. With no one else able to step in to collect information and make loans, adverse selection and moral hazard problems increased in the credit markets, leading to a slowing of the U.S. economy and rising unemployment levels.

FYI   Canada's Asset-Backed Commercial Paper Saga

As we noted in Chapter 2, commercial paper is short-term, unsecured debt issued by corporations, typically for financing accounts receivable and inventories. Asset-backed commercial paper, like traditional commercial paper, is also a short-term security (with a maturity that is typically less than nine months). It is issued by conduits (that is, bankruptcy-remote Special Purpose Vehicles), but instead of being an unsecured promissory note, is backed by physical assets such as mortgages, trade receivables, credit card receivables, automobile loans and leases, and other types of assets. Because of this backing, the quality of the ABCP depends on the underlying securities and thus ABCP could be very risky. For example, if there are negative developments in the underlying markets, the risk of ABCP will increase and investors will switch out of ABCP and into safer money market instruments such as traditional commercial paper, bankers' acceptances, and Treasury bills. As a result, conduits will not be able to roll over their ABCP and will face a liquidity crunch.

The ABCP market in Canada expanded very rapidly from the 1990s to 2007. As at July 31, 2007, the size of the Canadian ABCP market was $115 billion (equal to about 32.5% of the Canadian money market), of which $80 billion was bank-sponsored and $35 billion was non-bank-sponsored. At the same time, the ABCP market in the United States was approximately US$1.2 trillion, equal to about 50% of the U.S. commercial paper market. Bank-sponsored ABCP conduits are invested in "plain vanilla" assets such as residential mortgages and credit card receivables. Non-bank-sponsored ABCP conduits are invested in structured finance assets such as collateralized debt obligations (CDOs) and subprime mortgages. Canadian banks are involved in the distribution of ABCP and also provide liquidity back-stop facilities to non-bank-sponsored ABCP conduits under the so-called "general market disruption" clause.

In August of 2007, investors in the Canadian ABCP market declined to roll over maturing notes because of concerns about exposure to the U.S. subprime mortgage sector in the underlying assets. As a result, the market was divided into those ABCP conduits that could honour their obligations (bank-sponsored) and those that could not honour their obligations (non-bank-sponsored). In the case of bank-sponsored ABCP, the Big Six banks took back onto their balance sheets significant amounts of their own sponsored ABCP. Moreover, valuation and fair-value issues led to significant write downs in the fourth quarter of 2007 and the first quarter of 2008. In the case of non-bank-sponsored ABCP, a number of conduits faced significant liquidity shortages, seeking liquidity funding support from their liquidity providers (banks). However, major liquidity providers denied requests for liquidity support, arguing that the "general market disruption" clause was not met. They interpreted the clause to mean that the majority of the conduits in the entire Canadian ABCP market would need to be unable to roll over before a liquidity provider had to step in. As a result, the Canadian non-bank-sponsored ABCP market froze and investors, including Quebec's huge pension fund, *Caisse de dépôt et placement du Québec*, Alberta's ATB Financial, the National Bank of Canada, and about 2000 individual small investors, had their cash frozen in non-bank-sponsored ABCP.

At the time, the Bank of Canada indicated that it would not accept ABCP as collateral for loans to banks and that a solution from participants in the ABCP market was deemed to be appropriate. As a result, major market participants, including non-bank-sponsored ABCP conduits, institutional investors, liquidity providers (ABN AMRO Group, HSBC, Deutsche Bank, Merrill Lynch, Barclays Capital), and the Affected Trusts, reached an agreement on August 16, 2007, known as the

Montreal Accord. Under the Montreal Accord, investors agreed to a standstill period (initially 60 days, to October 16, 2007, extended three times to February 22, 2008), with the objective of restructuring the frozen ABCP into long-term floating rate notes with maturities matching the maturities of the underlying assets in the conduits. However, the agreement had to be renegotiated again 16 months later, in December 2008, with the participation of the federal government and three provinces (Ontario, Quebec, and Alberta), where publicly owned institutions held over $20 billion of frozen non-bank-sponsored ABCP. Small investors (holding less than $1 million of the paper) were fully paid out in cash by the brokerage firms that had sold them the paper, whereas the larger investors were given bonds. The final cost of the ABCP restructuring was in excess of $200 million in fees, with the big investors footing the bill.

High-Profile Firms Fail

In March of 2008, Bear Stearns, the fifth-largest investment bank in the U.S., which had invested heavily in subprime-related securities, had a run on its funding and was forced to sell itself to J.P. Morgan for less than 5% of what it was worth just a year earlier. In order to broker the deal, the Federal Reserve had to take over US$30 billion of Bear Stearns' hard-to-value assets. In July, Fannie Mae and Freddie Mac, the two privately owned government-sponsored enterprises that together insured over US$5 trillion of mortgages or mortgage-backed assets, had to be propped up by the U.S. Treasury and the Federal Reserve after suffering substantial losses from their holdings of subprime securities. In early September 2008 they were then put into conservatorship (in effect run by the government).

Worse events were still to come. On Monday, September 15, 2008, after suffering losses in the subprime market, Lehman Brothers, the fourth-largest U.S. investment bank by asset size (with over $600 billion in assets and 25 000 employees), filed for bankruptcy, making it the largest bankruptcy filing in U.S. history. The day before, Merrill Lynch, the third-largest investment bank (which also suffered large losses on its holding of subprime securities), announced its sale to Bank of America for a price 60% below its price a year earlier. On Tuesday, September 16, AIG, an insurance giant with assets over US$1 trillion, suffered an extreme liquidity crisis when its credit rating was downgraded. It had written over US$400 billion of insurance contracts called credit default swaps that had to make payouts on possible losses from subprime mortgage securities. The Federal Reserve then stepped in with a US$85 billion loan to keep AIG afloat (later increased to US$150 billion).

Also on September 16, as a result of its losses from exposure to Lehman Brothers' debt, the Reserve Primary Fund, a large money market mutual fund with over US$60 billion of assets, "broke the buck"—that is, it could no longer redeem its shares at the par value of $1. A run on money market funds then ensued, with the U.S. Treasury putting in place a temporary guarantee for all money market mutual fund redemptions in order to stem withdrawals. On September 25, 2008, Washington Mutual (WAMU), the sixth-largest bank in the United States with over US$300 billion in assets, was put into receivership by the FDIC and sold to J.P. Morgan, making it the largest bank failure in U.S. history.

Bailout Package Debated

The financial crisis then took an even more virulent turn after the U.S. House of Representatives, fearing the wrath of constituents who were angry about bailing out Wall Street, voted down a US$700 billion bailout package proposed by the Bush administration on Monday, September 29, 2008. The Emergency Economic Stabilization Act was finally passed on Friday, October 3. The stock market crash accelerated, with the week beginning on October 6 showing the worst weekly decline in U.S. history. Credit spreads went through the roof over the next three weeks, with the U.S. Treasury bill-to-Eurodollar rate spread going to over 450 basis points (4.50 percentage points), the highest value in its history (see Figure 9-2). The crisis then spread to Europe with a string of failures of financial institutions.

Recovery in Sight?

The increased uncertainty from the failures of so many financial institutions, the deterioration in financial institutions' balance sheets, and the decline in the stock market of over 40% from its peak all increased the severity of adverse selection and moral hazard problems in the credit markets. The resulting decline in lending led to the U.S. unemployment rate rising to 7% by the end of 2008, with worse likely to come. The financial crisis led to a slowing of economic growth worldwide and massive government bailouts of financial institutions (see the Global box, The U.S. Treasury Asset Relief Plan and Government Bailouts Throughout the World).

Subprime Mortgages in Canada

The subprime mortgage crisis in the United States dominated news headlines, but there is also the Canadian version of subprime mortgages. High-risk, long-term (40-year), zero-down mortgages proliferated in Canada in 2007 and 2008 after the Conservative government opened up the Canadian mortgage market to big U.S. players in its first budget in May of 2006. This created the Canadian version of subprime mortgages. How did Canadian regulators allow the entry into Canada of U.S.-style subprime mortgages?

The Canadian mortgage insurance market is the second largest and one of the most lucrative mortgage insurance markets in the world. For over 50 years, since revisions in the National Housing Act and the Bank Act in 1954 allowed chartered banks to make insured mortgage loans, the business of mortgage insurance was mainly the domain of the Canada Mortgage and Housing Corporation (CMHC). CMHC insured the mortgages of those home buyers that could not make a 25% down payment, charging them an insurance premium, with the federal government backing the CMHC's insurance policies with a 100% federal guarantee.

In May of 2006, however, after years of orchestrated lobbying the Department of Finance and Office of the Superintendent of Financial Institutions by U.S. insurance companies, the government allowed big U.S. players such as AIG to enter the Canadian mortgage insurance market and also committed to guarantee their business up to $200 billion. In February of 2006, in an attempt to protect its business in anticipation of the entry of the big U.S. insurers, CMHC announced that it would insure 30-year mortgages. Two weeks later, Genworth Mortgage Insurance Co., the Canadian mortgage subsidiary of the U.S. conglomerate General Electric and the only other (private) mortgage insurer in Canada at that time (with an estimated market share of about 30%), announced that it would insure 35-year mortgages. By October of 2006, AIG, CMHC, and Genworth were competing in the Canadian mortgage insurance market by insuring 40-year mortgages.

The U.S. Treasury Asset Relief Plan and Government Bailouts Throughout the World

The Economic Recovery Act of 2008 in the United States had several provisions to promote recovery from the subprime financial crisis. The most important was the Treasury Asset Relief Plan (TARP), which authorized the U.S. Treasury to spend US$700 billion purchasing subprime mortgage assets from troubled financial institutions or to inject capital into banking institutions. The hope was that by buying subprime assets, their price would rise above fire-sale prices, thus creating a market for them, while at the same time increasing capital in financial institutions. Along with injections of capital, this would enable these institutions to start lending again. In addition, the Act raised the federal deposit insurance limit temporarily from US$100 000 to US$250 000 in order to limit withdrawals from banks and required the U.S. Treasury, as the owner of these assets, to encourage the servicers of the underlying mortgages to restructure them to minimize foreclosures. Shortly thereafter, the Federal Deposit Insurance Corporation (FDIC) put in place a guarantee for certain debt newly issued by banks, and the Treasury guaranteed money market mutual fund shares at par value for one year.

The spreading bank failures in Europe in the fall of 2008 led to bailouts of financial institutions: the Netherlands, Belgium, and Luxembourg injected US$16 billion to prop up Fortis, a major European bank; the Netherlands injected US$13 billion into ING, a banking and insurance giant; Germany provided a US$50 billion rescue package for Hypo Real Estate Holdings; and Iceland took over its three largest banks after the banking system collapsed. Ireland's government guaranteed all the deposits of its commercial banks as well as interbank lending, as did Greece. Spain implemented a bailout package similar to the United States' to buy up to 50 billion euros of assets in their banks in order to encourage them to lend. The U.K. Treasury set up a bailout plan with a similar price tag to that of the U.S. Treasury's plan of 400 billion pounds. It guaranteed 250 billion pounds of bank liabilities, added 100 billion pounds to a facility that swaps these assets for government bonds, and allowed the U.K. government to buy up to 50 billion pounds of equity stakes in British banks. Bailout plans to the tune of over US$100 billion in South Korea, US$200 billion in Sweden, US$400 billion in France, and US$500 billion in Germany, all of which guaranteed debt of their banks as well as injecting capital into them, then followed. Both the scale of these bailout packages and the degree of international coordination was unprecedented.

In response to the subprime meltdown in the United States, the Canadian government banned subprime mortgages in Canada in the summer of 2008. Although there are currently no publicly available figures, it is estimated that more than half of the total new mortgages approved by Canadian financial institutions during this period (worth over $50 billion) were risky, 40-year mortgages, and that 10% of these mortgages (worth over $10 billion) were taken out with zero money down.

At the time of writing, it is not clear how this brief experiment with U.S.-style subprime lending will affect the Canadian economy and the country's otherwise prudent mortgage landscape.

Why Canada's Banking System Is the Envy of the World

Canadian banks also had their problems during the recent turbulent financial conditions. Their shares fell by almost 50% and some of them experienced huge losses in derivatives trading; for example, CIBC lost $2.1 billion in derivatives trading in 2008. However, while governments in the United States and Europe have been working on full scale banking bailouts and rescue packages (in the trillions of dollars), the Canadian government did not have to bail out any banks.

One reason that Canada's banks have fared better than banks in other countries is the structure of the Canadian mortgage market. Unlike banks in the United States that sold the bulk of their mortgages, banks in Canada held a large proportion of their mortgages on their balance sheets. This practice gave Canadian banks an incentive to make sure that their mortgage loans were good loans. In addition, law in Canada allows banks to go after other assets when a consumer walks away from a mortgage, thereby making it difficult for consumers to do so.

Another reason is that Canada's big banks have been more conservative in their lending and acquisition practices in comparison with major banks around the world. Also, Canada's top banking regulator, the Office of the Superintendent of Financial Institutions (OSFI), has been more conservative than banking regulators in the United States and Europe. For example, at the beginning of the financial crisis, Canada's banks had higher capital requirements than their global peers. As a result, they had stronger reserves to cushion potential losses. Although this conservative regulatory regime enabled Canadian banks to withstand the financial crisis better than banks in other countries, it has been argued that it makes the Canadian banking sector less competitive because of the lower leverage and a lower rate of return on capital than in other jurisdictions.

Moreover, the activities of Canada's banks are well diversified and are not limited to traditional retail banking. In particular, the federal government's decision in the late 1980s to allow banks to acquire investment brokers on Bay Street and to engage in the mutual fund and insurance businesses created a more diversified financial services marketplace for Canada's banks. In addition, these arm's-length institutions are subject to the same strict rules and regulations as the banks, unlike investment dealers in the United States that had been subject to very relaxed and minimal regulation from the Securities and Exchange Commission.

Overall, in the aftermath of the global economic meltdown, Canada's banking system has been viewed as the soundest in the world. In fact, many countries around the world are now considering Canadian-style reforms of their financial markets.

DYNAMICS OF FINANCIAL CRISES IN EMERGING-MARKET ECONOMIES

Before the subprime crisis in the United States, economists looked in other countries for recent examples of financial crises. Emerging-market economies, economies in an earlier stage of market development that have recently opened up to the flow of goods, services, and capital from the rest of the world, are particularly vulnerable. With the opening up of their economies to markets, emerging-market economies have been no stranger to devastating financial crises in recent years. The dynamics of financial crises in emerging-market economies have many of the same elements as those found in Canada and the United States, but with some important differences. Figure 9-3 outlines the key stages and sequence of events in financial crises in these economies that we will address in this section.

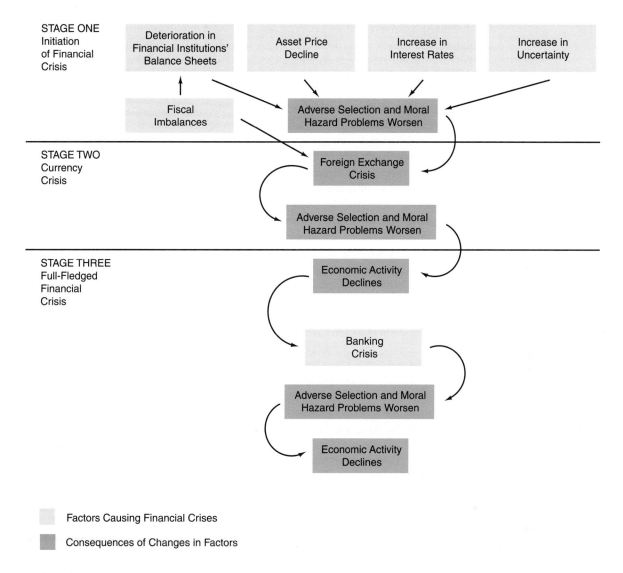

FIGURE 9-3 Sequence of Events in Emerging-Market Financial Crises

The arrows trace the sequence of events during financial crises.

Stage One: Initiation of Financial Crisis

Financial crises in emerging-market countries develop along two basic paths: one involving the mismanagement of financial liberalization and globalization, and the other involving severe fiscal imbalances.

PATH ONE: MISMANAGEMENT OF FINANCIAL LIBERALIZATION AND GLOBALIZATION As occurred in the United States during the subprime financial crisis of 2007–2008, the seeds of a financial crisis in emerging-market countries are often sown when countries liberalize their financial systems. Liberalization occurs when restrictions on domestic financial institutions and markets are eliminated and the economy is opened up to flows of capital and financial firms from other nations. This is a process called **financial globalization**.

Emerging-market countries typically have very weak supervision by bank regulators and a lack of expertise in the screening and monitoring of borrowers by banking institutions. Consequently, the lending boom that results after a financial liberalization often leads to even riskier lending than is typical in advanced countries like Canada and the United States, and enormous loan losses result. The financial globalization process adds fuel to the fire because it allows domestic banks to borrow abroad. The banks pay high interest rates to attract foreign capital and so can rapidly increase their lending. The capital inflow is further stimulated by government policies that keep exchange rates fixed to the dollar, which give foreign investors a sense of lower risk.

At some point, all of the highly risky lending starts producing high loan losses, which then lead to deterioration in bank balance sheets and banks cut back on their lending. Just as in advanced countries like Canada and the United States, the lending boom ends in a lending crash. In emerging-market countries, banks play an even more important role in the financial system than in advanced countries because securities markets and other financial institutions are not as well developed. The decline in bank lending thus means that there are really no other players to solve adverse selection and moral hazard problems (as shown by the arrow pointing from the first factor in the top row of Figure 9-3). The deterioration in bank balance sheets therefore has even more negative impacts on lending and economic activity than in advanced countries.

The story told so far suggests that a lending boom and crash are inevitable outcomes of financial liberalization and globalization in emerging-market countries, but this is not the case. They only occur when there is an institutional weakness that prevents the nation from successfully handling the liberalization and globalization process. More specifically, if prudential regulation and supervision to limit excessive risk-taking were strong, the lending boom and bust would not happen. Why does regulation and supervision instead end up being weak? The answer is the principal–agent problem, discussed in the previous chapter, which encourages powerful domestic business interests to pervert the financial liberalization process. Politicians and prudential supervisors are ultimately agents for voter-taxpayers (principals); that is, the goal of politicians and prudential supervisors is, or should be, to protect the taxpayers' interest. Taxpayers almost always bear the cost of bailing out the banking sector if losses occur.

Once financial markets have been liberalized, powerful business interests that own banks will want to prevent the supervisors from doing their jobs properly. Powerful business interests that contribute heavily to politicians' campaigns are often able to persuade politicians to weaken regulations that restrict their banks from engaging in high-risk/high-payoff strategies. After all, if bank owners achieve growth and expand bank lending rapidly, they stand to make a fortune. But if the bank gets in trouble, the government is likely to bail it out and the taxpayer foots the bill. In addition, these business interests can also make sure that the supervisory agencies, even in the presence of tough regulations, lack the resources to effectively monitor banking institutions or to close them down.

Powerful business interests also have acted to prevent supervisors from doing their jobs properly in advanced countries like Canada and the United States. The weaker institutional environment in emerging-market countries makes this perversion of the financial liberalization process even worse. In emerging-market economies, business interests are far more powerful than they are in advanced economies where a better-educated public and a free press monitor (and punish) politicians and bureaucrats who are not acting in the public interest. Not surprisingly, then, the cost to the society of the principal–agent problem is particularly high in emerging-market economies.

PATH TWO: SEVERE FISCAL IMBALANCES The second path through which emerging-market countries experience a financial crisis is government fiscal imbalances that entail substantial budget deficits that need to be financed. The recent financial crisis in Argentina in 2001–2002 was of this type; other recent crises, for example in Russia in 1998, Ecuador in 1999, and Turkey in 2001, also have some elements of deficit-driven fiscal imbalances.

When Willie Sutton, a famous bank robber, was asked why he robbed banks, he answered, "Because that's where the money is." Governments in emerging-market countries have the same attitude. When they face large fiscal imbalances and cannot finance their debt, they often cajole or force banks to purchase government debt. Investors who lose confidence in the ability of the government to repay this debt unload the bonds, which causes their prices to plummet. Now the banks that are holding this debt have a big hole on the asset side of their balance sheets, with a huge decline in their net worth. The deterioration in bank balance sheets then causes a decline in bank lending and can even lead to a bank panic. Severe fiscal imbalances spill over into and weaken the banking system, which leads to a worsening of adverse selection and moral hazard problems.

ADDITIONAL FACTORS Other factors also play a role in the first stage in some crises. For example, another precipitating factor in some crises is a rise in interest rates that comes from events abroad, such as a tightening of monetary policy. When interest rates rise, riskier firms are most willing to pay the higher interest rates, so the adverse selection problem is more severe. In addition, the higher interest rates reduce firms' cash flows, forcing them to seek funds in external capital markets in which asymmetric problems are greater. Increases in interest rates abroad that raise domestic interest rates can then increase adverse selection and moral hazard problems (as shown by the arrow from the third factor in the top row of Figure 9-3).

Because asset markets are not as large in emerging-market countries as they are in advanced countries, they play a less prominent role in financial crises. Asset-price declines in the stock market do, nevertheless, decrease the net worth of firms and so increase adverse selection problems. There is less collateral for lenders to grab on to, so moral hazard problems increase because with lower net worth the owners of firms have less to lose if they engage in riskier activities. Asset-price declines can therefore have some role in worsening adverse selection and moral hazard problems directly (as shown by the arrow pointing from the second factor in the first row of Figure 9-3) as well as indirectly by causing a deterioration in banks' balance sheets from asset write-downs.

As in advanced countries, when an emerging-market economy is in a recession or a prominent firm fails, people become more uncertain about the returns on investment projects. In emerging-market countries, another source of uncertainty can come from the political systems, which are often notoriously unstable. When uncertainty increases, it becomes harder for lenders to screen out good credit risks from bad and to monitor the activities of firms to whom they have loaned money, so that adverse selection and moral hazard problems worsen (as shown by the arrow pointing from the last factor in the first row of Figure 9-3).

Stage Two: Currency Crisis

As the effects of any or all of the factors at the top of the diagram in Figure 9-3 build on each other, participants in the foreign exchange market sense an opportunity: they can make huge profits if they bet on a depreciation of the currency. As we will describe in more detail in Chapter 20, a currency that is fixed against the U.S. dollar now becomes subject to a **speculative attack**, in which speculators engage in massive sales of the currency. As the currency sales flood the market, supply far outstrips demand, the value of the currency collapses, and a currency crisis ensues (see the Stage Two section of Figure 9-3). High interest rates abroad, increases in uncertainty, and falling asset prices all play a role. The deterioration in bank balance sheets and severe fiscal imbalances, however, are the two key factors that trigger speculative attacks and plunge an economy into a full-scale, vicious, downward spiral of currency crisis, financial crisis, and meltdown.

HOW DETERIORATION OF BANK BALANCE SHEETS TRIGGERS CURRENCY CRISES   When banks and other financial institutions are in trouble, governments have a limited number of options. Defending their currencies by raising interest rates should encourage capital inflows. If the government raises interest rates, banks must pay more to obtain funds. This increase in costs decreases bank profitability, which may lead them to insolvency. Thus, when the banking system is in trouble, the government and central bank are between a rock and a hard place: If they raise interest rates too much they will destroy their already weakened banks. If they don't raise interest rates, they can't maintain the value of their currency.

Speculators in the market for foreign currency are able to recognize the troubles in a country's financial sector and realize when the government's ability to defend the currency is limited. They will seize an almost sure-thing bet because the currency has only one way to go—downward in value. Speculators engage in a selling frenzy and sell the currency in anticipation of its decline, which provides them with huge profits. These sales rapidly use up the country's holdings of reserves of foreign currency because the country has to sell its reserves to buy the domestic currency and keep it from falling in value. Once the country's central bank has exhausted its holdings of foreign currency reserves, the cycle ends. It no longer has the resources to intervene in the foreign exchange market and must let the value of the domestic currency fall. That is, the government must allow a devaluation.

HOW SEVERE FISCAL IMBALANCES TRIGGER CURRENCY CRISES   We have seen that severe fiscal imbalances can lead to the deterioration of bank balance sheets, and so can help produce a currency crisis along the lines just described. Fiscal imbalances can also directly trigger a currency crisis. When government budget deficits spin out of control, foreign and domestic investors begin to suspect that the country may not be able to pay back its government debt and so will start pulling money out of the country and selling the domestic currency. Recognition that the fiscal situation is out of control thus results in a speculative attack against the currency, which eventually results in its collapse.

Stage Three: Full-Fledged Financial Crisis

When debt contracts are denominated in foreign currency (U.S. dollars), as is typically the case in emerging-market countries, and there is an unanticipated depreciation or devaluation of the domestic currency (for example, pesos), the debt burden of domestic firms increases in terms of domestic currency. That is, it takes more pesos to pay back the dollarized debt. Since the goods and services produced by most firms are priced in the domestic currency, the firms' assets do not rise in value in terms of pesos, while the debt does. The depreciation of the domestic currency increases the value of debt relative to assets, and the firm's net worth declines. The decline in net worth then increases adverse selection and moral hazard problems. A decline in investment and economic activity then follows (as shown by the Stage Three section of Figure 9-3).

We now see how the institutional structure of debt markets in emerging-market countries interacts with the currency devaluations to propel the economies into full-fledged financial crises. Economists often call a concurrent currency and financial crisis the "twin crises."

The collapse of a currency also can lead to higher inflation. The central banks in most emerging-market countries have little credibility as inflation fighters. Thus, a sharp depreciation of the currency after a currency crisis leads to immediate upward pressure on import prices. A dramatic rise in both actual and expected inflation will likely follow. The resulting increase in interest payments causes reductions in firms' cash flows, which lead to increased asymmetric information problems since firms are now more dependent on external funds to finance their investment. As the asymmetric information analysis suggests, the resulting increase in adverse selection and moral hazard problems leads to a reduction in investment and economic activity.

As shown in Figure 9-3, further deterioration in the economy occurs. The collapse in economic activity and the deterioration of cash flow and balance sheets of firms and households means that many are no longer able to pay off their debts, resulting in substantial losses for banks. Sharp rises in interest rates also have a negative effect on banks' profitability and balance sheets. Even more problematic for the banks is the sharp increase in the value of their foreign-currency-denominated liabilities after a devaluation. Thus, bank balance sheets are squeezed from both sides—the value of their assets falls as the value of their liabilities rises.

Under these circumstances, the banking system will often suffer a banking crisis in which many banks are likely to fail (as happened in the United States during the Great Depression). The banking crisis and the contributing factors in the credit markets explain a further worsening of adverse selection and moral hazard problems and a further collapse of lending and economic activity in the aftermath of the crisis.

APPLICATION | **Financial Crises in Mexico, 1994–1995; East Asia, 1997–1998; and Argentina, 2001–2002**

When emerging-market countries opened up their markets to the outside world in the 1990s, they had high hopes that globalization would stimulate economic growth and eventually make them rich. Instead of leading to high economic growth and reduced poverty, however, many of them experienced financial crises that were every bit as devastating as the Great Depression was in the United States and other countries.

The most dramatic of these crises were the Mexican crisis, which started in 1994; the East Asian crisis, which started in July 1997; and the Argentine crisis, which started in 2001. We now apply the asymmetric information analysis of the dynamics of financial crises to explain why a developing country can shift dramatically from a path of high growth before a financial crisis—as was true in

Mexico and particularly the East Asian countries of Thailand, Malaysia, Indonesia, the Philippines, and South Korea—to a sharp decline in economic activity.[2]

Before their crises, Mexico and the East Asian countries had achieved sound fiscal policies. The East Asian countries ran budget surpluses and Mexico ran a budget deficit of less than 1% of GDP, a number that most advanced countries would be thrilled to have today. The key precipitating factor driving these crises was the deterioration in banks' balance sheets because of increasing loan losses. When financial markets in these countries were liberalized and opened to foreign capital markets in the early 1990s, lending booms ensued. Bank credit to the private nonfinancial business sector accelerated sharply, with lending expanding at 15% to 30% per year. Because of weak supervision by bank regulators, aided and abetted by powerful business interests (see the Global box, The Perversion of the Financial Liberalization/Globalization Process: Chaebols and the South Korean Crisis) and a lack of expertise in screening and monitoring borrowers at banking institutions, losses on loans began to mount, causing an erosion of banks' net worth (capital). As a result of this erosion, banks had fewer resources to lend. This lack of lending led to a contraction of economic activity, as outlined in the previous section.

In contrast to Mexico and the East Asian countries, Argentina had a well-supervised banking system, and a lending boom did not occur before the crisis. The banks were in surprisingly good shape before the crisis, even though a severe recession had begun in 1998. This recession led to declining tax revenues and a widening gap between government expenditures and taxes. The subsequent severe fiscal imbalances were so large that the government had trouble getting both domestic residents and foreigners to buy enough of its bonds, so it coerced banks into absorbing large amounts of government debt. Investors soon lost confidence in the ability of the Argentine government to repay this debt. The price of the debt plummeted, leaving big holes in banks' balance sheets. This weakening led to a decline in lending and a contraction of economic activity, as in Mexico and East Asia.

Consistent with the Canadian experience in the nineteenth and early twentieth centuries, another precipitating factor in the Mexican and Argentine (but not East Asian) financial crises was a rise in interest rates abroad. Before the Mexican crisis in February 1994, and before the Argentine crisis in mid-1999, the Federal Reserve in the United States began a cycle of raising the federal funds rate to head off inflationary pressures. Although the Fed's monetary policy actions were successful in keeping U.S. inflation in check, they put upward pressure on interest rates in both Mexico and Argentina. The rise in interest rates in Mexico and Argentina added to the already increased adverse selection and moral hazard problems in their financial markets. As discussed earlier, it was more likely that the parties willing to take on the most risk would seek loans, and the higher interest payments led to a decline in firms' cash flows.

---

[2] This application does not examine the four recent crises in Russia, Brazil, Ecuador, and Turkey. Russia's financial crisis in August 1998 can also be explained with the asymmetric information story here, but it is more appropriate to view it as a symptom of a wider breakdown in the economy. The Brazilian crisis in January 1999 has features of a more traditional balance-of-payments crisis (see Chapter 20) rather than a financial crisis. Ecuador's crisis of 1999 and the Turkish crisis of 2001 have features of both types of emerging-market financial crises discussed in the Application, with mismanagement of financial liberalization and globalization and severe fiscal imbalances playing a prominent role.

GLOBAL

The Perversion of the Financial Liberalization and Globalization Process: Chaebols and the South Korean Crisis

Although similarities exist in the perversion of the financial liberalization and globalization process that has occurred in many emerging-market economies, South Korea exhibited some particularly extraordinary elements because of the unique role of the chaebols (large, family-owned conglomerates). Because of their massive size—sales of the top five chaebols were nearly 50% of GDP right before South Korea's crisis—the chaebols were politically very powerful. The chaebols' influence extended the government safety net far beyond the financial system because the government had a long-standing policy of viewing the chaebols as being "too big to fail." With this policy in place, the chaebols would receive direct government assistance or directed credit if they got into trouble. Not surprisingly, given this guarantee, chaebols borrowed like crazy and were highly leveraged.

In the 1990s, the chaebols were in trouble: they weren't making any money. From 1993 to 1996, the return on assets for the top 30 chaebols was never much more than 3% (a comparable figure for Canadian and U.S. corporations is 15–20%). In 1996, right before the crisis hit, the rate of return on assets had fallen to 0.2%. Furthermore, only the top five chaebols had any profits: the lower-ranked chaebols never had a rate of return on assets much above 1% and in many years had negative rates of return. With this poor profitability and the already high amount of leverage, any banker would hesitate to lend to these conglomerates *if* there were no government safety net. Yet because the banks knew the government would make good on the chaebols' loans if they were in default, the opposite occurred: banks continued to lend to the chaebols, evergreened their loans, and, in effect, threw good money after bad.

Even though the chaebols were getting substantial financing from commercial banks, it was not enough to feed their insatiable appetite for more credit. The chaebols decided that the way out of their troubles was to pursue growth, and they needed massive amounts of funds to do it. Even with the vaunted Korean national savings rate of over 30%, there just were not enough loanable funds to finance the chaebols' planned expansion. Where could they get funds? The answer was in the international capital markets.

The chaebols encouraged the Korean government to accelerate the process of opening up Korean financial markets to foreign capital as part of the liberalization process. In 1993, the government expanded the ability of domestic banks to make loans denominated in foreign currency by expanding the types of loans for which this was possible. At the same time, the Korean government effectively allowed unlimited short-term foreign borrowing by financial institutions, but maintained quantity restrictions on long-term borrowing as a means of managing capital flows into the country. Opening up to short-term but not long-term foreign capital flows made no economic sense. It is short-term capital flows that make an emerging-market economy financially fragile: *short-term* capital can fly out of the country extremely rapidly if there is any whiff of a crisis.

Opening up primarily to short-term capital, however, made complete political sense: the chaebols needed the money and it is much easier to borrow short-term funds at lower interest rates in the international market because long-term lending is much riskier for foreign creditors. Keeping restrictions on long-term international borrowing, however, allowed the government to say that it was still restricting foreign capital inflows and to claim that it was opening up to foreign capital in a prudent manner. In the aftermath of these changes, Korean banks opened 28 branches in foreign countries that gave them access to foreign funds.

Although Korean financial institutions now had access to foreign capital, the chaebols still had a problem. They were not allowed to own commercial banks and so the chaebols might not get all of the bank loans that they needed. What was the answer? The chaebols needed to get their hands on financial institutions that they could own, that were allowed to borrow abroad, and that were subject to very little regulation. The financial institution could then engage in connected lending by borrowing foreign funds and then lending them to the chaebols who owned the institution.

An existing type of financial institution specific to South Korea perfectly met the chaebols' requirements: the merchant bank. Merchant banking corporations were wholesale financial institutions that engaged in underwriting securities, leasing, and short-term lending to the corporate sector. They obtained funds for these loans by issuing bonds and commercial paper and by borrowing from inter-bank and foreign markets.

At the time of the Korean crisis, merchant banks were allowed to borrow abroad and were virtually unregulated. The chaebols saw their opportunity. Government officials, often lured with bribery and kickbacks, allowed many finance companies (some already owned by the chaebols) that were not allowed to borrow abroad to be converted into merchant banks, which could. In 1990 there were only six merchant banks and all of them were foreign affiliated. By 1997, after the chaebols had exercised their political influence, there were thirty merchant banks, sixteen of which were owned by chaebols, two of which were foreign owned but in which chaebols were major shareholders, and twelve of which were independent of the chaebols, but Korean owned. The chaebols were now able to exploit connected lending with a vengeance: the merchant banks channelled massive amounts of funds to their chaebol owners, where they flowed into unproductive investments in steel, automobile production, and chemicals. When the loans went sour, the stage was set for a disastrous financial crisis.

Also, stock market declines and increases in uncertainty initiated and contributed to full-blown financial crises in Mexico, Thailand, South Korea, and Argentina. (The stock market declines in Malaysia, Indonesia, and the Philippines, on the other hand, occurred simultaneously with the onset of these crises.) The Mexican economy was hit by political shocks in 1994 (specifically, the assassination of the ruling party's presidential candidate, Luis Colosio, and an uprising in the southern state of Chiapas) that created uncertainty, while the ongoing recession increased uncertainty in Argentina. Right before their crises, Thailand and South Korea experienced major failures of financial and nonfinancial firms that increased general uncertainty in financial markets.

As we have seen, an increase in uncertainty and a decrease in net worth as a result of a stock market decline increase asymmetric information problems. It becomes harder to screen out good from bad borrowers. The decline in net worth decreases the value of firms' collateral and increases their incentives to make risky investments because there is less equity to lose if the investments are unsuccessful. The increase in uncertainty and stock market declines that occurred before the crises, along with the deterioration in banks' balance sheets, worsened adverse selection and moral hazard problems and made the economies ripe for a serious financial emergency.

At this point, full-blown speculative attacks developed in the foreign exchange market, plunging these countries into a full-scale crisis. With the Colosio assassination, the Chiapas uprising, and the growing weakness in the banking sector, the Mexican peso came under attack. Even though the Mexican central bank intervened in the foreign exchange market and raised interest rates sharply, it was unable to stem the attack and was forced to devalue the peso on December 20, 1994. In the case of Thailand, concerns about the large current account deficit and weakness in the Thai financial system, culminating with the failure of a major finance company, Finance One, led to a successful speculative attack. The Thai central bank was forced to allow the baht to depreciate in July 1997. Soon thereafter, speculative attacks developed against the other countries in the region, leading to the collapse of the Philippine peso, the Indonesian rupiah, the Malaysian ringgit, and the South Korean won. In Argentina, a full-scale bank panic began in October–November 2001. This, along with realization that the government was going to default on its debt, also led to a speculative attack on the Argentine peso, resulting in its collapse on January 6, 2002.

The institutional structure of debt markets in Mexico and East Asia now interacted with the currency devaluations to propel the economies into full-fledged financial crises. Because so many firms in these countries had debt denominated in foreign currencies like the U.S. dollar and the yen, depreciation of their currencies resulted in increases in their indebtedness in domestic currency terms, even though the value of their assets remained unchanged. When the peso lost half its value by March 1995 and the Thai, Philippine, Malaysian, and South Korean currencies lost between one-third and one-half of their value by the beginning of 1998, firms' balance sheets took a big negative hit, causing dramatic exacerbation of adverse selection and moral hazard problems. This negative shock was especially severe for Indonesia and Argentina, which saw the value of their currencies fall by more than 70%, resulting in insolvency for firms with substantial amounts of debt denominated in foreign currencies.

The collapse of currencies also led to a rise in actual and expected inflation in these countries. Market interest rates rose sky-high (to around 100% in Mexico and Argentina). The resulting increase in interest payments caused reductions in household and firm cash flows. A feature of debt markets in emerging-market countries, like those in Mexico, East Asia, and Argentina, is that debt contracts have very short durations, typically less than one month. Thus the rise in short-term interest rates in these countries made the effect on cash flow, and hence on balance sheets, substantial. As our asymmetric information analysis suggests, this deterioration in households' and firms' balance sheets increased adverse selection and moral hazard problems in the credit markets, making domestic and foreign lenders even less willing to lend.

Consistent with the theory of financial crises outlined in this chapter, the sharp decline in lending in the countries discussed contributed to the collapse of economic activity, with real GDP growth falling sharply. Further economic deterioration occurred because the collapse in economic activity and the deterioration in the cash flow and balance sheets of both firms and households worsened banking crises. Many firms and households were no longer able to pay off their debts, resulting in substantial losses for banks. Even more problematic for banks were their many short-term liabilities denominated in foreign currencies. The sharp increase in the value of these liabilities after domestic currency devaluation led to further deterioration in bank balance sheets. Under these circumstances, the banking systems would have collapsed in the absence of a government safety net—as occurred in the United States during the Great Depression. With the assistance of the International Monetary Fund, these countries were in some cases able to protect depositors and avoid a bank panic. However, given the loss of bank capital and the need for the government to intervene to prop up the banks, the banks' ability to lend was nevertheless sharply curtailed. As we have seen, a banking crisis of this type hinders the ability of the banks to lend and also makes adverse selection and moral hazard problems worse in financial markets, because banks are less capable of playing their traditional financial intermediation role. The banking crisis, along with other factors that increased adverse selection and moral hazard problems in the credit markets of Mexico, East Asia, and Argentina, explains the collapse of lending, and hence economic activity, in the aftermath of the crises.

Following their crises, Mexico began to recover in 1996, while the crisis countries in East Asia tentatively began to recover in 1999, with stronger recovery later. Argentina was still in a severe depression in 2003, but subsequently the economy bounced back. In all these countries, the economic hardship caused by the financial crises was tremendous. Unemployment rose sharply, poverty increased substantially, and even the local social fabric was stretched thin. For example, after their financial crises, Mexico City and Buenos Aires became crime-ridden, while Indonesia experienced waves of ethnic violence.

SUMMARY

1. A financial crisis occurs when a disruption in the financial system causes an increase in asymmetric information that makes adverse selection and moral hazard problems far more severe, thereby rendering financial markets incapable of channelling funds to households and firms with productive investment opportunities, and causing a sharp contraction in economic activity. Six categories of factors play an important role in financial crises: asset market effects on balance sheets, deterioration in financial institutions' balance sheets, banking crisis, increases in uncertainty, increases in interest rates, and government fiscal imbalances.

2. There are several possible ways that financial crises can start in advanced countries like Canada and the United States: mismanagement of financial liberalization and innovation, asset-price booms and busts, spikes in interest rates, or a general increase in uncertainty when there are failures of major financial institutions. The result is substantial worsening of adverse selection and moral hazard problems that leads to contraction of lending and decline in eco-

nomic activity. The worsening business conditions and deterioration in bank balance sheets then triggers the second stage of crisis, the simultaneous failure of many banking institutions: a banking crisis. The resulting decline in the number of banks causes a loss of their information capital, leading to a further decline in lending and a downward spiral in the economy. In some instances, the resulting economic downturn leads to a sharp decline in prices, which increases the real liabilities of firms and therefore lowers their net worth, leading to debt deflation. The decline in firms' net worth worsens adverse selection and moral hazard problems so that lending, investment spending, and aggregate economic activity remain depressed for a long time.

3. The financial crisis of 2007–2008 in the United States that led to a number of banking crises throughout the world was triggered by mismanagement of financial innovations involving subprime residential mortgages and the bursting of a housing-price bubble.

4. Financial crises in emerging-market countries develop along two basic paths: one involving the mismanage-

ment of financial liberalization and globalization that weakens bank balance sheets, and the other involving severe fiscal imbalances. Both lead to a speculative attack on the currency, and eventually to a currency crisis in which there is a sharp decline in the value of the domestic currency. The decline in the value of the domestic currency causes a sharp rise in the debt burden of domestic firms, which leads to a decline in firms' net worth, as well as increases in inflation and interest rates. Adverse

selection and moral hazard problems then worsen, leading to the collapse of lending and economic activity. The worsening economic conditions and increases in interest rates result in substantial losses for banks, leading to a banking crisis, which further depresses lending and aggregate economic activity.

5. The financial crises in Mexico in 1994–1995, East Asia in 1997–1998, and Argentina in 2001–2002 led to great economic hardship and weakened the social fabric of these countries.

KEY TERMS

alt-A mortgages, p. 204

asset-price bubble, p. 202

bank panic, p. 198

collateralized debt obligations (CDOs), p. 205

credit boom, p. 200

debt deflation, p. 203

deleveraging, p. 200

financial engineering, p. 205

financial globalization, p. 213

financial liberalization, p. 200

mortgage-backed securities, p. 205

originate-to-distribute model, p. 205

securitization, p. 204

speculative attack, p. 216

structured credit products, p. 205

structured investment vehicles (SIVs), p. 207

subprime mortgages, p. 204

QUESTIONS

You will find the answers to the questions marked with an asterisk in the Textbook Resources section of your MyEconLab.

*1. How can the bursting of an asset-price bubble in the stock market help trigger a financial crisis?

2. How does an unanticipated decline in the price level cause a drop in lending?

*3. When can a decline in the value of a country's currency exacerbate adverse selection and moral hazard problems? Why?

4. How can a decline in real estate prices cause deleveraging and a decline in lending?

*5. How does deterioration in balance sheets of financial institutions and simultaneous failures of these institutions cause a decline in economic activity?

6. How does a general increase in uncertainty as a result of a failure of a major financial institution lead to an increase in adverse selection and moral hazard problems?

*7. What are the two ways that spikes in interest rates lead to an increase in adverse selection and moral hazard problems?

8. How can government fiscal imbalances lead to a financial crisis?

*9. How can financial liberalization lead to financial crises?

10. What role does weak financial regulation and supervision play in causing financial crises?

*11. Why do debt deflations occur in advanced countries but not in emerging-market countries?

12. What technological innovations led to the development of the subprime mortgage market?

*13. Why is the originate-to-distribute business model subject to the principal–agent problem?

14. True, false, or uncertain: Financial engineering always leads to a more efficient financial system. Explain your answer.

*15. How did a decline in housing prices help trigger the subprime financial crisis of 2007–2008?

16. How can opening up to capital flows from abroad lead to a financial crisis?

*17. Why are more resources not devoted to adequate prudential supervision of the financial system to limit excessive risk taking when it is clear that this supervision is needed to prevent financial crises?

18. Why does the "twin crisis" phenomenon of currency and banking crises occur in emerging-market countries?

*19. How can a currency crisis lead to higher interest rates?

20. How can deterioration in bank balance sheets lead to a currency crisis?

WEB EXERCISES

1. This chapter discusses how an understanding of adverse selection and moral hazard can help us better understand financial crises. The greatest financial crisis was the Great Depression of 1929–1933. Go to **www.amatecon.com/greatdepression.html**. This site contains a brief discussion of the factors that led to the Great Depression. Write a one-page summary explaining how adverse selection and moral hazard contributed to the Great Depression.

2. Go to the International Monetary Fund's Financial Crisis page **at www.imf.org/external/np/exr/key/finstab.htm**. Report on the most recent three countries that the IMF has given emergency loans to in response to a financial crisis. According to the IMF, what caused the crisis in each country?

3. One of the countries hardest hit by the global financial crisis of 2008 was Iceland. Go to **http://assets.opencrs.com/rpts/RS22988_20081120.pdf** and summarize the causes and events that led to the crisis in Iceland.

Be sure to visit the MyEconLab website at **www.myeconlab.com**. This online homework and tutorial system puts you in control of your own learning with study and practice tools directly correlated to this chapter content.

CHAPTER 10

Economic Analysis of Financial Regulation

LEARNING OBJECTIVES

After studying this chapter you should be able to

1. explain bank regulation in the context of asymmetric information problems
2. characterize how the CDIC handles failed banks and detail recent CDIC developments
3. outline the banking crises that have occurred in Canada and other countries throughout the world

PREVIEW

As we have seen in the previous chapters, the financial system is among the most heavily regulated sectors of the economy, and banks are among the most heavily regulated of financial institutions. In this chapter we develop an economic analysis of why regulation of the financial system takes the form it does.

Unfortunately, the regulatory process may not always work very well, as evidenced by the recent subprime meltdown in the United States and other financial crises, not only in Canada but also in many countries throughout the world. Here we also use our economic analysis of financial regulation to explain the worldwide crises in banking and how the regulatory system can be reformed to prevent future disasters.

ASYMMETRIC INFORMATION AND FINANCIAL REGULATION

In earlier chapters we have seen how asymmetric information, the fact that different parties in a financial contract do not have the same information, leads to adverse selection and moral hazard problems that have an important impact on our financial system. The concepts of asymmetric information, adverse selection, and moral hazard are especially useful in understanding why government has chosen the form of financial regulation we see in Canada and in other countries. There are nine basic categories of financial regulation: the government safety net, restrictions on asset holdings, capital requirements, prompt corrective action, chartering and examination, assessment of risk management, disclosure requirements, consumer protection, and restrictions on competition.

Government Safety Net

As we saw in Chapter 8, financial intermediaries, like banks, are particularly well suited to solving adverse selection and moral hazard problems because they make private loans that help avoid the free-rider problem. However, this solution to the free-rider problem creates another asymmetric information problem, because depositors lack information about the quality of these private loans. This asymmetric information problem leads to several reasons why the financial system might not function well.

BANK PANICS AND THE NEED FOR DEPOSIT INSURANCE   Before the CDIC started operations in 1967, a **bank failure** (in which a bank is unable to meet its obligations to pay its depositors and other creditors and so must go out of business) meant that depositors would have to wait to get their deposit funds until the bank was liquidated (until its assets had been turned into cash); at that time, they would be paid only a fraction of the value of their deposits. Unable to learn if bank managers were taking on too much risk or were outright crooks, depositors would be reluctant to put money in the bank, thus making financial institutions less viable. Depositors' lack of information about the quality of bank assets can lead to bank panics, which, as we saw in Chapter 9, can have serious harmful consequences for the economy. To see this, consider the following situation. There is no deposit insurance, and an adverse shock hits the economy. As a result of the shock, 5% of the banks have such large losses on loans that they become insolvent (have a negative net worth and so are bankrupt). Because of asymmetric information, depositors are unable to tell whether their bank is a good bank or one of the 5% that are insolvent. Depositors at bad *and* good banks recognize that they may not get back 100 cents on the dollar for their deposits and will want to withdraw them. Indeed, because banks operate on a "sequential service constraint" (a first-come, first-served basis), depositors have a very strong incentive to show up at the bank first because if they are last in line, the bank may have run out of funds and they will get nothing. Uncertainty about the health of the banking system in general can lead to runs on banks both good and bad, and the failure of one bank can hasten the failure of others (referred to as the *contagion effect*). If nothing is done to restore the public's confidence, a bank panic can ensue.

A government safety net for depositors can short-circuit runs on banks and bank panics, and by providing protection for the depositor, it can overcome reluctance to put funds in the banking system. One form of the safety net is deposit insurance, a guarantee such as that provided by the Canada Deposit Insurance Corporation (CDIC) in which depositors are paid off in full on the first $100 000 they have deposited in the bank no matter what happens to the bank. With fully insured deposits, depositors don't need to run to the bank to make withdrawals—even if they are worried about the bank's health—because their deposits will be worth 100 cents on the dollar no matter what.

The CDIC uses two primary methods to handle a failed bank. In the first, called the *payoff method,* the CDIC allows the bank to fail and pays off deposits up to the $100 000 insurance limit (with funds acquired from the insurance premiums paid by the banks that have bought CDIC insurance). After the bank has been liquidated, the CDIC lines up with other creditors of the bank and is paid its share of the proceeds from the liquidated assets. Typically, when the payoff method is used, account holders with deposits in excess of the $100 000 limit get back more than 90 cents on the dollar, although the process can take several years to complete.

In the second method, called the *purchase and assumption method,* the CDIC reorganizes the bank, typically by finding a willing merger partner who assumes (takes over) all of the failed bank's liabilities so that no depositor or other creditor loses a penny. The CDIC often sweetens the pot for the merger partner by providing it with subsidized loans or by buying some of the failed bank's weaker loans. The net effect of the purchase and assumption method is that the CDIC has guaranteed *all* of a bank's deposits, not just those under the $100 000 limit.

In recent years, government deposit insurance has been growing in popularity and has spread to many countries throughout the world. Whether this trend is desirable is discussed in the Global box, The Spread of Government Deposit Insurance Throughout the World: Is It a Good Thing?

OTHER FORMS OF THE GOVERNMENT SAFETY NET Deposit insurance is not the only form of government safety net. In other countries, governments have often stood ready to provide support to domestic banks facing runs even in the absence of explicit deposit insurance. Furthermore, banks are not the only financial intermediaries that can pose a systemic threat to the financial system, as our discussion of financial crises in Chapter 9 has illustrated. When financial institutions are very large or highly interconnected with other financial institutions or markets, their failure has the potential to bring down the entire financial system. Indeed, as we saw in Chapter 9, this is exactly what happened in the United States when Bear Stearns and Lehman Brothers, two investment banks, and AIG, an insurance company, got into trouble during the subprime financial crisis in 2008.

One way governments provide support is through lending from the central bank to troubled institutions, as the Bank of Canada did during the recent financial crisis (more on this in Chapter 17). This form of support is often referred to as

---

| **GLOBAL** | **The Spread of Government Deposit Insurance Throughout the World: Is It a Good Thing?** |

Government deposit insurance has taken off throughout the world because of growing concern about the health of banking systems, particularly after the increasing number of banking crises in recent years (documented at the end of the chapter). Has this spread of deposit insurance been a good thing? Has it helped improve the performance of the financial system and prevent banking crises?

The answer seems to be no under many circumstances. Research at the World Bank has found that on average, the adoption of explicit government deposit insurance is associated with less banking sector stability and a higher incidence of banking crises.* Furthermore, on average it seems to retard financial development. However, the negative effects of deposit insurance appear only in countries with weak institutional environments: an absence of rule of law, ineffective regulation and supervision of the financial sector, and high corruption. This is exactly what might be expected because, as we will see later in this chapter, a strong institutional environment is needed to limit the moral hazard incentives for banks to engage in the excessively risky behaviour encouraged by deposit insurance. The problem is that developing a strong institutional environment may be very difficult to achieve in many emerging-market countries. This leaves us with the following conclusion: adoption of deposit insurance may be exactly the wrong medicine for promoting stability and efficiency of banking systems in emerging-market countries.

*See World Bank, *Finance for Growth: Policy Choices in a Volatile World* (Oxford: World Bank and Oxford University Press, 2001).

the "lender of last resort" role of the central bank. In other cases, funds are provided directly to troubled institutions as was done by the government of Canada through the Canada Mortgage and Housing Corporation (CMHC), the U.S. Treasury, and by other governments in 2008 during the most virulent phase of the subprime financial crisis. Governments also take over (nationalize) troubled institutions and guarantee that all creditors will be repaid their loans in full.

MORAL HAZARD AND THE GOVERNMENT SAFETY NET   Although a government safety net can help protect depositors and other creditors and prevent or ameliorate financial crises, it is a mixed blessing. The most serious drawback of the government safety net stems from moral hazard, the incentives of one party to a transaction to engage in activities detrimental to the other party. Moral hazard is an important concern in insurance arrangements in general because the existence of insurance provides increased incentives for taking risks that might result in an insurance payoff. For example, some drivers who have automobile collision insurance with a low deductible might be more likely to drive recklessly, because if they get into an accident, the insurance company pays most of the costs for damage and repairs.

Moral hazard is a prominent concern in government arrangements to provide a safety net. With a safety net depositors or creditors know that they will not suffer losses if a financial institution fails, so they do not impose the discipline of the marketplace on financial institutions by withdrawing funds when they suspect that the financial institution is taking on too much risk. Consequently, financial institutions with a government safety net have an incentive to take on greater risks than they otherwise would, with taxpayers paying the bill if the bank subsequently goes belly up. Financial institutions have been given the following bet: "Heads I win, tails the taxpayer loses."

ADVERSE SELECTION AND THE GOVERNMENT SAFETY NET   A further problem with a government safety net like deposit insurance arises because of adverse selection, the fact that the people who are most likely to produce the adverse outcome insured against (bank failure) are those who most want to take advantage of the insurance. For example, bad drivers are more likely than good drivers to take out automobile collision insurance with a low deductible. Because depositors and creditors protected by a government safety net have little reason to impose discipline on financial institutions, risk-loving entrepreneurs might find the financial industry a particularly attractive one to enter—they know that they will be able to engage in highly risky activities. Even worse, because protected depositors and creditors have so little reason to monitor the financial institution's activities, without government intervention outright crooks might also find finance an attractive industry for their activities because it is easy for them to get away with fraud and embezzlement.

"TOO BIG TO FAIL"   The moral hazard created by a government safety net and the desire to prevent financial failures has presented financial regulators with a particular quandary. Because the failure of a very large financial institution makes it more likely that a major financial disruption will occur, financial regulators are naturally reluctant to allow a big institution to fail and cause losses to its depositors and creditors.

One problem with the too-big-to-fail policy is that it increases the moral hazard incentives for big banks. If the CDIC were willing to close a bank using the payoff method, paying depositors only up to the $100 000 limit, large depositors with more than $100 000 would suffer losses if the bank failed. Thus they would have an incentive to monitor the bank by examining the bank's activities closely and pulling their money out if the bank was taking on too much risk. To prevent such a loss of deposits, the bank would be more likely to engage in less-risky activities. However, once large depositors know that a bank is too big to fail, they have no incentive to monitor the bank and pull out their deposits when it takes on too much risk: no matter what the bank does, large depositors will not suffer any losses. The result of the too-big-to-fail policy is that big banks might take on even greater risks, thereby making bank failures more likely.

Similarly, the too-big-to-fail policy increases the moral hazard incentives for nonbank financial institutions that are extended a government safety net. Knowing that the financial institution will get bailed out, creditors have little incentive to monitor the institution and pull their money out when the institution is taking on excessive risk. As a result, large or interconnected financial institutions will be more likely to engage in high-risk activities, making it more likely that a financial crisis will occur.

FINANCIAL CONSOLIDATION AND THE GOVERNMENT SAFETY NET   Financial consolidation has been proceeding at a rapid pace, leading to both larger and more complex financial organizations. Financial consolidation poses two challenges to financial regulation because of the existence of the government safety net. First, the increased size of financial institutions as a result of financial consolidation increases the too-big-to-fail problem, because there will now be more large institutions whose failure exposes the financial system to systemic (system-wide) risk. Thus more financial institutions are likely to be treated as too big to fail, and the increased moral hazard incentives for these large institutions to take on greater risk can then increase the fragility of the financial system. Second, financial consolidation of banks with other financial services firms means that the government safety net may be extended to new activities such as securities underwriting, insurance, or real estate activities, as occurred in the United States during the subprime financial crisis in 2008. This increases incentives for greater risk taking in these activities that can also weaken the fabric of the financial system. Limiting the moral hazard incentives for the larger, more complex financial organizations that have arisen as a result of recent changes in legislation will be one of the key issues facing financial regulators in the aftermath of the subprime financial crisis in the United States.

Restrictions on Asset Holdings   As we have seen, the moral hazard associated with a government safety net encourages too much risk taking on the part of financial institutions. Financial regulations that restrict asset holdings are directed at minimizing this moral hazard, which can cost the taxpayers dearly.

Even in the absence of a government safety net, financial institutions still have the incentive to take on too much risk. Risky assets may provide a financial institution with higher earnings when they pay off; but if they do not pay off and the institution fails, depositors are left holding the bag. If depositors and creditors were able to monitor the institution easily by acquiring information on its risk-taking activities, they would immediately withdraw their funds if the institution was taking on too much risk. To prevent such a loss of funds, the institution would be more likely to reduce its risk-taking activities. Unfortunately, acquiring information on an institution's activities to learn how much risk the institution is taking can be a difficult task. Hence, most depositors and creditors are incapable of imposing discipline that might prevent financial institutions from engaging in risky activities. A strong rationale for government regulation to reduce risk taking on the part of financial institutions therefore existed even before the establishment of deposit insurance.

Because banks are most prone to panics, they are subjected to strict regulations to restrict their holding of risky assets such as common stocks. Bank regulations also promote diversification, which reduces risk by limiting the amount of loans given in particular categories or to individual borrowers. With the extension of the government safety net during the 2007–2008 financial crisis, it is likely that non-bank financial institutions (to be discussed in detail in Chapter 12) may face greater restrictions on their holdings of risky assets. There is a danger, however, that these restrictions may become so onerous that the efficiency of the financial system will be impaired.

Capital Requirements

Government-imposed capital requirements are another way of minimizing moral hazard at financial institutions. When a financial institution is forced to hold a large amount of equity capital, the institution has more to lose if it fails and is thus more likely to pursue lower-risk activities. In addition, as will be illustrated in Chapter 13, capital functions as a cushion when bad shocks occur, making it less likely that a financial institution will fail, thereby directly adding to the safety and soundness of financial institutions.

Capital requirements for banks take two forms. The first type is based on the **leverage ratio**, the amount of capital divided by the bank's total assets. To be classified as well capitalized, a bank's leverage ratio must exceed 5%; a lower leverage ratio, especially one below 3%, triggers increased regulatory restrictions on the bank.

In the past decade, regulators in Canada and the rest of the world have become increasingly worried about banks' holdings of risky assets and about the increase in banks' **off-balance-sheet activities**, activities that involve trading financial instruments and generating income from fees, which do not appear on bank balance sheets but nevertheless expose banks to risk. An agreement among banking officials from industrialized nations has set up the **Basel Committee on Bank Supervision** (because it meets under the auspices of the Bank for International Settlements in Basel, Switzerland), which has implemented the **Basel Accord** that deals with a second type of capital requirement, risk-based capital requirements. The Basel Accord, which required that banks hold as capital at least 8% of their risk-weighted assets, has been adopted by more than 100 countries, including Canada and the United States. Assets and off-balance-sheet activities were allocated into four categories, each with a different weight to reflect the degree of credit risk. The first category carried a zero weight and included items that have little default risk, such as reserves and government securities issued by the Organisation for Economic Co-operation and Development (OECD—industrialized) countries. The second category has a 20% weight and includes claims on banks in OECD countries. The third category has a weight of 50% and includes municipal bonds and residential mortgages. The fourth category has the maximum weight of 100% and includes debts to consumers and corporations. Off-balance-sheet activities are treated in a similar manner by assigning a credit-equivalent percentage that converts them to on-balance-sheet items to which the appropriate risk weight applies. The 1996 Market Risk Amendment to the Basel Accord set minimum capital requirements for risks in banks' trading accounts.

Over time, limitations of the Basel Accord have become apparent, because the regulatory measure of bank risk as stipulated by the risk weights can differ substantially from the actual risk the bank faces. This has resulted in what is known as **regulatory arbitrage**, a practice in which banks keep on their books assets that have the same risk-based capital requirements but are relatively risky, such as a loan to a company with a very low credit rating, while taking off their books low-risk assets such as a loan to a company with a very high credit rating. The Basel Accord could thus lead to increased risk taking, the opposite of its intent. To address these limitations, the Basel Committee on Bank Supervision proposed a new capital accord, often referred to as Basel 2, but it is not clear if it is workable (see the Global box, Basel 2: How Well Will It Work?).

The Basel Committee's work on bank capital requirements is never-ending. Indeed, with the extension of the government safety net to nonbank financial institutions during the subprime financial crisis in the United States, capital requirements for these other financial institutions will receive more scrutiny in the future. As the financial industry changes, regulation of capital must change with it to ensure the safety and soundness of financial institutions. It is increasingly likely that the Basel Committee will have an even greater role in exploring capital requirements for a wider range of financial institutions in the future.

Prompt Corrective Action

If the amount of a financial institution's capital falls to low levels, there are two serious problems. First, the bank is more likely to fail because it has a smaller capital cushion if it suffers loan losses or other asset write-downs. Second, with less capital, a financial institution has less "skin in the game" and is therefore more likely to take on excessive risks. In other words, the moral hazard problem becomes more severe, making it more likely that the institution will fail and the taxpayer will be left holding the bag. To prevent this, the CDIC adopted prompt corrective action provisions that require the CDIC to intervene earlier and more vigorously when a bank gets into trouble (see the Application Evaluating CDIC and Other Proposed Reforms of the Banking Regulatory System on page 244).

Financial Supervision: Chartering and Examination

Overseeing who operates financial institutions and how they are operated, referred to as **financial supervision** or **prudential supervision**, is an important method for reducing adverse selection and moral hazard in the financial industry. Because financial institutions can be used by crooks or overambitious entrepreneurs to engage in highly speculative activities, such undesirable people would be eager to run a financial institution. Chartering financial institutions is one method for preventing this adverse selection problem; through chartering, proposals for new institutions are screened to prevent undesirable people from controlling them.

Regular on-site examinations, which allow regulators to monitor whether an institution is complying with capital requirements and restrictions on asset holdings, also function to limit moral hazard. Bank examiners give banks a *CAMELS rating* (the acronym is based on the six areas assessed: capital adequacy, asset quality, management, earnings, liquidity, and sensitivity to market risk). With this information about a bank's activities, regulators can enforce regulations by taking such formal actions as *cease and desist orders* to alter the bank's behaviour or even close a bank if its CAMELS rating is sufficiently low. Actions taken to reduce moral hazard by restricting banks from taking on too much risk help reduce the adverse selection problem further, because with less opportunity for risk taking, risk-loving entrepreneurs will be less likely to be attracted to the banking industry. Note that the methods regulators use to cope with adverse selection and moral hazard have their counterparts in private financial markets (see Chapters 8 and 9). Chartering is

GLOBAL   Basel 2: How Well Will It Work?

Starting in June 1999, the Basel Committee on Banking Supervision released several proposals to reform the original 1988 Basel Accord. These efforts have culminated in what bank supervisors refer to as Basel 2, which is based on three pillars:

1. Pillar 1 links capital requirements for large, internationally active banks more closely to three types of actual risk: market risk, credit risk, and operational risk. It does so by specifying many more categories of assets with different risk weights in its standardized approach. Alternatively, it allows sophisticated banks to pursue an internal ratings-based approach that permits banks to use their own models of credit risk.
2. Pillar 2 focuses on strengthening the supervisory process, particularly in assessing the quality of risk management in financial institutions and evaluating whether these institutions have adequate procedures to determine how much capital they need.
3. Pillar 3 focuses on improving market discipline through increased disclosure of details about banks' credit exposures, amounts of reserves and capital, officials who control the banks, and the effectiveness of their internal rating systems.

Although Basel 2 makes great strides toward limiting excessive risk taking by internationally active financial institutions, it greatly increases the complexity of the accord. The document describing the original Basel Accord was 26 pages, while the final draft of Basel 2 exceeded 500 pages. The original timetable called for the completion of the final round of consultation by the end of 2001, with the new rules taking effect by 2004. However, criticism from banks, trade associations, and national regulators led to several postponements. The final draft was not published until June 2004 and Basel 2 started to be implemented at the end of 2007 by the "Big Six" internationally active banks in Canada, and at the beginning of 2008 by European banks. American banks submitted plans for compliance with Basel 2 in 2008, but full implementation did not occur until 2009. Only the dozen or so largest U.S. banks are subject to Basel 2: all others will be allowed to use a simplified version of the standards it imposes.

There are several serious criticisms of Basel 2 that cast doubts on how well it will work. First, its complexity could make it unworkable. Second, risk weights in the standardized approach are heavily reliant on credit ratings. Since these credit ratings have proved to be very unreliable on subprime mortgage products during the recent financial crisis, there are serious doubts that the standardized approach will produce reliable risk weights. Third, Basel 2 is very procyclical. That is, it demands that banks hold less capital when times are good, but more when times are bad, thereby exacerbating credit cycles. Because the probability of default and expected losses for different classes of assets rises during bad times, Basel 2 may require more capital at exactly the time when capital is most short. This has been a particularly serious concern in the aftermath of the subprime financial crisis. As a result of this crisis, banks' capital balances eroded, leading to a cutback on lending that was a big drag on the economy. Basel 2 may make such cutbacks in lending even worse, doing even more harm to an economy.

similar to the screening of potential borrowers, regulations restricting risky asset holdings are similar to restrictive covenants that prevent borrowing firms from engaging in risky investment activities, capital requirements act like restrictive covenants that require minimum amounts of net worth for borrowing firms, and regular examinations are similar to the monitoring of borrowers by lending institutions.

A chartered bank obtains a charter either by an Act of Parliament or through application to the Minister of Finance, who has the authority to issue a charter. To obtain a charter, the people planning to organize the bank must submit an application that shows how they plan to operate the bank. In evaluating the application, the regulatory authority looks at whether the bank is likely to be sound by examining the quality of the bank's intended management, the likely earnings of the bank, and the amount of the bank's initial capital. Moreover, the chartering agency typically explores the issue of whether the community needs a new bank. Often a new bank charter would not be granted if existing banks in a community would be hurt by its presence. Today this anticompetitive stance (justified by the desire to prevent bank failures of existing banks) is no longer as strong.

Once a bank has been chartered, it is required to file periodic (usually quarterly) *call reports* that reveal the bank's assets and liabilities, income and dividends, ownership, foreign exchange operations, and other details. The bank is also subject to examination by the bank regulatory agencies to ascertain its financial condition at least once a year. To avoid duplication of effort, the three federal agencies work together and usually accept each other's examinations. This means that, typically, chartered banks are examined by the OSFI, the CDIC, and the Bank of Canada.

Bank examinations are conducted by bank examiners, who study a bank's books to see whether it is complying with the rules and regulations that apply to its holdings of assets. If a bank is holding securities or loans that are too risky, the bank examiner can force the bank to get rid of them. If a bank examiner decides that a loan is unlikely to be repaid, the examiner can force the bank to declare the loan worthless (to write off the loan, which reduces the bank's capital). If, after examining the bank, the examiner feels that it does not have sufficient capital or has engaged in dishonest practices, the bank can be declared a "problem bank" and will be subject to more frequent examinations.

Assessment of Risk Management

Traditionally, on-site examinations have focused primarily on assessment of the quality of a financial institution's balance sheet at a point in time and whether it complies with capital requirements and restrictions on asset holdings. Although the traditional focus is important for reducing excessive risk taking by financial institutions, it is no longer felt to be adequate in today's world, in which financial innovation has produced new markets and instruments that make it easy for financial institutions and their employees to make huge bets easily and quickly. In this new financial environment, a financial institution that is healthy at a particular point in time can be driven into insolvency extremely rapidly from trading losses, as forcefully demonstrated by the failure of Barings in 1995 (discussed in Chapter 13). Thus an examination that focuses only on a financial institution's position at a point in time may not be effective in indicating whether it will, in fact, be taking on excessive risk in the near future.

This change in the financial environment for financial institutions has resulted in a major shift in thinking about the prudential supervisory process throughout the world. Bank examiners, for example, are now placing far greater emphasis on evaluating the soundness of a bank's management processes with regard to controlling risk. This shift in thinking is now reflected in a new focus on risk management in the guidelines to examiners on trading and derivatives activities. Now bank examiners focus on four elements of sound risk management: (1) the quality of oversight provided by the board of directors and senior management, (2) the adequacy of policies and limits for all activities that present significant risks, (3) the quality of the risk measurement and monitoring systems, and (4) the adequacy of internal controls to prevent fraud or unauthorized activities on the part of employees.

This shift toward focusing on management processes is also reflected in recent guidelines adopted by the Canadian bank regulatory authorities to deal with interest-rate risk. These guidelines require the bank's board of directors to establish interest-rate risk limits, appoint officials of the bank to manage this risk, and monitor the bank's risk exposure. The guidelines also require that senior management of a bank develop formal risk-management policies and procedures to ensure that the board of directors' risk limits are not violated and to implement internal controls to monitor interest-rate risk and compliance with the board's directives. Particularly important is the implementation of *stress testing*, which calculates losses under dire scenarios, or value-at-risk (VaR) calculations, which measure the size of the loss on a trading portfolio that might happen 1% of the time—say over a two-week period. In addition to these guidelines, bank examiners will continue to consider interest-rate risk in deciding a bank's capital requirements.

Disclosure Requirements

The free-rider problem described in Chapter 8 indicates that individual depositors and creditors will not have enough incentive to produce private information about the quality of a financial institution's assets. To ensure that there is better information in the marketplace, regulators can require that financial institutions adhere to certain standard accounting principles and disclose a wide range of information that helps the market assess the quality of an institution's portfolio and the amount of its exposure to risk. More public information about the risks incurred by financial institutions and the quality of their portfolios can better enable stockholders, creditors, and depositors to evaluate and monitor financial institutions and so act as a deterrent to excessive risk taking.

Disclosure requirements are a key element of financial regulation. Basel 2 puts a particular emphasis on disclosure requirements with one of its three pillars focusing on increasing market discipline by mandating increased disclosure of credit exposure, amount of reserves, and capital. Provincial securities commissions, the most significant being the Ontario Securities Commission (OSC), also impose disclosure requirements on all corporations, including financial institutions, that issue publicly traded securities. In addition, it has required financial institutions to provide additional disclosure regarding their off-balance-sheet positions and more information about how they value their portfolios.

Regulation to increase disclosure is needed to limit incentives to take on excessive risk, and it also improves the quality of information in the marketplace so that investors can make informed decisions, thereby improving the ability of financial markets to allocate capital to its most productive uses. The efficiency of markets is assisted by the OSC's disclosure requirements mentioned above, as well as its regulation of brokerage firms, mutual funds, exchanges, and credit-rating agencies to ensure that they produce reliable information and protect investors. Bill 198, introduced by the Ontario government in October 2002 in response to the Sarbanes-Oxley Act in the United States, took disclosure of information even further by increasing the incentives to produce accurate audits of corporate income statements and balance sheets, and put in place regulations to limit conflicts of interest in the financial services industry.

Particularly controversial in the wake of the subprime financial crisis is the move to **mark-to-market accounting** (also called **fair-value accounting**), in which assets are valued on the balance sheet at what they could sell for in the market (see the FYI box, Mark-to-Market Accounting and Financial Stability).

Consumer Protection

The existence of asymmetric information also suggests that consumers may not have enough information to protect themselves fully. Consumer protection regulation has taken several forms. First is "truth in lending," which requires all lenders, not just banks, to provide information to consumers about the cost of borrowing including a standardized interest rate (called the *annual percentage rate, or APR*) and the total finance charges on the loan. Legislation also requires creditors, especially credit card issuers, to provide information on the method of assessing finance charges and requires that billing complaints be handled quickly.

The subprime mortgage crisis in the United States and Canada's short experiment with subprime lending have illustrated the need for greater consumer protection because so many borrowers ended up taking out loans that they could not understand and which were well beyond their means to repay. The result was millions of foreclosures, with many households losing their homes. Because weak consumer protection regulation played a prominent role in this crisis, there have been increasing demands to beef up this regulation, not only in the United States but in other countries as well, as is discussed in the FYI box, The Subprime Mortgage Crisis and Consumer Protection Regulation.

Restrictions on Competition

Increased competition can also increase moral hazard incentives for financial institutions to take on more risk. Declining profitability as a result of increased competition could tip the incentives of financial institutions toward assuming greater risk in an effort to maintain former profit levels. Thus governments in many countries have instituted regulations to protect financial institutions from competition. These regulations have taken different forms in the past, one being preventing nonbank institutions from competing with banks by engaging in banking business.

Although restricting competition propped up the health of banks, restrictions on competition also had serious disadvantages: they led to higher charges to consumers and decreased the efficiency of financial institutions, which did not have to compete as vigorously. Thus, although the existence of asymmetric information provided a rationale for anticompetitive regulations, it did not mean that they would be beneficial. Indeed, in recent years, the impulse of governments in industrialized countries to restrict competition has been waning.

Summary

Asymmetric information analysis explains what types of financial regulations are needed to reduce moral hazard and adverse selection problems in the financial system. However, understanding the theory behind regulation does not mean that regulation and supervision of the financial system are easy in practice. Getting regulators and supervisors to do their job properly is difficult for several reasons. First, financial institutions have strong incentives to avoid existing regulations by exploiting loopholes. Thus, regulation applies to a moving target: Regulators are continually playing cat-and-mouse with financial institutions—financial institutions think up clever ways to avoid regulations, which then lead regulators to modify their regulation activities. Regulators continually face new challenges in a dynamically changing financial system—and unless they can respond rapidly to change, they may not be able to keep financial institutions from taking on excessive risk. This problem can be exacerbated if regulators and supervisors do not have the

FYI   Mark-to-Market Accounting and Financial Stability

The controversy over mark-to-market accounting has made accounting a hot topic. Mark-to-market accounting was made standard practice in the accounting industry in the United States in 1993. U.S. Generally Accepted Accounting Principles (GAAP) established a number of ways for measuring fair value, depending on whether a financial instrument is traded on an active market or in the absence of an active market. Canadian GAAP are similar to U.S. GAAP, as well as to standards in effect in those countries (approximately 110) that have adopted a set of global standards, known as International Financial Reporting Standards (IFRS), developed by the International Accounting Standards Board (IASB).

The rationale behind mark-to-market accounting is that market prices provide a better basis for estimating the true value of assets, and hence capital, in the firm. Before mark-to-market accounting, firms relied on the traditional historical-cost (book value) basis in which the value of an asset is set at its initial purchase price. The problem with historical-cost accounting is that changes in the value of assets and liabilities because of changes in interest rates or default are not reflected in the calculation of the firm's equity capital. Yet changes in the market value of assets and liabilities—and hence changes in the market value of equity capital—are what indicates if a firm is in good shape, or alternatively, if it is getting into trouble and may therefore be more susceptible to moral hazard.

Mark-to-market accounting, however, is subject to a major flaw. At times markets stop working, as occurred during the subprime financial crisis. The price of an asset sold at a time of financial distress does not reflect its fundamental value. That is, the fire-sale liquidation value of an asset can at times be well below the present value of its expected future cash flows. Many people, particularly bankers, criticized mark-to-market accounting during the subprime financial crisis, claiming that it was an important factor driving the crisis. They claim that the seizing up of the markets led to market prices being well below fundamental values. Since mark-to-market accounting requires that the financial firms' assets be marked down in value, this markdown creates a shortfall in capital that leads to a cutback in lending, which causes a further deterioration in asset prices, which in turn causes a further cutback in lending. The resulting adverse feedback loop can then make a financial crisis even worse. Although the criticisms of mark-to-market accounting have some validity, some of the criticism by bankers is self-serving. The criticism was made only when asset values were falling, when mark-to-market accounting was painting a bleaker picture of banks' balance sheets, as opposed to when asset prices were booming and it made banks' balance sheets look very good.

In the aftermath of the subprime meltdown in the United States, the criticisms of mark-to-market accounting led the International Accounting Standards Board to form an advisory panel to enhance its guidance on valuing financial instruments in inactive markets in times of crisis. Moreover, in the United States there was a Congressional focus on fair value accounting which led to a provision in the Emergency Economic Stabilization Act of 2008, discussed in Chapter 9, that required the SEC, in consultation with the Federal Reserve and the U.S. Treasury, to submit a study of mark-to-market accounting applicable to financial institutions. Who knew that accounting could get even politicians worked up!

FYI	The Subprime Mortgage Crisis and Consumer Protection Regulation

Because of the principal–agent problem inherent in the originate-to-distribute model for subprime mortgages discussed in Chapter 9, there were weak incentives for mortgage originators, typically mortgage brokers who were virtually unregulated, to ensure that subprime borrowers had the ability to pay back their loans. After all, mortgage brokers earned large fees from mortgage originators, even if sometime down the road the borrowers defaulted on their loan and lost their homes. With these incentives, mortgage brokers weakened their underwriting standards, leading to subprime mortgage products such as "no-doc loans," more pejoratively referred to as "liar loans," in which borrowers did not have to produce documentation about their assets or income. A particularly infamous variant of no-doc loans was dubbed the NINJA loan, because it was issued to borrowers with No Income, No Job, and No Assets.

Mortgage brokers also had incentives to put households into very complicated mortgage products that borrowers could not understand and which they couldn't afford to pay. In some cases, mortgage brokers even engaged in fraud by falsifying information on a borrower's mortgage application in order to qualify them for mortgage loans.

Lax consumer protection regulation was an important factor in producing the subprime mortgage crisis in the United States. Mortgage originators were not required to disclose information to borrowers that would have helped them better understand complicated mortgage products and whether they could afford to repay them. Outrage over the surge of foreclosures in the United States has been an important stimulus for new regulation to provide better information to mortgage borrowers and to ban unfair and deceptive practices.

resources or expertise to keep up with clever people in financial institutions seeking to circumvent the existing regulations.

Financial regulation and supervision are difficult for two other reasons. In the regulation and supervision game, the devil is in the details. Subtle differences in the details may have unintended consequences; unless regulators get the regulation and supervision just right, they may be unable to prevent excessive risk taking. In addition, regulated firms may lobby politicians to lean on regulators and supervisors to go easy on them. For all these reasons, there is no guarantee that regulators and supervisors will be successful in promoting a healthy financial system. These same problems bedevil financial regulators in other countries, as the Global box, International Financial Regulation, indicates. Indeed, as we will see, financial regulation and supervision have not always worked well, leading to banking crises throughout the world.

Because so many laws regulating the financial system have been passed in Canada, it is hard to keep track of them all. As a study aid, Table 10-1 lists the major financial legislation in the twentieth century and its key provisions.

THE 1980s CANADIAN BANKING CRISIS

The period from 1923 (when the Home Bank failed) to 1985 was one in which the failure of Canadian chartered banks was thought to be impossible. During the same period, failures of deposit-taking financial institutions in the United States were aver-

TABLE 10-1 Major Financial Legislation in Canada

Bank of Canada Act (1934)

Created the Bank of Canada following the recommendations of the Macmillan Commission

Bank Act of 1936

Prohibited banks from issuing banknotes

Imposed reserve requirements on depository institutions to be held with the Bank of Canada

Bank Act of 1954

Increased reserve requirements on depository institutions

Allowed chartered banks to offer mortgages issued under the National Housing Act

Canada Deposit Insurance Corporation Act (1967)

Created the CDIC to insure deposits with all federally chartered banks and near banks

Bank Act of 1967

Removed the 6% loan interest rate ceiling

Restricted foreign competition

Imposed secondary reserve requirements on depository institutions

Put chartered banks and near banks on equal footing regarding mortgage lending

Bank Act of 1981

Created the Canadian Payments Association to operate the national payments system and plan its development

Lowered reserve requirements on Canadian-dollar deposits

Increased competition by introducing a less-complicated procedure for obtaining a licence to operate as a bank

Allowed foreign banks to establish subsidiaries in Canada, subject to reciprocal treatment of Canadian banks

Extended banks' business powers to include financial leasing, factoring, and data processing

Redesigned corporate clauses to ensure consistency between the Bank Act and the Canada Business Corporations Act

Provided a simpler incorporation method for new banks (letters patent) while retaining incorporation through a special Act of Parliament

Office of the Superintendent of Financial Institutions Act (1987)

Created the OSFI to succeed two separate federal regulatory bodies (the Department of Insurance and the Inspector General of Banks) in the supervision of financial institutions

Financial Institutions and Deposit Insurance System Amendment Act (1987)

Allowed chartered banks to own investment banking subsidiaries, thereby initiating the merging of the four pillars

Savings and Credit Union Act of the Province of Québec (1988)

Set rules for credit unions, federations, and confederations, with specific reference to the *Mouvement Desjardins*

Bank Act of 1992

Comprehensive banking law

Allowed chartered banks to own trust companies

Allowed trust companies to make commercial loans

Made provisions for the phasing out of reserve requirements

(Continued)

TABLE 10-1 (Continued)

Set rules regarding the supervisory role of the Bank of Canada and the OSFI with respect to chartered banks

Reset the "sunset" clause from 10 years to 5 years to address the changing Canadian financial services marketplace

Cooperative Credit Associations Act (1992)

Replaced the Cooperative Credit Association Act of 1952–1953 and set rules for federally chartered credit unions

Followed the same format as the Bank Act

Insurance Companies Act (1992)

Replaced the Canadian and British Insurance Companies Act and the Foreign Insurance Companies Act, both passed in 1932

Set rules for life insurance companies and property and casualty (P&C) insurance companies

Allowed insurance companies to own Schedule II chartered banks

Followed the same format as the Bank Act

Trust and Loan Companies Act (1992)

Replaced the Trust Companies Act and the Loan Companies Act, both passed in 1914

Set rules for federally incorporated TMLs and provincially incorporated TMLs reporting to the OSFI

Required large, formerly closely held TMLs to become 35% widely held

Followed the same format as the Bank Act

Bank Act of 1997

Yielded minor changes because the government was waiting for the recommendations of the MacKay Task Force

Bank Act Reform of 2001

Set new ownership rules

Established a process for reviewing mergers involving large banks

Allowed bank financial groups to organize under a holding company structure

Allowed greater flexibility for bank involvement in the information technology area

Allowed non–deposit-taking financial institutions access to the payments and clearance systems

---

aging about 20 a year. In the mid-1980s, however, the situation in Canada changed dramatically with the failure of two chartered banks and the financial difficulties of a large number of other financial institutions. Why did this happen? How did a stable banking system that seemed to be working well find itself in trouble?

Early Stage of the Crisis

The story starts with the oil boom in western Canada in the 1970s. It led to the creation of several western banks, including two Alberta-based Schedule I banks, the Canadian Commercial Bank and the Northland Bank, both formed in 1975. Unfortunately, the managers of these banks did not have the expertise that would have enabled them to manage risk appropriately; they excessively concentrated in a few borrowers in western Canada and placed a large percentage of their total loans in real estate.

The existence of deposit insurance increased moral hazard for the Canadian Commercial and Northland banks, because insured depositors had little incentive

GLOBAL   International Financial Regulation

Because asymmetric information problems in the banking industry are a fact of life throughout the world, financial regulation in other countries is similar to that in Canada. Financial institutions are chartered and supervised by government regulators, just as they are in Canada. Disclosure requirements for financial institutions and corporations issuing securities are similar in other developed countries. Deposit insurance is also a feature of the regulatory systems in most other countries, although its coverage is different than in Canada and is intentionally not advertised. We have also seen that capital requirements are in the process of being standardized across countries with agreements like the Basel Accord. Accounting and financial reporting are also in the process of being standardized across countries by moving to IFRS, a set of global standards developed by the IASB.

Particular problems in financial regulation occur when financial institutions operate in many countries and thus can readily shift their business from one country to another. Financial regulators closely examine the domestic operations of financial institutions in their country, but they often do not have the knowledge or ability to keep a close watch on operations in other countries, either by domestic institutions' foreign affiliates or by foreign institutions with domestic branches. In addition, when a financial institution operates in many countries, it is not always clear which national regulatory authority should have primary responsibility for keeping the institution from engaging in overly risky activities.

The difficulties inherent in international financial regulation were highlighted by the collapse of the Bank of Credit and Commerce International (BCCI). BCCI, which was operating in more than 70 countries including the United States and the United Kingdom, was supervised by Luxembourg, a tiny country unlikely to be up to the task. When massive fraud was discovered, the Bank of England closed BCCI down, but not before depositors and stockholders were exposed to huge losses. Cooperation among regulators in different countries and standardization of regulatory requirements provide potential solutions to the problems of international financial regulation. The world has been moving in this direction through agreements like the Basel Accord and oversight procedures announced by the Basel Committee in July 1992, which require a bank's worldwide operations to be under the scrutiny of a single home-country regulator with enhanced powers to acquire information on the bank's activities. Also, the Basel Committee ruled that regulators in other countries can restrict the operations of a foreign bank if they feel that it lacks effective oversight. Whether agreements of this type will solve the problem of international financial regulation in the future is an open question.

to keep the banks from taking on too much risk. Regardless of how much risk the banks were taking, deposit insurance guaranteed that depositors would not suffer any losses.

Canadian Commercial and Northland pursued rapid growth and took on risky projects, attracting the necessary funds by issuing large denomination certificates of deposit with high interest rates. Without deposit insurance, high interest rates would not have induced depositors to provide the high-rolling banks with funds because of the realistic expectation that they might not get the funds back. But with deposit insurance, the government was guaranteeing that the deposits were safe, so depositors were more than happy to make deposits in the Canadian Commercial and Northland banks with the higher interest rates.

As already noted, the managers of Canadian Commercial and Northland did not have the required expertise to manage risk in the permissive atmosphere of western Canada. Even if the required expertise was available initially, rapid credit growth may have outstripped the available information resources of the banking institution, resulting in excessive risk taking. Also, the lending boom meant that the activities of Canadian Commercial and Northland were expanding in scope and were becoming more complicated, requiring an expansion of regulatory resources to monitor these activities appropriately. Unfortunately, regulators of chartered banks at the Inspector General of Banks (the predecessor of the Office of the Superintendent of Financial Institutions) had neither the expertise nor the resources that would have enabled them to sufficiently monitor the activities of Canadian Commercial and Northland. Given the lack of expertise in both the banks and the Inspector General of Banks, the weakening of the regulatory apparatus, and the moral hazard incentives provided by deposit insurance, it is no surprise that Canadian Commercial and Northland took on excessive risks, which led to huge losses on bad loans.

In addition, the incentives of moral hazard were increased dramatically by a historical accident: the combination of sharp increases in interest rates from late 1979 until 1981 and a severe recession in 1981–1982, both of which were engineered by the Federal Reserve in the United States to bring down inflation. The sharp rise in interest rates produced rapidly rising costs of funds for the banks that were not matched by higher earnings on their principal asset, long-term residential mortgages (whose rates had been fixed at a time when interest rates were far lower). The 1981–1982 recession and a collapse in the prices of energy and farm products hit the economy of Alberta very hard. As a result, there were defaults on many loans. Losses for Canadian Commercial and Northland mounted and the banks had negative net worths and were thus insolvent by the beginning of 1985.

Later Stage of the Crisis: Regulatory Forbearance

At this point, a logical step might have been for the regulators—the Bank of Canada and the Inspector General of Banks—to close the insolvent banks. Instead, the regulators adopted a stance of **regulatory forbearance**: they refrained from exercising their regulatory right to put the insolvent Canadian Commercial Bank and Northland Bank out of business.

There were two main reasons why the Bank of Canada and the Inspector General of Banks opted for regulatory forbearance. First, the CDIC did not have sufficient funds in its insurance fund to close the insolvent banks and pay off their deposits. Second, because bureaucrats do not like to admit that their own agency is in trouble, the regulators preferred to sweep their problems under the rug in the hope that they would go away.

When Canadian Commercial and Northland were declared insolvent in September of 1985, rumours of financial trouble caused many large depositors to withdraw large deposits from the Bank of British Columbia, Mercantile Bank, and Continental Bank. By the time Mercantile was acquired by the National Bank of Canada, Bank of British Columbia by the Hongkong Bank of Canada, and Continental by Lloyds Bank of Canada (a subsidiary of a U.K.-based banking powerhouse), the Bank of Canada had lent over $5 billion.

The loss of public confidence in the Canadian banking system led to the financial reforms of 1987–1992 (see Table 10-1) and the consolidating of financial institution supervision under the Office of the Superintendent of Financial Institutions.

CDIC DEVELOPMENTS

The Canada Deposit Insurance Corporation (CDIC) insures each depositor at member institutions up to a loss of $100 000 per account. All federally incorporated financial institutions and all provincially incorporated trust and mortgage loan companies are members of the CDIC. Insurance companies, credit unions, *caisses populaires*, and investment dealers are not eligible for CDIC membership; the Québec Deposit Insurance Board (QDIB) insures provincially incorporated financial institutions in Québec, and the other provinces have deposit insurance corporations that insure the deposits of credit unions in their jurisdiction, on terms similar to the CDIC's.

The CDIC is allowed to insure only deposits in Canadian currency and payable in Canada; foreign currency deposits, such as accounts in U.S. dollars, are not insured. Moreover, not all deposits and investments offered by CDIC member institutions are insurable. Insurable deposits include savings and chequing accounts, term deposits with a maturity date of less than five years, money orders and drafts, certified drafts and cheques, and traveller's cheques. The CDIC does not insure term deposits with an initial maturity date of more than five years, treasury bills, bonds and debentures issued by governments and corporations (including the chartered banks), and investments in stocks, mutual funds, and mortgages.

The primary rationale for deposit insurance is protecting depositors from bank insolvency and thus ensuring financial stability. Deposit insurance could also promote competition among financial institutions by removing barriers to entry for new deposit-taking institutions. In the absence of deposit insurance it is difficult for new banks to attract deposits. Most depositors, for example, are not capable of making appropriate risk calculations to assess the risk of a new bank. Those depositors would tend to place their deposits in banks that are considered too big to fail, thereby producing significant barriers to entry and unfair disadvantages for small new entrants. By insuring deposits at all deposit-taking financial institutions, the CDIC effectively removes barriers to entry for new deposit takers.

Differential Premiums

Until recently, CDIC premium revenue was not tied to the risk profile of financial institutions; the premium rate was the same for all deposit-taking institutions, irrespective of their risk profile. For example, in the 1998–1999 fiscal year, the flat-rate insurance premium was 1/6 of 1%, or 0.1667%, meaning that each deposit-taking financial institution paid an insurance premium of close to 17 cents per $100. This was one of the reasons that the Big Six, represented by the Canadian Bankers Association, vigorously opposed the establishment of the CDIC in 1967; it was argued that deposit insurance would be a subsidy to small banks paid by the big banks.

Over the years, the Canadian Bankers Association strongly promoted the reform of the Canadian deposit insurance system. As a result, the CDIC developed the Differential Premiums By-law, which came into effect for the premium year beginning May 1, 1999. The bylaw undergoes regular reviews and has been amended a number of times. The important feature of this legislation is its implicit, prompt corrective action provisions, which require the CDIC to intervene earlier and more vigorously when a bank gets into trouble. CDIC member institutions are now classified into four premium groups based on their risk profile. An institution's risk profile is determined using a variety of quantitative and qualitative criteria, including capital adequacy, profitability, asset concentration, income volatility, regulatory ratings, and adherence to CDIC's Standards of Sound Business and Financial Practices, with capital adequacy dominating the criteria, accounting for 20% of the score.

Under the new system the premium rates for CDIC member institutions are those shown in Table 10-2; they vary from 1 cent to 11 cents per $100. Group 1, classified as "best," is well-capitalized banks that significantly exceed minimum requirements. On the other hand, banks in group 4, classified as "worst," are significantly (and perhaps critically) undercapitalized and the insurance premium that they pay is 11 basis points, the maximum allowed under the CDIC Act. In addition, for group 4 banks, the CDIC is required to take prompt corrective actions such as requiring them to submit a capital restoration plan, restrict their asset growth, and seek regulatory approval to open new branches or develop new lines of business. Today, over 90% of CDIC member institutions are classified in categories 1 and 2, but as in other countries, the premium category and related supervisory information applicable to individual CDIC members are confidential.

Opting-Out

Another interesting recent development is the Opting-Out By-law that came into effect on October 15, 1999. This legislation permits Schedule III banks that accept primarily wholesale deposits (defined as $150 000 or more) to opt out of CDIC membership and therefore to operate without deposit insurance. The new legislation, however, includes provisions to protect depositors who hold deposits eligible for CDIC protection. In particular, it requires an opted-out bank to inform all depositors, by posting notices in its branches, that their deposits will not be protected by the CDIC, and not to charge any early withdrawal penalties for depositors who choose to withdraw.

Probably the most important feature of the opting-out legislation is its minimization of CDIC exposure to uninsured deposits. This represents a significant departure from past practices, when the CDIC showed generosity to uninsured depositors. For example, in the Canadian Commercial and Northland failures of the mid-1980s, the CDIC paid 100 cents on the dollar to all depositors, both insured and uninsured. By compensating only the insured depositors rather than all depositors, the opting-out legislation increases the incentives of uninsured depositors to monitor the risk-taking activities of banks, thereby reducing moral hazard risk.

TABLE 10-2 Premium Structure and Rates for CDIC Member Institutions	
Premium Category	**Premium Rate (as a % of Insured Deposits)**
1	1/72 of 1%, or 0.01389%
2	1/36 of 1%, or 0.02778%
3	1/18 of 1%, or 0.05556%
4	1/9 of 1%, or 0.11111%

Source: CDIC website: www.cdic.ca. Reprinted with permission of the Canada Deposit Insurance Corporation.

APPLICATION	**Evaluating CDIC and Other Proposed Reforms of the Banking Regulatory System**

The new system of risk-based premiums and opting-out rules is a major step in reformulating the financial regulatory system. How well will it work to solve the adverse selection and moral hazard problems of the bank regulatory system? Let's use the analysis in the chapter to evaluate the new legislation to answer this question.

Limits on the Scope of Deposit Insurance

CDIC's reductions of the scope of deposit insurance by limiting insurance to insured deposits might have increased the incentives for uninsured depositors to monitor banks and to withdraw funds if the bank is taking on too much risk. Because banks might now fear the loss of deposits when they engage in risky activities, they might have less incentive to take on too much risk.

Although the cited new elements of deposit insurance strengthen the incentive of depositors to monitor banks, some critics would take these limitations on the scope of deposit insurance even further. Some suggest that deposit insurance should be eliminated entirely or should be reduced in amount from the current $100 000 limit to, say, $20 000 or $10 000. Another proposed reform would institute a system of **coinsurance** in which only a percentage of a deposit, say 90%, would be covered by insurance. In this system, the insured depositor would suffer a percentage of the losses along with the deposit insurance agency. Because depositors facing a lower limit on deposit insurance or coinsurance would suffer losses if the bank went broke, they would have an incentive to monitor the bank's activities.

However, other experts do not believe that depositors are capable of monitoring banks and imposing discipline on them. The basic problem with reducing the scope of deposit insurance even further is that banks would be subject to runs, sudden withdrawals by nervous investors. Such runs could by themselves lead to bank failures. In addition to protecting individual depositors, the purpose of deposit insurance is to prevent a large number of bank failures, which would lead to an unstable banking system and an unstable economy. From this perspective, deposit insurance has been a resounding success. Bank panics, in which there are simultaneous failures of many banks and consequent disruption of the financial system, have not occurred since deposit insurance was established.

Eliminating the too-big-to-fail policy altogether would also cause some of the same problems that would occur if deposit insurance were eliminated or reduced: the probability of bank panics would increase. If a bank were allowed to fail, the repercussions in the financial system might be immense. Other banks with a correspondent relationship with the failed bank (those that have deposits at the bank in exchange for services) would suffer large losses and might fail in turn, leading to full-scale panic. In addition, the problem of liquidating the big bank's loan portfolio might create a major disruption in the financial system.

Prompt Corrective Action

The prompt corrective action provisions of CDIC should also substantially reduce incentives for bank risk taking and reduce taxpayer losses. CDIC uses a carrot-and-stick approach to get banks to hold more capital. If they are well capitalized, they receive better ratings and are placed in a better premium rate category (see Table 10-2); if their capital ratio falls, they are subject to more and more onerous regulation. Increased bank capital reduces moral hazard for the bank because the bank now has more to lose if it fails and so is less likely to take on too much risk. In addition, encouraging banks to hold more capital reduces potential losses for the CDIC because increased bank capital is a cushion that makes bank failure less likely.

Prompt corrective action, which requires regulators to intervene early when bank capital begins to fall, is a serious attempt to reduce the principal–agent problem for politicians and regulators. With prompt corrective action provisions, regulators no longer have the option of regulatory forbearance, which, as we have seen, can greatly increase moral hazard incentives for banks.

Risk-Based Insurance Premiums

Under the Differential Premiums By-law, banks deemed to be taking on greater risk, in the form of lower capital or riskier assets, are subjected to higher insurance premiums, as can be seen in Table 10-2. Risk-based insurance premiums consequently reduce the moral hazard incentives for banks to take on higher risk. In addition, the fact that risk-based premiums drop as the bank's capital increases encourages the banks to hold more capital, which has the benefits already mentioned.

One problem with risk-based premiums is that the scheme for determining the amount of risk the bank is taking may not be very accurate. For example, it might be hard for regulators to determine when a bank's loans are risky. Some critics have also pointed out that the classification of banks by such measures as the Basel risk-based capital standard solely reflects credit risk and does not take sufficient account of interest-rate risk. The regulatory authorities, however, are encouraged to modify existing risk-based standards to include interest-rate risk.

Other CDIC Provisions

CDIC's requirements that regulators perform frequent bank examinations and member institutions file a Standards report at least once a year are necessary for monitoring banks' compliance with bank capital requirements and asset restrictions. As the Canadian Commercial and Northland debacles illustrate, frequent supervisory examinations of banks are necessary to keep them from taking on too much risk or committing fraud. Similarly, beefing up the ability of the regulators to monitor foreign banks might help dissuade international banks from engaging in these undesirable activities.

The stricter and more burdensome reporting requirements for banks have the advantage of providing more information to regulators to help them monitor bank activities. However, these reporting requirements have been criticized by banks, which claim that the requirements make it harder to lend to small businesses. As a result, the CDIC developed the Modernized Standards By-law, adopted in early 2001, which enables the CDIC to determine the frequency of a member institution's reporting based on its categorization under the Differential Premiums By-law.

The Modernized Standards By-law allows CDIC discretion in examining the performance of problem member institutions. Under the new regime, well-capitalized, category 1 banks will be required to file a Standards report every five years. However, banks in categories 3 and 4 may be subjected to special examination at any time, the cost of which will be chargeable to the institution. The Modernized Standards By-law, in addition to increasing the regulatory supervision of problem banks, also increases the accountability of the CDIC. Moreover, it decreases the incentives of banks to take on excessive risk and increases their incentives to hold capital.

Other Proposed Changes in Banking Regulations

REGULATORY CONSOLIDATION   The current bank regulatory system in Canada has financial institutions supervised by three federal agencies: the Bank of Canada, the Office of the Superintendent of Financial Institutions, and the CDIC. Critics of this system of multiple regulatory agencies with overlapping jurisdictions believe it creates a system that is too complex and too costly because it is rife with duplication. For example, although the CDIC has no direct supervisory role, its Standards of Sound Business and Financial Practices overlap with those of the OSFI.

The MacKay Task Force, named after its chairman Harold MacKay and set up by the government in 1996 to review the financial services sector and propose a framework for its future, considered whether the CDIC and the OSFI should be amalgamated. Although the task force recommended that the regulator (OSFI) and the insurer (CDIC) should not be combined in a single institution, it proposed that the CDIC's mandate be amended to remove the overlap with the OSFI's mandate.

Overall Evaluation

The recent CDIC developments appear to be an important step in the right direction because they increase the incentives for banks to hold capital and decrease their incentives to take on excessive risk. However, more could be done to improve the incentives for banks to limit their risk taking. Yet eliminating deposit insurance and the too-big-to-fail policy altogether may be going too far because these proposals might make the banking system too prone to a banking panic.

BANKING CRISES THROUGHOUT THE WORLD

Because misery loves company, it may make you feel better to know that Canada has by no means been alone in suffering banking crises. Indeed, as Table 10-3 and Figure 10-1 (page 248) illustrate, banking crises have struck a large number of countries throughout the world, and many of them have been substantially worse than the one we experienced in the 1980s.

"Déjà Vu All Over Again"

In the banking crises in different countries, history keeps repeating itself. The parallels between banking crisis episodes in various countries are remarkably similar, creating a feeling of déjà vu. They all started with financial liberalization or innovation with weak bank regulatory systems and a government safety net. Although financial liberalization is generally a good thing because it promotes competition and can make a financial system more efficient, it can lead to an increase in moral hazard, with more risk-taking on the part of banks if there is lax regulation and supervision; the result can then be banking crises.[1]

However, the banking crisis episodes listed in Table 10-3 do differ in that deposit insurance has not played an important role in many of the countries experiencing banking crises. For example, the size of the Japanese equivalent of the CDIC, the Deposit Insurance Corporation, was so tiny that it did not play a promi-

---

[1] An appendix to this chapter on this book's MyEconLab at **www.pearsoned.ca/myeconlab** discusses many of the episodes of banking crises listed in Table 10-3 in more detail.

TABLE 10-3 The Cost of Rescuing Banks in Several Countries

Date	Country	Cost as a Percentage of GDP
1980–1982	Argentina	55
1997–2002	Indonesia	55
1990s–ongoing	China	47
1996–2000	Jamaica	44
1981–1983	Chile	42
1997–2002	Thailand	35
1993–1994	Macedonia	32
2000–ongoing	Turkey	31
1977–1983	Israel	30
1997–2002	South Korea	28
1988–1991	Cote d'Ivoire	25
1991–ongoing	Japan	24
1994–1995	Venezuela	22
1998–2001	Ecuador	20
1994–2000	Mexico	19
1997–2001	Malaysia	16
1992–1994	Slovenia	15
1998–ongoing	Philippines	13
1994–1999	Brazil	13
1995–2000	Paraguay	13
1989–1991	Czech Republic	12
1997–1998	Taiwan	12
1991–1994	Finland	11
1989–1990	Jordan	10
1991–1995	Hungary	10
1990–1993	Norway	8
1991–1994	Sweden	4
1988–1991	United States	3

Source: Gerard Caprio, Daniela Klingebiel, Luc Laeven and Guillermo Noguera, *Banking Crises Database* (updated October 2003), www.worldbook.org/finance/html/database_sfd.html.

nent role in the banking system and exhausted its resources almost immediately with the first bank failures. This example indicates that deposit insurance is not to blame for some of these banking crises. However, what is common to all the countries discussed here is the existence of a government safety net, in which the government stood ready to bail out banks whether deposit insurance was an important feature of the regulatory environment or not. It is the existence of a government safety net, and not deposit insurance per se, that increases moral hazard incentives for excessive risk taking on the part of banks.

FIGURE 10-1 Banking Crises Throughout the World Since 1970

Source: Gerard Caprio and Daniela Klingebiel, "Episodes of Systemic and Borderline Financial Crises" mimeo, World Bank, October 1999.

WHITHER FINANCIAL REGULATION AFTER THE SUBPRIME FINANCIAL CRISIS?

The recent subprime financial crisis has led to banking crises throughout the world, and it is too soon to tell how large the costs of rescuing the banks will be as a result of this episode (which is why they are not listed in Table 10-3). Given the size of the bailouts and the nationalization of so many financial institutions, the system of financial regulation will surely never be the same. Here we can speculate on where financial regulation might be heading as a result of this crisis.

The financial innovations of subprime and Alt-A mortgages and structured credit products like collateralized debt obligations helped trigger the crisis. Although these innovations have the positive potential for promoting the "democratization of credit," that is, increasing the access of poorer members of society to credit, they went horribly wrong because of the agency problems of the originate-to-distribute business model. Future regulation will surely focus on limiting these agency problems to make the originate-to-distribute model and the financial system overall work better. Eight types of regulation likely to be seen in the future are described below.

Increased Regulation of Mortgage Brokers

Mortgage brokers, who did not have proper incentives to make sure that borrowers could afford to pay back mortgages and were virtually unregulated, are now likely to be subjected to more regulatory scrutiny. Licensing requirements for mortgage originators are likely to be tightened up, and more regulations will require them to disclose mortgage terms more clearly and prevent them from encouraging borrowers to take on more debt than they can afford.

Fewer Subprime Mortgage Products

Some of the complex mortgage products that were offered to subprime borrowers may be banned by regulation. Even with full disclosure of these products' characteristics, they may still be so complicated that subprime borrowers, who are unlikely to be financially sophisticated, cannot understand them and make informed choices. Government ban or regulation of certain mortgage products might help prevent subprime borrowers from "getting in over their heads" again in the future.

Regulation Compensation

Compensation schemes for all the parties in the chain from origination of mortgages to the eventual distribution of mortgage-related securities may be constrained by government regulation. The high fees and executive compensation that have so outraged the public created incentives for the financial industry to push out securities that turned out to be much more risky than advertised and proved to be disastrous.

Higher Capital Requirements

Regulation and supervision of financial institutions to ensure that they have enough capital to cope with the amount of risk they take are likely to be strengthened. Given the risks they were taking, investment banks did not have enough capital relative to their assets and their risky activities. Similarly the capital at AIG was not sufficient to cover the high risk it was taking by issuing credit insurance. Capital requirements will almost surely be beefed up for these institutions. Capital requirements at banks are also likely to be tightened up, particularly for some of their off-balance-sheet activities. Banks' sponsoring of structured investment vehicles (SIVs), which were supposedly off-balance-sheet but came back on the balance sheet once the SIVs got into trouble, indicate that some off-balance-sheet activities should be treated as though they were on the balance sheet.

Additional Regulation of Privately Owned Government-Sponsored Enterprises

New regulations are needed to rein in privately owned government-sponsored enterprises such as Fannie Mae and Freddie Mac in the United States. There are four routes that the U.S. government might take here:

1. Fully privatize them by taking away their government sponsorship, thereby removing the implicit backing for their debt.
2. Completely nationalize them by taking away their private status and make them government agencies.
3. Leave them as privately owned government-sponsored enterprises, but strengthen regulations to restrict the amount of risk they take and to impose higher capital standards.
4. Leave them as privately owned government-sponsored enterprises, but force them to shrink dramatically in size so they no longer expose taxpayers to huge losses or pose a systemic risk to the financial system when they fail.

Heightened Regulation to Limit Financial Institutions' Risk Taking

With the extension of the government safety net to a wider range of financial institutions, regulation will be needed to limit risk taking by financial firms. This will require stricter regulation of investment banks—some of this will automatically occur because the largest ones that have survived are now part of bank holding companies and thus will be regulated and supervised like banks—as well as insurance companies, which, as the AIG example suggests, can threaten the health of the entire financial system when they take on excessive risk.

Increased Regulation of Credit-Rating Agencies

Regulations to restrict conflicts of interest at credit-rating agencies and to give them greater incentives to provide reliable ratings have already been strengthened, but even more is likely to be done. The inaccurate ratings provided by credit-rating agencies helped promote risk taking throughout the financial system and led to investors not having the information they needed to make informed choices about their investments. The reliance on credit ratings in the Basel 2 capital requirements may also have to be rethought, given the poor performance of credit-rating agencies in recent years.

Additional Regulation of Derivatives

More regulations both on disclosure and how derivatives are traded are likely to be put in place, particularly on derivatives such as credit-default swaps. These derivatives ended up being "weapons of mass destruction" that helped lead to a financial meltdown when AIG had to be rescued after making overly extensive use of them. Preventing this from happening again will be a high priority.

The Danger of Overregulation

As a result of the subprime financial crisis, the world of financial regulation will never be the same. Although it is clear that more regulation is needed to prevent such a crisis from ever occurring again, there is a substantial danger that too much or poorly designed regulation could hamper the efficiency of the financial system. If new regulations choke off financial innovation that can benefit both households and businesses, economic growth in the future will suffer.

SUMMARY

1. The concepts of asymmetric information, adverse selection, and moral hazard help explain the nine types of financial regulation that we see in Canada and other countries: the government safety net, restrictions on asset holdings, capital requirements, prompt corrective action, chartering and examination, assessment of risk management, disclosure requirements, consumer protection, and restrictions on competition.

2. Because of financial innovation, deregulation, and a set of historical accidents, adverse selection and moral hazard problems increased in the 1980s and resulted in huge losses for the Canadian banking industry and for taxpayers.

3. The Canadian deposit insurance system has recently been reformed by the introduction of the differential premiums and opting-out by-laws. The former is designed to increase the incentive for banks to hold capital and the latter aims to decrease their incentive to take on excessive risk.

4. The parallels between the banking crisis episodes that have occurred in countries throughout the world are striking, indicating that similar forces are at work.

KEY TERMS

bank failure,   p. 226

Basel Accord,   p. 230

Basel Committee on Bank
  Supervision,   p. 230

coinsurance,   p. 244

fair-value accounting,   p. 235

financial supervision (prudential
  supervision),   p. 231

leverage ratio,   p. 230

mark-to-market accounting,
  p. 235

off-balance-sheet activities,   p. 230

regulatory arbitrage,   p. 231

regulatory forbearance,   p. 241

QUESTIONS

You will find the answers to the questions marked with an asterisk in the Textbook Resources section of your MyEconLab.

1. Give one example each of moral hazard and adverse selection in private insurance arrangements.

*2. If property and casualty insurance companies provided fire insurance without any restrictions, what kind of adverse selection and moral hazard problems might result?

3. What financial regulation is designed to reduce adverse selection problems for deposit insurance? Will it always work?

*4. What financial regulations are designed to reduce moral hazard problems created by deposit insurance? Will they completely eliminate the moral hazard problem?

5. What are the costs and benefits of a too-big-to-fail policy?

*6. Why did Canada's bank crisis not occur until the 1980s?

7. Why is regulatory forbearance a dangerous strategy for a deposit insurance agency?

*8. The Differential Premiums By-law, introduced in 1999, is designed to increase the incentives for Canadian banks to hold more capital. Describe its major features.

9. What steps were taken in recent CDIC legislation to improve the functioning of deposit insurance?

*10. What are the advantages and disadvantages of the CDIC's risk-based insurance premiums?

11. How can the 1980s Canadian banking crisis be blamed on the principal–agent problem?

*12. Do you think that eliminating or limiting the amount of deposit insurance would be a good idea? Explain your answer.

13. Should the overlap between the OSFI and CDIC be eliminated? Why or why not?

*14. How could higher deposit insurance premiums for banks with riskier assets benefit the economy?

15. How could market-value accounting for bank capital requirements benefit the economy? How difficult would it be to implement?

WEB EXERCISES

1. Go to **www.cdic.ca** and click on "International Work." Write an essay summarizing how globalization and international financial integration affect Canada's financial sector safety net.

2. Go to **www.fdic.gov/regulations/laws/important/ index.html.** This site reports on the most significant pieces of legislation affecting U.S. banks since the 1800s. Summarize the most recently enacted bank regulation listed on this site.

Be sure to visit the MyEconLab website at **www.myeconlab.com**. This online homework and tutorial system puts you in control of your own learning with study and practice tools directly correlated to this chapter content.

On the MyEconLab website you will find the following appendix for this chapter:
Appendix 10.1: Banking Crises Throughout the World

CHAPTER 11

Banking Industry: Structure and Competition

LEARNING OBJECTIVES

After studying this chapter you should be able to

1. chronicle the historical development of the Canadian banking industry and its current structure
2. describe the globalization of banking, the international activities of Canadian banks, and the role of foreign banks in Canada
3. differentiate between chartered banks and near banks (i.e., trust and mortgage loan companies, and credit unions and *caisses populaires*)
4. assess why the recent financial sector legislation is expected to lead to larger and increasingly complex financial groups engaging in a full gamut of financial activities

PREVIEW

The operations of individual banks (how they acquire, use, and manage funds to make a profit) are roughly similar throughout the world. In all countries, banks are financial intermediaries in the business of earning profits. When you consider the structure and operation of the banking industry as a whole, however, Canada is in a class by itself, with a comparatively concentrated banking industry and small financial institutions. Unlike the United States, where there are over 7000 commercial banks, over 1200 savings and loan associations, 400 mutual savings banks, and over 8000 credit unions, Canada has six large commercial banks, commonly called chartered banks, that typically dominate the banking industry.[1]

Is fewer better? Does it mean that the Canadian banking system is more stable and competitive and therefore more economically efficient and sound than banking systems in other countries? What in the Canadian economic and political system explains this small number of banking institutions? In this chapter we try to answer these questions by examining the historical trends in the banking industry and its overall structure.

We start by examining the historical development of the banking system and how financial innovation has increased the competitive environment for the banking industry and is causing fundamental changes in it. We then go on to look at

---

[1] Commercial banks in Canada are called chartered banks, because they can be established only by charter granted either in a special act of the federal Parliament or by the Minister of Finance.

the chartered banking industry in detail and then discuss the near-banking industry, which includes trust and mortgage loan companies, and credit unions and *caisses populaires*. We spend more time on chartered banks because they are by far the largest depository institutions, accounting for over two-thirds of the deposits in the banking system. In addition to looking at our domestic banking system, we also examine forces behind the growth in international banking to see how it has affected us in Canada.

HISTORICAL DEVELOPMENT OF THE CANADIAN BANKING SYSTEM

The modern Canadian banking industry began with the creation of the Bank of Montreal in 1817 by nine merchants in Montreal. Initially, the Bank of Montreal was without statutory authority, but a charter was approved by the legislature of Lower Canada and confirmed by royal assent in 1822. Meanwhile, other banks opened for business, and the Canadian banking industry was off and running; the Bank of New Brunswick received royal assent in 1820 and the Chartered Bank of Upper Canada in York (Toronto) in 1821. (As a study aid, Figure 11-1 provides a timeline of the most important dates in the history of Canadian commercial banking before World War II.)

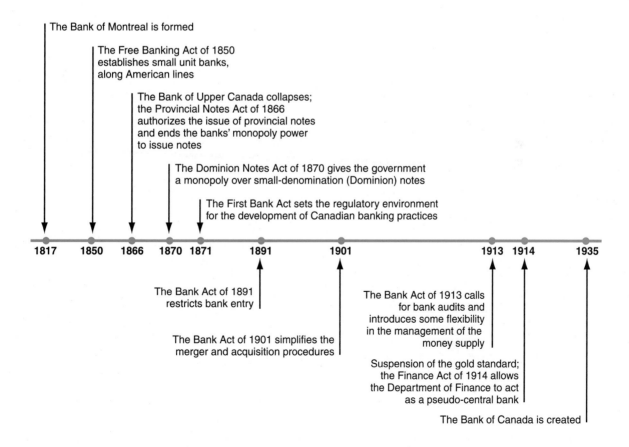

FIGURE 11-1 Timeline of the Early History of Commercial Banking in Canada

All these banks were authorized to issue notes (redeemable in specie, essentially British or American gold or silver coins, on demand), receive deposits, and lend for commercial purposes only; no bank was allowed to lend funds on mortgages, land, or real property. There were, however, some differences between the charters of these banks. For example, the terms of the charter of the Bank of New Brunswick followed the banking tradition of New England. The charter of the Bank of Montreal almost duplicated the terms governing the Bank of the United States (see the FYI box, The Dual Banking System in the United States), which had elements of both a private and a **central bank**, a government institution that has responsibility for the amount of money and credit supplied in the economy as a whole. Also, the Bank of New Brunswick had to submit regular annual statements to the government and was not allowed to open **branches** (additional offices for the conduct of banking operations), whereas the Bank of Montreal had to provide statements only on request and was allowed to open branches in any part of Upper or Lower Canada.

The Free Banking Experiment

Until 1850, no national currency existed in Canada, and banks obtained funds primarily by issuing *banknotes* (currency circulated by the banks that could be redeemed for gold). No banks failed, but because banking regulations were extremely lax banks regularly experienced substantial declines in bank capital due to business failures; their banknotes tended to become scarce. The government tried various schemes to guarantee the provision of stable money, including the issuing of its own notes, but it was significantly influenced by the concept of **free banking**, implemented in New York in 1837. This system, as the name suggests, permitted the organization of a bank by any group that met certain established criteria concerning the amount of equity capital and maintenance of reserves.

FYI   The Dual Banking System in the United States

The banking industry in the United States began when the Bank of North America was chartered in Philadelphia in 1782. A major controversy involving the U.S. banking industry in its early years was whether the federal government or the states should charter banks. The Federalists, particularly Alexander Hamilton, advocated greater centralized control of banking and federal chartering of banks. Their efforts led to the creation in 1791 of the Bank of the United States.

Until 1863, all commercial banks in the United States were chartered by the banking commission of the state in which they operated. No national currency existed, and banks obtained funds primarily by issuing banknotes. Because banking regulations were extremely lax in many states, banks regularly failed due to fraud or lack of sufficient bank capital; their banknotes became worthless.

To eliminate the abuses of the state-chartered banks (called **state banks**), the National Bank Act of 1863 (and subsequent amendments to it) created a new banking system of federally chartered banks (called **national banks**). This legislation was originally intended to dry up sources of funds to state banks by imposing a prohibitive tax on their banknotes while leaving the banknotes of the federally chartered banks untaxed. The state banks cleverly escaped extinction by acquiring funds through deposits. As a result, today the United States has a **dual banking system** in which banks supervised by the federal government and banks supervised by the states operate side by side.

The Free Banking Act was passed in Canada in 1850, with the purpose of facilitating the entry of small unit banks along American lines. It allowed the establishment of a bank, without a legislative charter, by any group that met the lax requirements set out in the free banking legislation. Under this legislation, the minimum amount of net worth to organize a bank was $100 000, branching was not allowed, and although the banknotes of the free banks were untaxed, the amount of note issue was limited to the amount of government debt held by the banks. The move to free banking was a step in the right direction, but Canada's experience with free banking was a failure. It did not lead to the establishment of a large number of new banks; only five new banks were established, two of which soon failed, and the other three converted to legislative charters.

The restriction on branching and the issue of banknotes based on government debt, rather than on commercial loans, were blamed for the failure of Canada's free banking experiment. The most important factor, however, was the fact that the option of a legislative charter was still available, unlike the situation in the United States where the provision of a legislative charter was simultaneously abolished in those states where free banking was established. In Canada, free banking with its restrictive provisions, particularly the restriction on branches and the less-liberal provision for note issue, proved to be less profitable than banking under legislative charters.

In 1850, there were fifteen chartered banks in Canada; eight in Central Canada and seven in what was to become Atlantic Canada. From 1850 until Confederation in 1867, and except for a short period after 1857, the Canadian provinces experienced an economic expansion and thirty new banks were established. However, eleven of these failed or closed their doors for other reasons, leaving thirty-four chartered banks with a total of 127 branches at the end of 1867.

The Provincial Notes Act, 1866

In the years before Confederation, governments were anxious about the chartered banks' control of the note issue. They believed that the best way to protect the public from some of the consequences of bank failures would be to separate the currency of the country from the banking interests. In 1860, Alexander Galt, finance minister of the Province of Canada, proposed the substitution of a government-issued paper currency for banknotes. His proposal, however, was defeated by his critics, especially the chartered banks, for obvious reasons; the substitution of interest-free government debt for interest-free bank debt would have directly reduced their profits.

In the midst of a minor financial crisis in 1866, with the collapse of the Bank of Upper Canada (Canada's first chartered bank failure), the proponents of government-issued paper money finally achieved their objective with the enactment of the Provincial Notes Act. The Act authorized the issue of provincial notes, which because of their legal reserve status could be substituted for specie. With the cooperation of the Bank of Montreal, which had become the government's fiscal agent in 1864 by replacing the Bank of Upper Canada, the banks began to hold the new currency, thereby surrendering their power to issue notes.

The Dominion Notes Act, 1870

Canada was created by the Constitution (formerly the British North America Act) in 1867. The Act granted the new federal government of Canada exclusive jurisdiction over all matters pertaining to currency and banking, and the first problem to be tackled was the issue of paper money. With the failure in 1867 of the Chartered Bank of Canada (the second chartered bank failure in Canadian history), the Dominion Notes Act was passed in 1870. The Act confirmed the rights of banks to issue banknotes on their own credit, but restricted to large-denomination (over

$5) notes, thereby giving the government a monopoly over small-denomination ($1 and $2) notes, the Dominion notes.

Although the Dominion Notes Act of 1870 did not set any reserve requirements, it required banks to hold at least half of their reserves in Dominion notes, thereby giving the government a share of the profits from the issuance of money, which is called **seignorage**. The Dominion notes themselves were fractionally backed by gold, and in this sense the Dominion Notes Act of 1870 confirmed that Canada would operate under the **gold standard**, meaning that its currency was convertible directly into gold.

Canada operated under the gold standard, keeping its currency backed by and convertible into gold, until World War I. During the years 1870–1935, Dominion notes increased in importance, but they never accounted for a major fraction of currency in circulation. They were superseded, together with the banknotes, by Bank of Canada notes, soon after the creation of the Bank of Canada (Canada's central bank) in 1935.

The First Bank Act, 1871

The first Bank Act came into effect in 1871. It was to be revised every 10 years, in light of experience and changing conditions; this "sunset" clause has effectively ensured that governments over the years paid periodic attention to banking reform. The Bank Act set the regulatory environment for Canadian chartered banks and for the future development of Canadian banking practices.

The Act continued the legislative chartering of banks, with each charter running for a ten-year period, then to be reviewed and renewed. New banks had to meet minimum capital requirements: $100 000 paid up before they opened for business against a total of $500 000. The banks' note issue continued to be restricted to large-denomination (over $5) notes and limited to the amount of their paid-up capital plus reserves. There were no reserve requirements, but one-third of a bank's cash reserves were required to be in the form of Dominion notes.

The Act continued the prohibition against mortgage lending and real estate loans, but it reinforced the commercial nature of banking by allowing banks to make loans on the security of most kinds of merchandise. Also, for the greater security of the public, bank shareholders were liable for double the amount of their subscription. Finally, each bank was required to submit a detailed statement to the government on a monthly basis, but there was no provision for government inspection or audit.

The Bank Act, 1881–1913

A depression followed Confederation and lasted from 1873 to 1879. During the depression years, the banks were hard hit and thirteen bank failures (four in 1878, five in 1887, and another four in 1890) wiped out the savings of many noteholders. To prevent future losses from such failures, the early decennial revisions of the Bank Act, in 1881, 1891, 1901, and 1913 (postponed since 1911), were intended to provide better protection for the holders of banknotes, but the Act was not substantially changed.

In particular, in the Bank Act revision of 1891, the capital requirement was increased to $250 000 paid up, thereby restricting entry into the industry. The proportion of Dominion notes in bank cash reserves was increased to 40%, and the notes of a failed bank were made a first charge against its assets in the event of liquidation. Moreover, in the Bank Act revision of 1891, a Bank Circulation Redemption Fund was created, each bank contributing an amount equal to 5% of its average note circulation, to insure noteholders against loss.

In the years between mid-1890 and the outbreak of World War I, the Canadian economy experienced a phenomenal economic expansion. While bank entry was restrained (due to the increase in capital requirements in the Bank Act of 1891), the Bank Act revision of 1901 simplified the merger and acquisition procedures, by requiring only approval of Cabinet; previously a special Act of Parliament was required for all mergers. As a result of these legislative changes, thirteen mergers took place before the end of 1914, relative to only six in the previous thirty-three-year period, and the number of banks declined from forty-one in 1890 to twenty-two in 1914. Over the same period, however, the number of bank branches increased from 426 to over 3000.

Another important legislative change occurred in the 1913 revision of the Bank Act. The Act called for a *bank audit*: annual, independent verification of the financial statements of the banks, with the results distributed to the shareholders and the Minister of Finance. The objective was to limit adverse selection and moral hazard problems that had increased over the years and been found to be the cause of a number of bank failures, particularly the failure of the Farmers Bank in 1910.

An additional noteworthy change was the excess circulation provision that introduced some flexibility in the management of the money supply. The economic expansion in the period after mid-1890 caused banknote issues to reach the ceiling that the Bank Act of 1871 had fixed at the amount of paid-up capital plus reserves. The banks did not increase their capital (and thus their note-issuing capacity), producing a shortage of currency. In order to achieve expansion in the money supply with the growth of economic activity, the Bank Act of 1913 allowed for the issuing of banknotes in excess of a bank's paid-up capital plus reserves.

The Finance Act, 1914

At the end of July 1914, less than a year after the revision of the Bank Act in 1913, World War I looked more and more inescapable. Canada's established banking legislation appeared to be inadequate and the immediate problem was to preserve the stability and liquidity of the financial system. Panic had taken hold, with depositors converting their money into gold for hoarding, and the banks and the government being concerned about their ability to convert money into gold on demand, since their gold reserves were a small fraction of their combined monetary liabilities. In light of these developments, on August 3, 1914, the government suspended the convertibility of Dominion notes and banknotes into gold, thereby ending the gold standard that had emerged over 40 years earlier in 1870. The gold standard was re-established in 1926 and suspended again in 1929, when the Great Depression hit the world.

A major legislative change, following the suspension of the gold standard, was the Finance Act of 1914. Patterned on the episode of 1907, during which banks could obtain cash reserves from the Department of Finance to prevent bank runs (which were triggered by bank failures in the United States), the Finance Act allowed the Department of Finance to act as a **lender of last resort**, that is, to provide Dominion notes to banks (on the pledge of approved securities) when no one else would, thereby preventing bank and financial panics. The Finance Act foreshadowed the increased flexibility in the management of the money supply that was provided by the Bank of Canada in 1935. We will examine in detail the economic forces that led to the creation of the Bank of Canada in Chapter 15.

FINANCIAL INNOVATION AND THE GROWTH OF THE "SHADOW BANKING SYSTEM"

Although banking institutions are still the most important financial institutions in the Canadian economy, in recent years the traditional banking business of making loans that are funded by deposits has been in decline. Some of this business has been replaced by the **shadow banking system**, in which bank lending has been replaced by lending via the securities markets.

To understand how the banking industry has evolved over time, we must first understand the process of financial innovation, which has transformed the entire financial system. Like other industries, the financial industry is in business to earn profits by selling its products. If a soap company perceives that there is a need in the marketplace for a laundry detergent with fabric softener, it develops a product to fit the need. Similarly, to maximize their profits, financial institutions develop new products to satisfy their own needs as well as those of their customers; in other words, innovation—which can be extremely beneficial to the economy—is driven by the desire to get (or stay) rich. This view of the innovation process leads to the following simple analysis: *a change in the financial environment will stimulate a search by financial institutions for innovations that are likely to be profitable.*

Starting in the 1960s, individuals and financial institutions operating in financial markets were confronted with drastic changes in the economic environment: inflation and interest rates climbed sharply and became harder to predict, a situation that changed demand conditions in financial markets. The rapid advance in computer technology changed supply conditions. In addition, financial regulations became more burdensome. Financial institutions found that many of the old ways of doing business were no longer profitable; the financial services and products they had been offering to the public were not selling. Many financial intermediaries found that they were no longer able to acquire funds with their traditional financial instruments, and without these funds they would soon be out of business. To survive in the new economic environment, financial institutions had to research and develop new products and services that would meet customer needs and prove profitable, a process referred to as financial engineering. In their case, necessity was the mother of innovation.

Our discussion of why financial innovation occurs suggests that there are three basic types of financial innovation: responses to changes in demand conditions, responses to changes in supply conditions, and avoidance of regulations. These three motivations often interact in producing particular financial innovations. Now that we have a framework for understanding why financial institutions produce innovations, let's look at examples of how financial institutions in their search for profits have produced financial innovations of the three basic types.

Responses to Changes in Demand Conditions: Interest Rate Volatility

The most significant change in the economic environment that altered the demand for financial products in recent years has been the dramatic increase in the volatility of interest rates. In the 1950s, the interest rate on three-month treasury bills fluctuated between 1.0% and 5.5%; in the 1970s, it fluctuated between 3% and 14%; in the 1980s, it ranged from 7% to over 20%. Large fluctuations in interest rates lead to substantial capital gains or losses and greater uncertainty about returns on investments. Recall that the risk that is related to the uncertainty about interest-rate movements and returns is called *interest-rate risk,* and high volatility of interest rates, such as we saw in the 1970s and 1980s, leads to a higher level of interest-rate risk.

We would expect the increase in interest-rate risk to increase the demand for financial products and services that could reduce that risk. This change in the economic environment would thus stimulate a search for profitable innovations by financial institutions that meet this new demand and would spur the creation of new financial instruments that help lower interest-rate risk. Two examples of financial innovations that appeared in the 1970s confirm this prediction: the development of adjustable-rate mortgages and financial derivatives.

ADJUSTABLE-RATE MORTGAGES Like other investors, financial institutions find that lending is more attractive if interest-rate risk is lower. They would not want to make a mortgage loan at a 10% interest rate and two months later find that they could obtain 12% in interest on the same mortgage. To reduce interest-rate risk, financial institutions began to issue adjustable-rate mortgages, that is, mortgage loans on which the interest rate changes when a market interest rate (usually the treasury bill rate) changes. Initially, an adjustable-rate mortgage might have a 5% interest rate. In six months, this interest rate might increase or decrease by the amount of the increase or decrease in, say, the six-month treasury bill rate, and the mortgage payment would change. Because adjustable-rate mortgages allow mortgage-issuing institutions to earn higher interest rates on mortgages when rates rise, profits are kept higher during these periods. This was the case in the early 1980s when the three-month T-bill rate exceeded 20%.

This attractive feature of adjustable-rate mortgages has encouraged mortgage-issuing institutions to issue adjustable-rate mortgages with lower initial interest rates than on conventional fixed-rate mortgages, making them popular with many households. However, because the mortgage payment on an adjustable-rate mortgage can increase, many households continue to prefer fixed-rate mortgages. Hence, both types of mortgages are widespread.

FINANCIAL DERIVATIVES Given the greater demand for the reduction of interest-rate risk, commodity exchanges such as the Chicago Board of Trade recognized that if they could develop a product that would help investors and financial institutions to protect themselves from, or to **hedge**, interest-rate risk, then they could make profits by selling this new instrument. **Futures contracts**, in which the seller agrees to provide a certain standardized commodity to the buyer on a specific future date at an agreed-on price, had been around for a long time. Officials at the Chicago Board of Trade realized that if they created futures contracts in financial instruments, which are called **financial derivatives** because their payoffs are linked to (i.e., derived from) previously issued securities, they could be used to hedge risk. Thus in 1975, financial derivatives were born. We will study financial derivatives in Chapter 14.

Responses to Changes in Supply Conditions: Information Technology

The most important source of the changes in supply conditions that stimulate financial innovation has been the improvement in computer and telecommunications technology. This technology, called *information technology*, has had two effects. First, it has lowered the cost of processing financial transactions, making it profitable for financial institutions to create new financial products and services for the public. Second, it has made it easier for investors to acquire information, thereby making it easier for firms to issue securities. The rapid developments in information technology have resulted in many new financial products and services that we examine here.

BANK CREDIT AND DEBIT CARDS   Credit cards have been around since well before World War II. Many individual stores (Sears, Eaton's, the Bay) institutionalized charge accounts by providing customers with credit cards that allowed them to make purchases at these stores without cash. Nationwide credit cards were not established until after World War II, when Diners Club developed one to be used in restaurants. Similar credit card programs were started by American Express and Carte Blanche, but because of the high cost of operating these programs, cards were issued only to selected persons and businesses that could afford expensive purchases.

A firm issuing credit cards earns income from loans it makes to credit card holders and from payments made by stores on credit card purchases (a percentage of the purchase price, say 5%). A credit card program's costs arise from loan defaults, stolen cards, and the expense involved in processing credit card transactions.

Seeing the success of Diners Club, American Express, and Carte Blanche, bankers wanted to share in the profitable credit card business. Several chartered banks attempted to expand the credit card business to a wider market in the 1950s, but the cost per transaction of running these programs was so high that their early attempts failed.

In the late 1960s, improved computer technology, which lowered the transaction costs for providing credit card services, made it more likely that bank credit card programs would be profitable. The banks tried to enter this business again, and this time their efforts led to the creation of two successful bank credit card programs: Visa and MasterCard. These programs have become phenomenally successful; more than 200 million of their cards are in use. Indeed, bank credit cards have been so profitable that nonfinancial institutions such as Sears (which launched the Discover card), General Motors, and Walmart have also entered the credit card business. Consumers have benefited because credit cards are more widely accepted than cheques to pay for purchases (particularly abroad), and they allow consumers to take out loans more easily.

The success of bank credit cards led these institutions to come up with a new financial innovation, *debit cards*. Debit cards often look just like credit cards and can be used to make purchases in an identical fashion. However, in contrast to credit cards, which extend the purchaser a loan that does not have to be paid off immediately, a debit card purchase is immediately deducted from the cardholder's bank account. Debit cards depend even more on low costs of processing transactions, since their profits are generated entirely from the fees paid by merchants on debit card purchases at their stores. Debit cards have grown increasingly popular in recent years.

ELECTRONIC BANKING   The wonders of modern computer technology have also enabled banks to lower the cost of bank transactions by having customers interact with electronic banking (e-banking) facilities rather than with human beings. One important form of an e-banking facility is the **automated teller machine (ATM)**, an electronic machine that allows customers to get cash, make deposits, transfer funds from one account to another, and check balances. The ATM has the advantage that it does not have to be paid overtime and never sleeps, thus being available for use 24 hours a day. Not only does this result in cheaper transactions for the bank, but it also provides more convenience for customers. Because of their low cost, ATMs can be put at locations other than a bank or its branches, further increasing customer convenience. The low cost of ATMs has meant that they have sprung up everywhere. Furthermore, it is now as easy to get foreign currency from an ATM when you are travelling in Europe as it is to get cash from your local bank.

With the drop in the cost of telecommunications, banks developed another financial innovation, *home banking*. It is now cost-effective for banks to set up an electronic banking facility in which the bank's customer is linked up with the bank's computer to carry out transactions by using either a telephone or a personal computer. Now a bank's customers can conduct many of their bank transactions without ever leaving the comfort of home. The advantage for customers is the convenience of home banking, while banks find that the cost of transactions is substantially less than having customers come to the bank.

With the decline in the price of personal computers and their increasing presence in the home, we have seen a further innovation in the home banking area, the appearance of the **virtual bank**, a bank that has no physical location but rather exists only in cyberspace. In 1995, Security First Network Bank, based in Atlanta but now owned by Royal Bank of Canada, became the first virtual bank, offering an array of banking services on the Internet—accepting chequing account and savings deposits, selling certificates of deposit, issuing ATM cards, providing bill-paying facilities, and so on. The virtual bank thus takes home banking one step further, enabling customers to have a full set of banking services at home 24 hours a day. In 1996, Bank of America and Wells Fargo entered the virtual banking market, to be followed by many others, with Bank of America now being the largest Internet bank in the United States. Will virtual banking be the predominant form of banking in the future? (See the Global box, Will "Clicks" Dominate "Bricks" in the Banking Industry?)

JUNK BONDS Before the advent of computers and advanced telecommunications, it was difficult to acquire information about the financial situation of firms that might want to sell securities. Because of the difficulty in screening out bad from good credit risks, the only firms that were able to sell bonds were very well-established corporations that had high credit ratings.[2] Before the 1980s, then, only corporations that could issue bonds with ratings of BBB or above could raise funds by selling newly issued bonds. Some firms that had fallen on bad times, so-called *fallen angels,* had previously issued long-term corporate bonds that now had ratings that had fallen below BBB, bonds that were pejoratively dubbed "junk bonds."

With the improvement in information technology in the 1970s, it became easier for investors to acquire financial information about corporations, making it easier to screen out bad from good credit risks. With easier screening, investors were more willing to buy long-term debt securities from less well-known corporations with lower credit ratings. With this change in supply conditions, we would expect that some smart individual would pioneer the concept of selling new public issues of junk bonds, not for fallen angels but for companies that had not yet achieved investment-grade status. This is exactly what Michael Milken of Drexel Burnham Lambert, an investment-banking firm, started to do in 1977. Junk bonds became an important factor in the corporate bond market. Although there was a sharp slowdown in activity in the junk bond market after Milken was indicted for securities law violations in 1989, it heated up again in the 1990s and 2000.

---

[2] The discussion of adverse selection problems in Chapter 8 provides a more detailed analysis of why only well-established firms with high credit ratings were able to sell securities.

GLOBAL   Will "Clicks" Dominate "Bricks" in the Banking Industry?

With the advent of virtual banks ("clicks") and the convenience they provide, a key question is whether they will become the primary form in which banks do their business, eliminating the need for physical bank branches ("bricks") as the main delivery mechanism for banking services. Indeed, will stand-alone Internet banks be the wave of the future?

The answer seems to be no. Internet-only banks such as Wingspan (owned by Bank One), First-e (Dublin-based), and Egg (a British Internet-only bank owned by Prudential) have had disappointing revenue growth and profits. The result is that pure online banking has not been the success that proponents had hoped for. Why has Internet banking been a disappointment?

There are several strikes against Internet banking. First, bank depositors want to know that their savings are secure, so are reluctant to put their money into new institutions without a long track record. Second, customers worry about the security of their online trans-actions and whether their transactions will truly be kept private. Traditional banks are viewed as being more secure and trustworthy in terms of releasing private information. Third, customers may prefer services provided by physical branches. For example, banking customers seem to prefer to purchase long-term savings products face-to-face. Fourth, Internet banking still has run into technical problems—server crashes, slow connections, mistakes in conducting transactions—that will probably diminish over time as technology improves.

The wave of the future thus does not appear to be pure Internet banks. Instead it looks like "clicks and bricks" will be the predominant form of banking, in which online banking is used to complement the services provided by traditional banks. Nonetheless, the delivery of banking services is undergoing massive changes, with more and more banking services delivered over the Internet and the number of physical bank branches likely to decline in the future.

COMMERCIAL PAPER MARKET   Recall that *commercial paper* is a short-term debt security issued by large banks and corporations. The commercial paper market has undergone tremendous growth since 1970, with commercial paper being one of the fastest-growing money market instruments.

Improvements in information technology also help provide an explanation for the rapid rise of the commercial paper market. We have seen that the improvement in information technology made it easier for investors to screen out bad from good credit risks, thus making it easier for corporations to issue debt securities. Not only did this make it easier for corporations to issue long-term debt securities as in the junk bond market, but it also meant that they could raise funds by issuing short-term debt securities like commercial paper more easily. Many corporations that used to do their short-term borrowing from banks now frequently raise short-term funds in the commercial paper market instead.

The development of money market mutual funds has been another factor in the rapid growth in the commercial paper market. Because money market mutual funds need to hold liquid, high-quality, short-term assets such as commercial paper, the growth of assets in these funds has created a ready market in commercial paper. The growth of pension and other large funds that invest in commercial paper has also stimulated the growth of this market.

SECURITIZATION   An important example of a financial innovation arising from improvements in both transaction and information technology is securitization, one of the most important financial innovations in the past two decades, which played an especially prominent role in the development of the subprime mortgage market in the mid 2000s. Securitization is the process of transforming otherwise illiquid financial assets (such as residential mortgages), which have typically been the bread and butter of banking institutions, into marketable capital market securities. As we have seen, improvements in the ability to acquire information have made it easier to sell marketable capital market securities. In addition, with low transaction costs because of improvements in computer technology, financial institutions find that they can cheaply bundle together a portfolio of loans (such as mortgages) with varying small denominations (often less than $100 000), collect the interest and principal payments on the mortgages in the bundle, and then "pass them through" (pay them out) to third parties. By dividing the portfolio of loans into standardized amounts, the financial institution can then sell the claims to these interest and principal payments to third parties as securities. The standardized amounts of these securitized loans make them liquid securities, and the fact that they are made up of a bundle of loans helps diversify risk, making them desirable. The financial institution selling the securitized loans makes a profit by servicing the loans (collecting the interest and principal payments and paying them out) and charging a fee to the third party for this service.

Avoidance of Existing Regulations

The process of financial innovation we have discussed so far is much like innovation in other areas of the economy: it occurs in response to changes in demand and supply conditions. However, because the financial industry is more heavily regulated than other industries, government regulation is a much greater spur to innovation in this industry. Government regulation leads to financial innovation by creating incentives for firms to skirt regulations that restrict their ability to earn profits. Edward Kane, an economist at Boston College, describes this process of avoiding regulations as "loophole mining." The economic analysis of innovation suggests that when the economic environment changes such that regulatory constraints are so burdensome that large profits can be made by avoiding them, loophole mining and innovation are more likely to occur.

Because banking is one of the most heavily regulated industries, loophole mining is especially likely to occur. The rise in inflation and interest rates from the late 1960s to 1980 made the regulatory constraints imposed on this industry even more burdensome, leading to financial innovation.

Two sets of regulations have seriously restricted the ability of U.S. banks to make profits: reserve requirements that force banks to keep a certain fraction of their deposits as reserves (deposits in the Federal Reserve System) and restrictions on the interest rates that can be paid on deposits. For the following reasons, these regulations have been major forces behind financial innovation.

1. *Reserve requirements.* The key to understanding why reserve requirements led to financial innovation is to recognize that they acted, in effect, as a tax on deposits. Because up until 2008 the Fed did not pay interest on reserves, the opportunity cost of holding them was the interest that a bank could otherwise have earned by lending the reserves out. For each dollar of deposits, reserve requirements therefore imposed a cost on the bank equal to the interest rate, i, that could have been earned if the reserves were lent out, times the fraction of deposits required as reserves, r. The cost of $i \times r$ imposed on the bank was just like a tax on bank deposits of $i \times r$ per dollar of deposits.

As you will learn in Chapter 17, the current Canadian situation is that banks earn interest on positive settlement balances with the Bank of Canada. The interest rate is typically the bank rate less 50 basis points. There is still an opportunity cost for Canadian banks, but not of the same order of magnitude as when the central bank does not pay any interest on bank reserves.

It is a great tradition to avoid taxes if possible, and banks also play this game. Just as taxpayers look for loopholes to lower their tax bills, banks seek to increase their profits by mining loopholes and by producing financial innovations that allow them to escape the tax on deposits imposed by reserve requirements.

2. *Restrictions on interest paid on deposits.* Although Canadian banks have never been subject to deposit rate ceilings, for decades after 1933, U.S. banks were prohibited from paying interest on chequing accounts. In addition, until 1986, the U.S. Federal Reserve System had the power under **Regulation Q** to set maximum interest rates that banks could pay on time deposits. To this day, banks are not allowed to pay interest on corporate chequing accounts. The desire to avoid these **deposit rate ceilings** also led to financial innovations.

If market interest rates rose above the maximum rates that banks paid on time deposits under Regulation Q, depositors withdrew funds from banks to put them into higher-yielding securities. This loss of deposits from the banking system restricted the amount of funds that banks could lend (called **disintermediation**) and thus limited bank profits. Banks had an incentive to get around deposit rate ceilings because by so doing, they could acquire more funds to make loans and earn higher profits.

We can now look at how the desire to avoid restrictions on interest payments and the tax effect of reserve requirements led to two important financial innovations.

MONEY MARKET MUTUAL FUNDS   Money market mutual funds issue shares that are redeemable at a fixed price (usually $1). For example, if you buy 5000 shares for $5000, the money market fund uses these funds to invest in short-term money market securities (treasury bills, certificates of deposit, commercial paper) that provide you with interest payments. Although money market fund shares effectively function as deposits that earn interest, they are not legally deposits and so are not insured by the CDIC.

In the U.S., money market mutual funds also offer chequing privileges, effectively functioning as chequing account deposits. For this reason, money market mutual funds in that country have experienced extraordinary growth since 1971, when they first appeared. Currently, their assets are around US$3 trillion. As consumers shift to mutual funds, deposit-taking financial institutions (throughout the world) risk losing a low-cost source of funds.

The first money market mutual fund was created by two Wall Street mavericks, Bruce Bent and Henry Brown, in 1970. In a supreme irony, risky investments by a money market mutual fund founded by Bruce Brent almost brought down the money market mutual fund industry in the United States during the subprime financial crisis in 2008 (see the FYI box, Bruce Bent and the Money Market Mutual Fund Panic of 2008).

SWEEP ACCOUNTS   Another innovation that enables banks to pay interest on corporate chequing accounts is the **sweep account**. In this type of arrangement, any balances above a certain amount in a chequing account at the end of a business day are "swept out" of the account and invested in overnight securities that

FYI | Bruce Bent and the Money Market Mutual Fund Panic of 2008

Bruce Bent, one of the originators of money market mutual funds, almost brought down the industry during the subprime financial crisis in the fall of 2008. Mr. Bent told his shareholders in a letter written in July 2008 that the fund was managed on a basis of "unwavering discipline focused on protecting your principal." He also wrote the U.S. Securities and Exchange Commission in September 2007, "When I first created the money market fund back in 1970, it was designed with the tenets of safety and liquidity." He added that these principles had "fallen to the wayside as portfolio managers chased the highest yield and compromised the integrity of the money fund." Alas, he did not follow his own advice, and his fund, the Reserve Primary Fund, bought risky assets so that its yield was higher than the industry average.

When Lehman Brothers went into bankruptcy on September 15, 2008, the Reserve Primary Fund, with assets of over $60 billion, was caught holding the bag on $785 million of Lehman's debt, which then had to be marked down to zero. The resulting losses meant that on September 16, Bent's fund could no longer afford to redeem its shares at the par value of $1, a situation known as "breaking the buck." Bent's shareholders began to pull their money out of the fund, causing it to lose 90% of its assets.

The fear that this could happen to other money market mutual funds led to a classic panic in which shareholders began to withdraw their funds at an alarming rate. The whole money market mutual fund industry looked like it could come crashing down. To prevent this, the Federal Reserve and the U.S. Treasury rode to the rescue on September 19, 2008. The Fed set up a facility to make loans to purchase commercial paper from money market mutual funds so they could meet the demands for redemptions from their investors. The U.S. Treasury then put in a temporary guarantee for all money market mutual fund redemptions and the panic subsided.

Not surprisingly, given the extension of a government safety net to the money market mutual fund industry, there are calls to regulate this industry more heavily. The money market mutual fund industry will never be the same.

pay interest. Moreover, in banking systems with reserve requirements because the "swept out" funds are no longer classified as chequable deposits, they are not subject to reserve requirements and thus are not "taxed." Sweep accounts have become so popular in recent years that reserve requirements are not even binding for most banking institutions.

The financial innovations of sweep accounts and money market mutual funds are particularly interesting because they were stimulated not only by the desire to avoid a costly regulation, but also by a change in supply conditions—in this case information technology. Without low-cost computers to process inexpensively the additional transactions required by these innovations, they would not have been profitable and therefore would not have been developed. Technological factors often combine with other incentives, such as the desire to get around a regulation, to produce innovation.

Financial Innovation and the Decline of Traditional Banking

The traditional financial intermediation role of banking has been to make long-term loans and fund them by issuing short-term deposits, a process of asset transformation commonly referred to as "borrowing short and lending long." Here we examine how financial innovations have created a more competitive environment for the banking industry, causing the industry to change dramatically, with its traditional banking business going into decline.

In recent years, the traditional financial intermediation role of banking, whereby banks make loans that are funded with deposits, is no longer as important in our financial system. However, the decline in the market share of banks in total lending and total financial intermediary assets does not necessarily indicate that the banking industry is in decline. There is no evidence of a declining trend in bank profitability. However, overall bank profitability is not a good indicator of the profitability of traditional banking, because it includes an increasing amount of income from nontraditional off-balance-sheet activities, discussed in Chapter 13. Noninterest income derived from off-balance-sheet activities, as a share of total banking income, increased from around 7% in 1980 to around 30% of total bank income today. Given that the overall profitability of banks has not risen, the increase in income from off-balance-sheet activities implies that the profitability of traditional banking business has declined. This decline in profitability then explains why banks have been reducing their traditional business.

To understand why traditional banking business has declined in size, we need to look at how the financial innovations described earlier have caused banks to suffer declines in their cost advantages in acquiring funds—that is, on the liabilities side of their balance sheet—while at the same time they have lost income advantages on the assets side of their balance sheet. The simultaneous decline of cost and income advantages has resulted in reduced profitability of traditional banking and an effort by banks to leave this business and engage in new and more profitable activities.

DECLINE IN COST ADVANTAGES IN ACQUIRING FUNDS (LIABILITIES) Until 1980, banks were paying low interest rates on chequable deposits. This worked to the banks' advantage because their major source of funds was chequable deposits. Unfortunately, this cost advantage for banks did not last. The rise in inflation from the late 1960s on led to higher interest rates, which made investors more sensitive to yield differentials on different assets. The result was the *disintermediation* process, in which people began to take their money out of banks, with their low interest rates on both chequable and time deposits, and began to seek out higher-yielding investments. Also, as we have seen, at the same time, financial innovation led to money market mutual funds, which put the banks at an even further disadvantage because depositors could now obtain deposit-like services while earning high interest on their money market mutual fund accounts. One manifestation of these changes in the financial system was that the low-cost source of funds declined dramatically in importance for banks.

DECLINE IN INCOME ADVANTAGES ON USES OF FUNDS (ASSETS) The loss of cost advantages on the liabilities side of the balance sheet for Canadian banks is one reason that they have become less competitive, but they have also been hit by a decline in income advantages on the assets side from the financial innovations we discussed earlier—junk bonds, securitization, and the rise of the commercial paper market. The resulting loss of income advantages for banks relative to these innovations has resulted in a loss of market share and has led to the growth of the shadow banking system, which has made use of these innovations to enable borrowers to bypass the traditional banking system.

We have seen that improvements in information technology have made it easier for firms to issue securities directly to the public. This has meant that instead of going to banks to finance short-term credit needs, many of the banks' best business customers now find it cheaper to go instead to the commercial paper market for funds.

Also, the emergence of the junk bond market has eaten into banks' loan business. Improvements in information technology have made it easier for corporations to sell their bonds to the public directly, thereby bypassing banks. Although well-established companies started taking this route in the 1970s, now lower-quality corporate borrowers are using banks less often because they have access to the junk bond market.

We have also seen that improvements in computer technology have led to securitization, whereby illiquid financial assets such as bank loans and mortgages are transformed into marketable securities. Computers enable other financial institutions to originate loans because they can now accurately evaluate credit risk with statistical methods, while computers have lowered transaction costs, making it possible to bundle these loans and sell them as securities. When default risk can be easily evaluated with computers, banks no longer have an advantage in making loans. Without their former advantages, banks have lost loan business to other financial institutions even though the banks themselves are involved in the process of securitization.

BANKS' RESPONSES   Canadian banks have sought to maintain former profit levels by pursuing new off-balance-sheet activities that are more profitable. They have, in effect, embraced the shadow banking system. This strategy, however, has generated concerns about what are proper activities for banks. Nontraditional bank activities can be riskier, and therefore result in excessive risk-taking by banks. Indeed, they led to a substantial weakening of bank balance sheets during the subprime financial crisis, as was discussed in Chapter 9.

The decline of banks' traditional business has thus meant that the banking industry has been driven to seek out new lines of business. This could be beneficial because by so doing, banks can keep vibrant and healthy. Indeed, bank profitability was high up until 2007, and nontraditional, off-balance-sheet activities played an important role in the high bank profits. However, the new directions in banking have led to increased risk taking, and thus the decline in traditional banking has required regulators to be more vigilant. It also poses new challenges for bank regulators, who as we saw in Chapter 10 must now be far more concerned about banks' off-balance sheet activities.

DECLINE OF TRADITIONAL BANKING IN OTHER INDUSTRIALIZED COUNTRIES   Forces similar to those in Canada and the United States have been leading to the decline of traditional banking in other industrialized countries. The loss of banks' monopoly power over depositors has occurred outside Canada and the United States as well. Financial innovation and deregulation are occurring worldwide and have created attractive alternatives for both depositors and borrowers. In Japan, deregulation opened a wide array of new financial instruments to the public, causing a disintermediation process similar to that in Canada and the United States. In European countries, innovations have steadily eroded the barriers that have traditionally protected banks from competition.

In other countries, banks also face increased competition from the expansion of securities markets and the growth of the shadow banking system. Both financial deregulation and fundamental economic forces in other countries have improved the availability of information in securities markets, making it easier and less costly for firms to finance their activities by issuing securities rather than going to banks. Further, even in countries where securities markets have not grown, banks have still lost loan business because their best corporate customers have had increasing access to foreign and offshore capital markets, such as the Eurobond market. In smaller economies, like Australia, which still do not have well-developed corporate bond or commercial paper markets, banks have lost loan business to international securities markets.

In addition, the same forces that drove the securitization process in Canada and the U.S. have been at work in other countries and have undercut the profitability of traditional banking in these countries as well. Canada and the U.S. have not been unique in seeing their banks face a more difficult competitive environment. Thus, although the decline of traditional banking occurred earlier in North America than elsewhere, the same forces have caused a decline in traditional banking in other countries.

STRUCTURE OF THE CANADIAN CHARTERED BANKING INDUSTRY

As of January 2009, there were seventy-three banks in Canada with over 8000 branches and over 257 000 employees. As Table 11-1 indicates, however, the six largest chartered banks, the Royal Bank of Canada, Canadian Imperial Bank of Commerce (CIBC), Bank of Montreal, Scotiabank, TD Canada Trust, and the National Bank of Canada, together hold over 90% of the assets in the industry.

Schedule I, Schedule II, and Schedule III Banks

The Big Six, together with the Laurentian Bank of Canada, the Canadian Western Bank, and another twelve domestic banks, are Canada's **Schedule I** banks. The remaining fifty-three banks are **Schedule II** banks (foreign bank subsidiaries, controlled by eligible foreign institutions) and **Schedule III** banks (foreign bank branches of foreign institutions).

Until 1981, foreign banks were not allowed to operate in Canada and there was no distinction between Schedule I and Schedule II banks. The 1981 revisions to the Bank Act focused on introducing more competition into the Canadian financial services industry. Domestic Canadian banks became Schedule I banks and subsidiaries of foreign banks became Schedule II banks.

Schedule I and Schedule II banks have identical powers; the only difference between them is the ownership structure permitted. In particular, according to current ownership policy, all Schedule I banks must be widely held: no individual can own more than 10% of any class of shares. Schedule II banks, however, are exceptions to this rule, if small. In fact, there are three categories of exception. The first exception is that widely held foreign banks can own 100% of a Canadian bank subsidiary. The second exception is that a Schedule II bank may have a significant shareholder (more than 10%) for up to ten years after chartering, as a transition measure to becoming a Schedule I bank. The third exception, introduced in the 1992 revision of the Bank Act, is that any widely held and regulated Canadian financial institution, other than a bank, may own 100% of a bank. In the case of large Schedule II banks (those with over $5 billion in equity capital), the same widely held ownership rule that applies to Schedule I banks applies.

With the 2001 Bank Act Reform (to be discussed in detail later in this chapter), a foreign bank may enter the Canadian banking industry as either a Schedule II or

TABLE 11-1 Canadian Banks (as of March 31, 2009)

Bank	Date of Establishment	Assets ($ millions)	Percent (%) of Bank Assets
The Big Six			
RBC Financial Group	1869	725 704	23.12
Canadian Imperial Bank of Commerce	1961	357 714	11.40
BMO Financial Group	1822	472 813	15.07
Scotiabank	1832	522 921	16.66
TD Bank Financial Group	1955	603 913	19.24
National Bank of Canada	1980	143 815	4.58
Big Six Subtotal		2 826 880	90.07
Laurentian Bank of Canada	1987	20 488	0.65
Canadian Western Bank	1988	11 460	0.37
Eight Domestic Banks Subtotal		2 858 828	91.09
Other Banks			
Domestic Banks		166 048	5.29
Foreign Banks		113 561	3.62
Total		3 138 437	100.00

Source: OSFI website www.osfi-bsif.gc.ca. Reprinted with permission.

a Schedule III bank. The difference between Schedule II and Schedule III banks is that a Schedule II bank is a Canadian subsidiary of a foreign bank whereas a Schedule III bank is a foreign bank allowed to branch directly into Canada, under certain restrictions (to be discussed later in the chapter).

Competition and Technology

Although Canada has a small number of banks relative to other countries, Canadians enjoy one of the most dynamic and competitive financial services industries. Besides chartered banks, there are over 4000 financial institutions providing financial services. These include trust and mortgage loan companies, credit unions and *caisses populaires*, government savings institutions, insurance companies, pension funds, mutual funds, and investment dealers.

New technology and the Internet have also helped in the development of a more competitive and innovative banking system in Canada. They have enabled new entrants to come into the Canadian financial services market and provide increased competition to the Big Six. For example, ING Canada, a Canadian banking subsidiary of a major Netherlands banking and insurance conglomerate, and Citizen Bank, a subsidiary of Vancouver City Savings Credit Union, are virtual banks offering an array of banking services on the Internet. In addition, U.S. credit card banks, such as MBNA and Capital One Financial Corporation, are now offering specialized credit card products in Canada, and Wells Fargo, one of the largest banks in the United States, provides loans to Canadian small businesses from the United States.

Moreover, the 2001 changes to bank ownership laws encouraged the establishment of new banks. For example, Canadian Tire established a banking subsidiary (Canadian Tire Bank), as has Loblaws (President's Choice Bank). Western Financial Group, a holding company for a network of insurance agencies, created Bank West, and the Wheaton Group, a chain of car dealerships, launched a new bank called General Bank of Canada. In addition, a large number of private-sector competitors (for example, General Motors Acceptance Corporation, Ford Credit, GE Capital Group, CIT Group, and Dell Financial Services) participate in Canada's financial services market and offer similar products and services as Canada's banks, including credit cards, residential and commercial mortgages, equipment leasing, and motor vehicle financing.

COMPARISON WITH THE UNITED STATES

The structure of the commercial banking industry in Canada, although similar to that in many other industrialized countries, is radically different from that in the United States. There are approximately 7100 commercial banks in the United States, far more than in any other country in the world. Japan, for example, has fewer than 100 commercial banks—a mere fraction of the number of banks in the United States, even though its economy and population are half the size of the United States—and, as already noted, Canada has seventy-three banks. Moreover, as Table 11-2 indicates, the United States has an extraordinary number of small banks; 40% of its commercial banks have less than US$100 million in assets, and the 10 largest U.S. banks (listed in Table 11-3) together hold just over 50% of the assets in the industry.

The presence of so many commercial banks in the United States reflects past regulations that restricted the ability of these financial institutions to open branches. The result was that many small banks stayed in existence because a large bank capable of driving them out of business was often restricted from opening a branch nearby. Indeed, it was often easier for a U.S. bank to open a branch in a foreign country than to open one in another state in the United States! In fact, most industries in the United States have far fewer firms than the commercial banking industry. For example, Microsoft dominates the computer software industry and General Motors, Ford, Chrysler, Toyota, and Honda dominate the automobile industry.

TABLE 11-2 Size Distribution of Insured Commercial Banks in the U.S., September 30, 2008

Assets	Number of Banks	Share of Banks (%)	Share of Assets Held (%)
Less than US$100 million	2882	40.3	1.9
US$100 million–US$1 billion	3755	52.5	11.4
US$1 billion–US$10 billion	425	6.0	12.8
More than US$10 billion	84	1.2	73.9
Total	7146	100.0	100.0

Source: Federal Deposit Insurance Corporation, "FDIC Quarterly Banking Profile," www2.fdic.gov/qbp/2008sep/cb4.html.

TABLE 11-3 Ten Largest U.S. Banks, December 30, 2008

Bank	Assets (US$ millions)	Share of All Commercial Bank Assets (%)
1. JPMorgan Chase, Columbus, OH	1 746 242	14.06
2. Bank of America Corp., Charlotte, NC	1 471 631	11.85
3. Citibank, Las Vegas, NV	1 227 040	9.88
4. Wachovia Bank Held By Wells Fargo & Co., Charlotte, NC	635 476	5.12
5. Wells Fargo, Sioux Falls, SD	538 958	4.34
6. U.S. Bank, Cincinnati, OH	261 776	2.11
7. Bank of NY Mellon, New York, NY	195 164	1.57
8. Suntrust Bank, Atlanta, GA	185 099	1.49
9. HSBC Bank USA, McLean, VA	181 604	1.46
10. State Street B&T Corp., Boston, MA	171 228	1.38
Total	6 614 218	53.26

Source: Federal Reserve Statistics Release, "Assets and Liabilities of Commercial Banks in the United States," December 29, 2008, www.federalreserve.gov/releases/h8/20081229.

Does the large number of banks in the commercial banking industry in the United States and the absence of a few dominant firms suggest that commercial banking is more competitive than other industries? Advocates of restrictive state branching regulations in the United States argued that regulations foster competition by keeping so many banks in business. But the existence of large numbers of banks in the United States should be seen as an indication of a *lack* of competition, *not* the presence of vigorous competition. Inefficient banks were able to remain in business because their customers could not find a conveniently located branch of another bank.

Response to Branching Restrictions in the United States

An important feature of the U.S. banking industry is that competition can be repressed by regulation but not completely quashed. As we saw earlier in the chapter, the existence of restrictive regulation stimulates financial innovations that get around these regulations in the banks' search for profits. Regulations restricting branching have stimulated similar economic forces and have promoted the development of two financial innovations: bank holding companies and automated teller machines.

BANK HOLDING COMPANIES   A **bank holding company** is a corporation that owns several different companies. This form of corporate ownership has important advantages for banks in that it has allowed them to circumvent restrictive branching regulations, because the holding company can own a controlling interest in several banks even if branching is not permitted. Furthermore, a bank holding company can engage in other activities related to banking, such as the provision of investment advice, data processing and transmission services, leasing, credit card services, and servicing of loans in other states.

The growth of the bank holding companies in the United States has been dramatic over the past three decades. Today bank holding companies own almost all large banks, and more than 90% of all commercial bank deposits are held in banks owned by holding companies.

AUTOMATED TELLER MACHINES   Another financial innovation that avoided the restrictions on branching is the automated teller machine (ATM). Banks realized that if they did not own or rent the ATM, but instead let it be owned by someone else and paid for each transaction with a fee, the ATM would probably not be considered a branch of the bank and thus would not be subject to branching regulations. This is exactly what the regulatory agencies and courts in most states in the United States concluded. Because they enable banks to widen their markets, a number of these shared facilities (such as Cirrus and NYCE) have been established nationwide. Furthermore, even when an ATM is owned by a bank, states typically have special provisions that allow wider establishment of ATMs than is permissible for traditional "brick and mortar" branches.

As we saw earlier in the chapter, avoiding regulation was not the only reason for the development of the ATM. The advent of cheaper computer and telecommunications technology enabled banks to provide ATMs at low cost, making them a profitable innovation. This example further illustrates that technological factors often combine with incentives such as the desire to avoid restrictive regulations like branching restrictions to produce financial innovations.

COMPETITION ACROSS ALL FOUR PILLARS

Another important feature of the structure of the banking industry in Canada until recently was the separation of the banking and other financial services industries—such as securities, insurance, and real estate. Regulations enforced the separation of institutions according to their core financial service, and only four distinct types of financial services were identified: banking, brokerage, trusts, and insurance. This approach to regulation by institution (versus regulation by function) has been known as the **four-pillar approach**. The separation of the four pillars prohibited chartered banks from engaging in insurance and real estate activities. In turn, it prevented investment banks and insurance companies from engaging in commercial banking activities and thus protected banks from competition.

Convergence

In recent years, however, financial markets have opened up and Canada's traditional four-pillar system has changed. Despite the prohibitions in the legislation, the pursuit of profits and financial innovation stimulated both banks and other financial institutions to bypass the intent of the legislation and encroach on each other's traditional territory. For example, credit unions long offered insurance to their members and brokerage firms engaged in the traditional banking business of issuing deposit instruments with the development of money market mutual funds and cash management accounts.

Not surprisingly, the regulatory barriers between banking and other financial services markets have been coming down in response to these forces. Before the 1950s, for example, legislation allowed chartered banks to make loans for commercial purposes only and prohibited them from making residential mortgage loans. It was only after the 1967 revision of the Bank Act that banks were allowed to make conventional residential mortgage loans, thereby directly competing with trust and mortgage loan companies, and credit unions and *caisses populaires*.

In the 1980s, the Bank Act was amended to allow Canadian and foreign financial institutions to own up to 100% of securities firms. Moreover, the 1990s revisions to the Bank Act allowed cross-ownership via subsidiaries between financial institutions. Chartered banks, for example, can either buy independent investment dealers or expand on their own into capital raising, brokerage, and other securities activities. As a result, the Big Six now dominate the investment banking industry through their investment brokerage subsidiaries; they hold about a 70% share in the business.

As a result of these recent legislative changes, Canada's traditional four pillars of financial services—banking, brokerage, trusts, and insurance—have now converged into a single financial services marketplace. Similar trends are also appearing in the United States as old rules and laws are overturned. With the merger in 1998 of Citicorp (the second-largest bank in the United States) and Travelers Group (an insurance company that also owned the third-largest securities firm in the country, Salomon Smith Barney), the Gramm-Leach-Bliley Financial Services Modernization Act of 1999 overturned the Glass-Steagall separation of the banking and securities industries. This allowed securities firms and insurance companies to purchase banks and banks to underwrite insurance and securities and engage in real estate activities.

Not surprisingly, the advent of the web and improved computer technology is another factor driving bank consolidation. Economies of scale have increased because large upfront investments are required to set up many information technology platforms for financial institutions. To take advantage of these economies of scale, banks have needed to get bigger, and this development has led to additional consolidation. Information technology has also been increasing economies of scope, the ability to use one resource to provide many different products and services. For example, details about the quality and creditworthiness of firms not only inform decisions about whether to make loans to them, but also can be useful in determining at what price their shares should trade. Similarly, once you have marketed one financial product to an investor, you probably know how to market another. Business people describe economies of scope by saying that there are "synergies" between different lines of business, and information technology is making these synergies more likely. The result is that consolidation is taking place not only to make financial institutions bigger, but also to increase the combination of products and services they can provide. This consolidation has had two consequences. First, different types of financial intermediaries are encroaching on each other's territory, making them more alike. Second, consolidation has led to the development of what has been named **large, complex banking organizations (LCBOs)**.

Implications for Financial Consolidation

As we have seen, recent legislation has stimulated consolidation of the banking industry. The financial consolidation process will even further speed up in the future, because the way is now open to consolidation in terms not only of the number of banking institutions, but also across financial service activities. Given that information technology is increasing economies of scope, mergers of banks with other financial service firms like that of Citicorp and Travelers in the United States should become increasingly common, and more mega-mergers are likely to be on the way. Banking institutions are becoming not only larger, but also increasingly complex organizations, engaging in the full gamut of financial service activities. The trend toward larger and more complex banking organizations was accelerated by the subprime financial crisis of 2007–2008 (see the FYI box, The Subprime Financial Crisis and the Demise of Large, Free-Standing Investment Banks.)

FYI   **The Subprime Financial Crisis and the Demise of Large, Free-Standing Investment Banks**

Although the move toward bringing financial service activities into larger, complex banking organizations was inevitable after the demise of Glass-Steagall, no one expected it to occur as rapidly as it did in 2008. Over a six month period from March to September of 2008, all five of the largest, free-standing investment banks in the United States ceased to exist in their old form. When Bear Stearns, the fifth largest investment bank, revealed its large losses from investments in subprime mortgage securities, it had to be bailed out by the Federal Reserve in March 2008; the price it paid was a forced sale to J.P. Morgan for less than one-tenth what it had been worth only a year or so before. The Bear Stearns bailout made it clear that the government safety net had been extended to investment banks. The tradeoff is that investment banks will be subject to more regulation, along the lines for commercial banks, in the future.

Next to go was Lehman Brothers, the fourth largest investment bank, which declared bankruptcy on September 15, 2008. Only one day before, Merrill Lynch, the third-largest investment bank, which also suffered large losses on its holdings of subprime securities, announced its sale to Bank of America for less than half of its year-earlier price. Within a week Goldman Sachs and Morgan Stanley, the first- and second-largest investment banks, both of which had smaller exposure to subprime securities, nevertheless saw the writing on the wall. They realized that they would soon become regulated on a similar basis and decided to become bank holding companies so they could access insured deposits, a more stable funding base.

It was the end of an era. Large, free-standing investment banking firms in the U.S. are now a thing of the past.

Separation of Banking and Other Financial Services Industries Throughout the World

Not many other countries in the aftermath of the Great Depression followed the lead of Canada and the United States in separating the banking and other financial services industries. In fact, in the past this separation was the most prominent difference between banking regulation in Canada and the United States versus regulation in other countries. Around the world, there are three basic frameworks for the banking and securities industries.

The first framework is *universal banking*, which exists in Germany, the Netherlands, and Switzerland. It provides no separation at all between the banking and securities industries. In a universal banking system, commercial banks provide a full range of banking, securities, real estate, and insurance services, all within a single legal entity. Banks are allowed to own sizable equity shares in commercial firms, and often they do.

The *British-style universal banking system*, the second framework, is found in the United Kingdom and countries with close ties to it, such as Australia, Canada, and now the United States. The British-style universal bank engages in securities underwriting, but it differs from the German-style universal bank in three ways: separate legal subsidiaries are more common, bank equity holdings of commercial firms are less common, and combinations of banking and insurance firms are less common.

The third framework features some legal separation of the banking and other financial services industries, as in Japan. A major difference between British-style and Japanese banking systems is that Japanese banks are allowed to hold substantial equity stakes in commercial firms, whereas British-style universal banks cannot. Although the banking and securities industries are legally separated in Japan under Section 65 of the Japanese Securities Act, commercial banks are increasingly being allowed to engage in securities activities and are thus becoming more like British-style universal banks.

THE NEAR BANKS: REGULATION AND STRUCTURE

Not surprisingly, the regulation and structure of the near banks (trust and mortgage loan companies, and credit unions and *caisses populaires*) closely parallel the regulation and structure of the chartered banking industry.

Trust Companies

Over the years, the Bank Acts have denied to chartered banks the power to function as corporate **trustees** (or fiduciaries). Unlike the situation in the United States, legislators in Canada reasoned that deposit-taking financial institutions might face a conflict of interest if they were to act as both financial fiduciaries and banks. So beginning in 1843, trust companies were established, under a variety of provincial and federal laws, and specialized in the provision of fiduciary services. As financial fiduciaries, trust companies administer estates, trusts, and agencies (i.e., assets that belong to someone else), for a fee, and under conditions prescribed in a contract.

Over the years, the structure of the trust industry has changed significantly and the trust companies became closely associated with the chartered banks. In the early 1900s, the trust companies were also allowed to act as financial intermediaries. In this role, trust companies borrow funds by issuing deposit liabilities and then use these funds to make loans and purchase assets. Moreover, over the years the Bank Acts have allowed regulated federal financial institutions (domestic chartered banks and life insurance companies) to own trust companies. As a result, and with the acquisition of Canada Trust (Canada's largest trust company) by the Toronto Dominion Bank in early 2000, trust companies now constitute a relatively small market segment.

Mortgage Loan Companies

The development of trust companies was paralleled by the growth of mortgage loan companies. The concept of mortgage loan companies came from the building societies in the United Kingdom (during the early part of the nineteenth century), whose purpose was to enable members to acquire land, build homes, or develop farms. Today's mortgage loan companies take deposits and primarily make residential mortgage loans. They do not act as trustees, unless they are licensed specifically for that purpose. Over the years, the mortgage loan companies together with the trust companies formed the second pillar of the traditional financial services industry in Canada. However, as you can see in this chapter, financial innovation, competition, and regulatory evolution significantly changed the competitive position of financial institutions in recent years.

Trust and mortgage loan companies (TMLs) operate under a charter issued by either the federal government or one of the provincial governments. Federally incorporated TMLs come under the federal Trust and Loan Companies Act and are regulated and supervised by the Office of the Superintendent of Financial Institutions Canada (OSFI). They must also register in all of the provinces in which they operate and must conform to the regulations of those provinces. In the case of trust companies, the fiduciary component of their business is only subject to provincial legislation, even if the company is federally incorporated. Deposit insurance for TMLs outside Québec is provided by the CDIC (up to $100 000 per account). The Québec Deposit Insurance Board (QDIB) insures deposits for Québec TMLs on terms similar to the CDIC's.

Trust and mortgage loan companies are funded almost entirely by chequable and nonchequable savings deposits, term deposits, guaranteed investment certificates, and debentures; together, they account for about 85% of the balance sheet. Their risk asset portfolio is made up mostly by residential mortgages and personal loans; together they account for about 60% of assets. The low-risk assets are largely in short-term paper and Canadian bonds.

Cooperative Banks: Credit Unions and *Caisses Populaires*

Cooperative banks are small lending institutions organized around a particular group of individuals with a common bond (union members or employees of a particular firm). Alphonse Desjardins formed Canada's first cooperative bank in 1900 in Québec, and it was based on the cooperative movements in Europe, which, among other things, stressed the provision of credit to the "little man." Today, there are two cooperative financial systems in Canada: the *caisses populaires* system in Québec and the credit union system in other parts of the country.

There are about 1000 credit unions and *caisses populaires* in Canada, with almost 10 million members and more than 60 000 employees, carrying on retail financial services businesses. Because their members share a common goal, credit unions and *caisses populaires* are typically quite small; most are about the size of a single bank branch and hold less than $10 million of assets, with the largest being VanCity Savings with assets close to $6 billion. The credit unions and *caisses populaires* are established under provincial legislation and are non–profit-seeking financial institutions. Unlike chartered banks that accept deposits from and lend funds to the general public, the cooperative banks accept deposits from and lend funds only to their members. Members have voting rights and elect a board of directors, which determines the union's lending and investment policies.

As member-owned, independent financial firms, credit unions and *caisses populaires* constitute an alternative financial system, different from the profit-seeking banking system. They have also developed their own set of institutions, including central banking and deposit insurance arrangements. In particular, each province has a central credit union, owned by the member credit unions, that provides financial services to individual credit unions. All central credit unions outside Québec are members of the Credit Union Central of Canada (CUCC), also known as Canadian Central. The Canadian Central serves as the third tier for the credit union movement; it coordinates various functions and provides cheque-clearing services for all provincial central credit unions.

In Québec, *caisses populaires* are assembled under a single federation, the *Fédération des caisses Desjardins du Québec*, which has a similar structure to the provincial central credit unions in the rest of Canada but with considerably broader regulatory responsibilities. The federation dominates retail and corporate financial intermediation in Québec. It owns a major P&C insurance group, *Desjardins General Insurance;* a life and health insurance company, *Desjardins Financial Security;* a venture capital firm, *Desjardins Venture Capital;* and an investment dealer and discount brokerage, *Desjardins Securities and Disnat.* It also owns *Caisse centrale Desjardins,* which functions as a central bank, as the CUCC does for the rest of Canada.

Credit unions and *caisses populaires* are not directly covered by the CDIC. However, each provincial government has an agency, commonly called a stabilization fund, which has a line of credit with the provincial treasury and provides deposit guarantees for credit unions. Deposits in New Brunswick and Prince Edward Island are insured up to $60 000 per account, in Ontario and British

Columbia up to $100 000, in Nova Scotia and Newfoundland and Labrador up to $250 000, and in Alberta, Saskatchewan, and Manitoba there are no limits on the amount of coverage provided. In Québec, the Québec Deposit Insurance Board, the same provincial government agency that insures deposits in other deposit-taking financial institutions in Québec, also provides deposit guarantees for *caisses populaires*, on terms similar to the CDIC's.

The main source of funds of credit unions and *caisses populaires* is deposits—they account for almost 85% of liabilities—followed by members' equity (about 7% of liabilities). Their asset portfolio is made up largely by residential and nonresidential mortgages (close to 55% of the balance sheet) and cash loans to members (about 13%). Low-risk assets, such as cash and deposits (primarily with central credit unions) also represent a significant proportion of the balance sheet (close to 15%). The rest of the balance sheet consists of fixed assets, and shares in central credit unions.

Government Savings Institutions

In addition to the near banks (trust and mortgage loan companies and credit unions and *caisses populaires*), there are some government-operated deposit-taking institutions such as the Province of Ontario Savings Office and the Alberta Treasury Branches.

The Province of Ontario Savings Office was established in 1921 with the objective to gather funds from the public and lend them to farmers. Today, however, the Savings Office only lends funds to the Treasurer of Ontario for provincial government purposes. In fact, its deposit liabilities are a debt of the province of Ontario and are guaranteed by the province. In 2003, the Province of Ontario Savings Office was sold to Desjardins Credit Union.

The province of Alberta established Treasury branches back in 1938 in response to Albertans' needs in remote areas. Today, there are 162 branches in 244 communities across the province operating in three target markets: individual financial services, agricultural operations, and independent business. Alberta Treasury Branches (with assets in excess of $16 billion) are funded almost entirely by demand, notice, and fixed-term deposits, and their risk asset portfolio is made up largely of residential mortgages and personal, commercial, and agricultural loans.

INTERNATIONAL BANKING

Canadian banks have a well-developed presence in the global financial services marketplace, which varies among the individual institutions. From its inception, for example, the Bank of Montreal found some of its best opportunities in international operations and was soon joined by the Canadian Imperial Bank of Commerce and the Bank of Nova Scotia. The spectacular growth in international banking can be explained by three factors.

First is the rapid growth in international trade and multinational (worldwide) corporations that has occurred in recent years. When Canadian firms operate abroad, they need banking services in foreign countries to help finance international trade. For example, they might need a loan in a foreign currency to operate a factory abroad. And when they sell goods abroad, they need to have a bank exchange the foreign currency they have received for their goods into Canadian dollars. Although these firms could use foreign banks to provide them with these international banking services, many of them prefer to do business with the Canadian banks with which they have established long-term relationships and which understand Canadian business customs and practices. As international trade has grown, international banking has grown with it.

Second, Canadian banks have been able to earn substantial profits by being very active in global investment banking, in which they underwrite foreign securities. They also sell insurance abroad, and they derive substantial profits from these investment banking and insurance activities.

Third, Canadian banks have wanted to tap into the large pool of Eurocurrencies—currencies deposited in banks outside the home country. To understand the structure of Canadian banking overseas, let us first look at the Eurocurrencies market, an important source for international banking.

Eurocurrencies Market

The most important of the Eurocurrencies are Eurodollars, which originated after World War II with U.S.-dollar deposits in European banks. They were created when deposits in accounts in the United States were transferred to a bank outside the United States and were kept in the form of U.S. dollars. For example, if Rolls-Royce PLC deposits a US$1 million cheque, written on an account at an American bank, in its bank in London—specifying that the deposit be payable in U.S. dollars—$1 million in Eurodollars is created.[3] More than 90% of Eurodollar deposits are time deposits, more than half of them certificates of deposit with maturities of thirty days or more. The total amount of Eurodollars outstanding is on the order of US$5.2 trillion, making the Eurodollar market (which was born in an ironic way—see the Global box, Ironic Birth of the Eurodollar Market) one of the most important financial markets in the world economy.

Although most offshore deposits are denominated in U.S. dollars, some are also denominated in other currencies. Collectively, these offshore deposits are referred to as Eurocurrencies. A Canadian dollar–denominated deposit held in London, for example, is called a Euro Canadian dollar, and a Japanese yen–denominated deposit held in London is called a Euroyen. Why would companies such as Rolls-Royce want to hold Eurocurrencies? First, some currencies are widely used in international trade, so Rolls-Royce might want to hold deposits in these currencies to

---

GLOBAL   Ironic Birth of the Eurodollar Market

One of capitalism's great ironies is that the Eurodollar market, one of the most important financial markets used by capitalists, was fathered by the Soviet Union. In the early 1950s, during the height of the Cold War, the Soviets had accumulated a substantial amount of dollar balances held by banks in the United States. Because the Russians feared that the U.S. government might freeze these assets in the United States, they wanted to move the deposits to Europe, where they would be safe from expropriation. (This fear was not unjustified—consider the U.S. freeze on Iranian assets in 1979 and Iraqi assets in 1990.) However, they also wanted to keep the deposits in dollars so that they could be used in their international transactions. The solution to the problem was to transfer the deposits to European banks but to keep the deposits denominated in dollars. When the Soviets did this, the Eurodollar was born.

---

[3] Note that the bank in London keeps the $1 million on deposits at the American bank, so the creation of Eurodollars has not caused a reduction in the amount of bank deposits in the United States.

conduct its international transactions. Second, Eurocurrencies are "offshore" deposits—they are held in countries that will not subject them to regulations such as reserve requirements or restrictions (called *capital controls*) on taking the deposits outside the country.

The main centre of the Eurocurrencies market is London, a major international financial centre for hundreds of years. Eurocurrencies are also held outside Europe in locations that provide offshore status to these deposits—for example, Singapore, the Bahamas, and the Cayman Islands.

The minimum transaction in the Eurocurrencies market is typically $1 million, and approximately 75% of Eurocurrency deposits are held by banks. Plainly, you and I are unlikely to come into direct contact with Eurocurrencies. The Eurocurrencies market is, however, an important source of funds to Canadian banks. Rather than using an intermediary and borrowing all the deposits from foreign banks, Canadian banks decided that they could earn higher profits by opening their own branches abroad to attract these deposits. Consequently, the Eurocurrencies market has been an important stimulus to Canadian banking overseas.

Canadian Banking Overseas

Canadian banks have been present in international financial markets for over 100 years, providing services to Canadians and multinational businesses. As Table 11-4 shows, the international presence of the Big Six varies among the individual institutions. In particular, the Bank of Montreal, the Canadian Imperial Bank of Commerce, and TD Canada Trust have a significant presence in the United States, whereas Scotiabank has established a presence in South America, and the Royal Bank in Europe and Asia.

During the 1970s and early 1980s a large proportion of the banks' foreign lending was in **sovereign loans**; loans to foreign governments and their agencies in the less-developed countries (LDCs), particularly Mexico, Brazil, Venezuela, Argentina, and Chile. Most of this activity in international lending was unregulated, with near disastrous consequences. One example is the international debt crisis, which had its origin in the oil price shocks of the 1970s. In particular, the 1973–1974 increase in the price of oil was a bonanza for some oil-exporting countries like Mexico, but a disaster for oil-importing countries like Brazil, which had to either cut their living standards or borrow massively abroad in order to pay their higher oil bills. At the time, real interest rates were very low (in fact negative) and the oil importers couldn't resist the temptation to borrow abroad.

TABLE 11-4   International Activity of the Big Six (as of March 31, 2009)

Bank	Primary Focus	International Assets ($ millions)	Percent of International Assets in Total Assets
Bank of Montreal	United States, Mexico	246 618	52%
CIBC	United States	97 794	27%
Bank of Nova Scotia	South America, Mexico	247 682	47%
Toronto Dominion	United States	295 267	49%
Royal Bank	Europe, Asia	369 121	51%
National Bank	No significant international presence	21 177	14%

Source: OSFI website, www.osfi-bsif.gc.ca, and authors' calculations.

At the same time, the oil exporters were depositing huge sums in banks and as a result the banks were lending not only to the oil-importing countries but also to the oil-exporting countries, because the latter had large oil reserves and seemed like good credit risks. The banks underestimated the **indebtedness** of these countries—the total amount these countries had borrowed from banks—and, as a result, were severely punished in the early 1980s when the recession hit and real interest rates increased significantly. With Argentina, Brazil, Mexico, and Peru threatening to default on their loans, the banks had two choices: to reschedule their loans and make more loans to these countries (to enable them to pay the interest on the debt), or to declare these countries in default and acknowledge large losses on their balance sheets. The banks chose to make more loans, because in many cases the losses would have been large enough to destroy them.

Today, the LDC debt is no longer a significant threat to the international banking system, because of other arrangements as well. In recent years, for example, a variety of debt conversion schemes have been proposed to alleviate the debt service obligations of the major indebted LDCs. There are three main forms of debt conversion: **debt-debt swaps** (where banks holding the debt of one LDC exchange it for the debt of another LDC), **debt-currency swaps** (where the debt denominated in foreign currency is converted into domestic currency), and **debt-equity swaps** (where the debt is converted into the equity of public and private domestic enterprises). The main impetus of all these debt conversion schemes has been the recognition that the true value of the sovereign debt is well below its face value.

As a result of their lending experience in Latin America, the Big Six have withdrawn from certain countries and focused more of their international activities in the United States. Moreover, the international activities of Canadian banking organizations are now regulated, primarily by the Office of the Superintendent of Financial Institutions Canada (OSFI), created in 1987 to succeed two separate regulatory bodies: the Inspector General of Banks and the Department of Insurance. In particular, in 1991, the OSFI asked the chartered banks to set up special reserves in the amount of 35%–45% of their exposure to a number of LDCs.

Foreign Banks in Canada

The growth in international trade not only has encouraged Canadian banks to open offices overseas but also has encouraged foreign banks to establish offices in Canada. Foreign banks have been extremely successful in Canada. Over the past 20 years, since the 1981 revision to the Bank Act, globally prominent foreign banks have set up and expanded banking subsidiaries in Canada. Foreign banks are a highly fragmented group and currently hold about 8% of total Canadian bank assets, with HSBC Bank Canada (the former Hongkong and Shanghai Banking Corp.) enjoying a national market share of over 3%. It should be noted, however, that these institutions target specific groups, achieving a higher representation within their target groups than their national share would suggest. For example, HSBC, the largest of the Schedule II banks, enjoys a strong presence and success in the Chinese communities of British Columbia and Ontario.

Foreign banks may enter the Canadian financial services industry as either Schedule II or Schedule III banks. As already noted, Schedule II banks don't have to be widely held if small. If, however, their equity capital exceeds $1 billion, then at least 35% of it must be widely held. In the case that their equity capital exceeds $5 billion, then the same widely held ownership rule applies as for Schedule I banks. The major difference between Schedule II and Schedule III banks is that Schedule III banks can branch directly into Canada, following authorization by the Minister of Finance, whereas Schedule II banks can add branches to their initial branch only with

TABLE 11-5   Largest Banks in the World, at Fiscal 2008

Bank	Country	Asset Rank	Assets ($ millions)
Royal Bank of Scotland	UK	1	4 287 263
Deutsche Bank	Germany	2	3 753 775
Barclays Bank	UK	3	3 664 838
BNP Paribas	France	4	3 537 536
HSBC Holdings	UK	5	2 961 123
Crédit Agricole Group	France	6	2 742 333
JPMorgan Chase & Co.	USA	7	2 663 569
Mitsubishi UFJ Financial Group	Japan	8	2 480 831
Citigroup	USA	9	2 373 850
UBS	Switzerland	10	2 319 910
Royal Bank of Canada	Canada	33	883 128
Toronto-Dominion Bank	Canada	47	684 336
Scotiabank	Canada	48	614 290
Bank of Montreal	Canada	53	504 033
CIBC	Canada	60	427 677

Source: The Banker, July 2009, www.thebanker.com.

ministerial approval. However, Schedule III banks cannot take retail deposits (i.e., deposits less than $150 000) and, as a result, have the advantage of not being subject to regulations that apply to full-service banks (such as requirements for CDIC insurance). Given that most Schedule II banks do little retail deposit gathering, it is likely that in the future many Schedule II banks will become Schedule III banks.

The internationalization of banking, both by Canadian banks going abroad and by foreign banks entering Canada, has meant that financial markets throughout the world have become more integrated. As a result, there is a growing trend toward international coordination of bank regulation, one example of which is the 1988 Basel agreement to standardize minimum capital requirements in industrialized countries. Financial market integration has also encouraged bank consolidation abroad, culminating in the creation of the first trillion-dollar bank with the merger of the Industrial Bank of Japan, Dai-Ichi Kangyo Bank, and Fuji Bank, announced in August 1999, but which took place in 2002. Another development has been the importance of foreign banks in international banking. As is shown in Table 11-5, in 2008, thirty-two of the largest banks in the world were foreign. The implications of this financial market integration for the operation of our economy is examined further in Chapter 20 when we discuss the international financial system in more detail.

THE 2001 BANK ACT REFORM

We have seen that fundamental structural changes make possible new financial products and services, increasing the competitive environment in the financial services industry and changing the financial intermediation role of banking at Internet speed. It is against this backdrop of phenomenal change that the federal government introduced legislation reforming the policy framework of the Canadian financial services sector.[4] This legislation took effect in October of 2001, when Bill C-8 came into force, and is generically known as **Bank Act Reform**. The new legislation is mostly based on the Report of the Task Force on the Future of the Canadian Financial Services Sector, also known as the MacKay Report, and it has been called one of the most significant revisions to the Bank Act in Canadian history.

In what follows we provide an overview of the key elements of the new regulatory environment for financial institutions that has the potential to dramatically change the face of competition in Canada's financial services marketplace.[5] As you will see, the new laws establish the regulatory framework to accelerate changes already taking place throughout the Canadian and world economies and introduce new opportunities for strategic alliances and partnerships, with the objective of fostering more competition and providing more innovative products and services to Canadians.

Bank Holding Companies

Before Bank Act Reform, the organizational structure of Canada's bank financial groups was based on the "bank-as-parent" model, where all banking functions and all subsidiaries of the bank are subject to the same regulation. Under the new legislation, bank financial groups have the option of organizing themselves under a holding company.[6] A holding company is a corporation that owns several different companies. For example, under a holding company structure, a bank financial group may have a banking subsidiary, an insurance subsidiary, a securities subsidiary, and another subsidiary for its unregulated businesses.

Most developed countries permit holding company structures, and the growth of holding companies has been dramatic over the past three decades. Today, in the United States, for example, holding companies own almost all large banks, and over 90% of all commercial bank deposits are held in banks owned by holding companies. In fact, the Gramm-Leach-Bliley Act of 1999 modernized the holding company rules in the United States (which had been in place since 1956) to allow a new and more flexible holding company model—the financial holding company.

The holding company form of corporate ownership has important advantages for bank financial groups in that (1) it allows them to engage in other activities related to banking, such as the provision of investment advice, data processing and transmission services, leasing, and credit card services; (2) a holding company structure allows for lighter regulation throughout the bank financial group because certain activities (those not involving retail deposit-taking and insurance) can be

---

[4] Since 1992, the practice of reviewing legislation governing Canada's chartered banks has been extended to reviewing legislation governing all federal financial institutions.

[5] See also Fred Daniel, "Recent Changes to Canada's Financial Sector Legislation," *Bank of Canada Review*, Winter 2002–2003: 3–16.

[6] The new legislation introduced a holding company regime for Canada's insurance companies as well. Under the legislation, insurance holding companies are required to have an investment in at least one life insurance company and are regulated under the Insurance Companies Act. Bank holding companies are regulated under the Bank Act and are required to have an investment in at least one bank.

undertaken by less-regulated, non–bank-affiliated companies held by the holding company parent rather than the regulated operating bank; and (3) the holding company model provides bank financial groups increased flexibility to achieve economies of scale and scope through strategic partnerships, alliances, and joint ventures.[7]

The big advantage of the new regime for establishing holding companies is that financial groups will be able to move parts of their heavily regulated business into less-regulated affiliates under a common holding company. The holding company, however, would be a viable option for financial groups, if the transition to a holding company would be tax-neutral and without increased costs or regulatory burdens. If, for example, additional taxes or heavier regulation were to arise as a result of a restructuring into a holding company, then the holding company option wouldn't be feasible. For this reason, the new legislation also provides a set of transitional rules to address unintended cost consequences that would be triggered by the transition to a holding company.

Permitted Investments

A second item of the 2001 legislation pertains to the type of investments federally regulated financial institutions are allowed to make. At present, there is a restrictive list of activities beyond banking that banks, for example, can get involved in. The new legislation, however, provides greater flexibility for bank involvement in the information technology area (and, in particular, the Internet and wireless technology). It permits bank financial groups to establish and operate information services entities utilizing recent advances in Internet and wireless banking and voice recognition technologies.

New information technologies are critical to the ability of Canadian banks and insurance companies to provide new financial products and services and adapt to the changing marketplace. Although bank and insurance company involvement in the information technology area is subject to regulation, the new permitted investment regime will enhance the ability of banks and insurance companies to pursue strategic alliances and joint ventures and will further accelerate the technological advances that are already taking place and revolutionize the financial services sector.

Ownership Rules

A third policy measure that can significantly change the face of competition in Canada's financial services marketplace is the new ownership regime that enables investors to take a greater equity interest in widely held bank financial groups, by expanding the definition of "widely held." In particular, the 2001 legislation increased the limit (that was in place since 1967) a single shareholder can own of a widely held financial institution (either a bank holding company or a bank subsidiary under the holding company) from 10% of any class of shares to 20% of voting shares and 30% of nonvoting shares. The new legislation, however, does not permit a single shareholder to own more than 10% of both a bank holding company and a bank subsidiary under the holding company at the same time. Moreover, acquisitions of more than 10% are subject to approval by the Minister of Finance based on a "fit and proper person" test.

The new legislation also includes a three-tiered ownership regime. Small banks (those with equity capital under $1 billion) don't have to be widely held and can be wholly owned (have one particular investor own 100% of their shares).

---

[7] Recently, for example, the British-based banking group HSBC entered into a joint venture with the U.S.-based securities dealer Merrill Lynch, to create a global online banking and investment company, called Merrill Lynch HSBC.

Medium-sized banks (and bank holding companies) with shareholders' equity between $1 billion and $5 billion can be closely held provided that there is a 35% public float (that is, they could have a single shareholder own up to 65% of their shares). Large banks (and bank holding companies), those with shareholders' equity in excess of $5 billion, are required to be widely held.

The new ownership regime, together with other provisions in the legislation, such as the lowering of the capital needed to create a bank from $10 million to $5 million and the allowance of domestic and foreign commercial enterprises (such as department stores and grocery chains) to establish small and medium-sized banks, will fundamentally change Canada's financial sector.

The CP Act and Access to the Payments and Clearance System

Before the 2001 financial sector legislation, membership in the Canadian Payments Association (CPA), a nonprofit organization formed in 1980 by an Act of Parliament to operate Canada's payments systems, was limited to the Bank of Canada and the deposit-taking financial institutions—chartered banks, trust and mortgage loan companies, and credit unions and *caisses populaires*. The 2001 legislation introduced some important changes for the Canadian Payments Association and also renamed the Canadian Payments Association Act to Canadian Payments Act (CP Act).

In particular, the CP Act extends eligibility for membership in the Canadian Payments Association—and therefore access to Canada's two domestic payments systems, the Large Value Transfer System (LVTS) and the Automated Clearing Settlement System (ACSS), both to be discussed in detail in Chapter 17—to non–deposit-taking financial institutions, such as life insurance companies, securities dealers, and money market mutual funds. This regulatory change will significantly affect Canada's financial services sector, since it will allow these organizations to provide bank-like services, such as chequing accounts and debit cards, without being banks, thereby directly competing with banks, trust and mortgage loan companies, and credit unions and *caisses populaires*.

Expanding access to the payments and clearance system, by allowing non–deposit-taking financial institutions to participate, will further accelerate the process of the blurring of distinction between deposit-taking and non–deposit-taking financial institutions. As already noted, this process started in 1987, when securities dealers were allowed to own banks, and was reinforced by the 1992 federal financial reforms that permitted cross-ownership of financial institutions.

Merger Review Policy

The government has also issued a statement establishing a process for reviewing mergers involving large banks—banks like the Bank of Montreal and CIBC with shareholder equity in excess of $5 billion. By doing so, the government acknowledges that mergers are a legitimate business option that should be available to Canadian bank financial groups. The bank merger review process, however, unlike those in other countries such as the United States and the United Kingdom, is political, having Parliament directly involved in it.

Under the new merger review policy, the merger partners are required to submit a public interest impact assessment (PIIA), covering various effects of the merger, such as the impact on the structure and competition of the banking industry, branch closures, and job losses. The merger proposal would then be submitted to the House of Commons Standing Committee on Finance and the Standing Senate Committee on Banking, Trade, and Commerce for consideration and public hearings. Each of these committees will report to the Minister of Finance, who would make these reports public, together with a report from the Competition Bureau on the competitive aspects of the proposed merger and a report from the

Office of the Superintendent of Financial Institutions Canada on the prudential aspects of the proposed merger. The Minister of Finance will decide whether the proposed merger will be allowed to proceed.

The government has also indicated that it will not allow mergers between large banks and large demutualized life insurance companies such as Manulife and Sun Life. We would note, however, that in other countries such as Australia, Germany, the Netherlands, Switzerland, the United Kingdom, and the United States, mergers of banks, insurance companies, and other financial services providers are not prohibited.

The National Financial Services OmbudService

Another recent significant achievement is the creation of a National Financial Services OmbudService (NFSO) that began operations on July 1, 2002. This service has been created, with the support of the federal and provincial governments, by the banking sector (through the Canadian Bankers Association), the insurance sector (through the Insurance Bureau of Canada and the Canadian Life and Health Association of Canada), and the securities sector (through the Investment Dealers Association of Canada, the Mutual Funds Dealers Association, and the Investment Funds Institute of Canada). The NFSO provides Canadian consumers and small businesses access to dispute-resolution services regarding their dealings with financial institutions.

The creation of the NFSO has been viewed as a first step towards building a national regulatory system and eliminating the overlaps among the many federal, provincial, and territorial departments and agencies that currently regulate the different industries of the Canadian financial services sector.

Implications for the Canadian Banking Industry

A bank holding company structure (as an alternative to the current "bank-as-parent" structure), new ownership rules, expanded permitted investments, expanded access to the payments and clearance system, and a transparent merger review policy, offer new opportunities for strategic alliances and joint ventures that have the potential to reshape the Canadian financial services marketplace. These developments, together with new information technologies, make possible new financial products and services and a more vibrant and dynamic market for financial services.

As we have seen, the 1991 federal financial reforms have stimulated consolidation of the Canadian banking industry. The financial consolidation process will be even further sped up by the 2001 legislation, because the way is now open to both mergers and acquisitions, and strategic alliances, partnerships, and joint ventures. As already noted, bank financial groups will become not only larger, but also increasingly complex organizations, engaging in a full gamut of financial activities.

SUMMARY

1. The history of banking in Canada has left us with a small number of banks chartered by the federal government. Multiple agencies regulate chartered banks: the Office of the Superintendent of Financial Institutions (OSFI), the Bank of Canada, and the Canada Deposit Insurance Corporation (CDIC).

2. The Big Six (the Royal Bank of Canada, Canadian Imperial Bank of Commerce, Bank of Montreal, Scotiabank, TD Canada Trust, and the National Bank of Canada) together with the *Desjardins Institutions* dominate the deposit-taking industry in Canada.

3. In the United States there is a dual banking system, with commercial banks chartered by the states and the federal government. Restrictive state-branching regulations that prohibited branching across state lines led to a large number of small commercial banks in the United States. The large number of commercial banks in the United States reflects the past *lack* of competition, not the presence of vigorous competition.

4. A change in the economic environment will stimulate financial institutions to search for financial innovations. Changes in demand conditions, especially the rise in

interest-rate risk; changes in supply conditions, especially improvements in information technology; and the desire to avoid costly regulations have been major driving forces behind financial innovation. Financial innovation has caused banks to suffer declines in cost advantages in acquiring funds and in income advantages on their assets. The resulting squeeze has hurt profitability in banks' traditional line of business and has led to a decline in traditional banking.

5. The regulation and structure of the near banks (trust and mortgage loan companies, and credit unions and *caisses populaires*) parallel closely the regulation and structure of the chartered banks. Federally incorporated near banks are regulated and supervised by the OSFI. They must also register in all the provinces in which they do business and must conform to the regulations of those provinces.

6. With the rapid growth of world trade since 1960, international banking has grown dramatically. Canadian banks engage in international banking activities by opening branches abroad and owning controlling interests in foreign banks. Foreign banks operate in Canada by owning a subsidiary Canadian bank or by operating branches or agency offices in Canada.

7. Until 1981, foreign banks were not allowed to operate in Canada. Today, we have 53 foreign bank subsidiaries and branches, operating as Schedule II and III banks. They have the same powers as the domestic banks but differ in the ownership structure permitted. That is, all Schedule I banks must be widely held, whereas Schedule II and III banks can be closely held if small.

8. The 2001 Bank Act Reform introduced a bank holding company structure, new ownership rules, expanded access to the payments and clearance system, and new opportunities for strategic alliances and joint ventures. These changes are reshaping the financial services marketplace in Canada by making it easier to introduce new financial products and services and increasing the competitive environment in the industry.

KEY TERMS

automated teller machine (ATM), p. 260

Bank Act Reform, p. 282

bank holding companies, p. 271

branches, p. 254

central bank, p. 254

debt-currency swaps, p. 280

debt-debt swaps, p. 280

debt-equity swaps, p. 280

deposit rate ceiling, p. 264

disintermediation, p. 264

dual banking system, p. 254

financial derivatives, p. 259

four-pillar approach, p. 272

free banking, p. 254

futures contracts, p. 259

gold standard, p. 256

hedge, p. 259

indebtedness, p. 280

large, complex banking organizations (LCBOs), p. 273

lender of last resort, p. 257

national banks, p. 254

Regulation Q, p. 264

Schedule I banks, p. 268

Schedule II banks, p. 268

Schedule III banks, p. 268

seignorage, p. 256

shadow banking system, p. 258

sovereign loans, p. 279

state banks, p. 254

sweep account, p. 264

trustees, p. 275

virtual bank, p. 261

QUESTIONS

You will find the answers to the questions marked with an asterisk in the Textbook Resources section of your MyEconLab.

1. Describe how the 2001 Bank Act Reform attempted to introduce more competiton in Canada's financial services marketplace.

*2. Which regulatory agency has the primary responsibility for supervising the following categories of financial institutions?
   a. chartered banks
   b. trust and mortgage loan companies
   c. credit unions and *caisses populaires*

3. "The commercial banking industry in Canada is less competitive than the commercial banking industry in the United States because in Canada only a few large banks dominate the industry, while in the United States there are around 7100 commercial banks." Is this statement true, false, or uncertain? Explain your answer.

*4. How did new technology cause banks' traditional lending activities to decline in balance-sheet importance?

5. Contrast the activities of a Schedule I bank, a Schedule II bank, a trust company, and a credit union.

*6. Explain how sovereign loans in the 1970s and early 1980s caused problems for the Big Six.

7. Explain how the early development of chartered banks in Canada differed from the development of commercial banks in the United States.

*8. What incentives do Canadian regulatory agencies have to encourage the establishment of foreign banks in Canada?

9. Explain how securitization can be used to change illiquid assets into liquid assets.

*10. If the bank at which you keep your chequing account is owned by Saudi Arabians, should you worry that your deposits are less safe than if Canadians owned the bank?

11. What are the essential differences between chartered banks, trust and mortgage loan companies, and credit unions and *caisses populaires*?

*12. Why have banks been losing cost advantages in acquiring funds in recent years?

13. "If inflation had not risen in the 1960s and 1970s, the banking industry might be healthier today." Is this statement true, false, or uncertain? Explain your answer.

*14. Why have banks been losing income advantages on their assets in recent years?

15. "The invention of the computer is the major factor behind the decline of the banking industry." Is this statement true, false, or uncertain? Explain your answer.

WEB EXERCISES

1. Go to the Canadian Bankers Association website at **www.cba.ca** and search for an article called "Automated Banking Machine Market in Canada." Write a short essay on ABM transactions in Canada and bank access points. According to the trends, does the public appear to have more or less access to banking facilities?

2. Despite the regulations that protect banks from failure, some do fail. Go to **www2.fdic.gov/hsob/**. Select the tab labelled "Failures and Assistance Transactions." How many bank failures occurred in the U.S. during the most recent complete calendar year? What were the total assets held by the banks that failed? How many U.S. banks failed in 1937?

 Be sure to visit the MyEconLab website at **www.myeconlab.com**. This online homework and tutorial system puts you in control of your own learning with study and practice tools directly correlated to this chapter content.

On the MyEconLab website you will find the following mini-case for this chapter:
Mini-Case 11.1: The Changing Landscape for Domestic and Global Financial Markets

CHAPTER 12

Nonbank Financial Institutions

LEARNING OBJECTIVES

After studying this chapter you should be able to

1. identify the difference between banks and nonbank financial institutions (insurance companies, pension funds, finance companies, mutual funds, and investment banks)
2. explain the regulation of nonbank financial institutions in the context of asymmetric information problems
3. report how recent financial-sector legislation is expected to lead to larger and increasingly complex financial groups, engaging in a full gamut of financial activities

PREVIEW

Banking is not the only type of financial intermediation you are likely to encounter. You might decide to purchase insurance, take out an instalment loan, or buy a share of stock. In each of these transactions you will be engaged in nonbank finance and will deal with nonbank financial institutions. In our economy, nonbank finance also plays an important role in channelling funds from lender-savers to borrower-spenders. Furthermore, the process of financial innovation we discussed in Chapter 11 has increased the importance of nonbank finance and is blurring the distinction between different financial institutions. This chapter examines in more detail how institutions engaged in nonbank finance operate, how they are regulated, and recent trends in nonbank finance.

INSURANCE

Every day we face the possibility of the occurrence of certain catastrophic events that could lead to large financial losses. A spouse's earnings might disappear due to death or illness; a car accident might result in costly repair bills or payments to an injured party. Because financial losses from crises could be large relative to our financial resources, we protect ourselves against them by purchasing insurance coverage that will pay a sum of money if catastrophic events occur. Life insurance companies sell policies that provide income if a person dies, is incapacitated by illness, or retires. Property and casualty companies specialize in policies that pay for losses incurred as a result of accidents, fire, or theft.

Life Insurance

As you can see in Table 12-1, there are currently 94 life insurance companies in Canada, which are organized as either stock companies or mutuals. Shareholders own stock companies; mutuals are technically similar to credit unions, owned by the policyholders. Prior to 1999, half of the life insurance companies in Canada were organized as mutuals. In 1999, however, five large mutual life insurance companies, Canada Life, Clarica, Manulife Financial, Sun Life, and Industrial-Alliance, started a process called **demutualization**, and have now converted to stock companies.

Life insurance company regulation is the responsibility of the OSFI and Assuris, formerly known as the Canadian Life and Health Insurance Compensation Corporation (CompCorp). OSFI regulation is directed at sales practices, the provision of adequate liquid assets to cover losses, and restrictions on the amount of risky assets (such as common stock) the companies can hold. In other words, OSFI performs the same oversight functions as it does for banks and near banks. Assuris has no regulatory role in overseeing individual life insurance companies. It is a federally incorporated private, not-for-profit corporation established and funded by the Canadian life and health insurance industry to provide liability insurance to policyholders: it compensates policyholders if the issuing company goes bankrupt.

Because death rates for the population as a whole are predictable with a high degree of certainty, life insurance companies can accurately predict what their payouts to policyholders will be in the future. Consequently, they hold long-term assets that are not particularly liquid—corporate bonds (about 60% of assets) and commercial mortgages (15% of assets) as well as some corporate stock. Actuarial liabilities make up about 70% of the liabilities of the Canadian life insurance industry. These are the present values of expected claims of policyholders.

There are two basic classes of life insurance, distinguished by the way they are sold: individual life insurance and group life insurance. **Individual life insurance**, as its name implies, is sold one policy at a time, whereas **group life insurance** is sold to a group of people under a single policy. There are two principal forms of individual life insurance policies: **permanent life insurance** (such

TABLE 12-1 Relative Shares of OSFI-Regulated Financial Intermediary Assets (as at March 31, 2008)

Financial Institution Company	Number of Companies	Total Assets (in millions)	Percent (%)
Insurance Companies			
Life Insurance	94	479 299	12.54
Property and Casualty	196	109 129	2.85
Pension Plans	1 350	131 765	3.45
Depository Institutions			
Banks	73	2 815 426	73.64
Trust and Loan Companies	70	266 455	6.97
Cooperative Associations	8	21 152	0.55
Total		3 823 226	100.00

Source: Office of the Superintendent of Financial Institutions Canada, OSFI Annual Report 2007–2008, www.osfi-bsif.gc.ca/app/DocRepository/1/RA/0708/eng/index_e.html.

as the traditional whole life insurance) and **temporary life insurance** (such as term insurance). Permanent life insurance policies have a constant premium throughout the life of the policy. In the early years of the policy, the size of this premium exceeds the amount needed to insure against death because the probability of death is low. Thus the policy builds up a cash value in its early years, but in later years the cash value declines because the constant premium falls below the amount needed to insure against death, the probability of which is now higher. The policyholder can borrow against the cash value of the permanent life policy or can claim it by cancelling the policy. For this reason, permanent insurance is also called **endowment insurance**.

Term insurance, by contrast, has a premium that is matched every year to the amount needed to insure against death during the period of the term (such as one year or five years). As a result, term policies have premiums that rise over time as the probability of death rises (or level premiums with a decline in the amount of death benefits). Term policies have no cash value and thus, in contrast to permanent life policies, provide insurance only, with no savings aspect.

Beginning in the mid-1970s, life insurance companies began to restructure their business to become managers of assets for pension funds. Now more than half of the assets managed by life insurance companies are for pension funds and not for life insurance. Insurance companies have also begun to sell investment vehicles for retirement such as **annuities**, arrangements whereby the customer pays an annual premium in exchange for a future stream of annual payments beginning at a set age, say 65, and continuing until death.

Property and Casualty Insurance

There are 196 property and casualty (P&C) or "general" insurance companies in Canada (see Table 12-1), and about 40% of the industry, measured by assets held, is foreign-controlled. Most property and casualty insurance companies in Canada are federally registered and subject to regulation by OSFI and the Property and Casualty Insurance Compensation Corporation (PACICC). PACICC was set up in 1988 and performs the same role for property and casualty companies as Assuris does for life insurance companies. Some lines of P&C insurance, for example auto insurance, are also subject to provincial laws and regulations.

Property insurance covers losses of real property and casualty insurance protects against legal liability exposures. Although property and casualty insurance companies have seen a slight increase in their share of total financial intermediary assets since 1960, in recent years they have not fared well, and insurance rates have skyrocketed. With the high interest rates in the 1970s, insurance companies had high investment income that enabled them to keep insurance rates low. Since then, however, investment income has fallen with the decline in interest rates, while the growth in lawsuits involving property and casualty insurance and the explosion in amounts awarded in such cases have produced substantial losses for companies.

To return to profitability, insurance companies have raised their rates dramatically—sometimes doubling or even tripling premiums—and have refused to provide coverage for some people. They have also campaigned actively for limits on insurance payouts, particularly for medical malpractice. In the search for profits, insurance companies are also branching out into uncharted territory by insuring the payment of interest on corporate bonds and mortgage-backed securities. One worry is that the insurance companies may be taking on excessive risk in order to boost their profits. One result of the concern about the health of the property and casualty insurance industry is that insurance regulators have proposed new rules that would impose capital requirements on these companies based on the riskiness of their assets and operations.

The investment policies of these companies are affected by the fact that property losses are very uncertain. In fact, because property losses are more uncertain than the death rate in a population, these insurers are less able to predict how much they will have to pay policyholders than life insurance companies are. Natural disasters such as the ice storm of 1998 and the Calgary hailstorm of 1991 exposed the property and casualty insurance companies to billions of dollars of losses.[1] Therefore, property and casualty insurers hold more liquid assets than life insurers: cash, due and accrued investment income, money market instruments, and receivables amount to over a third of their assets, and most of the remainder is held in bonds, debentures, and stocks. Their largest liability relates to unpaid claims and adjustment expenses, followed by unearned premiums (premiums representing the unexpired part of policies).

Property and casualty insurance companies will insure against losses from almost any type of event, including fire, theft, negligence, malpractice, earthquakes, and automobile accidents. If a possible loss being insured is too large for any one firm, several firms may join together to write a policy in order to share the risk. Insurance companies may also reduce their risk exposure by obtaining **reinsurance**. Reinsurance allocates a portion of the risk to another company in exchange for a portion of the premium and is particularly important for small insurance companies. You can think of reinsurance as insurance for the insurance company. The most famous risk-sharing operation is Lloyd's of London, an association in which different insurance companies can underwrite a fraction of an insurance policy. Lloyd's of London has claimed that it will insure against any contingency—for a price.

Credit Insurance

In recent years, insurance companies have also entered into the business of supplying credit insurance. There are two ways they have done this.

CREDIT DEFAULT SWAPS One way insurance companies can in effect provide credit insurance is by selling a traded derivative called a **credit default swap (CDS)** in which the seller is required to make a payment to the holder of the CDS if there is a *credit event* for that instrument such as a bankruptcy or downgrading of the firm's credit rating. (Credit derivatives are discussed more extensively in Chapter 14.) Issuing a CDS is thus tantamount to providing insurance on the debt instrument because, just like insurance, it makes a payment to the holder of the CDS when there is a negative credit event. Major insurance companies have entered the CDS market in recent years, sometimes to their great regret (see the FYI box, The AIG Blowup).

MONOLINE INSURANCE Another way of providing credit insurance is to supply it directly, just as with any insurance policy. However, insurance regulations do not allow property/casualty insurance companies, life insurance companies, or insurance companies with multiple lines of business to underwrite credit insurance. **Monoline insurance companies**, which specialize in credit insurance

---

[1] For example, the freezing rains of January 1998 triggered about 840 000 insurance claims. As a result, Canadian P&C insurers paid out over $1.44 billion. Similar disasters in the United States, such as the Los Angeles earthquake in 1994, Hurricane Katrina, which devasted New Orleans in 2005, Hurricane Ike, which devastated Galveston in 2008, and the September 11, 2001 destruction of the World Trade Center, exposed the U.S. property and casualty insurance companies to billions of dollars of losses.

FYI   The AIG Blowup

American International Group, better known as AIG, was a trillion-dollar insurance giant and before 2008 was one of the twenty largest companies in the world. A small separate unit, AIG's Financial Products division, went into the credit default swap business in a big way, insuring over US$400 billion of securities, of which US$57 billion were debt securities backed by subprime mortgages. Lehman Brothers' troubles and eventual bankruptcy on September 15, 2008, revealed that subprime securities were worth much less than they were being valued at and investors came to the realization that AIG's losses, which had already been substantial in the first half of the year, could bankrupt the company. Lenders to AIG then pulled back with a vengeance, and AIG could not raise enough capital to stay afloat.

On September 16, the Federal Reserve and the U.S. Treasury decided to rescue AIG because its failure was deemed potentially catastrophic for the financial system. Banks

and mutual funds were large holders of AIG's debt, plus the bankruptcy of AIG would have rendered all the credit default swaps it had sold worthless, thereby imposing huge losses on financial institutions that had bought them. The Federal Reserve set up an US$85 billion credit facility (with the total loan from the Fed and the government increased to US$173 billion) to provide liquidity to AIG. The rescue did not come cheap, however: AIG was charged a very high interest rate on the loans from the Fed and the government was given the rights to an 80% stake in the company if it survived. Maurice Greenberg, the former CEO of the company, described the government's actions as a "nationalization" of AIG.

Insurance companies have never been viewed as posing a risk to the financial system as a whole. Because the problems at AIG nearly brought down the U.S. financial system, this view is no longer tenable. The insurance industry will never be the same.

---

alone, are therefore the only insurance companies that are allowed to provide insurance that guarantees the timely repayment of bond principal and interest when a debt issuer defaults. These insurance companies have become particularly important in the municipal bond market, where they insure a large percentage of these securities. When a municipal security with a lower credit rating, say an A rating, has an insurance policy from a monoline insurer, it takes on the credit rating of the monoline insurer, say AAA. This lowers the interest cost for the municipality and so makes it worthwhile for the municipality to pay premiums for this insurance policy. Of course, to do this, the monoline insurers need to have a very high credit rating.

The New Legislative Framework

As noted in Chapter 11, in 2001 the government passed legislation reforming the regulatory framework governing Canada's financial services sector. The new legislation allows demutualized life and health insurance companies to restructure under a holding company structure, to enter into joint ventures and strategic alliances, and to access the Canadian payments and clearance systems, in an attempt to bring the sector in line with the banking sector. However, the new legislation does not allow mergers involving large banks and large demutualized life and health insurance companies. Moreover, the new legislation requires that large life and health insurance companies (those with equity over $5 billion) be widely held, in the sense that an individual or firm cannot own more than 20% of the voting shares. Small demutualized companies (those with equity under $1 billion) are eligible to be closely held.

APPLICATION	**Insurance Management**

Insurance, like banking, is the financial intermediation business of transforming one type of asset into another for the public. Insurance providers use the premiums paid on policies to invest in assets such as bonds, stocks, mortgages, and other loans; the earnings from these assets are then used to pay out claims on the policies. In effect, insurers transform assets such as bonds, stocks, and loans into insurance policies that provide a set of services (for example, claim adjustments, savings plans, friendly insurance agents). If the insurer's production process of asset transformation efficiently provides its customers with adequate insurance services at low cost and if it can earn high returns on its investments, it will make profits; if not, it will suffer losses.

The economic concepts of adverse selection and moral hazard discussed in Chapter 8 also apply to the lending activities of insurers. Here we apply the adverse selection and moral hazard concepts to explain many management practices specific to insurance.

In the case of an insurance policy, moral hazard arises when the existence of insurance encourages the insured party to take risks that increase the likelihood of an insurance payoff. For example, a person covered by burglary insurance might not take as many precautions to prevent a burglary because the insurance company will reimburse most of the losses if a theft occurs. Adverse selection holds that the people most likely to receive large insurance payoffs are the ones who will want to purchase insurance the most. For example, a person suffering from a terminal disease would want to take out the biggest life and medical insurance policies possible, thereby exposing the insurance company to potentially large losses. Both adverse selection and moral hazard can result in large losses to insurance companies because they lead to higher payouts on insurance claims. Lowering adverse selection and moral hazard to reduce these payouts is therefore an extremely important goal for insurance companies, and this goal explains the insurance practices we will discuss here.

Information Collection and Screening

To reduce adverse selection, insurance providers try to screen out good insurance risks from poor ones. Effective information collection procedures are therefore an important principle of insurance management.

When you apply for auto insurance, the first thing your insurance agent does is ask you questions about your driving record (number of speeding tickets and accidents), the type of car you are insuring, and certain personal matters (age, marital status). If you are applying for life insurance, you go through a similar grilling, but you are asked even more personal questions about such things as your health, smoking habits, and drug and alcohol use. The life insurer even orders a medical evaluation (usually done by an independent company) that involves taking blood and urine samples. Just as a bank calculates a credit score to evaluate a potential borrower, the insurer uses the information you provide to allocate you to a risk class—a statistical estimate of how likely you are to have an insurance claim.

Based on this information, the insurer can decide whether to accept you for the insurance or to turn you down because you pose too high a risk and thus would be an unprofitable customer.

Risk-Based Premiums

Charging insurance premiums on the basis of how much risk a policyholder poses for the insurance provider is a time-honoured principle of insurance management. Adverse selection explains why this principle is so important to insurance company profitability.

To understand why an insurance provider finds it necessary to have risk-based premiums, let's examine an example of risk-based insurance premiums that at first glance seems unfair. Harry and Sally, both college students with no accidents or speeding tickets, apply for auto insurance. Normally, Harry will be charged a much higher premium than Sally. Insurance companies do this because young males have a much higher accident rate than young females. Suppose, though, that one insurer did not base its premiums on a risk classification but rather just charged a premium based on the average combined risk for males and females. Then Sally would be charged too much and Harry too little. Sally could go to another insurer and get a lower rate, while Harry would sign up for the insurance. Because Harry's premium isn't high enough to cover the accidents he is likely to have, on average the insurer would lose money on Harry. Only with a premium based on a risk classification, so that Harry is charged more, can the insurance company make a profit.[2]

Restrictive Provisions

Restrictive provisions in policies are an insurance management tool for reducing moral hazard. Such provisions discourage policyholders from engaging in risky activities that make an insurance claim more likely. For example, life insurers have provisions in their policies that eliminate death benefits if the insured person commits suicide within the first two years that the policy is in effect. Restrictive provisions may also require certain behaviour on the part of the insured. A company renting motor scooters may be required to provide helmets for renters in order to be covered for any liability associated with the rental. The role of restrictive provisions is not unlike that of restrictive covenants on debt contracts described in Chapter 8. Both serve to reduce moral hazard by ruling out undesirable behaviour.

Prevention of Fraud

Insurance providers also face moral hazard because an insured person has an incentive to lie to the insurer and seek a claim even if the claim is not valid. For example, a person who has not complied with the restrictive provisions of an insurance contract may still submit a claim. Even worse, a person may file claims for events that did not actually occur. Thus an important management principle for insurance providers is conducting investigations to prevent fraud so that only policyholders with valid claims receive compensation.

Cancellation of Insurance

Being prepared to cancel policies is another insurance management tool. Insurers can discourage moral hazard by threatening to cancel a policy when the insured person engages in activities that make a claim more likely. If your auto insurance company makes it clear that coverage will be cancelled if a driver gets too many speeding tickets, you will be less likely to speed.

---

[2] Note that the example here is in fact the lemons problem described in Chapter 8.

Deductibles

The **deductible** is the fixed amount by which the insured's loss is reduced when a claim is paid off. A $250 deductible on an auto policy, for example, means that if you suffer a loss of $1000 because of an accident, the insurer will pay you only $750. Deductibles are an additional management tool that helps insurance companies reduce moral hazard. With a deductible, you experience a loss along with the insurer when you make a claim. Because you also stand to lose when you have an accident, you have an incentive to drive more carefully. A deductible thus makes a policyholder act more in line with what is profitable for the insurer; moral hazard has been reduced. And because moral hazard has been reduced, the insurance provider can lower the premium by more than enough to compensate the policyholder for the existence of the deductible. Another function of the deductible is to eliminate the administrative costs of handling small claims by forcing the insured to bear these losses.

Coinsurance

When a policyholder shares a percentage of the losses along with the insurer, their arrangement is called coinsurance. For example, some medical insurance plans provide coverage for 80% of medical bills, and the insured person pays 20% after a certain deductible has been met. Coinsurance works to reduce moral hazard in exactly the same way that a deductible does. A policyholder who suffers a loss along with the insurer has less incentive to take actions, such as going to a specialist unnecessarily, that involve higher claims. Coinsurance is thus another useful management tool for insurance providers.

Limits on the Amount of Insurance

Another important principle of insurance management is that there should be limits on the amount of insurance provided, even though a customer is willing to pay for more coverage. The higher the insurance coverage, the more the insured person can gain from risky activities that make an insurance payoff more likely and hence the greater the moral hazard. For example, if Zelda's car were insured for more than its true value, she might not take proper precautions to prevent its theft, such as making sure that the key is always removed or putting in an alarm system. If it were stolen, she would come out ahead because the excessive insurance payment would allow her to buy an even better car. By contrast, when the insurance payments are lower than the value of her car, she will suffer a loss if it is stolen and will thus take precautions to prevent this from happening. Insurance providers must always make sure that their coverage is not so high that moral hazard leads to large losses.

Summary

Effective insurance management requires several practices: information collection and screening of potential policyholders, risk-based premiums, restrictive provisions, prevention of fraud, cancellation of insurance, deductibles, coinsurance, and limits on the amount of insurance. All of these practices reduce moral hazard and adverse selection by making it harder for policyholders to benefit from engaging in activities that increase the amount and likelihood of claims. With smaller benefits available, the poor insurance risks (those who are more likely to engage in the activities in the first place) see less benefit from the insurance and are thus less likely to seek it out.

PENSION FUNDS

In performing the financial intermediation function of asset transformation, pension funds provide the public with another kind of protection: income payments on retirement. Employers, unions, or private individuals can set up pension plans, which acquire funds through contributions paid in by the plan's participants or their employees. Pension plans have grown in importance in recent years, with their share of total financial intermediary assets rising significantly. Federal tax policy has been a major factor behind the rapid growth of pension funds because employer contributions to employee pension plans are tax-deductible. Furthermore, tax policy has also encouraged employee contributions to pension funds by making them tax-deductible as well and enabling self-employed individuals to open up their own tax-sheltered pension plans.

Because the benefits paid out of the pension fund each year are highly predictable, pension funds invest in long-term securities, with the bulk of their asset holdings in bonds, stocks, and long-term mortgages. The key management issues for pension funds revolve around asset management. Pension fund managers try to hold assets with high expected returns and to lower risk through diversification. The investment strategies of pension plans have changed radically over time. In the aftermath of World War II, most pension fund assets were held in government bonds. However, the strong performance of stocks in the 1950s and 1960s afforded pension plans higher returns, causing them to shift their portfolios into stocks, currently on the order of over 50% of their assets. As a result, pension plans now have a much stronger presence in the stock market.

Although the purpose of all pension plans is the same, they can differ in a number of attributes. First is the method by which payments are made: if the benefits are determined by the contributions into the plan and their earnings, the pension is a **defined-contribution plan**; if future income payments (benefits) are set in advance (usually based on the highest average salary and the number of years of pensionable service), the pension is a **defined-benefit plan**. In the case of a defined-benefit plan, a further attribute is related to how the plan is funded. A defined-benefit plan is **fully funded** if the contributions into the plan and their earnings over the years are sufficient to pay out the defined benefits when they come due. If the contributions and earnings are not sufficient, the plan is **underfunded**. For example, if Jane Brown contributes $100 per year into her pension plan (at the beginning of each year) and the interest rate is 10%, after ten years the contributions and their earnings would be worth $1753.[3] If the defined benefit on her pension plan pays her $1753 or less after ten years, the plan is fully funded because her contributions and earnings will fully pay for this payment. But if the defined benefit is $2000, the plan is underfunded because her contributions and earnings do not cover this amount.

A second characteristic of pension plans is their *vesting*, the length of time that a person must be enrolled in the pension plan (by being a member of a union or an employee of a company) before being entitled to receive benefits. Typically,

---

[3] The $100 contributed in year 1 would be worth $100 \times (1 + 0.10)^{10} = \$259.37$ at the end of ten years; the $100 contributed in year 2 would be worth $100 \times (1 + 0.10)^9 = \$235.79$; and so on until the $100 contributed in year 10 would be worth $100 \times (1 + 0.10) = \$110$. Adding these together, we get the total value of these contributions and their earnings at the end of ten years:

$$\$259.37 + \$235.79 + \$214.36 + \$194.87 + \$177.16$$
$$+ \$161.05 + \$146.41 + \$133.10 + \$121.00 + \$110.00 = \$1753.11$$

firms require that an employee work two years for the company before being vested and qualifying to receive pension benefits; if the employee leaves the firm before the two years are up, either by quitting or being fired, all rights to benefits are lost.

Registered Pension Plans (RPPs)

Registered pension plans (RPPs) are voluntary, employer-sponsored plans, with the contributions usually shared between employer and employee. They are also referred to as **private pension plans** to differentiate them from the public Canada and Quebec Pension Plans. Private pension plans are registered with the federal or a provincial pension regulatory authority as well as with the Canada Revenue Agency (CRA) for tax purposes.

Trusteed pension plans account for the majority of registered pension plans in Canada. Typically, a pension plan sponsor (such as a government or private-sector employer) will hire a bank, a life insurance company, or a pension fund manager to manage the fund, for the benefit of the plan members. The largest trusteed pension funds in Canada are the Ontario Teachers' Pension Plan Board and the Ontario Municipal Employees' Retirement Board. Among the largest pension fund managers are the *Caisse de dépôt et placement du Québec* and Royal Trust, a subsidiary of the Royal Bank.

Many private pension plans are underfunded because they plan to meet their pension obligations out of current earnings when the benefits come due. As long as companies have sufficient earnings, underfunding creates no problems, but if not, they may not be able to meet their pension obligations. Because of potential problems caused by corporate underfunding, mismanagement, fraudulent practices, and other abuses of private pension funds, these funds are heavily regulated. As with insurance companies, the regulatory system governing pension funds is split between OSFI and provincial superintendents of pensions. Pension funds administered for people working in businesses that are federal in scope (for example, railways, air transport, telecommunications, and banking) are the responsibility of OSFI. However, most trusteed pension funds are registered under provincial acts. These acts and regulations tend to be similar across provinces. They establish minimum standards for the reporting and disclosure of information, set rules for vesting and the degree of underfunding, and place restrictions on investment practices.

Social Security and Public Pension Plans

The most important government-administered pension plan is the Old Age Security (OAS) program, which also includes the Guaranteed Income Supplement (GIS) and Spouse's Allowance (SPA) programs. The OAS guarantees a minimum income to all Canadians aged 65 and over and in some cases also pays income to persons before age 65. In particular, it makes monthly flat payments (out of federal government revenues) to retired or disabled workers or their surviving spouses.

Other government-administered pension plans are the Canada Pension Plan (CPP) and in Quebec the Quebec Pension Plan (QPP), both intended for persons who hold a job. They are supported by contributions from employees and their employers and cover almost all workers in Canada (the participation of workers aged 18 and over is compulsory). The accumulated funds of the CPP are managed by an investment board, called the CPP Investment Board, and those of the QPP are managed by the *Caisse de dépôt et placement du Québec*.

When the government pension plans were established, the federal government intended to operate them like private pension plans. However, unlike private pension plans, benefits are typically paid out from current contributions, not tied closely to a participant's past contributions. This "pay-as-you-go" system led to a massive underfunding. The problems of the public pension plans could become worse in the future because of the growth in the number of retired people relative to the working population. The government has been grappling with the problems of the public pension plans for years, but the prospect of a huge bulge of new retirees has resulted in calls for radical surgery (see the FYI box, Should Public Pension Plans Be Privatized?). In 1999, for example, the CPP was given authority to sharply increase contribution rates from 5.6% in 1999 to 9.9% in 2003. It was also given the authority to invest its accumulated assets in the market in order to earn a higher return so that future increases in contribution levels will not be needed.

FYI Should Public Pension Plans Be Privatized?

In recent years, public confidence in the public pension plans has reached a new low. Some surveys suggest that young people have more confidence in the existence of flying saucers than they do in the government's promise to pay them their public pension plan benefits. Without some overhaul of the system, public pension plans will not be able to meet their future obligations. The government has set up advisory commissions and has been holding hearings to address this problem.

Currently, the assets of the public pension plans, which reside in trust funds, are all invested in government securities. Because stocks and corporate bonds have higher returns than government securities, many proposals to save the public pension plans suggest investing part of the trust fund in corporate securities and thus partially privatizing the systems.

Suggestions for privatization take three basic forms:

1. *Government investment of trust fund assets in corporate securities.* This plan has the advantage of possibly improving the trust funds' overall return, while minimizing transaction costs because it exploits the economies of scale of the trust funds. Critics warn that government ownership of private assets could lead to increased government intervention in the private sector.

2. *Shift of trust fund assets to individual accounts that can be invested in private assets.* This option has the advantage of possibly increasing the return on investments and does not involve the government in the ownership of private assets. However, critics warn that it might expose individuals to greater risk and to transaction costs on individual accounts that might be very high because of the small size of many of these accounts.

3. *Individual accounts in addition to those in the trust funds.* This option has advantages and disadvantages similar to those of option 2 and may provide more funds to individuals at retirement. However, some increase in contributions would be required to fund these accounts.

Whether some privatization of the public pension plans occurs is an open question. In the short term public pension plan reform is likely to involve an increase in contributions, a reduction in benefits, or both. For example, under the 1997 changes to the CPP Act, the percentage of liabilities of CPP that are funded is expected to increase from the current 8% to 20% by 2018.

Provincial and local governments and the federal government, like private employers, have also set up pension plans for their employees. These plans are almost identical in operation to private pension plans and hold similar assets. Underfunding of the plans is also prevalent, and some investors in municipal bonds worry that it may lead to future difficulties in the ability of provincial and local governments to meet their debt obligations.

Personal Pension Plans

An alternative to both public pension plans and private pension plans is **personal pension plans**. These are the Registered Retirement Savings Plans (RRSPs) that Canadians set up with financial institutions. They provide tax-sheltered, self-financed retirement funds. Upon retirement, an RRSP must be converted into an annuity or a Registered Retirement Income Fund (RRIF), which provides taxable annuity payments. Since RRIFs are less popular than annuities, which may only be offered by insurance companies, the insurance industry has benefited from the introduction of the RRSP.

FINANCE COMPANIES

Finance companies are non–deposit-taking financial institutions that acquire funds by issuing commercial paper or stocks and bonds or borrowing from banks, and that use the proceeds to make loans (often for small amounts) that are particularly well suited to consumer and business needs. The financial intermediation process of finance companies can be described by saying that they borrow in large amounts but often lend in small amounts—a process quite different from that of banking institutions, which collect deposits in small amounts and then often make large loans. Renamed in 1998, finance companies became known as *non-depository credit intermediaries*, under the industry classification system.

A key feature of finance companies is that although they lend to many of the same customers that borrow from banks, they are virtually unregulated compared to chartered banks and near banks. Provinces regulate the maximum amount they can loan to individual consumers and the terms of the debt contract, but there are no restrictions on branching, the assets they hold, or how they raise their funds. The lack of restrictions enables finance companies to tailor their loans to customer needs better than banking institutions can.

There are three types of finance companies: sales, consumer, and business.

1. *Sales finance companies* are owned by a particular retailing or manufacturing company and make loans to consumers to purchase items from that company. Sears Roebuck Acceptance Corporation, for example, finances consumer purchases of all goods and services at Sears stores, and General Motors Acceptance Corporation finances purchases of GM cars. Sales finance companies compete directly with banks for consumer loans and are used by consumers because loans can frequently be obtained faster and more conveniently at the location where an item is purchased.

2. *Consumer finance companies* make loans to consumers to buy particular items such as furniture or home appliances, to make home improvements, or to help refinance small debts. Consumer finance companies are separate corporations or are owned by banks. Typically, these companies charge higher interest rates and make loans to consumers who cannot obtain credit from other sources.

3. *Business finance companies* provide specialized forms of credit to businesses by making loans and purchasing accounts receivable (bills owed to the firm) at a discount; this provision of credit is called *factoring*. For example, a

dressmaking firm might have outstanding bills (accounts receivable) of $100 000 owed by the retail stores that have bought its dresses. If this firm needs cash to buy 100 new sewing machines, it can sell its accounts receivable for, say, $90 000 to a finance company, which is now entitled to collect the $100 000 owed to the firm. Besides factoring, business finance companies also specialize in leasing equipment (such as railroad cars, jet planes, and computers), which they purchase and then lease to businesses for a set number of years.

SECURITIES MARKET OPERATIONS

The smooth functioning of securities markets, in which bonds and stocks are traded, involves several financial institutions, including securities brokers and dealers, investment banks, and organized exchanges. None of these institutions were included in our list of financial intermediaries in Chapter 2 because they do not perform the intermediation function of acquiring funds by issuing liabilities and then using the funds to acquire financial assets. Nonetheless, they are important in the process of channelling funds from savers to spenders and can be thought of as "financial facilitators."

First, however, we must recall the distinction between primary and secondary securities markets discussed in Chapter 2. In a primary market, new issues of a security are sold to buyers by the corporation or government agency borrowing the funds. A secondary market then trades the securities that have been sold in the primary market (and so are secondhand). *Investment banks* (also called *investment dealers*) assist in the initial sale of securities in the primary market; *securities brokers* and *dealers* assist in the trading of securities in the secondary markets, some of which are organized into exchanges.

Investment Banking

When a corporation wishes to borrow (raise) funds, it normally hires the services of an investment banker to help sell its securities. Despite its name, an investment banker is not a banker in the ordinary sense; that is, it is not engaged in financial intermediation that takes in deposits and then lends them out. Some of the well-known Canadian investment banking firms are ScotiaMcLeod, RBC Dominion Securities, and BMO Nesbitt Burns.

Investment bankers assist in the sale of securities as follows. First, they advise the corporation on whether it should issue bonds or stock. If they suggest that the corporation issue bonds, investment bankers give advice on what the maturity and interest payments on the bonds should be. If they suggest that the corporation should sell stock, they give advice on what the price should be. This is fairly easy to do if the firm has prior issues currently selling in the market, called **seasoned issues**. However, when a firm issues stock for the first time in what is called an initial public offering (IPO), it is more difficult to determine what the correct price should be. All the skills and expertise of the investment-banking firm then need to be brought to bear to determine the most appropriate price. IPOs have become very important in the Canadian economy because they are a major source of financing for Internet companies, which became all the rage on Bay Street in the late 1990s. Not only have IPOs helped these companies to acquire capital to substantially expand their operations, but they have also made the original owners of these firms very rich. Many a nerdy 20- to 30-year-old became an instant millionaire when his stake in his Internet company was given a high valuation after the initial public offering of shares in the company. However, with the bursting of the tech bubble in 2000, many of them lost much of their wealth when the value of their shares came tumbling down to earth.

When the corporation decides which kind of financial instrument it will issue, it offers them to **underwriters**—investment bankers that guarantee the corporation a price on the securities and then sell them to the public. If the issue is small, only one investment-banking firm underwrites it (usually the original investment banking firm hired to provide advice on the issue). If the issue is large, several investment-banking firms form a syndicate to underwrite the issue jointly, thus limiting the risk that any one investment bank must take. The underwriters sell the securities to the general public by contacting potential buyers, such as banks and insurance companies, directly and by placing advertisements in newspapers like the *National Post* and the *Globe and Mail.*

The activities of investment bankers and the operation of primary markets are heavily regulated by the provinces and the federal government. The Ontario Securities Commission (OSC), for example, is responsible for administering the Ontario Securities Act, Canada's first provincial securities act passed in 1945. Other provinces and territories have generally tended to follow Ontario's lead and passed Securities Acts regulating investment banking and the trading of securities. Canada doesn't have a Securities Act, but portions of the Criminal Code of Canada specifically apply to securities trading.

Securities Brokers and Dealers

Securities brokers and dealers conduct trading in secondary markets. Brokers are pure intermediaries who act as agents for investors in the purchase or sale of securities. Their function is to match buyers with sellers, a function for which they are paid brokerage commissions. In contrast to brokers, dealers link buyers and sellers by standing ready to buy and sell securities at given prices. Therefore, dealers hold inventories of securities and make their living by selling these securities for a slightly higher price than they paid for them—that is, on the "spread" between the asked price and the bid price. This can be a high-risk business because dealers hold securities that can rise or fall in price; in recent years, several firms specializing in bonds have collapsed. Brokers, by contrast, are not as exposed to risk because they do not own the securities involved in their business dealings.

Brokerage firms engage in all three securities market activities, acting as brokers, dealers, and investment bankers. That is, the same investment banks that handle the sale of securities in the primary markets also are involved in the retail business of trading for clients on the stock exchanges. However, the provinces and the federal government regulate the investment banking operation of the firms and also restrict brokers and dealers from misrepresenting securities and from trading on *insider information*, nonpublic information known only to the management of a corporation.

Organized Exchanges

As discussed in Chapter 2, secondary markets can be organized either as over-the-counter markets, in which trades are conducted using dealers, or as organized exchanges, in which trades are conducted in one central location. The largest of the organized stock exchanges in Canada is the Toronto Stock Exchange. It was established on October 25, 1861 as a nonprofit organization, and now boasts the fourth most active stock exchange in North America, after the New York Stock Exchange (NYSE), the American Stock Exchange (AMEX), and NASDAQ.

Before 1999, the Canadian capital markets landscape consisted of the Toronto Stock Exchange and small regional exchanges in Vancouver, Calgary, and Montreal. In 1999, however, the Calgary and Vancouver exchanges consolidated to form the Canadian Dealing Network Exchange (CDNX), which dealt with emerging companies and the venture capital market. The Montréal Exchange (ME) was left to provide for the derivatives market, and the Toronto Stock Exchange was the singular market left for senior stocks.

The Toronto Stock Exchange has undergone many significant changes in the last decade. It ditched the original initials TSE in favour of TSX, mainly in order to eliminate confusion with the Tokyo Stock Exchange. On May 1, 2001 the TSX bought the CDNX, forming the new joint venture called the TMX Group of Companies. The TMX Group of Companies encompasses the Toronto Stock Exchange, the TSX Venture Exchange, and its own regulatory arm, TSX Market Regulation Services.

Organized stock exchanges actually function as a hybrid of an auction market (in which buyers and sellers trade with each other in a central location) and a dealer market (in which dealers make the market by buying and selling securities at given prices). Securities are traded on the floor of the exchange with the help of a special kind of dealer-broker called a **specialist**. A specialist matches buy and sell orders submitted at the same price and so performs a brokerage function. However, if buy and sell orders do not match up, the specialist buys stocks or sells from a personal inventory of securities, in this manner performing a dealer function. By assuming both functions, the specialist maintains orderly trading of the securities for which he or she is responsible.

Organized exchanges are also heavily regulated. In particular, government regulatory bodies, such as the Ontario Securities Commission, impose regulations that govern the behaviour of brokers and dealers involved with exchanges. Furthermore, recent advances in computers and telecommunications, which reduce the costs of linking these markets, have encouraged the expansion of a national market system. We thus see that legislation and modern computing technology are leading the way to a more-competitive securities industry. Another development is the growing importance of the Internet in securities markets.

The growing internationalization of capital markets has encouraged another trend in securities trading. Increasingly, Canadian companies are being listed on U.S. stock exchanges, and the markets are moving toward trading stocks internationally, 24 hours a day.

MUTUAL FUNDS

Mutual funds are financial intermediaries that pool the resources of many small investors by selling them shares and using the proceeds to buy securities. Through the asset transformation process of issuing shares in small denominations and buying large blocks of securities, mutual funds can take advantage of volume discounts on brokerage commissions and purchase diversified holdings (portfolios) of securities. Mutual funds allow the small investor to obtain the benefits of lower transaction costs in purchasing securities and to take advantage of the reduction of risk by diversifying the portfolio of securities held. Many mutual funds are run by brokerage firms, but others are run by banks or independent investment advisers such as Fidelity or Investors Group.

Mutual funds have seen a large increase in their market share since 1980, due primarily to the booming stock market during the 1990s. Another source of growth has been mutual funds that specialize in debt instruments, which first appeared in the 1970s. Before 1970, mutual funds invested almost solely in common stocks. Funds that purchase common stocks may specialize even further and invest solely in foreign securities or in specialized industries, such as energy or high technology. Funds that purchase debt instruments may specialize further in corporate, government, or municipal bonds or in long-term or short-term securities.

Mutual funds are held by households, financial institutions, and nonfinancial businesses. Mutual funds have become increasingly important in household savings. By the beginning of 2007, mutual funds made up over $750 billion, or about 30% of Canadians' financial wealth. Today, close to 50% of Canadian households hold mutual fund shares. The age group with the greatest participation in mutual fund ownership includes individuals between 50 and 70, which makes sense because they are the most interested in saving for retirement. Interestingly, 18 to 30 is the second most active age group in mutual fund ownership, suggesting that they have a greater tolerance for investment risk than those who are somewhat older.

The growing importance of mutual funds and pension funds, so-called **institutional investors**, has resulted in their controlling a large share of total financial sector assets. They are also the predominant players in the stock markets, with over 70% of the total daily volume in the stock market due to their trading. Increased ownership of stocks has also meant that institutional investors have more clout with corporate boards, often forcing changes in leadership or in corporate policies. Particularly controversial in recent years has been a type of institutional investor called **sovereign wealth funds**, state-owned investment funds that invest in foreign assets (see the FYI box, Sovereign Wealth Funds: Are They a Danger?).

Mutual funds are structured in two ways. The more common structure is an **open-end fund**, from which shares can be redeemed at any time at a price that is tied to the asset value of the fund. Mutual funds also can be structured as **closed-end funds**, in which a fixed number of nonredeemable shares are sold at an initial offering and are then traded like a common stock. The market price of these shares fluctuates with the value of the assets held by the fund. In contrast to the open-end fund, however, the price of the shares may be above or below the value of the assets held by the fund, depending on factors such as the liquidity of the shares or the quality of the management. The greater popularity of the open-end funds is explained by the greater liquidity of their redeemable shares relative to that of the nonredeemable shares of closed-end funds.

Originally, shares of most open-end mutual funds were sold by salespeople (usually brokers) who were paid a commission. Since this commission is paid at the time of purchase and is immediately subtracted from the redemption value of the shares, these funds are called **load funds**. Most mutual funds are currently **no-load funds**; they are sold directly to the public with no sales commissions. In both types of funds, the managers earn their living from management fees paid by the shareholders. These fees amount to approximately 0.5% of the asset value of the fund per year.

Mutual funds are regulated by a variety of agencies. As securities distributed by investment dealers and financial advisers, they fall within provincial jurisdiction. As services provided by financial institutions, they fall under the Bank Act, Trust and Loan Companies Act, Insurance Companies Act, etc., and are the responsibility of OSFI. Regulations require periodic disclosure of information on these funds to the public and restrictions on the methods of soliciting business.

FYI   Sovereign Wealth Funds: Are They a Danger?

Sovereign wealth funds have been around a long time: The first, the Kuwait Investment Authority, was established in 1953. When governments accumulate a substantial amount of foreign exchange earnings, as has happened in oil-rich countries, they often recognize that these earnings would be better put into investments in foreign countries rather than kept at home. The largest sovereign wealth funds are the Abu Dhabi Investment Authority, Government Pension Fund of Norway, Government of Singapore Investment Corporation, Kuwait Investment Authority, China Investment Corporation, the Stabilization Fund of the Russian Federation, and Singapore's Temasek Holdings. Canada's Alberta Heritage Savings Trust Fund, established in 1976, is a small fund with about $20 billion of assets under management. In 2007, there were about 40 sovereign wealth funds with estimated assets under management between $2.5 trillion and $3.5 trillion, representing about 2.5% of global assets.*

Up until recently these funds have been relatively uncontroversial because they were comparatively small and primarily invested in government bonds issued by industrialized countries. In recent years, however, they have grown in size—they now hold over $3 trillion in assets—and, in the search for higher returns, invest in a much broader set of assets. This shift in size and focus has led to serious concerns about them in industrialized countries.

One concern is that as the size of these funds increases, they may play a more important role in asset markets, and since some of them are very large (the Abu Dhabi fund has close to $1 trillion of assets) the decision of one fund to pull out of a particular asset market could cause market instability. Sovereign wealth funds also raise national security issues, because they might use their investments for political purposes. They might buy up strategically important industries or use their clout to get political concessions. This is a particular concern, because the governments of Russia, China, and Arab countries control many of the largest of these funds. A third concern is that many of these funds, with the exception of the Norwegian fund, provide very little information about their operations and the assets in which they invest.

Although sovereign wealth funds do pose some dangers, they are probably overplayed. Xenophobia often plays well in politics, and foreign purchase of domestic assets is often prevented under the banner of national security in order to protect domestic companies from unwanted takeovers. The lack of transparency for some of these large funds is a serious problem, however. This is why organizations like the International Monetary Fund (IMF) and the Organisation for Economic Co-operation and Development (OECD) proposed rules to increase the amount of information these funds disclose to the markets.

*For more details on sovereign wealth funds see Tamara Gomes, "The Impact of Sovereign Wealth Funds on the International Financial System," *Bank of Canada Financial System Review* (June 2008): 41–44.

The industry also has a national association, the Investment Funds Institute of Canada (IFIC). The IFIC, however, has no regulatory role; its main function is to reflect the industry's concerns and to distribute information regarding the industry. The Investment Dealers Association of Canada (IDA), the Mutual Funds Dealers Association of Canada (MFDA), established in 2000, and the stock exchanges are the self-regulatory organizations for the distribution end of the mutual funds industry.

Money Market Mutual Funds

An important addition to the family of mutual funds resulting from the financial innovation process described in earlier chapters is the money market mutual fund. Recall that this type of mutual fund invests in short-term debt (money market) instruments of very high quality, such as treasury bills, commercial paper, and bank certificates of deposit. There is some fluctuation in the market value of these securities, but because their maturity is typically less than six months, the change in the market value is small enough that these funds allow their shares to be redeemed at a fixed value. Changes in the market value of the securities are figured into the interest paid out by the fund.

In the United States, many money market mutual funds allow their shareholders to redeem shares by writing cheques on the funds' account at a commercial bank. In this way, shares in money market mutual funds effectively function as chequable deposits that earn market interest rates on short-term debt securities. For this reason, in the United States the share of money market mutual funds in total financial intermediary assets has increased to nearly 6% and currently money market mutual funds account for around one-quarter of the asset value of all mutual funds.

Hedge Funds

Hedge funds are a special type of investment fund, with estimated assets of more than $1 trillion. Hedge funds have received considerable attention recently due to the shock to the financial system resulting from the near collapse of Long-Term Capital Management, once one of the most important hedge funds (see the FYI box, The Long-Term Capital Management Debacle). Well-known hedge funds in the United States include Moore Capital Management and the Quantum group of funds associated with George Soros. Investors in hedge funds, who are limited partners, give their money to managing (general) partners to invest on their behalf. Several features distinguish hedge funds from mutual funds. Hedge funds have a minimum investment requirement between $100 000 and $20 million, with the typical minimum investment being $1 million. Long-Term Capital Management required a $10 million minimum investment. In the United States, federal law limits hedge funds to have no more than 99 investors (limited partners) who must have steady annual incomes of $200 000 or more or a net worth of $1 million, excluding their homes. These restrictions are aimed at allowing hedge funds to be largely unregulated, on the theory that the rich can look out for themselves. Many of the 4000 U.S. hedge funds are located offshore to escape regulatory restrictions.

Hedge funds also differ from traditional mutual funds in that they usually require that investors commit their money for long periods of time, often several years. The purpose of this requirement is to give managers breathing room to pursue long-run strategies. Hedge funds also typically charge large fees to investors. The typical fund charges a 2% annual fee on the assets it manages plus 20% of profits.

The term *hedge fund* is highly misleading because the word hedge typically is used to indicate strategies to avoid risk. As the near failure of Long-Term Capital illustrates, despite their name, these funds can and do take big risks. Many hedge funds engage in what are called "market-neutral" strategies where they buy a security, such as a bond, that seems cheap and sell an equivalent amount of a similar security that appears to be overvalued. If interest rates as a whole go up or down, the fund is hedged because the decline in value of one security is matched by the rise in value of the other. However, the fund is speculating on whether the spread between the prices on the two securities moves in the direction predicted by the fund managers. If the fund bets wrong, it can lose a lot of

FYI   The Long-Term Capital Management Debacle

Long-Term Capital Management was a hedge fund with a star cast of managers, including twenty-five Ph.D.s, two Nobel Prize winners in economics (Myron Scholes and Robert Merton), a former vice-chairman of the Federal Reserve System (David Mullins), and one of Wall Street's most successful bond traders (John Meriwether). It made headlines in September 1998 because its near-collapse roiled markets and required a private rescue plan organized by the Federal Reserve Bank of New York.

The experience of Long-Term Capital demonstrates that hedge funds are far from risk-free, despite their use of market-neutral strategies. Long-Term Capital got into difficulties when it thought that the high spread between prices on long-term Treasury bonds and long-term corporate bonds was too high, and bet that this "anomaly" would disappear and the spread would narrow. In the wake of the collapse of the Russian financial system in August 1998, investors increased their assessment of the riskiness of corporate securities and the spread between corporates and Treasuries rose rather than narrowed as Long-Term Capital had predicted. The result was that Long-Term Capital took big losses on its positions, eating up much of its equity position.

By mid-September, Long-Term Capital was unable to raise sufficient funds to meet the demands of its creditors. With Long-Term Capital facing the potential need to liquidate its portfolio of $80 billion in securities and more than $1 trillion of notional value in derivatives (discussed in Chapter 14), the Federal Reserve Bank of New York stepped in on September 23 and organized a rescue plan with its creditors. The Fed's rationale for stepping in was that a sudden liquidation of Long-Term Capital's portfolio would create unacceptable systemic risk. Tens of billions of dollars of illiquid securities would be dumped on an already jittery market, causing potentially huge losses to numerous lenders and other institutions. The rescue plan required creditors, banks, and investment banks to supply an additional $3.6 billion of funds to Long-Term Capital in exchange for much tighter management control of funds and a 90% reduction in the managers' equity stake. In the middle of 1999, John Meriwether began to wind down the fund's operations.

Even though no public funds were expended, the Fed's involvement in organizing the rescue of Long-Term Capital was highly controversial. Some critics argue that the Fed intervention increased moral hazard by weakening discipline imposed by the market on fund managers because future Fed interventions of this type would be expected. Others think that the Fed's action was necessary to prevent a major shock to the financial system that could have provoked a financial crisis. The debate on whether the Fed should have intervened is likely to go on for some time.

money, particularly if it has leveraged up its positions, that is, has borrowed heavily against these positions so that its equity stake is small relative to the size of its portfolio. When Long-Term Capital was rescued it had a leverage ratio of 50 to 1, that is, its assets were fifty times larger than its equity, and even before it got into trouble it was leveraged 20 to 1.

In the wake of the near collapse of Long-Term Capital, many U.S. politicians have called for regulation of these funds. However, because these funds operate offshore in places like the Cayman Islands and are outside U.S. jurisdiction, they would be extremely hard to regulate. What U.S. regulators can do is ensure that

U.S. banks and investment banks have clear guidelines on the amount of lending they can provide to hedge funds and require that these institutions get the appropriate amount of disclosure from hedge funds as to the riskiness of their positions.

PRIVATE EQUITY AND VENTURE CAPITAL FUNDS

Another type of investment fund is the **private equity fund**, which makes long-term investments in companies that are not traded in public markets and has a similar structure to hedge funds. In a private equity fund, investors who are limited partners (e.g., high-wealth individuals, pension funds, financial institutions, and university endowments) place their money with the managing (general) partners who make the private equity investments. Private equity funds are of two types. **Venture capital funds** make investments in new startup businesses, often in the technology industry. **Capital buyout funds** instead make investments in established businesses, and in many cases buy publicly traded firms through a so-called **leveraged buyout (LBO)**, in which the publicly traded firm is taken private by buying all of its shares, while financing the purchase by increasing the leverage (debt) of the firm.

Private equity has several advantages over investing in publicly traded companies. First, private companies are not subject to controversial and costly regulations. Second, managers of private companies do not feel under pressure to produce immediate profits, as do those at publicly traded companies, and thus can manage their company with their eyes on longer-term profitability. Third, because private equity funds give managers of these companies larger stakes in the firm than is usually the case in publicly traded corporations, they have greater incentives to work hard to maximize the value of the firm. Fourth, private equity overcomes the free-rider problem that we discussed in Chapter 8. In contrast to publicly traded companies, which have a diverse set of owners who are happy to free-ride off of each other, venture capital and capital buyout funds are able to garner almost all the benefits of monitoring the firm and therefore have incentive to make sure the firm is run properly.

In both venture capital and capital buyout funds, once the startup or the purchased company is successful, the fund earns its returns by either selling the firm to another company or by selling it off to the public through an initial public offering (IPO). The managing partners of private equity funds are well compensated for their activities: Like hedge funds, they typically earn around a 2% fee for management of the equity fund investments and earn 20% of the profits, which is called **carried interest**.

Both venture capital and capital buyout funds have been highly profitable. Venture capital firms have been an especially important driver of economic growth in recent years because they have funded so many successful high-tech firms, including Apple Computer, Cisco Systems, Genentech, Microsoft, and Sun Microsystems.

GOVERNMENT FINANCIAL INTERMEDIATION

The government has become involved in financial intermediation in two basic ways: First, by supplying government guarantees for private loans, and second by setting up government-sponsored enterprises that directly engage in financial intermediation.

Crown Finance Companies

To promote housing and community development, the government has created the Canada Mortgage and Housing Corporation (CMHC) to provide funds to the mortgage market by borrowing from the federal government and also from the private sector by issuing mortgage-backed securities. The CMHC is not a bank; it doesn't take deposits and is not governed by the Bank Act, but as a financial intermediary makes direct loans and investments primarily for social housing.

Agriculture is another area in which government financial intermediation plays an important role. Farm Credit Canada (FCC), headquartered in Regina, was set up as a Crown corporation in 1959 and is the successor of the Canadian Farm Loan Board, which was established in 1927 to help Canadian farmers. It makes direct loans to new and established farmers for any agricultural or farm-related operation, including the purchase of land, equipment, and livestock. It sources its funds from the federal government and from selling its notes to domestic and foreign capital markets.

To stimulate the export of Canadian goods and services, Export Development Canada (EDC) was established in 1969 as the successor to the Export Credits Insurance Corporation, which dated from 1944. The EDC is a Crown corporation wholly owned by the Canadian government. With its head office in Ottawa, the EDC provides loans to Canadian exporters to finance the working capital buildup associated with international trade. It also provides intermediate-term, low-interest-rate loans to foreign concerns for the purchase of Canadian goods, equipment, and services.

To promote and assist in the establishment and development of business enterprises in Canada, in 1995 the government created the Business Development Bank of Canada (BDC), headquartered in Montreal. It is the successor to the Federal Business Development Bank (FBDB), which had been set up in 1975 to succeed the Industrial Development Bank (IDB), which dated from 1944. The BDC issues notes in domestic and foreign financial markets and then uses the proceeds to make loans to small and medium-sized businesses.

Government-Sponsored Enterprises in the United States

The U.S. government has also created a number of government agencies that provide funds, either directly or indirectly, to the mortgage market. Three agencies—the Government National Mortgage Association (GNMA, or "Ginnie Mae"), the Federal National Mortgage Association (FNMA or "Fannie Mae"), and the Federal Home Loan Mortgage Corporation (FHLMC, or "Freddie Mac") provide funds to the U.S. mortgage market by selling bonds and using the proceeds to buy mortgages or mortgage-backed securities. Except for Ginnie Mae, which is a federal agency and thus is an entity of the U.S. government (like CMHC, FCC, EDC, and BDC are in Canada), the other agencies, known as **government-sponsored enterprises (GSEs)**, are federally sponsored agencies that function as private corporations with close ties to the government. Although the U.S. government does not explicitly back the debt of the GSEs, as is the case for government-sponsored Treasury bonds, in practice the federal government in the United States has not allowed a default on their securities.

Unfortunately, the implicit government backing of GSE debt leads to moral hazard problems similar to those that led to financial crises discussed in Chapters 8 and 9. Because the U.S. government in effect guarantees GSE debt, market discipline to limit excessive risk taking by GSEs is quite weak. The GSEs therefore have incentives to take on excessive risk, and this is exactly what they have done in the United States, with the taxpayer left holding the bag. The recent bailout of Fannie Mae and Freddie Mac by the U.S. government involved US$200 billion of government funds (see the FYI box, The Subprime Financial Crisis and the Bailout of Fannie Mae and Freddie Mac).

Because it encouraged excessive risk taking, the peculiar structure of Fannie Mae and Freddie Mac—private companies sponsored by the U.S. government—was an accident waiting to happen. Earlier editions of this textbook, as well as many economists, predicted exactly what came to pass: a government bailout of both companies, with huge potential losses for American taxpayers.

As we learned in Chapter 10, when there is a government safety net for financial institutions, there needs to be appropriate government regulation and supervision to make sure these institutions do not take on excessive risk. Fannie and Freddie were given a federal regulator and supervisor, the Office of Federal Housing Oversight (OFHEO), as a result of legislation in 1992, but this regulator was quite weak with only a limited ability to rein them in. The outcome was not surprising: These GSEs had strong incentives to resist effective regulation and supervision because it would cut into their profits. This is exactly what they did: Fannie and Freddie were legendary for their lobbying machine in the U.S. Congress, and they were not apologetic about it. In 1999, Franklin Raines, at the time Fannie's CEO, said, "We manage our political risk with the same intensity that we manage our credit and interest rate risks."* Between 1998 and 2008, Fannie and Freddie jointly spent over US$170 million on lobbyists, and from 2000 to 2008, they and their employees made over US$14 million of political campaign contributions.

Their lobbying efforts paid off. Attempts to strengthen their regulator, OFHEO, in both the Clinton and Bush administrations came to naught, and remarkably this was even true after major accounting scandals at both firms were revealed in 2003 and 2004, in which they cooked the books to smooth out earnings. It was only in July of 2008, after the cat was let out of the bag and Fannie and Freddie were in serious trouble, that legislation was passed to put into place a stronger regulator, the Federal Housing Finance Agency, to supersede OFHEO.

With a weak regulator and strong incentives to take on risk, Fannie and Freddie grew like crazy, and by 2008 had purchased or were guaranteeing over US$5 trillion in mortgages or mortgage-backed securities. The accounting scandals might have even pushed them to take on more risk. In the 1992 legislation, Fannie and Freddie had been given a mission to promote affordable housing. What better way to do this than to purchase subprime and Alt-A mortgages or mortgage-backed securities (discussed in Chapter 9)? The accounting scandals made this motivation even stronger because they weakened the political support for Fannie and Freddie, giving them even greater incentives to please the U.S. Congress and support affordable housing through the purchase of these assets. By the time the subprime financial crisis hit in force, they had over US$1 trillion of subprime and Alt-A assets on their books. Furthermore, they had extremely low ratios of capital relative to their assets: Indeed their capital ratios were far lower than for other financial institutions like commercial banks.

By 2008, after many subprime mortgages went into default, Fannie and Freddie had booked large losses. Their small capital buffer meant that they had little cushion to withstand these losses, and investors started to pull their money out. With Fannie and Freddie playing such a dominant role in mortgage markets, the U.S. government could not afford to have them go out of business because this would have had a disastrous effect on the availability of mortgage credit, which would have had further devastating effects on the housing market. With bankruptcy imminent, the U.S. Treasury stepped in with a pledge to provide up to US$200 billion of taxpayer money to the companies if

(continued)

needed. This largesse did not come for free. The federal government in effect took over these companies by putting them into conservatorship, requiring that their CEOs step down, and by having their regulator, the Federal Housing Finance Agency, oversee the companies' day-to-day operations. In addition the U.S. government received around US$1 billion of senior preferred stock and the right to purchase 80% of the common stock if the companies recovered. After the bailout, the prices of both companies' common stocks was less than 2% of what they had been worth only a year earlier.

It is not yet clear how much the government bailout of Fannie and Freddie will cost the American taxpayer. The ultimate fate of these two companies is also unclear. The sad saga of Fannie Mae and Freddie Mac illustrates how dangerous it was for the U.S. government to set up GSEs that were exposed to a classic conflict-of-interest problem: They were supposed to serve two masters. As publicly traded corporations, they were expected to maximize profits for their shareholders, but as government agencies, they were obliged to work in the interests of the public. In the end, neither the public nor the shareholders were well served.

*Quoted in Nile Stephen Campbell, "Fannie Mae Officials Try to Assuage Worried Investors," *Real Estate Finance Today*, May 10, 1999.

SUMMARY

1. Insurance providers, which are regulated by the OSFI and the provinces, acquire funds by selling policies that pay out benefits if catastrophic events occur. Property and casualty insurance companies hold more liquid assets than life insurance companies because of greater uncertainty regarding the benefits they will have to pay out. All insurers face moral hazard and adverse selection problems that explain the use of insurance management tools, such as information collection and screening of potential policyholders, risk-based premiums, restrictive provisions, prevention of fraud, cancellation of insurance, deductibles, coinsurance, and limits on the amount of insurance.

2. Pension plans provide income payments to people when they retire after contributing to the plans for many years. Pension funds have experienced very rapid growth as a result of encouragement by federal tax policy and now play an important role in the stock market. Many pension plans are underfunded, which means that in future years they will have to pay out higher benefits than the value of their contributions and earnings. The problem of underfunding is especially acute for public pension plans such as the CPP.

3. Finance companies raise funds by issuing commercial paper and stocks and bonds and use the proceeds to make loans that are particularly suited to consumer and business needs. Virtually unregulated in comparison to chartered banks and near banks, finance companies have been able to tailor their loans to customer needs very quickly and have grown rapidly.

4. Investment bankers assist in the initial sale of securities in primary markets, whereas securities brokers and dealers assist in the trading of securities in the secondary markets, some of which are organized into exchanges. The provinces and the federal government regulate the financial institutions in the securities markets and ensure that adequate information reaches prospective investors.

5. Mutual funds sell shares and use the proceeds to buy securities. Open-end funds issue shares that can be redeemed at any time at a price tied to the asset value of the firm. Closed-end funds issue nonredeemable shares, which are traded like common stock. They are less popular than open-end funds because their shares are not as liquid. Money market mutual funds hold only short-term, high-quality securities, allowing shares to be redeemed at a fixed value.

6. Private equity funds make long-term investments in companies that are not traded publicly and are of two types: venture capital funds, which make investments in startups, and capital buyout funds, which make investments in established companies, often taking publicly traded firms private.

7. To provide credit to residential housing and agriculture, the U.S. government has created a number of government agencies. Particularly important are government-sponsored enterprises (GSEs), which are federally sponsored agencies that function as private corporations with close ties to the government. Because the government provides an implicit guarantee for GSE debt, market discipline to limit excessive risk-taking by GSEs is weak. The resulting moral hazard problem has led to major taxpayer bailouts, especially the recent bailout of Fannie Mae and Freddie Mac, which involved US$200 billion of government funds.

KEY TERMS

annuities, p. 290

brokerage firms, p. 301

carried interest, p. 307

capital buyout fund, p. 307

closed-end fund, p. 303

credit default swap (CDS), p. 291

deductible, p. 295

defined-benefit plan, p. 296

defined-contribution plan, p. 296

demutualization, p. 289

endowment insurance, p. 290

fully funded, p. 296

government-sponsored enterprises (GSE), p. 308

group life insurance, p. 289

hedge fund, p. 305

individual life insurance, p. 289

institutional investors, p. 303

leveraged buyout (LBO), p. 307

load funds, p. 303

monoline insurance companies, p. 291

no-load funds, p. 303

open-end fund, p. 303

permanent life insurance, p. 289

personal pension plans, p. 299

private equity fund, p. 307

private pension plans, p. 297

reinsurance, p. 291

seasoned issue, p. 300

sovereign wealth funds, p. 303

specialist, p. 302

temporary life insurance, p. 290

underfunded, p. 296

underwriters, p. 301

venture capital funds, p. 307

QUESTIONS

You will find the answers to the questions marked with an asterisk in the Textbook Resources section of your MyEconLab.

*1. If death rates were to become less predictable than they are, how would life insurance companies change the types of assets they hold?

2. Why do property and casualty insurance companies have large holdings of liquid assets but life insurance companies do not?

*3. Why are all defined contribution pension plans fully funded?

4. How can favourable tax treatment of pension plans encourage saving?

*5. "In contrast to private pension plans, government pension plans are rarely underfunded." Is this statement true, false, or uncertain? Explain your answer.

6. What explains the widespread use of deductibles in insurance policies?

*7. Why might insurance companies restrict the amount of insurance a policyholder can buy?

8. Why are restrictive provisions a necessary part of insurance policies?

*9. If you needed to take out a loan, why might you first go to your local bank rather than to a finance company?

10. Explain why shares in closed-end mutual funds typically sell for less than the market value of the stocks they hold.

*11. Why might you buy a no-load mutual fund instead of a load fund?

12. Why can a money market mutual fund allow its shareholders to redeem shares at a fixed price but other mutual funds cannot?

*13. Why might government loan guarantees be a high-cost way for the government to subsidize certain activities?

14. If you like to take risks, would you rather be a dealer, a broker, or a specialist? Why?

*15. Is investment banking a good career for someone who is afraid of taking risks? Why or why not?

16. How do hedge funds differ from mutual funds?

*17. How do private equity funds escape the free-rider problem?

18. What are the four advantages of private equity funds?

*19. How have GSEs in the United States exposed taxpayers to large losses?

WEB EXERCISES

1. The Office of the Superintendent of Financial Institutions (OSFI) maintains extensive data on insurers. Go to **www.osfi-bsif.gc.ca** and click on "Life Insurance Companies & Fraternals" and then on "Financial Data—Life Insurance Companies."
   a. Do life insurance companies make more mortgage loans than they invest in bonds and debentures?
   b. Which type of asset has grown most rapidly over the last five years?
   c. Repeat (a) and (b) for property and casualty insurers.

2. OSFI also maintains extensive data on nondepository credit intermediaries (known as finance companies). Go to its website at the address above, locate the data, and answer the following questions.
   a. Do finance companies make more personal loans than business loans?
   b. Do they borrow more from the money market than the bond market?
   c. Which type of asset has grown most rapidly over the last five years?

Be sure to visit the MyEconLab website at **www.myeconlab.com**. This online homework and tutorial system puts you in control of your own learning with study and practice tools directly correlated to this chapter content.

CRISIS AND RESPONSE: CANADIAN BANKS ARE THE WORLD'S BEST

During the subprime financial crisis the value of mortgage-backed securities held by financial institutions plummeted and governments in the United States and Europe worked on full-scale banking bailouts and rescue packages in the trillions of dollars. Canada, however, did not have to bail out any banks, although Canadian banks also had their problems. Their shares fell by almost 50% and some of them experienced huge losses; for example, the CIBC suffered writedowns in excess of $6 billion in 2008 because of significant exposure to the U.S. capital and real estate markets.

One reason Canadian banks have done much better than their U.S. and European counterparts is because Canada's banking regulator, the Office of the Superintendent of Financial Institutions (OSFI), has been more conservative than banking regulators in other countries. As a result, Canadian banks have lower leverage and more conservative lending and acquisition practices. In fact, in the aftermath of the subprime recession, Canada's banking system has been viewed as the soundest in the world, with many countries considering Canadian-style reforms of their financial markets.

Managing banks is not an easy task, and the subprime crisis highlights that it has become even more difficult because of increased complexity in the financial services marketplace. In Chapter 13 we look at the business and process of banking and in Chapter 14 we study financial derivatives and how managers of financial institutions use derivatives to manage different types of risk.

CHAPTER 13

Banking and the Management of Financial Institutions

LEARNING OBJECTIVES

After studying this chapter you should be able to

1. outline a bank's sources and uses of funds
2. specify how banks make profits by accepting deposits and making loans
3. discuss how bank managers manage credit risk and interest-rate risk
4. explain gap analysis and duration analysis
5. illustrate how off-balance-sheet activities affect bank profits

PREVIEW

Because banking plays such a major role in channelling funds to borrowers with productive investment opportunities, this financial activity is important in ensuring that the financial system and the economy run smoothly and efficiently. In Canada and other countries, banks (depository institutions) provide loans to businesses, help us finance our postsecondary educations or the purchase of a new car or home, and provide us with services such as chequing and savings accounts. Managing banks, however, has never been an easy task, and recently it has become even more difficult because of greater complexity and uncertainty in the economic environment. Asset prices and interest rates have become much more volatile, resulting in substantial fluctuations in profits and in the value of assets and liabilities held by financial institutions.

In this chapter, we examine how banking is conducted to earn the highest profits possible, how and why banks make loans, how they acquire funds and manage their assets and liabilities (debts), and how they earn income. We also examine how banks cope with credit risk, the risk arising because borrowers may default on their obligations, and with interest-rate risk, the risk arising from fluctuations in interest rates.

Although we focus on commercial banking, because this is the most important financial intermediary activity, many of the same principles are applicable to other types of financial intermediation.

THE BANK BALANCE SHEET

To understand how banking works, we start by looking at the bank **balance sheet**, a list of the bank's assets and liabilities. As the name implies, this list balances; that is, it has the characteristic that

$$\text{Total assets} = \text{total liabilities} + \text{capital}$$

A bank's balance sheet is also a list of its *sources* of bank funds (liabilities) and *uses* to which the funds are put (assets). Banks obtain funds by borrowing and by issuing other liabilities such as deposits. They then use these funds to acquire assets such as securities and loans. Banks make profits by earning an interest rate on their holdings of securities and loans that is higher than the expenses on their liabilities. The balance sheet of all banks in Canada, as of January 31, 2009, appears in Table 13-1.

Liabilities

A bank acquires funds by issuing (selling) liabilities such as deposits, which are the *sources of funds* the bank uses. The funds obtained from issuing liabilities are used to purchase income-earning assets. Banks have three main sources of funds: deposits, borrowings, and equity. Table 13-1 shows that deposits make about 64% of bank liabilities, borrowings 31%, and equity 5%.

DEMAND AND NOTICE DEPOSITS   Demand deposits are payable on demand; that is, if a depositor shows up at the bank and requests payment by making a withdrawal, the bank must pay the depositor immediately. Similarly, if a person who receives a cheque written on an account from a bank presents that cheque at the bank, the bank must pay the funds out immediately (or credit them to that person's account). Notice deposits are more important as a source of funds for the banks than are demand deposits. Although notice deposits have a notice requirement in the contractual agreement with the client, the banks rarely enforce this clause, and so in fact most notice deposits are really just like demand deposits in this sense.

Demand deposits and notice deposits are bank accounts that allow the owner to write cheques to third parties. Table 13-1 shows that this category of chequable deposits is an important low-cost source of bank funds, making up close to 26% of bank liabilities. Once, chequable deposits were the most important source of bank funds, but with the appearance of new, more attractive financial instruments, the share of chequable deposits in total bank liabilities has shrunk over time.

A chequable deposit is an asset for the depositor because it is part of his or her wealth. Conversely, because the depositor can withdraw from an account funds that the bank is obligated to pay, chequable deposits are a liability for the bank.

TABLE 13-1   Balance Sheet of All Banks in Canada (items as a percentage of the total, January 31, 2009)

Assets (Uses of Funds)*		Liabilities (Sources of Funds)	
Reserves and cash items	4.56	Demand and notice deposits	25.67
Securities	23.16	Fixed-term deposits	38.02
Loans		Advances from the Bank of Canada	0.01
Non-mortgage loans	33.07	Borrowings	31.39
Mortgages	17.87	Bank capital	4.91
Other assets	21.34		
Total	100.00	Total	100.00

*In order of decreasing liquidity.

Source: OSFI website, www.osfi-bsif.gc.ca

They are usually the lowest-cost source of bank funds because depositors are willing to forgo some interest in order to have access to a liquid asset that can be used to make purchases. The bank's costs of maintaining chequable deposits include interest payments and the costs incurred in servicing these accounts—processing and storing cancelled cheques, preparing and sending out monthly statements, providing efficient tellers (human or otherwise), maintaining an impressive building and conveniently located branches, and advertising and marketing to entice customers to deposit their funds with a given bank.

FIXED-TERM DEPOSITS   Fixed-term deposits are the primary source of bank funds (over 38% of bank liabilities in Table 13-1). Owners (retail customers, small and medium-sized businesses, large corporations, governments, and other financial institutions) cannot write cheques on fixed-term deposits, but the interest rates are usually higher than those on chequable deposits. There are two main types of fixed-term deposits: savings accounts and time deposits (also called certificates of deposit, or CDs).

Savings accounts were once the most common type of fixed-term deposit. In these accounts, to which funds can be added or from which funds can be withdrawn at any time, transactions and interest payments are recorded in a monthly statement or in a small book (the passbook) held by the owner of the account.

Time deposits have a fixed maturity length, ranging from several months to over five years, and have substantial penalties for early withdrawal (the forfeiture of several months' interest). Small-denomination time deposits (deposits of less than $100 000) are less liquid for the depositor than passbook savings, earn higher interest rates, and are a more costly source of funds for the banks.

Large-denomination time deposits (CDs) are available in denominations of $100 000 or over and are typically bought by corporations or other banks. Large-denomination CDs are negotiable; like bonds, they can be resold in a secondary market before they mature. For this reason, negotiable CDs are held by corporations, money market mutual funds, and other financial institutions as alternative assets to treasury bills and other short-term bonds. Since 1964, when they first appeared in Canada, negotiable CDs have become an important source of bank funds.

BORROWINGS   Banks obtain funds by borrowing from the Bank of Canada, other banks, and corporations. Borrowings from the Bank of Canada are called **overdraft loans** (also known as **advances**). Banks also borrow reserves overnight in the overnight market from other banks and financial institutions. Banks borrow funds overnight to have enough **settlement balances** at the Bank of Canada to facilitate the clearing of cheques and other transfers (these clearing and settlement processes will be investigated in detail in Chapter 17). Other sources of borrowed funds are loan arrangements with corporations (such as repurchase agreements) and borrowings of Eurodollars (deposits denominated in dollars residing in foreign banks or foreign branches of Canadian banks). Borrowings have become a more important source of bank funds over time: in 1960, they made up only a small fraction of bank liabilities; currently, they are over 30% of bank liabilities.

BANK CAPITAL   The final category on the liabilities side of the balance sheet is bank capital, the bank's net worth, which equals the difference between total assets and liabilities (close to 5% of total bank assets in Table 13-1). The funds are raised by selling new equity (stock) or from retained earnings. Bank capital is a cushion against a drop in the value of its assets, which could force the bank into insolvency (having liabilities in excess of assets, meaning that the bank can be forced into liquidation).

Assets

A bank uses the funds that it has acquired by issuing liabilities to purchase income-earning assets. Bank assets are thus naturally referred to as *uses of funds,* and the interest payments earned on them are what enable banks to make profits.

RESERVES   All banks hold some of the funds they acquire as deposits in an account at the Bank of Canada, in the form of settlement balances. **Reserves** are these settlement balances plus currency that is physically held by banks (called **vault cash** because it is stored in bank vaults overnight). Although Canadian banks are not required to hold reserves in some proportion to their deposits (Canada removed all such legal requirements in June 1994) and there is a requirement of zero settlement balances with the Bank of Canada at the end of each banking day, banks hold some reserves, which we call **desired reserves**.

Banks hold reserves because of their desire to manage their own short-term liquidity requirements and respond to predictable clearing drains and predictable across-the-counter and automated banking machine drains. Moreover, banks hold reserves in order to meet unpredictable and potentially large withdrawals by their liability holders. The risk that net cash withdrawals might be negative is known as **banker's risk**, and from the perspective of this risk, banks hold reserves to meet unpredictable cash and clearing drains. We will refer to the fraction of deposits banks hold in the form of reserves as the **desired reserve ratio**.

CASH ITEMS IN PROCESS OF COLLECTION   Suppose that a cheque written on an account at another bank is deposited in your bank and the funds for this cheque have not yet been received (collected) from the other bank. The cheque is classified as a cash item in process of collection, and it is an asset for your bank because it is a claim on another bank for funds that will be paid within a few days. Items in process of collection are also called **items in transit** or **bank float**.

DEPOSITS AT OTHER BANKS   Many small banks hold deposits in larger banks in exchange for a variety of services, including cheque collection, foreign exchange transactions, and help with securities purchases. These deposits are known as **interbank deposits**.

Collectively, reserves, cash items in process of collection, and deposits at other banks are referred to as *cash items*. In Table 13-1 they constitute close to 5% of total assets, and their importance has been shrinking over time: in 1960, for example, they accounted for over 20% of total assets.

SECURITIES   A bank's holdings of securities are an important income-earning asset: securities (made up entirely of debt instruments for commercial banks because banks are not allowed to hold stock) account for more than 23% of bank assets in Table 13-1. These securities can be classified into three categories: government of Canada, provincial and municipal securities, and other securities. The government of Canada securities are the most liquid because they can be easily traded and converted into cash with low transaction costs. Because of their high liquidity, short-term Canadian government securities (such as treasury bills) are called **secondary reserves**.

Provincial and municipal government securities are desirable for banks to hold primarily because provincial and municipal governments are more likely to do business with banks that hold their securities. Provincial and municipal government and other securities are less marketable (hence less liquid) and are also riskier than government of Canada securities, primarily because of default risk: there is some possibility that the issuer of the securities may not be able to make its interest payments or pay back the face value of the securities when they mature.

LOANS   Banks make their profits primarily by issuing loans. In Table 13-1, some 50% of bank assets are in the form of loans, and in recent years they have generally produced more than half of bank revenues. A loan is a liability for the individual or corporation receiving it but an asset for a bank because it provides income to the bank. Loans are typically less liquid than other assets because they cannot be turned into cash until the loan matures. If the bank makes a one-year loan, for example, it cannot get its funds back until the loan comes due in one year. Loans also have a higher probability of default than other assets. Because of the lack of liquidity and higher default risk, the bank earns its highest return on loans.

As you can see in Table 13-1, the largest categories of loans for banks are non-mortgage loans (commercial and industrial loans made to businesses, consumer loans, and interbank loans) and mortgages. The balance sheet in Table 13-1 shows that non-mortgage loans exceed mortgage loans (33% versus 18% of bank assets). This is so because a larger portion of the foreign activities of Canadian banks is in corporate loans rather than mortgages. In fact, the major difference in the balance sheets of the various depository institutions is primarily the type of loan they specialize in. Trust and mortgage loan companies and credit unions and *caisses populaires*, for example, specialize in residential mortgages.

OTHER ASSETS   Bankers' acceptances and the physical capital (bank buildings, computers, and other equipment) owned by the banks are included in this category.

BASIC BANKING

Before proceeding to a more detailed study of how a bank manages its assets and liabilities in order to make the highest profit, you should understand the basic operation of a bank.

In general terms, banks make profits by selling liabilities with one set of characteristics (a particular combination of liquidity, risk, size, and return) and using the proceeds to buy assets with a different set of characteristics. This process is often referred to as *asset transformation*. For example, a savings deposit held by one person can provide the funds that enable the bank to make a mortgage loan to another person. The bank has, in effect, transformed the savings deposit (an asset held by the depositor) into a mortgage loan (an asset held by the bank). Another way this process of asset transformation is described is to say that the bank "borrows short and lends long" because it makes long-term loans and funds them by issuing short-dated deposits.

The process of transforming assets and providing a set of services (cheque clearing, record keeping, credit analysis, and so forth) is like any other production process in a firm. If the bank produces desirable services at low cost and earns substantial income on its assets, it earns profits; if not, the bank suffers losses.

To make our analysis of the operation of a bank more concrete, we use a tool called a **T-account**. In this case we will use it like a simplified balance sheet, with lines in the form of a T, which lists only the changes that occur in balance sheet items starting from some initial balance sheet position.

The key characteristic of banks is their ability to buy assets by issuing their own deposit liabilities. Suppose that the First Bank has found some profitable loans that it wants to add to its portfolio. It makes a loan in the amount of $100 to a business and credits the business's chequable deposit in that amount. The business accepts the First Bank's deposit liabilities because they have the characteristic of being the medium of exchange and are accepted as money by others. The T-accounts for the First Bank and the business look like these:

First Bank			Business		
Assets	Liabilities		Assets	Liabilities	
Loans +$100	Chequable deposits +$100		Chequable deposits +$100	Bank loans +$100	

Note that the transaction is simply an exchange of assets and liabilities, with no change in the net worth of both the First Bank and the business. The bank's act of making a new loan to the business increases chequable deposits, and thus the money supply, by the amount of the loan. Note, however, that the bank's objective is not to create deposits and increase the money supply; ***the bank is in the business of making a profit for its shareholders and the creation of deposits occurs as a byproduct of the bank's financing decisions.***

Acquiring income-producing assets is not the only way in which the First Bank can create new chequable deposits. Let's say that Jane Brown has heard that the First Bank provides excellent service, so she opens a chequing account with a $100 bill. She now has a $100 chequable deposit at the bank, which shows up as a $100 liability on the bank's balance sheet. The bank now puts her $100 bill into its vault so that the bank's assets rise by the $100 increase in vault cash. The T-account for the bank looks like this:

First Bank	
Assets	Liabilities
Vault cash +$100	Chequable deposits +$100

Because vault cash is also part of the bank's reserves, we can rewrite the T-account as follows:

Assets	Liabilities
Reserves +$100	Chequable deposits +$100

Note that Jane Brown's opening of a chequing account leads to ***an increase in the bank's reserves equal to the increase in chequable deposits.***

If Jane had opened her account with a $100 cheque written on an account at another bank, say, the Second Bank, we would get the same result. The initial effect on the T-account of the First Bank is as follows:

Assets		Liabilities	
Cash items in process of collection	+$100	Chequable deposits	+$100

Chequable deposits increase by $100 as before, but now the First Bank is owed $100 by the Second Bank. This asset for the First Bank is entered in the T-account as $100 of cash items in process of collection because the First Bank will now try to collect the funds that it is owed. It could go directly to the Second Bank and ask for payment of the funds, but if the two banks are in separate provinces, that would be a time-consuming and costly process. Instead, the First Bank deposits the cheque in its account at the Bank of Canada, and the Bank of Canada collects the funds from the Second Bank. The result is that the Bank of Canada transfers $100 of reserves from the Second Bank to the First Bank, and the final balance sheet positions of the two banks are as follows:

First Bank

Assets		Liabilities	
Reserves	+$100	Chequable deposits	+$100

Second Bank

Assets		Liabilities	
Reserves	−$100	Chequable deposits	−$100

The process initiated by Jane Brown can be summarized as follows: when a cheque written on an account at one bank is deposited in another, the bank receiving the deposit gains reserves equal to the amount of the cheque, while the bank on which the cheque is written sees its reserves fall by the same amount. Therefore, **when a bank receives additional deposits, it gains an equal amount of reserves; when it loses deposits, it loses an equal amount of reserves.**

Now that you understand how banks gain and lose reserves, we can examine how a bank rearranges its balance sheet to make a profit when it experiences a change in its deposits. Let's return to the situation when the First Bank has just received the extra $100 of chequable deposits. As you know, the bank wants to keep a certain fraction of its chequable deposits as reserves. If the fraction (the desired reserve ratio) is 10%, the First Bank's desired reserves have increased by $10, and we can rewrite its T-account as follows:

First Bank

Assets		Liabilities	
Desired reserves	+$10	Chequable deposits	+$100
Excess reserves	+$90		

Let's see how well the bank is doing as a result of the additional chequable deposits. While reserves earn little interest, servicing the extra $100 of chequable deposits is costly because the bank must keep records, pay tellers, pay for cheque clearing, and so forth. The bank is making a loss! The situation is even worse if the bank makes interest payments on the deposits. If it is to make a profit, the bank must put to productive use all or part of the $90 of excess reserves it has available.

One way to do this is to invest in securities. The other is to make loans; as we have seen, loans account for approximately 50% of the total value of bank assets (uses of funds). Because lenders are subject to the asymmetric information problems of adverse selection and moral hazard (discussed in Chapter 8), banks take steps to reduce the incidence and severity of these problems. Bank loan officers evaluate potential borrowers using what are called the "five C's"—character, capacity (ability to repay), collateral, conditions (in the local and national economies), and capital (net worth)—before they agree to lend (a more detailed discussion of the methods banks use to reduce the risk involved in lending appears later in this chapter).

Let us assume that the bank chooses not to hold any excess reserves but to make loans instead. Assuming that the bank gives up its cash directly, the T-account then looks like this:

Assets		Liabilities	
Desired reserves	+$10	Chequable deposits	+$100
Loans	+$90		

The bank is now making a profit because it holds short-term liabilities such as chequable deposits and uses the proceeds to buy longer-term assets such as loans with higher interest rates. As mentioned earlier, this process of asset transformation is frequently described by saying that banks are in the business of "borrowing short and lending long." For example, if the loans have an interest rate of 10% per year, the bank earns $9 in income from its loans over the year. If the $100 of chequable deposits is in an account with a 5% interest rate and it costs another $3 per year to service the account, the cost per year of these deposits is $8. The bank's profit on the new deposits is then $1 per year, plus any interest that is paid on reserves.

GENERAL PRINCIPLES OF BANK MANAGEMENT

Now that you have some idea of how a bank operates, let's look at how a bank manages its assets and liabilities in order to earn the highest possible profit. The bank manager has four primary concerns. The first is to make sure that the bank has enough ready cash to pay its depositors when there are **deposit outflows**, that is, when deposits are lost because depositors make withdrawals and demand payment. To keep enough cash on hand, the bank must engage in **liquidity management**, the acquisition of sufficiently liquid assets to meet the bank's obligations to depositors. Second, the bank manager must pursue an acceptably low level of risk by acquiring assets that have a low rate of default and by diversifying asset holdings (**asset management**). The third concern is to acquire funds at low cost (**liability management**). Finally, the manager must decide the amount of capital the bank should maintain and then acquire the needed capital (**capital adequacy management**).

To understand bank and other financial institution management fully, we must go beyond the general principles of bank asset and liability management described next and look in more detail at how a financial institution manages its assets. The two sections following this one provide an in-depth discussion of how a financial institution manages **credit risk**, the risk arising because borrowers may default, and how it manages **interest-rate risk**, the riskiness of earnings and returns on bank assets that results from interest-rate changes.

Liquidity Management and the Role of Reserves

Let us see how a typical bank, the First Bank, can deal with deposit outflows that occur when its depositors withdraw cash from chequing or savings accounts or write cheques that are deposited in other banks. In the example that follows, we assume that the bank has ample excess reserves and that all deposits have the same desired reserve ratio of 10% (the bank wants to keep 10% of its time and chequable deposits as reserves). Suppose that the First Bank's initial balance sheet is as follows:

Assets		Liabilities	
Reserves	$20 million	Deposits	$100 million
Loans	$80 million	Bank capital	$ 10 million
Securities	$10 million		

The bank's desired reserves are 10% of $100 million, or $10 million. Given that it holds $20 million of reserves, the First Bank has excess reserves of $10 million. If a deposit outflow of $10 million occurs, the bank's balance sheet becomes

Assets		Liabilities	
Reserves	$10 million	Deposits	$90 million
Loans	$80 million	Bank capital	$10 million
Securities	$10 million		

The bank loses $10 million of deposits *and* $10 million of reserves, but because its desired reserves are now 10% of only $90 million ($9 million), its reserves still exceed this amount by $1 million. In short, ***if a bank has ample reserves, a deposit outflow does not necessitate changes in other parts of its balance sheet.***

The situation is quite different when a bank holds insufficient reserves. Let's assume that instead of initially holding $10 million in excess reserves, the First Bank makes additional loans of $10 million, so that it holds no excess reserves. Its initial balance sheet would be

Assets		Liabilities	
Reserves	$10 million	Deposits	$100 million
Loans	$90 million	Bank capital	$ 10 million
Securities	$10 million		

When it suffers the $10 million deposit outflow, its balance sheet becomes

Assets		Liabilities	
Reserves	$ 0 million	Deposits	$90 million
Loans	$90 million	Bank capital	$10 million
Securities	$10 million		

After $10 million has been withdrawn from deposits and hence reserves, the bank has a problem: its desired reserves are 10% of $90 million, or $9 million, but it has no reserves! To eliminate this shortfall, the bank has four basic options. One is to acquire reserves to meet a deposit outflow by borrowing them from other banks in the overnight market or by borrowing from corporations.[1] If the First Bank acquires the $9 million shortfall in reserves by borrowing it from other banks or corporations, its balance sheet becomes

Assets		Liabilities	
Reserves	$ 9 million	Deposits	$90 million
Loans	$90 million	Borrowings	
Securities	$10 million	from other	
		banks or	
		corporations	$ 9 million
		Bank capital	$10 million

The cost of this activity is the interest rate on these loans, such as the overnight interest rate.

A second alternative is for the bank to sell some of its securities to help cover the deposit outflow. For example, it might sell $9 million of its securities and deposit the proceeds with the Bank of Canada, resulting in the following balance sheet:

Assets		Liabilities	
Reserves	$ 9 million	Deposits	$90 million
Loans	$90 million	Bank capital	$10 million
Securities	$ 1 million		

The bank incurs some brokerage and other transaction costs when it sells these securities. The government of Canada securities that the bank holds are very liquid, so the transaction costs of selling them are quite modest. However, the other securities the bank holds are less liquid, and the transaction costs can be appreciably higher.

---

[1] One way that the First Bank can borrow from other banks and corporations is by selling negotiable certificates of deposit. This method for obtaining funds is discussed in the section on liability management.

A third way that the bank can meet a deposit outflow is to acquire reserves by borrowing from the Bank of Canada. In our example, the First Bank could leave its security and loan holdings the same and borrow $9 million in advances from the Bank of Canada. Its balance sheet would be

Assets		Liabilities	
Reserves	$ 9 million	Deposits	$90 million
Loans	$90 million	Advances	
Securities	$10 million	from the	
		Bank of	
		Canada	$ 9 million
		Bank capital	$10 million

The cost associated with advances from the Bank of Canada is the interest rate that must be paid to the Bank of Canada (called the **bank rate**).

Finally, a bank can acquire the $9 million of reserves to meet the deposit outflow by reducing its loans by this amount and depositing the $9 million it then receives with the Bank of Canada, thereby increasing its reserves by $9 million. This transaction changes the balance sheet as follows:

Assets		Liabilities	
Reserves	$ 9 million	Deposits	$90 million
Loans	$81 million	Bank capital	$10 million
Securities	$10 million		

The First Bank is once again in good shape because its $9 million of reserves satisfies the reserve requirement.

However, this process of reducing its loans is the bank's costliest way of acquiring reserves when there is a deposit outflow. If the First Bank has numerous short-term loans renewed at fairly short intervals, it can reduce its total amount of loans outstanding fairly quickly by *calling in* loans—that is, by not renewing some loans when they come due. Unfortunately for the bank, this is likely to antagonize the customers whose loans are not being renewed because they have not done anything to deserve such treatment. Indeed, they are likely to take their business elsewhere in the future, a very costly consequence for the bank.

A second method for reducing its loans is for the bank to sell them off to other banks. Again, this is very costly because other banks do not personally know the customers who have taken out the loans and so may not be willing to buy the loans at their full value (this is just the lemons adverse selection problem discussed in Chapter 8).

The foregoing discussion explains why banks hold reserves even though loans or securities earn a higher return. When a deposit outflow occurs, holding reserves allows the bank to escape the costs of (1) borrowing from other banks or corporations, (2) selling securities, (3) borrowing from the Bank of Canada, or (4) calling in or selling off loans. ***Reserves are insurance against the costs associated with deposit outflows. The higher the costs associated with deposit outflows, the more reserves banks will want to hold.***

Just as you and I would be willing to pay an insurance company to insure us against a casualty loss such as the theft of a car, a bank is willing to pay the cost of holding reserves (the opportunity cost, the earnings forgone by not holding income-earning assets such as loans or securities) to insure against losses due to deposit outflows. Because reserves, like insurance, have a cost, banks also take other steps to protect themselves; for example, they might shift their holdings of assets to more liquid securities (secondary reserves).

Asset Management

Now that you understand why a bank has a need for liquidity, we can examine the basic strategy a bank pursues in managing its assets. To maximize its profits, a bank must simultaneously seek the highest returns possible on loans and securities, reduce risk, and make adequate provisions for liquidity by holding liquid assets. Banks try to accomplish these three goals in four basic ways.

First, banks try to find borrowers who will pay high interest rates and are unlikely to default on their loans. They seek out loan business by advertising their borrowing rates and by approaching corporations directly to solicit loans. It is up to the bank's loan officer to decide if potential borrowers are good credit risks who will make interest and principal payments on time (i.e., engage in screening to reduce the adverse selection problem). Typically, banks are conservative in their loan policies; the default rate is usually less than 1%. It is important, however, that banks not be so conservative that they miss out on attractive lending opportunities that earn high interest rates.

Second, banks try to purchase securities with high returns and low risk. Third, in managing their assets, banks must attempt to lower risk by diversifying. They accomplish this by purchasing many different types of assets (short- and long-term, government of Canada, and municipal bonds) and approving many types of loans to a number of customers. Banks that have not sufficiently sought the benefits of diversification often come to regret it later. For example, banks that had overspecialized in making loans to energy companies, real estate developers, or farmers suffered huge losses in the 1980s with the slump in energy, property, and farm prices. Indeed, some of these banks (e.g., the Canadian Commercial Bank and the Northland Bank) went broke because they had "put too many eggs in one basket."

Finally, the bank must manage the liquidity of its assets so that it can pay depositors when there are deposit outflows without bearing huge costs. This means that it will hold liquid securities even if they earn a somewhat lower return than other assets. In addition, it will want to hold government securities so that even if a deposit outflow forces some costs on the bank, these will not be terribly high. Again, it is not wise for a bank to be too conservative. If it avoids all costs associated with deposit outflows by holding only reserves, the bank suffers losses because reserves earn little interest, while the bank's liabilities are costly to maintain. The bank must balance its desire for liquidity against the increased earnings that can be obtained from less liquid assets such as loans.

Liability Management

Before the 1960s, liability management was a staid affair: for the most part, banks took their liabilities as fixed and spent their time trying to achieve an optimal mix of assets. There were two main reasons for the emphasis on asset management. First, a large part of the sources of bank funds was obtained through demand deposits that did not pay any interest. Thus banks could not actively compete with one another for these deposits, and so their amount was effectively a given for an individual bank. Second, because the markets for making overnight loans between banks were not well developed, banks rarely borrowed from other banks to meet their reserve needs.

Starting in the 1960s, however, large banks (called **money centre banks**) began to explore ways in which the liabilities on their balance sheets could provide them with reserves and liquidity. This led to an expansion of overnight loan markets, such as the federal funds market in the United States and the overnight funds market in Canada, and the development of new financial instruments such as negotiable CDs (first developed in 1961), which enabled money centre banks to acquire funds quickly.[2]

This new flexibility in liability management meant that banks could take a different approach to bank management. They no longer needed to depend on chequable deposits as the primary source of bank funds and as a result no longer treated their sources of funds (liabilities) as given. Instead, they aggressively set target goals for their asset growth and tried to acquire funds (by issuing liabilities) as they were needed.

For example, today, when a money centre bank finds an attractive loan opportunity, it can acquire funds by selling a negotiable CD. Or if it has a reserve shortfall, funds can be borrowed from another bank in the overnight market without incurring high transaction costs. The overnight market can also be used to finance loans. Because of the increased importance of liability management, most banks now manage both sides of the balance sheet together in an *asset–liability management (ALM) committee.*

The emphasis on liability management explains some of the important changes over the past three decades in the composition of banks' balance sheets. While negotiable CDs and bank borrowings have greatly increased in importance as a source of bank funds in recent years, chequable deposits have decreased in importance. Newfound flexibility in liability management and the search for higher profits have also stimulated banks to increase the proportion of their assets held in loans, which earn higher income.

Capital Adequacy Management

Banks have to make decisions about the amount of capital they need to hold for three reasons. First, bank capital helps prevent *bank failure,* a situation in which the bank cannot satisfy its obligations to pay its depositors and other creditors and so goes out of business. Second, the amount of capital affects returns for the owners (equity holders) of the bank. Third, a minimum amount of bank capital (bank capital requirements) is required by regulatory authorities.

HOW BANK CAPITAL HELPS PREVENT BANK FAILURE   Let's consider two banks with identical balance sheets, except that the High Capital Bank has a ratio of capital to assets of 10% while the Low Capital Bank has a ratio of 4%.

High Capital Bank				Low Capital Bank			
Assets		Liabilities		Assets		Liabilities	
Reserves	$10 million	Deposits	$90 million	Reserves	$10 million	Deposits	$96 million
Loans	$90 million	Bank capital	$10 million	Loans	$90 million	Bank capital	$ 4 million

[2] Because small banks are not as well known as money centre banks and so might be a higher credit risk, they find it harder to raise funds in the negotiable CD market. Hence, they do not engage nearly as actively in liability management.

Suppose that both banks got caught up in the euphoria of the real estate market in 2006 and 2007, only to find that $5 million of their real estate loans became worthless. When these bad loans are written off (valued at zero), the total value of assets declines by $5 million. As a consequence, bank capital, which equals total assets minus liabilities, also declines by $5 million. The balance sheets of the two banks now look like this:

High Capital Bank				Low Capital Bank			
Assets		Liabilities		Assets		Liabilities	
Reserves	$10 million	Deposits	$90 million	Reserves	$10 million	Deposits	$96 million
Loans	$85 million	Bank		Loans	$85 million	Bank	
		capital	$ 5 million			capital	−$1 million

The High Capital Bank takes the $5 million loss in stride because its initial cushion of $10 million in capital means that it still has a positive net worth (bank capital) of $5 million after the loss. The Low Capital Bank, however, is in big trouble. The value of its assets has fallen below its liabilities, and its net worth is now −$1 million. Because the bank has a negative net worth, it is insolvent: it does not have sufficient assets to pay off all holders of its liabilities. When a bank becomes insolvent, government regulators close the bank, its assets are sold off, and its managers are fired. Since the owners of the Low Capital Bank will find their investment wiped out, they would clearly have preferred the bank to have had a large enough cushion of bank capital to absorb the losses, as was the case for the High Capital Bank. We therefore see an important rationale for a bank to maintain a sufficient level of capital: ***a bank maintains bank capital to lessen the chance that it will become insolvent.***

HOW THE AMOUNT OF BANK CAPITAL AFFECTS RETURNS TO EQUITY HOLDERS

Because owners of a bank must know whether their bank is being managed well, they need good measures of bank profitability. A basic measure of bank profitability is the **return on assets** (*ROA*), the net profit after taxes per dollar of assets:

$$ROA = \frac{\text{net profit after taxes}}{\text{assets}}$$

The return on assets provides information on how efficiently a bank is being run, because it indicates how much profit is generated on average by each dollar of assets.

However, what the bank's owners (equity holders) care about most is how much the bank is earning on their equity investment. This information is provided by the other basic measure of bank profitability, the **return on equity** (*ROE*), the net profit after taxes per dollar of equity capital:

$$ROE = \frac{\text{net profit after taxes}}{\text{equity capital}}$$

There is a direct relationship between the return on assets (which measures how efficiently the bank is run) and the return on equity (which measures how well the owners are doing on their investment). This relationship is determined by the **equity multiplier** (*EM*), the amount of assets per dollar of equity capital:

$$EM = \frac{\text{assets}}{\text{equity capital}}$$

To see this, we note that

$$\frac{\text{net profit after taxes}}{\text{equity capital}} = \frac{\text{net profit after taxes}}{\text{assets}} \times \frac{\text{assets}}{\text{equity capital}}$$

which, using our definitions, yields

$$ROE = ROA \times EM \tag{1}$$

The formula in Equation 1 tells us what happens to the return on equity when a bank holds a smaller amount of capital (equity) for a given amount of assets. As we have seen, the High Capital Bank initially has $100 million of assets and $10 million of equity, which gives it an equity multiplier of 10 (= $100 million/$10 million). The Low Capital Bank, by contrast, has only $4 million of equity, so its equity multiplier is higher, equalling 25 (= $100 million/$4 million). Suppose that these banks have been equally well run so that they both have the same return on assets, 1%. The return on equity for the High Capital Bank equals 1% × 10 = 10%, while the return on equity for the Low Capital Bank equals 1% × 25 = 25%. The equity holders in the Low Capital Bank are clearly a lot happier than the equity holders in the High Capital Bank because they are earning more than twice as high a return. We now see why owners of a bank may not want it to hold a lot of capital. ***Given the return on assets, the lower the bank capital, the higher the return for the owners of the bank.***

TRADE-OFF BETWEEN SAFETY AND RETURNS TO EQUITY HOLDERS   We now see that bank capital has benefits and costs. Bank capital benefits the owners of a bank in that it makes their investment safer by reducing the likelihood of bankruptcy. But bank capital is costly because the higher it is, the lower will be the return on equity for a given return on assets. In determining the amount of bank capital, managers must decide how much of the increased safety that comes with higher capital (the benefit) they are willing to trade off against the lower return on equity that comes with higher capital (the cost).[3]

In more uncertain times, when the possibility of large losses on loans increases, bank managers might want to hold more capital to protect the equity holders. Conversely, if they have confidence that loan losses won't occur, they might want to reduce the amount of bank capital, have a high equity multiplier, and thereby increase the return on equity.

BANK CAPITAL REQUIREMENTS   Banks also hold capital because they are required to do so by regulatory authorities. Because of the high costs of holding capital for the reasons just described, bank managers often want to hold less bank capital relative to assets than is required by the regulatory authorities. In this case, the amount of bank capital is determined by the bank capital requirements.

---

[3] Managers of financial institutions also need to know how well their banks are doing at any point in time. A web appendix to this chapter discusses how bank performance is measured, and is available on this book's MyEconLab at **www.pearsoned.ca/myeconlab**.

| APPLICATION | **Strategies for Managing Bank Capital** |

Suppose that as the manager of the First Bank, you have to make decisions about the appropriate amount of bank capital. Looking at the balance sheet of the bank, which like the High Capital Bank has a ratio of bank capital to assets of 10% ($10 million of capital and $100 million of assets), you are concerned that the large amount of bank capital is causing the return on equity to be too low. You conclude that the bank has a capital surplus and should increase the equity multiplier to increase the return on equity. What should you do?

To lower the amount of capital relative to assets and raise the equity multiplier, you can do any of three things: (1) you can reduce the amount of bank capital by buying back some of the bank's stock; (2) you can reduce the bank's capital by paying out higher dividends to its stockholders, thereby reducing the bank's retained earnings; (3) you can keep bank capital constant but increase the bank's assets by acquiring new funds, say, by issuing CDs, and then seeking out loan business or purchasing more securities with these new funds. Because you think that it would enhance your position with the stockholders, you decide to pursue the second alternative and raise the dividend on the First Bank stock.

Now suppose that the First Bank is in a similar situation to the Low Capital Bank and has a ratio of bank capital to assets of 4%. You now worry that the bank is short on capital relative to assets because it does not have a sufficient cushion to prevent bank failure. To raise the amount of capital relative to assets, you now have the following three choices: (1) you can raise capital for the bank by having it issue equity (common stock); (2) you can raise capital by reducing the bank's dividends to shareholders, thereby increasing retained earnings that it can put into its capital account; (3) you can keep capital at the same level but reduce the bank's assets by making fewer loans or by selling off securities and then using the proceeds to reduce its liabilities. Suppose that raising bank capital is not easy to do at the current time because capital markets are tight or because shareholders will protest if their dividends are cut. Then you might have to choose the third alternative and decide to shrink the size of the bank.

In the aftermath of the subprime mortgage crisis in the United States, many banks experienced capital shortfalls and had to restrict asset growth, as you might have had to do if the First Bank were short of capital. The important consequences of this for the credit markets are discussed in the Application that follows.

| APPLICATION | **How a Capital Crunch Caused a Credit Crunch in 2008** |

In the wake of the financial crisis of 2007–2008, there occurred a dramatic slow-down in the growth of credit, triggered by a "credit crunch" in which credit was hard to get, and as a result the performance of the economy in 2008 and 2009 was very poor. What caused the credit crunch?

Our analysis of how a bank manages bank capital explains why a credit crunch occurred in 2008 and that it was caused, at least in part, by the capital crunch, in which shortfalls of bank capital led to slower credit growth.

As we discussed in the previous chapter, there was a major boom and bust in the U.S. housing market that led to huge losses for banks around the world from their holdings of securities backed by U.S. residential mortgages. In addition, banks had to take back onto their balance sheets many of the structured investment vehicles (SIVs) they had sponsored. The losses reduced bank capital and increased the need for more capital to support the assets coming back onto bank balance sheets. This led to capital shortfalls: banks had to either raise new capital or restrict asset growth by cutting back on lending. Banks did raise some capital but with the growing weakness of the world economy, raising new capital was extremely difficult, so the banks chose the latter course. Banks tightened their lending standards and restricted lending, both of which helped produce a weak economy in 2008 and 2009.

MANAGING CREDIT RISK

As seen in the earlier discussion of general principles of asset management, banks and other financial institutions must make successful loans that are paid back in full (and so subject the institution to little credit risk) if they are to earn high profits. The economic concepts of adverse selection and moral hazard discussed in Chapters 2 and 8 provide a framework for understanding the principles that financial institutions have to follow to reduce credit risk and make successful loans.

Adverse selection in loan markets occurs because bad credit risks (those most likely to default) are the ones who usually line up for loans—in other words, those who are most likely to produce an *adverse* outcome are the most likely to be *selected*. Borrowers with very risky investment projects have much to gain if their projects are successful, and so they are the most eager to obtain loans. Clearly, however, they are the least desirable borrowers because of the greater possibility that they will be unable to pay back their loans.

Moral hazard is a problem in loan markets because borrowers may have incentives to engage in activities that are undesirable from the lender's point of view. In such situations, it is more likely that the lender will be exposed to the *hazard* of default. Once borrowers have obtained a loan, they are more likely to invest in high-risk investment projects—projects that pay high returns to the borrowers if successful. The high risk, however, makes it less likely that they will be able to pay the loan back.

To be profitable, financial institutions must overcome the adverse selection and moral hazard problems that make loan defaults more likely. The attempts of financial institutions to solve these problems help explain a number of principles for managing credit risk: screening and monitoring, establishment of long-term customer relationships, loan commitments, collateral and compensating balance requirements, and credit rationing.

Screening and Monitoring

Asymmetric information is present in loan markets because lenders have less information about the investment opportunities and activities of borrowers than borrowers do. This situation leads to two information-producing activities by financial institutions: screening and monitoring.

SCREENING   Adverse selection in loan markets requires that financial institutions screen out the bad credit risks from the good ones so that loans will be profitable to them. To accomplish effective screening, lenders must collect reliable information from prospective borrowers. Effective screening and information collection together form an important principle of credit risk management.

When you apply for a consumer loan (such as a car loan or a mortgage to purchase a house), the first thing you are asked to do is fill out forms that elicit a great deal of information about your personal finances. You are asked about your salary, bank accounts, other assets (such as cars, insurance policies, and furnishings), and your outstanding loans; your record of loan, credit card, and charge account repayments; and the number of years you've worked and who your employers have been. You also are asked personal questions such as your age, marital status, and number of children. The lender uses this information to evaluate how good a credit risk you are by calculating your credit score, a statistical measure derived from your answers that predicts whether you are likely to have trouble making your loan payments. Deciding on how good a risk you are cannot be entirely scientific, so the lender must also use judgement. A loan officer, whose job is to decide whether you should be given the loan, might call your employer or talk to some of the personal references you supplied. The officer might even make a judgement based on your demeanour or your appearance (this is why most people dress neatly and conservatively when they go to a bank to apply for a loan).

The process of screening and collecting information is similar when a financial institution makes a business loan. It collects information about the company's profits and losses (income) and about its assets and liabilities. The lender also has to evaluate the likely future success of the business. So in addition to obtaining information on such items as sales figures, a loan officer might ask questions about the company's future plans, the purpose of the loan, and the competition in the industry. The officer might even visit the company to obtain a firsthand look at its operations. The bottom line is that, whether for personal or business loans, bankers and other financial institutions need to be nosy.

SPECIALIZATION IN LENDING   One puzzling feature of bank lending is that a bank often specializes in lending to local firms or to firms in particular industries, such as energy. In one sense, this behaviour appears surprising because it means that the bank is not diversifying its portfolio of loans and is therefore exposing itself to more risk. But from another perspective, such specialization makes perfect sense. The adverse selection problem requires that banks screen out bad credit risks. It is easier for a bank to collect information about local firms and determine their creditworthiness than to collect similar information on firms that are far away. Similarly, by concentrating its lending on firms in specific industries, the bank becomes more knowledgeable about these industries and is therefore better able to predict which firms will be able to make timely payments on their debt.

MONITORING AND ENFORCEMENT OF RESTRICTIVE COVENANTS   Once a loan has been made, the borrower may have an incentive to engage in risky activities that make it less likely that the loan will be repaid. To reduce this moral hazard, financial institutions must adhere to the principle for managing credit risk that a lender should write provisions (restrictive covenants) into loan contracts that prevent borrowers from engaging in overly risky activities. By monitoring borrowers' activities to see whether they are complying with the restrictive covenants and by enforcing the covenants if they are not, lenders can make sure that borrowers are not taking on risks at the institution's expense. The need for banks and other financial institutions to engage in screening and monitoring explains why they spend so much money on auditing and information-collecting activities.

Long-Term Customer Relationships

An additional way for banks and other financial institutions to obtain information about borrowers is through long-term customer relationships, another important principle of credit risk management.

If a prospective borrower has had a chequing or savings account or other loans with a bank over a long period of time, a loan officer can look at past activity in the accounts and learn quite a bit about the borrower. The balances in the chequing and savings accounts tell the banker how liquid the potential borrower is and at what time of year the borrower has a strong need for cash. A review of the cheques the borrower has written reveals the borrower's suppliers. If the borrower has borrowed previously from the bank, the bank has a record of the loan payments. Thus, long-term customer relationships reduce the costs of information collection and make it easier to screen out bad credit risks.

The need for monitoring by lenders adds to the importance of long-term customer relationships. If the borrower has borrowed from the bank before, the bank has already established procedures for monitoring that customer. Therefore, the costs of monitoring long-term customers are lower than those for new customers.

Long-term relationships benefit the customers as well as the bank. A firm with a previous relationship will find it easier to obtain a loan at a low interest rate because the bank has an easier time determining if the prospective borrower is a good credit risk and incurs fewer costs in monitoring the borrower.

A long-term customer relationship has another advantage for the bank. No bank can think of every contingency when it writes a restrictive covenant into a loan contract; there will always be risky borrower activities that are not ruled out. However, what if a borrower wants to preserve a long-term relationship with a bank because it will be easier to get future loans at low interest rates? The borrower then has incentive to avoid risky activities that would upset the bank, even if restrictions on these risky activities are not specified in the loan contract. Indeed, if a bank doesn't like what a borrower is doing even when the borrower isn't violating any restrictive covenants, it has some power to discourage the borrower from such activity: the bank can threaten not to let the borrower have new loans in the future. Long-term customer relationships therefore enable banks to deal with even unanticipated moral hazard contingencies.

Loan Commitments

Banks also create long-term relationships and gather information by issuing **loan commitments** to commercial customers. A loan commitment is a bank's commitment (for a specified future period of time) to provide a firm with loans up to a given amount at an interest rate that is tied to some market interest rate. The majority of commercial and industrial loans are made under the loan commitment arrangement. The advantage for the firm is that it has a source of credit when it needs it. The advantage for the bank is that the loan commitment promotes a long-term relationship, which in turn facilitates information collection. In addition, provisions in the loan commitment agreement require that the firm continually supply the bank with information about the firm's income, asset and liability position, business activities, and so on. A loan commitment arrangement is a powerful method for reducing a bank's costs for screening and information collection.

Collateral and Compensating Balances

Collateral requirements for loans are important credit risk management tools. Collateral, which is property promised to the lender as compensation if the borrower defaults, lessens the consequences of adverse selection because it reduces the lender's losses in the case of a loan default. It also reduces moral hazard, because the borrower has more to lose from a default. If a borrower defaults on a loan, the lender can sell the collateral and use the proceeds to make up for its losses on the loan. One particular form of collateral required when a bank makes commercial loans is called **compensating balances**: A firm receiving a loan must keep a required minimum amount of funds in a chequing account at the bank. For example, a business getting a $10 million loan may be required to keep compensating balances of at least $1 million in its chequing account at the bank. The $1 million in compensating balances can be taken by the bank to make up some of the losses on the loan if the borrower defaults.

Besides serving as collateral, compensating balances help increase the likelihood that a loan will be paid off. They do this by helping the bank monitor the borrower and consequently reduce moral hazard. Specifically, by requiring the borrower to use a chequing account at the bank, the bank can observe the firm's cheque payment practices, which may yield a great deal of information about the borrower's financial condition. For example, a sustained drop in the borrower's chequing account balance may signal that the borrower is having financial trouble, or account activity may suggest that the borrower is engaging in risky activities; perhaps a change in suppliers means that the borrower is pursuing new lines of business. Any significant change in the borrower's payment procedures is a signal to the bank that it should make inquiries. Compensating balances therefore make it easier for banks to monitor borrowers more effectively and are consequently another important credit risk management tool.

Credit Rationing

Another way in which financial institutions deal with adverse selection and moral hazard is through **credit rationing**: refusing to make loans even though borrowers are willing to pay the stated interest rate or even a higher rate. Credit rationing takes two forms. The first occurs when a lender refuses to make a loan of *any amount* to a borrower, even if the borrower is willing to pay a higher interest rate. The second occurs when a lender is willing to make a loan but restricts the size of the loan to less than the borrower would like.

At first you might be puzzled by the first type of credit rationing. After all, even if the potential borrower is a credit risk, why doesn't the lender just extend the loan but at a higher interest rate? The answer is that adverse selection prevents this solution. Individuals and firms with the riskiest investment projects are exactly those that are willing to pay the highest interest rates. If a borrower took on a high-risk investment and succeeded, the borrower would become extremely rich. But a lender wouldn't want to make such a loan precisely because the credit risk is high; the likely outcome is that the borrower will *not* succeed and the lender will not be paid back. Charging a higher interest rate just makes adverse selection worse for the lender; that is, it increases the likelihood that the lender is lending to a bad credit risk. The lender would therefore rather not make any loans at a higher interest rate; instead, it would engage in the first type of credit rationing and would turn down loans.

Financial institutions engage in a second type of credit rationing to guard against moral hazard: They grant loans to borrowers, but not loans as large as the borrowers want. Such credit rationing is necessary because the larger the loan, the greater the benefits from moral hazard. If a bank gives you a $1000 loan, for example, you are likely to take actions that enable you to pay it back because you don't want to hurt your credit rating for the future. However, if the bank lends you $10 million, you are more likely to fly off to Rio to celebrate. The larger your loan, the greater your incentives to engage in activities that make it less likely that you will repay the loan. Because more borrowers repay their loans if the loan amounts are small, financial institutions ration credit by providing borrowers with smaller loans than they seek.

MANAGING INTEREST-RATE RISK

With the increased volatility of interest rates that occurred in the 1980s, banks and other financial institutions became more concerned about their exposure to interest-rate risk, the riskiness of earnings and returns that is associated with changes in interest rates. To see what interest-rate risk is all about, let's take a look at the balance sheet of the First Bank:

First Bank

Assets		Liabilities	
Rate-sensitive assets	$20 million	Rate-sensitive liabilities	$50 million
Variable-rate and		Variable-rate CDs	
short-term loans			
Short-term securities			
Fixed-rate assets	$80 million	Fixed-rate liabilities	$50 million
Reserves		Chequable deposits	
Long-term loans		Savings deposits	
Long-term securities		Long-term CDs	
		Equity capital	

A total of $20 million of its assets are rate-sensitive, with interest rates that change frequently (at least once a year), and $80 million of its assets are fixed-rate, with interest rates that remain unchanged for a long period (over a year). On the liabilities side, the First Bank has $50 million of rate-sensitive liabilities and $50 million of fixed-rate liabilities. Suppose that interest rates rise by 5 percentage points on average, from 10% to 15%. The income on the assets increases by $1 million (= 5% × $20 million of rate-sensitive assets), while the payments on the liabilities increase by $2.5 million (= 5% × $50 million of rate-sensitive liabilities). The First Bank's profits now decline by $1.5 million (= $1 million − $2.5 million). Conversely, if interest rates fall by 5 percentage points, similar reasoning tells us that the First Bank's profits increase by $1.5 million. This example illustrates the following point: *If a bank has more rate-sensitive liabilities than assets, a rise in interest rates will reduce bank profits and a decline in interest rates will raise bank profits.*

Gap Analysis   One simple and quick approach to measuring the sensitivity of bank income to changes in interest rates is **gap analysis** (also called **income gap analysis**), in which the amount of rate-sensitive liabilities is subtracted from the amount of rate-sensitive assets. This calculation, *GAP*, can be written as

$$GAP = RSA - RSL \tag{2}$$

where
$$RSA = \text{rate-sensitive assets}$$
$$RSL = \text{rate-sensitive liabilities}$$

In our example, the bank manager calculates *GAP* to be

$$GAP = \$20 \text{ million} - \$50 \text{ million} = -\$30 \text{ million}$$

Multiplying *GAP* times the change in the interest rate immediately reveals the effect on bank income:

$$\Delta I = GAP \times \Delta i \tag{3}$$

where
$$\Delta I = \text{change in bank income}$$
$$\Delta i = \text{change in interest rates}$$

APPLICATION   Gap Analysis

Using the $-\$30$-million gap calculated using Equation 2, what is the change in income if interest rates rise by 1%?

Solution   The change in income is $-\$300\ 000$.

$$\Delta I = GAP \times \Delta i$$

where

$$GAP = RSA - RSL \qquad = -\$30 \text{ million}$$
$$\Delta i = \text{change in interest rate} = 0.01$$

Thus

$$\Delta I = -\$30 \text{ million} \times 0.01 = -\$300\ 000$$

The analysis we just conducted is known as *basic gap analysis*, and it suffers from the problem that many of the assets and liabilities that are not classified as rate-sensitive have different maturities. One refinement to deal with this problem, the *maturity bucket approach*, is to measure the gap for several maturity subintervals, called *maturity buckets*, so that effects of interest-rate changes over a multiyear period can be calculated. The second refinement, called *standardized gap analysis*, accounts for the differing degrees of rate sensitivity for different rate-sensitive assets and liabilities.

Duration Analysis

The gap analysis we have examined so far focuses only on the effect of interest-rate changes on income. Clearly, owners and managers of banks care not only about the effect of changes in interest rates on income but also about the effect of changes in interest rates on the market value of the net worth of the bank.[4]

An alternative method for measuring interest-rate risk, called **duration analysis**, examines the sensitivity of the market value of the bank's net worth to changes in interest rates. Duration analysis is based on Macaulay's concept of *duration*, which measures the average lifetime of a security's stream of payments (described in the Web Appendix to Chapter 4). Recall that duration is a useful concept because it provides a good approximation, particularly when interest-rate changes are small, of the sensitivity of a security's market value to a change in its interest rate using the following formula:

$$\%\Delta P = -DUR \times \frac{\Delta i}{1 + i} \qquad (4)$$

where

$\%\Delta P = (P_{t+1} - P_t)/P_t$ = percent change in market value of security

DUR = duration

i = interest rate

After having determined the duration of all assets and liabilities on the bank's balance sheet, the bank manager could use this formula to calculate how the market value of each asset and liability changes when there is a change in interest rates and then calculate the effect on net worth. There is, however, an easier way to go about doing this, derived from the basic fact about duration we learned in the Web Appendix to Chapter 4: Duration is additive; that is, the duration of a portfolio of securities is the weighted average of the durations of the individual securities, with the weights reflecting the proportion of the portfolio invested in each. What this means is that the bank manager can figure out the effect that interest-rate changes will have on the market value of net worth by calculating the average duration for assets and for liabilities and then using those figures to estimate the effects of interest-rate changes.

To see how a bank manager would do this, let's return to the balance sheet of the First Bank. Suppose that the average duration of its assets is three years (that is, the average lifetime of the stream of payments is three years), while the average duration of its liabilities is two years. In addition, the First Bank has $100 million of assets and, say, $90 million of liabilities, so its bank capital is 10% of assets. With a 5-percentage-point increase in interest rates, the market value of the bank's assets falls by 15% (= −5% × 3 years), a decline of $15 million on the $100 million of assets. However, the market value of the liabilities falls by 10% (= −5% × 2 years), a decline of $9 million on the $90 million of liabilities. The net result is that the net worth (the market value of the assets minus the liabilities) has declined by $6 million, or 6% of the total original asset value. Similarly, a 5-percentage-point decline in interest rates increases the net worth of the First Bank by 6% of the total asset value.

---

[4] Note that accounting net worth is calculated on a historical-cost (book-value) basis, meaning that the value of assets and liabilities is based on their initial price. However, book-value net worth does not give a complete picture of the true worth of a firm; the market value of net worth provides a more accurate measure. This is why duration gap analysis focuses on what happens to the market value of net worth, and not on book value, when interest rates change.

APPLICATION   **Duration Analysis**

Suppose that a bank's average duration of assets is 2.70 years and its average duration of liabilities is 1.03 years. The bank manager wants to know what happens when interest rates rise from 10% to 11%. The total asset value is $100 million, and the total liability value is $95 million. Use Equation 4 to calculate the change in the market value of the assets and liabilities.

Solution

With a total asset value of $100 million, the market value of assets falls by $2.5 million ($100 million × 0.025 = $2.5 million).

$$\%\Delta P = -DUR \times \frac{\Delta i}{1 + i}$$

where

DUR = duration = 2.70
Δi = change in interest rate = 0.11 − 0.10 = 0.01
i = interest rate = 0.10

Thus

$$\%\Delta P = -2.70 \times \frac{0.01}{1 + 0.10} = -0.025 = -2.5\%$$

With total liabilities of $95 million, the market value of liabilities falls by $0.9 million ($95 million × 0.009 = −$0.9 million).

$$\%\Delta P = -DUR \times \frac{\Delta i}{1 + i}$$

where

DUR = duration = 1.03
Δi = change in interest rate = 0.11 − 0.10 = 0.01
i = interest rate = 0.10

Thus

$$\%\Delta P = -1.03 \times \frac{0.01}{1 + 0.10} = -0.009 = -0.9\%$$

The result is that the net worth of the bank would decline by $1.6 million (−$2.5 million − [−$0.9 million] = −$2.5 million + $0.9 million = −$1.6 million).

The bank manager could have gotten to the answer even more quickly by first calculating what is called a duration gap, which is defined as follows:

$$DUR_{gap} = DUR_a - \left(\frac{L}{A} \times DUR_l\right) \tag{5}$$

where
DUR_a = average duration of assets
DUR_l = average duration of liabilities
L = market value of liabilities
A = market value of assets

Then, to estimate what will happen if interest rates change, the bank manager uses the DUR_{gap} calculation in Equation 4 to obtain the change in the market value of net worth as a percentage of total assets. In other words, the change in the market value of net worth as a percentage of assets is calculated as

$$\frac{\Delta NW}{A} = -DUR_{gap} \times \frac{\Delta i}{1 + i} \tag{6}$$

APPLICATION | Duration Gap Analysis

Based on the information provided in the previous Application, use Equation 5 to determine the duration gap for the First Bank and then use equation 6 to determine the change in the market value of net worth as a percentage of assets if interest rates rise from 10% to 11%.

Solution

The duration gap for First Bank is 1.72 years.

$$DUR_{gap} = DUR_a - \left(\frac{L}{A} \times DUR_l\right)$$

where
DUR_a = average duration of assets   = 2.70,
L = market value of liabilities   = 95
A = market value of assets   = 100
DUR_l = average duration of liabilities = 1.03

Thus

$$DUR_{gap} = 2.70 - \left(\frac{95}{100} \times 1.03\right) = 1.72 \text{ years}$$

Hence, a rise in interest rates from 10% to 11% would lead to a change in the market value of net worth as a percentage of assets of -1.6%

$$\frac{\Delta NW}{A} = -DUR_{gap} \times \frac{\Delta i}{1 + i}$$

where

DUR_{gap} = duration gap   = 1.72

Δi = change in interest rate = $0.11 - 0.10 = 0.01$

i = interest rate   = 0.10

Thus

$$\frac{\Delta NW}{A} = -1.72 \times \frac{0.01}{1 + 0.10} = -0.016 = -1.6\%$$

With assets totalling \$100 million, this Application indicates a fall in the market value of net worth of \$1.6 million, which is the same figure that we found in the previous Application.

As our example makes clear, both gap analysis and duration analysis indicate that First Bank will suffer if interest rates rise, but will gain if they fall. Duration analysis and gap analysis are thus useful tools for telling a financial institution manager the institution's degree of exposure to interest-rate risk.[5]

APPLICATION   Strategies for Managing Interest-Rate Risk

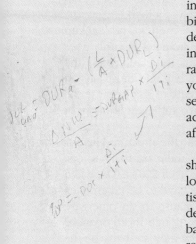

Suppose that as the manager of the First Bank, you have done a duration and gap analysis for the bank as discussed in the text. Now you need to decide which alternative strategies you should pursue to manage the interest-rate risk.

If you firmly believe that interest rates will fall in the future, you may be willing to take no action because you know that the bank has more rate-sensitive liabilities than rate-sensitive assets and so will benefit from the expected interest-rate decline. However, you also realize that the First Bank is subject to substantial interest-rate risk because there is always a possibility that interest rates will rise rather than fall. What should you do to eliminate this interest-rate risk? One thing you could do is to shorten the duration of the bank's assets to increase their rate sensitivity. Alternatively, you could lengthen the duration of the liabilities. By this adjustment of the bank's assets and liabilities, the bank's income will be less affected by interest-rate swings.

One problem with eliminating the First interest-rate risk by altering the balance sheet is that doing so might be very costly in the short run. The bank may be locked into assets and liabilities of particular durations because of where its expertise lies. Fortunately, recently developed financial instruments known as financial derivatives—financial forwards and futures, options, and swaps—can help the bank reduce its interest-rate risk exposure but do not require that the bank rearrange its balance sheet.

---

[5] Gap analysis and duration analysis apply equally to other financial institutions. A second web appendix to this chapter applies gap and duration analyses to a nonbank financial institution; it can be found on the book's MyEconLab at **www.pearsoned.ca/myeconlab**.

OFF-BALANCE-SHEET ACTIVITIES

Although asset and liability management has traditionally been the major concern of banks, in the more competitive environment of recent years banks have been aggressively seeking out profits by engaging in off-balance-sheet activities. Off-balance-sheet activities involve trading financial instruments and generating income from fees and loan sales, activities that affect bank profits but do not appear on bank balance sheets. Indeed, off-balance-sheet activities have been growing in importance for banks: the income from these activities as a percentage of assets has nearly doubled since 1980.

Loan Sales

One type of off-balance-sheet activity that has grown in importance in recent years involves income generated by loan sales. A **loan sale**, also called a *secondary loan participation,* involves a contract that sells all or part of the cash stream from a specific loan so that it no longer is an asset on the bank's balance sheet. Banks earn profits by selling loans for an amount slightly greater than the amount of the original loan. Because the high interest rate on these loans makes them attractive, institutions are willing to buy them even though the higher price means that they earn a slightly lower interest rate than the original interest rate on the loan, usually on the order of 0.15 percentage points.

Generation of Fee Income

Another type of off-balance-sheet activity involves the generation of income from fees that banks receive for providing specialized services to their customers, such as making foreign exchange trades on a customer's behalf, servicing a mortgage-backed security by collecting interest and principal payments and then paying them out, guaranteeing debt securities such as banker's acceptances (by which the bank promises to make interest and principal payments if the party issuing the security cannot), and providing backup lines of credit. There are several types of backup lines of credit. The most important is the loan commitment, under which for a fee the bank agrees to provide a loan at the customer's request, up to a given dollar amount, over a specified period of time. Credit lines are also now available to bank depositors with "overdraft privileges"—these bank customers can write cheques in excess of their deposit balances and, in effect, write themselves a loan.

Off-balance-sheet activities involving guarantees of securities and backup credit lines increase the risk a bank faces. Even though a guaranteed security does not appear on a bank balance sheet, it still exposes the bank to default risk: if the issuer of the security defaults, the bank is left holding the bag and must pay off the security's owner. Backup credit lines also expose the bank to risk because the bank may be forced to provide loans when it does not have sufficient liquidity or when the borrower is a very poor credit risk.

Banks also earn fees by creating financial instruments like the structured investment vehicles (SIVs) mentioned in Chapter 9 and selling them off to investors. However, as became clear during the subprime financial crisis of 2007–2008, when they decline in value, many of these financial instruments have to be taken back onto the balance sheet of the bank sponsoring them, because to do otherwise would severely damage the reputation of the bank. Even though these financial instruments at first appear to be off-balance-sheet, in reality they are back on the balance sheet if they are subject to large losses. To their regret, banks ended up taking large losses on these financial instruments during the subprime financial crisis, indicating that these off-balance-sheet vehicles exposed banks to just as much risk as if they had been part of the balance sheet at the outset.

**Trading
Activities
and Risk-
Management
Techniques**

We have already mentioned that banks' attempts to manage interest-rate risk led them to trading in financial futures, options for debt instruments, and interest-rate swaps. Banks engaged in international banking also conduct transactions in the foreign exchange market. All transactions in these markets are off-balance-sheet activities because they do not have a direct effect on the bank's balance sheet. Although bank trading in these markets is often directed toward reducing risk or facilitating other bank business, banks also try to outguess the markets and engage in speculation. This speculation can be a very risky business and indeed has led to bank insolvencies, the most dramatic being the failure of Barings, a British bank, in 1995.

Trading activities, although often highly profitable, are dangerous because they make it easy for financial institutions and their employees to make huge bets quickly. A particular problem for management of trading activities is that the principal–agent problem, discussed in Chapter 8, is especially severe. Given the ability to place large bets, a trader (the agent), whether she trades in bond markets, in foreign exchange markets, or in financial derivatives, has an incentive to take on excessive risks: if her trading strategy leads to large profits, she is likely to receive a high salary and bonuses, but if she takes large losses, the financial institution (the principal) will have to cover them. As the Barings Bank failure in 1995 so forcefully demonstrated, a trader subject to the principal–agent problem can take an institution that is quite healthy and drive it into insolvency very fast (see the Global box, Barings, Daiwa, Sumitomo, and Société Générale: Rogue Traders and the Principal–Agent Problem).

To reduce the principal–agent problem, managers of financial institutions must set up internal controls to prevent debacles like the one at Barings. Such controls include complete separation of the people in charge of trading activities from those in charge of the bookkeeping for trades. In addition, managers must set limits on the total amount of traders' transactions and on the institution's risk exposure. Managers must also scrutinize risk assessment procedures using the latest computer technology. One such method involves the value-at-risk approach. In this approach, the institution develops a statistical model with which it can calculate the maximum loss that its portfolio is likely to sustain over a given time interval, dubbed the value at risk, or VAR. For example, a bank might estimate that the maximum loss it would be likely to sustain over one day with a probability of 1 in 100 is $1 million; the $1 million figure is the bank's calculated value at risk. Another approach is called "stress testing." In this approach, a manager determines what would happen if a doomsday scenario occured; that is, she looks at the losses the institution would sustain if an unusual combination of bad events occurred. With the value-at-risk approach and stress testing, a financial institution can assess its risk exposure and take steps to reduce it.

Regulators have become concerned about the increased risk that banks are facing from their off-balance-sheet activities, and, as we saw in Chapter 10, are encouraging banks to pay increased attention to risk management. In addition, the Bank for International Settlements is developing additional bank capital requirements based on value-at-risk calculations for a bank's trading activities.

GLOBAL

Barings, Daiwa, Sumitomo, and Société Générale: Rogue Traders and the Principal—Agent Problem

The demise of Barings, a venerable British bank over a century old, is a sad morality tale of how the principal–agent problem operating through a rogue trader can take a financial institution that has a healthy balance sheet one month and turn it into an insolvent tragedy the next.

In July 1992, Nick Leeson, Barings's new head clerk at its Singapore branch, began to speculate on the Nikkei, the Japanese version of the Dow Jones index. By late 1992, Leeson had suffered losses of US$3 million, which he hid from his superiors by stashing the losses in a secret account. He even fooled his superiors into thinking he was generating large profits, thanks to a failure of internal controls at his firm that allowed him to execute trades on the Singapore exchange *and* oversee the book-keeping of those trades. (As anyone who runs a cash business, such as a bar, knows, there is always a lower likelihood of fraud if more than one person handles the cash. Similarly for trading operations, you never mix management of the back room with management of the front room; this principle was grossly violated by Barings management.)

Things didn't get better for Leeson, who by late 1994 had losses exceeding US$250 million. In January and February 1995, he bet the bank. On January 17, 1995, the day of the earthquake in Kobe, Japan, he lost US$75 million, and by the end of the week had lost more than US$150 million. When the stock market declined on February 23, leaving him with a further loss of US$250 million, he called it quits and fled Singapore. Three days later, he turned himself in at the Frankfurt airport. By the end of his wild ride, Leeson's losses, US$1.3 billion in all, ate up Barings's capital and caused the bank to fail. Leeson was subsequently convicted and sent to jail in Singapore for his activities. He was released in 1999 and apologized for his actions.

Our asymmetric information analysis of the principal–agent problem explains Leeson's behaviour and the danger of Barings's management lapse. By letting Leeson control both his own trades and the back room, it increased asymmetric information because it reduced the principal's (Barings's) knowledge about Leeson's trading activities. This lapse increased the moral hazard incentive for him to take risks at the bank's expense, as he was now less likely to be caught. Furthermore, once he had experienced large losses, he had even greater incentives to take on even higher risk because if his bets worked out, he could reverse his losses and keep in good standing with the company, whereas if his bets soured, he had little to lose since he was out of a job anyway. Indeed, the bigger his losses, the more he had to gain by placing bigger bets, which explains the escalation of the amount of his trades as his losses mounted. If Barings's managers had understood the principal–agent problem, they would have been more vigilant at finding out what Leeson was up to, and the bank might still be here today.

Unfortunately, Nick Leeson is no longer a rarity in the rogue traders' billionaire club, those who have lost more than US$1 billion. Over 11 years, Toshihide Iguchi, an officer in the New York branch of Daiwa Bank, also had control of both the bond trading operation and the back room, and he racked up US$1.1 billion in losses over the period. In July 1995, Iguchi disclosed his losses to his superiors, but the management of the bank did not disclose them to its regulators. The result was that Daiwa was slapped with a US$340 million fine and the bank was thrown out of the country by U.S. bank regulators. Yasuo Hamanaka is also a member of the billionaire club. In July 1996, he topped Leeson's and Iguchi's record, losing US$2.6 billion for his employer, the Sumitomo Corporation, one of Japan's top trading companies. Jerome Kerriel's loss for his bank, Société Générale, in January 2008 set the all-time record for a rogue trader: his unauthorized trades cost the bank US$7.2 billion.

The moral of these stories is that management of firms engaged in trading activities must reduce the principal–agent problem by closely monitoring their traders' activities, or the rogues' gallery will continue to grow.

SUMMARY

1. The balance sheet of commercial banks can be thought of as a list of the sources and uses of bank funds. The bank's liabilities are its sources of funds, which include chequable deposits, time deposits, advances from the Bank of Canada, borrowings from other banks and corporations, and bank capital. The bank's assets are its uses of funds, which include cash reserves, cash items in process of collection, deposits at other banks, securities, loans, and other assets (mostly physical capital).

2. Banks make profits through the process of asset transformation: they borrow short (accept deposits) and lend long (make loans). When a bank takes in additional deposits, it gains an equal amount of reserves; when it pays out deposits, it loses an equal amount of reserves.

3. Although more-liquid assets tend to earn lower returns, banks still desire to hold them. Specifically, banks hold reserves because they provide insurance against the costs of a deposit outflow. Banks manage their assets to maximize profits by seeking the highest returns possible on loans and securities while at the same time trying to lower risk and making adequate provisions for liquidity. Although liability management was once a staid affair, large (money centre) banks now actively seek out sources of funds by issuing liabilities such as negotiable CDs or by actively borrowing from other banks and corporations. Banks manage the amount of capital they hold to prevent

bank failure and to meet bank capital requirements set by the regulatory authorities. However, they do not want to hold too much capital because by so doing they will lower the returns to equity holders.

4. The concepts of adverse selection and moral hazard explain the origin of many credit risk management principles involving loan activities, including screening and monitoring, development of long-term customer relationships, loan commitments, collateral, compensating balances, and credit rationing.

5. With the increased volatility of interest rates that occurred in recent years, financial institutions became more concerned about their exposure to interest-rate risk. Gap and duration analyses tell a financial institution if it has fewer rate-sensitive assets than liabilities (in which case a rise in interest rates will reduce income and a fall in interest rates will raise it) or more rate-sensitive assets than liabilities (in which case a rise in interest rates will raise income and a fall in interest rates will reduce it). Financial institutions can manage interest-rate risk by modifying their balance sheets and by making use of new financial instruments.

6. Off-balance-sheet activities consist of trading financial instruments and generating income from fees and loan sales, all of which affect bank profits but are not visible on bank balance sheets. Because these off-balance-sheet activities expose banks to increased risk, bank management must pay particular attention to risk assessment procedures and internal controls to restrict employees from taking on too much risk.

KEY TERMS

asset management, p. 321

balance sheet, p. 314

bank rate, p. 324

banker's risk, p. 317

capital adequacy management, p. 321

compensating balance, p. 333

credit rationing, p. 333

credit risk, p. 322

deposit outflows, p. 321

desired reserves, p. 317

desired reserve ratio, p. 317

duration analysis, p. 336

equity multiplier (EM), p. 327

gap analysis (income gap analysis), p. 334

interbank deposits, p. 317

interest-rate risk, p. 322

items in transit (bank float), p. 317

liability management, p. 321

liquidity management, p. 321

loan commitment, p. 332

loan sale, p. 340

money centre banks, p. 326

overdraft loans (advances), p. 316

reserves, p. 317

return on assets (ROA), p. 327

return on equity (ROE), p. 327

secondary reserves, p. 317

settlement balances, p. 316

T-account, p. 318

vault cash, p. 317

QUESTIONS

You will find the answers to the questions marked with an asterisk in the Textbook Resources section of your MyEconLab.

1. Why might a bank be willing to borrow funds from the Bank of Canada at a higher rate than it can borrow from other banks?

*2. Rank the following bank assets from most to least liquid:
   a. Commercial loans
   b. Securities
   c. Reserves
   d. Physical capital

3. Why has the development of overnight loan markets made it more likely that banks will hold fewer reserves?

*4. If the bank you own has no excess reserves and a sound customer comes in asking for a loan, should you automatically turn the customer down, explaining that you don't have any excess reserves to lend out? Why or why not? What options are available for you to provide the funds your customer needs?

5. If a bank finds that its *ROE* is too low because it has too much bank capital, what can it do to raise its *ROE*?

*6. If a bank is falling short of meeting its capital requirements by $1 million, what three things can it do to rectify the situation?

7. If a bank doubles the amount of its capital and *ROA* stays constant, what will happen to *ROE*?

*8. What does the net interest margin measure, and why is it important to bank managers?

9. Which components of operating expenses experience the greatest fluctuations? Why?

10. Can a financial institution keep borrowers from engaging in risky activities if there are no restrictive covenants written into the loan agreement?

*11. Why are secured loans an important method of lending for financial institutions?

12. "If more customers want to borrow funds at the prevailing interest rate, a financial institution can increase its profits by raising interest rates on its loans." Is this statement true, false, or uncertain? Explain your answer.

*13. Why is being nosy a desirable trait for a banker?

14. A bank almost always insists that the firms it lends to keep compensating balances at the bank. Why?

*15. "Because diversification is a desirable strategy for avoiding risk, it never makes sense for a financial institution to specialize in making specific types of loans." Is this statement true, false, or uncertain? Explain your answer.

QUANTITATIVE PROBLEMS

1. Using the T-accounts of the First Bank and the Second Bank, describe what happens when Jane Brown writes a $50 cheque on her account at the First Bank to pay her friend Joe Green, who in turn deposits the cheque in his account at the Second Bank.

*2. What happens to reserves at the First Bank if one person withdraws $1000 of cash and another person deposits $500 of cash? Use T-accounts to explain your answer.

3. The bank you own has the following balance sheet:

Assets		Liabilities	
Reserves	$ 75 million	Deposits	$500 million
Loans	$525 million	Bank capital	$100 million

If the bank suffers a deposit outflow of $50 million and has a desired reserve ratio on deposits of 10%, what actions must you take to keep your bank from failing?

*4. If a deposit outflow of $50 million occurs, which balance sheet would a bank rather have initially, the balance sheet in Problem 3 or the following balance sheet? Why?

Assets		Liabilities	
Reserves	$100 million	Deposits	$500 million
Loans	$500 million	Bank capital	$100 million

For Problems 5–9, assume that the First Bank initially has the balance sheet shown on page 334. Also assume that the average duration of its assets is three years, that of its liabilities is two years, that interest rates are initially at 10%, and that the bank's equity capital is $10 million.

5. If the First Bank sells $10 million of its fixed-rate assets and replaces them with rate-sensitive assets, what is the income gap for the bank? What will happen to profits next year if interest rates fall by 3 percentage points?

6. If the First bank decides to convert $5 million of its fixed-rate assets into rate-sensitive assets, what will happen to its interest-rate risk? Explain using gap analysis.

7. What happens to the market value of the bank's assets if the interest rate increases by 2 percentage points?

8. What happens to the market value of the bank's liabilities if the interest rate falls by 2 percentage points?

9. What will happen to the bank's net worth if interest rates rise by 10 percentage points? Will the bank stay in business? Why or why not?

10. WestBank just started operations with $6 million in capital. On the first day of operations, it received $100 million in chequable deposits and issued $25 million non-mortgage loans and another $25 million in mortgages.
   a. If the desired reserve ratio is 8%, what does the bank's balance sheet look like?
   b. On the second day of operations, the bank decides to invest $45 million in 30-day T-bills, traded at $4986.70 per $5000 face value. How many T-bills does the bank purchase? How does the bank's balance sheet look after the purchase of these T-bills?
   c. On the third day of operations, deposits fall by $5 million. What does the balance sheet look like? Are there any problems? If yes, how can the bank address the problems?

WEB EXERCISES

1. It is relatively easy to find up-to-date information on banks because of their extensive reporting requirements. Go to **www.osfi-bsif.gc.ca**. This site is sponsored by the Office of the Superintendent of Financial Institutions Canada (OSFI). You will find balance sheet data on domestic banks as well as on foreign bank subsidiaries.
   a. Have bank loans been increasing or decreasing over the last few years?
   b. Has bank capital been increasing? How does it compare to the figure reported in Table 13-1 (p. 315)?

2. Table 13-1 reports the balance sheet of all commercial banks based on aggregate data found in the OSFI's website. Compare this table to the balance sheet information reported (under Financial Highlights) by CIBC at **www.cibc.com /ca/inside-cibc/fin-higlights. html**. Does CIBC have more or less of its portfolio in loans than the average Canadian bank?

3. This chapter discussed the need financial institutions have to control credit risk by lending to creditworthy borrowers. If you allow your credit to deteriorate, you may find yourself unable to borrow when you need to. Go to **www.quicken.com/cms/viewers/article/ banking/39654** and assess your own creditworthiness. What can you do to improve your appeal to lenders?

4. The CDIC is extremely concerned with risk management in banks. High-risk banks are more likely to fail and cost the CDIC money. The CDIC regularly examines banks and rates them using a system called CAMELS. Go to **www.fdic.gov/regulations/ safety/manual/index.html.** What does the acronym CAMELS stand for? Go to Part II. 7.1 and review the discussion of Market Risk. Summarize the interest-rate risk-measurement methods.

Be sure to visit the MyEconLab website at **www.myeconlab.com**. This online homework and tutorial system puts you in control of your own learning with study and practice tools directly correlated to this chapter content.

On the MyEconLab website you will find the following appendices and mini-cases for this chapter:

Appendix 13.1: Measuring Bank Performance
Appendix 13.2: Nonbanking Financial Institutions and Duration Analysis
Mini-Case 13.1: Bank Performance Analysis
Mini-Case 13.2: Calculating and Comparing Gap, Duration, and Risk Management Alternatives

CHAPTER 14

Risk Management with Financial Derivatives

LEARNING OBJECTIVES

After studying this chapter you should be able to

1. distinguish among forwards, futures, options, swaps, and credit derivatives
2. discuss the success of the financial derivatives market
3. explain how managers of financial institutions use financial derivatives to manage interest-rate and foreign exchange risk
4. outline the dangers of derivatives

PREVIEW

Starting in the 1970s and increasingly in the 1980s and 1990s, the world became a riskier place for financial institutions. Swings in interest rates widened, and the bond and stock markets went through some episodes of increased volatility. As a result of these developments, managers of financial institutions have become more concerned with reducing the risk their institutions face. Given the greater demand for risk reduction, the process of financial innovation came to the rescue by producing new assets that help financial institution managers manage risk better. These assets, called financial derivatives, have payoffs that are linked to previously issued securities and are extremely useful risk reduction tools.

In this chapter we look at the most important financial derivatives that managers of financial institutions use to reduce risk: forward contracts, financial futures, options, and swaps. We examine not only how markets for each of these financial derivatives work but also how each can be used by financial institution managers to reduce risk. We also study financial derivatives because they have become an important source of profits for financial institutions, particularly larger banks.

HEDGING

Financial derivatives are so effective in reducing risk because they enable financial institutions to hedge, that is, engage in a financial transaction that reduces or eliminates risk. When a financial institution has bought an asset, it is said to have taken a **long position**, and this exposes the institution to risk if the returns on the asset are uncertain. On the other hand, if it has sold an asset that it has agreed to deliver to another party at a future date, it is said to have taken a **short position**, and this can also expose the institution to risk. Financial derivatives can be used to reduce risk by invoking the following basic principle of hedging: ***Hedging risk involves engaging in a financial transaction that offsets a long position by taking an***

additional short position, or offsets a short position by taking an additional long position. In other words, if a financial institution has *bought* a security and has therefore taken a long position, it conducts a hedge by contracting to *sell* that security (take a short position) at some future date. Alternatively, if it has taken a short position by *selling* a security that it needs to deliver at a future date, then it conducts a hedge by contracting to *buy* that security (take a long position) at a future date. We first look at how this principle can be applied using forward contracts.

FORWARD CONTRACTS AND MARKETS

Forward contracts are agreements by two parties to engage in a financial transaction at a future (forward) point in time. Here we focus on forward contracts that are linked to debt instruments, called **interest-rate forward contracts**; later in the chapter we discuss forward contracts for foreign currencies.

Interest-Rate Forward Contracts

Interest-rate forward contracts involve the future sale (or purchase) of a debt instrument and have several dimensions: (1) specification of the actual debt instrument that will be delivered at a future date, (2) amount of the debt instrument to be delivered, (3) price (interest rate) on the debt instrument when it is delivered, and (4) date on which delivery will take place. An example of an interest-rate forward contract might be an agreement for the First Bank to sell to the Rock Solid Insurance Company, one year from today, $5 million face value of the 6s of 2030 Canada bonds (coupon bonds with a 6% coupon rate that mature in 2030) at a price that yields the same interest rate on these bonds as today's, say, 6%. Because Rock Solid will buy the securities at a future date, it has taken a long position, while the First Bank, which will sell the securities, has taken a short position.

APPLICATION   **Hedging with Interest-Rate Forward Contracts**

Why would the First Bank want to enter into this forward contract with Rock Solid Insurance Company in the first place? To understand, suppose that you are the manager of the First Bank and have previously bought $5 million of the 6s of 2030 Canada bonds, which currently sell at par value and so their yield to maturity is also 6%. Because these are long-term bonds, you recognize that you are exposed to substantial interest-rate risk and worry that if interest rates rise in the future, the price of these bonds will fall, resulting in a substantial capital loss that may cost you your job. How do you hedge this risk?

Knowing the basic principle of hedging, you see that your long position in these bonds must be offset by a short position with a forward contract. That is, you need to contract to sell these bonds at a future date at the current par value price. As a result you agree with another party, in this case, Rock Solid Insurance Company, to sell them the $5 million of the 6s of 2030 Canada bonds at par one year from today. By entering into this forward contract, you have locked in the future price and so have eliminated the price risk the First Bank faces from interest-rate changes. In other words, you have successfully hedged against interest-rate risk.

Why would the Rock Solid Insurance Company want to enter into the forward contract with the First Bank? Rock Solid expects to receive premiums of $5 million

in one year's time that it will want to invest in the 6s of 2030 but worries that interest rates on these bonds will decline between now and next year. By using the forward contract, it is able to lock in the 6% interest rate on the Canada bonds (which
will be sold to it by the First Bank).

**Pros and Cons
of Forward
Contracts**

The advantage of forward contracts is that they can be as flexible as the parties
involved want them to be. This means that an institution like the First Bank may
be able to hedge completely the interest-rate risk for the exact security it is holding in its portfolio, just as it has in our example.

However, forward contracts suffer from two problems that severely limit their
usefulness. The first is that it may be very hard for an institution like the First Bank
to find another party (called a *counterparty*) to make the contract with. There are
brokers to facilitate the matching up of parties like the First Bank with the Rock
Solid Insurance Company, but there may be few institutions that want to engage
in a forward contract specifically for the 6s of 2030. This means that it may prove
impossible to find a counterparty when a financial institution like the First Bank
wants to make a specific type of forward contract. Furthermore, even if the First
Bank finds a counterparty, it may not get as high a price as it wants because there
may not be anyone else to make the deal with. A serious problem for the market
in interest-rate forward contracts, then, is that it may be difficult to make the financial transaction or that it will have to be made at a disadvantageous price; in the
parlance of the financial world, this market suffers from a *lack of liquidity*. (Note
that this use of the term *liquidity* when it is applied to a market is somewhat
broader than its use when it is applied to an asset. For an asset, liquidity refers to
the ease with which the asset can be turned into cash, whereas for a market, liquidity refers to the ease of carrying out financial transactions.)

The second problem with forward contracts is that they are subject to default
risk. Suppose that in one year's time, interest rates rise so that the price of the
6s of 2030 falls. The Rock Solid Insurance Company might then decide that it
would like to default on the forward contract with the First Bank because it can
now buy the bonds at a price lower than the agreed price in the forward contract.
Or perhaps Rock Solid may not have been rock solid and will have gone bust
during the year and so is no longer available to complete the terms of the forward contract. Because there is no outside organization guaranteeing the contract, the only recourse is for the First Bank to go to the courts to sue Rock Solid,
but this process will be costly. Furthermore, if Rock Solid is already bankrupt, the
First Bank will suffer a loss; the bank can no longer sell the 6s of 2030 at the price
it had agreed with Rock Solid but instead will have to sell at a price well below
that because the price of these bonds has fallen.

The presence of default risk in forward contracts means that parties to these
contracts must check each other out to be sure that the counterparty is both financially sound and likely to be honest and live up to its contractual obligations.
Because this is a costly process and because all the adverse selection and moral
hazard problems discussed in earlier chapters apply, default risk is a major barrier
to the use of interest-rate forward contracts. When the default risk problem is
combined with a lack of liquidity, we see that these contracts may be of limited
usefulness to financial institutions. Although there is a market for interest-rate forward contracts, particularly in mortgage-backed and Canada securities, it is not
nearly as large as the financial futures market, to which we turn next.

FINANCIAL FUTURES CONTRACTS AND MARKETS

Given the default risk and liquidity problems in the interest-rate forward market, another solution to hedging interest-rate, stock market, and foreign exchange risks was needed. This solution was provided by the development of financial futures contracts by the Chicago Board of Trade starting in 1975.

Financial futures are classified as (1) interest-rate futures, (2) stock index futures, and (3) currency futures. In Canada, such contracts are traded on the Montreal Exchange (ME) that maintains active markets in short- and long-term Canada bond futures and stock index futures (see the FYI box, The Montreal Exchange and the Canadian Derivatives Clearing Corporation (CDCC)). In what follows, we discuss interest-rate and stock index futures. Later in the chapter, we also discuss currency futures.

Interest-Rate Futures Contracts

An **interest-rate futures contract** is similar to an interest-rate forward contract in that it specifies that a financial instrument must be delivered by one party to another on a stated future date. However, it differs from an interest-rate forward contract in several ways that overcome some of the liquidity and default problems of forward markets.

To understand what interest-rate futures contracts are all about, let's look at one of the most widely traded futures contracts, that for 10-year Canada bonds, which are traded on the Montreal Exchange. (An illustration of how prices on these contracts are quoted can be found in the Financial News box, Interest-Rate Futures.)

FYI | **The Montreal Exchange and the Canadian Derivatives Clearing Corporation (CDCC)**

The Montreal Exchange (ME) is Canada's oldest exchange, founded in 1874. In 1975 the ME became the first exchange in Canada to list equity derivatives (equity futures and options) and in December 2001 it became the first fully automated derivatives exchange in North America. Today, the Montreal Exchange is a world-class derivatives exchange, offering market participants a range of equity, interest rate, and index derivative products.

For example, in addition to offering equity futures and options, the Montreal Exchange also offers a large number of interest rate futures such as the BAX (3-month Canadian Bankers' Acceptances futures), the CGB (10-year Government of Canada Bond futures), and the ONX (30-day Overnight Repo Rate futures), as well as options on BAX and options on CGB. The ME also offers index derivatives based on the S&P/TSX 60 index, such as the SXF (S&P Canada 60 Index futures) and the SXO (S&P Canada 60 Index options), as well as index derivatives based on a large number of sectorial indices. Finally, the Montreal Exchange offers sponsored options—financial derivatives instruments issued by its wholly owned subsidiary, the Canadian Derivatives Clearing Corporation (CDCC), and sponsored by financial institutions.

The CDCC is the issuer, clearinghouse, and guarantor of all exchange-traded derivative products traded in Canada. Until recently, the CDCC was a nonprofit organization and therefore not subject to taxation by the Canada Revenue Agency. Effective January 1, 2001, however, the CDCC changed its articles of association and is now a profit-oriented corporation and therefore subject to corporate income taxes.

FINANCIAL NEWS

Interest-Rate Futures

The prices for interest-rate futures contracts are available on the Montreal Exchange's website.   An excerpt is reproduced here.

3-Month Canadian Bankers' Acceptances Futures (BAX)

Month	Open	High	Low	Last	Net Chg.	Volume	Op. Int.
JN 10	98.460	98.460	98.400	98.460	−0.050	1067	3440
SE 10	98.250	98.250	98.190	98.220	−0.150	153	827

30-Day Overnight Repo Rate Futures (ONX)

Month	Open	High	Low	Last	Net Chg.	Volume	Op. Int.
SE 09	0.000	0.000	0.000	98.050	0.000	0	0
DE 09	0.000	0.000	0.000	98.150	0.000	0	0

10-Year Government of Canada Bond Futures (CGB)

Month	Open	High	Low	Last	Net Chg.	Volume	Op. Int.
MR 09	125.020	125.300	124.230	125.250	0.020	11415	134779

Source: TMX Montreal Exchange, "Intra-Session Summary," www.m-x.ca/nego_intra_en.php.

The following information is included in each column. The Montreal Exchange's contract for delivery of 10-year Canadian government bonds in March 2009 is used as an example.

Month: Maturity month of the futures contract.

Open: Opening price—125.020 is $125 020 for the March contract.

High: Highest traded price that day—125.300 is $125 300 for the March contract.

Low: Lowest traded price that day—124.230 is $124 230 for the March contract.

Last: The closing price that day—125.250 is $125 250 for the March contract.

Net Chg: Change in the settlement price from the previous day—0.020 is $20.

Volume: Number of contracts traded that day: 11 415.

Op. Int.: Number of contracts outstanding—134 779 for the March contract, with a face value of (134 779 × $100 000).

The contract value is for $100 000 face value of bonds. Prices are quoted in points, with each point equal to $1000, and the smallest change in price is one hundredth of a point ($10). This contract specifies that the bonds to be delivered must have at least 10 years to maturity at the delivery date. If the Canada bonds delivered to settle the futures contract have a coupon rate different from (say) the 6% specified in the futures contract, the amount of bonds to be delivered is adjusted to reflect the difference in value between the delivered bonds and the 6% coupon bond. In line with the terminology used for forward contracts, parties who have bought a futures contract and thereby agreed to buy (take delivery of) the bonds are said to have taken a *long position*, and parties who have sold a futures contract and thereby agreed to sell (deliver) the bonds have taken a *short position*.

To make our understanding of this contract more concrete, let's consider what happens when you buy or sell one of these Canada bond futures contracts. Let's say that on January 1, you sell one $100 000 March contract at a price of 115 (that is, $115 000). By selling this contract, you agree to deliver $100 000 face value of the long-term Canada bonds to the contract's counterparty at the end of March for $115 000. By buying the contract at a price of 115, the buyer has agreed to pay $115 000 for the $100 000 face value of bonds when you deliver them at the end of March. If interest rates on long-term bonds rise so that when the contract matures at the end of March the price of these bonds has fallen to 110 ($110 000 per $100 000 of face value), the buyer of the contract will have lost $5000 because he or she paid $115 000 for the bonds but can sell them only for the market price of $110 000. But you, the seller of the contract, will have gained $5000 because you can now sell the bonds to the buyer for $115 000 but have to pay only $110 000 for them in the market.

It is even easier to describe what happens to the parties who have purchased futures contracts and those who have sold futures contracts if we recognize the following fact: ***At the expiration date of a futures contract, the price of the contract is the same as the price of the underlying asset to be delivered.*** To see why this is the case, consider what happens on the expiration date of the March contract at the end of March when the price of the underlying $100 000 face value Canada bond is 110 ($110 000). If the futures contract is selling below 110, say, at 109, a trader can buy the contract for $109 000, take delivery of the bond, and immediately sell it for $110 000, thereby earning a quick profit of $1000. Because earning this profit involves no risk, it is a great deal that everyone would like to get in on. That means that everyone will try to buy the contract, and as a result, its price will rise. Only when the price rises to 110 will the profit opportunity cease to exist and the buying pressure disappear. Conversely, if the price of the futures contract is above 110, say, at 111, everyone will want to sell the contract. Now the sellers get $111 000 from selling the futures contract but have to pay only $110 000 for the Canada bonds that they must deliver to the buyer of the contract, and the $1000 difference is their profit. Because this profit involves no risk, traders will continue to sell the futures contract until its price falls back down to 110, at which price there are no longer any profits to be made. The elimination of riskless profit opportunities in the futures market is referred to as **arbitrage**, and it guarantees that the price of a futures contract at expiration equals the price of the underlying asset to be delivered.[1]

Armed with the fact that a futures contract at expiration equals the price of the underlying asset makes it even easier to see who profits and loses from such a contract when interest rates change. When interest rates have risen so that the price of the Canada bond is 110 on the expiration day at the end of March, the March Canada bond futures contract will also have a price of 110. Thus if you bought the contract for 115 in January, you have a loss of 5 points, or $5000 (5% of $100 000). But if you sold the futures contract at 115 in January, the decline in price to 110 means that you have a profit of 5 points, or $5000.

---

[1] In actuality, futures contracts sometimes set conditions for delivery of the underlying assets that cause the price of the contract at expiration to differ slightly from the price of the underlying assets. Because the difference in price is extremely small, we ignore it in this chapter.

APPLICATION   **Hedging with Interest-Rate Futures**

As the manager of the First Bank, you can also use interest-rate futures to hedge the interest-rate risk on its holdings of $5 million of the 6s of 2030 (Canada bonds with a 6% coupon rate that mature in 2030).

To see how to do this, suppose that in March 2010, the 6s of 2030 are the long-term bonds that would be delivered in the Montreal Exchange's Canada bond futures contract expiring one year in the future, in March 2011. Also suppose that the interest rate on these bonds is expected to remain at 6% over the next year so that both the 6s of 2030 and the futures contract are selling at par (i.e., the $5 million of bonds is selling for $5 million and the $100 000 futures contract is selling for $100 000). The basic principle of hedging indicates that you need to offset the long position in these bonds with a short position, so you have to sell the futures contract. But how many contracts should you sell? The number of contracts required to hedge the interest-rate risk is found by dividing the amount of the asset to be hedged by the dollar value of each contract, as is shown in Equation 1 below.

$$NC = VA/VC \tag{1}$$

where

NC = number of contracts for the hedge
VA = value of the asset
VC = value of each contract

Given that the 6s of 2030 are the long-term bonds that would be delivered in the Montreal Exchange's Canada bond futures contract expiring one year in the future and that the interest rate on these bonds is expected to remain at 6% over the next year, so that both the 6s of 2030 and the futures contract are selling at par, how many contracts must First Bank sell to remove its interest-rate exposure from its $5 million holdings of the 6s of 2030?[2]

If

$$VA = \$5 \text{ million}$$
$$VC = \$100\ 000$$

Then

$$NC = \$5 \text{ million}/\$100\ 000 = 50$$

You therefore hedge the interest-rate risk by selling 50 of the Canada bond futures contracts.

Now suppose that over the next year, interest rates increase to 8% due to an increased threat of inflation. The value of the 6s of 2030 that the First Bank is holding will then fall to $4 039 640 in March 2011.[3] Thus, the loss from the long position in these bonds is $960 360 as shown below:

---

[2] In the real world, designing a hedge is somewhat more complicated than the example here because the bond that is most likely to be delivered might not be a 6s of 2030.

[3] The value of the bonds can be calculated using a financial calculator as follows: FV = $5 000 000, PMT = $300 000, I = 8%, N = 19, PV = $4 039 640.

Value in March 2011 @ 8% interest rate	$4 039 640
Value in March 2010 @ 6% interest rate	−$5 000 000
Loss	−$ 960 360

However, the short position in the 50 futures contracts that obligate you to deliver $5 million of the 6s of 2030 in March 2011 has a value equal to $4 039 640, the value of the $5 million of bonds after the interest rate has risen to 8%. Yet when you sold the futures contract, the buyer was obligated to pay you $5 million on the maturity date. Thus the gain from the short position on these contracts is also $960 360:

Amount paid to you in March 2011, agreed in March 2010	$5 000 000
Cost of bonds delivered in March 2011 @ 8% interest rate	−$4 039 640
Gain	$ 960 360

Therefore, the net gain for the First Bank is zero, showing that the hedge has been conducted successfully.

The hedge just described is called a **micro hedge** because the financial institution is hedging the interest-rate risk for a specific asset it is holding. A second type of hedge that financial institutions engage in is called a **macro hedge**, in which the hedge is for the institution's entire portfolio. For example, if a bank has more rate-sensitive liabilities than assets, a rise in interest rates will cause the value of the bank to decline. By selling interest-rate future contracts that will yield a profit when interest rates rise, the bank can offset the losses on its overall portfolio from an interest-rate rise and thereby hedge its interest-rate risk.

Organization of Trading in Financial Futures Markets

Financial futures contracts are traded on organized exchanges such as the Chicago Board of Trade, the Chicago Mercantile Exchange, the Montreal Exchange, the London International Financial Futures Exchange, and the Marché à Terme International de France. These futures exchanges are highly competitive with one another, and each organization tries to design contracts and set rules that will increase the amount of futures trading on its exchange. The exchanges are also regulated to ensure that prices in the market are not being manipulated. The most widely traded financial futures contracts in the U.S. and the exchanges where they are traded (along with the number of contracts outstanding, called **open interest**, in January 2009) are listed in Table 14-1.

Given the globalization of other financial markets in recent years, it is not surprising that increased international competition has been occurring in financial futures markets as well.

The Globalization of Financial Futures Markets

Because futures exchanges in the United States were the first to develop financial futures, they dominated the trading of financial futures in the early 1980s. For example, in 1985, all of the top ten futures contracts were traded on exchanges in the United States. With the rapid growth of financial futures markets and the resulting high profits made by the American exchanges, exchanges in other countries saw a profit opportunity and began to enter the business. By the 1990s, Eurodollar contracts traded on the London International Financial

TABLE 14-1   Widely Traded Financial Futures Contracts in the United States

Type of Contract	Contract Size	Open Interest January 2009
Interest Rate Contracts		
Treasury bonds	$100 000	715 939
Treasury notes	$100 000	1 060 707
Five-year Treasury notes	$100 000	926 329
Two-year Treasury notes	$200 000	482 940
Thirty-day Fed funds rate	$5 million	416 967
One-month LIBOR	$3 million	23 128
Eurodollar	$4 million	6 802 183
Euroyen	$100 million	10 295
Stock Index Contracts		
Standard & Poor's 500 Index	$250 × index	556 751
Standard & Poor's MIDCAP 400	$500 × index	3 941
NASDAQ 100	$100 × index	26 798
Nikkei 225 Stock Average	$5 × index	37 591
Currency Contracts		
Yen	12 500 000 yen	64 480
Euro	125 000 euros	144 993
Canadian dollar	100 000 Canadian $	26 619
British pound	100 000 pounds	41 882
Swiss franc	125 000 francs	5 575
Mexican peso	500 000 new pesos	33 465

Source: www.cmegroup.com/market-data/volume-open-interest/index.html, click on "CME Group Open Interest Report"

Futures Exchange, Japanese government bond contracts and Euroyen contracts traded on the Tokyo Stock Exchange, French government bond contracts traded on the Marché à Terme International de France, and Nikkei 225 contracts traded on the Osaka Securities Exchange all became among the most widely traded futures contracts in the world. Even developing countries are getting into the act. In 1996, seven developing countries (also referred to as *emerging-market countries*) established futures exchanges, and this number is expected to double within a few years.

International competition has also spurred knockoffs of the most popular financial futures contracts initially developed in the United States. These contracts traded on financial futures exchanges in other countries are virtually identical to those traded in the United States and have the advantage that they can be traded when the American exchanges are closed. The movement to 24-hour-a-day trading in financial futures has been further stimulated by the development of the Globex electronic trading platform, which allows traders throughout the world to trade futures even when the exchanges are not officially open. Financial futures trading is thus well on the way to being completely internationalized, and competition between U.S. and foreign exchanges is now intense.

Explaining the Success of Futures Markets

There are several differences between financial futures and forward contracts and in the organization of their markets that help explain why financial futures markets, like those for Canada bonds, have been so successful.

Several features of futures contracts were designed to overcome the liquidity problem inherent in forward contracts. The first feature is that, in contrast to forward contracts, the quantities delivered and the delivery dates of futures contracts are standardized, making it more likely that different parties can be matched up in the futures market, thereby increasing the liquidity of the market. In the case of the 10-year Canada bond futures contract, the quantity delivered is $100 000 face value of bonds, and the delivery dates are set to be the last business day of March, June, September, and December. The second feature is that after the futures contract has been bought or sold, it can be traded (bought or sold) again at any time until the delivery date. In contrast, once a forward contract is agreed on, it typically cannot be traded. The third feature is that in a futures contract, not just one specific type of Canada bond is deliverable on the delivery date, as in a forward contract. Instead, any Canada bond that matures in more than 10 years and is not callable for 10 years is eligible for delivery. Allowing continuous trading also increases the liquidity of the futures market, as does the ability to deliver a range of Canada bonds rather than one specific bond.

Another reason why futures contracts specify that more than one bond is eligible for delivery is to limit the possibility that someone might corner the market and "squeeze" traders who have sold contracts. To corner the market, someone buys up all the deliverable securities so that investors with a short position cannot obtain from anyone else the securities that they contractually must deliver on the delivery date. As a result, the person who has cornered the market can set exorbitant prices for the securities that investors with a short position must buy to fulfill their obligations under the futures contract. The person who has cornered the market makes a fortune, but investors with a short position take a terrific loss. Clearly, the possibility that corners might occur in the market will discourage people from taking a short position and might therefore decrease the size of the market. By allowing many different securities to be delivered, the futures contract makes it harder for anyone to corner the market because a much larger amount of securities would have to be purchased to establish the corner. Corners are more than a theoretical possibility, as the FYI box, The Hunt Brothers and the Silver Crash, indicates, and are a concern to both regulators and the organized exchanges that design futures contracts.

Trading in the futures market has been organized differently from trading in forward markets to overcome the default risk problems arising in forward contracts. In both types, for every contract there must be a buyer who is taking a long position and a seller who is taking a short position. However, the buyer and seller of a futures contract make their contract not with each other but with the clearinghouse associated with the futures exchange. This setup means that the buyer of the futures contract does not need to worry about the financial health or trustworthiness of the seller, or vice versa, as in the forward market. As long as the clearinghouse is financially solid, buyers and sellers of futures contracts do not have to worry about default risk.

To make sure that the clearinghouse is financially sound and does not run into financial difficulties that might jeopardize its contracts, buyers or sellers of futures contracts must put an initial deposit, called a **margin requirement**, of perhaps $2000 per Canada bond contract into a margin account kept at their brokerage firm. Futures contracts are then **marked to market** every day. What

FYI   The Hunt Brothers and the Silver Crash

In early 1979, two Texas billionaires, W. Herbert Hunt and his brother, Nelson Bunker Hunt, decided that they were going to get into the silver market in a big way. Herbert stated his reasoning for purchasing silver as follows: "I became convinced that the economy of the United States was in a weakening condition. This reinforced my belief that investment in precious metals was wise . . . because of rampant inflation." Although the Hunts' stated reason for purchasing silver was that it was a good investment, others felt that their real motive was to establish a corner in the silver market. Along with other associates, several of them from the Saudi royal family, the Hunts purchased close to 300 million ounces of silver in the form of either actual bullion or silver futures contracts. The result was that the price of silver rose from US$6 an ounce to over US$50 an ounce by January 1980.

Once the regulators and the futures exchanges got wind of what the Hunts were up to, they decided to take action to eliminate the possibility of a corner by limiting to 2000 the number of contracts that any single trader could hold. This limit, which was equivalent to 10 million ounces, was only a small fraction of what the Hunts were holding, and so they were forced to sell. The silver market collapsed soon afterward, with the price of silver declining back to below US$10 an ounce. The losses to the Hunts were estimated to be in excess of US$1 billion, and they soon found themselves in financial difficulty. They had to go into debt to the tune of US$1.1 billion, mortgaging not only the family's holdings in the Placid Oil Company but also 75 000 head of cattle, a stable of thoroughbred horses, paintings, jewellery, and even such mundane items as irrigation pumps and lawn mowers. Eventually both Hunt brothers were forced into declaring personal bankruptcy, earning them the dubious distinction of declaring the largest personal bankruptcies ever in the United States.

Nelson and Herbert Hunt paid a heavy price for their excursion into the silver market, but at least Nelson retained his sense of humour. When asked right after the collapse of the silver market how he felt about his losses, he said, "A billion dollars isn't what it used to be."

Source: G. Christian Hill, "Dynasty's Decline: The Current Question About the Hunts of Dallas: How Poor Are They?" *Wall Street Journal*, November 14, 1984, p. C28. Republished by permission of Dow Jones, Inc. via Copyright Clearance Center, Inc. © 2002 Dow Jones and Company, Inc. All rights reserved worldwide.

this means is that at the end of every trading day, the change in the value of the futures contract is added to or subtracted from the margin account. Suppose that after buying the Canada bond contract at a price of 115 on Wednesday morning, its closing price at the end of the day, the *settlement price*, falls to 114. You now have a loss of 1 point, or $1000, on the contract, and the seller who sold you the contract has a gain of 1 point, or $1000. The $1000 gain is added to the seller's margin account, making a total of $3000 in that account, and the $1000 loss is subtracted from your account, so you now only have $1000 in your account. If the amount in this margin account falls below the maintenance margin requirement (which can be the same as the initial requirement but is usually a little less), the trader is required to add money to the account. For example, if the maintenance margin requirement is also $2000, you would have to add $1000 to your account to bring it up to $2000. Margin requirements and marking to market make it far less likely that a trader will default on a contract, thus protecting the futures exchange from losses.

A final advantage that futures markets have over forward markets is that most futures contracts do not result in delivery of the underlying asset on the expiration date, whereas forward contracts do. A trader who sold a futures contract is allowed to avoid delivery on the expiration date by making an offsetting purchase of a futures contract. Because the simultaneous holding of the long and short positions means that the trader would in effect be delivering the bonds to itself, under the exchange rules the trader is allowed to cancel both contracts. Allowing traders to cancel their contracts in this way lowers the cost of conducting trades in the futures market relative to the forward market in that a futures trader can avoid the costs of physical delivery, which is not so easy with forward contracts.

APPLICATION	Hedging Foreign Exchange Risk

As we discussed in Chapter 1, foreign exchange rates have been highly volatile in recent years. The large fluctuations in exchange rates subject financial institutions and other businesses to significant foreign exchange risk because they generate substantial gains and losses. Luckily for financial institution managers, the financial derivatives discussed in this chapter—forward and financial futures contracts—can be used to hedge foreign exchange risk.

To understand how financial institution managers manage foreign exchange risk, let's suppose that in January, the First Bank's customer Frivolous Luxuries, Inc. is due a payment of 10 million euros in two months for $14 million worth of goods it has just sold in Germany. Frivolous Luxuries is concerned that if the value of the euro falls substantially from its current value of $1.40, the company might suffer a large loss because the 10 million euro payment will no longer be worth $14 million. So Sam, the CEO of Frivolous Luxuries, calls up his friend Mona, the manager of the First Bank, and asks her to hedge this foreign exchange risk for his company. Let's see how the bank manager does this using forward and financial futures contracts.

Hedging Foreign Exchange Risk with Forward Contracts

Forward markets in foreign exchange have been highly developed by commercial banks and investment banking operations that engage in extensive foreign exchange trading and so are widely used to hedge foreign exchange risk. Mona knows that she can use this market to hedge the foreign exchange risk for Frivolous Luxuries. Such a hedge is quite straightforward for her to execute. Because the payment of euros in two months means that at that time Sam would hold a long position in euros, Mona knows that the basic principle of hedging indicates that she should offset this long position by a short position. Thus, she just enters a forward contract that obligates her to sell 10 million euros two months from now in exchange for dollars at the current forward rate of $1.40 per euro.[4]

---

[4] The forward exchange rate will probably differ slightly from the current spot rate of $1.40 per euro because the interest rates in Europe and Canada may not be equal. In that case, as we will see in Chapter 19, the future expected exchange rate will not equal the current spot rate and neither will the forward rate. However, since interest differentials have typically been less than 6% at an annual rate (1% bimonthly), the expected appreciation or depreciation of the euro over a two-month period has always been less than 1%. Thus the forward rate is always close to the current spot rate, and so our assumption in the example that the forward rate and the spot rate are the same is a reasonable one.

In two months, when her customer receives the 10 million euros, the forward contract ensures that it is exchanged for dollars at an exchange rate of $1.40 per euro, thus yielding $14 million. No matter what happens to future exchange rates, Frivolous Luxuries will be guaranteed $14 million for the goods it sold in Germany. Mona calls up her friend Sam to let him know that his company is now protected from any foreign exchange movements, and he thanks her for her help.

Hedging Foreign Exchange Risk with Futures Contracts

As an alternative, Mona could have used the currency futures market to hedge the foreign exchange risk. In this case, she would see that the Chicago Mercantile Exchange has a euro contract with a contract amount of 125 000 euros and a price of $1.40 per euro. To do the hedge, Mona must sell euros as with the forward contract, to the tune of $14 million of the March futures. How many of the Chicago Mercantile Exchange March euro contracts must Mona sell in order to hedge the 10 million euro payment due in March?

Using Equation 1 with

$$VA = 10 \text{ million euros}$$
$$VC = 125\ 000 \text{ euros}$$

we have

$$NC = 10 \text{ million}/125\ 000 = 80$$

Thus, Mona can hedge the 10 million euros by selling 80 of the CME euro contracts. Given the $1.40 per euro price, the sale of the contract yields $80 \times 125\ 000$ euros = $14 million. The futures hedge thus again enables her to lock in the exchange rate for Frivolous Luxuries so that it gets its payment of $14 million.

One advantage of using the futures market is that the contract size of 125 000 euros, worth $175 000, is quite a bit smaller than the minimum size of a forward contract, which is usually $1 million or more. However, in this case, the bank manager is making a large enough transaction that she can use either the forward or the futures market. Her choice depends on whether the transaction costs are lower in one market than in the other. If the First Bank is active in the forward market, that market would probably have the lower transaction costs, but if First Bank rarely deals in foreign exchange forward contracts, the bank manager may do better by sticking with the futures market.

STOCK INDEX FUTURES

As we have seen, interest rate futures markets can be useful in hedging interest-rate risk. However, financial institution managers, particularly those who manage mutual funds, pension funds, and insurance companies, also worry about **stock market risk**, the risk that occurs because stock prices fluctuate. Stock index futures were developed in 1982 to meet the need to manage stock market risk, and they have become among the most widely traded of all futures contracts. The futures trading in stock price indexes is now controversial (see the FYI box, Program Trading and Portfolio Insurance: Were They to Blame for the Stock Market Crash of 1987?) because critics assert that it has led to substantial increases in market volatility, especially in such episodes as 1987's stock market crash.

FYI	Program Trading and Portfolio Insurance: Were They to Blame for the Stock Market Crash of 1987?

In the aftermath of the Black Monday crash on October 19, 1987, in which the U.S. stock market declined by over 20% and the Canadian market by 11% in one day, trading strategies involving stock price index futures markets have been accused of being culprits in the market collapse. One such strategy, called program trading, involves computer-directed trading between the stock index futures and the stocks whose prices are reflected in the stock price index. Program trading is a form of arbitrage conducted to keep stock index futures and stock prices in line with each other. For example, when the price of the stock index futures contract is far below the prices of the underlying stocks in the index, program traders buy index futures, thereby increasing their price, and sell the stocks, thereby lowering their price. Critics of program trading assert that the sharp fall in stock index futures prices on Black Monday led to massive selling in the stock market to keep stock prices in line with the stock index futures prices.

Some experts also blame portfolio insurance for amplifying the crash because they feel that when the stock market started to fall, uncertainty in the market increased, and the resulting increased desire to hedge stocks led to massive selling of stock index futures. The resulting large price declines in stock index futures contracts then led to massive selling of stocks by program traders to keep prices in line.

Because they view program trading and portfolio insurance as causes of the October 1987 market collapse, critics of stock index futures have advocated restrictions on their trading. In response, certain brokerage firms, as well as organized exchanges, have placed limits on program trading. For example, the New York Stock Exchange has curbed computerized program trading when the Dow Jones Industrial Average moves by more than 50 points in one day. However, some prominent finance scholars (among them Nobel laureate Merton Miller of the University of Chicago) do not accept the hypothesis that program trading and portfolio insurance provoked the stock market crash. They believe that the prices of stock index futures primarily reflect the same economic forces that move stock prices—changes in the market's underlying assessment of the value of stocks.

Stock Index Futures Contracts

To understand stock index futures contracts, let's look at the Standard & Poor's 500 Index futures contract (shown in the Financial News box, Stock Index Futures), the most widely traded stock index futures contract in North America. (The S&P 500 Index measures the value of 500 of the most widely traded stocks in the United States.) Stock index futures contracts differ from most other financial futures contracts in that they are settled with a cash delivery rather than with the delivery of a security. Cash settlement gives these contracts the advantage of a high degree of liquidity and also rules out the possibility of anyone cornering the market. In the case of the S&P 500 Index contract, at the final settlement date, the cash delivery due is US$250 times the index, so if the index is at 1000 on the final settlement date, $250 000 would be the amount due. The price quotes for this contract are also quoted in terms of index points, so a change of 1 point represents a change of $250 in the contract's value.

To understand what all this means, let's look at what happens when you buy or sell this futures contract. Suppose that on January 1, you sell one March contract at a price of 1000 (that is, $250 000). By selling the contract, you agree to a delivery amount due of $250 times the S&P 500 Index on the expiration date

FINANCIAL NEWS

Stock Index Futures

The prices for stock index futures contracts are published daily. In the *Wall Street Journal*, these prices are found in the "Futures" column. An excerpt is reproduced here.

S&P 500 Index (CME)-$250 × Index

	Open	High	Low	Settle	Change	Open Interest
March	840.10	848.00	813.00	839.30	−0.50	509 850

Information for each contract is given in columns, as follows. (The March contract is used as an example.)

Open: Opening price; each point corresponds to $250 times the index—840.10; that is, 840.10 × $250 = $210 025 per contract

High: Highest traded price that day—848.00, or $212 000 per contract

Low: Lowest traded price that day—813.00, or $203 250 per contract

Settle: Settlement price, the closing price that day—839.30, or $209 825 per contract

Change: Change in the settlement price from the previous trading day—−0.50 points, or −$125 per contract

Open Interest: Number of contracts outstanding—509 850, or a total value of $107 billion ($509 850 × $209 825).

Source: Wall Street Journal, January 16, 2009, p. C5.

at the end of March. By buying the contract at a price of 1000, the buyer has agreed to pay $250 000 for the delivery amount due of $250 times the S&P 500 Index at the expiration date at the end of March. If the stock market falls so that the S&P 500 Index declines to 900 on the expiration date, the buyer of the contract will have lost $25 000 because he or she has agreed to pay $250 000 for the contract but has a delivery amount due of $225 000 (900 × $250). But you, the seller of the contract, will have a profit of $25 000 because you agreed to receive a $250 000 purchase price for the contract but have a delivery amount due of only $225 000. Because the amounts payable and due are netted out, only $25 000 will change hands; you, the seller of the contract, will receive $25 000 from the buyer.

| APPLICATION | Hedging with Stock Index Futures |

Financial institution managers can use stock index futures contracts to reduce stock market risk.

Suppose that in March 2010, Mort, the portfolio manager of the Rock Solid Insurance Company, has a portfolio of stocks valued at $100 million that moves percentagewise one-for-one with the S&P Index. Suppose also that the March 2011 S&P 500 Index contracts are currently selling at a price of 1000. How many of these contracts should Mort sell so that he hedges the stock market risk of this portfolio over the next year?

Because Mort is holding a long position, using the basic principle of hedging, he must offset it by taking a short position in which he sells S&P futures. To calculate the number of contracts he needs to sell, he uses Equation 1.

$$VA = \$100 \text{ million}$$

$$VC = \$250 \times 1000 = \$250\ 000$$

Thus,

$$NC = \$100 \text{ million}/\$250\ 000 = 400$$

Mort's hedge therefore involves selling 400 S&P March 2011 futures contracts.

If the S&P Index falls 10% to 900, the $100 million portfolio will suffer a $10 million loss. At the same time, however, Mort makes a profit of $100 \times \$250 = \$25\ 000$ per contract because he agreed to be paid $250 000 for each contract at a price of 1000, but at a price of 900 on the expiration date he has a delivery amount of only $225 000 (900 $\times$ $250). Multiplied by 400 contracts, the $25 000 profit per contract yields a total profit of $10 million. The $10 million profit on the futures contract exactly offsets the loss on Rock Solid's stock portfolio, so Mort has been successful in hedging the stock market risk.

Why would Mort be willing to forgo profits when the stock market rises? One reason is that he might be worried that a bear market was imminent, so he wants to protect Rock Solid's portfolio from the coming decline (and so protect his job).

OPTIONS

Another vehicle for hedging interest-rate, foreign exchange, and stock market risk involves the use of options on assets. **Options** are contracts that give the purchaser the option, or *right*, to buy or sell the underlying asset at a specified price, called the **exercise price** or **strike price**, within a specific period of time (the *term to expiration*). The seller (sometimes called the *writer*) of the option is *obligated* to buy or sell the asset to the purchaser if the owner of the option exercises the right to sell or buy. These option contract features are important enough to be emphasized: The *owner* or buyer of an option does not have to exercise the option; he or she can let the option expire without using it. Hence the *owner* of an option is *not obligated* to take any action but rather has the *right* to exercise the contract if he or she so chooses. The *seller* of an option, by contrast, has no choice in the matter; he or she *must* buy or sell the asset if the owner exercises the option.

Because the right to buy or sell an asset at a specified price has value, the owner of an option is willing to pay an amount for it called a **premium**. There are two types of option contracts: **American options** can be exercised *at any time up to* the expiration date of the contract, and **European options** can be exercised only *on* the expiration date.

Option contracts written on individual stocks are called **stock options**, and such options have existed for a long time. However, option contracts can also be written on assets. Options on financial futures called **financial futures options** or, more commonly, **futures options**, were developed in 1982 and have become the most widely traded option contracts.

You might wonder why option contracts are more likely to be written on financial futures than on underlying financial instruments such as bonds. As you saw earlier in the chapter, at the expiration date, the price of the futures contract and of the deliverable debt instrument will be the same because of arbitrage. So it would seem that investors should be indifferent about having the option written on the asset or on the futures contract. However, financial futures contracts have been so well designed that their markets are often more liquid than the markets in the underlying assets. Investors would rather have the option contract written on the more liquid instrument, in this case the futures contract. That explains why the most popular futures options are written on many of the same futures contracts listed in Table 14-1.

In Canada, the regulation of option markets is the responsibility of the Canadian Derivatives Clearing Corporation (CDCC), a firm that is jointly owned by Canada's stock exchanges: the Toronto Stock Exchange, the TSX Venture Exchange, and the Montreal Exchange. The regulation of U.S. option markets is split between the Securities and Exchange Commission (SEC), which regulates stock options, and the Commodity Futures Trading Commission (CFTC), which regulates futures options. Regulation focuses on ensuring that writers of options have enough capital to make good on their contractual obligations and on overseeing traders and exchanges to prevent fraud and ensure that the market is not being manipulated.

Stock Options

To understand option contracts more fully, let's first discuss stock options (options on individual stocks) before we turn to the more complicated futures options (that is, options on financial futures).

PROFITS AND LOSSES ON CALLS   A **call option** is a contract that gives the owner the right (but not the obligation) to *buy* a stock (from the option writer) at the exercise price within a specific period of time. Since a call represents an option to buy, the purchase of a call is undertaken if the price of the underlying stock is expected to go up. The buyer of a call is said to be **long in a call** and the writer of a call is said to be **short in a call**. The buyer of a call option will have to pay a premium, called a **call premium**, in order to get the writer to sign the contract and assume the risk.

To illustrate the profitability of a call option, suppose you hold a European call option on an equity security with an exercise price of X (say $100) and a call premium of α (say $5), as shown in Figure 14-1. If at the expiration date, the price of the underlying asset, S, is less than X, the call will not be exercised, resulting in a loss of the premium. At a price above X, the call will be exercised. In particular,

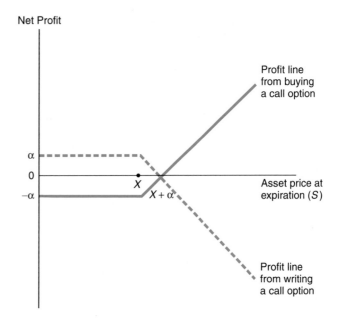

FIGURE 14-1   Profits from Buying and Writing a Call Option

at a price between X and $X + \alpha$, the gain would be insufficient to cover the cost of the premium, while at a price above $X + \alpha$ the call will yield a net profit. In fact, at a price above $X + \alpha$, each \$1 rise in the price of the asset will cause the profit of the call option to increase by \$1.

The payoff function from writing the call option is the mirror image of the payoff function from buying the call and is represented by the dashed line in Figure 14-1. Note that the writer of the call receives the call premium α up front and must stand ready to sell the underlying asset to the buyer of the call at the exercise price X, if the buyer exercises the option to buy.

In general, the value of a call option C at expiration with asset price S (at that time) and exercise price X is

$$C = \max(0, S - X)$$

In other words, the value of a call option at maturity (also known as the **intrinsic value**) is the difference between the current asset price and the exercise price, $S - X$, or zero, whichever is greater. If the stock price happens to be greater than the exercise price ($S > X$), the call is said to be **in the money**, and the owner will exercise it for a net profit of $C - \alpha$. If the asset price happens to be less than the exercise price ($S < X$), the call is said to be **out of the money** and will expire worthless. A call with $S = X$ is said to be **at the money** or **trading at par**.

PROFIT AND LOSSES ON PUTS   As already noted, a second type of option contract is the put option. A **put option** is a contract that gives the owner the right (but not the obligation) to *sell* an asset (to the option writer) at the specified exercise price within a specific period of time. As a put represents an option to sell rather than buy, it is worth buying a put when the price of the underlying asset is expected to fall. As with calls, the buyer of a put is said to be **long in a put** and the writer of a put is said to be **short in a put**. Also, as with calls, the buyer of a put option will have to pay a premium, called a **put premium**, in order to get the writer to sign the contract and assume the risk.

The solid line in Figure 14-2 illustrates the profit line from buying a put with an exercise price of X and a premium of β. At a price of X or higher, the put will not be exercised, resulting in a loss of the premium. At a price below $X - \beta$, the put is sufficiently deep in the money to cover the option premium and yield a net profit. In fact, between $X - \beta$ and X, the put will be exercised, but the gain is insufficient to cover the cost of the premium.

The payoff function from writing a put is the mirror image of that from buying a put and is represented by the dashed line in Figure 14-2. As with writing a call, the writer of a put receives the put premium β up front and must sell the asset underlying the option if the buyer of the put exercises the option to sell.

In general, the value of a put option P at the expiration date with exercise price X and asset price S (at that time) is

$$P = \max (X - S, 0)$$

That is, the value of a put at maturity is the difference between the exercise price of the option and the price of the asset underlying the option, $X - S$, or zero, whichever is greater. If the stock price happens to be greater than the exercise price ($S > X$), the put is said to be out of the money and will expire worthless. If the asset price happens to be less than the exercise price ($S < X$), the put is said to be in the money and the owner will exercise it for a net profit of $P - \beta$. If $S = X$, the put is said to be at the money.

Remembering which is a call option and which is a put option is not always easy. To keep them straight, just remember that having a *call* option to *buy* an asset is the same as having the option to *call in* the asset for delivery at a specified price. Having a *put* option to *sell* an asset is the same as having the option to *put up* an asset for the other party to buy.

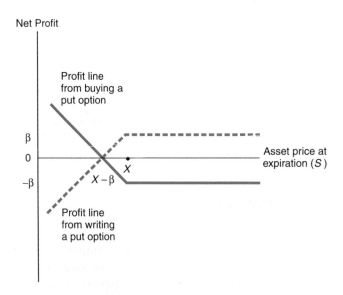

FIGURE 14-2   Profits from Buying and Writing a Put Option

**Futures
Options**

To understand option contracts on financial futures, let's examine the option on a June Canada bond futures contract. If you buy this futures contract at a price of 115 (that is, $115 000), you have agreed to pay $115 000 for $100 000 face value of long-term Canada bonds when they are delivered to you at the end of June. If you sold this futures contract at a price of 115, you agreed, in exchange for $115 000, to deliver $100 000 face value of the long-term Canada bonds at the end of June. An option contract on the Canada bond futures contract has several key features: (1) It has the same expiration date as the underlying futures contract, (2) it is an American option and so can be exercised at any time before the expiration date, and (3) the premium (price) of the option is quoted in points that are the same as in the futures contract, so each point corresponds to $1000. If, for a premium of $2000, you buy one call option contract on the June Canada bond contract with an exercise price of 115, you have purchased the right to buy (call in) the June Canada bond futures contract for a price of 115 ($115 000 per contract) at any time through the expiration date of this contract at the end of June. Similarly, when for $2000 you buy a put option on the June Canada bond contract with an exercise price of 115, you have the right to sell (put up) the June Canada bond futures contract for a price of 115 ($115 000 per contract) at any time until the end of June.

Futures option contracts are somewhat complicated, so to explore how they work and how they can be used to hedge risk, let's first examine how profits and losses on the call option on the June Canada bond futures contract occur. In February, our old friend Irving the Investor buys, for a $2000 premium, a call option on the $100 000 June Canada bond futures contract with a strike price of 115. (We assume that if Irving exercises the option, it is on the expiration date at the end of June and not before.) On the expiration date at the end of June, suppose that the underlying Canada bond for the futures contract has a price of 110. Recall that on the expiration date, arbitrage forces the price of the futures contract to be the same as the price of the underlying bond, so it too has a price of 110 on the expiration date at the end of June. If Irving exercises the call option and buys the futures contract at an exercise price of 115, he will lose money by buying at 115 and selling at the lower market price of 110. Because Irving is smart, he will not exercise the option, but he will be out the $2000 premium he paid. In such a situation, in which the price of the underlying financial instrument is below the exercise price, a call option is said to be "out of the money." At the price of 110 (less than the exercise price), Irving thus suffers a loss on the option contract of the $2000 premium he paid. This loss is plotted as point A in panel (a) of Figure 14-3.

On the expiration date, if the price of the futures contract is 115, the call option is "at the money," and Irving is indifferent whether he exercises his option to buy the futures contract or not, since exercising the option at 115 when the market price is also at 115 produces no gain or loss. Because he has paid the $2000 premium, at the price of 115 his contract again has a net loss of $2000, plotted as point B.

If the futures contract instead has a price of 120 on the expiration day, the option is "in the money," and Irving benefits from exercising the option: He would buy the futures contract at the exercise price of 115 and then sell it for 120, thereby earning a 5% gain ($5000 profit) on the $100 000 Canada bond futures contract. Because Irving paid a $2000 premium for the option contract, however, his net profit is $3000 ($5000 − $2000). The $3000 profit at a price of 120 is plotted as point C. Similarly, if the price of the futures contract rose to 125, the option contract would yield a net profit of $8000 ($10 000 from

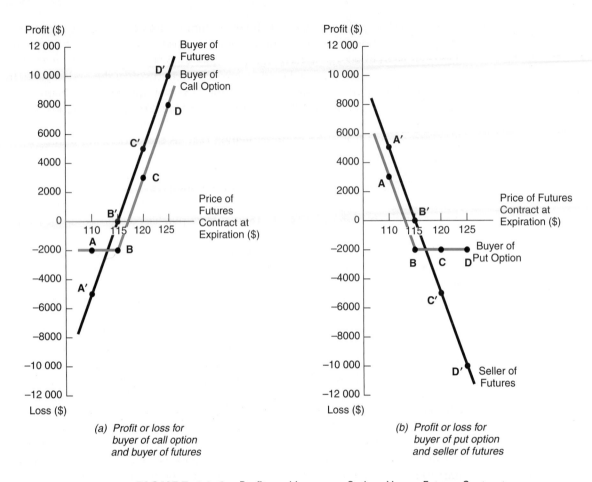

FIGURE 14-3   Profits and Losses on Options Versus Futures Contracts

The futures contract is the $100 000 June Canada bond contract, and the option contracts are written on this futures contract with an exercise price of 115. Panel (a) shows the profits and losses for the buyer of the call option and the buyer of the futures contract, and panel (b) shows the profits and losses for the buyer of the put option and the seller of the futures contract.

exercising the option minus the $2000 premium), plotted as point D. Plotting these points, we get the kinked profit curve for the call option that we see in panel (a).

Suppose that instead of purchasing the futures *option* contract in February, Irving decides to buy the $100 000 June Canada bond *futures* contract at the price of 115. If the price of the bond on the expiration day at the end of June declines to 110, meaning that the price of the futures contract also falls to 110, Irving suffers a loss of 5 percentage points, or $5000. The loss of $5000 on the futures contract at a price of 110 is plotted as point A′ in panel (a). At a price of 115 on the expiration date, Irving would have a zero profit on the futures contract, plotted as point B′. At a price of 120, Irving would have a profit on the contract of 5 percentage points, or $5000 (point C′), and at a price of 125, the profit would be 10 percentage points, or $10 000 (point D′). Plotting these points, we get the linear (straight-line) profit curve for the futures contract that appears in panel (a).

Now we can see the major difference between a futures contract and an option contract. As the profit curve for the futures contract in panel (a) indicates, the futures contract has a linear profit function: Profits grow by an equal dollar amount for every point increase in the price of the underlying asset. By contrast, the kinked profit curve for the option contract is nonlinear, meaning that profits do not always grow by the same amount for a given change in the price of the underlying asset. The reason for this nonlinearity is that the call option protects Irving from having losses that are greater than the amount of the $2000 premium. In contrast, Irving's loss on the futures contract is $5000 if the price on the expiration day falls to 110, and if the price falls even further, Irving's loss will be even greater. This insurance-like feature of option contracts explains why their purchase price is referred to as a premium. Once the underlying asset's price rises above the exercise price, however, Irving's profits grow linearly. Irving has given up something by buying an option rather than a futures contract. As we see in panel (a), when the price of the underlying asset rises above the exercise price, Irving's profits are always less than that on the futures contract by exactly the $2000 premium he paid.

Panel (b) plots the results of the same profit calculations if Irving buys not a call but a put option (an option to sell) with an exercise price of 115 for a premium of $2000 and if he sells the futures contract rather than buying one. In this case, if on the expiration date the Canada bond futures have a price above the 115 exercise price, the put option is "out of the money." Irving would not want to exercise the put option and then have to sell the futures contract he owns as a result of exercising the put option at a price below the market price and lose money. He would not exercise his option, and he would be out only the $2000 premium he paid. Once the price of the futures contract falls below the 115 exercise price, Irving benefits from exercising the put option because he can sell the futures contract at a price of 115 but can buy it at a price below this. In such a situation, in which the price of the underlying asset is below the exercise price, the put option is "in the money," and profits rise linearly as the price of the futures contract falls. The profit function for the put option illustrated in panel (b) of Figure 14-3 is kinked, indicating that Irving is protected from losses greater than the amount of the premium he paid. The profit curve for the sale of the futures contract is just the negative of the profit for the futures contract in panel (a) and is therefore linear.

Panel (b) of Figure 14-3 confirms the conclusion from panel (a) that profits on option contracts are nonlinear but profits on futures contracts are linear.

Two other differences between futures and option contracts must be mentioned. The first is that the initial investment on the contracts differs. As we saw earlier in the chapter, when a futures contract is purchased, the investor must put up a fixed amount, the margin requirement, in a margin account. But when an option contract is purchased, the initial investment is the premium that must be paid for the contract. The second important difference between the contracts is that the futures contract requires money to change hands daily when the contract is marked to market, whereas the option contract requires money to change hands only when it is exercised.

Earlier in the chapter, we saw how a financial institution manager like Mona, the manager of the First Bank, could hedge the interest-rate risk on its $5 million holdings of 6s of 2030 by selling $5 million of Canada bond futures (50 contracts). A rise in interest rates and the resulting fall in bond prices and bond futures contracts would lead to profits on the bank's sale of the futures contracts that would exactly offset the losses on the 6s of 2030 the bank is holding.

As panel (b) of Figure 14-3 (p. 366) suggests, an alternative way for the manager to protect against a rise in interest rates and hence a decline in bond prices is to buy $5 million of put options written on the same Canada bond futures. Because the size of the options contract is the same as the futures contract ($100 000 of bonds), the number of put options contracts bought is the same as the number of futures contracts sold, that is, 50. As long as the exercise price is not too far from the current price as in panel (b), the rise in interest rates and decline in bond prices will lead to profits on the futures and the futures put options, profits that will offset any losses on the $5 million of Canada bonds.

The one problem with using options rather than futures is that the First Bank will have to pay premiums on the options contracts, thereby lowering the bank's profits in order to hedge the interest-rate risk. Why might the bank manager be willing to use options rather than futures to conduct the hedge? The answer is that the option contract, unlike the futures contract, allows the First Bank to gain if interest rates decline and bond prices rise. With the hedge using futures contracts, the First Bank does not gain from increases in bond prices because the profits on the bonds it is holding are offset by the losses from the futures contracts it has sold. However, as panel (b) of Figure 14-3 indicates, the situation when the hedge is conducted with put options is quite different: Once bond prices rise above the exercise price, the bank does not suffer additional losses on the option contracts. At the same time, the value of the Canada bonds the bank is holding will increase, thereby leading to a profit for the bank. Thus using options rather than futures to conduct the micro hedge allows the bank to protect itself from rises in interest rates but still allows the bank to benefit from interest-rate declines (although the profit is reduced by the amount of the premium).

Similar reasoning indicates that the bank manager might prefer to use options to conduct a macro hedge to immunize the entire bank portfolio from interest-rate risk. Again, the strategy of using options rather than futures has the disadvantage that the First Bank has to pay the premiums on these contracts up front. By contrast, using options allows the bank to keep the gains from a decline in interest rates (which will raise the value of the bank's assets relative to its liabilities) because these gains will not be offset by large losses on the option contracts.

In the case of a macro hedge, there is another reason why the bank might prefer option contracts to futures contracts. Profits and losses on futures contracts can cause accounting problems for banks because such profits and losses are not allowed to be offset by unrealized changes in the value of the rest of the bank's portfolio. Consider the case when interest rates fall. If First Bank sells futures contracts to conduct the macro hedge, then when interest rates fall and the prices of the Canada bond futures contracts rise, it will have large losses on these contracts. Of course, these losses are offset by unrealized profits in the rest of the bank's portfolio, but the bank is not allowed to offset these losses in its accounting statements. So even though the macro hedge is serving its intended purpose of immunizing the bank's portfolio from interest-rate risk, the bank would experience large accounting losses when interest rates fall. Indeed, bank managers have lost their jobs when perfectly sound hedges with interest-rate futures have led to large accounting losses. Not surprisingly, bank managers might shrink from using financial futures to conduct macro hedges for this reason.

Futures options, however, can come to the rescue of the managers of banks and other financial institutions. Suppose that First Bank conducted the macro hedge by buying put options instead of selling Canada bond futures. Now if interest rates fall and bond prices rise well above the exercise price, the bank will not have large losses on the option contracts because it will just decide not to exercise its options. The bank will not suffer the accounting problems produced by hedging with financial futures. Because of the accounting advantages of using futures options to conduct macro hedges, option contracts have become important to financial institution managers as tools for hedging interest-rate risk.

Factors Affecting the Prices of Option Premiums	There are several interesting facts about how the premiums on option contracts are priced. The first fact is that when the strike (exercise) price for a contract is set at a higher level, the premium for the call option is lower and the premium for the put option is higher. For example, in going from a contract with a strike price of 110 to one with 115, the premium for the February call option might fall from 1 39/64 to 1/64, and the premium for the March put option might rise from 15/64 to 3 28/64.

Our understanding of the profit function for option contracts illustrated in Figure 14-3 helps explain this fact. As we saw in panel (a), a higher price for the underlying asset (in this case a Canada bond futures contract) relative to the option's exercise price results in higher profits on the call (buy) option. Thus the lower the strike price, the higher the profits on the call option contract and the greater the premium that investors like Irving are willing to pay. Similarly, we saw in panel (b) that a higher price for the underlying asset relative to the exercise price lowers profits on the put (sell) option, so that a higher strike price increases profits and thus causes the premium to increase.

The second thing is that as the period of time over which the option can be exercised (the term to expiration) gets longer, the premiums for both call and put options usually rise. For example, at a strike price of 114, the premium on the call option might increase from 1/64 in February to 4/64 in March and to 7/64 in April. Similarly, the premium on the put option at a strike price of 111 might increase from 8/64 in February to 32/64 in March and to 1 13/64 in April. The fact that premiums increase with the term to expiration is also explained by the nonlinear profit function for option contracts. As the term to expiration lengthens, there is a greater chance that the price of the underlying asset will be very high or very low by the expiration date. If the price becomes very high and goes well above the exercise price, the call (buy) option will yield a high profit, but if the price becomes very low and goes well below the exercise price, the losses will be small because the owner of the call option will simply decide not to exercise the option. The possibility of greater variability of the underlying asset as the term to expiration lengthens raises profits on average for the call option.

Similar reasoning tells us that the put (sell) option will become more valuable as the term to expiration increases because the possibility of greater price variability of the underlying financial instrument increases as the term to expiration increases. The greater chance of a low price increases the chance that profits on the put option will be very high. But the greater chance of a high price does not produce substantial losses for the put option because the owner will again just decide not to exercise the option.

Another way of thinking about this reasoning is to recognize that option contracts have an element of "heads, I win; tails, I don't lose too badly." The greater variability of where the prices might be by the expiration date increases the value of both kinds of options. Since a longer term to the expiration date leads to greater variability of where the prices might be by the expiration date, a longer term to expiration raises the value of the option contract.

The reasoning that we have just developed also explains another important fact about option premiums. When the volatility of the price of the underlying asset is great, the premiums for both call and put options will be higher. Higher volatility of prices means that for a given expiration date, there will again be greater variability of where the prices might be by the expiration date. The "heads, I win; tails, I don't lose too badly" property of options then means that the greater variability of possible prices by the expiration date increases average profits for the option and thus increases the premium that investors are willing to pay.

Summary

Our analysis of how profits on options are affected by price movements for the underlying asset leads to the following conclusions about the factors that determine the premium on an option contract:

1. The higher the strike price, everything else being equal, the lower the premium on call (buy) options and the higher the premium on put (sell) options.

2. The greater the term to expiration, everything else being equal, the higher the premiums for both call and put options.

3. The greater the volatility of prices of the underlying asset, everything else being equal, the higher the premiums for both call and put options.

The results we have derived here appear in more formal models, such as the Black-Scholes model, which analyze how the premiums on options are priced. You might study such models in other finance courses.

SWAPS

In addition to forwards, futures, and options, financial institutions use one other important financial derivative to manage risk. **Swaps** are financial contracts that obligate each party to the contract to exchange (swap) a set of payments it owns for another set of payments owned by another party. There are two basic kinds of swaps: **Currency swaps** involve the exchange of a set of payments in one currency for a set of payments in another currency. **Interest-rate swaps** involve the exchange of one set of interest payments for another set of interest payments, all denominated in the same currency. We focus on interest-rate swaps.

Interest-Rate Swap Contracts

Interest-rate swaps are an important tool for managing interest-rate risk, and they first appeared in the United States in 1982 when there was an increase in the demand for financial instruments that could be used to reduce interest-rate risk. The most common type of interest-rate swap (called the *plain vanilla swap*) specifies (1) the interest rate on the payments that are being exchanged; (2) the type of interest payments (variable or fixed-rate); (3) the amount of **notional principal**, which is the amount on which the interest is being paid; and (4) the time period over which the exchanges continue to be made. There are many other more complicated versions of swaps, including forward swaps and swap options (called *swaptions*), but here we will look only at the plain vanilla swap. Figure 14-4 illustrates an interest-rate swap between First Trust and the Friendly Finance Company. First Trust agrees to pay Friendly Finance a fixed rate of 7% on $1 million of notional principal for the next ten years, and Friendly Finance agrees to pay First Trust the one-year treasury bill rate plus 1% on $1 million of notional principal for the same period. Thus, as shown in Figure 14-4, every year First Trust would be paying the Friendly Finance Company 7% on $1 million while Friendly Finance would be paying First Trust the one-year T-bill rate plus 1% on $1 million.

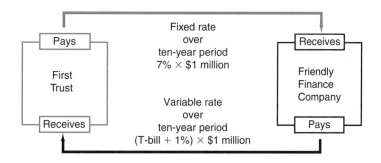

FIGURE 14-4   Interest-Rate Swap Payments

In this swap arrangement, with a notional principal of $1 million and a term of ten years, First Trust pays a fixed rate of 7% × $1 million to the Friendly Finance Company, which in turn agrees to pay the one-year treasury bill rate plus 1% × $1 million to First Trust.

APPLICATION   **Hedging with Interest-Rate Swaps**

You might wonder why the managers of the two financial institutions find it advantageous to enter into this swap agreement. The answer is that it may help both of them hedge interest-rate risk.

Suppose that First Trust, which tends to borrow short-term and then lend long-term in the mortgage market, has $1 million less of rate-sensitive assets than it has of rate-sensitive liabilities. As we learned in Chapter 13, this situation means that as interest rates rise, the rise in the cost of funds (liabilities) is greater than the rise in interest payments it receives on its assets, many of which are fixed-rate. The result of rising interest rates is thus a shrinking of First Trust's net interest margin and a decline in its profitability. As we saw in Chapter 13, to avoid this interest-rate risk, the manager of First Trust would like to convert $1 million of its fixed-rate assets into $1 million of rate-sensitive assets, in effect making rate-sensitive assets equal to rate-sensitive liabilities, thereby eliminating the gap. This is exactly what happens when she engages in the interest-rate swap. By taking $1 million of its fixed-rate income and exchanging it for $1 million of rate-sensitive treasury bill income, she has converted income on $1 million of fixed-rate assets into income on $1 million of rate-sensitive assets. Now when interest rates increase, the rise in rate-sensitive income on its assets exactly matches the rise in the rate-sensitive cost of funds on its liabilities, leaving the net interest margin and bank profitability unchanged.

The manager of the Friendly Finance Company, which issues long-term bonds to raise funds and uses them to make short-term loans, finds that he is in exactly the opposite situation to First Trust: He has $1 million more of rate-sensitive assets than of rate-sensitive liabilities. He is therefore concerned that a fall in interest rates, which will result in a larger drop in income from its assets than the decline in the cost of funds on its liabilities, will cause a decline in profits. By doing the interest-rate swap, the manager eliminates this interest-rate risk because he has converted $1 million of rate-sensitive income into $1 million of fixed-rate income. Now the manager of the Friendly Finance Company finds that when interest rates fall, the decline in rate-sensitive income is smaller and so is matched by the decline in the rate-sensitive cost of funds on its liabilities, leaving profitability unchanged.

Advantages of Interest-Rate Swaps

To eliminate interest-rate risk, both First Trust and the Friendly Finance Company could have rearranged their balance sheets by converting fixed-rate assets into rate-sensitive assets, and vice versa, instead of engaging in an interest-rate swap. However, this strategy would have been costly for both financial institutions for several reasons. The first is that financial institutions incur substantial transaction costs when they rearrange their balance sheets. Second, different financial institutions have informational advantages in making loans to certain customers who may prefer certain maturities. Thus, adjusting the balance sheet to eliminate interest-rate risk may result in a loss of these informational advantages, which the financial institution is unwilling to give up. Interest-rate swaps solve these problems for financial institutions because in effect they allow the institutions to convert fixed-rate assets into rate-sensitive assets without affecting the balance sheet. Large transaction costs are avoided, and the financial institutions can continue to make loans where they have an informational advantage.

We have seen that financial institutions can also hedge interest-rate risk with other financial derivatives such as futures contracts and futures options. Interest-rate swaps have one big advantage over hedging with these other derivatives: They can be written for very long horizons, sometimes as long as 20 years, whereas financial futures and futures options typically have much shorter horizons, not much more than a year. If a financial institution needs to hedge interest-rate risk for a long horizon, financial futures and option markets may not do it much good. Instead it can turn to the swap market.

Disadvantages of Interest-Rate Swaps

Although interest-rate swaps have important advantages that make them very popular with financial institutions, they also have disadvantages that limit their usefulness. Swap markets, like forward markets, can suffer from a lack of liquidity. Let's return to looking at the swap between First Trust and the Friendly Finance Company. As with a forward contract, it might be difficult for First Trust to link up with the Friendly Finance Company to arrange the swap. In addition, even if First Trust could find a counterparty like the Friendly Finance Company, it might not be able to negotiate a good deal because it couldn't find any other institution to negotiate with.

Swap contracts also are subject to the same default risk that we encountered for forward contracts. If interest rates rise, the Friendly Finance Company would love to get out of the swap contract because the fixed-rate interest payments it receives are less than it could get in the open market. It might then default on the contract, exposing First Trust to a loss. Alternatively, the Friendly Finance Company could go bust, meaning that the terms of the swap contract would not be fulfilled.

It is important to note that the default risk of swaps is not the same as the default risk on the full amount of the notional principal because the notional principal is never exchanged. If the Friendly Finance Company goes broke because $1 million of its one-year loans default and it cannot make its interest payment to First Trust, First Trust will stop sending its payment to Friendly Finance. If interest rates have declined, this will suit First Trust just fine because it would rather keep the 7% fixed-rate interest payment, which is at a higher rate, than receive the rate-sensitive payment, which has declined. Thus a default on a swap contract does not necessarily mean that there is a loss to the other party. First Trust will suffer losses from a default only if interest rates have risen when the default occurs. Even then, the loss will be far smaller than the amount of the notional principal because interest payments are far smaller than the amount of the notional principal.[5]

Financial Intermediaries in Interest-Rate Swaps

As we have just seen, financial institutions do have to be aware of the possibility of losses from a default on swaps. As with a forward contract, each party to a swap must have a lot of information about the other party to make sure that the contract is likely to be fulfilled. The need for information about counterparties and the liquidity problems in swap markets could limit the usefulness of these markets. However, when informational and liquidity problems crop up in a market, financial intermediaries come to the rescue. That is exactly what happens in swap markets. Intermediaries such as investment banks and especially large banks have the ability to acquire information cheaply about the creditworthiness and reliability of parties to swap contracts and are also able to match up parties to a swap. Hence, large banks and investment banks have set up swap markets in which they act as intermediaries.

---

[5] The actual loss will equal the present value of the difference in the interest payments that the bank would have received if the swap were still in force as compared to interest payments it receives otherwise.

CREDIT DERIVATIVES

In recent years, a new type of derivative has come on the scene to hedge credit risk. Like other derivatives, **credit derivatives** offer payoffs on previously issued securities, but ones that bear credit risk. In the past ten years, the markets in credit derivatives have grown at an outstanding pace and the notional amounts of these derivatives now number in the trillions of dollars. These credit derivatives take several forms.

Credit Options

Credit options work just like the options discussed earlier in the chapter: For a fee, the purchaser gains the right to receive profits that are tied either to the price of an underlying security or to an interest rate. Suppose you buy $1 million of General Motors bonds but worry that a potential slowdown in the sale of SUVs might lead a credit-rating agency to downgrade (lower the credit rating on) GM bonds. As we saw in Chapter 6, such a downgrade would cause the price of GM bonds to fall. To protect yourself, you could buy an option for, say, $15 000 to sell the $1 million of bonds at a strike price that is the same as the current price. With this strategy, you would not suffer any losses if the value of the GM bonds declined because you could exercise the option and sell them at the price you paid for them. In addition, you would be able to reap any gains that occurred if GM bonds rose in value.

The second type of credit option ties profits to changes in an interest rate such as a credit spread (the interest rate on the average bond with a particular credit rating minus the interest rate on default-free bonds such as those issued by the Canadian goverment). Suppose that your company, which has a BAA credit rating, plans to issue $10 million of one-year bonds in three months and expects to have a credit spread of 1 percentage point (i.e., it will pay an interest rate that is 1 percentage point higher than the one-year T-bill rate). You are concerned that the market might start to think that BAA companies in general will become riskier in the coming months. If this were to happen by the time you are ready to issue your bonds in three months, you would have to pay a higher interest rate than the 1 percentage point in excess of the T-bill rate and your cost of issuing the bonds would increase. To protect yourself against these higher costs, you could buy for, say, $20 000 a credit option on $10 million of BAA bonds that would pay you the difference between the average BAA credit spread in the market minus the 1 percentage point credit spread on $10 million. If the credit spread jumps to 2 percentage points, you would receive $100 000 from the option (= [2% − 1%] × $10 million), which would exactly offset the $100 000 higher interest costs from the 1 percentage point higher interest rate you would have to pay on your $10 million of bonds.

Credit Swaps

Suppose you manage a bank in Calgary called Oil Drillers' Bank (ODB), which specializes in lending to a particular industry in your local area, oil drilling companies. Another bank, Potato Farmers Bank (PFB), specializes in lending to potato farmers in Charlottetown. Both ODB and PFB have a problem because their loan portfolios are not sufficiently diversified. To protect ODB against a collapse in the oil market, which would result in defaults on most of its loans made to oil drillers, you could reach an agreement to have the loan payments on, say, $100 million worth of your loans to oil drillers paid to the PFB in exchange for PFB paying you the loan payments on $100 million of its loans to potato farmers. Such a transaction, in which risky payments on loans are swapped for each other, is called a **credit swap**. As a result of this swap, ODB and PFB have increased their diversification and lowered the overall risk of their loan portfolios because some of the loan payments to each bank are now coming from a different type of loans.

Another form of credit swap is, for arcane reasons, called a credit default swap, although it functions more like insurance. With a credit default swap, one party who wants to hedge credit risk pays a fixed payment on a regular basis, in return for a contingent payment that is triggered by a credit event such as the bankruptcy of a particular firm or the downgrading of the firm's credit rating by a credit-rating agency. For example, you could use a credit default swap to hedge the $1 million of General Motors bonds that you are holding by arranging to pay an annual fee of $1000 in exchange for a payment of $10 000 if the GM bonds' credit rating is lowered. If a credit event happens and GM's bonds are downgraded so that their price falls, you will receive a payment that will offset some of the loss you suffer if you sell the bonds at this lower price.

Credit-Linked Notes

Another type of credit derivative, the **credit-linked note**, is a combination of a bond and a credit option. Just like any corporate bond, the credit-linked note makes periodic coupon (interest) payments and a final payment of the face value of the bond at maturity. If a key financial variable specified in the note changes, however, the issuer of the note has the right (option) to lower the payments on the note. For example, General Motors could issue a credit-linked note that pays a 5% coupon rate, with the specification that if a national index of SUV sales falls by 10%, then GM has the right to lower the coupon rate by 2 percentage points to 3%. In this way, GM can lower its risk because when it is losing money as SUV sales fall, it can offset some of these losses by making smaller payments on its credit-linked notes.

APPLICATION

Lessons from the Subprime Financial Crisis: When Are Financial Derivatives Likely to Be a Worldwide Time Bomb?

Although financial derivatives can be useful in hedging risk, the AIG blowup discussed in Chapter 12 illustrates that they can pose a real danger to the financial system. Indeed, Warren Buffett warned about the dangers of financial derivatives by characterizing them as "financial weapons of mass destruction." Particularly scary are the notional amounts of derivatives contracts—more than $500 trillion worldwide. What does the recent subprime financial crisis tell us about when financial derivatives are likely to be a time bomb that could bring down the world financial system?

There are two major concerns about financial derivatives. The first is that financial derivatives allow financial institutions to increase their leverage; that is, these institutions can in effect hold an amount of the underlying asset that is many times greater than the amount of money they have had to put up. Increasing their leverage enables them to take huge bets, which, if they are wrong, can bring down the institution. This is exactly what AIG did, to its great regret, when it plunged into the credit default swap (CDS) market. Even more of a problem was that AIG's speculation in the CDS market had the potential to bring down the whole financial system. An important lesson from the subprime financial crisis is that having one player take huge positions in a derivatives market is highly dangerous.

A second concern is that banks have holdings of huge notional amounts of financial derivatives, particularly interest-rate and currency swaps, that greatly exceed the amount of bank capital, and so these derivatives expose the banks to serious risk of failure. Banks are indeed major players in the financial derivatives markets, particularly in the interest-rate and currency swaps market, where our earlier analysis has shown that they are the natural market-makers because they can act as intermediaries between two counterparties who would not make the swap without their involvement. However, looking at the notional amount of interest-rate and currency swaps at banks gives a very misleading picture of their risk exposure. Because banks act as intermediaries in the swap markets, they are typically exposed only to credit risk—a default by one of their counterparties. Furthermore, these swaps, unlike loans, do not involve payments of the notional amount but rather the much smaller payments that are based on the notional amounts. For example, in the case of a 7% interest rate, the payment is only $70 000 for a $1 million swap. Estimates of the credit exposure from swap contracts indicate that they are on the order of only 1% of the notional value of the contracts and that credit exposure at banks from derivatives is generally less than a quarter of their total credit exposure from loans. Banks' credit exposures from their derivative positions are thus not out of line with other credit exposures they face. Indeed, during the recent subprime financial crisis, in which the financial system was put under great stress, derivatives exposure at banks was not a serious problem.

The conclusion is that recent events indicate that financial derivatives pose serious dangers to the financial system, but some of these dangers have been overplayed. The biggest danger occurs in trading activities of financial institutions, and this is particularly true for credit derivatives, as was illustrated by AIG's activities in the CDS market. As discussed in Chapter 10, regulators have been paying increased attention to this danger and are continuing to develop new disclosure requirements and regulatory guidelines for how derivatives trading should be done. Of particular concern is the need for financial institutions to disclose their exposure in derivatives contracts, so that regulators can make sure that a large institution is not playing too large a role in these markets and does not have too large an exposure to derivatives relative to its capital, as was the case for AIG. Another concern is that derivatives, particularly credit derivatives, need to have a better clearing mechanism so that the failure of one institution does not bring down many others whose net derivatives positions are small, even though they have many offsetting positions. Better clearing could be achieved either by having these derivatives traded in an organized exchange like a futures market, or by having one clearing organization net out trades.

The credit risk exposure posed by interest-rate derivatives, by contrast, seems to be manageable with standard methods of dealing with credit risk, both by managers of financial institutions and the institutions' regulators.

New regulations for derivatives markets are sure to come in the wake of the subprime financial crisis. The industry has also had a wake up call as to where the dangers in derivatives products might lie. There is now the hope that the time bomb arising from derivatives can be defused with appropriate effort on the part of the markets and regulators.

SUMMARY

1. Interest-rate forward contracts, which are agreements to sell a debt instrument at a future (forward) point in time, can be used to hedge interest-rate risk. The advantage of forward contracts is that they are flexible, but the disadvantages are that they are subject to default risk and their market is illiquid.

2. A financial futures contract is similar to an interest-rate forward contract in that it specifies that a debt instrument must be delivered by one party to another on a stated future date. However, it has advantages over a forward contract in that it is not subject to default risk and is more liquid. Forward and futures contracts can be used by financial institutions to hedge (protect against) interest-rate risk.

3. Stock index futures are financial futures whose underlying financial instrument is a stock market index. Stock index futures can be used to hedge stock market risk by reducing systematic risk in portfolios or by locking in stock prices.

4. An option contract gives the purchaser the right to buy (call option) or sell (put option) a security at the exercise (strike) price within a specific period of time. The profit function for options is nonlinear—profits do not always grow by the same amount for a given change in the price of the underlying asset. The nonlinear profit function for options explains why their value (as reflected by the premium paid for them) is negatively related to the exercise price for call options, positively related to the exercise price for put options, positively related to the term to expiration for both call and put options, and positively related to the volatility of the prices of the underlying asset for both call and put options. Financial institutions use futures options to hedge

interest-rate risk in a similar fashion to the way they use financial futures and forward contracts. Futures options may be preferred for macro hedges because they suffer from fewer accounting problems than financial futures.

5. Interest-rate swaps involve the exchange of one set of interest payments for another set of interest payments and have default risk and liquidity problems similar to those of forward contracts. As a result, interest-rate swaps often involve intermediaries such as large banks and investment banks that make a market in swaps. Financial institutions find that interest-rate swaps are useful ways to hedge interest-rate risk. Interest-rate swaps have one big advantage over financial futures and options: They can be written for very long horizons.

6. Credit derivatives are a new type of derivative that offer payoffs on previously issued securities that have credit risk. These derivatives—credit options, swaps, and credit-linked notes—can be used to hedge credit risk.

7. There are two major concerns about the dangers of derivatives: They allow financial institutions to more easily increase their leverage and take big bets (by effectively enabling them to hold a larger amount of the underlying assets than the amount of money put down), and they expose financial institutions to large credit risks because the huge notional amounts of derivative contracts greatly exceed the capital of these institutions. The second danger seems to be overplayed, but the danger from increased leverage using derivatives is very real, as events in the subprime financial crisis revealed.

KEY TERMS

American option, p. 362

arbitrage, p. 351

at the money (trading at par) option, p. 363

call option, p. 362

call premium, p. 362

credit derivatives, p. 374

credit-linked note, p. 375

credit options, p. 374

credit swap, p. 375

currency swaps, p. 370

European option, p. 362

exercise price (strike price), p. 361

financial futures, p. 349

financial futures option (futures option), p. 362

forward contracts, p. 347

in the money option, p. 363

interest-rate forward contract, p. 347

interest-rate futures contract, p. 349

interest-rate swaps, p. 370

intrinsic value, p. 363

long in a call, p. 362

long in a put, p. 364

long position, p. 346

macro hedge, p. 353

margin requirement, p. 355

marked to market, p. 355

micro hedge, p. 353

notional principal, p. 371

open interest, p. 353

option, p. 361

out of the money option, p. 363

premium, p. 362

put option, p. 363

put premium, p. 364

QUESTIONS

You will find the answers to the question marked with an asterisk in the Textbook Resources section of your MyEconLab.

1. Explain why greater volatility or a longer term to maturity leads to a higher premium on both call and put options.

*2. Why does a lower strike price imply that a call option will have a higher premium and a put option a lower premium?

QUANTITATIVE PROBLEMS

1. If the pension fund you manage expects to have an inflow of $120 million six months from now, what forward contract would you seek to enter into to lock in current interest rates?

*2. If the portfolio you manage is holding $25 million of 8s of 2030 Canada bonds with a price of 110, what forward contract would you enter into to hedge the interest-rate risk on these bonds over the coming year?

3. If at the expiration date, the deliverable Canada bond is selling for 101 but the Canada bond futures contract is selling for 102, what will happen to the futures price? Explain your answer.

*4. If you buy a $100 000 June Canada bond contract for 108 and the price of the deliverable Canada bond at the expiration date is 102, what is your profit or loss on the contract?

5. Suppose that the pension you are managing is expecting an inflow of funds of $100 million next year and you want to make sure that you will earn the current interest rate of 8% when you invest the incoming funds in long-term bonds. How would you use the futures market to do this?

*6. How would you use the options market to accomplish the same thing as in Problem 5? What are the advantages and disadvantages of using an options contract rather than a futures contract?

7. If you buy a put option on a $100 000 Canada bond futures contract with an exercise price of 95 and the price of the Canada bond is 120 at expiration, is the contract in the money, out of the money, or at the money? What is your profit or loss on the contract if the premium was $4000?

*8. Suppose that you buy a call option on a $100 000 Canada bond futures contract with an exercise price

of 110 for a premium of $1500. If on expiration the futures contract has a price of 111, what is your profit or loss on the contract?

9. If the finance company you manage has a gap of +$5 million (rate-sensitive assets greater than rate-sensitive liabilities by $5 million), describe an interest-rate swap that would eliminate the company's income gap.

*10. If the bank you manage has a gap of −$42 million, describe an interest-rate swap that would eliminate the bank's income risk from changes in interest rates.

11. If your company has a payment of 200 million euros due one year from now, how would you hedge the foreign exchange risk in this payment with a 125 000 euro futures contract?

*12. If your company has to make a 10 million euro payment to a German company three months from now, how would you hedge the foreign exchange risk in this payment with a 125 000 euro futures contract?

13. Suppose that your company will be receiving 30 million euros six months from now and the euro is currently selling for 1.4 Canadian dollars. If you want to hedge the foreign exchange risk in this payment, what kind of forward contract would you want to enter into?

14. A swap agreement calls for Rocky Industries to pay interest annually based on a rate of 2% over the one-year T-bill rate, currently 3%. In return, Rocky Industries receives interest at a rate of 4% on a fixed-rate basis. The notional principal for the swap is $100 000. What is Rocky's net interest for the year after the agreement?

WEB EXERCISES

1. Visit the Montreal Exchange's website at **www. m-x.ca**. Under "Trading Tools," click on the "Options Calculator." Use the calculator to price an American equity option maturing in 60 days with a strike price of $80, on a non-dividend paying stock, with a current price of $90, annual volatility of 15%, and risk free annual interest rate of 3% on the 90-day period.

2. Visit the Montreal Exchange's website (as above). Under "Trading Tools," click on the "ONX Simulator." Use the simulator to compute the probability of an upcoming Bank of Canada rate move as reflected in the ONX futures price.

3. We have discussed various stock markets in detail throughout this text. Another market that is less well known is the TSX Venture Exchange. Here con-tracts on a wide variety of commodities are traded on a daily basis. Go to **www.tmx.com** to find some information about the origin and purpose of this exchange. Write a one-page summary discussing the information you obtained.

4. We leave the details of pricing option contracts to another course. However, the following site can be used to demonstrate how the features of an option affect the option's prices. Go to **www.intrepid.com/ ~robertl/option-pricer4.html**. Indicate what happens to the price of an option under each of the following situations:
   a. The strike price increases.
   b. Interest rates increase.
   c. Volatility increases.
   d. The time until the option matures increases.

Be sure to visit the MyEconLab website at **www.myeconlab.com**. This online homework and tutorial system puts you in control of your own learning with study and practice tools directly correlated to this chapter content.

On the MyEconLab website you will find the following mini-case for this chapter:
Mini-Case 14.1: Micro Hedge, Macro Hedge, Managing Interest Rate Risk, and Duration

PART V

Central Banking and the Conduct of Monetary Policy

CRISIS AND RESPONSE: THE BANK OF CANADA'S MONETARY POLICY AND LIQUIDITY PROVISION DURING THE FINANCIAL CRISIS

The onset of the subprime financial crisis in August 2007 was a curve ball for central banks around the world. The crisis, described by former Federal Reserve Chairman Alan Greenspan as a "once-in-a-century credit tsunami," had the potential to devastate the world economy.

The Bank of Canada resolved to come to the rescue of the Canadian economy. Starting in September of 2007, the Bank of Canada enacted monetary policy at a rapid rate by reducing the overnight interest rate. Specifically, the Bank lowered the overnight rate target in December by 25 basis points (0.25 percentage points) from 4.50% to 4.25%, and eventually drove the overnight rate target down to 0.25% by April of 2009.

At the same time, the Bank of Canada implemented large liquidity injections into the credit markets to try to get them lending again. Over the course of the crisis, the Bank broadened its provision of liquidity to the financial system well outside of its traditional lending to depository institutions. The number of new Bank of Canada instruments over the course of the crisis spawned a whole new terminology, including term PRAs, quantitative easing, and credit easing, making the Bank of Canada sound like the military with code-named initiatives and weapons. Like the military, the Bank of Canada was fighting a war, although its weapons were financial rather than physical.

The recent financial crisis has demonstrated the importance of central banks like the Bank of Canada to the health of the financial system and the economy. Chapter 15 outlines what central banks are trying to achieve, what motivates them, and how they are set up. Chapter 16 describes how the money supply is determined. In Chapter 17, we look at the tools that central banks like the Bank of Canada have at their disposal and how they use them. Chapter 18 extends the discussion of how monetary policy is conducted to focus on the broader picture of central banks' strategies and tactics.

CHAPTER 15

Central Banks and the Bank of Canada

LEARNING OBJECTIVES

After studying this chapter you should be able to

1. classify the institutional structure of the Bank of Canada as well as four of the most important foreign central banks
2. identify the Bank of Canada's functions and degree of independence and specify the arguments for and against an independent central bank
3. describe the relationship between central bank independence and macroeconomic performance

PREVIEW

Among the most important players in financial markets throughout the world are central banks, the government authorities in charge of monetary policy. Central banks' actions affect interest rates, the amount of credit, and the money supply, all of which have direct impacts not only on financial markets but also on aggregate output and inflation. To understand the role that central banks play in financial markets and the overall economy, we need to understand how these organizations work. Who controls central banks and determines their actions? What motivates their behaviour? Who holds the reins of power?

In this chapter, we look at the goals and institutional structure of major central banks, and focus particularly on the Bank of Canada, Canada's central bank, often just called the Bank. We start by examining what central banks are trying to do, and then focus on the elements of the Bank of Canada's institutional structure that determine where the true power within the Bank of Canada lies. By understanding who makes the decisions, we will have a better idea of how they are made. We then look at several other major central banks, particularly the Federal Reserve System in the United States—the most important central bank in the world—and the European Central Bank, and see how they are organized. Finally, we examine what explains central bank behaviour and whether it is a good idea to make central banks independent by insulating them from politicians. With this context in place, we will be prepared to comprehend the actual conduct of monetary policy described in the following chapters.

ORIGINS OF THE BANK OF CANADA

The devastation of the Great Depression was of fundamental importance in the creation of the Bank of Canada. From 1929 to 1933, Canadian real GDP fell by almost 30% and the unemployment rate increased sevenfold from less than 3% to close to 20%. The Great Depression involved not only the largest decline in the level of economic activity in the history of Canada, but was also followed by an extremely slow recovery. Being such a cataclysmic event, the Great Depression contributed to significant changes in government policy, including fiscal policy, monetary policy, banking policy, and international policy.

In particular, as the depth of the Great Depression was blamed on the operation of the monetary system, in 1933 the federal Conservative government established a royal commission to study the problems of the Great Depression. Based on a recommendation of the royal commission, Parliament passed the Bank of Canada Act in 1934 and the newly founded Bank of Canada started operations on March 11, 1935. By this time, most other countries already had a central bank (see the Global box, Establishment of Selected Central Banks). Although the primary motivation for the formation of the Bank of Canada was economic (or monetary), other motives within the government included the need for Canada to reflect its growing political independence from Britain and the need to coordinate its international economic policy.

Initially the Bank of Canada was a private institution but was nationalized in 1938, so it is now a national institution with headquarters in Ottawa. The Bank also has regional offices in Toronto (for Ontario), Vancouver (for British Columbia and the Yukon), Calgary (for the Prairies, Northwest Territories, and Nunavut), Montreal (for Quebec), and Halifax (for Atlantic Canada), and in 2002 the Bank also established a post in New York to enhance communication with the world's largest financial community. Unlike a private bank that operates in pursuit of profit, the Bank of Canada is responsible for the country's monetary policy and for the regulation of Canada's deposit-based financial institutions.

GLOBAL   Establishment of Selected Central Banks

Canada did not have a central bank for almost the first 70 years after Confederation. By the time the Bank of Canada began operations in 1935, most other countries already had a central bank. In fact, as you can see in the table, Sweden and the United Kingdom created their central banks back in the seventeenth century. These early central banks, however, were initially privately owned and gradually evolved into modern publicly owned central banks.

Country	Year central bank was established
Sweden	1656
United Kingdom	1694
France	1800
Belgium	1850
Germany	1875
Japan	1882
Italy	1893
Switzerland	1905
United States	1913
Canada	1935

Source: Forrest H. Capie, Terence C. Mills, and Geoffrey E. Wood, "Central Bank Dependence and Inflation Performance: An Exploratory Data Analysis," in *Varieties of Monetary Reform: Lessons and Experiences on the Road to Monetary Union,* ed. Pierre L. Siklos (Dordrecht, The Netherlands: Kluwer Academic Publishers, 1994), pp. 95–132. Reprinted with permission of the publisher.

FORMAL STRUCTURE OF THE BANK OF CANADA

The overall responsibility for the operation of the Bank of Canada rests with a **Board of Directors**, which consists of fifteen members—the governor, the senior deputy governor, the deputy minister of finance, and twelve outside directors. The Board appoints the governor and senior deputy governor with the government's approval, for a renewable term of seven years. The outside directors are appointed by the minister of finance, with Cabinet approval, for a three-year term, and they are required to come from all regions of Canada representing a variety of occupations with the exception of banking. The governor of the Bank is the chief executive officer and chairman of the Board of Directors. Currently, the governor of the Bank of Canada is Mark Carney (see the Inside the Central Bank box, The Political Environment and the Bank of Canada).

In 1994 the Board of Directors made some changes in the internal organization of the Bank. Most prominently the Board established a new senior decision-making authority within the Bank called the **Governing Council**. The Council is chaired by the governor and is composed of the senior deputy governor and four deputy governors. Since this change, the six members of the Governing Council of the Bank collectively assume responsibility for the Bank's new semi-annual *Monetary Policy Report*, published in April and October, and its *Update*, published in January and July. This system of "collective responsibility" ensures that the Bank's governor is not personally identified with the Bank's policy.

THE FUNCTIONS OF THE BANK OF CANADA

In the words of the preamble of the Bank of Canada Act, the functions of the Bank of Canada are

> "to regulate credit and currency in the best interests of the economic life of the nation, to control and protect the external value of the national monetary unit and to mitigate by its influence fluctuations in the general level of production, trade, prices and employment, so far as may be possible within the scope of monetary action, and generally to promote the economic and financial welfare of Canada."

INSIDE THE CENTRAL BANK

The Political Environment and the Bank of Canada

Since the inception of the Bank of Canada there have been eight governors:

1935–1954, Graham Towers

1955–1961, James Coyne

1961–1973, Louis Rasminsky

1973–1987, Gerald Bouey

1987–1994, John Crow

1994–2000, Gordon Thiessen

2001–2007, David Dodge

2008–   , Mark Carney

It is interesting to note that during the same period, Canadians went to the polls more than twenty times to elect a federal government. The Bank of Canada is not completely independent from the government. For example, the government can directly influence the Bank by not renewing the governor's appointment when it expires, as the Liberal government did in 1994 when it didn't renew the appointment of John Crow, who was appointed by the Conservative government in 1987.

This is a vague mandate, leaving a lot of room for interpretation. To explore this subject, we discuss four functions of the Bank of Canada as they are mentioned in the Bank's webpage:

- bank note issue
- government debt and asset management services
- central banking services, and
- monetary policy management.

Bank Note Issue

Before the creation of the Bank of Canada, the federal government and the early banks issued notes designed to circulate as currency. The day it began operations, the Bank replaced the outstanding issue of federal government notes and provision was also made for the gradual removal of notes issued by banks. By 1945 the Bank had a monopoly over note issue. Although the original Bank Act required the Bank to redeem its notes in gold, this provision was never used. In fact, it was removed with the 1967 revision of the Bank Act, thereby providing the Bank with unlimited powers to issue legal tender.

The Bank also conducts ongoing research, working closely with private-sector partnerships and note-issuing authorities in other countries, in order to improve cost-effectiveness, increase the durability of bank notes, and reduce counterfeiting. In its role as provider of paper money, the Bank's overall objective is to preserve the integrity and safety of Canadian currency in the most economical and efficient manner possible.

Government Debt and Asset Management Services

In its role as the federal government's fiscal agent, the Bank of Canada provides debt-management services for the federal government such as advising on borrowings, managing new debt offerings, and servicing outstanding debt. Before 1995 these services were provided for all of the federal government's debt. In 1995, however, a special agency of the Department of Finance was created, known as Canada Investment and Savings, to be responsible for the federal government's debt held by individuals, commonly known as retail debt.

Canada Investment and Savings handles government of Canada securities such as Canada Savings Bonds, treasury bills, and marketable bonds, and is also responsible for the development of new investment products and marketing initiatives. The Bank of Canada, however, continues to be responsible for all of the government's securities after they are issued, administering millions of bondholder accounts and making payments on behalf of the federal government for interest and debt redemption.

In its role as fiscal agent, the Bank of Canada also manages the government's foreign exchange reserves held by the **Exchange Fund Account** of the Department of Finance. In particular, the Bank assists the Department of Finance in investing these foreign reserves and in borrowing when necessary to maintain an adequate level of reserves. The Bank also engages in international financial transactions, on behalf of the government, in order to influence exchange rates. (We discuss the Bank's foreign exchange interventions more formally in Chapter 20.)

Central Banking Services

The Bank of Canada serves as the lender of last resort if a deposit-taking financial institution faces a liquidity crisis. Because of its unique power to create base money, the Bank can ease the liquidity problems of any financial institution by extending advances, and therefore deter bank runs and panics. **Base money** (also called **monetary base**) consists of the monetary liabilities of the central bank and, as you will see in the next chapter, is an important part of the money supply, because changes in it lead to multiple changes in the money supply. Of course, lender-of-last-resort lending is closely coordinated with the two federal regulatory agencies that are set up specifically to regulate financial institutions— the Office of the Superintendent of Financial Institutions Canada and the Canada Deposit Insurance Corporation.[1] Moreover, such lending is done judiciously, explicitly considering the effects on other financial institutions, the money supply, and government policy.

The Bank of Canada also plays a central role in Canada's national payments system (to be discussed in some detail in Chapter 17). This is essentially an electronic system that clears and settles payments and transactions including securities and foreign exchange, currently handling 15 times our gross domestic product per year. Although this system is operated by the Canadian Payments Association, federal legislation that came into force in 1996 gave the Bank explicit responsibility for the regulatory oversight of this system. The Bank's main concern is whether problems that affect one participant in the clearing and settlement system will spread to other participants.

Finally, the Bank of Canada acts as the holder of deposit accounts of the federal government, the directly clearing members of the Canadian Payments Association, international organizations such as the International Monetary Fund, and other central banks. As the federal government's banker, the Bank is also responsible for the government's operating accounts. In this role, as you will see in Chapter 17, the Bank shifts government balances between the government's transactions account with the Bank and the government's non-transactions accounts with the banks, using twice-daily auctions of government term deposits.

Monetary Policy

The Bank of Canada employs such tools as **open market buyback operations** (the purchase and sale of government securities that affect both interest rates and the amount of reserves in the banking system) and, to a lesser extent, the shifting of government balances between it and the directly clearing members of the Canadian Payments Association to implement changes in the money supply. The Bank's ultimate objective is to keep inflation low. The Bank has a staff of professional economists, which provides economic analysis that the Board of Directors uses in making its decisions (see the Inside the Central Bank box, Role of the Bank's Research Staff).

The Bank's goal of low inflation is closely related to the goal of steady economic growth, because businesses are more likely to invest in capital equipment to increase productivity and economic growth when inflation is low. Low inflation is also desirable because it protects the purchasing power of pensioners and those on fixed incomes.[2]

Although the Bank determines monetary policy, in the following section you will learn that the ultimate responsibility for policy rests with the government,

---

[1] The Office of the Superintendent of Financial Institutions Canada was created in 1987 to succeed the Department of Insurance and the Inspector General of Banks, whereas the Canada Deposit Insurance Corporation was created by an act of Parliament in 1967 to insure deposits, currently up to $100 000 per account, of member deposit-taking institutions.

[2] See the Web Appendix to Chapter 15 on this book's MyEconLab (**www.pearsoned.ca/myeconlab**) for a discussion of the Bank of Canada's goal of price stability and the monetary policy used to achieve it.

INSIDE THE CENTRAL BANK

Role of the Bank's Research Staff

The Bank of Canada is the largest employer of economists in Canada. What do all these economists do?

The most important task of the Bank's economists is to follow the incoming data from government agencies and private sector organizations on the economy and provide guidance to policymakers on where the economy may be heading and what the impact of monetary policy actions on the economy might be. Moreover, the Bank's economists maintain large econometric models (models whose equations are estimated with statistical procedures) that help them produce forecasts of the national economy, and brief the governor and the senior management of the Bank on their forecasts for the Canadian economy.

Because of the increased influence of developments in foreign countries on the Canadian economy, the research staff produces reports on the major foreign economies. They also conduct research on developments in the foreign exchange market because of its growing importance in the monetary policy process and to

support the activities of the Bank's foreign exchange desk.

Staff economists also engage in basic research on the effects of monetary policy on output and inflation, developments in the labour markets, international trade, international capital markets, banking and other financial institutions, financial markets, and regional economy, among other topics. This research is published widely in academic journals and in Bank of Canada publications. Bank of Canada publications, such as the *Annual Report* (published in March each year), the *Bank of Canada Review* (published quarterly), the *Financial System Review* (published in June and December), the *Bank of Canada Banking and Financial Statistics* (published monthly), the *Monetary Policy Report* (published in April and October), and the *Monetary Policy Report Update* (published in January and July) are good sources of supplemental material for money and banking students.

Another important activity of the research staff is in the public education area. Staff economists are called on frequently to make presentations to the public.

since it is the government that must answer to Parliament. This system of "joint responsibility" dates back to 1967 when the Bank of Canada Act was amended to give responsibility for monetary policy to the government.

HOW INDEPENDENT IS THE BANK OF CANADA?

When we look, in the next three chapters, at how the Bank of Canada conducts monetary policy, we will want to know why it decides to take certain policy actions but not others. To understand its actions, we must understand the incentives that motivate the Bank's behaviour. How free is the Bank from the whims of the government? Do economic, bureaucratic, or political considerations guide it? Is the Bank truly independent of outside pressures?

Stanley Fischer, who was a professor at MIT and is now governor of the Bank of Israel, has defined two different types of independence of central banks: **instrument independence**, the ability of the central bank to set monetary policy instruments, and **goal independence**, the ability of the central bank to set the goals of monetary policy. Unlike the U.S. Federal Reserve and the European Central Bank that have both types of independence and are remarkably free of political pressures that influence other government agencies, the Bank of Canada has instrument independence but not goal independence.

The Bank's degree of independence has evolved over time, in part because of changing circumstances, and in part because a clear division of authority was not established in the original Bank of Canada Act. Initially, the Bank of Canada was privately owned, with about 12 000 individual shareholders, and so was largely free of political pressures. It was also free of private interference, because of regulations regarding who could hold how much stock in the Bank. The Conservative government in office at the time of the Bank's creation believed that the Bank should possess a large share of the responsibility for the development of monetary policy.

Significant changes in the balance of power occurred with the election of a majority Liberal government in the fall of 1935. The Liberals moved the Bank in the direction of public ownership, culminating in its complete nationalization by 1938. This was done to further isolate the Bank from the pressures of the private system. However, the nationalization of the Bank did tilt the balance of authority for monetary policy back towards the federal Cabinet and Parliament. The Liberals believed that the Bank should have discretion in internal management and in implementing monetary policy yet the policies being implemented should be in harmony with the views of the government.

In June 1954, the first governor of the Bank of Canada, Graham Towers, retired after 19 years of service. Graham Towers was replaced by James Coyne (see the Inside the Central Bank box, The Political Environment and the Bank of Canada, on page 383). Like many Canadians at the time, James Coyne was concerned about the level of foreign ownership and the increase in consumer prices during the Korean War. He was convinced that the solution to these problems was a tighter monetary policy stance. A decline in the supply of bank reserves would increase interest rates, thereby raising national savings and reducing Canada's dependence on foreign capital inflows. The tighter monetary policy led to rising unemployment and weak output growth. As a result, the Bank's policies were criticized by commentary in the popular press and by most of the academic community. In fact, thirty economists signed a letter to the minister of finance calling for Coyne's dismissal.[3]

James Coyne, however, did not change his mind. He was convinced that there was no long-run relationship between inflation and unemployment, despite the publication of a famous paper in 1958 by the British economist A. W. Phillips, showing that higher inflation was typically associated with a lower unemployment rate.[4] Although the Phillips hypothesis attracted widespread support in Canada and was replicated with Canadian data, Coyne was anticipating the pathbreaking work by Milton Friedman and Edmund Phelps on the vertical Phillips curve, to be published 10 years later in 1968.[5] But as a former governor of the Bank of Canada, Gordon Thiessen, put it in a recent speech,

> "[t]here was one critical area, however, where Coyne and many other policy analysts, both within and outside the Bank, appear to have been misguided. Those who had questioned the effectiveness of monetary policy in earlier years had failed to

---

[3] See H. S. Gordon, *The Economists versus the Bank of Canada* (Toronto: The Ryerson Press, 1961): v–vi.

[4] A. W. Phillips, "The Relation between Unemployment and the Rate of Change of Money Wages in the United Kingdom," *Economica* 24 (1958): 283–299.

[5] Milton Friedman, "The Role of Monetary Policy," *American Economic Review* 58 (1968): 1–17; Edmund Phelps, "Money-Wage Dynamics and Labour Market Equilibrium," *Journal of Political Economy* 76 (1968): 678–711.

appreciate that it was likely to be much stronger than fiscal policy under a flexible exchange rate system, especially when capital was highly mobile. The large capital movements triggered by any change in interest rates would put significant pressure on the exchange rate, amplifying the effects of monetary policy while undercutting the effects of any opposing fiscal policy. Coyne did not realize that, for similar reasons, it was unlikely that a tighter monetary policy would ever raise national savings or reduce foreign investment inflows."[6]

To avoid accepting blame for this state of affairs, the Liberal government in office reversed its previous stand and disavowed its position that the government was responsible for monetary policy. The government was criticized for this reversal and the new hands-off approach to monetary policy. When the government changed hands on June 10, 1957 and Donald Fleming became the federal minister of finance, the stage was set for a confrontation with the governor of the Bank, James Coyne. After a long and acrimonious debate, the so-called "Coyne Affair" was resolved in 1961 with the resignation of Governor Coyne.

On July 24, 1961, Louis Rasminsky accepted the position as the third governor of the Bank of Canada on the condition that the relationship between the government and the Bank be clearly defined. Soon after he assumed office, he issued a public statement containing two main principles reflecting his views on that relationship

> "...(1) in the ordinary course of events, the Bank has the responsibility for monetary policy, and (2) if the government disapproves of the monetary policy being carried out by the Bank, it has the right and the responsibility to direct the Bank as to the policy which the Bank is to carry out."[7]

A royal commission, whose appointment was partly initiated by the Coyne Affair, accepted Governor Rasminsky's views regarding the relationship between the Bank and the government. The commission recommended a system of joint responsibility under which the Bank has considerable autonomy in the conduct of day-to-day monetary policy but the government must accept full responsibility for the policy being followed.

The Bank of Canada Act was amended in 1967 to confirm the joint responsibility system, and this state of affairs regarding monetary policy has generally remained in order to this day. Under this joint responsibility system, the governor of the Bank of Canada and the minister of finance, acting on behalf of the government, consult regularly and, in the event of a serious disagreement over the conduct of monetary policy, the government has the right to override the Bank's decisions. In particular, the minister of finance can issue a directive to the Bank indicating the specific policy changes that the Bank must follow. The directive, however, must be published indicating not only the new policy that the Bank is supposed to undertake but also the period during which it is to apply.

Hence, ultimate responsibility for monetary policy rests with the democratically elected government. However, because of the consequences of issuing a directive, it is unlikely that such a directive would be issued, and none has been issued to date.

---

[6] Gordon Thiessen, "Can a Bank Change? The Evolution of Monetary Policy at the Bank of Canada 1935–2000," Lecture to the Faculty of Social Science, University of Western Ontario.

[7] Bank of Canada, *Annual Report*, 1961, p. 3.

THE CHANGING FACE OF THE BANK OF CANADA

The legislation governing the Bank of Canada's responsibility for monetary policy has remained relatively unchanged since the Bank Act of 1967. Over the past decade, however, the Bank has undertaken a broad range of initiatives and made significant institutional changes to the way it operates. The impetus for change came from the interaction of experience and economic theory, the desire to explain and build confidence in the Bank's actions, and (to a smaller extent) from technological change and globalization.

Clarifying objectives is an important starting point for any successful monetary policy framework. The legislation by which the Bank of Canada is governed does not facilitate a clear understanding of objectives. For example, the preamble to legislation governing the Bank refers to multiple, and potentially inconsistent, policy objectives. Over the past few decades, however, the performance of the Canadian economy, together with the evolution of economic theory, led to the view that price stability is the most important goal of monetary policy. As John Crow put it, in his January 1988 Hanson Memorial Lecture at the University of Alberta,

> "[t]heory and experience—much of this experience not overly cheerful but certainly instructive—both point to a very clear answer. Monetary policy should be conducted so as to achieve a pace of monetary expansion that promotes stability in the value of money. This means pursuing a policy aimed at achieving and maintaining stable prices."[8]

The Hanson lecture was designed to explicitly identify price stability as the objective of Bank of Canada policy. This message was reinforced on February 26, 1991, through a joint announcement by the governor of the Bank and the minister of finance regarding the establishment of formal inflation targets (to be discussed in detail in Chapter 18). Clearly defined targets can be appealed as an institutional way of improving the macroeconomic outcomes of monetary policy.

The effectiveness of such an institutional framework, however, depends on two fundamental requirements: "independence" and "accountability." Although the Bank of Canada has not been given "goal independence"—the goal of price stability has been set jointly by the Bank and the Department of Finance—over the last decade the Bank placed increased emphasis on its responsibility to achieve the goal of price stability and its greater freedom to take whatever action is needed to do so. This freedom is referred to as "operational" (or "instrument") independence and, although it hasn't been explicitly legislated, it exists in practice. Increased operational independence has also raised the standards for accountability. As already noted, for example, the governor of the Bank has delegated the authority for monetary policy decisions to a committee—the six-member internal Governing Council. Moreover, it has become a de facto standard for the governor to appear before a parliamentary committee following the release of the Bank's *Monetary Policy Report*.

The Bank of Canada has also improved its communications activities by moving towards greater transparency in its operations and objectives. In 1999, for example, the Bank started a twice-yearly *Update* to the *Monetary Policy Report*, both published by the Bank's Governing Council. The *Monetary Policy Report* is published every April and October while the *Update* is published every January and July, giving an account of the Bank's management of monetary policy. Moreover, the Bank has noticeably increased the number of press conferences, press releases, and speeches, and also reorganized its regional offices in 1996–1997 with the objective of improv-

---

[8]John Crow, "The Work of Canadian Monetary Policy," The Eric J. Hanson Memorial Lecture, University of Alberta, Edmonton, Alberta. *Bank of Canada Review* (1988): 3–17.

ing communication, transparency, and its assessment of economic conditions across Canada. For example, the Bank's regional offices, by maintaining contact with provincial governments, industries, and the general public, present quarterly "grassroots" assessments of current and prospective economic developments to the Bank's Governing Council—information that complements economic projections prepared by the Bank's staff. Finally, the Bank of Canada maintains a comprehensive website (at **www.bankofcanada.ca**) to disseminate information regarding financial statistics, publications, the transmission of monetary policy, and Bank-related material.[9]

The direction taken in the recent evolution of the monetary policy framework in Canada has been heavily influenced by the role that the institutional monetary structure plays in influencing the monetary conduct.[10] As the Bank's former governor, Gordon Thiessen, put it in his October 17, 2000, speech to the Faculty of Social Science of the University of Western Ontario,

> "[t]he Bank tries to work with the markets, rather than against them, to avoid surprising them with unexpected actions. Greater transparency facilitates the policy-transmission process by conditioning market expectations, and helps avoid unnecessary confusion about the reasons for our actions."[11]

From Opaqueness to Accountability and Transparency

The Bank of Canada did not release information regarding its guidelines or resulting consequences during the 1960s and 1970s. As a general rule, the Bank wanted to remain nontransparent, keeping its monetary policy approaches secret. The use of multiple instruments and goals, vague statements about its policies, and moral suasion with banks, resulted in an unnecessary level of secrecy. Due to this instrument and goal opaqueness, the public was not able to question or comprehend the Bank's actions, allowing the accountability of the Bank of Canada to deteriorate.

Over the past decade, however, the Bank of Canada has rejected multiple policy instruments by adopting the overnight interest rate as the centrepiece of its monetary policy implementation and by focusing on an explicit inflation-control target. The goal of the Bank's current monetary policy is to keep the inflation rate within a target range of 1% to 3%, with the midpoint of the inflation target range, 2%, being the most desirable outcome; the 1% to 3% target range for inflation applies until the end of 2011. By announcing a target overnight interest rate, establishing planned dates for policy changes, and implementing the Governing Council for making decisions and disclosing information, the Bank of Canada has moved towards greater accountability and transparency.

The Bank's move towards accountability and transparency was motivated by a number of recent trends in society and the economy. For example, the shift from fixed to flexible exchange rates removed an obstacle to openness. The experience with inflation in the 1970s and the recession in the early 1980s allowed the Bank

---

[9] An inside view of how the Bank interacts with the public and the politicians can be found in John Crow, *Making Money: An Insider's Perspective on Finance, Politics, and Canada's Central Bank* (John Wiley: Toronto, 2002).

[10] For a discussion of similar changes implemented by other central banks around the world, see Graydon Paulin, "The Changing Face of Central Banking in the 1990s," *Bank of Canada Review* (Summer 2000): 3–13.

[11] Gordon Thiessen, "Can a Bank Change? The Evolution of Monetary Policy at the Bank of Canada 1935–2000." Lecture to the Faculty of Social Science, University of Western Ontario.

of Canada to reconsider its analysis of inflation and its costs. In addition, economic comprehension about interest rates, developments about targets and inflation, and greater openness in the government also contributed to the accountability and transparency of the Bank of Canada.[12]

STRUCTURE AND INDEPENDENCE OF FOREIGN CENTRAL BANKS

In contrast to the Bank of Canada, which is a centralized unit owned by the government, central banks in other industrialized countries have a more decentralized structure. Here we examine the structure and degree of independence of four of the most important foreign central banks: the Federal Reserve System of the United States, the European Central Bank, the Bank of England, and the Bank of Japan.

Federal Reserve System

Of all the central banks in the world, the **Federal Reserve System** of the United States (also called simply **the Fed**) probably has the most unusual structure. It includes the following entities: the **Board of Governors of the Federal Reserve System**, the **Federal Reserve Banks**, the **Federal Open Market Committee (FOMC)**, the Federal Advisory Council, and around 2900 member commercial banks. Figure 15-1 outlines the relationships of these entities to one another and to the three policy tools of the Fed—open market operations, the discount rate (the U.S. equivalent of the bank rate in Canada), and reserve requirements.

BOARD OF GOVERNORS OF THE FEDERAL RESERVE SYSTEM   At the head of the Federal Reserve System is the seven-member Board of Governors, headquartered in Washington, D.C. Each governor is appointed by the president of the United States and confirmed by the Senate. To limit the president's control over the Fed and insulate the Fed from other political pressures, the governors can serve one nonrenewable fourteen-year term plus part of another term, with one governor's term expiring every other January. The chairman of the Board of Governors is chosen from among the seven governors and serves a four-year term. It is expected that once a new chairman is chosen, the old chairman resigns from the Board of Governors, even if there are many years left to his or her term as a governor.

FEDERAL RESERVE BANKS   Each of the twelve Federal Reserve districts has one main Federal Reserve bank, which may have branches in other cities in the district. The locations of these districts, the Federal Reserve banks, and their branches are shown in Figure 15-2. The three largest Federal Reserve banks in terms of assets are those of New York, Chicago, and San Francisco—combined they hold more than 50% of the assets (discount loans, securities, and other holdings) of the Federal Reserve System. The New York bank, with around one-quarter of the assets, is the most important of the Federal Reserve banks (see the Inside the Central Bank box, The Special Role of the Federal Reserve Bank of New York on page 394).

---

[12] For more details regarding the Bank's recent move towards openness and accountability, see John Chant, "The Bank of Canada: Moving Towards Transparency," *Bank of Canada Review* (Spring 2003): 5–13. Also, regarding Canada's experience with central banking, see Michael D. Bordo and Angela Redish, "70 Years of Central Banking: The Bank of Canada in an International Context, 1935–2005," *Bank of Canada Review* (Winter 2005–2006): 7–14, and David Laidler, "Free Banking and the Bank of Canada," *Bank of Canada Review* (Winter 2005–2006): 15–24.

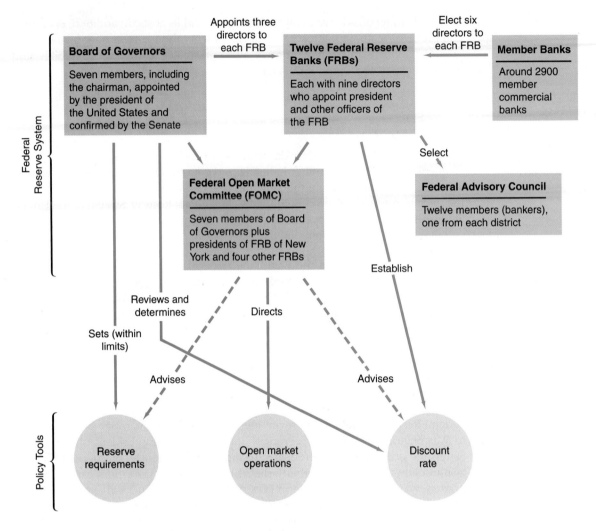

FIGURE 15-1   Structure and Responsibility for Policy Tools in the Federal Reserve System

Dashed lines indicate that the FOMC "advises" on the setting of reserve requirements and the discount rate.

FEDERAL OPEN MARKET COMMITTEE (FOMC)   The twelve Federal Reserve banks and the Board of Governors are actively involved in decisions concerning the conduct of monetary policy. In particular, all seven governors are voting members of the FOMC together with the president of the Federal Reserve Bank of New York and presidents of four other Federal Reserve banks. The FOMC usually meets eight times a year (about every six weeks) and makes decisions regarding the conduct of monetary policy in the United States. Indeed, the FOMC is often referred to as the "Fed" in the press: for example, when the media say that the Fed is meeting, they actually mean that the FOMC is meeting.

HOW INDEPENDENT IS THE FED?   The Federal Reserve appears to be remarkably free of the political pressures that influence other government agencies in the United States. Yet it is still subject to the influence of the president of the United States, since the president appoints members to the Board of Governors. The power of the

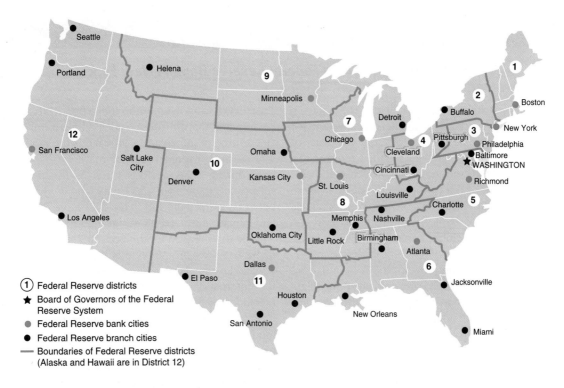

(1) Federal Reserve districts
★ Board of Governors of the Federal
  Reserve System
● Federal Reserve bank cities
● Federal Reserve branch cities
— Boundaries of Federal Reserve districts
  (Alaska and Hawaii are in District 12)

FIGURE 15-2   Federal Reserve System

Source: Federal Reserve Bulletin

United States president in appointing members to the Board of Governors is limited, however. Because the term of the chairman of the Board of Governors is not necessarily concurrent with that of the president of the United States, a president may have to deal with a chairman of the Board of Governors appointed by a previous administration. Alan Greenspan, for example, was appointed chairman in 1987 by President Ronald Reagan and was reappointed to another term by another Republican president, George Bush, in 1992. When Bill Clinton, a Democrat, became president in 1993, Greenspan had several years left to his term. Clinton was put under tremendous pressure to reappoint Greenspan when his term expired and did so in 1996 and again in 2000, even though Greenspan is a Republican.[13] George W. Bush, a Republican, then reappointed Greenspan in 2004.

You can see that the Federal Reserve has extraordinary independence for a government agency. Nonetheless, the Fed is not free from political pressures. Indeed, to understand the Fed's behaviour, we must recognize that public support for the actions of the Federal Reserve plays a very important role.[14]

---

[13] Similarly, William McChesney Martin Jr., the chairman from 1951 to 1970, was appointed by President Truman (Dem.) but was reappointed by Presidents Eisenhower (Rep.), Kennedy (Dem.), and Nixon (Rep.). Also Paul Volcker, the chairman from 1979 to 1987, was appointed by President Carter (Dem.) but was reappointed by President Reagan (Rep.).

[14] An inside view of how the Fed interacts with the public and the politicians can be found in Bob Woodward, *Maestro: Greenspan's Fed and the American Boom* (New York: Simon and Schuster, 2000).

INSIDE THE CENTRAL BANK

The Special Role of the Federal Reserve Bank of New York

The Federal Reserve Bank of New York plays a special role in the Federal Reserve System for several reasons. First, its district contains many of the largest commercial banks in the United States, the safety and soundness of which are paramount to the health of the U.S. financial system. The Federal Reserve Bank of New York conducts examinations of bank holding companies and state-chartered member banks in its district, making it the supervisor of some of the most important financial institutions in the U.S. financial system. Not surprisingly, given this responsibility, the bank supervision group is one of the largest units of the New York Fed and is by far the largest bank supervision group in the Federal Reserve System.

The second reason for the New York Fed's special role is its active involvement in the bond and foreign exchange markets. The New York Fed houses the open market desk, which conducts open market operations—the purchase and sale of bonds—that determine the amount of reserves in the banking system. Because of this involvement in the Treasury securities market, as well as its walking-distance location near the New York and American Stock Exchanges, the officials at the Federal Reserve Bank of New York are in constant contact with the major financial markets in the United States. In addition, the Federal Reserve Bank of New York houses the foreign exchange desk, which conducts foreign exchange interventions on behalf of the Federal Reserve System and the U.S.

Treasury. Its involvement in these financial markets means that the New York Fed is an important source of information on what is happening in U.S. and foreign financial markets, particularly during crisis periods, such as the recent subprime meltdown, as well as a liaison between officials in the Federal Reserve System and private participants in the markets.

The third reason for the Federal Reserve Bank of New York's prominence is that it is the only Federal Reserve bank to be a member of the Bank for International Settlements (BIS). Thus the president of the New York Fed, along with the chairman of the Board of Governors, represents the Federal Reserve System in its regular monthly meetings with other major central bankers at the BIS. This close contact with foreign central bankers and interaction with foreign exchange markets means that the New York Fed has a special role in international relations, both with other central bankers and with private market participants. Adding to its prominence in international circles is that the New York Fed is the repository for more than US$100 billion of the world's gold, an amount greater than the gold at Fort Knox.

Finally, the president of the Federal Reserve Bank of New York is the only permanent member of the FOMC among the Federal Reserve bank presidents, serving as the vice-chairman of the committee. Thus he and the chairman and vice-chairman of the Board of Governors are the three most important officials in the Federal Reserve System.

European Central Bank

Until recently, the Federal Reserve had no rivals in terms of importance in the central banking world. However, this situation changed in January 1999 with the start-up of the European Central Bank (ECB)—the central bank of the sixteen euro area countries— which now conducts monetary policy for countries that are members of the European Monetary Union. These countries, taken together, have a population that exceeds that in the United States and a GDP comparable to that of the United States. The Maastricht Treaty, which established the ECB and the **European System of Central Banks (ESCB)**, patterned these institutions after the Federal Reserve, in that central banks for each country (referred to as *National Central Banks*, or *NCBs*) have a similar role to that of the Federal Reserve Banks. The European Central Bank and the national central banks of the countries that have adopted the euro are referred to as the **Eurosystem** (note that Slovenia adopted the euro on January 1, 2007, Cyprus and Malta in January 1, 2008, and Slovakia on January 1, 2009). The Eurosystem excludes the central banks of the European Union countries that have not yet adopted the euro. The Eurosystem should not be confused with the European System of Central Banks, the term used to refer to the European Central Bank and the national central banks of all twenty-seven European Union (EU) member countries— when all EU member countries adopt the euro, the Eurosystem and the European System of Central Banks will become one entity.

The European Central Bank, which is housed in Frankfurt, Germany, has an Executive Board that is similar in structure to the Board of Governors of the Federal Reserve; it is made up of the president, the vice president, and four other members, who are appointed to eight-year, nonrenewable terms. The Governing Council, which comprises the Executive Board and the presidents of the National Central Banks, is similar to the FOMC and makes the decisions on monetary policy. While the presidents of the National Central Banks are appointed by their countries' respective governments, the members of the Executive Board are appointed by a committee consisting of the heads of state of all the countries that are part of the European Monetary Union.

DIFFERENCES BETWEEN THE EUROPEAN SYSTEM OF CENTRAL BANKS AND THE FEDERAL RESERVE SYSTEM   In the popular press, the European System of Central Banks is usually referred to as the European Central Bank (ECB), even though it would be more accurate to refer to it as the Eurosystem, just as it would be more accurate to refer to the Federal Reserve System rather than the Fed. Although the structure of the Eurosystem is similar to that of the Federal Reserve System, some important differences distinguish the two. First, the budgets of the Federal Reserve Banks are controlled by the Board of Governors, while the National Central Banks control their own budgets *and* the budget of the ECB in Frankfurt. The ECB in the Eurosystem therefore has less power than does the Board of Governors in the Federal Reserve System. Second, the monetary operations of the Eurosystem are conducted by all the National Central Banks in each country, so monetary operations are not centralized as they are in the Federal Reserve System. Third, in contrast to the Federal Reserve, the ECB is not involved in supervision and regulation of financial institutions; these tasks are left to the individual countries in the European Monetary Union.

GOVERNING COUNCIL   Just as there is a focus on meetings of the FOMC in the United States, there is a similar focus in Europe on meetings of the Governing Council, which meets monthly at the ECB in Frankfurt to make decisions on monetary policy. Currently, fifteen countries are members of the European Monetary Union, and the head of each of the fifteen National Central Banks has one vote in the Governing Council; each of the six Executive Board members has one vote. In contrast to FOMC meetings, which staff from both the Board of Governors and individual Federal Reserve Banks attend, only the twenty-one members of the Governing Council attend the meetings with no staff present.

The Governing Council has decided that although its members have the legal right to vote, no formal vote is actually taken; instead the Council operates by consensus. One reason the Governing Council has decided not to take votes is because of worries that the casting of individual votes might lead to heads of National Central Banks supporting a monetary policy that would be appropriate for their individual countries, but not necessarily for the countries in the European Monetary Union as a whole. This problem is less severe for the Federal Reserve: Although Federal Reserve Bank presidents do live in different regions of the country, all have the same nationality and are more likely to take a national view in monetary policy decisions rather than a regional view.

Just as the Federal Reserve releases the FOMC's decision on the setting of the policy interest rate (the federal funds rate) immediately after the meeting is over, the ECB does the same after the Governing Council meeting concludes (announcing the target for a similar short-term interest rate for interbank loans). However, whereas the Fed simply releases a statement about the setting of the monetary policy instruments, the ECB goes further by having a press conference in which the president and vice president of the ECB take questions from the news media. Holding such a press conference so soon after the meeting is tricky because it requires the president and vice president to be quick on their feet in dealing with the press. The first president of the ECB, Willem F. Duisenberg, put his foot in his mouth at some of these press conferences, and the ECB came under some sharp criticism. His successor, Jean-Claude Trichet, a more successful communicator, has encountered fewer problems in this regard.

Although currently only sixteen countries in the European Monetary Union have representation on the Governing Council, this situation is likely to change in the future. Three countries in the European Community already qualify for entering the European Monetary Union: the United Kingdom, Sweden, and Denmark. Six other countries in the European Community (the Czech Republic, Estonia, Hungary, Latvia, Lithuania, and Poland) might enter the European Monetary Union once they qualify, which may not be too far in the future. The possible expansion of membership in the Eurosystem presents a particular dilemma. The current size of the Governing Council (twenty-one voting members) is substantially larger than the FOMC (twelve voting members). Many commentators have wondered whether the Governing Council is already too unwieldy—a situation that would get considerably worse as more countries join the European Monetary Union. To deal with this potential problem, the Governing Council has decided on a complex system of rotation, somewhat like that for the FOMC, in which National Central Banks from the larger countries will vote more often than National Central Banks from smaller countries.

HOW INDEPENDENT IS THE ECB?   Although the Federal Reserve is a highly independent central bank, the Maastricht Treaty, which established the Eurosystem, has made the latter the most independent central bank in the world. Like the Board of Governors, the members of the Executive Board have long terms (eight years), while heads of National Central Banks are required to have terms at least five years long. Like the Fed, the Eurosystem determines its own budget, and the governments of the member countries are not allowed to issue instructions to the ECB. These elements of the Maastricht Treaty make the ECB highly instrument-independent.

The Maastricht Treaty specifies that the overriding, long-term goal of the ECB is price stability, which means that the goal for the Eurosystem is more clearly specified than it is for the Federal Reserve System. However, the Maastricht Treaty did not specify exactly what "price stability" means. The Eurosystem has defined the quantitative goal for monetary policy to be an inflation rate slightly less than 2%, so from this perspective, the ECB is slightly less goal-independent than the Fed. The Eurosystem is, however, much more goal-independent than the Federal Reserve System in another way: The Eurosystem's charter cannot be changed by legislation; it can be changed only by revision of the Maastricht Treaty—a difficult process, because *all* signatories to the treaty must agree to accept any proposed change.

Bank of England

Founded in 1694, the Bank of England is one of the oldest central banks. The Bank Act of 1946 gave the government statutory authority over the Bank of England. The Court (equivalent to a board of directors) of the Bank of England is made up of the governor and two deputy governors, who are appointed for five-year terms, and 16 nonexecutive directors, who are appointed for three-year terms.

Until 1997, the Bank of England was the least independent of the central banks examined in this chapter because the decision to raise or lower interest rates resided not within the Bank of England but with the chancellor of the exchequer (the equivalent of the Canadian minister of finance). All of this changed when the new Labour government came to power in May 1997. At this time, the new chancellor of the exchequer, Gordon Brown, made a surprise announcement that the Bank of England would henceforth have the power to set interest rates. However, the Bank was not granted total instrument independence. The government can overrule the Bank and set rates "in extreme economic circumstances" and "for a limited period." Nonetheless, as in Canada, because overruling the Bank would be so public and is supposed to occur only in highly unusual circumstances and for a limited time, it is likely to be a rare occurrence.

Because the United Kingdom is not a member of the European Monetary Union, the Bank of England makes its monetary policy decisions independently from the European Central Bank. The decision to set interest rates resides in the Monetary Policy Committee, made up of the governor, two deputy governors, two members appointed by the governor after consultation with the chancellor (normally central bank officials), plus four outside economic experts appointed by the chancellor. (Surprisingly, two of the four outside experts initially appointed to this committee were not British citizens—one was Dutch and the other American, although both were residents of the United Kingdom.) The inflation target for the Bank of England is set by the chancellor of the exchequer, so the Bank of England has as much goal independence as the Bank of Canada, but is less goal-independent than the Fed.

Bank of Japan

The Bank of Japan (Nippon Ginko) was founded in 1882 during the Meiji Restoration. Monetary policy is determined by the Policy Board, which is composed of the governor, two vice governors, and six outside members appointed by the cabinet and approved by the parliament, all of whom serve for five-year terms.

Until recently, the Bank of Japan was not formally independent of the government, with the ultimate power residing with the Ministry of Finance. However, the new Bank of Japan Law, which took effect in April 1998 and was the first major change in the powers of the Bank of Japan in 55 years, has changed this. In addition to stipulating that the objective of monetary policy is to attain price stability, the law granted greater instrument and goal independence to the Bank of Japan. Before this, the government had two voting members on the Policy Board, one from the Ministry of Finance and the other from the Economic Planning Agency. Now the government may send two representatives from these agencies to board meetings, but they no longer have voting rights, although they do have the ability to request delays in monetary policy decisions. In addition, the Ministry of Finance lost its authority to oversee many of the operations of the Bank of Japan, particularly the right to dismiss senior officials. However, the Ministry of Finance continues to have control over the part of the Bank's budget that is unrelated to monetary policy, which might limit its independence to some extent.

The Trend Toward Greater Independence

As our survey of the structure and independence of the major central banks indicates, in recent years we have been seeing a remarkable trend toward increasing independence. It used to be that the Federal Reserve was substantially more independent than almost all other central banks, with the exception of those in Germany and Switzerland. Now the newly established European Central Bank is far more independent than the Fed, and greater independence has been granted to central banks like the Bank of England and the Bank of Japan, putting them more on a par with the Fed, as well as to central banks in such diverse countries as New Zealand, Sweden, and the euro nations. Both theory and experience suggest that more independent central banks produce better monetary policy, thus providing an impetus for this trend.

EXPLAINING CENTRAL BANK BEHAVIOUR

One view of government bureaucratic behaviour is that bureaucracies serve the public interest (this is the *public interest view*). Yet some economists have developed a theory of bureaucratic behaviour that suggests other factors that influence how bureaucracies operate. The *theory of bureaucratic behaviour* suggests that the objective of a bureaucracy is to maximize its own welfare, just as a consumer's behaviour is motivated by the maximization of personal welfare and a firm's behaviour is motivated by the maximization of profits. The welfare of a bureaucracy is related to its power and prestige. Thus this theory suggests that an important factor affecting a central bank's behaviour is its attempt to increase its power and prestige.

What predictions does this view of a central bank like the Bank of Canada suggest? One is that the Bank of Canada will fight vigorously to preserve its autonomy, a prediction verified time and time again as the Bank of Canada has continually counterattacked attempts to control its functions. Another prediction is that the Bank of Canada will try to avoid conflict with powerful groups that may threaten to curtail its power and reduce its autonomy. The Bank's behaviour may take several forms. One possible factor explaining why the Bank is sometimes slow to increase interest rates and so smoothes out their fluctuations is that it wishes to avoid a conflict with the government over increases in interest rates. The desire to avoid conflict may also explain why some central banks devised clever stratagems to avoid blame for their mistakes.

The theory of bureaucratic behaviour seems applicable to the Bank of Canada's actions, but we must recognize that this view of the Bank as being solely concerned with its own self-interest is too extreme. Maximizing one's welfare does not rule out altruism. (You might give generously to a charity because it makes you feel good about yourself, but in the process you are helping a worthy cause.) The Bank is surely concerned that it conducts monetary policy in the public interest. However, much uncertainty and disagreement exist over what monetary policy should be.[15] When it is unclear what is in the public interest, other motives may influence the Bank's behaviour. In these situations, the theory of bureaucratic behaviour may be a useful guide to predicting what motivates the Bank of Canada and other central banks.

---

[15] One example of the uncertainty over how best to conduct monetary policy was discussed in Chapter 3: economists are not sure how to measure money. So even if economists agreed that controlling the quantity of money is the appropriate way to conduct monetary policy (a controversial position, as we will see in later chapters), the Bank of Canada cannot be sure which monetary aggregate it should control.

SHOULD THE BANK OF CANADA BE INDEPENDENT?

As we have seen, the Bank of Canada is probably the most independent government agency in Canada. Every few years, the question arises whether the independence given to the Bank of Canada should be curtailed. Politicians who strongly oppose a Bank policy often want to bring it under their supervision in order to impose a policy more to their liking. Should the Bank of Canada be independent, or would we be better off with a central bank under the control of the government?

The Case for Independence

The strongest argument for an independent Bank of Canada rests on the view that subjecting the Bank to more political pressures would impart an inflationary bias to monetary policy. In the view of many observers, politicians in a democratic society are shortsighted because they are driven by the need to win their next election. With this as the primary goal, they are unlikely to focus on long-run objectives, such as promoting a stable price level. Instead, they will seek short-run solutions to problems, like high unemployment and high interest rates, even if the short-run solutions have undesirable long-run consequences. For example, we saw in Chapter 5 that high money growth might lead initially to a drop in interest rates but might cause an increase later as inflation heats up. Would a Bank of Canada under the control of the government be more likely to pursue a policy of excessive money growth when interest rates are high, even though it would eventually lead to inflation and even higher interest rates in the future? The advocates of an independent central bank say yes. They believe that a politically insulated central bank is more likely to be concerned with long-run objectives and thus be a defender of a sound dollar and a stable price level.

A variation on the preceding argument is that the political process in Canada could lead to a **political business cycle**, in which just before an election, expansionary policies are pursued to lower unemployment and interest rates. After the election, the bad effects of these policies—high inflation and high interest rates—come home to roost, requiring contractionary policies that politicians hope the public will forget before the next election. Although the issue has not been completely settled, research indicates that there is no credible evidence that such a political business cycle exists in Canada (see the FYI box, Economics and Politics).

Putting the Bank of Canada under the control of the government is also considered dangerous because the Bank can be used to facilitate government financing of large budget deficits by its purchases of government bonds in the open market. Such open-market purchases by the Bank of Canada increase the money supply and lead to inflation. Government pressure on the Bank of Canada to "help out" might lead to a more inflationary bias in the economy. An independent Bank of Canada is better able to resist this pressure from the government.

Another argument for Bank of Canada independence is that control of monetary policy is too important to leave to politicians, a group that has repeatedly demonstrated a lack of expertise at making hard decisions on issues of great economic importance, such as reducing the budget deficit or reforming the banking system. Another way to state this argument is in terms of the principal–agent problem discussed in Chapters 8 9, and 10. Both the Bank of Canada and politicians are agents of the public (the principals), and as we have seen, both politicians and the Bank of Canada have incentives to act in their own interest rather than in the interest of the public. The argument supporting Bank of Canada independence is that the principal–agent problem is worse for politicians than for the Bank of Canada because politicians have fewer incentives to act in the public interest.

FYI   **Economics and Politics**

Recent politico-institutional approaches to the theory of economic policy emphasize the incentives of rational and maximizing policymakers in explaining movements in macroeconomic variables. Central to this perspective is the general assumption that policymakers respond to incentives and constraints just like the rest of the economic agents. As a consequence, the actual policies of government give rise to political cycles, which on the basis of the primary motivational force involved are distinguished into opportunistic and partisan cycles.

In opportunistic (or electoral) business cycle models, politicians maximize their popularity or their probability of re-election by following pre-election expansionary fiscal policies in order to please the fiscally knowledgeable voters. As a consequence, their actual policies give rise to **electoral business cycles**, that is, persistent cyclical patterns of key policy and target variables across electoral terms, regardless of the political orientation of the incumbent government. In particular, models of opportunistic cycles

predict pre-election high growth and low unemployment, increasing inflation around the election time, and a post-election contraction, regardless of the political party in power.

In the more accepted partisan cycle models, politicians are ideological; that is, they represent the interests of different pressure groups and, when in office, follow policies which are favourable to their supporting groups. For example, the left-wing parties pursue expansionary policies in order to reduce unemployment, while the right-wing parties tend to induce post-election contractions in economic performance in order to reduce inflation. The outcome, therefore, is **partisan business cycles**, that is, systematic and permanent differences in macroeconomic outcomes that differ by political party.

Work by Apostolos Serletis and Panos Afxentiou of the University of Calgary indicates that there is no credible evidence that such a political business cycle exists in Canada.*

---

* Apostolos Serletis and Panos C. Afxentiou, "Electoral and Partisan Cycle Regularities in Canada," *Canadian Journal of Economics* 31 (1998): 28–46.

Indeed, some politicians may prefer to have an independent Bank of Canada, which can be used as a public scapegoat to take some of the heat off their backs. It is possible that a politician who in private opposes an inflationary monetary policy will be forced to support such a policy in public for fear of not being re-elected. An independent Bank of Canada can pursue policies that are politically unpopular yet in the public interest.

The Case Against Independence

Proponents of a Bank of Canada under the control of the government argue that it is undemocratic to have monetary policy (which affects almost everyone in the economy) controlled by an elite group responsible to no one. The current lack of de facto accountability of the Bank of Canada has serious consequences: if the Bank performs badly, there is no provision for replacing members (as there is with politicians). True, the Bank of Canada needs to pursue long-run objectives, but elected government officials vote on long-run issues also (foreign policy, for example). If we push the argument further that policy is always performed better by elite groups like the Bank of Canada, we end up with such conclusions as the Canada Revenue Agency should set tax policies with no oversight from the government. Would you advocate this degree of independence for the Canada Revenue Agency?

The public holds government responsible for the economic well-being of the country, yet it lacks control over the government agency that may well be the most important factor in determining the health of the economy. In addition, to achieve a cohesive program that will promote economic stability, monetary policy must be coordinated with fiscal policy (management of government spending and taxation). Only by placing monetary policy under the control of the politicians who also control fiscal policy can these two policies be prevented from working at cross-purposes.

There is no consensus on whether Bank of Canada independence is a good thing, although public support for independence of the central bank seems to have been growing in both Canada and abroad. As you might expect, people who like the Bank's policies are more likely to support its independence, while those who dislike its policies advocate a less-independent Bank of Canada.

Global Central Bank Independence and Macroeconomic Performance

We have seen that advocates of **central bank independence** believe that macroeconomic performance will be improved by making the central bank more independent. Recent research seems to support this conjecture: when central banks are ranked from least independent to most independent, inflation performance is found to be the best for countries with the most independent central banks.[16] Although a more independent central bank appears to lead to a lower inflation rate, this is not achieved at the expense of poorer real economic performance. Countries with independent central banks are no more likely to have high unemployment or greater output fluctuations than countries with less-independent central banks.

SUMMARY

1. The Bank of Canada was created by an act of Parliament in 1934 and began operations on March 11, 1935. Initially it was privately owned but became a Crown corporation in 1938.

2. The overall responsibility for the operation of the Bank of Canada rests with a Board of Directors, consisting of the governor, the senior deputy governor, the deputy minister of finance, and twelve outside directors. The Bank's governor (currently Mark Carney) is the chief executive officer and chairman of the Board of Directors.

3. Although on paper the Bank of Canada is an arm of the government, in practice the Bank has more independence than the Bank of Canada Act suggests.

4. The Bank of Canada is more independent than most agencies of the Canadian government, but it is still subject to political pressures. The theory of bureaucratic behaviour indicates that one factor driving the Bank's behaviour is its attempt to increase its power and prestige. This view explains many of the Bank's actions, although the agency may also try to act in the public interest.

5. The case for an independent Bank of Canada rests on the view that curtailing the Bank's independence and subjecting it to more political pressures would impart an inflationary bias to monetary policy. An independent Bank of Canada can afford to take the long view and not respond to short-run problems that will result

---

[16] Alberto Alesina and Lawrence H. Summers, "Central Bank Independence and Macroeconomic Performance: Some Comparative Evidence," *Journal of Money, Credit and Banking* 25 (1993): 151–162. However, Adam Posen, "Central Bank Independence and Disinflationary Credibility: A Missing Link," *Oxford Economic Papers* 50 (1998): 335–359, has cast some doubt on whether the causality runs from central bank independence to improved inflation performance.

in expansionary monetary policy and a political business cycle. The case against an independent Bank of Canada holds that it is undemocratic to have monetary policy (so important to the public) controlled by an elite group that is not accountable to the public. An independent Bank of Canada also makes the coordination of monetary and fiscal policy difficult.

6. The Federal Reserve System was created in 1913 to lessen the frequency of bank panics. Because of public hostility to central banks and the centralization of power, the Federal Reserve System was created with many checks and balances to diffuse power.

7. The formal structure of the Federal Reserve System consists of twelve regional Federal Reserve banks, around 2900 member commercial banks, the Board of Governors of the Federal Reserve System, the Federal Open Market Committee, and the Federal Advisory Council.

8. Although on paper the Federal Reserve appears to be decentralized, in practice it has come to function as a unified central bank controlled by the Board of Governors, especially the board's chairman.

9. The European Central Bank is the central bank of the euro area—a common currency area, currently consisting of sixteen countries: Austria, Belgium, Cyprus, Finland, France, Germany, Greece, Ireland, Italy, Luxembourg, Malta, the Netherlands, Portugal, Slovakia, Slovenia, and Spain. The ECB is based in Frankfurt, Germany, and came into being on January 1, 1999.

10. The Eurosystem is the term used to refer to the European Central Bank and the national central banks of the sixteen countries that have adopted the euro. The Eurosystem excludes the central banks of the European Union countries that have not yet adopted the euro. These countries continue to pursue national monetary policies and have no input into the decisions related to the single monetary policy for the euro area.

11. The European System of Central Banks (ESCB) is the term used to refer to the European Central Bank and the national central banks of all twenty-seven European Union (EU) member countries—when all EU member countries adopt the euro, the Eurosystem and the European System of Central Banks will become one entity.

KEY TERMS

base money (monetary base), p. 384

Board of Directors, p. 383

Board of Governors of the Federal Reserve System, p. 391

central bank independence, p. 401

electoral business cycles, p. 400

European System of Central Banks (ESCB), p. 394

Eurosystem, p. 395

Exchange Fund Account, p. 384

Federal Open Market Committee (FOMC), p. 391

Federal Reserve Banks, p. 391

Federal Reserve System (the Fed), p. 391

goal independence, p. 386

Governing Council, p. 383

instrument independence, p. 386

open market buyback operations, p. 385

partisan business cycles, p. 400

political business cycle, p. 399

QUESTIONS

You will find the answers to the questions marked with an asterisk in the Textbook Resources section of your MyEconLab.

*1. What political realities might explain the creation of the Bank of Canada in 1934?

2. In what ways can the government influence the conduct of monetary policy?

*3. Who is responsible for monetary policy in Canada?

4. Do you think that the seven-year renewable term for the governor of the Bank of Canada effectively insulates the Bank from political pressure?

*5. How did the "Coyne Affair" motivate the current system of joint responsibility for monetary policy?

6. Over time, which entities have gained power in the conduct of monetary policy in Canada and which have lost power? Why do you think this has happened?

*7. "The strongest argument for an independent Bank of Canada rests on the view that subjecting the Bank of Canada to more political pressures would impart an inflationary bias to monetary policy." Is this statement true, false, or uncertain? Explain your answer.

8. The Bank of Canada is the most independent of all Canadian government agencies. What is the main difference between it and other government agencies that explains its greater independence?

*9. How can the government directly influence the Bank of Canada?

10. How is the responsibility for monetary policy shared in the Eurosystem?

*11. "The theory of bureaucratic behaviour indicates that the Bank of Canada never operates in the public interest." Is this statement true, false, or uncertain? Explain your answer.

12. Why might eliminating the Bank's independence lead to a more-pronounced political business cycle?

*13. "The independence of the Bank of Canada leaves it completely unaccountable for its actions." Is this statement true, false, or uncertain? Explain your answer.

14. "The independence of the Bank of Canada has meant that it takes the long view and not the short view." Is this statement true, false, or uncertain? Explain your answer.

*15. Why did Canada show little interest in the establishment of a central bank during the first 60 or so years of Confederation?

WEB EXERCISES

1. Go to **www.bankofcanada.ca** and click on "About the Bank." Choose "Management and Corporate Governance." Write a short essay about the diversity of the twelve outside directors of the Bank of Canada's Board of Directors.

2. Go to **www.federalreserve.gov** and click on "About The Fed." Then click on "The Federal Reserve System" and then on "Structure." According to the Federal Reserve, what is the most important responsibility of the Board of Governors?

3. Go to the above site and click on "Monetary Policy." Then click on "Reports" and then choose "Beige Book." According to the summary of the most recently published book, is the U.S. economy weakening or recovering?

Be sure to visit the MyEconLab website at **www.myeconlab.com**. This online homework and tutorial system puts you in control of your own learning with study and practice tools directly correlated to this chapter content.

On the MyEconLab website you will find the following appendix for this chapter:
Appendix 15.1: The Price Stability Goal and the Nominal Factor

CHAPTER 16

The Money Supply Process

LEARNING OBJECTIVES

After studying this chapter you should be able to

1. summarize the Bank of Canada's balance sheet and the monetary base
2. discern who controls the monetary base and what causes it to change
3. explain how the banking system creates deposits
4. utilize a simple model of multiple deposit creation, showing how the central bank can control the level of deposits by setting the level of reserves

PREVIEW

As we saw in Chapter 5 and will see in later chapters on monetary theory, movements in the money supply affect interest rates and the overall health of the economy and thus affect us all. Because of its far-reaching effects on economic activity, it is important to understand how the money supply is determined. Who controls it? What causes it to change? How might control of it be improved? In this and subsequent chapters we answer these questions by providing a detailed description of the *money supply process*, the mechanism that determines the level of the money supply.

Because deposits at banks are by far the largest component of the money supply, understanding how these deposits are created is the first step in understanding the money supply process. This chapter provides an overview of how the banking system creates deposits. In addition, it outlines the basic building blocks needed in later chapters for you to understand in greater depth how the money supply is determined.

THREE PLAYERS IN THE MONEY SUPPLY PROCESS

The "cast of characters" in the money supply story is as follows:

1. The central bank—the government agency that oversees the banking system and is responsible for the conduct of monetary policy; in Canada, the Bank of Canada

2. Banks (depository institutions)—the financial intermediaries that accept deposits from individuals and institutions and make loans: chartered banks and near banks

3. Depositors—individuals and institutions that hold deposits in banks

Of the three players, the central bank, the Bank of Canada, is the most important. Its conduct of monetary policy involves actions that affect its balance sheet (holdings of assets and liabilities), to which we turn now.

THE BANK OF CANADA'S BALANCE SHEET

The operation of the Bank of Canada and its monetary policy involve actions that affect its balance sheet, its holdings of assets and liabilities. Here we discuss a simplified balance sheet that includes just four items that are essential to our understanding of the money supply process.[1]

Bank of Canada

Assets	Liabilities
Government securities	Notes in circulation
Advances to banks	Reserves

Liabilities

The two liabilities on the balance sheet, notes in circulation and reserves, are often referred to as the *monetary liabilities* of the Bank of Canada. They are an important part of the money supply story, because increases in either or both will lead to an increase in the money supply (everything else being constant). The sum of the Bank's monetary liabilities (notes in circulation and reserves) and the Canadian Mint's monetary liabilities (coins in circulation) is called the **monetary base**. When discussing the monetary base, we will focus only on the monetary liabilities of the Bank of Canada because the monetary liabilities of the Canadian Mint account for a very small fraction of the base.[2]

1. *Notes in circulation.* The Bank of Canada issues notes (those blue, purple, green, red, and brown pieces of paper in your wallet that say "Bank of Canada"). The Bank of Canada notes in circulation is the amount of these notes that is in the hands of the public and the depository institutions. Coins issued by the Canadian Mint are not a liability of the Bank of Canada. The coins and Bank of Canada notes that we use in Canada today are collectively known as currency.

   Bank of Canada notes are IOUs from the Bank to the bearer and are also liabilities, but unlike most liabilities, they promise to pay back the bearer solely with Bank of Canada notes; that is, they pay off IOUs with other IOUs. Accordingly, if you bring a $100 bill to the Bank of Canada and demand payment, you will receive two $50s, five $20s, ten $10s, or twenty $5 bills.

   People are more willing to accept IOUs from the Bank of Canada than from you or me because Bank of Canada notes are a recognized medium of exchange; that is, they are accepted as a means of payment and so function as *money*.

---

[1] A detailed discussion of the Bank's balance sheet and the factors that affect the monetary base can be found in the appendix to this chapter on this book's MyEconLab at **www.pearsoned.ca/myeconlab.**

[2] It is also safe to ignore the Canadian Mint's monetary liabilities when discussing the monetary base because the Canadian Mint cannot actively supply its monetary liabilities to the economy because of legal restrictions.

Unfortunately, neither you nor I can convince people that our IOUs are worth anything more than the paper they are written on.[3]

2. *Reserves.* All banks that participate in the Large Value Transfer System (LVTS), to be discussed in detail in Chapter 17, have an account at the Bank of Canada in which they hold deposits (also called settlement balances).[4] Reserves consist of settlement balances at the Bank of Canada plus currency that is physically held by banks (called vault cash, because it is held in bank vaults, cash tills, and automated banking machines). Reserves are assets for the banks but liabilities for the Bank of Canada because the banks can demand payment on them at any time and the Bank of Canada is required to satisfy its obligation by paying Bank of Canada notes. As you will see, an increase in reserves leads to an increase in the level of deposits and hence in the money supply.

As already noted in Chapter 13, Canadian banks are no longer required to hold reserves (see the Global box, The Worldwide Decline in Reserve Requirements). Banks, however, hold some reserves in order to manage their own short-term liquidity requirements and respond to predictable clearing drains and across-the-counter and automated banking machine drains. We call these reserves prudential or desired reserves. For example, banks might desire that for every dollar of deposits, a certain fraction (say, 5 cents) must be held as reserves. This fraction (5%) is called the desired reserve ratio. Reserves in excess of the desired amounts are called unwanted or excess reserves.

Assets

The two assets on the Bank of Canada's balance sheet are important for two reasons. First, changes in the asset items lead to changes in reserves and consequently to changes in the money supply. Second, because these assets (government securities and advances to banks) earn interest while the liabilities (notes in circulation and settlement balances) in general do not, the Bank of Canada makes millions of dollars every year—its assets earn income and its liabilities cost little. Although it returns most of its earnings to the federal government, the Bank does spend some of it on "worthy causes," such as supporting economic research.

1. *Government securities.* This category of assets covers the Bank of Canada's holdings of securities issued by the Canadian government. As you will see, one way the Bank of Canada can provide reserves to the banking system is by purchasing government securities, thereby increasing its holdings of these assets. In fact, the total amount of securities is controlled by open market operations (the

---

[3] The notes item on our balance sheet refers only to notes in circulation—that is, the amount in the hands of the public. Notes that have been printed are not automatically a liability of the Bank. For example, consider the importance of having $1 million of your own IOUs printed up. You give out $100 worth to other people and keep the other $999 900 in your pocket. The $999 900 of IOUs does not make you richer or poorer and does not affect your indebtedness. You care only about the $100 of liabilities from the $100 of circulated IOUs. The same reasoning applies for the Bank of Canada in regard to its notes.

For similar reasons, the currency component of the money supply, no matter how it is defined, includes only currency in circulation. It does not include any additional currency that is not yet in the hands of the public. The fact that currency has been printed but is not circulating means that it is not anyone's asset or liability and thus cannot affect anyone's behaviour. Therefore, it makes sense not to include it in the money supply.

[4] There are fourteen LVTS participants in addition to the Bank of Canada: the Big Six, Alberta Treasury Branches, Bank of America National Association, BNP Paribas, Caisse Centrale Desjardins du Québec, Credit Union Central of Canada, HSBC Bank Canada, Laurentian Bank of Canada, and State Street Bank and Trust Company.

GLOBAL   The Worldwide Decline in Reserve Requirements

In order to meet the demand for withdrawals by depositors or to pay the cheques drawn on depositors' accounts, depository institutions need to keep sufficient reserves on hand. In most countries, banks hold a certain amount of non–interest-bearing reserves because of legally imposed reserve requirements. These reserves are called **required reserves**. The rationale for reserve requirements is that reserves are necessary for monetary control purposes and, to a lesser extent, for the protection of depositors and the stability of the banking system.

In recent years, however, central banks in many countries in the world have been reducing or eliminating their reserve requirements. In the euro area the required reserve ratio is 2% of bank deposits, while in the United States it is 3% (rising to 10% for large deposits). Canada has gone a step further: financial market legislation in June 1992 eliminated all reserve requirements over a two-year period. The central banks of Switzerland, New Zealand, and Australia have also eliminated reserve requirements entirely. What explains the downward trend in reserve requirements in most countries?

You may recall from Chapter 11 that reserve requirements act as a tax on banks. Because central banks typically do not pay interest on reserves, the bank earns nothing on them and loses the interest that could have been earned if the bank held loans instead. The cost imposed on banks from reserve requirements means that banks, in effect, have a higher cost of funds than other deposit-based financial institutions not subject to reserve requirements, making them less competitive. Central banks have thus been reducing reserve requirements to make banks more competitive and stronger.

Although central banks have been reducing or eliminating their reserve requirements, banks still want to hold reserves to protect themselves against predictable and unpredictable cash and clearing drains. Hence, "desired reserves" is the appropriate term to describe the reserves of deposit-taking financial institutions in a system without reserve requirements.

Bank's purchase and sale of these securities). Government securities are by far the Bank's largest category of assets, accounting for over 80% of the balance sheet.

2. *Advances.* The second way the Bank of Canada can provide reserves to the banking system is by making advances (loans) to banks. For the banks, the Bank of Canada advances they have taken out are referred to as *borrowing from the Bank of Canada* or, alternatively, as **borrowed reserves**. There is a big difference between normal advances and extraordinary advances (to be discussed in detail later) lent by the Bank of Canada to troubled banks to prevent bank and financial panics. Normal advances are fully collateralized and generally overnight in duration. The interest rate charged banks for these loans is called the *bank rate*.

CONTROL OF THE MONETARY BASE

The *monetary base* (also called **high-powered money**) equals currency in circulation C plus the total reserves in the banking system R.[5] The monetary base MB can be expressed as

$$MB = C + R$$

The Bank of Canada exercises control over the monetary base through its purchases or sale of government securities in the open market, called open market operations, and through its extension of loans to banks.

Bank of Canada Open Market Operations

The primary way in which the Bank of Canada can cause changes in the monetary base is through its open market operations. A purchase of bonds by the Bank is called an **open market purchase**, and a sale of bonds by the Bank is called an **open market sale**.

OPEN MARKET PURCHASE FROM A BANK   Suppose that the Bank of Canada purchases $100 of bonds from a bank and pays for them with a $100 cheque. The bank will either deposit the cheque in its account with the Bank of Canada (thereby increasing its settlement balances) or cash it in for currency, which will be counted as vault cash. To understand what occurs as a result of this transaction, we look at *T-accounts*, which list only the changes that occur in balance sheet items starting from the initial balance sheet position. Either action means that the bank will find itself with $100 more reserves and a reduction in its holdings of securities of $100. The T-account for the banking system, then, is

Banking System			
Assets		**Liabilities**	
Securities	−$100		
Reserves	+$100		

The Bank of Canada meanwhile finds that its liabilities have increased by the additional $100 of settlement balances, while its assets have increased by the $100 of additional securities that it now holds. Its T-account is

Bank of Canada			
Assets		**Liabilities**	
Securities	+$100	Settlement balances	+$100

The net result of this open market purchase is that reserves have increased by $100, the amount of the open market purchase. Because bank reserves have increased and there has been no change of currency in circulation, the monetary base has also risen by $100.

---

[5] Here currency in circulation includes both Bank of Canada notes and Canadian Mint coins.

OPEN MARKET PURCHASE FROM THE NONBANK PUBLIC   To understand what happens when there is an open market purchase from the nonbank public, we must look at two cases. First, let's assume that the person or corporation that sells the $100 of bonds to the Bank of Canada deposits the Bank's cheque in the local bank. The nonbank public's T-account after this transaction is

Nonbank Public		
Assets		Liabilities
Securities	−$100	
Chequable deposits	+$100	

When the bank receives the cheque, it credits the depositor's account with the $100 and then deposits the cheque in its account with the Bank of Canada, thereby increasing its settlement balances and adding to its reserves. The banking system's T-account becomes

Banking System		
Assets		Liabilities
Reserves	+$100	Chequable deposits +$100

The effect on the Bank of Canada's balance sheet is that it has gained $100 of securities in its assets column, while it has an increase of $100 of settlement balances in its liabilities column:

Bank of Canada		
Assets		Liabilities
Securities	+$100	Settlement balances +$100

As you can see in the previous T-account, when the Bank of Canada's cheque is deposited in a bank, the net result of the Bank of Canada's open market purchase from the nonbank public is identical to the effect of its open market purchase from a bank. Reserves increase by the amount of the open market purchase, and the monetary base increases by the same amount.

If, however, the person or corporation selling the bonds to the Bank of Canada cashes the Bank's cheque at a local bank, the effect on reserves is different.[6]

---

[6] If the bond seller cashes the cheque at the local bank, its balance sheet will be unaffected because the $100 of vault cash that it pays out will be exactly matched by the deposit of the $100 cheque at the Bank of Canada. Thus its reserves will remain the same, and there will be no effect on its T-account. That is why a T-account for the banking system does not appear here.

This seller will receive currency of $100 while reducing holdings of securities by $100. The bond seller's T-account will be

Nonbank Public

Assets		Liabilities
Securities	−$100	
Currency	+$100	

The Bank of Canada now finds that it has exchanged $100 of currency for $100 of securities, so its T-account is

Bank of Canada

Assets		Liabilities	
Securities	+$100	Currency in circulation	+$100

The net effect of the open market purchase in this case is that reserves are unchanged, while currency in circulation increases by the $100 of the open market purchase. Thus the monetary base increases by the $100 amount of the open market purchase, while reserves do not. This contrasts with the case in which the seller of the bonds deposits the Bank of Canada's cheque in a bank; in that case, reserves increase by $100, and so does the monetary base.

This analysis reveals that **the effect of an open market purchase on reserves depends on whether the seller of the bonds keeps the proceeds from the sale in currency or in deposits.** If the proceeds are kept in currency, the open market purchase has no effect on reserves; if the proceeds are kept as deposits, reserves increase by the amount of the open market purchase.

The effect of an open market purchase on the monetary base, however, is always the same (the monetary base increases by the amount of the purchase) whether the seller of the bonds keeps the proceeds in deposits or in currency. The impact of an open market purchase on reserves is much more uncertain than its impact on the monetary base.

OPEN MARKET SALE If the Bank of Canada sells $100 of bonds to a bank or the nonbank public, the monetary base will decline by $100. For example, if the Bank of Canada sells the bonds to an individual who pays for them with currency, the buyer exchanges $100 of currency for $100 of bonds, and the resulting T-account is

Nonbank Public

Assets		Liabilities
Securities	+$100	
Currency	−$100	

The Bank of Canada, for its part, has reduced its holdings of securities by $100 and has also lowered its monetary liability by accepting the currency as payment for its bonds, thereby reducing the amount of currency in circulation by $100:

Bank of Canada			
Assets		Liabilities	
Securities	−$100	Currency in circulation	−$100

The effect of the open market sale of $100 of bonds is to reduce the monetary base by an equal amount, although reserves remain unchanged. Manipulations of T-accounts in cases in which the buyer of the bonds is a bank or the buyer pays for the bonds with a cheque written on a chequable deposit account at a local bank lead to the same $100 reduction in the monetary base, although the reduction occurs because the level of reserves has fallen by $100.

The following conclusion can now be drawn from our analysis of open market purchases and sales. ***The effect of open market operations on the monetary base is much more certain than the effect on reserves.*** Therefore, the Bank of Canada can control the monetary base with open market operations more effectively than it can control reserves.

Open market operations can also be done in other assets besides government bonds and have the same effects on the monetary base we have described here.

Although open market operations are the most important monetary policy tool for most central banks around the world, in 1994 the Bank of Canada stopped conducting open market operations in Government of Canada bills and bonds. Since then, the Bank's most common open market operations involve repurchase transactions, either SPRAs or SRAs. More recently, and in response to the subprime financial crisis, the Bank of Canada introduced term PRAs, which are similar to special PRAs. As we will discuss in detail in Chapter 17, the Bank of Canada is currently conducting repurchase transactions to reinforce its operating target—the midpoint of the operating band for the overnight interest rate—and to address liquidity issues at times of financial instability. The Bank, however, neutralizes the effect on settlement balances of SPRAs and SRAs, so that at the end of the day there is no change in the level of settlement balances in the banking system.

Shifts from Deposits into Currency

Even if the Bank of Canada does not conduct open market operations, including repurchase transactions, a shift from deposits to currency will affect the reserves in the banking system. However, such a shift will have no effect on the monetary base, another reason why the Bank has more control over the monetary base than over reserves.

Let's suppose that Jane Brown (who opened a $100 chequing account at the First Bank in Chapter 13) decides that tellers are so abusive in all banks that she closes her account by withdrawing the $100 balance in cash and vows never to deposit it in a bank again. The effect on the T-account of the nonbank public is

Nonbank Public

Assets		Liabilities
Chequable deposits	−$100	
Currency	+$100	

The banking system loses $100 of deposits and hence $100 of reserves:

Banking System

Assets		Liabilities	
Reserves	−$100	Chequable deposits	−$100

For the Bank of Canada, Jane Brown's action means that there is $100 of additional currency circulating in the hands of the public, while reserves in the banking system have fallen by $100. The Bank's T-account is

Bank of Canada

Assets		Liabilities	
		Currency in circulation	+$100
		Reserves	−$100

The net effect on the monetary liabilities of the Bank of Canada is a wash; the monetary base is unaffected by Jane Brown's disgust at the banking system. But reserves are affected. Random fluctuations of reserves can occur as a result of random shifts into currency and out of deposits, and vice versa. The same is not true for the monetary base, making it a more stable variable.

Bank of Canada Advances

In this chapter so far we have seen changes in the monetary base solely as a result of open market operations. However, the monetary base is also affected when the Bank of Canada makes a loan to a bank. When the Bank makes a $100 loan to the First Bank, the bank is credited with $100 of reserves (settlement balances) from the proceeds of the loan. The effects on the balance sheet of the banking system and the Bank of Canada are illustrated by the following T-accounts:

Banking System				**Bank of Canada**			
Assets		Liabilities		Assets		Liabilities	
Reserves	+$100	Advances	+$100	Advances	+$100	Reserves	+$100

The monetary liabilities of the Bank have now increased by $100, and the monetary base, too, has increased by this amount. However, if a bank pays off a loan from the Bank of Canada, thereby reducing its borrowings from the Bank by $100, the T-accounts of the banking system and the Bank are as follows:

Banking System				Bank of Canada			
Assets		Liabilities		Assets		Liabilities	
Reserves	−$100	Advances	−$100	Advances	−$100	Reserves	−$100

The net effect on the monetary liabilities of the Bank of Canada, and hence on the monetary base, is then a reduction of $100. We see that the monetary base changes one-for-one with the change in the borrowings from the Bank of Canada.

Other Factors That Affect the Monetary Base

So far in this chapter, it seems as though the Bank of Canada has complete control of the monetary base through its open market operations and advances to banks. However, the world is a little bit more complicated for the Bank. Two important items that are not controlled by the Bank but affect the monetary base are *float* and *government deposits at the Bank of Canada*. When the Bank clears cheques for banks, it often credits the amount of the cheque to a bank that has deposited it (increases the bank's settlement balances) but only later debits (decreases the settlement balances of) the bank on which the cheque is drawn. The resulting temporary net increase in the total amount of settlement balances in the banking system (and hence in the monetary base) occurring from the Bank's cheque-clearing process is called float. Also, certain federal government flows (for example, federal government receipts and disbursements) affect *government deposits at the Bank of Canada*. In particular, net government receipts lead to a rise in government deposits at the Bank, causing a deposit outflow at the banks like that shown in Chapter 13 and thus causing reserves in the banking system and the monetary base to fall. Thus *float* (affected by random events such as the weather, which affects how quickly cheques are presented for payment) and *government deposits at the Bank of Canada* (determined by the federal government's actions) both affect the monetary base but are not controlled by the Bank of Canada at all.

Overview of the Bank's Ability to Control the Monetary Base

Our discussion above indicates that there are two primary factors that determine the monetary base: open market operations and Bank of Canada lending. Whereas the amount of open market purchases or sales is completely controlled by the Bank's placing orders with dealers in bond markets, the central bank lacks complete control over the monetary base because it cannot unilaterally determine, and therefore perfectly predict, the amount of borrowing by banks from the Bank. The Bank of Canada sets the bank rate (interest rate on advances) by setting the operating band for the overnight interest rate, and then banks make decisions about whether to borrow. The amount of advances, though influenced by the Bank's setting of the bank rate, is not completely controlled by the Bank; banks' decisions play a role, too.

Therefore, we might want to split the monetary base into two components: one that the Bank of Canada can control completely and another that is less tightly controlled. The less tightly controlled component is the amount of the base that is created by advances from the Bank. The remainder of the base (called the

nonborrowed monetary base) is under the Bank's control because it results primarily from open market operations.[7] The nonborrowed monetary base is formally defined as the monetary base minus advances from the Bank of Canada, which are referred to as borrowed reserves.

$$MB_n = MB - BR$$

where
MB_n = nonborrowed monetary base
MB = monetary base
BR = borrowed reserves from the Bank of Canada

Factors not controlled at all by the Bank of Canada undergo substantial short-run variations and can be important sources of fluctuations in the monetary base over time periods as short as a week. However, these fluctuations are quite predictable and so can be offset through open market operations. ***Although technical and external factors complicate control of the monetary base, they do not prevent the Bank of Canada from accurately controlling it.***

MULTIPLE DEPOSIT CREATION: A SIMPLE MODEL

With our understanding of how the Bank of Canada controls the monetary base and how banks operate (Chapter 13), we now have the tools necessary to explain how deposits are created. When the Bank supplies the banking system with $1 of additional reserves, deposits increase by a multiple of this amount—a process called **multiple deposit creation**.

Deposit Creation: The Single Bank

Suppose that the $100 open market purchase described earlier was conducted with the First Bank. After the Bank of Canada has bought the $100 bond from the First Bank, the bank finds that it has an increase in reserves of $100. To analyze what the bank will do with these additional reserves, assume that the bank does not want to hold more reserves because it earns no interest on them. We begin the analysis with the following T-account:

First Bank		
Assets		Liabilities
Securities	−$100	
Reserves	+$100	

Because the bank has no increase in its chequable deposits, desired reserves remain the same, and the bank finds that its additional $100 of reserves means that its excess reserves (reserves in excess of desired reserves) have increased by $100. Let's say that the bank decides to make a loan equal in amount to the $100 increase in excess reserves. When the bank makes the loan, it sets up a chequing account

---

[7] Actually, there are other items on the Bank's balance sheet (discussed in the appendix on the website) that affect the magnitude of the nonborrowed monetary base. Because their effects on the nonborrowed base relative to open market operations are both small and predictable, these other items do not present the Bank with difficulties in controlling the nonborrowed base.

for the borrower and puts the proceeds of the loan into this account. In this way, the bank alters its balance sheet by increasing its liabilities with $100 of chequable deposits and at the same time increasing its assets with the $100 loan. The resulting T-account looks like this:

First Bank				
Assets			Liabilities	
Securities	−$100		Chequable deposits	+$100
Reserves	+$100			
Loans	+$100			

The bank has created chequable deposits by its act of lending. Because chequable deposits are part of the money supply, the bank's act of lending has, in fact, created money.

In its current balance sheet position, the First Bank still has excess reserves and so might want to make additional loans. However, these reserves will not stay at the bank for very long. The borrower took out a loan not to leave $100 idle at the First Bank but to purchase goods and services from other individuals and corporations. When the borrower makes these purchases by writing cheques, they will be deposited at other banks, and the $100 of reserves will leave the First Bank. ***A bank cannot safely make loans for an amount greater than the excess reserves it has before it makes the loan.***

The final T-account of the First Bank is

First Bank				
Assets			Liabilities	
Securities	−$100			
Loans	+$100			

The increase in reserves of $100 has been converted into additional loans of $100 at the First Bank, plus an additional $100 of deposits that have made their way to other banks. (All the cheques written on accounts at the First Bank are deposited in banks rather than converted into cash because we are assuming that the public does not want to hold any additional currency.) Now let's see what happens to these deposits at the other banks.

Deposit Creation: The Banking System

To simplify the analysis, let us assume that the $100 of deposits created by First Bank's loan is deposited at Bank A and that this bank and all other banks hold no excess reserves. Bank A's T-account becomes

Bank A				
Assets			Liabilities	
Reserves	+$100		Chequable deposits	+$100

If the desired reserve ratio is 10%, this bank will now find itself with a $10 increase in desired reserves, leaving it $90 of excess reserves. Because Bank A (like the First Bank) does not want to hold on to excess reserves, it will make loans for the entire amount. Its loans and chequable deposits will then increase by $90, but when the borrower spends the $90 of chequable deposits, they and the reserves at Bank A will fall back down by this same amount. The net result is that Bank A's T-account will look like this:

Bank A			
Assets		Liabilities	
Reserves	+$10	Chequable deposits	+$100
Loans	+$90		

If the money spent by the borrower to whom Bank A lent the $90 is deposited in another bank, such as Bank B, the T-account for Bank B will be

Bank B			
Assets		Liabilities	
Reserves	+$90	Chequable deposits	+$90

The chequable deposits in the banking system have increased by another $90, for a total increase of $190 ($100 at Bank A plus $90 at Bank B). In fact, the distinction between Bank A and Bank B is not necessary to obtain the same result on the overall expansion of deposits. If the borrower from Bank A writes cheques to someone who deposits them at Bank A, the same change in deposits would occur. The T-accounts for Bank B would just apply to Bank A, and its chequable deposits would increase by the total amount of $190.

Bank B will want to modify its balance sheet further. It must keep 10% of $90 ($9) as desired reserves and has 90% of $90 ($81) in excess reserves and so can make loans of this amount. Bank B will make an $81 loan to a borrower, who spends the proceeds from the loan. Bank B's T-account will be

Bank B			
Assets		Liabilities	
Reserves	+$ 9	Chequable deposits	+$90
Loans	+$81		

The $81 spent by the borrower from Bank B will be deposited in another bank (Bank C). Consequently, from the initial $100 increase of reserves in the banking system, the total increase of chequable deposits in the system so far is $271 (= $100 + $90 + $81).

TABLE 16-1 Creation of Deposits (assuming a 10% desired reserve ratio and a $100 increase in reserves)

Bank	Increase in Deposits ($)	Increase in Loans ($)	Increase in Reserves ($)
First Bank	0.00	100.00	0.00
A	100.00	90.00	10.00
B	90.00	81.00	9.00
C	81.00	72.90	8.10
D	72.90	65.61	7.29
E	65.61	59.05	6.56
F	59.05	53.14	5.91
.	.	.	.
.	.	.	.
.	.	.	.
Total for all banks	1000.00	1000.00	100.00

Following the same reasoning, if all banks make loans for the full amount of their excess reserves, further increments in chequable deposits will continue (at Banks C, D, E, and so on), as depicted in Table 16-1. Therefore, the total increase in deposits from the initial $100 increase in reserves will be $1000. The increase is tenfold, the reciprocal of the 10% (0.10) desired reserve ratio.

If the banks choose to invest their excess reserves in securities, the result is the same. If Bank A had taken its excess reserves and purchased securities instead of making loans, its T-account would have looked like this:

Bank A

Assets		Liabilities	
Reserves	+$10	Chequable deposits	+$100
Securities	+$90		

When the bank buys $90 of securities, it writes a $90 cheque to the seller of the securities, who in turn deposits the $90 at a bank such as Bank B. Bank B's chequable deposits rise by $90, and the deposit expansion process is the same as before. ***Whether a bank chooses to use its excess reserves to make loans or to purchase securities, the effect on deposit expansion is the same.***

You can now see the difference in deposit creation for the single bank versus the banking system as a whole. Because a single bank can safely create deposits equal only to the amount of its excess reserves, it cannot by itself generate multiple deposit expansion. A single bank cannot make loans greater in amount than its excess reserves because the bank will lose these reserves as the deposits created by the loan find their way to other banks. However, the banking system as a whole can generate a multiple expansion of deposits because when a bank loses its excess reserves, these reserves do not leave the banking system even though they are lost to the individual bank. So as each bank makes a loan and creates deposits, the reserves find their way to another bank, which uses them to make additional loans and create additional deposits. As you have seen, this process continues until the initial increase in reserves results in a multiple increase in deposits.

The multiple increase in deposits generated from an increase in the banking system's reserves is called the **simple deposit multiplier**.[8] In our example, with a 10% desired reserve ratio, the simple deposit multiplier is 10. More generally, the simple deposit multiplier equals the reciprocal of the desired reserve ratio, expressed as a fraction (10 = 1/0.10), so the formula for the multiple expansion of deposits can be written as

$$\Delta D = \frac{1}{r} \times \Delta R \qquad (1)$$

where ΔD = change in total chequable deposits in the banking system
r = desired reserve ratio (0.10 in the example)
ΔR = change in reserves for the banking system ($100 in the example)[9]

Deriving the Formula for Multiple Deposit Creation

The formula for the multiple creation of deposits can also be derived directly using algebra. We obtain the same answer for the relationship between a change in deposits and a change in reserves, but more quickly.

Our assumption that banks do not hold on to any excess reserves means that the total amount of desired reserves for the banking system DR will equal the total reserves in the banking system R:

$$DR = R$$

The total amount of desired reserves equals the desired reserve ratio r times the total amount of chequable deposits D:

$$DR = r \times D$$

Substituting $r \times D$ for DR in the first equation,

$$r \times D = R$$

and dividing both sides of the preceding equation by r gives us

$$D = \frac{1}{r} \times R$$

---

[8] This multiplier should not be confused with the Keynesian multiplier, which is derived through a similar step-by-step analysis. That multiplier relates an increase in income to an increase in investment, whereas the simple deposit multiplier relates an increase in deposits to an increase in reserves.

[9] A formal derivation of this formula follows. Using the reasoning in the text, the change in chequable deposits is $100 (= $\Delta R \times 1$) plus $90 [= $\Delta R \times (1 - r)$] plus $81 [= $\Delta R \times (1 - r)^2$] and so on, which can be rewritten as

$$\Delta D = \Delta R \times [1 + (1 - r) + (1 - r)^2 + (1 - r)^3 + \cdots]$$

Using the formula for the sum of an infinite series found in footnote 3 in Chapter 4, this can be rewritten as

$$\Delta D = \Delta R \times \frac{1}{1 - (1 - r)} = \frac{1}{r} \times \Delta R$$

Taking the change in both sides of this equation and using delta to indicate a change gives

$$\Delta D = \frac{1}{r} \times \Delta R$$

which is the same formula for deposit creation found in Equation 1.

   This derivation provides us with another way of looking at the multiple creation of deposits, because it forces us to look directly at the banking system as a whole rather than one bank at a time. For the banking system as a whole, deposit creation (or contraction) will stop only when all excess reserves in the banking system are gone; that is, the banking system will be in equilibrium when the total amount of desired reserves equals the total amount of reserves, as seen in the equation $DR = R$. When $r \times D$ is substituted for DR, the resulting equation $R = r \times D$ tells us how high chequable deposits will have to be in order for desired reserves to equal total reserves. Accordingly, a given level of reserves in the banking system determines the level of chequable deposits when the banking system is in equilibrium (when excess reserves, ER, equal 0); put another way, the given level of reserves supports a given level of chequable deposits.

   In our example, the desired reserve ratio is 10%. If reserves increase by $100, chequable deposits must rise to $1000 in order for total desired reserves also to increase by $100. If the increase in chequable deposits is less than this, say $900, then the increase in desired reserves of $90 remains below the $100 increase in reserves, so there are still excess reserves somewhere in the banking system. The banks with the excess reserves will now make additional loans, creating new deposits, and this process will continue until all reserves in the system are used up. This occurs when chequable deposits have risen to $1000.

   We can also see this by looking at the T-account of the banking system as a whole (including the First Bank) that results from this process:

Banking System

Assets		Liabilities	
Securities	−$ 100	Chequable deposits	+$1000
Reserves	+$ 100		
Loans	+$1000		

   The procedure of eliminating excess reserves by loaning them out means that the banking system (First Bank and Banks A, B, C, D, and so on) continues to make loans up to the $1000 amount until deposits have reached the $1000 level. In this way, $100 of reserves supports $1000 (ten times the quantity) of deposits.

Critique of the Simple Model

Our model of multiple deposit creation seems to indicate that the Bank of Canada is able to exercise complete control over the level of chequable deposits by setting the level of reserves. The actual creation of deposits is much less mechanical than the simple model indicates. If proceeds from Bank A's $90 loan are not deposited but are kept in currency, nothing is deposited in Bank B and the deposit creation process ceases. The total increase in the money supply is now the $90 increase in currency plus the initial $100 of deposits deposited at Bank A, for a total of only $190—considerably less than the $1000 we calculated with the simple model above. Another way of saying this is that currency has no multiple deposit expansion, while deposits do. Thus, if some proceeds from loans are used to raise the holdings of currency, there is less multiple expansion overall, and the money supply will not increase by as much as our simple model of multiple deposit creation tells us.

Another situation ignored in our model is one in which banks do not make loans or buy securities in the full amount of their excess reserves. If Bank A decides to hold on to all $90 of its excess reserves, no deposits would be made in Bank B, and this would also stop the deposit creation process. The total increase in deposits would again be only $100 and not the $1000 increase in our example. Hence, if banks choose to hold all or some of their excess reserves, the full expansion of deposits predicted by the simple model of multiple deposit creation again does not occur.

Our examples indicate that the Bank of Canada is not the only player whose behaviour influences the level of deposits and therefore the money supply. Depositors' decisions regarding how much currency to hold and banks' decisions regarding the amount of reserves to hold can cause the money supply to change.

FACTORS THAT DETERMINE THE MONEY SUPPLY

Our critique of the simple model shows how we can expand on it to discuss all the factors that affect the money supply. Let's look at changes in each factor in turn, holding all other factors constant.

Changes in the Nonborrowed Monetary Base, MB_n

As shown earlier in the chapter, the Bank of Canada's open market purchases increase the nonborrowed monetary base, and its open market sales decrease it. Holding all other variables constant, an increase in MB_n arising from an open market purchase increases the amount of the monetary base and reserves, so that multiple deposit creation occurs and the money supply increases. Similarly, an open market sale that decreases MB_n shrinks the amount of the monetary base and reserves, thereby causing a multiple contraction of deposits and the money supply decreases. We have the following result: ***The money supply is positively related to the nonborrowed monetary base, MB_n.***

Changes in Borrowed Reserves (*BR*) from the Bank of Canada

An increase in advances from the Bank of Canada provides additional borrowed reserves, and thereby increases the amount of the monetary base and reserves, so that multiple deposit creation occurs and the money supply increases. If banks reduce the level of their loans from the Bank of Canada, all other variables held constant, the monetary base and amount of reserves fall, and the money supply would decrease. The result is this: ***The money supply is positively related to the level of borrowed reserves, BR, from the Bank of Canada.***

Changes in the Desired Reserve Ratio, *r*

If the desired reserve ratio on chequable deposits increases while all other variables, such as the monetary base, stay the same, we have seen that there is less multiple deposit expansion, and hence the money supply falls. If, on the other hand, the desired reserve ratio falls, multiple deposit expansion would be higher and the money supply would rise. We now have the following result: ***The money supply is negatively related to the desired reserve ratio, r.***

Recall that in Chapter 13, the primary benefit to a bank of holding reserves is that they provide insurance against losses due to deposit outflows; that is, they enable the bank experiencing deposit outflows to escape the costs of calling in loans, selling securities, borrowing from the Bank of Canada or other corporations, or bank failure. If banks fear that deposit outflows are likely to increase (that is, if expected deposit outflows increase), they will want more insurance against this possibility and desired reserves will increase.

Changes in Currency Holdings

As shown before, chequable deposits undergo multiple expansions while currency does not. Hence, when chequable deposits are converted into currency, holding the monetary base and other variables constant, there is a switch from a component of the money supply that undergoes multiple expansion to one that does not. The overall level of multiple expansion declines and the money supply falls. On the other hand, if currency holdings fall there is a switch into chequable deposits, which undergo multiple deposit expansion, so the money supply rises. This analysis suggests the following result: ***The money supply is negatively related to currency holdings.***

OVERVIEW OF THE MONEY SUPPLY PROCESS

We now have a model of the money supply process in which all three of the players—the Bank of Canada, depositors, and banks—directly influence the money supply. As a study aid, Table 16-2 charts the money supply response to the three factors discussed above and gives a brief synopsis of the reasoning behind them.

The variables are grouped by the player or players who are the primary influence behind the variable. The Bank of Canada, for example, influences the money supply by controlling the first two variables (called tools of the Bank of Canada). Depositors influence the money supply through their decisions about their holdings of currency, while banks influence the money supply by their decisions about desired reserves. However, because depositors' behaviour influences bankers' expectations about deposit outflows, which as we have seen affects banks' decisions to hold reserves, depositors are also listed as a player determining desired reserves.

TABLE 16-2   Money Supply Response

Player	Variable	Change in Variable	Money Supply Response	Reason
Bank of Canada	Nonborrowed monetary base, MB_n	↑	↑	More *MB* for deposit creation
	Borrowed reserves, *BR*	↑	↑	More *MB* for deposit creation
Depositors	Currency holdings	↑	↓	Less multiple deposit expansion
Depositors and banks	Desired reserves	↑	↓	Less loans and deposit creation

Note: Only increases (↑) in the variables are shown. The effects of decreases on the money supply would be the opposite of those indicated in the "Response" column.

THE MONEY MULTIPLIER

The intuition in the section above is sufficient for you to understand how the money supply process works. For those of you who are more mathematically inclined, we can derive all of the above results using a concept called the **money multiplier**, denoted by m, which tells us how much the money supply changes for a given change in the monetary base. The relationship among the money supply, the money multiplier, and the monetary base is described by the following equation:

$$M = m \times MB \tag{2}$$

The money multiplier m tells us what multiple of the monetary base is transformed into the money supply. Because the money multiplier is larger than 1, the alternative name for the monetary base, *high-powered money*, is logical: a $1 change in the monetary base leads to more than a $1 change in the money supply.

Deriving the Money Multiplier

Let's assume that the desired holdings of currency C, like desired reserves DR, grows proportionally with chequable deposits D; in other words, we assume that the ratios of these items to chequable deposits are constants in equilibrium:

$$c = \text{currency ratio, } C/D$$
$$r = \text{desired reserve ratio, } DR/D$$

We will now derive a formula that describes how the currency ratio desired by depositors c and the reserves ratio desired by banks r affect the money multiplier m. We begin the derivation of the model of the money supply with the equation

$$R = DR$$

which states that the total amount of reserves in the banking system R equals desired reserves DR. (Note that this equation corresponds to the equilibrium condition $DR = R$, where excess reserves were assumed to be zero.)

The total amount of desired reserves equals the desired reserve ratio r times the amount of chequable deposits D:

$$DR = r \times D$$

Substituting $r \times D$ for DR in the first equation yields an equation that links reserves in the banking system to the amount of chequable deposits they can support:

$$R = r \times D$$

A key point here is that banks set the desired reserve ratio r to be less than 1. Thus $1 of reserves can support more than $1 of deposits, and the multiple expansion of deposits can occur.

Let's see how this works in practice. If the desired reserve ratio is $r = 0.05$, and the level of chequable deposits in the banking system is $800 billion, the amount of reserves needed to support these deposits is $40 billion ($= 0.05 \times \$800$ billion). The $40 billion of reserves can support twenty times this amount in chequable deposits, because multiple deposit creation will occur.

Because the monetary base MB equals currency C plus reserves R, we can generate an equation that links the amount of monetary base to the levels of chequable deposits and currency by adding currency to both sides of the equation:

$$MB = C + R = C + (r \times D)$$

Another way of thinking about this equation is to recognize that it reveals the amount of the monetary base needed to support the existing amounts of currency and chequable deposits.

To derive the money multiplier formula in terms of the currency ratio c and the desired reserve ratio, we rewrite the last equation, specifying C as $c \times D$:

$$MB = (c \times D) + (r \times D)$$
$$= (c + r) \times D$$

We next divide both sides of the equation by the term inside the parentheses to get an expression linking chequable deposits D to the monetary base MB:

$$D = \frac{1}{c + r} \times MB \qquad (3)$$

Using the definition of the money supply as currency plus chequable deposits ($M = C + D$) and again specifying C as $c \times D$

$$M = (c \times D) + D$$
$$= (1 + c) \times D$$

Substituting in this equation the expression for D from Equation 3, we have

$$M = \frac{1 + c}{c + r} \times MB \qquad (4)$$

Finally, we have achieved our objective of deriving an expression in the form of our earlier Equation 2. As you can see, the ratio that multiplies MB is the money multiplier that tells how much the money supply changes in response to a given change in the monetary base (high-powered money). The money multiplier m is thus

$$m = \frac{1 + c}{c + r} \qquad (4)$$

It is a function of the currency ratio set by depositors c and the desired reserve ratio set by banks r.

Intuition Behind the Money Multiplier

To get a feel for what the money multiplier means, let us construct a numerical example with realistic numbers for the following variables:

r = desired reserve ratio = 0.05
C = currency in circulation = $40 billion
D = chequable deposits = $160 billion
M = money supply (M1+) = $C + D$ = $200 billion

From these numbers we can calculate the value for the currency ratio c:

$$c = \frac{\$40 \text{ billion}}{\$160 \text{ billion}} = 0.25$$

The resulting value of the money multiplier is

$$m = \frac{1 + 0.25}{0.25 + 0.05} = \frac{1.25}{0.3} = 4.2$$

The money multiplier of 4.2 tells us that given the behaviour of depositors as represented by $c = 0.25$ and banks as represented by $r = 0.05$, a $1 increase in the monetary base leads to a $4.20 increase in the money supply.

An important characteristic of the money multiplier is that it is less than the simple deposit multiplier of 10 found earlier in the chapter. The key to understanding this result is to realize that ***although there is multiple expansion of deposits, there is no such expansion for currency.*** Thus, if some portion of the increase in high-powered money finds its way into currency, this portion does not undergo multiple deposit expansion. In our simple model earlier in the chapter, we did not allow for this possibility, and so the increase in reserves led to the maximum amount of multiple deposit creation. However, in our current model of the money multiplier, the level of currency does increase when the monetary base MB and chequable deposits D increase because c is greater than zero. As previously stated, any increase in MB that goes into an increase in currency is not multiplied, so only part of the increase in MB is available to support chequable deposits that undergo multiple expansion. The overall level of multiple deposit expansion must be lower, meaning that the increase in M, given an increase in MB, is smaller than the simple model earlier in the chapter indicated.

Money Supply Response to Changes in the Factors

By recognizing that the monetary base $MB = MB_n + BR$, we can rewrite Equation 2 as:

$$M = m \times (MB_n \times BR) \tag{6}$$

Now we can show algebraically all the results in Table 16-2, which shows the money supply response to the changes in the factors.

As you can see from Equation 6, a rise in MB_n or BR raises the money supply M by a multiple amount because the money multiplier m is greater than one. We can see that a rise in the desired reserve ratio lowers the money supply by calculating what happens to the value of the money multiplier using Equation 5 in our numerical example when r increases from 5% to 10% (leaving all other variables unchanged). The money multiplier then falls from 4.2 to

$$m = \frac{1 + 0.25}{0.25 + 0.10} = \frac{1.25}{0.35} = 3.6$$

which, as we would expect, is less than 4.2.[10]

Similarly, we can see in our numerical example that a rise in currency lowers the money supply by calculating what happens to the money multiplier when c is raised from 0.25 to 0.30. The money multiplier becomes

$$m = \frac{1 + 0.30}{0.30 + 0.05} = \frac{1.30}{0.35} = 3.7$$

---

[10]All the above results can be derived more generally from Equation 5 as follows. When r increases, the denominator of the money multiplier increases, and therefore the money multiplier must decrease. As long as r is less than 1 (as is the case using the realistic numbers we have used), an increase in c raises the denominator of the money multiplier proportionally by more than it raises the numerator. The increase in c causes the multiplier to fall. Recall that the money multiplier in Equation 5 is for the M1+ definition of money. A second appendix to this chapter on the book's MyEconLab at **www. pearsoned.ca/myeconlab** discusses how the multiplier for M2+ is determined.

APPLICATION **The Great Depression Bank Panics, 1930–1933**

We can also use our money supply model to help us understand major movements in the money supply that have occurred in the past. In this application, we use the model to explain the monetary contraction that occurred in the United States during the Great Depression. In Chapter 9 we discussed bank panics and saw that they could harm the economy by making asymmetric information problems more severe in credit markets, as they did during the Great Depression. Here we can see that another consequence of bank panics is that they can cause a substantial reduction in the money supply. As we will see in the chapters on monetary theory later in the book, such reductions can also cause severe damage to the economy.

Figure 16-1 traces the bank crisis during the Great Depression by showing the volume of deposits at failed commercial banks from 1929 to 1933. In their classic book *A Monetary History of the United States, 1867–1960*, Milton Friedman and Anna Schwartz describe the onset of the first banking crisis in late 1930 as follows:

> Before October 1930, deposits of suspended [failed] commercial banks had been somewhat higher than during most of 1929 but not out of line with experience during the preceding decade. In November 1930, they were more than double the highest value recorded since the start of monthly data in 1921. A crop of bank failures, particularly in Missouri, Indiana, Illinois, Iowa, Arkansas, and North Carolina, led to widespread attempts to convert chequable and time deposits into currency, and also, to a much lesser extent, into postal savings deposits. A contagion of fear

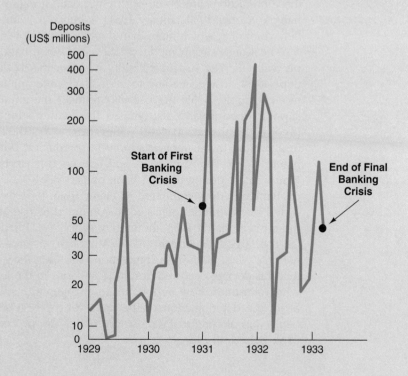

FIGURE 16-1 Deposits of Failed Commercial Banks, 1929–1933

Source: Milton Friedman and Anna Jacobson Schwartz, *A Monetary History of the United States, 1867–1960* (Princeton, N.J.: Princeton University Press, 1963), p. 309.

spread among depositors, starting from the agricultural areas, which had experienced the heaviest impact of bank failures in the twenties. But failure of 256 banks with $180 million [in U.S. dollars] of deposits in November 1930 was followed by the failure of 532 with over $370 million of deposits in December (all figures seasonally unadjusted), the most dramatic being the failure on December 11 of the Bank of the United States with over $200 million of deposits. That failure was especially important. The Bank of the United States was the largest commercial bank, as measured by volume of deposits, ever to have failed up to that time in U.S. history. Moreover, though it was just an ordinary commercial bank, the Bank of the United States's name had led many at home and abroad to regard it somehow as an official bank, hence its failure constituted more of a blow to confidence than would have been administered by the fall of a bank with a less distinctive name.[11]

The first bank panic, from October 1930 to January 1931, is clearly visible in Figure 16-1 at the end of 1930, when there is a rise in the amount of deposits at failed banks. Because there was no deposit insurance at the time (the FDIC wasn't established until 1934), when a bank failed, depositors would receive only partial repayment of their deposits. Therefore, when banks were failing during a bank panic, depositors knew that they would be likely to suffer substantial losses on deposits and thus the expected return on deposits would be negative. The theory of asset demand predicts that with the onset of the first bank crisis, depositors would shift their holdings from chequable deposits to currency by withdrawing currency from their bank accounts, and c would rise. Our earlier analysis of reserves suggests that the resulting surge in deposit outflows would cause the banks to protect themselves by substantially increasing their desired reserves ratio r.[12] Both of these predictions are borne out by the data in Figure 16-2. During the first bank panic (October 1930–January 1931), c began to climb. Even more striking is the behaviour of r, which more than doubled from November 1930 to January 1931.

The money supply model predicts that when r and c increase, the money supply will fall. The rise in c results in a decline in the overall level of multiple deposit expansion, leading to a smaller money multiplier and a decline in the money supply, while the rise in r reduces the amount of reserves available to support deposits and also causes the money supply to fall. Thus our model predicts that the rise in r and c after the onset of the first bank crisis would result in a decline in the money supply—a prediction borne out by the evidence in Figure 16-3. The money supply declined sharply in December 1930 and January 1931 during the first bank panic.

Banking crises continued to occur from 1931 to 1933, and the pattern predicted by our model persisted: c continued to rise, and so did r. By the end of the crisis in March 1933, the money supply (M1) had declined by over 25%—by far the largest decline in all of American history—and it coincided with the nation's worst economic contraction (see Chapter 9). Even more remarkable is that this decline occurred despite a 20% rise in the level of the monetary base—which illustrates how important the changes in c and r during bank panics can be in the determination of the money supply. It also illustrates that a central bank's job of conducting monetary policy can be complicated by depositor and bank behaviour.

---

[11] Milton Friedman and Anna Jacobson Schwartz, *A Monetary History of the United States, 1867–1960* (Princeton, N.J.: Princeton University Press, 1963), pp. 308–311.

[12] In this Application we use the term *desired reserves* to mean reserves in excess of required reserves.

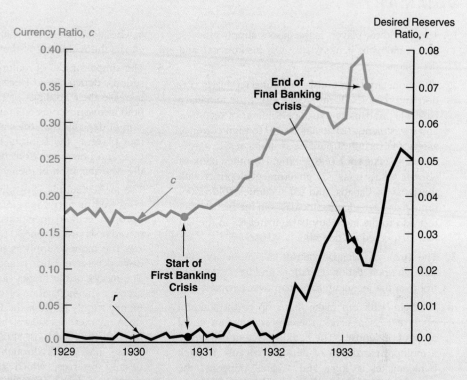

FIGURE 16-2   Desired Reserves Ratio and Currency Ratio, 1929–1933

Source: Federal Reserve *Bulletin*; Milton Friedman and Anna Jacobson Schwartz, *A Monetary History of the United States, 1867–1960* (Princeton, N.J.: Princeton University Press, 1963), p. 333.

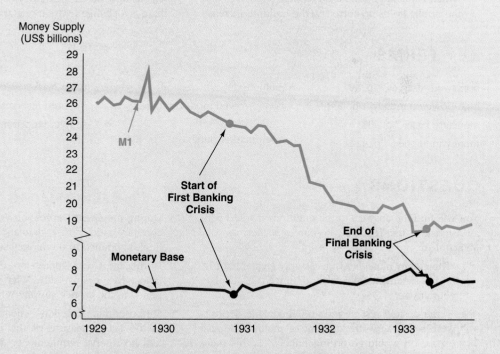

FIGURE 16-3   M1 and the Monetary Base, 1929–1933

Source: Milton Friedman and Anna Jacobson Schwartz, *A Monetary History of the United States, 1867–1960* (Princeton, N.J.: Princeton University Press, 1963), p. 333.

SUMMARY

1. There are three players in the money supply process: the central bank, banks (depository institutions), and depositors.

2. The monetary base consists of currency in circulation and reserves. Eight factors affect the monetary base: (1) the Bank of Canada's holdings of securities and investments, (2) advances, (3) foreign currency assets, (4) securities purchased under resale agreements, (5) currency outstanding, (6) other Bank of Canada assets (net), (7) government deposits with the Bank of Canada, and (8) securities sold under repurchase agreements. Increases in the first six factors add to the monetary base; increases in the last two factors reduce the monetary base.

3. The Bank of Canada controls the monetary base through open market operations and has better control over the monetary base than over reserves.

4. A single bank can make loans up to the amount of its excess reserves, thereby creating an equal amount of deposits. The banking system can create a multiple expansion of deposits because as each bank makes a loan and creates deposits, the reserves find their way to another bank, which uses them to make loans and create additional deposits. In the simple model of multiple deposit creation in which banks do not hold on to excess reserves and the public holds no currency, the multiple increase in chequable deposits (simple deposit multiplier) equals the reciprocal of the desired reserve ratio.

5. The simple model of multiple deposit creation has serious deficiencies. Decisions by depositors to increase their holdings of currency or of banks to hold excess reserves will result in a smaller expansion of deposits than the simple model predicts. All four players—the Bank of Canada, banks, depositors, and borrowers from banks—are important in the determination of the money supply.

6. The money supply is positively related to the nonborrowed monetary base MB_n, which is determined by open market operations, and the level of borrowed reserves (advances) from the bank of Canada, BR. The money supply is negatively related to the desired reserve ratio, r, and holdings of currency. The model of the money supply process takes into account the behaviour of all three players in the money supply process: the Bank of Canada through open market operations and lending; depositors through their decision about their holding of currency; and banks through their decisions about desired reserves, which are also influenced by depositors' decisions about deposit outflows.

7. The monetary base is linked to the money supply using the concept of the money multiplier, which tells us how much the money supply changes when there is a change in the monetary base.

KEY TERMS

borrowed reserves,   p. 407

high-powered money,   p. 408

monetary base,   p. 405

money multiplier,   p. 422

multiple deposit creation,   p. 414

nonborrowed monetary base,
   p. 414

open market purchase,   p. 408

open market sale,   p. 408

required reserves,   p. 407

simple deposit multiplier,   p. 418

QUESTIONS

You will find the answers to the questions marked with an asterisk in the Textbook Resources section of your MyEconLab.

*1. "The money multiplier is necessarily greater than 1." Is this statement true, false, or uncertain? Explain your answer.

2. "If the desired reserve ratio on chequable deposits were set at zero, the amount of multiple deposit expansion would go on indefinitely." Is this statement true, false, or uncertain? Explain.

*3. During the Great Depression years 1930–1933, the currency ratio c rose dramatically. What do you think happened to the money supply? Why?

4. During the Great Depression, the desired reserves ratio r rose dramatically. What do you think happened to the money supply? Why?

*5. Suppose that travellers' cheques were included in the M1+ measure of the money supply and had no reserve requirements. When people travel during the summer and convert some of their chequing account deposits into travellers' cheques, what would happen to the money supply? Why?

6. If Jane Brown closes her account at the First Bank and uses the money instead to open a money market mutual fund account, what happens to M1+ and M2++? Why?

*7. What happens to M2+ when chequable deposits are converted into time deposits?

8. Why might the procyclical behaviour of interest rates (rising during business cycle expansions and falling during recessions) lead to procyclical movements in the money supply?

Using Economic Analysis to Predict the Future

*9. The Bank of Canada buys $100 million of bonds from the public and banks lower r. What will happen to the money supply?

10. If the Bank of Canada paid interest on bank reserves, what would happen to r?

*11. If the Bank of Canada sells $1 million of bonds and banks reduce their borrowing from the Bank of Canada by $1 million, predict what will happen to the money supply.

12. Predict what will happen to the money supply if there is a sharp rise in the currency ratio.

*13. What do you predict would happen to the money supply if expected inflation suddenly increased?

14. If the economy starts to boom and loan demand picks up, what do you predict will happen to the money supply?

*15. Milton Friedman once suggested that central bank lending should be abolished. Predict what would happen to the money supply if Friedman's suggestion were put into practice.

QUANTITATIVE PROBLEMS

1. If the Bank of Canada sells $2 million of bonds to the First Bank, what happens to reserves and the monetary base? Use T-accounts to explain your answer.

*2. If the Bank of Canada sells $2 million of bonds to Irving the Investor, who pays for the bonds with a briefcase filled with currency, what happens to reserves and the monetary base? Use T-accounts to explain your answer.

*3. If the Bank of Canada lends five banks an additional total of $100 million but depositors withdraw $50 million and hold it as currency, what happens to reserves and the monetary base? Use T-accounts to explain your answer.

4. The First Bank receives an extra $100 of reserves but decides not to lend any of these reserves out. How much deposit creation takes place for the entire banking system?

Unless otherwise noted, the following assumptions are made in all the remaining problems: the desired reserve ratio on chequable deposits is 10%, banks do not hold on to excess reserves, and the public's holdings of currency do not change.

*5. Using T-accounts, show what happens to chequable deposits in the banking system when the Bank of Canada lends an additional $1 million to the First Bank.

6. Using T-accounts, show what happens to chequable deposits in the banking system when the Bank of Canada sells $2 million of bonds to the First Bank.

*7. Suppose that the Bank of Canada buys $1 million of bonds from the First Bank. If the First Bank and all other banks use the resulting increase in reserves to purchase securities only and not to make loans, what will happen to chequable deposits?

8. If the Bank of Canada buys $1 million of bonds from the First Bank, but an additional 10% of any deposit is held as excess reserves, what is the total increase in chequable deposits? (*Hint:* Use T-accounts to show what happens at each step of the multiple expansion process.)

*9. If a bank depositor withdraws $1000 of currency from an account, what happens to reserves and chequable deposits?

10. If reserves in the banking system increase by $1 billion as a result of advances of $1 billion and chequable deposits increase by $9 billion, why isn't the banking system in equilibrium? What will continue to happen in the banking system until equilibrium is reached? Show the T-account for the banking system in equilibrium.

*11. If the Bank of Canada reduces reserves by selling $5 million worth of bonds to the banks, what will the T-account of the banking system look like when the banking system is in equilibrium? What will have happened to the level of chequable deposits?

12. If the desired reserve ratio on chequable deposits increases to 20%, how much multiple deposit creation will take place when reserves are increased by $100?

*13. If a bank decides that it wants to hold $1 million of excess reserves, what effect will this have on chequable deposits in the banking system?

14. If a bank sells $10 million of bonds back to the Bank of Canada in order to pay back $10 million on the advances it owes, what will be the effect on the level of chequable deposits?

*15. If you decide to hold $100 less cash than usual and therefore deposit $100 in cash in the bank, what effect will this have on chequable deposits in the banking system if the rest of the public keeps its holdings of currency constant?

CANSIM Questions

16. An important aspect of the money supply process is the money multiplier. Get monthly data from 1968 to 2009 on Statistics Canada CANSIM II series V37145 (monetary base), V37152 (M1++ (gross)), and V41552801 (M2++ (gross)) from the Textbook Resources area of the MyEconLab.
    a. Calculate the M1++ money multiplier. What is its average value over your sample period?
    b. Calculate the M2++ money multiplier. What is its average value?
    c. Compare the two money multipliers.
    d. Does it appear that the money multipliers are increasing or decreasing?

17. Continuing from the previous question, compute the growth rates of M1 and M2.
    a. What is the average M1 growth rate? Its variance?
    b. What is the average M2 growth rate? Its variance?
    c. Which monetary aggregate is more variable?

WEB EXERCISES

1. An important aspect of the supply of money is bank deposits with the Bank of Canada. Go to **www.osfi-bsif.gc.ca** and locate financial data for banks. This site reports the consolidated balance sheet for all banks.

    a. What is the current level of bank deposits with the Bank of Canada?
    b. What is the change in bank deposits with the Bank of Canada since a year ago?
    c. Based on (a) and (b), does it appear that bank reserves with the Bank of Canada are increasing or decreasing?

2. Go to **www.bankofcanada.ca** and click on "Rates and Statistics," then "Indicators," and then choose "Summary of Key Monetary Policy Variables."

    a. What is the 12-month growth rate of M2 (gross), M1++, and M2++?
    b. What is the change in the 12-month growth rate in M2 (gross), M1++, and M2++ since a year ago?

Be sure to visit the MyEconLab website at **www.myeconlab.com**. This online homework and tutorial system puts you in control of your own learning with study and practice tools directly correlated to this chapter content.

On the MyEconLab website you will find the following appendices for this chapter:
Appendix 16.1: The Bank of Canada's Balance Sheet and the Monetary Base
Appendix 16.2: The M2+ Money Multiplier

CHAPTER 17

Tools of Monetary Policy

LEARNING OBJECTIVES

After studying this chapter you should be able to

1. characterize the framework for the implementation of monetary policy in Canada (the LVTS, the target and the operating band for the overnight interest rate, and the Bank of Canada's standing liquidity facilities)
2. explain the market for reserves and the channel/corridor system for setting the overnight interest rate in Canada
3. identify the Bank of Canada's approach to monetary policy and the tools of policy (open market operations, settlement balances management, and Bank of Canada lending)

PREVIEW

In the chapters describing the structure of the Bank of Canada and the money supply process, we mentioned three policy tools that the Bank can use to manipulate interest rates and the money supply: open market operations, settlement balances management, and Bank of Canada advances. Because the Bank's use of these tools has such an important impact on interest rates and economic activity, it is important to understand how the Bank wields them in practice and how relatively useful each tool is.

In recent years, the Bank of Canada has increased its focus on the **overnight rate**, the interest rate on overnight loans of reserves from one bank to another, as the primary instrument of monetary policy. Since December 2000, the Bank of Canada has announced an overnight rate target eight times throughout the year, an announcement that is watched closely by market participants because it affects interest rates throughout the economy. Thus to fully understand how the Bank's tools are used in the conduct of monetary policy, we must understand their direct effects on the overnight interest rate.

This chapter begins with the institutional framework within which the Bank of Canada conducts monetary policy, followed by a supply and demand analysis of the market for reserves, where the overnight interest rate is determined.

We then go on to look in more detail at the tools of monetary policy—open market operations, settlement balances management, and Bank of Canada lending—to see how they are used in practice.

THE FRAMEWORK FOR THE IMPLEMENTATION OF MONETARY POLICY

The tools used by the Bank of Canada to implement monetary policy are closely linked to the institutional arrangements regarding the clearing and settlement systems in the Canadian economy. Understanding the tools of monetary policy therefore requires that we know the key features of the framework for the implementation of monetary policy. As you will see, this framework has been designed to encourage deposit-taking financial institutions to deal directly with the market, rather than with the Bank of Canada.[1]

The Large Value Transfer System (LVTS)

The core of the Canadian payments system is the **Large Value Transfer System (LVTS)**, introduced by the Canadian Payments Association on February 4, 1999. The LVTS is an electronic, real-time net settlement network, designed to provide immediate finality and settlement to time-critical transactions. In addition to the Bank of Canada there are fourteen **LVTS participants**.[2] A financial institution can participate directly in the LVTS if it is a member of the Canadian Payments Association, uses the SWIFT telecommunications network, maintains a settlement account at the Bank of Canada, and has agreements regarding borrowing from the Bank of Canada and pledging eligible collateral. All other members of the Canadian Payments Association that are not direct participants in the LVTS (110 members) are able to arrange LVTS payments through the LVTS participants.

The LVTS has been put in place in order to eliminate **systemic risk**—the risk to the entire payments system due to the inability of one financial institution to fulfill its payment obligations in a timely fashion. In fact, each LVTS payment is subject to real-time risk-control tests to confirm that sufficient collateral is available, and is final and irrevocable in real time. In particular, LVTS participants can make a payment only if they have, in real time (right now), either positive settlement balances in their accounts with the Bank of Canada, or posted collateral (such as Government of Canada treasury bills and bonds), or explicit lines of credit with other participants. As a result, the system will settle at the end of each day even in the face of risk and liquidity problems.

Of course, it is not just Canada that is concerned about systemic risk. Real-time settlement systems were implemented by Sweden in 1986, Germany and Switzerland in 1987, Japan in 1988, Italy in 1989, Belgium and the United Kingdom in 1996, and France, Hong Kong, and the Netherlands in 1997. Moreover, the central banks of the G-10 countries, through the Bank for International Settlements, have developed minimum standards for the operation of the global payment network for large-value funds transfers.

In Canada's LVTS, participants know in real time their large-value, wholesale transactions (over $50 000). Although these transactions account for less than 1% of the total number of transactions, they account for about 94% of the value of transac-

---

[1] For more details, see Donna Howard, "A Primer on the Implementation of Monetary Policy in the LVTS Environment," *Bank of Canada Review* (Autumn, 1998): 57–66; Kevin Clinton, "Implementation of Monetary Policy in a Regime with Zero Reserve Requirements," Bank of Canada Working Paper 97–8; and "The Framework for the Implementation of Monetary Policy in the Large Value Transfer System Environment," *Bank of Canada Release,* March 31, 1999.

[2] These are the Big Six (Bank of Montreal, Bank of Nova Scotia, Canadian Imperial Bank of Commerce, National Bank of Canada, Royal Bank of Canada, and the Toronto Dominion Bank), Alberta Treasury Branches, Bank of America National Association, BNP Paribas, Caisse centrale Desjardins du Québec, Credit Union Central of Canada, HSBC Bank Canada, Laurentian Bank of Canada, and State Street Bank and Trust Company.

tions. For example, the LVTS is used to settle over 20 000 payments daily, with a value of over $185 billion. This information eliminates most of the uncertainty from settlement balance prediction—the largest reason for financial institutions not being able to hit their target settlement balances with the Bank of Canada in the pre-LVTS system. Settlement of payment obligations among LVTS participants takes place, at the end of each banking day, through the transfer of funds in their settlement accounts at the Bank of Canada. The LVTS uses **multilateral netting**, in which only the net credit or debit position of each participant vis-à-vis all other participants is calculated for settlement, thereby reducing the need for a large amount of settlement balances.

Non-LVTS (ACSS) Transactions

Although the LVTS eliminates the uncertainty from daily wholesale settlement balances prediction, there is still a residual stochastic element in settlement balances from non-LVTS paper-based payments items (such as paper cheques, travellers' cheques, gift certificates, and money orders), and electronic payments items (such as pre-authorized debits and fund transfers, direct deposit items, and debit card transactions). Those items are cleared through the Automated Clearing Settlement System (ACSS), an electronic payments system also operated by the Canadian Payments Association, but without the vigorous risk controls of the LVTS. The ACSS aggregates interbank payments and calculates the net amounts to be transferred from and to each participant's settlement account with the Bank of Canada. The Bank completes the settlement the next day (at midday) through the LVTS.

Regarding the smaller value of ACSS settlements, **direct clearers** with positive clearing balances in the ACSS (that is, with net credit positions) receive an interest payment (calculated daily by the Canadian Payments Association, at the Bank of Canada's target overnight interest rate) to cover their cost of crediting their customers' accounts on the business day before receiving funds in settlement. On the other hand, direct clearers with net debit positions in the ACSS make payments (also at the Bank's target overnight interest rate) to offset their benefit of debiting the accounts of their customers on the day before paying funds in settlement. Interest compensation is included in the clearing balances settled at the Bank of Canada using LVTS funds.[3]

The Bank of Canada's Policy Rate

The overnight market in Canada is the key market for finance and monetary policy. This market is very liquid, with a broad range of participants, the most active of which are deposit-taking institutions and their investment dealer affiliates.[4] The interest rate at which participants borrow and lend overnight funds to each other in the money market is called the **overnight interest rate**. This rate is the shortest-term rate available and forms the base of any term structure of interest rates relation.

The Bank of Canada signals its monetary policy stance by announcing a target for the overnight interest rate (the overnight interest rate is known as the **reference rate**). The target for the overnight rate, known as the **policy rate**, is the main tool the Bank uses to conduct monetary policy. This rate refers to collateralized, market-based overnight transactions. The implementation of the stance of monetary policy is more successful when the reference rate is closer to the

---

[3] There are eleven ACSS direct clearers in addition to the Bank of Canada—the Big Six, Alberta Treasury Branches, La Caisse centrale Desjardins du Québec, Credit Union Central of Canada, HSBC Bank Canada, and the Laurentian Bank of Canada. Direct clearers maintain a settlement account at the Bank of Canada and participate directly in the ACSS.

[4] See Eugene Lundrigan and Sari Toll, "The Overnight Market in Canada," *Bank of Canada Review* (Winter 1997–1998): 27–42, for details regarding the evolution of the overnight market.

policy rate; that is, the closer the overnight rate is to the target for the overnight interest rate.

The Operating Band for the Overnight Interest Rate

The Bank of Canada implements monetary policy by changing the policy rate, in order to influence other short-term interest rates and the exchange rate. In fact, in normal times the Bank's operational objective is to keep the overnight rate within an **operating band** (also known as a channel or corridor) of 50 basis points (1/2 of 1%). Recently, however, and in response to the subprime financial crisis, the Bank of Canada temporarily narrowed the operating band for the overnight interest rate to 25 basis points (1/4 of 1%).

As Figure 17-1 shows, the upper limit of the operating band defines the bank rate i_b. The bank rate is the interest rate the Bank charges LVTS participants that require an overdraft loan (advance) to cover negative settlement balances on the books of the Bank at the end of the banking day. The lower limit of the operating band is the rate the Bank pays to LVTS participants with positive settlement balances at the end of the day. The midpoint of the operating band is the Bank of Canada's target for the overnight rate, the operating target of the Bank of Canada's monetary policy. When, for example, the operating band is from 3.5% to 4.0%, the bank rate is 4.0%, the rate the Bank pays on deposits to LVTS participants is 3.5%, and the Bank's target for the overnight interest rate is 3.75%.

Since December 2000, the Bank of Canada has operated under a system of eight "fixed" dates throughout the year for announcing any changes to the target and the operating band for the overnight rate, and has reserved the option of acting between the fixed dates in "extraordinary circumstances." Early in the morning (at 9:00 a.m.) on each of the eight announcement dates, the Bank of Canada announces the target and an operating band of 50 basis points for the overnight interest rate (see the FYI box, "Monetary Policy Implementation in the LVTS Environment").

This channel/corridor system for setting the overnight interest rate is also used by other central banks that, like the Bank of Canada, no longer have reserve requirements—for example, the Reserve Bank of Australia and the Reserve Bank of New Zealand (see the FYI box, The Worldwide Decline in Reserve Requirements and the Channel/Corridor System for Setting Interest Rates).

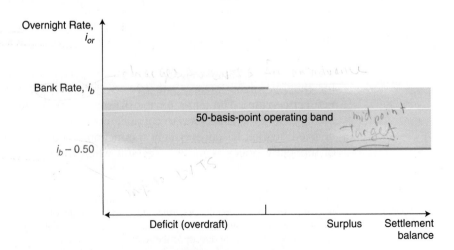

FIGURE 17-1 Operating Band for the Overnight Interest Rate

FYI
Monetary Policy Implementation in the LVTS Environment

In the LVTS environment, the Bank of Canada operates under a system of eight fixed dates throughout the year for announcing, via a press release (at 9:00 a.m.), the target and the operating band for the overnight interest rate. The upper limit of the operating band defines the bank rate at which the Bank provides overdraft loans to LVTS participants at the end of the day and the lower limit is the rate the Bank pays to LVTS participants with positive settlement balances at the end of the day.

The operating band for the overnight rate, reinforced by the Bank's standing liquidity facilities, and a target level of settlement balances (of roughly $50 million) are currently the framework within which the Bank of Canada implements monetary policy. The midpoint of the operating band, the policy rate, is the operating target of the Bank's monetary policy.

In targeting the midpoint of the operating band, the Bank of Canada will intervene in the overnight market at 11:45 a.m. to conduct open market buyback operations at the target overnight interest rate, if required. In particular, the Bank will use SPRAs if overnight funds are traded above the target for the overnight rate and SRAs if overnight funds are traded below the target for the overnight rate. There will be no Bank of Canada intervention in the overnight market if the overnight rate is around the target rate.

To maintain the desired level of settlement balances, the Bank of Canada must neutralize the net impact of its open market buyback operations and of certain federal government and Bank of Canada flows that potentially affect settlement balances. The neutralization is effected through the shifting (transfer) of federal government deposits (balances) between the government's account at the Bank of Canada and the participants in the auction of government cash balances. The shifting is made through the twice-daily auctions of Receiver General (federal government) balances (the first at 9:15 a.m. and the second at 4:15 p.m.).

The LVTS has a pre-settlement trading period of half an hour, at the end of the banking day (6–6:30 p.m.), to permit participating financial institutions to adjust positions with each other (in the overnight market) at a better return than can be achieved at the Bank of Canada's standing facilities. LVTS participants with settlement imbalances at the end of the banking day use the Bank of Canada's standing facilities to bring their settlement balances to the target level. That is, LVTS participants that require an overdraft loan to cover negative settlement balances on the books of the Bank borrow from the Bank at the bank rate. LVTS participants with positive settlement balances at the end of the day earn the bank rate less 50 basis points.

The Market Timetable

9:00 a.m.	Bank of Canada announces changes (if any) to the target and the operating band for the overnight rate
9:15 a.m.	Auction for (federal) government cash balances
11:45 a.m.	Open market buyback operations (if required)
4:15 p.m.	Auction for (federal) government cash balances
6:00 p.m.	Close of LVTS for client transactions
6:00–6:30 p.m.	Pre-settlement period
8:00 p.m. or earlier	Settlement of LVTS balances at the Bank of Canada

Source: Donna Howard, "A Primer on the Implementation of Monetary Policy in the LVTS Environment," *Bank of Canada Review* (Autumn, 1998): 57–66; "The Framework for the Implementation of Monetary Policy in the Large Value Transfer System Environment," *Bank of Canada Release*, March 31, 1999. Reprinted with permission.

The Bank of Canada's Standing Facilities

At the end of each banking day, each LVTS participant must bring its settlement balance with the Bank of Canada close to zero. Of course, it can scarcely be expected that LVTS participants will always be successful in ending up with near-zero settlement balances. The Bank of Canada therefore stands ready (with what we call **standing liquidity facilities**) to lend to or borrow from a participant to bring their settlement balances to zero at the end of the banking day. As already noted, participants also know with certainty the rates applicable to positive and negative settlement balances with the Bank of Canada (see the FYI box, Monetary Policy Implementation in the LVTS Environment, and Figure 17-1).

To permit participating financial institutions to adjust positions with each other (i.e., reduce the costs of either positive or negative positions), the LVTS has a pre-settlement trading period of half an hour, at the end of the banking day (6–6:30 p.m.). The purpose of the pre-settlement trading period is to allow LVTS participants to reduce their LVTS positions (which resulted during the day from their own transactions and those of their clients) at interest rates better than those at the Bank of Canada's standing liquidity facilities. That is, to provide a window for those participants with excess positions to trade with those in deficit, at a better return than can be achieved at the Bank's facilities, to the advantage of both. In fact, the typical bid–ask spread on overnight funds in the interbank market has been less than 1/8%. This is significantly less than the spread of 50 basis points between the rate charged on overdrafts and that paid on deposits by the Bank of Canada after settlement of LVTS multilateral positions.

In general, pre-settlement trading among participants will achieve a zero settlement balance for each participant on wholesale transactions. However, if at the end of the settlement day a participant has a negative balance on the books of the Bank

---

FYI   The Worldwide Decline in Reserve Requirements and the Channel/Corridor System for Setting Interest Rates

As already noted, central banks in many countries have been reducing or eliminating their reserve requirements. For example, there are no reserve requirements in Australia, Canada, New Zealand, Switzerland, and the U.K., while in the euro area the reserve ratio is 2% and in the U.S. 3%, rising to 10% for large deposit holdings. The fall in reserve requirements has elicited the concern that if the demand for reserves falls to zero, then a central bank may not be able to exercise control over interest rates.

However, the so-called channel or corridor system for conducting monetary policy—which has been adopted by Canada, Australia, and New Zealand—shows that central banks can continue to effectively set overnight, interbank interest rates like the overnight interest rate in Canada. How the channel/corridor system works is discussed in detail in this chapter.[5]

The important point of this analysis is that the channel/corridor approach enables the central bank to set the overnight policy rate whatever the demand for reserves, including zero demand. Thus in the future, continuing declines in the demand for reserves may eventually lead central banks to follow in the footsteps of the central banks of Canada, Australia, and New Zealand and to adopt the channel/corridor system for conducting monetary policy.

---

[5] See also Michael Woodford, "Monetary Policy in the Information Economy," in *Symposium on Economic Policy for the Information Economy* (Federal Reserve Bank of Kansas City: 2001).

of Canada, the deficit will be financed by a collateralized advance at the bank rate. Participants with positive settlement balances at the end of the day are paid interest at the bank rate less 50 basis points (i.e., the bottom of the operating band). Hence, as long as the bank rate is set so that the market bid-ask spread is within the operating band, participants will resolve their nonzero settlement balances among themselves rather than through the Bank of Canada's standing facilities. In fact, in a fully competitive market, participants would be expected to trade at the midpoint of the operating band for the overnight interest rate.

Clearly, the LVTS and the Bank of Canada's standing liquidity facilities have been set up in such a way so as to ensure a determinate demand for settlement balances, treating the costs of deficits and surpluses symmetrically. That is, the cost of holding excess settlement balances (an opportunity cost of 25 basis points) equals the cost of holding deficit levels of settlement balances (a premium of 25 basis points for an overdraft loan). These cost incentives are very important in the absence of reserve requirements; they encourage banks to target zero settlement balances at the Bank of Canada and in doing so to deal directly with the market rather than to rely on the Bank's automatic standing liquidity facilities.

The Bank of Canada's Implementation of the Operating Band for the Overnight Interest Rate

It is through its lending and taking deposits from LVTS participants that the Bank of Canada implements its target band for the overnight interest rate. **If the overnight rate increases towards the upper limit of the operating band, then the Bank will lend at the bank rate to put a ceiling on the overnight rate.** The bank rate is the ceiling on the overnight rate in the money market for LVTS participants, because they are unlikely to borrow overnight funds at a higher interest rate, since they can borrow at the bank rate from the Bank of Canada.

If the overnight rate *declines* towards the lower limit of the operating band, then the Bank will accept deposits from LVTS participants at the bank rate less 50 basis points, to put a floor on the overnight rate. The bank rate less 50 basis points is the floor on the overnight rate because LVTS participants are unlikely to lend overnight funds at a lower rate, since they can leave funds on deposit at this rate at the Bank of Canada.

THE MARKET FOR SETTLEMENT BALANCES AND THE CHANNEL/CORRIDOR SYSTEM FOR SETTING THE OVERNIGHT INTEREST RATE

The market for settlement balances (reserves) is where the overnight interest rate is determined, and this is why we turn to a supply and demand analysis of this market to analyze how the tools of monetary policy affect the overnight rate. Our analysis of the market for reserves proceeds in a similar fashion to the analysis of the bond market we conducted in Chapter 4 and describes determination of the overnight interest rate in a channel/corridor system of interest-rate control such as that in Canada, Australia, New Zealand, and the euro area.

We derive a demand and supply curve for reserves. Then the market equilibrium in which the quantity of reserves demanded equals the quantity of reserves supplied determines the overnight rate, the interest rate charged on the loans of these reserves.

Demand Curve

To derive the demand curve for reserves, we need to ask what happens to the quantity of reserves demanded, holding everything else constant, as the overnight interest rate, i_{or}, changes. Recall that banks in Canada are no longer required to hold reserves. Banks, however, hold some reserves in order to manage their own short-term liquidity requirements. We called these reserves *desired reserves*.

Desired reserves are insurance against deposit outflows, and the cost of holding these reserves is their opportunity cost, the interest rate that could have been earned on lending these reserves out, which is the overnight interest rate. Thus, as the overnight interest rate decreases, the opportunity cost of holding desired reserves falls and, holding everything else constant, the quantity of reserves demanded rises. Consequently, the demand curve for reserves, R^d, slopes downward in Figure 17-2.

Supply Curve

The Bank of Canada's standing liquidity facilities (lending and deposit facilities) define an effective supply curve for settlement balances, shown in Figure 17-2. In particular, with a standing lending facility, the Bank of Canada does not limit the amount of borrowing by banks, but always stands ready to make collateralized overdraft loans (advances) at the lending rate, i_b. Thus the quantity of reserves supplied is flat (infinitely elastic) at i_b, as shown in Figure 17-2, because if the overnight interest rate, denoted by i_{or}, begins to rise above i_b, banks would just keep borrowing from the Bank of Canada indefinitely.

On the other hand, the Bank of Canada's deposit facility pays banks a fixed interest rate, $i_b - 0.50$ on any reserves (deposits) they would like to keep at the Bank of Canada. The quantity of reserves supplied is also flat at $i_b - 0.50$, because if the overnight rate begins to fall below this rate, banks would not lend in the overnight market. Instead, they would keep increasing the amount of their deposits in the Bank of Canada (effectively lending to the Bank of Canada), and would thereby keep lowering the quantity of reserves the Bank of Canada is supplying.

In between $i_b - 0.50$ and i_b, banks will not borrow from the Bank of Canada and *borrowed reserves* (BR) will be zero, because borrowing in the overnight market is cheaper. Thus, between $i_b - 0.50$ and i_b, the quantity of reserves supplied

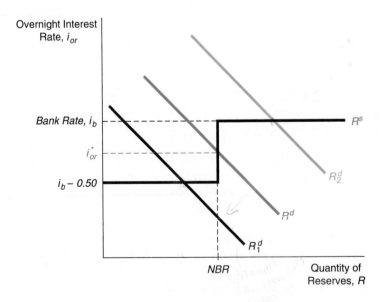

FIGURE 17-2 Equilibrium in the Market for Reserves in the Channel/Corridor System for Setting the Overnight Interest Rate

In the channel/corridor system, standing liquidity facilities result in a step function supply curve, R^s. Equilibrium occurs at the intersection of the supply curve R^s and the demand curve R^d at an interest rate of i_{or}^*. Then if the demand curve shifts between R_1^d and R_2^d, the overnight interest rate i_{or} always remains between $i_b - 0.50$ and i_b.

equals *nonborrowed reserves* (*NBR*), the amount of reserves that are supplied by the Bank of Canada's open market operations. Nonborrowed reserves are set to zero if the demand for reserves is also expected to be zero. Initially, the Bank of Canada targeted a daily level of settlement balances of zero, but subsequently the target level of settlement balances varied considerably depending on pressures on the overnight rate; the Bank's target level of balances for a given day is always announced the previous day. Assuming here that the Bank is targeting a level of settlement balances of zero, the supply curve for reserves R^s is thus the step function depicted in Figure 17-2.

Equilibrium in the Market for Reserves

Market equilibrium occurs where the quantity of reserves demanded equals the quantity supplied. In terms of Figure 17-2, equilibrium occurs at the intersection of the vertical supply curve and the demand curve at the Bank of Canada's target level of reserves. More in-depth analysis shows that banks will set the demand for reserves so that the demand curve is expected to intersect the supply curve at the announced target overnight rate of i^*_{or}, with the result that deviations from the announced target are fairly small.[6]

The equilibrium overnight interest rate is necessarily within the operating band. For example, when the demand curve shifts to the left to R^d_1, the overnight interest rate never falls below $i_b - 0.50$, while if the demand curve shifts to the right to R^d_2, the overnight interest rate never rises above i_b. Thus the channel/corridor system enables the Bank of Canada to keep the overnight interest rate in between the narrow channel/corridor with an upper limit of i_b and a lower limit of $i_b - 0.50$.

The important point of this analysis is that the channel/corridor approach enables the Bank of Canada to set the overnight policy rate, whatever the demand for reserves, including zero demand.

THE BANK OF CANADA'S APPROACH TO MONETARY POLICY

The goal of the Bank of Canada's current monetary policy is to keep the inflation rate within a target range of 1% to 3%, with the midpoint of the inflation target range, 2%, being the most desirable outcome. In setting its inflation targets, the Bank of Canada uses the rate of change in the consumer price index (CPI), because it is the most commonly used and understood price measure in Canada. Although the Bank's targets are specified in terms of "headline CPI" (all items), the Bank uses "core CPI," which excludes volatile components such as food, energy, and the effect of indirect taxes. Core CPI inflation is useful in assessing whether trend inflation is on track for the medium term. Also, defining the inflation targets in terms of ranges provides the Bank of Canada sufficient flexibility to deal with supply shocks beyond those already taken care of by the exclusion of volatile components from core inflation.

Figure 17-3 shows what has happened to the Canadian inflation rate since February 26, 1991, after the Bank's governor and the minister of finance jointly announced a series of declining inflation targets, with a band of plus and minus one percentage point around them. In what follows, we examine the tools used by the Bank of Canada to implement monetary policy, leaving a detailed analysis of the Bank's monetary policy for Chapter 18.

---

[6] See Michael Woodford, "Monetary Policy in the Information Economy," in *Symposium on Economic Policy for the Information Economy* (Federal Reserve Bank of Kansas City: 2001), pp. 297–370.

How Monetary Policy Affects the Economy

The Bank of Canada affects interest rates and the level of economic activity by changing the target and operating band for the overnight interest rate. As we saw in Chapter 6, interest rates on different assets tend to move together over time. Hence, changes in the target for the overnight interest rate (and thus the bank rate, i_b) influence other rates, such as the prime rate (the interest rate banks charge to their best customers) and the interest rates on bank deposits and mortgages. These changes in interest rates may also lead to changes in the exchange rate. The level of short-term interest rates and the exchange rate of the Canadian dollar determine the **monetary conditions** in which the economy operates.

The concept of monetary conditions, introduced by the Bank of Canada in its conduct of monetary policy in the early 1990s, focuses on the effect on the economy of both short-term interest rates and the exchange rate. Changes in monetary conditions affect the economy and the Bank's ultimate objective, the inflation rate, only indirectly and are usually felt over a period of several months to several years. This means that the Bank of Canada must always be forward looking in its conduct of monetary policy, anticipating the level of monetary conditions needed today to achieve its ultimate goal of low and stable inflation in the future.

As an example, suppose that the Bank of Canada expects the economy to slow down and wishes to ease monetary conditions. It lowers the target and operating band for the overnight interest rate.[7] As you can see in Figure 17-4, this reduces interest rates and the value of the dollar and leads to an increase in the supply of money, aggregate demand, and the price level, thereby preventing the inflation rate from falling below the target range of 1% to 3%.

In the opposite case, if the Bank expects the economy to be exceeding its capacity at some point in the future, it raises the operating band in order to prevent inflationary pressures from building. The consequent increase in interest rates and the value of the dollar lead to a decline in the supply of money, aggregate demand, and the price level, thereby preventing the inflation rate from moving above the Bank's target range of 1% to 3%—see Figure 17-5.

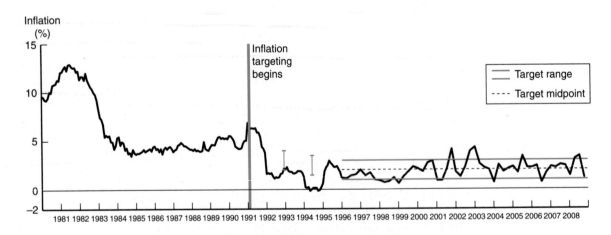

FIGURE 17-3 Inflation Rates and Inflation Targets for Canada, 1980–2008

Source: Ben S. Bernanke, Thomas Laubach, Frederic S. Mishkin, and Adam S. Posen, *Inflation Targeting: Lessons from the International Experience* (Princeton, NJ: Princeton University Press, 2001) and updates from the same source.

---

[7] For example, the Bank might lower the operating band by 25 basis points from 3.5% to 4.0% to 3.25% to 3.75%.

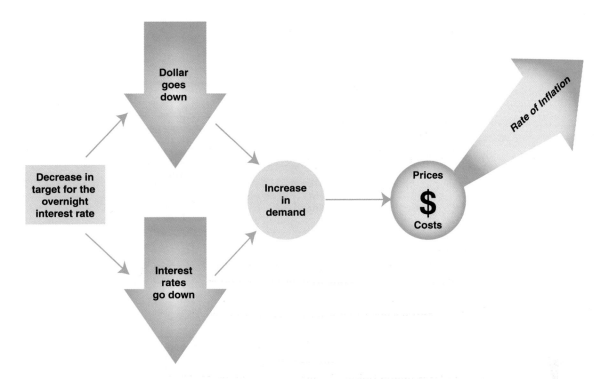

FIGURE 17-4 How the Bank of Canada Keeps the Rate of Inflation from Falling Below the Target Range

Source: Bank of Canada website: www.bankofcanada.ca. Reprinted with permission.

Hence, by changing the target and operating band for the overnight rate, the Bank of Canada sends a signal regarding the direction that it would like interest rates and the money supply to take. A rise in the target and operating band, and thus the bank rate, is a signal that the Bank would like to see higher interest rates and less money in the economy. A fall in the target and operating band is a signal that the Bank would like lower interest rates and more money.

Nominal Interest Rates and Monetary Policy

The Bank of Canada uses the *nominal* overnight interest rate as its operating instrument, but as you will learn in Chapter 25, the effects of monetary policy on economic activity stem from how the *real* interest rate, i_r, rather than the nominal interest rate, i, affects consumption and investment spending. In fact, the current interest rate targeting approach is based on the belief that it is the real *long-term* interest rate, and not the real short-term interest rate, that affects consumer and business decisions.

How is it that changes in short-term nominal interest rates (such as the Bank of Canada's overnight rate) affect short- and long-term real interest rates? Under the "new Keynesian" assumption of *sticky* prices (that is, under the assumption that prices do not adjust instantaneously to clear the markets), an expansionary monetary policy that lowers the short-term nominal interest rate will also lower the short-term real interest rate, since the aggregate price level adjusts slowly over time and there is not much change in the inflation rate. Moreover, according to the expectations hypothesis of the term structure of interest rates (discussed in detail in Chapter 6), the decline in short-term interest rates will also lead to a decline in long-term interest rates and ultimately to increases in consumer and investment spending.

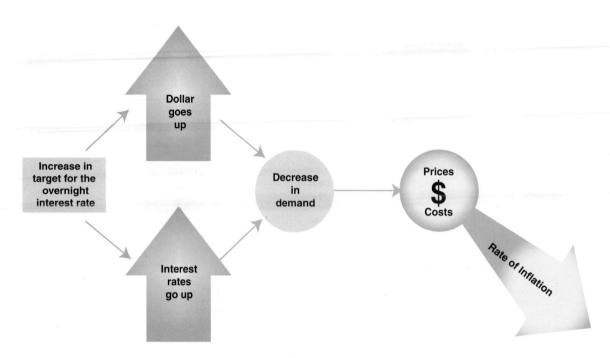

FIGURE 17-5   How the Bank of Canada Keeps the Rate of Inflation from Moving Above the Target Range

Source: Bank of Canada website: www.bankofcanada.ca. Reprinted with permission.

This transmission mechanism works well even when the short-term nominal interest rate is at or close to zero. With a nominal interest rate of zero, a commitment by the central bank to expansionary monetary policy raises the expected inflation rate, $i_r = i - \pi^e$, reduces the real interest rate, π^e, and leads to a rise in aggregate output. Thus, expansionary monetary policy could stimulate spending even when the short-term nominal interest rate is at zero. In fact, this mechanism is the key element in monetarist discussions of why an expansionary monetary policy could have prevented the sharp decline in output in the United States during the Great Depression, why it would have helped the Japanese economy when nominal interest rates fell to near zero in the late 1990s, and why it could help cope with the recent financial crisis and the global economic meltdown.

However, the collapse of stable relationships in financial markets may be causing the term structure of interest rate relationships on which the Keynesian transmission mechanism depends to loosen. For example, the U.S. Federal Reserve raised the target federal funds rate in seventeen consecutive meetings from June 2004 to July 2006, from 1% to 5.25%, but long-term interest rates in the United States and around the world declined for most of this period. It has been argued that the reason long-term interest rates did not respond over this period of monetary tightening was the adoption of an inflation-targeting approach to monetary policy by many countries and increased competition from China and India in labour and product markets that contributed to price stability and put downward pressure on long-term interest rates by reducing inflationary expectations.

Similarly, the recent decline in the federal funds rate to its current range of 0% to 0.25% from 5.25% in August of 2007 has not led to the desired decline in long-term interest rates. Why? Because the turmoil in the financial markets has increased risk premiums, thereby keeping long-term nominal interest rates high. Moreover, with collapsing asset prices (stock and real estate prices), there has been an increase in deflationary expectations, which led to a rise in real interest rates. This has the potential to make monetary policy highly contractionary, despite falling short-term nominal interest rates.

Now that we understand how the overnight rate is determined and the Bank of Canada's approach to monetary policy, we can examine how changes in the three tools of monetary policy—open market operations, settlement balances management, and Bank of Canada lending—affect the market for reserves and the equilibrium overnight interest rate.

OPEN MARKET OPERATIONS

Open market operations are an important monetary policy tool for many central banks around the world, because they are the primary determinants of changes in interest rates and the monetary base, the main source of fluctuations in the money supply. Open market purchases expand bank reserves and the monetary base, thereby lowering short-term interest rates and raising the money supply. Open market sales shrink bank reserves and the monetary base, raising short-term interest rates and lowering the money supply.

The Bank of Canada, however, stopped conducting open market operations in Government of Canada treasury bills and bonds in 1994, and its most common operations since then have been repurchase transactions with **primary dealers** (formerly known as jobbers)—the Big Six and the major investment dealers. In particular, the Bank uses **repos**, which in Canada are known as **special Purchase and Resale Agreements (special PRAs or SPRAs)**, as a tool to reduce undesired upward pressure on the overnight interest rate, and **reverse repos**, known in Canada as **Sale and Repurchase Agreements (SRAs),** as a tool to reduce undesired downward pressure on the overnight rate.

Let's see how the Bank of Canada uses special PRAs and SRAs in order to reinforce the target for the overnight interest rate during the course of a day.

Special PRAs

Assume that the operating band for the overnight interest rate is 3.5% to 4% and that the Bank of Canada is targeting the overnight rate at the midpoint of the band, at 3.75%. If overnight funds are traded at a rate higher than the target rate of 3.75%, then the Bank of Canada enters into special PRAs, typically at 11:45 at a price that works out to a 3.75% interest rate, the midpoint of the operating band. That is, the Bank purchases Government of Canada treasury bills or bonds, with an agreement that the seller will repurchase them one business day later (see Figure 17-6 regarding the mechanics of a special PRA).

Since the securities are placed with the Canadian Depository for Securities (CDS), Canada's central securities depository owned and operated by the financial community, the title of the securities changes hands by electronic instruction. The balance sheets of the Bank of Canada and the primary dealers look like this:

Bank of Canada				Primary Dealers			
Assets		Liabilities		Assets		Liabilities	
Government securities	+$100	Settlement balances	+$100	Settlement balances	+$100	SPRAs	+$100

Today

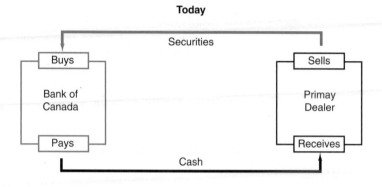

Next Day

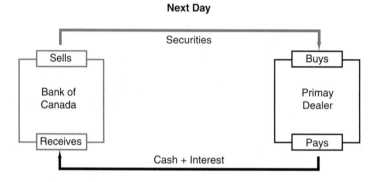

FIGURE 17-6   The Mechanics of a Special PRA Operation

Note: In a special PRA (SPRA), the Bank of Canada buys securities from a primary dealer in exchange for cash and the primary dealer agrees to buy the securities back (repurchase them) the next day at the original price plus interest, regardless of what happens in the market. In that arrangement, the primary dealer gets an overnight collateralized loan and the Bank of Canada gets some interest.

Hence, **repos, also known as special Purchase and Resale Agreements (SPRAs), relieve undesired upward pressure on the overnight interest rate.**

SRAs

If on the other hand overnight funds are traded at a rate below the target rate of 3.75%, then the Bank of Canada enters into SRAs, in which the Bank sells government securities and the buyer agrees to sell them back to the Bank one business day later. The balance sheets of the Bank of Canada and the direct clearers now look like this:

Bank of Canada			Primary Dealers		
Assets	Liabilities		Assets		Liabilities
	Settlement balances	−$100	Settlement balances	−$100	
	SRAs	+$100	Government securities	+$100	

Hence, ***reverse repos, also known as Sale and Repurchase Agreements (SRAs), alleviate undesired downward pressure on the overnight financing rate.***

Because the effects on settlement balances of SPRAs and SRAs are reversed on the day the agreement matures, SPRAs and SRAs are actually temporary open market operations. Moreover, as you will see in the next section, because the effects on settlement balances of SPRAs and SRAs are typically neutralized by the end of the day by the Bank of Canada, there is no change at the end of the day in the level of settlement balances in the system.

Advantages of SPRAs and SRAs

The Bank of Canada's repurchase transactions, either special PRAs or SRAs, have several advantages over other tools of monetary policy. They occur at the initiative of the Bank of Canada, which has complete control over their volume, and are easily reversed. Moreover, the Bank of Canada can enter into multiple rounds of open-market-buyback operations and can also conduct these operations outside of the regular timeframe.

However, open-market-buyback operations tend to be infrequent and small, because the channel/corridor system for setting the overnight interest rate requires a minimal amount of such operations. As can be seen in Figure 17-7, which shows special PRAs and SRAs over the 1999 to 2008 period, the Bank of Canada conducted repurchase transactions on about 70 days per year (on average) over this period.

SETTLEMENT BALANCES MANAGEMENT

In addition to targeting the overnight interest rate at the mid-point of the operating band, the Bank of Canada also targets the level of settlement balances in the system. Typically, the target level of settlement balances is announced the previous day. Initially, the Bank targeted a daily level of settlement balances of zero or greater (usually $25 million), but recently, because of pressures on the overnight rate, the Bank made several adjustments to the target level of settlement balances

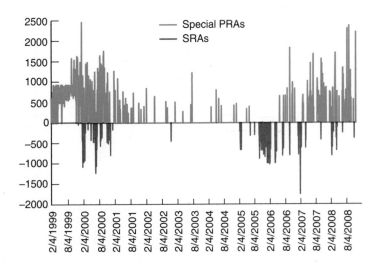

FIGURE 17-7 Special PRA and SRA Operations

Source: Bank of Canada website, www.bankofcanada.ca.

(as shown in Figure 17-8) over, for example, the period from May 18, 2007 to October 15, 2008.

However, in targeting the overnight interest rate at the mid-point of the operating band, the Bank of Canada usually neutralizes the impact on settlement balances of any open-market-buyback operations. For example, the Bank neutralizes special PRA operations, so as not to leave the system in a surplus position at the end of the day, in which case at least one LVTS participant would end up holding positive settlement balances with the Bank of Canada earning the bank rate less 50 basis points, $i_b - 0.50$. Similarly, the Bank of Canada neutralizes SRA operations, so as not to leave the system in a deficit position, in which case at least one LVTS participant would end up holding negative settlement balances with the Bank paying the bank rate, i_b.

Moreover, being the federal government's fiscal agent, the Bank of Canada usually neutralizes the net impact on settlement balances of certain federal government payment flows and Bank of Canada transactions.

The neutralization of the effects of open-market-buyback operations and of public sector flows on the level of settlement balances, and the adjustment of the level of settlement balances are effected through shifts (transfers) of government deposits (balances) between the government's account at the Bank of Canada and the government's accounts at the LVTS participants. In particular, the Bank of Canada uses twice-daily auctions of federal government (Receiver General) balances, the first at 9:15 a.m. (which are collateralized) and the second at 4:15 p.m. (which are uncollateralized), when all the flows affecting the Bank of Canada's balance sheet are known. This neutralizes the effect of market buyback operations and of public sector flows, and also adjusts the level of settlement balances.

Receiver General Auctions

To illustrate the process for neutralizing public sector flows using auctions of Receiver General balances, suppose that there is a net government receipt of $100 (i.e., the government's receipts from the public exceed its payments to the public by $100). Net receipts are drawn on the government's deposits at the LVTS participants, creating claims on the LVTS participants in favour of the Bank of Canada

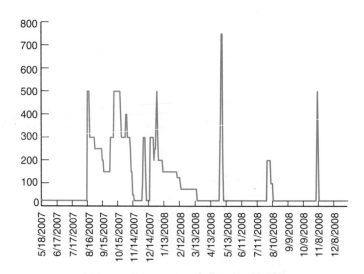

FIGURE 17-8   Target Level of Settlement Balances (in millions)

Source: Bank of Canada website, www.bankofcanada.ca.

and ultimately reducing settlement balances by an amount equal to the government's net receipts. In the absence of any offsetting transactions by the Bank of Canada, through the workings of supply and demand, a decline in settlement balances will normally cause an increase in the overnight interest rate, as many LVTS participants would have to borrow more to meet their settlement obligations.

However, in targeting the overnight interest rate, the Bank of Canada will neutralize the net government receipt by arranging a net increase of $100 in the government deposit auctions to leave the system unchanged. This procedure results in the following balance sheets for the Bank and the LVTS participants:

Bank of Canada				LVTS Participants			
Assets		Liabilities		Assets		Liabilities	
		Government deposits	−100	Settlement balances	+100	Government deposits	+100
		Settlement balances	+100				

Note that government deposits at the Bank of Canada are reduced by $100 and at the same time the settlement balances of the LVTS participants are increased by $100.

If instead of a net receipt by the government, there was a net disbursement of $100 (i.e., the government's payments to the public exceed its receipts from the public by $100), then the financial system's settlement balances would increase by the same amount. This would prompt a fall in the overnight interest rate, as many LVTS participants would have to borrow less to meet their settlement obligations. The Bank's neutralization process would prevent a decline in the overnight rate by reducing the banking system's settlement balances. This would involve LVTS transfers of $100 (i.e., the difference between the total amount of government balances maturing and the total amount of government balances auctioned) from the government's accounts at the participating institutions to the government's account at the Bank. This procedure results in the following T-accounts:

Bank of Canada				LVTS Participants			
Assets		Liabilities		Assets		Liabilities	
		Government deposits	+100	Settlement balances	−100	Government deposits	−100
		Settlement balances	−100				

In this case government deposits at the Bank of Canada are increased by $100 and at the same time the clearing balances of the participants are reduced by $100.

Swaps with the Exchange Fund Account

When the Bank of Canada transfers government balances, it usually brings onto its balance sheet Exchange Fund Account assets to back its liabilities. It does so by arranging a swap with the Exchange Fund Account, which holds the country's foreign exchange reserves. This involves a spot purchase and a simultaneous forward sale of foreign exchange. To illustrate the operation, assume that the Bank temporarily buys $100 of foreign currency assets from the Exchange Fund Account. It credits the government's account on its own books and the operation results in the following balance sheets for the Bank and the government:

Bank of Canada				Government of Canada		
Assets		Liabilities		Assets		Liabilities
Foreign exchange	+100	Government deposits	+100	Exchange Fund Account	−100	
				Deposits at the Bank of Canada	+100	

We see that government deposit balances at the Bank of Canada increase and these balances can then be transferred to participants to increase settlement balances, as we saw earlier.

Although the spot transaction adds to the government deposits at the Bank of Canada and enables the Bank to auction government balances, the forward contract between the Bank and the Exchange Fund Account does not affect the settlement balances of participating financial institutions. The Bank simply sells foreign exchange to the Exchange Fund Account in the future at a price agreed upon today. The advantage to the Bank of Canada of using swap transactions with the Exchange Fund Account is that it can bring a temporary change in the level of settlement balances or respond to some event that the Bank thinks will have a significant but not long-lived effect.

As we will learn in Chapter 20, the foreign exchange reserves held in the Exchange Fund Account can also be used by the Bank of Canada in international financial transactions to prevent undesirable movements in the exchange rate. For example, a Bank of Canada sale of domestic currency and corresponding purchase of foreign assets in the foreign exchange market leads to a gain in international reserves, an increase in the monetary base and the money supply, and a depreciation of the domestic currency. A Bank purchase of domestic currency and corresponding sale of foreign exchange leads to a loss of international reserves, a decline in the monetary base and the money supply, and an appreciation of the domestic currency. We shall discuss such foreign exchange interventions in detail in Chapter 20.

The Target Level of Settlement Balances

In addition to the auctions of Receiver General balances, the Bank of Canada can also adjust the target level of settlement balances if warranted by conditions in the overnight market. That is, the Bank retains the right to adjust the targeted level of settlement balances higher or lower than the typical setting, depending on pressures on the overnight rate.

The Bank of Canada, however, is not always able to completely neutralize special PRA and SRA operations and public sector flows so that the actual level of settlement balances ends up being higher or lower than the target level. As an example, Figure 17-9 shows the difference between the actual level of settlement balances and the target level of settlement balances over the period (from May 18, 2007 to October 15, 2008). However, deviations of the actual level of settlement balances from the target level appear to have insignificant effects on the overnight

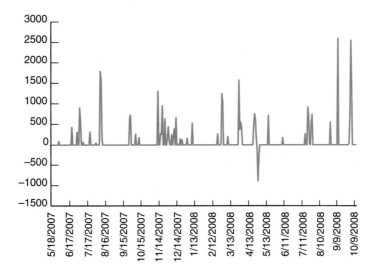

FIGURE 17-9   Deviations of the Actual Level of Settlement Balances from the Target Level of Settlement Balances (in millions)

Source: Bank of Canada website, www.bankofcanada.ca.

interest rate the day that they occur, unlike pre-announced changes to the target level of settlement balances, which appear to have a significant effect on the overnight interest rate.

Monetary Control in the Channel/Corridor System

Suppose that the operating band is 4.5% to 5% and the Bank of Canada expects the economy to exceed its capacity in the near future. To prevent inflationary pressures from building, the Bank wishes to tighten monetary policy by raising the target and operating band by 25 basis points. In one of the eight fixed days for announcing changes to the target and operating band for the overnight rate, the Bank announces, at 9:00 a.m., that it is adjusting the target and operating band up from 4.5% to 5% to 4.75% to 5.25%. From this announcement, LVTS participants know that the bank rate shifts from 5% to 5.25%, the rate on positive settlement balances shifts from 4.5% to 4.75%, and that the Bank of Canada's new target overnight rate, the midpoint of the operating band, shifts from 4.75% to 5%.

Later in the day, at 11:45 a.m., if overnight funds are trading below the target overnight rate (the midpoint of the operating band), the Bank of Canada enters into SRAs to enforce the new target for the overnight rate. That is, it sells government securities to primary dealers, who pay for the securities with settlement balances and agree to sell the securities back to the Bank of Canada on the next business day, at a price that works out to an annual interest rate of 5%—the midpoint of the new operating band. Assuming that the Bank of Canada enters into SRAs in the amount of $100, the T-accounts of the Bank of Canada and the primary dealers will be

Bank of Canada				Primary Dealers			
Assets		Liabilities		Assets		Liabilities	
		Settlement balances	−100	Settlement balances	−100		
		SRAs	+100	Government securities	+100		

The clearing banks find that their settlement balances have declined by $100, and because they had not been holding any excess reserves, their holdings of settlement balances are $100 short of the desired amount. Assuming that no other transactions occur during the day, at 4:15 p.m., the Bank of Canada neutralizes the effect on aggregate settlement balances of its issue of SRAs by auctioning off government deposits. The Bank's neutralization process involves auctioning off $100 of government deposits and paying those LVTS participants taking government deposits with settlement balances, bringing the amount of aggregate settlement balances back to zero. The balance sheets of the Bank of Canada and the LVTS participants now look like this:

Bank of Canada				LVTS Participants			
Assets		Liabilities		Assets		Liabilities	
		Settlement balances	+100	Settlement balances	+100	Government deposits	+100
		Government deposits	−100				

The Bank of Canada's monetary tightening has been effected through the management of settlement balances, during the course of the day, with no change in the aggregate settlement balances of deposit-taking institutions. As already noted, the change in the overnight rate will influence other interest rates and the level of monetary conditions in which the economy operates.

Monetary Policy at the Effective Lower Bound for the Overnight Rate

On April 21, 2009, the Bank of Canada lowered the overnight rate target by 0.25 of a percentage point to 0.25% and also made some changes to its operating framework for the implementation of monetary policy. In particular, the Bank narrowed the operating band for the overnight interest rate to 25 basis points, from 0.25% to 0.5%, with 0.5% being the bank rate and 0.25% being the deposit rate. The Bank also announced that the target for the overnight rate will be the bottom of the operating band (that is, 0.25%) rather than the midpoint of the operating band, thus setting an effective lower bound for the overnight rate.

As the policy rate has reached the effective lower bound, the Bank of Canada has lost its usual ability to signal policy changes via changes in the policy rate. Moreover, with short-term interest rates close to zero, the Bank of Canada has also lost its ability to lower long-term interest rates by lowering short-term interest rates.

For these reasons, many central banks around the world, including the Bank of Japan, the U.S. Federal Reserve, and the Bank of England, have departed from the traditional interest-rate targeting approach to monetary policy and are focusing on their balance sheet instead, using quantitative measures of monetary policy. The Bank of Canada is also considering such quantitative measures and has recently identified three alternative instruments that it would consider using in an environment with low short-term (nominal) interest rates: conditional statements about the future path of the policy rate, quantitative easing, and credit easing.

CONDITIONAL STATEMENTS   Because the Bank of Canada has lost its ability to influence long-term interest rates using conventional monetary policy tools, recently the Bank started making conditional statements about the future path of its policy rate in order to influence long-term interest rates. The objective of such conditional commitments regarding the operating band for the overnight interest rate is to align market expectations of future short-term interest rates with those of the Bank to achieve desirable outcomes in interest rates throughout the term structure.

For example, on April 21, 2009, the Bank of Canada lowered the policy rate by 0.25 of a percentage point to 0.25%, and it also committed to holding the policy rate at 0.25% until the second quarter of 2010, conditional on the outlook for inflation. Such a conditional commitment by the Bank of Canada to keep the policy rate at 25 basis points for a long period is expected to shape market expectations of future short-term interest rates and lower long-term interest rates, since long-term rates are averages of current and expected future short-term interest rates (plus risk premiums).

QUANTITATIVE EASING   Quantitative easing refers to the purchase of financial assets by the central bank through the creation of excess reserves (settlement balances in the Canadian case) for banks. This is the same as open market operations, but extends to include private financial assets such as corporate bonds and commercial paper. By buying financial assets, the central bank affects the cost of borrowing by pushing up the price of the purchased assets and reducing their yields. Moreover, by creating excess reserves for banks, the central bank encourages banks to lend more to households and businesses, thereby increasing the level of economic activity.

Quantitative easing is regarded as an unconventional form of monetary policy, very different from interest-rate targeting that central banks and the financial markets around the world have used over the last twenty years. It targets the amount of liquidity provided by the central bank instead of targeting the price of liquidity (as interest-rate targeting does). The Bank of Japan used it during the early 2000s, as did the Federal Reserve and the Bank of England during the recent global financial crisis. Quantitative easing, however, is a high-risk monetary policy tool as it runs the risk of going too far, pumping too much money into the economy and possibly creating inflation and even hyperinflation.

CREDIT EASING   Credit easing refers to the purchase of private sector assets by the central bank in critical markets that are considered important for the effective functioning of the economy. The objective of credit easing is to reduce risky spreads and improve liquidity and trading in these markets, thereby stimulating the level of economic activity. Unlike quantitative easing, which leads to an expansion in the monetary base through the creation of excess reserves, the effects of credit easing on the monetary base could be sterilized, for example, by reducing the central bank's holdings of other assets.

The effectiveness of credit easing is judged by reduction in risk premiums and this depends on the substitutability between asset classes. If the degree of substitutability between asset classes is high, any given effect will be transmitted more broadly across assets, but their yields will not be significantly affected, leaving risky spreads unchanged. If, however, the degree of substitutability is low, the effect on the yields of the purchased assets will be greater, although the pass-through to the interest rates on other asset classes will be low. Since the substitutability between asset classes changes over time, the effects of credit easing on credit flows and aggregate demand are likely to be uncertain.

SUMMARY   The Bank of Canada and other central banks around the world are switching from the "one tool, one target" mode of operation and are searching for new tools to steer their economies in an environment with interest rates at or near zero. In Canada, the one tool was the overnight interest rate and the target was an inflation rate around 2%. However, with an effective lower bound of 25 basis points for the overnight interest rate, a decoupling of long- and short-term interest rates, and the possibility of a deflationary trap (that is, extremely low nominal interest rates and sustained deflation), the Bank of Canada is now considering new tools to steer the economy (see the Inside the Central Bank box, Monetary Policy at Times of Crisis).

BANK OF CANADA LENDING

The facility at which banks can borrow reserves from the Bank of Canada is called the **standing lending facility**. The easiest way to understand how the Bank of Canada affects the volume of borrowed reserves is by looking at how the standing lending facility operates.

Operation of the Standing Lending Facility

As already noted, the Bank of Canada offers a lending facility, standing ready to lend (upon presentation of suitable collateral) overnight settlement balances to LVTS participants with negative clearing balances at the end of the business day. The lending rate is the bank rate, denoted by i_b in Figure 17-2 (on page 438), and is 25 basis points higher than the target overnight interest rate, so as to penalize participants for not using the overnight interbank market. LVTS participants know with certainty the lending rate applicable to their negative settlement balances with the Bank of Canada.

To see how the standing lending facility works, let's see what happens if there is a large increase in the demand for reserves, say because deposits have surged unexpectedly and have led to an increase in desired reserves. This situation is analyzed in Figure 17-10. Suppose that initially the demand and supply curves for reserves intersect at point 1 so that the overnight rate is at its target level, i_{or}^*. Now the increase in desired reserves shifts the demand curve to R_2^d and the equilibrium moves to point 2. The result is that borrowed reserves increase from zero to BR and the overnight rate rises to i_b and can rise no further. The standing lending facility has thus put a ceiling on the overnight interest rate of i_{or}.

INSIDE THE CENTRAL BANK

Monetary Policy at Times of Crisis

At times of turmoil in financial markets, central banks face a number of challenges. In the Canadian case, for example, challenges involve keeping the overnight rate near the policy rate, keeping spreads in the term interbank market low by influencing interbank term rates, and deciding how to respond to the potential macroeconomic effects of the crisis by changing the monetary policy stance (that is, the target and operating band for the overnight rate).

Against the backdrop of the recent turmoil in financial markets, the Bank of Canada faced widening spreads and increased volatility in the term interbank market and took extraordinary measures to stabilize the financial system. In its efforts to influence interbank term rates, the Bank introduced term PRAs and increased the frequency and size of its discretionary liquidity operations. Moreover, the Bank expanded its list of acceptable collateral (for both its standing

lending facility as well as for its term PRA operations) to include bank-sponsored asset-backed commercial paper and U.S. Treasuries.

These discretionary liquidity operations do not represent a change in the stance of monetary policy. However, in order to support the Canadian economy, the Bank of Canada, acting in concert with other major central banks, also changed its policy stance by lowering the target and operating band for the overnight interest rate in a series of announcements. In fact, in the first ten months of 2008 alone, the policy rate was reduced by 300 basis points to 1.5% by the end of 2008 and then to 0.25% by April 2009. Moreover, the Bank is now considering quantitative measures of monetary policy, and has identified alternative instruments that it would consider using at the effective lower bound for the overnight interest rate.

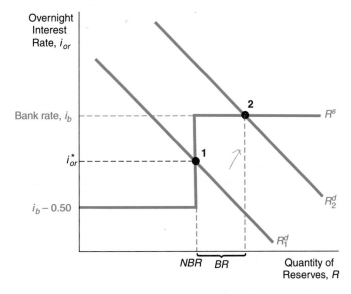

FIGURE 17-10   How the Standing Lending Facility Puts a Ceiling on the Overnight Interest Rate

The rightward shift of the demand curve for reserves from R_1^d to R_2^d moves the equilibrium from point 1 to point 2 where $i_{or} = i_b$ and borrowed reserves incease from zero to BR.

Lender of Last Resort

In addition to its use as a standing liquidity facility to reinforce the operating band for the overnight interest rate, Bank of Canada lending is also important in preventing financial panics. In fact, one of the Bank's most important roles is to be the lender of last resort in the Canadian economy.[8] It provides emergency lending assistance (against eligible collateral) for a maximum period of six months (which can be extended for periods up to six months as many times as the Bank judges) to solvent (but illiquid) deposit-taking institutions to prevent bank failures from spinning further out of control, thereby preventing bank and financial panics. The rate that the Bank normally charges on these loans is the bank rate, although the Bank has discretion to charge a higher rate. In providing emergency lending assistance, the Bank always makes a judgement with respect to the trade-off between morally hazardous behaviour and the costs in terms of financial stability. Last-resort lending is a particularly effective way to provide reserves to the banking system during a banking crisis because reserves are immediately channelled to the banks that need them most.

Avoiding financial panics by performing the role of lender of last resort is an extremely important requirement of successful monetary policymaking. As we demonstrated with our money supply analysis in Chapter 16, the bank panics in the United States in the 1930–1933 period were the cause of the sharpest decline in the money supply in U.S. history, which many economists see as the driving force behind the collapse of the world economy during the Great Depression. Financial panics can also severely damage the economy because they interfere with the ability of financial intermediaries and markets to move funds to people with productive investment opportunities (see Chapter 8).

At first glance, it might appear as though the presence of the CDIC, which insures depositors from losses due to a bank's failure up to a limit of $100 000 per account, would make the lender-of-last-resort function of the Bank of Canada superfluous. (The CDIC is described in detail in Chapter 10.) There are two reasons why this is not the case. First, it is important to recognize that the CDIC's insurance fund amounts to a small fraction of the amount of deposits outstanding. If a large number of bank failures occurred, the CDIC would not be able to cover all the depositors' losses. Indeed, the failures of deposit-based financial institutions in the 1980s and early 1990s in Canada, described in Chapter 10, led to large losses and a shrinkage in the CDIC's insurance fund, which reduced the CDIC's ability to cover depositors' losses. This fact has not weakened the confidence of small depositors in the banking system because the Bank of Canada has been ready to stand behind the banks to provide whatever reserves are needed to prevent bank panics. Second, the large-denomination deposits in the banking system are not guaranteed by the CDIC because they exceed the $100 000 limit. A loss of confidence in the banking system could still lead to runs on banks from the large-denomination depositors, and bank panics could still occur despite the existence of the CDIC.

The importance of the Bank of Canada's role as lender of last resort is, if anything, more important today because of the bank failures experienced in Canada in the 1980s and early 1990s. Figure 17-11, which shows Bank of Canada advances to members of the Canadian Payments Association, reveals that the Bank of Canada advanced considerable funds in the recent past to financial institutions facing liquidity crises. Unfortunately, the Bank of Canada's lending policy has not

---

[8] Regarding the policy framework that governs the Bank of Canada's lender-of-last-resort activities, see Daniel Fred and Walter Engert, "The Bank of Canada as Lender of Last Resort," *Bank of Canada Review* (Winter 2004–2005).

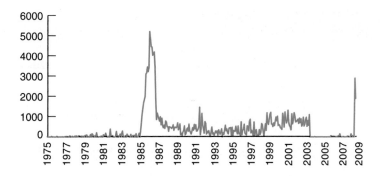

FIGURE 17-11 Bank of Canada Advances to Members of the Canadian Payments Association, 1975–2008 (in millions of dollars)

Source: Statistics Canada CANSIM II Series V36663.

always been successful in preventing financial crises. Two examples of the use of the Bank's lending weapon to avoid bank panics are the provisions of huge loans to the Canadian Commercial Bank and the Northland Bank in 1985 (see the Inside the Central Bank box, Emergency Lending Assistance to Troubled Banks).

Discretionary Liquidity Operations

Not only can the central bank be a lender of last resort to banks, but it can also play the same role for the financial system as a whole. In fact, under the Bank of Canada Act, under extreme conditions on a financial market or financial system, the Bank of Canada has the authority to provide liquid funds to any (financial or nonfinancial) Canadian or foreign entities, for the purpose of promoting the stability of the financial system. Such central bank intervention can help prevent financial panics that are not triggered by bank failures, as was the case in the United States during the recent financial crisis that started in August 2007 (see the Inside the Central Bank box, Federal Reserve Lender-of-Last-Resort Facilities During the Subprime Financial Crisis).

Recently, central banks around the world have been facing significant challenges in implementing monetary policy because of the financial-market turmoil and the subprime credit crisis in the United States. In response to these challenges, central banks have been improving and refining their financial infrastructures to address turmoil in the financial markets. Although there are differences across countries in institutional arrangements for the conduct of monetary policy, most central banks have responded to the recent financial turbulence in a similar fashion, providing liquidity directly to the financial system, called aggregate system or macro liquidity.

To address market failure and financial instability at times of crisis, central banks rely on discretionary liquidity operations, the maturity of which depends on their objective, independent of the maturity of the reference rate. The Bank of Canada, for example, recently introduced new facilities to address aggregate system liquidity at times of financial instability. In particular, the Bank introduced term repos, known in Canada as term Purchase and Resale Agreements (PRAs), and term securities lending.[9]

Let's see how these new facilities are used in providing liquidity to specific markets as opposed to lending directly to banks.

---

[9] For more details, see Walter Engert, Jack Selody, and Carolyn Wilkins, "Financial Market Turmoil and Central Bank Intervention," *Financial System Review* (June 2008), 71–78.

INSIDE THE CENTRAL BANK

Emergency Lending Assistance to Troubled Banks

Canadian Commercial and Northland. In 1985, there was public concern over the quality of the assets of two small Alberta-based banks—the Canadian Commercial Bank and the Northland Bank—which had made many bad loans. Larger depositors, whose accounts exceeded the $60 000 limit insured (at that time) by the CDIC, began to withdraw their deposits, and the failure of the banks was imminent. Because the immediate failure of Canadian Commercial and Northland would have had repercussions on other vulnerable banks, the Bank of Canada, under the advice from the Inspector General of Banks (the predecessor of the Office of the Superintendent of Financial Institutions Canada) made extraordinary advances. Total emergency lending assistance amounted to $1.8 billion so that depositors, including the largest, would not suffer any losses.

In doing this, the Bank of Canada was following the precedent established in 1984 by the Federal Reserve's rescue of Continental Illinois National Bank. Continental Illinois had made bad loans (primarily to businesses in the energy industry and to foreign countries), and rumours of financial trouble in early May 1984 caused large depositors to withdraw over US$10 billion of deposits from the bank. The Federal Deposit Insurance Corporation (FDIC) arranged a rescue effort in

July 1984 that culminated in a US$4.5 billion commitment of funds to save the bank. Still the Fed had to lend Continental Illinois over US$5 billion—making the Bank of Canada's $1.8 billion advances to Canadian Commercial and Northland look like small potatoes! Although Continental Illinois was taken over by the FDIC, the Fed's action prevented further bank failures, and a potential bank panic was averted.

The Bank of Canada, however, was not as successful in preventing a bank crisis. With the failure of Canadian Commercial and Northland, rumours of financial trouble caused many large depositors to withdraw large deposits from the Bank of British Columbia, Mercantile Bank, and Continental Bank. By the time Mercantile was acquired by the National Bank of Canada, the Bank of British Columbia by the Hongkong Bank of Canada, and Continental by Lloyds Bank of Canada, the Bank of Canada had provided emergency lending assistance of more than $5 billion (see Figure 17-11). The loss of public confidence in the Canadian banking system led to the financial reforms of 1987–1992 and the consolidating of financial institution supervision under the Office of the Superintendent of Financial Institutions Canada.

TERM PRAS Term PRAs are similar to special PRAs (see Figure 17-6), but have a term longer than one business day, typically a term of 28 business days. They are offered to primary dealers and used at times of crisis, when asymmetric information among market participants impairs their ability to buy and sell an asset class or maturity, thereby distorting liquidity premiums in the money market.

For example, against the backdrop of widening spreads and increased volatility in the term interbank market in the second half of 2008, the Bank of Canada announced that it would enter into a series of 28-day PRA transactions, thereby injecting huge amounts of liquidity into the markets. Moreover, the Bank expanded its list of acceptable collateral to include bank-sponsored asset-backed commercial paper and U.S. Treasuries. It also expanded its list of eligible counterparties. In engaging in these trades, the Bank takes securities onto its books in exchange for borrowings from the Bank's standing lending facility.

TERM SECURITIES LENDING   This mechanism is designed to increase the supply of high-quality securities that could be used for collateral by banks. It can also be used to swap less-liquid securities for more-liquid securities that the banks are putting up as collateral. It is also designed to partially offset the temporary increase in assets in the Bank's books associated with the term purchase and resale transactions.

Advantages and Disadvantages of the Bank's Lending Policy

Although the Bank of Canada's role as the lender of last resort has the benefit of preventing bank and financial panics, it does have a cost. If a bank expects that the Bank of Canada will provide it with advances when it gets into trouble, it will be willing to take on more risk knowing that the Bank of Canada will come to the rescue. The Bank of Canada's lender-of-last-resort role has thus created a moral hazard problem similar to the one created by deposit insurance (discussed in Chapter 11). Banks take on more risk, thus exposing the deposit insurance agency, and hence taxpayers, to greater losses. The moral hazard problem is most severe for large banks, which may believe that the Bank of Canada and the CDIC view them as "too big to fail"; that is, they will always receive Bank of Canada emergency lending assistance when they are in trouble because their failure would be likely to precipitate a bank panic.

Similarly, Bank of Canada actions to prevent financial panic may encourage financial institutions other than banks to take on greater risk. They, too, expect the Bank of Canada to ensure that they could get loans if a financial panic seemed imminent. When the Bank of Canada considers using the lending weapon to prevent panics, it therefore needs to consider the trade-off between the moral hazard cost of its role as lender of last resort and the benefit of preventing financial panics. This trade-off explains why the Bank of Canada must be careful not to perform its role as lender of last resort too frequently.

The most important advantage of the Bank of Canada's lending policy is that the Bank can use it to perform its role of lender of last resort and stabilize the financial system in times of stress. Experiences in the 1980s and early 1990s, the Black Monday crash, the terrorist destruction of the World Trade Center, and the recent global financial crisis indicate that this role has become more important in the past couple of decades.

In the past, Bank of Canada advances were used as a tool of monetary policy, with the bank rate changed to affect interest rates and the money supply. However, because the decisions to take out loans are made by banks and are therefore not completely controlled by the Bank of Canada (while open-market-buyback operations are completely controlled by the Bank of Canada), using lending policy to conduct monetary policy has advantages. This is why the Bank of Canada moved to the current channel/corridor system of monetary control in which the bank rate is not used to set the overnight rate, but is only a backup facility to prevent the overnight interest rate from moving outside the operating band.

INSIDE THE CENTRAL BANK

Federal Reserve Lender-of-Last-Resort Facilities During the Subprime Financial Crisis

In the U.S., the onset of the subprime financial crisis in August of 2007 led to a massive increase in Federal Reserve lender-of-last-resort facilities to contain the crisis.

In mid-August 2007, the Federal Reserve lowered the discount rate to just 50 basis points (0.5 percentage points) above the federal funds rate target from the normal 100 basis points. In March 2008, it narrowed the spread further by setting the discount rate at only 25 basis points above the federal funds rate target. In September 2007 and March 2008, it extended the term of discount loans: Before the crisis they were overnight or very short-term loans; in September the maturity of discount loans was extended to 30 days and to 90 days in March.

In December 2007, the Fed set up a temporary Term Auction Facility (TAF) in which it made discount loans at a rate determined through competitive auctions. This facility carried less of a stigma for banks than the normal discount window facility. It was more widely used than the discount window facility because it enabled banks to borrow at a rate less than the discount rate and because the rate was determined competitively, rather than being set at a penalty rate. While the TAF was a new facility for the Fed, the European Central Bank already had a similar facility. The TAF auctions started at amounts of $20 billion, but as the crisis worsened, the amounts were raised dramatically, with a total outstanding of over $400 billion.

On March 11, 2008, the Fed created the Term Securities Lending Facility (TSLF), in which it would lend Treasury securities to primary dealers for terms longer than overnight, as in existing lending programs, with the primary dealers pledging other securities. The TSLF's purpose was to supply more Treasury securities to primary dealers so they had sufficient Treasury securities to act as collateral, thereby helping the orderly functioning of financial markets. On the same day, the Fed authorized increases in reciprocal currency arrangements known as swap lines, in which it lent dollars to foreign central banks (in this case, the European Central Bank and the Swiss National Bank) in exchange for foreign currencies so that these central banks could in turn make dollar loans to their domestic banks. These swap lines were enlarged even further during the course of the crisis.

On March 14, 2008, as liquidity dried up for Bear Stearns, the Fed announced that it would in effect buy up $30 billion of Bear Stearns's mortgage-related assets in order to facilitate the purchase of Bear Stearns by J.P. Morgan.* The Fed took this extraordinary action because it believed that Bear Stearns was so interconnected with other financial institutions that its failure would have caused a massive fire-sale of assets and a complete seizing up of credit markets. The Fed took this action under an obscure provision of the Federal Reserve Act, section 13(3), that was put into the act during the Great Depression. It allowed the Fed under "unusual and exigent circumstances" to lend money to any individual, partnership, or corporation, as long as certain requirements were met. This broadening of the Fed's lender-of-last-resort actions outside of its traditional lending to depository institutions was described by Paul Volcker, a former chairman of the Federal Reserve, as the Fed going to the "very edge of its lawful and implied powers."

The broadening of the Fed's lender-of-last-resort activities using section 13(3) grew as the crisis deepened. On March 16, 2008, the Federal Reserve announced a new temporary credit facility, the Primary Dealer Credit Facility (PDCF), under which primary dealers, many of them investment banks, could borrow on similar terms to depository institutions using the traditional discount window facility. On September 19, 2008, after money market mutual funds were subject to large amounts of redemptions by investors, the Fed announced another tempo-

(continued)

rary facility, the Asset-Backed Commercial Paper Money Market Mutual Fund Liquidity Facility (AMLF), in which the Fed would lend to primary dealers so that they could purchase asset-backed commercial paper from money market mutual funds. By so doing, money market mutual funds would be able to unload their asset-backed commercial paper when they needed to sell it to meet the demands for redemptions from their investors. A similar facility, the Money Market Investor Funding Facility (MMIFF), was set up on October 21, 2008, to lend to special-purpose vehicles that could buy a wider range of money market mutual funds assets. On October 7, 2008, the Fed announced another liquidity facility to promote the smooth functioning of the commercial paper market that had also begun to seize up, the Commercial Paper Funding Facility (CPFF). With this facility, the Fed could buy commercial paper directly from issuers at a rate 100 basis points above the expected federal funds rate over the term of the commercial paper. To restrict the facility to rolling over existing commercial paper, the Fed stipulated that each issuer could sell only an amount of commercial paper that was less than or equal to its average amount outstanding in August 2008. Then on November 25, 2008, the Fed announced two new liquidity facilities, the Term Asset-Backed Securities Loan Facility (TALF), in which it committed to the financing of $200 billion (later raised to $1 trillion) of asset-backed

securities for a one-year period, and a Government Sponsored Entities Purchase Program, in which the Fed made a commitment to buy $100 billion of debt issued by Fannie Mae and Freddie Mac and other government-sponsored enterprises (GSEs), as well as $500 billion of mortgage-backed securities guaranteed by these GSEs.

In the aftermath of the Lehman Brothers failure, the Fed also extended large amounts of credit directly to financial institutions that needed to be bailed out. In late September, the Fed agreed to lend over $100 billion to prop up AIG and also authorized the Federal Reserve Bank of New York to purchase mortgage-backed and other risky securities from AIG to pump more liquidity into the company. In November, the Fed committed over $200 billion to absorb 90% of losses resulting from the federal government's guarantee of Citigroup's risky assets; in January it did the same thing for Bank of America, committing over $80 billion.

The expansion of the Fed's lender-of-last-resort programs during the subprime financial crisis was indeed remarkable, expanding the Fed's balance sheet by over $1 trillion by the end of 2008, with expectations that the balance-sheet expansion would be far higher. The unprecedented expansion in the Fed's balance sheet demonstrated the Fed's commitment to get the financial markets working again.

---

*Technically, the purchase of these assets was in effect done with a non-recourse loan of $30 billion to J.P. Morgan, with the Fed bearing all the downside risk except for the first $1 billion, while getting all the gains if the assets were eventually sold for more than $30 billion. The effective purchase of commercial paper under the Asset-Backed Commercial Paper Money Market Mutual Fund Liquidity Facility, the Commercial Paper Funding Facility, and the Government Sponsored Entities Purchase Program was also done with non-recourse loans. Purchasing assets in this way conforms to section 13(3), which allows the Fed to make loans, but not purchase assets directly.

SUMMARY

1. The Bank of Canada views the overnight interest rate as the centrepiece of its monetary policy implementation. At 9:00 a.m. on the fixed action date, the Bank announces an operating band of 50 basis points for the overnight rate. The upper limit of the operating band is the bank rate—the rate the Bank charges LVTS participants that require an overdraft loan to cover negative settlement balances. The lower limit is the rate the Bank pays LVTS participants with positive settlement balances.

2. The Bank of Canada targets the value of the overnight interest rate within its operating band, at the midpoint of the band. In doing so, the Bank intervenes in the overnight market using open-market buyback operations at the target rate. If the overnight rate is trading above the target rate, the Bank uses repos in which it purchases Government of Canada securities from primary dealers with an agreement to resell them on the next business day. If the overnight rate is too low relative to the target rate, the Bank uses reverse repos in which it sells Government of Canada securities to primary dealers with an agreement to buy them back on the next day.

3. The Bank uses government deposit shifting to neutralize public sector flows that affect LVTS participants' settlement balances—this in effect is a cash setting, a cash setting that is typically $25 million. Because its holdings of Government of Canada securities are often much smaller than its monetary liabilities, the Bank brings onto its balance sheet Exchange Fund Account assets to back its liabilities. These amounts are adjusted daily, depending on factors such as the level of financial institution borrowings and/or deposits.

4. In neutralizing the effects of open-market-buyback operations and of public sector flows on the level of settlement balances, and also in adjusting the level of settlement balances, the Bank of Canada uses transfers of government deposits (balances) between the government's account at the Bank of Canada and the government's accounts at the LVTS participants. These transfers are effected by twice daily auctions of federal government (Receiver General) balances, the first at 9:15 a.m. (which are collateralized) and the second at 4:15 p.m. (which are uncollateralized).

5. In normal times, the Bank of Canada relies mainly on its traditional monetary policy tools—standing liquidity facilities (lending and deposit facilities), settlement balances management, and lender-of-last-resort arrangements. At times of crisis, however, to address market failure and financial instability the Bank of Canada relies on discretionary liquidity operations whose maturity depends on their objective, independent of the maturity of the reference rate. For example, the Bank of Canada recently introduced new facilities to address aggregate system liquidity at times of financial instability—term PRAs and term securities lending.

6. A supply and demand analysis of the market for reserves in the United States yields the following results. When the Fed makes an open market purchase or lowers reserve requirements, the federal funds rate declines. When the Fed makes an open market sale or raises reserve requirements, the federal funds rate rises. Changes in the discount rate may also affect the federal funds rate.

KEY TERMS

direct clearers,   p. 433

Large Value Transfer System (LVTS),
   p. 432

LVTS participants,   p. 432

monetary conditions,   p. 440

multilateral netting,   p. 433

operating band,   p. 434

overnight interest rate (reference
   rate),   p. 433

overnight rate,   p. 431

policy rate,   p. 433

primary dealers,   p. 443

repos,   p. 443

reverse repos,   p. 443

Sale and Repurchase Agreements
   (SRAs),   p. 443

Special Purchase and Resale
   Agreements (SPRAs),   p. 443

standing lending facility,   p. 452

standing liquidity facilities,   p. 436

systemic risk,   p. 432

QUESTIONS

You will find the answers to the questions marked with an asterisk in the Textbook Resources section of your MyEconLab.

*1. If government deposits at the Bank of Canada are predicted to increase, what open market operations could be undertaken to neutralize the effect on settlement balances?

2. During the holiday season, when the public's holdings of currency increase, what open market operations typically occur? Why?

*3. If the government has just paid for major computer upgrades and as a result its deposits with the Bank of Canada fall, what open market operations could be undertaken?

4. "In the LVTS environment, government deposit shifting is effected by auctions of government balances." Discuss.

*5. Most open market operations are currently repurchase agreements. What does this tell us about the likely volume of open market operations relative to dynamic open market operations?

6. "The only way that the Bank of Canada can affect the level of advances is by adjusting the bank rate." Is this statement true, false, or uncertain? Explain your answer.

*7. If the Bank of Canada did not administer the operating band what do you predict would happen to the money supply if the bank rate were several percentage points below the overnight rate?

8. Discuss how the operating band affects interest rates and the money supply in the economy.

*9. "Last-resort lending is no longer needed because the presence of the CDIC eliminates the possibility of bank panics." Discuss.

10. The benefits of using last-resort lending to prevent bank panics are straightforward. What are the costs?

*11. You often read in the newspaper that the Bank of Canada has just lowered the target overnight rate. Does this signal that the Bank is moving to a more expansionary monetary policy? Why or why not?

12. How can the procyclical movement of interest rates (rising during business cycle expansions and falling during business cycle contractions) lead to a procyclical movement in the money supply as a result of the Bank of Canada's lending policy? Why might this movement of the money supply be undesirable?

*13. Explain how repos and reverse repos affect the overnight rate.

14. "The channel/corridor system for setting interest rates enables the Bank of Canada to set the overnight rate whatever the demand for reserves, including zero demand." Discuss.

*15. Compare the use of open market operations and government deposit shifting to control the money supply, using the following criteria: flexibility, reversibility, effectiveness, and speed of implementation.

QUANTITATIVE PROBLEM

CANSIM Question

1. Get the daily CANSIM data from January 2, 1996, to November 11, 2009, for the bank rate (series V39078) and the target overnight rate (series V39079) from the Textbook Resources area of the MyEconLab.
   a. What is the difference between the two series?
   b. Plot the two series.

   c. Calculate the upper and lower bounds of the operating band and plot the time path of the operating band.
   d. What does the time path of the operating band say about the easiness of monetary policy over this period?

WEB EXERCISES

1. Go to **www.bankofcanada.ca** and click on "Media Room" and then "Press Releases." Scroll down and click on the release regarding recent changes in the overnight rate of interest. Summarize the statement in one paragraph. Be sure to note whether the bank rate was increased or decreased. Now review the changes in the operating band for the overnight interest rate in the previous two press releases

regarding this issue. Has the stance of monetary policy changed?

2. Refer to Figure 17-1 on page 434. Go to **www.bankofcanada.ca** and scroll down on "Rates and Statistics." What is the current overnight rate target? What is the overnight rate? Is the difference between them what you would expect it to be?

Be sure to visit the MyEconLab website at **www.myeconlab.com**. This online homework and tutorial system puts you in control of your own learning with study and practice tools directly correlated to this chapter content.

CHAPTER 18

The Conduct of Monetary Policy: Strategy and Tactics

LEARNING OBJECTIVES

After studying this chapter you should be able to

1. assess the different types of monetary policy strategy
2. list the advantages and disadvantages of inflation targeting
3. specify the role of a nominal anchor in the conduct of monetary policy
4. outline Bank of Canada policy procedures from a historical perspective

PREVIEW

Getting monetary policy right is crucial to the health of the economy. Overly expansionary monetary policy leads to high inflation, which decreases the efficiency of the economy and hampers economic growth. Monetary policy that is too tight can produce serious recessions in which output falls and unemployment rises. It can also lead to deflation, a fall in the price level, such as occurred in the United States during the Great Depression and in Japan more recently. As we saw in Chapter 9, deflation can be especially damaging to an economy, because it promotes financial instability and can trigger financial crises.

Now that we understand the tools that central banks such as the Bank of Canada use to conduct monetary policy, we can consider how central banks *should* conduct monetary policy. To explore this subject, we first examine three monetary policy strategies, all of which focus on price stability as the primary, long-run goal of monetary policy. We then look at tactics, that is, the choice and setting of the monetary policy instrument in use. After examining the strategies and tactics, we can evaluate the Bank of Canada's conduct of monetary policy in the past, with the hope that it will give us some clues to where monetary policy may head in the future.

MONETARY TARGETING STRATEGY

In pursuing a strategy of **monetary targeting,** the central bank announces that it will achieve a certain value (the target) of the annual growth rate of a monetary aggregate, such as a 5% growth rate of M1+ or a 6% growth rate of M2+. The central bank then is accountable for hitting the target.

Monetary Targeting in the United States, Canada, Japan, and Germany

In the 1970s, monetary targeting was adopted by several countries—most notably, Germany, Switzerland, Canada, the United Kingdom, Japan, and the United States. Monetary targeting as practised during this decade was quite different from Milton Friedman's suggestion that the chosen monetary aggregate be targeted to grow at a constant rate. Indeed, in all of these countries, the central banks never adhered to strict, ironclad rules for monetary growth. In some of these countries, monetary targeting was not pursued very seriously.

UNITED STATES   In 1970, Arthur Burns was appointed chairman of the Board of Governors of the Federal Reserve, and soon thereafter the Fed stated that it was committing itself to the use of monetary targets to guide monetary policy. In 1975, in response to a congressional resolution, the Fed began to announce publicly its targets for money supply growth, though it often missed them. In October 1979, two months after Paul Volcker became chairman of the Board of Governors, the Fed switched to an operating procedure that focused more on nonborrowed reserves and control of the monetary aggregates and less on the federal funds rate. Despite the change in focus, the performance in hitting monetary targets was even worse: In all three years of the 1979–1982 period, the Fed missed its M1 growth target ranges. What went wrong?

There are several possible answers to this question. The first is that the U.S. economy was exposed to several shocks during this period that made monetary control more difficult: the acceleration of financial innovation and deregulation, which added new categories of deposits such as NOW (negotiable order of withdrawal) accounts to the measures of monetary aggregates; the imposition by the Fed of credit controls from March to July 1980, which restricted the growth of consumer and business loans; and the back-to-back recessions of 1980 and 1981–1982.[1]

A more persuasive explanation for poor monetary control, however, is that controlling the money supply was never really the intent of Volcker's policy shift. Despite Volcker's statements about the need to target monetary aggregates, he was not committed to these targets. Rather, he was far more concerned with using interest-rate movements to wring inflation out of the economy. Volcker's primary reason for changing the Fed's operating procedure was to free his hand to manipulate interest rates and thereby fight inflation. It was necessary to abandon interest-rate targets if Volcker were to be able to raise interest rates sharply when a slowdown in the economy was required to dampen inflation. This view of Volcker's strategy suggests that the Fed's announced attachment to monetary aggregate targets may have been a smokescreen to keep the Fed from being blamed for the high interest rates that would result from the new interest-rate policy.

In 1982, with inflation in check, the Fed decreased its emphasis on monetary targets. In July 1993, Board of Governors Chairman Alan Greenspan testified in Congress that the Fed would no longer use any monetary aggregates as a guide for conducting monetary policy.

CANADA   The Bank of Canada also made commitments to monetary targets around the same time as the Federal Reserve and had similar experiences to that in the United States. By the 1980s, it found that monetary aggregates were not a

---

[1] Another explanation focuses on the technical difficulties of monetary control when using a nonborrowed reserves operating target under a system of lagged reserve requirements, in which required reserves for a given week are calculated on the basis of the level of deposits two weeks earlier. See David Lindsey, "Nonborrowed Reserve Targeting and Monetary Control," in *Improving Money Stock Control*, ed. Laurence Meyer (Boston: Kluwer-Nijhoff, 1983), pp. 3–41.

reliable guide to monetary policy and, like the Federal Reserve, abandoned monetary targeting. Gerald Bouey, the governor of the Bank of Canada, described the Bank of Canada's experience colourfully by saying, "We didn't abandon monetary aggregates; they abandoned us." A more detailed description of monetary targeting in Canada is provided later in this chapter.

JAPAN The increase in oil prices in late 1973 was a major shock for Japan, which experienced a huge jump in the inflation rate, to greater than 20% in 1974—a surge facilitated by money growth in 1973 in excess of 20%. The Bank of Japan, like the other central banks discussed here, began to pay more attention to money supply growth rates. In 1978, the Bank of Japan began to announce "forecasts" at the beginning of each quarter for M2 + CDs. Although the Bank of Japan was not officially committed to monetary targeting, monetary policy appeared to be more money-focused after 1978. For example, after the second oil price shock in 1979, the Bank of Japan quickly reduced M2 + CDs growth, rather than allowing it to shoot up as occurred after the first oil shock. The Bank of Japan now conducts monetary policy with operating procedures that are similar in many ways to those of the Federal Reserve. It uses the interest rate in the Japanese inter-bank market (similar to the federal funds market) as its daily operating target, just as the Fed does.

The Bank of Japan's monetary policy performance during the 1978–1987 period was much better than the Fed's. Money growth in Japan slowed gradually, beginning in the mid-1970s, and was much less variable than in the United States. The outcome was a more rapid braking of inflation and a lower average inflation rate. In addition, these excellent results on inflation were achieved with lower variability in real output than in the United States.

In parallel with the United States and Canada, financial innovation and deregulation in Japan began to reduce the usefulness of the M2 + CDs monetary aggregate as an indicator of monetary policy. Because of concerns about the appreciation of the yen, the Bank of Japan significantly increased the rate of money growth from 1987 to 1989. Many observers blame speculation in Japanese land and stock prices (the *bubble economy*) on the increase in money growth. To reduce this speculation, in 1989 the Bank of Japan switched to a tighter monetary policy aimed at slower money growth. The aftermath was a substantial decline in land and stock prices and the collapse of the bubble economy.

As a result, the Japanese economy was in a slump for ten years, often referred to as the "lost decade." The collapse of land and stock prices helped provoke a severe banking crisis, discussed in Chapter 11, that was a severe drag on the economy. The resulting weakness of the economy even led to deflation, promoting further financial instability. The outcome was an economy that stagnated for over a decade. Many critics believe that the Bank of Japan has pursued overly tight monetary policy and needs to substantially increase money growth in order to lift the economy out of its stagnation.

GERMANY Starting in the mid-1970s and continuing through the next two decades, both Germany and Switzerland engaged in monetary targeting. The success of monetary targeting in controlling inflation in these two countries explains why monetary targeting still has strong advocates and is an element of the official policy regime for the European Central Bank (see the Global box, The European Central Bank's Monetary Policy Strategy). Because the success of the German monetary targeting regime in producing low inflation has received the most attention, we'll concentrate on Germany's experience.

GLOBAL   **The European Central Bank's Monetary Policy Strategy**

The European Central Bank (ECB) pursues a hybrid monetary policy strategy that has elements in common with the monetary-targeting strategy previously used by the Bundesbank but also includes some elements of inflation targeting.* Like inflation targeting, the ECB has an announced goal for inflation over the medium term of "below, but close to, 2%." The ECB's strategy has two key "pillars." First, monetary and credit aggregates are assessed for "their implications for future inflation and economic growth." Second, many other economic variables are used to assess the future economic outlook. (Until 2003, the ECB employed something closer to a monetary

target, setting a "reference value" for the growth rate of the M3 monetary aggregate.)

The ECB's strategy is somewhat unclear and has been subject to criticism for this reason. Although the "below, but close to, 2%" goal for inflation sounds like an inflation target, the ECB has repeatedly stated that it does not have an inflation target. This central bank seems to have decided to try to "have its cake and eat it, too" by not committing too strongly to either a monetary-targeting strategy or an inflation-targeting strategy. The resulting difficulty of assessing the ECB's strategy has the potential to reduce the accountability of the institution.

* For a description of the ECB's monetary policy strategy, go to the ECB's website at **www.ecb.int**.

Germany's central bank, the Bundesbank, chose to focus on a narrow monetary aggregate called *central bank money*, the sum of currency in circulation and bank deposits weighted by the 1974 required reserve ratios. In 1988, the Bundesbank switched targets from central bank money to M3.

The key fact about the monetary targeting regime in Germany is that it was not a Friedman-type monetary targeting rule in which a monetary aggregate is kept on a constant-growth-rate path and is the primary focus of monetary policy. The Bundesbank allowed growth outside of its target ranges for periods of two to three years, and overshoots of its targets were subsequently reversed. Monetary targeting in Germany was instead primarily a method of communicating the strategy of monetary policy focused on long-run considerations and the control of inflation.

The calculation of monetary target ranges puts great stress on making policy transparent (clear, simple, and understandable) and on regular communication with the public. First and foremost, a numerical inflation goal was prominently featured in the setting of target ranges. Second, monetary targeting, far from being a rigid policy rule, was flexible in practice. The target ranges for money growth were missed about 50% of the time in Germany, often because of the Bundesbank's concern about other objectives, including output and exchange rates. Furthermore, the Bundesbank demonstrated its flexibility by allowing its inflation goal to vary over time and to converge gradually to the long-run inflation goal.

The monetary targeting regime in Germany demonstrated a strong commitment to clear communication of the strategy to the general public. The money growth targets were continually used as a framework to explain the monetary policy strategy, and the Bundesbank expended tremendous effort in its publications and in frequent speeches by central bank officials to communicate to the public what the central bank was trying to achieve. Given that the Bundesbank frequently missed its money growth targets by significant amounts, its monetary targeting framework is best viewed as a mechanism for transparently communicating how monetary policy is being directed to achieve inflation goals and as a means for increasing the accountability of the central bank.

There are two key lessons to be learned from our discussion of German monetary targeting. First, a monetary targeting regime can restrain inflation in the longer run, even when the regime permits substantial target misses. Thus adherence to a rigid policy rule is not necessary to obtain good inflation outcomes. Second, the key reason why monetary targeting was reasonably successful, despite frequent target misses, is that the objectives of monetary policy were clearly stated and the central bank actively engaged in communicating the strategy of monetary policy to the public, thereby enhancing the transparency of monetary policy and the accountability of the central bank.

As we will see in the next section, these key elements of a successful monetary-targeting regime—flexibility, transparency, and accountability—are also important elements in inflation-targeting regimes. German monetary policy was actually closer in practice to inflation targeting than it was to Friedman-like monetary targeting, and thus might best be thought of as "hybrid" inflation targeting.

Advantages of Monetary Targeting

One advantage of monetary targeting is that information on whether the central bank is achieving its target is known almost immediately—figures for monetary aggregates are typically reported within a couple of weeks. Thus monetary targets can send almost immediate signals to the public and markets about the stance of monetary policy and the intentions of the policymakers to keep inflation in check. In turn, these signals help fix inflation expectations and produce less inflation. Monetary targets also allow almost immediate accountability for monetary policy to keep inflation low, thus helping to constrain the monetary policymaker from falling into the time-inconsistency trap.

Disadvantages of Monetary Targeting

All of the above advantages of monetary aggregate targeting depend on a big *if*: There must be a strong and reliable relationship between the goal variable (inflation or nominal income) and the targeted monetary aggregate. If the relationship between the monetary aggregate and the goal variable is weak, monetary aggregate targeting will not work; this seems to have been a serious problem in the United States and other countries that pursued monetary targets. The weak relationship implies that hitting the target will not produce the desired outcome on the goal variable and thus the monetary aggregate will no longer provide an adequate signal about the stance of monetary policy. As a result, monetary targeting will not help fix inflation expectations and will not be a good guide for assessing central bank accountability. In addition, an unreliable relationship between monetary aggregates and goal variables makes it difficult for monetary targeting to serve as a communications device that increases the transparency of monetary policy and makes the central bank accountable to the public.

INFLATION TARGETING

Given the breakdown of the relationship between monetary aggregates and goal variables such as inflation, many countries have recently adopted inflation targeting as their monetary policy strategy to achieve price stability. New Zealand was the first country to formally adopt inflation targeting in 1990, followed by

Canada in 1991, the United Kingdom in 1992, Sweden and Finland in 1993, and Australia and Spain in 1994. Israel, Chile, and Brazil, among others, have also adopted a form of inflation targeting.

Inflation targeting involves several elements: (1) public announcement of medium-term numerical targets for inflation; (2) an institutional commitment to price stability as the primary, long-run goal of monetary policy and a commitment to achieve the inflation goal; (3) an information-inclusive approach in which many variables (not just monetary aggregates) are used in making decisions about monetary policy; (4) increased transparency of the monetary policy strategy through communication with the public and the markets about the plans and objectives of monetary policymakers; and (5) increased accountability of the central bank for attaining its inflation objectives.

Inflation Targeting in New Zealand, Canada, and the United Kingdom

We begin our look at inflation targeting with New Zealand, because it was the first country to adopt it. We then go on to look at the experiences in Canada and the United Kingdom, which were next to adopt this strategy.[2]

NEW ZEALAND As part of a general reform of the government's role in the economy, the New Zealand parliament passed a new Reserve Bank of New Zealand Act in 1989, which became effective on February 1, 1990. Besides increasing the independence of the central bank, moving it from being one of the least independent to one of the most independent among the developed countries, the act committed the Reserve Bank to a sole objective of price stability. The act stipulated that the minister of finance and the governor of the Reserve Bank should negotiate and make public a Policy Targets Agreement, a statement that sets out the targets by which monetary policy performance will be evaluated, specifying numerical target ranges for inflation and the dates by which they are to be reached. An unusual feature of the New Zealand legislation is that the governor of the Reserve Bank is held highly accountable for the success of monetary policy. If the goals set forth in the Policy Targets Agreement are not satisfied, the governor is subject to dismissal.

The first Policy Targets Agreement, signed by the minister of finance and the governor of the Reserve Bank on March 2, 1990, directed the Reserve Bank to achieve an annual inflation rate within a 3–5% range. Subsequent agreements lowered the range to 0–2% until the end of 1996, when the range was changed to 0–3% and later to 1–3% in 2002. As a result of tight monetary policy, the inflation rate was brought down from above 5% to below 2% by the end of 1992 (see Figure 18-1, panel a), but at the cost of a deep recession and a sharp rise in unemployment. Since then, inflation has typically remained within the targeted range, with the exception of a brief period in 1995 when it exceeded the range by a few tenths of a percentage point. (Under the Reserve Bank Act, the governor, Donald Brash, could have been dismissed, but after parliamentary debate he was retained in his job.) Since 1992, New Zealand's growth rate has

---

[2] For further discussion of experiences with inflation targeting, particularly in other countries, see Leonardo Leiderman and Lars E. O. Svensson, *Inflation Targeting* (London: Centre for Economic Policy Research, 1995); Frederic S. Mishkin and Adam Posen, "Inflation Targeting: Lessons from Four Countries," Federal Reserve Bank of New York, *Economic Policy Review* 3 (August 1997), pp. 9–110; and Ben S. Bernanke, Thomas Laubach, Frederic S. Mishkin, and Adam S. Posen, *Inflation Targeting: Lessons from the International Experience* (Princeton: Princeton University Press, 1999).

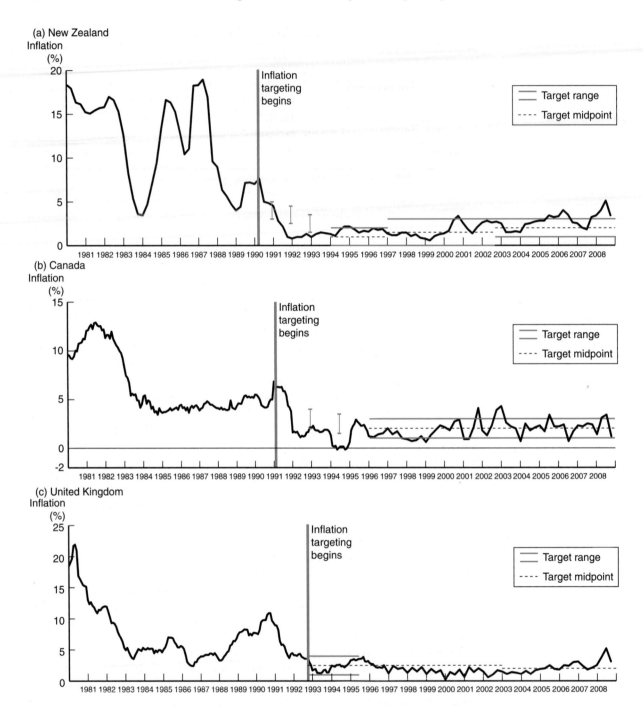

FIGURE 18-1   Inflation Rates and Inflation Targets for New Zealand, Canada, and the United Kingdom, 1980–2008

(a) New Zealand; (b) Canada; (c) United Kingdom

Source: Ben S. Bernanke, Thomas Laubach, Frederic S. Mishkin, and Adam S. Posen, *Inflation Targeting: Lessons from the International Experience* (Princeton: Princeton University Press, 1999), updates from the same sources, and **www.rbnz.govt.nz/statistics/econind/a3/ha3.xls**.

generally been high, with some years exceeding 5%, and unemployment has come down significantly.

CANADA   On February 26, 1991, a joint announcement by the minister of finance and the governor of the Bank of Canada established formal inflation targets. The target ranges were 2–4% by the end of 1992, 1.5–3.5% by June 1994, and 1–3% by December 1996. After the new government took office in late 1993, the target range was set at 1–3% from December 1995 until December 1998 and has been kept at this level. Canadian inflation has also fallen dramatically since the adoption of inflation targets, from above 5% in 1991, to a 0% rate in 1995, and to between 1 and 2% in the late 1990s (see Figure 18-1, panel b). As was the case in New Zealand, however, this decline was not without cost: Unemployment soared to above 10% from 1991 until 1994, but then declined substantially. A more detailed discussion of inflation targeting in Canada is provided later in this chaper.

UNITED KINGDOM   In October 1992, the United Kingdom adopted an inflation target as its nominal anchor, and the Bank of England began to produce an *Inflation Report*, a quarterly report on the progress being made in achieving that target. The inflation target range was initially set at 1–4% until the next election (spring 1997 at the latest), with the intent that the inflation rate should settle down to the lower half of the range (below 2.5%). In May 1997, the inflation target was set at 2.5% and the Bank of England was given the power to set interest rates henceforth, granting it a more independent role in monetary policy.

Before the adoption of inflation targets, inflation had already been falling in the United Kingdom, with a peak of 9% at the beginning of 1991 and a rate of 4% at the time of adoption (see Figure 18-1, panel c). After a small upward movement in early 1993, inflation continued to fall. By the third quarter of 1994, it was at 2.2%, within the intended range. Subsequently inflation rose, climbing slightly above the 2.5% level by 1996, but has remained close to the target since then. In December 2003, the target was changed to 2.0% for a slightly different measure of inflation. Meanwhile, growth of the U.K. economy has been strong, causing a substantial reduction in the unemployment rate.

Advantages of Inflation Targeting

Inflation targeting has several advantages over monetary targeting as a strategy for the conduct of monetary policy. With inflation targeting, stability in the relationship between money and inflation is not critical to its success, because it does not rely on this relationship. An inflation target allows the monetary authorities to use all available information, not just one variable, to determine the best settings for monetary policy.

Inflation targeting also has the key advantage that it is readily understood by the public and is thus highly transparent. Monetary targets, in contrast, are less likely to be easily understood by the public, and if the relationship between the growth rates of monetary aggregates and the inflation goal variable is subject to unpredictable shifts, as has occurred in many countries, monetary targets lose their transparency because they are no longer able to accurately signal the stance of monetary policy.

Because an explicit numerical inflation target increases the accountability of the central bank, inflation targeting has the potential to reduce the likelihood that the central bank will fall into the time-inconsistency trap of trying to expand output and employment in the short run by pursuing overly expansionary monetary policy. A key advantage of inflation targeting is that it can help focus the political debate on what a central bank can do in the long run—that is, control inflation, rather than what it cannot do, permanently increase economic growth and the number of jobs through expansionary monetary policy. Thus inflation targeting has the potential to reduce political pressures on the central bank to pursue inflationary monetary policy and thereby to reduce the likelihood of the time-inconsistency problem.

Inflation-targeting regimes also put great stress on making policy transparent and on regular communication with the public. Inflation-targeting central banks have frequent communications with the government, some mandated by law and some in response to informal inquiries, and their officials take every opportunity to make public speeches on their monetary policy strategy. While these techniques are also commonly used in countries that have not adopted inflation targeting, inflation-targeting central banks have taken public outreach a step further: Not only do they engage in extended public information campaigns, including the distribution of glossy brochures, but they also publish documents like the Bank of England's *Inflation Report*. The publication of these documents is particularly noteworthy, because they depart from the usual dull-looking, formal reports of central banks and use fancy graphics, boxes, and other eye-catching design elements to engage the public's interest.

The above channels of communication are used by central banks in inflation-targeting countries to explain the following concepts to the general public, financial market participants, and the politicians: (1) the goals and limitations of monetary policy, including the rationale for inflation targets; (2) the numerical values of the inflation targets and how they were determined; (3) how the inflation targets are to be achieved, given current economic conditions; and (4) reasons for any deviations from targets. These communications have improved private sector planning by reducing uncertainty about monetary policy, interest rates, and inflation; they have promoted public debate of monetary policy, in part by educating the public about what a central bank can and cannot achieve; and they have helped clarify the responsibilities of the central bank and of politicians in the conduct of monetary policy.

Another key feature of inflation-targeting regimes is the tendency toward increased accountability of the central bank. Indeed, transparency and communication go hand in hand with increased accountability. The strongest case of accountability of a central bank in an inflation-targeting regime is in New Zealand, where the government has the right to dismiss the Reserve Bank's governor if the inflation targets are breached, even for one quarter. In other inflation-targeting countries, the central bank's accountability is less formalized. Nevertheless, the transparency of policy associated with inflation targeting has tended to make the central bank highly accountable to the public and the government. Sustained success in the conduct of monetary policy as measured against a pre-announced and well-defined inflation target can be instrumental in building public support for a central bank's independence and for its policies. This building of public support and accountability occurs even in the absence of a rigidly defined and legalistic standard of performance evaluation and punishment.

The performance of inflation-targeting regimes has been quite good. Inflation-targeting countries seem to have significantly reduced both the rate of inflation and inflation expectations beyond what would likely have occurred in the absence of inflation targets. Furthermore, once down, inflation in these countries has stayed down; following disinflations, the inflation rate in targeting countries has not bounced back up during subsequent cyclical expansions of the economy.

Disadvantages of Inflation Targeting

Critics of inflation targeting cite four disadvantages of this monetary policy strategy: delayed signalling, too much rigidity, the potential for increased output fluctuations, and low economic growth. We look at each in turn and examine the validity of these criticisms.

DELAYED SIGNALLING   In contrast to exchange rates and monetary aggregates, inflation is not easily controlled by the monetary authorities. Furthermore, because of the long lags in the effects of monetary policy, inflation outcomes are revealed only after a substantial lag. Thus an inflation target is unable to send immediate signals to both the public and markets about the stance of monetary policy. However, we have seen that the signals provided by monetary aggregates may not be very strong. Hence, it is not at all clear that monetary targeting is superior to inflation targeting on these grounds.

TOO MUCH RIGIDITY   Some economists have criticized inflation targeting because they believe it imposes a rigid rule on monetary policymakers and limits on their ability to respond to unforeseen circumstances. However, useful policy strategies exist that are "rule-like," in that they involve forward-looking behaviour that limits policymakers from systematically engaging in policies with undesirable long-run consequences. Such policies avoid the time-inconsistency problem and would best be described as "constrained discretion."

Indeed, inflation targeting can be described exactly in this way. Inflation targeting, as actually practised, is far from rigid. First, inflation targeting does not prescribe simple and mechanical instructions on how the central bank should conduct monetary policy. Rather, it requires the central bank to use all available information to determine which policy actions are appropriate to achieve the inflation target. Unlike simple policy rules, inflation targeting never requires the central bank to focus solely on one key variable. Second, inflation targeting as practised contains a substantial degree of policy discretion. Inflation targets have been modified depending on economic circumstances, as we have seen. Moreover, central banks under inflation-targeting regimes have left themselves considerable scope to respond to output growth and fluctuations through several devices.

POTENTIAL FOR INCREASED OUTPUT FLUCTUATIONS   An important criticism of inflation targeting is that a sole focus on inflation may lead to monetary policy that is too tight when inflation is above target and thus may lead to larger output fluctuations. Inflation targeting does not, however, require a sole focus on inflation—in fact, experience has shown that inflation targeters display substantial concern about output fluctuations. All the inflation targeters have set their inflation targets above zero.[3] For example, currently New Zealand has the lowest midpoint for an inflation target, 1.5%, while Canada and Sweden set the midpoint of their inflation target at 2%; the United Kingdom and Australia currently have their midpoints at 2.5%.

The decision by inflation targeters to choose inflation targets above zero reflects the concern of monetary policymakers that particularly low inflation can have substantial negative effects on real economic activity. Deflation (negative inflation in which the price level actually falls) is especially to be feared because of the possibility that it may promote financial instability and precipitate a severe economic contraction (Chapter 9). The deflation in Japan in recent years has been an important factor in the weakening of the Japanese financial system and economy. Targeting inflation rates of above zero makes periods of deflation less likely. This

---

[3] Consumer price indexes have been found to have an upward bias in the measurement of true inflation, so it is not surprising that inflation targets would be chosen to exceed zero. However, the actual targets have been set to exceed the estimates of this measurement bias, indicating that inflation targeters have decided to have targets for inflation that exceed zero even after measurement bias is accounted for.

is one reason why some economists both within and outside of Japan have been calling on the Bank of Japan to adopt an inflation target at levels of 2% or higher.

Inflation targeting also does not ignore traditional stabilization goals. Central bankers in inflation-targeting countries continue to express their concern about fluctuations in output and employment, and the ability to accommodate short-run stabilization goals to some degree is built into all inflation-targeting regimes. All inflation-targeting countries have been willing to minimize output declines by gradually lowering medium-term inflation targets toward the long-run goal.

LOW ECONOMIC GROWTH   Another common concern about inflation targeting is that it will lead to low growth in output and employment. Although inflation reduction has been associated with below-normal output during disinflationary phases in inflation-targeting regimes, once low inflation levels were achieved, output and employment returned to levels at least as high as they were before. A conservative conclusion is that once low inflation is achieved, inflation targeting is not harmful to the real economy. Given the strong economic growth after disinflation in many countries (such as New Zealand) that have adopted inflation targets, a case can be made that inflation targeting promotes real economic growth, in addition to controlling inflation.

MONETARY POLICY WITH AN IMPLICIT NOMINAL ANCHOR

In recent years, the United States has achieved excellent macroeconomic performance (including low and stable inflation) without using an explicit nominal anchor such as a monetary aggregate or an inflation target. Although the Federal Reserve has not articulated an explicit strategy, a coherent strategy for the conduct of monetary policy exists nonetheless. This strategy involves an implicit but not an explicit nominal anchor in the form of an overriding concern by the Federal Reserve to control inflation in the long run. In addition, it involves forward-looking behaviour in which there is careful monitoring for signs of future inflation using a wide range of information, coupled with periodic "pre-emptive strikes" by monetary policy against the threat of inflation.

As emphasized by Milton Friedman, monetary policy effects have long lags. In industrialized countries with a history of low inflation, the inflation process seems to have tremendous inertia: Estimates from large macroeconometric models of the U.S. economy, for example, suggest that monetary policy takes over a year to affect output and over two years to have a significant impact on inflation. For countries that have experienced highly variable inflation, and therefore have more flexible prices, the lags may be shorter.

The presence of long lags means that monetary policy cannot wait to respond until inflation has begun. If the central bank waits until overt signs of inflation appear, it will already be too late to maintain stable prices, at least not without a severe tightening of policy: Inflation expectations will already be embedded in the wage- and price-setting process, creating an inflation momentum that will be hard to halt. Inflation becomes much harder to control once it has been allowed to gather momentum, because higher inflation expectations become ingrained in various types of long-term contracts and pricing agreements.

To prevent inflation from getting started, therefore, monetary policy needs to be forward-looking and pre-emptive. That is, depending on the lags from monetary policy to inflation, monetary policy needs to act long before inflationary pressures appear in the economy. For example, suppose it takes roughly two years for monetary policy to have a significant impact on inflation. In this case, even if inflation is currently low but policymakers believe inflation will rise over the next two years with an unchanged stance of monetary policy, they must tighten monetary policy *now* to prevent the inflationary surge.

Under Alan Greenspan, the Federal Reserve was successful in pursuing a pre-emptive monetary policy. For example, the Fed raised interest rates from 1994 to 1995 before a rise in inflation got a toehold. As a result, inflation not only did not rise, but fell slightly. This pre-emptive monetary policy strategy is clearly also a feature of inflation-targeting regimes, because monetary policy instruments are adjusted to take account of the long lags in their effects in an effort to hit future inflation targets. However, the Fed's policy regime might best be described as a "just do it" policy and differs from inflation targeting in that it does not officially have a nominal anchor and is much less transparent in its monetary policy strategy.

Advantages of the "Just Do It" Approach

The Fed's "just do it" approach, which has some of the key elements of inflation targeting, has many of the same advantages. It also does not rely on a stable money–inflation relationship. As with inflation targeting, the central bank uses many sources of information to determine the best settings for monetary policy. The Fed's forward-looking behaviour and stress on price stability also help to discourage overly expansionary monetary policy, thereby ameliorating the time-inconsistency problem.

Another key argument for the "just do it" strategy is its demonstrated success. The Federal Reserve has been able to reduce inflation in the United States from double-digit levels in 1980 to an average rate close to 3% over the last fifteen years, which is arguably consistent with the price-stability goal. At the same time, economic growth has been high, averaging around 3% over the same period, with relatively steady growth up until the subprime financial crisis hit the economy hard. Indeed, up until recently, the performance of the U.S. economy has been the envy of the industrialized world.

Disadvantages of the "Just Do It" Approach

Given the success of the "just do it" strategy in the United States, why should the United States consider other monetary policy strategies? (If it ain't broke, why fix it?) The answer is that the "just do it" strategy has some disadvantages that may cause it to work less well in the future.

One disadvantage of the strategy is its lack of transparency. The Fed's close-mouthed approach about its intentions gives rise to a constant guessing game about what it is going to do. This high level of uncertainty leads to unnecessary volatility in financial markets and creates doubt among producers and the general public about the future course of inflation and output. Furthermore, the opacity of its policymaking makes it hard to hold the Federal Reserve accountable to Congress and the general public: The Fed can't be held accountable if there are no predetermined criteria for judging its performance. Low accountability may make the central bank more susceptible to the time-inconsistency problem, whereby it may pursue short-term objectives at the expense of long-term ones.

Probably the most serious problem with the "just do it" approach is its strong dependence on the preferences, skills, and trustworthiness of the individuals in charge of the central bank. In recent years in the United States, Federal Reserve chairmen Alan Greenspan and Ben Bernanke and other Federal Reserve officials have emphasized forward-looking policies and inflation control, with great success. The Fed's prestige and credibility with the public have risen accordingly. But the Fed's leadership will periodically change, and there is no guarantee that it will be committed to the same approach. Nor is there any guarantee that the relatively good working relationship that has existed between the Fed and the executive branch will always continue. In a different economic or political environment, the Fed might face strong pressure to engage in over-expansionary policies, raising the possibility that time inconsistency may become a more serious problem. In the past, after a successful period of low inflation, the Federal Reserve has reverted to inflationary monetary policy—the 1970s are one example—and without an explicit nominal anchor, this could certainly happen again.

Another disadvantage of the "just do it" approach is that it has some inconsistencies with democratic principles. As described in Chapter 15, there are good reasons—notably, insulation from short-term political pressures—for the central bank to have some degree of independence, as the Federal Reserve currently does, and the evidence does generally support central bank independence. Yet the practical economic arguments for central bank independence coexist uneasily with the presumption that government policies should be made democratically, rather than by an elite group.

In contrast, inflation targeting can make the institutional framework for the conduct of monetary policy more consistent with democratic principles and avoid some of the above problems. The inflation-targeting framework promotes the accountability of the central bank to elected officials, who are given some responsibility for setting the goals for monetary policy and then monitoring the economic outcomes. However, under inflation targeting as it has generally been practised, the central bank has complete control over operational decisions, so that it can be held accountable for achieving its assigned objectives.

The Fed's monetary policy strategy may move more toward inflation targeting in the future, particularly with the appointment of Ben Bernanke, who has been an advocate of inflation targeting (see the Inside the Central Bank box, Chairman Bernanke and Inflation Targeting). As a study aid, the advantages and disadvantages of monetary targeting and the other monetary policy strategies are listed in Table 18-1.

TABLE 18-1 Advantages and Disadvantages of Different Monetary Policy Strategies

	Monetary Targeting	Inflation Targeting	Implicit Nominal Anchor
Advantages	Immediate signal on achievement of target	Simplicity and clarity of target	Does not rely on stable money–inflation relationship
		Does not rely on stable money–inflation relationship	Demonstrated success in United States
		Increased accountability of central bank	
		Reduced effects of inflationary shocks	
Disadvantages	Relies on stable money–inflation relationship	Delayed signal about achievement of target	Lack of transparency
		Could impose rigid rule (though has not in practice)	Success depends on individuals
		Larger output fluctuations if sole focus on inflation (though not in practice)	Low accountability

INSIDE THE CENTRAL BANK

Chairman Bernanke and Inflation Targeting

Ben Bernanke, a former professor at Princeton University, became the new Federal Reserve Chairman in February 2006, after serving as a member of the Board of Governors from 2002–2005 and then the chairman of the Council of Economic Advisors. Bernanke is a world-renowned expert on monetary policy and while an academic wrote extensively on inflation targeting, including articles and a book written with one of the authors of this text.*

Bernanke's writings suggest that he is a strong proponent of inflation targeting and increased transparency in central banks. In an important speech given at a conference at the Federal Reserve Bank of St. Louis in 2004 he described how the Federal Reserve might approach a movement toward inflation targeting.** Bernanke suggested that the Fed should announce a numerical value for its long-run inflation goal. Bernanke emphasized that announcing a numerical objective for inflation would be completely consistent with the Fed's dual mandate of achieving price stability and maximum employment, and therefore might be called a *mandate-consistent inflation objective*, because it would be set above zero to avoid deflations, which have harmful effects on employment. In addition, it would not be intended to be a short-run target that might lead to excessively tight control of inflation at the expense of overly high employment fluctuations.

Since becoming Fed Chairman, Bernanke has made it clear that any movement toward inflation targeting must result from a consensus within the Federal Open Market Committee (FOMC). After Chairman Bernanke set up a subcommittee to discuss Federal Reserve communication, which included discussions about announcing a specific numerical inflation objective, the FOMC made a partial step in the direction of inflation targeting in November 2007 when it announced a new communication strategy that lengthened the horizon for FOMC participants' inflation projections to three years. In many cases, the three-year horizon will be sufficiently long so that the projection for inflation under "appropriate policy" will reflect each participant's inflation objective because at that horizon inflation should converge with the long-run objective. A couple of relatively minor modifications could move the Fed even further toward inflation targeting. The first modification requires lengthening the horizon for the inflation projection. The goal would be to set a time sufficiently far off so that inflation would almost surely converge with its long-run value by then. Second, the FOMC participants would need to be willing to reach a consensus on a single value for the mandate-consistent inflation objective. With these two modifications, the longer-run inflation projections would in effect be an announcement of a specific numerical objective for the inflation rate and so serve as a flexible version of inflation targeting.*** Whether the U.S. Federal Reserve will move in this direction in the future is still highly uncertain.

*Ben S. Bernanke and Frederic S. Mishkin, "Inflation Targeting: A New Framework for Monetary Policy," *Journal of Economic Perspectives,* vol. 11, no. 2 (1997), Ben S. Bernanke, Frederic S. Mishkin and Adam S. Posen, "Inflation Targeting: Fed Policy After Greenspan," *Milken Institute Review* (Fourth Quarter, 1999): 48–56, Ben S. Bernanke, Frederic S. Mishkin and Adam S. Posen, "What Happens When Greenspan Is Gone," *Wall Street Journal,* January 5, 2000: p. A22, and Ben S. Bernanke, Thomas Laubach, Frederic S. Mishkin and Adam S. Posen, *Inflation Targeting: Lessons from the International Experience* (Princeton, NJ.: Princeton University Press, 1999).

**Ben S. Bernanke, "Inflation Targeting," Federal Reserve Bank of St. Louis, *Review,* vol 86, no. 4 (July/August 2004), pp. 165–168.

***See Frederic S. Mishkin, "Whither Federal Reserve Communications," speech given at the Petersen Institute for International Economics, Washington, D.C., July 28, 2008, available at **www.federalreserve.gov/newsevents/speech/mishkin20080728a.htm**.

TACTICS: CHOOSING THE POLICY INSTRUMENT

Now that we are familiar with the overall strategies for monetary policy, let's look at how monetary policy is conducted on a day-to-day basis. Central banks directly control the tools of monetary policy—open market operations, government deposit shifting, last-resort lending, and the overnight interest rate—but knowing the tools and the strategies for implementing a monetary policy does not tell us whether it is easy or tight. The **policy instrument** (also called an **operating instrument**) is a variable that responds to the central bank's tools and indicates the stance (easy or tight) of monetary policy. A central bank like the Bank of Canada has at its disposal two basic types of policy instruments: reserve aggregates (total reserves, nonborrowed reserves, the monetary base, and the nonborrowed base) and interest rates (overnight interest rate and other short-term interest rates). (Central banks in small countries can choose another policy instrument, the exchange rate, but we leave this topic to Chapter 20.) The policy instrument might be linked to an **intermediate target**, such as a monetary aggregate or a long-term interest rate. Intermediate targets stand between the policy instrument and the goals of monetary policy (e.g., price stability, output growth); they are not as directly affected by the tools of monetary policy, but might be more closely linked to the goals of monetary policy. As a study aid, Figure 18-2 shows a schematic of the linkages between the tools of monetary policy, policy instruments, intermediate targets, and the goals of monetary policy.

As an example, suppose the central bank's employment and inflation goals are consistent with a nominal GDP growth rate of 5%. The central bank might believe that the 5% nominal GDP growth rate will be achieved by a 4% growth rate for M2 (an intermediate target), which will in turn be achieved by a growth rate of 3% for nonborrowed reserves (the policy instrument). Alternatively, the central bank might believe that the best way to achieve its objectives would be to set the overnight interest rate (a policy instrument) at, say, 4%. Can the central bank choose to target both the nonborrowed-reserves and the overnight-interest-rate policy instruments at the same time? The answer is no. The application of supply and demand analysis to the market for reserves we developed in Chapter 17 explains why a central bank must choose one or the other.

Let's first see why an aggregate target involves losing control of the interest rate. Figure 18-3 contains a supply and demand diagram for the market for reserves. Although the central bank expects the demand curve for reserves to be at R^{d*}, it fluctuates between $R^{d'}$ and $R^{d''}$ because of changes in banks' desire to hold reserves. If the central bank has a nonborrowed-reserves target of NBR^* (say, because it has a

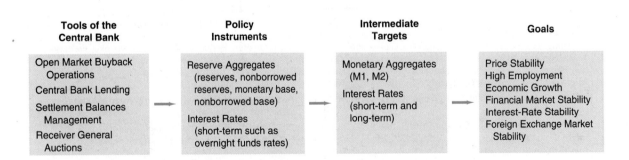

Tools of the Central Bank	Policy Instruments	Intermediate Targets	Goals
Open Market Buyback Operations Central Bank Lending Settlement Balances Management Receiver General Auctions	Reserve Aggregates (reserves, nonborrowed reserves, monetary base, nonborrowed base) Interest Rates (short-term such as overnight funds rates)	Monetary Aggregates (M1, M2) Interest Rates (short-term and long-term)	Price Stability High Employment Economic Growth Financial Market Stability Interest-Rate Stability Foreign Exchange Market Stability

FIGURE 18-2   Linkages Among Central Bank Tools, Policy Instruments, Intermediate Targets, and Goals of Monetary Policy

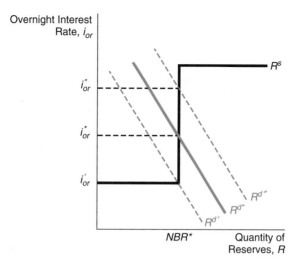

FIGURE 18-3   Result of Targeting on Nonborrowed Reserves

Targeting on nonborrowed reserves of NBR^* will lead to fluctuations in the overnight funds rate between i'_{or} and i''_{or} because of fluctuations in the demand for reserves between $R^{d'}$ and $R^{d''}$.

target growth rate of the money supply of 4%), it expects that the overnight funds rate will be i^*_{or}. However, as the figure indicates, the fluctuations in the reserves demand curve between $R^{d'}$ and $R^{d''}$ will result in a fluctuation in the overnight funds rate between i'_{or} and i''_{or}. Pursuing an aggregate target implies that interest rates will fluctuate.

The supply and demand diagram in Figure 18-4 shows the consequences of an interest-rate target set at i^*_{or}. Again the central bank expects the reserves demand curve to be at R^{d*}, but it fluctuates between $R^{d'}$ and $R^{d''}$ due to unexpected changes in banks' desire to hold reserves. If the demand curve rises to $R^{d''}$, the overnight funds rate will begin to rise above i^*_{or} and the central bank will

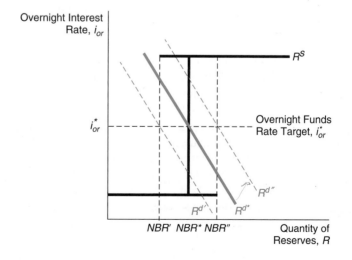

FIGURE 18-4   Result of Targeting on the Overnight Funds Rate

Targeting on the interest rate i^*_{or} will lead to fluctuation on nonborrowed reserves because of fluctuations in the demand for reserves between $R^{d'}$ and $R^{d''}$.

engage in SPRAs (repos) until it raises the supply of nonborrowed reserves to NBR'', at which point the equilibrium overnight funds rate is again at i^*_{or}. Conversely, if the demand curve falls to $R^{d'}$ and lowers the overnight funds rate, the central bank would keep entering into SRAs (reverse repos) until nonborrowed reserves fall to NBR' and the overnight funds rate is i^*_{or}. The central bank's adherence to the interest-rate target thus leads to a fluctuating quantity of nonborrowed reserves and the money supply.

The conclusion from the supply and demand analysis is that interest-rate and reserve (monetary) aggregate targets are incompatible. A central bank can hit one or the other, but not both. Because a choice between them has to be made, we need to examine what criteria should be used to select a policy instrument.

Criteria for Choosing the Policy Instrument

Three criteria apply when choosing a policy instrument: The instrument must be observable and measurable, it must be controllable by the central bank, and it must have a predictable effect on goals.

OBSERVABILITY AND MEASURABILITY   Quick observability and accurate measurement of a policy instrument is necessary, because it will be useful only if it signals the policy stance rapidly. Reserve aggregates like nonborrowed reserves are straightforward to measure, but there is still some lag in reporting of reserve aggregates (a delay of two weeks). Short-term interest rates like the overnight funds rate, by contrast, not only are easy to measure, but also are observable immediately. Thus, it seems that interest rates are more observable and measurable than are reserves and, therefore, are a better policy instrument.

However, as we learned in Chapter 4, the interest rate that is easiest to measure and observe is the nominal interest rate. It is typically a poor measure of the real cost of borrowing, which indicates with more certainty what will happen to the real GDP. This real cost of borrowing is more accurately measured by the real interest rate—that is, the interest rate adjusted for expected inflation ($i_r = i - \pi^e$). Unfortunately, real interest rates are extremely difficult to measure, because we do not have a direct way to measure expected inflation. Given that both interest rates and aggregates have observability and measurability problems, it is not clear whether one should be preferred to the other as a policy instrument.

CONTROLLABILITY   A central bank must be able to exercise effective control over a variable if it is to function as a useful policy instrument. If the central bank cannot control the policy instrument, knowing that it is off track does little good, because the central bank has no way of getting it back on track.

Because of shifts in and out of currency, even reserve aggregates such as nonborrowed reserves are not completely controllable. Conversely, the Bank of Canada can control short-term interest rates such as the overnight funds rate very tightly. It might appear, therefore, that short-term interest rates would dominate reserve aggregates on the controllability criterion. However, a central bank cannot set short-term real interest rates because it does not have control over expectations of inflation. Once again, a clear-cut case cannot be made that short-term interest rates are preferable to reserve aggregates as a policy instrument, or vice versa.

PREDICTABLE EFFECT ON GOALS   The most important characteristic of a policy instrument is that it must have a predictable effect on a goal. If a central bank can accurately and quickly measure the price of tea in China and can completely control its price, what good will that do? The central bank cannot use the price of tea in China to affect unemployment or the price level in its country. Because the ability to affect goals is so critical to the usefulness of any policy instrument, the tightness of the link from reserve or monetary aggregates to goals (output, employment, and inflation) or, alternatively, from interest rates to these goals, is a matter of much debate. In recent years, most central banks have concluded that the link between interest rates and goals such as inflation is tighter than the link between aggregates and inflation. For this reason, central banks throughout the world now generally use short-term interest rates as their policy instrument.

TACTICS: THE TAYLOR RULE

As we have seen, the Bank of Canada and most other central banks currently conduct monetary policy by setting a target for short-term interest rates like the overnight funds rate. But how should this target be chosen?

John Taylor of Stanford University has come up with an answer, called the **Taylor rule.** The Taylor rule indicates that the overnight rate should be set equal to the inflation rate plus an "equilibrium" real overnight rate, $\bar{i}_{or}$ (the real overnight rate that is consistent with full employment in the long run), plus a weighted average of two parts: (1) an inflation gap—current inflation, π, minus a target rate, π^*, and (2) an output gap—the percentage deviation of real GDP, y, from an estimate of its potential full employment level, $\bar{y}$.[4] This rule can be written as follows:

$$i_{or} = \pi + \bar{i}_{or} + \frac{1}{2}(\pi - \pi^*) + \frac{1}{2}(y - \bar{y})$$

where $\pi - \pi^*$ is the inflation gap and $y - \bar{y}$ is the output gap. Taylor has assumed that the equilibrium and overnight funds rate is 2% and that an appropriate target for inflation would also be 2%, with equal weights of 0.5% on the inflation and output gaps.

For an example of the Taylor rule in practice, suppose that the inflation rate is at 3%, leading to a positive inflation gap of 1% (= 3% − 2%), and real GDP is 1% above its potential, resulting in a positive output gap of 1%. Then the Taylor rule suggests that the overnight rate should be set at 6%,

$$i_{or} = 3\% + 2\% + \frac{1}{2}(1\% \text{ inflation gap}) + \frac{1}{2}(1\% \text{ output gap}) = 6\%$$

An important feature of the Taylor rule is that the coefficient on the inflation gap is positive and equal to 0.5. If the inflation rate rises by 1 percentage point, then the overnight interest-rate target is raised by 1.5 percentage points, and so by more than one-to-one. In other words, a rise in inflation by 1 percentage point leads to a real overnight rate increase of 0.5 percent. The principle that the monetary authorities should raise nominal interest rates by more than the increase in the inflation rate has been named the Taylor rule, and it is critical to the success of monetary policy. Suppose the Taylor rule is not followed and nominal rates rise by *less* than the rise in the inflation rate so that real interest rates *fall* when inflation rises. There will then be serious instability, because a rise in inflation leads to

[4] John B. Taylor, "Discretion Versus Policy Rules in Practice," *Carnegie-Rochester Conference Series on Public Policy* 39 (1993): 195–214. A more intuitive discussion with a historical perspective can be found in John B. Taylor, "A Historical Analysis of Monetary Policy Rules," in *Monetary Policy Rules,* ed. John B. Taylor (Chicago: University of Chicago Press, 1999), pp. 319–341.

an effective easing of monetary policy, which then leads to even higher inflation in the future.

The presence of an output gap in the Taylor rule might indicate that the Bank of Canada should care not only about keeping inflation under control, but also about minimizing business cycle fluctuations of output around its potential. Caring about both inflation and output fluctuations is consistent with many statements by Bank of Canada officials that controlling inflation and stabilizing real output are important concerns of the Bank of Canada.

An alternative interpretation of the presence of the output gap in the Taylor rule is that the output gap is an indicator of future inflation as stipulated in **Phillips curve theory.** Phillips curve theory indicates that changes in inflation are influenced by the state of the economy relative to its productive capacity, as well as to other factors. This productive capacity can be measured by potential GDP, which is a function of the natural rate of unemployment, the rate of unemployment consistent with full employment. A related concept is the **NAIRU**, the **nonaccelerating inflation rate of unemployment,** the rate of unemployment at which there is no tendency for inflation to change.[5] Simply put, the theory states that when the unemployment rate is above NAIRU with output below potential, inflation will come down, but if it is below NAIRU with output above potential, inflation will rise. Prior to 1995, the NAIRU was thought to reside around 8%. However, with the decline in unemployment in the late 1990s, with no increase in inflation and even a slight decrease, some critics have questioned the value of Phillips curve theory. Either they claim that it just doesn't work any more or alternatively believe that there is great uncertainty about the value of NAIRU. Phillips curve theory is now highly controversial, and many economists believe that it should not be used as a guide for the conduct of monetary policy.

As Figure 18-5 shows, the Taylor rule does a pretty good job of describing the Bank of Canada's setting of the overnight rate. Does this mean that the Bank of Canada should fire all its economists and put a computer in charge that just has to compute the Taylor rule setting for the overnight interest rate? This would certainly save taxpayers a lot of money.

There are several reasons why the answer is no. First, monetary policy has long lags, that is, it takes a long time for policy actions to affect the economy. Therefore, monetary policy necessarily needs to be forward looking. Good monetary policy requires that the Bank of Canada forecast where inflation and economic activity are going to be in the future, and then adjust the policy instrument accordingly. The Bank of Canada will therefore look at a much wider range of information than just the current inflation rate and output gap in setting policy, as is done in the Taylor rule. Second, no one really knows what the true model of the economy is. Monetary policymakers therefore need to apply a lot of judgement in deciding what the appropriate stance of monetary policy should be. In other words, the conduct of monetary policy is as much an art as it is a science. The Taylor rule leaves out all the art, and so is unlikely to produce the best monetary policy outcomes. Third, the economy is changing all the time, so the Taylor rule coefficients would be unlikely to stay constant. Fourth, financial crises such as the recent

---

[5] There are, however, subtle differences between the two concepts, as is discussed in Arturo Estrella and Frederic S. Mishkin, "The Role of NAIRU in Monetary Policy: Implications of Uncertainty and Model Selection," in *Monetary Policy Rules,* ed. John Taylor (Chicago: University of Chicago Press, 1999): 405–430.

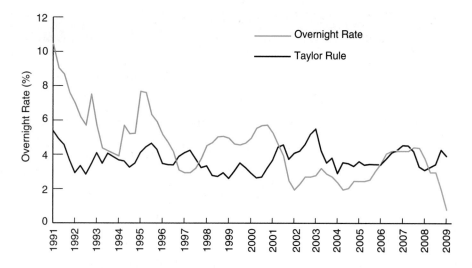

FIGURE 18-5   The Taylor Rule for the Overnight Interest Rate, 1991–2009

Source: Statistics Canada CANSIM II Series V41690926, V122514, and V41707125, and authors' calculations.

subprime meltdown may require very different monetary policy, because changes in credit spreads may alter the relationship between the overnight rate and other interest rates more relevant to investment decisions, and therefore to economic activity. The bottom line is that putting monetary policy on autopilot with a Taylor rule with fixed coefficients would be a bad idea.

Given the above reasons, it is no surprise that the Taylor rule does not explain all the movements in the overnight rate shown in Figure 18-5. For this reason, financial institutions hire central bank watchers, as described in the Inside the Central Bank box, Bank of Canada Watching. The Taylor rule is, however, useful as a guide to monetary policy. If the setting of the policy instrument is very different from what the Taylor rule suggests, then policymakers should ask whether they have a good reason for deviating from this rule. If they don't, then they might be making a mistake.

CENTRAL BANKS' RESPONSE TO ASSET-PRICE BUBBLES: LESSONS FROM THE SUBPRIME CRISIS

Over the centuries, economies have been periodically subject to asset-price bubbles, pronounced increases in asset prices that depart from fundamental values, which eventually crash resoundingly. The story of the subprime financial crisis in the United States, discussed in Chapter 9, indicates how costly these bubbles can be. The bursting of the asset-price bubble in the U.S. housing market brought down the financial system, leading to an economic downturn, a rise in unemployment, disrupted communities, and direct hardship for families forced to leave their homes after foreclosures.

The high cost of asset-price bubbles raises the question: What should central banks do about them? Should they use monetary policy to try to pop bubbles? Are there regulatory measures they can take to rein in asset-price bubbles? To answer these questions, we need to ask whether there are different kinds of bubbles that require different types of response.

INSIDE THE CENTRAL BANK

Bank of Canada Watching

As we have seen, the most important player in the determination of the Canadian money supply and interest rates is the Bank of Canada. When the Bank wants to inject reserves into the system, it conducts open market purchases of bonds, which cause the bond prices to increase and their interest rates to fall, at least in the short term. If the Bank withdraws reserves from the system, it sells bonds, thereby depressing their price and raising their interest rates. From a longer-run perspective, if the Bank pursues an expansionary monetary policy with high money growth, inflation will rise and, as we saw in Chapter 5, interest rates will rise as well. Contractionary monetary policy is likely to lower inflation in the long run and lead to lower interest rates.

Knowing what actions the Bank of Canada might be taking can thus help investors and financial institutions to predict the future course of interest rates with greater accuracy. Because, as we have seen, changes in interest rates have a major impact on investors' and financial institutions' profits, they are particularly interested in scrutinizing the Bank's behaviour. To assist in this task, financial institutions hire so-called *Bank of Canada watchers,* experts on Bank of Canada behaviour who may have worked in the Bank and so have an insider's view of Bank operations. A Bank of Canada watcher who can accurately predict the course of monetary policy is a very valuable commodity, and successful Bank of Canada watchers therefore often earn very high salaries, well into the six-figure range and sometimes even higher.

Two Types of Asset-Price Bubbles

There are two types of asset-price bubbles: those driven by credit and those driven purely by overly optimistic expectations (which former chairman of the Federal Reserve Alan Greenspan referred to as "irrational exuberance").

CREDIT-DRIVEN BUBBLES   When a credit boom begins, it can spill over into an asset-price bubble: Easier credit terms can be used to purchase particular assets and thereby raise their prices. The rise in asset values in turn encourages further lending for these assets, either because it increases the value of collateral, making it easier to borrow, or because it raises the value of capital at financial institutions, which gives them more capacity to lend. The lending for these assets then can increase demand for them further and hence raise their prices even more. This feedback loop—in which a credit boom drives up asset prices, which in turn fuels the credit boom, which drives asset prices even higher, and so on—can generate a bubble in which asset prices rise well above their fundamental values.

Credit-driven bubbles are particularly dangerous, as the recent subprime financial crisis has demonstrated. When asset prices come back down to earth and the bubble bursts, the collapse in asset prices then leads to a reversal of the feedback loop in which loans go sour, lenders cut back on the credit supply, the demand for assets declines further, and prices drop even more. These were exactly the dynamics in housing markets during the subprime financial crisis. Driven by a credit boom in subprime lending, housing prices rose way above fundamental values; but when housing prices crashed, credit shrivelled up and housing prices plummeted.

The resulting losses on subprime loans and securities eroded the balance sheets of financial institutions, causing a decline in credit (deleveraging) and a sharp fall in business and household spending, and therefore in economic activity. As we saw during the subprime financial crisis, the interaction between housing prices and the health of financial institutions following the collapse of the housing price bubble endangered the operation of the financial system as a whole and had dire consequences for the economy.

BUBBLES DRIVEN SOLELY BY IRRATIONAL EXUBERANCE   Bubbles that are driven solely by overly optimistic expectations, but which are not associated with a credit boom, pose much less risk to the financial system. For example, the bubble in technology stocks in the late 1990s (described in Chapter 7) was not fuelled by credit, and the bursting of the tech-stock bubble was not followed by a marked deterioration in financial institution balance sheets. The bursting of the tech-stock bubble thus did not have a very severe impact on the economy and the recession that followed was quite mild. Bubbles driven solely by irrational exuberance are therefore far less dangerous than those driven by credit booms.

Should Central Banks Respond to Bubbles?

One view is that central banks should not respond to bubbles. It is argued that bubbles are nearly impossible to identify. If central banks or government officials knew that a bubble was in progress, why wouldn't market participants know as well? If so, then a bubble would be unlikely to develop, because market participants would know that prices were getting out of line with fundamentals. This argument applies very strongly to asset-price bubbles that are driven by irrational exuberance, as is often the case for bubbles in the stock market. Unless central bank or government officials are smarter than market participants, which is unlikely given the especially high wages that savvy market participants garner, they will be unlikely to identify when bubbles of this type are occurring. There is then a strong argument for not responding to these kinds of bubbles.

On the other hand, when asset-price bubbles are rising rapidly at the same time that credit is booming, there is a greater likelihood that asset prices are deviating from fundamentals, because laxer credit standards are driving asset prices upward. In this case, central bank or government officials have a greater likelihood of identifying that a bubble is in progress; this was indeed the case during the housing market bubble in the United States because these officials did have information that lenders had weakened lending standards and that credit extension in the mortgage markets was rising at abnormally high rates.

Should Monetary Policy Try to Prick Asset-Price Bubbles?

Not only are credit-driven bubbles possible to identify, but as we saw above, they are the ones that are capable of doing serious damage to the economy. There is thus a strong case for central banks to respond to possible credit-driven bubbles. But what is the appropriate response? Should monetary policy be used to try to prick a possible asset-price bubble that is associated with a credit boom by raising interest rates above what is desirable for keeping the economy on an even keel? Or are there other measures that are more suited to deal with credit-driven bubbles?

There are three strong arguments against using monetary policy to prick bubbles by raising interest rates more than is necessary for achieving price stability and minimizing economic fluctuations. First, even if an asset-price bubble is of the credit-driven variety and so can be identified, the effect of raising interest rates on asset prices is highly uncertain. Although some economic analysis suggests that raising interest rates can diminish rises in asset prices, raising interest rates may be very ineffective in restraining the bubble, because market participants expect such high rates of return from buying bubble-driven assets. Furthermore, raising interest rates has often been found to cause a bubble to burst more severely, thereby increasing the damage to the economy. Another way of saying this is that bubbles are departures from normal behaviour, and it is unrealistic to expect that the usual tools of monetary policy will be effective in abnormal conditions.

Second, there are many different asset prices, and at any one time a bubble may be present in only a fraction of assets. Monetary policy actions are a very blunt instrument in such cases, as such actions would be likely to affect asset prices in general, rather than the specific assets that are experiencing a bubble.

Third, monetary policy actions to prick bubbles can have harmful effects on the aggregate economy. If interest rates are raised significantly to curtail a bubble, the economy will slow, people will be thrown out of work, and inflation can fall below its desirable level. Indeed, as the first two arguments suggest, the rise in interest rates necessary to prick a bubble may be so high that it can only be done at great cost to workers and the economy. This is not to say that monetary policy should not respond to asset prices per se. As we will see in Chapter 25, the level of asset prices does affect aggregate demand and thus the evolution of the economy. Monetary policy should react to fluctuations in asset prices to the extent that they affect inflation and economic activity.

Although it is controversial, the basic conclusion from the above reasoning is that monetary policy should not be used to prick bubbles.

Are Other Types of Policy Responses Appropriate?

As argued above, there is a case for responding to credit-driven bubbles because they are more identifiable and can do great damage to the economy, but monetary policy does not seem to be the way to do it. Regulatory policy to affect what is happening in credit markets in the aggregate, referred to as **macroprudential regulation**, on the other hand, does seem to be the right tool for the job of reining in credit-driven bubbles.

Financial regulation and supervision, either by central banks or other government entities which have the usual elements of a well-functioning prudential regulatory and supervisory system described in Chapter 10, can prevent excessive risk-taking that can trigger a credit boom, which in turn leads to an asset-price bubble. These elements include adequate disclosure and capital requirements, prompt corrective action, close monitoring of financial institutions' risk-management procedures, and close supervision to enforce compliance with regulations. More generally, regulation should focus on preventing future feedback loops from credit booms to asset prices, asset prices to credit booms, and so on. As the subprime financial crisis in the United States demonstrated, the rise in asset prices that accompanied the credit boom resulted in higher capital buffers at financial institutions, supporting further lending in the context of unchanging capital requirements; in the bust, the value of the capital dropped precipitously, leading to a cut in lending. Capital requirements that are countercyclical, that is, adjusted upward during a boom and downward during a bust, might help eliminate the pernicious feedback loops that promote credit-driven bubbles.

A rapid rise in asset prices accompanied by a credit boom provides a signal that market failures or poor financial regulation and supervision might be causing a bubble to form. Central banks and other government regulators could then consider implementing policies to rein in credit growth directly or implement measures to make sure credit standards are sufficiently high.

An important lesson from the subprime financial crisis is that central banks and other regulators should not have a laissez-faire attitude and let credit-driven bubbles proceed without any reaction. Appropriate macroprudential regulation can help limit credit-driven bubbles and improve the performance of both the financial system and the economy.

BANK OF CANADA POLICY PROCEDURES: HISTORICAL PERSPECTIVE

The well-known adage "The road to hell is paved with good intentions" applies as much to the Bank of Canada as it does to human beings. Understanding a central bank's goals and the strategies it can use to pursue them cannot tell us how monetary policy is actually conducted. To understand the practical results of the theoretical underpinnings, we have to look at how the Bank of Canada has actually conducted policy in the past. This historical perspective not only will show us how our central bank carries out its duties but also will help us interpret the Bank's activities and see where Canadian monetary policy may be heading in the future.

The Early Years

From the end of World War II in 1945 until the early 1970s, the world economy operated under a system of fixed exchange rates, known as the Bretton Woods system (to be discussed in detail in Chapter 20). Initially, Canada opted out of this system, but joined in 1962 and participated with the exchange rate fixed at 92.5 U.S. cents. Even before 1962, Canadian monetary policy had been driven by the goal of maintaining a stable exchange rate with the United States and the Bank of Canada therefore kept short-term interest rates more or less in step with U.S. interest rates. This meant that short-term interest rates, or the differential between U.S. and Canadian rates, were the intermediate target of monetary policy. As a result, inflation rates and interest rates followed generally similar patterns in the two countries (see, for example, Figure 18-6).

In 1971, Canada switched to a flexible exchange rate regime, but the Bank of Canada continued to adjust short-term interest rates to keep the foreign exchange and domestic bonds markets functioning smoothly, and paid no attention to the growth rate of money. As a result, monetary policy was quite expansionary in the early 1970s and the inflation rate increased to double digits—in fact, the price level increased by 11% in 1974 compared to only 3% in 1971. By the mid-1970s there was little doubt that one consequence of the policy of using interest rates as the intermediate target was that the Bank of Canada did not concern itself with the rate of growth of the money supply, as measured by the monetary aggregates.

By the end of this period there was also a wide consensus among central banks around the world that fluctuations in money contained useful information about income and prices. This evidence contributed to the rise of **monetarism,** a theory that emphasizes a steady, predictable rate of growth in the monetary aggregates, to be discussed in Chapter 24. It led the Bank of Canada and many other central banks, including the Federal Reserve, the Bank of England, the Bundesbank, the Swiss National Bank, and the Bank of Japan, to adopt key monetary aggregates as the intermediate targets of monetary policy.

Monetary Targeting, 1975–1981

In response to rising inflation in the early 1970s, in 1975 the Bank of Canada introduced a program of "monetary gradualism," under which M1 growth would be controlled within a gradually falling target range (see Table 18-2). The change in monetary strategy did not extend to a change in operating procedures—the Bank continued to use an interest rate as its operating target. The idea was to announce

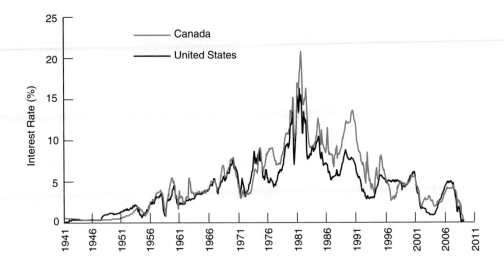

FIGURE 18-6   Interest Rates (90-Day T-bills), Canada and the United States, 1941–2009

Source: Statistics Canada CANSIM II Series V122541, and Federal Reserve Economic Data (FRED).

(about one year) in advance the target path for the growth of M1 and then adjust policy during the course of the year to make the actual growth rate lie within the target range. The rationale for announcing the monetary policy targets in advance was to influence people's expectations, with the hope that this would help bring down actual inflation faster than otherwise. Moreover, the Bank decided to target M1 because it was the most prominent measure of money with a very stable demand.

As can be seen from Table 18-2, the Bank of Canada was successful at keeping actual M1 growth within the target range, and the goal of reducing M1 growth

TABLE 18-2   Canadian M1 Target Ranges and Actual Growth Rates for 1975–1980

Announcement Date	Base Period	M1 Growth Target (%)	Outcome (%)
November 1975	April–June 1975	10–15	9.3
August 1976	February–April 1976	8–12	7.7
October 1977	June 1977	7–11	9.3
September 1978	June 1978	6–10	5.1
December 1979	April–June 1979	5–9	5.9
February 1981	August–October 1980	4–8	0.4

Notes: Outcomes are annualized growth rates (%) of seasonally adjusted M1 between the base period and the next announcement of new targets. For example, the outcome corresponding to the November 1975 announcement is the annualized growth rate of M1 between April and June 1975 and August 1976.

Source: Ben Bernanke and Frederic Mishkin, "Central Bank Behaviour and the Strategy of Monetary Policy: Observations from Six Industrialised Countries." *NBER Macroeconomics Annual* (1992): 183–228. Reprinted with permission of the authors.

was achieved by the end of the decade. However, the inflation rate accelerated, and by the end of the 1970s, it was almost at the same level as when monetary gradualism was introduced in 1975. What went wrong? Why did the inflation rate remain high? The answers to these questions lie in a series of financial innovations that reduced the demand for M1 balances. In particular, the introduction of new kinds of bank deposit accounts, and the development of cash management techniques for corporate accounts, motivated individuals and firms to move out of demand deposits—part of M1—into new chequable savings deposits—part of M2. This increased the growth rate of M2 and reduced the growth rate of M1 at the same time that M1 growth was being targeted, thereby rendering what seemed like tight anti-inflationary policy one that was in fact accommodating inflation.

By 1978, only three years after monetary targeting had begun, the Bank of Canada began to distance itself from this strategy out of concern for the nominal exchange rate, which had been depreciating. In particular, when interest rates in the United States increased sharply in late 1979, the Bank of Canada had to choose between allowing Canadian rates to increase to prevent an outflow of financial capital or allowing the exchange rate to depreciate to accommodate the spread in interest rates between the two countries. The Bank responded with an extremely restrictive monetary policy to resist depreciation of the Canadian dollar and the possible inflationary shock from import prices. Not surprisingly, M1 growth was negative in 1981 even though the target range was for growth between 4% and 8% (see Table 18-2), and Canadian interest rates increased to unprecedented levels (see Figure 18-6). The cost was the very deep 1981–1982 recession, the most severe since the 1930s.

Because of the conflict with exchange rate goals, as well as the uncertainty about M1 as a reliable guide to monetary policy, monetary targeting was formally abandoned in November 1982.

The Checklist Approach, 1982–1988

The period following 1982 was one of groping. With the abandonment of M1 targets, the Bank of Canada switched its focus to a range of broader monetary aggregates, such as M2 and M2+, but no aggregate was found that would be suitable as a guide for conducting monetary policy. As a result, the Bank adopted what came to be called the "checklist" approach to policy, meaning that it looked at a list of factors in order to design and implement monetary policy. The Bank's checklist included the interest rate, the exchange rate, and with less weight attached to it, the money supply. The goal of monetary policy was inflation containment in the short term and price stability in the long term.

The Bank's anti-inflation policy during the 1982–1988 period can be viewed as one where the interest rate became the operating target and the exchange rate was the intermediate target. Throughout most of the period the Bank targeted interest rates, resisting depreciation of the Canadian dollar (fearing that depreciation would worsen inflation). The Bank's policy, however, had been undertaken against the backdrop of a persistent federal budget deficit that led to higher interest rates, making it difficult for the Bank to control money growth and inflation. In fact inflation had begun to increase again and the Bank responded with a dramatic reversal of its ad hoc monetary strategy. It announced early in 1988 that short-term issues would henceforth guide policy less and that price stability would be the Bank's long-term objective of monetary policy.

Inflation Targeting, 1989–Present

The adoption of inflation targets in Canada followed a three-year campaign by the Bank of Canada to promote price stability as the long-term goal of monetary policy. Beginning with the Hanson Lecture at the University of Alberta in January 1988, the newly appointed Bank of Canada governor, John Crow, announced that the Bank would subsequently pursue an objective of price stability (or zero inflation).[6] Initially, the policy of zero inflation took the form of a return to the high interest rates of the early 1980s. For example, during 1987 through 1989, interest rates increased and the Canadian dollar appreciated by more than would have normally been expected under previous regimes. The idea was that higher interest rates and a stronger dollar would lower aggregate demand and eventually bring inflation down.

In this most recent attempt at lowering inflation, the Bank of Canada, however, followed a different strategy, by announcing explicit targets for its ultimate goal—the inflation rate—rather than for an intermediate variable such as money growth. In particular, in February 1991 the Bank's governor and the minister of finance jointly announced a series of declining inflation targets, with a band of plus and minus one percentage point around them. The targets were 3% by the end of 1992, falling to 2% by the end of 1995, to remain within a range of 1% to 3% thereafter. The 1% to 3% target range for inflation was renewed in December 1995, in early 1998, May 2001, and again in November 2006, to apply until the end of 2011.[7] The midpoint of the current inflation target range, 2%, is regarded as the most desirable outcome.

In setting its inflation targets, the Bank uses the rate of change in the CPI because of its "headline" quality—it is the most commonly used and understood price measure in Canada. Moreover, the CPI comes out monthly and without revisions, whereas other price indexes, such as the GDP deflator, are frequently revised. However, because headline CPI (all items) includes volatile components such as food, energy, and the effect of indirect taxes, the Bank, in order to avoid responses to short-run fluctuations, prefers to use and report inflation in "core CPI," which excludes volatile components. A core inflation rate is useful in assessing whether trend inflation is on track for the medium term. Also, defining the inflation targets in terms of ranges provides the Bank sufficient flexibility to deal with supply shocks beyond those already taken care of by the exclusion of volatile components from core inflation.

The move to targeting directly a goal of policy rather than an intermediate variable represented a significant shift in Bank of Canada policy procedures. An implication of this change was that the Bank had to broaden its information gathering to include variables containing significant information about future inflation. It has since used the overnight interest rate as the operating target and indicated that a range of monetary aggregates is useful in guiding policy along with an index of monetary conditions based on interest rates and exchange rates. The main purpose of this index is to capture the two key monetary policy transmission mechanisms in an open economy—the one operating through interest rates and the one operating through exchange rates.

What are the results of Canada's inflation-targeting monetary policy? Figure 18-1 (panel B) on page 468 plots the Canadian inflation rate for each year since 1980 and shows the Bank's target range since 1996. Clearly, inflation has fallen dramatically since the adoption of inflation targets, from above the 5% level in 1991 to a 1% rate in 1998, being most of the time in the lower half of the target range. However, this decline was not without cost: unemployment soared to above the 10% level from 1991 until 1994 but has since fallen. What is difficult to say is whether explicit inflation targets are the only way to achieve good macroeconomic outcomes. As the Bank's former governor, Gordon Thiessen, put it, "It is too early to draw very strong conclusions

---

[6] Zero inflation should be interpreted as a small positive rate of measured inflation.

[7] The 1995 and 1998 inflation-control agreements between the Bank of Canada and the government had a three-year horizon. However, the 2006 agreement, like the 2001 agreement, has a five-year horizon, reflecting the wide acceptance of the targets after over fifteen years of operation.

about the impact of inflation targets on actual economic performance in Canada. We really do require a longer period of time for targets to demonstrate their ability to deal successfully with the peak of an economic upturn without the trend of inflation moving persistently outside the target range."[8]

From Opaqueness to Openness and Accountability

The historical record of the Bank of Canada's conduct of monetary policy reveals that during the 1960s and 1970s, the Bank operated in an environment characterized by instrument and goal opaqueness. The use of multiple instruments and goals tended to shield the Bank from scrutiny and accountability; the public was not able to comprehend the Bank's actions, allowing the accountability of the Bank of Canada to deteriorate.

Over the past decade, however, as John Chant, a former Special Adviser at the Bank of Canada, recently put it ". . . the Bank of Canada has transformed its conduct of monetary policy by focusing on an explicit inflation-control target, establishing a Governing Council for decision-making, announcing a target overnight interest rate, and adopting fixed action dates for making policy changes."[9] These changes (and in particular the adoption of inflation targets) have moved the Bank away from opaqueness, towards openness and accountability.

Pre-emptive Strikes Against Economic Downturns and Financial Disruptions

The recognition that monetary policy needs to be more forward looking has prompted the Bank of Canada to be more pre-emptive. The Bank has not only engaged in pre-emptive strikes against a rise in inflation, but it has acted pre-emptively against negative shocks to aggregate demand and especially to those associated with financial disruptions.

With the onset of the financial crisis in August 2007, the Bank of Canada began to ease policy even in the face of a strong economy with growth close to 3% in the third quarter of 2007, unemployment below 6%, and inflation rising because of the increase in energy prices. The potential for the financial disruption to weaken the economy and to produce an adverse feedback loop—in which credit markets would worsen and weaken economic activity, which in turn would further weaken credit markets—encouraged the Bank of Canada to take pre-emptive action, cutting the overnight interest rate by 25 basis points in December of 2007 to 4.25%. Subsequent easing of monetary policy lowered the overnight funds rate to 0.25% by April of 2009. At the same time, the Bank of Canada implemented large liquidity injections into the credit markets to try to get them working again (as discussed in the previous chapter).

These pre-emptive attacks against negative shocks to aggregate demand were particularly successful in the past in keeping economic fluctuations very mild. The magnitude of the financial disruption during the recent financial crisis, however, was so great that the pre-emptive actions by the Bank of Canada were not enough to contain the crisis, and the economy suffered accordingly.

---

[8] Gordon G. Thiessen, "The Canadian Experience with Targets for Inflation Control," *Canadian Public Policy* 24 (1998), p. 425. For a more detailed discussion of Canada's experience with inflation targets, see also Charles Freedman, "Inflation Targeting and the Economy: Lessons from Canada's First Decade," *Contemporary Economic Policy* 19 (2001), pp. 2–19, and Ben Bernanke, Thomas Laubach, Frederic Mishkin, and Adam Posen, *Inflation Targeting: Lessons from the International Experience* (Princeton: Princeton University Press, 1998).

[9] John Chant, "The Bank of Canada: Moving Towards Transparency," *Bank of Canada Review* (Spring 2003): 5–13.

International Considerations

The growing integration and interdependence of national economies (a process known as **globalization**) has brought international considerations to the forefront of Bank of Canada policymaking in recent years. With integrated financial markets, the Bank of Canada's monetary policy is also influenced by developments outside Canada. This is not a bad thing, but requires international policy cooperation to reduce potential disruptions to domestic policymaking and promote greater stability in financial markets. International cooperation has been encouraged by the process of **international policy coordination** (in which countries agree to enact policies cooperatively).

International considerations also played a role in the initiatives recently undertaken by the International Monetary Fund and the Bank for International Settlements, following the G-7 Halifax Summit in 1995, to improve the functioning of international financial markets. These initiatives seek to maximize the benefits of financial globalization, reduce the risks of financial instability that unrestrained capital flows may cause, and develop mechanisms for support in times of financial crisis. For example, the issue of international financial stability played a role in the Federal Reserve's decision to lower the federal funds rate by 3/4 of a percentage point in the fall of 1998. Concerns about the potential for worldwide financial crisis in the wake of the collapse of the Russian financial system at that time and weakness in other economies, particularly in Asia, stimulated the Fed to take a dramatic step to calm down markets.

International considerations, although not the primary focus of the Bank of Canada, are also likely to be a major factor in the conduct of Canadian monetary policy in the future.

SUMMARY

1. Monetary targeting has the advantage that information on whether the central bank is achieving its target is known almost immediately. Monetary targeting suffers from the disadvantage that it works well only if there is a reliable relationship between the monetary aggregate and the goal variable, inflation—a relationship that has often not held in various countries.

2. Inflation targeting has several advantages: (1) It enables monetary policy to focus on domestic considerations; (2) stability in the relationship between money and inflation is not critical to its success; (3) it is readily understood by the public and is highly transparent; (4) it increases accountability of the central bank; and (5) it appears to ameliorate the effects of inflationary shocks. It does have some disadvantages, however: (1) Inflation is not easily controlled by the monetary authorities, so that an inflation target is unable to send immediate signals to both the public and markets; (2) it might impose a rigid rule on policymakers, although this has not been the case in practice; and (3) a sole focus on inflation may lead to larger output fluctuations, although this has also not been the case in practice.

3. The Federal Reserve has a strategy of having an implicit, not an explicit, nominal anchor. This strategy

has the following advantages: (1) It enables monetary policy to focus on domestic considerations; (2) it does not rely on a stable money–inflation relationship; and (3) it has had demonstrated success, producing low inflation with the longest business-cycle expansion in U.S. history. However, it does have some disadvantages: (1) It has a lack of transparency; (2) it is strongly dependent on the preferences, skills, and trustworthiness of individuals in the central bank and the government; and (3) it has some inconsistencies with democratic principles, because the central bank is not highly accountable.

4. Because interest-rate and aggregate policy instruments are incompatible, a central bank must choose between them on the basis of three criteria: measurability, controllability, and the ability to affect goal variables predictably. Unfortunately, these criteria do not establish an overwhelming case for one set of policy instruments over another.

5. The Taylor rule indicates that the overnight funds rate should be set equal to the inflation rate plus an "equilibrium" real funds rate plus a weighted average of two gaps: (1) an inflation gap, current inflation minus a target rate, and (2) an output gap, the percentage deviation of real GDP from an estimate of its potential full employment level. The output gap in

the Taylor rule could represent an indicator of future inflation as stipulated in Phillips curve theory. However, this theory is controversial, because high output relative to potential as measured by low unemployment has not seemed to produce higher inflation in recent years.

6. There are two types of bubbles: credit-driven bubbles, which are highly dangerous and so deserve a response from central banks; and bubbles driven solely by irrational exuberance, which do not warrant central bank response. Although there are

strong arguments against using monetary policy to attempt to prick bubbles, appropriate macroprudential regulation to rein in credit-driven bubbles can improve the performance of both the financial system and the economy.

7. The historical record of the Bank of Canada's conduct of monetary policy reveals that the Bank has switched its operating targets many times, returning to an overnight interest rate target in recent years, with pre-emptive strikes against both inflation and economic downturns.

KEY TERMS

globalization,   p. 490

inflation targeting,   p. 467

intermediate target,   p. 476

international policy coordination,   p. 490

macroprudential regulation,   p. 484

monetarism,   p. 485

monetary targeting,   p. 462

nonaccelerating inflation rate of unemployment (NAIRU),   p. 480

Phillips curve theory,   p. 480

policy instrument (operating instrument),   p. 476

Taylor rule,   p. 479

QUESTIONS

You will find the answers to the questions marked with an asterisk in the Textbook Resources section of your MyEconLab.

*1. "Unemployment is a bad thing, and the government should make every effort to eliminate it." Do you agree or disagree? Explain your answer.

2. Classify each of the following as either a policy instrument or an intermediate target, and explain why.
   a. The three-month treasury bill rate
   b. The monetary base
   c. M2+

*3. "If the demand for reserves did not fluctuate, the Bank of Canada could pursue both a money supply target and an interest-rate target at the same time." Is this statement true, false, or uncertain? Explain your answer.

4. If the Bank of Canada has an interest-rate target, why will an increase in the demand for reserves lead to a rise in the money supply?

*5. What procedures can the Bank of Canada use to control the overnight funds rate? Why does control of this interest rate imply that the Bank will lose control of nonborrowed reserves?

6. Compare the monetary base to M2+ on the grounds of controllability and measurability. Which do you prefer as an intermediate target? Why?

*7. "Interest rates can be measured more accurately and more quickly than reserve aggregates. Hence an

interest rate is preferred over the reserve aggregates as a policy instrument." Do you agree or disagree? Explain your answer.

8. What are the benefits of using a nominal anchor for the conduct of monetary policy?

9. Give an example of the time-inconsistency problem that you experience in your everyday life.

10. What incentives arise for a central bank to fall into the time-inconsistency trap of pursuing overly expansionary monetary policy?

*11. What are the advantages of monetary targeting as a strategy for the conduct of monetary policy?

12. What is the big *if* necessary for the success of monetary targeting? Does the experience with monetary targeting suggest that the big *if* is a problem?

*13. What methods have inflation-targeting central banks used to increase communication with the public and increase the transparency of monetary policymaking?

14. Why might inflation targeting increase support for the independence of the central bank to conduct monetary policy?

*15. "Because the public can see whether a central bank hits its monetary targets almost immediately, whereas it takes time before the public can see whether an inflation target is achieved, monetary targeting makes central banks more accountable than inflation targeting does." Is this statement true, false, or uncertain? Explain your answer.

16. "Because inflation targeting focuses on achieving the inflation target, it will lead to excessive output fluctuations." Is this statement true, false, or uncertain? Explain your answer.

*17. What are the most important advantages and disadvantages of nominal GDP targeting over inflation targeting?

18. "The failure of the Bank of Canada to control the money supply in the 1970s and 1980s suggests that the Bank is not able to control the money supply." Do you agree or disagree? Explain your answer.

*19. What is the advantage that monetary targeting, inflation targeting, and a monetary strategy with an implicit, but not an explicit, nominal anchor have in common?

20. How can bank behaviour and the Bank of Canada's behaviour cause money supply growth to be procyclical (rising in booms and falling in recessions)?

WEB EXERCISES

1. Go to **www.bankofcanada.ca**, and click on "About the Bank" and then "What We Do."
   a. Review the Bank of Canada's main functions.
   b. How does the Bank's monetary policy contribute to rising living standards for Canadians?

2. It is possible to access other central bank websites to learn about their structure. One example is the European Central Bank. Go to **www.ecb.int/index. html**. On the ECB home page, locate the current exchange rate between the euro and the U.S. dollar. It was initially set at 1 to 1. What is it now?

3. Many countries have central banks that are responsible for their nation's monetary policy. Go to **www.bis.org/cbanks.htm** and select one of the central banks (for example, Norway). Review that bank's website to determine its policies regarding application of monetary policy. How does this bank's policies compare to those of the Bank of Canada?

Be sure to visit the MyEconLab website at **www.myeconlab.com**. This online homework and tutorial system puts you in control of your own learning with study and practice tools directly correlated to this chapter content.

PART VI

International Finance and Monetary Policy

CRISIS AND RESPONSE: FOREIGN EXCHANGE MARKET TURMOIL AND THE IMF

From 2002 until 2008, the Canadian dollar steadily increased in value relative to the U.S. dollar. With the credit markets seizing up in September and October of 2008, however, the U.S. dollar appreciated sharply. The same "flight to quality" that led investors to step up their purchases of U.S. Treasury securities also led them to want to hold more U.S. dollars, thereby bidding up the dollar's value relative to other currencies, including the Canadian dollar.

This good news for the U.S. dollar was often bad news for other currencies. Many countries in Latin America and Eastern Europe found their currencies in free fall. The International Monetary Fund (IMF) stepped in and set up a new lending facility to make loans to distressed countries with fewer strings attached than was true for the IMF's previous lending programs. The IMF started making loans to the tune of billions of dollars. The IMF, which had looked like it was on the sidelines as the subprime financial crisis spread worldwide, now was moving to front and centre.

The subprime crisis has demonstrated that events in the United States have worldwide ramifications and that international financial institutions like the IMF have an important role in responding to make sure that the international financial system continues to work well. Chapter 19 outlines how the foreign exchange market functions and how exchange rates between different countries' currencies are determined. In Chapter 20, we examine how the international financial system operates and how it affects monetary policy.

CHAPTER 19

The Foreign Exchange Market

LEARNING OBJECTIVES

After studying this chapter you should be able to

1. summarize the basic function performed by the foreign exchange market
2. identify the factors that lead to changes in the exchange rate in the long run
3. identify the factors that lead to changes in the exchange rate in the short run
4. explain why changes in the money supply lead to *exchange rate overshooting* (causing the exchange rate to change by more in the short run than in the long run)

PREVIEW

In the late 1980s and early 1990s, Canadian businesses became less competitive with their counterparts in the United States; afterwards their competitiveness increased. Did this swing in competitiveness occur primarily because Canadian management fell down on the job in the late 1980s and early 1990s and then got its act together afterwards? Not really. Canadian business became less competitive in the late 1980s and early 1990s because Canadian dollars became worth more in terms of U.S. dollars, making Canadian goods more expensive relative to U.S. goods. By the late 1990s and early 2000s, the value of the Canadian dollar had fallen appreciably from its highs in the late 1980s, making Canadian goods cheaper and Canadian businesses more competitive.

The price of one currency in terms of another (say euros per Canadian dollar) is called the **exchange rate**. As you can see in Figure 19-1, exchange rates are highly volatile. The exchange rate affects the economy and our daily lives because when the Canadian dollar becomes more valuable relative to foreign currencies, foreign goods become cheaper for Canadians and Canadian goods become more expensive for foreigners. When the Canadian dollar falls in value, foreign goods become more expensive for Canadians and Canadian goods become cheaper for foreigners.

Fluctuations in the exchange rate also affect both inflation and output, and are an important concern to monetary policymakers. When the Canadian dollar falls in value, the higher prices of imported goods feed directly into a higher price level and inflation. A declining Canadian dollar, which makes Canadian goods cheaper for foreigners, increases the demand for Canadian goods and leads to higher production and output.

We begin our study of international finance by examining the **foreign exchange market**, the financial market where exchange rates are determined.

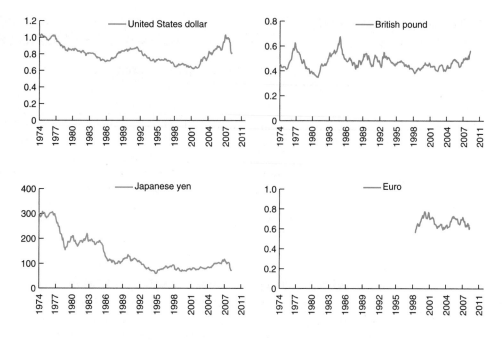

FIGURE 19-1   Canadian Exchange Rates, 1974–2009

Canadian dollar prices of selected foreign currencies (monthly averages). Note that a decline in these plots means a weakening of the Canadian dollar, and an increase indicates a strengthening of the Canadian dollar.

Source: Statistics Canada CANSIM II Series V37426, V37430, V37456, and V21570998.

FOREIGN EXCHANGE MARKET

Most countries of the world have their own currencies: Canada has its dollar; the European Monetary Union, its euro; Brazil, its real; and China, its yuan. Trade between countries involves the mutual exchange of different currencies (or, more usually, assets denominated in different currencies). When a Canadian firm buys foreign goods, services, or financial assets, for example, Canadian dollars (typically, assets denominated in Canadian dollars) must be exchanged for foreign currency (assets denominated in the foreign currency).

The trading of currency and assets denominated in particular currencies takes place in the foreign exchange market. Transactions conducted in the foreign exchange market determine the rates at which currencies are exchanged, which in turn determine the cost of purchasing foreign goods and financial assets.

What Are Foreign Exchange Rates?

There are two kinds of exchange rate transactions. The predominant ones, called **spot transactions**, involve the immediate (two-day) exchange of assets. **Forward transactions** involve the exchange of assets at some specified future date. The **spot exchange rate** is the exchange rate for the spot transaction, and the **forward exchange rate** is the exchange rate for the forward transaction.

When a currency increases in value, it experiences **appreciation**; when it falls in value and is worth fewer Canadian dollars, it undergoes **depreciation**. At the beginning of 1999, for example, the euro was valued at 1.76 Canadian dollars, and (as indicated in the Financial News box, Foreign Exchange Rates)

FINANCIAL NEWS

Foreign Exchange Rates

Foreign exchange rates are published daily in the financial pages of newspapers and on the web. The entries from Bloomberg, shown here, are explained in the text.

The entry for the Canadian dollar (CAD) gives the cross rate for several currencies on November 18, 2009. For example, we find that the Canadian dollar per euro (EUR) exchange rate is $1.5798 by looking across the Canadian dollar row for the euro column. To find the U.S. dollar (USD) price of euros, we look across the U.S. dollar row for the euro column and see that USD/euro = USD 1.494.

By dividing USD/euro by CDN/euro, we find the implied cross rate for USD = 0.9457, which is the same as the rate that we find by looking across the U.S. dollar row for the Canadian dollar column.

	USD	EUR	JPY	GPB	CHF	CAD	AUD	HKD
HKD	7.75	11.5789	0.0866	12.958	7.6625	7.3294	7.185	
AUD	1.0786	1.6115	0.0121	1.8035	1.0665	1.0201		0.1392
CAD	1.0574	1.5798	0.0118	1.768	1.0455		0.9803	0.1364
CHF	1.0114	1.5111	0.0113	1.6911		0.9565	0.9377	0.1305
GBP	0.5981	0.8936	0.0067		0.5913	0.5656	0.5545	0.0772
JPY	89.48	133.6876		149.6106	88.4697	84.6235	82.9569	11.5458
EUR	0.6693		0.0075	1.1191	0.6618	0.633	0.6205	0.0864
USD		1.494	0.0112	1.672	0.9887	0.9457	0.9271	0.129

Source: Reprinted from Bloomberg.com with permission on November 18, 2009.

on November 18, 2009, it was valued at 1.5798 dollars. The euro *depreciated* by 10.24%: (1.5798 − 1.76)/1.76 = −10.24%. Equivalently, we could say that the Canadian dollar, which went from a value of 0.57 euros per dollar at the beginning of 1999 to a value of 0.63 euros per dollar on November 18, 2009, *appreciated* by 10.53%: (0.63 − 0.57)/0.57 = 10.53%

Why Are Exchange Rates Important?

Exchange rates are important because they affect the relative price of domestic and foreign goods. The dollar price of French goods to a Canadian is determined by the interaction of two factors: the price of French goods in euros and the euro/dollar exchange rate.

Suppose that Wanda the Winetaster, a Canadian, decides to buy a bottle of 1961 (a very good year) Château Lafite Rothschild to complete her wine cellar. If the price of the wine in France is 1000 euros and the exchange rate is $1.32 to the euro, the wine will cost Wanda $1320 (1000 euros × $1.32/euro).[1]

---

[1] Throughout this book we use the symbol $ for the Canadian dollar. We denote the United States dollar using the symbol US$.

Now suppose that Wanda delays her purchase by two months, at which time the dollar has appreciated to $1.50 per euro. If the domestic price of the bottle of Lafite Rothschild remains 1000 euros, its dollar cost will have risen from $1320 to $1500.

The same currency appreciation, however, makes the price of foreign goods in that country less expensive. At an exchange rate of $1.32 per euro, a Dell computer priced at $2000 costs Pierre the Programmer 1515 euros; if the exchange rate increases to $1.50 per euro, the computer will cost him only 1333 euros.

A depreciation of the euro lowers the cost of French goods in Canada but raises the cost of Canadian goods in France. If the euro drops in value to $1.20, Wanda's bottle of Lafite Rothschild will cost her only $1200 instead of $1320, and the Dell computer will cost Pierre 1667 euros rather than 1515.

Such reasoning leads to the following conclusion: ***when a country's currency appreciates (rises in value relative to other currencies), the country's goods abroad become more expensive and foreign goods in that country become cheaper (holding domestic prices constant in the two countries). Conversely, when a country's currency depreciates, its goods abroad become cheaper and foreign goods in that country become more expensive.***

Depreciation of a currency makes it easier for domestic manufacturers to sell their goods abroad and makes foreign goods less competitive in domestic markets. From 2002 to 2008, the appreciating Canadian dollar hurt Canadian industries trying to sell more goods, but helped Canadian consumers because foreign goods were less expensive. The price of French wine and cheese and the cost of vacationing abroad fell as a result of the strong Canadian dollar.

How Is Foreign Exchange Traded?

You cannot go to a centralized location to watch exchange rates being determined; currencies are not traded on exchanges such as the Toronto Stock Exchange. Instead, the foreign exchange market is organized as an over-the-counter market in which several hundred dealers (mostly banks) stand ready to buy and sell assets denominated in foreign currencies. Because these dealers are in constant telephone and computer contact, the market is very competitive; in effect, it functions no differently from a centralized market.

An important point to note is that while banks, companies, and governments talk about buying and selling currencies in foreign exchange markets, they do not take a fistful of dollars and sell them for British pound notes. Rather, most trades involve the buying and selling of assets denominated in different currencies. So when we say that a bank is buying euros in the foreign exchange market, what we actually mean is that the bank is buying *assets denominated in euros.* The volume in this market is colossal, exceeding $1 trillion per day.

Trades in the foreign exchange market consist of transactions in excess of $1 million. The market that determines the exchange rates shown in the Financial News box is not where one would buy foreign currency for a trip abroad. Instead, we buy foreign currency in the retail market from dealers such as Thomas Cook or from banks. Because retail prices are higher than wholesale, when we buy foreign exchange, we obtain fewer units of foreign currency per dollar than exchange rates in the box indicate.

EXCHANGE RATES IN THE LONG RUN

Like the price of any good or asset in a free market, exchange rates are determined by the interaction of supply and demand. To simplify our analysis of exchange rates in a free market, we divide it into two parts. First, we examine how exchange rates are determined in the long run; then we use our knowledge of the long-run determinants of the exchange rate to help us understand how they are determined in the short run.

Law of One Price

The starting point for understanding how exchange rates are determined is a simple idea called the **law of one price**: if two countries produce an identical good, and transportation costs and trade barriers are very low, the price of the good should be the same throughout the world no matter which country produces it.

Suppose that Canadian steel costs $100 per tonne and identical Japanese steel costs 10 000 yen per tonne. For the law of one price to hold true, the exchange rate between the yen and the dollar must be 100 yen per dollar ($0.01 per yen) so that one tonne of Canadian steel sells for 10 000 yen in Japan (the price of Japanese steel) and one tonne of Japanese steel sells for $100 in Canada (the price of Canadian steel). If the exchange rate were 200 yen to the dollar, Japanese steel would sell for $50 per tonne in Canada or half the price of Canadian steel, and Canadian steel would sell for 20 000 yen per tonne in Japan, twice the price of Japanese steel. Because Canadian steel would be more expensive than Japanese steel in both countries and is identical to Japanese steel, the demand for Canadian steel would go to zero. Given a fixed dollar price for Canadian steel, the resulting excess supply of Canadian steel will be eliminated only if the exchange rate falls to 100 yen per dollar, making the price of Canadian steel and Japanese steel the same in both countries.

APPLICATION   Law of One Price

Recently, the yen price of Japanese steel has increased by 10% (to 11 000 yen) relative to the dollar price of Canadian steel (unchanged at $100). By what amount must the dollar increase or decrease in value for the law of one price to hold true?

Solution

For the law of one price to hold, the exchange rate must rise to 110 yen per dollar, which is a 10% appreciation of the dollar.

The exchange rate rises to 110 yen so that the price of Japanese steel in dollars remains unchanged at $100 (=11 000 yen/110 yen per dollar). In other words, the 10% depreciation of the yen (10% appreciation of the dollar) just offsets the 10% increase in the yen price of the Japanese steel.

**Theory of
Purchasing
Power Parity**

One of the most prominent theories of how exchange rates are determined is the **theory of purchasing power parity (PPP)**. It states that exchange rates between any two currencies will adjust to reflect changes in the price levels of the two countries. The theory of PPP is simply an application of the law of one price to national price levels rather than to individual prices.

As the Application above illustrates, if the law of one price holds, a 10% rise in the yen price of Japanese steel results in a 10% appreciation of the dollar. Applying the law of one price to the price levels in the two countries produces the theory of purchasing power parity, which maintains that if the Japanese price level rises 10% relative to the Canadian price level, the dollar will appreciate by 10%. As our Canadian/Japanese application illustrates, *the theory of PPP suggests that if one country's price level rises relative to another's, its currency should depreciate (the other country's currency should appreciate).*

Another way of thinking about purchasing power parity is through a concept called the **real exchange rate**, the rate at which domestic goods can be exchanged for foreign goods. In effect, it is the price of domestic goods relative to the price of foreign goods denominated in the domestic currency. For example, if a basket of goods in Toronto costs $50, while the cost of the same basket of goods in Tokyo costs $75 because it costs 7500 yen while the exchange rate is at 100 yen per dollar, then the real exchange rate is 0.66 (= $50/$75). The real exchange rate is below 1.0, indicating that it is cheaper to buy a basket of goods in Canada than in Japan. It is the real exchange rate that indicates whether a currency is relatively cheap or not. Another way of describing PPP is to say that the real exchange rate is always equal to 1.0, so that the purchasing power of the dollar is the same as the purchasing power of other currencies such as the yen or the euro.

As our Canadian/Japanese example demonstrates, the theory of PPP suggests that if one country's price level rises relative to another's, its currency should depreciate (the other country's currency should appreciate). As you can see in Figure 19-2, this prediction is borne out in the long run. Yet, as the same figure indicates, PPP theory often has little predictive power in the short run. So even though PPP theory provides some guidance to the long-run movement of exchange rates, it is not perfect and in the short run is a particularly poor predictor (see the FYI box, The Purchasing Power Parity Puzzle). What explains PPP theory's failure to predict well?

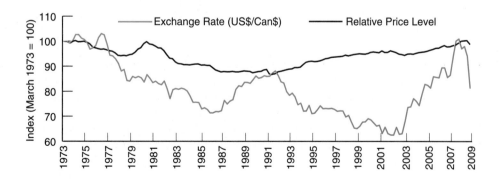

FIGURE 19-2   Purchasing Power Parity, Canada/United States, 1973–2008

Source: International Monetary Fund, *International Financial Statistics.* Reprinted with permission.

FYI   The Purchasing Power Parity Puzzle

The theory of purchasing power parity has attracted a great deal of attention and has been explored extensively in the recent literature using recent advances in the field of applied econometrics. Based on the law of one price, the theory asserts that relative goods prices are not affected by exchange rates—or, equivalently, that exchange rate changes will be proportional to relative inflation. The relationship is important not only because it has been a cornerstone of exchange rate models in international economics, but also because of its policy implications—it provides a benchmark exchange rate and therefore has some practical appeal for policymakers and exchange rate arbitragers.

Empirical studies generally fail to find support for long-run purchasing power parity, especially during the recent floating exchange rate period. In fact, the empirical consensus is that purchasing power parity does not hold over this period. But there are also studies covering different groups of countries as well as studies covering periods of long duration or country pairs experiencing large differentials in price movements that report evidence consistent with the theory of purchasing power parity. For an excellent discussion of the purchasing power parity puzzle, see Kenneth Rogoff, "The Purchasing Power Parity Puzzle," *Journal of Economic Literature* 34 (1996): 647–668.

Why the Theory of Purchasing Power Parity Cannot Fully Explain Exchange Rates

The PPP conclusion that exchange rates are determined solely by changes in relative price levels rests on the assumption that all goods are identical in both countries and that transportation costs and trade barriers are very low. When this assumption is true, the law of one price states that the relative prices of all these goods (that is, the relative price level between the two countries) will determine the exchange rate. The assumption that goods are identical may not be too unreasonable for Canadian and Japanese steel, but is it a reasonable assumption for Canadian and Japanese cars? Is a Toyota the equivalent of a Chevrolet?

Because Toyotas and Chevys are obviously not identical, their prices do not have to be equal. Toyotas might be more expensive relative to Chevys and both Canadians and Japanese will still purchase Toyotas. Because the law of one price does not hold for all goods, a rise in the price of Toyotas relative to Chevys will not necessarily mean that the yen must depreciate by the amount of the relative price increase of Toyotas over Chevys.

PPP theory furthermore does not take into account that many goods and services (whose prices are included in a measure of a country's price level) are not traded across borders. Housing, land, and services such as restaurant meals, haircuts, and golf lessons are not traded goods. So even though the prices of these items might rise and lead to a higher price level relative to another country's, there would be little direct effect on the exchange rate.

Factors That Affect Exchange Rates in the Long Run

Our analysis indicates that in the long run, four major factors affect the exchange rate: relative price levels, trade barriers, preferences for domestic versus foreign goods, and productivity. We examine how each of these factors affects the exchange rate while holding the others constant.

The basic reasoning proceeds along the following lines: anything that increases the demand for domestically produced goods that are traded relative to foreign-traded goods tends to appreciate the domestic currency because domestic goods will continue to sell well even when the value of the domestic currency is higher. Similarly, anything that increases the demand for foreign goods relative to domestic goods tends to depreciate the domestic currency because domestic goods will continue to sell well only if the value of the domestic currency is lower. In other words, ***if a factor increases the demand for domestic goods relative to foreign goods, the domestic currency will appreciate; if a factor decreases the relative demand for domestic goods, the domestic currency will depreciate***.

RELATIVE PRICE LEVELS In line with PPP theory, when prices of Canadian goods rise (holding prices of foreign goods constant), the demand for Canadian goods falls and the dollar tends to depreciate so that Canadian goods can still sell well. By contrast, if prices of Japanese goods rise so that the relative prices of Canadian goods fall, the demand for Canadian goods increases, and the dollar tends to appreciate because Canadian goods will continue to sell well even with a higher value of the domestic currency. ***In the long run, a rise in a country's price level (relative to the foreign price level) causes its currency to depreciate, and a fall in the country's relative price level causes its currency to appreciate.***

TRADE BARRIERS Barriers to free trade such as **tariffs** (taxes on imported goods) and **quotas** (restrictions on the quantity of foreign goods that can be imported) can affect the exchange rate. Suppose that Canada increases its tariff or puts a lower quota on Japanese cars. These increases in trade barriers increase the demand for Canadian cars, and the dollar tends to appreciate because Canadian cars will still sell well even with a higher value of the dollar. ***Increasing trade barriers cause a country's currency to appreciate in the long run.***

PREFERENCES FOR DOMESTIC VERSUS FOREIGN GOODS If the Japanese develop an appetite for Canadian goods—say, for Bombardier's high-speed trains and Canadian beef and pork—the increased demand for Canadian goods (exports) tends to appreciate the dollar because the Canadian goods will continue to sell well even at a higher value for the dollar. Likewise, if Canadians decide that they prefer Japanese cars to Canadian cars, the increased demand for Japanese goods (imports) tends to depreciate the dollar. ***Increased demand for a country's exports causes its currency to appreciate in the long run; conversely, increased demand for imports causes the domestic currency to depreciate.***

PRODUCTIVITY When productivity in a country rises, it tends to rise in domestic sectors that produce traded goods rather than nontraded goods. Higher productivity is therefore associated with a decline in the price of domestically produced traded goods relative to foreign-traded goods. As a result, the demand for domestic traded goods rises, and the domestic currency tends to appreciate. If, however, a country's productivity lags behind that of other countries, its traded goods become relatively more expensive, and the currency tends to depreciate. ***In the long run, as a country becomes more productive relative to other countries, its currency appreciates.*** [2]

Our long-run theory of exchange rate behaviour is summarized in Table 19-1. We use the convention that the exchange rate E is quoted so that an appreciation of the currency corresponds to a rise in the exchange rate. In the case of Canada, this means that we are quoting the exchange rate as units of foreign currency per dollar (say, euros per dollar). [3]

EXCHANGE RATES IN THE SHORT RUN: A SUPPLY AND DEMAND ANALYSIS

We have developed a theory of the long-run behaviour of exchange rates. However, because factors driving long-run changes in exchange rates move slowly over time, if we are to understand why exchange rates exhibit such large changes (sometimes several percent) from day to day, we must develop a supply and demand analysis of how current exchange rates (spot exchange rates) are determined in the short run.

The key to understanding the short-run behaviour of exchange rates is to recognize that an exchange rate tells us the price at which domestic assets (those denominated in the domestic currency, which includes domestic bank deposits) trade for foreign assets (those denominated in the foreign currency, which includes foreign bank deposits). Because the exchange rate is the price of one asset in terms of another, the natural way to investigate the short-run

TABLE 19-1   Factors That Affect Exchange Rates in the Long Run

Factor	Change in Factor	Response of the Exchange Rate, E*
Domestic price level†	↑	↓
Trade barriers	↑	↑
Import demand	↑	↓
Export demand	↑	↑
Productivity†	↑	↑

*Units of foreign currency per Canadian dollar: ↑ indicates domestic currency appreciation; ↓, depreciation.

†Relative to other countries.

Note: Only increases (↑) in the factors are shown; the effects of decreases in the variables on the exchange rate are the opposite of those indicated in the "Response" column.

[2] A country might be so small that a change in productivity or the preferences for domestic or foreign goods would have no effect on prices of these goods relative to foreign goods. In this case changes in productivity or changes in preferences for domestic or foreign goods affect the country's income but will not necessarily affect the value of the currency. In our analysis, we are assuming that these factors can affect relative prices and consequently the exchange rate.

[3] Exchange rates can be quoted either as units of foreign currency per domestic currency or alternatively as units of domestic currency per foreign currency. In professional writing, many economists quote exchange rates as units of domestic currency per foreign currency so that an appreciation of the domestic currency is portrayed as a fall in the exchange rate. The opposite convention is used in the text here because it is more intuitive to think of an appreciation of the domestic currency as a rise in the exchange rate.

determination of exchange rates is to use an asset market approach that relies heavily on the theory of asset demand developed in Chapter 5. As you will see, however, the long-run determinants of the exchange rate we have just outlined also play an important role in the short-run asset market approach.[4]

In the past, supply and demand approaches to exchange rate determination emphasized the role of import and export demand. The more modern asset market approach used here emphasizes stocks of assets rather than the flows of exports and imports over short periods, because export and import transactions are quite small relative to the amount of domestic and foreign assets at any given time. For example, foreign exchange transactions in Canada each year are well over 25 times greater than the amount of Canadian exports and imports. Thus over short periods such as a year, decisions to hold domestic or foreign assets play a much greater role in exchange rate determination than the demand for exports and imports does.

Supply Curve for Domestic Assets

We start by discussing the supply curve. In this analysis we treat Canada as the home country, so domestic assets are denominated in Canadian dollars. For simplicity, we use euros to stand for any foreign country's currency, so foreign assets are denominated in euros.

The quantity of dollar assets supplied is primarily the quantity of bank deposits, bonds, and equities in Canada and for all practical purposes we can take this amount as fixed with respect to the exchange rate. The quantity supplied at any exchange rate does not change, so the supply curve, S, is vertical, as shown in Figure 19-3.

Demand Curve for Domestic Assets

The demand curve traces out the quantity demanded at each current exchange rate by holding everything else constant, particularly the expected future value of the exchange rate. We write the current exchange rate (the spot exchange rate) as E_t, and the expected exchange rate for the next period as E_{t+1}^e. As the theory of asset demand suggests, the most important determinant of the quantity of domestic (dollar) assets demanded is the relative expected return of domestic assets. Let's see what happens as the current exchange rate, E_t, falls.

Suppose we start at point A in Figure 19-3 where the current exchange rate is at E_2. With the future expected value of the exchange rate held constant at E_{t+1}^e, a lower value of the exchange rate, say at E^*, implies that the dollar is more likely to rise in value, that is appreciate. The greater the expected rise (appreciation) of the dollar, the higher is the relative expected return on dollar (domestic) assets. The theory of asset demand then tells us that because dollar assets are now more desirable to hold, the quantity of dollar assets demanded will rise, as is shown by point B in Figure 19-3. If the current exchange rate falls even further to E_1, there is an even higher expected appreciation of the dollar, a higher expected return, and therefore an even greater quantity of dollar assets demanded. This is shown in point C in Figure 19-3. The resulting demand curve, D, which connects these points, is downward sloping, indicating that at lower current values of the dollar (everything else equal), the quantity demanded of dollar assets is higher.

---

[4] For a further description of the modern asset market approach to exchange rate determination that we use here, see Paul Krugman and Maurice Obstfeld, *International Economics*, 8th ed. (Reading, Mass.: Addison Wesley Longman, 2009).

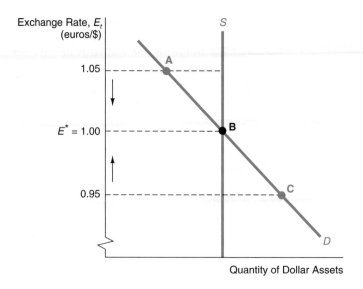

FIGURE 19-3   Equilibrium in the Foreign Exchange Market

Equilibrium in the foreign exchange market occurs at point B, the intersection of the demand curve *D* and the supply curve *S* at an exchange rate of E^*.

Equilibrium in the Foreign Exchange Market

As in the usual supply and demand analysis, the market is in equilibrium when the quantity of dollar assets demanded equals the quantity supplied. In Figure 19-3, equilibrium occurs at point B, the intersection of the demand and supply curves. At point B, the exchange rate is E^*.

Suppose that the exchange rate is at E_2, which is higher than the equilibrium exchange rate of E^*. As we can see in Figure 19-3, the quantity of dollar assets supplied is then greater than the quantity demanded, a condition of excess supply. Given that more people want to sell dollar assets than want to buy them, the value of the dollar will fall. As long as the exchange rate remains above the equilibrium exchange rate, there will continue to be an excess supply of dollar assets, and the dollar will fall in value until it reaches the equilibrium exchange rate of E^*.

Similarly, if the exchange rate is less than the equilibrium exchange rate at E_1, the quantity of dollar assets demanded will exceed the quantity supplied, a condition of excess demand. Given that more people want to buy dollar assets than want to sell them, the value of the dollar will rise until the excess demand disappears and the value of the dollar is again at the equilibrium exchange rate of E^*.

EXPLAINING CHANGES IN EXCHANGE RATES

The supply and demand analysis of the foreign exchange market illustrates how and why exchange rates change. We can simplify this analysis by assuming the amount of dollar assets is fixed: The supply curve is vertical at a given quantity and does not shift. Under this assumption, we need look at only those factors that shift the demand curve for dollar assets to explain how exchange rates change over time.

Shifts in the Demand for Domestic Assets

As we have seen, the quantity of domestic (dollar) assets demanded depends on the relative expected return of dollar assets. To see how the demand curve shifts, we need to determine how the quantity demanded changes, holding the current exchange rate, E_t, constant, when other factors change.

For insight into which direction the demand curve shifts, suppose you are an investor who is considering putting funds into domestic (dollar) assets. When a factor changes, decide whether at a given level of the current exchange rate, holding all other variables constant, you would earn a higher or lower expected return on dollar assets versus foreign assets. This decision tells you whether you want to hold more or fewer dollar assets and thus whether the quantity demanded increases or decreases at each level of the exchange rate. Knowing the direction of the change in the quantity demanded at each exchange rate tells you which way the demand curve shifts. In other words, if the relative expected return of dollar assets rises holding the current exchange rate constant, the demand curve shifts to the right. If the relative expected return falls, the demand curve shifts to the left.

DOMESTIC INTEREST RATE, i^D   Suppose that dollar assets pay an interest rate of i^D. When the domestic interest rate on dollar assets i^D rises, holding the current exchange rate E_t and everything else constant, the return on dollar assets increases relative to foreign assets, so people will want to hold more dollar assets. The quantity of dollar assets demanded increases at every value of the exchange rate, as shown by the rightward shift of the demand curve in Figure 19-4 from D_1 to D_2. The new equilibrium is reached at point 2, the intersection of D_2 and S, and the equilibrium exchange rate rises from E_1 to E_2. ***An increase in the domestic interest rate i^D shifts the demand curve for domestic assets, D, to the right and causes the domestic currency to appreciate (E ↑).***

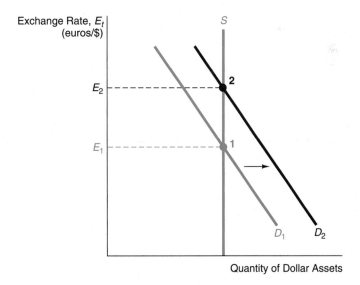

FIGURE 19-4   Response to an Increase in the Domestic Interest Rate, i^D

When the domestic interest rate i^D increases, the relative expected return on domestic (dollar) assets increases and the demand curve shifts to the right. The equilibrium exchange rate rises from E_1 to E_2.

Conversely, if i^D falls, the relative expected return on dollar assets falls, the demand curve shifts to the left, and the exchange rate falls. ***A decrease in the domestic interest rate i^D shifts the demand curve for domestic assets, D, to the left and causes the domestic currency to depreciate (E ↓).***

FOREIGN INTEREST RATE, I^F   Suppose that the foreign asset pays an interest rate of i^F. When the foreign interest rate i^F rises, holding the current exchange rate and everything else constant, the return on foreign assets rises relative to dollar assets. Thus the relative expected return on dollar assets falls. Now people want to hold fewer dollar assets, and the quantity demanded decreases at every value of the exchange rate. This scenario is shown by the leftward shift of the demand curve in Figure 19-5 from D_1 to D_2. The new equilibrium is reached at point 2, when the value of the dollar has fallen. Conversely, a decrease in i^F raises the relative expected return on dollar assets, shifts the demand curve to the right, and raises the exchange rate. To summarize, ***an increase in the foreign interest rate i^F shifts the demand curve D to the left and causes the domestic currency to depreciate; a fall in the foreign interest rate i^F shifts the demand curve D to the right and causes the domestic currency to appreciate***.

CHANGES IN THE EXPECTED FUTURE EXCHANGE RATE, E^e_{t+1}   Expectations about the future value of the exchange rate play an important role in shifting the current demand curve, because the demand for domestic assets, like the demand for any durable good, depends on the future resale price. Any factor that causes the expected future exchange rate, E^e_{t+1}, to rise increases the expected appreciation of the dollar. The result is a higher relative expected return on dollar assets, which increases the demand for dollar assets at every exchange rate, thereby shifting the demand curve to the right in Figure 19-6 from D_1 to D_2. The equilibrium exchange rate rises to point 2 at the intersection of the D_2 and S curves.

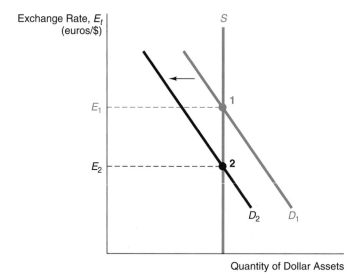

FIGURE 19-5   Response to an Increase in the Foreign Interest Rate, i^F

When the foreign interest rate i^F increases, the relative expected return on domestic (dollar) assets falls and the demand curve shifts to the left. The equilibrium exchange rate falls from E_1 to E_2.

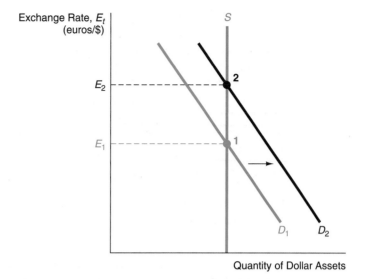

FIGURE 19-6   Response to an Increase in the Expected Future Exchange Rate, E_{t+1}^e

When the expected future exchange rate increases, the relative expected return on domestic (dollar) assets rises and the demand curve shifts to the right. The equilibrium exchange rate rises from E_1 to E_2.

A rise in the expected future exchange rate, E_{t+1}^e, shifts the demand curve to the right and causes an appreciation of the domestic currency. Using the same reasoning, *a fall in the expected future exchange rate, E_{t+1}^e, shifts the demand curve to the left and causes a depreciation of the currency*.

Earlier in the chapter we discussed the determinants of the exchange rate in the long run: the relative price level, relative trade barriers, import and export demand, and relative productivity (refer to Table 19-1). These four factors influence the expected future exchange rate. The theory of purchasing power parity suggests that if a higher Canadian price level relative to the foreign price level is expected to persist, the dollar will depreciate in the long run. A higher expected relative Canadian price level should thus have a tendency to lower E_{t+1}^e, lower the relative expected return on dollar assets, shift the demand curve to the left, the lower the current exchange rate.

Similarly, the other long-run determinants of the exchange rate can influence the relative expected return on dollar assets and the current exchange rate. Briefly, the following changes, all of which increase the demand for domestic goods relative to foreign goods, will raise E_{t+1}^e: (1) expectations of a fall in the Canadian price level relative to the foreign price level; (2) expectations of higher Canadian trade barriers relative to foreign trade barriers; (3) expectations of lower Canadian import demand; (4) expectations of higher foreign demand for Canadian exports; and (5) expectations of higher Canadian productivity relative to foreign productivity. By increasing E_{t+1}^e, all of these changes increase the relative expected return on dollar assets, shift the demand curve to the right, and cause an appreciation of the domestic currency, the dollar.

**Recap:
Factors That
Change the
Exchange
Rate**

Table 19-2 outlines all the factors that shift the demand curve for domestic assets and thereby cause the exchange rate to change. Shifts in the demand curve occur when one factor changes, holding everything else constant, including the current exchange rate. Again, the theory of asset demand tells us that changes in the relative expected return on dollar assets are the source of shifts in the demand curve.

Let's review what happens when each of the seven factors in Table 19-2 changes. Remember that to understand which direction the demand curve shifts, consider what happens to the relative expected return on dollar assets when the factor changes. If the relative expected return rises, holding the current exchange rate constant, the demand curve shifts to the right. If the relative expected return falls, the demand curve shifts to the left.

1. When the interest rates on domestic assets i^D rise, the expected return on dollar assets rises at each exchange rate and so the quantity demanded increases. The demand curve therefore shifts to the right, and the equilibrium exchange rate rises, as is shown in the first row of Table 19-2.

2. When the foreign interest rate i^F rises, the return on foreign assets rises, so the relative expected return on dollar assets falls. The quantity demanded of dollar assets then falls, the demand curve shifts to the left, and the exchange rate declines, as in the second row of Table 19-2.

3. When the expected price level is higher, our analysis of the long-run determinants of the exchange rate indicates that the value of the dollar will fall in the future. The expected return on dollar assets thus falls, the quantity demanded declines, the demand curve shifts to the left, and the exchange rate falls, as in the third row of Table 19-2.

4. With higher expected trade barriers, the value of the dollar is higher in the long run and the expected return on dollar assets is higher. The quantity demanded of dollar assets thus rises, the demand curve shifts to the right, and the exchange rate rises, as in the fourth row of Table 19-2.

5. When expected import demand rises, we expect the exchange rate to depreciate in the long run, so the expected return on dollar assets falls. The quantity demanded of dollar assets at each value of the current exchange rate therefore falls, the demand curve shifts to the left, and the exchange rate declines, as in the fifth row of Table 19-2.

6. When expected export demand rises, the opposite occurs because the exchange rate is expected to appreciate in the long run. The expected return on dollar assets rises, the demand curve shifts to the right, and the exchange rate rises, as in the sixth row of Table 19-2.

7. With higher expected domestic productivity, the exchange rate is expected to appreciate in the long run, so the expected return on domestic assets rises. The quantity demanded at each exchange rate therefore rises, the demand curve shifts to the right, and the exchange rate rises, as in the seventh row of Table 19-2.

TABLE 19-2 Factors That Shift the Demand Curve for Domestic Assets and Affect the Exchange Rate

Factor	Change in Factor	Change in Quantity Demanded of Domestic Assets at Each Exchange Rate	Response of Exchange Rate, E_t	
Domestic interest rate, i^D	↑	↑	↑	E_t S_A E_2 E_1 D_1 D_2 Dollar Assets
Foreign interest rate, i^F	↑	↓	↓	E_t S_A E_1 E_2 D_2 D_1 Dollar Assets
Expected domestic price level*	↑	↓	↓	E_t S_A E_1 E_2 D_2 D_1 Dollar Assets
Expected trade barriers*	↑	↑	↑	E_t S_A E_2 E_1 D_1 D_2 Dollar Assets
Expected import demand	↑	↓	↓	E_t S_A E_1 E_2 D_2 D_1 Dollar Assets
Expected export demand	↑	↑	↑	E_t S_A E_2 E_1 D_1 D_2 Dollar Assets
Expected productivity*	↑	↑	↑	E_t S_A E_2 E_1 D_1 D_2 Dollar Assets

*Relative to other countries.

Note: Only increases (↑) in the factors are shown; the effects of decreases in the variables on the exchange rate are the opposite of those indicated in the "Response" column.

APPLICATION   **Changes in the Equilibrium Exchange Rate: Two Examples**

Our analysis has revealed the factors that affect the value of the equilibrium exchange rate. Now we use this analysis to take a closer look at the response of the exchange rate to changes in interest rates and money growth.

Changes in Interest Rates

Changes in domestic interest rates i^D are often cited as a major factor affecting exchange rates. For example, we see headlines in the financial press like this one: "Dollar Recovers as Interest Rates Edge Upward." But is the view presented in this headline always correct?

Not necessarily, because to analyze the effects of interest rate changes, we must carefully distinguish the sources of the changes. The Fisher equation (Chapter 4) states that a nominal interest rate such as i^D equals the *real* interest rate plus expected inflation: $i = i_r + \pi^e$. The Fisher equation thus indicates that the interest rate i^D can change for two reasons: Either the real interest rate i_r changes or the expected inflation rate π^e changes. The effect on the exchange rate is quite different, depending on which of these two factors is the source of the change in the nominal interest rate.

Suppose that the domestic real interest rate increases so that the nominal interest rate i^D rises while expected inflation remains unchanged. In this case, it is reasonable to assume that the expected appreciation of the dollar will be unchanged because expected inflation is unchanged. In this case, the increase in i^D increases the relative expected return on dollar assets, increases the quantity of dollar assets demanded at each level of the exchange rate, and shifts the demand curve to the right. We end up with the situation depicted in Figure 19-4, which analyzes an increase in i^D, holding everything else constant. Our model of the foreign exchange market produces the following result: ***When domestic real interest rates rise, the domestic currency appreciates***.

When the nominal interest rate rises because of an increase in expected inflation, we get a different result from the one shown in Figure 19-4. The rise in expected domestic inflation leads to a decline in the expected appreciation of the dollar, which is typically thought to be larger than the increase in the domestic interest rate i^D.[5] As a result, at any given exchange rate, the relative expected return on domestic (dollar) assets falls, the demand curve shifts to the left, and the exchange rate falls from E_1 to E_2 as shown in Figure 19-7. Our analysis leads to this conclusion: ***When domestic interest rates rise due to an expected increase in inflation, the domestic currency depreciates***.

Because this conclusion is completely different from the one reached when the rise in the domestic interest rate is associated with a higher real interest rate, we must always distinguish between *real* and *nominal* measures when analyzing the effects of interest rates on exchange rates.

---

[5] This conclusion is standard in asset market models of exchange rate determination; see Rudiger Dornbusch, "Expectations and Exchange Rate Dynamics," *Journal of Political Economy* 84 (1976): 1061–1076. It is also consistent with empirical evidence that suggests that nominal interest rates do not rise one-for-one with increases in expected inflation. See Frederic S. Mishkin, "The Real Interest Rate: An Empirical Investigation," *Carnegie-Rochester Conference Series on Public Policy* 15 (1981): 151–200; and Lawrence Summers, "The Nonadjustment of Nominal Interest Rates: A Study of the Fisher Effect," in *Macroeconomics, Prices and Quantities*, ed. James Tobin (Washington, DC: Brookings Institution, 1983), pp. 201–240.

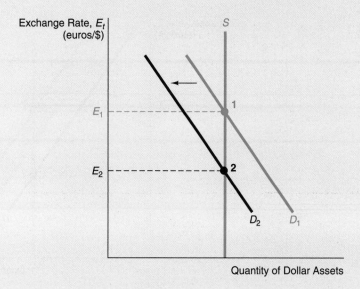

FIGURE 19-7   Effect of a Rise in the Domestic Interest Rate as a Result of an Increase in Expected Inflation

Because a rise in domestic expected inflation leads to a decline in expected dollar appreciation that is larger than the increase in the domestic interest rate, the relative expected return on domestic (dollar) assets falls. The demand curve shifts to the left, and the equilibrium exchange rate falls from E_1 to E_2.

Changes in the Money Supply

Suppose that the Bank of Canada decides to increase the level of the money supply in an attempt to reduce unemployment, which it believes to be excessive. The higher money supply will lead to a higher Canadian price level in the long run (as we will see in Chapter 24) and hence to a lower expected future exchange rate. The resulting decline in the expected appreciation of the dollar lowers the quantity of dollar assets demanded at each level of the exchange rate and shifts the demand curve to the left. In addition, the higher money supply will lead to a higher real money supply M/P, because the price level does not immediately increase in the short run. As suggested in Chapter 5, the resulting rise in the real money supply causes the domestic interest rate to fall, which also lowers the relative expected return on dollar assets, providing a further reason why the demand curve shifts to the left. As we can see in Figure 19-8, the demand curve shifts to D_2, and the exchange rate declines from E_1 to E_2. The conclusion: ***A higher domestic money supply causes the domestic currency to depreciate***.

Exchange Rate Over-shooting

Our analysis of the effect of an increase in the money supply on the exchange rate is not yet over—we still need to look at what happens to the exchange rate in the long run. A basic proposition in monetary theory, called **monetary neutrality**, states that in the long run, a one-time percentage rise in the money supply is matched by the same one-time percentage rise in the price level, leaving unchanged the real money supply and all other economic variables such as interest rates. An intuitive way to understand this proposition is to think of what would happen if our government announced overnight that an old dollar would now be worth 100 new dollars. The money supply in new dollars would be 100 times its

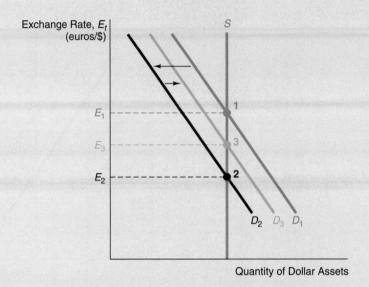

FIGURE 19-8   Effect of a Rise in the Money Supply

A rise in the money supply leads to a higher domestic price level, which in turn leads to a lower expected future exchange rate. In addition, the higher money supply leads to a decline in domestic interest rates. The decline in both the expected appreciation of the dollar and the domestic interest rate lowers the relative expected return on dollar assets, shifting the demand curve leftward from D_1 to D_2. In the short run, the equilibrium exchange rate falls from E_1 to E_2. In the long run, however, the interest rate rises back up again to its initial level and the demand curve shifts rightward to D_3. The exchange rate rises from E_2 to E_3 in the long run.

old value and the price level would also be 100 times higher, but nothing in the economy would really have changed: Real and nominal interest rates and the real money supply would remain the same. Monetary neutrality tells us that in the long run, the rise in the money supply would not lead to a change in the domestic interest rate so it would rise back to its old level. The demand curve would shift to the right to D_3, but not all the way back to D_1, because the price level will still be higher in the long run. As we can see in Figure 19-8, this means that the exchange rate would rise from E_2 to E_3 in the long run.

The phenomenon we have described here in which the exchange rate falls by more in the short run than it does in the long run when the money supply increases is called **exchange rate overshooting**. It is important because, as we will see in the following application, it can help explain why exchange rates exhibit so much volatility.

Another way of thinking about why exchange rate overshooting occurs is to recognize that when the domestic interest rate falls in the short run, equilibrium in the foreign exchange market means that the expected return on foreign deposits must be lower. With the foreign interest rate given, this lower expected return on foreign deposits means that there must be an expected appreciation of the dollar (depreciation of the euro) for the expected return on foreign deposits to decline when the domestic interest rate falls. This can occur only if the current exchange rate falls below its long-run value.

APPLICATION   Why Are Exchange Rates So Volatile?

The high volatility of foreign exchange rates surprises many people. Thirty or so years ago, economists generally believed that allowing exchange rates to be determined in the free market would not lead to large fluctuations in their values. Recent experience has proved them wrong. If we return to Figure 19-1, we see that exchange rates over the 1974–2009 period have been very volatile.

The asset market approach to exchange rate determination that we have outlined in this chapter gives a straightforward explanation of volatile exchange rates. Because expected appreciation of the domestic currency affects the expected return on foreign deposits, expectations about the price level, inflation, trade barriers, productivity, import demand, export demand, and the money supply play important roles in determining the exchange rate. When expectations about any of these variables change, as they do—and often at that—our model indicates that there will be an immediate effect on the expected return on foreign deposits and therefore on the exchange rate. Because expectations on all these variables change with just about every bit of news that appears, it is not surprising that the exchange rate is volatile. In addition, we have seen that our exchange rate analysis produces exchange rate overshooting when the money supply increases. Exchange rate overshooting is an additional reason for the high volatility of exchange rates.

Because earlier models of exchange rate behaviour focused on goods markets rather than asset markets, they did not emphasize changing expectations as a source of exchange rate movements, and so these earlier models could not predict substantial fluctuations in exchange rates. The failure of earlier models to explain volatility is one reason why they are no longer so popular. The more modern approach developed here emphasizes that the foreign exchange market is like any other asset market in which expectations of the future matter. The foreign exchange market, like other asset markets such as the stock market, displays substantial price volatility, and foreign exchange rates are notoriously hard to forecast.

APPLICATION   The Subprime Crisis and the U.S. Dollar

With the start of the subprime financial crisis in August 2007, the U.S. dollar began an accelerated decline in value, falling by 9% against the euro until mid-July of 2008, and 6% against a wider basket of currencies. After hitting an all-time low against the euro on July 11, the U.S. dollar suddenly shot upward, by over 20% against the euro by the end of October and 15% against a wider basket of currencies. What is the relationship between the subprime crisis and these large swings in the value of the U.S. dollar?

During 2007, the negative effects of the subprime crisis on economic activity were mostly confined to the United States. The Federal Reserve acted aggressively to lower interest rates to counter the contractionary effects, decreasing the federal funds rate target by 325 basis points from September of 2007 to April of 2008. In contrast, other central banks like the ECB did not see the need to lower interest rates, particularly because high energy prices had led to a surge in inflation. The relative expected return on dollar assets thus declined, shifting the demand curve for dollar assets to the left, as in Figure 19-5, leading to a decline in the equilibrium exchange rate. Our analysis of the foreign exchange market thus explains why the early phase of the subprime crisis led to a decline in the value of the dollar.

We now turn to the rise in the value of the U.S. dollar. Starting in the summer of 2008, the effects of the subprime crisis on economic activity began to spread more widely throughout the world. Foreign central banks started to cut interest rates, with the expectation that further rate cuts would follow, as indeed did occur. The expected decline in foreign interest rates then increased the relative expected return of U.S. dollar assets, leading to a rightward shift in the demand curve, and a rise in the value of the U.S. dollar, as shown in Figure 19-4. Another factor driving the U.S. dollar upwards was the "flight to quality" when the subprime financial crisis reached a particularly virulent stage in September and October. Both Americans and foreigners wanted to put their money in the safest assets possible: U.S. Treasury securities. The resulting increase in the demand for U.S. dollar assets provided an additional reason for the demand curve for U.S. dollar assets to shift out to the right, thereby helping to produce a sharp appreciation of the U.S. dollar.

APPLICATION   Reading the *Wall Street Journal*: The "Currency Trading" Column

Now that we have an understanding of how exchange rates are determined, we can use our analysis to understand discussions about developments in the foreign exchange market reported in the financial press.

Every day, the *Wall Street Journal* reports on developments in the foreign exchange market on the previous business day in its "Currency Trading" column, an example of which is presented in the Financial News box, The "Currency Trading" Column.

The column states that the euro gained against the U.S. dollar because traders were willing to take on more risk and because confidence indices rose in Europe but fell in the United States. Our analysis of the foreign exchange market explains why these developments led to a stronger euro.

Because the U.S. dollar is considered a safe haven, when traders were willing to take on more risk, they were more willing to hold assets denominated in other currencies such as the euro. As a result, the demand for euro assets increased at each value of the exchange rate, causing the demand curve for euros to shift out to the right, and the value of the euro to rise.

The rise in confidence in Europe relative to the United States' economy suggested that Europe would be stronger relative to the United States so that, as the analysis in Chapter 5 indicates, real interest rates in Europe would be relatively higher. The resulting higher relative expected return on euro assets caused the demand for them to increase at each value of the exchange rate, shifting the demand curve to the right, providing a further reason why the euro appreciated.

FINANCIAL NEWS

The "Currency Trading" Column

The "Currency Trading" column appears daily in the *Wall Street Journal*; an example is presented here. It is usually found in the third section, "Money and Investing."

Euro Gains on Dollar; Pound Above $1.40

BY RIVA FROYMOVICH

The euro gained against the dollar Tuesday as stock markets rose, encouraging traders to take on more risk and sell the dollar. The dollar is **CURRENCY TRADING** considered a safe haven because it is the world's reserve currency.

The euro and pound also were supported by stronger-than-expected European data, which overnight sent both currencies to one-week highs.

Late Tuesday in New York, the euro was at $1.3189 from $1.3176 late Monday, while the dollar was flat at 89.02 yen. The euro was at 117.40 yen from 117.30 yen, and the U.K. pound was at $1.4166 from $1.3973. The dollar was at 1.1399 Swiss francs from 1.1370 francs.

The Ifo German business con-fidence index slightly rebounded in January, beating economists' forecasts. Still, with the index just above record lows, officials at the research institute cautioned against calling this a recovery. Meanwhile, in the U.K., sales volumes at retailers recovered slightly in January.

The pound was able to hold above the key $1.40 level throughout the session. The euro, however, fell to intraday lows of $1.3118 and 116.12 yen after the U.S. Conference Board reported its January consumer-confidence index fell to a historic low. The yen also is considered a haven due to Japan's large foreign-exchange reserves and current-account surplus.

Currency analysts said the lifetime of the current revival of risk appetite depends on the outcome of the Federal Reserve's policy meeting Wednesday.

Source: Wall Street Journal, Wednesday, January 28, 2009, p. C12.

SUMMARY

1. Foreign exchange rates (the price of one country's currency in terms of another's) are important because they affect the price of domestically produced goods sold abroad and the cost of foreign goods bought domestically.

2. The theory of purchasing power parity suggests that long-run changes in the exchange rate between two countries' currencies are determined by changes in the relative price levels in the two countries. Other factors that affect exchange rates in the long run are tariffs and quotas, import demand, export demand, and productivity.

3. In the short run, exchange rates are determined by changes in the relative expected return on domestic assets, which cause the demand curve to shift. Any factor that changes the relative expected return on

domestic assets will lead to changes in the exchange rate. Such factors include changes in the interest rates on domestic and foreign assets as well as changes in any of the factors that affect the long-run exchange rate and hence the expected future exchange rate. Changes in the money supply lead to exchange rate overshooting, causing the exchange rate to change by more in the short run than in the long run.

4. The asset market approach to exchange rate determination can explain both the volatility of exchange rates and the rise of the dollar in the 1980–1984 period and its subsequent fall.

KEY TERMS

appreciation,   p. 495

depreciation,   p. 495

exchange rate,   p. 494

exchange rate overshooting,
    p. 512

foreign exchange market,   p. 494

forward exchange rate,   p. 495

forward transaction,   p. 495

law of one price,   p. 498

monetary neutrality,   p. 511

quotas,   p. 501

real exchange rate,   p. 499

spot exchange rate,   p. 495

spot transaction,   p. 495

tariffs,   p. 501

theory of purchasing power parity
    (PPP),   p. 499

QUESTIONS

You will find the answers to the questions marked with an asterisk in the Textbook Resources section of your MyEconLab.

1. When the euro appreciates, are you more likely to drink Canadian or French wine?

*2. "A country is always worse off when its currency is weak (falls in value)." Is this statement true, false, or uncertain? Explain your answer.

3. In a newspaper, check the exchange rates for the foreign currencies listed in the Financial News box, Foreign Exchange Rates, on page 496. Which of these currencies have appreciated and which have depreciated since January 2009?

*4. If the Japanese price level rises by 5% relative to the price level in Canada, what does the theory of purchasing power parity predict will happen to the value of the Japanese yen in terms of dollars?

5. If the demand for a country's exports falls at the same time that tariffs on imports are raised, will the country's currency tend to appreciate or depreciate in the long run?

*6. In the mid- to late-1970s, the yen appreciated relative to the U.S. dollar even though Japan's inflation rate was higher than America's. How can this be explained by an improvement in the productivity of Japanese industry relative to American industry?

Predicting the Future

Answer the remaining questions by drawing the appropriate exchange market diagrams.

7. The governor of the Bank of Canada announces that he will reduce inflation with a new anti-inflation program. If the public believes him, predict what will happen to the Canadian dollar exchange rate.

*8. If the British central bank prints money to reduce unemployment, what will happen to the value of the pound in the short run and the long run?

9. If the Indian government unexpectedly announces that it will be imposing higher tariffs on foreign goods one year from now, what will happen to the value of the Indian rupee today?

*10. If nominal interest rates in Canada rise but real interest rates fall, predict what will happen to the Canadian exchange rate.

11. If Canadian auto companies make a breakthrough in automobile technology and are able to produce a car that gets 100 kilometres to the litre, what will happen to the Canadian exchange rate?

*12. If Canadians go on a spending spree and buy twice as much French perfume, Japanese TVs, English sweaters, Swiss watches, and Italian wine, what will happen to the value of the Canadian dollar?

13. If expected inflation drops in Europe so that interest rates fall there, predict what will happen to the exchange rate for the Canadian dollar.

*14. If the European Central Bank decides to contract the money supply in order to fight inflation, what will happen to the value of the Canadian dollar?

15. If there is a strike in France, making it harder to buy French goods, what will happen to the value of the euro?

QUANTITATIVE PROBLEMS

*1. The current exchange rate between Canada and Britain is £0.5268 per Canadian dollar. The three-month forward rate between the British pound and the Canadian dollar is £0.4968 per dollar. What is the percentage difference between current three-month Canadian and British interest rates?

2. An Italian sports car is selling for 70 000 euros. What is the Canadian dollar price for the Italian car if the exchange rate is 0.60 euros per Canadian dollar? What is the U.S. dollar price for the Italian car if the exchange rate is 0.80 euros per U.S. dollar?

*3. The current exchange rate between the Canadian dollar and the euro is 0.60 euros per Canadian dollar. If the Canadian dollar is expected to appreciate by 10% relative to the euro, what is the new expected exchange rate?

4. If the price level recently fell by 5% in Canada while increasing by 20% in Europe, how much must the exchange rate change if PPP holds? Assume that the current exchange rate is 0.60 euros per Canadian dollar.

CANSIM Question

5. Get the CANSIM monthly data from 1974 to 2009 on the Canadian-dollar-per-U.S.-dollar exchange rate (series V37426), the Canadian-dollar-per-British-pound exchange rate (series V37430), the Canadian-dollar-per-Japanese-yen exchange rate (series V37456), and the Canadian-dollar-per-euro exchange rate (series V21570998) from the Textbook Resources area of the MyEconLab.
   a. Present a time series plot of each of these series and compare it to Figure 19-1.
   b. Calculate the mean and standard deviation as well as the maximum and minimum values for each series over the sample period.
   c. Which were the worst and best decades in terms of exchange rate volatility against each of the four foreign currencies?

WEB EXERCISES

1. The Bank of Canada maintains a website that lists the exchange rate between the Canadian dollar and many other currencies. Go to **www.bankofcanada.ca/en/rates/exchange-look.html**. Find the exchange rate between the Canadian dollar and the euro for the past 40 weeks.
   a. What has the percentage change in the euro–dollar exchange rate been in the past 40 weeks?
   b. What has been the annual percentage change in the euro–dollar exchange rate for each year since the euro's introduction?

2. Visit the website of the Bank of Canada, at the address above. Click *Rates and Statistics* and then *Exchange Rates*.
   a. What are the fundamental determinants of exchange rates?
   b. What are the different ways that a foreign exchange rate can be quoted?

   c. What is the difference between spot and forward exchange rates?
   d. Go to the CANSIM website and get series V37456. Present a time series plot of the observations of the yen-per-Canadian-dollar and the Canadian-dollar-per-yen exchange rates. Did the yen appreciate or depreciate in 2008? By how much?

3. International travellers and businesspeople frequently need to accurately convert from one currency to another. It is often easy to find the rate needed to convert the Canadian dollar into another currency. It can be more difficult to find exchange rates between two non-Canadian currencies. Go to **www.oanda.com/convert/classic**. This site lets you convert from any currency into any other currency. How many Lithuanian Litas can you currently buy with one Chilean Peso?

Be sure to visit the MyEconLab website at **www.myeconlab.com**. This online homework and tutorial system puts you in control of your own learning with study and practice tools directly correlated to this chapter content.

On the MyEconLab website you will find the following appendix and mini-case for this chapter:
Appendix 19.1: The Interest Parity Condition
Mini-Case 19.1: The Foreign Exchange Market and Financial Derivatives

CHAPTER 20

The International Financial System

LEARNING OBJECTIVES

After studying this chapter you should be able to

1. describe central bank intervention in the foreign exchange market and its effects on the money supply and the exchange rate
2. discuss international financial transactions and the balance of payments
3. summarize the arguments for and against capital controls
4. depict the role of the IMF as an international lender of last resort

PREVIEW

As the Canadian economy and the economies of the rest of the world grow more interdependent, a country's monetary policy can no longer be conducted without taking international considerations into account. In this chapter we examine how international financial transactions and the structure of the international financial system affect monetary policy. We also examine the evolution of the international financial system during the past half-century and consider where it may be heading in the future.

INTERVENTION IN THE FOREIGN EXCHANGE MARKET

In Chapter 19 we analyzed the foreign exchange market as if it were a completely free market that responds to all market pressures. Like many other markets, however, the foreign exchange market is not free of government intervention; central banks regularly engage in international financial transactions called **foreign exchange interventions** in order to influence exchange rates. In our current international environment, exchange rates fluctuate from day to day, but central banks attempt to influence their countries' exchange rates by buying and selling currencies. We can use the exchange rate analysis we developed in Chapter 19 to explain the impact of central bank intervention on the foreign exchange market.

Foreign Exchange Intervention and the Money Supply

The first step in understanding how central bank intervention in the foreign exchange market affects exchange rates is to see the impact on the monetary base from a central bank sale in the foreign exchange market of some of its holdings of assets denominated in a foreign currency (called **international reserves**). Suppose that the Bank of Canada decides to sell $1 billion of its foreign assets in exchange for $1 billion of Canadian currency. The Bank's purchase of dollars has two effects.

First, it reduces the Bank's holding of international reserves by $1 billion. Second, because the Bank's purchase of currency removes it from the hands of the public, currency in circulation falls by $1 billion. We can see this in the following T-account for the Bank of Canada:

Bank of Canada

Assets	Liabilities
Foreign assets (inter- national reserves) −$1 billion	Currency in circulation −$1 billion

Because the monetary base is made up of currency in circulation plus reserves, this decline in currency implies that the monetary base has fallen by $1 billion.

If instead of paying for the foreign assets sold by the Bank of Canada with currency the persons buying the foreign assets pay for them by cheques written on accounts at domestic banks, then the Bank deducts the $1 billion from the deposit accounts these banks have with the Bank of Canada. The result is the deposits with the Bank of Canada (reserves) decline by $1 billion, as shown in the following T-account:

Bank of Canada

Assets	Liabilities
Foreign assets (inter- national reserves) −$1 billion	Deposits with the Bank of Canada (reserves) −$1 billion

In this case, the outcome of the Bank of Canada sale of foreign assets and the purchase of dollar deposits is a $1 billion decline in reserves and, as before, a $1 billion decline in the monetary base because reserves are also a component of the monetary base.

We now see that the outcome for the monetary base is exactly the same when a central bank sells foreign assets to purchase domestic bank deposits or domestic currency. This is why when we say that a central bank has purchased its domestic currency, we do not have to distinguish whether it actually purchased currency or bank deposits denominated in the domestic currency. We have thus reached an important conclusion: ***A central bank's purchase of domestic currency and corresponding sale of foreign assets in the foreign exchange market leads to an equal decline in its international reserves and the monetary base.***

We could have reached the same conclusion by a more direct route. A central bank sale of a foreign asset is no different from an open market sale of a government bond. We learned in our exploration of the money supply process that an open market sale leads to an equal decline in the monetary base; therefore, a sale of foreign assets also leads to an equal decline in the monetary base. By similar reasoning, a central bank purchase of foreign assets paid for by selling domestic currency, like an open market purchase, leads to an equal rise in the monetary base. Thus we reach the following conclusion: ***A central bank's sale of domestic currency to purchase foreign assets in the foreign exchange market results in an equal rise in its international reserves and the monetary base.***

The intervention we have just described, in which a central bank allows the purchase or sale of domestic currency to have an effect on the monetary base, is called an **unsterilized foreign exchange intervention**. But what if the central bank does not want the purchase or sale of domestic currency to affect the monetary base? All it has to do is to counter the effect of the foreign exchange intervention by conducting an offsetting open market operation in the government bond market. For example, in the case of a $1 billion purchase of dollars by the Bank of Canada and a corresponding $1 billion sale of foreign assets, which we have seen would decrease the monetary base by $1 billion, the Bank can conduct an open market purchase of $1 billion of government bonds, which would increase the monetary base by $1 billion. The resulting T-account for the foreign exchange intervention and the offsetting open market operation leaves the monetary base unchanged:

Bank of Canada

Assets		Liabilities	
Foreign assets (international reserves)	−$1 billion	Monetary base (reserves)	0
Government bonds	+$1 billion		

A foreign exchange intervention with an offsetting open market operation that leaves the monetary base unchanged is called a **sterilized foreign exchange intervention**.

Now that we understand that there are two types of foreign exchange interventions, unsterilized and sterilized, let's look at how each affects the exchange rate.

Unsterilized Intervention

Your intuition might lead you to suspect that if a central bank wants to lower the value of the domestic currency, it should sell its currency in the foreign exchange market and purchase foreign assets. Indeed, this intuition is correct for the case of an unsterilized intervention.

Recall that in an unsterilized intervention, if the Bank of Canada decides to sell dollars so that it can buy foreign assets in the foreign exchange market, this works just like an open market purchase of bonds to increase the monetary base. Hence the sale of dollars leads to an increase in the money supply, and we find ourselves analyzing a similar situation to that described in Figure 19-8 (page 512), which is reproduced here as Figure 20-1.[1] The higher money supply leads to a higher Canadian price level in the long run and so to a lower expected future exchange rate. The resulting decline in the expected appreciation of the dollar lowers the relative expected return on dollar assets and shifts the demand curve to the left. In addition, the increase in the money supply will

---

[1] An unsterilized intervention in which the Bank of Canada sells dollars increases the amount of dollar assets slightly because it leads to an increase in the monetary base while leaving the amount of government bonds in the hands of the public unchanged. The curve depicting the supply of dollar assets would thus shift to the right slightly, which also works toward lowering the exchange rate, yielding the same conclusion derived from Figure 20-1. Because the resulting increase in the monetary base would be only a minuscule fraction of the total amount of dollar assets outstanding, the supply curve would shift by an imperceptible amount. This is why Figure 20-1 is drawn with the supply curve unchanged.

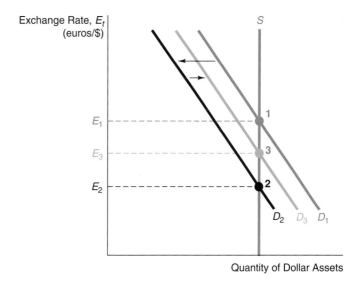

FIGURE 20-1   Effect of a Sale of Dollars and a Purchase of Foreign Assets

A sale of dollars and the consequent open market purchase of foreign assets increase the monetary base. The resulting rise in the money supply leads to a decline in domestic interest rates and a higher domestic price level in the long run, which produces a lower expected future exchange rate. The decline in both the expected appreciation of the dollar and the domestic interest rate lowers the relative expected return on dollar assets, shifting the demand curve leftward from D_1 to D_2. In the short run, the equilibrium exchange rate falls from E_1 to E_2. In the long run, the interest rate rises back to its initial level and the demand curve shifts rightward to D_3. The exchange rate rises from E_2 to E_3 in the long run.

lead to a higher real money supply in the short run, which causes the interest rate on dollar assets to fall, also lowering the relative expected return on dollar assets, and providing another reason for the demand curve to shift to the left. The demand curve shifts from D_1 to D_2, and the exchange rate falls to E_2. Because the domestic interest rate will rise back to its initial level in the long run, the relative expected return of dollar assets will increase somewhat, sending the demand curve to D_3, but not all the way back to D_1 because the price level will still be higher in the long run. The exchange rate thus rises from E_2 to E_3, which is still below the initial value of E_1. The result is the same one we found in the previous chapter, in which there is exchange rate overshooting—that is, the exchange rate falls by more in the short run than in the long run.

Our analysis leads us to the following conclusion about unsterilized interventions in the foreign exchange market: ***An unsterilized intervention in which domestic currency is sold to purchase foreign assets leads to a gain in international reserves, an increase in the money supply, and a depreciation of the domestic currency.***

The reverse result is found for an unsterilized intervention in which domestic currency is purchased by selling foreign assets. The purchase of domestic currency by selling foreign assets (reducing international reserves) works like an open market sale to reduce the monetary base and the money supply. The decrease in the money supply raises the interest rate on dollar assets and lowers the long-run price level, thereby increasing the future expected exchange rate. The resulting increase in the relative expected return on dollar assets means that people will buy more dollar assets, so the demand curve shifts to the right and the exchange rate rises. ***An unsterilized intervention in which domestic currency is purchased by selling foreign assets leads to a drop in international reserves, a decrease in the money supply, and an appreciation of the domestic currency.***

Sterilized Intervention

The key point to remember about a sterilized intervention is that the central bank engages in offsetting open market operations, so that there is no impact on the monetary base and the money supply. In the context of the model of exchange rate determination we have developed here, it is straightforward to show that a sterilized intervention has almost *no effect* on the exchange rate. A sterilized intervention leaves the money supply unchanged and so has no direct way of affecting interest rates or the expected future exchange rate.[2] Because the relative expected return on dollar assets is unaffected, the demand curve would remain at D_1 in Figure 20-1, and the exchange rate would remain unchanged at E_1.

At first it might seem puzzling that a central bank purchase or sale of domestic currency that is sterilized does not lead to a change in the exchange rate. A central bank purchase of domestic currency cannot raise the exchange rate, because with no effect on the domestic money supply or interest rates, any resulting rise in the exchange rate would mean that there would be an excess supply of dollar assets. With more people willing to sell dollar assets than to buy them, the exchange rate would have to fall back to its initial equilibrium level, where the demand and supply curves intersect.

BALANCE OF PAYMENTS

Because international financial transactions such as foreign exchange interventions have considerable effects on monetary policy, it is worth knowing how these transactions are measured. The **balance of payments** is a bookkeeping system for recording all receipts and payments that have a direct bearing on the movement of funds between a nation (private sector and government) and foreign countries.

Here we examine the key items in the balance of payments that you often hear about in the media.[3]

The **current account** shows international transactions that involve currently produced goods and services. The difference between merchandise exports and imports, the net receipts from trade, is called the **trade balance**. When exports

---

[2] A sterilized intervention changes the amount of foreign securities relative to domestic securities in the hands of the public, called a *portfolio balance effect*. Through this effect, the central bank might be able to affect the interest differential between domestic and foreign assets, which in turn affects the relative expected return of domestic assets. Empirical evidence has not revealed this portfolio balance effect to be significant. However, a sterilized intervention *could* indicate what central banks want to happen to the future exchange rate and so might provide a signal about the course of future monetary policy. In this way a sterilized intervention could lead to shifts in the demand curve for domestic assets and ultimately affect the exchange rate. However, the future change in monetary policy—not the sterilized intervention—is the source of the exchange rate effect. For a further discussion of the signalling and portfolio balance effects and the possible differential effects of sterilized versus unsterilized intervention, see Paul Krugman and Maurice Obstfeld, *International Economics,* 7th ed. (Boston: Addison-Wesley, 2006).

[3] A Web Appendix to this chapter on this book's MyEconLab at **www.pearsoned.ca/myeconlab** discusses the Canadian balance of payments in more detail.

are greater than imports as in 2007 by $28.8 billion, we have a trade surplus; if imports are greater than exports, we have a trade deficit.

Additional items included in the current account are the net receipts (cash flows received from abroad minus cash flows sent abroad) from three categories: investment income, service transactions, and unilateral transfers (gifts, pensions, and foreign aid). In 2007, for example, net investment income was minus $14.2 billion for Canada because Canadians received less investment income from abroad than they paid out. Since Canadians made more unilateral transfers to foreign countries than foreigners made to Canada, net unilateral transfers were minus $1 billion. The sum of the previous two items plus the trade balance is the current account balance, which in 2007 showed a surplus of $13.6 billion.

Another important item in the balance of payments is the **capital account**, the net receipts from capital transactions. In 2007 the capital account was $4.2 billion, indicating that $4.2 billion more capital came into Canada than left Canada. Another way of saying this is that Canada had a net capital inflow of $4.2 billion.[4] The sum of the current account and the capital account equals the **official reserve transactions balance**, which was $21.9 billion in 2007. When economists refer to a surplus or deficit in the balance of payments, they actually mean a surplus or deficit in the official reserve transactions balance.

Because the balance of payments must balance, the official reserve transactions balance, which equals the current account plus the capital account, tells us the net amount of international reserves that must move between governments (as represented by their central banks) to finance international transactions. The relationship between the current account, the capital account, and the change in net government international reserves can thus be expressed as:

Current account + capital account = net change in government international reserves

This equation shows us why the current account receives so much attention from economists and the media. The current account balance tells us whether Canada (private sector and government combined) is increasing or decreasing its claims on foreign wealth. A surplus indicates that Canada is increasing its claims on foreign wealth, and thus is increasing its holdings of foreign assets (both good things for Canadians), and a deficit indicates that Canada is reducing its holdings of foreign assets and foreign countries are increasing their claims on Canada.[5]

For example, the rapid growth in the U.S. current account deficit in recent years, which is nearing US$1 trillion, has raised serious concerns that these large deficits may have negative consequences for the U.S. economy (see the Global box, Why the Large U.S. Current Account Deficit Worries Economists).

---

[4] Note that the capital account balance number reported above includes a statistical discrepancy item that represents errors due to unrecorded transactions involving smuggling and other capital flows ($4.1 billion in 2007). Many experts believe that the statistical discrepancy item, which keeps the balance of payments in balance, is primarily the result of large hidden capital flows, and this is why it is included in the capital account balance reported above.

[5] The current account balance can also be viewed as showing by how much total saving exceeds private sector and government investment in Canada. We can see this by noting that total Canadian saving equals the increase in total wealth held by the Canadian private sector and government. Total investment equals the increase in the Canadian capital stock (wealth physically in Canada). The difference between them is the increase in Canadian claims on foreign wealth.

| GLOBAL | Why the Large U.S. Current Account Deficit Worries Economists |

The massive U.S. current account deficit in recent years, which now exceeds 6% of GDP, the highest level reached over the past century, worries economists for several reasons. First, it says that at current values of the exchange rate, foreigners' demand for U.S. exports is far less than Americans' demand for imports. As we saw in the previous chapter, low demand for U.S. exports and high U.S. demand for imports may lead to a future decline in the value of the U.S. dollar. Some economists estimate that the decline could be very large, with the U.S. dollar depreciating by as much as 50%.

Second, the current account deficit means that foreigners' claims on U.S. assets are rising, and these claims will have to be paid back. Americans are thus mortgaging their future to foreigners, and when the bill comes due, Americans will be poorer. Furthermore, if Americans have a greater preference for U.S. dollar assets than foreigners, the movement of American wealth to foreigners can decrease the demand for U.S. dollar assets over time and provide another reason why the U.S. dollar might depreciate.

The hope is that the eventual decline of the U.S. dollar resulting from the large U.S. current account deficit will be a gradual one, occurring over a period of several years. If however, the decline is precipitous, it could potentially disrupt financial markets and hurt the U.S. economy.

EXCHANGE RATE REGIMES IN THE INTERNATIONAL FINANCIAL SYSTEM

Exchange rate regimes in the international financial system are of two basic types: fixed and floating. In a **fixed exchange rate regime**, the value of a currency is pegged relative to the value of one other currency (called the **anchor currency**), so that the exchange rate is fixed in terms of the anchor country. In a **floating exchange rate regime**, the value of a currency is allowed to fluctuate against all other currencies. When countries intervene in foreign exchange markets in an attempt to influence their exchange rates by buying and selling foreign assets, the regime is referred to as a **managed float regime** (or a **dirty float**).

In examining past exchange rate regimes, we start with the gold standard of the late nineteenth and early twentieth centuries.

Gold Standard   Before World War I, the world economy operated under the gold standard, a fixed exchange rate regime in which most currencies were convertible directly into gold at fixed rates, so exchange rates between countries were also fixed. Canadian dollar bills, for example, could be exchanged for approximately 1/20 ounce of gold. Likewise, the British Treasury would exchange 1/4 ounce of gold for £1. Because a Canadian could convert $20 into 1 ounce of gold, which could be used to buy £4, the exchange rate between the pound and the Canadian dollar was effectively fixed at approximately $5 to the pound. The fixed exchange rates under the gold standard had the important advantage of encouraging world trade by eliminating the uncertainty that occurs when exchange rates fluctuate.

As long as countries abided by the rules under the gold standard and kept their currencies backed by and convertible into gold, exchange rates remained fixed. However, adherence to the gold standard meant that a country had no control over its monetary policy because its money supply was determined by gold flows between countries. Furthermore, monetary policy throughout the world was greatly influenced by the production of gold and gold discoveries. When gold production was low in the 1870s and 1880s, the money supply throughout the world grew slowly and did not keep pace with the growth of the world economy. The result was deflation (falling price levels). Gold discoveries in Alaska and South Africa in the 1890s greatly expanded gold production, causing money supplies to increase rapidly and price levels to rise (inflation) until World War I.

The Bretton Woods System

After World War II, the victors set up a fixed exchange rate system that became known as the **Bretton Woods system**, after the New Hampshire town in which the agreement was negotiated in 1944. The Bretton Woods system was in effect until 1971.

The Bretton Woods agreement created the **International Monetary Fund (IMF)**, headquartered in Washington, D.C., which had 30 original member countries in 1945 and currently has 180. The IMF was given the task of promoting the growth of world trade by setting rules for the maintenance of fixed exchange rates and by making loans to countries that were experiencing balance-of-payments difficulties. As part of its role of monitoring the compliance of member countries with its rules, the IMF also took on the job of collecting and standardizing international economic data.

The Bretton Woods agreement also set up the International Bank for Reconstruction and Development, commonly referred to as the **World Bank**, also headquartered in Washington, D.C., which provides long-term loans to help developing countries build dams, roads, and other physical capital that would contribute to their economic development. The funds for these loans are obtained primarily by issuing World Bank bonds, which are sold in the capital markets of the developed countries. In addition, the General Agreement on Tariffs and Trade (GATT), headquartered in Geneva, was set up to monitor rules for the conduct of trade between countries (tariffs and quotas) and the GATT has evolved into the **World Trade Organization (WTO)**.

Because the United States emerged from World War II as the world's largest economic power, with over half of the world's manufacturing capacity and the greater part of the world's gold, the Bretton Woods system of fixed exchange rates was based on the convertibility of U.S. dollars into gold (for foreign governments and central banks only) at US$35 per ounce. The fixed exchange rates were to be maintained by intervention in the foreign exchange market by central banks in countries besides the United States who bought and sold U.S. dollar assets, which they held as international reserves. The U.S. dollar, which was used by other countries to denominate the assets that they held as international reserves, was called the **reserve currency**. Thus an important feature of the Bretton Woods system was the establishment of the United States as the reserve currency country. Even after the breakup of the Bretton Woods system, the U.S. dollar has kept its position as the reserve currency in which most international financial transactions are conducted. However, with the creation of the euro in 1999, the supremacy of the U.S. dollar may be subject to a serious challenge (see the Global box, The Euro's Challenge to the U.S. Dollar).

GLOBAL   The Euro's Challenge to the U.S. Dollar

With the creation of the European Monetary Union and the euro in 1999, the U.S. dollar is facing a challenge to its position as the key reserve currency in international financial transactions. Adoption of the euro increases integration of Europe's financial markets, which could help them rival those in the United States. The resulting increase in the use of euros in financial markets will make it more likely that international transactions are carried out in the euro. The economic clout of the European Union rivals that of the United States; both have a similar share of world GDP (around 20%) and world exports (around 15%). If the European Central Bank can make sure that inflation remains low so that the euro becomes a sound currency, this should bode well for the euro.

However, for the euro to eat into the U.S. dollar's position as a reserve currency, the European Union must function as a cohesive political entity that can exert its influence on the world stage. There are serious doubts on this score, however, particularly with the "no" votes on the European constitution by France and the Netherlands in 2005, and most analysts think it will be a long time before the euro beats out the U.S. dollar in international financial transactions.

The fixed exchange rate dictated by the Bretton Woods system was abandoned in 1971. From 1979 to 1990, however, the European Union instituted among its members a fixed exchange rate system, the European Monetary System (EMS). In the *exchange rate mechanism* (ERM) in this system, the exchange rate between any pair of currencies of the participating countries was not supposed to fluctuate outside narrow limits, called the "snake." In practice, all of the countries in the EMS pegged their currencies to the German mark.

How a Fixed Exchange Rate Regime Works

Figure 20-2 shows how a fixed exchange rate regime works in practice by using the supply and demand analysis of the foreign exchange market we learned in the previous chapter. Panel (a) describes a situation in which the domestic currency is fixed relative to an anchor currency at E_{par}, while the demand curve has shifted left to D_1, perhaps because foreign interest rates have risen, thereby lowering the relative expected return of domestic assets. At E_{par}, the exchange rate is now *overvalued*: The demand curve D_1 intersects the supply curve at an exchange rate E_1, which is lower than the fixed (par) value of the exchange rate E_{par}. To keep the exchange rate at E_{par}, the central bank must intervene in the foreign exchange market to purchase domestic currency by selling foreign assets. This action, like an open market sale, means that both the monetary base and the money supply decline, driving up the interest rate on domestic assets, i^{D}.[6] This increase in the domestic interest rate raises the relative expected return on domestic assets, shifting the demand curve to the right. The central bank will continue purchasing domestic currency until the demand curve reaches D_2 and the equilibrium exchange rate is at E_{par} at point 2 in panel (a).

---

[6] Because the exchange rate will continue to be fixed at E_{par}, the expected future exchange rate remains unchanged and so does not need to be addressed in the analysis.

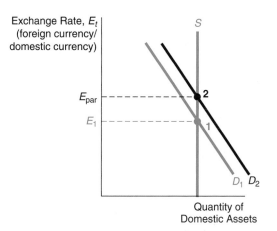

(a) Intervention in the case of an overvalued exchange rate

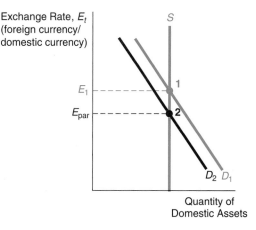

(b) Intervention in the case of an undervalued exchange

FIGURE 20-2   Intervention in the Foreign Exchange Rate Market Under a Fixed Exchange Rate Regime

In panel (a), the exchange rate at E_{par} is overvalued. To keep the exchange rate at E_{par} (point 2), the central bank must purchase domestic currency to shift the demand curve to D_2. In panel (b), the exchange rate at E_{par} is undervalued, so the central bank must sell domestic currency to shift the demand curve to D_2 and keep the exchange rate at E_{par} (point 2).

We have thus come to the conclusion that ***when the domestic currency is overvalued, the central bank must purchase domestic currency to keep the exchange rate fixed, but as a result it loses international reserves.***

Panel (b) in Figure 20-2 describes the situation in which the demand curve has shifted to the right to D_1 because the relative expected return on domestic assets has risen and hence the exchange rate is undervalued: The initial demand curve D_1 intersects the supply curve at exchange rate E_1, which is above E_{par}. In this situation, the central bank must sell domestic currency and purchase foreign assets. This action works like an open market purchase to increase the money supply and lower the interest rate on domestic assets i^D. The central bank keeps selling domestic currency and lowering i^D until the demand curve shifts all the way to D_2, where the equilibrium exchange rate is at E_{par}—point 2 in panel (b). Our analysis thus leads us to the following result: ***When the domestic currency is undervalued, the central bank must sell domestic currency to keep the exchange rate fixed, but as a result it gains international reserves.***

As we have seen, if a country's currency is overvalued, its central bank's attempts to keep the currency from depreciating will result in a loss of international reserves. If the country's central bank eventually runs out of international reserves, it cannot keep its currency from depreciating, and a **devaluation** must occur, in which the par exchange rate is reset at a lower level.

If, by contrast, a country's currency is undervalued, its central bank's intervention to keep the currency from appreciating leads to a gain of international reserves. As we will see shortly, the central bank might not want to acquire these international reserves, and so it might want to reset the par value of its exchange rate at a higher level (a **revaluation**).

If there is perfect capital mobility—that is, if there are no barriers to domestic residents purchasing foreign assets or foreigners purchasing domestic assets—then a sterilized exchange rate intervention cannot keep the exchange rate at E_{par}

because, as we saw earlier in the chapter, the relative expected return of domestic assets is unaffected. For example, if the exchange rate is overvalued, a sterilized purchase of domestic currency will leave the relative expected return and the demand curve unchanged—so pressure for a depreciation of the domestic currency is not removed. If the central bank keeps purchasing its domestic currency but continues to sterilize, it will just keep losing international reserves until it finally runs out of them and is forced to let the value of the currency seek a lower level.

One important implication of the foregoing analysis is that a country that ties its exchange rate to an anchor currency of a larger country loses control of its monetary policy. If the larger country pursues a more contractionary monetary policy and decreases its money supply, this would lead to lower expected inflation in the larger country, thus causing an appreciation of the larger country's currency and a depreciation of the smaller country's currency. The smaller country, having locked in its exchange rate to the anchor currency, will now find its currency overvalued and will therefore have to sell the anchor currency and buy its own to keep its currency from depreciating. The result of this foreign exchange intervention will then be a decline in the smaller country's international reserves, a contraction of its monetary base, and thus a decline in its money supply. Sterilization of this foreign exchange intervention is not an option because this would just lead to a continuing loss of international reserves until the smaller country was forced to devalue its currency. The smaller country no longer controls its monetary policy, because movements in its money supply are completely determined by movements in the larger country's money supply.

Another way to see that when a country fixes its exchange rate to a larger country's currency it loses control of its monetary policy through the interest parity condition discussed in Web Appendix 19.1. There we saw that when there is capital mobility, the domestic interest rate equals the foreign interest rate minus the expected appreciation of the domestic currency. With a fixed exchange rate, expected appreciation of the domestic currency is zero, so that the domestic interest rate equals the foreign interest rate. Therefore, changes in the monetary policy in the large anchor country that affect its interest rate are directly transmitted to interest rates in the smaller country. Furthermore, because the monetary authorities in the smaller country cannot make their interest rate deviate from that of the larger country, they have no way to use monetary policy to affect their economy.

APPLICATION   How Did China Accumulate Nearly US$2 Trillion of International Reserves?

By the end of 2008, China had accumulated nearly US$2 trillion of international reserves. How did the Chinese get their hands on this vast amount of foreign assets? After all, China is not yet a rich country.

The answer is that China pegged its exchange rate to the U.S. dollar at a fixed rate of 8.28 yuan (also called renminbi) to the U.S. dollar in 1994. Because of China's rapidly growing productivity and an inflation rate that is lower than in the United States, the long-run value of the yuan has increased, leading to a higher relative expected return for yuan assets and a rightward shift of the demand for yuan assets. As a result, the Chinese have found themselves in the situation depicted in panel (b) of Figure 20-2, in which the yuan is undervalued. To keep the yuan from appreciating above E_{par} to E_1 in the figure, the Chinese central bank has been engaging in massive purchases of U.S. dollar assets. Today the Chinese government is one of the largest holders of U.S. government bonds in the world.

The pegging of the yuan to the U.S. dollar has created several problems for Chinese authorities. First, the Chinese now own a lot of U.S. assets, particularly U.S. Treasury securities, which have very low returns. Second, the undervaluation of the yuan has meant that Chinese goods are so cheap abroad that many countries have threatened to erect trade barriers against these goods if the Chinese government does not allow an upward revaluation of the yuan. Third, as we learned earlier in the chapter, the Chinese purchase of U.S. dollar assets has resulted in a substantial increase in the Chinese monetary base and money supply, which has the potential to produce high inflation in the future. Because the Chinese authorities have created substantial roadblocks to capital mobility, they have been able to sterilize most of their exchange rate interventions while maintaining the exchange rate peg. Nevertheless, they still worry about inflationary pressures. In July 2005, China finally made its peg somewhat more flexible by letting the value of the yuan rise 2.1% and subsequently allowed it to appreciate at a gradual pace. The central bank also indicated that it would no longer fix the yuan to the U.S. dollar, but would instead maintain its value relative to a basket of currencies.

Why did the Chinese authorities maintain this exchange rate peg for so long despite the problems? One answer is that they wanted to keep their export sector humming by keeping the prices of their export goods low. A second answer might be that they wanted to accumulate a large amount of international reserves as a "war chest" that could be sold to buy yuan in the event of a speculative attack against the yuan at some future date. Given the pressure on the Chinese government to further revalue its currency from government officials in the United States and Europe, there are likely to be further adjustments in China's exchange rate policy in the future.

HOW THE BRETTON WOODS SYSTEM WORKED   Under the Bretton Woods system, exchange rates were supposed to change only when a country was experiencing a "fundamental disequilibrium"—that is, large persistent deficits or surpluses in its balance of payments. To maintain fixed exchange rates when countries had balance-of-payments deficits and were losing international reserves, the IMF would loan deficit countries international reserves contributed by other members. As a result of its power to dictate loan terms to borrowing countries, the IMF could encourage deficit countries to pursue contractionary monetary policies that would strengthen their currency or eliminate their balance-of-payments deficits. If the IMF loans were not sufficient to prevent depreciation of a currency, the country was allowed to devalue its currency by setting a new, lower exchange rate.

A notable weakness of the Bretton Woods system was that although deficit countries losing international reserves could be pressured into devaluing their currencies or pursuing contractionary policies, the IMF had no way to force surplus countries to revise their exchange rates upward or pursue more expansionary policies. Particularly troublesome in this regard was the fact that the reserve currency country, the United States, could not devalue its currency under the Bretton Woods system even if the U.S. dollar was overvalued. When the United States attempted to reduce domestic unemployment in the 1960s by pursuing an inflationary monetary policy, a fundamental disequilibrium of an overvalued dollar developed. Because surplus countries were not willing to revise their exchange rates upward, adjustment in the Bretton Woods system did not take place, and the system collapsed in 1971. Attempts to patch up the Bretton Woods system with the Smithsonian Agreement in December 1971 proved unsuccessful, and by 1973, the United States and its trading partners had agreed to allow exchange rates to float.

Managed Float

Although most exchange rates are currently allowed to change daily in response to market forces, central banks have not been willing to give up their option of intervening in the foreign exchange market. Preventing large changes in exchange rates makes it easier for firms and individuals purchasing or selling goods abroad to plan into the future. Furthermore, countries with surpluses in their balance of payments frequently do not want to see their currencies appreciate because it makes their goods more expensive abroad and foreign goods cheaper in their country. Because an appreciation might hurt sales for domestic businesses and increase unemployment, surplus countries have often sold their currency in the foreign exchange market and acquired international reserves.

Countries with balance-of-payments deficits do not want to see their currency lose value because it makes foreign goods more expensive for domestic consumers and can stimulate inflation. To keep the value of the domestic currency high, deficit countries have often bought their own currency exchange in the foreign exchange market and given up international reserves.

The current international financial system is a hybrid of a fixed and a flexible exchange rate system. Rates fluctuate in response to market forces but are not determined solely by them. Furthermore, many countries continue to keep the value of their currency fixed against other currencies, as was the case in the European Monetary System (to be described shortly).

Another important feature of the current system is the continuing de-emphasis of gold in international financial transactions. Not only has the United States suspended convertibility of dollars into gold for foreign central banks, but also since 1970 the IMF has been issuing a paper substitute for gold, called **special drawing rights (SDRs)**. Like gold in the Bretton Woods system, SDRs function as international reserves. Unlike gold, whose quantity is determined by gold discoveries and the rate of production, SDRs can be created by the IMF whenever it decides that there is a need for additional international reserves to promote world trade and economic growth.

The use of gold in international transactions was further de-emphasized by the IMF's elimination of the official gold price in 1975 and the sale of gold by the U.S. Treasury and the IMF to private investors in order to demonetize it. Currently, the price of gold is determined in a free market. Investors who want to speculate in it are able to purchase and sell at will, as are jewellers and dentists who use gold in their businesses.

European Monetary System (EMS)

In March 1979, eight members of the European Economic Community (Germany, France, Italy, the Netherlands, Belgium, Luxembourg, Denmark, and Ireland) set up an exchange rate union, the European Monetary System (EMS), in which they agreed to fix their exchange rates vis-à-vis one another and to float jointly against the U.S. dollar. Spain joined the EMS in June 1989, the United Kingdom in October 1990, and Portugal in April 1992. The EMS created a new monetary unit, the *European currency unit* (ECU), whose value was tied to a basket of specified amounts of European currencies.

The exchange rate mechanism (ERM) of the European Monetary System worked as follows. The exchange rate between every pair of currencies of the participating countries was not allowed to fluctuate outside narrow limits around a fixed exchange rate. (The limits were typically ±2.25% but were raised to ±15% in August 1993.) When the exchange rate between two countries' currencies moved outside these limits, the central banks of both countries were supposed to intervene in the foreign exchange market. If, for example, the French franc depreciated below its lower limit against the German mark, the Bank of France was required to buy francs and sell marks, thereby giving up international reserves. Similarly, the German central bank was also required to intervene to sell marks and buy francs and consequently increase its international reserves. The EMS thus required that intervention be symmetric when a currency fell outside the limits, with the central bank with the weak currency giving up international reserves and the one with the strong currency gaining them. Central bank intervention was also very common even when the exchange rate was within the limits, but in this case, if one central bank intervened, no others were required to intervene as well.

A serious shortcoming of fixed exchange rate systems such as the Bretton Woods system or the European Monetary System is that they can lead to foreign exchange crises involving a "speculative attack" on a currency—massive sales of a weak currency or purchases of a strong currency that cause a sharp change in the exchange rate. In the following application, we use our model of exchange rate determination to understand how the September 1992 exchange rate crisis that rocked the European Monetary System came about.

APPLICATION	The Foreign Exchange Crisis of September 1992

In the aftermath of German reunification in October 1990, the German central bank, the Bundesbank, faced rising inflationary pressures, with inflation having accelerated from below 3% in 1990 to near 5% by 1992. To get monetary growth under control and to dampen inflation, the Bundesbank raised German interest rates to near double-digit levels. Figure 20-3 shows the consequences of these actions by the Bundesbank in the foreign exchange market for British pounds. Note that in the diagram, the pound is the domestic currency and the German mark (deutsche mark, DM, Germany's currency before the advent of the euro in 1999) is the foreign currency.

The increase in German interest rates i^F lowered the relative expected return of British pound assets and shifted the demand curve to D_2 in Figure 20-3. The intersection of the supply and demand curves at point 2 was now below the lower exchange rate limit at that time (2.778 marks per pound, denoted E_{par}). To increase the value of the pound relative to the mark and to restore the mark/pound exchange rate to within the exchange rate mechanism limits, one of two things had to happen. The Bank of England would have to pursue a contractionary monetary policy, thereby raising British interest rates sufficiently to shift the demand curve back to D_1 so that the equilibrium would remain at point 1, where the exchange rate would remain at E_{par}. Alternatively, the Bundesbank would have to pursue an expansionary monetary policy, thereby lowering German interest rates. Lower German interest rates would raise the relative expected return on British assets and shift the demand curve back to D_1 so the exchange rate would be at E_{par}.

The catch was that the Bundesbank, whose primary goal was fighting inflation, was unwilling to pursue an expansionary monetary policy, and the British, who were facing their worst recession in the postwar period, were unwilling to pursue a contractionary monetary policy to prop up the pound. This impasse became clear when in response to great pressure from other members of the EMS, the Bundesbank was willing to lower its lending rates by only a token amount on September 14 after a speculative attack was mounted on the currencies of the Scandinavian countries. So at some point in the near future, the value of the pound would have to decline to point 2. Speculators now knew that the depreciation of

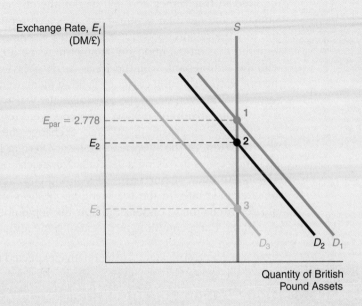

FIGURE 20-3   Foreign Exchange Market for British Pounds in 1992

The realization by speculators that the United Kingdom would soon devalue the pound decreased the relative expected return on British pound assets, resulting in a leftward shift of the demand curve from D_2 to D_3. The result was the need for a much greater purchase of pounds by the British central bank to raise the interest rate so that the demand curve would shift back to D_1 and keep the exchange rate E_{par} at 2.778 German marks per pound.

the pound was imminent. As a result, the relative expected return of the pound fell sharply, shifting the demand curve left to D_3 in Figure 20-3.

As a result of the large leftward shift of the demand curve, there was now a huge excess supply of pound assets at the par exchange rate E_{par}, which caused a massive sell-off of pounds (and purchases of marks) by speculators. The need for the British central bank to intervene to raise the value of the pound now became much greater and required a huge rise in British interest rates. After a major intervention effort on the part of the Bank of England, which included a rise in its lending rate from 10% to 15%, which still wasn't enough, the British were finally forced to give up on September 16: They pulled out of the ERM indefinitely and allowed the pound to depreciate by 10% against the mark.

Speculative attacks on other currencies forced devaluation of the Spanish peseta by 5% and the Italian lira by 15%. To defend its currency, the Swedish central bank was forced to raise its daily lending rate to the astronomical level of 500%! By the time the crisis was over, the British, French, Italian, Spanish, and Swedish central banks had intervened to the tune of US$100 billion; the Bundesbank alone had laid out US$50 billion for foreign exchange intervention. Because foreign exchange crises lead to large changes in central banks' holdings of international reserves and thus significantly affect the official reserve asset items in the balance of payments, these crises are also referred to as **balance-of-payments crises**.

The attempt to prop up the European Monetary System was not cheap for these central banks. It is estimated that they lost US$4 billion to US$6 billion as a result of exchange rate intervention during the crisis. What the central banks lost, the speculators gained. A speculative fund run by George Soros ran up US$1 billion of profits during the crisis, and Citibank traders reportedly made US$200 million. When an exchange rate crisis comes, life can certainly be sweet for exchange rate speculators.

| APPLICATION | **Recent Foreign Exchange Crises in Emerging Market Countries: Mexico 1994, East Asia 1997, Brazil 1999, and Argentina 2002** |

Major currency crises in emerging market countries have been a common occurrence in recent years. We can use Figure 20-3 to understand the sequence of events during the currency crises in Mexico in 1994, East Asia in 1997, Brazil in 1999, and Argentina in 2002. To do so, we just need to recognize that United States dollars are the foreign currency, while the domestic currency was either pesos, baht, or reals. (Note that the exchange rate label on the vertical axis would be in terms of U.S. dollars/domestic currency and that the label on the horizontal axis would be the quantity of domestic currency (say, pesos) assets.)

In Mexico in March 1994, political instability (the assassination of the ruling party's presidential candidate) sparked investors' concerns that the peso might be devalued. The result was that the relative expected return on peso assets fell, thus moving the demand curve from D_1 to D_2 in Figure 20-3. In the case of Thailand in May 1997, the large current account deficit and the weakness of the Thai financial system raised similar concerns about the devaluation of the domestic currency, with the same effect on the demand curve. In Brazil in late 1998 and Argentina in 2001, concerns about fiscal situations that could lead to the printing of money to finance the deficit, and thereby raise inflation, also meant that a devaluation was more likely to occur. The concerns thus lowered the relative expected return on domestic assets and shifted the demand curve from D_1 to D_2. In all of these cases, the result was that the intersection of the supply and demand curves was below the pegged value of the domestic currency at E_{par}.

To keep their domestic currencies from falling below E_{par}, these countries' central banks needed to buy the domestic currency and sell U.S. dollars to raise interest rates and shift the demand curve to the right, in the process losing international reserves. At first, the central banks were successful in containing the speculative attacks. However, when more bad news broke, speculators became even more confident that these countries could not defend their currencies. (The bad news was everywhere: In Mexico, there was an uprising in Chiapas and revelations about problems in the banking system; in Thailand, there was a major failure of a financial institution; Brazil had a worsening fiscal situation, along with a threat by a governor to default on his state's debt; and in Argentina, a full-scale bank panic and an actual default on the government debt occurred.) As a result, the relative expected returns on domestic assets fell further, the demand curve moved much farther to the left to D_3, and the central banks lost even more international reserves. Given the stress on the economy from rising interest rates and the loss of reserves, eventually the monetary authorities could no longer continue to defend the currency and were forced to give up and let their currencies depreciate. This scenario happened in Mexico in December 1994, in Thailand in July 1997, in Brazil in January 1999, and in Argentina in January 2002.

Concerns about similar problems in other countries then triggered speculative attacks against them as well. This contagion occurred in the aftermath of the Mexican crisis (jauntily referred to as the "Tequila effect") with speculative attacks on other Latin American currencies, but there were no further currency collapses. In the East Asian crisis, however, fears of devaluation spread throughout the region, leading to a scenario akin to that depicted in Figure 20-3. Consequently, one by one, Indonesia, Malaysia, South Korea, and the Philippines were forced to devalue sharply. Even Hong Kong, Singapore, and Taiwan were subjected to speculative attacks, but because these countries had healthy financial systems, the attacks were successfully averted.

As we saw in Chapter 8, the sharp depreciations in Mexico, East Asia, and Argentina led to full-scale financial crises that severely damaged these countries' economies. The foreign exchange crisis that shocked the European Monetary System in September 1992 cost central banks a lot of money, but the public in European countries were not seriously affected. By contrast, the public in Mexico, Argentina, and the crisis countries of East Asia were not so lucky: The collapse of these currencies triggered by speculative attacks led to the financial crises described in Chapter 8, producing severe depressions that caused hardship and political unrest.

CAPITAL CONTROLS

Because capital flows were an important element in the currency crises in Mexico and East Asia, politicians and some economists have advocated that emerging-market countries avoid financial instability by restricting capital mobility. Are capital controls a good idea?

Controls on Capital Outflows

Capital outflows can promote financial instability in emerging-market countries because when domestic residents and foreigners pull their capital out of a country, the resulting capital outflow forces a country to devalue its currency. This is why recently some politicians in emerging-market countries have found capital controls particularly attractive. For example, Prime Minister Mahathir of Malaysia instituted capital controls in 1998 to restrict outflows in the aftermath of the East Asian crisis.

Although these controls sound like a good idea, they suffer from several disadvantages. First, empirical evidence indicates that controls on capital outflows are seldom effective during a crisis because the private sector finds ingenious ways to evade them and has little difficulty moving funds out of the country.[7] Second, the evidence suggests that capital flight may even increase after controls are put into place because confidence in the government is weakened. Third, controls on capital outflows often lead to corruption, as government officials get paid off to look the other way when domestic residents are trying to move funds abroad. Fourth, controls on capital outflows may lull governments into thinking they do not have to take the steps to reform their financial systems to deal with the crisis, with the result that opportunities to improve the functioning of the economy are lost.

Controls on Capital Inflows

Although most economists find the arguments against controls on capital outflows persuasive, controls on capital inflows receive more support. Supporters reason that if speculative capital cannot come in, then it cannot go out suddenly and create a crisis. Our analysis of the financial crises in East Asia in Chapter 8 provides support

---

[7] See Sebastian Edwards, "How Effective Are Capital Controls?" *Journal of Economic Perspectives,* Winter 2000; vol. 13, no. 4, pp. 65–84.

for this view by suggesting that capital inflows can lead to a lending boom and excessive risk taking on the part of banks, which then helps trigger a financial crisis.

However, controls on capital inflows have the undesirable feature that they may block from entering a country funds that would be used for productive investment opportunities. Although such controls may limit the fuel supplied to lending booms through capital flows, over time they produce substantial distortions and misallocation of resources as households and businesses try to get around them. Indeed, just as with controls on capital outflows, controls on capital inflows can lead to corruption. There are serious doubts whether capital controls can be effective in today's environment, in which trade is open and where there are many financial instruments that make it easier to get around these controls.

On the other hand, there is a strong case for improving bank regulation and supervision so that capital inflows are less likely to produce a lending boom and encourage excessive risk taking by banking institutions. For example, restricting banks in how fast their borrowing can grow might substantially limit capital inflows. Supervisory controls that focus on the sources of financial fragility, rather than the symptoms, can enhance the efficiency of the financial system rather than hamper it.

THE ROLE OF THE IMF

The International Monetary Fund was originally set up under the Bretton Woods system to help countries deal with balance-of-payments problems and stay with the fixed exchange rates by lending to deficit countries. When the Bretton Woods system of fixed exchange rates collapsed in 1971, the IMF took on new roles.

The IMF continues to function as a data collector and provides technical assistance to its member countries. Although the IMF no longer attempts to encourage fixed exchange rates, its role as an international lender has become more important recently. This role first came to the fore in the 1980s during the third-world debt crisis, in which the IMF assisted developing countries in repaying their loans. The financial crises in Mexico in 1994–1995 and in East Asia in 1997–1998 led to huge loans by the IMF to these and other affected countries to help them recover from their financial crises and to prevent the spread of these crises to other countries. This role, in which the IMF acts like an international lender of last resort to cope with financial instability, is indeed highly controversial.

Should the IMF Be an International Lender of Last Resort?

As we saw in Chapter 17, when a financial crisis occurs in industrialized countries and the financial system threatens to seize up, domestic central banks can address matters with a lender-of-last-resort operation to limit the degree of instability in the banking system. In emerging markets, however, where the credibility of the central bank as an inflation fighter may be in doubt and debt contracts are typically short-term and in foreign currencies, a lender-of-last-resort operation becomes a double-edged sword—as likely to exacerbate the financial crisis as to alleviate it. For example, when the U.S. Federal Reserve engaged in a lender-of-last-resort operation during the 1987 stock market crash and after the 2001 terrorist destruction of the World Trade Center, there was almost no sentiment in the markets that there would be substantially higher inflation. However, for a central bank with less inflation-fighting credibility than the Fed, central bank lending to the financial system in the wake of a financial crisis—even under the lender-of-last-resort rhetoric—may well arouse fears of inflation spiraling out of control, causing an even greater currency depreciation and still greater deterioration of balance sheets. The resulting increase in moral hazard and adverse selection problems in financial markets, along the lines discussed in Chapter 8, would only make the financial crisis worse.

Central banks in emerging-market countries therefore have only a very limited ability to successfully engage in a lender-of-last-resort operation. However, liquidity provided by an international lender of last resort does not have these undesirable consequences, and in helping to stabilize the value of the domestic currency it strengthens domestic balance sheets. Moreover, an international lender of last resort may be able to prevent contagion, the situation in which a successful speculative attack on one emerging-market currency leads to attacks on other emerging-market currencies, spreading financial and economic disruption. Since a lender of last resort for emerging-market countries is needed at times, and since it cannot be provided domestically, there is a strong rationale for an international institution to fill this role. Indeed, since Mexico's financial crisis in 1994, the International Monetary Fund and other international agencies have stepped into the lender-of-last-resort role and provided emergency lending to countries threatened by financial instability.

However, support from an international lender of last resort brings risks of its own, especially the risk that the perception it is standing ready to bail out irresponsible financial institutions may lead to excessive risk taking of the sort that makes financial crises more likely. In the Mexican and East Asian crises, governments in the crisis countries used IMF support to protect depositors and other creditors of banking institutions from losses. This safety net creates a well-known moral hazard problem because the depositors and other creditors have less incentive to monitor these banking institutions and withdraw their deposits if the institutions are taking on too much risk. The result is that these institutions are encouraged to take on excessive risks. Indeed, critics of the IMF—most prominently the U.S. Congressional Commission headed by Professor Alan Meltzer of Carnegie-Mellon University—contend that IMF lending in the Mexican crisis, which was used to bail out foreign lenders, set the stage for the East Asian crisis. They argue that these lenders expected to be bailed out if things went wrong and thus provided funds that were used to fuel excessive risk taking.[8]

An international lender of last resort must find ways to limit this moral hazard problem, or it can actually make the situation worse. The international lender of last resort can make it clear that it will extend liquidity only to governments that put the proper measures in place to prevent excessive risk taking. In addition, it can reduce the incentives for risk taking by restricting the ability of governments to bail out stockholders and large uninsured creditors of domestic financial institutions. Some critics of the IMF believe that the IMF has not put enough pressure on the governments to which it lends to contain the moral hazard problem.

One problem that arises for international organizations like the IMF engaged in lender-of-last-resort operations is that they know that if they don't come to the rescue, the emerging-market country will suffer extreme hardship and possible political instability. Politicians in the crisis country may exploit these concerns and engage in a game of chicken with the international lender of last resort: they resist necessary reforms, hoping that the IMF will cave in. Elements of this game were present in the Mexican crisis of 1995 and were also a particularly important feature of the negotiations between the IMF and Indonesia during the Asian crisis.

---

[8] See International Financial Institution Advisory Commission, *Report* (IFIAC: Washington, D.C., 2000).

How Should the IMF Operate?

The IMF would produce better outcomes if it made it clear that it will not play this game. Just as giving in to ill-behaved children may be the easy way out in the short run but supports a pattern of poor behaviour in the long run, some critics worry that the IMF may not be tough enough when confronted by short-run humanitarian concerns. For example, they have been particularly critical of the IMF's lending to the Russian government, which has resisted adopting appropriate reforms to stabilize its financial system.

The IMF has also been criticized for imposing on the East Asian countries so-called austerity programs that focus on tight macroeconomic policies rather than on microeconomic policies to fix the crisis-causing problems in the financial sector. Such programs are likely to increase resistance to IMF recommendations, particularly in emerging-market countries. Austerity programs allow politicians in these countries to label institutions such as the IMF as being anti-growth, rhetoric that helps the politicians mobilize the public against the IMF and avoid doing what they really need to do to reform the financial system in their country. IMF programs that are focused instead on reforms of the financial sector would increase the likelihood that the IMF will be seen as a helping hand in the creation of a more efficient financial system.

An important historical feature of successful lender-of-last-resort operations is that the faster the lending is done, the lower is the amount that actually has to be lent. An excellent example involving the Federal Reserve occurred in the aftermath of the stock market crash on October 19, 1987. At the end of that day, in order to service their customers' accounts, securities firms needed to borrow several billion dollars to maintain orderly trading. However, given the unprecedented developments, banks were nervous about extending further loans to these firms. Upon learning this, the U.S. Federal Reserve engaged in an immediate lender-of-last-resort operation, making it clear that it would provide liquidity to banks making loans to the securities industry. What is striking about this episode is that the extremely quick intervention of the Fed not only resulted in a negligible impact of the stock market crash on the economy, but also meant that the amount of liquidity that the Fed needed to supply to the economy was not very large.

The ability of the Fed to engage in a lender-of-last-resort operation within a day of a substantial shock to the financial system is in sharp contrast to the amount of time it has taken the IMF to supply liquidity during the recent crises in emerging-market countries. Because IMF lending facilities were originally designed to provide funds after a country was experiencing a balance-of-payments crisis and because the conditions for the loan had to be negotiated, it took several months before the IMF made funds available. By this time, the crises had gotten much worse—and much larger sums of funds were needed to cope with the crises, often stretching the resources of the IMF. One reason central banks can lend so much more quickly than the IMF is that they have set up procedures in advance to provide loans, with the terms and conditions for this lending agreed upon beforehand. The need for quick provision of liquidity to keep the loan amount manageable argues for similar credit facilities at the international lender of last resort, so that funds can be provided quickly as long as the borrower meets conditions such as properly supervising its banks or keeping budget deficits low.

The flaws in IMF lending programs discussed above led to countries avoiding borrowing from the IMF in recent years. Countries did not want to be subjected to harsh austerity programs and also were unhappy with IMF delays in disbursing funds during a crisis. As an alternative to the IMF, countries built up substantial cushions of international reserves to deal with balance-of-payments problems on their own. IMF lending therefore shrank to very low levels, even creating a shortfall of revenue for its operations because it was no longer earning income by making loans. The IMF was at risk of becoming irrelevant—until the subprime financial crisis. With the subprime financial crisis, the IMF's role as an international lender of last resort returned, as can be seen in the Global box, The Subprime Financial Crisis and the IMF.

The debate on whether the world will be better off with the IMF operating as an international lender of last resort is currently a hot one. Much attention is being focused on making the IMF more effective in performing this role, and redesign of the IMF is at the centre of proposals for a new international financial architecture to help reduce international financial instability.

GLOBAL   The Subprime Financial Crisis and the IMF

Because financial institutions in emerging-market countries had limited exposure to subprime mortgages, the early stages of the subprime financial crisis had little impact on their economies. However, when the subprime crisis became more virulent in October of 2008, a number of emerging-market countries, as well as Iceland and former communist countries, found that foreigners were pulling funds out of their financial systems, putting not only domestic banks under stress, but also causing a sharp depreciation of their currencies.

The role of the IMF as an international lender of last resort now came to the fore. Toward the end of October, the IMF extended $25 billion in loans to Hungary, $16.5 billion to the Ukraine, and $2 billion to Iceland. These loans stipulated that the countries would have to undergo belt-tightening in order to get their fiscal houses in order.

The IMF recognized, however, that, as the Managing Director of the IMF, Dominique Strauss-Kahn, put it, "exceptional times call for an exceptional response," and that a new type of lending program was needed to overcome the reluctance of countries to borrow from it during the crisis at hand. The IMF created a new lending program at the end of October 2008 called the Short-Term Liquidity Facility, with $100 billion of funds. It provides three-month loans to countries whose economies are judged by the IMF to be basically sound, but under stress. These condition-free loans could be disbursed very quickly. In addition, these loans would not have austerity programs attached to them, making them far more attractive to potential borrowing countries.

In 1999, the IMF tried to implement a similar facility called the Contingent Credit Line, but it was unsuccessful because it required preapproval from the IMF, and countries were reluctant to apply for it because doing so might suggest that they were likely to get into trouble. The new Short-Term Liquidity Facility does not require countries to apply for it. The IMF can just determine that a country has access and give them a loan if they need it. It is too soon to determine whether this new lending facility will overcome some of the criticisms levelled against previous IMF lending programs, but it does appear to be a step in the right direction.

INTERNATIONAL CONSIDERATIONS AND MONETARY POLICY

Our analysis in this chapter so far has suggested several ways in which monetary policy can be affected by international matters. Awareness of these effects can have significant implications for the way monetary policy is conducted.

Direct Effects of the Foreign Exchange Market on the Money Supply

When central banks intervene in the foreign exchange market, they acquire or sell off international reserves, and their monetary base is affected. When a central bank intervenes in the foreign exchange market, it gives up some control of its money supply. For example, in the early 1970s, the German central bank faced a dilemma. In attempting to keep the German mark from appreciating too much against the U.S. dollar, the Germans acquired huge quantities of international reserves, leading to a rate of money growth that the German central bank considered inflationary.

The Bundesbank could have tried to halt the growth of the money supply by stopping its intervention in the foreign exchange market and reasserting control over its own money supply. Such a strategy has a major drawback when the central bank is under pressure not to allow its currency to appreciate: the lower price of imports and higher price of exports as a result of an appreciation in its currency will hurt domestic producers and increase unemployment.

The ability to conduct monetary policy is typically easier when a country's currency is a reserve currency. For example, because the U.S. dollar has been a reserve currency, the U.S. monetary base and money supply have been less affected by developments in the foreign exchange market. As long as other central banks, rather than the Fed, intervene to keep the value of the dollar from changing, U.S. holdings of international reserves are unaffected. However, the central bank of a reserve currency country must worry about a shift away from the use of its currency for international reserves.

Balance-of-Payments Considerations

Under the Bretton Woods system, balance-of-payments considerations were more important than they are under the current managed float regime. When a non–reserve-currency country is running balance-of-payments deficits, it necessarily gives up international reserves. To keep from running out of these reserves, under the Bretton Woods system it had to implement contractionary monetary policy to strengthen its currency. This is exactly what occurred in the United Kingdom before its devaluation of the pound in 1967. When policy became expansionary, the balance of payments deteriorated, and the British were forced to "slam on the brakes" by implementing a contractionary policy. Once the balance of payments improved, policy became more expansionary until the deteriorating balance of payments again forced the British to pursue a contractionary policy. Such on-again, off-again actions became known as a "stop-go" policy, and the domestic instability it created was criticized severely.

Because the United States is a major reserve currency country, it can run large balance-of-payments deficits without losing huge amounts of international reserves. This does not mean, however, that the Federal Reserve is never influenced by developments in the U.S. balance of payments. Current account deficits in the United States suggest that American businesses may be losing some of their ability to compete because the value of the dollar is too high. In addition, large U.S. balance-of-payments deficits lead to balance-of-payments surpluses in other countries, which can in turn lead to large increases in their holdings of international reserves (this was especially true under the Bretton Woods system). Because such increases put a strain on the international financial system and may stimulate world inflation, the Fed worries about U.S. balance-of-payments and current account deficits. To help shrink these deficits, the Fed might pursue a more contractionary monetary policy.

Exchange Rate Considerations

Unlike balance-of-payments considerations, which have become less important under the current managed float system, exchange rate considerations now play a greater role in the conduct of monetary policy. If a central bank does not want to see its currency fall in value, it may pursue a more contractionary monetary policy of reducing the money supply to raise the domestic interest rate, thereby strengthening its currency. Similarly, if a country experiences an appreciation in its currency, domestic industry may suffer from increased foreign competition and may pressure the central bank to pursue a higher rate of money growth in order to lower the exchange rate.

TO PEG OR NOT TO PEG: EXCHANGE-RATE TARGETING AS AN ALTERNATIVE MONETARY POLICY STRATEGY

In Chapter 18, we discussed several monetary policy strategies that could be followed to promote price stability, including monetary targeting and inflation targeting. One other strategy also uses a strong nominal anchor to promote price stability: *exchange-rate targeting* (sometimes referred to as an *exchange-rate peg*).

Targeting the exchange rate is a monetary policy strategy with a long history. It can take the form of fixing the value of the domestic currency to a commodity such as gold, the key feature of the gold standard described earlier in the chapter. More recently, fixed exchange-rate regimes have involved fixing the value of the domestic currency to that of a large, low-inflation country like the United States or Germany (*the anchor country*). Another alternative is to adopt a *crawling target* or *peg,* in which a currency is allowed to depreciate at a steady rate so that the inflation rate in the pegging country can be higher than that of the anchor country.

Advantages of Exchange-Rate Targeting

Exchange-rate targeting has several advantages. First, the nominal anchor of an exchange-rate target directly contributes to keeping inflation under control by tying the inflation rate for internationally traded goods to that found in the anchor country. It does this because the foreign price of internationally traded goods is set by the world market, while the domestic price of these goods is fixed by the exchange-rate target. For example, until 2002 in Argentina the exchange rate for the Argentine peso was exactly one to the U.S. dollar, so that a bushel of wheat traded internationally at five U.S. dollars had its price set at five pesos. If the exchange-rate target is credible (i.e., expected to be adhered to), the exchange-rate target has the added benefit of anchoring inflation expectations to the inflation rate in the anchor country.

Second, an exchange-rate target provides an automatic rule for the conduct of monetary policy that helps mitigate the time-inconsistency problem described in the Web Appendix to Chapter 15. As we saw earlier, an exchange-rate target forces a tightening of monetary policy when there is a tendency for the domestic currency to depreciate or a loosening of policy when there is a tendency for the domestic currency to appreciate, so that discretionary monetary policy is less of an option. The central bank will therefore be constrained from falling into the time-inconsistency trap of trying to expand output and employment in the short run by pursuing overly expansionary monetary policy.

Third, an exchange-rate target has the advantage of simplicity and clarity, which makes it easily understood by the public. A "sound currency" is an easy-to-understand rallying cry for monetary policy. In the past, for example, this aspect was important in France, where an appeal to the "franc fort" (strong franc) was often used to justify tight monetary policy.

Given its advantages, it is not surprising that exchange-rate targeting has been used successfully to control inflation in industrialized countries. Both France and the United Kingdom, for example, successfully used exchange-rate targeting to lower inflation by tying the values of their currencies to the German mark. In 1987, when France first pegged its exchange rate to the mark, its inflation rate was 3%, two percentage points above the German inflation rate. By 1992, its inflation rate had fallen to 2%, a level that can be argued is consistent with price stability, and was even below that in Germany. By 1996, the French and German inflation rates had converged, to a number slightly below 2%. Similarly, after pegging to the German mark in 1990, the United Kingdom was able to lower its inflation rate from 10% to 3% by 1992, when it was forced to abandon the exchange rate mechanism (ERM).

Exchange-rate targeting has also been an effective means of reducing inflation quickly in emerging-market countries. For example, before the devaluation in Mexico in 1994, its exchange-rate target enabled it to bring inflation down from levels above 100% in 1988 to below 10% in 1994.

Disadvantages of Exchange-Rate Targeting

Despite the inherent advantages of exchange-rate targeting, there are several serious criticisms of this strategy. The problem (as we saw earlier in the chapter) is that with capital mobility the targeting country can no longer pursue its own independent monetary policy and use it to respond to domestic shocks that are independent of those hitting the anchor country. Furthermore, an exchange-rate target means that shocks to the anchor country are directly transmitted to the targeting country, because changes in interest rates in the anchor country lead to a corresponding change in interest rates in the targeting country.

A striking example of these problems occurred when Germany was reunified in 1990. In response to concerns about inflationary pressures arising from reunification and the massive fiscal expansion required to rebuild East Germany, long-term German interest rates rose until February 1991 and short-term rates rose until December 1991. This shock to the anchor country in the exchange rate mechanism (ERM) was transmitted directly to the other countries in the ERM whose currencies were pegged to the mark, and their interest rates rose in tandem with those in Germany. Continuing adherence to the exchange-rate target slowed economic growth and increased unemployment in countries such as France that remained in the ERM and adhered to the exchange-rate peg.

A second problem with exchange-rate targets is that they leave countries open to speculative attacks on their currencies. Indeed, one aftermath of German reunification was the foreign exchange crisis of September 1992. As we saw earlier, the tight monetary policy in Germany following reunification meant that the countries in the ERM were subjected to a negative demand shock that led to a decline in economic growth and a rise in unemployment. It was certainly feasible for the governments of these countries to keep their exchange rates fixed relative to the mark in these circumstances, but speculators began to question whether these countries' commitment to the exchange-rate peg would weaken. Speculators reasoned that these countries would not tolerate the rise in unemployment resulting from keeping interest rates high enough to fend off attacks on their currencies.

At this stage, speculators were, in effect, presented with a one-way bet, because the currencies of countries like France, Spain, Sweden, Italy, and the United Kingdom could go in only one direction and depreciate against the mark. Selling these currencies before the likely depreciation occurred gave speculators an attractive profit opportunity with potentially high expected returns. The result was the speculative attack in September 1992. Only in France was the commitment to the fixed exchange rate strong enough so that France did not devalue. The governments in the other countries were unwilling to defend their currencies at all costs and eventually allowed their currencies to fall in value.

The different responses of France and the United Kingdom after the September 1992 exchange-rate crisis illustrates the potential cost of an exchange-rate target. France, which continued to peg its currency to the mark and was thus unable to use monetary policy to respond to domestic conditions, found that economic growth remained slow after 1992 and unemployment increased. The United Kingdom, on the other hand, which dropped out of the ERM exchange-rate peg and adopted inflation targeting, had much better economic performance: Economic growth was higher, the unemployment rate fell, and yet its inflation was not much worse than France's.

In contrast to industrialized countries, emerging-market countries (including the transition countries of Eastern Europe) may not lose much by giving up an independent monetary policy when they target exchange rates. Because many emerging-market countries have not developed the political or monetary institutions that allow the successful use of discretionary monetary policy, they may have little to gain from an independent monetary policy, but a lot to lose. Thus they would be better off by, in effect, adopting the monetary policy of a country like the United States through targeting exchange rates than by pursuing their own independent policy. This is one of the reasons that so many emerging-market countries have adopted exchange-rate targeting.

Nonetheless, exchange-rate targeting is highly dangerous for these countries, because it leaves them open to speculative attacks that can have far more serious consequences for their economies than for the economies of industrialized countries. Indeed, the successful speculative attacks in Mexico in 1994, East Asia in 1997, and Argentina in 2002 plunged their economies into full-scale financial crises that devastated their economies.

An additional disadvantage of an exchange-rate target is that it can weaken the accountability of policymakers, particularly in emerging-market countries. Because exchange-rate targeting fixes the exchange rate, it eliminates an important signal that can help constrain monetary policy from becoming too expansionary and thereby limit the time-inconsistency problem. In industrialized countries, particularly in the United States, the bond market provides an important signal about the stance of monetary policy. Overly expansionary monetary policy or strong political pressure to engage in overly expansionary monetary policy produces an inflation scare in which inflation expectations surge, interest rates rise because of the Fisher effect (described in Chapter 5), and there is a sharp decline in long-term bond prices. Because both central banks and the politicians want to avoid this kind of scenario, overly expansionary monetary policy will be less likely.

In many countries, particularly emerging-market countries, the long-term bond market is essentially nonexistent. Under a floating exchange rate regime, however, if monetary policy is too expansionary, the exchange rate will depreciate. In these countries the daily fluctuations of the exchange rate can, like the bond market in Canada and the United States, provide an early warning signal that monetary policy is too expansionary. Just as the fear of a visible inflation scare in the bond market constrains central bankers from pursuing overly expansionary monetary policy and constrains politicians from putting pressure on the central bank to engage in overly expansionary monetary policy, fear of exchange-rate depreciations can make overly expansionary monetary policy, and the time-inconsistency problem, less likely.

The need for signals from the foreign exchange market may be even more acute for emerging-market countries, because the balance sheets and actions of their central banks are not as transparent as they are in industrialized countries. Targeting the exchange rate can make it even harder to ascertain a central bank's policy actions. The public is less able to keep watch on the central bank and the politicians pressuring it, which makes it easier for monetary policy to become too expansionary.

When Is Exchange-Rate Targeting Desirable for Industrialized Countries?

Given the above disadvantages with exchange-rate targeting, when might it be an appropriate strategy?

In industrialized countries, the biggest cost to exchange-rate targeting is the loss of an independent monetary policy to deal with domestic considerations. If an independent, domestic monetary policy can be conducted responsibly, this can be a serious cost indeed, as the comparison between the post-1992 experiences of France and the United Kingdom indicates. However, not all industrialized countries have found that they are capable of conducting their own monetary policy successfully, either because the central bank is not independent or because political pressures on the central bank lead to an inflationary bias in monetary policy. In these cases, giving up independent control of domestic monetary policy may not be a great loss, while the gain of having monetary policy determined by a better-performing central bank in the anchor country can be substantial.

Italy provides an example: It was not a coincidence that the Italian public had the most favourable attitude of all those in Europe toward the European Monetary Union. The past record of Italian monetary policy was not good, and the Italian public recognized that having monetary policy controlled by more responsible outsiders had benefits that far outweighed the costs of losing the ability to focus monetary policy on domestic considerations.

A second reason why industrialized countries might find targeting exchange rates useful is that it encourages integration of the domestic economy with its neighbours. Clearly, this was the rationale for long-standing pegging of the exchange rate to the deutsche mark by countries such as Austria and the Netherlands, and the more recent exchange-rate pegs that preceded the European Monetary Union.

To sum up, exchange-rate targeting for industrialized countries is probably not the best monetary policy strategy to control the overall economy unless (1) domestic monetary and political institutions are not conducive to good monetary policy-making or (2) there are other important benefits of an exchange-rate target that have nothing to do with monetary policy.

When Is Exchange-Rate Targeting Desirable for Emerging-Market Countries?

In countries in which political and monetary institutions are particularly weak and which therefore have been experiencing continued bouts of hyperinflation, a characterization that applies to many emerging-market (including transition) countries, exchange-rate targeting may be the only way to break inflationary psychology and stabilize the economy. In this situation, exchange-rate targeting is the stabilization policy of last resort. However, if the exchange-rate targeting regimes in emerging-market countries are not always transparent, they are more likely to break down, often resulting in disastrous financial crises.

Are there exchange-rate strategies that make it less likely that the exchange-rate regime will break down in emerging-market countries? Two such strategies that have received increasing attention in recent years are currency boards and dollarization.

Currency Boards

One solution to the problem of lack of transparency and commitment to the exchange-rate target is the adoption of a **currency board**, in which the domestic currency is backed 100% by a foreign currency (say, U.S. dollars or euros) and in which the note-issuing authority, whether the central bank or the government, establishes a fixed exchange rate to this foreign currency and stands ready to exchange domestic currency for the foreign currency at this rate whenever the public requests it. A currency board is just a variant of a fixed exchange-rate target in which the commitment to the fixed exchange rate is especially strong because the conduct of monetary policy is in effect put on autopilot, taken completely out of the hands of the central bank and the government. In contrast, the typical fixed or pegged exchange-rate regime does allow the monetary authorities some discretion in their conduct of monetary policy because they can still adjust interest rates or print money.

A currency board arrangement thus has important advantages over a monetary policy strategy that just uses an exchange-rate target. First, the money supply can expand only when foreign currency is exchanged for domestic currency at the central bank. Thus the increased amount of domestic currency is matched by an equal increase in foreign exchange reserves. The central bank no longer has the ability to print money and thereby cause inflation. Second, the currency board involves a stronger commitment by the central bank to the fixed exchange rate and may therefore be effective in bringing down inflation quickly and in decreasing the likelihood of a successful speculative attack against the currency.

Although they solve the transparency and commitment problems inherent in an exchange-rate target regime, currency boards suffer from some of the same shortcomings: the loss of an independent monetary policy and increased exposure of the economy to shocks from the anchor country, and the loss of the central bank's ability to create money and act as a lender of last resort. Other means must therefore be used to cope with potential banking crises. Also, if there is a speculative attack on a currency board, the exchange of the domestic currency for foreign currency leads to a sharp contraction of the money supply, which can be highly damaging to the economy.

Currency boards have been established in countries such as Hong Kong (1983), Argentina (1991), Estonia (1992), Lithuania (1994), Bulgaria (1997), and Bosnia (1998). Argentina's currency board, which operated from 1991 to 2002 and required the central bank to exchange U.S. dollars for new pesos at a fixed exchange rate of 1 to 1, is one of the most interesting. For more on this subject, see the Global box, Argentina's Currency Board.

Dollarization

Another solution to the problems created by a lack of transparency and commitment to the exchange-rate target is **dollarization**, the adoption of a sound currency, like the U.S. dollar, as a country's money. Indeed, dollarization is just another variant of a fixed exchange-rate target with an even stronger commitment mechanism than a currency board provides. A currency board can be abandoned, allowing a change in the value of the currency, but a change of value is impossible with dollarization: A U.S. dollar bill is always worth one U.S. dollar, whether it is held in the United States or outside of it.

Dollarization has been advocated as a monetary policy strategy for emerging-market countries: It was discussed actively by Argentine officials in the aftermath

GLOBAL   Argentina's Currency Board

Argentina has had a long history of monetary instability, with inflation rates fluctuating dramatically and sometimes surging to beyond 1000% per year. To end this cycle of inflationary surges, Argentina decided to adopt a currency board in April 1991. The Argentine currency board worked as follows. Under Argentina's convertibility law, the peso/U.S. dollar exchange rate was fixed at one to one, and a member of the public could go to the Argentine central bank and exchange a peso for a U.S. dollar, or vice versa, at any time.

The early years of Argentina's currency board looked stunningly successful. Inflation, which had been running at an 800% annual rate in 1990, fell to less than 5% by the end of 1994, and economic growth was rapid, averaging almost 8% per year from 1991 to 1994. In the aftermath of the Mexican peso crisis, however, concern about the health of the Argentine economy resulted in the public pulling money out of the banks (deposits fell by 18%) and exchanging pesos for U.S. dollars, thus causing a contraction of the Argentine money supply. The result was a sharp drop in Argentine economic activity, with real GDP shrinking by more than 5% in 1995 and the unemployment rate jumping above 15%. Only in 1996 did the economy begin to recover.

Because the central bank of Argentina had no control over monetary policy under the currency board system, it was relatively helpless to counteract the contractionary monetary policy stemming from the public's behaviour. Furthermore, because the currency board did not allow the central bank to create pesos and lend them to the banks, it had very little capability to act as a lender of last resort. With help from international agencies, such as the IMF, the World Bank, and the Interamerican Development Bank, which lent Argentina more than US$5 billion in 1995 to help shore up its banking system, the currency board survived.

However, in 1998 Argentina entered another recession, which was both severe and very long lasting. By the end of 2001, unemployment reached nearly 20%, a level comparable to that experienced in the United States during the Great Depression of the 1930s. The result has been civil unrest and the fall of the elected government, as well as a major banking crisis and a default on nearly US$150 billion of government debt. Because the Central Bank of Argentina had no control over monetary policy under the currency board system, it was unable to use monetary policy to expand the economy and get out of its recession. Furthermore, because the currency board did not allow the central bank to create pesos and lend them to banks, it had very little capability to act as a lender of last resort. In January 2002, the currency board finally collapsed and the peso depreciated by more than 70%. The result was the full-scale financial crisis described in Chapter 9, with inflation shooting up and an extremely severe depression. Clearly, the Argentine public is not as enamoured of its currency board as it once was.

of the devaluation of the Brazilian real in January 1999 and was adopted by Ecuador in March 2000. Dollarization's key advantage is that it completely avoids the possibility of a speculative attack on the domestic currency (because there is none). (Such an attack is still a danger even under a currency board arrangement.)

Dollarization is subject to the usual disadvantages of an exchange-rate target (the loss of an independent monetary policy, increased exposure of the economy to shocks from the anchor country, and the inability of the central bank to create money and act as a lender of last resort). Dollarization has one additional disadvantage not characteristic of currency boards or other exchange-rate target regimes. Because a country adopting dollarization no longer has its own currency, it loses the revenue that a government receives by issuing money, which is called seignorage. Because governments (or their central banks) do not have to pay interest on their currency, they earn revenue (seignorage) by using this currency to purchase income-earning assets such as bonds. In the case of the Federal Reserve in the United States, this revenue is on the order of US$30 billion per year. If an emerging-market country dollarizes and gives up its currency, it needs to make up this loss of revenue somewhere, which is not always easy for a poor country.

SUMMARY

1. An unsterilized central bank intervention in which the domestic currency is sold to purchase foreign assets leads to a gain in international reserves, an increase in the money supply, and a depreciation of the domestic currency. Available evidence suggests, however, that sterilized central bank interventions have little long-term effect on the exchange rate.

2. The balance of payments is a bookkeeping system for recording all payments between a country and foreign countries that have a direct bearing on the movement of funds between them. The official reserve transactions balance is the sum of the current account balance plus the items in the capital account. It indicates the amount of international reserves that must be moved between countries to finance international transactions.

3. Before World War I, the gold standard was predominant. Currencies were convertible into gold, thus fixing exchange rates between countries. After World War II, the Bretton Woods system and the IMF were established to promote a fixed exchange rate system in which the U.S. dollar was convertible into gold. The Bretton Woods system collapsed in 1971. We now have an international financial system that has elements of a managed float and a fixed exchange rate system. Some exchange rates fluctuate from day to day, although central banks intervene in the foreign exchange market, while other exchange rates are fixed.

4. Controls on capital outflows receive support because they may prevent domestic residents and foreigners from pulling capital out of a country during a crisis and make devaluation less likely. Controls on capital inflows make sense under the theory that if speculative capital cannot flow in, then it cannot go out suddenly and create a crisis. However, capital controls suffer from several disadvantages: They are seldom effective, they lead to corruption, and they may allow governments to avoid taking the steps needed to reform their financial systems to deal with the crises.

5. The IMF has recently taken on the role of an international lender of last resort. Because central banks in emerging-market countries are unlikely to be able to perform a lender-of-last-resort operation successfully, an international lender of last resort like the IMF is needed to prevent financial instability. However, the IMF's role as an international lender of last resort creates a serious moral hazard problem that can encourage excessive risk taking and make a financial crisis more likely, but refusing to lend may be politically hard to do. In addition, it needs to be able to provide liquidity quickly during a crisis to keep manageable the amount of funds lent.

6. Three international considerations affect the conduct of monetary policy: direct effects of the foreign exchange market on the money supply, balance-of-payments considerations, and exchange rate considerations. Inasmuch as the United States has been a reserve currency country in the post–World War II period, U.S. monetary policy has been less affected by developments in the foreign exchange market and its balance of payments than is true for other countries. However, in recent years, exchange rate considerations have been playing a more prominent role in influencing U.S. monetary policy.

7. Exchange-rate targeting has the following advantages as a monetary policy strategy: (1) It directly keeps inflation under control by tying the inflation rate for internationally traded goods to that found in the anchor country to which its currency is pegged; (2) it provides an automatic rule for the conduct of monetary policy that helps mitigate the time-inconsistency problem; and (3) it is simple and clear. Exchange-rate targeting also has serious disadvantages: (1) It results in a loss of independent monetary policy; (2) it leaves the country open to speculative attacks; and (3) it can weaken the accountability of policymakers because the exchange-rate signal is lost. Two strategies that make it less likely that the exchange-rate regime will break down are currency boards, in which the central bank stands ready to automatically exchange domestic for foreign currency at a fixed rate, and dollarization, in which a sound currency like the U.S. dollar is adopted as the country's money.

KEY TERMS

anchor currency, p. 524

balance of payments, p. 522

balance-of-payments crisis, p. 532

Bretton Woods system, p. 525

capital account, p. 523

currency board, p. 544

current account, p. 522

devaluation, p. 527

dollarization, p. 544

fixed exchange rate regime, p. 524

floating exchange rate regime, p. 524

foreign exchange interventions, p. 518

International Monetary Fund (IMF), p. 525

international reserves, p. 518

managed float regime (dirty float), p. 524

official reserve transactions balance, p. 523

reserve currency, p. 525

revaluation, p. 527

special drawing rights (SDRs), p. 530

sterilized foreign exchange intervention, p. 520

trade balance, p. 522

unsterilized foreign exchange intervention, p. 520

World Bank, p. 525

World Trade Organization (WTO), p. 525

QUESTIONS

You will find the answers to the questions marked with an asterisk in the Textbook Resources section of your MyEconLab.

1. If the Bank of Canada buys Canadian dollars in the foreign exchange market but conducts an offsetting open market operation to sterilize the intervention, what will be the impact on international reserves, the money supply, and the exchange rate?

*2. If the Bank of Canada buys Canadian dollars in the foreign exchange market but does not sterilize the intervention, what will be the impact on international reserves, the money supply, and the exchange rate?

3. For each of the following, identify in which part of the balance-of-payments account it appears (current account, capital account, or method of financing) and whether it is a receipt or a payment.
   a. A British subject's purchase of a share of Air Canada stock
   b. A Canadian's purchase of an airline ticket from Air France
   c. The Swiss government's purchase of Canadian treasury bills.
   d. A Japanese's purchase of Canadian salmon
   e. $50 million of foreign aid to Honduras
   f. A loan by a Canadian bank to Mexico
   g. A Canadian bank's borrowing of Eurodollars

*4. Why does a balance-of-payments deficit for Canada have a different effect on its international reserves than a balance-of-payments deficit for the United States?

5. Under the gold standard, if Britain became more productive relative to Canada, what would happen to the money supply in the two countries? Why would the changes in the money supply help preserve a fixed exchange rate between Canada and Britain?

*6. What is the exchange rate between dollars and Swiss francs if one dollar is convertible into $\frac{1}{20}$ ounce of gold and one Swiss franc is convertible into $\frac{1}{40}$ ounce of gold?

7. If a country's par exchange rate was undervalued during the Bretton Woods fixed exchange rate regime, what kind of intervention would that country's central bank be forced to undertake, and what effect would it have on its international reserves and the money supply?

*8. How can a large balance-of-payments surplus contribute to the country's inflation rate?

9. "If a country wants to keep its exchange rate from changing, it must give up some control over its money supply." Is this statement true, false, or uncertain? Explain your answer.

*10. Why can balance-of-payments deficits force some countries to implement a contractionary monetary policy?

11. "Balance-of-payments deficits always cause a country to lose international reserves." Is this statement true, false, or uncertain? Explain your answer.

*12. How can persistent U.S. balance-of-payments deficits stimulate world inflation?

13. "Inflation is not possible under the gold standard." Is this statement true, false, or uncertain? Explain your answer.

*14. Why is it that in a pure flexible exchange rate system, the foreign exchange market has no direct effects on the money supply? Does this mean that the foreign exchange market has no effect on monetary policy?

15. "The abandonment of fixed exchange rates after 1973 has meant that countries have pursued more independent monetary policies." Is this statement true, false, or uncertain? Explain your answer.

*16. What are the key advantages of exchange-rate targeting as a monetary policy strategy?

17. Why did the exchange-rate peg lead to difficulties for the countries in the ERM when German reunification occurred?

*18. How can exchange-rate targets lead to a speculative attack on a currency?

19. Why may the disadvantage of exchange-rate targeting of not having an independent monetary policy be less of an issue for emerging-market countries than for industrialized countries?

*20. How can the long-term bond market help reduce the time-inconsistency problem for monetary policy? Can the foreign exchange market also perform this role?

21. When is exchange-rate targeting likely to be a sensible strategy for industrialized countries? When is exchange-rate targeting likely to be a sensible strategy for emerging-market countries?

*22. What are the advantages and disadvantages of a currency board over a monetary policy that just uses an exchange-rate target?

23. What are the key advantages and disadvantages of dollarization over other forms of exchange-rate targeting?

QUANTITATIVE PROBLEMS

*1. The Bank of Canada purchases $1 million of foreign assets for $1 million. Show the effect of this open market operation on the Bank's T-account.

2. The Bank of Canada purchases $1 million of foreign assets by selling $1 million in T-bills. Show the effect of this open market operation on the Bank's T-account.

*3. The Bank of Canada sells $1 million of foreign assets for $1 million. Show the effect of this open market operation on the Bank's T-account.

4. If the balance in the current account increases by $1 billion while the capital account is off by $2 billion, what is the impact on governmental international reserves?

CANSIM Question

5. Visit the website of the Bank of Canada, at **www.bankofcanada.ca**. Click on *Rates and Statistics* and then *Exchange Rates*.
   a. What is the Canadian-dollar effective exchange rate index (CERI)?
   b. How many foreign countries are included in the index?
   c. What are the weights of the included countries? Which country has the highest weight? Which has the lowest?
   d. Get the daily CANSIM data from January 1, 1982, to November 10, 2009, for the Canadian-dollar effective exchange rate index (series V41589522) from the Textbook Resources area of the MyEconLab. Present a time series plot of the (daily) observations. Did the Canadian dollar appreciate or depreciate in 2008? By how much?

WEB EXERCISES

1. The U.S. Federal Reserve publishes information online that explains the workings of the foreign exchange market. One such publication can be found at **www.newyorkfed.org/education/addpub/usfxm/**. Review the table of contents and open Chapter 10, Evolution of the International Monetary System. Read this chapter and write a one-page summary that discusses why each monetary standard was dropped in favour of the succeeding one.

2. The International Monetary Fund stands ready to help nations facing monetary crises. Go to **www.imf.org**. Click on the tab labelled "About the IMF." What is the stated purpose of the IMF? How many nations participate and when was it established?

 Be sure to visit the MyEconLab website at **www.myeconlab.com**. This online homework and tutorial system puts you in control of your own learning with study and practice tools directly correlated to this chapter content.

On the MyEconLab website you will find the following appendix for this chapter:
Appendix 20.1: The Canadian Balance of Payments

CRISIS AND RESPONSE: THE PERFECT STORM OF ADVERSE SHOCKS

In 2007 and 2008, the Canadian economy was hit by a perfect storm of formidable shocks. Higher demand for oil from rapidly growing developing countries like China and India and slowing of production in places like Mexico, Russia, and Nigeria drove up oil prices sharply from around the US$60 per barrel level at the beginning of 2007. By the end of the year, oil prices had risen to US$100 per barrel and reached a peak of over US$140 in July of 2008. The oil price shock was both contractionary and inflationary, and as a result led to both higher inflation and unemployment—and many unhappy drivers at gas pumps.

If this supply shock were not bad enough, the subprime financial crisis in the United States hit the world economy starting in August of 2007 and caused a contraction in both household and business spending. This shock led to a further rise in unemployment, with some weakening of inflationary pressure further down the road.

The result of this perfect storm of adverse shocks was a rise in unemployment from the 6% level in 2006 and 2007 to over 8% by the beginning of 2009. Inflation also accelerated from 2.6% in 2007 to over 5% by the middle of 2008, but with the increase in the unemployment rate and the decline of oil and other commodity prices by the beginning of 2009, inflation rapidly came back down again.

Although the Bank of Canada's aggressive monetary policy aimed to address the contractionary forces in the economy, the government of Canada also took action in a coordinated response to the global financial crisis with the Group of 20 (G20) countries. Although this policy response helped stimulate household spending, it was overwhelmed by the continued worsening of the financial crisis, and the economy went into a tailspin.

The impact of the perfect storm of adverse shocks highlights that we need to understand how monetary and other government policies affect the price level and economic activity. Chapter 21 discusses how theories of the demand for money have evolved. Chapters 22 and 23 outline the ISLM model, which explains how interest rates and total output in the economy are determined. In Chapter 24, we develop a basic tool, aggregate supply and demand analysis, that will enable us to study the effect of monetary policy on output and prices. Chapter 25 outlines how monetary policy affects the aggregate economy. In Chapter 26, we expand on aggregate supply and demand analysis in order to understand the inflation process. Chapter 27 examines the rational expectations revolution in monetary theory and what it implies for analyzing the impact of monetary policy on inflation and economic activity.

CHAPTER 21

The Demand for Money

LEARNING OBJECTIVES

After studying this chapter you should be able to

1. describe how the demand for money is determined
2. define the theories of the demand for money (classical and Keynesian theories and Milton Friedman's reformulation of the quantity theory of money)
3. present empirical evidence on how the demand for money is affected by changes in interest rates and the level of income

PREVIEW

In earlier chapters we spent a lot of time and effort learning what the money supply is, how it is determined, and what role the Bank of Canada plays in it. Now we are ready to explore the role of the money supply in determining the price level and total production of goods and services (aggregate output) in the economy. The study of the effect of money on the economy is called **monetary theory,** and we examine this branch of economics in the chapters of Part VII.

When economists mention *supply,* the word *demand* is sure to follow, and the discussion of money is no exception. The supply of money is an essential building block in understanding how monetary policy affects the economy because it suggests the factors that influence the quantity of money in the economy. Not surprisingly, another essential part of monetary theory is the demand for money.

This chapter describes how the theories of the demand for money have evolved. We begin with the classical theories refined at the start of the twentieth century by economists such as Irving Fisher, Alfred Marshall, and A. C. Pigou; then we move on to the Keynesian theories of the demand for money. We end with Milton Friedman's modern quantity theory.

A central question in monetary theory is whether or to what extent the quantity of money demanded is affected by changes in interest rates. Because this issue is crucial to how we view money's effects on aggregate economic activity, we focus on the role of interest rates in the demand for money.[1]

---

[1] In Chapter 23 we will see that the responsiveness of the quantity of money demanded to changes in interest rates has important implications for the relative effectiveness of monetary policy and fiscal policy in influencing aggregate economic activity.

QUANTITY THEORY OF MONEY

Developed by the classical economists in the nineteenth and early twentieth centuries, the quantity theory of money is a theory of how the nominal value of aggregate income is determined. Because it also tells us how much money is held for a given amount of aggregate income, it is also a theory of the demand for money. The most important feature of this theory is that it suggests that interest rates have no effect on the demand for money.

Velocity of Money and Equation of Exchange

The clearest exposition of the classical theory approach is found in the work of the American economist Irving Fisher, in his influential book *The Purchasing Power of Money*, published in 1911. Fisher wanted to examine the link between the total quantity of money M (the money supply) and the total amount of spending on final goods and services produced in the economy $P \times Y$, where P is the price level and Y is aggregate output (income). (Total spending $P \times Y$ is also thought of as aggregate nominal income for the economy or as nominal GDP.) The concept that provides the link between M and $P \times Y$ is called the **velocity of money** (often reduced simply to *velocity*), the average number of times per year (turnover) that a dollar is spent in buying the total amount of goods and services produced in the economy. Velocity V is defined more precisely as total spending $P \times Y$ divided by the quantity of money M:

$$V = \frac{P \times Y}{M} \tag{1}$$

If, for example, nominal GDP ($P \times Y$) in a year is $5 trillion and the quantity of money is $1 trillion, velocity is 5, meaning that the average dollar bill is spent five times in purchasing final goods and services in the economy.

By multiplying both sides of this definition by M, we obtain the **equation of exchange**, which relates nominal income to the quantity of money and velocity:

$$M \times V = P \times Y \tag{2}$$

The equation of exchange thus states that the quantity of money multiplied by the number of times that this money is spent in a given year must equal nominal income (the total nominal amount spent on goods and services in that year).[2]

As it stands, Equation 2 is nothing more than an identity—a relationship that is true by definition. It does not tell us, for instance, that when the money supply M changes, nominal income ($P \times Y$) changes in the same direction; a rise in M, for example, could be offset by a fall in V that leaves $M \times V$ (and therefore $P \times Y$) unchanged. To convert the equation of exchange (*an identity*) into a *theory* of how nominal income is determined requires an understanding of the factors that determine velocity.

---

[2] Fisher actually first formulated the equation of exchange in terms of the nominal value of transactions in the economy PT:

$$MV_T = PT$$

where P = average price per transaction
   T = number of transactions conducted in a year
   $V_T = PT/M$ = transactions velocity of money

Because the nominal value of transactions T is difficult to measure, the quantity theory has been formulated in terms of aggregate output Y, as follows: T is assumed to be proportional to Y so that $T = vY$, where v is a constant of proportionality. Substituting vY for T in Fisher's equation of exchange yields $MV_T = vPY$, which can be written as Equation 2 in the text in which $V = V_T/v$.

Irving Fisher reasoned that velocity is determined by the institutions in an economy that affect the way individuals conduct transactions. If people use charge accounts and credit cards to conduct their transactions, as they can today, and consequently use money less often when making purchases, less money is required to conduct the transactions generated by nominal income (M falls relative to $P \times Y$), and velocity ($P \times Y$)$/M$ will increase. Conversely, if it is more convenient for purchases to be paid for with cash or cheques (both of which are money), more money is used to conduct the transactions generated by the same level of nominal income, and velocity will fall. Fisher took the view that the institutional and technological features of the economy would affect velocity only slowly over time, so velocity would normally be reasonably constant in the short run.

Quantity Theory of Money

Fisher's view that velocity is fairly constant in the short run transforms the equation of exchange into the **quantity theory of money**, which states that nominal income is determined solely by movements in the quantity of money. When the quantity of money M doubles, $M \times V$ doubles and so must $P \times Y$, the value of nominal income. To see how this works, let's assume that velocity is 5, nominal income (GDP) is initially $5 trillion, and the money supply is $1 trillion. If the money supply doubles to $2 trillion, the quantity theory of money tells us that nominal income will double to $10 trillion (= 5 × $2 trillion).

Because the classical economists (including Fisher) thought that wages and prices were completely flexible, they believed that the level of aggregate output Y produced in the economy during normal times would remain at the full-employment level, so Y in the equation of exchange could also be treated as reasonably constant in the short run. The quantity theory of money then implies that if M doubles, P must also double in the short run because V and Y are constant. In our example, if aggregate output is $5 trillion, the velocity of 5 and a money supply of $1 trillion indicate that the price level equals 1 because 1 times $5 trillion equals the nominal income of $5 trillion. When the money supply doubles to $2 trillion, the price level must also double to 2 because 2 times $5 trillion equals the nominal income of $10 trillion.

For the classical economists, the quantity theory of money provided an explanation of movements in the price level. ***Movements in the price level result solely from changes in the quantity of money.***

Quantity Theory of Money Demand

Because the quantity theory of money tells us how much money is held for a given amount of aggregate income, it is in fact a theory of the demand for money. We can see this by dividing both sides of the equation of exchange by V, thus rewriting it as

$$M = \frac{1}{V} \times PY$$

where nominal income $P \times Y$ is written as PY. When the money market is in equilibrium, the quantity of money M that people hold equals the quantity of money demanded M^d, so we can replace M in the equation with M^d. Using k to represent the quantity $1/V$ (a constant because V is a constant), we can rewrite the equation as

$$M^d = k \times PY \tag{3}$$

Equation 3 tells us that because k is a constant, the level of transactions generated by a fixed level of nominal income PY determines the quantity of money M^d that people demand. Therefore, Fisher's quantity theory of money suggests that the demand for money is purely a function of income, and interest rates have no effect on the demand for money.[3]

Fisher came to this conclusion because he believed that people hold money only to conduct transactions and have no freedom of action in terms of the amount they want to hold. The demand for money is determined (1) by the level of transactions generated by the level of nominal income PY and (2) by the institutions in the economy that affect the way people conduct transactions that determine velocity and hence k.

APPLICATION	Testable Theoretical Implications of the Quantity Theory of Money Demand

A convenient linearization of Equation 3 is achieved if we write it in logarithmic form as (ignoring the d superscript here)

$$\log M = \log k + \log (PY)$$
$$= \alpha + \log P + \log Y, \qquad \text{(3-A)}$$

where $\alpha = \log k$. Using Equation 3-A, we can clearly see the testable theoretical implications of the quantity theory of money demand.

In particular, Equation 3-A implies that the price level elasticity of the demand for nominal money balances, denoted $\eta (M, P)$, is

$$\eta(M, P) = \frac{d \log M}{d \log P} = 1,$$

and that the real income elasticity of the demand for real money balances, denoted $\eta (M/P, Y)$, is

$$\eta \left(\frac{M}{P}, Y \right) = \frac{d \log (M/P)}{d \log Y} = 1.$$

Equation 3-A also suggests that the demand for money is purely a function of income and that interest rates have no effect on the demand for money. In other words, the (nominal) interest rate elasticity of the demand for real money balances, denoted $\eta (M/P, i)$, is

$$\eta \left(\frac{M}{P}, i \right) = \frac{d \log (M/P)}{d \log i} = 0.$$

These are the testable theoretical implications of the quantity theory of money demand.*

* Regarding the testable implications of some of the other money demand theories discussed in this chapter, see Apostolos Serletis, *The Demand for Money: Theoretical and Empirical Approaches* (Springer, 2007).

---

[3] While Fisher was developing his quantity theory approach to the demand for money, a group of classical economists in Cambridge, England, came to similar conclusions, although with slightly different reasoning. They derived Equation 3 by recognizing that two properties of money motivate people to hold it: its utility both as a medium of exchange and as a store of wealth.

IS VELOCITY A CONSTANT?

The classical economists' conclusion that nominal income is determined by movements in the money supply rested on their belief that velocity *PY/M* could be treated as reasonably constant.[4] Is it reasonable to assume that velocity is constant? To answer this, let's look at Figure 21-1, which shows four-quarter (short-run) percentage changes in velocity from 1968 to 2008 (nominal income is represented by nominal GDP and the money supply by M2++ (gross)).

What we see in Figure 21-1 is that even in the short run, velocity fluctuates too much to be viewed as a constant. Prior to 1980, velocity exhibited large swings up and down. This may reflect the substantial instability of the economy in this period. After 1980, velocity appears to have more moderate fluctuations, yet there are large differences in the growth rate of velocity from year to year. Velocity actually falls, or at least its rate of growth declines, in years when recessions are taking place.

Until the Great Depression, economists did not recognize that velocity declines sharply during severe economic contractions. Why did the classical economists not recognize this fact? Unfortunately, accurate data on GDP and the money supply did not exist before World War II. (Only after the war did the government start to collect these data.) Economists had no way of knowing that their view of velocity as a constant was demonstrably false. The decline in velocity during the Great Depression years was so great, however, that even the crude data available to economists at that time suggested that velocity was not constant. This explains why, after the Great Depression, economists began to search for other factors influencing the demand for money that might help explain the large fluctuations in velocity.

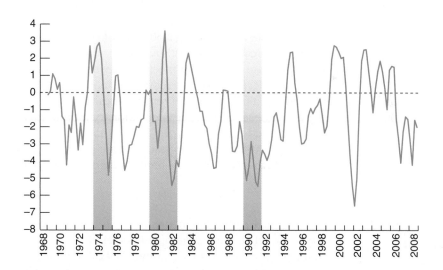

FIGURE 21-1 Change in the Velocity of M2++ (gross), 1968–2008

Shaded areas indicate recessions.

Source: Statistics Canada CANSIM II series V41552801, V41707150, and V1997756.

---

[4] Actually, the classical conclusion still holds if velocity grows at some uniform rate over time that reflects changes in transaction technology. Hence the concept of a constant velocity should more accurately be thought of here as a lack of upward and downward fluctuations in velocity.

Let us now examine the theories of money demand that arose from this search for a better explanation of the behaviour of velocity.

KEYNES'S LIQUIDITY PREFERENCE THEORY

In his famous 1936 book *The General Theory of Employment, Interest, and Money,* John Maynard Keynes abandoned the classical view that velocity was a constant and developed a theory of money demand that emphasized the importance of interest rates. Keynes, at Cambridge at the time, naturally enough followed the approach developed by his Cambridge predecessors. His theory of the demand for money, which he called the **liquidity preference theory,** also asked the question, why do individuals hold money? But Keynes was far more precise than his predecessors regarding what influences individuals' decisions. He postulated that there are three motives behind the demand for money: the transactions motive, the precautionary motive, and the speculative motive.

Transactions Motive

In the classical approach, individuals are assumed to hold money because it is a medium of exchange that can be used to carry out everyday transactions. Following the classical tradition, Keynes emphasized that this component of the demand for money is determined primarily by the level of people's transactions. Because he believed that these transactions were proportional to income, like the classical economists he took the transactions component of the demand for money to be proportional to income.

Precautionary Motive

Keynes went beyond the classical analysis by recognizing that in addition to holding money to carry out current transactions, people hold money as a cushion against an unexpected need. Suppose that you've been thinking about buying a fancy stereo; you walk by a store that is having a 50%-off sale on the one you want. If you are holding money as a precaution for just such an occurrence, you can purchase the stereo right away; if you are not holding precautionary money balances, you cannot take advantage of the sale. Precautionary money balances also come in handy if you are hit with an unexpected bill, say for car repair or health needs not covered by insurance.

Keynes believed that the precautionary money balances people want to hold are determined primarily by the level of transactions that they expect to make in the future and that these transactions are proportional to income. Therefore, he postulated, the demand for precautionary money balances is proportional to income.

Speculative Motive

If Keynes had ended his theory with the transactions and precautionary motives, income would be the only important determinant of the demand for money, and he would not have added much to the classical approach. However, Keynes took the view that people also hold money as a store of wealth. He called this reason for holding money the *speculative motive.* Since he believed that wealth is tied closely to income, the speculative component of money demand would be related to income. However, Keynes looked more carefully at the factors that influence the decisions regarding how much money to hold as a store of wealth, especially interest rates.

Keynes divided the assets that can be used to store wealth into two categories: money and bonds. He then asked the following question: why would individuals decide to hold their wealth in the form of money rather than bonds?

Thinking back to the discussion of the theory of asset demand (Chapter 5), you would want to hold money if its expected return was greater than the expected return from holding bonds. Keynes assumed that the expected return on money was zero because in his time, unlike today, most chequable deposits did not earn interest. For bonds, there are two components of the expected return: the interest payment and the *expected* rate of capital gains.

You learned in Chapter 4 that when interest rates rise, the price of a bond falls. If you expect interest rates to rise, you expect the price of the bond to fall and therefore suffer a negative capital gain—that is, a capital loss. If you expect the rise in interest rates to be substantial enough, the capital loss might outweigh the interest payment, and your *expected* return on the bond might be negative. In this case, you would want to store your wealth as money because its expected return is higher; its zero return exceeds the negative return on the bond.

Keynes assumed that individuals believe that interest rates gravitate to some normal value (an assumption less plausible in today's world). If interest rates are below this normal value, individuals expect the interest rate on bonds to rise in the future and so expect to suffer capital losses on them. As a result, individuals will be more likely to hold their wealth as money rather than bonds, and the demand for money will be high.

What would you expect to happen to the demand for money when interest rates are above the normal value? In general, people will expect interest rates to fall, bond prices to rise, and capital gains to be realized. At higher interest rates, they are more likely to expect the return from holding a bond to be positive, thus exceeding the expected return from holding money. They will be more likely to hold bonds than money, and the demand for money will be quite low. From Keynes's reasoning we can conclude that as interest rates rise, the demand for money falls, and therefore ***money demand is negatively related to the level of interest rates.***

Putting the Three Motives Together

In putting the three motives for holding money balances together into a demand for money equation, Keynes was careful to distinguish between nominal quantities and real quantities. Money is valued in terms of what it can buy. If, for example, all prices in the economy double (the price level doubles), the same nominal quantity of money will be able to buy only half as many goods. Keynes thus reasoned that people want to hold a certain amount of **real money balances** (the quantity of money in real terms)—an amount that his three motives indicated would be related to real income Y and to interest rates i. Keynes wrote down the following demand for money equation, known as the *liquidity preference function,* which says that the demand for real money balances M^d/P is a function of (related to) i and Y.[5]

$$\frac{M^d}{P} = f(\underset{-}{i}, \underset{+}{Y}) \tag{4}$$

The minus sign below i in the liquidity preference function means that the demand for real money balances is negatively related to the interest rate i, and the plus sign below Y means that the demand for real money balances and real income Y are positively related. The money demand function in Equation 4 is the same one used

---

[5] The classical economists' money demand equation can also be written in terms of real money balances by dividing both sides of Equation 3 by the price level P to obtain

$$\frac{M^d}{P} = k \times Y$$

in our analysis of money demand in Chapter 5 and in Chapter 22 that describes the *ISLM* model. Because money demand is negatively related to the interest rate, a fall in i leads to a rise in the quantity of money demanded M^d, and so the money demand curve is downward sloping as in Figure 5-8 (page 98). Keynes's conclusion that the demand for money is related not only to income but also to interest rates is a major departure from Fisher's view of money demand, in which interest rates have no effect on the demand for money.

By deriving the liquidity preference function for velocity PY/M, we can see that Keynes's theory of the demand for money implies that velocity is not constant but instead fluctuates with movements in interest rates. The liquidity preference equation can be rewritten as

$$\frac{P}{M^d} = \frac{1}{f(i, Y)}$$

Multiplying both sides of this equation by Y and recognizing that M^d can be replaced by M because they must be equal in money market equilibrium, we solve for velocity:

$$V = \frac{PY}{M} = \frac{Y}{f(i, Y)} \tag{5}$$

We know that the demand for money is negatively related to interest rates; when i goes up, $f(i, Y)$ declines, and therefore velocity rises. In other words, a rise in interest rates encourages people to hold lower real money balances for a given level of income; therefore, the rate at which money turns over (velocity) must be higher. This reasoning implies that because interest rates have substantial fluctuations, the liquidity preference theory of the demand for money indicates that velocity has substantial fluctuations as well.

An interesting feature of Equation 5 is that it explains some of the velocity movements in Figure 21-1 (page 555), in which we noted that when recessions occur, velocity falls or its rate of growth declines. What fact regarding the cyclical behaviour of interest rates that we discussed in Chapter 5 might help us explain this phenomenon? You might recall that interest rates are procyclical, rising in expansions and falling in recessions. The liquidity preference theory indicates that a rise in interest rates will cause velocity to rise also. The procyclical movements of interest rates should induce procyclical movements in velocity, and that is exactly what we see in Figure 21-1.

Keynes's model of the speculative demand for money provides another reason why velocity might show substantial fluctuations. What would happen to the demand for money if the view of the normal level to which interest rates gravitate changes? For example, what if people expect the future normal interest rate to be higher than the current normal interest rate? Because interest rates are then expected to be higher in the future, more people will expect the prices of bonds to fall and will anticipate capital losses. The expected returns from holding bonds will decline, and money will become more attractive relative to bonds. As a result, the demand for money will increase. This means that $f(i, Y)$ will increase and so velocity will fall. Velocity will change as expectations about future normal levels of interest rates change, and unstable expectations about future movements in normal interest rates can lead to instability of velocity. This is one more reason why Keynes rejected the view that velocity could be treated as a constant.

To sum up, Keynes's liquidity preference theory postulated three motives for holding money: the transactions motive, the precautionary motive, and the speculative motive. Although Keynes took the transactions and precautionary components of the demand for money to be proportional to income, he reasoned that the speculative motive would be negatively related to the level of interest rates.

Keynes's model of the demand for money has the important implication that velocity is not constant but instead is positively related to interest rates, which fluctuate substantially. His theory also rejected the constancy of velocity because changes in people's expectations about the normal level of interest rates would cause shifts in the demand for money that would cause velocity to shift as well. Thus Keynes's liquidity preference theory casts doubt on the classical quantity theory that nominal income is determined primarily by movements in the quantity of money.

FURTHER DEVELOPMENTS IN THE KEYNESIAN APPROACH

After World War II, economists began to take the Keynesian approach to the demand for money even further by developing more precise theories to explain the three Keynesian motives for holding money. Because interest rates were viewed as a crucial element in monetary theory, a key focus of this research was to understand better the role of interest rates in the demand for money.

Transactions Demand

William Baumol and James Tobin independently developed similar demand for money models, which demonstrated that even money balances held for transactions purposes are sensitive to the level of interest rates.[6] In developing their models, they considered a hypothetical individual who receives a payment once a period and spends it over the course of this period. In their model, money, which earns zero interest, is held only because it can be used to carry out transactions.

To refine this analysis, let's say that Grant Smith receives $1000 at the beginning of the month and spends it on transactions that occur at a constant rate during the course of the month. If Grant keeps the $1000 in cash in order to carry out his transactions his money balances follow the sawtooth pattern displayed in panel (a) of Figure 21-2. At the beginning of the month he has $1000, and by the end of month he has no cash left because he has spent it all. Over the course of the month, his holdings of money will on average be $500 (his holdings at the beginning of the month, $1000, plus his holdings at the end of the month, $0, divided by 2).

At the beginning of the next month, Grant receives another $1000 payment, which he holds as cash, and the same decline in money balances begins again. This process repeats monthly, and his average money balance during the course of the year is $500. Since his yearly nominal income is $12 000 and his holdings of money average $500, the velocity of money ($V = PY/M$) is $12 000/$500 = 24.

Suppose that as a result of taking a money and banking course, Grant realizes that he can improve his situation by not always holding cash. In January, then, he decides to hold part of his $1000 in cash and puts part of it into an income-earning security such as bonds. At the beginning of each month, Grant keeps

---

[6] William J. Baumol, "The Transactions Demand for Cash: An Inventory Theoretic Approach," *Quarterly Journal of Economics* 66 (1952): 545–556; James Tobin, "The Interest Elasticity of the Transactions Demand for Cash," *Review of Economics and Statistics* 38 (1956): 241–247.

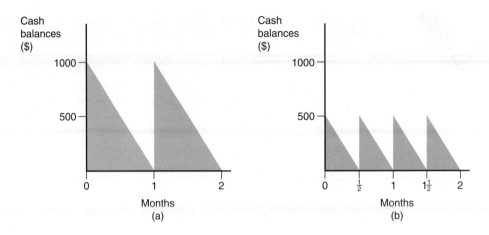

FIGURE 21-2   Cash Balances in the Baumol-Tobin Model

In panel (a), the $1000 payment at the beginning of the month is held entirely in cash and is spent at a constant rate until it is exhausted by the end of the month. In panel (b), half of the monthly payment is put into cash and the other half into bonds. At the middle of the month, cash balances reach zero and bonds must be sold to bring balances up to $500. By the end of the month, cash balances again dwindle to zero.

$500 in cash and uses the other $500 to buy a Canada bond. As you can see in panel (b), he starts out each month with $500 of cash and $500 of bonds, and by the middle of the month, his cash balance has run down to zero. Because bonds cannot be used directly to carry out transactions, Grant must sell them and turn them into cash so that he can carry out the rest of the month's transactions. At the middle of the month, then, Grant's cash balance rises back up to $500. By the end of the month, the cash is gone. When he again receives his next $1000 monthly payment, he again divides it into $500 of cash and $500 of bonds, and the process continues. The net result of this process is that the average cash balance held during the month is $500/2 = $250—just half of what it was before. Velocity has doubled to $12 000/$250 = 48.

What has Grant Smith gained from his new stategy? He has earned interest on $500 of bonds that he held for half the month. If the interest rate is 1% per month, he has earned an additional $2.50 ($= \frac{1}{2} \times \$500 \times 1\%$) per month.

Sounds like a pretty good deal, doesn't it? In fact, if he had kept $333.33 in cash at the beginning of the month, he would have been able to hold $666.67 in bonds for the first third of the month. Then he could have sold $333.33 of bonds and held on to $333.34 of bonds for the next third of the month. Finally, two-thirds of the way through the month, he would have had to sell the remaining bonds to raise cash. The net result of this is that Grant would have earned $3.33 per month $\left[= \left(\frac{1}{3} \times \$666.67 \times 1\% \right) + \left(\frac{1}{3} \times \$333.34 \times 1\% \right) \right]$. This is an even better deal. His average cash holdings in this case would be $333.33/2 = $166.67. Clearly, the lower his average cash balance, the more interest he will earn.

As you might expect, there is a catch to all this. In buying bonds, Grant incurs transaction costs of two types. First, he must pay a straight brokerage fee for the buying and selling of the bonds. These fees increase when average cash balances are lower because Grant will be buying and selling bonds more often. Second, by holding less cash, he will have to make more trips to the bank to get the cash, once he has sold some of his bonds. Because time is money, this must also be counted as part of the transaction costs.

Grant faces a trade-off. If he holds very little cash, he can earn a lot of interest on bonds, but he will incur greater transaction costs. If the interest rate is high, the benefits of holding bonds will be high relative to the transaction costs, and he will hold more bonds and less cash. Conversely, if interest rates are low, the transaction costs involved in holding a lot of bonds may outweigh the interest payments, and Grant would then be better off holding more cash and fewer bonds.

The conclusion of the Baumol-Tobin analysis may be stated as follows: as interest rates increase, the amount of cash held for transactions purposes will decline, which in turn means that velocity will increase as interest rates increase.[7] Put another way, the ***transactions component of the demand for money is negatively related to the level of interest rates.***

The basic idea in the Baumol-Tobin analysis is that there is an opportunity cost of holding money—the interest that can be earned on other assets. There is also a benefit to holding money—the avoidance of transaction costs. When interest rates increase, people will try to economize on their holdings of money for transactions purposes because the opportunity cost of holding money has increased. By using simple models, Baumol and Tobin revealed something that we might not otherwise have seen: that the transactions demand for money, and not just the speculative demand, will be sensitive to interest rates. The Baumol-Tobin analysis presents a nice demonstration of the value of economic modelling.[8]

The idea that as interest rates increase, the opportunity cost of holding money increases so that the demand for money falls can be stated equivalently with the terminology of expected returns used in Chapter 5. As interest rates increase, the expected return on the other asset, bonds, increases, causing the relative expected return on money to fall, thereby lowering the demand for money. These two explanations are in fact identical because as we saw in Chapter 5, changes in the opportunity cost of an asset are just a description of what is happening to the relative expected return. Baumol and Tobin used the opportunity cost terminology in their work on the transactions demand for money, and that is why we use this terminology.

Precautionary Demand

Models that explore the precautionary motive of the demand for money have been developed along lines similar to the Baumol-Tobin framework, so we will not go into great detail about them here. We have already discussed the benefits of holding precautionary money balances, but weighed against these benefits must be the opportunity cost of the interest forgone by holding money. We therefore have a trade-off similar to the one of transactions balances. As interest rates rise, the opportunity cost of holding precautionary balances rises, and so the holdings of these money balances fall. We then have a result similar to the one

---

[7] Similar reasoning leads to the conclusion that as brokerage fees increase, the demand for transactions money balances increases as well. When these fees rise, the benefits from holding transactions money balances increase because by holding these balances an individual will not have to sell bonds as often, thereby avoiding these higher brokerage costs. The greater benefits to holding money balances relative to the opportunity cost of interest forgone, then, lead to a higher demand for transactions balances.

[8] The mathematics behind the Baumol-Tobin model can be found in an appendix to this chapter on this book's MyEconLab at **www.pearsoned.ca/myeconlab**.

found for the Baumol-Tobin analysis.[9] ***The precautionary demand for money is negatively related to interest rates.***

Speculative Demand

Keynes's analysis of the speculative demand for money was open to several serious criticisms. It indicated that an individual holds only money as a store of wealth when the expected return on bonds is less than the expected return on money and holds only bonds when the expected return on bonds is greater than the expected return on money. Solely in the rare instance when people have expected returns on bonds and money that are exactly equal would they hold both. Keynes's analysis therefore implies that practically no one holds a diversified portfolio of bonds and money simultaneously as a store of wealth. Since diversification is apparently a sensible strategy for choosing which assets to hold, the fact that it rarely occurs in Keynes's analysis is a serious shortcoming of his theory of the speculative demand for money.

Tobin developed a model of the speculative demand for money that attempted to avoid this criticism of Keynes's analysis.[10] His basic idea was that not only do people care about the expected return on one asset versus another when they decide what to hold in their portfolio, but they also care about the riskiness of the returns from each asset. Specifically, Tobin assumed that most people are risk-averse—that they would be willing to hold an asset with a lower expected return if it is less risky. An important characteristic of money is that its return is certain; Tobin assumed it to be zero. Bonds, by contrast, can have substantial fluctuations in price, and their returns can be quite risky and sometimes negative. So even if the expected returns on bonds exceed the expected return on money, people might still want to hold money as a store of wealth because it has less risk associated with its return than bonds do.

The Tobin analysis also shows that people can reduce the total amount of risk in a portfolio by diversifying, that is, by holding both bonds and money. The model suggests that individuals will hold bonds and money simultaneously as stores of wealth. Since this is probably a more realistic description of people's behaviour than Keynes's, Tobin's rationale for the speculative demand for money seems to rest on more solid ground.

Tobin's attempt to improve on Keynes's rationale for the speculative demand for money was only partly successful, however. It is still not clear that the speculative demand even exists. What if there are assets that have no risk—like money—but earn a higher return? Will there be any speculative demand for money? No, because an individual will always be better off holding such an asset rather than money. The resulting portfolio will enjoy a higher expected return yet has no higher risk. Do such assets exist in the Canadian economy? The answer is yes. Canadian treasury bills, money market mutual fund shares, and other assets that have no default risk provide certain returns that are greater than those available on money. Therefore, why would anyone want to hold money balances as a store of wealth (ignoring for the moment transactions and precautionary reasons)?

---

[9] These models of the precautionary demand for money also reveal that as uncertainty about the level of future transactions grows, the precautionary demand for money increases. This is so because greater uncertainty means that individuals are more likely to incur transaction costs if they are not holding precautionary balances. The benefit of holding such balances then increases relative to the opportunity cost of forgone interest, and so the demand for them rises.

[10] James Tobin, "Liquidity Preference as Behavior Towards Risk," *Review of Economic Students* 25 (1958): 65–86.

Although Tobin's analysis did not explain why money is held as a store of wealth, it was an important development in our understanding of how people should choose among assets. Indeed, his analysis was an important step in the development of the academic field of finance, which examines asset pricing and portfolio choice (the decision to buy one asset over another).

To sum up, further developments of the Keynesian approach have attempted to give a more precise explanation for the transactions, precautionary, and speculative demands for money. The attempt to improve Keynes's rationale for the speculative demand for money has been only partly successful; it is still not clear that this demand even exists. However, the models of the transactions and precautionary demands for money indicate that these components of money demand are negatively related to interest rates. Hence Keynes's proposition that the demand for money is sensitive to interest rates—suggesting that velocity is not constant and that nominal income might be affected by factors other than the quantity of money—is still supported.

FRIEDMAN'S MODERN QUANTITY THEORY OF MONEY

In 1956, Milton Friedman developed a theory of the demand for money in a famous article, "The Quantity Theory of Money: A Restatement."[11] Although Friedman frequently refers to Irving Fisher and the quantity theory, his analysis of the demand for money is actually closer to that of Keynes.

Like his predecessors, Friedman pursued the question of why people choose to hold money. Instead of analyzing the specific motives for holding money, as Keynes did, Friedman simply stated that the demand for money must be influenced by the same factors that influence the demand for any asset. Friedman then applied the theory of asset demand to money.

The theory of asset demand (Chapter 5) indicates that the demand for money should be a function of the resources available to individuals (their wealth) and the expected returns on other assets relative to the expected return on money. Like Keynes, Friedman recognized that people want to hold a certain amount of real money balances (the quantity of money in real terms). From this reasoning, Friedman expressed his formulation of the demand for money as follows:

$$\frac{M^d}{P} = f(\underset{+}{Y_p},\ \underset{-}{r_b - r_m},\ \underset{-}{r_e - r_m},\ \underset{-}{\pi^e - r_m}) \tag{6}$$

where M^d/P = demand for real money balances
Y_p = Friedman's measure of wealth, known as *permanent income* (technically, the present discounted value of all expected future income, but more easily described as expected average long-run income)
r_m = expected return on money
r_b = expected return on bonds
r_e = expected return on equity (common stocks)
π^e = expected inflation rate

[11] Milton Friedman, "The Quantity Theory of Money: A Restatement," in *Studies in the Quantity Theory of Money,* ed. Milton Friedman (Chicago: University of Chicago Press, 1956), pp. 3–21.

and the signs underneath the equation indicate whether the demand for money is positively (+) related or negatively (−) related to the terms that are immediately above them.[12]

Let us look in more detail at the variables in Friedman's money demand function and what they imply for the demand for money.

Because the demand for an asset is positively related to wealth, money demand is positively related to Friedman's wealth concept, permanent income (indicated by the plus sign beneath it). Unlike our usual concept of income, permanent income (which can be thought of as expected average long-run income) has much smaller short-run fluctuations because many movements of income are transitory (short-lived). For example, in a business cycle expansion, income increases rapidly, but because some of this increase is temporary, average long-run income does not change very much. Hence in a boom, permanent income rises much less than income. During a recession, much of the income decline is transitory, and average long-run income (hence permanent income) falls less than income. One implication of Friedman's use of the concept of permanent income as a determinant of the demand for money is that the demand for money will not fluctuate much with business cycle movements.

An individual can hold wealth in several forms besides money; Friedman categorized them into three types of assets: bonds, equity (common stocks), and goods. The incentives for holding these assets rather than money are represented by the expected return on each of these assets relative to the expected return on money, the last three terms in the money demand function. The minus sign beneath each indicates that as each term rises, the demand for money will fall.

The expected return on money r_m, which appears in all three terms, is influenced by two factors:

1. The services provided by banks on deposits included in the money supply, such as provision of receipts in the form of cancelled cheques or the automatic paying of bills. When these services are increased, the expected return from holding money rises.

2. The interest payments on money balances. Deposits that are included in the money supply currently pay interest. As these interest payments rise, the expected return on money rises.

The terms $r_b - r_m$ and $r_e - r_m$ represent the expected return on bonds and equity relative to money; as they rise, the relative expected return on money falls, and the demand for money falls. The final term, $\pi^e - r_m$, represents the expected return on goods relative to money. The expected return from holding goods is the expected rate of capital gains that occurs when their prices rise and hence is equal to the expected inflation rate π^e. If the expected inflation rate is 10%, for example, then goods' prices are expected to rise at a 10% rate, and their expected return is 10%. When $\pi^e - r_m$ rises, the expected return on goods relative to money rises, and the demand for money falls.

---

[12] Friedman also added to his formulation a term h that represented the ratio of human to nonhuman wealth. He reasoned that if people had more permanent income coming from labour income and thus from their human capital, they would be less liquid than if they were receiving income from financial assets. In this case, they might want to hold more money because it is a more liquid asset than the alternatives. The term h plays no essential role in Friedman's theory and has no important implications for monetary theory. That is why we ignore it in the money demand function.

DISTINGUISHING BETWEEN THE FRIEDMAN AND KEYNESIAN THEORIES

There are several differences between Friedman's theory of the demand for money and the Keynesian theories. One is that by including many assets as alternatives to money, Friedman recognized that more than one interest rate is important to the operation of the aggregate economy. Keynes, for his part, lumped financial assets other than money into one big category—bonds—because he felt that their returns generally move together. If this is so, the expected return on bonds will be a good indicator of the expected return on other financial assets, and there will be no need to include them separately in the money demand function.

Also in contrast to Keynes, Friedman viewed money and goods as substitutes; that is, people choose between them when deciding how much money to hold. That is why Friedman included the expected return on goods relative to money as a term in his money demand function. The assumption that money and goods are substitutes indicates that changes in the quantity of money may have a direct effect on aggregate spending.

In addition, Friedman stressed two issues in discussing his demand for money function that distinguish it from Keynes's liquidity preference theory. First, Friedman did not take the expected return on money to be a constant, as Keynes did. When interest rates rise in the economy, banks make more profits on their loans, and they want to attract more deposits to increase the volume of their now more profitable loans. If there are no restrictions on interest payments on deposits, banks attract deposits by paying higher interest rates on them. Because the industry is competitive, the expected return on money held as bank deposits then rises with the higher interest rates on bonds and loans. The banks compete to get deposits until there are no excess profits, and in doing so they close the gap between interest earned on loans and interest paid on deposits. The net result of this competition in the banking industry is that $r_b - r_m$ stays relatively constant when the interest rate i rises.[13]

What if there are restrictions on the amount of interest that banks can pay on their deposits? Will the expected return on money be a constant? As interest rates rise, will $r_b - r_m$ rise as well? Friedman thought not. He argued that although banks might be restricted from making pecuniary payments on their deposits, they could still compete on the quality dimension. For example, they can provide more services to depositors by hiring more tellers, paying bills automatically, or making more cash machines available at more accessible locations. The result of these improvements in money services is that the expected return from holding deposits will rise. So despite the restrictions on pecuniary interest payments, we might still find that a rise in market interest rates will raise the expected return on money sufficiently so that $r_b - r_m$ will remain relatively constant. ***Unlike Keynes's theory, which indicates that interest rates are an important determinant of the demand for money, Friedman's theory suggests that changes in interest rates should have little effect on the demand for money.***

---

[13] Friedman does suggest that there is some increase in $r_b - r_m$ when i rises because part of the money supply (especially currency) is held in forms that cannot pay interest in a pecuniary or nonpecuniary form. See, for example, Milton Friedman, "Why a Surge of Inflation Is Likely Next Year," *Wall Street Journal,* September 1, 1983. p. 24.

Therefore, Friedman's money demand function is essentially one in which permanent income is the primary determinant of money demand, and his money demand equation can be approximated by

$$\frac{M^d}{P} = f(Y_p) \tag{7}$$

In Friedman's view, the demand for money is insensitive to interest rates—not because he viewed the demand for money as insensitive to changes in the incentives for holding other assets relative to money but rather because changes in interest rates should have little effect on these incentive terms in the money demand function. The incentive terms remain relatively constant because any rise in the expected returns on other assets as a result of the rise in interest rates would be matched by a rise in the expected return on money.

The second issue Friedman stressed is the stability of the demand for money function. In contrast to Keynes, Friedman suggested that random fluctuations in the demand for money are small and that the demand for money can be predicted accurately by the money demand function. When combined with his view that the demand for money is insensitive to changes in interest rates, this means that velocity is highly predictable. We can see this by writing down the velocity that is implied by the money demand equation (Equation 7):

$$V = \frac{Y}{f(Y_p)} \tag{8}$$

Because the relationship between Y and Y_p is usually quite predictable, a stable money demand function (one that does not undergo pronounced shifts so that it predicts the demand for money accurately) implies that velocity is predictable as well. If we can predict what velocity will be in the next period, a change in the quantity of money will produce a predictable change in aggregate spending. Even though velocity is no longer assumed to be constant, the money supply continues to be the primary determinant of nominal income as in the quantity theory of money. Therefore, Friedman's theory of money demand is indeed a restatement of the quantity theory because it leads to the same conclusion about the importance of money to aggregate spending.

You may recall that we said that the Keynesian liquidity preference function (in which interest rates are an important determinant of the demand for money) can explain the procyclical movement of velocity that we find in the data. Can Friedman's money demand formulation explain this procyclical velocity phenomenon as well?

The key clue to answering this question is the presence of permanent income rather than measured income in the money demand function. What happens to permanent income in a business cycle expansion? Because much of the increase in income will be transitory, permanent income rises much less than income. Friedman's money demand function then indicates that the demand for money rises only a small amount relative to the rise in measured income, and as Equation 8 indicates, velocity rises. Similarly, in a recession, the demand for money falls less than income because the decline in permanent income is small relative to income, and velocity falls. In this way we have the procyclical movement in velocity.

To summarize, Friedman's theory of the demand for money used a similar approach to that of Keynes and the earlier Cambridge economists but did not go into detail about the motives for holding money. Instead, Friedman made use of the theory of asset demand to indicate that the demand for money will be a function of permanent income and the expected returns on alternative assets relative to the expected return on money. There are two major differences between Friedman's theory and Keynes's. Friedman believed that changes in interest rates have little effect on the expected returns on other assets relative to money. Thus, in contrast to Keynes, he viewed the demand for money as insensitive to interest rates. In addition, he differed from Keynes in stressing that the money demand function does not undergo substantial shifts and so is stable. These two differences also indicate that velocity is predictable, yielding a quantity theory conclusion that money is the primary determinant of aggregate spending. The conclusion that money is the primary determinant of aggregate spending was the basis of monetarism, the view that the money supply is the primary source of movements in the price level and aggregate output.

EMPIRICAL EVIDENCE ON THE DEMAND FOR MONEY

As we have seen, the alternative theories of the demand for money can have very different implications for our view of the role of money in the economy. Which of these theories is an accurate description of the real world is an important question, and it is the reason why evidence on the demand for money has been at the centre of many debates on the effects of monetary policy on aggregate economic activity. Here we examine the empirical evidence in the United States and Canada on the two primary issues that distinguish the different theories of money demand and affect their conclusions about whether the quantity of money is the primary determinant of aggregate spending. Is the demand for money sensitive to changes in interest rates, and is the demand for money function stable over time?[14]

---

[14] If you are interested in a more detailed discussion of the empirical research on the demand for money, you can find it in an appendix to this chapter on this book's MyEconLab at **www.pearsoned.ca/ myeconlab**.

APPLICATION   **Empirical Estimation of Money Demand Functions**

To see what empirical estimation of money demand functions is all about, suppose that we want to estimate the quantity theory of money demand function and test its theoretical implications.* That is, test the hypotheses that the price level elasticity of the demand for nominal money balances, $\eta\ (M, P)$, equals 1 and that the real income elasticity of the demand for real money balances, $\eta\ (M/P,\ Y)$, equals 1.

The hypothesis $\eta\ (M, P) = 1$ can easily be tested by reformulating Equation 3-A and estimating the following regression equation

$$\log P_t = -\ \alpha - \beta \log Y_t + \gamma \log M_t + \epsilon_t$$

using time series data, and testing the hypothesis

$$H_0: \gamma = 1.$$

Moreover, the implication of a unitary income elasticity can be tested by reformulating Equation 3-A as

$$\log\left(\frac{M}{P}\right)_t = \alpha + \beta \log Y_t + \epsilon_t$$

and (using time series data) testing the null hypothesis

$$H_0{:}\beta = 1.$$

---

* Regarding other empirical approaches to the demand for money, see Apostolos Serletis, *The Demand for Money: Theoretical and Empirical Approaches* (Springer, 2007).

Interest Rates and Money Demand

Earlier in the chapter we saw that if interest rates do not affect the demand for money, velocity is more likely to be a constant—or at least predictable—so that the quantity theory view that aggregate spending is determined by the quantity of money is more likely to be true. However, the more sensitive the demand for money is to interest rates, the more unpredictable velocity will be, and the less clear the link between the money supply and aggregate spending will be. Indeed, there is an extreme case of ultrasensitivity of the demand for money to interest rates, called the *liquidity trap,* in which monetary policy has no direct effect on aggregate spending because a change in the money supply has no effect on interest rates. (If the demand for money is ultrasensitive to interest rates, a tiny change in interest rates produces a very large change in the quantity of money demanded. Hence in this case, the demand for money is completely flat in the supply and demand diagrams of Chapter 5. Therefore, a change in the money supply that shifts the money supply curve to the right or left results in it intersecting the flat money demand curve at the same unchanged interest rate.)

The evidence on the interest sensitivity of the demand for money found by different researchers for different countries is remarkably consistent. Neither extreme case is supported by the data. In situations in which nominal interest rates have not hit a floor of zero, the demand for money is sensitive to interest rates, and there is little evidence that a liquidity trap has ever existed. However, as we saw in Chapter 4, when interest rates fall to zero, they can go no lower. In this situation, a liquidity trap has occurred because the demand for money is now completely flat. Indeed, Japan has been experiencing a liquidity trap of this type in recent years, and this is one reason why it has been difficult for the monetary authorities to stimulate the economy.

Stability of Money Demand

If the money demand function, like Equation 4 or 6, is unstable and undergoes substantial unpredictable shifts, as Keynes thought, then velocity is unpredictable, and the quantity of money may not be tightly linked to aggregate spending, as it is in the modern quantity theory. The stability of the money demand function is also crucial to whether the central bank should target interest rates or the money supply (see Chapter 23). Thus it is important to look at the question of whether or not the money demand function is stable because it has important implications for how monetary policy should be conducted.

By the early 1970s, evidence strongly supported the stability of the money demand function. However, after 1973, the rapid pace of financial innovation (which changed what items could be counted as money) led to substantial instability in estimated money demand functions.

The recent instability of the money demand function calls into question whether our theories and empirical analyses are adequate.[15] It also has important implications for the way monetary policy should be conducted because it casts doubt on the usefulness of the money demand function as a tool to provide guidance to policymakers. In particular, because the money demand function has become unstable, velocity is now harder to predict, and, as discussed in Chapter 18, setting rigid money supply targets in order to control aggregate spending in the economy may not be an effective way to conduct monetary policy.

SUMMARY

1. Irving Fisher developed a transactions-based theory of the demand for money in which the demand for real balances is proportional to real income and is insensitive to interest-rate movements. An implication of his theory is that velocity, the rate of turnover of money, is constant. This generates the quantity theory of money, which implies that aggregate spending is determined solely by movements in the quantity of money.

2. The classical Cambridge approach tried to answer the question of how much money individuals want to hold. This approach also viewed the demand for real balances as proportional to real income, but it differs from Fisher's analysis in that it does not rule out interest-rate effects on the demand for money.

3. The classical view that velocity can be effectively treated as a constant is not supported by the data. The nonconstancy of velocity became especially clear to the economics profession after the sharp drop in velocity during the years of the Great Depression.

4. John Maynard Keynes extended the classical approach by suggesting three motives for holding money: the transactions motive, the precautionary motive, and the speculative motive. His resulting liquidity preference theory views the transactions and precautionary components of money demand as proportional to income. However, the speculative component of money demand is viewed as sensitive to interest rates as well as to expectations about the

future movements of interest rates. This theory, then, implies that velocity is unstable and cannot be treated as a constant.

5. Further developments in the Keynesian approach provided a better rationale for the three Keynesian motives for holding money. Interest rates were found to be important to the transactions and precautionary components of money demand as well as to the speculative component.

6. Milton Friedman's theory of money demand used a similar approach to that of Keynes and the classical economists. Treating money like any other asset, Friedman used the theory of asset demand to derive a demand for money that is a function of the expected returns on other assets relative to the expected return on money and permanent income. In contrast to Keynes, Friedman believed that the demand for money is stable and insensitive to interest-rate movements. His belief that velocity is predictable (though not constant) in turn leads to the quantity theory conclusion that money is the primary determinant of aggregate spending.

7. There are two main conclusions from the research on the demand for money. The demand for money is sensitive to interest rates, but there is little evidence that it is or has been ultrasensitive (liquidity trap). Since 1973, money demand has been found to be unstable, with the most likely source of the instability being the rapid pace of financial innovation.

---

[15] For example, William Barnett, Douglas Fisher, and Apostolos Serletis, "Consumer Theory and the Demand for Money," *Journal of Economic Literature* 30 (1992): 2086–2119; William Barnett and Apostolos Serletis, *The Theory of Monetary Aggregation,* (Amsterdam: North-Holland, 2000); and Apostolos Serletis, *The Demand for Money: Theoretical and Empirical Approaches* (Springer, 2007) are especially critical of the use of simple-sum monetary aggregates in the empirical research on the demand for money.

KEY TERMS

equation of exchange,   p. 552   monetary theory,   p. 557   real money balances,   p. 557

liquidity preference theory,   p. 556   quantity theory of money,   p. 553   velocity of money,   p. 552

QUESTIONS

You will find the answers to the questions marked with an asterisk in the Textbook Resources section of your MyEconLab.

*1. "Considering that both Fisher and the classical economists ended with the same equation for the demand for money, $M^d = k \times PY$, their theories are equivalent." Is this statement true, false, or uncertain? Explain your answer.

2. Explain how the velocity of money is affected by changes in the nominal interest rate, i, and real GDP, Y.

*3. In Keynes's analysis of the speculative demand for money, what will happen to money demand if people suddenly decide that the normal level of the interest rate has declined? Why?

4. Why is Keynes's analysis of the speculative demand for money important to his view that velocity will undergo substantial fluctuations and thus cannot be treated as constant?

*5. If interest rates on bonds go to zero, what does the Baumol-Tobin analysis suggest Grant Smith's average holdings of money balances should be?

6. If brokerage fees go to zero, what does the Baumol-Tobin analysis suggest Grant Smith's average holdings of money should be?

*7. "In Tobin's analysis of the speculative demand for money, people will hold both money and bonds, even if bonds are expected to earn a positive return." Is this statement true, false, or uncertain? Explain your answer.

8. Both Keynes's and Friedman's theories of the demand for money suggest that as the relative expected return on money falls, demand for it will fall. Why does Friedman think that money demand is unaffected by changes in interest rates? Why did Keynes think that money demand is affected by changes in interest rates?

*9. Why does Friedman's view of the demand for money suggest that velocity is predictable, whereas Keynes's view suggests the opposite?

QUANTITATIVE PROBLEMS

*1. The money supply M has been growing at 10% per year, and nominal GDP PY has been growing at 20% per year. The data are as follows (in billions of dollars):

	2007	2008	2009
M	100	110	121
PY	1000	1200	1440

Calculate the velocity in each year. At what rate is velocity growing?

2. Calculate what happens to nominal GDP if velocity remains constant at 5 and the money supply increases from $200 billion to $300 billion.

*3. What happens to nominal GDP if the money supply grows by 20% but velocity declines by 30%?

4. If credit cards were made illegal by government legislation, what would happen to velocity? Explain your answer.

*5. If velocity and aggregate output are reasonably constant (as the classical economists believed), what

happens to the price level when the money supply increases from $1 trillion to $4 trillion?

6. If velocity and aggregate output remain constant at 5 and 1000, respectively, what happens to the price level if the money supply declines from $400 billion to $300 billion?

*7. Suppose that the demand for money is given by

$$\log \left(\frac{M}{P} \right) = \alpha + \beta i + \log Y$$

where M is nominal balances, P the price level, i the nominal interest rate, and Y is real income. α and β, are parameters.

a. Explain how a constant rate of increase in the price level affects the demand for money.

b. What is the definition of the velocity of money? Use the concept of velocity to explain how a given quantity of money balances can be used to pay for a relatively large volume of consumption expenditure over a year.

8. Suppose that the demand for money is given by

$$\log\left(\frac{M}{P}\right) = \alpha + \beta i + \log Y$$

where M is nominal balances, P the price level, i the nominal interest rate, and Y is real income. α and β are parameters. For given values of i and Y, state whether the following statements are true, false, or uncertain.
   a. An agricultural society has lower real money demand than an industrial society.
   b. Real money demand is higher in dictatorships than in democracies.

CANSIM Questions

9. Refer to Figure 21-1 on page 555. Get the quarterly CANSIM data from 1968 to 2009 for the real GDP (series V41707150), GDP deflator (series V1997756), and M2 (gross; series V41552801) from the Textbook Resources area of the MyEconLab.
   a. Compute the velocity of money (don't forget to calculate the nominal GDP!), plot this series, and comment on its long-term behaviour.

   b. Compare the calculated velocity of money to its level in 2005. Has it risen or fallen? Suggest reasons for its change since that time.

10. Get the quarterly data from 1962 to 2009 on real GDP (CANSIM series 41707150), the GDP deflator (series V1997756), the monetary base (series V37145), and the three-month T-Bill rate (series V122531) from the Textbook Resources area of the MyEconLab. Run a regression of real money balances on a constant real GDP and the nominal interest rate.
   a. Comment on the fit of the regression.
   b. What is the estimated income elasticity of the demand for real money balances? What is the estimated interest rate elasticity?
   c. Are your estimates in (b) statistically significant?
   d. Is your evidence consistent with the Baumol-Tobin model or with the quantity theory of money?
   e. Is the money demand relationship stable?

WEB EXERCISE

1. John Maynard Keynes is among the most well known of early economic theorists. Go to **http://en.wikipedia.org/wiki/John_Maynard_Keynes** and write a one-page summary of his life and contributions.

Be sure to visit the MyEconLab website at **www.myeconlab.com**. This online homework and tutorial system puts you in control of your own learning with study and practice tools directly correlated to this chapter content.

On the MyEconLab website you will find the following appendices for this chapter:
Appendix 21.1: A Mathematical Treatment of the Baumol-Tobin and Tobin Mean Variance Models
Appendix 21.2: Empirical Evidence on the Demand for Money

CHAPTER 22

The *ISLM* Model

LEARNING OBJECTIVES

After studying this chapter you should be able to

1. utilize the Keynesian cross model for the determination of aggregate output
2. employ the Keynesian *ISLM* model for the determination of aggregate output
3. evaluate how fiscal policy variables (spending and taxes) and monetary policy variables (the money supply and the interest rate) enter into these models

PREVIEW

In the media, you often see forecasts of GDP and interest rates by economists and government agencies. At times, these forecasts seem to come from a crystal ball, but economists actually make their predictions using a variety of economic models. One model widely used by economic forecasters is the *ISLM* model, which was developed by Sir John Hicks in 1937 and is based on the analysis in John Maynard Keynes's influential book *The General Theory of Employment, Interest, and Money*, published in 1936.[1] The *ISLM* model explains how interest rates and total output produced in the economy (aggregate output or, equivalently, aggregate income) are determined, given a fixed price level (a reasonable assumption in the short run).

The *ISLM* model is valuable not only because it can be used in economic forecasting but also because it provides a deeper understanding of how government policy can affect aggregate economic activity. In Chapter 23 we use it to evaluate the effects of monetary and fiscal policy on the economy and to learn some lessons about how monetary policy might best be conducted.

In this chapter we begin by developing the simplest framework for determining aggregate output, in which all economic actors (consumers, firms, and others) except the government play a role. Government fiscal policy (spending and taxes) is then added to the framework to see how it can affect the determination of aggregate output. Finally, we achieve a complete picture of the *ISLM* model by adding monetary policy variables: the money supply and the interest rate.

DETERMINATION OF AGGREGATE OUTPUT

Keynes was especially interested in understanding movements of aggregate output because he wanted to explain why the Great Depression had occurred and how government policy could be used to increase employment in a similar economic

---

[1]John Hicks, "Mr. Keynes and the Classics: A Suggested Interpretation," *Econometrica* (1937): 147–159.

situation. Keynes's analysis started with the recognition that the total quantity demanded of an economy's output was the sum of four types of spending: (1) **consumer expenditure** (*C*), the total demand for consumer goods and services (hamburgers, stereos, rock concerts, and so on); (2) **planned investment spending** (*I*), the total planned spending by businesses on new physical capital (machines, computers, factories, raw materials, and the like) plus planned spending on new homes; (3) **government spending** (*G*), the spending by all levels of government on goods and services (aircraft carriers, government workers, red tape, and so forth); and (4) **net exports** (*NX*), the net foreign spending on domestic goods and services, equal to exports minus imports.[2] The total quantity demanded of an economy's output, called **aggregate demand** (Y^{ad}), can be written as

$$Y^{ad} = C + I + G + NX \tag{1}$$

Using the commonsense concept from supply and demand analysis, Keynes recognized that equilibrium would occur in the economy when total quantity of output supplied (aggregate output produced), *Y*, equals quantity of output demanded, Y^{ad}, that is, when

$$Y = Y^{ad} \tag{2}$$

When this equilibrium condition is satisfied, producers are able to sell all of their output and have no reason to change their production. Keynes's analysis explains two things: (1) why aggregate output is at a certain level (which involves understanding what factors affect each component of aggregate demand) and (2) how the sum of these components can add up to an output smaller than the economy is capable of producing, resulting in less than full employment of resources.

Keynes was especially concerned with explaining the low level of output and employment during the Great Depression. Because inflation was not a serious problem during this period, he assumed that output could change without causing a change in prices. ***Keynes's analysis assumes that the price level is fixed***; that is, dollar amounts for variables such as consumer expenditure, investment, and aggregate output do not have to be adjusted for changes in the price level to tell us how much the real quantities of these variables change. Because the price level is assumed to be fixed, when we talk in this chapter about changes in nominal quantities, we are talking about changes in real quantities as well.

Our discussion of Keynes's analysis begins with a simple framework of aggregate output determination in which the role of government, net exports, and the possible effects of money and interest rates are ignored. Because we are assuming that government spending and net exports are zero (*G* = 0 and *NX* = 0), we need only examine consumer expenditure and investment spending to explain how aggregate output is determined. This simple framework is unrealistic because both government and monetary policy are left out of the picture and because it makes other simplifying assumptions, such as a fixed price level. Still, the model is worth studying because its simplified view helps us understand the key factors that explain how the economy works. It also clearly illustrates the Keynesian idea that the economy can come to rest at a level of aggregate output below the full employment level. Once you understand this simple framework, we can proceed to more complex and more realistic models.

---

[2] Imports are subtracted from exports in arriving at the net exports component of the total quantity demanded of an economy's output because imports are already counted in *C, I,* and *G* but do not add to the demand for the economy's output.

Consumer Expenditure and the Consumption Function

Ask yourself what determines how much you spend on consumer goods and services. Your likely response is that your income is the most important factor because if your income rises, you will be willing to spend more. Keynes reasoned similarly that consumer expenditure is related to **disposable income,** the total income available for spending, equal to aggregate income (which is equivalent to aggregate output) minus taxes $(Y - T)$. He called this relationship between disposable income Y_D and consumer expenditure C the **consumption function** and expressed it as

$$C = a + (mpc \times Y_D) \tag{3}$$

The term *mpc*, the **marginal propensity to consume,** is the slope of the consumption function line $(\Delta C / \Delta Y_D)$ and reflects the change in consumer expenditure that results from an additional dollar of disposable income. Keynes assumed that *mpc* was a constant between the values of 0 and 1. If, for example, a $1.00 increase in disposable income leads to an increase in consumer expenditure of $0.50, then $mpc = 0.5$.

The term *a* stands for **autonomous consumer expenditure,** the amount of consumer expenditure that is independent of disposable income. It tells us how much consumers will spend when disposable income is 0 (they still must have food, clothing, and shelter). If *a* is $200 billion when disposable income is 0, consumer expenditure will equal $200 billion.[3]

A numerical example of a consumption function using the values of $mpc = 0.5$ and $a = 200$ will clarify the preceding concept. The $200 billion of consumer expenditure at a disposable income of 0 is listed in the first row of Table 22-1 and is plotted as point E in Figure 22-1. (Remember that throughout this chapter, dollar amounts for all variables in the figures correspond to real quantities because Keynes assumed that the price level is fixed.) Because $mpc = 0.5$, when disposable income increases by $400 billion, the change in consumer expenditure ΔC in

TABLE 22-1   Consumption Function: Schedule of Consumer Expenditure C When $mpc = 0.5$ and $a = 200$ ($ billions)

Point in Figure 22-1	Disposable Income Y_D (1)	Change in Disposable Income ΔY_D (2)	Change in Consumer Expenditure ΔC $(0.5 \times \Delta Y_D)$ (3)	Consumer Expenditure C (4)
E	0	—	—	200 (= a)
F	400	400	200	400
G	800	400	200	600
H	1200	400	200	800

---

[3] Consumer expenditure can exceed income if people have accumulated savings to tide them over bad times. An alternative is to have parents who will give you money for food (or to pay for school) when you have no income. The situation in which consumer expenditure is greater than disposable income is called *dissaving*.

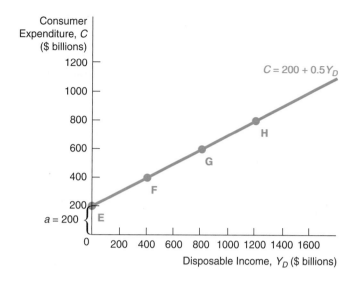

FIGURE 22-1 Consumption Function

The consumption function plotted here is from Table 22-1; *mpc* = 0.5 and *a* = 200.

column 3 of Table 22-1 is $200 billion (0.5 × $400 billion). Thus when disposable income is $400 billion, consumer expenditure is $400 billion (initial value of $200 billion when income is 0 plus the $200 billion change in consumer expenditure). This combination of consumer expenditure and disposable income is listed in the second row of Table 22-1 and is plotted as point F in Figure 22-1. Similarly, at point G, where disposable income has increased by another $400 billion to $800 billion, consumer expenditure will rise by another $200 billion to $600 billion. By the same reasoning, at point H, at which disposable income is $1200 billion, consumer expenditure will be $800 billion. The line connecting these points in Figure 22-1 graphs the consumption function.

Investment Spending

It is important to understand that there are two types of investment. The first type, **fixed investment,** is the spending by firms on equipment (machines, computers, airplanes) and structures (factories, office buildings, shopping centres) and planned spending on residential housing. The second type, **inventory investment,** is spending by firms on additional holdings of raw materials, parts, and finished goods, calculated as the change in holdings of these items in a given time period, say, a year. (The FYI box explains how economists' use of the word *investment* differs from everyday use of the term.)

Suppose that Dell, a company that produces personal computers, has 100 000 computers sitting in its warehouses on December 31, 2009, ready to be shipped to dealers. If each computer has a wholesale price of $1000, Dell has an inventory worth $100 million. If by December 31, 2010, its inventory of personal computers has risen to $150 million, its inventory investment in 2010 is $50 million, the *change* in the level of its inventory over the course of the year ($150 million minus $100 million). Now suppose that there is a drop in the level of inventories; inventory investment will then be negative.

Dell may also have additional inventory investment if the level of raw materials and parts that it is holding to produce these computers increases over the

FYI	Meaning of the Word Investment

Economists use the word *investment* somewhat differently from other people. When people say that they are making an investment, they are normally referring to the purchase of common stocks or bonds, purchases that do not necessarily involve newly produced goods and services. But when economists speak of investment spending, they are referring to the purchase of *new* physical assets such as new machines or new houses—purchases that add to aggregate demand.

course of the year. If on December 31, 2009, it holds $20 million of computer chips used to produce its computers and on December 31, 2010, it holds $30 million, it has an additional $10 million of inventory investment in 2010.

An important feature of inventory investment is that—in contrast to fixed investment, which is always planned—some inventory investment can be unplanned. Suppose that the reason Dell finds itself with an additional $50 million of computers on December 31, 2010, is that $50 million less of its computers were sold in 2010 than expected. This $50 million of inventory investment in 2010 was unplanned. In this situation, Dell is producing more computers than it can sell and will cut production.

Planned investment spending, a component of aggregate demand Y^{ad}, is equal to planned fixed investment plus the amount of inventory investment *planned* by firms. Keynes mentioned two factors that influence planned investment spending: interest rates and businesses' expectations about the future. How these factors affect investment spending is discussed later in this chapter. For now, planned investment spending will be treated as a known value. At this stage, we want to see how aggregate output is determined for a given level of planned investment spending; once we understand this, we can examine how interest rates and business expectations influence aggregate output by affecting planned investment spending.

Equilibrium and the Keynesian Cross Diagram

We have now assembled the building blocks (consumer expenditure and planned investment spending) that will enable us to see how aggregate output is determined when we ignore the government. Although unrealistic, this stripped-down analysis clarifies the basic principles of output determination. In another section, government enters the picture and makes our model more realistic.

The diagram in Figure 22-2, known as the *Keynesian cross diagram*, shows how aggregate output is determined. The vertical axis measures aggregate demand, and the horizontal axis measures the level of aggregate output. The 45° line shows all the points at which aggregate output Y equals aggregate demand Y^{ad}; that is, it shows all the points at which the equilibrium condition $Y = Y^{ad}$ is satisfied. Since government spending and net exports are zero ($G = 0$ and $NX = 0$), aggregate demand is

$$Y^{ad} = C + I$$

Because there is no government sector to collect taxes, there are none in our simplified economy; disposable income Y_D then equals aggregate output Y (remember that aggregate income and aggregate output are equivalent; see the Web Appendix to Chapter 1). Thus the consumption function with $a = 200$ and

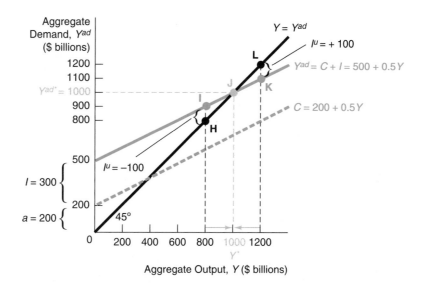

FIGURE 22-2 Keynesian Cross Diagram

When $I = 300$ and $C = 200 + 0.5Y$, equilibrium output occurs at $Y^* = 1000$, where the aggregate demand function $Y^{ad} = C + I$ intersects with the 45° line $Y = Y^{ad}$.

$mpc = 0.5$ plotted in Figure 22-1 can be written as $C = 200 + 0.5Y$ and is plotted in Figure 22-2. Given that planned investment spending is $300 billion, aggregate demand can then be expressed as

$$Y^{ad} = C + I = 200 + 0.5Y + 300 = 500 + 0.5Y$$

This equation, plotted in Figure 22-2, represents the quantity of aggregate demand at any given level of aggregate output and is called the **aggregate demand function**.

The aggregate demand function $Y^{ad} = C + I$ is the vertical sum of the consumption function line ($C = 200 + 0.5Y$) and planned investment spending ($I = 300$). The point at which the aggregate demand function crosses the 45° line $Y = Y^{ad}$ indicates the equilibrium level of aggregate demand and aggregate output. In Figure 22-2, equilibrium occurs at point J, with both aggregate output Y^* and aggregate demand Y^{ad*} at $1000 billion.

As you learned in Chapter 5, the concept of equilibrium is useful only if there is a tendency for the economy to settle there. To see whether the economy heads toward the equilibrium output level of $1000 billion, let's first look at what happens if the amount of output produced in the economy is above the equilibrium level, at $1200 billion. At this level of output, aggregate demand is $1100 billion (point K), $100 billion less than the $1200 billion of output (point L on the 45° line). Since output exceeds aggregate demand by $100 billion, firms are saddled with $100 billion of unsold inventory. To keep from accumulating unsold goods, firms will cut production. As long as it is above the equilibrium level, output will exceed aggregate demand and firms will cut production, sending aggregate output toward the equilibrium level.

Another way to observe a tendency of the economy to head toward equilibrium at point J is from the viewpoint of inventory investment. When firms do not sell all output produced, they add unsold output to their holdings of inventory, and inventory investment increases. At an output level of $1200 billion, for instance, the $100 billion of unsold goods leads to $100 billion of unplanned inventory investment, which firms do not want. Companies will decrease production to reduce inventory to the desired level, and aggregate output will fall (indicated by the arrow near the horizontal axis). This viewpoint means that unplanned inventory investment for the entire economy I^u equals the excess of output over aggregate demand. In our example, at an output level of $1200 billion, $I^u = $100 billion. If I^u is positive, firms will cut production and output will fall. Output will stop falling only when it has returned to its equilibrium level at point J, where $I^u = 0$.

What happens if aggregate output is below the equilibrium level of output? Let's say output is $800 billion. At this level of output, aggregate demand at point I is $900 billion, $100 billion higher than output (point H on the 45° line). At this level, firms are selling $100 billion more goods than they are producing, so inventory falls below the desired level. The negative unplanned inventory investment ($I^u = -$100 billion) will induce firms to increase their production in order to raise inventory to desired levels. As a result, output rises toward the equilibrium level, shown by the arrow in Figure 22-2. As long as output is below the equilibrium level, unplanned inventory investment will remain negative, firms will continue to raise production, and output will continue to rise. We again see the tendency for the economy to settle at point J, where aggregate demand Y equals output Y^{ad} and unplanned inventory investment is zero ($I^u = 0$).

Expenditure Multiplier

Now that we understand that equilibrium aggregate output is determined by the position of the aggregate demand function, we can examine how different factors shift the function and consequently change aggregate output. We will find that either a rise in planned investment spending or a rise in autonomous consumer expenditure shifts the aggregate demand function upward and leads to an increase in aggregate output.

OUTPUT RESPONSE TO A CHANGE IN PLANNED INVESTMENT SPENDING Suppose that a new electric motor is invented that makes all factory machines three times more efficient. Because firms are suddenly more optimistic about the profitability of investing in new machines that use this new motor, planned investment spending increases by $100 billion from an initial level of $I_1 = $300 billion to $I_2 = $400 billion. What effect does this have on output?

The effects of this increase in planned investment spending are analyzed in Figure 22-3 using a Keynesian cross diagram. Initially, when planned investment spending I_1 is $300 billion, the aggregate demand function is Y_1^{ad}, and equilibrium occurs at point 1, where output is $1000 billion. The $100 billion increase in planned investment spending adds directly to aggregate demand and shifts the aggregate demand function upward to Y_2^{ad}. Aggregate demand now equals output at the intersection of Y_2^{ad} with the 45° line $Y = Y^{ad}$ (point 2). As a result of the $100 billion increase in planned investment spending, equilibrium output rises by $200 billion to $1200 billion ($Y_2$). For every dollar increase in planned investment spending, aggregate output has increased twofold.

The ratio of the change in aggregate output to a change in planned investment spending, $\Delta Y/\Delta I$, is called the **expenditure multiplier.** (This multiplier should not be confused with the money supply multiplier developed in Chapter 16, which measures the ratio of the change in the money supply to a change in the monetary base.) In Figure 22-3, the expenditure multiplier is 2.

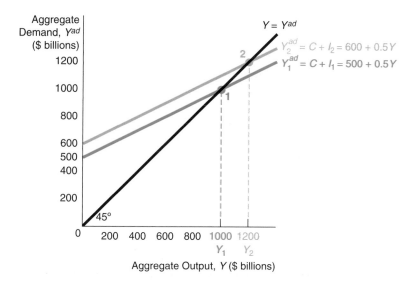

FIGURE 22-3   Response of Aggregate Output to a Change in Planned Investment

A \$100 billion increase in planned investment spending from $I_1 = 300$ to $I_2 = 400$ shifts the aggregate demand function upward from Y_1^{ad} to Y_2^{ad}. The equilibrium moves from point 1 to point 2, and equilibrium output rises from $Y_1 = 1000$ to $Y_2 = 1200$.

Why does a change in planned investment spending lead to an even larger change in aggregate output so that the expenditure multiplier is greater than 1?

The expenditure multiplier is greater than 1 because an increase in planned investment spending, which raises output, also leads to an additional increase in consumer expenditure ($mpc \times \Delta Y$). The increase in consumer expenditure in turn raises aggregate demand and output further, resulting in a multiple change of output from a given change in planned investment spending. This conclusion can be derived algebraically by solving for the unknown value of Y in terms of a, mpc, and I, resulting in the following equation:[4]

$$Y = \frac{1}{1 - mpc} \times (a + I) \tag{4}$$

Because I is multiplied by the term $1/(1 - mpc)$, this equation tells us that a \$1 change in I leads to a $\$1/(1 - mpc)$ change in aggregate output; thus $1/(1 - mpc)$ is the expenditure multiplier. When $mpc = 0.5$, the change in output for a \$1 change in

---

[4] Substituting the consumption function $C = a + mpc \times Y$ into the aggregate demand function $Y^{ad} = C + I$ yields

$$Y^{ad} = a + mpc \times Y + I$$

In equilibrium, where aggregate output equals aggregate demand,

$$Y = Y^{ad} = a + mpc \times Y + I$$

Subtracting the term $mpc \times Y$ from both sides of this equation in order to collect the terms involving Y on the left side, we have

$$Y - mpc \times Y = (1 - mpc)Y = a + I$$

Dividing both sides by $1 - mpc$ to solve for Y leads to Equation 4 in the text.

I is $2 [= 1/(1 − 0.5)]$; if *mpc* = 0.8, the change in output for a $1 change in *I* is $5. The larger the marginal propensity to consume, the higher the expenditure multiplier.

RESPONSE TO CHANGES IN AUTONOMOUS SPENDING   Because *a* is also multiplied by the term $1/(1 − mpc)$ in Equation 4, a $1 change in autonomous consumer expenditure *a* also changes aggregate output by $1/(1 − mpc)$, the amount of the expenditure multiplier. Therefore, we see that the expenditure multiplier applies equally well to changes in autonomous consumer expenditure. In fact, Equation 4 can be rewritten as

$$Y = \frac{1}{1 - mpc} \times A \qquad (5)$$

in which *A* = autonomous spending = *a* + *I*.

This rewritten equation tells us that any change in autonomous spending, whether from a change in *a*, in *I*, or in both, will lead to a multiplied change in *Y*. If both *a* and *I* decrease by $100 billion each, so that *A* decreases by $200 billion, and *mpc* = 0.5, the expenditure multiplier is 2 [= $1/(1 − 0.5)$], and aggregate output *Y* will fall by 2 × $200 billion = $400 billion. Conversely, a rise in *I* by $100 billion that is offset by a $100 billion decline in *a* will leave autonomous spending *A*, and hence *Y*, unchanged. The expenditure multiplier $1/(1 − mpc)$ can therefore be defined more generally as the ratio of the change in aggregate output to a change in autonomous spending ($\Delta Y/\Delta A$).

Another way to reach this conclusion—that any change in autonomous spending will lead to a multiplied change in aggregate output—is to recognize that the shift in the aggregate demand function in Figure 22-3 did not have to come from an increase in *I*; it could also have come from an increase in *a*, which directly raises consumer expenditure and therefore aggregate demand. Alternatively, it could have come from an increase in both *a* and *I*. Changes in the attitudes of consumers and firms about the future, which cause changes in their spending, will result in multiple changes in aggregate output.

APPLICATION   **The Collapse of Autonomous Consumer Expenditure and the Great Depression in the United States**

From 1929 to 1933, the U.S. economy experienced the largest percentage decline in investment spending ever recorded. One explanation for the investment collapse was the ongoing set of financial crises during this period, described in Chapter 8. In 2000 dollars, investment spending fell from US$232 billion to US$38 billion—a decline of over 80%. What does the Keynesian analysis developed so far suggest should have happened to aggregate output in this period?

Figure 22-4 demonstrates how the US$194 billion drop in planned investment spending would shift the aggregate demand function downward from Y_1^{ad} to Y_2^{ad}, moving the economy from point 1 to point 2. Aggregate output would then fall sharply; real GDP actually fell by US$352 billion (a multiple of the US$194 billion drop in investment spending), from US$1184 billion to US$832 billion (in 2000 U.S. dollars). Because the economy was at full employment in 1929, the fall in output resulted in massive unemployment, with over 25% of the labour force unemployed in 1933.

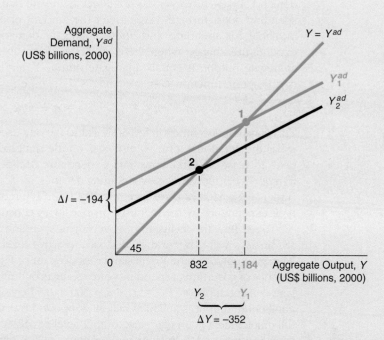

FIGURE 22-4   Response of Aggregate Output to the Collapse of Investment Spending, 1929–1933

The decline of US$194 billion (in 2000 U.S. dollars) in planned investment spending from 1929 to 1933 shifted the aggregate demand function down from Y_1^{ad} to Y_2^{ad} and caused the economy to move from point 1 to point 2, where output fell by US$352 billion.

Source: *Economic Report of the President.*

Keynes believed that changes in autonomous spending are dominated by unstable fluctuations in planned investment spending, which is influenced by emotional waves of optimism and pessimism—factors he labelled "**animal spirits**." His view was coloured by the collapse in investment spending during the Great Depression, which he saw as the primary reason for the economic contraction. We examine the consequences of this fall in investment spending in the above application.

Government's Role

After witnessing the events in the Great Depression, Keynes took the view that an economy would continually suffer major output fluctuations because of the volatility of autonomous spending, particularly planned investment spending. He was especially worried about sharp declines in autonomous spending, which would inevitably lead to large declines in output and an equilibrium with high unemployment. If autonomous spending fell sharply, as it did during the Great Depression, how could an economy be restored to higher levels of output and more reasonable levels of unemployment? Not by an increase in autonomous spending, since the business outlook was so grim. Keynes's answer to this question involved looking at the role of government in determining aggregate output.

Keynes realized that government spending and taxation could also affect the position of the aggregate demand function and hence be manipulated to restore the economy to full employment. As shown in the aggregate demand equation $Y^{ad} = C + I + G + NX$, government spending G adds directly to aggregate demand. Taxes, however, do not affect aggregate demand directly, as government spending does. Instead, taxes lower the amount of income that consumers have available for spending and affect aggregate demand by influencing consumer expenditure; that is, when there are taxes, disposable income Y_D does not equal aggregate output; it equals aggregate output Y minus taxes T: $Y_D = Y - T$. The consumption function $C = a + mpc \times Y_D$ can be rewritten as follows:

$$C = a + mpc \times (Y - T) = a + mpc \times Y - mpc \times T \qquad (6)$$

This consumption function looks similar to the one used in the absence of taxes, but it has the additional term $- mpc \times T$ on the right side. This term indicates that if taxes increase by $100, consumer expenditure declines by mpc times this amount; if $mpc = 0.5$, consumer expenditure declines by $50. This occurs because consumers view $100 of taxes as equivalent to a $100 reduction in income and reduce their expenditure by the marginal propensity to consume times this amount.

To see how the inclusion of government spending and taxes modifies our analysis, first we will observe the effect of a positive level of government spending on aggregate output in the Keynesian cross diagram of Figure 22-5. Let's say that in the absence of government spending or taxes, the economy is at point 1, where the aggregate demand function $Y_1^{ad} = C + I = 500 + 0.5Y$ crosses the 45° line $Y = Y^{ad}$. Here equilibrium output is at $1000 billion. Suppose, however, that the economy reaches full employment at an aggregate output level of $1800 billion. How can government spending be used to restore the economy to full employment at $1800 billion of aggregate output?

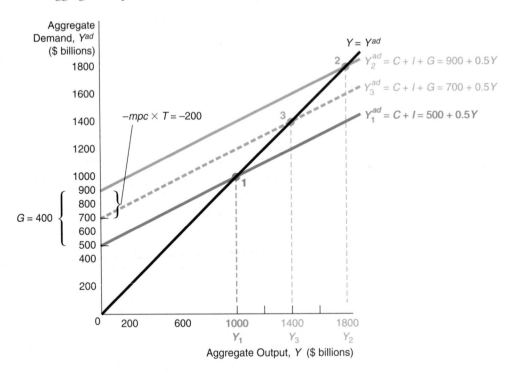

FIGURE 22-5   Response of Aggregate Output to Government Spending and Taxes

With no government spending or taxes, the aggregate demand function is Y_1^{ad}, and equilibrium output is $Y_1 = 1000$. With government spending of $400 billion, the aggregate demand function shifts upward to Y_2^{ad}, and aggregate output rises by $800 billion to $Y_2 = 1800$ billion. Taxes of $400 billion lower consumer expenditure and the aggregate demand function by $200 billion from Y_2^{ad} to Y_3^{ad}, and aggregate output falls by $400 billion to $Y_3 = 1400$ billion.

If government spending is set at $400 billion, the aggregate demand function shifts upward to $Y_2^{ad} = C + I + G = 900 + 0.5Y$. The economy moves to point 2, and aggregate output rises by $800 billion to $1800 billion. Figure 22-5 indicates that aggregate output is positively related to government spending and that a change in government spending leads to a multiplied change in aggregate output, equal to the expenditure multiplier, $1/(1 - mpc) = 1/(1 - 0.5) = 2$. Therefore, declines in planned investment spending that produce high unemployment (as occurred during the Great Depression) can be offset by raising government spending.

What happens if the government decides that it must collect taxes of $400 billion to balance the budget? Before taxes are raised, the economy is in equilibrium at the same point 2 found in Figure 22-5. Our discussion of the consumption function (which allows for taxes) indicates that taxes T reduce consumer expenditure by $mpc \times T$ because there is T less income now available for spending. In our example, $mpc = 0.5$, so consumer expenditure and the aggregate demand function shift downward by $200 billion (= 0.5 \times 400)$; at the new equilibrium, point 3, the level of output has declined by twice this amount (the expenditure multiplier) to $1400 billion.

Although you can see that aggregate output is negatively related to the level of taxes, it is important to recognize that the change in aggregate output from the $400 billion increase in taxes ($\Delta Y = -\$400$ billion) is smaller than the change in aggregate output from the $400 billion increase in government spending ($\Delta Y = \$800$ billion). If both taxes and government spending are raised equally, by $400 billion, as occurs in going from point 1 to point 3 in Figure 22-5, aggregate output will rise.

The Keynesian framework indicates that the government can play an important role in determining aggregate output by changing the level of government spending or taxes. If the economy enters a deep recession, in which output drops severely and unemployment climbs, the analysis we have just developed provides a prescription for restoring the economy to health. The government might raise aggregate output by increasing government spending, or it could lower taxes and reverse the process described in Figure 22-5 (that is, a tax cut makes more income available for spending at any level of output, shifting the aggregate demand function upward and causing the equilibrium level of output to rise).

Role of International Trade

International trade also plays a role in determining aggregate output because net exports (exports minus imports) are a component of aggregate demand. To analyze the effect of net exports in the Keynesian cross diagram of Figure 22-6, suppose that initially net exports are equal to zero ($NX_1 = 0$) so that the economy is at point 1, where the aggregate demand function $Y_1^{ad} = C + I + G + NX_1 = 500 + 0.5Y$ crosses the 45° line $Y = Y_1^{ad}$. Equilibrium output is again at $1000 billion. Now foreigners suddenly get an urge to buy more Canadian products so that net exports rise to $100 billion ($NX_2 = 100$). The $100 billion increase in net exports adds directly to aggregate demand and shifts the aggregate demand function upward to $Y_2^{ad} = C + I + G + NX_2 = 600 + 0.5Y$. The economy moves to point 2, and aggregate output rises by $200 billion to $1200 billion ($Y_2$). Figure 22-6 indicates that just as we found for planned investment spending and government spending, a rise in net exports leads to a multiplied rise in aggregate output, equal to the expenditure multiplier, $1/(1 - mpc) = 1/(1 - 0.5) = 2$. Therefore, changes in net exports can be another important factor affecting fluctuations in aggregate output.

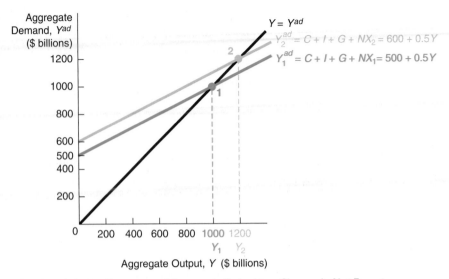

FIGURE 22-6   Response of Aggregate Output to a Change in Net Exports

A $100 billion increase in net exports from $NX_1 = 0$ to $NX_2 = 100$ shifts the aggregate demand function upward from Y_1^{ad} to Y_2^{ad}. The equilibrium moves from point 1 to point 2, and equilibrium output rises from $Y_1 = \$1000$ billion to $Y_2 = \$1200$ billion.

Summary of the Determinants of Aggregate Output

Our analysis of the Keynesian framework so far has identified five autonomous factors (factors independent of income) that shift the aggregate demand function and hence the level of aggregate output:

1. Changes in autonomous consumer expenditure (a)

2. Changes in planned investment spending (I)

3. Changes in government spending (G)

4. Changes in taxes (T)

5. Changes in net exports (NX)

The effects of changes in each of these variables on aggregate output are summarized in Table 22-2 and discussed next in the text.

CHANGES IN AUTONOMOUS CONSUMER SPENDING (*a*)   A rise in autonomous consumer expenditure a (say, because consumers become more optimistic about the economy when the stock market booms) directly raises consumer expenditure and shifts the aggregate demand function upward, resulting in an increase in aggregate output. A decrease in a causes consumer expenditure to fall, leading ultimately to a decline in aggregate output. Therefore, ***aggregate output is positively related to autonomous consumer expenditure* a.**

CHANGES IN PLANNED INVESTMENT SPENDING (*I*)   A rise in planned investment spending adds directly to aggregate demand, thus raising the aggregate demand function and aggregate output. A fall in planned investment spending lowers aggregate demand and causes aggregate output to fall. Therefore, ***aggregate output is positively related to planned investment spending* I.**

CHANGES IN GOVERNMENT SPENDING (*G*)   A rise in government spending also adds directly to aggregate demand and raises the aggregate demand function, increasing aggregate output. A fall directly reduces aggregate demand, lowers the

TABLE 22-2 Response of Aggregate Output *Y* to Autonomous Changes in *a, I, G, T,* and *NX*

Variable	Change in Variable	Response of Aggregate Output, *Y*	
Autonomous consumer expenditure, *a*	↑	↑	
Investment, *I*	↑	↑	
Government spending, *G*	↑	↑	
Taxes, *T*	↑	↓	
Net exports, *NX*	↑	↑	

Note: Only increases (↑) in the variables are shown; the effects of decreases in the variables on aggregate output would be the opposite of those indicated in the "Response" column.

aggregate demand function, and causes aggregate output to fall. Therefore, ***aggregate output is positively related to government spending* G.**

CHANGES IN TAXES (*T*) A rise in taxes does not affect aggregate demand directly but does lower the amount of income available for spending, reducing consumer expenditure. The decline in consumer expenditure then leads to a fall in the aggregate demand function, resulting in a decline in aggregate output. A lowering of taxes makes more income available for spending, raises consumer expenditure, and leads to higher aggregate output. Therefore, ***aggregate output is negatively related to the level of taxes* T.**

CHANGES IN NET EXPORTS (NX)   A rise in net exports adds directly to aggregate demand and raises the aggregate demand function, increasing aggregate output. A fall directly reduces aggregate demand, lowers the aggregate demand function, and causes aggregate output to fall. Therefore, ***aggregate output is positively related to net exports* NX.**

SIZE OF THE EFFECTS FROM THE FIVE FACTORS   The aggregate demand function in the Keynesian cross diagrams shifts vertically by the full amount of the change in *a, I, G,* or *NX,* resulting in a multiple effect on aggregate output through the effects of the expenditure multiplier, $1/(1 - mpc)$. A change in taxes has a smaller effect on aggregate output because consumer expenditure changes only by *mpc* times the change in taxes ($-mpc \times \Delta T$), which in the case of $mpc = 0.5$ means that aggregate demand shifts vertically by only half of the change in taxes.

If there is a change in one of these autonomous factors that is offset by a change in another (say, *I* rises by \$100 billion, but *a, G,* or *NX* falls by \$100 billion or *T* rises by \$200 billion when $mpc = 0.5$), the aggregate demand function will remain in the same position, and aggregate output will remain unchanged.[5]

THE *ISLM* MODEL

So far our analysis has excluded monetary policy. We now include money and interest rates in the Keynesian framework to develop the more intricate *ISLM* model of how aggregate output is determined, in which monetary policy plays an important role. Why another complex model? The *ISLM* model is versatile and allows us to understand economic phenomena that cannot be analyzed with the simpler Keynesian cross framework used earlier. The *ISLM* model will help you understand how monetary policy affects economic activity and interacts with fiscal policy (changes in government

---

[5] These results can be derived algebraically as follows. Substituting the consumption function allowing for taxes (Equation 6) into the aggregate demand function (Equation 1), we have

$$Y^{ad} = a - mpc \times T + mpc \times Y + I + G + NX$$

If we assume that taxes *T* are unrelated to income, we can define autonomous spending in the aggregate demand function to be

$$A = a - mpc \times T + I + G + NX$$

The expenditure equation can be rewritten as

$$Y^{ad} = A + mpc \times Y$$

In equilibrium, aggregate demand equals aggregate output,

$$Y = A + mpc \times Y$$

which can be solved for *Y.* The resulting equation,

$$Y = \frac{1}{1 - mpc} \times A$$

is the same equation that links autonomous spending and aggregate output in the text (Equation 5), but it now allows for additional components of autonomous spending in *A.* We see that any increase in autonomous expenditure leads to a multiple increase in output. Thus any component of autonomous spending that enters *A* with a positive sign (*a, I, G,* and *NX*) will have a positive relationship with output, and any component with a negative sign ($-mpc \times T$) will have a negative relationship with output. This algebraic analysis also shows us that any rise in a component of *A* that is offset by a movement in another component of *A*, leaving *A* unchanged, will also leave output unchanged.

spending and taxes) to produce a certain level of aggregate output; how the level of interest rates is affected by changes in investment spending as well as by changes in monetary and fiscal policy; how best to conduct monetary policy; and how the *ISLM* model generates the aggregate demand curve, an essential building block for the aggregate supply and demand analysis used in Chapter 24 and thereafter.

Like our simplified Keynesian model, the full *ISLM* model examines an equilibrium in which aggregate output produced equals aggregate demand, and since it assumes a fixed price level, real and nominal quantities are the same. The first step in constructing the *ISLM* model is to examine the effect of interest rates on planned investment spending and hence on aggregate demand. Next we use a Keynesian cross diagram to see how the interest rate affects the equilibrium level of aggregate output. The resulting relationship between equilibrium aggregate output and the interest rate is known as the **IS curve**.

Just as a demand curve alone cannot tell us the quantity of goods sold in a market, the *IS* curve by itself cannot tell us what the level of aggregate output will be because the interest rate is still unknown. We need another relationship, called the **LM curve**, to describe the combinations of interest rates and aggregate output for which the quantity of money demanded equals the quantity of money supplied. When the *IS* and *LM* curves are combined in the same diagram, the intersection of the two determines the equilibrium level of aggregate output as well as the interest rate. Finally, we will have obtained a more complete analysis of the determination of aggregate output in which monetary policy plays an important role.

Equilibrium in the Goods Market: The *IS* Curve

In Keynesian analysis, the primary way that interest rates affect the level of aggregate output is through their effects on planned investment spending and net exports. After explaining why interest rates affect planned investment spending and net exports, we will use Keynesian cross diagrams to learn how interest rates affect equilibrium aggregate output.[6]

INTEREST RATES AND PLANNED INVESTMENT SPENDING   Businesses make investments in physical capital (machines, factories, and raw materials) as long as they expect to earn more from the physical capital than the interest cost of a loan to finance the investment. When the interest rate is high, few investments in physical capital will earn more than the cost of borrowed funds, so planned investment spending is low. When the interest rate is low, many investments in physical capital will earn more than the interest cost of borrowed funds. Therefore, when interest rates are lower, business firms are more likely to undertake an investment in physical capital, and planned investment spending will be higher.

Even if a company has surplus funds and does not need to borrow to undertake an investment in physical capital, its planned investment spending will be affected by the interest rate. Instead of investing in physical capital, it could purchase a security, such as a bond. If the interest rate on this security is high, the opportunity cost (forgone interest earnings) of an investment is high, and planned investment spending will be low because the firm would probably prefer to purchase the security than to invest in physical capital. As the interest rate and the opportunity cost of invest-

---

[6] More modern Keynesian approaches suggest that consumer expenditure, particularly for consumer durables (cars, furniture, appliances), is influenced by the interest rate. This interest sensitivity of consumer expenditure can be allowed for in the model here by defining planned investment spending more generally to include the interest-sensitive component of consumer expenditure.

ing fall, planned investment spending will increase because investments in physical capital are more likely than the security to earn greater income for the firm.

The relationship between the amount of planned investment spending and any given level of the interest rate is illustrated by the investment schedule in panel (a) of Figure 22-7. The downward slope of the schedule reflects the negative relationship between planned investment spending and the interest rate. At a low interest rate i_1, the level of planned investment spending I_1 is high; for a high interest rate i_3, planned investment spending I_3 is low.

INTEREST RATES AND NET EXPORTS   As discussed in more detail in Chapter 19, when interest rates rise in Canada (with the price level fixed), Canadian-dollar bank deposits become more attractive relative to deposits denominated in foreign currencies, thereby causing a rise in the value of dollar deposits relative to other currency deposits, that is, a rise in the exchange rate. The higher value of the dollar resulting from the rise in interest rates makes domestic goods more expensive than foreign goods, thereby causing a fall in net exports. The resulting negative relationship between interest rates and net exports is shown in panel (b) of Figure 22-7. At a low interest rate i_1, the exchange rate is low and net exports NX_1 are high; at a high interest rate i_3, the exchange rate is high and net exports NX_3 are low.

DERIVING THE *IS* CURVE   We can now use what we have learned about the relationship of interest rates to planned investment spending and net exports in panels (a) and (b) to examine the relationship between interest rates and the equilibrium level of aggregate output (holding government spending and autonomous consumer expenditure constant). The three levels of planned investment spending and net exports in panels (a) and (b) are represented in the three aggregate demand functions in the Keynesian cross diagram of panel (c). The lowest interest rate i_1 has the highest level of both planned investment spending i_1 and net exports NX_1 and hence the highest aggregate demand function Y_1^{ad}. Point 1 in panel (d) shows the resulting equilibrium level of output Y_1, which corresponds to interest rate i_1. As the interest rate rises to i_2, both planned investment spending and net exports fall, to I_2 and NX_2, so equilibrium output falls to Y_2. Point 2 in panel (d) shows the lower level of output Y_2, which corresponds to interest rate i_2. Finally, the highest interest rate i_3 leads to the lowest level of planned investment spending and net exports and hence the lowest level of equilibrium output, which is plotted as point 3.

The line connecting the three points in panel (d), the *IS* curve, shows the combinations of interest rates and equilibrium aggregate output for which aggregate output produced equals aggregate demand. The negative slope indicates that higher interest rates result in lower planned investment spending and net exports and hence lower equilibrium output.

WHAT THE *IS* CURVE TELLS US   The *IS* curve traces out the points at which the total quantity of goods produced equals the total quantity of goods demanded. It describes points at which the goods market is in equilibrium. For each given level of the interest rate, the *IS* curve tells us what aggregate output must be for the goods market to be in equilibrium. As the interest rate rises, planned investment spending and net exports fall, which in turn lowers aggregate demand; aggregate output must be lower in order for it to equal aggregate demand and satisfy goods market equilibrium.

The *IS* curve is a useful concept because output tends to move toward points on the curve that satisfy goods market equilibrium. If the economy is located in

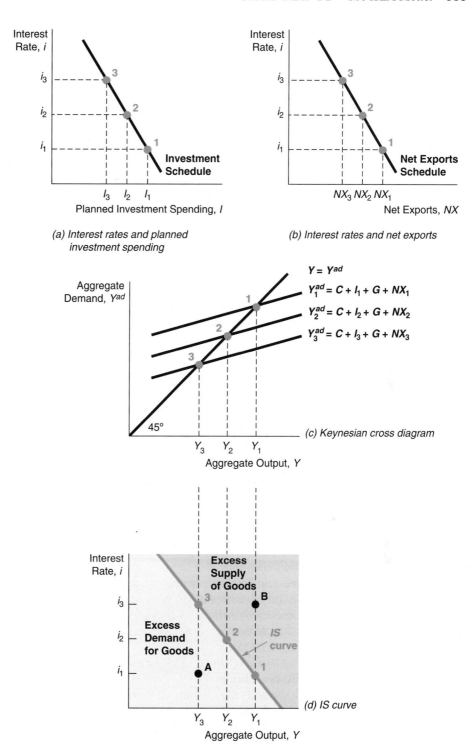

FIGURE 22-7 Deriving the *IS* Curve

The investment schedule in panel (a) shows that as the interest rate rises from i_1 to i_2 to i_3, planned investment spending falls from I_1 to I_2 to I_3, and panel (b) shows that net exports also fall from NX_1 to NX_2 to NX_3 as the interest rate rises. Panel (c) then indicates the levels of equilibrium output Y_1, Y_2, and Y_3 that correspond to those three levels of planned investment and net exports. Finally, panel (d) plots the level of equilibrium output corresponding to each of the three interest rates; the line that connects these points is the *IS* curve.

the area to the right of the *IS* curve, it has an excess supply of goods. At point B, for example, aggregate output Y_1 is greater than the equilibrium level of output Y_3 on the *IS* curve. This excess supply of goods results in unplanned inventory accumulation, which causes output to fall toward the *IS* curve. The decline stops only when output is again at its equilibrium level on the *IS* curve.

If the economy is located in the area to the left of the *IS* curve, it has an excess demand for goods. At point A, aggregate output Y_3 is below the equilibrium level of output Y_1 on the *IS* curve. The excess demand for goods results in an unplanned decrease in inventory, which causes output to rise toward the *IS* curve, stopping only when aggregate output is again at its equilibrium level on the *IS* curve.

Significantly, equilibrium in the goods market does not produce a unique equilibrium level of aggregate output. Although we now know where aggregate output will head for a given level of the interest rate, we cannot determine aggregate output because we do not know what the interest rate is. To complete our analysis of aggregate output determination, we need to introduce another market that produces an additional relationship that links aggregate output and interest rates. The market for money fulfills this function with the *LM* curve. When the *LM* curve is combined with the *IS* curve, a unique equilibrium that determines both aggregate output and the interest rate is obtained.

Equilibrium in the Market for Money: The *LM* Curve

Just as the *IS* curve is derived from the equilibrium condition in the goods market (aggregate output equals aggregate demand), the *LM* curve is derived from the equilibrium condition in the market for money, which requires that the quantity of money demanded equal the quantity of money supplied. The main building block in Keynes's analysis of the market for money is the demand for money he called *liquidity preference*. Let us briefly review his theory of the demand for money (discussed at length in Chapters 5 and 21).

Keynes's liquidity preference theory states that the demand for money in real terms M^d/P depends on income Y (aggregate output) and interest rates i. The demand for money is positively related to income for two reasons. First, a rise in income raises the level of transactions in the economy, which in turn raises the demand for money because it is used to carry out these transactions. Second, a rise in income increases the demand for money because it increases the wealth of individuals who want to hold more assets, one of which is money. The opportunity cost of holding money is the interest sacrificed by not holding other assets (such as bonds) instead. As interest rates rise, the opportunity cost of holding money rises, and the demand for money falls. According to the liquidity preference theory, the demand for money is positively related to aggregate output and negatively related to interest rates.

DERIVING THE *LM* CURVE   In Keynes's analysis, the level of interest rates is determined by equilibrium in the market for money (when the quantity of money demanded equals the quantity of money supplied). Figure 22-8 depicts what happens to equilibrium in the market for money as the level of output changes. Because the *LM* curve is derived holding the money supply at a fixed level, it is fixed at the level of $\overline{M}$, in panel (a).[7] Each level of aggregate output has its own money demand curve because as aggregate output changes, the level of transactions in the economy changes, which in turn changes the demand for money.

---

[7] As pointed out in earlier chapters on the money supply process, the money supply is positively related to interest rates, and so the M^s curve in panel (a) should actually have a positive slope. The M^s curve is assumed to be vertical in panel (a) in order to simplify the graph, but allowing for a positive slope leads to identical results.

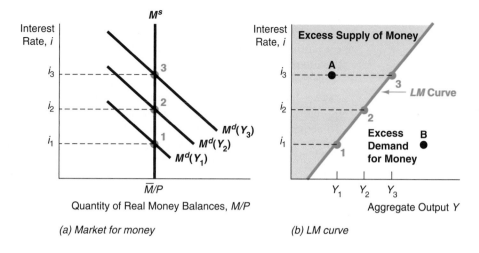

FIGURE 22-8   Deriving the *LM* Curve

Panel (a) shows the equilibrium levels of the interest rate in the market for money that arise when aggregate output is at Y_1, Y_2, and Y_3. Panel (b) plots the three levels of the equilibrium interest rate i_1, i_2, and i_3 corresponding to these three levels of output; the line that connects these points is the *LM* curve.

When aggregate output is Y_1, the money demand curve is $M^d(Y_1)$. It slopes downward because a lower interest rate means that the opportunity cost of holding money is lower, so the quantity of money demanded is higher. Equilibrium in the market for money occurs at point 1, at which the interest rate is i_1. When aggregate output is at the higher level Y_2, the money demand curve shifts rightward to $M^d(Y_2)$ because the higher level of output means that at any given interest rate, the quantity of money demanded is higher. Equilibrium in the market for money now occurs at point 2, at which the interest rate is at the higher level of i_2. Similarly, a still higher level of aggregate output, Y_3, results in an even higher level of the equilibrium interest rate, i_3.

Panel (b) plots the equilibrium interest rates that correspond to the different output levels, with points 1, 2, and 3 corresponding to the equilibrium points 1, 2, and 3 in panel (a). The line connecting these points is the *LM* curve, which shows the combinations of interest rates and output for which the market for money is in equilibrium. The positive slope arises because higher output raises the demand for money and thus raises the equilibrium interest rate.

WHAT THE *LM* CURVE TELLS US   The *LM* curve traces out the points that satisfy the equilibrium condition that the quantity of money demanded equals the quantity of money supplied. For each given level of aggregate output, the *LM* curve tells us what the interest rate must be for there to be equilibrium in the market for money. As aggregate output rises, the demand for money increases and the interest rate rises, so that money demanded equals money supplied and the market for money is in equilibrium.

Just as the economy tends to move toward the equilibrium points represented by the *IS* curve, it also moves toward the equilibrium points on the *LM* curve. If the economy is located in the area to the left of the *LM* curve, there is an excess supply of money. At point A, for example, the interest rate is i_3 and aggregate output is Y_1. The interest rate is above the equilibrium level, and people are holding more money than they want to. To eliminate their excess money balances, they will purchase bonds, which causes the price of the bonds to rise and their interest rate to fall. (The inverse relationship between the price of a bond and its interest rate is discussed in Chapter 4.) As long as an excess supply of money exists, the interest rate will fall until it comes to rest on the *LM* curve.

If the economy is located in the area to the right of the *LM* curve, there is an excess demand for money. At point B, for example, the interest rate i_1 is below the equilibrium level, and people want to hold more money than they currently do. To acquire this money, they will sell bonds and drive down bond prices, and the interest rate will rise. This process will stop only when the interest rate rises to an equilibrium point on the *LM* curve.

ISLM APPROACH TO AGGREGATE OUTPUT AND INTEREST RATES

Now that we have derived the *IS* and *LM* curves, we can put them into the same diagram (Figure 22-9) to produce a model that enables us to determine both aggregate output and the interest rate. The only point at which the goods market and the market for money are in simultaneous equilibrium is at the intersection of the *IS* and *LM* curves, point E. At this point, aggregate output equals aggregate demand (*IS*) and the quantity of money demanded equals the quantity of money supplied (*LM*). At any other point in the diagram, at least one of these equilibrium conditions is not satisfied, and market forces move the economy toward the general equilibrium, point E.

To learn how this works, let's consider what happens if the economy is at point A, which is on the *IS* curve but not the *LM* curve. Even though at point A the goods market is in equilibrium, so that aggregate output equals aggregate demand, the

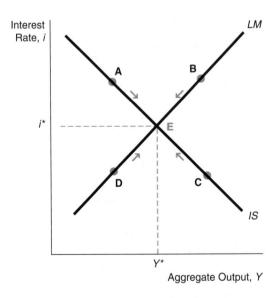

FIGURE 22-9   *ISLM* Diagram: Simultaneous Determination of Output and the
Interest Rate

Only at point E, where the interest rate is *i** and output is *Y**, is there equilibrium simultaneously in both the goods market (as measured by the *IS* curve) and the market for money (as measured by the *LM* curve). At other points, such as A, B, C, or D, one of the two markets is not in equilibrium, and there will be a tendency to head toward the equilibrium, point E.

interest rate is above its equilibrium level, so the demand for money is less than the supply. Because people have more money than they want to hold, they will try to get rid of it by buying bonds. The resulting rise in bond prices causes a fall in interest rates, which in turn causes both planned investment spending and net exports to rise, and thus aggregate output rises. The economy then moves down along the *IS* curve, and the process continues until the interest rate falls to i^* and aggregate output rises to Y^*—that is, until the economy is at equilibrium point E.

If the economy is on the *LM* curve but off the *IS* curve at point B, it will also head toward the equilibrium at point E. At point B, even though money demand equals money supply, output is higher than the equilibrium level and exceeds aggregate demand. Firms are unable to sell all their output, and unplanned inventory accumulates, prompting them to cut production and lower output. The decline in output means that the demand for money will fall, lowering interest rates. The economy then moves down along the *LM* curve until it reaches equilibrium point E.

We have finally developed a model, the *ISLM* model, which tells us how both interest rates and aggregate output are determined when the price level is fixed. Although we have demonstrated that the economy will head toward an aggregate output level of Y^*, there is no reason to assume that at this level of aggregate output the economy is at full employment. If the unemployment rate is too high, government policymakers might want to increase aggregate output to reduce it. The *ISLM* apparatus indicates that they can do this by manipulating monetary and fiscal policy. We will conduct an *ISLM* analysis of how monetary and fiscal policy can affect economic activity in the next chapter.

SUMMARY

1. In the simple Keynesian framework in which the price level is fixed, output is determined by the equilibrium condition in the goods market that aggregate output equals aggregate demand. Aggregate demand equals the sum of consumer expenditure, planned investment spending, government spending, and net exports. Consumer expenditure is described by the consumption function, which indicates that consumer expenditure will rise as disposable income increases. Keynes's analysis shows that aggregate output is positively related to autonomous consumer expenditure, planned investment spending, government spending, and net exports and negatively related to the level of taxes. A change in any of these factors leads, through the expenditure multiplier, to a multiple change in aggregate output.

2. The *ISLM* model determines aggregate output and the interest rate for a fixed price level using the *IS* and *LM* curves. The *IS* curve traces the combinations of the interest rate and aggregate output for which the goods market is in equilibrium, and the *LM* curve traces the combinations for which the market for money is in equilibrium. The *IS* curve slopes downward because higher interest rates lower planned investment spending and so lower equilibrium output. The *LM* curve slopes upward because higher aggregate output raises the demand for money and so raises the equilibrium interest rate.

3. The simultaneous determination of output and interest rates occurs at the intersection of the *IS* and *LM* curves, where both the goods market and the market for money are in equilibrium. At any other level of interest rates and output, at least one of the markets will be out of equilibrium, and forces will move the economy toward the general equilibrium point at the intersection of the *IS* and *LM* curves.

KEY TERMS

aggregate demand,   p. 573

aggregate demand function,
   p. 577

"animal spirits,"   p. 581

autonomous consumer
   expenditure,   p. 574

consumer expenditure,   p. 573

consumption function,   p. 574

disposable income,   p. 574

expenditure multiplier,   p. 578

fixed investment,   p. 575

government spending,   p. 573

inventory investment,   p. 575

IS curve,   p. 587

LM curve,   p. 587

marginal propensity to consume,
   p. 574

net exports,   p. 573

planned investment spending,
   p. 573

QUESTIONS

You will find the answers to the questions marked with an asterisk in the Textbook Resources section of your MyEconLab.

1. If the marginal propensity to consume were 0.5, how much would government spending have to rise in order to raise output by $1000 billion?

*2. Suppose that government policymakers decide that they will change taxes to raise aggregate output by $400 billion, and *mpc* = 0.5. By how much will taxes have to be changed?

3. What happens to aggregate output if both taxes and government spending are lowered by $300 billion and *mpc* = 0.5? Explain your answer.

*4. Will aggregate output rise or fall if an increase in autonomous consumer expenditure is matched by an equal increase in taxes?

5. If a change in the interest rate has no effect on planned investment spending, trace out what happens to the equilibrium level of aggregate output as interest rates fall. What does this imply about the slope of the *IS* curve?

*6. Using a supply and demand diagram for the market for money, show what happens to the equilibrium level of the interest rate as aggregate output falls. What does this imply about the slope of the *LM* curve?

7. "If the point describing the combination of the interest rate and aggregate output is not on either the *IS* or the *LM* curve, the economy will have no tendency to head toward the intersection of the two curves." Is this statement true, false, or uncertain? Explain your answer.

QUANTITATIVE PROBLEMS

1. Calculate the value of the consumption function at each level of disposable income in Table 22-1 (page 574) if *a* = 100 and *mpc* = 0.9.

*2. Why do companies cut production when they find that their unplanned inventory investment is greater than zero? If they didn't cut production, what effect would this have on their profits? Why?

3. Plot the consumption function $C = 100 + 0.75Y$ on graph paper.
   a. Assuming no government sector, if planned investment spending is 200, what is the equilibrium level of aggregate output? Show this equilibrium level on the graph you have drawn.
   b. If businesses become more pessimistic about the profitability of investment and planned investment spending falls by 100, what happens to the equilibrium level of output?

*4. If the consumption function is $C = 100 + 0.8Y$ and planned investment spending is 200, what is the

equilibrium level of output? If planned investment falls by 100, how much does the equilibrium level of output fall?

5. Why are the multipliers in Problems 3 and 4 different? Explain intuitively why one is higher than the other.

*6. If firms suddenly become more optimistic about the profitability of investment and planned investment spending rises by $100 billion, while consumers become more pessimistic and autonomous consumer spending falls by $100 billion, what happens to aggregate output?

7. "A rise in planned investment spending by $100 billion at the same time that autonomous consumer expenditure falls by $50 billion has the same effect on aggregate output as a rise in autonomous consumer expenditure alone by $50 billion." Is this statement true, false, or uncertain? Explain your answer.

*8. If the consumption function is $C = 100 + 0.75Y$, $I = 200$, and government spending is 200, what will be the equilibrium level of output? Demonstrate your answer with a Keynesian cross diagram. What happens to aggregate output if government spending rises by 100?

9. Consider a closed economy ($NX = 0$) and assume the following functions

$$C = a + mpc \times (Y + TR - TA)$$
$$I = \bar{I} - bi_r$$
$$G = \bar{G}$$

where $\bar{I}$ is autonomous investment expenditure; i_r is the real interest rate, $b > 0$; TR denotes transfers, which are assumed to be exogenous; and TA denotes taxes, which are given by $TA = t \times Y$, where t is the tax rate on income.
   a. Derive the aggregate demand function.
   b. Derive the equation for the IS curve.

c. What is the slope of the IS curve?
d. Discuss how the slope of the IS curve is affected by b, t, and mpc.

*10. Consider the following money demand function (in real terms)

$$\frac{M}{P} = kY - hi$$

where k is the income elasticity and h is the (nominal) interest rate elasticity of real money balances. Assume that $k > 0$ and that $h > 0$. Further assume that the quantity of nominal money balances is fixed by the Bank of Canada at $\bar{M}$ and that the price level, P, is also fixed at $\bar{P}$.
   a. Derive the equation for the LM curve.
   b. What is the slope of the LM curve?
   c. Discuss how the slope of the LM curve is affected by k and h.

WEB EXERCISES

1. Go to **www.fgn.unisg.ch/eurmacro/Tutor/ keynesiancross.html**. Make sure the following settings are used: $t = 0$, $G = 200$; $c = 0.8$, and $m = 0.0$. Click on the "memorize" button. Note the value of equilibrium output. Now decrease G by 50. What is the value of equilibrium output? What is the implied multiplier?

2. Go to **www.fgn.unisg.ch/eurmacro/Tutor/ keynesiancrss.html**. Make sure the following settings are used: $t = 0.25$, $G = 400$; $c = 0.8$, and $m = 0.0$. Click on the "memorize" button. Note the value of equilibrium output. Now decrease G by 50. What is the value of equilibrium output? What is the implied multiplier? Compare your answer with the answer to Web Exercise Question 1.

Be sure to visit the MyEconLab website at **www.myeconlab.com**. This online homework and tutorial system puts you in control of your own learning with study and practice tools directly correlated to this chapter content.

CHAPTER 23

Monetary and Fiscal Policy in the *ISLM* Model

LEARNING OBJECTIVES

After studying this chapter you should be able to

1. apply the *ISLM* framework for the determination of aggregate output and the interest rate
2. explain how the *ISLM* model can be used to address questions about the effectiveness of monetary and fiscal policy
3. determine how fiscal policy should be conducted (by changing government spending or taxes)
4. analyze how monetary policy should be conducted (by changing the money supply or interest rates)
5. illustrate how the *ISLM* model generates the aggregate demand curve featured in the aggregate demand and supply framework (examined in Chapter 24)

PREVIEW

Since World War II, government policymakers have tried to promote high employment without causing inflation. If the economy experiences a recession such as the one that occurred at the time of Iraq's invasion of Kuwait in 1990, policymakers have two principal sets of tools that they can use to affect aggregate economic activity: *monetary policy,* the control of interest rates or the money supply, and *fiscal policy,* the control of government spending and taxes.

The *ISLM* model can help policymakers predict what will happen to aggregate output and interest rates if they decide to increase the money supply or increase government spending. In this way, *ISLM* analysis enables us to answer some important questions about the usefulness and effectiveness of monetary and fiscal policy in influencing economic activity.

But which is better? When is monetary policy more effective than fiscal policy at controlling the level of aggregate output, and when is it less effective? Will fiscal policy be more effective if it is conducted by changing government spending rather than changing taxes? Should the monetary authorities conduct monetary policy by manipulating the money supply or interest rates?

In this chapter we use the *ISLM* model to help answer these questions and to learn how the model generates the aggregate demand curve featured prominently in the aggregate demand and supply framework (examined in Chapter 24), which is used to understand changes not only in aggregate output but in the price level as well. Our analysis will show why economists focus so much attention on topics such as the stability of the demand for money function and whether the demand for money is strongly influenced by interest rates.

First, however, let's examine the *ISLM* model in more detail to see how the *IS* and *LM* curves developed in Chapter 22 shift and the implications of these shifts. (We continue to assume that the price level is fixed so that real and nominal quantities are the same.)

FACTORS THAT CAUSE THE *IS* CURVE TO SHIFT

You have already learned that the *IS* curve describes equilibrium points in the goods market—the combinations of aggregate output and interest rate for which aggregate output produced equals aggregate demand. The *IS* curve shifts whenever a change in autonomous factors (factors independent of aggregate output) occurs that is unrelated to the interest rate. (A change in the interest rate that affects equilibrium aggregate output only causes a movement along the *IS* curve.) We have already identified five candidates as autonomous factors that can shift aggregate demand and hence affect the level of equilibrium output. We can now ask how changes in each of these factors affect the *IS* curve.

1. *Changes in Autonomous Consumer Expenditure.* A rise in autonomous consumer expenditure shifts aggregate demand upward and shifts the *IS* curve to the right (Figure 23-1). To see how this shift occurs, suppose that the *IS* curve is initially at IS_1 in panel (a) and a huge oil field is discovered in Alberta, perhaps containing more oil than fields in Saudi Arabia. Consumers now become more optimistic about the future health of the economy, and autonomous consumer expenditure rises. What happens to the equilibrium level of aggregate output as a result of this rise in autonomous consumer expenditure when the interest rate is held constant at i_A?

    The IS_1 curve tells us that equilibrium aggregate output is at Y_A when the interest rate is at i_A (point A). Panel (b) shows that this point is an equilibrium in the goods market because the aggregate demand function Y_1^{ad} at an interest rate i_A crosses the 45° line $Y = Y^{ad}$ at an aggregate output level of Y_A. When autonomous consumer expenditure rises because of the oil discovery, the aggregate demand function shifts upward to Y_2^{ad} and equilibrium output rises to $Y_{A'}$. This rise in equilibrium output from Y_A to $Y_{A'}$ when the interest rate is i_A is plotted in panel (a) as a movement from point A to point A′. The same analysis can be applied to every point on the initial IS_1 curve; therefore, the rise in autonomous consumer expenditure shifts the *IS* curve to the right from IS_1 to IS_2 in panel (a).

    A decline in autonomous consumer expenditure reverses the direction of the analysis. For any given interest rate, the aggregate demand function shifts downward, the equilibrium level of aggregate output falls, and the *IS* curve shifts to the left.

2. *Changes in Investment Spending Unrelated to the Interest Rate.* In Chapter 22 we learned that changes in the interest rate affect planned investment spending and hence the equilibrium level of output. This change in investment spending merely causes a movement along the *IS* curve and not a shift. A rise in planned investment spending unrelated to the interest rate (say, because companies become more confident about investment profitability after the Alberta oil discovery) shifts the aggregate demand function upward, as in panel (b) of Figure 23-1. For any given interest rate, the equilibrium level of aggregate output rises, and the *IS* curve will shift to the right, as in panel (a).

    A decrease in investment spending because companies become more pessimistic about investment profitability shifts the aggregate demand function

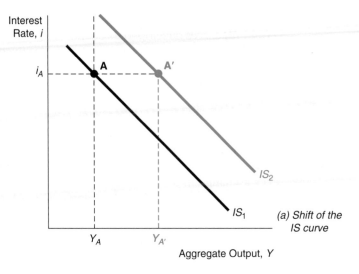

(a) Shift of the
IS curve

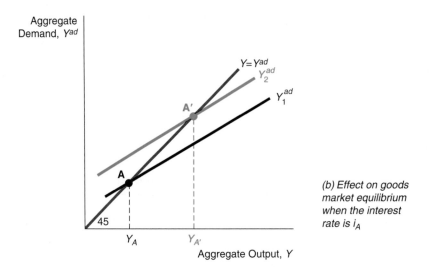

(b) Effect on goods
market equilibrium
when the interest
rate is i_A

FIGURE 23-1   Shift in the *IS* curve

The *IS* curve will shift from IS_1 to IS_2 as a result of (1) an increase in autonomous consumer spending, (2) an increase in planned investment spending due to business optimism, (3) an increase in government spending, (4) a decrease in taxes, or (5) an increase in net exports that is unrelated to interest rates. Panel (b) shows how changes in these factors lead to the rightward shift in the *IS* curve using a Keynesian cross diagram. For any given interest rate (here i_A), these changes shift the aggregate demand function upward and raise equilibrium output Y_A to $Y_{A'}$.

downward for any given interest rate; the equilibrium level of aggregate output falls, shifting the *IS* curve to the left.

3. *Changes in Government Spending.* An increase in government spending will also cause the aggregate demand function at any given interest rate to shift upward, as in panel (b). The equilibrium level of aggregate output rises at any given interest rate, and the *IS* curve shifts to the right. Conversely, a decline in government spending shifts the aggregate demand function downward, and the equilibrium level of output falls, shifting the *IS* curve to the left.

4. *Changes in Taxes.* Unlike changes in other factors that directly affect the aggregate demand function, a decline in taxes shifts the aggregate demand function by raising consumer expenditure and shifting the aggregate demand function upward at any given interest rate. A decline in taxes raises the equilibrium level of aggregate output at any given interest rate and shifts the *IS* curve to the right (as in Figure 23-1). Recall, however, that a change in taxes has a smaller effect on aggregate demand than an equivalent change in government spending. So for a given change in taxes, the *IS* curve will shift less than for an equal change in government spending.

A rise in taxes lowers the aggregate demand function and reduces the equilibrium level of aggregate output at each interest rate. Therefore, a rise in taxes shifts the *IS* curve to the left.

5. *Changes in Net Exports Unrelated to the Interest Rate.* As with planned investment spending, changes in net exports arising from a change in interest rates merely cause a movement along the *IS* curve and not a shift. An autonomous rise in net exports unrelated to the interest rate—say because Canadian-made clothes become more chic than French-made clothes—shifts the aggregate demand function upward and causes the *IS* curve to shift to the right, as in Figure 23-1. Conversely, an autonomous fall in net exports shifts the aggregate demand function downward, and the equilibrium level of output falls, shifting the *IS* curve to the left.

FACTORS THAT CAUSE THE *LM* CURVE TO SHIFT

The *LM* curve describes the equilibrium points in the market for money—the combinations of aggregate output and interest rate for which the quantity of money demanded equals the quantity of money supplied. Whereas five factors can cause the *IS* curve to shift (changes in autonomous consumer expenditure, planned investment spending unrelated to the interest rate, government spending, taxes, and net exports unrelated to the interest rate), only two factors can cause the *LM* curve to shift: autonomous changes in money demand and changes in the money supply. How do changes in these two factors affect the *LM* curve?

1. *Changes in the Money Supply.* A rise in the money supply shifts the *LM* curve to the right, as shown in Figure 23-2. To see how this shift occurs, suppose that the *LM* curve is initially at LM_1 in panel (a) and the Bank of Canada conducts open market purchases that increase the money supply. If we consider point A, which is on the initial LM_1 curve, we can examine what happens to the equilibrium level of the interest rate, holding output constant at Y_A.

Panel (b), which contains a supply and demand diagram for the market for money, depicts the equilibrium interest rate initially as i_A at the intersection of the supply curve for money M_1^s and the demand curve for money M^d. The rise in the quantity of money supplied shifts the supply curve to M_2^s, and, holding output constant at Y_A, the equilibrium interest rate falls to $i_{A'}$. In panel (a), this decline in the equilibrium interest rate from i_A to $i_{A'}$ is shown as a movement from point A to point A'. The same analysis can be applied to every point on the initial LM_1 curve, leading to the conclusion that at any given level of aggregate output, the equilibrium interest rate falls when the money supply increases. Thus LM_2 is below and to the right of LM_1.

Reversing this reasoning, a decline in the money supply shifts the *LM* curve to the left. A decline in the money supply results in a shortage of money at points on the initial *LM* curve. This condition of excess demand for money can

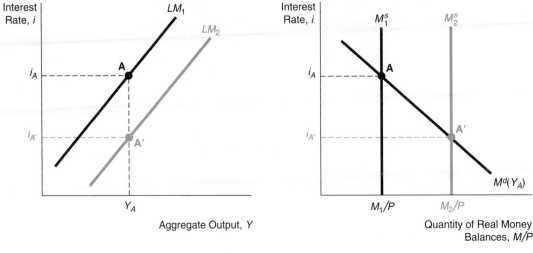

FIGURE 23-2 Shift in the *LM* Curve from an Increase in the Money Supply

The *LM* curve shifts to the right from LM_1 to LM_2 when the money supply increases because, as indicated in panel (b), at any given level of aggregate output (say, Y_A), the equilibrium interest rate falls (point A to A').

be eliminated by a rise in the interest rate, which reduces the quantity of money demanded until it again equals the quantity of money supplied.

2. *Autonomous Changes in Money Demand.* The theory of asset demand outlined in Chapter 5 indicates that there can be an autonomous rise in money demand (that is, a change not caused by a change in the price level, aggregate output, or the interest rate). For example, an increase in the volatility of bond returns would make bonds riskier relative to money and would increase the quantity of money demanded at any given interest rate, price level, or amount of aggregate output. The resulting autonomous increase in the demand for money shifts the *LM* curve to the left, as shown in Figure 23-3. Consider point A on the initial LM_1 curve. Suppose that a massive financial panic occurs, sending many companies into bankruptcy. Because bonds have become a riskier asset, people want to shift from holding bonds to holding money; they will hold more money at all interest rates and output levels. The resulting increase in money demand at an output level of Y_A is shown by the shift of the money demand curve from M_1^d to M_2^d in panel (b). The new equilibrium in the market for money now indicates that if aggregate output is constant at Y_A, the equilibrium interest rate will rise to $i_{A'}$, and the point of equilibrium moves from A to A'.

Conversely, an autonomous decline in money demand would lead to a rightward shift in the *LM* curve. The fall in money demand would create an excess supply of money, which is eliminated by a rise in the quantity of money demanded from a decline in the interest rate.

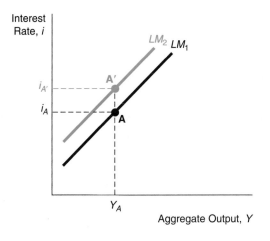

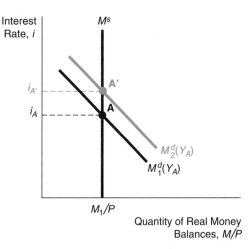

(a) Shift in the LM curve

(b) Effect on the market for money when aggregate output is constant at Y_A

FIGURE 23-3   Shift in the *LM* Curve When Money Demand Increases

The *LM* curve shifts to the left from LM_1 to LM_2 when money demand increases because, as indicated in panel (b), at any given level of aggregate output (say, Y_A), the equilibrium interest rate rises (point A to A′).

CHANGES IN EQUILIBRIUM LEVEL OF THE INTEREST RATE AND AGGREGATE OUTPUT

You can now use your knowledge of factors that cause the *IS* and *LM* curves to shift for the purpose of analyzing how the equilibrium levels of the interest rate and aggregate output change in response to changes in monetary and fiscal policies.

Response to a Change in Monetary Policy

Figure 23-4 illustrates the response of output and the interest rate to an increase in the money supply. Initially, the economy is in equilibrium for both the goods market and the market for money at point 1, the intersection of IS_1 and LM_1. Suppose that at the resulting level of aggregate output Y_1, the economy is suffering from an unemployment rate of 10%, and the Bank of Canada decides it should try to raise output and reduce unemployment by raising the money supply. Will the Bank's change in monetary policy have the intended effect?

The rise in the money supply causes the *LM* curve to shift rightward to LM_2, and the equilibrium point for both the goods market and the market for money moves to point 2 (intersection of IS_1 and LM_2). As a result of an increase in the money supply, the interest rate declines to i_2, as we found in Figure 23-2, and aggregate output rises to Y_2; the Bank's policy has been successful in improving the health of the economy.

For a clear understanding of the way aggregate output rises and the interest rate declines, think about exactly what has happened in moving from point 1 to point 2. When the economy is at point 1, the increase in the money supply (rightward shift of the *LM* curve) creates an excess supply of money, resulting in a decline in the interest rate. The decline causes investment spending and net exports to rise, which in turn raises aggregate demand and causes aggregate output to rise. The excess supply of money is eliminated when the economy reaches point 2 because both the rise in output and the fall in the interest rate have raised the quantity of money demanded until it equals the new higher level of the money supply.

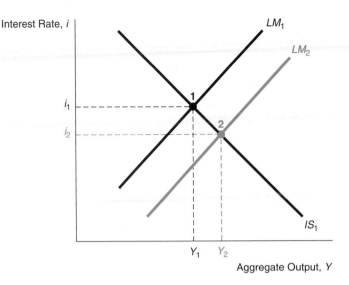

FIGURE 23-4   Response of Aggregate Output and the Interest Rate to an Increase in the Money Supply

The increase in the money supply shifts the *LM* curve to the right from LM_1 to LM_2; the economy moves to point 2, where output has increased to Y_2 and the interest rate has declined to i_2.

A decline in the money supply reverses the process; it shifts the *LM* curve to the left, causing the interest rate to rise and output to fall. Accordingly, ***aggregate output is positively related to the money supply***; aggregate output expands when the money supply increases and falls when it decreases.

Response to a Change in Fiscal Policy

Suppose that the Bank of Canada is not willing to increase the money supply when the economy is suffering from a 10% unemployment rate at point 1. Can the federal government come to the rescue and manipulate government spending and taxes to raise aggregate output and reduce the massive unemployment?

The *ISLM* model demonstrates that it can. Figure 23-5 depicts the response of output and the interest rate to an expansionary fiscal policy (increase in government spending or decrease in taxes). An increase in government spending or a decrease in taxes causes the *IS* curve to shift to IS_2, and the equilibrium point for both the goods market and the market for money moves to point 2 (intersection of IS_2 with LM_1). The result of the change in fiscal policy is a rise in aggregate output to Y_2 and a rise in the interest rate to i_2. Note the difference in the effect on the interest rate between an expansionary fiscal policy and an expansionary monetary policy. In the case of an expansionary fiscal policy, the interest rate rises, whereas in the case of an expansionary monetary policy, the interest rate falls.

Why does an increase in government spending or a decrease in taxes move the economy from point 1 to point 2, causing a rise in both aggregate output and the interest rate? An increase in government spending raises aggregate demand directly; a decrease in taxes makes more income available for spending and raises aggregate demand by raising consumer expenditure. The resulting increase in aggregate demand causes aggregate output to rise. The higher level of aggregate output raises the quantity of money demanded, creating an excess demand for money, which in turn causes the interest rate to rise. At point 2, the excess demand

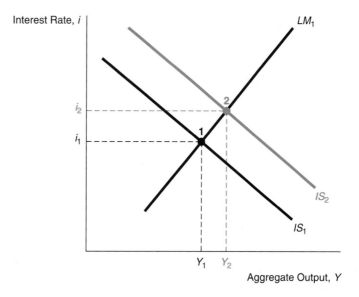

FIGURE 23-5   Response of Aggregate Output and the Interest Rate to an Expansionary Fiscal Policy

Expansionary fiscal policy (a rise in government spending or a decrease in taxes) shifts the *IS* curve to the right from IS_1 to IS_2; the economy moves to point 2, aggregate output increases to Y_2, and the interest rate rises to i_2.

for money created by a rise in aggregate output has been eliminated by a rise in the interest rate, which lowers the quantity of money demanded.

A contractionary fiscal policy (decrease in government spending or increase in taxes) reverses the process described in Figure 23-5; it causes aggregate demand to fall, which shifts the *IS* curve to the left and causes both aggregate output and the interest rate to fall. ***Aggregate output and the interest rate are positively related to government spending and negatively related to taxes.***

As a study aid, Table 23-1 indicates the effect on aggregate output and interest rates of a change in the seven factors that shift the *IS* and *LM* curves.

EFFECTIVENESS OF MONETARY VERSUS FISCAL POLICY

Our discussion of the effects of fiscal and monetary policy suggests that a government can easily lift an economy out of a recession by implementing any of a number of policies (changing the money supply, government spending, or taxes). But how can policymakers decide which of these policies to use if faced with too much unemployment? Should they decrease taxes, increase government spending, raise the money supply, or do all three? And if they decide to increase the money supply, by how much should it be increased? Economists do not pretend to have all the answers, and although the *ISLM* model will not clear the path to aggregate economic bliss, it can help policymakers decide which policies may be most effective under certain circumstances.

TABLE 23-1   Effects from Factors That Shift the *IS* and *LM* Curves

Factor	Autonomous Change in Factor	Response	Reason	
Consumer expenditure, C	↑	$Y\uparrow, i\uparrow$	$C\uparrow \Rightarrow Y^{ad}\uparrow \Rightarrow$ IS shifts right	
Investment, I	↑	$Y\uparrow, i\uparrow$	$I\uparrow \Rightarrow Y^{ad}\uparrow \Rightarrow$ IS shifts right	
Government spending, G	↑	$Y\uparrow, i\uparrow$	$G\uparrow \Rightarrow Y^{ad}\uparrow \Rightarrow$ IS shifts right	
Taxes, T	↑	$Y\downarrow, i\downarrow$	$T\uparrow \Rightarrow C\downarrow \Rightarrow Y^{ad}\downarrow \Rightarrow$ IS shifts left	
Net exports, NX	↑	$Y\uparrow, i\uparrow$	$NX\uparrow \Rightarrow Y^{ad}\uparrow \Rightarrow$ IS shifts right	
Money supply, M^s	↑	$Y\uparrow, i\downarrow$	$M^s\uparrow \Rightarrow i\downarrow \Rightarrow$ LM shifts right	
Money demand, M^d	↑	$Y\downarrow, i\uparrow$	$M^d\uparrow \Rightarrow i\uparrow \Rightarrow$ LM shifts left	

Note: Only increases (↑) in the factors are shown; the effect of decreases in the factors would be the opposite of those indicated in the "Response" column.

APPLICATION   The Policy Mix and German Unification

So far we have looked at fiscal and monetary policy in isolation and showed how each one works. In practice, however, fiscal and monetary policies are used together and the combination of the two is known as the **policy mix**.

For example, following the 1990 unification of West Germany and East Germany, the German government sharply increased government spending and transfers in order to revive eastern Germany. In terms of the *ISLM* model of Figure 23-6, this resulted in a large rightward shift of the *IS* curve from IS_1 to IS_2 and moved the German economy from point 1 to point 2, thereby raising aggregate output.

The German central bank (Bundesbank) saw these developments and feared that they would result in inflation. The Bundesbank concluded that economic activity should be slowed and adopted accordingly a tight monetary policy. In terms of the *ISLM* model of Figure 23-6, it shifted the *LM* curve to the left from LM_1 to LM_2 in order to increase interest rates and slow down the level of activity. Thus, the policy mix moved the German economy to point 3 and resulted in fast growth (from the fiscal expansion) and high interest rates (from the tight monetary policy).

In fact, due to its financial leadership the Bundesbank was accused of forcing interest rates to higher levels than they might otherwise have been in Europe as well as in the rest of the world.

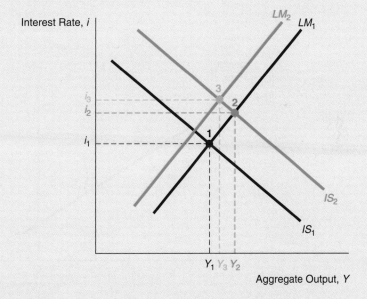

FIGURE 23-6   The Policy Mix and German Unification

The fiscal expansion led to a rightward shift of the *IS* curve from IS_1 to IS_2 and moved the German economy from point 1 to point 2, thereby raising both the interest rate and aggregate output. The Bundesbank's tight money policy led to a leftward shift of the *LM* curve from LM_1 to LM_2 and moved the economy to point 3. Thus, the policy mix resulted in fast growth and high interest rates.

Monetary Policy Versus Fiscal Policy: The Cases of Complete Crowding Out

The *ISLM* model developed so far in this chapter shows that both monetary and fiscal policy affect the level of aggregate output. To understand when monetary policy is more effective than fiscal policy, we will examine a special case of the *ISLM* model in which money demand is unaffected by the interest rate (money demand is said to be interest-inelastic) so that monetary policy affects output but fiscal policy does not.

Consider the slope of the *LM* curve if the demand for money is unaffected by changes in the interest rate. If point 1 in panel (a) of Figure 23-7 is such that the quantity of money demanded equals the quantity of money supplied, then it is

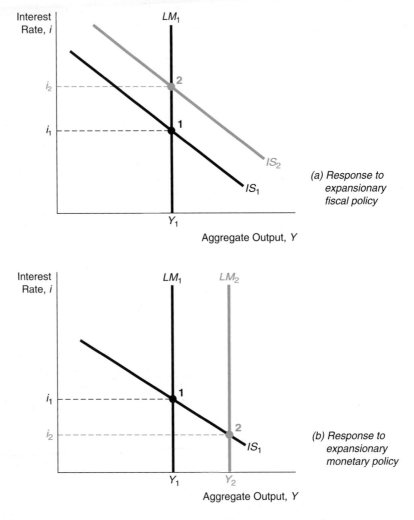

(a) Response to expansionary fiscal policy

(b) Response to expansionary monetary policy

FIGURE 23-7 Effectiveness of Monetary and Fiscal Policy When Money Demand Is Unaffected by the Interest Rate

When the demand for money is unaffected by the interest rate, the *LM* curve is vertical. In panel (a), an expansionary fiscal policy (increase in government spending or a cut in taxes) shifts the *IS* curve from IS_1 to IS_2 and leaves aggregate output unchanged at Y_1. In panel (b), an increase in the money supply shifts the *LM* curve from LM_1 to LM_2 and raises aggregate output from Y_1 to Y_2. Therefore, monetary policy is effective, but fiscal policy is not.

on the *LM* curve. If the interest rate rises to, say, i_2, the quantity of money demanded is unaffected, and it will continue to equal the *unchanged* quantity of money supplied only if aggregate output remains *unchanged* at Y_1 (point 2). Equilibrium in the market for money will occur at the same level of aggregate output regardless of the interest rate, and the *LM* curve will be vertical, as shown in both panels of Figure 23-7.

Suppose that the economy is suffering from a high rate of unemployment, which policymakers try to eliminate with either expansionary fiscal or monetary policy. Panel (a) depicts what happens when an expansionary fiscal policy (increase in government spending or cut in taxes) is implemented, shifting the *IS* curve to the right from IS_1 to IS_2. As you can see in panel (a), the fiscal expansion has no effect on output; aggregate output remains at Y_1 when the economy moves from point 1 to point 2.

In our earlier analysis, expansionary fiscal policy always increased aggregate demand and raised the level of output. Why doesn't that happen in panel (a)? The answer is that because the *LM* curve is vertical, the rightward shift of the *IS* curve raises the interest rate to i_2, which causes investment spending and net exports to fall enough to offset completely the increased spending of the expansionary fiscal policy. Put another way, increased spending that results from expansionary fiscal policy has *crowded out* investment spending and net exports, which decrease because of the rise in the interest rate. This situation in which expansionary fiscal policy does not lead to a rise in output is frequently referred to as a case of **complete crowding out**.[1]

Panel (b) shows what happens when the Bank of Canada tries to eliminate high unemployment through an expansionary monetary policy (increase in the money supply). Here the *LM* curve shifts to the right from LM_1 to LM_2 because at each interest rate, output must rise so that the quantity of money demanded rises to match the increase in the money supply. Aggregate output rises from Y_1 to Y_2 (the economy moves from point 1 to point 2), and expansionary monetary policy does affect aggregate output in this case.

We conclude from the analysis in Figure 23-7 that if the demand for money is unaffected by changes in the interest rate (money demand is interest-inelastic), monetary policy is effective but fiscal policy is not. An even more general conclusion can be reached: ***the less interest-sensitive money demand is, the more effective monetary policy is relative to fiscal policy.***[2]

Because the interest sensitivity of money demand is important to policymakers' decisions regarding the use of monetary or fiscal policy to influence economic activity, the subject has been studied extensively by economists and has been the focus of many debates. Findings on the interest sensitivity of money demand were discussed in Chapter 21.

---

[1] When the demand for money is affected by the interest rate, the usual case in which the *LM* curve slopes upward but is not vertical, some crowding out occurs. The rightward shift of the *IS* curve also raises the interest rate, which causes investment spending and net exports to fall somewhat. However, as Figure 23-5 indicates, the rise in the interest rate is not sufficient to reduce investment spending and net exports to the point where aggregate output does not increase. Thus expansionary fiscal policy increases aggregate output, and only partial crowding out occurs.

[2] This result and many others in this and the previous chapter can be obtained more directly by using algebra. An algebraic treatment of the *ISLM* model can be found in an appendix to this chapter on this book's MyEconLab at **www.pearsoned.ca/myeconlab**.

In the 1970s and early 1980s, central banks in many countries pursued a strategy of monetary targeting—that is, they used their policy tools to make the money supply equal a target value. However, as we saw in Chapter 18, many of these central banks abandoned monetary targeting in the 1980s to pursue interest-rate targeting instead, because of the breakdown of the stable relationship between the money supply and economic activity. The *ISLM* model has important implications for which variable a central bank should target and we can apply it to explain why central banks have abandoned monetary targeting for interest-rate targeting.[3]

As we saw in Chapter 18, when the Bank of Canada attempts to hit a money supply target, it cannot at the same time pursue an interest-rate target; it can hit one target or the other but not both. Consequently, it needs to know which of these two targets will produce more accurate control of aggregate output.

In contrast to the textbook world you have been inhabiting, in which the *IS* and *LM* curves are assumed to be fixed, the real world is one of great uncertainty in which *IS* and *LM* curves shift because of unanticipated changes in autonomous spending and money demand. To understand whether the Bank of Canada should use a money supply target or an interest-rate target, we need to look at two cases: first, one in which uncertainty about the *IS* curve is far greater than uncertainty about the *LM* curve, and another in which uncertainty about the *LM* curve is far greater than uncertainty about the *IS* curve.

The *ISLM* diagram in Figure 23-8 illustrates the outcome of the two targeting strategies for the case in which the *IS* curve is unstable and uncertain and so it fluctuates around its expected value of IS^* from IS' and IS'', while the *LM* curve is stable and certain so it stays at LM^*. Since the central bank knows that the expected position of the *IS* curve is at IS^* and desires aggregate output of Y^*, it will set its interest-rate target at i^* so that the expected level of output is Y^*. This policy of targeting the interest rate at i^* is labelled "Interest-Rate Target."

How would the central bank keep the interest rate at its target level of i^*? Recall from Chapter 18 that the central bank can hit its interest-rate target by buying and selling bonds when the interest rate differs from i^*. When the *IS* curve shifts out to IS'', the interest rate would rise above i^*, with the money supply unchanged. To counter this rise in interest rates, however, the central bank would need to buy bonds just until their price is driven back up so that the interest rate comes back down to i^*. (The result of these open market purchases, as we have seen in Chapter 16, is that the monetary base and the money supply rise until the *LM* curve shifts to the right to intersect the IS'' curve at i^*—not shown in the diagram for simplicity.) When the interest rate is below i^*, the central bank needs to sell bonds to lower their price and raise the interest rate back up to i^*. (These open market sales reduce the monetary base and the money supply until the *LM* curve shifts to the left to intersect the IS' curve at i^*—again not shown in the diagram.) The result of pursuing the interest-rate target is that aggregate output fluctuates between Y_I' and Y_I'' in Figure 23-8.

---

[3] The classic paper on this topic is William Poole, "The Optimal Choice of Monetary Policy Instruments in a Simple Macro Model," *Quarterly Journal of Economics* 84 (1970): 192–216. A less mathematical version of his analysis, far more accessible to students, is contained in William Poole, "Rules of Thumb for Guiding Monetary Policy," in *Open Market Policies and Operating Procedures: Staff Studies* (Washington, D.C.: Board of Governors of the Federal Reserve System, 1971).

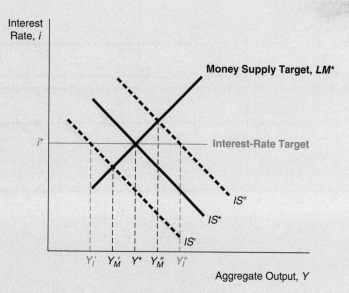

FIGURE 23-8   Money Supply and Interest-Rate Targets When the *IS* Curve Is Unstable and the *LM* Curve Is Stable

The unstable *IS* curve fluctuates between *IS'* and *IS"*. The money supply target produces smaller fluctuations in output (Y'_M to Y''_M) than the interest-rate targets (Y'_I to Y''_I). Therefore, the money supply target is preferred.

If, instead, the central bank pursues a money supply target, it will set the money supply so that the resulting *LM* curve *LM** intersects the *IS** curve at the desired output level of Y^*. This policy of targeting the money supply is labelled "Money Supply Target." Because it is not changing the money supply and so keeps the *LM* curve at *LM**, aggregate output will fluctuate between Y'_M and Y''_M for the money supply target policy.

As you can see in the figure, the money supply target leads to smaller output fluctuations around the desired level than the interest-rate target. A rightward shift of the *IS* curve to *IS"*, for example, causes the interest rate to rise, given a money supply target, and this rise in the interest rate leads to a lower level of investment spending and net exports and hence to a smaller increase in aggregate output than occurs under an interest-rate target. Because smaller output fluctuations are desirable, the conclusion is that ***if the* IS *curve is more unstable than the* LM *curve, a money supply target is preferred.***

The outcome of the two targeting strategies for the case of a stable *IS* curve and an unstable *LM* curve caused by unanticipated changes in money demand is illustrated in Figure 23-9. Again, the interest-rate and money supply targets are set so that the expected level of aggregate output equals the desired level Y^*. Because the *LM* curve is now unstable, it fluctuates between *LM'* and *LM"* even when the money supply is fixed, causing aggregate output to fluctuate between Y'_M and Y''_M. The interest-rate target, by contrast, is not affected by uncertainty about the *LM* curve because it is set by the central bank's adjusting the money supply whenever the interest rate tries to depart from i^*. When the interest rate begins to rise above i^* because of an increase in money demand, the central bank again just buys bonds, driving up their price and bringing the interest rate back down to i^*. The result of these open market purchases is a rise in the monetary base and the money supply. Similarly, if the interest rate falls below i^*, the central bank sells bonds to lower their price and raise the interest rate

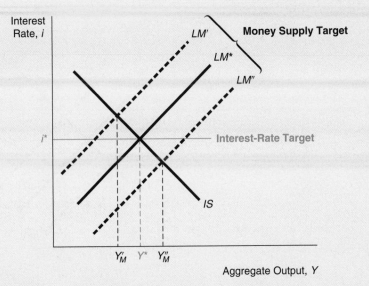

FIGURE 23-9 Money Supply and Interest-Rate Targets When the *LM* Curve Is Unstable and the *IS* Curve Is Stable

The unstable *LM* curve fluctuates between *LM'* and *LM"*. The money supply target then produces bigger fluctuations in output (Y'_M to Y''_M) than the interest-rate target (which leaves output fixed at Y^*). Therefore, the interest-rate target is preferred.

back to i^*, thereby causing a decline in the monetary base and the money supply. The only effect of the fluctuating *LM* curve, then, is that the money supply fluctuates more as a result of the interest-rate target policy. The outcome of the interest-rate target is that output will be exactly at the desired level with no fluctuations.

Since smaller output fluctuations are desirable, the conclusion from Figure 23-9 is that ***if the LM curve is more unstable than the IS curve, an interest-rate target is preferred.***

We can now see why many central banks decided to abandon monetary targeting for interest-rate targeting in the 1980s. With the rapid proliferation of new financial instruments whose presence can affect the demand for money (see Chapter 21), money demand (which is embodied in the *LM* curve) became highly unstable in many countries. Thus central banks in these countries recognized that they were more likely to be in the situation in Figure 23-9 and decided that they would be better off with an interest-rate target than a money supply target.[4]

---

[4] It is important to recognize, however, that the crucial factor in deciding which target is preferred is the *relative* instability of the IS and LM curves. Although the LM curve has been unstable recently, the evidence supporting a stable IS curve is also weak. Instability in the money demand function does not automatically mean that money supply targets should be abandoned for interest-rate targets. Furthermore, the analysis so far has been conducted assuming that the price level is fixed. More realistically, when the price level can change so that there is uncertainty about expected inflation, the case for an interest-rate target is less strong. As we learned in Chapters 4 and 5, the interest rate that is more relevant to investment decisions is not the nominal interest rate but the real interest rate (the nominal interest rate minus expected inflation). Hence when expected inflation rises, at each given nominal interest rate, the real interest rate falls and investment and net exports rise, shifting the IS curve to the right. Similarly, a fall in expected inflation raises the real interest rate at each given nominal interest rate, lowers investment and net exports, and shifts the IS curve to the left. Since in the real world expected inflation undergoes large fluctuations, the IS curve in Figure 23-9 will also have substantial fluctuations, making it less likely that the interest-rate target is preferable to the money supply target.

ISLM MODEL IN THE LONG RUN

So far in our *ISLM* analysis, we have been assuming that the price level is fixed so that nominal values and real values are the same. This is a reasonable assumption for the short run, but in the long run the price level does change. To see what happens in the *ISLM* model in the long run, we make use of the concept of the **natural rate level of output** (denoted by Y_n), which is the rate of output at which wages and the price level have no tendency to rise or fall (this is the full employment level of output). When output is above the natural rate level, the booming economy will cause prices to rise; when output is below the natural rate level, the slack in the economy will cause prices to fall.

Because we now want to examine what happens when the price level changes, we can no longer assume that real and nominal values are the same. The spending variables that affect the *IS* curve (consumer expenditure, investment spending, government spending, and net exports) describe the demand for goods and services and are *in real terms*; they describe the physical quantities of goods that people want to buy. Because these quantities do not change when the price level changes, a change in the price level has no effect on the *IS* curve, which describes the combinations of the interest rate and aggregate output *in real terms* that satisfy goods market equilibrium.

Figure 23-10 shows what happens in the *ISLM* model when output rises above the natural rate level, which is marked by a vertical line at Y_n. Suppose that initially the *IS* and *LM* curves intersect at point 1, where output $Y = Y_n$. Panel (a) examines what happens to output and interest rates when there is a rise in the

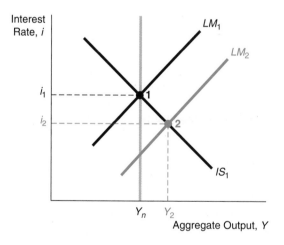

(a) *Response to a rise in the money supply M*

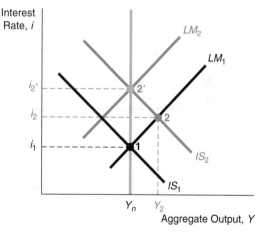

(b) *Response to a rise in government spending G*

FIGURE 23-10 The *ISLM* Model in the Long Run

In panel (a), a rise in the money supply causes the *LM* curve to shift rightward to LM_2, and the equilibrium moves to point 2, where the interest rate falls to i_2 and output rises to Y_2. Because output at Y_2 is above the natural rate level Y_n, the price level rises, the real money supply falls, and the *LM* curve shifts back to LM_1; the economy has returned to the original equilibrium at point 1. In panel (b), an increase in government spending shifts the *IS* curve to the right to IS_2, and the economy moves to point 2, at which the interest rate has risen to i_2 and output has risen to Y_2. Because output at Y_2 is above the natural rate level Y_n, the price level begins to rise, real money balances M/P begin to fall, and the *LM* curve shifts to the left to LM_2. The long-run equilibrium at point 2′ has an even higher interest rate at $i_{2'}$ and output has returned to Y_n.

612   PART VII   *Monetary Theory*

money supply. As we saw in Figure 23-2 (page 600), the rise in the money supply causes the *LM* curve to shift to LM_2, and the equilibrium moves to point 2 (the intersection of IS_1 and LM_2), where the interest rate falls to i_2 and output rises to Y_2. However, as we can see in panel (a), the level of output at Y_2 is greater than the natural rate level Y_n, and so the price level begins to rise.

In contrast to the *IS* curve, which is unaffected by a rise in the price level, the *LM* curve is affected by the price level rise because the liquidity preference theory states that the demand for money *in real terms* depends on real income and interest rates. This makes sense because money is valued in terms of what it can buy. However, the money supply that you read about in newspapers is not the money supply in real terms; it is a nominal quantity. As the price level rises, the quantity of money *in real terms* falls, and the effect on the *LM* curve is identical to a fall in the nominal money supply with the price level fixed. The lower value of the real money supply creates an excess demand for money, causing the interest rate to rise at any given level of aggregate output, and the *LM* curve shifts back to the left. As long as the level of output exceeds the natural rate level, the price level will continue to rise, shifting the *LM* curve to the left, until finally output is back at the natural rate level Y_n. This occurs when the *LM* curve has returned to LM_1, where real money balances M/P have returned to the original level and the economy has returned to the original equilibrium at point 1. The result of the expansion in the money supply in the long run is that the economy has the same level of output and interest rates.

The fact that the increase in the money supply has left output and interest rates unchanged in the long run is referred to as **long-run monetary neutrality.** The only result of the increase in the money supply is a higher price level, which has increased proportionally to the increase in the money supply so that real money balances M/P are unchanged. Long-run monetary neutrality is generally consistent with time series data from actual economies (see the Global box, International Evidence on Long-Run Monetary Neutrality).

Panel (b) looks at what happens to output and interest rates when there is expansionary fiscal policy such as an increase in government spending. As we saw earlier, the increase in government spending shifts the *IS* curve to the right to IS_2, and in the short run the economy moves to point 2 (the intersection of IS_2 and LM_1), where the interest rate has risen to i_2 and output has risen to Y_2. Because output at Y_2 is above the natural rate level Y_n, the price level begins to rise, real money balances M/P begin to fall, and the *LM* curve shifts to the left. Only when the *LM* curve has shifted to LM_2 and the equilibrium is at point 2′, where output is again at the natural rate level Y_n, does the price level stop rising and the *LM* curve come to rest. The resulting long-run equilibrium at point 2′ has an even higher interest rate at $i_{2'}$ and output has not risen from Y_n. Indeed, what has occurred in the long run is complete crowding out. The rise in the price level, which has shifted the *LM* curve to LM_2, has caused the interest rate to rise to $i_{2'}$, causing investment and net exports to fall enough to offset the increased government spending completely. What we have discovered is that even though complete crowding out does not occur in the short run in the *ISLM* model (when the *LM* curve is not vertical), it does occur in the long run.

Our conclusion from examining what happens in the *ISLM* model from an expansionary monetary or fiscal policy is that ***although monetary and fiscal policy can affect output in the short run, neither affects output in the long run.*** Clearly, an important issue in deciding on the effectiveness of monetary and fiscal policy to raise output is how soon the long run occurs. This is a topic that we explore in the next chapter.

GLOBAL	International Evidence on Long-Run Monetary Neutrality

Over the years, the long-run neutrality proposition has been investigated in a large number of studies, often with conflicting results. Apostolos Serletis and Zisimos Koustas argue that meaningful long-run monetary neutrality tests depend on the time series properties of the variables, and they test the long-run neutrality of money proposition using recent advances in the field of applied econometrics.* In doing so, they use the Backus and Kehoe data set, consisting of over one hundred years of annual observations on real output and money for ten countries: Australia, Canada, Denmark, Germany, Italy, Japan, Norway, Sweden, the United Kingdom, and the United States.

The results show that the data are supportive of the proposition that money is neutral in the long run. The same authors find support for the long-run neutrality of money using weighted monetary aggregates for the U.S. economy.** As already noted in Chapter 3, weighted monetary aggregates represent a significant advance over simple sum measures of money.

However, international evidence on another important long-run neutrality proposition, the Fisher effect, seems to provide little support to the hypothesis that fully anticipated inflation has a unit effect on nominal interest rates.*** The preponderance of the evidence suggests that anticipated inflation has less than a unit effect on nominal interest rates, and thus reduces real interest rates even in the longest of runs.

The apparent contradiction of the two types of long-run neutrality results represents a puzzle that needs to be addressed by future theoretical and empirical research.

* See Apostolos Serletis and Zisimos Koustas, "International Evidence on the Neutrality of Money," *Journal of Money, Credit and Banking* 30 (1998): pp. 1–25. For details regarding the Backus and Kehoe data set, see David K. Backus and Patrick J. Kehoe, "International Evidence on the Historical Properties of Business Cycles," *American Economic Review* 82 (1992): pp. 864–888.

** See Apostolos Serletis and Zisimos Koustas, "Monetary Aggregation and the Neutrality of Money," *Economic Inquiry* 39 (2001): pp. 124–138.

*** See Zisimos Koustas and Apostolos Serletis, "On the Fisher Effect," *Journal of Monetary Economics* 44 (1999): pp. 105–130.

ISLM MODEL AND THE AGGREGATE DEMAND CURVE

We now examine further what happens in the *ISLM* model when the price level changes. When we conduct the *ISLM* analysis with a changing price level, we find that as the price level falls, the level of aggregate output rises. Thus we obtain a relationship between the price level and quantity of aggregate output for which the goods market and the market for money are in equilibrium, called the *aggregate demand curve*. This aggregate demand curve is a central element in the aggregate supply and demand analysis of Chapter 24, which allows us to explain changes not only in aggregate output but also in the price level.

Deriving the Aggregate Demand Curve

Now that you understand how a change in the price level affects the *IS* and *LM* curves, we can analyze what happens in the *ISLM* diagram when the price level changes. This exercise is carried out in Figure 23-11. Panel (a) contains an *ISLM* diagram for a given value of the nominal money supply. Let us first consider a price level of P_1. The *LM* curve at this price level is $LM(P_1)$, and its intersection with the

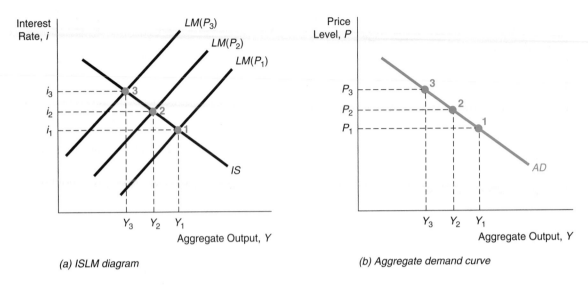

FIGURE 23-11   Deriving the Aggregate Demand Curve

The *ISLM* diagram in panel (a) shows that as the price level rises from P_1 to P_2 to P_3, the *LM* curve shifts to the left, and equilibrium output falls. The combinations of the price level and equilibrium output from panel (a) are then plotted in panel (b), and the line connecting them is the aggregate demand curve *AD*.

IS curve is at point 1, where output is Y_1. The equilibrium output level Y_1 that occurs when the price level is P_1 is also plotted in panel (b) as point 1. If the price level rises to P_2, then *in real terms* the money supply has fallen. The effect on the *LM* curves is identical to a decline in the nominal money supply when the price level is fixed. The *LM* curve will shift leftward to $LM(P_2)$. The new equilibrium level of output has fallen to Y_2 because planned investment and net exports fall when the interest rate rises. Point 2 in panel (b) plots this level of output for price level P_2. A further increase in the price level to P_3 causes a further decline in the real money supply, leading to a further decline in planned investment and net exports, and output declines to Y_3. Point 3 in panel (b) plots this level of output for price level P_3.

The line that connects the three points in panel (b) is the aggregate demand curve *AD*, and it indicates the level of aggregate output consistent with equilibrium in the goods market and the market for money at any given price level. This aggregate demand curve has the usual downward slope because a higher price level reduces the money supply in real terms, raises interest rates, and lowers the equilibrium level of aggregate output.

Factors That Cause the Aggregate Demand Curve to Shift

ISLM analysis demonstrates how the equilibrium level of aggregate output changes for a given price level. A change in any factor (except a change in the price level) that causes the *IS* or *LM* curve to shift causes the aggregate demand curve to shift. To see how this works, let's first look at what happens to the aggregate demand curve when the *IS* curve shifts.

SHIFTS IN THE *IS* CURVE   Five factors cause the *IS* curve to shift: changes in autonomous consumer spending, changes in investment spending related to business confidence, changes in government spending, changes in taxes, and autonomous changes in net exports. How changes in these factors lead to a shift in the aggregate demand curve is examined in Figure 23-12.

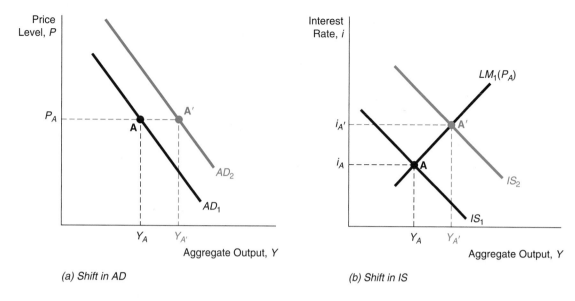

FIGURE 23-12   Shift in the Aggregate Demand Curve from a Shift in the *IS* Curve

Expansionary fiscal policy, a rise in net exports, or more optimistic consumers and firms shift the *IS* curve to the right in panel (b), and at a price level of P_A equilibrium output rises from Y_A to $Y_{A'}$. This change in equilibrium output is shown as a movement from point A to point A' in panel (a); hence the aggregate demand curve shifts to the right, from AD_1 to AD_2.

Suppose that initially the aggregate demand curve is at AD_1 and there is a rise, for example, in government spending. The *ISLM* diagram in panel (b) shows what then happens to equilibrium output, holding the price level constant at P_A. Initially, equilibrium output is at Y_A at the intersection of IS_1 and LM_1. The rise in government spending (holding the price level constant at P_A) shifts the *IS* curve to the right and raises equilibrium output to $Y_{A'}$. In panel (a), this rise in equilibrium output is shown as a movement from point A to point A', and the aggregate demand curve shifts to the right (to AD_2).

The conclusion from Figure 23-12 is that **any factor that shifts the IS curve shifts the aggregate demand curve in the same direction.** Therefore, "animal spirits" that encourage a rise in autonomous consumer spending or planned investment spending, a rise in government spending, a fall in taxes, or an autonomous rise in net exports—all of which shift the *IS* curve to the right—will also shift the aggregate demand curve to the right. Conversely, a fall in government spending, a rise in taxes, or a fall in net exports will cause the aggregate demand curve to shift to the left.

SHIFTS IN THE LM CURVE   Shifts in the *LM* are caused by either an autonomous change in money demand (not caused by a change in *P, Y,* or *i*) or a change in the money supply. Figure 23-13 shows how either of these changes leads to a shift in the aggregate demand curve. Again, we are initially at the AD_1 aggregate demand curve, and we look at what happens to the level of equilibrium output when the price level is held constant at P_A. A rise in the money supply shifts the *LM* curve to the right and raises equilibrium output to $Y_{A'}$. This rise in equilibrium output is shown as a movement from point A to point A' in panel (a), and the aggregate demand curve shifts to the right.

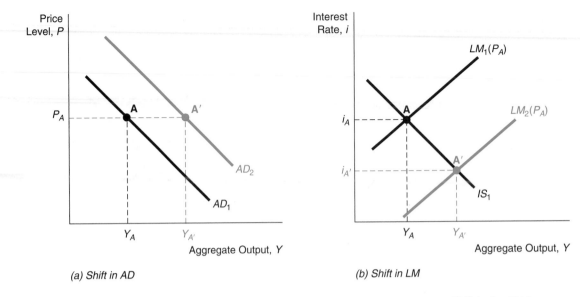

FIGURE 23-13 Shift in the Aggregate Demand Curve from a Shift in the *LM* Curve

A rise in the money supply or a fall in money demand shifts the *LM* curve to the right in panel (b), and at a price level of P_A, equilibrium output rises from Y_A to $Y_{A'}$. This change in equilibrium output is shown as a movement from point A to point A' in panel (a); hence the aggregate demand curve shifts to the right, from AD_1 to AD_2.

Our conclusion from Figure 23-13 is similar to that of Figure 23-12. ***Holding the price level constant, any factor that shifts the* LM *curve shifts the aggregate demand curve in the same direction.*** Therefore, a decline in money demand and an increase in the money supply, both of which shift the *LM* curve to the right, also shift the aggregate demand curve to the right. The aggregate demand curve will shift to the left, however, if the money supply declines or money demand rises.

You have now derived and analyzed the aggregate demand curve—an essential element in the aggregate demand and supply framework that we examine in Chapter 24. The aggregate demand and supply framework is particularly useful because it demonstrates how the price level is determined and enables us to examine factors that affect aggregate output when the price level varies.

SUMMARY

1. The *IS* curve is shifted to the right by a rise in autonomous consumer spending, a rise in planned investment spending related to business confidence, a rise in government spending, a fall in taxes, or an autonomous rise in net exports. A movement in the opposite direction of these five factors will shift the *IS* curve to the left.

2. The *LM* curve is shifted to the right by a rise in the money supply or an autonomous fall in money demand; it is shifted to the left by a fall in the money supply or an autonomous rise in money demand.

3. A rise in a money supply raises equilibrium output but lowers the equilibrium interest rate. Expansionary fiscal policy (a rise in government spending or a fall in taxes) raises equilibrium output but, in contrast to expansionary monetary policy, also raises the interest rate.

4. The less interest-sensitive money demand is, the more effective monetary policy is relative to fiscal policy.

5. The *ISLM* model provides the following conclusion about the conduct of monetary policy. When the *IS*

curve is more unstable than the *LM* curve, pursuing a money supply target provides smaller output fluctuations than pursuing an interest-rate target and is preferred; when the *LM* curve is more unstable than the *IS* curve, pursuing an interest-rate target leads to smaller output fluctuations and is preferred.

6. The conclusion from examining what happens in the *ISLM* model from an expansionary monetary or fiscal policy is that although monetary and fiscal policy can affect output in the short run, neither affects output in the long run.

7. The aggregate demand curve tells us the level of aggregate output consistent with equilibrium in the goods market and the market for money for any given price level. It slopes downward because a lower price level creates a higher level of the real money supply, lowers the interest rate, and raises equilibrium output. The aggregate demand curve shifts in the same direction as a shift in the *IS* or *LM* curve; hence it shifts to the right when government spending increases, taxes decrease, "animal spirits" encourage consumer and business spending, autonomous net exports increase, the money supply increases, or money demand decreases.

KEY TERMS

complete crowding out, p. 607

long-run monetary neutrality, p. 612

natural rate level of output, p. 611

policy mix, p. 605

QUESTIONS

You will find the answers to the questions marked with an asterisk in the Textbook Resources section of your MyEconLab.

1. If taxes and government spending rise by equal amounts, what will happen to the position of the *IS* curve? Explain this with a Keynesian cross diagram.

*2. What happened to the *IS* curve during the Great Depression when investment spending collapsed? Why?

3. What happens to the position of the *LM* curve if the Bank of Canada decides that it will decrease the money supply to fight inflation and if, at the same time, the demand for money falls?

*4. "An excess demand for money resulting from a rise in the demand for money can be eliminated only by a rise in the interest rate." Is this statement true, false, or uncertain? Explain your answer.

In questions 5–13, demonstrate your answers with an *ISLM* diagram.

5. Suppose that the Bank of Canada wants to keep interest rates from rising when the government sharply increases military spending. How can the Bank do this?

*6. Evidence indicates that lately the demand for money has become quite unstable. Why is this finding important to monetary policymakers?

7. "As the price level rises, the equilibrium level of output determined in the *ISLM* model also rises." Is this statement true, false, or uncertain? Explain your answer.

*8. What will happen to the position of the aggregate demand curve if the money supply is reduced when government spending increases?

9. An equal rise in government spending and taxes will have what effect on the position of the aggregate demand curve?

*10. If money demand is unaffected by changes in the interest rate, what effect will a rise in government spending have on the position of the aggregate demand curve?

Predicting the Future

11. Predict what will happen to interest rates and output if a stock market crash causes autonomous consumer expenditure to fall.

*12. Predict what will happen to interest rates and aggregate output when there is an autonomous export boom.

13. If a series of defaults in the bond market make bonds riskier and as a result the demand for money rises, predict what will happen to interest rates and aggregate output.

QUANTITATIVE PROBLEMS

*1. Assume that the price level is fixed (so that $i = i_r$) and consider the following *ISLM* model

$$Y = \alpha \times (\bar{A} - bi)$$

$$i = \frac{1}{b} \times \left(k \times Y - \frac{\bar{M}}{P} \right)$$

where

$$\alpha = \frac{1}{1 - (1 - t) \times mpc}$$

$\bar{A}$ is autonomous expenditure, b is the interest elasticity of investment expenditure, k is the income elasticity of money demand, h is the interest elasticity of money demand, t is the tax rate, and mpc is the marginal propensity to consume.

a. Solve for the equilibrium level of income, Y_0.

b. How does the equilibrium level of income depend on $\bar{A}$ and $\bar{M}/P$?

2. Continuing from the above problem,

a. What is the autonomous expenditure multiplier for this *ISLM* model?

b. What is the money multiplier?

WEB EXERCISES

1. An excellent way to learn about how changes in various factors affect the IS and LM curves is to visit **www.fgn.unisg.ch/eurmacro/tutor/islm.html**. This site, sponsored by the World Bank, allows you to make changes and to observe immediately their impact on the *ISLM* model.

a. Increase *G* from 200 to 500. What happens to the interest rate?

b. Reduce *t* to 0.1. What happens to aggregate output *Y*?

c. Increase *M* to 450. What happens to the interest rate and aggregate output?

2. Looking at the same site as you used in Question 1, **www.fgn.unisg.ch/eurmacro/tutor/islm.html**, the exogenous parameters in this simulation are the MPC (c), the sensitivity of money demand to income (k), the sensitivity of money demand to the interest rate (h), and the sensitivity of investment to the interest rate (b). For each of these parameters, explain what happens in the *ISLM* graph when they are *increased*. What happens to the equilibrium output and the equilibrium level of the interest rate?

Be sure to visit the MyEconLab website at **www.myeconlab.com**. This online homework and tutorial system puts you in control of your own learning with study and practice tools directly correlated to this chapter content.

On the MyEconLab website you will find the following appendix for this chapter:
Appendix 23.1: Algebra of the *ISLM* Model

CHAPTER 24

Aggregate Demand and Supply Analysis

LEARNING OBJECTIVES

After studying this chapter you should be able to

1. discern between monetarist and Keynesian views of aggregate demand
2. interpret the aggregate demand and supply framework for the determination of aggregate output and the price level
3. differentiate between short-run and long-run equilibria in the context of the aggregate demand and supply framework

PREVIEW

In earlier chapters we focused considerable attention on monetary policy because it touches our everyday lives by affecting the prices of the goods we buy and the quantity of available jobs. In this chapter we develop a basic tool, aggregate demand and supply analysis, which will enable us to study the effects of monetary policy on output and prices. **Aggregate demand** is the total quantity of an economy's final goods and services demanded at different price levels. **Aggregate supply** is the total quantity of final goods and services that firms in the economy want to sell at different price levels. As with other supply and demand analyses, the actual quantity of output and the price level are determined by equating aggregate demand and aggregate supply.

Aggregate demand and supply analysis will enable us to explore how aggregate output and the price level are determined. (The Financial News box, Aggregate Output, Unemployment, and the Price Level, indicates where and how often data on aggregate output and the price level are published.) Not only will the analysis help us interpret recent episodes in the business cycle, but it will also enable us to understand the debates on how economic policy should be conducted.

AGGREGATE DEMAND

The first building block of aggregate supply and demand analysis is the aggregate demand curve, which describes the relationship between the quantity of aggregate output demanded and the price level when all other variables are held constant.

Aggregate demand is made up of four component parts: **consumer expenditure**, the total demand for consumer goods and services; **planned investment spending**,[1] the total planned spending by business firms on new machines, facto-

---

[1] Recall that economists restrict use of the word *investment* to the purchase of new physical capital, such as a new machine or a new house, which adds to expenditure.

FINANCIAL NEWS

Aggregate Output, Unemployment, and the Price Level

Newspapers and Internet sites periodically report data that provide information on the level of aggregate output, unemployment, and the price level. Here is a list of the relevant data series, their frequency, and when they are published.

Aggregate Output and Unemployment

Real GDP: Quarterly; published about two months after the end of a quarter.

Industrial production: Monthly. Industrial production is not as comprehensive a measure of aggregate output as real GDP because it measures only manufacturing output: the estimate for the previous month is reported after about two months.

Unemployment rate: Monthly; the estimate for a month is reported two months later.

Price Level

GDP deflator: Quarterly. This comprehensive measure of the price level (described in the Web Appendix to Chapter 1) is published at the same time as the real GDP data.

Consumer price index (CPI): Monthly. The CPI is a measure of the price level for consumers (also described in the Web Appendix to Chapter 1); the value for the previous month is published in the third or fourth week of the following month.

Producer price index (PPI): Monthly. The PPI is a measure of the average level of wholesale prices charged by producers and is published in the third or fourth week of the following month.

---

ries, and other inputs to production, plus planned spending on new homes; **government spending**, spending by all levels of government (federal, provincial, and local) on goods and services (paper clips, computers, computer programming, missiles, government workers, and so on); and **net exports**, the net foreign spending on domestic goods and services, equal to exports minus imports. Using the symbols C for consumer expenditure, I for planned investment spending, G for government spending, and NX for net exports, we can write the following expression for aggregate demand Y^{ad}:

$$Y^{ad} = C + I + G + NX \qquad (1)$$

Deriving the Aggregate Demand Curve

Examining the effects of changes in the price level on individual components of aggregate demand is one way to derive the aggregate demand curve. The aggregate demand curve is downward-sloping because a lower price level ($P\downarrow$), holding the nominal quantity of money (M) constant, leads to a larger quantity of money in real terms (in terms of the goods and services that it can buy, $M/P\uparrow$). The larger quantity of money in real terms ($M/P\uparrow$) that results from the lower price level causes interest rates to fall ($i\downarrow$), as suggested in Chapter 5. The resulting lower cost of financing purchases of new physical capital makes investment more profitable and stimulates planned investment spending ($I\uparrow$). Because, as shown in Equation 1, the increase in planned investment spending adds directly to aggregate demand ($Y^{ad}\uparrow$), the lower price level leads to a higher level of the quantity of aggregate output demanded ($P\downarrow \Rightarrow Y^{ad}\uparrow$), and so the aggregate demand curve slopes down as in Figure 24-1. Schematically, we can write the mechanism just described as follows:

$$P\downarrow \Rightarrow M/P\uparrow \Rightarrow i\downarrow \Rightarrow I\uparrow \Rightarrow Y^{ad}\uparrow$$

Another mechanism that generates a downward-sloping aggregate demand curve operates through international trade. Because a lower price level ($P\downarrow$) leads to a larger quantity of money in real terms ($M/P\uparrow$) and lower interest rates ($i\downarrow$), Canadian-dollar assets become less attractive relative to assets denominated in foreign currencies, thereby causing a fall in the value of dollar assets relative to other currency assets (a decline in the exchange rate, denoted by $E\downarrow$). The lower value of the dollar, which makes domestic goods cheaper relative to foreign goods, then causes net exports to rise ($NX\uparrow$), which in turn increases aggregate demand ($Y^{ad}\uparrow$):

$$P\downarrow \Rightarrow M/P\uparrow \Rightarrow i\downarrow \Rightarrow E\downarrow \Rightarrow NX\uparrow \Rightarrow Y^{ad}\uparrow$$

The fact that the aggregate demand curve is downward sloping can also be derived from the quantity theory of money analysis in Chapter 21. The equation of exchange, $MV = PY$, indicates that if velocity stays constant, a constant money supply (M) implies that nominal aggregate spending (PY) is also constant. When the price level falls ($P\downarrow$), aggregate demand must necessarily rise ($Y^{ad}\uparrow$) to keep aggregate spending at the same level.

Factors That Shift the Aggregate Demand Curve

The quantity theory analysis shows that an increase in the money supply ($M\uparrow$) shifts the demand curve to the right, because with velocity constant the higher money supply raises nominal aggregate spending ($PY\uparrow$) and hence at a given price level the quantity of aggregate demand increases ($Y^{ad}\uparrow$). An increase in the quantity of money increases the quantity of aggregate demand at each price level and shifts the aggregate demand curve to the right from AD_1 to AD_2 in Figure 24-1. A components approach to aggregate demand also indicates that changes in the money supply cause the aggregate demand curve to shift via the two mechanisms shown in the schematics above. For a given price level, a rise in the money supply causes the real money supply to increase ($M/P\uparrow$), which leads to a decline in interest rates ($i\downarrow$), an increase in investment and net exports (I, $NX\uparrow$), and an

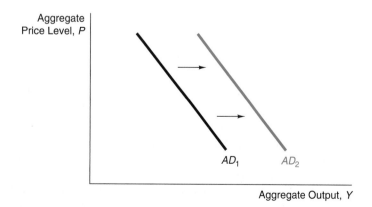

FIGURE 24-1   Aggregate Demand Curve

A decrease in taxes ($T\downarrow$) or an increase in the money supply ($M\uparrow$), government expenditure ($G\uparrow$), net exports ($NX\uparrow$), or business or consumer optimism ($C\uparrow$, $I\uparrow$) increases aggregate demand at each aggregate price level and shifts the aggregate demand curve from AD_1 to AD_2

increase in the quantity of aggregate demand ($Y^{ad}\uparrow$), shifting the aggregate demand curve to the right from AD_1 to AD_2.[2]

In contrast to the quantity theory, the components approach suggests that other factors (manipulation of government spending and taxes, changes in net exports, and changes in consumer and business spending) are also important causes of shifts in the aggregate demand curve. For instance, if the government spends more ($G\uparrow$) or net exports increase ($NX\uparrow$), the quantity of aggregate output demanded at each price level rises, and the aggregate demand curve shifts to the right. A decrease in government taxes ($T\downarrow$) leaves consumers with more income to spend, so consumer expenditure rises ($C\uparrow$). The quantity of aggregate output demanded at each price level also rises, and the aggregate demand curve shifts to the right. Finally, if consumer and business optimism increases, consumer expenditure and planned investment spending rise *($C\uparrow$, $I\uparrow$)*, again shifting the aggregate demand curve to the right. John Maynard Keynes described these waves of optimism and pessimism as "animal spirits" and considered them a major factor affecting the aggregate demand curve and an important source of business cycle fluctuations.

Summary

You have seen that both the quantity theory and components approaches to aggregate demand agree that the aggregate demand curve slopes downward and shifts in response to changes in the money supply. However, in the quantity theory approach there is only one important source of movements in the aggregate demand curve—changes in the money supply. The components approach suggests that other factors—fiscal policy, net exports, and "animal spirits"—are equally important sources of shifts in the aggregate demand curve. Our discussion of quantity theory and components approaches indicates that six factors can shift the aggregate demand curve: the money supply, government spending, net exports, taxes, consumer optimism, and business optimism—the last two ("animal spirits") affecting willingness to spend. The possible effect on the aggregate demand curve of these six factors (often referred to as **demand shocks**) is summarized in Table 24-1.

AGGREGATE SUPPLY

To complete our analysis we need to derive an **aggregate supply curve**, the relationship between the quantity of output supplied and the price level. In the typical supply and demand analysis, we have only one supply curve, but because prices and wages take time to adjust to their long-run level, the aggregate supply curve differs in the short and the long runs. First, we examine the long-run aggregate supply curve. We then derive the short-run aggregate supply curve and see how it shifts over time as the economy moves from the short run to the long run.

Long-Run Aggregate Supply Curve

The amount of output that can be produced in the economy in the long run is determined by the amount of capital in the economy, the amount of labour supplied at full employment, and the available technology. As discussed in Chapter 18, some unemployment cannot be helped because it is either frictional or structural. Thus full employment is not at zero, but is rather at a level above zero at which the demand for labour equals the supply of labour. This **natural rate of unemployment** is

---

[2] A complete demonstration of the components approach to the aggregate demand curve is given in Chapters 22 and 23.

TABLE 24-1 Factors That Shift the Aggregate Demand Curve

Factor	Change	Shift in the Aggregate Demand Curve
Money supply, M	↑	AD_1 → AD_2
Government spending, G	↑	AD_1 → AD_2
Taxes, T	↑	AD_2 ← AD_1
Net exports, NX	↑	AD_1 → AD_2
Consumer optimism, C	↑	AD_1 → AD_2
Business optimism, I	↑	AD_1 → AD_2

Note: Only increases (↑) in the factors are shown. The effect of decreases in the factors would be the opposite of those indicated in the "Shift" column. Note that the quantity theory approach views the money supply as an important cause of shifts in the aggregate demand curve.

where the economy gravitates to in the long run.[3] Many economists believe that the natural rate of unemployment is currently around 6%.

---

[3] A related concept is the **nonaccelerating inflation rate of unemployment (NAIRU)**, the rate of unemployment at which there is no tendency for inflation to change.

The level of aggregate output produced at the natural rate of unemployment is called the **natural rate of output**; it is where the economy settles in the long run for any price level. Hence the long-run aggregate supply curve (*LRAS*) is vertical at the natural rate of output, denoted by Y_n, as drawn in Figure 24-2.

Short-Run Aggregate Supply Curve

Because wages and prices take time to adjust to economic conditions, a process described by saying that wages and prices are *sticky*, the aggregate supply curve (AS_1) in the short run is upward-sloping, as depicted in Figure 24-3. To understand why the short-run aggregate supply curve is upward-sloping, we have to look at the factors that cause the quantity of output supplied to change. Because the goal of business is to maximize profits, the quantity of output supplied is determined by the profit made on each unit of output. If profit rises, more output will be produced, and the quantity of output supplied will increase; if it falls, less output will be produced, and the quantity of aggregate output supplied will fall.

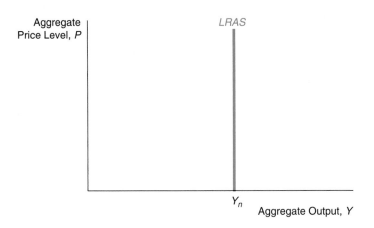

FIGURE 24-2 Long-Run Aggregate Supply Curve

The amount of aggregate output supplied at any given price level goes to the natural rate level of output in the long run, so that the long-run aggregate supply curve *LRAS* is a vertical line at Y_n.

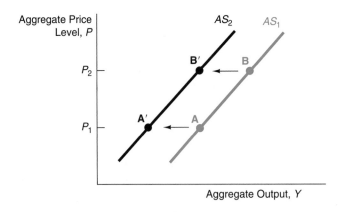

FIGURE 24-3 Aggregate Supply Curve in the Short Run

A rise in the costs of production shifts the short-run supply curve leftward from AS_1 to AS_2.

Profit on a unit of output equals the price for the unit minus the costs of producing it. In the short run, costs of many factors that go into producing goods and services are fixed; wages, for example, are often fixed for periods of time by labour contracts, and raw materials are often bought by firms under long-term contracts that fix the price. Because these costs of production are fixed in the short run, when the overall price level rises, the price for a unit of output will rise relative to the costs of producing it, and the profit per unit will rise. Because the higher price level results in higher profits in the short run, firms increase production, and the quantity of aggregate output supplied rises, resulting in an upward-sloping short-run aggregate supply curve.

Frequent mention of the *short run* in the preceding paragraph hints that the relationship between the price level and aggregate output embodied in the upward-sloping, short-run aggregate supply curve (AS_1 in Figure 24-3) may not remain fixed as time passes. To see what happens over time, we need to understand what makes the aggregate supply curve shift.

Shifts in the Short-Run Aggregate Supply Curve

We have seen that the profit on a unit of output determines the quantity of output supplied. If the cost of producing a unit of output rises, profit on a unit of output falls, and the quantity of output supplied at each price level falls. To learn what this implies for the position of the aggregate supply curve, let's consider what happens at a price level of P_1 when the costs of production increase. Now that firms are earning a lower profit per unit of output, they reduce production at that price level, and the quantity of aggregate output supplied falls from point A to point A′. Applying the same reasoning at point B indicates that the quantity of aggregate output supplied falls to point B′. What we see is that ***the short-run aggregate supply curve shifts to the left when costs of production increase and to the right when costs decrease.***

Factors That Shift the Short-Run Aggregate Supply Curve

The factors that cause the short-run aggregate supply curve to shift are the ones that affect the costs of production: (1) tightness of the labour market, (2) expectations of inflation, (3) workers' attempts to push up their real wages, and (4) changes in production costs that are unrelated to wages (such as energy costs). The first three factors shift the short-run aggregate supply curve by affecting wage costs: the fourth affects other costs of production.

TIGHTNESS OF THE LABOUR MARKET   If the economy is booming and the labour market is tight ($Y > Y_n$), employers may have difficulty hiring qualified workers and may even have a hard time keeping their present employees. Because the demand for labour now exceeds supply in this tight labour market, employers will raise wages to attract needed workers, and the costs of production will rise. The higher costs of production lower the profit per unit of output at each price level, and the short-run aggregate supply curve shifts to the left (see Figure 24-3).

By contrast, if the economy enters a recession and the labour market is slack ($Y < Y_n$), because the demand for labour is less than the supply, workers who cannot find jobs will be willing to work for lower wages. In addition, employed workers may be willing to make wage concessions to keep their jobs. Therefore, in a slack labour market in which the quantity of labour demanded is less than the quantity supplied, wages and hence costs of production will fall, the profit per unit of output will rise, and the short-run aggregate supply curve will shift to the right.

The effects of tightness of the labour market on the short-run aggregate supply curve can be summarized as follows: ***When aggregate output is above the*** *natural rate, the short-run aggregate supply curve shifts to the left; when aggregate output is below the natural rate, the short-run aggregate supply curve shifts to the right.*

EXPECTED PRICE LEVEL   Workers and firms care about wages in real terms—that is, in terms of the goods and services that wages can buy. When the price level increases, a worker earning the same nominal wage will be able to buy fewer goods and services: A worker who expects the price level to rise will thus demand a higher nominal wage to keep the real wage from falling. For example, if Chuck the Construction Worker expects prices to increase by 5%, he will want a wage increase of at least 5% (more, if he thinks he deserves an increase in real wages). Similarly, if Chuck's employer knows that the houses he is building will rise in value at the same rate as inflation (5%), his employer will be willing to pay Chuck 5% more. An increase in the expected price level leads to higher wages, which in turn raise the costs of production, lower the profit per unit of output at each price level, and shift the aggregate supply curve to the left (see Figure 24-3). Therefore, *a rise in the expected price level causes the aggregate supply curve to shift to the left; the greater the expected increase in price level (that is, the higher the expected inflation), the larger the shift.*

WAGE PUSH   Suppose that Chuck and his fellow construction workers decide to strike and succeed in obtaining higher real wages. This wage push will then raise the costs of production, and the aggregate supply curve will shift leftward. *A successful wage push by workers will cause the aggregate supply curve to shift to the left.*

CHANGES IN PRODUCTION COSTS UNRELATED TO WAGES   Changes in technology and in the supply of raw materials (called **supply shocks**) can also shift the aggregate supply curve. A negative supply shock, such as a reduction in the availability of raw materials (like oil), which raises their price, increases production costs and shifts the aggregate supply curve leftward. A positive supply shock, such as unusually good weather that leads to a bountiful harvest and lowers the cost of food, will reduce production costs and shift the aggregate supply curve rightward. Similarly, the development of a new technology that lowers production costs, perhaps by raising worker productivity, can be considered a positive supply shock that shifts the aggregate supply curve to the right.

The effect on the aggregate supply curve of changes in production costs unrelated to wages (referred to as **aggregate supply shocks**) can be summarized as follows: *A negative supply shock that raises production costs shifts the aggregate supply curve to the left; a positive supply shock that lowers production costs shifts the aggregate supply curve to the right.*[4] As a study aid, factors that shift the short-run aggregate supply curve are listed in Table 24-2.

---

[4] Developments in the foreign exchange market can also shift the aggregate supply curve by changing domestic production costs. As discussed in more detail in Chapter 19, an increase in the value of the dollar makes foreign goods cheaper in Canada. The decline in prices of foreign goods and hence foreign factors of production lowers Canadian production costs and thus raises the profit per unit of output at each price level in Canada. An increase in the value of the dollar therefore shifts the aggregate supply curve to the right. Conversely, a decline in the value of the dollar, which makes foreign factors of production more expensive, shifts the aggregate supply curve to the left.

TABLE 24-2 Factors That Shift the Short-Run Aggregate Supply Curve

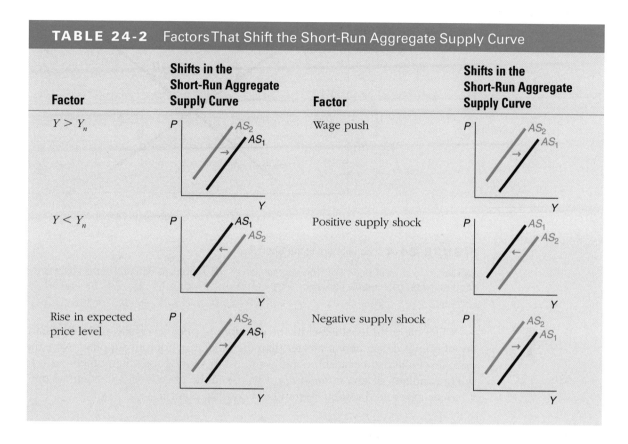

Factor	Shifts in the Short-Run Aggregate Supply Curve	Factor	Shifts in the Short-Run Aggregate Supply Curve
$Y > Y_n$		Wage push	
$Y < Y_n$		Positive supply shock	
Rise in expected price level		Negative supply shock	

EQUILIBRIUM IN AGGREGATE SUPPLY AND DEMAND ANALYSIS

The equilibrium level of aggregate output and the price level will occur at the point where the quantity of aggregate output demanded equals the quantity of aggregate output supplied. However, in the context of aggregate supply and demand analysis, there are two types of equilibrium: short-run and long-run.

Equilibrium in the Short Run

Figure 24-4 illustrates a short-run equilibrium in which the quantity of aggregate output demanded equals the quantity of output supplied, that is, where the aggregate demand curve *AD* and the short-run aggregate supply curve *AS* intersect at point E. The equilibrium level of aggregate output equals Y^*, and the equilibrium price level equals P^*.

As in our earlier supply and demand analyses, equilibrium is a useful concept only if there is a tendency for the economy to head toward it. We can see that the economy heads toward the equilibrium at point E by first looking at what happens when we are at a price level above the equilibrium price level P^*. If the price level is at P'', the quantity of aggregate output supplied at point D is greater than the quantity of aggregate output demanded at point A. Because people want to sell more goods and services than others want to buy (a condition of *excess supply*), the prices of goods and services will fall, and the aggregate price level will drop. This decline in the price level will continue until it has reached its equilibrium level of P^* at point E.

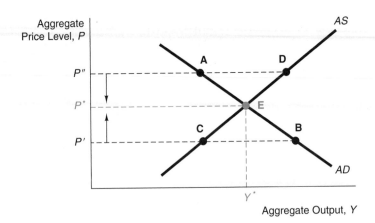

FIGURE 24-4   Equilibrium in the Short Run

Equilibrium occurs at point E at the intersection of the aggregate demand curve *AD* and the short-run aggregate supply curve *AS*.

When the price level is below the equilibrium price level, say at P', the quantity of output demanded is greater than the quantity of output supplied. Now the price level will rise because people want to buy more goods than others want to sell (a condition of *excess demand*). This rise in the price level will continue until it has again reached its equilibrium level of P^* at point E.

Equilibrium in the Long Run

Usually in supply and demand analysis, once we find the equilibrium at which the quantity demanded equals the quantity supplied, there is no need for additional discussion. In *aggregate* supply and demand analysis, however, that is not the case. Even when the quantity of aggregate output demanded equals the quantity supplied, forces operate that can cause the equilibrium to move over time. To understand why, we must remember that if costs of production change, the aggregate supply curve will shift.

As we saw earlier, the short-run aggregate supply curve will not remain stationary when aggregate output and unemployment differs from its natural rate: when $Y > Y_n$, labour markets are tight, production costs rise at any given price level, and the short-run aggregate supply curve shifts to the left; while when $Y < Y_n$, labour markets are slack, production costs fall at any given price level, and the aggregate supply curve shifts to the right. Only when aggregate output and unemployment are at their natural rates is there no pressure from the labour market for wages to rise or fall; under these conditions, there is no reason for the short-run aggregate supply to shift.

We look at how the short-run equilibrium changes over time in response to two situations: when equilibrium is initially below the natural rate level and when it is initially above the natural rate level.

In panel (a) of Figure 24-5, the initial equilibrium occurs at point 1, the intersection of the aggregate demand curve *AD* and the initial short-run aggregate supply curve AS_1. Because the level of equilibrium output Y_1 is greater than the natural rate level Y_n, unemployment is less than the natural rate, and excessive tightness exists in the labour market. This tightness drives wages up, raises production costs, and shifts the aggregate supply curve to AS_2. The equilibrium is now at point 2, and output falls to Y_2. Because aggregate output Y_2 is still above the natural rate

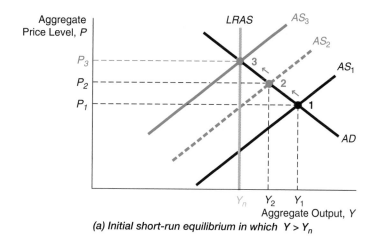

(a) Initial short-run equilibrium in which Y > Y_n

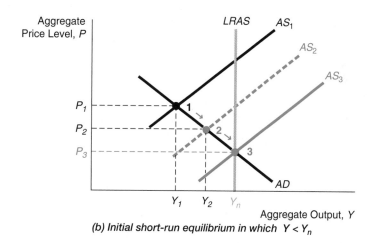

(b) Initial short-run equilibrium in which Y < Y_n

FIGURE 24-5   Adjustment to Long-Run Equilibrium in Aggregate Supply and Demand Analysis

In both panels, the initial equilibrium is at point 1 at the intersection of *AD* and *AS_1*. In panel (a), $Y_1 > Y_n$, so the short-run aggregate supply curve keeps shifting to the left until it reaches *AS_3*, where output has returned to Y_n. In panel (b), $Y_1 < Y_n$, so the short-run aggregate supply curve keeps shifting to the right until output is again returned to Y_n. Hence in both cases, the economy displays a self-correcting mechanism that returns it to the natural rate level of output.

level, Y_n, wages continue to be driven up, eventually shifting the aggregate supply curve to AS_3. The equilibrium reached at point 3 is on the vertical long-run aggregate supply curve (*LRAS*) at Y_n and is a long-run equilibrium. Because output is at the natural rate level, there is no further pressure on wages to rise and thus no further tendency for the aggregate supply curve to shift.

The movements in panel (a) indicate that the economy will not remain at a level of output higher than the natural rate level because the short-run aggregate supply curve will shift to the left, raise the price level, and cause the economy (equilibrium) to slide upward along the aggregate demand curve until it comes to rest at a point on the **long-run aggregate supply curve** at the natural rate level of output Y_n.

In panel (b), the initial equilibrium at point 1 is one at which output Y_1 is below the natural rate level. Because unemployment is higher than the natural rate, wages begin to fall, shifting the short-run aggregate supply curve rightward until it comes to rest at AS_3. The economy (equilibrium) slides downward along the aggregate demand curve until it reaches the long-run equilibrium point 3, the intersection of the aggregate demand curve AD and the long-run aggregate supply curve (*LRAS*) at Y_n. Here, as in panel (a), the economy comes to rest when output has again returned to the natural rate level.

A striking feature of both panels of Figure 24-5 is that regardless of where output is initially, it returns eventually to the natural rate level. This feature is described by saying that the economy has a **self-correcting mechanism**.

An important issue for policymakers is how rapidly this self-correcting mechanism works. Many economists believe that the self-correcting mechanism takes a long time, so the approach to long-run equilibrium is slow. This view is reflected in Keynes's often quoted remark, "In the long run, we are all dead." These economists view the self-correcting mechanism as slow because wages are inflexible, particularly in the downward direction when unemployment is high. The resulting slow wage and price adjustments mean that the aggregate supply curve does not move quickly to restore the economy to the natural rate of unemployment. Hence when unemployment is high, these economists, many of whom are followers of Keynes and are thus known as **Keynesians**, are more likely to see the need for active government policy to restore the economy to full employment.

Other economists believe that wages are sufficiently flexible that the wage and price adjustment process is reasonably rapid. As a result of this flexibility, adjustment of the aggregate supply curve to its long-run position and the economy's return to the natural rate levels of output and unemployment will occur quickly. Thus these economists see much less need for active government policy to restore the economy to the natural rate levels of output and unemployment when unemployment is high. Indeed, Milton Friedman and his followers, known as **monetarists**, advocate the use of a rule whereby the money supply or the monetary base grows at a constant rate so as to minimize fluctuations in aggregate demand that might lead to output fluctuations. We will return in Chapter 26 to the debate about whether government policy should react in a discretionary fashion to keep the economy near full employment.

Changes in the Equilibrium Caused by Aggregate Demand Shocks

With an understanding of the distinction between short-run and long-run equilibria, you are now ready to analyze what happens when an economy's aggregate demand curve shifts. Figure 24-6 depicts the effect of a rightward shift in the aggregate demand curve due to positive demand shocks: an increase in the money supply ($M\uparrow$), an increase in government spending ($G\uparrow$), an increase in net exports ($NX\uparrow$), a decrease in taxes ($T\downarrow$), or an increase in the willingness of consumers and businesses to spend because they become more optimistic ($C\uparrow$, $I\uparrow$). The figure has been drawn so that the economy initially is in long-run equilibrium at point 1, where the initial aggregate demand curve AD_1 intersects the short-run aggregate supply AS_1 curve at Y_n. When the aggregate demand curve shifts rightward to AD_2, the economy moves to point 1' and both output and the price level rise. However, the economy will not remain at point 1' in the long run because output at Y_1, is above the natural rate level. Wages will rise, increasing the costs of production at all price levels and the short-run aggregate supply curve will eventually shift leftward to AS_2, where it finally comes to rest. The economy (equilibrium) thus slides up the aggregate demand curve from point 1' to point 2, which is the point of long-run equilibrium at the intersection of AD_2 and the long-run aggregate supply curve (*LRAS*) at Y_n. ***Although the initial short-run effect***

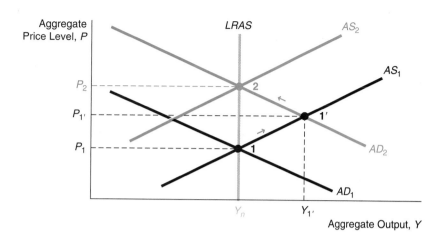

FIGURE 24-6   Response of Output and the Price Level to a Shift in the Aggregate Demand Curve

A shift in the aggregate demand curve from AD_1 to AD_2 moves the economy from point 1 to point 1'. Because $Y_{1'} > Y_n$, the short-run aggregate supply curve begins to shift leftward, eventually reaching AS_2, where output returns to Y_n and the price level has risen to P_2.

of the rightward shift in the aggregate demand curve is a rise in both the price level and output, the ultimate long-run effect is only a rise in the price level.

Changes in the Equilibrium Caused by Aggregate Supply Shocks

Our understanding of the distinction between short-run and long-run equilibria allows us to analyze what happens when there are aggregate supply shocks that shift the short-run aggregate supply curve. Suppose that the economy is initially at the natural rate level of output at point 1 when the short-run aggregate supply curve shifts from AS_1 to AS_2 in Figure 24-7, because of a negative supply shock (a sharp rise in energy prices, for example). The economy will move from point 1 to point 2, where the price level rises but aggregate output *falls*. A situation of a rising price level but a falling level of aggregate output, as pictured in Figure 24-7, has been labelled *stagflation* (a combination of the words *stagnation* and *inflation*). At point 2, output is below the natural rate level, so wages fall and shift the short-run aggregate supply curve back to where it was initially at AS_1. The result is that the economy slides down the aggregate demand curve AD_1 (assuming that the aggregate demand curve remains in the same position), and the economy returns to the long-run equilibrium at point 1. *Although a leftward shift in the short-run aggregate supply curve initially raises the price level and lowers output, the ultimate effect is that output and price level are unchanged (holding the aggregate demand curve constant).*

Shifts in the Long-Run Aggregate Supply Curve: Real Business Cycle Theory and Hysteresis

To this point we have assumed that the natural rate level of output Y_n and hence the long-run aggregate supply curve are given. However, over time, the natural rate level of output increases as a result of economic growth. If the productive capacity of the economy is growing at a steady rate of 3% per year, for example, this means that every year Y_n will grow by 3% and the long-run aggregate supply curve at Y_n will shift to the right by 3%. To simplify the analysis when Y_n grows at a steady rate, Y_n and the long-run aggregate supply curve are drawn as fixed in the aggregate demand and supply diagrams. Keep in mind, however, that the level of aggregate output pictured in

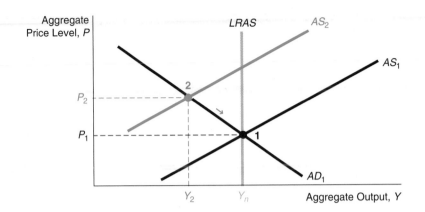

FIGURE 24-7   Response of Output and the Price Level to a Shift in Short-Run
Aggregate Supply

A shift in the short-run aggregate supply curve from AS_1 to AS_2 moves the economy from point 1
to point 2. Because $Y_2 < Y_n$, the short-run aggregate supply curve begins to shift back to the
right, eventually returning to AS_1, where the economy is again at point 1.

these diagrams is actually best thought of as the level of aggregate output relative to
its normal rate of growth (trend).

The usual assumption when conducting aggregate demand and supply analysis
is that shifts in either the aggregate demand or aggregate supply curve have no effect
on the natural rate level of output (which grows at a steady rate). Movements of
aggregate output around the Y_n level in the diagram then describe short-run (business cycle) fluctuations in aggregate output. However, some economists take issue
with the assumption that Y_n is unaffected by aggregate demand and supply shocks.

One group, led by Edward Prescott of the University of Minnesota, has developed a theory of aggregate economic fluctuations called **real business cycle
theory** in which aggregate supply (real) shocks do affect the natural rate level of
output Y_n. This theory views shocks to tastes (workers' willingness to work, for
example) and technology (productivity) as the major driving forces behind short-
run fluctuations in the business cycle because these shocks lead to substantial
short-run fluctuations in Y_n. Shifts in the aggregate demand curve, say as a result
of changes in monetary policy, by contrast, are not viewed as being particularly
important to aggregate output fluctuations. Because real business cycle theory
views most business cycle fluctuations as resulting from fluctuations in the natural rate level of output, it does not see much need for government intervention
to eliminate high unemployment. Real business cycle theory is highly controversial and is the subject of intensive research.[5]

Another group of economists disagrees with the assumption that the natural
rate level of output Y_n is always at the full employment level and is unaffected by
aggregate demand shocks. These economists contend that the natural rate level
of unemployment and output are subject to **hysteresis**, a departure from full
employment levels as a result of past high unemployment.[6] When unemployment

---

[5] See Charles Plosser, "Understanding Real Business Cycles," *Journal of Economic Perspectives* (1989):
51–77, for a nontechnical discussion of real business cycle theory.

[6] For a further discussion of hysteresis, see Olivier Blanchard and Lawrence Summers, "Hysteresis in
the European Unemployment Problem," *NBER Macroeconomics Annual*, 1986, 1, ed. Stanley Fischer
(Cambridge, Mass.: M.I.T. Press, 1986), pp. 15–78.

rises because of a reduction of aggregate demand that shifts the *AD* curve inward, the natural rate of unemployment is viewed as rising above the full employment level. This could occur because the unemployed become discouraged and fail to look hard for work or because employers may be reluctant to hire workers who have been unemployed for a long time, seeing it as a signal that the worker is undesirable. The outcome is that the natural rate of unemployment shifts upward after unemployment has become high, and Y_n falls below the full employment level. In this situation, the self-correcting mechanism will be able to return the economy only to the natural rate levels of output and unemployment, not to the full employment level. Only with expansionary policy to shift the aggregate demand curve to the right and raise aggregate output can the natural rate of unemployment be lowered (Y_n raised) to the full employment level. Proponents of hysteresis are thus more likely to promote governmemnt intervention and expansionary policies to restore the economy to full employment.

Conclusions

Aggregate demand and supply analysis yields the following conclusions (under the usual assumption that the natural rate level of output is unaffected by aggregate demand and supply shocks):

1. A shift in the aggregate demand curve—which can be caused by changes in monetary policy (the money supply), fiscal policy (government spending or taxes), international trade (net exports), or "animal spirits" (business and consumer optimism)—affects output only in the short run and has no effect in the long run. Furthermore, the initial change in the price level is less than is achieved in the long run, when the aggregate supply curve has fully adjusted.

2. A shift in the aggregate supply curve—which can be caused by changes in expected inflation, workers' attempts to push up real wages, or a supply shock—affects output and prices only in the short run and has no effect in the long run (holding the aggregate demand curve constant).

3. The economy has a self-correcting mechanism, which will return it to the natural rate levels of unemployment and aggregate output over time.

APPLICATION **Explaining Past Business Cycle Episodes**

Aggregate supply and demand analysis is an extremely useful tool for analyzing aggregate economic activity; we will apply it to several business cycle episodes. To simplify our analysis, we always assume that aggregate output is initially at the natural rate level.

The United States During the Vietnam War Buildup, 1964–1970

America's involvement in Vietnam began to escalate in the early 1960s, and after 1964, the United States was fighting a full-scale war. Beginning in 1965, the resulting increases in military expenditure raised government spending, while at the same time the Federal Reserve increased the rate of money growth in an attempt to keep interest rates from rising. What does aggregate supply and demand analysis suggest should have happened to aggregate output and the price level in the United States as a result of the Vietnam War buildup?

The rise in government spending and the higher rate of money growth would shift the aggregate demand curve to the right (shown in Figure 24-6 on page 631).

As a result, aggregate output would rise, unemployment would fall, and the price level would rise. Table 24-3 demonstrates that this is exactly what happened. The unemployment rate fell steadily from 1964 to 1969, remaining well below what economists now think was the natural rate of unemployment during that period (around 5%), and inflation began to rise. As Figure 24-6 predicts, unemployment would eventually begin to return to the natural rate level because of the economy's self-correcting mechanism. This is exactly what we saw occurring in 1970, when the inflation rate rose even higher and unemployment increased.

TABLE 24-3   Unemployment and Inflation in the United States During the Vietnam War Buildup, 1964–1970

Year	Unemployment Rate (%)	Inflation (Year to Year) (%)
1964	5.0	1.3
1965	4.4	1.6
1966	3.7	2.9
1967	3.7	3.1
1968	3.5	4.2
1969	3.4	5.5
1970	4.8	5.7

Source: Economic Report of the President.

Negative Supply Shocks in Canada, 1973–1975 and 1978–1980

In 1973, the Canadian and world economies were hit by a series of negative supply shocks. As a result of the oil embargo stemming from the Arab–Israeli war of 1973, the Organization of the Petroleum Exporting Countries (OPEC) was able to engineer a quadrupling of oil prices by restricting oil production. In addition, a series of crop failures throughout the world led to a sharp increase in food prices. These events caused the aggregate supply curve in Canada to shift sharply leftward, and as the aggregate demand and supply diagram in Figure 24-7 (page 632) predicts, both the price level and unemployment began to rise dramatically (see Table 24-4).

TABLE 24-4   Unemployment and Inflation in Canada During the Negative Supply Shock Periods, 1973–1975 and 1978–1980

Year	Unemployment Rate (%)	Inflation (Year to Year) (%)	Year	Unemployment Rate (%)	Inflation (Year to Year) (%)
1973	5.6	9.4	1978	8.3	6.5
1974	5.3	14.6	1979	7.4	9.5
1975	6.9	10.3	1980	7.5	10.9

Source: Statistics Canada, CANSIM Series D44950 and D15612.

The 1978–1980 period was almost an exact replay of the 1973–1975 period. By 1978, the economy had just about fully recovered from the 1973–1974 supply shocks when poor harvests and a doubling of oil prices (as a result of the overthrow of the shah of Iran) again led to another sharp leftward shift of the aggregate supply curve. The pattern predicted by Figure 24-7 played itself out again—inflation and unemployment both shot upward (see Table 24-4).

The Perfect Storm of 2007–2008: Negative Supply Shocks in Canada and the Financial Crisis

Higher demand for oil from rapidly growing developing countries like China and India and the slowing of production in places like Mexico, Russia, and Nigeria drove up oil prices sharply from around the US$60 per barrel level at the beginning of 2007. By the end of the year, oil prices had risen to US$100 per barrel and reached a peak of over US$140 in July of 2008. The run up of oil prices along with other commodity prices caused the aggregate supply curve to shift sharply leftward. As the aggregate demand and supply diagram in Figure 24-7 indicates, the result was a rise in both unemployment and inflation.

If this supply shock were not bad enough, the subprime financial crisis hit the economy in August of 2007, and reached a more virulent phase in the fall of 2008. As discussed in Chapter 9, the financial crisis caused a contraction in both household and business spending, leading to a drop in aggregate demand and a shift of the aggregate demand curve to the left, the exact opposite of the situation depicted in Figure 24-6. Aggregate demand and supply analysis indicates that this would lead to a rise in unemployment, with some weakening of inflationary pressure. As our aggregate demand and supply analysis predicts, and as Table 24-5 shows, the result of this perfect storm of negative shocks was a rise in unemployment from the 6% level in the third quarter of 2007 to 6.1% in the third quarter of 2008 and to 8.4% in the second quarter of 2009. Also, as the aggregate demand and supply analysis predicts, inflation accelerated from 2.6% in the third quarter of 2007 to 5.8% in the third quarter of 2008, but with the increase in the unemployment rate and the decline of oil and other commodity prices by the fall of 2008, inflation began to fall back down again to 0.1% in the second quarter of 2009.

TABLE 24-5   Unemployment and Inflation During the Perfect Storm of 2007–2008

Year	Unemployment Rate (%)	Inflation Rate, Based on the Chain Price Index for GDP (%)
2007, Q3	6.0	2.6
2008, Q3	6.1	5.8
2009, Q2	8.4	0.1

Source: Bank of Canada's website.

SUMMARY

1. The aggregate demand curve indicates the quantity of aggregate output demanded at each price level, and it is downward-sloping. The primary source of shifts in the aggregate demand curve are changes in the money supply, fiscal policy (government spending and taxes), net exports, and the willingness of consumers and businesses to spend ("animal spirits").

2. The long-run aggregate supply curve is vertical at the natural rate level of output. The short-run aggregate supply curve slopes upward, because a rise in the price level raises the profit earned on each unit of production, and the quantity of output supplied rises. Four factors can cause the aggregate supply curve to shift: tightness of the labour market as represented by unem-

ployment relative to the natural rate, expectations of inflation, workers' attempts to push up their real wages, and supply shocks unrelated to wages that affect production costs.

3. Equilibrium in the short run occurs at the point where the aggregate demand curve intersects the short-run aggregate supply curve. Although this is where the economy heads temporarily, it has a self-correcting mechanism, which leads it to settle permanently at the long-run equilibrium where aggregate output is at its natural rate level. Shifts in either the aggregate demand or the short-run aggregate supply curve can produce changes in aggregate output and the price level.

KEY TERMS

aggregate demand, p. 619

aggregate supply, p. 619

aggregate supply curve, p. 622

aggregate supply shock, p. 626

consumer expenditure, p. 619

demand shocks, p. 622

government spending, p. 620

hysteresis, p. 632

Keynesian, p. 630

long-run aggregate supply curve, p. 629

monetarist, p. 630

natural rate of output, p. 624

natural rate of unemployment, p. 622

net exports, p. 620

nonaccelerating inflation rate of unemployment (NAIRU), p. 623

planned investment spending, p. 619

real business cycle theory, p. 632

self-correcting mechanism, p. 630

supply shock, p. 626

QUESTIONS

You will find the answers to the questions marked with an asterisk in the Textbook Resources section of your MyEconLab.

1. If exports fall while imports rise, what happens to the aggregate demand curve?

*2. If government expenditure goes down while taxes are raised to balance the budget, what happens to the aggregate demand curve?

3. Suppose that government spending is raised at the same time that the money supply is lowered. What will happen to the position of the aggregate demand curve?

*4. Why does the aggregate demand curve shift when "animal spirits" change?

5. If the dollar increases in value relative to foreign currencies so that foreign goods become cheaper in Canada, what will happen to the position of the short-run aggregate supply curve? The aggregate demand curve?

*6. "Profit-maximizing behaviour on the part of firms explains why the short-run aggregate supply curve is upward-sloping." Is this statement true, false, or uncertain? Explain your answer.

7. If huge budget deficits cause the public to think that there will be higher inflation in the future, what is likely to happen to the short-run aggregate supply curve when budget deficits rise?

*8. If a pill were invented that made workers twice as productive but their wages did not change, what would happen to the position of the short-run aggregate supply curve?

9. When aggregate output is below the natural rate level, what will happen to the price level over time if the aggregate demand curve remains unchanged? Why?

*10. Show how aggregate supply and demand analysis can explain why both aggregate output and the price level fell sharply when investment spending collapsed during the Great Depression.

11. "An important difference between Keynesians and monetarists rests on how long they think the long run actually is." Is this statement true, false, or uncertain? Explain your answer.

Predicting the Future

*12. Predict what will happen to aggregate output and the price level if the Bank of Canada increases the money supply at the same time that the government implements an income tax cut.

13. Suppose that the public believes that a newly announced anti-inflation program will work and so lowers its expectations of future inflation. What will happen to aggregate output and the price level in the short run?

*14. Predict the effect of an increase in the goods and services tax (GST) on both the aggregate supply and demand curves and on aggregate output and the price level.

15. When there is a decline in the value of the dollar, some experts expect this to lead to a dramatic improvement in the ability of Canadian firms to compete abroad. Predict what would happen to output and the price level in Canada as a result.

QUANTITATIVE PROBLEMS

1. Consider the following *ISLM* model.

$$Y = \alpha \times (\bar{A} - bi)$$

$$i = \frac{1}{b} \times \left(k \times Y - \frac{\overline{M}}{P} \right)$$

where

$$\alpha = \frac{1}{1 - (1 - t) \times mpc}$$

$\bar{A}$ is autonomous expenditure, b is the interest elasticity of investment expenditure, k is the income elasticity of money demand, b is the interest elasticity of money demand, t is the tax rate, and mpc is the marginal propensity to consume.
   a. Derive the equation for aggregate demand.
   b. Is the aggregate demand curve upward or downward sloping?

*2. Continuing from the above problem,
   a. How does an increase in $\overline{M}/\overline{P}$ shift the aggregate demand curve?
   b. How do increases in $\bar{G}$ and declines in transfers shift the aggregate demand curve?

WEB EXERCISES

1. As this book goes to press, the Canadian economy was in a recession with an increasing unemployment rate. Go to **www.bankofcanada.ca** and follow the link to employment statistics. What has happened to the unemployment rate since the last reported figure in Table 24-5?

2. As the CPI inflation rate in Canada fell close to 1% at the beginning of 2009, Bank of Canada policymakers were beginning to be concerned about deflation. Go to **www.bankofcanada.ca**, and follow the link to the inflation statistics.
   a. What has happened to the inflation rate since then?
   b. Does deflation still appear to be a threat?

 Be sure to visit the MyEconLab website at **www.myeconlab.com**. This online homework and tutorial system puts you in control of your own learning with study and practice tools directly correlated to this chapter content.

CHAPTER 25

Transmission Mechanisms of Monetary Policy: The Evidence

LEARNING OBJECTIVES

After studying this chapter you should be able to

1. express the different types of empirical evidence
2. distinguish between *structural model evidence* and *reduced-form evidence*
3. identify the early Keynesian and monetarist evidence regarding the role of money in the economy
4. outline the transmission mechanisms of monetary policy (the interest-rate and exchange-rate channels, Tobin's q theory, and the credit view channels)

PREVIEW

Since 1980, the Canadian economy has been on a roller coaster, with output, unemployment, and inflation undergoing drastic fluctuations. At the start of the 1980s, inflation was running at double-digit levels, and the recession of 1980 was followed by one of the shortest economic expansions on record. After a year, the economy plunged into the 1981–1982 recession, the most severe economic contraction in the postwar era—the unemployment rate climbed to over 10%, and only then did the inflation rate begin to come down to around the 5% level by early 1984.

For several years following 1984, the Canadian economy enjoyed robust growth, with the inflation rate falling to around 3% and the unemployment rate to around 8% by early 1990. With the Iraqi invasion of Kuwait in the summer of 1990 and the collapse in consumer confidence in the United States, the Canadian economy again plunged into recession. The recovery that began in 1992 was initially weak, not only by historical standards but also by comparison with the robust recovery of the U.S. economy. However, subsequent growth in the Canadian economy sped up, lowering the unemployment rate to less than 7% in 2005, although it jumped again to over 8% in early 2009 in the aftermath of the subprime financial crisis. In light of large fluctuations in aggregate output (reflected in the unemployment rate) and inflation, and the economic instability that accompanies them, policymakers face the following dilemma: what policy or policies, if any, should be implemented to reduce fluctuations in output and inflation in the future?

To answer this question, monetary policymakers must have an accurate assessment of the timing and effect of their policies on the economy. To make this assessment, they need to understand the mechanisms through which monetary policy affects the economy. In this chapter we examine empirical evidence on the effect of monetary policy on economic activity. We first look at a framework for evaluating empirical evidence and then use this framework to understand why there are still deep disagreements on the importance of monetary policy to the economy. We then go on to examine the transmission mechanisms of monetary policy and evaluate the empirical evidence on them to better understand the role that monetary policy plays in the economy. We will see that these monetary transmission mechanisms emphasize the link between the financial system (which we studied in the first three parts of this book) and monetary theory, the subject of this part.

FRAMEWORK FOR EVALUATING EMPIRICAL EVIDENCE

To develop a framework for understanding how to evaluate empirical evidence, we need to recognize that there are two basic types of empirical evidence in economics and other scientific disciplines. **Structural model evidence** examines whether one variable affects another by using data to build a model that explains the channels through which this variable affects the other; **reduced-form evidence** examines whether one variable has an effect on another simply by looking directly at the relationship between the two variables.

Suppose that you were interested in whether drinking coffee leads to heart disease. Structural model evidence would involve developing a model that analyzed data on how coffee is metabolized by the human body, how it affects the operation of the heart, and how its effects on the heart lead to heart attacks. Reduced-form evidence would involve looking directly at whether coffee drinkers tend to experience heart attacks more frequently than non–coffee drinkers.

How you look at evidence—whether you focus on structural model evidence or reduced-form evidence—can lead to different conclusions. This is particularly true for the debate on the importance of monetary policy to economic fluctuations.

Structural Model Evidence

The components analysis of aggregate demand discussed in Chapter 24 is specific about the channels through which the money supply affects economic activity (called the **transmission mechanisms of monetary policy**). This approach typically examines the effect of changes in the money supply on economic activity by building a **structural model**, a description of how the economy operates using a collection of equations that describe the behaviour of firms and consumers in many sectors of the economy. These equations then show the channels through which monetary and fiscal policy affect aggregate output and spending. A structural model might have behavioural equations that describe the workings of monetary policy with the following schematic diagram:

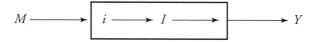

$$M \longrightarrow \boxed{i \longrightarrow I \longrightarrow} \longrightarrow Y$$

The model describes the transmission mechanism of monetary policy as follows: the change in the money supply M affects interest rates i, which in turn affect investment spending I, which in turn affects aggregate output or aggregate spending Y. Structural model evidence on the relationship between M and Y looks at empirical evidence on the specific channels of monetary influence, such as the link between interest rates and investment spending.

Reduced-Form Evidence

The quantity theory approach to aggregate demand does not describe specific ways in which the money supply affects aggregate spending. Instead, it suggests that the effect of money on economic activity should be examined by looking at whether movements in Y are tightly linked to (have a high correlation with) movements in M. Reduced-form evidence analyzes the effect of changes in M on Y as if the economy were a black box whose workings cannot be seen. The reduced-form way of looking at the evidence can be represented by the following schematic diagram, in which the economy is drawn as a black box with a question mark:

Advantages and Disadvantages of Structural Model Evidence

The structural model approach has the advantage of giving us an understanding of how the economy works. If the structure is correct—if it contains all the transmission mechanisms and channels through which monetary policy can affect economic activity—the structural model approach has three major advantages over the reduced-form approach.

1. Because we can evaluate each transmission mechanism separately to see whether it is plausible, we can gather more evidence on whether monetary policy has an important effect on economic activity. If we find that monetary policy significantly affects economic activity, for example, we will have more confidence that changes in monetary policy actually cause the changes in economic activity; that is, we will have more confidence in the direction of causation between M and Y.

2. Knowing how changes in monetary policy affect economic activity may help us predict the effect of changes in M on Y more accurately. For example, expansions in the money supply might be found to be less effective when interest rates are low. Then, when interest rates are higher, we would be able to predict that an expansion in the money supply would have a larger impact on Y than would otherwise be the case.

3. By knowing how the economy operates, we may be able to predict how institutional changes in the economy might affect the link between changes in M and Y. Because of the rapid pace of financial innovation, the advantage of being able to predict how institutional changes affect the link between changes in M and Y may be more important now than in the past.

These three advantages of the structural model approach suggest that it is better than the reduced-form approach *if we know the correct structure of the model.* Put another way, structural model evidence is only as good as the structural model it is based on; it is best only if all the transmission mechanisms are fully understood. This is a big *if*, as failing to include one or two relevant transmission mechanisms for monetary policy in the structural model might result in a serious misjudgement about the impact of changes in M on Y.

However, structural models may ignore the transmission mechanisms for monetary policy that are most important. For example, if the most important monetary transmission mechanisms involve consumer spending rather than investment spending, the structural model (such as the $M\uparrow \Rightarrow i\downarrow \Rightarrow I\uparrow \Rightarrow Y\uparrow$ one we used earlier), which focuses on investment spending for its monetary transmission mechanism, may underestimate the importance of an increase in the money supply to economic activity.

Advantages and Disadvantages of Reduced-Form Evidence

The main advantage of reduced-form evidence over structural model evidence is that no restrictions are imposed on the way monetary policy affects the economy. If we are not sure that we know what all the monetary transmission mechanisms are, we may be more likely to spot the full effect of changes in M on Y by looking at whether movements in Y correlate highly with movements in M.

The most notable objection to reduced-form evidence is that it may misleadingly suggest that changes in M cause changes in Y when that is not the case. A basic principle applicable to all scientific disciplines, including economics, states that ***correlation does not necessarily imply causation***. The fact that the movement of one variable is linked to another doesn't necessarily mean that movement in one variable *causes* movement in the other.

Suppose, for example, you notice that wherever criminal activity abounds, more police patrol the street. Should you conclude from this evidence that police patrols cause criminal activity and recommend pulling police off the street to lower the crime rate? The answer is clearly no, because police patrols do not cause criminal activity; criminal activity causes police patrols. This situation is called **reverse causation** and can lead to misleading conclusions when interpreting correlations (see the FYI box, Perils of Reverse Causation: A Russian Folk Tale).

The reverse causation problem may be present when examining the link between changes in money and aggregate output or spending. Our discussion of the conduct of monetary policy in Chapter 18 suggested that when the Bank of Canada has an interest-rate target, higher output might lead to a higher money supply. If most of the correlation between M and Y occurs because of the Bank's interest-rate target, controlling the money supply will not help control aggregate output because it is actually changes in Y that are causing changes in M, rather than the other way around.

Another facet of the correlation–causation question is that an outside factor, yet unknown, could be the driving force behind two variables that move together. Coffee drinking might be associated with heart disease not because coffee drinking causes heart attacks but because coffee drinkers tend to be people who are under a lot of stress and the stress causes heart attacks. Getting people to stop drinking coffee, then, would not lower the incidence of heart disease. Similarly, if there is an unknown outside factor that causes M and Y to move together, controlling M will not improve control of Y.

Conclusions

No clear-cut case can be made that reduced-form evidence is preferable to structural model evidence or vice versa. The structural model approach offers an understanding of how the economy works. If the structure is correct, it predicts the effect of monetary policy more accurately, allows predictions of the effect of monetary

---

FYI   **Perils of Reverse Causation: A Russian Folk Tale**

A Russian folk tale illustrates the problems that can arise from reverse causation. As the story goes, there once was a severe epidemic in the Russian countryside and many doctors were sent to the towns where the epidemic was at its worst. The peasants in the towns noticed that wherever doctors went, many people were dying. So to reduce the death rate, they killed all the doctors.

Were the peasants better off? Clearly not.

policy when institutions change, and provides more confidence in the direction of causation between M and Y. If the structure of the model is not correctly specified because it leaves out important transmission mechanisms of monetary policy, it could be very misleading.

The reduced-form approach does not restrict the way monetary policy affects the economy and may be more likely to spot the full effect of changes in M on Y. However, reduced-form evidence cannot rule out reverse causation, whereby changes in output cause changes in money, or the possibility that an outside factor drives changes in both output and money. A high correlation of money and output might then be misleading because controlling the money supply would not help control the level of output.

Armed with the framework to evaluate empirical evidence we have outlined here, we can now use it to evaluate the empirical debate on the importance of monetary policy to economic fluctuations.

APPLICATION	The Debate on the Importance of Monetary Policy to Economic Fluctuations

We can apply our understanding of the advantages and disadvantages of structural model versus reduced-form evidence to a debate that has been ongoing for over seventy years: how important is monetary policy to economic fluctuations? The followers of Milton Friedman, known as monetarists, tended to focus on reduced-form evidence and found that changes in the money supply are very important to economic fluctuations. Early followers of John Maynard Keynes, known as Keynesians, focused on structural model evidence based on the components approach to determination of aggregate demand, which was less likely to find that monetary policy is important. We evaluate the evidence that monetarists and Keynesians brought to bear on the importance of monetary policy using the analysis we developed in the previous section.

Early Keynesian Evidence on the Importance of Money

Although Keynes proposed his theory for analyzing aggregate economic activity in 1936, his views reached their peak of popularity among economists in the 1950s and early 1960s, when the majority of economists had accepted his framework. Although most Keynesians currently believe that monetary policy has important effects on economic activity, the early Keynesians of the 1950s and early 1960s characteristically held the view that *monetary policy does not matter at all* to movements in aggregate output and hence to the business cycle.

Their belief in the ineffectiveness of monetary policy stemmed from three pieces of structural model evidence:

1. During the Great Depression, interest rates on Canadian and U.S. government securities fell to extremely low levels. Early Keynesians believed monetary policy affected aggregate demand solely through its effect on nominal interest rates, which in turn affected investment spending; they believed that low interest rates during the Depression indicated that monetary policy was easy because it encouraged investment spending and so could not have played a contractionary role during this period. Since monetary policy was not capable of explaining why the worst economic contraction in history had taken place,

early Keynesians concluded that changes in the money supply have no effect on aggregate output—in other words, that money doesn't matter.

2. Early empirical studies found no linkage between movements in nominal interest rates and investment spending. Because early Keynesians saw this link as the channel through which changes in the money supply affect aggregate demand, finding that the link was weak also led them to the conclusion that changes in the money supply have no effect on aggregate output.

3. Surveys of businesspeople revealed that their decisions on how much to invest in new physical capital were not influenced by market interest rates. This evidence further confirmed that the link between interest rates and investment spending was weak, strengthening the conclusion that money doesn't matter. The result of this interpretation of the evidence was that most economists paid only scant attention to monetary policy before the mid-1960s.

Objections to Early Keynesian Evidence

While Keynesian economics was reaching its ascendancy in the 1950s and 1960s, a small group of economists at the University of Chicago, led by Milton Friedman, adopted what was then the unfashionable view that money *does* matter to aggregate demand. Friedman and his disciples, who later became known as monetarists, objected to the early Keynesian interpretation of the evidence on the grounds that the structural model used by the early Keynesians was severely flawed. Because structural model evidence is only as good as the model it is based on, the monetarist critique of this evidence needs to be taken seriously.

In 1963, Friedman and Anna Schwartz, a researcher at the National Bureau of Economic Research, published their classic monetary history of the United States, which showed that contrary to the early Keynesian beliefs, monetary policy during the Great Depression was not easy; indeed, it had never been more contractionary.[1] Friedman and Schwartz documented the massive bank failures of this period and the resulting decline in the money supply—the largest ever experienced in the United States. Hence monetary policy could explain the worst economic contraction in U.S. history, and the Great Depression could not be singled out as a period that demonstrates the ineffectiveness of monetary policy.

A Keynesian could still counter Friedman and Schwartz's argument that money was contractionary during the Great Depression by citing the low level of interest rates. But were these interest rates really so low? Although interest rates on government securities and high-grade corporate bonds were low during the Great Depression, interest rates on lower-grade bonds rose to unprecedented high levels during the sharpest part of the contraction phase (1930–1933). By the standard of these lower-grade bonds, then, interest rates were high and monetary policy was tight.

There is a moral to this story. Although much aggregatge economic analysis proceeds as though there is only *one* interest rate, we must always be aware that there are *many* interest rates, which may tell different stories. During normal times, most interest rates move in tandem, so lumping them all together and looking at one representative interest rate may not be too misleading. But that is not always so. Unusual periods (like the Great Depression) when interest rates on different securities begin to diverge, do occur. This is exactly the kind of situation in which a structural model (like the early Keynesians') that looks at only the interest rates on a low-risk security such as a Canadian government treasury bill or bond can be very misleading.

---

[1] Milton Friedman and Anna Jacobson Schwartz, *A Monetary History of the United States, 1867–1960* (Princeton, N.J.: Princeton University Press, 1963).

There is a second, potentially more important reason why the early Keynesian structural model's focus on nominal interest rates provides a misleading picture of the tightness of monetary policy during the Great Depression. In a period of deflation, when there is a declining price level, low *nominal* interest rates do not necessarily indicate that the cost of borrowing is low and that monetary policy is easy—in fact, the cost of borrowing could be quite high. If, for example, the public expects the price level to decline at a 10% rate, then even though nominal interest rates are at zero, the real cost of borrowing would be as high as 10%. (Recall from Chapter 4 that the real rate equals the nominal rate, 0, minus the expected rate of inflation, −10%, so the real rate equals $0 - (-10\%) = 10\%$.)

You can see in Figure 25-1 that this is exactly what happened during the Great Depression in the United States. Real interest rates on U.S. treasury bills were far higher during the 1931–1933 contraction phase of the Depression than was the case throughout the next 40 years.[2] As a result, movements of *real* interest rates

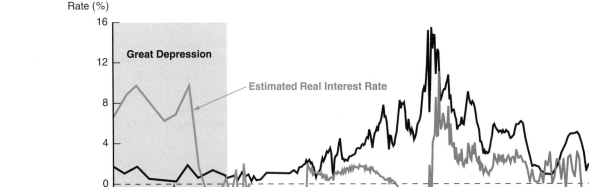

FIGURE 25-1   Real and Nominal Interest Rates on Three-Month Treasury Bills, 1931–2008

Sources: Nominal rates from **www.federalreserve.gov/releases/h15/update/**. The real rate is constructed using the procedure outlined in Frederic S. Mishkin, "The Real Interest Rate: An Empirical Investigation," *Carnegie-Rochester Conference Series on Public Policy* 15 (1981): 151–200. This involves estimating expected inflation as a function of past interest rates, inflation, and time trends and then subtracting the expected inflation measure from the nominal interest rate.

---

[2] In the 1980s, real interest rates rose to exceedingly high levels, approaching those of the Great Depression period. Research has tried to explain this phenomenon, some of which points to monetary policy as the source of high real rates in the 1980s. For example, see Olivier J. Blanchard and Lawrence H. Summers, "Perspectives on High World Interest Rates," *Brookings Papers on Economic Activity* 2 (1984): 273–324; and John Huizinga and Frederic S. Mishkin, "Monetary Policy Regime Shifts and the Unusual Behavior of Real Interest Rates," *Carnegie-Rochester Conference Series on Public Policy* 24 (1986): 231–274.

indicate that contrary to the early Keynesians' beliefs, monetary policy was extremely tight during the Great Depression. Because an important role for monetary policy during this depressed period could no longer be ruled out, most economists were forced to rethink their position regarding whether money matters.

Monetarists also objected to the early Keynesian structural model's view that a weak link between nominal interest rates and investment spending indicates that investment spending is unaffected by monetary policy. A weak link between *nominal* interest rates and investment spending does not rule out a strong link between *real* interest rates and investment spending. As depicted in Figure 25-1, nominal interest rates are often a very misleading indicator of real interest rates—not only during the Great Depression but in later periods as well. Because real interest rates more accurately reflect the true cost of borrowing, they should be more relevant to investment decisions than nominal interest rates. Accordingly, the two pieces of early Keynesian evidence indicating that nominal interest rates have little effect on investment spending do not rule out a strong effect of changes in the money supply on investment spending and hence on aggregate demand.

Monetarists also asserted that interest-rate effects on investment spending might be only one of many channels through which monetary policy affects aggregate demand. Monetary policy could then have a major impact on aggregate demand even if interest-rate effects on investment spending are small, as was suggested by the early Keynesians.

Early Monetarist Evidence on the Importance of Money

In the early 1960s, Milton Friedman and his followers published a series of studies based on reduced-form evidence that promoted the case for a strong effect of money on economic activity. In general, reduced-form evidence can be broken down into three categories: *timing evidence*, which looks at whether the movements in one variable typically occur before another; *statistical evidence*, which performs formal statistical tests on the correlation of the movements of one variable with another; and *historical evidence*, which examines specific past episodes to see whether movements in one variable appear to cause another. Let's look at the monetarist evidence on the importance of money that falls into each of these three categories.

TIMING EVIDENCE   Monetarist timing evidence reveals how the rate of money supply growth moves relative to the business cycle. The evidence on this relationship was first presented by Friedman and Schwartz in a famous paper published in 1963.[3] Friedman and Schwartz found that in every business cycle they studied over nearly a century, the money growth rate always turned down before output did. On average, the peak in the rate of money growth occurred 16 months before the peak in the level of output. However, this lead-time could vary, ranging from a few months to more than two years. The conclusion that these authors reached on the basis of this evidence is that money growth causes business cycle fluctuations, but its effect on the business cycle operates with "long and variable lags."

Timing evidence is based on the philosophical principle first stated in Latin as *post hoc, ergo propter hoc,* which means that if one event occurs after another, the second event must have been caused by the first. This principle is valid only if we know that the first event is an *exogenous* event, an event occurring as a result of

---

[3] Milton Friedman and Anna Jacobson Schwartz, "Money and Business Cycles," *Review of Economics and Statistics* 45, Suppl. (1963): 32–64.

an independent action that could not possibly be caused by the event following it or by some outside factor that might affect both events. If the first event is exogenous, when the second event follows the first we can be more confident that the first event is causing the second.

An example of an exogenous event is a controlled experiment. A chemist mixes two chemicals; suddenly his lab blows up and he with it. We can be absolutely sure that the cause of his demise was the act of mixing the two chemicals together. The principle of *post hoc, ergo propter hoc* is extremely useful in scientific experimentation.

Unfortunately, economics does not enjoy the precision of hard sciences like physics or chemistry. Often we cannot be sure that an economic event, such as a decline in the rate of money growth, is an exogenous event—it could have been caused, itself, by an outside factor or by the event it is supposedly causing. When another event (such as a decline in output) typically follows the first event (a decline in money growth), we cannot conclude with certainty that one caused the other. Timing evidence is clearly of a reduced-form nature because it looks directly at the relationship of the movements of two variables. Money growth could lead output, or both could be driven by an outside factor.

Because timing evidence is of a reduced-form nature, there is also the possibility of reverse causation, in which output growth causes money growth. How can this reverse causation occur while money growth still leads output? There are several ways in which this can happen, but we will deal with just one example.[4]

Suppose that you are in a hypothetical economy with a very regular business cycle movement, plotted in panel (a) of Figure 25-2, that is four years long (four years from peak to peak). Let's assume that in our hypothetical economy, there is reverse causation from output to the money supply, so movements in the money supply and output are perfectly correlated; that is, the money supply M and output Y move upward and downward at the same time. The result is that the peaks and troughs of the M and Y series in panels (a) and (b) occur at exactly the same time; therefore, no lead or lag relationship exists between them.

Now let's construct the rate of money supply growth from the money supply series in panel (b). This is done in panel (c). What is the rate of growth of the money supply at its peaks in years 1 and 5? At these points, it is not growing at all; the rate of growth is zero. Similarly, at the trough in year 3, the growth rate is zero. When the money supply is declining from its peak in year 1 to its trough in year 3, it has a negative growth rate, and its decline is fastest sometime between years 1 and 3 (year 2). Translating to panel (c), the rate of money growth is below zero from years 1 to 3, with its most negative value reached at year 2. By similar reasoning, you can see that the growth rate of money is positive in years 0 to 1 and 3 to 5, with the highest values reached in years 0 and 4. When we connect all these points together, we get the money growth series in panel (c), in which the peaks are at years 0 and 4, with a trough in year 2.

Now let's look at the relationship of the money growth series of panel (c) with the level of output in panel (a). As you can see, the money growth series consistently

---

[4] A famous article by James Tobin, "Money and Income: *Post Hoc, Ergo Propter Hoc,*" *Quarterly Journal of Economics* 84 (1970): 301–317, describes an economic system in which changes in aggregate output cause changes in the growth rate of money but changes in the growth rate of money have no effect on output. Tobin shows that such a system with reverse causation could yield timing evidence similar to that found by Friedman and Schwartz.

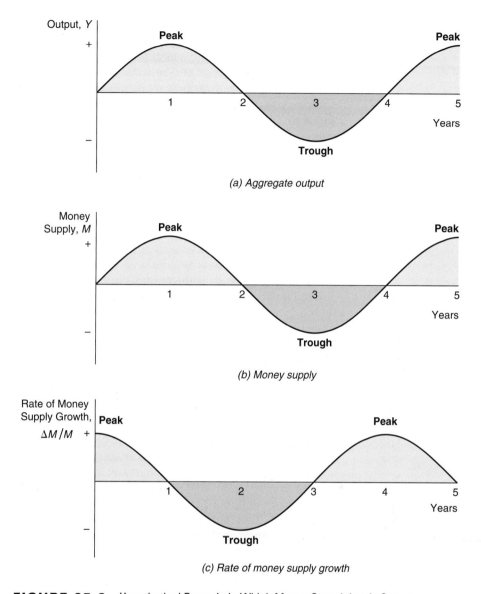

FIGURE 25-2 Hypothetical Example in Which Money Growth Leads Output

Although neither M nor Y leads the other (that is, their peaks and troughs coincide), ΔM/M has its peaks and troughs one year ahead of M and Y, thus leading both series. (Note that M and Y in the panels are drawn as movements around a positive average value; a plus sign indicates a value above the average, and a minus sign indicates a value below the average, not a negative value.)

has its peaks and troughs exactly one year before the peaks and troughs of the output series. We conclude that in our hypothetical economy, the rate of money growth always decreases one year before output does. This evidence does not, however, imply that money growth *drives* output. In fact, by assumption, we know that this economy is one in which causation actually runs from output to the level of money supply, and there is no lead or lag relationship between the two. Only by our judicious choice of using the *growth rate* of the money supply rather than its *level* have we found a leading relationship.

This example shows how easy it is to misinterpret timing relationships. Furthermore, by searching for what we hope to find, we might focus on a variable, such as a growth rate, rather than a level, which suggests a misleading relationship. Timing evidence can be a dangerous tool for deciding on causation.

Stated even more forcefully, "one person's lead is another person's lag." For example, you could just as easily interpret the relationship of money growth and output in Figure 25-2 to say that the money growth rate lags output by three years—after all, the peaks in the money growth series occur three years after the peaks in the output series. In short, you could say that output leads money growth.

We have seen that timing evidence is extremely hard to interpret. Unless we can be sure that changes in the leading variable are exogenous events, we cannot be sure that the leading variable is actually causing the following variable. And it is all too easy to find what we seek when looking for timing evidence. Perhaps the best way of describing this danger is to say, "timing evidence may be in the eyes of the beholder."

STATISTICAL EVIDENCE   Monetarist statistical evidence examined the correlations between money and aggregate output or aggregate spending by performing formal statistical tests. Again in 1963 (obviously a vintage year for the monetarists), Milton Friedman and David Meiselman published a paper that proposed the following test of a monetarist model against a model used by early Keynesians.[5] In the Keynesian framework, investment and government spending were sources of fluctuations in aggregate demand, so Friedman and Meiselman constructed a "Keynesian" autonomous expenditure variable A equal to investment spending plus government spending. They characterized the Keynesian model as saying that A should be highly correlated with aggregate spending Y, while the money supply M should not. In the monetarist model, the money supply is the source of fluctuations in aggregate spending, and M should be highly correlated with Y, while A should not.

A logical way to find out which model is better would be to see which is more highly correlated with Y: M or A. When Friedman and Meiselman conducted this test for many different periods of U.S. data, they discovered that *the monetarist model wins!*[6] They concluded that monetarist analysis gives a better description than Keynesian analysis of how aggregate spending is determined.

Several objections were raised against the Friedman–Meiselman evidence:

1. The standard criticisms of this reduced-form evidence are the ones we have already discussed. Reverse causation could occur, or an outside factor might drive both series.

2. The test may not be fair because the Keynesian components model is characterized too simplistically. Keynesian structural models commonly include hundreds of equations. The one-equation "Keynesian" model that Friedman–Meiselman tested may not adequately capture the effects of autonomous expenditure. Furthermore, Keynesian models usually include the effects of other variables. By ignoring them, the effect of monetary

[5] Milton Friedman and David Meiselman, "The Relative Stability of Monetary Velocity and the Investment Multiplier," in *Stabilization Policies,* ed. Commission on Money and Credit (Upper Saddle River, N.J.: Prentice-Hall, 1963), pp. 165–268.

[6] Friedman and Meiselman did not actually run their tests using the Y variable because they felt that this gave an unfair advantage to the Keynesian model in that A is included in Y. Instead, they subtracted A from Y and tested for the correlation of $Y - A$ with M or A.

policy might be overestimated and the effect of autonomous expenditure underestimated.

3. The Friedman–Meiselman measure of autonomous expenditure *A* might be constructed poorly, preventing the "Keynesian" model from performing well. For example, orders for military hardware affect aggregate demand before they appear as spending in the autonomous expenditure variable that Friedman and Meiselman used. A more careful construction of the autonomous expenditure variable should take account of the placing of orders for military hardware. When the autonomous expenditure variable was constructed more carefully by critics of the Friedman–Meiselman study, they found that the results were reversed: The "Keynesian" model won.[7] A more recent study on the appropriateness of various ways of determining autonomous expenditure does not give a clear-cut victory to either the "Keynesian" or the monetarist model.[8]

HISTORICAL EVIDENCE The monetarist historical evidence, found in Friedman and Schwartz's *A Monetary History,* has been very influential in gaining support for the monetarist position. We have already seen that the book was extremely important as a criticism of early Keynesian thinking, showing as it did that the Great Depression was not a period of easy monetary policy and that the depression could be attributed to the sharp decline in the money supply from 1930 to 1933 resulting from bank panics. In addition, the book documented in great detail that the growth rate of money leads business cycles because it declines before every recession. This timing evidence is, of course, subject to all the criticisms raised earlier.

The historical evidence contains one feature, however, that makes it different from other monetarist evidence we have discussed so far. Several episodes occur in which changes in the money supply appear to be exogenous events. These episodes are almost like controlled experiments, so the *post hoc, ergo propter hoc* principle is far more likely to be valid. If the decline in the growth rate of the money supply is soon followed by a decline in output in these episodes, much stronger evidence is presented that money growth is the driving force behind the business cycle.

One of the best examples of such an episode is the increase in reserve requirements in the United States in 1936–1937, which led to a sharp decline in the money supply and in its rate of growth. The increase in reserve requirements was implemented because the Federal Reserve wanted to improve its control of monetary policy; it was not implemented in response to economic conditions. We can thus rule out reverse causation from output to the money supply. Also, it is hard to think of an outside factor that could have driven the Fed to increase reserve requirements and that could also have directly affected output. Therefore, the decline in the money supply in this episode can probably be classified as an exogenous event with the characteristics of a controlled experiment. Soon after this experiment, the very severe U.S. recession of 1937–1938 occurred. We can conclude with confidence that in this episode, the change in the money supply due to the Fed's increase in reserve requirements was indeed the source of the business cycle contraction that followed.

---

[7] See, for example, Albert Ando and Franco Modigliani, "The Relative Stability of Monetary Velocity and the Investment Multiplier," *American Economic Review* 55 (1965): 693–728.

[8] See William Poole and Edith Kornblith, "The Friedman–Meiselman CMC Paper: New Evidence on an Old Controversy," *American Economic Review* 63 (1973): 908–917.

A Monetary History also documented other historical episodes, such as the bank panic of 1907 and other years in which the decline in money growth again appears to have been an exogenous event. The fact that recessions have frequently followed apparently exogenous declines in money growth is very strong evidence that changes in the growth rate of the money supply do have an impact on aggregate output. Recent work by Christina and David Romer, both of the University of California, Berkeley, applies the historical approach to more recent data using more sophisticated statistical techniques and also finds that monetary policy shifts have had an important impact on the aggregate economy.[9]

Overview of the Monetarist Evidence

Where does this discussion of the monetarist evidence leave us? We have seen that because of reverse causation and outside-factor possibilities, there are some serious doubts about the conclusions that can be drawn from timing and statistical evidence alone. However, some of the historical evidence in which exogenous declines in money growth are followed by business cycle contractions does provide stronger support for the monetarist position. When historical evidence is combined with timing and statistical evidence, the conclusion that monetary policy does matter seems warranted.

As you can imagine, the economics profession was shaken by the appearance of the monetarist evidence, because up to that time most economists believed that money does not matter at all. Monetarists had demonstrated that this early Keynesian position was probably wrong, and it won them a lot of converts. Recognizing the fallacy of the position that money does not matter does not necessarily mean that we must accept the position that money is *all* that matters. Many Keynesian economists shifted their views toward the monetarist position, but not all the way. Instead, they adopted an intermediate position: They allowed that money, fiscal policy, net exports, and "animal spirits" all contributed to fluctuations in aggregate demand. The result has been a convergence of the views on the importance of monetary policy to economic activity. However, proponents of a new theory of aggregate fluctuations called *real business cycle theory* are more critical of the monetarist reduced-form evidence that money is important to business cycle fluctuations because they believe there is reverse causation from the business cycle to money (see the FYI box, Real Business Cycle Theory and the Debate on Money and Economic Activity).

TRANSMISSION MECHANISMS OF MONETARY POLICY

After the successful monetarist attack on the early Keynesian position, economic research went in two directions. One direction was to use more sophisticated monetarist reduced-form models to test for the importance of money to economic activity.[10] The second direction was to pursue a structural model approach and to

---

[9] Christina Romer and David Romer, "Does Monetary Policy Matter? A New Test in the Spirit of Friedman and Schwartz," *NBER Macroeconomics Annual, 1989,* 4, ed. Stanley Fischer (Cambridge, Mass.: M.I.T. Press, 1989), 121–170.

[10] The most prominent example of more sophisticated reduced-form research is the St. Louis model, which was developed at the Federal Reserve Bank of St. Louis in the late 1960s and early 1970s. It provided support for the monetarist position but is subject to the same criticisms of reduced-form evidence outlined in the text. The St. Louis model was first outlined in Leonall Andersen and Jerry Jordan, "Monetary and Fiscal Actions: A Test of Their Relative Importance in Economic Stabilization," *Federal Reserve Bank of St. Louis Review* 50 (November 1968): 11–23.

FYI	**Real Business Cycle Theory and the Debate on Money and Economic Activity**

New entrants to the debate on money and economic activity are advocates of *real business cycle theory,* which states that real shocks to tastes and technology (rather than monetary shocks) are the driving forces behind business cycles. Proponents of this theory are critical of the monetarist view that money matters to business cycles because they believe that the correlation of output with money reflects reverse causation; that is, the business cycle drives money, rather than the other way around. An important piece of evidence they offer to support the reverse causation argument is that almost none of the correlation between money and output comes from the monetary base, which is controlled by the monetary authorities.* Instead, the money–output correlation stems from other sources of money supply movements that, as we saw in Chapter 16, are affected by the actions of banks, depositors, and borrowers from banks and are more likely to be influenced by the business cycle.

* Robert King and Charles Plosser, "Money, Credit and Prices in a Real Business Cycle," *American Economic Review* 74 (1984): 363–380; Charles Plosser, "Understanding Real Business Cycles," *Journal of Economic Perspectives* 3 (Summer 1989): 51–78.

develop a better understanding of channels (other than interest-rate effects on investment) through which monetary policy affects aggregate demand. In this section we examine some of these channels, or *transmission mechanisms,* beginning with interest-rate channels because they are the key monetary transmission mechanism in the *ISLM* and *AD/AS* models you have seen in Chapters 22, 23, and 24.

Traditional Interest-Rate Channels

The traditional components view of the monetary transmission mechanism can be characterized by the following schematic, which shows the effect of expansionary monetary policy:

$$\text{Expansionary monetary policy} \Rightarrow i_r\downarrow \Rightarrow I\uparrow \Rightarrow Y\uparrow \qquad (1)$$

where an expansionary monetary policy leads to a fall in real interest rates ($i_r\downarrow$), which in turn lowers the cost of capital, causing a rise in investment spending ($I\uparrow$), thereby leading to an increase in aggregate demand and a rise in output ($Y\uparrow$).

Although Keynes originally emphasized this channel as operating through businesses' decisions about investment spending, the search for new monetary transmission mechanisms recognized that consumers' decisions about housing and **consumer durable expenditure** (spending by consumers on durable items such as automobiles and refrigerators) also are investment decisions. Thus the interest-rate channel of monetary transmission outlined in Equation 1 applies equally to consumer spending, in which I also represents residential housing and consumer durable expenditure.

An important feature of the interest-rate transmission mechanism is its emphasis on the *real* rather than the nominal interest rate as the rate that affects consumer and business decisions. In addition, it is often the real *long*-term interest rate and not the real short-term interest rate that is viewed as having the major impact on spending. How is it that changes in the short-term nominal interest rate induced by a central bank result in a corresponding change in the real interest rate on both short- and long-term bonds? The key is the phenomenon known as *sticky prices,* the fact that the aggregate price level adjusts slowly over time, meaning that expansionary monetary policy, which lowers the short-term nominal interest rate, also lowers the short-term *real* interest rate. The expectations hypothesis of the term structure described in Chapter 6, which states that the long-term interest rate is an average of expected future short-term interest rates, suggests that a lower real short-term interest rate, as long as it persists, leads to a fall in the real long-term interest rate. These lower real interest rates then lead to rises in business fixed investment, residential housing investment, inventory investment, and consumer durable expenditure, all of which produce the rise in aggregate output.

That it is the real interest rate rather than the nominal rate that affects spending provides an important mechanism for how monetary policy can stimulate the economy, even if nominal interest rates hit a floor of zero during a deflationary episode. With nominal interest rates at a floor of zero, a commitment to future expansionary monetary policy can raise the expected price level ($P^e\uparrow$) and hence expected inflation ($\pi^e\uparrow$), thereby lowering the real interest rate ($i_r = i - \pi^e \downarrow$) even when the nominal interest rate is fixed at zero and stimulating spending through the interest-rate channel:

$$\text{Expansionary monetary policy} \Rightarrow P^e\uparrow \Rightarrow \pi^e\uparrow \Rightarrow i_r\downarrow \Rightarrow I\uparrow \Rightarrow Y\uparrow \quad (2)$$

This mechanism thus indicates that monetary policy can still be effective even when nominal interest rates have already been driven down to zero by the monetary authorities. Indeed, this mechanism is a key element in monetarist discussions of why actual economies were not stuck in a liquidity trap (in which increases in the money supply may not be sufficient to lower interest rates, discussed in Chapter 21) during the Great Depression and why expansionary monetary policy could have prevented the sharp decline in output during that period.

Some economists, such as John Taylor of Stanford University, take the position that there is strong empirical evidence for substantial interest-rate effects on consumer and investment spending through the cost of capital, making the interest-rate monetary transmission mechanism a strong one. His position is highly controversial, and many researchers, including Ben Bernanke, the chairman of the Fed, and Mark Gertler of New York University, believe that the empirical evidence does not support strong interest-rate effects operating through the cost of capital.[11] Indeed, these researchers see the empirical failure of traditional interest-rate monetary transmission mechanisms as having provided the stimulus for the search for other transmission mechanisms of monetary policy.

These other transmission mechanisms fall into two basic categories: those operating through asset prices other than interest rates and those operating through asymmetric information effects on credit markets (the so-called **credit view**). (All these mechanisms are summarized in the schematic diagram in Figure 25-3).

---

[11] See John Taylor, "The Monetary Transmission Mechanism: An Empirical Framework," *Journal of Economic Perspectives* 9 (Fall 1995): 11–26, and Ben Bernanke and Mark Gertler, "Inside the Black Box: The Credit Channel of Monetary Policy Transmission," *Journal of Economic Perspectives* 9 (Fall 1995): 27–48.

653

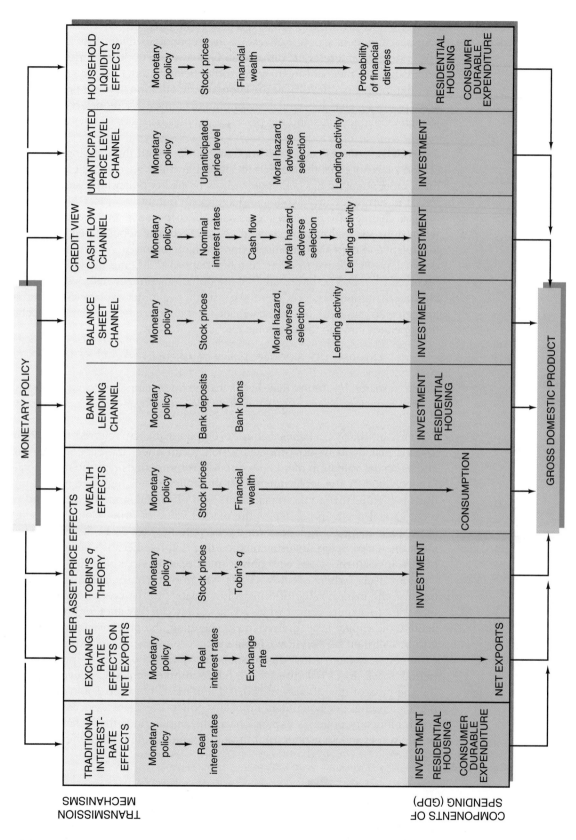

FIGURE 25-3 The Link Between Monetary Policy and GDP: Monetary Transmission Mechanisms

Other Asset Price Channels

As we saw earlier in the chapter, a key monetarist objection to the Keynesian analysis of monetary policy effects on the economy is that it focuses on only one asset price, the interest rate, rather than on many asset prices. Monetarists envision a transmission mechanism in which other relative asset prices and real wealth transmit monetary effects onto the economy. In addition to bond prices, two other asset prices receive substantial attention as channels for monetary policy effects: foreign exchange rates and the prices of equities (stocks).

EXCHANGE RATE EFFECTS ON NET EXPORTS   With the growing internationalization of economies throughout the world and the advent of flexible exchange rates, more attention has been paid to how monetary policy affects exchange rates, which in turn affect net exports and aggregate output.

This channel also involves interest-rate effects because, as we saw in Chapter 19, when domestic real interest rates fall, domestic dollar deposits become less attractive relative to deposits denominated in foreign currencies. As a result, the value of dollar deposits relative to other currency deposits falls, and the dollar depreciates (denoted by $E\downarrow$). The lower value of the domestic currency makes domestic goods cheaper than foreign goods, thereby causing a rise in net exports ($NX\uparrow$) and hence in aggregate output ($Y\uparrow$). The schematic for the monetary transmission mechanism that operates through the exchange rate is

$$\text{Expansionary monetary policy} \Rightarrow i_r\downarrow \Rightarrow E\downarrow \Rightarrow NX\uparrow \Rightarrow Y\uparrow \tag{3}$$

Recent research has found that this exchange rate channel plays an important role in how monetary policy affects the domestic economy.[12]

TOBIN'S *q* THEORY   James Tobin developed a theory, referred to as *Tobin's q Theory,* that explains how monetary policy can affect the economy through its effects on the valuation of equities (stock). Tobin defines q as the market value of firms divided by the replacement cost of capital. If q is high, the market price of firms is high relative to the replacement cost of capital, and new plant and equipment capital is cheap relative to the market value of firms. Companies can then issue stock and get a high price for it relative to the cost of the facilities and equipment they are buying. Investment spending will rise because firms can buy a lot of new investment goods with only a small issue of stock.

Conversely, when q is low, firms will not purchase *new* investment goods because the market value of firms is low relative to the cost of capital. If companies want to acquire capital when q is low, they can buy another firm cheaply and acquire old capital instead. Investment spending, the purchase of new investment goods, will then be very low. Tobin's q theory gives a good explanation for the extremely low rate of investment spending during the Great Depression. In that period, stock prices collapsed and q fell to unprecedented low levels.

The crux of this discussion is that a link exists between Tobin's q and investment spending. But how might monetary policy affect stock prices? Quite simply, when monetary policy is expansionary, the public finds that it has more money than it wants and so gets rid of it through spending. One place the public spends

---

[12] For example, see Ralph Bryant, Peter Hooper, and Catherine Mann, *Evaluating Policy Regimes: New Empirical Research in Empirical Macroeconomics* (Washington, D.C.: Brookings Institution, 1993); and John B. Taylor, *Macroeconomic Policy in a World Economy: From Econometric Design to Practical Operation* (New York: Norton, 1993).

is in the stock market, increasing the demand for stocks and consequently raising their prices.[13] Combining this with the fact that higher stock (equity) prices (P_e) will lead to a higher q and thus higher investment spending I leads to the following transmission mechanism of monetary policy:[14]

$$\text{Expansionary monetary policy} \Rightarrow P_e \uparrow \Rightarrow q \uparrow \Rightarrow I \uparrow \Rightarrow Y \uparrow \qquad (4)$$

(Note that P_e represents the price of equity, whereas P^e, in an earlier schematic, represents the expected price level.)

WEALTH EFFECTS   In their search for new monetary transmission mechanisms, researchers also looked at how consumers' balance sheets might affect their spending decisions. Franco Modigliani was the first to take this tack, using his famous life cycle hypothesis of consumption. **Consumption** is spending by consumers on nondurable goods and services.[15] It differs from *consumer expenditure* in that it does not include spending on consumer durables. The basic premise of Modigliani's theory is that consumers smooth out their consumption over time. Therefore, what determines consumption spending is the lifetime resources of consumers, not just today's income.

An important component of consumers' lifetime resources is their financial wealth, a major component of which is common stocks. When stock prices rise, the value of financial wealth increases, thereby increasing the lifetime resources of consumers, and consumption should rise. Considering that, as we have seen, expansionary monetary policy can lead to a rise in stock prices, we now have another monetary transmission mechanism:

$$\text{Expansionary monetary policy} \Rightarrow P_e \uparrow \Rightarrow \text{wealth} \uparrow \Rightarrow \text{consumption} \uparrow \Rightarrow Y \uparrow \quad (5)$$

Modigliani's research found this relationship to be an extremely powerful mechanism that adds substantially to the potency of monetary policy.[16]

The wealth and Tobin's q channels allow for a general definition of equity, so the Tobin q framework can also be applied to the housing market, where housing is equity. An increase in house prices, which raises their prices relative to replacement cost, leads to a rise in Tobin's q for housing, thereby stimulating its production. Similarly, housing and land prices are extremely important components of wealth, and so rises in these prices increase wealth, thereby raising consumption. Monetary expansion, which raises land and housing prices through the Tobin's q and wealth mechanisms described here, thus leads to a rise in aggregate demand.

---

[13] See James Tobin, "A General Equilibrium Approach to Monetary Theory," *Journal of Money, Credit, and Banking* 1 (1969): 15–29. A somewhat more Keynesian story with the same outcome is that the increase in the money supply lowers interest rates on bonds so that the yields on alternatives to stocks fall. This makes stocks more attractive relative to bonds, so demand for them increases, raises their price, and thereby lowers their yield.

[14] An alternative way of looking at the link between stock prices and investment spending is that higher stock prices lower the yield on stocks and reduce the cost of financing investment spending through issuing equity. This way of looking at the link between stock prices and investment spending is formally equivalent to Tobin's q approach; see Barry Bosworth, "The Stock Market and the Economy," *Brookings Papers on Economic Activity* 2 (1975): 267–290.

[15] Consumption also includes another small component, the services that a consumer receives from the ownership of housing and consumer durables.

[16] See Franco Modigliani, "Monetary Policy and Consumption," in *Consumer Spending and Money Policy: The Linkages* (Boston: Federal Reserve Bank, 1971), pp. 9–84.

Credit View

Dissatisfaction with the conventional stories that interest-rate effects explain the impact of monetary policy on expenditures on durable assets has led to a new explanation based on the problem of asymmetric information in financial markets (see Chapter 8). This explanation, referred to as the *credit view,* proposes that two types of monetary transmission channels arise as a result of information problems in credit markets: those that operate through effects on bank lending and those that operate through effects on firms' and households' balance sheets.[17]

BANK LENDING CHANNEL   The bank lending channel is based on the analysis in Chapter 8, which demonstrated that banks play a special role in the financial system because they are especially well suited to solve asymmetric information problems in credit markets. Because of banks' special role, certain borrowers will not have access to the credit markets unless they borrow from banks. As long as there is no perfect substitutability of retail bank deposits with other sources of funds, the bank lending channel of monetary transmission operates as follows. Expansionary monetary policy, which increases bank reserves and bank deposits, increases the quantity of bank loans available. Because many borrowers are dependent on bank loans to finance their activities, this increase in loans will cause investment (and possibly consumer) spending to rise. Schematically, the monetary policy effect is

$$\begin{matrix}\text{Expansionary} \\ \text{monetary policy}\end{matrix} \Rightarrow \text{bank deposits} \uparrow \Rightarrow \text{bank loans} \uparrow \Rightarrow I\uparrow \Rightarrow Y\uparrow \qquad (6)$$

An important implication of the credit view is that monetary policy will have a greater effect on expenditure by smaller firms, which are more dependent on bank loans, than it will on large firms, which can get funds directly through stock and bond markets (and not only through banks).

BALANCE SHEET CHANNEL   Like the bank lending channel, the balance sheet channel also arises from the presence of asymmetric information problems in credit markets. In Chapter 8, we saw that the lower the net worth of business firms, the more severe the adverse selection and moral hazard problems in lending to these firms. Lower net worth means that lenders in effect have less collateral for their loans, and so potential losses from adverse selection are higher. A decline in net worth, which raises the adverse selection problem, thus leads to decreased lending to finance investment spending. The lower net worth of businesses also increases the moral hazard problem because it means that owners have a lower equity stake in their firms, giving them more incentive to engage in risky investment projects. Since taking on riskier investment projects makes it more likely that lenders will not be paid back, a decrease in businesses' net worth leads to a decrease in lending and hence in investment spending.

Monetary policy can affect firms' balance sheets in several ways. Expansionary monetary policy, which causes a rise in equity prices ($P_e\uparrow$) along lines described earlier, raises the net worth of firms and so leads to higher investment spending ($I\uparrow$) and aggregate demand ($Y\uparrow$) because of the decrease in adverse selection and

---

[17] Recent surveys of the credit view can be found in Ben Bernanke, "Credit in the Macroeconomy," Federal Reserve Bank of New York *Quarterly Review,* Spring 1993, pp. 50–70; Ben Bernanke and Mark Gertler, "Inside the Black Box: The Credit Channel of Monetary Policy Transmission," *Journal of Economic Perspectives* 9 (Fall 1995): 27–48; Stephen G. Cecchetti, "Distinguishing Theories of the Monetary Transmission Mechanism," Federal Reserve Bank of St. Louis *Review* 77 (May–June 1995): 83–97; and R. Glenn Hubbard, "Is There a 'Credit Channel' for Monetary Policy?" Federal Reserve Bank of St. Louis *Review* 77 (May–June 1995): 63–74.

moral hazard problems. This leads to the following schematic for one balance sheet channel of monetary transmission:

$$\text{Expansionary monetary policy} \Rightarrow P_e \uparrow \Rightarrow$$
$$\text{adverse selection} \downarrow, \text{moral hazard} \downarrow \Rightarrow \text{lending} \uparrow \Rightarrow I \uparrow \Rightarrow Y \uparrow \qquad (7)$$

CASH FLOW CHANNEL   Another balance sheet channel operates by affecting *cash flow*, the difference between cash receipts and cash expenditures. Expansionary monetary policy, which lowers nominal interest rates, also causes an improvement in firms' balance sheets because it raises cash flow. The rise in cash flow causes an improvement in the balance sheet because it increases the liquidity of the firm (or household) and thus makes it easier for lenders to know whether the firm (or household) will be able to pay its bills. The result is that adverse selection and moral hazard problems become less severe, leading to an increase in lending and economic activity. The following schematic describes this additional balance sheet channel:

$$\text{Expansionary monetary policy} \Rightarrow i \downarrow \Rightarrow \text{cash flow} \uparrow \Rightarrow$$
$$\text{adverse selection} \downarrow, \text{moral hazard} \downarrow \Rightarrow \text{lending} \uparrow \Rightarrow I \uparrow \Rightarrow Y \uparrow \qquad (8)$$

An important feature of this transmission mechanism is that it is *nominal* interest rates that affect firms' cash flow. Thus this interest-rate mechanism differs from the traditional interest-rate mechanism discussed earlier, in which the real interest rate affects investment. Furthermore, the short-term interest rate plays a special role in this transmission mechanism because it is interest payments on short-term rather than long-term debt that typically have the greatest impact on households' and firms' cash flow.

A related mechanism involving adverse selection through which expansionary monetary policy that lowers interest rates can stimulate aggregate output involves the credit-rationing phenomenon. As we discussed in Chapter 13, credit rationing occurs in cases where borrowers are denied loans even when they are willing to pay a higher interest rate. This is because individuals and firms with the riskiest investment projects are exactly the ones who are willing to pay the highest interest rates, for if the high-risk investment succeeds, they will be the primary beneficiaries. Thus higher interest rates increase the adverse selection problem, and lower interest rates reduce it. When expansionary monetary policy lowers interest rates, less risk-prone borrowers make up a higher fraction of those demanding loans, and so lenders are more willing to lend, raising both investment and output, along the lines of parts of the schematic in Equation 8.

UNANTICIPATED PRICE LEVEL CHANNEL   A third balance sheet channel operates through monetary policy effects on the general price level. Because in industrialized countries debt payments are contractually fixed in nominal terms, an unanticipated rise in the price level lowers the value of firms' liabilities in real terms (decreases the burden of the debt) but should not lower the real value of the firms' assets. Monetary expansion that leads to an unanticipated rise in the price level ($P \uparrow$) therefore raises real net worth, which lowers adverse selection and moral hazard problems, thereby leading to a rise in investment spending and aggregate output as in the following schematic:

$$\text{Expansionary monetary policy} \Rightarrow \text{unanticipated } P \uparrow \Rightarrow$$
$$\text{adverse selection} \downarrow, \text{moral hazard} \downarrow \Rightarrow \text{lending} \uparrow \Rightarrow I \uparrow \Rightarrow Y \uparrow \qquad (9)$$

The view that unanticipated movements in the price level affect aggregate demand has a long tradition in economics. It is the key feature in the debt-deflation view of the Great Depression outlined in Chapter 9.

HOUSEHOLD LIQUIDITY EFFECTS   Although most of the literature on the credit channel focuses on spending by businesses, the credit view should apply equally well to consumer spending, particularly on consumer durables and housing. Declines in bank lending induced by a monetary contraction should cause a decline in durables and housing purchases by consumers who do not have access to other sources of credit. Similarly, increases in interest rates cause a deterioration in household balance sheets because consumers' cash flow is adversely affected.

Another way of looking at how the balance sheet channel may operate through consumers is to consider liquidity effects on consumer durable and housing expenditures—found to have been important factors during the Great Depression.[18] In the liquidity effects view, balance sheet effects work through their impact on consumers' desire to spend rather than on lenders' desire to lend. Because of asymmetric information about their quality, consumer durables and housing are very illiquid assets. If, as a result of a bad income shock, consumers needed to sell their consumer durables or housing to raise money, they would expect a big loss because they could not get the full value of these assets in a distress sale. (This is just a manifestation of the lemons problem described in Chapter 8.) In contrast, if consumers held financial assets (such as money in the bank, stocks, or bonds), they could easily sell them quickly for their full market value and raise the cash. Hence if consumers expect a higher likelihood of finding themselves in financial distress, they would rather be holding fewer illiquid consumer durable or housing assets and more liquid financial assets.

A consumer's balance sheet should be an important influence on his or her estimate of the likelihood of suffering financial distress. Specifically, when consumers have a large amount of financial assets relative to their debts, their estimate of the probability of financial distress is low, and they will be more willing to purchase consumer durables or housing. When stock prices rise, the value of financial assets rises as well; consumer durable expenditure will also rise because consumers have a more secure financial position and a lower estimate of the likelihood of suffering financial distress. This leads to another transmission mechanism for monetary policy, operating through the link between money and equity prices:[19]

$$\text{Expansionary monetary policy} \Rightarrow P_e \uparrow \Rightarrow \text{value of financial assests } \uparrow \Rightarrow$$
$$\text{likelihood of financial distress } \downarrow \Rightarrow$$
$$\text{consumer durable and housing expenditure } \uparrow \Rightarrow Y \uparrow \qquad (10)$$

The illiquidity of consumer durable and housing assets provides another reason why a monetary expansion, which lowers interest rates and thereby raises cash flow to consumers, leads to a rise in spending on consumer durables and housing. A rise in consumer cash flow decreases the likelihood of financial distress, which increases the desire of consumers to hold durable goods or housing,

---

[18] Frederic S. Mishkin, "The Household Balance Sheet and the Great Depression," *Journal of Economic History* 38 (1978): 918–937.

[19] See Frederic S. Mishkin, "What Depressed the Consumer? The Household Balance Sheet and the 1973–1975 Recession," *Brookings Papers on Economic Activity* 1 (1977): 123–164.

thus increasing spending on them and hence aggregate output. The only difference between this view of cash flow effects and that outlined in Equation 8 is that it is not the willingness of lenders to lend to consumers that causes expenditure to rise but the willingness of consumers to spend.

Why Are Credit Channels Likely to Be Important?

There are three reasons to believe that credit channels are important monetary transmission mechanisms. First, a large body of evidence on the behaviour of individual firms supports the view that credit market imperfections of the type crucial to the operation of credit channels do affect firms' employment and spending decisions.[20] Second, there is evidence that small firms (which are more likely to be credit-constrained) are hurt more by tight monetary policy than large firms, which are unlikely to be credit-constrained.[21] Third, and maybe most compelling, the asymmetric information view of credit market imperfections at the core of the credit channel analysis is a theoretical construct that has proved useful in explaining many other important phenomena, such as why many of our financial institutions exist, why our financial system has the structure that it has, and why financial crises are so damaging to the economy (all topics discussed in Chapters 8 and 9). The best support for a theory is its demonstrated usefulness in a wide range of applications. By this standard, the asymmetric information theory supporting the existence of credit channels as an important monetary transmission mechanism has much to recommend it.

APPLICATION

National Monetary Policy and Differential Regional Effects

Our analysis thus far has assumed a uniform national monetary effect. In reality, however, there are quite pronounced regional disparities across a geographically large and diversified country like Canada, meaning that monetary policy actions may have differential effects on regional economic activity. In fact, as Gerald Carlino and Robert DeFina (1998) argue, regional differences in the mix of interest-sensitive industries and in the proportion of large and small borrowers underscores the complexity of conducting a national monetary policy.[22]

There is, at present, little evidence on the issue of whether Canadian monetary policy has differential effects on regional economic activity. Empirical evidence on this issue may aid policymakers in their consideration of regional economic conditions in the formulation of national monetary policy.

---

[20] For a survey of this evidence, see Hubbard, "Is There a 'Credit Channel' for Monetary Policy?" (note 17).

[21] See Mark Gertler and Simon Gilchrist, "Monetary Policy, Business Cycles, and the Behavior of Small Manufacturing Firms," *Quarterly Journal of Economics* 109 (May 1994): 309–340.

[22] Gerald Carlino and Robert DeFina, "The Differential Regional Effects of Monetary Policy," *The Review of Economics and Statistics* 80 (November 1998): 572–587.

APPLICATION   The Subprime Recession

With the advent of the subprime financial crisis in the United States in the summer of 2007, the Fed and many other central banks around the world, including the Bank of Canada, began very aggressive easing of monetary policy. For example, the Fed dropped the target federal funds rate from 5.25% to between 0% and 0.25% over a fifteen-month period from September 2007 to December 2008. At first, it appeared that the Fed's actions would keep the growth slowdown mild and prevent a recession. However, the U.S. economy proved to be weaker than the Fed or private forecasters expected, and a recession began in December of 2007. Why did the economy become so weak despite this unusually rapid reduction in the Fed's policy instrument?

The subprime meltdown led to negative effects on the economy from many of the channels we have outlined above. The rising level of subprime mortgage defaults, which led to a decline in the value of mortgage-backed securities and CDOs, led to large losses on the balance sheets of financial institutions. With weaker balance sheets, these financial institutions began to deleverage and cut back on their lending. With no one else to collect information and make loans, adverse selection and moral hazard problems increased in credit markets, leading to a slowdown of the economy. Credit spreads also went through the roof with the increase in uncertainty from failures of so many financial markets. The decline in the stock market and housing prices also weakened the U.S. economy, because it lowered household wealth. The decrease in household wealth led to restrained consumer spending and weaker investment, because of the resulting drop in Tobin's *q*.

With all these channels operating, it is no surprise that despite the Fed's aggressive lowering of the federal funds rate, the U.S. economy still took a big hit.

LESSONS FOR MONETARY POLICY

What useful implications for central banks' conduct of monetary policy can we draw from the analysis in this chapter? There are four basic lessons to be drawn.

1. ***It is always dangerous to associate the easing or tightening of monetary policy with a fall or a rise in short-term nominal interest rates.***
    Because most central banks use short-term nominal interest rates, typically the interbank rate, as the key operating instrument for monetary policy, there is a danger that central banks and the public will focus too much on short-term nominal interest rates as an indicator of the stance of monetary policy. Indeed, it is quite common to see statements that always associate monetary tightenings with a rise in the interbank rate and monetary easings with a decline in the rate. This view is highly problematic because movements in nominal interest rates do not always correspond to movements in real interest rates, and yet it is typically the real and not the nominal interest rate that is an element in the channel of monetary policy transmission. For example, we have seen that during the contraction phase of the Great Depression in the United States, short-term interest rates fell to near zero and yet real interest rates were extremely

high. Short-term interest rates that are near zero therefore do not indicate that monetary policy is easy if the economy is undergoing deflation, as was true during the contraction phase of the Great Depression. As Milton Friedman and Anna Schwartz have emphasized, the period of near-zero short-term interest rates during the contraction phase of the Great Depression was one of highly contractionary monetary policy rather than the reverse.

2. ***Other asset prices besides those of short-term debt instruments contain important information about the stance of monetary policy because they are important elements in various monetary policy transmission mechanisms.*** As we have seen in this chapter, economists have come a long way in understanding that other asset prices besides interest rates have major effects on aggregate demand. As we saw in Figure 25-3 (page 653), other asset prices, such as stock prices, foreign exchange rates, and housing and land prices, play an important role in monetary transmission mechanisms. Furthermore, the discussion of such additional channels as those operating through the exchange rate, Tobin's *q*, and wealth effects provides additional reasons why other asset prices play such an important role in the monetary transmission mechanisms. Although there are strong disagreements among economists about which channels of monetary transmission are the most important—not surprising, given that economists, particularly those in academia, always like to disagree—they do agree that other asset prices play an important role in the way monetary policy affects the economy.

   The view that other asset prices besides short-term interest rates matter has important implications for monetary policy. When we try to assess the stance of policy, it is critical that we look at other asset prices in addition to short-term interest rates. For example, if short-term interest rates are low or even zero and yet stock prices are low, land prices are low, and the value of the domestic currency is high, monetary policy is clearly tight, *not* easy.

3. ***Monetary policy can be highly effective in reviving a weak economy even if short-term interest rates are already near zero.*** We have recently entered a world where inflation is not always the norm. Japan, for example, recently experienced a period of deflation, when the price level was actually falling. One common view is that when a central bank has driven down short-term nominal interest rates to near zero, there is nothing more that monetary policy can do to stimulate the economy. The transmission mechanisms of monetary policy described here indicate that this view is false. As our discussion of the factors that affect the monetary base in Chapter 16 indicated, expansionary monetary policy to increase liquidity in the economy can be conducted with open market purchases, which do not have to be solely in short-term government securities. For example, purchases of foreign currencies, like purchases of government bonds, lead to an increase in the monetary base and in the money supply. This increased liquidity and a commitment to future expansionary monetary policy helps revive the economy by raising general price-level expectations and by reflating other asset prices, which then stimulate aggregate demand through the channels outlined here. Therefore, monetary policy can be a potent force for reviving economies that are undergoing deflation and have short-term interest rates near zero. Indeed, because of the lags inherent in fiscal policy and the political constraints on its use, expansionary monetary policy is the key policy action required to revive an economy experiencing deflation.

4. ***Avoiding unanticipated fluctuations in the price level is an important objective of monetary policy, thus providing a rationale for price stability as the primary long-run goal for monetary policy.*** As we saw in Chapter 18, central banks in recent years have been putting greater emphasis on price stability as the primary long-run goal for monetary policy. Several rationales have been proposed for this goal, including the undesirable effects of uncertainty about the future price level on business decisions and hence on productivity, distortions associated with the interaction of nominal contracts and the tax system with inflation, and increased social conflict stemming from inflation. The discussion here of monetary transmission mechanisms provides an additional reason why price stability is so important. As we have seen, unanticipated movements in the price level can cause unanticipated fluctuations in output, an undesirable outcome. Particularly important in this regard is that, as we saw in Chapter 9, price deflations can be an important factor leading to a prolonged financial crisis, as occurred during the Great Depression. An understanding of the monetary transmission mechanisms thus makes it clear that the goal of price stability is desirable because it reduces uncertainty about the future price level. Thus the price stability goal implies that a negative inflation rate is at least as undesirable as too high an inflation rate. Indeed, because of the threat of financial crises, central banks must work very hard to prevent price deflations.

APPLICATION	Applying the Monetary Policy Lessons to Japan

Until 1990, it looked as if Japan might overtake the U.S. in per capita income. Since then the Japanese economy has been stagnating, with deflation and low growth. As a result, Japanese living standards have been falling behind those in the United States. Many economists take the view that Japanese monetary policy is in part to blame for the poor performance of the Japanese economy. Could applying the four lessons outlined in the previous section have helped Japanese monetary policy to perform better?

The first lesson suggests that it is dangerous to think that declines in interest rates always mean that monetary policy is easing. In the mid-1990s, when short-term interest rates began to decline (falling to near zero in the late 1990s and early 2000s) the monetary authorities in Japan took the view that monetary policy was sufficiently expansionary. Now, it is widely recognized that this view was incorrect because the falling—and eventually negative—inflation rates in Japan meant that real interest rates were actually quite high and that monetary policy was tight, not easy. If the monetary authorities in Japan had followed the advice of the first lesson, they might have pursued a more expansionary monetary policy, which would have helped to boost the economy.

The second lesson suggests that monetary policymakers should pay attention to other asset prices in assessing the stance of monetary policy. At the same time interest rates were falling in Japan, stock and real estate prices were collapsing, thus providing another indication that Japanese monetary policy was not easy. Recognizing the second lesson might have led Japanese monetary policymakers to recognize sooner that they needed a more expansionary monetary policy.

The third lesson indicates that monetary policy can still be effective even if short-term interest rates are near zero. Officials at the Bank of Japan frequently claimed to be helpless in stimulating the economy because short-term interest rates had fallen to near zero. Recognizing that monetary policy can still be effective even when interest rates are near zero, as the third lesson suggests, would have helped them to take monetary policy actions to stimulate aggregate demand by raising other asset prices and inflationary expectations.

The fourth lesson indicates that unanticipated fluctuations in the price level should be avoided. If the Japanese monetary authorities had adhered to this lesson, they might have recognized that allowing deflation to occur could be very damaging to the economy and would be inconsistent with the goal of price stability. Indeed, critics of the Bank of Japan have suggested that the Bank should announce an inflation target in order to promote the price stability objective, but the Bank has resisted this suggestion.

Heeding the advice from the four lessons in the previous section might have led to a far more successful conduct of monetary policy in Japan in recent years.[23]

---

[23] For a more detailed critique of recent monetary policy in Japan, see Takatoshi Ito and Frederic S. Mishkin, "Two Decades of Japanese Monetary Policy and the Deflation Problem," National Bureau of Economic Research Working Paper No. 10878 (November, 2004).

SUMMARY

1. There are two basic types of empirical evidence: structural model evidence and reduced-form evidence. Both have advantages and disadvantages. The main advantage of structural model evidence is that it provides us with an understanding of how the economy works and gives us more confidence in the direction of causation between money and output. However, if the structure is not correctly specified because it ignores important monetary transmission mechanisms, it could seriously underestimate the effectiveness of monetary policy. Reduced-form evidence has the advantage of not restricting the way monetary policy affects economic activity and so may be more likely to capture the full effects of monetary policy. However, reduced-form evidence cannot rule out the possibility of reverse causation or an outside driving factor, which could lead to misleading conclusions about the importance of money.

2. The early Keynesians believed that money does not matter because they found weak links between interest rates and investment and because low interest rates on government securities convinced them that monetary policy was easy during the worst economic contraction in history, the Great Depression. Monetarists objected to this interpretation of the evidence on the grounds that (a) the focus on nominal rather than real interest rates may have obscured any link between interest rates and investment, (b) interest-rate effects on investment might be only one of many channels through which monetary policy affects aggregate demand, and (c) by the standards of real interest rates, monetary policy was extremely contractionary during the Great Depression.

3. Early monetarist evidence falls into three categories: timing, statistical, and historical. Because of reverse causation and outside-factor possibilities, some serious doubts exist regarding conclusions that can be drawn from timing and statistical evidence alone. However, some of the historical evidence in which exogenous declines in money growth are followed by recessions provides stronger support for the monetarist position that money matters. As a result of empirical research, Keynesian and monetarist opinion has converged to the view that money does matter to aggregate economic activity and the price level. However, Keynesians do not agree with the monetarist position that money is *all* that matters.

4. The transmission mechanisms of monetary policy include traditional interest-rate channels that operate through the cost of capital and affect investment; other asset price channels such as exchange rate effects, Tobin's *q* theory, and wealth effects; and the credit view channels—the bank lending channel, the balance sheet channel, the cash flow channel, the unanticipated price level channel, and household liquidity effects.

5. Four lessons for monetary policy can be drawn from this chapter: (a) It is dangerous always to associate monetary policy easing or tightening with a fall or a rise in short-term nominal interest rates; (b) other asset prices besides those on short-term debt instruments contain important information about the stance of monetary policy because they are important elements in the monetary policy transmission mechanisms; (c) monetary policy can be highly effective in reviving a weak economy even if short-term interest rates are already near zero; and (d) avoiding unanticipated fluctuations in the price level is an important objective of monetary policy, thus providing a rationale for price stability as the primary long-run goal for monetary policy.

KEY TERMS

consumer durable expenditure, p. 651

consumption, p. 655

credit view, p. 652

reduced-form evidence, p. 639

reverse causation, p. 641

structural model, p. 639

structural model evidence, p. 639

transmission mechanisms of monetary policy, p. 639

QUESTIONS

You will find the answers to the questions marked with an asterisk in the Textbook Resources section of your MyEconLab.

1. Suppose that a researcher is trying to determine whether jogging is good for a person's health. She examines this question in two ways. In method A, she looks to see whether joggers live longer than nonjoggers. In method B, she looks to see whether jogging reduces cholesterol in the bloodstream and lowers blood pressure; then she asks whether lower cholesterol and blood pressure prolong life. Which of these two methods will produce reduced-form evidence and which will produce structural model evidence?

2. If research indicates that joggers do not have lower cholesterol and blood pressure than nonjoggers, is it still possible that jogging is good for your health? Give a concrete example.

3. If research indicates that joggers live longer than nonjoggers, is it possible that jogging is not good for your health? Give a concrete example.

*4. Suppose that you plan to buy a car and want to know whether a General Motors car is more reliable than a Ford. One way to find out is to ask owners of both cars how often their cars go into the shop for repairs. Another way is to visit the factory producing the cars and see which one is built better. Which procedure will provide reduced-form evidence and which structural model evidence?

*5. If the GM car you plan to buy has a better repair record than a Ford, does this mean that the GM car is necessarily more reliable? (GM car owners might, for example, change their oil more frequently than Ford owners.)

*6. Suppose that when you visit the Ford and GM car factories to examine how the cars are built, you only have time to see how well the engine is put together. If Ford engines are better built than GM engines, does that mean that the Ford will be more reliable than the GM car?

7. How might bank behaviour (described in Chapter 16) lead to causation running from output to the money supply? What does this say about evidence that finds a strong correlation between money and output?

*8. What operating procedures of the Bank of Canada (described in Chapter 18) might explain how movements in output might cause movements in the money supply?

9. "In every business cycle in the past 100 years, the rate at which the money supply is growing always decreases before output does. Therefore, the money supply causes business cycle movements." Do you agree? What objections can you raise against this argument?

*10. How did the research strategies of Keynesian and monetarist economists differ after they were exposed to the earliest monetarist evidence?

11. In the 1973–1975 recession, the value of common stocks in real terms fell by nearly 50%. How might this decline in the stock market have affected aggregate demand and thus contributed to the severity of this recession? Be specific about the mechanisms through which the stock market decline affected the economy.

*12. "The cost of financing investment is related only to interest rates; therefore, the only way that monetary policy can affect investment spending is through its effects on interest rates." Is this statement true, false, or uncertain? Explain your answer.

13. Predict what will happen to stock prices if the money supply rises. Explain why you are making this prediction.

*14. Franco Modigliani found that the most important transmission mechanisms of monetary policy involve consumer expenditure. Describe how at least two of these mechanisms work.

15. "The monetarists have demonstrated that the early Keynesians were wrong in saying that money doesn't matter at all to economic activity. Therefore, we should accept the monetarist position that money is all that matters." Do you agree? Why or why not?

WEB EXERCISES

1. Figure 25-1 on page 644 shows the relationship between estimated real rates and nominal rates for the United States. Go to **www.martincapital.com** and click on "charts and data" and then on "nominal versus real market rates" to find data showing the spread between real rates and nominal rates. Discuss the current spread difference compared to that shown most recently in Figure 25-1. What are the implications of this change?

2. Figure 25-2 on page 647 discusses business cycles. While peaks and troughs of economic activity are a normal part of the business cycle, recessions are not. They represent a failure of economic policy. Go to **www.econlib.org/library/Enc1/Recessions.html** and review the material reported on recessions.
   a. What is the formal definition of a recession?
   b. What are the problems with the definition?
   c. What are the three D's used by the National Bureau of Economic Research (NBER) to define a recession?
   d. Review chart 1. What trend is apparent about the length of recessions?

Be sure to visit the MyEconLab website at **www.myeconlab.com**. This online homework and tutorial system puts you in control of your own learning with study and practice tools directly correlated to this chapter content.

CHAPTER 26

Money and Inflation

LEARNING OBJECTIVES

After studying this chapter you should be able to

1. define *inflation*
2. discern between monetarist and Keynesian views of inflation
3. explain Milton Friedman's famous proposition that "inflation is always and everywhere a monetary phenomenon"
4. characterize the *activist versus nonactivist* and *rules versus discretion* policy debates

PREVIEW

Since the early 1960s, when the inflation rate hovered between 1% and 2%, the economy has suffered from higher and more variable rates of inflation. By the late 1960s, the inflation rate had climbed beyond 4%, and by 1974, it reached the double-digit level. After moderating somewhat during the 1975–1978 period, it shot above 10% in 1980 and 1981, slowed to around 3% from 1982 to 1990, declined further to around 2% in the late 1990s, and remained around that level through 2008. Inflation, the condition of a continually rising price level, has become a major concern of politicians and the public, and how to control it frequently dominates the discussion of economic policy.

How do we prevent the inflationary fire from igniting and end the roller-coaster ride in the inflation rate of the past 40 years? Milton Friedman provides an answer in his famous proposition that "inflation is always and everywhere a monetary phenomenon." He postulates that the source of all inflation episodes is a high growth rate of the money supply: simply by reducing the growth rate of the money supply to low levels, inflation can be prevented.

In this chapter we use aggregate demand and supply analysis from Chapter 24 to reveal the role of monetary policy in creating inflation. You will find that as long as inflation is defined as the condition of a continually and rapidly rising price level, almost all economists agree with Friedman's proposition that inflation is a monetary phenomenon.

But what *causes* inflation? How does inflationary monetary policy come about? You will see that inflationary monetary policy is an offshoot of other government policies: the attempt to hit high employment targets or the running of large budget deficits. Examining how these policies lead to inflation will point us toward ways of preventing it at minimum cost in terms of unemployment and output loss.

MONEY AND INFLATION: EVIDENCE

The evidence for Friedman's statement is straightforward. ***Whenever a country's inflation rate is extremely high for a sustained period of time, its rate of money supply growth is also extremely high.*** Indeed, this is exactly what we saw in Figure 1-5 (page 8), which shows that the countries with the highest inflation rates have also had the highest rates of money growth.

Evidence of this type seems to support the proposition that extremely high inflation is the result of a high rate of money growth. Keep in mind, however, that you are looking at reduced-form evidence, which focuses solely on the correlation of two variables: money growth and the inflation rate. As with all reduced-form evidence, reverse causation (inflation causing money supply growth) or an outside factor that drives both money growth and inflation could be involved.

How might you rule out these possibilities? First, you might look for historical episodes in which an increase in money growth appears to be an exogenous event; a high inflation rate for a sustained period following the increase in money growth would provide strong evidence that high money growth is the driving force behind the inflation. Luckily for our analysis, such clear-cut episodes—hyperinflations (extremely rapid inflations with inflation rates exceeding 50% per month)—have occurred, the most notorious being the German hyperinflation of 1921–1923.

German Hyperinflation, 1921–1923

In 1921, the need to make reparations and reconstruct the economy after World War I caused the German government's expenditures to greatly exceed revenues. The government could have obtained revenues to cover these increased expenditures by raising taxes, but that solution was, as always, politically unpopular and would have taken much time to implement. The government could also have financed the expenditure by borrowing from the public, but the amount needed was far in excess of its capacity to borrow. There was only one route left: the printing press. The government could pay for its expenditures simply by printing more currency (increasing the money supply) and using it to make payments to the individuals and companies that were providing it with goods and services. As shown in Figure 26-1, this is exactly what the German government did; in late 1921, the money supply began to increase rapidly, and so did the price level.

In 1923, the budgetary situation of the German government deteriorated even further. Early that year, the French invaded the Ruhr because Germany had failed to make its scheduled reparations payments. A general strike in the region then ensued to protest the French action, and the German government actively supported this "passive resistance" by making payments to striking workers. As a result, government expenditures climbed dramatically, and the government printed currency at an even faster rate to finance this spending. As displayed in Figure 26-1, the result of the explosion in the money supply was that the price level blasted off, leading to an inflation rate for 1923 that exceeded 1 million percent!

The invasion of the Ruhr and the printing of currency to pay striking workers fit the characteristics of an exogenous event. Reverse causation (that the rise in the price level caused the French to invade the Ruhr) is highly implausible, and it is hard to imagine a third factor that could have been a driving force behind both inflation and the explosion in the money supply. Therefore, the German hyperinflation qualifies as a "controlled experiment" that supports Friedman's proposition that inflation is a monetary phenomenon.

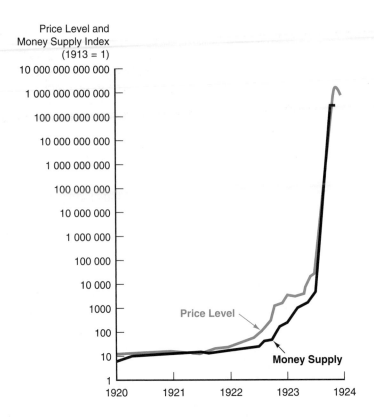

FIGURE 26-1   Money Supply and Price Level in the German Hyperinflation

Source: Frank D. Graham, *Exchange, Prices and Production in Hyperinflation: Germany, 1920–25* (Princeton, N.J.: Princeton University Press, 1930), pp. 105–106.

Recent Episodes of Rapid Inflation

Only one country has recently topped Germany in the high inflation league. In 2008, Zimbabwe's inflation rate went to over 2 million percent officially (but unofficially over 10 million percent). In July, the Zimbabwean central bank issued a new $100 billion bank note. That's a lot of zeros.

The explanation for Zimbabwe's hyperinflation is the same as Germany's during its hyperinflation: extremely high money growth because the weak government of Robert Mugabe was unwilling to finance government expenditures by raising taxes, which led to a very high budget deficit financed by money creation.

Note that the inflation rate is high in all cases in which the high rate of money growth can be classified as an exogenous event. This is strong evidence that high money growth causes high inflation.

MEANING OF INFLATION

You may have noticed that all the empirical evidence on the relationship of money growth and inflation discussed so far looks only at cases in which the price level is continually rising at a rapid rate and so inflation is persistent. It is this definition of inflation that Friedman and other economists use when they make statements such as "Inflation is always and everywhere a monetary phenomenon." This is not what your friendly newscaster means when reporting the monthly inflation rate on the nightly news. The newscaster is only telling you how much, in percentage terms, the price level has changed from the previous month. For example, when you hear that the monthly inflation rate is 1% (12% annual rate), this indicates only that the price level has risen by 1% in that month. This could be a one-shot change, in which the high inflation rate is merely temporary, not sustained. Only if the inflation rate remains high persistently (greater than 1% per month say for several years) will economists say that inflation has been high.

Accordingly, Milton Friedman's proposition actually says that upward movements in the price level are a monetary phenomenon *only* if this is a sustained process. When *inflation* is defined as a persistent and rapid rise in the price level, almost all economists agree with Friedman's proposition that money alone is to blame.

VIEWS OF INFLATION

Now that we understand what Friedman's proposition means, we can use the aggregate supply and demand analysis learned in Chapter 24 to show that large and persistent upward movements in the price level (high inflation) can occur only if there is a continually growing money supply.

How Money Growth Produces Inflation

First, let's look at the outcome of a continually growing money supply (Figure 26-2). Initially, the economy is at point 1, with output at the natural rate level and the price level at P_1 (the intersection of the aggregate demand curve AD_1 and the short-run aggregate supply curve AS_1). If the money supply increases steadily over the course of the year, the aggregate demand curve shifts rightward to AD_2. At first, for a very brief time, the economy may move to point 1′ and output may increase above the natural rate level to Y', but the resulting decline in unemployment below the natural rate level will cause wages to rise, and the short-run aggregate supply curve will quickly begin to shift leftward. It will stop shifting only when it

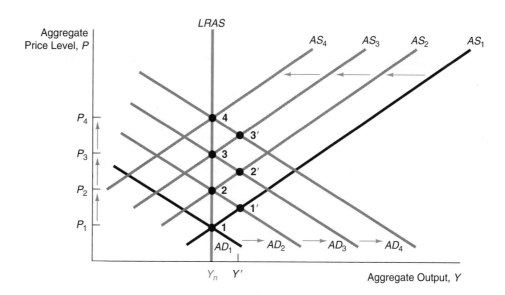

FIGURE 26-2   Response to a Continually Rising Money Supply

A continually rising money supply shifts the aggregate demand curve to the right from AD_1 to AD_2 to AD_3 to AD_4, while the supply curve shifts to the left from AS_1 to AS_2 to AS_3 to AS_4. The result is that the price level rises continually from P_1 to P_2 to P_3 to P_4.

reaches AS_2, at which time the economy has returned to the natural rate level of output on the long-run aggregate supply curve.[1] At the new equilibrium, point 2, the price level has increased from P_1 to P_2.

If the money supply increases the next year, the aggregate demand curve will shift to the right again to AD_3, and the short-run aggregate supply curve will shift from AS_2 to AS_3; the economy will then move to point 2' and then to point 3, where the price level has risen to P_3. If the money supply continues to grow in subsequent years, the economy will continue to move to higher and higher price levels. As long as the money supply grows, this process will continue, and inflation will occur. ***High money growth produces high inflation.***

Can Other Factors Besides Money Growth Produce a Sustained Inflation?

In the aggregate demand and supply analysis of Chapter 24, you learned that other factors besides changes in the money supply (such as fiscal policy and supply shocks) can affect the aggregate demand and supply curves. Doesn't this suggest that these other factors can generate persistent high inflation? The answer, surprisingly, is no. To see why high inflation is always a monetary phenomenon, let's dig a little deeper into aggregate demand and supply analysis to see whether other factors can generate high inflation in the absence of a high rate of money growth.

CAN FISCAL POLICY BY ITSELF PRODUCE INFLATION? To examine this question, let's look at Figure 26-3, which demonstrates the effect of a one-shot permanent increase in government expenditure (say, from $500 billion to $600 billion) on aggregate output and the price level. Initially, we are at point 1, where output is at the natural rate level and the price level is P_1. The increase in government expenditure shifts the aggregate demand curve to AD_2, and we move to point 1', where output is above the natural rate level at Y_1. The short-run aggregate supply curve will begin to shift leftward, eventually reaching AS_2, where it intersects the aggregate demand curve AD_2 at point 2, at which output is again at the natural rate level and the price level has risen to P_2.

The net result of a one-shot permanent increase in government expenditure is a one-shot permanent increase in the price level. What happens to the inflation rate? When we move from point 1 to 1' to 2, the price level rises, and we have a positive inflation rate. But when we finally get to point 2, the inflation rate returns to zero. We see that the one-shot increase in government expenditure leads to only a *temporary* increase in the inflation rate, not to persistent inflation in which the price level is continually rising.

If government spending increases continually, however, we *could* get a continuing rise in the price level. It appears, then, that aggregate demand and supply analysis could reject Friedman's proposition that inflation is always the result of money growth. The problem with this argument is that a continually increasing level of government expenditure is not a feasible policy. There is a limit on the total amount of possible government expenditure; the government cannot spend more than 100% of GDP. In fact, well before this limit is reached, the political process would stop the increases in government spending. As revealed in the continual debates over balanced budgets and government spending, both the

---

[1] There is a possibility that the short-run aggregate supply curve may immediately shift in toward AS_2 because workers and firms may expect the increase in the money supply, so expected inflation will be higher. In this case, the movement to point 2 will be very rapid, and output need not rise above the natural rate level. (Some support for this scenario, from the theory of rational expectations, is discussed in Chapter 27.)

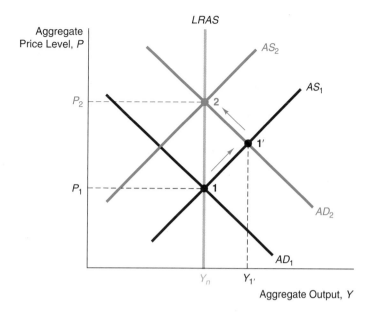

FIGURE 26-3 Response to a One-Shot Permanent Increase in Government Expenditure

A one-shot permanent increase in government expenditure shifts the aggregate demand curve rightward from AD_1 to AD_2, moving the economy from point 1 to point 1'. Because output now exceeds the natural rate level Y_n, the short-run aggregate supply curve eventually shifts leftward to AS_2, and the price level rises from P_1 to P_2, a one-shot permanent increase but not a continuing increase.

public and politicians have a particular target level of government spending they deem appropriate; although small deviations from this level might be tolerated, large deviations would not. Indeed, public and political perceptions impose tight limits on the degree to which government expenditures can increase.

What about the other side of fiscal policy—taxes? Could continual tax cuts generate inflation? Again the answer is no. The analysis in Figure 26-3 also describes the price and output response to a one-shot decrease in taxes. There will be a one-shot increase in the price level, but the increase in the inflation rate will be only temporary. We can increase the price level by cutting taxes even more, but this process would have to stop—once taxes reach zero, they can't be reduced further. We must conclude, then, that ***persistent high inflation cannot be driven by fiscal policy alone.***[2]

CAN SUPPLY-SIDE PHENOMENA BY THEMSELVES PRODUCE INFLATION? Because supply shocks and workers' attempts to increase their wages can shift the short-run aggregate supply curve leftward, you might suspect that these supply-side phenomena by themselves could stimulate inflation. Again, we can show that this suspicion is incorrect.

---

[2] The argument here demonstrates that "animal spirits" also cannot be the source of inflation. Although consumer and business optimism, which stimulates their spending, can produce a one-shot shift in the aggregate demand curve and temporary inflation, it cannot produce continuing shifts in the aggregate demand curve and persistent inflation. The reasoning is the same as before: Consumers and businesses cannot continue to raise their spending without limit because their spending cannot exceed 100% of GDP.

Suppose that there is a negative supply shock—for example, an oil embargo—that raises oil prices (or workers could have successfully pushed up their wages). As displayed in Figure 26-4, the negative supply shock shifts the short-run aggregate supply curve from AS_1 to AS_2. If the money supply remains unchanged, leaving the aggregate demand curve at AD_1, we move to point 1′, where output $Y_{1'}$ is below the natural rate level and the price level $P_{1'}$ is higher. The short-run aggregate supply curve will now shift back to AS_1 because unemployment is above the natural rate, and the economy slides down AD_1 from point 1′ to point 1. The net result of the supply shock is that we return to full employment at the initial price level, and there is no continuing inflation. Additional negative supply shocks that again shift the short-run aggregate supply curve leftward will lead to the same outcome. The price level will rise temporarily, but persistent inflation will not result. The conclusion that we have reached is the following: ***supply-side phenomena cannot be the source of persistent high inflation.***[3]

Summary

Our aggregate demand and supply analysis shows that persistent high inflation can occur only with a high rate of money growth. As long as we recognize that inflation refers to a *continuing* increase in the price level at a rapid rate, we now see why Milton Friedman was correct when he said that "inflation is always and everywhere a monetary phenomenon."

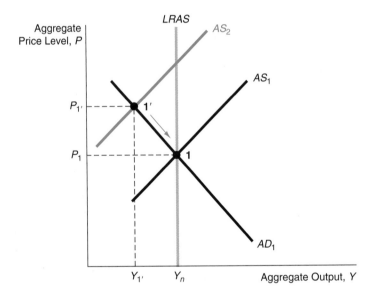

FIGURE 26-4   Response to a Supply Shock

A negative supply shock (or a wage push) shifts the short-run aggregate supply curve leftward to AS_2 and results in high unemployment at point 1′. As a result, the short-run aggregate supply curve shifts back to the right to AS_1, and the economy returns to point 1, where the price level has returned to P_1.

---

[3] Supply-side phenomena that alter the natural rate level of output (and shift the long-run aggregate supply curve at Y_n) can produce a permanent one-shot change in the price level. However, this resulting one-shot change results in only temporary inflation, not a continuing rise in the price level.

ORIGINS OF INFLATIONARY MONETARY POLICY

Although we now know *what* must occur to generate persistent rapid inflation—a high rate of money growth—we still can't understand *why* persistent high inflation occurs until we have learned how and why inflationary monetary policies come about. If everyone agrees that inflation is not a good thing for an economy, why do we see so much of it? Why do governments pursue inflationary monetary policies? Since there is nothing intrinsically desirable about inflation and since we know that a high rate of money growth doesn't happen of its own accord, it must follow that in trying to achieve other goals, governments end up with a high money growth rate and high inflation. In this section we will examine the government policies that are the most common sources of inflation.

High Employment Targets and Inflation

The first goal most governments pursue that often results in inflation is high employment. Two types of inflation can result from an activist stabilization policy to promote high employment: **cost-push inflation**, which occurs because of negative supply shocks or a push by workers to get higher wages, and **demand-pull inflation**, which results when policymakers pursue policies that shift the aggregate demand curve to the right. We will now use aggregate demand and supply analysis to examine how a high employment target can lead to both types of inflation.

COST-PUSH INFLATION In Figure 26-5, the economy is initially at point 1, the intersection of the aggregate demand curve AD_1 and the short-run aggregate supply curve AS_1. Suppose that workers decide to seek higher wages either because they want to increase their real wages (wages in terms of the goods and services they can buy) or because they expect inflation to be high and wish to keep up

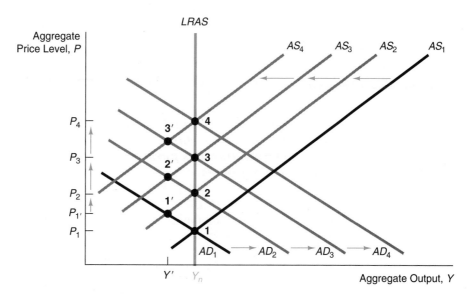

FIGURE 26-5 Cost-Push Inflation with an Activist Policy to Promote High Employment

In a cost-push inflation, the leftward shifts of the short-run aggregate supply curve from AS_1 to AS_2 to AS_3 and so on cause a government with a high employment target to shift the aggregate demand curve to the right continually to keep unemployment and output at their natural rate levels. The result is a continuing rise in the price level from P_1 to P_2 to P_3 and so on.

with inflation. The effect of such an increase (similar to a negative supply shock) is to shift the short-run aggregate supply curve leftward to AS_2.[4] If government fiscal and monetary policy remains unchanged, the economy would move to point 1' at the intersection of the new short-run aggregate supply curve AS_2 and the aggregate demand curve AD_1. Output would decline to below its natural rate level Y_n, and the price level would rise to $P_{1'}$.

What would policymakers with a high employment target do if this situation developed? Because of the drop in output and resulting increase in unemployment, they would implement policies to raise the aggregate demand curve to AD_2 so that we would return to the natural rate level of output at point 2 and price level P_2. The workers who have increased their wages have not fared too badly. The government has stepped in to make sure that there is no excessive unemployment, and they have achieved their goal of higher wages. Because the government has, in effect, given in to the demands of workers for higher wages, policy with a high employment target is often referred to as an **accommodating policy**.

The workers, having had their cake and eaten it too, might be encouraged to seek even higher wages. In addition, other workers might now realize that their wages have fallen relative to their fellow workers', and because they don't want to be left behind, these workers will seek to increase their wages. The result is that the short-run aggregate supply curve shifts leftward again, to AS_3. Unemployment develops again when we move to point 2', and policies will once more be used to shift the aggregate demand curve rightward to AD_3 and return the economy to full employment at a price level of P_3. If this process continues, the result will be a continuing increase in the price level—a persistent cost-push inflation.

What role does monetary policy play in a cost-push inflation? A cost-push inflation can occur only if the aggregate demand curve is shifted continually to the right. The first shift of the aggregate demand curve to AD_2 could be achieved by a one-shot increase in government expenditure or a one-shot decrease in taxes. But what about the next required rightward shift of the aggregate demand curve to AD_3, and the next, and the next? The limits on the maximum level of government expenditure and the minimum level of taxes would prevent the use of this expansionary fiscal policy for very long. Hence it cannot be used continually to shift the aggregate demand curve to the right. But the aggregate demand curve *can* be shifted continually rightward by continually increasing the money supply, that is, by going to a higher rate of money growth. Therefore, *a persistent cost-push inflation is a monetary phenomenon because it cannot occur without the monetary authorities pursuing an accommodating policy of a higher rate of money growth.*

DEMAND-PULL INFLATION The goal of high employment can lead to inflationary monetary policy in another way. Even at full employment, some unemployment is always present because of frictions in the labour market, which make it difficult to immediately match unemployed workers with employers. An unemployed autoworker in Windsor may not know about a job opening in the oil industry in Calgary or, even if he or she did, may not want to move or be retrained. So the unemployment rate when there is full employment (the natural rate of unemployment) will be greater than zero. If policymakers set a target for unemployment

---

[4] The cost-push inflation we describe here might also occur as a result of either firms' attempts to obtain higher prices or negative supply shocks.

that is too low because it is less than the natural rate of unemployment, this can set the stage for a higher rate of money growth and a resulting persistent inflation. Again we can show how this can happen using an aggregate supply and demand diagram (Figure 26-6).

If policymakers have an unemployment target (say 4%) that is below the natural rate (estimated to be 6% currently), they will try to achieve an output target greater than the natural rate level of output. This target level of output is marked Y_T in Figure 26-6. Suppose that we are initially at point 1; the economy is at the natural rate level of output but below the target level of output Y_T. To hit the unemployment target of 4%, policymakers enact policies to increase aggregate demand, and the effects of these policies shift the aggregate demand curve until it reaches AD_2 and the economy moves to point 1′. Output is at Y_T, and the 4% unemployment rate goal has been reached.

If the targeted unemployment rate were at the natural rate level, there would be no problem. However, because at Y_T the 4% unemployment rate is below the natural rate level, wages will rise and the short-run aggregate supply curve will shift leftward to AS_2, moving the economy from point 1′ to point 2. The economy is back at the natural rate of unemployment but at a higher price level of P_2. We could stop there, but because unemployment is again higher than the target level, policymakers would again shift the aggregate demand curve rightward to AD_3 to hit the output target at point 2′, and the whole process would continue to drive the economy to point 3 and beyond. The overall result is a steadily rising price level—persistent inflation.

How can policymakers continually shift the aggregate demand curve rightward? We have already seen that they cannot do it through fiscal policy because of the limits on raising government expenditures and reducing taxes. Instead they

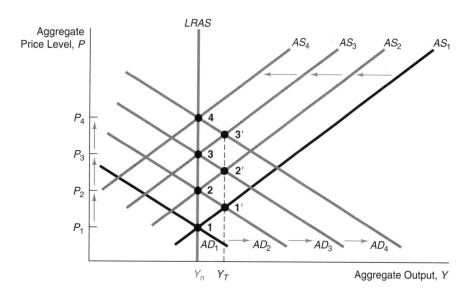

FIGURE 26-6 Demand-Pull Inflation: The Consequence of Setting Too Low an Unemployment Target

Too low an unemployment target (too high an output target of Y_T) causes the government to shift the aggregate demand curve rightward from AD_1 to AD_2 to AD_3 and so on, while the short-run aggregate supply curve shifts leftward from AS_1 to AS_2 to AS_3 and so on. The result is a continuing rise in the price level known as a demand-pull inflation.

will have to resort to expansionary monetary policy: a continuing increase in the money supply and hence a high money growth rate.

Pursuing too high an output target or, equivalently, too low an unemployment rate is the source of inflationary monetary policy in this situation, but it seems senseless for policymakers to do this. They have not gained the benefit of a permanently higher level of output but have generated the burden of an inflation. If, however, they do not realize that the target rate of unemployment is below the natural rate, the process that we see in Figure 26-6 will be well under way before they realize their mistake.

Because the inflation described results from policymakers pursuing policies that shift the aggregate demand curve to the right, it is called a *demand-pull inflation*. In contrast, a *cost-push inflation* occurs when workers push their wages up. Is it easy to distinguish between them in practice? The answer is no. We have seen that both types of inflation will be associated with higher money growth, so we cannot distinguish them on this basis. Yet as Figures 26-5 and 26-6 demonstrate, demand-pull inflation will be associated with periods when unemployment is below the natural rate level, whereas cost-push inflation is associated with periods when unemployment is above the natural rate level. To decide which type of inflation has occurred, we can look at whether unemployment has been above or below its natural rate level. This would be easy if economists and policymakers actually knew how to measure the natural rate of unemployment; unfortunately, this difficult research question is still not fully resolved by the economics profession. In addition, the distinction between cost-push and demand-pull inflation is blurred because a cost-push inflation can be initiated by a demand-pull inflation. When a demand-pull inflation produces higher inflation rates, expected inflation will eventually rise and cause workers to demand higher wages so that their real wages do not fall. In this way, demand-pull inflation can eventually trigger cost-push inflation.

Budget Deficits and Inflation

Our discussion of the evidence on money and inflation suggest that budget deficits are another possible source of inflationary monetary policy. To see if this could be the case, we need to look at how a government finances its budget deficits.

GOVERNMENT BUDGET CONSTRAINT   Because the government has to pay its bills just as we do, it has a budget constraint. There are two ways we can pay for our spending: raise revenue (by working) or borrow. The government also enjoys these two options: raise revenue by levying taxes or go into debt by issuing government bonds. Unlike us, however, it has a third option. The government can create money and use it to pay for the goods and services it buys.

Methods of financing government spending are described by an expression called the **government budget constraint**, which states the following: the government budget deficit *DEF*, which equals the excess of government spending *G* over tax revenue *T*, must equal the sum of the change in the monetary base ΔMB and the change in government bonds held by the public ΔB. Algebraically, this expression can be written as

$$DEF = G - T = \Delta MB + \Delta B \tag{1}$$

To see what the government budget constraint means in practice, let's look at the case in which the only government purchase is a $100 million supercomputer. If the government convinces the electorate that such a computer is worth paying for, it will probably be able to raise the $100 million in taxes to pay for it, and the budget deficit will equal zero. The government budget constraint then tells us that no issue of money or bonds is needed to pay for the computer because the budget is balanced. If taxpayers think that supercomputers are too expensive and refuse to pay taxes for them, the budget constraint indicates that the government must pay for it by selling $100 million of new bonds to the public or by, in effect, printing $100 million of currency to pay for the computer. In either case, the budget constraint is satisfied; the $100 million deficit is balanced by the change in the stock of government bonds held by the public (ΔB = $100 million) or by the change in the monetary base (ΔMB = $100 million).

The government budget constraint thus reveals two important facts. ***If the government deficit is financed by an increase in bond holdings by the public, there is no effect on the monetary base and hence on the money supply. But, if the deficit is not financed by increased bond holdings by the public, the monetary base and the money supply increase.***

There are several ways to understand why a deficit leads to an increase in the monetary base when the public's bond holdings do not increase. The simplest case is when the government issues currency to finance its deficit. Financing the deficit is then very straightforward. The government just pays for the spending that is in excess of its tax revenues with new currency. Because this increase in currency adds directly to the monetary base, the monetary base rises and the money supply with it through the process of multiple deposit creation described in Chapter 16.

In Canada, however, and in many other countries, the government does not have the right to issue currency to pay for its bills. In this case, the government must finance its deficit by first issuing bonds to the public to acquire the extra funds to pay its bills. Yet if these bonds do not end up in the hands of the public, the only alternative is that they are purchased by the central bank. For the government bonds not to end up in the hands of the public, the central bank must conduct an open market purchase, which, as we saw in Chapter 16, leads to an increase in the monetary base and in the money supply. This method of financing government spending is called **monetizing the debt** because, as the two-step process described indicates, government debt issued to finance government spending has been removed from the hands of the public and has been replaced by high-powered money. This method of financing, or the more direct method when a government just issues the currency directly, is also, somewhat inaccurately, referred to as **printing money** because high-powered money (the monetary base) is created in the process. The use of the word *printing* is misleading because what is essential to this method of financing government spending is not the actual printing of money but rather the issuing of monetary liabilities to the public after the money has been printed.

We thus see that a budget deficit can lead to an increase in the money supply if it is financed by the creation of high-powered money. However, earlier in this chapter you have seen that persistent inflation can develop only when the stock of money grows continually. Can a budget deficit financed by printing money do this? The answer is yes, if the budget deficit persists for a substantial period of time. In the first period, if the deficit is financed by money creation, the money supply will rise, shifting the aggregate demand curve to the right and leading to a rise in the price level (see Figure 26-2 on page 669). If the budget deficit is still present in the next period, it has to be financed all over again. The money supply will rise again, and the aggregate demand curve will again shift to the right, causing the price level to rise further. As long as the deficit persists and the government resorts to printing money to pay for it, this process will continue. ***Financing a persistent deficit using money creation will lead to sustained inflation.***

A critical element in this process is that the deficit is persistent. If temporary, it would not produce inflation because the situation would then be similar to that shown in Figure 26-3 (page 671), in which there is a one-shot increase in government expenditure. In the period when the deficit occurs, there will be an increase in money to finance it, and the resulting rightward shift of the aggregate demand curve will raise the price level. If the deficit disappears next period, there is no longer a need to print money. The aggregate demand curve will not shift further, and the price level will not continue to rise. Hence the one-shot increase in the money supply from the temporary deficit generates only a one-shot increase in the price level, and persistent inflation does not develop.

To summarize, *a deficit can be the source of sustained inflation only if it is persistent rather than temporary and if the government finances it by creating money rather than by issuing bonds to the public.*

If inflation is the result, why do governments frequently finance persistent deficits by creating money? The answer is the key to understanding how budget deficits may lead to inflation.

BUDGET DEFICITS AND MONEY CREATION IN OTHER COUNTRIES   Although Canada has well-developed money and capital markets in which huge quantities of its government bonds, both short- and long-term, can be sold, this is not the situation in many developing countries. If developing countries run budget deficits, they cannot finance them by issuing bonds and must resort to their only other alternative, printing money. As a result, when they run large deficits relative to GDP, the money supply grows at substantial rates, and persistent inflation results.

Earlier we cited Germany in the 1920s, and Zimbabwe more recently, which had high inflation rates and high money growth as evidence that inflation is a monetary phenomenon. The countries that had high money growth are precisely the ones that had persistent and extremely large budget deficits relative to GDP. The only way to finance the deficits was to print more money, so the ultimate source of their high inflation rates was their large budget deficits.

In all episodes of hyperinflation, huge government budget deficits are also the ultimate source of inflationary monetary policies. The budget deficits during hyperinflations are so large that even if a capital market exists to issue government bonds, it does not have sufficient capacity to handle the quantity of bonds that the government wishes to sell. In this situation, the government must also resort to the printing press to finance the deficits.

BUDGET DEFICITS AND MONEY CREATION IN CANADA   So far we have seen why budget deficits in some countries must lead to money creation and inflation. Either the deficit is huge, or the country does not have sufficient access to capital markets in which it can sell government bonds. But neither of these scenarios seems to describe the situation in Canada. True, Canada's deficits were large in the 1980s and early 1990s, but even so, the magnitude of these deficits relative to GDP was small compared to the deficits of countries that have experienced hyperinflations. The federal government deficit as a percentage of GDP reached a peak of 6.5% in 1985, whereas Argentina's budget deficit, for example, sometimes exceeded 15% of GDP. Furthermore, since Canada has a well-developed government bond market, it can issue large quantities of bonds when it needs to finance its deficit.

Whether the budget deficit can influence the monetary base and the money supply or not depends critically on how the Bank of Canada chooses to conduct monetary policy. If the Bank pursues a policy goal of preventing high interest rates (a possibility, as we saw in Chapter 18), many economists contend that a budget deficit will lead to the printing of money. Their reasoning, using the supply and demand analysis of the bond market in Chapter 5, is as follows: when the government issues bonds to the public, the supply of bonds rises (from B_1^s to B_2^s in Figure 26-7), causing bond prices to fall from P_1 to P_2 and hence interest rates to rise. If the Bank of Canada considers the rise in interest rates undesirable, it will buy bonds to prop up bond prices and reduce interest rates. The net result is that the government budget deficit can lead to Bank of Canada open market purchases, which raise the monetary base (create high-powered money) and raise the money supply. If the budget deficit persists so that the quantity of bonds supplied keeps on growing, the upward pressure on interest rates will continue, the Bank will purchase bonds again and again, and the money supply will continually rise, resulting in persistent inflation.

Economists such as Robert Barro of Harvard University, however, do not agree that budget deficits influence the monetary base in the manner just described. Their analysis (which Barro named **Ricardian equivalence** after the nineteenth-century British economist David Ricardo) contends that when the government runs deficits and issues bonds, the public recognizes that it will be subject to higher taxes in the future to pay off these bonds. The public then saves more in anticipation of these future taxes, with the net result that the public demand for bonds increases to match the increased supply. The demand curve for bonds shifts rightward to B_R^d in Figure 26-7, leaving the bond price and interest rate unchanged. There is now no need for the Bank of Canada to purchase bonds to keep the interest rate from rising.

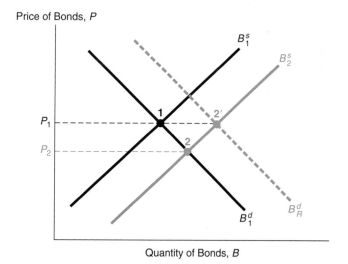

FIGURE 26-7 Interest Rates and the Government Budget Deficit

When the government issues bonds to finance the budget deficit, the supply curve for bonds shifts rightward from B_1^s to B_2^s. Many economists take the position that the equilibrium moves to point 2 because the bond demand curve remains unchanged, with the result that the bond price falls from P_1 to P_2 and the interest rate rises. Adherents of Ricardian equivalence, however, suggest that the demand curve for bonds also increases to B_R^d, moving the equilibrium to point 2', where the interest rate is unchanged at i_1.

To sum up, although persistent high inflation is "always and everywhere a monetary phenomenon" in the sense that it cannot occur without a high rate of money growth, there are reasons why inflationary monetary policy might come about. The two underlying reasons are the adherence of policymakers to a high employment target and the presence of persistent government budget deficits.

The Welfare Cost of Inflation

Although inflation has little effect on the long-run values of most real macroeconomic variables, such as output, consumption, and the real interest rate, there is one real variable (namely, real money balances, M/P) that depends negatively on the inflation rate and takes on different values with different rates of inflation. This suggests that there are welfare effects of inflation. In particular, as the inflation rate increases and the demand for real money balances declines (because of the subsequent increase in the nominal rate of interest), more time and energy must be devoted to shopping, for any given level of spending. This reduces the amount of leisure enjoyed by society's people and leads to lower utility levels (see the FYI box, Evidence on the Welfare Cost of Inflation).

APPLICATION   Explaining the Rise in Canadian Inflation, 1960–1980

Now that we have examined the underlying sources of inflation, let's apply this knowledge to understanding the causes of the rise in Canadian inflation from 1960 to 1980.

Figure 26-8 documents the rise in inflation in those years. At the beginning of the period, the inflation rate is less than 2% at an annual rate; by the late 1970s, it is averaging around 8%. How does the analysis of this chapter explain this rise in inflation?

The conclusion that inflation is a monetary phenomenon is given a fair amount of support by the period from 1960 through 1980. As Figure 26-8 shows, in this period there is a close correspondence between movements in the inflation rate and the monetary growth rate from two years earlier. (The money growth rates are from two years earlier because research indicates that a change in money growth takes that long to affect the inflation rate.) The rise in inflation from 1960 to 1980 can be attributed to the rise in the money growth rate over this period. But you have probably noticed that in 1979–1980, the inflation rate is well above the money growth rate from two years earlier. You may recall from Chapter 24 that temporary upward bursts of the inflation rate in those years can be attributed to supply shocks from oil and food price increases that occurred in 1978–1980.

However, the linkage between money growth and inflation after 1980 is not at all evident in Figure 26-8, and this explains why in 1982 the Bank of Canada announced that it would no longer use M1 as a basis to set monetary policy (see Chapter 18). The breakdown of the relationship between money growth and inflation is the result of substantial gyrations in velocity in the 1980s and 1990s (documented in Chapter 21). For example, the early 1980s was a period of rapid disinflation (a substantial fall in the inflation rate), yet the money growth rates in Figure 26-8 do not display a visible downward trend. (The disinflationary

FYI   Evidence on the Welfare Cost of Inflation

Robert E. Lucas Jr. of the University of Chicago recently provided estimates of the welfare cost of inflation in the United States, using data over the period from 1900 to 1994.[*] In doing so, he assumes an interest elasticity of money demand of −0.5 (as in the Baumol and Tobin model we discussed in Chapter 21) and estimates the welfare cost of inflation using tools from public finance and applied microeconomics. Lucas argues that reducing the interest rate from 3% to zero yields a benefit equivalent to an increase in real output of about 0.9% (or nine-tenths of one percent).

More recently, however, Apostolos Serletis and Kazem Yavari calculated the welfare cost of inflation for Canada and the United States over the post–World War II period (from 1948 to 2001), paying particular attention to the time series properties of the money demand variables and using recent advances in the field of applied econometrics to estimate the interest elasticity of money demand (instead of assuming that it is −0.5 as Lucas did).[**] Their estimates of the interest rate elasticity are −0.22 for Canada and −0.21 for the United States, much lower than the −0.5 value assumed by Lucas.

Based on this lower estimate of the interest elasticity of money demand, Serletis and Yavari conclude that the welfare cost of inflation is significantly lower than Lucas reported. In particular, for the United States, they find that reducing the interest rate from 3% to zero would yield a benefit equivalent to 0.0018 (less than two-tenths of one percent) of real income. This is much smaller than the 0.9% (nine-tenths of one percent) figure obtained by Lucas under the assumption that the interest elasticity of money demand is −0.5.

They also find that the welfare cost of inflation is marginally lower in Canada than it is in the United States, suggesting that varieties of monetary policy (such as attempts to stabilize interest rates rather than monetary aggregates, or monetary policy with an explicit rather than an implicit nominal anchor) have insignificant welfare effects on the North American economies. This is potentially important in the current debate in Canada of whether a floating currency is the right exchange rate regime or whether Canada should fix the exchange rate against the U.S. dollar, as in the 1962–1970 period, or consider a currency union with the United States.

[*] Robert E. Lucas Jr, "Inflation and Welfare," *Econometrica* 68 (2000): 247–274.

[**] Apostolos Serletis and Kazem Yavari, "The Welfare Cost of Inflation in Canada and the United States," *Economics Letters* 84 (2004): 199–204.

process in the 1980s will be discussed in another application later in this chapter.) Although some economists see the 1980s and 1990s as evidence against the money–inflation link, others view this as an unusual period characterized by large fluctuations in interest rates and by rapid financial innovation that made the correct measurement of money far more difficult (see Chapter 3). In their view, this period was an aberration, and the close correspondence of money and inflation is sure to reassert itself. However, this has not yet occurred.

What is the underlying cause of the increased rate of money growth that we see occurring from 1960 to 1980? We have identified two possible sources of inflationary monetary policy: government adherence to a high employment target and

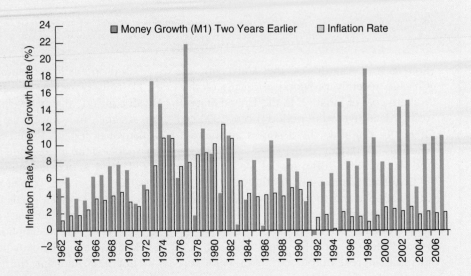

FIGURE 26-8   Inflation and Money Growth, 1960–2007

Source: IMF, *International Financial Statistics.*

budget deficits. Let's see if budget deficits can explain the move to an inflationary monetary policy by plotting the ratio of government debt to GDP in Figure 26-9. This ratio provides a reasonable measure of whether government budget deficits put upward pressure on interest rates. Only if this ratio is rising might there be a tendency for budget deficits to raise interest rates because the public is then being asked to hold more government bonds relative to their capacity to buy them. Surprisingly, over the course of the 20-year period from 1960 to 1980, this ratio was falling, not rising. Thus Canadian budget deficits in this period did not raise interest rates and so could not have encouraged the Bank of Canada to expand the money supply by buying bonds. Therefore, Figure 26-9 tells us that we can rule out budget deficits as a source of the rise in inflation in this period.

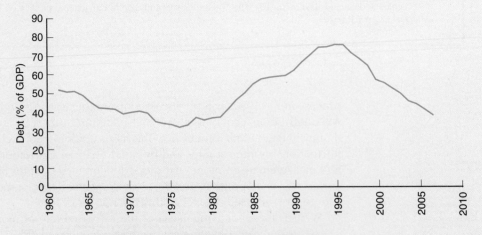

FIGURE 26-9   Government Debt-to-GDP Ratio, 1960–2007

Source: Statistics Canada, CANSIM II Series V34441 and V498086.

We have ruled out budget deficits as the instigator; what else could be the underlying cause of the higher rate of money growth and more rapid inflation in the 1960s and 1970s? Figure 26-10, which compares the actual unemployment rate to the natural rate of unemployment, shows that the economy was experiencing unemployment below the natural rate in all but three years between 1964 and 1974. This suggests that in 1964–1974, the Canadian economy was experiencing the demand-pull inflation described in Figure 26-6 (page 675).[5]

Policymakers apparently pursued policies that continually shifted the aggregate demand curve to the right in trying to achieve an output target that was too high, thus causing the continual rise in the price level outlined in Figure 26-6. This occurred because policymakers, economists, and politicians had become committed in the mid-1960s to full employment. Most economists today agree that the natural rate of unemployment was substantially higher in this period, on the order of 5% to 6%, as shown in Figure 26-10. The result of the inappropriate unemployment target was the beginning of the most sustained inflationary episode in Canadian history.

After 1975, the unemployment rate was regularly above the natural rate of unemployment, yet inflation continued. It appears that we have the phenomenon of a cost-push inflation described in Figure 26-5 on page 673 (the impetus for which was the earlier demand-pull inflation). The persistence of inflation can be explained by the public's knowledge that government policy continued to be concerned with achieving high employment. With a higher rate of expected inflation arising initially from the demand-pull inflation, the aggregate supply curve in Figure 26-5 continued to shift leftward, causing a rise in unemployment that policymakers would try to eliminate by shifting the aggregate demand curve to the right. The result was a continuation of the inflation that had started in the 1960s.

FIGURE 26-10   Unemployment and the Natural Rate of Unemployment, 1960–2008

Source: Historical Statistics of Canada, Second Edition, Catalogue 11-516, 1983; Statistics Canada, CANSIM II Series V2062815; and authors' calculations.

---

[5] Our estimates of the natural rate of unemployment are based on the methodology suggested by Finn E. Kydland and Edward C. Prescott, "Business Cycles: Real Facts and a Monetary Myth," Federal Reserve Bank of Minneapolis *Quarterly Review* (Spring 1990): 3–18. Although this method can produce reasonable estimates of the natural rate of unemployment, such estimates are subject to a great deal of uncertainty and disagreement amongst economists.

THE DISCRETIONARY/NONDISCRETIONARY POLICY DEBATE

All economists have similar policy goals—they want to promote high employment and price stability—and yet they often have very different views on how policy should be conducted. Advocates of **discretionary policy**, that is, policy to eliminate high unemployment whenever it appears, regard the self-correcting mechanism through wage and price adjustment (see Chapter 24) as very slow. Advocates of **nondiscretionary policy**, by contrast, believe that the performance of the economy would be improved if the government avoided discretionary policy reactions to eliminate unemployment. We will explore this policy debate by first looking at what the policy responses might be when the economy experiences high unemployment.

Responses to High Unemployment

Suppose that policymakers confront an economy that has moved to point 1′ in Figure 26-11. At this point, aggregate output $Y_{1'}$ is lower than the natural rate level, and the economy is suffering from high unemployment. Policymakers have two viable choices: If they are proponents of nondiscretionary policy and do nothing, the short-run aggregate supply curve will eventually shift rightward over time, driving the economy from point 1′ to point 1, where full employment is restored. The discretionary policy alternative is to try to eliminate the high unemployment by attempting to shift the aggregate demand curve rightward to AD_2 by pursuing expansionary policy (an increase in the money supply, increase in government spending, or lowering of taxes). If policymakers could shift the aggregate demand curve to AD_2 instantaneously, the economy would immediately move to point 2, where there is full employment. However, several types of lags prevent this immediate movement from occurring.

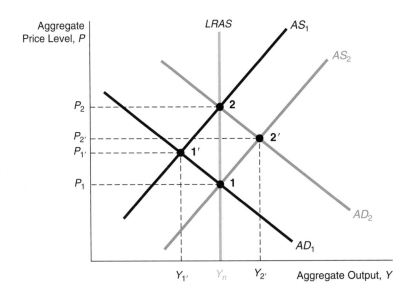

FIGURE 26-11 The Choice Between Discretionary and Nondiscretionary Policy

When the economy has moved to point 1′, the policymaker has two choices of policy: the nondiscretionary policy of doing nothing and letting the economy return to point 1 or the discretionary policy of shifting the aggregate demand curve to AD_2 to move the economy to point 2.

1. The *data lag* is the time it takes for policymakers to obtain the data that tell them what is happening in the economy. Accurate data on GDP, for example, are not available until several months after a given quarter is over.

2. The *recognition lag* is the time it takes for policymakers to be sure of what the data are signalling about the future course of the economy. For example, to minimize errors, the government will not declare the economy to be in recession until at least six months after it has determined that one has begun.

3. The *legislative lag* represents the time it takes to pass legislation to implement a particular policy. The legislative lag does not exist for most monetary policy actions such as open market operations. It is, however, important for the implementation of fiscal policy, when it can sometimes take six months to a year to get legislation passed to change taxes or government spending.

4. The *implementation lag* is the time it takes for policymakers to change policy instruments once they have decided on the new policy. Again, this lag is unimportant for the conduct of open market operations because the Bank of Canada's trading desk can purchase or sell bonds almost immediately upon being told to do so. Actually implementing fiscal policy may take time, however; for example, getting government agencies to change their spending habits takes time, as does changing tax tables.

5. The *effectiveness lag* is the time it takes for the policy actually to have an impact on the economy. An important argument against discretionary policy is that the effectiveness lag is long (often a year or longer) and variable (i.e., there is substantial uncertainty about how long this lag is).

Discretionary and Non-discretionary Positions

Now that we understand the considerations that affect decisions by policymakers on whether to pursue discretionary versus nondiscretionary policy, we can examine when each of these policies would be preferable.

CASE FOR A DISCRETIONARY POLICY Advocates of discretionary policies view the wage and price adjustment process as extremely slow. They believe that nondiscretionary policy is costly because the slow movement of the economy back to full employment results in a large loss of output. However, even though the five lags described above result in a delay of a year or two before the aggregate demand curve shifts to AD_2, the short-run aggregate supply curve moves very little during this time. The appropriate path for policymakers to pursue is thus a discretionary policy of moving the economy to point 2 in Figure 26-11.

CASE FOR A NONDISCRETIONARY POLICY Opponents of discretionary policy view the wage and price adjustment process as more rapid than advocates of discretionary policy do and consider nondiscretionary policy less costly because output is soon back at the natural rate level. They suggest that a discretionary policy of shifting the aggregate demand curve to AD_2 is costly because it produces more volatility in both the price level and output. The reason for this volatility is that the time it takes to shift the aggregate demand curve to AD_2 is substantial, whereas the wage and price adjustment process is more rapid. Hence before the aggregate demand curve shifts to the right, the short-run aggregate supply curve will have shifted rightward to AS_2, and the economy will have moved from point 1' to point 1, where it has returned to the natural rate level of output Y_n. After adjustment to the AS_2 curve is complete, the shift of the aggregate demand curve to AD_2 finally takes effect, leading the economy to point 2' at the intersection of AD_2 and AS_2.

Aggregate output at $Y_{2'}$ is now greater than the natural rate level ($Y_{2'} > Y_n$), so the short-run aggregate supply curve will now shift leftward back to AS_1, moving the economy to point 2, where output is again at the natural rate level.

Although the discretionary policy eventually moves the economy to point 2 as policymakers intended, it leads to a sequence of equilibrium points—1′, 1, 2′, and 2—at which both output and the price level have been highly variable. Output overshoots its target level of Y_n, and the price level falls from $P_{1'}$ to P_1 and then rises to $P_{2'}$ and eventually to P_2. Because this variability is undesirable, policymakers would be better off pursuing nondiscretionary policy, which just lets the economy move to point 1.

Expectations and Discretionary/ Non-discretionary Debate

Our analysis of inflation in the 1970s demonstrated that expectations about policy can be an important element in the inflation process. Allowing for expectations about policy to affect how wages are set (the wage-setting process) provides an additional reason for pursuing a nondiscretionary policy.

DO EXPECTATIONS FAVOUR A NONDISCRETIONARY POLICY?   Does the possibility that expectations about policy matter to the wage-setting process strengthen the case for nondiscretionary policy? The case for discretionary policy states that with slow wage and price adjustment, the discretionary policy returns the economy to full employment at point 2 far more quickly than it takes to get to full employment at point 1 if nothing is done. However, the argument for discretionary policy does not allow for the possibility (1) that expectations about policy matter to the wage-setting process and (2) that the economy might initially have moved from point 1 to point 1′ because of an attempt by workers to raise their wages or a negative supply shock shifted the short-run aggregate supply curve from AS_2 to AS_1. We must therefore ask the following question about discretionary policy: will the short-run aggregate supply curve continue to shift to the left after the economy has reached point 2, leading to cost-push inflation?

The answer to this question is yes *if* expectations about policy matter. Our discussion of cost-push inflation in Figure 26-5 (page 673) suggested that if workers know that policy will be accommodating in the future, they will continue to push their wages up, and the short-run aggregate supply curve will keep shifting leftward. As a result, policymakers are forced to accommodate the cost push by continuing to shift the aggregate demand curve to the right to eliminate the unemployment that develops. The accommodating, discretionary policy with its high employment target has the hidden cost or disadvantage that it may well lead to inflation.[6]

The main advantage of a nonaccommodating, nondiscretionary policy, in which policymakers do not try to shift the aggregate demand curve in response to the cost push, is that it will prevent inflation. As depicted in Figure 26-4 (page 672), the result of an upward push on wages in the face of a nonaccommodating, nonactivist policy will be a period of unemployment above the natural rate level, which will eventually shift the short-run aggregate supply curve and the price level back to their initial positions. The main criticism of this policy is that the economy will suffer protracted periods of unemployment when the short-run aggregate supply curve shifts leftward. Workers, however, would probably not

---

[6] The issue that is being described here is the time-inconsistency problem described in Chapter 18.

push for higher wages to begin with if they knew that policy would be nonaccommodating, because their wage gains would lead to a protracted period of unemployment. A nonaccommodating, nondiscretionary policy may have not only the advantage of preventing inflation but also the hidden benefit of discouraging leftward shifts in the short-run aggregate supply curve that lead to excessive unemployment.

In conclusion, ***if workers' opinions about whether policy is accommodating or nonaccommodating matter to the wage-setting process, the case for discretionary policy is much weaker.***

DO EXPECTATIONS ABOUT POLICY MATTER TO THE WAGE-SETTING PROCESS? The answer to this question is crucial to deciding whether discretionary or nondiscretionary policy is preferred and so has become a major topic of current research for economists, but the evidence is not yet conclusive. We can ask, however, whether expectations about policy do affect people's behaviour in other contexts. This information will help us know if expectations regarding whether or not policy is accommodating are important to the wage-setting process.

As any good negotiator knows, convincing your opponent that you will be nonaccommodating is crucial to getting a good deal. If you are bargaining with a car dealer over price, for example, you must convince him that you can just as easily walk away from the deal and buy a car from a dealer on the other side of town. This principle also applies to conducting foreign policy—it is to your advantage to convince your opponent that you will go to war (be nonaccommodating) if your demands are not met. Similarly, if your opponent thinks that you will be accommodating, he will almost certainly take advantage of you. Finally, anyone who has dealt with a two-year-old child knows that the more you give in (pursue an accommodating policy), the more demanding the child becomes. People's expectations about policy *do* affect their behaviour. Consequently, it is quite plausible that expectations about policy also affect the wage-setting process.[7]

Discretionary versus Non-discretionary: Conclusions

The following conclusions can be generated from our analysis. Advocates of discretionary policy believe in the use of policy to eliminate excessive unemployment whenever it develops because they view the wage and price adjustment process as sluggish and unresponsive to expectations about policy. Proponents of nondiscretionary policy, by contrast, believe that a discretionary policy that reacts to excessive unemployment is counterproductive, because wage and price adjustment is rapid and because expectations about policy can matter to the wage-setting process. Proponents of nondiscretionary policy thus advocate the use of a policy rule to keep the aggregate demand curve from fluctuating away from the trend rate of growth of the natural rate level of output. Monetarists, who oppose discretionary policy and who also see money as the sole source of fluctuations in the aggregate demand curve, in the past advocated

---

[7] A recent development in monetary theory, new classical macroeconomics, strongly suggests that expectations about policy are crucial to the wage-setting process and the movements of the aggregate supply curve. We will explore why new classical macroeconomics comes to this conclusion in Chapter 27, when we discuss the implications of the rational expectations hypothesis, which states that expectations are formed using all available information, including expectations about policy.

a policy rule whereby the Bank of Canada keeps the money supply growing at a constant rate. This monetarist rule is referred to as a **constant-money-growth-rate rule.** Because of the misbehaviour of velocity of M1 and M2, monetarists such as Bennett McCallum and Alan Meltzer of Carnegie-Mellon University now advocate a rule for the growth of the monetary base that is adjusted for past velocity changes.

As our analysis indicates, an important element for the success of a nonaccommodating policy rule is that it be *credible*. The public must believe that policymakers will be tough and not accede to a cost push by shifting the aggregate demand curve to the right to eliminate unemployment. In other words, government policymakers need credibility as inflation-fighters in the eyes of the public. Otherwise, workers will be more likely to push for higher wages, which will shift the aggregate supply curve leftward after the economy reaches full employment at a point such as point 2 in Figure 26-11 (page 684) and will lead to unemployment or inflation (or both). Alternatively, a credible, nonaccommodating policy rule has the benefit that it makes a cost push less likely and thus helps prevent inflation and potential increases in unemployment. The following application suggests that recent historical experience is consistent with the importance of credibility to successful policymaking.

APPLICATION   Importance of Credibility to the Bank of Canada's Victory over Inflation

In the period from 1965 through the 1970s, policymakers had little credibility as inflation-fighters—a well-deserved reputation, as they pursued a discretionary accommodating policy to achieve high employment. As we have seen, the outcome was not a happy one. Inflation soared to double-digit levels, while the unemployment rate remained high. To wring inflation out of the system, the Bank of Canada under governor Gerald Bouey put the economy through two back-to-back recessions in 1980 and 1981–1982. (The data on inflation, money growth, and unemployment in this period are shown in Figures 26-8 and 26-10 on pages 682 and 683.) Only after the 1981–1982 recession—the most severe in the postwar period, with unemployment above the 10% level—did Bouey establish credibility for the Bank of Canada's anti-inflation policy. By the end of 1983, inflation was running at a rate of less than 5%.

From November 1982 to January 1988, the primary objective of the Bank of Canada was price stability in the longer term and inflation containment in the shorter term. This policy, however, was carried out without intermediate targets or a specified path to the longer-term goal. In January 1988, John Crow, the governor of the Bank of Canada, announced that the Bank would subsequently pursue an objective of price stability. One indication of the Bank of Canada's credibility came in 1991 when the Bank and the Department of Finance jointly announced inflation targets. This convinced the public and the markets that if inflation reared its head, the Bank of Canada would pursue a nonaccommodating policy of quashing it. Workers and firms did not raise wages and prices, which would have led to both inflation and unemployment. The success of the Bank's anti-inflation policy has been continuing to date—the inflation rate has been running at a rate of less than 3%. The Bank of Canada's triumph over inflation was achieved because it obtained credibility the hard way: it earned it.

SUMMARY

1. Milton Friedman's famous proposition that "inflation is always and everywhere a monetary phenomenon" is supported by the following evidence. Every country that has experienced sustained, high inflation has also experienced a high rate of money growth.

2. Aggregate demand and supply analysis shows that Keynesian and monetarist views of the inflation process are not very different. Both believe that high inflation can occur only if there is a high rate of money growth. As long as we recognize that by inflation we mean a rapid and continuing increase in the price level, almost all economists agree with Friedman's proposition.

3. Although high inflation is "always and everywhere a monetary phenomenon" in the sense that it cannot

occur without a high rate of money growth, there are reasons why inflationary monetary policy comes about. The two underlying reasons are the adherence of policymakers to a high employment target and the presence of persistent government budget deficits.

4. Advocates of discretionary policy believe in the use of policy to eliminate excessive unemployment whenever it occurs because they view wage and price adjustment as sluggish and unresponsive to expectations about policy. Advocates of nondiscretionary policy take the opposite view and believe that discretionary policy is counterproductive. In addition, they regard the credibility of a nonaccommodating anti-inflation policy as crucial to its success.

KEY TERMS

accommodating policy,   p. 674

constant-money-growth-rate
   rule,   p. 688

cost-push inflation,   p. 673

demand-pull inflation,   p. 673

discretionary policy,   p. 684

government budget
   constraint,   p. 676

monetizing the debt,   p. 677

nondiscretionary policy,   p. 684

printing money,   p. 677

Ricardian equivalence,   p. 679

QUESTIONS

You will find the answers to the questions marked with an asterisk in the Textbook Resources section of your MyEconLab.

1. "There are frequently years when the inflation rate is high and yet money growth is quite low. Therefore, the statement that inflation is a monetary phenomenon cannot be correct." Comment.

*2. Why do economists focus on historical episodes of hyperinflation to decide whether inflation is a monetary phenomenon?

3. "Since increases in government spending raise the aggregate demand curve, fiscal policy by itself can be the source of inflation." Is this statement true, false, or uncertain? Explain your answer.

*4. "A cost-push inflation occurs as a result of workers' attempts to push up their wages. Therefore, inflation does not have to be a monetary phenomenon." Is this statement true, false, or uncertain? Explain your answer.

5. "Because government policymakers do not consider inflation desirable, their policies cannot be the source of inflation." Is this statement true, false, or uncertain? Explain your answer.

*6. "A budget deficit that is only temporary cannot be the source of inflation." Is this statement true, false, or uncertain? Explain your answer.

7. How can the Bank of Canada's desire to prevent high interest rates lead to inflation?

*8. "If the data and recognition lags could be reduced, discretionary policy would more likely be beneficial to the economy." Is this statement true, false, or uncertain? Explain your answer.

9. "The more sluggish wage and price adjustment is, the more variable output and the price level are when a discretionary policy is pursued." Is this statement true, false, or uncertain? Explain your answer.

*10. "If the public believes that the monetary authorities will pursue a discretionary policy, cost-push inflation is more likely to develop." Is this statement true, false, or uncertain? Explain your answer.

11. Why are discretionary policies to eliminate unemployment more likely to lead to inflation than nondiscretionary policies?

*12. "The less important expectations about policy are to movements of the aggregate supply curve, the stronger the case is for discretionary policy to eliminate unemployment." Is this statement true, false, or uncertain? Explain your answer.

13. If the economy's self-correcting mechanism works slowly, should the government necessarily pursue discretionary policy to eliminate unemployment?

*14. "To prevent inflation, the Bank of Canada should follow Teddy Roosevelt's advice: 'Speak softly and carry a big stick.'" What would the Bank's "big stick" be? What is the statement trying to say?

CANSIM Question

15. Figure 26-8 on page 682 reports the inflation rate from 1960 to 2008. As this chapter states, inflation continues to be a major factor in economic policy. Get the monthly data from 1960 to 2009 on the Consumer Price Index (CANSIM series V41690973) from the Textbook Resources area of the MyEconLab.

a. Graph these data and compare them to Figure 26-8.
b. Has inflation increased or decreased since the end of 2008?
c. When was inflation at its highest? When was inflation at its lowest?
d. Have we ever had a period of deflation? If so, when?
e. Have we ever had a period of hyperinflation? If so, when?

WEB EXERCISES

1. It can be interesting to compare the purchasing power of the dollar over different periods in history. Go to **www.bankofcanada.ca/en/rates.htm** and scroll down to the link to the "inflation calculator" to compute the following.

a. If a new house cost $10 000 in 1950, what would it have cost in 2009?
b. From (a), what is the percent change in the price of the house from 1950 to 2009?
c. What is the average annual rate of inflation?

Be sure to visit the MyEconLab website at **www.myeconlab.com**. This online homework and tutorial system puts you in control of your own learning with study and practice tools directly correlated to this chapter content.

CHAPTER 27

Rational Expectations: Implications for Policy

LEARNING OBJECTIVES

After studying this chapter you should be able to

1. describe the Lucas critique of policy evaluation
2. illustrate the new classical and new Keynesian aggregate demand and supply models
3. represent the effect of activist stabilization policy in a rational expectations world
4. recount the impact of the rational expectations revolution in macroeconomics

PREVIEW

After World War II, economists, armed with models (such as the *ISLM* model) that described how government policies could be used to manipulate employment and output, felt that discretionary policies could reduce the severity of business cycle fluctuations without creating inflation. In the 1960s and 1970s, these economists got their chance to put their policies into practice (see Chapter 26), but the results were not what they had anticipated. The economic record for that period is not a happy one. Inflation accelerated, the rate often climbing above 10%, while unemployment figures deteriorated from those of the 1950s.[1]

In the 1970s and 1980s, economists, including Robert Lucas of the University of Chicago and Thomas Sargent of Stanford University and the University of Chicago, used rational expectations theory to examine why discretionary policies appear to have performed so poorly. Their analysis cast doubt on whether macroeconomic models can be used to evaluate the potential effects of policy and on whether policy can be effective when the public *expects* that it will be implemented. Because the analysis of Lucas and Sargent has such strong implications for the way policy should be conducted, it has been labelled the *rational expectations revolution*.[2]

This chapter examines the analysis behind the rational expectations revolution. We start first with the Lucas critique, which indicates that because expectations are important in economic behaviour, it may be quite difficult to predict what the

---

[1] Some of the deterioration can be attributed to supply shocks in 1973–1975 and 1978–1980.

[2] Other economists who have been active in promoting the rational expectations revolution are Robert Barro of Harvard University, Bennett McCallum of Carnegie-Mellon University, Edward Prescott of the University of Minnesota, and Neil Wallace of Pennsylvania State University.

outcome of a discretionary policy will be. We then discuss the effect of rational expectations on the aggregate demand and supply analysis developed in Chapter 24 by exploring three models that incorporate expectations in different ways.

A comparison of all three models indicates that the existence of rational expectations makes discretionary policies less likely to be successful and raises the issue of credibility as an important element affecting policy outcomes. With rational expectations, an essential ingredient to a successful anti-inflation policy is the credibility of the policy in the eyes of the public. The rational expectations revolution is now at the centre of many of the current debates in monetary theory that have major implications for how monetary and fiscal policy should be conducted.

THE LUCAS CRITIQUE OF POLICY EVALUATION

In his famous paper "Econometric Policy Evaluation: A Critique," Robert Lucas presented an argument that had devastating implications for the usefulness of conventional **econometric models** (models whose equations are estimated with statistical procedures) for evaluating policy.[3] Economists developed these models for two purposes: to forecast economic activity and to evaluate the effects of different policies. Although Lucas's critique had nothing to say about the usefulness of these models as forecasting tools, he argued that they could not be relied on to evaluate the potential impact of particular policies on the economy.

Econometric Policy Evaluation

To understand Lucas's argument, we must first understand econometric policy evaluation: how econometric models are used to evaluate policy. For example, we can examine how the Bank of Canada uses its econometric model in making decisions about the future course of monetary policy. The model contains equations that describe the relationships among hundreds of variables. These relationships are assumed to remain constant and are estimated using past data. Let's say that the Bank wants to know the effect on unemployment and inflation of a decrease in the overnight rate from 3% to 2%. It feeds the new, lower overnight rate into a computer that contains the model, and the model then provides an answer about how much unemployment will fall as a result of the lower overnight rate and how much the inflation rate will rise. Other possible policies, such as a rise in the overnight rate by one percentage point, might also be fed into the model. After a series of these policies have been tried out, the policymakers at the Bank can see which policies produce the most desirable outcome for unemployment and inflation.

Lucas's challenge to this procedure for evaluating policies is based on a simple principle of rational expectations theory from Chapter 7: *The way in which expectations are formed (the relationship of expectations to past information) changes when the behaviour of forecasted variables changes.* So when policy changes, the relationship between expectations and past information will change, and because expectations affect economic behaviour, the relationships in the econometric model will change. The econometric model, which has been estimated with past data, is then no longer the correct model for evaluating the response to this policy change and may consequently prove highly misleading.

---

[3] *Carnegie-Rochester Conference Series on Public Policy* 1 (1976): 19–46.

**Example:
The Term
Structure of
Interest Rates**

The best way to understand Lucas's argument is to look at a concrete example involving only one equation typically found in econometric models: the term structure equation. The equation relates the long-term interest rate to current and past values of the short-term interest rate. It is one of the most important equations in macro econometric models because the long-term interest rate, not the short-term rate, is the one believed to have an impact on aggregate demand.

In Chapter 6 we learned that the long-term interest rate is related to an average of expected future short-term interest rates. Suppose that in the past, when the short-term rate rose, it quickly fell back down again; that is, any increase was temporary. Because rational expectations theory suggests that any rise in the short-term interest rate is expected to be only temporary, a rise should have only a minimal effect on the average of expected future short-term rates. It will cause the long-term interest rate to rise by a negligible amount. The term structure relationship estimated using past data would then show only a weak effect on the long-term interest rate of changes in the short-term rate.

Suppose the Bank of Canada wants to evaluate what will happen to the economy if it pursues a policy that is likely to raise the short-term interest rate from a current level of 5% to a permanently higher level of 8%. The term structure equation that has been estimated using past data will indicate that there will be just a small change in the long-term interest rate. However, if the public recognizes that the short-term rate is rising to a permanently higher level, rational expectations theory indicates that people will no longer expect a rise in the short-term rate to be temporary. Instead, when they see the interest rate rise to 8%, they will expect the average of future short-term interest rates to rise substantially, and so the long-term interest rate will rise greatly, not minimally as the estimated term structure equation suggests. You can see that evaluating the likely outcome of the change in Bank of Canada policy with an econometric model can be highly misleading.

The term structure example also demonstrates another aspect of the Lucas critique. The effects of a particular policy depend critically on the public's expectations about the policy. If the public expects the rise in the short-term interest rate to be merely temporary, the response of long-term interest rates, as we have seen, will be negligible. If, however, the public expects the rise to be more permanent, the response of long-term rates will be far greater. ***The Lucas critique points out not only that conventional econometric models cannot be used for policy evaluation but also that the public's expectations about a policy will influence the response to that policy.***

The term structure equation discussed here is only one of many equations in econometric models to which the Lucas critique applies. In fact, Lucas uses the examples of consumption and investment equations in his paper. One attractive feature of the term structure example is that it deals with expectations in a financial market, a sector of the economy for which the theory and empirical evidence supporting rational expectations are very strong. The Lucas critique should also apply, however, to sectors of the economy for which rational expectations theory is more controversial because the basic principle of the Lucas critique is not that expectations are always rational but rather that the formation of expectations changes when the behaviour of a forecasted variable changes. This less stringent principle is supported by the evidence in sectors of the economy other than financial markets.

NEW CLASSICAL MACROECONOMIC MODEL

We now turn to the implications of rational expectations for the aggregate demand and supply analysis we studied in Chapter 24. The first model we examine that views expectations as rational is the *new classical macroeconomic model* developed by Robert Lucas and Thomas Sargent, among others. In the new classical model, all wages and prices are completely flexible with respect to expected changes in the price level; that is, a rise in the expected price level results in an immediate and equal rise in wages and prices because workers try to keep their *real* wages from falling when they expect the price level to rise.

This view of how wages and prices are set indicates that a rise in the expected price level causes an immediate leftward shift in the short-run aggregate supply curve, which leaves real wages unchanged and aggregate output at the natural rate (full-employment) level if expectations are realized. This model then suggests that anticipated policy has no effect on aggregate output and unemployment; only unanticipated policy has an effect.

Effects of Unanticipated and Anticipated Policy

First, let us look at the short-run response to an unanticipated (unexpected) policy such as an unexpected increase in the money supply.

In Figure 27-1, the short-run aggregate supply curve AS_1 is drawn for an expected price level P_1. The initial aggregate demand curve AD_1 intersects AS_1 at point 1, where the realized price level is at the expected price level P_1 and aggregate output is at the natural rate level Y_n. Because point 1 is also on the long-run aggregate supply curve at Y_n, there is no tendency for the aggregate supply to shift. The economy remains in long-run equilibrium.

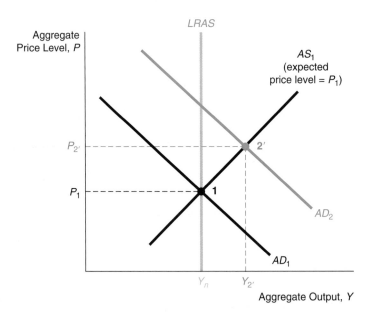

FIGURE 27-1   Short-Run Response to Unanticipated Expansionary Policy in the New Classical Model

Initially, the economy is at point 1 at the intersection of AD_1 and AS_1 (expected price level = P_1). An expansionary policy shifts the aggregate demand curve to AD_2, but because this is unexpected, the short-run aggregate supply curve remains fixed at AS_1. Equilibrium now occurs at point 2'—aggregate output has increased above the natural rate level to $Y_{2'}$, and the price level has increased to $P_{2'}$.

Suppose the Bank of Canada suddenly decides the unemployment rate is too high and so makes a large bond purchase that is unexpected by the public. The money supply increases, and the aggregate demand curve shifts rightward to AD_2. Because this shift is unexpected, the expected price level remains at P_1 and the short-run aggregate supply curve remains at AS_1. Equilibrium is now at point 2′, the intersection of AD_2 and AS_1. Aggregate output increases above the natural rate level to $Y_{2'}$ and the realized price level increases to $P_{2'}$.

If, by contrast, the public expects that the Bank of Canada will make these open market purchases in order to lower unemployment because they have seen it done in the past, the expansionary policy will be anticipated. The outcome of such anticipated expansionary policy is illustrated in Figure 27-2. Because expectations are rational, workers and firms recognize that an expansionary policy will shift the aggregate demand curve to the right and will expect the aggregate price level to rise to P_2. Workers will demand higher wages so that their real earnings will remain the same when the price level rises. The short-run aggregate supply curve then shifts leftward to AS_2 and intersects AD_2 at point 2, an equilibrium point where aggregate output is at the natural rate level Y_n and the price level has risen to P_2.

The new classical macroeconomic model demonstrates that aggregate output does not increase as a result of anticipated expansionary policy and that the economy immediately moves to a point of long-run equilibrium (point 2) where aggregate output is at the natural rate level. Although Figure 27-2 suggests why this occurs, we have not yet proved why an anticipated expansionary policy shifts the short-run aggregate supply curve to exactly AS_2 (corresponding to an expected price level of P_2) and hence why aggregate output *necessarily* remains at the natural rate level. The proof is somewhat difficult and is dealt with in the FYI box, Proof of the Policy Ineffectiveness Proposition.

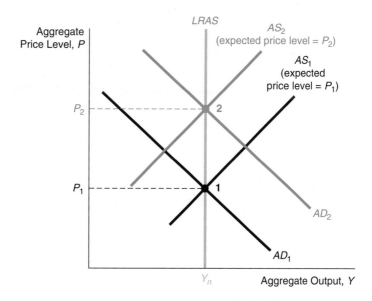

FIGURE 27-2 Short-Run Response to Anticipated Expansionary Policy in the New Classical Model

The expansionary policy shifts the aggregate demand curve rightward to AD_2, but because this policy is expected, the short-run aggregate supply curve shifts leftward to AS_2. The economy moves to point 2, where aggregate output is still at the natural rate level but the price level has increased to P_2.

FYI   **Proof of the Policy Ineffectiveness Proposition**

The proof that in the new classical macroeconomic model aggregate output *necessarily* remains at the natural rate level when there is anticipated expansionary policy is as follows. In the new classical model, the expected price level for the short-run aggregate supply curve occurs at its intersection with the long-run aggregate supply curve (see Figure 27-2). The optimal forecast of the price level is given by the intersection of the aggregate supply curve with the anticipated aggregate demand curve AD_2. If the short-run aggregate supply curve is to the right of AS_2 in Figure 27-2, it will intersect AD_2 at a price level lower than the expected level (which is the intersection of this aggregate supply curve and the

long-run aggregate supply curve). The optimal forecast of the price level will then not equal the expected price level, thereby violating the rationality of expectations. A similar argument can be made to show that when the short-run aggregate supply curve is to the left of AS_2, the assumption of rational expectations is violated. Only when the short-run aggregate supply curve is at AS_2 (corresponding to an expected price level of P_2) are expectations rational because the optimal forecast equals the expected price level. As we see in Figure 27-2, the AS_2 curve implies that aggregate output remains at the natural rate level as a result of the anticipated expansionary policy.

The new classical model has the word *classical* associated with it because when policy is anticipated, the new classical model has a property that is associated with the classical economists of the nineteenth and early twentieth centuries: aggregate output remains at the natural rate level. Yet the new classical model allows aggregate output to fluctuate away from the natural rate level as a result of *unanticipated* movements in the aggregate demand curve. The conclusion from the new classical model is a striking one: ***anticipated policy has no effect on the business cycle; only unanticipated policy matters.***[4]

This conclusion has been called the **policy ineffectiveness proposition** because it implies that one anticipated policy is just like any other; it has no effect on output fluctuations. You should recognize that this proposition does not rule out output effects from policy changes. If the policy is a surprise (unanticipated), it will have an effect on output.[5]

Can an Expansionary Policy Lead to a Decline in Aggregate Output?

Another important feature of the new classical model is that an expansionary policy, such as an increase in the rate of money growth, can lead to a *decline* in aggregate output if the public expects an even more expansionary policy than the one actually implemented. There will be a surprise in the policy, but it will be negative and drive output down. Policymakers cannot be sure if their policies will work in the intended direction.

---

[4] Note that the new classical view in which anticipated policy has no effect on the business cycle does not imply that anticipated policy has no effect on the overall health of the economy. For example, the new classical analysis does not rule out possible effects of anticipated policy on the natural rate of output Y_n, which can benefit the public.

[5] Thomas Sargent and Neil Wallace, "'Rational' Expectations, the Optimal Monetary Instrument, and the Optimal Money Supply Rule," *Journal of Political Economy* 83 (1975): 241–254, first demonstrated the full implications of the policy ineffectiveness proposition.

To see how an expansionary policy can lead to a decline in aggregate output, let us turn to the aggregate supply and demand diagram in Figure 27-3. Initially we are at point 1, the intersection of AD_1 and AS_1; output is Y_n, and the price level is P_1. Now suppose that the public expects the Bank of Canada to increase the money supply in order to shift the aggregate demand curve to AD_2. As we saw in Figure 27-2, the short-run aggregate supply curve shifts leftward to AS_2 because the price level is expected to rise to P_2. Suppose that the expansionary policy engineered by the Bank of Canada actually falls short of what was expected so that the aggregate demand curve shifts only to $AD_{2'}$. The economy will move to point 2', the intersection of the short-run aggregate supply curve AS_2 and the aggregate demand curve $AD_{2'}$. The result of the mistaken expectation is that output falls to $Y_{2'}$, while the price level rises to $P_{2'}$ rather than P_2. An expansionary policy that is less expansionary than anticipated leads to an output movement directly opposite to that intended.

Implications for Policymakers

The new classical model, with its policy ineffectiveness proposition, has two important lessons for policymakers. It illuminates the distinction between the effects of anticipated versus unanticipated policy actions, and it demonstrates that policymakers cannot know the outcome of their decisions without knowing the public's expectations regarding them.

At first you might think that policymakers can still use discretionary policy to stabilize the economy. Once they figure out the public's expectations, they can know what effect their policies will have. There are two catches to such a conclusion. First, it may be nearly impossible to find out what the public's expectations are, given that the public consists of more than 30 million citizens. Second, even if it were possible, policymakers would run into further difficulties because the public has

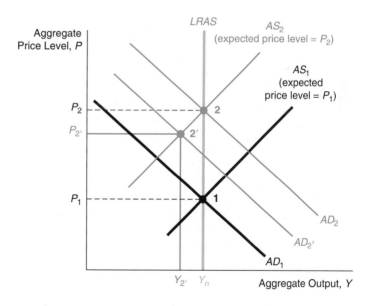

FIGURE 27-3   Short-Run Response to an Expansionary Policy That Is Less Expansionary Than Expected in the New Classical Model

Because the public expects the aggregate demand curve to shift to AD_2, the short-run aggregate supply curve shifts to AS_2 (expected price level = P_2). When the actual expansionary policy falls short of the public's expectation (the aggregate demand curve merely shifts to $AD_{2'}$), the economy ends up at point 2', at the intersection of $AD_{2'}$ and AS_2. Despite the expansionary policy, aggregate output falls to $Y_{2'}$.

rational expectations and will try to guess what policymakers plan to do. Public expectations do not remain fixed while policymakers are plotting a surprise—the public will revise its expectations, and policies will have no predictable effect on output.[6]

Where does this lead us? Should the Bank of Canada and other policymaking agencies pack up, lock the doors, and go home? In a sense, the answer is yes. The new classical model implies that discretionary stabilization policy cannot be effective and might have undesirable effects on the economy. Policymakers' attempts to use discretionary policy may create a fluctuating policy stance that leads to unpredictable policy surprises, which in turn cause undesirable fluctuations around the natural rate level of aggregate output. To eliminate these undesirable fluctuations, the central bank and other policymaking agencies should abandon discretionary policy and generate as few policy surprises as possible.

As we saw in Figure 27-2 on page 695, even though anticipated policy has no effect on aggregate output in the new classical model, it *does* have an effect on the price level. The new classical macroeconomists care about anticipated policy and suggest that policy rules be designed so that the price level will remain stable.

NEW KEYNESIAN MODEL

In the new classical model, all wages and prices are completely flexible with respect to expected changes in the price level; that is, a rise in the expected price level results in an immediate and equal rise in wages and prices. Many economists who accept rational expectations as a working hypothesis do not accept the characterization of wage and price flexibility in the new classical model. These critics of the new classical model, called *new Keynesians,* object to complete wage and price flexibility and identify factors in the economy that prevent some wages and prices from rising fully with a rise in the expected price level.

Long-term labour contracts are one source of rigidity that prevents wages and prices from responding fully to changes in the expected price level (called *wage–price stickiness*). For example, workers might find themselves at the end of the first year of a three-year wage contract that specifies the wage rate for the coming two years. Even if new information appeared that would make them raise their expectations of the inflation rate and the future price level, they could not do anything about it because they are locked into a wage agreement. Even with a high expectation about the price level, the wage rate will not adjust. In two years, when the contract is renegotiated, both workers and firms may build the expected inflation rate into their agreement, but they cannot do so immediately.

Another source of rigidity is that firms may be reluctant to change wages frequently even when there are no explicit wage contracts because such changes may affect the work effort of the labour force. For example, a firm may not want to lower workers' wages when unemployment is high because this might result in poorer worker performance. Price stickiness may also occur because firms engage in fixed-price contracts with their suppliers or because it is costly for firms to change prices frequently. All of these rigidities (which diminish wage and price flexibility), even if they are not present in all wage and price arrangements,

---

[6] This result follows from one of the implications of rational expectations. The forecast error of expectations about policy (the deviation of actual policy from expectations of policy) must be unpredictable. Because output is affected only by unpredictable (unanticipated) policy changes in the new classical model, policy effects on output must be unpredictable as well.

suggest that an increase in the expected price level might not translate into an immediate and complete adjustment of wages and prices.

Although the new Keynesians do not agree with the complete wage and price flexibility of the new classical macroeconomics, they nevertheless recognize the importance of expectations to the determination of short-run aggregate supply and are willing to accept rational expectations theory as a reasonable characterization of how expectations are formed. The model they have developed, the *new Keynesian model,* assumes that expectations are rational but does not assume complete wage and price flexibility; instead, it assumes that wages and prices are sticky. Its basic conclusion is that unanticipated policy has a larger effect on aggregate output than anticipated policy (as in the new classical model). However, in contrast to the new classical model, the policy ineffectiveness proposition does not hold in the new Keynesian model: anticipated policy *does* affect aggregate output and the business cycle.

Effects of Unanticipated and Anticipated Policy

In panel (a) of Figure 27-4, we look at the short-run response to an unanticipated expansionary policy for the new Keynesian model. The analysis is identical to that of the new classical model. We again start at point 1, where the aggregate demand curve AD_1 intersects the short-run aggregate supply curve AS_1 at the natural rate level of output and price level P_1. When the Bank of Canada pursues its expansionary policy of purchasing bonds and raising the money supply, the aggregate demand curve shifts rightward to AD_2. Because the expansionary policy is unanticipated, the expected price level remains unchanged, leaving the short-run aggregate supply curve unchanged. Thus the economy moves to point U, where aggregate output has increased to Y_U and the price level has risen to P_U.

In panel (b), we see what happens when the Bank's expansionary policy that shifts the aggregate demand curve from AD_1 to AD_2 is anticipated. Because the expansionary policy is anticipated and expectations are rational, the expected price level increases, causing wages to increase and the short-run aggregate supply curve to shift to the left. Because of rigidities that do not allow *complete* wage and price adjustment, the short-run aggregate supply curve does not shift all the way to AS_2 as it does in the new classical model. Instead, it moves to AS_A, and the economy settles at point A, the intersection of AD_2 and AS_A. Aggregate output has risen above the natural rate level to Y_A, while the price level has increased to P_A. *Unlike the new classical model, in the new Keynesian model anticipated policy does have an effect on aggregate output.*

We can see in Figure 27-4 that Y_U is greater than Y_A, meaning that the output response to unanticipated policy is greater than to anticipated policy. It is greater because the short-run aggregate supply curve does not shift when policy is unanticipated, causing a lower price level and hence a higher level of output. We see that *like the new classical model, the new Keynesian model distinguishes between the effects of anticipated versus unanticipated policy, with unanticipated policy having a greater effect.*

Implications for Policy-makers

Because the new Keynesian model indicates that anticipated policy has an effect on aggregate output, it does not rule out beneficial effects from discretionary stabilization policy, in contrast to the new classical model. It does warn the policymakers that designing such a policy will not be an easy task because the effects of anticipated and unanticipated policy can be quite different. As in the new classical model, to predict the outcome of their actions, policymakers must be aware of the public's expectations about those actions. Policymakers face similar difficulties in devising successful policies in both the new classical and new Keynesian models.

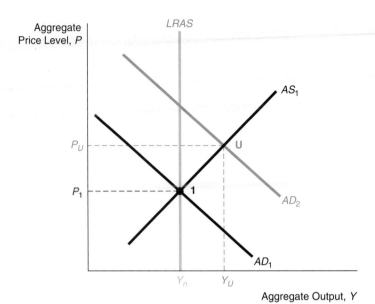

(a) Response to an unanticipated expansionary policy

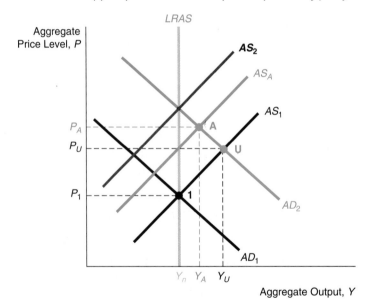

(b) Response to an anticipated expansionary policy

FIGURE 27-4   Short-Run Response to Expansionary Policy in the
New Keynesian Model

The expansionary policy that shifts aggregate demand to AD_2 has a bigger effect on output when it is unanticipated than when it is anticipated. When the expansionary policy is unanticipated in panel (a), the short-run aggregate supply curve does not shift, and the economy moves to point U so that aggregate output increases to Y_U and the price level rises to P_U. When the policy is anticipated in panel (b), the short-run aggregate supply curve shifts to AS_A (but not all the way to AS_2 because rigidities prevent complete wage and price adjustment), and the economy moves to point A so that aggregate output rises to Y_A (which is less than Y_U) and the price level rises to P_A (which is higher than P_U).

COMPARISON OF THE TWO NEW MODELS
WITH THE TRADITIONAL MODEL

To obtain a clearer picture of the impact of the rational expectations revolution on our analysis of the aggregate economy, we can compare the two rational expectations models (the new classical macroeconomic model and the new Keynesian model) to a model we call, for lack of a better name, the *traditional model.* In the traditional model, expectations are *not* rational. That model uses adaptive expectations (mentioned in Chapter 7), expectations based solely on past experience. The traditional model views expected inflation as an average of past inflation rates. This average is not affected by the public's predictions of future policy; hence predictions of future policy do not affect the short-run aggregate supply curve.

First we will examine the short-run output and price responses in the three models. Then we will examine the implications of these models for both stabilization and anti-inflation policies.

As a study aid, the comparison of the three models is summarized in Table 27-1. You may want to refer to the table as we proceed with the comparison.

Short-Run Output and Price Responses

Figure 27-5 compares the response of aggregate output and the price level to an expansionary policy in the three models. Initially, the economy is at point 1, the intersection of the aggregate demand curve AD_1 and the short-run aggregate supply curve AS_1. When the expansionary policy occurs, the aggregate demand curve

TABLE 27-1 The Three Models

Model	Response to Unanticipated Expansionary Policy	Response to Anticipated Expansionary Policy	Can Discretionary Policy Be Beneficial?	Response to Unanticipated Anti-Inflation Policy	Response to Anticipated Anti-Inflation Policy	Is Credibility Important to Successful Anti-Inflation Policy?
Traditional model	$Y\uparrow, P\uparrow$	$Y\uparrow, P\uparrow$ by same amount as when policy is unanticipated	Yes	$Y\downarrow, \pi\downarrow$	$Y\downarrow, \pi\downarrow$ by same amount as when policy is unanticipated	No
New classical macroeconomic model	$Y\uparrow, P\uparrow$	Y unchanged, $P\uparrow$ by more than when policy is unanticipated	No	$Y\downarrow, \pi\downarrow$	Y unchanged, $\pi\downarrow$ by more than when policy is unanticipated	Yes
New Keynesian model	$Y\uparrow, P\uparrow$	$Y\uparrow$ by less than when policy is unanticipated, $P\uparrow$ by more than when policy is unanticipated	Yes, but designing a beneficial policy is difficult	$Y\downarrow, \pi\downarrow$	$Y\downarrow$ by less than when policy is unanticipated, $\pi\downarrow$ by more than when policy is unanticipated	Yes

Note: π represents the inflation rate.

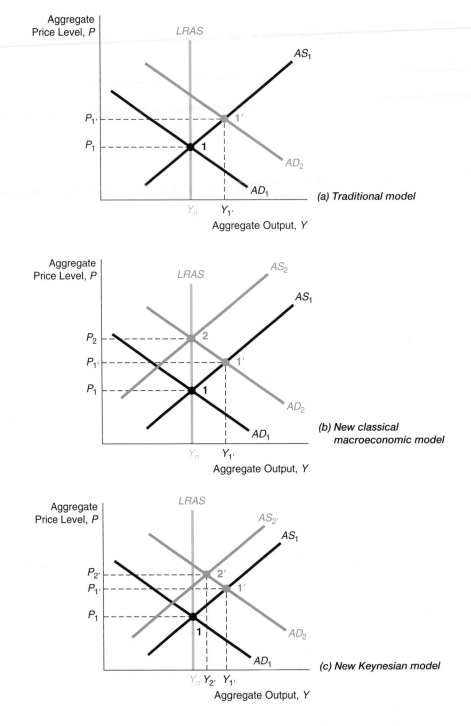

FIGURE 27-5   Comparison of the Short-Run Response to Expansionary Policy in the Three Models

Initially, the economy is at point 1. The expansionary policy shifts the aggregate demand curve from AD_1 to AD_2. In the traditional model, the expansionary policy moves the economy to point 1' whether the policy is anticipated or not. In the new classical model, the expansionary policy moves the economy to point 1' if it is unanticipated and to point 2 if it is anticipated. In the new Keynesian model, the expansionary policy moves the economy to point 1' if it is unanticipated and to point 2' if it is anticipated.

shifts to AD_2. If the expansionary policy is *unanticipated,* all three models show the same short-run output response. The traditional model views the short-run aggregate supply curve as given in the short run, while the other two view it as remaining at AS_1 because there is no change in the expected price level when the policy is a surprise. Hence when policy is *unanticipated,* all three models indicate a movement to point 1′, where the AD_2 and AS_1 curves intersect and where aggregate output and the price level have risen to $Y_{1'}$ and $P_{1'}$, respectively.

The response to the *anticipated* expansionary policy is, however, quite different in the three models. In the traditional model in panel (a), the short-run aggregate supply curve remains at AS_1 even when the expansionary policy is anticipated because adaptive expectations imply that anticipated policy has no effect on expectations and hence on aggregate supply. It indicates that the economy moves to point 1′, which is where it moved when the policy was unanticipated. The traditional model does not distinguish between the effects of anticipated and unanticipated policy: both have the same effect on output and prices.

In the new classical model in panel (b), the short-run aggregate supply curve shifts leftward to AS_2 when policy is anticipated because when expectations of the higher price level are realized, aggregate output will be at the natural rate level. Thus it indicates that the economy moves to point 2; aggregate output does not rise, but prices do, to P_2. This outcome is quite different from the move to point 1′ when policy is unanticipated. The new classical model distinguishes between the short-run effects of anticipated and unanticipated policies: anticipated policy has no effect on output, but unanticipated policy does. However, anticipated policy has a bigger impact than unanticipated policy on price level movements.

The new Keynesian model in panel (c) is an intermediate position between the traditional and new classical models. It recognizes that anticipated policy affects the short-run aggregate supply curve, but due to rigidities such as long-term contracts, wage and price adjustment is not as complete as in the new classical model. Hence the short-run aggregate supply curve shifts only to $AS_{2'}$ in response to anticipated policy, and the economy moves to point 2′, where output at $Y_{2'}$ is lower than the $Y_{1'}$ level reached when the expansionary policy is unanticipated. But the price level at $P_{2'}$ is higher than the level $P_{1'}$ that resulted from the unanticipated policy. Like the new classical model, the new Keynesian model distinguishes between the effects of anticipated and unanticipated policies: anticipated policy has a smaller effect on output than unanticipated policy but a larger effect on the price level. However, in contrast to the new classical model, anticipated policy does affect output fluctuations.

Stabilization Policy

The three models have different views of the effectiveness of *stabilization policy,* policy intended to reduce output fluctuations. Because the effects of anticipated and unanticipated policy are identical in the traditional model, policymakers do not have to concern themselves with the public's expectations. This makes it easier for them to predict the outcome of their policy, an essential matter if their actions are to have the intended effect. In the traditional model, it is possible for a discretionary policy to stabilize output fluctuations.

The new classical model takes the extreme position that discretionary stabilization policy serves to aggravate output fluctuations. In this model, only unanticipated policy affects output; anticipated policy does not matter. Policymakers can affect output only by surprising the public. Because the public is assumed to have rational expectations, it will always try to guess what policymakers plan to do.

In the new classical model, the conduct of policy can be viewed as a game in which the public and the policymakers are always trying to outfox each other by guessing the other's intentions and expectations. The sole possible outcome of this process is that discretionary stabilization policy will have no predictable effect on output and cannot be relied on to stabilize economic activity. Instead it may create a lot of uncertainty about policy that will increase random output fluctuations around the natural rate level of output. Such an undesirable effect is exactly the opposite of what the discretionary stabilization policy is trying to achieve. The outcome in the new classical view is that policy should promote as much certainty about policy actions as possible.

The new Keynesian model again takes an intermediate position between the traditional and the new classical models. Contrary to the new classical model, it indicates that anticipated policy *does* matter to output fluctuations. Policymakers can count on some output response from their anticipated policies and can use them to stabilize the economy.

In contrast to the traditional model, however, the new Keynesian model recognizes that the effects of anticipated and unanticipated policy will not be the same. Policymakers will encounter more uncertainty about the outcome of their actions because they cannot be sure to what extent the policy is anticipated or not. Hence discretionary policy is less likely to operate always in the intended direction and is less likely to achieve its goals. The new Keynesian model raises the possibility that discretionary policy could be beneficial, but uncertainty about the outcome of policies in this model may make the design of such a beneficial policy extremely difficult.

Anti-Inflation Policies

So far we have focused on the implications of these three models for policies whose intent is to eliminate fluctuations in output. By the end of the 1970s, the high inflation rate (then over 10%) helped shift the primary concern of policymakers to the reduction of inflation. What do these models have to say about anti-inflation policies designed to eliminate upward movements in the price level? The aggregate demand and supply diagrams in Figure 27-6 will help us answer the question.

Suppose that the economy has settled into a sustained 10% inflation rate caused by a high rate of money growth that shifts the aggregate demand curve so that it moves up by 10% every year. If this inflation rate has been built into wage and price contracts, the short-run aggregate supply curve rises at the same rate. We see this in Figure 27-6 as a shift in the aggregate demand curve from AD_1 in year 1 to AD_2 in year 2, while the short-run aggregate supply curve moves from AS_1 to AS_2. In year 1, the economy is at point 1 (intersection of AD_1 and AS_1); in the second year, the economy moves to point 2 (intersection of AD_2 and AS_2), and the price level has risen 10%, from P_1 to P_2. (Note that the figure is not drawn to scale.)

Now suppose that a new Bank of Canada governor is appointed who decides that inflation must be stopped. He convinces the Bank's Board of Directors to stop the high rate of money growth so that the aggregate demand curve will not rise from AD_1. The policy of halting money growth immediately could be costly if it led to a fall in output. Let's use our three models to explore the degree to which aggregate output will fall as a result of an anti-inflation policy.

First, look at the outcome of this policy in the traditional model's view of the world in panel (a). The movement of the short-run aggregate supply curve to AS_2 is already set in place and is unaffected by the new policy of keeping the

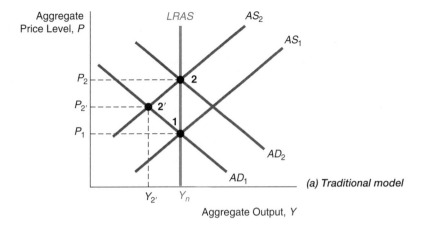

(a) Traditional model

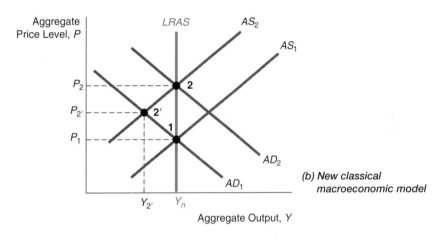

(b) New classical macroeconomic model

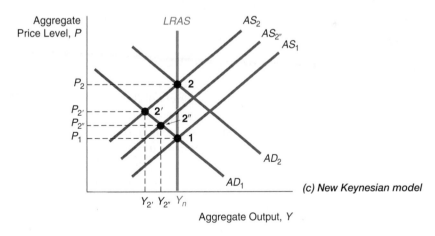

(c) New Keynesian model

FIGURE 27-6   Anti-Inflation Policy in the Three Models

With an ongoing inflation in which the economy is moving from point 1 to point 2, the aggregate demand curve is shifting from AD_1 to AD_2 and the short-run aggregate supply curve from AS_1 to AS_2. The anti-inflation policy, when implemented, prevents the aggregate demand curve from rising, holding it at AD_1. (a) In the traditional model, the economy moves to point 2′ whether the anti-inflation policy is anticipated or not. (b) In the new classical model, the economy moves to point 2′ if the policy is unanticipated and to point 1 if it is anticipated. (c) In the new Keynesian model, the economy moves to point 2′ if the policy is unanticipated and to point 2″ if it is anticipated.

aggregate demand curve at AD_1 (whether the effort is anticipated or not). The economy moves to point 2′ (the intersection of the AD_1 and AS_2 curves), and the inflation rate slows down because the price level increases only to $P_{2'}$ rather than P_2. The reduction in inflation has not been without cost: output has declined to $Y_{2'}$, which is well below the natural rate level.

In the traditional model, estimates of the cost in terms of lost output for each 1% reduction in the inflation rate are around 4% of a year's real GDP. The high cost of reducing inflation in the traditional model is one reason why some economists are reluctant to advocate an anti-inflation policy of the sort tried here. They question whether the cost of high unemployment is worth the benefits of a reduced inflation rate.

If you adhere to the new classical philosophy, you would not be as pessimistic about the high cost of reducing the inflation rate. If the public *expects* the monetary authorities to stop the inflationary process by ending the high rate of money growth, it will occur without any output loss. In panel (b), the aggregate demand curve will remain at AD_1, but because this is expected, wages and prices can be adjusted so that they will not rise, and the short-run aggregate supply curve will remain at AS_1 instead of moving to AS_2. The economy will stay put at point 1 (the intersection of AD_1 and AS_1), and aggregate output will remain at the natural rate level while inflation is stopped because the price level is unchanged.

An important element in the story is that the anti-inflation policy be anticipated by the public. If the policy is *not* expected, the aggregate demand curve remains at AD_1, but the short-run aggregate supply curve continues its shift to AS_2. The outcome of the unanticipated anti-inflation policy is a movement of the economy to point 2′. Although the inflation rate slows in this case, it is not entirely eliminated as it was when the anti-inflation policy was anticipated. Even worse, aggregate output falls below the natural rate level to $Y_{2'}$. An anti-inflation policy that is unanticipated, then, is far less desirable than one that is.

The new Keynesian model in panel (c) also leads to the conclusion that an unanticipated anti-inflation policy is less desirable than an anticipated one. If the policy of keeping the aggregate demand curve at AD_1 is *not* expected, the short-run aggregate supply curve will continue its shift to AS_2, and the economy moves to point 2′, at the intersection of AD_1 and AS_2. The inflation rate slows, but output declines to $Y_{2'}$, well below the natural rate level.

If, by contrast, the anti-inflation policy is *expected,* the short-run aggregate supply curve will not move all the way to AS_2. Instead it will shift only to $AS_{2''}$ because some wages and prices (but not all) can be adjusted, so wages and the price level will not rise at their previous rates. Instead of moving to point 2′ (as occurred when the anti-inflation policy was not expected), the economy moves to point 2″, the intersection of the AD_1 and $AS_{2''}$ curves. The outcome is more desirable than when the policy is unanticipated—the inflation rate is lower (the price level rises only to $P_{2''}$ and not $P_{2'}$), and the output loss is smaller as well ($Y_{2''}$ is higher than $Y_{2'}$).

Credibility in Fighting Inflation

Both the new classical and new Keynesian models indicate that for an anti-inflation policy to be successful in reducing inflation at the lowest output cost, the public must believe (expect) that it will be implemented. In the new classical view of the world, the best anti-inflation policy (when it is credible) is to go "cold turkey." The rise in the aggregate demand curve from AD_1 should be stopped immediately. Inflation would be eliminated at once with no loss of output *if the policy were credible*. In a new Keynesian world, the cold-turkey policy, *even if credible,* is not as desirable because it will produce some output loss.

John Taylor, a proponent of the new Keynesian model, has demonstrated that a more gradual approach to reducing inflation may be able to eliminate inflation without producing a substantial output loss.[7] An important catch here is that this gradual policy must somehow be made credible, which may be harder to achieve than a cold-turkey anti-inflation policy, which demonstrates immediately that the policymakers are serious about fighting inflation. Taylor's contention that inflation can be reduced with little output loss may be overly optimistic.

Incorporating rational expectations into aggregate supply and demand analysis indicates that a successful anti-inflation policy must be credible. Evidence that credibility plays an important role in successful anti-inflation policies is provided by the dramatic end of the Bolivian hyperinflation in 1985 (see the Global box, Ending the Bolivian Hyperinflation). But establishing credibility is easier said than done. You might think that an announcement by policymakers at the Bank of Canada that they plan to pursue an anti-inflation policy might do the trick. The public would expect this policy and would act accordingly. However, that conclusion implies that the public will believe the policymakers' announcement. Unfortunately, that is not how the real world works.

GLOBAL — Ending the Bolivian Hyperinflation: Case Study of a Successful Anti-Inflation Program

The most remarkable anti-inflation program in recent times was implemented in Bolivia. In the first half of 1985, Bolivia's inflation rate was running at 20 000% and rising. Indeed, the inflation rate was so high that the price of a movie ticket often rose while people waited in line to buy it. In August 1985, Bolivia's new president announced his anti-inflation program, the New Economic Policy. To rein in money growth and establish credibility, the new government took drastic actions to slash the budget deficit by shutting down many state-owned enterprises, eliminating subsidies, freezing public sector salaries, and collecting a new wealth tax. The finance ministry was put on a new footing; the budget was balanced on a day-by-day basis. Without exceptions, the finance minister would not authorize spending in excess of the amount of tax revenue that had been collected the day before.

The rule of thumb that a reduction of 1% in the inflation rate requires a 4% loss of a year's aggregate output indicates that ending the Bolivian hyperinflation would have required halving Bolivian aggregate output for 1600 years! Instead, the Bolivian inflation was stopped in its tracks within one month, and the output loss was minor (less than 5% of GDP).

Certain hyperinflations before World War II were also ended with small losses of output using policies similar to Bolivia's,* and a more recent anti-inflation program in Israel that also involved substantial reductions in budget deficits sharply reduced inflation without any clear loss of output. There is no doubt that credible anti-inflation policies can be highly successful in eliminating inflation.

* For an excellent discussion of the end of four hyperinflations in the 1920s, see Thomas Sargent, "The Ends of Four Big Inflations," in *Inflation: Causes and Consequences,* ed. Robert E. Hall (Chicago: University of Chicago Press, 1982), pp. 41–98.

[7] John Taylor, "The Role of Expectations in the Choice of Monetary Policy," in *Monetary Policy Issues in the 1980s* (Kansas City: Federal Reserve Bank, 1982), pp. 47–76.

Our historical review of Bank of Canada policymaking in the Web Appendix to Chapter 5 suggests that the Bank has not always done what it set out to do. In the early 1970s, the Bank accommodated inflationary shocks by raising the rate of growth of monetary aggregates, thereby forming expectations of rising inflation. When in 1975 the Bank adopted a gradual anti-inflation policy, the public had no reason to believe in such a policy. As Robert Lucas of the University of Saskatchewan argues, "For various reasons, including the caution of the Bank in moving too quickly for fear of generating large increases in the unemployment rate in the transition to lower inflation, the policy was a failure."[8]

Such episodes reduced the credibility of the Bank of Canada in the eyes of the public and, as predicted by the new classical and new Keynesian models, had serious consequences. For example, when the Bank embarked on a very restrictive monetary policy in the summer of 1981, following the Federal Reserve Board of the United States, it was successful in generating a significant decline in the inflation rate (from 12% to 4%), but it initiated the most severe recession in the post–World War II period. Clearly, unless some method of restoring credibility to anti-inflation policy is achieved, eliminating inflation will be a costly affair because such policy will be unanticipated.

Recently, however, the Bank of Canada acquired considerable credibility. When the Bank and the Department of Finance jointly announced inflation targets in 1991, they were clearly credible. In fact, as David Johnson of Wilfrid Laurier University argues, this particular announcement had little effect on the level of inflation in the short run, but the subsequent revision of inflation targets and the 1993 change in governor (from Governor Crow to Governor Thiessen) were handled in such a way that the Bank's anti-inflation policy turned out to be successful.[9]

The Canadian government can play an important role in establishing the credibility of anti-inflation policy. We have seen that large budget deficits may help stimulate inflationary monetary policy, and when the government and the Bank of Canada announce that they will pursue a restrictive anti-inflation policy, it is less likely that they will be believed *unless* the federal government demonstrates fiscal responsibility. Another way to say this is to use the old adage "Actions speak louder than words." When the government takes actions that will help the Bank of Canada adhere to anti-inflation policy, the policy will be more credible. Unfortunately, this lesson has sometimes been ignored by politicians in Canada and other countries.

---

[8] Robert F. Lucas, "The Bank of Canada and Zero Inflation: A New Cross of Gold?" *Canadian Public Policy* 15 (1989): 84–93.

[9] David R. Johnson, "Expected Inflation in Canada 1988–1995: An Evaluation of Bank of Canada Credibility and the Effect of Inflation Targets," *Canadian Public Policy* 23 (1997): 233–258.

APPLICATION   Credibility and Budget Deficits

The Reagan administration in the United States was strongly criticized for creating huge budget deficits by cutting taxes in the early 1980s. In the Keynesian framework, we usually think of tax cuts as stimulating aggregate demand and increasing aggregate output. Could the expectation of large budget deficits have helped create a more severe recession in 1981–1982 after the Federal Reserve implemented an anti-inflation monetary policy?

Some economists answer yes, using diagrams like panels (b) and (c) of Figure 27-6 on page 705. They claim that the prospect of large budget deficits made it harder for the public to believe that an anti-inflationary policy would actually be pursued when the Fed announced its intention to do so. Consequently, the short-run aggregate supply curve would continue to rise from AS_1 to AS_2 as in panels (b) and (c). When the Fed actually kept the aggregate demand curve from rising to AD_2 by slowing the rate of money growth in 1980–1981 and allowing interest rates to rise, the economy moved to a point like 2′ in panels (b) and (c), and much unemployment resulted. As our analysis in panels (b) and (c) of Figure 27-6 predicts, the inflation rate did slow substantially, falling below 5% by the end of 1982, but this was very costly: unemployment in the United States reached a peak of 10.7%.

If the Reagan administration had actively tried to reduce deficits instead of raising them by cutting taxes, what might have been the outcome of the anti-inflation policy? Instead of moving to point 2′, the economy might have moved to point 2″ in panel (c)—or even to point 1 in panel (b), if the new classical macroeconomists are right. Reduction of budget deficits thus could have led to an even more rapid reduction in inflation and a smaller loss of output.

Although many economists agree that the Fed's anti-inflation program lacked credibility, especially in its initial phases, not all of them agree that the Reagan budget deficits were the cause of that lack of credibility. The conclusion that the Reagan budget deficits helped create a more severe recession in 1981–1982 is controversial.

Reagan is not the only head of state who ran large budget deficits while espousing an anti-inflation policy. Britain's prime minister, Margaret Thatcher, preceded Reagan in this activity, and economists such as Thomas Sargent assert that the reward for her policy was a climb of unemployment in Britain to unprecedented levels.[10]

IMPACT OF THE RATIONAL EXPECTATIONS REVOLUTION

The theory of rational expectations has caused a revolution in the way most economists now think about the conduct of monetary and fiscal policies and their effects on economic activity. One result of this revolution is that economists are now far more aware of the importance of expectations to economic decision-making and to the outcome of particular policy actions. Although the rationality of expectations in all markets is still controversial, most economists now accept the following principle suggested by rational expectations: expectation formation will change when the behaviour of forecasted variables changes. As a result, the Lucas critique of policy evaluation using conventional econometric models is now taken seriously by most economists. The Lucas critique also demonstrates that the effect of a particular policy depends critically on the public's expectations about that policy. This observation has made economists much less certain that policies will have their intended effect. An important result of the rational expectations revolution is that economists are no longer as confident in the success of discretionary stabilization policies as they once were.

---

[10] Thomas Sargent, "Stopping Moderate Inflations: The Methods of Poincaré and Thatcher," in *Inflation, Debt, and Indexation,* ed. Rudiger Dornbusch and M. H. Simonsen (Cambridge, Mass.: MIT Press, 1983), pp. 54–96, discusses the problems that Thatcher's policies caused and contrasts them with more successful anti-inflation policies pursued by the Poincaré government in France during the 1920s.

Has the rational expectations revolution convinced economists that there is no role for discretionary stabilization policy? Those who adhere to the new classical macroeconomics think so. Because anticipated policy does not affect aggregate output, discretionary policy can lead only to unpredictable output fluctuations. Pursuing a nondiscretionary policy in which there is no uncertainty about policy actions is then the best we can do. Such a position is not accepted by many economists because the empirical evidence on the policy ineffectiveness proposition is mixed. Some studies find that only unanticipated policy matters to output fluctuations, while other studies find a significant impact of anticipated policy on output movements.[11] In addition, some economists question whether the degree of wage and price flexibility required in the new classical model actually exists.

The result is that many economists take an intermediate position that recognizes the distinction between the effects of anticipated versus unanticipated policy but believe that anticipated policy can affect output. They are still open to the possibility that discretionary stabilization policy can be beneficial, but they recognize the difficulties of designing it.

The rational expectations revolution has also highlighted the importance of credibility to the success of anti-inflation policies. Economists now recognize that if an anti-inflation policy is not believed by the public, it may be less effective in reducing the inflation rate when it is actually implemented and may lead to a larger loss of output than is necessary. Achieving credibility (not an easy task in that policymakers often say one thing but do another) should then be an important goal for policymakers. To achieve credibility, policymakers must be consistent in their course of action.

The rational expectations revolution has caused major rethinking about the way economic policy should be conducted and has forced economists to recognize that we may have to accept a more limited role for what policy can do for us. Rather than attempting to fine-tune the economy so that all output fluctuations are eliminated, we may have to settle for policies that create less uncertainty and thereby promote a more stable economic environment.

---

[11] Studies with findings that only unanticipated policy matters include Thomas Sargent, "A Classical Macroeconometric Model for the United States," *Journal of Political Economy* 84 (1976): 207–237; Robert J. Barro, "Unanticipated Money Growth and Unemployment in the United States," *American Economic Review* 67 (1977): 101–115; and Robert J. Barro and Mark Rush, "Unanticipated Money and Economic Activity," in *Rational Expectations and Economic Policy,* ed. Stanley Fischer (Chicago: University of Chicago Press, 1980), pp. 23–48. Studies that find a significant impact of anticipated policy are Frederic S. Mishkin, "Does Anticipated Monetary Policy Matter? An Econometric Investigation," *Journal of Political Economy* 90 (1982): 22–51, and Robert J. Gordon, "Price Inertia and Policy Effectiveness in the United States, 1890–1980," *Journal of Political Economy* 90 (1982): 1087–1117.

SUMMARY

1. The simple principle (derived from rational expectations theory) that expectation formation changes when the behaviour of forecasted variables changes led to the famous Lucas critique of econometric policy evaluation. Lucas argued that when policy changes, expectation formation changes; hence the relationships in an econometric model will change. An econometric model that has been estimated on the basis of past data will no longer be the correct model for evaluating the effects of this policy change and may prove to be highly misleading. The Lucas critique also points out that the effects of a particular policy depend critically on the public's expectations about the policy.

2. The new classical macroeconomic model assumes that expectations are rational and that wages and prices are completely flexible with respect to the expected price level. It leads to the policy ineffectiveness proposition that anticipated policy has no effect on output; only unanticipated policy matters.

3. The new Keynesian model also assumes that expectations are rational but views wages and prices as sticky. Like the new classical model, the new Keynesian model distinguishes between the effects of anticipated and unanticipated policy: anticipated policy has a smaller effect on aggregate output than unanticipated policy. However, anticipated policy does matter to output fluctuations.

4. The new classical model indicates that discretionary policy can only be counterproductive, while the new Keynesian model suggests that discretionary policy might be beneficial. However, since both indicate that there is uncertainty about the outcome of a par-ticular policy, the design of a beneficial discretionary policy may be very difficult. A traditional model in which expectations about policy have no effect on the short-run aggregate supply curve does not distinguish between the effects of anticipated or unanticipated policy. This model favours discretionary policy because the outcome of a particular policy is less uncertain.

5. If expectations about policy affect the short-run aggregate supply curve, as they do in the new classical and new Keynesian models, an anti-inflation policy will be more successful (will produce a faster reduction in inflation with smaller output loss) if it is credible.

6. The rational expectations revolution has forced economists to be less optimistic about the effective use of discretionary stabilization policy and has made them more aware of the importance of credibility to successful policymaking.

KEY TERMS

econometric model,   p. 692

policy ineffectiveness proposition,   p. 696

QUESTIONS

You will find the answers to the questions marked with an asterisk in the Textbook Resources section of your MyEconLab.

1. If the public expects the Bank of Canada to pursue a policy that is likely to raise short-term interest rates permanently to 12% but the Bank does not go through with this policy change, what will happen to long-term interest rates? Explain your answer.

*2. If consumer expenditure is related to consumers' expectations of their average income in the future, will an income tax cut have a larger effect on consumer expenditure if the public expects the tax cut to last for one year or for ten years?

Use an aggregate supply and demand diagram to illustrate your answer in all of the following questions.

3. Having studied the new classical model, the new governor of the Bank of Canada has thought up a surefire plan for reducing inflation and lowering unemployment. He announces that the Bank will lower the rate of money growth from 10% to 5%, but the Bank actually keeps the rate of money growth at 10%. If the new classical view of the world is correct, can his plan achieve the goals of lowering inflation and unemployment? How? Do you think his plan will work? If the traditional model's view of the world is correct, will the governor's surefire plan work?

*4. "The costs of fighting inflation in the new classical and new Keynesian models are lower than in the traditional model." Is this statement true, false, or uncertain? Explain your answer.

5. The new classical model is sometimes characterized as an offshoot of the monetarist model because the two models have similar views of aggregate supply. What are the differences and similarities between the monetarist and new classical views of aggregate supply?

*6. "The new classical model does not eliminate policymakers' ability to reduce unemployment because they can always pursue policies that are more expansionary than the public expects." Is this statement true, false, or uncertain? Explain your answer.

7. What principle of rational expectations theory is used to prove the proposition that stabilization policy can have no predictable effect on aggregate output in the new classical model?

*8. "The Lucas critique by itself casts doubt on the ability of discretionary stabilization policy to be beneficial." Is this statement true, false, or uncertain? Explain your answer.

9. "The more credible the policymakers who pursue an anti-inflation policy, the more successful that policy will be." Is this statement true, false, or uncertain? Explain your answer.

*10. Many economists are worried that a high level of budget deficits may lead to inflationary monetary policies in the future. Could these budget deficits have an effect on the current rate of inflation?

Predicting the Future

11. Suppose that a treaty is signed limiting armies throughout the world. The result of the treaty is that the public expects military and hence government spending to be reduced. If the new classical view of the economy is correct and government spending does affect the aggregate demand curve, predict what will happen to aggregate output and the price level when government spending is reduced in line with the public's expectations.

12. How would your prediction differ in Problem 11 if the new Keynesian model provides a more realistic description of the economy? What if the traditional model provides the most realistic description of the economy?

*13. The governor of the Bank of Canada announces that over the next year, the rate of money growth will be reduced from its current rate of 10% to a rate of 2%. If the governor is believed by the public but the Bank actually reduces the rate of money growth to 5%, predict what will happen to the inflation rate and aggregate output if the new classical view of the economy is correct.

*14. How would your prediction differ in Problem 13 if the new Keynesian model provides a more accurate description of the economy? What if the traditional model provides the most realistic description of the economy?

15. If, in a surprise victory, a new government is elected to office that the public believes will pursue inflationary policy, predict what might happen to the level of output and inflation even before the new government comes into power. Would your prediction differ depending on which of the three models—traditional, new classical, and new Keynesian—you believed in?

WEB EXERCISE

1. Robert Lucas won the Nobel Prize in economics. Go to **www.nobel.se/nobel_prizes/economics** and locate the press release on Robert Lucas. In what year and for what contribution to the study of economics was Lucas awarded the prize?

Be sure to visit the MyEconLab website at **www.myeconlab.com**. This online homework and tutorial system puts you in control of your own learning with study and practice tools directly correlated to this chapter content.

GLOSSARY

accommodating policy Economic policy in pursuit of a high employment target. **674**

adaptive expectations Expectations of a variable based on an average of past values of the variable. **147**

advances See *overdraft loans.*

adverse selection The problem created by asymmetric information *before* a transaction occurs: The people who are the most undesirable from the other party's point of view are the ones who are most likely to want to engage in the financial transaction. **32**

agency theory The analysis of how asymmetric information problems affect economic behaviour. **171**

aggregate demand The total quantity of output demanded in the economy at different price levels. **573, 619**

aggregate demand function The relationship between aggregate output and aggregate demand that shows the quantity of aggregate output demanded for each level of aggregate output. **577**

aggregate output The total production of final goods and services in the economy. **6**

aggregate price level The average price of goods and services in an economy. **7**

aggregate supply The quantity of aggregate output supplied by the economy at different price levels. **619**

aggregate supply curve The relationship between the quantity of output supplied in the short run and the price level. **622**

aggregate supply shock The effect on the aggregate supply curve of changes in production costs unrelated to wages. **626**

alt-A mortgages Mortgages for borrowers with higher expected default rates than prime borrowers, but with better credit records than subprime borrowers. **204**

American option An option that can be exercised at any time up to the expiration date of the contract. **362**

anchor currency A currency to which other countries' currencies are pegged. **524**

"animal spirits" Waves of optimism and pessimism that affect consumers' and businesses' willingness to spend. **581**

annuities Financial contracts under which a customer pays an annual premium in exchange for a future stream of annual payments beginning at a set age (say, 65) and ending when the person dies. **290**

appreciation Increase in a currency's value. **11, 495**

arbitrage Elimination of a riskless profit opportunity in a market. **153, 351**

asset A financial claim or piece of property that is a store of value. **3**

asset management The acquisition of assets that have a low rate of default and diversification of asset holdings to increase profits. **321**

asset market approach An approach of determining asset prices using stocks of assets rather than flows. **88**

asset-price bubbles Increases in asset prices in the stock and real estate markets that are driven well above their fundamental economic values by investor psychology. **202**

asset transformation See *risk sharing.* **32**

asymmetric information The unequal knowledge that each party to a transaction has about the other party. **32**

at the money (trading at par) option Option whose exercise price is just equal to the current asset price. **363**

audits Certification by accounting firms that a business is adhering to standard business principles. **174**

automated teller machine (ATM) An electronic machine that allows customers to get cash, make deposits, transfer funds from one account to another, and check balances. **260**

autonomous consumer expenditure The amount of consumer expenditure that is independent of disposable income. **574**

balance of payments A bookkeeping system for recording all payments that have a direct bearing on the movement of funds between a country and foreign countries. **522**

balance-of-payments crisis A foreign exchange crisis stemming from problems in a country's balance of payments. **532**

balance sheet A list of the assets and liabilities of a bank (or firm) that balances: Total assets equal total liabilities plus capital. **314**

Bank Act Reform The legislation that took effect in October of 2001 regarding the policy framework of the Canadian financial services sector. **282**

bank failure A situation in which a bank cannot satisfy its obligations to pay its depositors and other creditors and so goes out of business. **226**

bank holding companies Companies that own one or more banks. **271**

Bank of Canada (the Bank) Canada's central bank. **9**

bank panic The simultaneous failure of many banks, as during a financial crisis. **198**

bank rate The interest rate the Bank of Canada charges to members of the Canadian Payments Association. **324**

banker's risk The risk of not holding enough reserves to make immediate and larger than normal cash payments to liability holders. **317**

banks Financial institutions that accept money deposits and make loans (such as commercial banks, savings and loan associations, and credit unions). **5**

base money The sum of the Bank of Canada's monetary liabilities (notes outstanding and bank settlement balances) and coins outstanding. Also called *monetary base*. **384, 405**

Basel Accord An agreement adopted by more than 100 countries that requires banks to hold as capital at least 8% of their risk-weighted activities. **230**

Basel Committee on Bank Supervision A committee of banking officials from industrialized nations that meets under the auspices of the Bank for International Settlements in Basel, Switzerland to implement the Basel Accord. **230**

basis point One one-hundredth of a percentage point. **117**

bearer deposit notes CDs and GICs that can be traded and are in bearer form, meaning that whoever holds the instrument at maturity receives the principal and interest. **23**

behavioural finance The field of study that applies concepts from other social sciences, such as anthropology, sociology, and particularly psychology, to understand the behaviour of securities prices. **159**

Board of Directors of the Bank of Canada A board with fifteen members (including the governor) that is responsible for the management of the Bank. **383**

Board of Governors of the Federal Reserve System A board with seven governors (including the chairman) that plays an essential role in decision making within the Federal Reserve System. **391**

bond A debt security that promises to make payments periodically for a specified period of time. **3**

borrowed reserves The loans the central bank makes to deposit-based financial institutions. **407**

branches Additional offices of banks that conduct banking operations. **254**

Bretton Woods system The international monetary system in use from 1945 to 1971 in which exchange rates were fixed and the U.S. dollar was freely convertible into gold (by foreign governments and central banks only). **525**

brokerage firms Firms that participate in securities markets as brokers, dealers, and investment bankers. **301**

brokers Agents for investors who match buyers with sellers. **20**

bubble A situation in which the price of an asset differs from its fundamental market value. **159**

budget deficit The excess of government expenditure over tax revenues. **10**

budget surplus Excess of tax revenues over government expenditures for a particular time period. **10**

business cycles The upward and downward movement of aggregate output produced in the economy. **7**

call (redemption) A redemption feature allowing issues to be "called" on specified notice. **26**

call option An option contract that provides the right to buy a security at a specified price. **362**

call premium Price of a call option. **362**

Canada bonds (Canadas) Securities issued by the Government of Canada. **26**

capital account An account that describes the flow of capital between the U.S. and other countries. **523**

capital adequacy management A bank's decision about the amount of capital it should maintain and then acquisition of the needed capital. **321**

capital buyout fund A private equity fund that makes investments in established businesses. **307**

capital market A financial market in which longer-term debt (generally with original maturity of greater than one year) and equity instruments are traded. **21**

carried interest A share of the profit paid to a private equity fund. **307**

cash flow The difference between cash receipts and cash expenditures. **59, 141**

central bank The government agency that oversees the banking system and is responsible for the amount of money and credit supplied in the economy; in Canada, the Bank of Canada. **9, 254**

central bank independence Advocates of central bank independence find that inflation performance is found to be the best for countries with the most independent central banks. **401**

closed-end fund A mutual fund in which a fixed number of nonredeemable shares are sold at an initial offering, then traded in the over-the-counter market like common stock. **303**

coinsurance A situation in which only a portion of losses are covered by insurance, so that the insured suffers a percentage of the losses along with the insurance agency. **244**

collateral Property that is pledged to the lender to guarantee payment in the event that the borrower is unable to make debt payments. **169**

collateralized debt obligations (CDOs) Securities that pay out cash flows from subprime mortgage-backed securities in different tranches, with the highest tranche paying out first, while lower ones pay out less if there are losses. **205**

commodity money Money made up of precious metals or another valuable commodity. **48**

common stock A share of ownership in a corporation. **3**

compensating balance A required minimum amount of funds that a firm receiving a loan must keep in a chequing account at the lending bank. **333**

complete crowding out The situation in which expansionary fiscal policy, such as an increase in government spending, does not lead to a rise in output because there is an equal offsetting movement in private spending. **607**

conflict of interest A manifestation of the moral hazard in which one party in a financial contract has incentive to act in its own interest, rather than in the interests of the other party. **187**

consol (perpetuity) A perpetual bond with no maturity date and no repayment of principal that periodically makes fixed coupon payments. **67**

constant-money-growth-rate rule A policy rule advocated by monetarists whereby the central bank keeps the money supply growing at a constant rate. **688**

consumer durable expenditure Spending by consumers on durable items such as automobiles and household appliances. **651**

consumer expenditure The total demand for (spending on) consumer goods and services. **573, 619**

consumption Spending by consumers on nondurable goods and services (including services related to the ownership of homes and consumer durables). **655**

consumption function The relationship between disposable income and consumer expenditure. **574**

costly state verification Monitoring a firm's activities, an expensive process in both time and money. **178**

cost-push inflation Inflation that occurs because of the push by workers to obtain higher wages. **673**

coupon bond A credit market instrument that pays a fixed interest payment every year until the maturity date, when a specified final amount is repaid. **62**

coupon rate The dollar amount of the yearly coupon payment expressed as a percentage of the face value of a coupon bond. **62**

credit boom A lending spree when financial institutions expand their lending at a rapid pace. **200**

credit default swap (CDS) A traded derivative to which the seller is required to make a payment to the holder of the CDS if there is a credit event for that instrument such as a bankruptcy or downgrading of the firm's credit rating. **291**

credit derivatives Derivatives that have payoffs to previously issued securities, but ones that bear credit risk. **374**

credit-linked note A type of credit derivative that combines a bond and a credit option. **375**

credit options Options in which, for a fee, the purchaser has the right to get profits that are tied either to the price of an underlying risky security or to an interest rate. **374**

credit-rating agencies Investment advisory firms that rate the quality of corporate and government bonds in terms of the probability of default. **115**

credit rationing A lender's refusing to make loans even though borrowers are willing to pay the stated interest rate or even a higher rate, or restricting the size of loans made to less than the full amount sought. **333**

credit risk The risk arising from the possibility that the borrower will default. **322**

credit swap A transaction in which risky payments on loans are swapped for each other. **375**

credit view Monetary transmission mechanisms operating through asymmetric information effects on credit markets. **652**

currency The name applied collectively to the coins and notes issued by the central bank. **43**

currency board A monetary regime in which the domestic currency is backed 100% by a foreign currency (say dollars) and in which the note-issuing authority, whether the central bank or the government, establishes a fixed exchange rate to this foreign currency and stands ready to exchange domestic currency at this rate whenever the public requests it. **544**

currency swap The exchange of a set of payments in one currency for a set of payments in another currency. **370**

current account An account that shows international transactions involving currently produced goods and services. **522**

current yield An approximation of the yield to maturity that equals the yearly coupon payment divided by the price of a coupon bond. **68**

dealers People who link buyers with sellers by buying and selling securities at stated prices. **20**

debt-currency swap The form of debt conversion where the debt denominated in foreign currency is converted into domestic currency. **280**

debt-debt swap The form of debt conversion where banks holding the debt of one less developed country (LDC) exchange it for the debt of another LDC. **280**

debt deflation A situation in which a substantial decline in the price level sets in, leading to a further deterioration in firms' net worth because of the increased burden of indebtedness. **203**

debt-equity swap The form of debt conversion where the debt is converted into the equity of public and private domestic enterprises. **280**

deductible The fixed amount by which the insured party's loss is reduced when a claim is paid off. **295**

default A situation in which the party issuing a debt instrument is unable to make interest payments or pay off the amount owed when the instrument matures. **114**

default-free bonds Bonds with no default risk, such as Canada bonds. **114**

defined-benefit plan A pension plan in which benefits are set in advance. **296**

defined-contribution plan A pension plan in which benefits are determined by the contributions into the plan and their earnings. **296**

deleveraging When financial institutions cut back on their lending because they have less capital. **200**

demand curve A curve depicting the relationship between quantity demanded and price when all other economic variables are held constant. **85**

demand-pull inflation Inflation that results when policymakers pursue policies that shift the aggregate demand curve. **673**

demand shocks Shocks that can shift the aggregate demand curve, including changes in the money supply, changes in government expenditure and taxes, changes in net exports, and changes in consumer and business spending. **622**

demutualization The process of converting a life insurance company into a stock company. **289**

deposit outflows Losses of deposits when depositors make withdrawals or demand payment. **321**

deposit rate ceiling Restriction on the maximum interest rate payable on deposits. **264**

depreciation Decrease in a currency's value. **11, 495**

desired reserve ratio The fraction of deposits that banks desire to keep as reserves. **317**

desired reserves Reserves that are held to meet the banks' desire that for every dollar of deposits, a certain fraction should be kept as reserves. **317**

devaluation Resetting of the fixed value of a currency at a lower level. **527**

direct clearers Members of the Canadian Payments Association who participate directly in the Automated Clearing Settlement System (ACSS) and maintain a settlement account at the Bank of Canada. **433**

dirty float See *managed float regime.*

discount bond A credit market instrument that is bought at a price below its face value and whose face value is repaid at the maturity date; it does not make any interest payments. Also called a *zero-coupon bond.* **62**

discretionary policy Policy to eliminate high unemployment whenever it appears on a discretionary basis. **684**

disintermediation A reduction in the flow of funds into the banking system that causes the amount of financial intermediation to decline. **264**

disposable income Total income available for spending, equal to aggregate income minus taxes. **574**

diversification Investing in a collection of assets whose returns do not always move together, with the result that overall risk is lower than for individual assets. **32**

dividends Periodic payments made by equities to shareholders. **20, 141**

dollarization The adoption of a sound currency, like the U.S. dollar, as a country's money. **544**

dual banking system The system in the United States in which banks supervised by the federal government and banks supervised by the states operate side by side. **254**

duration analysis A measurement of the sensitivity of the market value of a bank's assets and liabilities to changes in interest rates. **336**

e-cash A form of electronic money that can be used on the Internet to purchase goods or services. **49**

econometric model A model whose equations are estimated using statistical procedures. **692**

economies of scale The reduction in transaction costs per dollar of transaction as the size (scale) of transactions increases. **31**

economies of scope The ability to use one resource to provide many different products and services. **187**

e-finance A new means of delivering financial services electronically. **6**

efficient market hypothesis The application of the theory of rational expectations to financial markets. **150**

electoral business cycles Persistent cyclical patterns of key policy and target variables across electoral terms. **400**

electronic money (e-money) Money that is stored electronically. **49**

endowment insurance See *permanent life insurance.*

equation of exchange The equation $MV = PY$, which relates nominal income to the quantity of money. **552**

equities Claims to share in the net income and assets of a corporation (such as common stock). **20**

equity capital See *net worth.*

equity multiplier (EM) The amount of assets per dollar of equity capital. **327**

error-learning hypothesis The expectations formation hypothesis that emphasizes the learning behaviour of economic agents. It postulates that expectations are corrected by some fraction of the past period's expectations error. **148**

Eurobonds Bonds denominated in a currency other than that of the country in which they are sold. **27**

Eurocurrencies A variant of the Eurobond, which are foreign currencies deposited in banks outside the home country. **27**

Eurodollars U.S. dollars that are deposited in foreign banks outside the United States or in foreign branches of U.S. banks. **27**

European option An option that can be exercised only at the expiration date of the contract. **362**

European System of Central Banks (ESCB) Refers to the European Central Bank and the national central banks of all European Union (EU) member countries; when all EU member countries adopt the euro, the Eurosystem and the European System of Central Banks will become one entity. **394**

Eurosystem Refers to the European Central Bank and the national central banks of the countries that have adopted the euro. **395**

excess demand A situation in which quantity demanded is greater than quantity supplied. **87**

excess supply A situation in which quantity supplied is greater than quantity demanded. **87**

Exchange Fund Account The fund that holds Canada's official foreign exchange assets. **384**

exchange rate The price of one currency in terms of another. **494**

exchange rate overshooting A phenomenon whereby the exchange rate changes by more in the short run than it does in the long run when the money supply changes. **512**

exchanges Secondary markets in which buyers and sellers of securities (or their agents or brokers) meet in one central location to conduct trades. **21**

exercise price (strike price) The price at which the purchaser of an option has the right to buy or sell the underlying financial instrument. **361**

expectations theory The proposition that the interest rate on a long-term bond will equal the average of the short-term interest rates that people expect to occur over the life of the long-term bond. **121**

expected return The return on an asset expected over the next period. **83**

expenditure multiplier The ratio of a change in aggregate output to a change in investment spending (or autonomous spending). **578**

face value A specified final amount paid to the owner of a coupon bond at the maturity date. Also called *par value.* **62**

fair-value accounting An accounting method in which assets are valued on the balance sheet at what they would sell for in the market (also called *mark-to-market accounting*). **235**

fallen angels Investment-grade securities whose rating has fallen to junk levels. **116**

Federal Open Market Committee (FOMC) The committee that makes decisions regarding the conduct of open market operations; composed of the seven members of the Board of Governors of the Federal Reserve System, the president of the Federal Reserve Bank of New York, and the presidents of four other Federal Reserve banks on a rotating basis. **391**

Federal Reserve Banks The twelve district banks in the Federal Reserve System. **391**

Federal Reserve System (the Fed) The central banking authority responsible for monetary policy in the United States. **391**

fiat money Paper currency decreed by a government as legal tender but not convertible into coins or precious metal. **48**

finance paper Short-term secured promissory notes issued by sales finance companies. **23**

financial crisis A major disruption in financial markets that is characterized by sharp declines in asset prices and the failures of many financial and nonfinancial firms. **6**

financial derivatives Instruments that have payoffs that are linked to previously issued securities, used as risk reduction tools. **259**

financial engineering The process of researching and developing new products and services that would meet customer needs and prove profitable. **205**

financial futures A futures contract in which the standardized commodity is a particular type of financial instrument. **349**

financial futures option An option in which the underlying instrument is a futures contract. Also called a *futures option.* **362**

financial globalization The process of economies opening up to flows of capital and financial firms from other nations. **213**

financial intermediaries Institutions (such as banks, insurance companies, mutual funds, pension funds, and finance companies) that borrow funds from people who have saved and then make loans to others. **5**

financial intermediation The process of indirect finance whereby financial intermediaries link lender-savers and borrower-spenders. **30**

financial liberalization The elimination of restrictions on financial markets. **200**

financial markets Markets in which funds are transferred from people who have a surplus of available funds to people who have a shortage of available funds. **2**

financial panic The widespread collapse of financial markets and intermediaries in an economy. **38**

financial supervision (prudential supervision) Overseeing who operates financial institutions and how they are operated. **231**

fiscal policy Decisions about government spending and taxation. **10**

Fisher effect The outcome that when expected inflation occurs, interest rates will rise; named after economist Irving Fisher. **95**

fixed exchange rate regime A regime in which central banks buy and sell their own currencies to keep their exchange rates fixed at a certain level. **524**

fixed investment Spending by firms on equipment (computers, airplanes) and structures (factories, office buildings) and planned spending on residential housing. **575**

fixed-payment loan A credit market instrument that provides a borrower with an amount of money that is repaid by making a fixed payment periodically (usually monthly) for a set number of years. Also called a *fully amortized loan.* **62**

float Funds in transit between the time a cheque is deposited and the time the payment is settled. **50**

floating exchange rate regime An exchange rate regime in which the value of currencies are allowed to fluctuate against one another. **524**

foreign bonds Bonds sold in a foreign country and denominated in that country's currency. **27**

foreign exchange intervention An international financial transaction in which a central bank buys or sells currency to influence foreign exchange rates. **518**

foreign exchange market The market in which exchange rates are determined. **11, 494**

foreign exchange rate The price of one country's currency in terms of another's. See also *exchange rate*. **11**

forward contract An agreement by two parties to engage in a financial transaction at a future (forward) point in time. **347**

forward rate The interest rate predicted by pure expectations theory of the term structure of interest rates to prevail in the future. **134**

forward exchange rate The exchange rate for a forward transaction. **495**

forward transaction A transaction that involves the exchange of bank deposits denominated in different currencies at some specified future date. **495**

four-pillar approach Regulation of the banking industry by institution (banking, brokerage, trusts, and insurance), versus regulation by function. **272**

free banking A system that permits the organization of a bank by any group that meets certain established criteria concerning the amount of equity capital and maintenance of reserves. **254**

free-rider problem The problem that occurs when people who do not pay for information take advantage of the information that other people have paid for. **173**

fully amortized loan See *fixed-payment loan.*

fully funded Describing a pension plan in which the contributions to the plan and their earnings over the years are sufficient to pay out the defined benefits when they come due. **296**

futures contracts The seller agrees to provide a certain standardized commodity to the buyer on a specific future date at an agreed-upon price. **259**

futures option See *financial futures option.*

gap analysis (income gap analysis) A measurement of the sensitivity of bank profits to changes in interest rates, calculated by subtracting the amount of rate-sensitive liabilities from the amount of rate-sensitive assets. **334**

generalized dividend model The current value of a share of stock can be calculated as simply the present value of the future dividend stream. **142**

globalization The growing integration and interdependence of national economies. **490**

goal independence The ability of the central bank to set the goals of monetary policy. **386**

gold standard A fixed exchange rate regime in which a currency is directly convertible into gold. **256**

Gordon growth model The generalized dividend valuation model that assumes constant dividend growth. **143**

Governing Council of the Bank of Canada A council with six members (including the governor) that is responsible for the management of the Bank. **383**

government budget constraint The requirement that the government budget deficit equal the sum of the change in the monetary base and the change in government bonds held by the public. **676**

government spending Spending by all levels of government on goods and services. **573, 620**

government-sponsored enterprises (GSEs) In the U.S., federally sponsored agencies that function as private corporations with close ties to the government. **308**

group life insurance Insurance sold to a group of people under a single policy. **289**

hedge To protect oneself against risk. **259**

hedge fund A special type of mutual fund that engages in "market-neutral strategies." **305**

high-powered money The monetary base. **408**

hyperinflation An extreme inflation in which the inflation rate exceeds 50% per month. **47**

hysteresis A departure from full employment levels as a result of past high unemployment. **632**

incentive-compatible Having the incentives of both parties to a contract in alignment. **181**

income The flow of earnings. **44**

indebtedness In describing a country, the total amount it has borrowed from banks. **280**

indexed bond A bond whose interest and principal payments are adjusted for changes in the price level, and whose interest rate thus provides a direct measure of a real interest rate. **79**

individual life insurance Insurance sold one policy at a time. **289**

inflation The condition of a continually rising price level. **7**

inflation rate The rate of change of the price level, usually measured as a percentage change per year. **8**

inflation targeting A monetary policy strategy to achieve price stability. **467**

initial public offering (IPO) A stock whose firm is issuing it for the first time. **188**

institutional investors Institutional investors—mutual funds and pension funds—are important players in Canadian financial markets; they are also the predominant players in the stock markets, with over 70% of the total daily volume in the stock market due to their trading. **303**

instrument independence The ability of the central bank to set monetary policy instruments. **386**

interbank deposits Deposits made at other banks. **317**

interest rate The cost of borrowing or the price paid for the rental of funds (usually expressed as a percentage per year). **3**

interest-rate forward contract A forward contract that is linked to a debt instrument. **347**

interest-rate futures contract A futures contract that is linked to a debt instrument. It is similar to an interest-rate forward contract.   **349**

interest-rate risk The possible reduction in returns associated with changes in interest rates.   **74, 322**

interest-rate swap A financial contract that allows one party to exchange (swap) a set of interest payments for another set of interest payments owned by another party.   **370**

intermediate target Any of a number of variables, such as monetary aggregates or interest rates, that have a direct effect on employment and the price level and that the central bank seeks to influence.   **476**

intermediate-term With reference to a debt instrument, having a maturity of one to ten years.   **20**

International Monetary Fund (IMF) The international organization created by the Bretton Woods agreement whose objective is to promote the growth of world trade by making loans to countries experiencing balance-of-payments difficulties.   **525**

international policy coordination Agreements among countries to enact policies cooperatively.   **490**

international reserves Central bank holdings of assets denominated in foreign currencies.   **518**

in the money option Option that would be profitable to exercise.   **363**

intrinsic value The value of an option at expiration.   **363**

inventory investment Spending by firms on additional holdings of raw materials, parts, and finished goods.   **575**

inverted yield curve A yield curve that is downward-sloping.   **120**

investment banks Firms that assist in the initial sale of securities in the primary market.   **20**

IS curve The relationship that describes the combinations of aggregate output and interest rates for which the total quantity of goods produced equals the total quantity demanded (goods market equilibrium).   **587**

items in transit (bank float) Items in the process of collection.   **317**

junk bonds Bonds with ratings below BAA (or BBB) that have a high default risk.   **116**

Keynesian A follower of John Maynard Keynes who believes that movements in the price level and aggregate output are driven by changes not only in the money supply but also in government spending and fiscal policy and who does not regard the economy as inherently stable.   **630**

large, complex banking organizations (LCBOs) Large, complex, banking organizations have developed through consolidation of financial institutions that has made them bigger and has increased the products and services they can provide.   **273**

Large Value Transfer System (LVTS) An electronic, net settlement system for the transfer of large-value payments.   **432**

law of one price The principle that if two countries produce an identical good, the price of this good should be the same throughout the world no matter which country produces it.   **498**

lender of last resort Provider of reserves to financial institutions when no one else will provide them, in order to prevent a financial crisis.   **257**

leverage ratio A bank's capital divided by its assets.   **230**

leveraged buyout (LBO) A purchase of a publicly traded firm by buying all of its shares, while financing the purchase by increasing the leverage (debt) of the firm.   **307**

liabilities IOUs or debts.   **18**

liability management The acquisition of funds at low cost to increase profits.   **321**

liquid Easily converted into cash.   **21**

liquidity The relative ease and speed with which an asset can be converted into cash.   **47, 83**

liquidity management The decisions made by a bank to maintain sufficient liquid assets to meet the bank's obligations to depositors.   **321**

liquidity preference framework A model developed by John Maynard Keynes that predicts the equilibrium interest rate on the basis of the supply of and demand for money.   **99**

liquidity preference theory John Maynard Keynes's theory of the demand for money.   **556**

liquidity premium theory The theory that the interest rate on a long-term bond will equal an average of short-term interest rates expected to occur over the life of the long-term bond plus a positive term (liquidity) premium.   **127**

liquidity services Services that make it easier for customers to conduct transactions.   **32**

LM curve The relationship that describes the combinations of interest rates and aggregate output for which the quantity of money demanded equals the quantity of money supplied.   **587**

load funds Open-end mutual funds sold by salespeople who receive a commission that is paid at the time of purchase and is immediately subtracted from the redemption value of the shares.   **303**

loan commitment A bank's commitment (for a specified future period of time) to provide a firm with loans up to a given amount at an interest rate that is tied to some market interest rate.   **332**

loan sale The sale under a contract (also called a secondary loan participation) of all or part of the cash stream from a specific loan, thereby removing the loan from the bank's balance sheet.   **340**

long in a call Purchase of a call option.   **362**

long in a put Purchase of a put option.   **364**

long position A contractual obligation to take delivery of an underlying financial instrument.   **346**

long-run aggregate supply curve The quantity of output supplied in the long run at any given price level.   **629**

long-run monetary neutrality See *monetary neutrality.*

long-term With reference to a debt instrument, having a maturity of ten years or more.   **20**

LVTS See *Large Value Transaction System.*

LVTS participants Members of the Canadian Payments Association (CPA) who participate in the LVTS and maintain a settlement account at the Bank of Canada.   **432**

M1+ Includes currency, personal chequing accounts, and current accounts, plus other assets that have cheque-writing features—all chequable notice deposits at chartered banks, TMLs, and CUCPs.   **52**

M1++ M1+, plus all nonchequable notice deposits at chartered banks, TMLs, and CUCPs.   **52**

M2 Adds to M1 money market deposit accounts, money market mutual fund shares, small-denomination time deposits, savings deposits, overnight repurchase agreements, and overnight Eurodollars.   **51**

M2+ Includes M2 plus deposits at near banks, life insurance company annuities, and money market mutual funds.   **52**

M2++ Adds to M2+ Canada Savings Bonds and non-money market mutual funds.   **52**

M3 Adds to M2 large-denomination time deposits, long-term repurchase agreements, and institutional money market fund shares.   **51**

macro hedge A hedge of interest-rate risk for a financial institution's entire portfolio.   **353**

macroprudential regulation Regulatory policy to affect what is happening in the credit markets in the aggregate.   **484**

managed float regime The current international financial environment in which exchange rates fluctuate from day to day but central banks attempt to influence their countries' exchange rates by buying and selling currencies. Also known as a *dirty float.*   **524**

margin requirement A sum of money that must be kept in an account (the margin account) at a brokerage firm.   **355**

marginal propensity to consume The slope of the consumption function line that measures the change in consumer expenditure resulting from an additional dollar of disposable income.   **574**

mark-to-market accounting An accounting method in which assets are valued on the balance sheet at what they would sell for in the market (also called *fair-value accounting*).   **235**

marked to market Repriced and settled in the margin account at the end of every trading day to reflect any change in the value of the future contract.   **355**

market equilibrium A situation occurring when the quantity that people are willing to buy (demand) equals the quantity that people are willing to sell (supply).   **87**

market fundamentals Items that have a direct impact on future income streams of a security.   **154**

maturity Time to the expiration date (maturity date) of a debt instrument.   **20**

medium of exchange Anything that is used to pay for goods and services.   **44**

micro hedge A hedge for a specific asset.   **353**

monetarism A theory that emphasizes the importance of money in the economy, but opposes the use of discretionary stabilization policy.   **485**

monetarist A follower of Milton Friedman who sees changes in the money supply as the primary source of movements in the price level and aggregate output and who views the economy as inherently stable.   **630**

monetary aggregates The various measures of the money supply used by the central bank (M1, M2, and M3).   **51**

monetary base See *base money.*

monetary conditions Determined by the level of short-term interest rates and the exchange rate of the Canadian dollar.   **440**

monetary neutrality A proposition that in the long run, a percentage rise in the money supply is matched by the same percentage rise in the price level, leaving unchanged the real money supply and all other economic variables such as interest rates.   **511, 612**

monetary policy The management of the money supply and interest rates.   **9**

monetary targeting A monetary policy strategy in which the central bank announces that it will achieve a certain value (the target) of the annual growth rate of a monetary aggregate.   **462**

monetary theory The theory that relates changes in the quantity of money to changes in aggregate economic activity and the price level.   **7, 557**

monetizing the debt A method of financing government spending whereby the government debt issued to finance government spending is removed from the hands of the public and is replaced by high-powered money instead. Also called *printing money.*   **677**

money Anything that is generally accepted in payment for goods or services or in the repayment of debts.   **6**

money centre banks Large banks in key financial centres.   **326**

money market A financial market in which only short-term debt instruments (generally those with original maturity of less than one year) are traded.   **21**

money multiplier A ratio that relates the change in the money supply to a given change in the monetary base.   **422**

monoline insurance companies Insurance companies that specialize in credit insurance alone.   **291**

moral hazard The risk that one party to a transaction will engage in behaviour that is undesirable from the other party's point of view. **33**

mortgage-backed securities Securities that cheaply bundle and quantify the default risk of the underlying high-risk mortgages. **205**

multilateral netting The LVTS process by which only the net credit or debit position of each participant vis-à-vis all other participants is calculated for settlement, thereby reducing the need for a large amount of settlement balances. **433**

multiple deposit creation The process whereby, when the Bank of Canada supplies the banking system with $1 of additional reserves, deposits increase by a multiple of this amount. **414**

municipal bonds (municipals) Bonds issued by cities and other government entities to raise money for public purposes, such as building schools, highways, hospitals, and other special projects. **26**

NAIRU (nonaccelerating inflation rate of unemployment) The rate of unemployment when demand for labour equals supply, consequently eliminating the tendency for the inflation rate to change. **480, 623**

national banks Federally chartered banks. **254**

natural rate level of output The level of aggregate output produced at the natural rate of unemployment at which there is no tendency for wages or prices to change. **611, 624**

natural rate of unemployment The rate of unemployment consistent with full employment at which the demand for labour equals the supply of labour. **622**

net exports Net foreign spending on domestic goods and services, equal to exports minus imports. **573, 620**

net worth The difference between a firm's assets (what it owns or is owed) and its liabilities (what it owes). Also called *equity capital*. **176**

no-load funds Mutual funds sold directly to the public on which no sales commissions are charged. **303**

nominal interest rate An interest rate that does not take inflation into account. **76**

nonaccelerating inflation rate of unemployment See *NAIRU*.

nonborrowed monetary base The monetary base minus discount loans. **414**

nondiscretionary policy Avoidance of the use of discretionary policy to eliminate unemployment. **684**

notional principal The amount on which interest is being paid in a swap arrangement. **371**

off-balance-sheet activities Bank activities that involve trading financial instruments and the generation of income from fees and loan sales, all of which affect bank profits but are not visible on bank balance sheets. **230**

official reserve transactions balance The current account balance plus items in the capital account. **523**

open-end fund A mutual fund from which shares can be redeemed at any time at a price that is tied to the asset value of the fund. **303**

open interest The number of contracts outstanding. **353**

open market buyback operations The Bank of Canada's buying or selling of bonds in the open market. **385**

open market purchase A purchase of bonds by the Bank of Canada. **408**

open market sale A sale of bonds by the Bank of Canada. **408, 417**

operating band The Bank's operational objective is to keep the overnight rate within an operating band of twenty-five basis points. **434**

opportunity cost The amount of interest (expected return) sacrificed by not holding an alternative asset. **100**

optimal forecast The best guess of the future using all available information. **148**

option A contract that gives the purchaser the option (right) to buy or sell the underlying financial instrument at a specified price, called the exercise price or strike price, within a specific period of time (the term to expiration). **361**

originate-to-distribute model A business model in which a mortgage is originated by a separate party, typically a mortgage broker, and then distributed to an investor as an underlying asset in a security. **205**

out of the money option An option that would not be profitable to exercise. **363**

over-the-counter (OTC) market A secondary market in which dealers at different locations who have an inventory of securities stand ready to buy and sell securities "over the counter" to anyone who comes to them and is willing to accept their prices. **21**

overdraft loans Borrowings from the Bank of Canada. Also called *advances*. **316**

overnight interest rate (reference rate) The interest rate at which participants borrow and lend overnight funds to each other in the money market. **24, 433**

overnight rate The interest rate on overnight (one-day) securities. **431**

par value See *face value*.

partisan business cycles Systematic and permanent differences in macroeconomic outcomes that differ by political party. **400**

payments system The method of conducting transactions in the economy. **47**

permanent life insurance An insurance policy that has a constant premium throughout the life of the policy. **289**

perpetuity See *consol.*

personal pension plans RRSPs that provide tax-sheltered, self-financed retirement funds. **299**

Phillips curve theory A theory suggesting that changes in inflation are influenced by the state of the economy relative to its production capacity, as well as to other factors. **480**

planned investment spending Total planned spending by businesses on new physical capital (machines, computers, apartment buildings) plus planned spending on new homes. **573, 619**

policy ineffectiveness proposition The conclusion from the new classical model that anticipated policy has no effect on output fluctuations. **696**

policy instrument (operating instrument) A variable that is very responsive to the central bank's tools and indicates the stance of monetary policy. **476**

policy mix The combination of fiscal and monetary policies used together. **605**

policy rate The target for the Bank of Canada's overnight interest rate. **433**

political business cycle A business cycle caused by expansionary policies before an election. **399**

portfolio A collection of assets. **32**

preferred habitat theory Assumes that investors have a preference for bonds of one maturity over another, a particular bond maturity (preferred habitat) in which they prefer to invest. **127**

premium The amount paid for an option contract. **362**

present discounted value See *present value.*

present value Today's value of a payment to be received in the future when the interest rate is *i*. **59**

price earnings ratio (PE) The ratio of a stock's price to its earnings per share. **144**

primary dealers Government securities dealers, operating out of private firms or commercial banks, with whom the Bank of Canada's open market desk trades. **443**

primary market A financial market in which new issues of a security are sold to initial buyers. **20**

principal–agent problem A moral hazard problem that occurs when the managers in control (the agents) act in their own interest rather than in the interest of the owners (the principals) due to different sets of incentives. **177**

printing money See *monetizing the debt.*

private equity fund A fund that makes long-term investments in companies that are not traded in public markets. **307**

private pension plans Voluntary, employer-sponsored plans, with the contributions usually shared between employer and employee. **297**

provincial bonds (provincials) Bonds issued by Canada's provincial governments. **26**

prudential supervision See *financial supervision.*

put option An option contract that provides the right to sell a security at a specified price. **363**

put premium Price of a put option. **364**

quantity theory of money The theory that nominal income is determined solely by movements in the quantity of money. **553**

quotas Restrictions on the quantity of foreign goods that can be imported. **501**

rate of capital gain The change in a security's price relative to the initial purchase price. **72**

rate of return See *return.*

rational expectations Expectations that reflect optimal forecasts (the best guess of the future) using all available information. **147**

real business cycle theory A theory that views real shocks to tastes and technology as the major driving force behind short-run business cycle fluctuations. **632**

real exchange rate The rate at which domestic goods can be exchanged for foreign goods; i.e., the price of domestic relative to foreign goods denominated in domestic currency. **499**

real interest rate The interest rate adjusted for expected changes in the price level (inflation) so that it more accurately reflects the true cost of borrowing. **76**

real money balances The quantity of money in real terms. **557**

real terms Terms reflecting actual goods and services one can buy. **77**

recession A period when aggregate output is declining. **7**

reduced-form evidence Evidence that examines whether one variable has an effect on another by simply looking directly at the relationship between the two variables. **639**

registered bonds Bonds recorded on the books of a company in the name of the owner. They can be transferred to someone else only with the owner's endorsement. **26**

Regulation Q The regulation under which the Federal Reserve System had the power to set maximum interest rates that banks can pay on time deposits. **264**

regulatory arbitrage Banks keep on their books assets that have the same risk-based capital requirements but are relatively risky, while taking off their books low-risk assets. **231**

regulatory forbearance Regulators' refraining from exercising their right to put an insolvent bank out of business. **241**

reinsurance An allocation of the portion of the insurance risk to another company in exchange for a portion of the insurance premium. **291**

repo See *special Purchase and Resale Agreements.*

required reserves Reserves that are held to meet the central bank's requirement that for every dollar of deposits at a bank, a certain fraction must be kept as reserves. **407**

reserve currency A currency, such as the U.S. dollar, that is used by other countries to denominate the assets they hold as international reserves. **525**

reserves Banks' settlement balances with the Bank of Canada plus currency that is physically held by banks (vault cash). **317**

residual claimant The stockholder receives whatever remains after all other claims against the firm's assets have been satisfied. **141**

restrictive covenants Provisions that restrict and specify certain activities that a borrower can engage in. **169**

return The payments to the owner of a security plus the change in the security's value, expressed as a fraction of its purchase price. More precisely called the *rate of return.* **71**

return on assets (ROA) Net profit after taxes per dollar of assets. **327**

return on equity (ROE) Net profit after taxes per dollar of equity capital. **327**

revaluation Resetting of the fixed value of a currency at a higher level. **527**

reverse causation A situation in which one variable is said to cause another variable when in reality the reverse is true. **641**

reverse repo See *Sale and Repurchase Agreements.*

Ricardian equivalence Named after the nineteenth-century British economist David Ricardo, it contends that when the government runs deficits and issues bonds, the public recognizes that it will be subject to higher taxes in the future in order to pay off these bonds. **679**

risk The degree of uncertainty associated with the return on an asset. **32, 83**

risk of default See *default.*

risk premium The spread between the interest rate on bonds with default risk and the interest rate on default-free bonds. **114**

risk sharing Financial intermediaries create and sell assets with risk characteristics that people are comfortable with, and the intermediaries then use the funds they acquire by selling these assets to purchase other assets that may have far more risk. Also called *asset transformation.* **32**

risk structure of interest rates The relationship among the various interest rates on bonds with the same term to maturity. **113**

Sale and Repurchase Agreements (SRAs) The Bank of Canada's sale of government securities to primary dealers with an agreement to repurchase them one business day later. **443**

Schedule I banks Comprised of the Big Six, together with the Laurentian Bank of Canada, the Canadian Western Bank, and another eight domestic banks. **268**

Schedule II banks Include three domestic Schedule II banks, Citizen Bank (owned by VanCity Savings), First Nations Bank (owned by the Toronto Dominion Bank), and Manulife Bank (owned by Manulife Insurance), and thirty-six subsidiaries (i.e., separate Canadian legal entities) of foreign banks. **268**

Schedule III banks Foreign banks allowed to branch directly into Canada, under certain restrictions. **268**

seasoned issue A stock issued for sale for which prior issues currently sell in the market. **300**

secondary market A financial market in which securities that have previously been issued (and are thus secondhand) can be resold. **20**

secondary reserves Short-term U.S. government and agency securities held by banks. **317**

secured debt Debt guaranteed by collateral. **169**

securitization The process of transforming illiquid financial assets into marketable capital market instruments. **204**

security A claim on the borrower's future income that is sold by the borrower to the lender. Also called a *financial instrument.* **3**

segmented markets theory A theory of term structure that sees markets for different-maturity bonds as completely separated and segmented such that the interest rate for bonds of a given maturity is determined solely by supply of and demand for bonds of that maturity. **126**

seignorage The revenue a government receives by issuing money. **256**

self-correcting mechanism A characteristic of the economy that causes output to return eventually to the natural rate level regardless of where it is initially. **630**

settlement balances Deposits held by directly clearing members of the Canadian Payments Association at the Bank of Canada. They are also known as *clearing balances.* **316**

shadow banking system A system in which bank lending is replaced by lending via the securities market. **258**

shareholders Those who hold stock in a corporation. **141**

short in a call Sale of a call option. **362**

short in a put Sale of a put option. **364**

short position A contractual obligation to deliver an underlying financial instrument. **346**

short sale Involves borrowing a security from an investor or another financial institution for a fixed time period and selling it in the market with the intention of repurchasing it when it is due to be returned to the lender. **160**

short-term With reference to a debt instrument, having a maturity of one year or less. **20**

simple deposit multiplier The multiple increase in deposits generated from an increase in the banking system's reserves in a simple model in which the behaviour of depositor and bank plays no role.   **418**

simple loan A credit market instrument providing the borrower with an amount of funds that must be repaid to the lender at the maturity date along with an additional payment (interest).   **59**

smart card A sophisticated stored-value card containing its own computer chip so that the owner can load it with digital cash from a bank account.   **49**

sovereign loans Loans to foreign governments and their agencies in the less developed countries.   **279**

sovereign wealth fund A state-owned investment fund that invests in foreign assets.   **303**

special drawing rights (SDRs) An IMF-issued paper substitute for gold that functions as international reserves.   **530**

special Purchase and Resale Agreements (SPRAs) The Bank of Canada's purchase of government securities from primary dealers with an agreement to resell them one business day later.   **443**

specialist A dealer-broker operating in an exchange who maintains orderly trading of the securities for which he or she is responsible.   **302**

speculative attack A situation in which speculators engage in massive sales of a currency.   **216**

spinning When an investment bank allocates shares of hot, but underpriced, initial public offerings to executives of other companies in return for their companies' future business with the investment bank.   **188**

spot exchange rate The exchange rate for a spot transaction.   **495**

spot rate The interest rate at a given moment.   **134**

spot transaction The predominant type of exchange rate transaction, involving the immediate exchange of bank deposits.   **495**

standing lending facility A lending facility in which healthy banks are allowed to borrow all they want from a central bank.   **452**

standing liquidity facilities Refers to the Bank of Canada standing ready to lend to or borrow from a participant to bring their settlement balances to zero at the end of the banking day.   **436**

state banks U.S. banks chartered by the states.   **185, 254**

sterilized foreign exchange intervention A foreign exchange intervention with an offsetting open market operation that leaves the monetary base unchanged.   **520**

stock market risk The risk associated with fluctuations in stock prices.   **358**

stock option An option on an individual stock.   **362**

store of value A repository of purchasing power over time.   **46**

strike price See *exercise price*.

structured credit products Securities that are derived from cash flows of underlying assets and are tailored to have particular risk characteristics that appeal to investors with different preferences.   **205**

structured investment vehicles (SIVs) Securities similar to CDOs in that they pay off cash flows from pools of assets such as mortgages; however, instead of being issued as long-term debt as in CDOs, they are issued as asset-backed commercial paper.   **207**

structural model A description of how the economy operates, using a collection of equations that describe the behaviour of firms and consumers in many sectors of the economy.   **639**

structural model evidence Evidence that examines whether one variable affects another by using data to build a model illustrating the channels through which this variable affects the other.   **639**

subprime mortgages Mortgages for borrowers with less-than-stellar credit records.   **204**

supply curve A curve depicting the relationship between quantity supplied and price when all other economic variables are held constant.   **86**

supply shock Any change in technology or the supply of raw materials that can shift the aggregate supply curve.   **626**

swap A financial contract that obligates one party to exchange (swap) a set of payments it owns for a set of payments owned by another party.   **370**

sweep account An arrangement in which any balances above a certain amount in a corporation's chequing account at the end of a business day are "swept out" of the account and invested in overnight repos that pay the corporation interest.   **264**

systemic risk The risk to the entire payments system due to the inability of one financial institution to fulfill its payment obligations in a timely fashion.   **432**

T-account A simplified balance sheet with lines in the form of a T that lists only the changes that occur in balance sheet items starting from some initial balance sheet position.   **318**

tariffs Taxes on imported goods.   **501**

Taylor rule Economist John Taylor's monetary policy rule that explains how the federal funds rate target is set.   **479**

term deposit receipts (term notes) Deposit instruments requiring a minimum investment at a predetermined interest rate for a stated term.   **23**

term structure of interest rates The relationship among interest rates on bonds with different terms to maturity but with the same risk of default.   **113**

temporary life insurance An insurance policy with a premium that is matched every year to the amount needed to insure against death during the period of the term.   **290**

theory of asset demand The theory that the quantity demanded of an asset is (1) usually positively related to wealth, (2) positively related to its expected return relative to alternative assets, (3) negatively related to the risk of its return relative to alternative assets, and (4) positively related to its liquidity relative to alternative assets. **84**

theory of efficient capital markets See *efficient market hypothesis.*

theory of purchasing power parity (PPP) The theory that exchange rates between any two currencies will adjust to reflect changes in the price levels of the two countries. **499**

total cash reserves See *reserves.*

trade balance The difference between merchandise exports and imports. **522**

transaction costs The time and money spent trying to exchange financial assets, goods, or services. **31**

transmission mechanisms of monetary policy The channels through which the money supply affects economic activity. **639**

trustee The representative of a person or corporation. **275**

underfunded Describing a pension plan in which the contributions and their earnings are not sufficient to pay out the defined benefits when they come due. **296**

underwriters Investment banks that guarantee prices on securities to corporations and then sell the securities to the public. **301**

underwriting Guaranteeing prices on securities to corporations and then selling the securities to the public. **20**

unemployment rate The percentage of the labour force not working. **6**

unexploited profit opportunity A situation in which an investor can earn a higher than normal return. **153**

unit of account Anything used to measure value in an economy. **45**

unsecured debt Debt not guaranteed by collateral. **169**

unsterilized foreign exchange intervention A foreign exchange intervention in which a central bank allows the purchase or sale of domestic currency to affect the monetary base. **520**

vault cash Currency that is physically held by banks and stored in vaults overnight. **317**

velocity of money The rate of turnover of money; the average number of times per year that a dollar is spent in buying the total amount of final goods and services produced in the economy. **552**

venture capital firm A financial intermediary that pools the resources of its partners and uses the funds to help entrepreneurs start up new businesses. **179**

venture capital fund A financial intermediary that pools the resources of its partners and uses the funds to help entrepreneurs start up new businesses. **307**

virtual bank A bank that has no building but rather exists only in cyberspace. **261**

wealth All resources owned by an individual, including all assets. **44, 83**

World Bank The International Bank for Reconstruction and Redevelopment, an international organization that provides long-term loans to assist developing countries in building dams, roads, and other physical capital that would contribute to their economic development. **525**

World Trade Organization (WTO) An organization headquartered in Geneva, Switzerland, that monitors rules for the conduct of trade between countries (tariffs and quotas). **525**

yield curve A plot of the interest rates for particular types of bonds with different terms to maturity. **119**

yield to maturity The interest rate that equates the present value of payments received from a credit market instrument with its value today. **63**

zero-coupon bond See *discount bond.*

INDEX

A

A-paper, 204
ABN AMRO Group, 208
Abu Dhabi Investment Authority, 304
accommodating policy, 674
accountability, 390–391
accounting firms, 188
accounting net worth, 336n
adaptive expectations, 147, 148
adjustable-rate mortgages, 259
advances, 316, 407, 412–413
adverse selection
    see also asymmetric information
    collateral, 176–177
    credit risk management, 330–334
    defined, 171
    described, 32–33
    financial intermediation, 175–176
    financial structure, influence on,
        171–177
    financial supervision and, 231
    free-rider problem, 173
    and government regulation to
        increase information, 174–175
    and government safety net, 228
    lemons problem, 171–177
    net worth, 176–177
    private production, 173
    sale of information, 173
    tools to help solve problems, 173–177
adverse shocks, 549
Affected Trusts, 208
after-tax real interest rate, 78n
Afxentiou, Panos, 400
agency problems, 205–206, 341
agency theory, 171
aggregate demand
    components of, 619–620
    defined, 619
    deriving the aggregate demand curve,
        620–622
    equation, 573
    equilibrium, 627–633
aggregate demand curve, 613–616,
    620–622
aggregate demand function, 577
aggregate demand shocks, 630–631
aggregate output
    aggregate demand, 573
    aggregate demand function, 577
    autonomous consumer expenditure,
        580–581, 584
    changes in equilibrium level of,
        601–603
    consumer expenditure, 573, 574–575
    consumption function, 574–575, 575f
    defined, 6
    determinants of, 572–586
    and expansionary policy, 696–697,
        701–703

expenditure multiplier, 578–581
fiscal policy, response to change in,
    602–603
government, role of, 581–583
government spending, 573, 581–583,
    584–585, 603
international trade, role of, 583
and *ISLM* model, 592–593, 592f
Keynesian cross diagram, 576–578
monetary policy, response to change
    in, 601–602
and money supply, 602
net exports, 573, 586
in new classical macroeconomic
    model, 696
planned investment spending, 573,
    575–576, 579, 579f, 584
and price level, 620
response of, 585t
taxes, 585, 603
and unemployment, 620
aggregate price level
    and aggregate output, 620
    defined, 7
    equilibrium interest rate, changes in,
        102
    and exchange rates, 501
    expansionary policy, response to,
        701–703
    expected price level, 626
    fixed, 573
    and the money supply, 8f
    unanticipated price level channel,
        657–658, 662
    unexpected decline, and balance
        sheets, 197
aggregate supply
    defined, 619
    deriving the aggregate supply curve,
        622–627
    equilibrium, 627–633
aggregate supply curve, 622–627
aggregate supply shocks, 631
AIG, 209, 210, 227, 292, 375
Akerlof, George, 172n
Alberta Heritage Savings Trust Fund, 304
Alberta Municipal Financing Corporation,
    27
Alberta Treasury Branches, 277, 406n,
    432n, 433n
Alesina, Alberto, 401n
alt-A mortgages, 204
American Express, 260
American International Group. *See* AIG
American options, 362
American Stock Exchange (AMEX), 301
anchor country, 540
anchor currency, 524
Ando, Albert, 649n
animal spirits, 581, 671n

annual percentage rate (APR), 235
annuities, 290
anti-inflation policies, 704–706
anticipated policy, 694–696, 699
appreciation, 11, 495, 497
Arab countries, and sovereign wealth
    funds, 304
arbitrage, 153, 231, 351
Argentina
    Central Bank of Argentina, 545
    currency, collapse of, 221
    currency board, 544, 545
    financial crises in, 217–222
    fiscal imbalances in, 199
    foreign exchange crisis, 533–534
    foreign lending to, 279, 280
Arthur Andersen, 188, 191
asset-backed commercial paper (ABCP)
    market, 207, 208–209
Asset-Backed Commercial Paper Money
    Market Mutual Fund Liquidity
    Facility, 459
asset demand
    determinants of, 83–85
    expected return, 83
    liquidity, 83, 84
    risk, 83–84
    theory of asset demand, 84, 84t
    wealth, 83
asset-liability management (ALM)
    committee, 326
asset management, 321, 325
asset market approach, 88, 88n, 503n,
    510n
asset market effects, and balance sheets,
    197–199
asset-price bubble, 202, 481–485
asset price channels, 654–655
asset transformation, 32
assets
    asset price boom and bust, 202
    on bank balance sheet, 317–318
    on Bank of Canada's balance sheet,
        406–407
    as collateral, 23
    defined, 3
    demand for. *See* asset demand
    of financial intermediaries, 39
    plain vanilla assets, 208
    portfolio, 32
    real assets, 91
    restrictions on asset holdings, 229–230
    risky assets, 229–230
    write-downs, and balance sheets, 198
asymmetric information
    see also adverse selection; moral
        hazard
    consumer protection, 235
    credit risk management, 330–334
    credit view, 652